Encyclopedia
of American
Gospel Music

Encyclopedia of American Gospel Music

W. K. McNeil, Editor

Routledge
Taylor & Francis Group
New York   London

This edition published in paperback in 2010

First edition published 2005
by Routledge
270 Madison Avenue, New York, NY 10016

Simultaneously published in the UK
by Routledge
2 Park Square, Milton Park, Abingdon, Oxon OX14 4RN

Routledge is an imprint of the Taylor & Francis Group, an informa business

© 2005, 2010 Taylor & Francis

Printed and bound in the United States of America on acid-free paper by Sheridan Books, Inc.

Library of Congress Cataloging in Publication Data
Encyclopedia of American gospel music / W.K. McNeil, editor.
    p. cm.
  Includes discographical and bibliographical references and index.
  ISBN 0-415-94179-2
  1. Gospel music–Encyclopedias. 2. Gospel music–Bio-bibliography. I. McNeil, W. K.
  ML102.G6E63 2005
  782.25′4′03–dc22 2005044994

ISBN 13: 978-0-415-94179-2 (hbk)
ISBN 13: 978-0-415-87569-1 (pbk)

ADVISORY BOARD

In memory of
W. K. McNeil

CONTENTS

LIST OF CONTRIBUTORS

Sarah Arthur
Florida State University

Scott Banville
The Ohio State University

John Bealle
Cincinnati, Ohio

David Beaudouin
Baltimore, Maryland

Drew Beisswenger
Southwest Missouri State University

Rob Bowman
York University

Mark Burford
Carnegie Hall

Melvin L. Butler
Dartmouth College

Richard Carlin
New York, New York

Henry L. Carrigan, Jr.
New York, New York

Rodney Clapp
Brazos Press, Wheaton, IL

Joe C. Clark
Albin O. Kuhn Library & Gallery,
University of Maryland,
Baltimore County

Donna M. Cox
University of Dayton

John Crenshaw
Hickory, North Carolina

Sarah E. Crest
Albert S. Cook Library, Towson University

Don Cusic
Belmont University

Robert Darden
Baylor University

Jacqueline Cogdell DjeDje
University of California, Los Angeles

Sherry Sherrod DuPree
The DuPree Holiness Pentecostal Collection,
Schomburg Center for Research in Black Culture,
New York Public Library

James I. Elliott
Belmont University

Margaret B. Fisher
New York, New York

Tom Fisher
Lawrence, Kansas

Kevin S. Fontenot
Tulane University

Theodore E. Fuller
Fayetteville, North Carolina

Andrea Gannaway
Gallipolis, Ohio

Becky Garrison
New York, New York

Luvenia A. George
Washington, DC

Bob Gersztyn
Salem, Oregon

Abby Gail Goodnite-Ehman
Gallipolis, Ohio

James E. Henry
Lindenwood University

LIST OF CONTRIBUTORS

Harold Jacobs
Emory University

Tamara J. Jaffe-Notier
Oak Park, Illinois

Melvin Klaudt
Atlanta, Georgia

Kip Lornell
Silver Spring, Maryland

Robert Marovich
Chicago, Illinois

Kenny Mathieson
Strathspey, Scotland

Ben McCorkle
The Ohio State University

W. K. McNeil
The Ozark Folk Center

Luigi Monge
Genova, Italy

Hilary Moore
Royal College of Music, London

Timothy J. Moore
Lakewood, Ohio

Jocelyn R. Neal
University of North Carolina, Chapel Hill

Per Notini
Enskede Gård, Sweden

William E. Plants
Gallipolis, Ohio

Mark Allan Powell
Trinity Lutheran Seminary, Columbus, Ohio

Emmett G. Price III
Northeastern University

Ronnie Pugh
Nashville Public Library

Charles F. Reese
Gospel Music Workshop of America, Inc.

Robert Sacré
University of Liège

Stephen Shearon
Middle Tennessee State University

Simmona E. Simmons-Hodo
Albin O. Kuhn Library & Gallery,
University of Maryland,
Baltimore County

Alphonso Simpson, Jr.
Western Illinois University

Erin Stapleton-Corcoran
University of Chicago

Lynda Rutledge Stephenson
Grand Rapids, MI

Evelyn M. E. Taylor
Kearneysville, West Virginia

Deanna L. Tribe
The Ohio State University

Ivan M. Tribe
University of Rio Grande and Rio Grande
Community College

Mel R. Wilhoit
Bryan College

David Willoughby
Elizabethtown, Pennsylvania

Charles K. Wolfe
Middle Tennessee State University

Elizabeth L. Wollman
Brooklyn, New York

LIST OF ENTRIES A-Z

A

Abernathy, Lee Roy
Ackley, Alfred
Ackley, Bentley DeForest
Acuff, Roy
Adams, Yolanda
Akers, Doris
Alexander, Charles McCallum
Allen, Rance
Allen, Richard
Anderson, Robert
Andrews Gospel Singers, The
Andrews, Inez
Andrus, Blackwood & Company
Angelic Gospel Singers
Anointed Pace Sisters
Archers, The
Armond Morales and the Imperials
Armstrong, Vanessa Bell
Arthur Smith and His Crossroads Quartet
Azusa Street Revival

B

Bagwell, Wendy
Bailes Brothers, The
Banjo
Barbershop Quartets
Barren Cross
Barrett Sisters
Barrows, Cliff
Bartlett, Eugene Monroe
Bass, Martha
Baxter, J. R., Jr.
Baylor, Helen
Beck, Elder Charles D.
Bennard, George
Bethlehem
Black Gospel Musicals
Blackwood Brothers
Bliss, Philip Paul
Blue Jay Singers
Blue Ridge Quartet

Blue Sky Boys (Bolick Brothers)
Bluegrass
Blues
Bobby Jones and New Life
Boones, The
Bostic, Joe
Boyer Brothers, The
Bradbury, William Batchelder
Bradford, Alex
Bradley, John Robert
Brewster, William Herbert
Brooklyn Tabernacle Choir
Brown's Ferry Four
Brumley, Albert Edward
Burnett, Reverend J. C.

C

Caesar, Shirley
Calvary Chapel, Costa Mesa
Campbell, Lucie
Canaan Records
Caravans
Carman
Carmichael, Ralph
Carson, James and Martha
Carson, Martha
Carter Family, The
Cash, Johnny
Cathedral Quartet
Catholic Church, Gospel in
Chapman, Gary
Charioteers, The
Charles E. Fuller and the Old
  Fashioned Revival Hour
Charles Fold Singers
Cheeks, Julius
Cheré, Tami (Tami Cheré Gunden)
Chestnut Grove Quartet
Chuck Wagon Gang, The
Church of God in Christ (COGIC)
Clark, Elbernita
Clawson, Cynthia
Cleveland, James
Coates, Dorothy Love

INTRODUCTION

Two questions frequently asked about gospel music are "What is it?" and "When did it start?" Some people would designate as gospel music any religious song, but that is not the definition scholars would use. They interpret the term as referring to songs reflecting the personal religious experience of people. Gospel song lyrics are often subjective, usually addressed to one's fellow human beings, and focus on a single theme that is emphasized through repetition of individual phrases and concludes by a refrain after each stanza. Texts deal with conversion, atonement through Christ, salvation, and heaven's pleasures. Stylistically, they range from meditative and devotional to instructive and even militant. Gospel songs rarely employ the technique of utilizing a single tune between texts, as often happens in other forms of popular music. Generally, gospel music is confined to Protestant evangelical groups, both black and white, but it can also be found in Roman Catholic churches.

Defining when gospel started is more problematic because there are many times one could select as gospel's starting point. It could be dated from the 1850s when these songs first appeared in religious revivals. Or it could be dated from the urban revivalism era of the late nineteenth century. Or it could be dated from 1874 when Philip Paul Bliss titled one of his collections *Gospel Songs*.

There are some other problems in dating gospel's origins, the major one being the divisions of white and black gospel. Although there has been considerable interplay between the two types of gospel, they have different starting points. Generally, white gospel is considered to be the older of the two, although both have roots extending back far beyond their actual origins. White gospel is usually dated from the second half of the nineteenth century, while black gospel's basic performance style dates from the first decade of the twentieth century.

This seems a good time to lay to rest an opinion that frequently crops up in discussions of gospel's origins, namely, that gospel music grew out of camp meeting spirituals. It is true that one can find similarities between camp meeting spirituals and gospel songs, but overall, marches and secular songs of the day were more influential and should be considered a greater source of derivation. Indeed, many early gospel composers, such as George F. Root, were also well known as producers of secular music.

How to Use This Book

The *Encyclopedia of American Gospel Music* comes at a time when there is a revival of interest in gospel music. It is designed to answer questions such as the definition and origins of gospel music and cover the subject in as broad a way as possible. In other words, it aims to answer the who, what, and why of gospel music. The work is intended to be a valuable reference for both scholars and the general reading public.

This encyclopedia has several points that should enhance its appeal. For one thing, it deals with both black and white gospel, something that is usually not attempted in reference works on gospel music. In fact, no form of music has traditionally been as segregated as gospel. In recent years this has started to change. Even so, most of the attempts to cover both in book form have been superficial and inadequate. It is the sincere hope of the editors and contributors that the present work will correct this trend.

Another important feature of the *Encyclopedia of American Gospel Music* is that it contains the most up-to-date information. This is due in large part to the contributors, who have been specially selected because of their expertise. In some cases, putting these entries together required conducting a good deal of independent research.

The entries in this work are arranged in an easily accessible A to Z format. Twenty photographs illustrate the text. Essays include cross references that direct interested readers to related entries throughout the text. Most essays include a bibliography and a discography. These are selective and intended as guidelines to further research. Bibliographies cite sources used by the authors and the discographies include recordings, usually in

CD or LP form, of significance or ones that are currently available. When no reference citation appears, it means that the information was taken from record liner notes.

Coverage

The list of entries was drawn up with the intention of covering every important aspect of the music. Admittedly, such a list is subjective, but it was not the work of only one person. The editor and associate editors and various consultants contributed to the final list. By this coverage we believed we would be representing every important aspect of gospel's history. Although in a work of this kind there can be differences of opinion about inclusion and exclusion and practical considerations now and then intervene to modify one's ideal plan, we believe that all major figures have been included and that the work overall represents an important step forward in the study of gospel.

One of the most difficult things to run down were birth and death dates for personalities. In some cases, such as the Deal Family, not even family members knew the birth and death dates of the act's members. They were, however, cooperative, with some family members even going so far as to search cemeteries for Deals in an effort to find the needed information. Ultimately, we came up with both birth and death dates for most and only death dates for others. But even this is more data than is given in other references that include the Deal Family.

The Deals recorded in the 1920s, so it is perhaps understandable that some biographical details about them would be forgotten. Less comprehensible is the lack of such information on currently active and popular acts. An example is Take 6, one of today's hottest gospel acts. It took a great deal of effort to find birth dates for the members of this group, but we finally succeeded. They were not trying to hide the information; apparently it was just not of great concern to them to make their birth dates widely known. Yet, it should be noted here that most performers were gracious with their time and understood our need to get the most accurate data we could.

Although the attempt was to provide birth and death dates for all performers, we were not always successful and had to settle for providing them when possible. For groups, we give birth and death dates wherever possible for the most significant members of the group, usually the original members or the ones belonging to the act when it was most popular. It was thought pointless, as well as probably impossible to discover, birth and death dates for everyone who belonged to a quartet that had frequent changes of personnel. For the same reason, all members of choirs or other large aggregations are not listed individually. Instead, only the leaders are supplied.

Included in this volume are

- Biographical profiles of numerous performers, such as Andrae Crouch, and influential figures in the development of gospel music, such as Isaac Watts. Coverage extends from the earliest names in gospel to the most contemporary. Birth and death dates are included wherever possible.
- Important events in the history of gospel such as the Azusa Street Revival.
- Broadcasting outlets, such as radio station WLAC AM, and record companies, such as Canaan Records, that were prominent in gospel's history.
- Publications, such as *The Singing News*, significant songbooks, such as *Gospel Pearls*, and noteworthy publishing companies, such as Lillenas, all of which helped popularize some of the best-known gospel songs.
- Thematic entries on topics ranging from instruments frequently used by gospel performers to types of performing groups, such as gospel quartets and gospel choirs, to the unique qualities of gospel as it is composed and performed in different regions around the United States, to the globalization of gospel.

Undoubtedly, the most important consideration is that this encyclopedia be read. Every effort has been expended in making the entries readable. Our contributors must be given credit for this. Carefully chosen not just for their expertise but also for their writing ability, they have produced a volume that is academically sound, readable, and mostly jargon-free. In short, they have produced a manuscript that will appeal not just to scholars but to interested lay readers as well. We hope, and think, that the *Encyclopedia of American Gospel Music* will be for some time the book that everyone turns to when they want to find out about any aspect of gospel music.

W. K. McNeil

A

ABERNATHY, LEE ROY

(b. August 13, 1913; d. May 25, 1993)

Lee Roy Abernathy, affectionately dubbed "Professor," was one of gospel music's more innovative and entrepreneurial performers. In a professional career that spanned more than sixty years, he organized quartets, taught voice and piano, and composed one of the all-time best-selling gospel songs. He grasped the importance of television in its early days, hosting his own daily gospel show in Atlanta and introducing other gospel musicians to a wider audience. In many ways, Abernathy broke the mold of the traditional gospel performer as he used his broad range of musical—and marketing—talents to succeed in the world of professional entertainment.

Gospel Roots in a North Georgia Textile Community

Abernathy was born on August 13, 1913, in the community of Atco in Bartow County, Georgia. He acquired his musical training early from his piano-playing mother, Clara, and his father, Dee, who taught singing in schools and wrote gospel songs while variously employed as a sharecropper and mill worker in the rural North Georgia textile community.

By the age of five, Abernathy sang first tenor in his father's weekend group, the Atco Quartet. He

was still singing five years later when the quartet recorded with Columbia. However, because of complications from impacted tonsils and throat surgery, he turned to playing the piano at the age of twelve and did not resume his singing career for another twenty years.

In the 1920s, the Abernathy family moved frequently around northwest Georgia in search of better employment prospects. They finally settled in Canton, about thirty-five miles north of Atlanta, which eventually became Abernathy's permanent home. As a young teenager, Abernathy was a member of his father's group, the Abernathy Quartet, and played piano for recordings of "I'm Redeemed" and "Don't Forget to Pray" for RCA Victor. He also started his own quartet, the Modern Mountaineers, a country band that played in local theaters and churches and at banquets. During the early 1930s, the group played occasionally on Atlanta's WSB radio, and they recorded a series of 78s for Bluebird.

Abernathy's lifelong involvement in music education began early. He studied under such legends of the shape-note gospel world as A. J. Showalter and Adger Pace. He also learned to read sheet music at Atlanta's Conservatory of Music. After marrying Louise Ammons, the daughter of a mill supervisor, and moving to nearby Dalton, he opened Lee Roy's Music Store, where he taught private music lessons. During this time, he and his father continued to collaborate, writing such songs as "Won't We Have a Good Time" and "My Labor Will Be O'er."

Professional Legacy

In the mid-1930s, Abernathy began to display the entrepreneurial range that would characterize the rest of his career. He introduced his "Radio School of Music" on Dalton radio station WBLJ in 1938. Several years earlier, he recorded one of the Speer Family's first records at his Dalton studio. He also wrote campaign songs ("Good Times Are Coming Soon") for Franklin D. Roosevelt's 1936 reelection and for Georgia Governor Eugene Talmadge ("$3-Dollar Tag Song"). Nearly twenty years later, Abernathy would be writing campaign songs for himself ("Lee Roy's the Boy") as a candidate for the 1958 Georgia gubernatorial race. He even followed this with a song to concede defeat after he finished a distant third with 33,099 votes.

In 1943, he became the first gospel musician to publish sheet music of compositions, in shaped notes, with the first song being his own "I'll Thank My Savior for It." This break from tradition earned him ridicule at a time when other gospel groups sold collections of their songs in annual convention books under the auspices of music publishers.

After moving to Chattanooga and organizing the Four Tones in 1943, Abernathy toured the country and performed gospel and popular songs in USO shows. When the group disbanded because of two members' draft status, he joined Billy Carrier, George Hughes, and Bill Lyles in the Swanee River Boys as part of a special wartime arrangement. He followed this with an interlude in Richmond, where he played piano for the Rangers Quartet on WRVA. In 1945, the enterprising businessman began offering piano lessons by mail order, once again garnering ridicule from his contemporaries but nevertheless finding a market for his efforts. After Atlanta's tragic Winecoff Hotel fire in December 1946, one of the nation's deadliest hotel fires with 119 victims, Abernathy displayed his versatility by writing a popular song that described the event, "The Burning of the Winecoff."

In 1947, he joined the Homeland Harmony Quartet, created by Connor Hall and including James McCoy, Shorty Bradford, and Aycel Soward. Early the next year the group recorded Abernathy's new song, "Everybody's Gonna Have a Wonderful Time Up There." Later known as the "Gospel Boogie," the song became a subject of controversy across the United States because of its jazzy, dance hall beat. The White Church Records version sold 200,000 copies. Months later, black gospel artists and country singers gave the song wider distribution with their renditions. Over the years, the song has been recorded (and frequently turned into *Billboard* hits) by Pat

Boone, Johnny Mathis, and Johnny Cash, eventually selling more than five million records.

In 1948, he wrote his now out-of-print book "*It*," a history of gospel music events and, according to Abernathy, a "handbook for the new professional quartets." A year later, in 1949, he and Shorty Bradford left the Homeland Harmony Quartet and formed the Happy Two, performing on television shows and doing backup work and commercials. Abernathy wrote some of TV's first singing commercials, including "You'd Better Get Wild Root Cream Oil, Charlie," as well as songs for shampoo and insect spray.

In 1951, with their rising popularity, Abernathy and Bradford began hosting a daily TV show on WAGA in Atlanta that would air for the next seven years. The show featured other gospel musicians and, at one point, was rated number three in the United States by Nielson. During this time, he also performed with other quartets, including the Miracle Men and the Lee Roy Abernathy Quartet.

During his later years, he invented a typesetting system for setting music and established his Hall of Fame School of Music located near his home in Canton. In 1973, he was inducted into the Gospel Music Hall of Fame. This was followed by his election to the Georgia Music Hall of Fame in 1989.

Abernathy died on May 25, 1993, as a result of complications after a stroke. He was survived by his wife Louise, a son, and two daughters.

HAROLD JACOBS

See also Hall, Connor; Homeland Harmony Quartet; Rangers Quartet; Showalter, Anthony Johnson; Speer Family, The; Swanee River Boys

Reference and Further Reading

Blackwell, Lois S. *The Wings of the Dove: The Story of Gospel Music in America.* Marceline, MO: Donning, 1978.

Goff, James R. *Close Harmony: A History of Southern Gospel.* Chapel Hill, NC: The University of North Carolina Press, 2002.

Miller, Zell. *They Heard Georgia Singing, Vol. 2.* Franklin Springs, GA: Advocate Press, 1984.

Discography

Lee Roy Abernathy with Homeland Harmony Quartet (and Happy Two where indicated), 78-rpm recordings:
"Burning of the Winecoff Hotel"/"Newborn Feeling" (White Church 1097); "Checking Up on My Payments"/"Sin Ain't Nothing but Blues" (White Church 1099); "Filled with Glory Divine"/"Jacob's Ladder" (Happy Two) (Quartet 1060); "Filled with Glory Divine"/"Television" (Quartet 0012); "Gospel Boogie (Everybody's Gonna Have a Wonderful Time Up

There)"/"You Can't Believe Everything You Hear" (King 4223); "Gospel Boogie (Everybody's Gonna Have a Wonderful Time Up There)"/"You Can't Believe Everything You Hear" (White Church 1084); "Hallelujah Boogie" (Happy Two)/"Georgia Boy" (Shorty Bradford) (Quartet 0020); "I Know the Lord"/"Tis So Sweet to Trust Him" (White Church 1098); "I Want to Know More"/"On That Judgement Day" (White Church 1082); "Oh What an Awful Day"/"Everybody Ought to Know" (White Church 1083); "Television"/"Shorty's Banjo" (Shorty Bradford) (Quartet 1061); "You Can't Believe Everything"/"Gospel Boogie" (Quartet 0013).

ACKLEY, ALFRED

(b. January 21, 1887, Spring Hill, PA; d. July 3, 1960, Whittier, CA)

Although a Presbyterian minister by calling, Alfred Henry Ackley is chiefly remembered as a composer of evangelical hymns that were widely admired in the 1930s. He is credited as the author of more than 1,500 religious and secular songs, many of which were published through his lifelong association with the Rodeheaver Publishing Company. (His older brother, Bentley DeForest Ackley [1872–1958], was also an accomplished composer and editor with the Rodeheaver Company and the author of more than 3,000 gospel songs.)

Ackley's own musical credentials were of a professional order. He received his first musical training as a child from his father and later studied composition at the Royal Academy of Music in London. Ackley was also known as a highly skilled cellist.

In 1914, he was ordained into the ministry following graduation from Westminster Theological Seminary in Maryland. After serving in pastorates in Pennsylvania and California, he worked for several years with the evangelist Billy Sunday. In recognition of his many contributions to the field of gospel music, Ackley was awarded an honorary doctor of sacred music degree from John Brown University in Arkansas.

Ackley's most famous song, "He Lives," remains a popular hymn today. Anecdotal evidence suggests that Ackley wrote the song in response to the query of a sincere young Jewish student who had asked Ackley, "Why should I worship a dead Jew?"

DAVID BEAUDOUIN

Reference and Further Reading

Ackley, Alfred Henry. http://www.cyberhymnal.org/bio/a/c/ackley_ah.htm.
Sanville, George. *Forty Gospel Hymn Stories*, 34–35. Winona Lake, IN: Rodeheaver-Hall Mack Co., 1945.

ACKLEY, BENTLEY DEFOREST

(b. September 27, 1872; d. September 3, 1958)

Prolific writer and editor of gospel hymns, reportedly producing over 2,000 songs. Born in Spring Hill, Pennsylvania, he was the older brother of Alfred Henry Ackley (1887–1960), who was also a prolific gospel songwriter, and the two worked together in Homer A. Rodeheaver's publishing company. As a child Bentley demonstrated a prodigious interest in music, becoming proficient on the melodeon, piano, reed organ, alto horn, cornet, piccolo, and clarinet. His first job, however, was as a stenographer in New York and Philadelphia; he acquired after these positions studying shorthand and typing.

During the 1890s, he published several secular songs, none of which found lasting success. In 1908 he became private secretary and pianist to evangelist Billy Sunday, remaining with him until 1915. During these seven years he began to compose gospel songs. In 1910 he joined with Rodeheaver in founding the Rodeheaver–Ackley publishing company in Chicago. He, his brother, and Charles H. Gabriel supplied a majority of the firm's copyrighted publications. B. D. Ackley remained with the firm until his death. The most popular of Ackley's gospel songs are "If Your Heart Keeps Right," "I Walk with the King," and "Sunrise." Some of his other songs include "Jesus, I Am Coming Home," "Mother's Prayers Have Followed Me," "I Would Be Like Jesus," "In the Service of the King," "Somebody Knows," "Jesus," "Surrender," and "God Understands."

W. K. McNEIL

Reference and Further Reading

McLoughlin, W. G. *Billy Sunday Was His Real Name*. Chicago: University of Chicago Press, 1955.
Porter, Thomas Henry. Homer Alvan Rodeheaver (1880–1955): Evangelistic Musician and Publisher. Ph.D. diss., New Orleans Baptist Theological Seminary, 1981.

ACUFF, ROY

(b. September 15, 1903, Maynardsville, TN; d. November 25, 1992)

Singer, composer, publisher, bandleader. Known to generations of fans as "the King of Country Music," Roy Claxton Acuff was for years the cornerstone of Nashville's Grand Ole Opry, where he served as a spokesman for country music. In the 1940s, his records were constantly on the best-seller charts, and his formation of the Acuff–Rose publishing company

Roy Acuff. Photo courtesy Frank Driggs Collection.

in mid-1942 launched the Nashville country music publishing industry. Although his own repertoire ranged from classics such as "Wabash Cannonball" and "The Precious Jewel" to modern songs such as Eddy Raven's "Back in the Country," he routinely performed, recorded, and wrote gospel songs, and these form the backbone of his musical legacy.

Born in Union County north of Knoxville, Acuff was early exposed to a rich variety of Appalachian music, from fiddle tunes to old ballads. His father was a lawyer and a Missionary Baptist preacher, and young Roy dutifully attended the rural singing schools sponsored by teachers employed by publishing companies such as Vaughan, Teacher's, and Showalter. His greater interest, though, lay in fiddling and singing, and soon he had landed a job on Knoxville radio station WROL, with his string band he called the Crazy Tennesseans.

One of the popular groups on the station was a gospel quartet called the Black Shirts, which was made up of young men from Bob Jones University in southeast Tennessee. They featured a song called "The Great Speckled Bird," an odd song based on a verse from Jeremiah, chapter 12, verse 9: "Mine heritage is unto me as a speckled bird." When Acuff learned the quartet was leaving the station, he paid them twenty-five cents to copy down the words for him, and he started using the song. The audience response was overwhelming, and in October 1936 the American Record Company offered him a recording contract, largely on the strength of the "Bird." Acuff later joked, "They didn't want me—they wanted the Great Speckled Bird." Under the misspelled title "Great Speckle Bird," it became Acuff's first release—released the same month it was recorded—and went on to become his career song and a gospel standard.

The authorship of the song is tangled and confused. It was picked up by radio singers throughout the South and was published in an M. M. Cole songbook in 1937 with composer credits to Reverend Guy Smith, a singing evangelist from Springfield, Missouri, and Smith is generally still given credit for the song today. However, recent research has suggested that the song was written by a Hurricane, West Virginia, songwriter named Sara Dillon, as early as 1926, and it was published as a single-sheet "ballet" that year and in a songbook in 1928 by the Church of God Publishing House in Cleveland. The Church of God operated Bob Jones University, where the Black Shirts were from, and the song specifically mentions "the great Church of God." Acuff used for his melody the folk tune "I Am Thinking Tonight of My Blue Eyes," although Smith and later recordings used a different melody similar to that of "Old Ties." The record sold so well that, in March 1937, Acuff

recorded "Great Speckle Bird #2," in which he used other stanzas from the Dillon song that he presumably got from the Black Shirts. In 1938, when he auditioned for the Grand Ole Opry, Acuff sang the song, and the audience response won him a place on the Opry roster.

Throughout the late 1930s, Acuff sprinkled his recording sessions with other gospel songs: "Tell Mother I Will Be There"; "The Automobile of Life" (1938), a 1925 song written by a woman from Kansas; "That Beautiful Picture" (1938), a favorite encore on the Opry; "Further Along" (1940), a singing convention song popularized in the mid-1930s; and "The Precious Jewel" (1940), a rewriting of "The Hills of Roane County." On most of these, Acuff did not use a quartet format but rather often sang verses solo, joined by Pete Kirby (Bashful Brother Oswald) doing what people of the time called a "screaming tenor."

For a time in the late 1930s and early 1940s, Acuff had a publishing arrangement with R. E. Winsett, a veteran shape-note convention book publisher from Dayton, Tennessee, and a number of his songs appeared in Winsett books of the time. Around 1940, Acuff also published his own little songbook, which he sold to fans for twenty-five cents; this also included many gospel songs, including a number that he was apparently singing at the time but did not get around to recording until years later. When his 1941 recording "Just Inside the Pearly Gates" was noted by *Billboard* magazine, making it one of the first country records to receive national trade paper attention, New York publishers began to offer him contracts. Always a shrewd businessman, Acuff felt if his song properties were that valuable, he could do better by organizing his own publishing company. This he did in 1942, in partnership with Fred Rose, an experienced publisher and songwriter who was located in Nashville. The result would become one of the largest publishing houses in the country, Acuff–Rose.

As Acuff's popularity soared in the 1940s, he began to rely on his new partner, Fred Rose, for new gospel songs written in the older style. This resulted in the 1944 chart hit "The Prodigal Son," the up-tempo "Wait for the Light to Shine" (1944), "I Heard a Silver Trumpet" (1943), and "I'll Reap My Harvest in Heaven" (1942). The 1945 hit "That Glory Bound Train" merged Acuff's two favorite themes: salvation and trains; it was written by Acuff with Odell McLeod. Perhaps the most lachrymose of these songs was "Wreck on the Highway" (1942), which described a scene where "whiskey and blood ran together" but "I didn't hear nobody pray." After some initial confusion, Acuff–Rose discovered the composer was a North Carolina textile worker named Dorsey Dixon.

The last of the great Acuff gospel songs was "I Saw the Light" (1947), written by Hank Williams from an old Chuck Wagon Gang song, "He Set Me Free." Acuff actually beat Williams in recording it first, and it became a show closer for him for the rest of his career. It actually charted again in 1971, when Acuff rerecorded it with the Nitty Gritty Dirt Band.

Throughout his long career, Roy Acuff remained a staunch defender of traditional country music, with its high harmonies and acoustic instrumentation. To the end, he considered gospel music a cornerstone of that musical style.

CHARLES K. WOLFE

Reference and Further Reading

Schlappi, Elizabeth. *Roy Acuff, Smoky Mountain Boy.* Reverend ed. Gretna, LA: Pelican, 1978.

Selected Discography

The Essential Roy Acuff (1936–1949).
Gospel Favorites.
King of Country Music (boxed set).

ADAMS, YOLANDA

(b. August 27, 1962, Houston, TX)

Singer Yolanda Adams was born into a family that ensured her exposure to a wide variety of musical genres. Her appreciation of a broad range of musical styles flourished as her mother, who had studied music in college, introduced Adams and her five siblings to jazz, gospel, and classical works. Today, Adams is one of the most prominent and versatile contemporary gospel artists in the world. It is difficult to categorize her performance style because she possesses the amazing ability to switch musical gears from song to song. From traditional gospel to a style heavily influenced by R&B, new jack, and jazz overtones, Adams delivers each with complete integrity in an emotionally charged delivery. She is credited with liberating gospel music's more formal, traditional image. In each recording she addresses social issues forthrightly. In the works of this former elementary teacher, the problems that plague the nation's youths are especially prevalent.

From the time she was thirteen Adams toured and performed with the Southeast Inspirational Choir. Composer/producer Thomas Whitfield recognized the genius in the young singer and offered her an opportunity to record her own solo album. The resultant project, *Just As I Am* (1988), was guided by

Whitfield and attracted widespread critical praise. Subsequent albums including *Through the Storm* (1991) and *More Than a Melody* (1995) established her as a force in gospel and R&B, and she won a host of awards including several Stellar Awards, two Soul Train Lady of Soul Award, two Grammys, and five NAACP Image Awards.

Adams soared to new heights with the 1999 release of *Mountain High . . . Valley Low*. The album featured the smash hit "Open My Heart" and spent much of the year at number one on *Billboard* magazine's Gospel and Contemporary Christian Charts, eventually selling over a million copies. Her subsequent albums, *Christmas with Yolanda Adams* (2000), the live release *The Experience* (2001), and *Believe* (2002), have further strengthened her position as one of gospel's best loved and most successful artists and one of the most talented singers in all of music. Since her debut in 1988, Adams has recorded an impressive number of projects.

DONNA M. COX

Discography

Through the Storm (1991, Verity Records); *Save the World* (1993, Verity Records); *More Than a Melody* (1995, Verity Records); *Live From Washington* (1996, Verity Records); *Songs from the Heart* (1996, Verity Records); *Mountain High . . . Valley Low* (1999, Elektra Records); *Christmas with Yolanda Adams* (2000, Elektra Records); *Believe* (2001, Elektra Records); *The Experience* (2001, Elektra Records); *Christmas with Yolanda and Clay Aiken* (2004, Atlantic Records); *Yolanda Adams Is Keeping the Faith* (2005, Atlantic Records); *Yolanda Adams Sings Praises in Celebration* (2005, Atlantic Records).

AKERS, DORIS

Doris Mae Akers (b. May 21, 1923, Brookfield, MO; d. July 26, 1995, Minneapolis, MN)

Highly regarded singer, choir director, music publisher, and composer of gospel music, sometimes referred to as "Mrs. Gospel Music." Akers showed an early aptitude for music, teaching herself to play piano by ear as a very small child and composing her first work, "Keep the Fire Burning in Me," a few years later. By her teens Akers had formed an ensemble called Dot Akers and Her Swingsters, which performed jazz and swing standards of the day. Akers moved to Los Angeles in the mid-1940s, and there she performed with the Sallie Martin Singers and later founded her own group, the Doris Akers Singers. In 1948 Akers and Dorothy Simmons formed the

Simmons–Akers Singers, which performed frequently and became one of the most important gospel groups of the late 1940s and 1950s.

Akers published hundreds of songs during her lifetime, and many of them may still be found in religious hymnals and songbooks of various religious denominations. Her first published composition was "A Double Portion of God's Love" in 1947, with Martin and Morris Music, and shortly thereafter Akers cofounded a publishing company with Simmons called the Simmons and Akers Music House. Beginning in the 1950s Akers also published with the white-owned publishing house Manna Music, effectively bridging the distinctly separate realms of black and white gospel music that were present at that time.

During the 1950s and 1960s Akers performed regularly as a solo artist and directed the Sky Pilot Choir. She was the creator of the so-called "Doris Akers/Sky Pilot sound," an innovative style of directing and arranging gospel choir music that continues to influence gospel music composition and direction today. Akers wrote or arranged many of the standards in gospel music from this period, and she recorded for the RCA, Capitol, and Christian Faith labels. Among her better-known compositions are "Sweet Sweet Spirit," "How Big Is God," "I Cannot Fail the Lord," and "Sweet Jesus," and she cowrote "Lord Don't Move That Mountain" with her long-time friend Mahalia Jackson. Several of Akers's songs were featured in movies or stage productions, including "Trouble" (*Praise House* and *Me and Bessie*) and "Lead Me Guide Me," which was sung by Elvis Presley in one of his final films. In the 1970s, Akers moved from Los Angeles but continued to perform gospel music in Columbus, Ohio. After relocating to Minneapolis in the 1980s, Akers served as choir director at Grace Temple Deliverance. In the late 1990s she was featured in gospel musician Bill Gaither's music videos *Old Friends* and *Turn Your Radio On*. Akers received several awards during her lifetime, including Gospel Composer of the Year (1961), and the Smithsonian Institution honored her songs and recordings with the accolade of "National Treasure." In 2001, Akers was posthumously inducted into the Gospel Music Association's Gospel Music Hall of Fame.

ERIN STAPLETON-CORCORAN

Reference and Further Reading

DjeDje, Jacqueline Cogdell. "Los Angeles Composers of African American Gospel Music: The First Generations." *American Music* 11, no. 4 (Winter 1993): 412–457.

Discography

Doris Akers/Sky Pilot Choir (1956, Sing).
Sing Praises Unto the Lord (1957, RCA Victor).
The Sky Pilot Choir, Vol. I (1958, Christian Faith Records).
The Sky Pilot Choir, Vol. II (1959, Christian Faith Records).
Doris Akers Sings (1960, Christian Faith).
Forever Faithful (1963, RCA Victor).

ALEXANDER, CHARLES McCALLUM

(b. October 24, 1867; d. October 13, 1920)

Charles "Charlie" McCallum Alexander was one of the two most important individuals—the other being Homer Rodeheaver—who established the model of the twentieth-century evangelistic musician and popularized gospel music around the world.

His connection with gospel music began in 1884 when he attended a revival service held by evangelist D. L. Moody and his song leader/soloist Ira Sankey. Six years later he matriculated at Moody Bible Institute in Chicago, the chief training ground for gospel musicians. After graduation he spent eight years with evangelist Milan B. Williams on the "Kerosene Circuit" of the Midwest, perfecting his approach to leading congregations in singing the popular religious music of the age: gospel songs.

In 1902 Alexander joined evangelist Reuben A. Torrey for a tour of Australia. There the gregarious and flamboyant Charlie with the distinctly Southern accent became a prominent feature of the revival meetings, holding popular "services of song" in which he treated the enthusiastic crowds of thousands like a well-trained choir.

Part of his success came from his association with pianist Robert Harkness, whom he met while in Australia. Harkness had no previous knowledge of how to play church music, and he began improvising accompaniments on the piano to make the gospel songs more interesting. Alexander quickly realized that Harkness had discovered a highly effective style for playing gospel music on the piano—an instrument that proved to be much better suited for accompanying gospel music than the traditional organ.

During the next decade the two men helped popularize a new paradigm for church music wherein singing was led by a highly visible song leader standing in front of the congregation, employing standard conducting patterns to coordinate the music of congregation, choir, and musical instruments, with the piano being prominent. This model clearly differed from the traditional approach wherein an organ, usually placed in a choir loft above and behind the congregation, led the singing (often with the help of a choir).

One of the reasons requiring this new approach was the nature of gospel songs. Whereas most of the hymns had been rhythmically more straightforward, many of the new gospel songs were much more fluid rhythmically, often requiring holds or tempo changes during the songs themselves. This newer style clearly required a leader to keep everything together, and Alexander proved to be the perfect combination of conductor, cheerleader, and master teacher.

In addition to his leading congregational singing, Alexander became involved in editing and publishing song collections for the revival meetings. *Alexander's Revival Songs* (1902) was the first of his productions and continued for nearly two decades, with *Alexander's Hymns Nos. 3* (1915) achieving worldwide fame and remaining in publication for nearly a century. Part of Alexander's success in gospel hymn publishing resulted from his relationship with songwriters such as Charlie Tillman and Charles Gabriel.

It was Gabriel's lilting "Glory Song" ("When all my labors and trials are o'er") that Alexander adopted as a kind of theme song and helped popularize literally around the world. For many of these songs Alexander obtained international publishing copyrights, thus ensuring his collections a long life.

Because a number of books were also published about the life and work of Alexander, his influence became a powerful model for future gospel musicians to emulate. For with Charlie, people loved to sing the gospel songs and hymns that he made come alive in a new and powerful way. His legacy helped spawn nearly a century of revivalism in which gospel hymnody was one of its most vital components.

MEL R. WILHOIT

Reference and Further Reading

Alexander, Helen Cadbury; J. Kennedy Maclean. *Charles M. Alexander: A Romance of Song and Soul-Winning.* New York: Marshall Brothers, Ltd., 1920.

Davis, George. *Twice Around the World with Alexander: Prince of Gospel Singers.* New York: The Christian Herald, 1907.

Wilhoit, Mel R. "Alexander the Great: Or, Just Plain Charlie." *The Hymn: A Journal of Congregational Song* 46, no. 2 (April 1995): 20–28.

Discography

Yesterday's Voices: The Actual Voices of Many of the World's Greatest Christian Leaders (Word Records #W3076-LP; complilation), side 2, band 9, with Alexander singing "Glory Song."

ALLEN, RANCE

(b. November 19, 1948, Monroe, MI)

Rance Allen fronted the first modern gospel group to take secular songs and secular performance practices and recast them with religious lyrics. In doing so, the Rance Allen Group was able to cross over to the soul charts and proved to be influential in what was referred to as the contemporary Christian music movement, epitomized by crossover artists such as the Winans and Andrae Crouch.

Raised in the Church of God in Christ (COGIC), Allen started playing piano at the age of seven. A few years later Allen took up guitar. At the time, Sister Rosetta Tharpe and Reverend Utah Smith were largely responsible for making the electric guitar the instrument of choice in the COGIC church. Allen's mother, Emma Pearl Allen, partially inspired by Rosetta Tharpe, also played the electric guitar and passed much of Tharpe's incendiary, church-wrecking style onto her son.

In the late 1960s, Allen began playing church programs in and around Detroit fronting the Rance Allen Group, which included his brothers Tom and Steve on drums and bass guitar. A third brother, Esau, would play percussion with the group at various times in the 1970s. In 1969 the Rance Allen Group recorded a single for a small independent label, Reflect Records, which is owned by their manager. Two years later, they entered a Detroit radio contest, where they won first prize singing Tharpe's "Up Above My Head." One of the judges was legendary black promotion man Dave Clark. Impressed by what he heard, Clark took Allen to the Memphis-based soul label Stax Records, whose vice president, Al Bell, proceeded to sign Allen and set up a gospel subsidiary, Gospel Truth, to release recordings by the Rance Allen Group.

The Rance Allen Group's three *Gospel Truth* albums, issued between 1972 and 1974, included gospel treatments of the Temptations' "Just My Imagination" (retitled "Just My Salvation"), Stevie Wonder's "For Once in My Life," and Archie Bell's "There's Gonna Be a Showdown." After Stax went bankrupt in 1975, the Rance Allen Group recorded for Capitol, a reconstituted Stax, Myrrh, Bellmark, and Tyscot. Along the way, the group placed five singles on the *Billboard* rhythm and blues charts. In 2004, the group was nominated for a Grammy for their *Live Experience* album, which featured guest appearances by contemporary gospel stars Fred Hammond, LaShun Pace, and Kirk Franklin.

ROB BOWMAN

Reference and Further Reading

Allen, Rance. Phone interview by author (tape recording). May 21, 2003.
———. Phone interview by author. December 27, 2004.

Discography

The Rance Allen Group (1972, Gospel Truth LP GT-14001).
Truth Is Where It's At (1973, Gospel Truth LP GT-2709).
Brothers (1974, Gospel Truth LP GT-3502).
A Soulful Experience (1975, Gospel Truth LP GT-4207).
Live Experience (2004, Tyscot CD).

ALLEN, RICHARD

(b. February 14, 1760, Philadelphia, PA; d. March 26, 1831, Philadelphia, PA)

African American religious leader, founder and first bishop of the African Methodist Episcopal (AME) Church, and hymnbook compiler, Richard Allen was one of the most influential figures in nineteenth century America for the black community.

Born in Philadelphia, Pennsylvania, on February 14, 1760, Richard Allen was the slave of distinguished lawyer and Chief Justice of the Commonwealth (1774–1777) Benjamin Chew. Allen was later sold to Stokley Sturgis, a farmer near Dover, Delaware, where he was brought up and converted to Methodism. Shortly afterwards, he began preaching, and as a result of his religious dedication and conviction, his master allowed Allen to preach in his house, where even he was converted under Allen's proselytizing. Once he was able to pay for his freedom, Allen and his brother found work cutting wood, working in a brickyard, and hauling salt during the Revolutionary War, all the while preaching and traveling to neighboring states whenever possible. Allen traveled to small towns and rural settlements in Pennsylvania, Delaware, New York, Maryland, and even as far south as South Carolina, bringing him into contact with other leaders and founders of early American Methodism.

In 1786 Allen began preaching regularly at St. George Methodist Church in Philadelphia, where the number of black worshippers attending services increased tenfold. The suggestion to establish a separate place of worship was made but was quickly rejected by the white majority congregation and elders. In 1787, fellow black minister Absalom Jones was asked to leave the altar of St. George and led the remainder of the congregation out of the church to worship independent of white oppression. This movement led to the formation of the Free African Society, one of the first black mutual aid societies in the United States, and the eventual construction of the African Episcopal Church of St. Thomas, which later fell under the direction of Absalom Jones.

Wanting to remain faithful to Methodist doctrines, Allen separated from the African Episcopal Church and established Bethel African Church in 1794. In 1799, Allen was ordained deacon, but despite having independent congregations, white elders still maintained control over the black church. After many years of struggling to achieve total separation, the church was granted independence in 1816. Later that year, several black Methodists came together and decided upon the title of African Methodist Episcopal Church, and Richard Allen was ordained the first bishop.

During this time of separation Allen wanted to publish his own hymnal specific to the worshipping needs of black Methodists. In 1801 Allen published *A Collection of Spiritual Songs and Hymns Selected from Various Authors*, the first hymnal published exclusively for use in the black church. While Allen could have easily adopted the Methodist hymnal, he instead collected hymns that appealed to black Americans. The first edition of Allen's 1801 hymnal contained fifty-four hymn texts, without musical notation, drawn mainly from the collections of Isaac Watts, Charles and John Wesley, and other popular hymnodists from Methodist and Baptist churches. Like many other hymnals of the time, Allen's collection was in the form of a "pocket" hymnal, without any guidelines to the tunes or melodies of the text, although it has been said that many of the hymns were sung to familiar tunes used in other churches and, in some cases, even originally composed or adapted from popular tunes. A second edition of the hymnal was released later in 1801, entitled *A Collection of Hymns and Spiritual Songs, from Various Authors*, which included ten more texts, some composed by Richard Allen himself.

In 1818 Allen published the first official hymnbook of the AME church, which was also the first published document produced by the oldest black-owned publishing company in the country, the AME Book Concern. The *African Methodist Pocket Hymn Book* contained 314 hymns, and, of those, only fifteen were carried over from the 1801 volume, not including Allen's own "See! How the Nations Rage Together." Following the publication of the 1818 hymnal, other hymnals were periodically published but without significant changes. It was not until the publication of the 1889 hymnal that musical notation was included.

The historical significance of the publication of Allen's early hymnals is an essential component to understanding the black church and the black religious experience in America. Although Methodist and Episcopal doctrines permeated much of early African Methodist Episcopal Church practices, the music was defined primarily by the African American experience. Richard Allen served at Bethel AME in Philadelphia until his death on March 26, 1831, and he was buried in Philadelphia.

SARAH ARTHUR

See also Jones, Absalom

Reference and Further Reading

Payne, Daniel A. *History of the African Methodist Episcopal Church*. Nashville, TN: Publishing House of the A.M.E. Sunday-School Union, [1891] 1968.
Southern, Eileen. *The Music of Black Americans: A History*. 3rd ed. New York: W. W. Norton and Company, 1997.
Wright, Richard R., Jr. *The Encyclopaedia of the African Methodist Episcopal Church* 2nd ed. [microform]. Philadelphia: Book Concern of the A.M.E. Church, 1947.

ANDERSON, ROBERT

(b. 1919, Chicago, IL; d. June 1995, Chicago, IL)

Anderson began singing in church as a boy and in the early 1930s was one of the first members of the Roberta Martin Singers considered as the best mixed (male–female) gospel group of the time in Chicago, thanks to Roberta Martin's gift for writing lyrical songs (she was also a great piano player). Anderson was probably her best singer, but he was also ambitious. In 1939, he left the group and began singing duets with R. L. Knowles, a Kansas City singer who was appointed the lead singer of the First Church of Deliverance, the famous Spiritualist church of Chicago led at the time by the flamboyant Reverend Clarence Cobb.

Knowles and Anderson are credited with bringing the "ad-lib" style to church singing, with jazz-influenced runs, free-spirited melisma, and influences of secular music, whether pop, blues, or swing. Anderson was even called the "Bing Crosby of gospel," because he was crooning and delivered an effortless phrasing; he also had a great sense of timing. Knowles and Anderson successfully toured California, and Anderson once mentioned that he even had played a small role in *Gone With the Wind*! He came back to Chicago to open a music studio, The Good Shepherd, where he instructed singers and musicians, publishing also his own compositions. In 1943 he stole the show at the National Baptist Convention with his own rendition of his song "Something Within." In 1946 he made a tour of the South and sang on the radio in Birmingham, Alabama, with a tremendous success.

Back in Chicago, he formed his own group modeled on Roberta Martin's, but he hired only female singers—the best he could find in Chicago and Gary, Indiana. First, he called them the Good Shepherd Singers (like his studio) and then the Gospel Caravans.

By the time he recorded for United Records, the group was composed of Albertina Walker, Elyse Yancey, Ora Lee Hopkins, and Nellie Grace Daniels. It was a very strong ensemble, whose only rivals were the Ward Singers and the Davis Sisters in Philadelphia. Each member could lead, and they influenced many groups and singers, such as Dorothy Love Coates and her Gospel Harmonettes, James Cleveland (who played piano for some years with Anderson), and quartet leads Sam Cooke, Johnnie Taylor, and Lou Rawls, who were trained by him and carried the Anderson style into pop music. He started a long friendship with Mahalia Jackson, who sang a lot of his compositions. In April 1952, he left the Caravans and Albertina Walker became the group's manager, leading it to stardom.

Anderson spent some years successfully leading a male group, but his popularity declined with the rise of Contemporary Gospel, and he went to work for a florist. In the 1980s he recorded for Spirit Feel. In early 1995 he entered the hospital for a by pass operation but it failed because he also had diabetes. He suffered a stroke and some months later, in June 1995, he died; the funeral was held at the Greater Harvest Baptist Church, the choir of which he had once conducted.

ROBERT SACRÉ

See also Caravans; Cleveland, James; Cooke, Sam; Jackson, Mahalia; Martin, Roberta; Walker, Albertina; Ward Trio (Ward Singers)

Reference and Further Reading

Boyer, Horace Clarence. *How Sweet the Sound: The Golden Age of Gospel*. Washington, DC: Elliott & Clark, 1995.
Hayes, J. Cedric; Laughton, Robert. *Gospel Records 1943–1969. A Black Music Discography*, 2 vols. London: Record Information Services, 1992.
Heilbut, Tony. *The Gospel Sound: Good News and Bad Times*. New York: Limelight, 1985.
Reagon, Bernice Johnson, ed. *We'll Understand It Better By and By. Pioneering African American Gospel Composers*. Washington, DC: Smithsonian Institution Press, 1992.

Discography

The Great Gospel Men (1993, Shanachie/Spirit Feel [USA] CD 6005); *Working the Road: The Golden Age of Chicago Gospel* (1997, Delmark CD 702).

ANDREWS GOSPEL SINGERS, THE

Ola Jean (b. December 12, 1929)
Myrta Sue (b. 1932)
Paula (b. 1934)
Sylvia (b. 1936)

In the early 1960s, the Andrews Gospel Singers and their leader Ola Jean Andrews represented what was called "progressive gospel." The term referred to elements of blues and jazz that imbued the music. As a popular performing group in the San Francisco Bay area, they were admired by the young Edwin Hawkins, who picked up on their modern, high, "fluted" sound. The style appealed to many white as well as black churchgoers. With her musical expertise and passion for an advanced gospel music, Ola Jean became an incentive also for Andrae Crouch. The Andrews Gospel Singers were, in turn, influenced by older groups such as the Clara Ward Singers and the Gospel Harmonettes; The Andrewses can therefore be regarded as a link between the traditional and the contemporary black gospel styles.

The nucleus of the Andrews Gospel Singers was four sisters: Ola Jean, Myrta Sue, Paula Marie, and Sylvia Lois. With the eldest, Ola Jean, as director and pianist, they were formed in 1950. Myrta Sue was eventually replaced by Jeanne King, and they were augmented with two cousins, Donna and Flora Daggao.

The Andrews sisters moved with their parents in 1939 from Eldorado, Arkansas, to the San Francisco Bay area. Mother Leceola Tobin Andrews was a singer and choir director, and their father Joseph Henry Andrews became a deacon and Sunday school superintendent at the Eighth and Peralta Church of God in Christ (COGIC). Ola Jean devoted herself most deeply to the church's music activities. At an early age she was encouraged by her parents to play the piano. She heard her uncle play honky-tonk music and also favored big band jazz and boogie-woogie pianists on the radio. At fifteen, Ola Jean decided to completely deliver herself to Christ. Of the other sisters, alto Myrta Sue played keyboard, Paula Marie was a Richard Williamson– trained soprano, and Sylvia Lois had sung from the age of seven.

The Andrews sisters started in a children's group called the Sunshine Band at Emmanuel Church of God in Christ. " . . . [W]e were asked to sing in other churches. We entered many contests, winning first place each time. One such contest was given by KDIA. As winners of that contest . . . we were awarded a fifteen-minute broadcast every Sunday afternoon (live) for three years."

Ola Jean's piano playing was influenced by Herbert "Pee Wee" Pickard of the Gospel Harmonettes, James Cleveland of the Caravans, and her greatest idol, Clara Ward. Ward often rehearsed in the Andrews home. By watching her, Ola Jean learned how to teach harmony. Ola Jean took private piano lessons and studied music at City College in San Francisco. She also became a music major graduate of Career Academy of Broadcasting.

During the 1950s, the Andrews sang at many important events arranged by the churches, and they soon became stars in the Bay Area. They appeared in the Bay Area Youth Fellowship under the direction of Herman Harper and at F. D. Haynes's Third Baptist Church in San Francisco. The sisters moved to Berkeley and in 1958 Ola Jean became principal choir director for the Choir of the Ephesians COGIC. Reid's Records in Berkeley sponsored choir competitions and the Andrews won the Best Group trophies several times. They also participated in the yearly gospel fests at Oakland Auditorium. The Andrewses opened one year for C. L. Franklin and his young daughter Aretha. The Clara Ward Singers were also on the program.

At the same time Ola Jean was developing music programs at the Ephesians COGIC—where the famous Hawkins family were members of the assembly— Edwin Hawkins often played organ for the Inspirational Choir. Hawkins adored the Andrewses and learned a lot from listening to them. The girls had appeared at the International Young Congress of the COGIC in Cincinnati, Ohio, in 1959. Then they were recruited to the A. A. Allen's revival meetings in Miracle Valley, Hereford, Arizona. The meetings were broadcast and recorded. The Andrews were featured on at least six Miracle Revival LPs in 1960–1961. They also appeared on television in Hollywood with their idols Dorothy Love Coates and the Gospel Harmonettes. A successful tour of the Eastern and Southern states followed. Another milestone in their career was their participation in drummer/jazz singer Jon Hendrick's show Evolution of the Blues at the Monterey Jazz Festival in 1960.

Several female gospel groups at this time—for example, the Clara Ward Singers, the Gospel Pearls, and the Meditation Singers—had adjusted their presentation for performances in night clubs. Some even forsook their gospel roots and became pop singers. The Andrews were approached by Columbia Records, who offered them a recording contract if they would only sing secular words to gospel melodies. They refused.

In 1961, the Andrewses sang on two gospel songs with folk/jazz singer Barbara Dane for Capitol Records. The company soon recorded the Andrewses on their own and in 1963 issued *Open Your Heart* (Capitol LP 1959). The album contains a tasteful mixture of Negro spirituals, gospel standards, and a few compositions by Herbert Pickard and Ola Jean. The record exposes the polished, immaculate, and yet exuberant and soulful sounds of the Andrews Gospel Singers.

Although they did several out-of-state tours, family affairs and commitments in their church took over, and the Andrews Gospel Singers dissolved in 1970. However, Ola Jean continued on her own. Between 1973 and 1978, she produced a half-hour morning program on radio station KRE, titled "The Happy Sounds of a Forever Life." From 1979 to 1981, she was music director of a church (Christlicher Zentrum) in Berlin, Germany. During the period from 1982 to 2004 Ola Jean was minister of music and psalmist in both Europe and the United States and an in-prison seminar instructor with Chuck Colson.

Ola Jean returns to her Berlin church every so often. Of the original group, Donna Daggao has passed away, but even in the twenty-first century the Andrews Gospel Singers come together now and then for reunion concerts.

PER NOTINI

Reference and Further Reading

Andrews, Ola Jean. "At a Glance—Who I Am and What I Do." Presentation, 2004. Capitol LP ST 1959. Liner notes, 1963.

DjeDje, Jacqueline Cogdell. "The California Black Gospel Music Tradition." In *California Soul—Music of African Americans in the West*, edited by Jacqueline Cogdell DjeDje and Eddie S. Meadows. Los Angeles: University of California Press, 1998.

Nations, Opal Louis. "Open Your Heart—The Story of Ola Jean Andrews & the Andrews Sisters." Essay, 2002.

Discography

The Andrews Sisters

He Lives (Miracle Revival LP 129). The Andrews Sisters (vocal) with David Davis (piano?), unknown (organ) Miracle Valley, Hereford, Arizona, 1960.

He's All Right (Miracle Revival LP 143). The Andrews Sisters (vocal), Ola Jean Andrews (piano/vocal) with Gene Martin (vocal) and David Davis (organ), Miracle Valley, Hereford, Arizona, 1961.

He's Coming Home Again (Miracle Revival LP 139). The Andrews Sisters (vocal) with Ola Jean Andrews (piano/vocal), unknown (organ), Miracle Valley, Hereford, Arizona, *I Shall Not Be Moved* (Miracle Revival LP 127). The Andrews Sisters (vocal) with Ola Jean Andrews (piano/vocal) and the A. A. Allen Revival Choir, Miracle Valley, Hereford, Arizona, 1960.

The Andrews Gospel Singers

Does Jesus Care (Capitol T/ST 1959); *He Satisfies; He's a Mighty God* (4995); *I Won't Turn Back* (4995); *If You Miss Me Here; Joshua Fit the Battle of Jericho; The Miracle; Open Your Heart; Soon I Will Be Done; Walk*

Over God's Heaven. Ola Jean Andrews (piano, vocal, arrangement), Sylvia Lois Andrews (lead vocal), Paula Marie Andrews (vocal), Donna Daggao (lead vocal), Flora Daggao, Norma J. King (vocal) unknown (bass, drums, tambourines); probably Los Angeles, May 1963.

Don't Forget to Pray; Faith (Capitol T/ST 1959). Same group as previous entry except organ player unknown; probably Los Angeles, January 1963.

ANDREWS, INEZ

(b. October 19, 1929/1935, Birmingham, AL)

This contralto lead vocalist, nicknamed "Songbird," was a main figure in gospel music for more than three decades, working with the Caravans as well as having a significant solo career. Andrews was known as much for her impeccable ability to blend with a choir as for her ability to be an aggressive lead vocalist. Her lead vocal sound is described as reverent, effusive, and sometimes "shrieking" with her passion for her music. She is most commonly recognized for her hits "Lord, Don't Move That Mountain," "The Need of Prayer," "The Healer," and "I'm Glad About It."

Andrews was a child prodigy but started her more formal singing career with the Raymond Raspberry Singers and the Original Gospel Harmonettes.

Andrews gained her wider appreciation singing with Albertina Walker's Caravans, one of the most popular touring gospel acts of the late 1950s and early 1960s. The Caravans featured a constant rotation of some of the best female gospel singers of the era, with Andrews joining in 1958. She and Shirley Caesar performed together as the lead voices, gaining immense popularity.

Andrews left the Caravans in 1962 to pursue solo initiatives. One of the most significant record-label owners and producers of the era, Don Robey, who gave her the nickname "Songbird," signed her to his new subsidiary of the same name (Songbird) part of Duke–Peacock (Gospel) Records. Her magnanimous vocal style helped forge the style of the label, which also signed other famous gospel acts such as the Jackson Southernaires, the Williams Brothers, the Pilgrim Outlets, and the Reverend Oris Mays.

Andrews recorded and performed regularly with her four backup singers, the Andrewettes, throughout the 1960s. In 1973, she had her first crossover breakthrough with the release of "Lord, Don't Move That Mountain," which hit #48 on the black singles chart.

Andrews exhibited the ultimate staying power as a recording artist, having top-ranked albums across various charts over three decades. In addition to "Lord, Don't Move That Mountain," she returned in 1988 with *If Jesus Came to Your Town Today,* which rose to #31 on the top gospel album chart. Her last major hit came in 1992 when she recorded with the Thompson Community Singers for the release of *Raise a Nation,* which made it to #30 on the top gospel album chart.

Andrews' style has influenced many, ranging from Shirley Brown to Vanessa Bell Armstrong to Cassietta George. And although Andrews has not won a Dove Award or been inducted into the Gospel Music Hall of Fame, her presence and contribution to the fabric of gospel music cannot be denied.

MARGARET B. FISHER

See also Caesar, Shirley; Caravans; Original Gospel Harmonettes; Williams Brothers

Reference and Further Reading

Ankeny, Jason. "All Music Guide: The Caravans." http://www.allmusic.com (2003).

Callahan, Mike and David Edwards. "Duke/Peacock/Back Beat Album Discographies." http://www.bsnpubs.com/robey.html (accessed September 4, 1997).

Callahan, Mike, and David Edwards. "Songbird Album Discographies." http://www.bsnpubs.com/songbird.html (accessed November 24, 2003).

Collins, Nikki, Bob Laughton, and Maureen Quinlan. *Black Gospel: Classic Recordings of the Gospel Sound.* 1985.

Wynn, Ron. "All Music Guide: Inez Andrews." http://www.allmusic.com (accessed 2003).

Discography

The Need Prayer (1963, Songbird SBLP-200); *Lord, Don't Move That Mountain* (1972, Jewel); *Jehovah Is His Name* (1986, Jewel); *The Two Sides of Inez Andrews* (1987, Shanachie LP 6019); *If Jesus Came to Your Town Today* (1988, Miracle); *I Made a Step in the Right Direction,* (1990, Savoy); *Inez Andrews* (1990, Savoy); *Raise Up a Nation* (1991, Word/Epic); *Shine On Me* (1991, MCA); *Headline News* (1999, MCA); *Close to Thee* (Songbird, SBLP-213); *Letter to Jesus* (Songbird SBLP-201).

ANDRUS, BLACKWOOD & COMPANY

Sherman Andrus (dates unknown)
Terry Blackwood (dates unknown)

Gospel group popular in the 1970s formed by Sherman Andrus and Terry Blackwood, former members of the Imperials. Blackwood had been the lead singer for both the Imperials and the reorganized Stamps Quartet. While with the Imperials, the two men had been experimenting together; their efforts resulted in the Imperials' increased popularity. After departing from that group, they formed their own band with

Karen Voegtin (vocalist), Bill Egtlin (keyboards and vocals), Bob Villareal (guitar and vocals), Tim Marsh (drums), and Rocky Laughlin (bass). This aggregation debuted on Greentree Records in 1977 with *Grand Opening.*

After this album became a hit on contemporary Christian music charts, it was followed in 1979 by *Following You,* which featured gospel songs by Phil Johnson and Reba and Dony McGuire, among others. Since the 1970s both men have remained active, Blackwood working with his sister Kaye in Memphis and Andrus performing as a solo act on college campuses in Oklahoma.

W. K. MCNEIL

Reference and Further Reading

Terrell, Bob. *The Music Men: The Story of Professional Gospel Quartet Singing.* Asheville, NC: 1990.

Discography

Grand Opening (1977, Greentree).
Following You (1979, Greentree).

ANGELIC GOSPEL SINGERS

Since 1944, the traditional Angelic Gospel Singers (the Angelics) have written and sung spiritually inspiring songs. The Angelic Gospel Singers are the longest consistently selling female gospel group in African American history. Margaret Wells Allison, her sister Josephine Wells McDowell, and friends Ella Mae Norris and Lucille Shird formed the group. Norris, Shird, and Allison had been members of the Spiritual Echoes of Philadelphia.

The Angelics started singing in the Philadelphia area. They performed at revivals, local churches, and conventions. These women wore robes for special occasions, over plain dresses or black skirts and white blouses. They accepted "free-will offerings." The Angelics never sang in nightclubs or wore flashy clothes. During the Golden era of gospel music (1945–1955), they began to perform for audiences that were willing to pay an admission. Male gospel groups were prominent and well received; however, women groups were told they needed to stay home with their families. The Angelics' travels outside Philadelphia began in Asheville, North Carolina, Shird's home town. They then traveled to Greenville, South Carolina, to Norris's home town. They traveled all over the South and to major cities such as Chicago, Detroit, Birmingham, Miami, Atlanta, Raleigh, and New York.

A 1949 recording on Gotham Records produced a hit written by Lucie Eddie Campbell (1885–1963), known as "Miss Lucie," of the National Baptist Convention. The rendition by the Angelics, "Touch Me, Lord Jesus," became a household song during the golden era, selling over a million copies the first year and receiving the *Billboard* Top Twenty Award. The gospel radio program "Ernie's Record Mart" on WLAC, Nashville, Tennessee, made this song its theme for over ten years. Accompanied by Allison's piano backup, "Touch Me, Lord Jesus," written by Campbell, has continued to be a gospel hit. It has not been published in as many hymnals as Thomas A. Dorsey's "Precious Lord," yet this song has received a reputation as a traditional gospel hymn in Baptist, Holiness, and Pentecostal audiences.

While under the Gotham Record label, the Angelics recorded "He Never Left Me Alone," "Jesus, When Troubles Burden Me Down," and the Christmas composition of "Glory to the Newborn King." In 1950, the Angelics teamed with the Dixie Hummingbirds quartet to record "Dear Lord Look Down Upon Me," "Left Me Standing on the Highway," "Wondering Which Way to Go," and other songs.

In 1951, Bernice Cole of New York joined the group. In 1953, Lucille Shird left the group to get married. In 1955, Ella Mae Norris also left the group to get married. In 1955, they remade "Touch Me, Lord Jesus," and "Sweet Home." The next remake of "Touch Me, Lord Jesus" included Allison's testimony under the Nashboro Label. In 1957, Bernice Cole left the group because of illness in her family. Allison and McDowell continued to sing. In 1961, the first male singer, Thomas Mobley, joined the group and stayed twelve years, until 1973. Geraldine Morris joined in 1973 and stayed until she died in 1974. In 1975, Bernice Cole returned to the group. In 1982, Pauline Turner of Franklin, Virginia, joined. In 1984, Darryl Richmond (bass guitarist) and John Richmond (lead guitarist) of Danville, Virginia, joined the group. Teresa Burton later joined.

In 1984, they released an anniversary album to commemorate forty years of gospel. The album featured "If you Can't help Me" and "Don't Stop at the Top of the Hill." Since 1984, the Angelics recorded these albums: *Out of the Depths, Lord, You Gave Me Another Chance, He's My Ever Present Help, I'll Live Again,* and *I've Weathered the Storm.* The Angelics were on the Nashboro Label for twenty-seven years. They then moved to Malaco Records in Jackson, Mississippi, in the 1980s. In December 1993, Malaco released an album of theirs entitled *Don't Stop Praying.*

The Angelics worked closely with the "queen of gospel," Mahalia Jackson (1911–1972), the Mighty Clouds of Joy, the Soul Stirrers, the Jackson Southernaires, Willie Banks and the Messengers, Brooklyn Allstars, Slim and the Supreme Angels, the Swanee Quintet, the Davis Sisters, evangelist Shirley Caesar, the CBS Trumpeters, and the Sensational Nightingales.

The Angelics are a traditional pioneer group who maintain the "down-home" style of expressing feelings in simple words. Although there were changes in personnel, the group still maintains the same style of music, dress, and mannerisms. A music video entitled *Angelic Gospel Singers: The Gospel in Motion,* produced by Xenon Pictures, Inc., describes what words can't explain. One can see and hear a unique barrelhouse piano style that echoes the lead singer. These strong female voices harmonize in a manner similar to the male quartet the Fairfield Four.

In May 2004, to a standing-room audience in Starke, Florida (a town north of Gainesville), the Angelics "brought the house down," meaning people were praising God, shouting, and singing. The featured songs were "Going Over Yonder," "Jesus Never Fails," "Touch Me, Lord Jesus," "Sweet Home," and "I'll Meet You on the Other Side of Jordan." The Angelics have been nominated for induction into the International Gospel Music Hall of Fame and Museum in Detroit, Michigan.

Margaret Wells Allison

The founder and leader of the Angelics, Allison was born on September 25, 1921, in McCormick, South Carolina, about fifty miles from Augusta, Georgia. In 1925, during the depression, when Margaret was four years old, the Wells family moved to Philadelphia for her father to obtain work. The Wells family attended the Little Temple Pentecostal Church in Philadelphia. The name "Angelic Gospel Singers" came to Margaret in a dream. She studied piano and at the age of twelve transferred her membership to the B. M. Oakley Memorial Church of God in Christ. The largest African American Holiness Pentecostal denomination in the world, the Church of God in Christ, was founded in 1907 and in 2004, it had over 5.6 million members in fifty-eight countries. Its historical headquarters are in Memphis, Tennessee.

SHERRY SHERROD DuPREE

Reference and Further Reading

"Angelic Gospel Singers in Concert." Agape Faith Worship Center, Starke, FL, May 23, 2004.

Boyer, Horace Clarence. *How Sweet the Sound: The Golden Age of Gospel.* Washington, DC: Elliott & Clark, 1995.

DuPree, Sherry Sherrod. *African-American Holiness Pentecostal Movement: An Annotated Bibliography.* Religious Information Systems Vol. 4; Garland Reference Library of Social Science Vol. 526. New York: Garland Publishing, 1996.

———. *Biographical Dictionary of African-American Holiness-Pentecostals 1880–1990.* Washington, DC: Middle Atlantic Regional Press, 1989.

DuPree, Sherry Sherrod; Herbert C. DuPree. *African-American Good News (Gospel) Music.* Washington, DC: Middle Atlantic Regional Press, 1993.

International Gospel Music Hall of Fame and Museum. http://www.gmhf.org (accessed August 28, 2004).

Discography

Touch Me, Lord Jesus (Malaco Records 4381).

ANOINTED PACE SISTERS

The nine sisters who comprise the Anointed Pace Sisters began singing informally in local talent shows in Georgia in the late 1960s. As children, the sisters experienced poverty and uncertain conditions in the Pool Creek neighborhood of southeast Atlanta. Reared in a strong Christian family, like many gospel singers, the sisters found release and safety in the church. Active in the Church of God in Christ (COGIC) music conventions, the sisters soon came under the direction of the famed choral director Dr. Mattie Moss Clark. In the early 1970s, they won an award for Best Gospel Group at the annual COGIC convention—a frequent stepping-stone for success in gospel music. Among their early supporters were the Reverend Clay Evans (who once told Clark that she would "pick up the torch left by Mahalia Jackson") and Edwin Hawkins. Dubbed the Anointed Pace Sisters, the group began actively touring with their uncle, evangelist Gene Martin, as part of the Action Revival Team.

The Anointed Pace Sisters, now dominated by the powerful voice of LaShun Pace, recorded two projects with the independent Faith label in Atlanta that enjoyed some regional success. The group's first recording for a nationally distributed label came in 1992, when they released *U-Know* for Savoy. *U-Know* remained on the *Billboard* charts for more than a year, eventually reaching the number two spot in the gospel charts. Several of the sisters shared writing duties, including Phyllis Pace ("U-Know") and LaShun Pace ("24-7"). A subsequent Savoy release recorded lived in Atlanta, *My Purpose,* did nearly as well in 1994 and produced the hit "Hands of God," featuring LaShun on vocals.

However, the sisters experienced various management and booking problems and did not record for several years. Still, recording as Shun Pace-Rhodes, LaShun's powerful performance of "In the House of the Lord" with Dr. Jonathan Greer and the Cathedral of Faith Choir brought her to the attention of Savoy Records in 1990. She released her first solo project, *He Lives,* in 1991, and she was the featured soloist for a variety of mass choirs, most notably the Gospel Music Workshop of America, Hawkins' Music & Arts Seminar Mass Choir, and the Central George State Choir. She was also featured in the Steve Martin movie *Leap of Faith* (directed by Richard Pearce, 1992) as one of the "Angels of Mercy Choir" and in the theatrical productions *The Living Cross* and *A Fool and His Money.*

Later releases, again under the name of LaShun Pace, include *Shekinah Glory: Live* (1993), *Wealthy Place* (1996), *Just Because God Said It: Live* (1998), and *God Is Faithful* (2001), all for Savoy. Anthony Heilbut's *The Gospel Sound* cites LaShun Pace as one of the great voices of modern gospel, able to "draw on folkloric traditions" as well as sing modern, funk-oriented gospel.

Finally freed from legal difficulties, the Anointed Pace Sisters released *It's Already Done* in 2004 for the independent Gospel Music label—ten years after their previous release, *My Purpose.* Like earlier recordings, *It's Already Done* is a mixture of traditional and contemporary gospel, featuring the songwriting talents of Melonda Pace, Latrice Pace-Speights, and Duranice Pace-Love.

LaShun signed with EMI Gospel in late 2004 and released her first CD with the label, *It's My Time,* in early 2005.

Both LaShun Pace and the Anointed Pace Sisters have received several Stellar and Grammy award nominations for their releases.

ROBERT DARDEN

See also Church of God in Christ (COGIC); Gospel Music Workshop of America; Mattie Moss Clark and the Southwest Michigan State Choir

Reference and Further Reading

Collins, Lisa. "In the Spirit." *Billboard* (June 25, 1994): 63.

Heilbut, Anthony. *The Gospel Sound: Good News and Bad Times.* New York: Limelight Editions, 1997.

Jones, Dr. Bobby; with Lesley Sussman. *Touched by God: Black Gospel Greats Share Their Stories of Finding God.* New York: Pocket Books, 1998.

Larkin, Colin, ed. *The Encyclopedia of Popular Music.* 3rd ed., Vol. 1. New York: MUZE, 1998.

Smith, Pepper. "Look Out for Shun Pace-Rhodes." *Rejoice!* (August/September 1992): 15–16.
Verna, Paul. "Just Because God Said It." *Billboard Magazine* (August 29, 1998): 28.

Discography

Anointed Pace Sisters

It's Already Done (Gospel Pace Music).
My Purpose: Live in Atlanta (Savoy).
U-Know (Savoy).

Shun Pace-Rhodes and LaShun Pace

God Is Faithful (Savoy).
He Lives (Savoy).
It's My Time (EMI Gospel).
Just Because God Said It: Live (Savoy).
Shekinah Glory: Live (Savoy).
Wealthy Place (Savoy).

ARCHERS, THE

Tim Archer
Steve Archer

Contemporary Christian gospel duo popular in the 1970s that grew to include their sister Janice on soprano. It was perhaps inevitable that the brothers would be involved in religious activities of some sort because their father spent thirty years in the ministry and two of Tim and Steve's brothers were pastors in California and Holland.

The Archers got their start participating in singing sessions in their father's church and then started performing in other churches throughout northern California. Encouraged by Ralph Carmichael and Andrae Crouch, among others, they added instrumentation to back up their voices. In 1972 they recorded their first album, for Charisma Records. Impact soon purchased Charisma and reissued the disc as *The Archers*. This repackaged album received great critical praise, which led to a booking at Expo '72 in Dallas. Subsequently, they toured with Pat Boone and worked in one of his films.

As their name became prominent and their album sales increased, the addition of Janice only made the group better. Their 1978 album *Fresh Surrender* was nominated for a Dove Award.

W. K. McNeil

Discography

Any Day Now (aka *The Archers*) (1972, Charisma).
Keep Singing That Love Song (1974, Impact).
Fresh Surrender (1978, Light).

ARMOND MORALES AND THE IMPERIALS

Armond Morales (b. February 25, 1932)
Jake Hess (b. December 24,1927)
Shaun Sherrill Nielsen (b. September 10, 1942)
Gary McSpadden (b. January 26, 1943)
Henry Slaughter (b. January 9, 1927).

The Imperials were first formed in 1963 by Jake Hess. Hess had been the lead singer for the Statesmen, a Southern gospel quartet, and he handpicked the best vocalists he could find to form the original group. Bass singer Armond Morales and pianist Henry Slaughter had both been members of another successful gospel quartet, the Weatherfords. Tenor Shaun Sherrill Nielsen came from the Speer Family, and Gary McSpadden was a member of both the Statesmen and the Oak Ridge Boys.

In 1964 their musical direction was impacted by the British music invasion of America, led by the Beatles. Their first album was released in 1964, on Impact Records, and was entitled *Jake Hess and the Imperials*. In 1967 Hess left the Imperials for health reasons, and Armond Morales took up the mantle as group leader.

During the next four decades, the Imperials would regularly change personnel and had nearly three dozen different members, some of whom—such as Larry Gatlin, Danny Ward, Jason Beddoe, Mark Addock, Brian Como, Peter Pankratz, and Bill Morris—never recorded with the group. Many former alumni, including Sherman Andrus, Terry Blackwood, Gary McSpadden, Henry Slaughter, Paul Smith, and Russ Taff, had successful solo careers after leaving the troupe. The only original member who continued to tour with the group was Armond Morales. Morales owned the name "Imperials," and he served as the group's manager.

By the late 1960s the Imperials had a new look and a new sound, which drew some criticism from old fans as they gained acceptance by new ones. In 1971 the Imperials broke down racial and musical barriers when they had Sherman Andrus join the group as its new lead singer. He was an original member of Andrae Crouch and the Disciples. By the end of his five-year stay with the group, the Imperials won a Grammy Award for best gospel album, with *No Shortage*.

In the early 1970s, they were in great demand and regularly appeared on a variety of television shows, including those of Mike Douglas, David Frost, Merv Griffin, and Joey Bishop. At the same time they made appearances in Las Vegas, Reno, and Lake Tahoe, where they shared the stage with artists as diverse as

Pat Boone, Carol Channing, Jimmy Dean, Elvis Presley, and Connie Smith. The Imperials collaborated with Elvis Presley on his *How Great Thou Art* and *He Touched Me* albums. They also toured with Presley and shared the stage as his backup singers from 1969 to 1971. They became regulars on Jimmy Dean's weekly TV show, as well as recording and touring with him. Being in the spotlight gave the Imperials the opportunity to cross over into secular music, like their contemporaries the Oak Ridge Boys, but they chose to stay with gospel.

They have recorded over forty albums during their four decades of performing. Fourteen of their songs hit number one on the CCM chart. They received fifty-eight Dove Award nominations, of which they won seventeen. They have been Group of the Year eight times. The secular recording industry recognized the Imperials with four Grammy Awards, and they were the first Christian act to perform on the Grammy Awards live telecast. The Imperials have appeared in concert in many countries around the world, including Canada, England, Finland, Haiti, Holland, Hong Kong, Israel, and the Philippines.

In the mid 1980s, they once again stirred up a certain amount of controversy and alienated many of their oldest fans when they abandoned Southern gospel for the techno-pop/hard rock sound of *This Year's Model.* Morales considers this period, which also included *Stir It Up* and *Love's Still Changing Hearts,* as a period when the band was going through an identity crisis. The band lost touch with its original direction and eventually returned to its initial purpose of ministering to the church with a joyful noise. It was during this period that Morales recruited Steve Ferguson and Jeff Walker, who were ordained ministers, to aid in helping the group get refocused. Throughout the 1990s the Imperials scaled down their musical focus from entertaining in concert halls to ministering in churches. In the late 1990s the group formed their own record label, Big God Records. The beginning of the twenty-first century saw the group still going strong under the direction of founding member Armond Morales and performing between a hundred and fifty and two hundred concerts a year. The twenty-first century Imperials configuration included Morales and his son Jason, Jeremie Hudson, and Shannon Smith.

BOB GERSZTYN

See also Andrus, Blackwood & Company; Crouch, Andrae; Jake Hess and the Imperials; Oak Ridge Boys; Presley, Elvis; Slaughter, Henry and Hazel; Speer Family, The; Weatherfords, The (Quartet and Trio)

Reference and Further Reading

CCM Magazine. http://www.ccmcom.com/ (accessed August 17, 2003).

"A Decade of Jesus Music." http://one-way.org/jesusmusic/index.html (accessed July 29, 2003).

GMA Gospel Music Hall of Fame. http://www.gospelmusic.org/hall_of_fame/inductee_bio.cfm?ID=362 (accessed July 29, 2003).

Hess, Jake. www.jakehess.com (accessed July 29, 2003).

Imperial Ministries. www.theimperials.com (accessed August 14, 2003).

The Weatherford's. http://www.geocities.com/Heartland/Prairie/6093/history.html (accessed July 29, 2003).

Discography

Jake Hess & the Imperials (1964, Impact); *New Dimensions* (1968, Impact); *Love Is the Thing* (1969, Impact); *Gospel's Alive & Well* (1970, Impact); *Time To Get It Together* (1971, Impact); *Song of Love* (1972, Impact); *A Thing Called Love* (1973, Vista); *Live* (1973, Impact); *Follow the Man with the Music* (1974, Impact); *No Shortage* (1975, Impact); *Just Because* (1976, Impact); *The Best of the Imperials* (1977, Impact); *Sail On* (1977, Dayspring/Word); *Live* (1978, Dayspring/Word); *Heed the Call* (1979, Dayspring/Word); *One More Song for You* (1979, Dayspring/Word); *Christmas with the Imperials* (1980, Word); *Very Best of* (1981, Dayspring/Word); *Stand By the Power* (1982, Dayspring/Word); *Side by Side* (1983, Dayspring/Word); *Let the Wind Blow* (1985, Myrrh/Word); *This Year's Model* (1987, Myrrh/Word); *Free the Fire* (1988, Myrrh/Word); *Love's Still Changing Hearts* (1990, StarSong); *Big God* (1991, StarSong); *Stir It Up* (1992, StarSong); *Til He Comes* (1994, Impact); *Treasures* (1994, StarSong); *Legacy* (1996, Word); *It's Still the Cross* (1997, Big God Records); *I Was Made for This* (2003, Big God Records).

ARMSTRONG, VANESSA BELL

(b. October 2, 1953, Detroit, MI)

Starting from a humble beginning singing in church at age four, Vanessa Bell Armstrong has built a career that exceeds the standard bounds of gospel performer, to encompass the full entertainment spectrum, from Broadway show appearances to television.

Dr. Mattie Moss Clark first noticed Armstrong at age thirteen in her local singing setting at church in Detroit, Michigan. By being in the presence of Clark during her formative years, Armstrong was able to work with and learn from some of the finest gospel talents of the era, including the Reverend James Cleveland, the Mighty Clouds of Joy, the Clark Sisters, and the Winans.

Her recording career commenced with her signing to Onyx, a division of Malaco, where she recorded two albums, *Peace Be Still* and *Chosen.* She later began recording with Jive Records/Zomba, where she sustained a prolific recording stint during the late 1980s and throughout the 1990s. She segued labels to Tommy Boy Gospel for the 2001 release of *Brand New Day*. She has a steady and building audience of fans, ranging from young to old alike, through her ability to connect with strong material, her vibrant vocal style, and her connection to mainstream media.

Her first major foray into mainstream recording happened in 1986 when she was selected to record the theme song for the NBC primetime television show *Amen*, starring Sherman Helmsley. She beat out both Aretha Franklin and Patti Labelle for the spot. During this creative period, she also made a Broadway appearance in *Don't Get God Started* in 1987, and she appeared in Oprah Winfrey's television movie *The Women of Brewster Place* in 1989. She has since appeared in more than a dozen television productions.

This broad expansion into mainstream media brought her fuller attention across contemporary gospel, urban, and traditional gospel music segments. She has influenced other contemporary gospel and urban recording artists, such as Sandra Crouch and Joe.

Overall, Armstrong has achieved strong commercial success with her urban contemporary, soul, and gospel vocal style. She has hit the *Billboard* top gospel charts ten times, with a #1 on *Chosen* and a #3 with her debut *Peace Be Still*. Her 1988 self-titled album *Vanessa Bell Armstrong* crossed over to the contemporary Christian charts as well, reaching #28. She took *Something on the Inside* and *Secret Is Out* to the R&B/hip-hop album charts. She also has charted on the R&B/hip-hop singles and tracks with 1987's "You Bring Out the Best in Me" (#80) and 1993's "Something on the Inside" (#94).

In recognition of her great career achievements, Armstrong was voted into the Gospel Music Hall of Fame in 2001.

Margaret B. Fisher

See also Cleveland, James; Mighty Clouds of Joy; Winans, The

Reference and Further Reading

Carpenter, Bil; Wynn, Ron. "All Music Guide—Vanessa Bell Armstrong." http://www.allmusic.com (accessed 2003).

De La Font, Richard. "Vanessa Bell Armstrong—Gospel Music Artists." http://www.delafont.com/music_acts/vanessa-bell-armstrong.htm (accessed 2003).

Discography

Peace Be Still (1983, Onyx); *Chosen* (1984, Onyx); *Vanessa Bell Armstrong* (1987, Jive); *Wonderful One* (1989, Jive); *The Truth About Christmas* (1990, Jive); *Something on the Inside* (1993, Jive); *Desire of My Heart: Live* (1998, Jive); *The Best of Vanessa Bell Armstrong* (1999, Jive); *Brand New Day* (2001, Tommy Boy Gospel); *The Secret Is Out* (Jive).

ARTHUR SMITH AND HIS CROSSROADS QUARTET

Arthur Smith (b. April 1, 1921)
Ralph Smith (b. Unknown; d. Early 1980s)
Sonny Smith (b. Unknown)
Tommy Faile (b. September 1928; d. ca. 1996)
Lois Atkins (b. Unknown)
Don Ange (b. Unknown; d. ca. 2004)
Wayne "Skeeter" Haas (b. ca. 1940)

Arthur Smith, best known for his jazzy-country guitar instrumentals, has experienced a long career in country music, including leadership of the popular Crossroads Quartet. A native of Clinton, South Carolina, he grew up in nearby Kershaw, where his father was music director at a textile mill. Initially interested in horn music, young Smith also developed dexterity on a number of stringed instruments as well, especially lead guitar. His brothers Ralph and Sonny also joined him, and they worked on radio at WSPA Spartanburg and recorded four numbers—two of them sacred—for Bluebird in 1938 as Smith's Carolina Crackerjacks.

Smith's ascent began about 1945 when he first recorded his classic instrumental "Guitar Boogie," originally for Superdisc, but the master was later leased to MGM, where most of his recordings appeared over the next decade when he became the leading musical figure at WBT radio and then at WBT-TV. The Crossroads Quartet developed as a featured act within his entourage and became quite popular, first recording for MGM in 1953. The original members were Arthur on guitar and baritone, Ralph Smith on tenor, Sonny Smith on lead, and Tommy Faile on bass vocal. Their best-known early recordings were "I Saw a Man" and "The Fourth Man," cut in 1954 and 1955, respectively. In all, the Quartet made some twenty-three sides for MGM and later did long-play albums for Dot and Starday as well as on Smith's country albums.

Membership in the Crossroads Quartet underwent some changes over the years. Sonny Smith retired from the group after the first few years, and Arthur did not always sing but still played guitar. When Sonny retired, Ralph took over the vocal leads, and several females were part of the quartet at times, most notably Lois Atkins. Later members included Don Ange, a blind pianist who could also sing, Wayne "Skeeter" Haas, and banjo picker David Deese. In addition to daily television in Charlotte, a weekly *Arthur Smith Show* was syndicated, sometimes in as many as sixty-eight markets, but usually about fifty, and the quartet was always a popular feature.

After Ralph Smith passed away the Crossroads Quartet performed less, and Arthur Smith also became less active musically, spending much of his time with a variety of business activities. He has been considered one of Charlotte's leading citizens for several decades.

IVAN M. TRIBE

Reference and Further Reading

Holt, George, ed. *The Charlotte Country Music Story.* Raleigh, NC: North Carolina Arts Council, 1985, 20–21, 28–29.

Discography

Arthur Smith & the Crossroads Quartet (1962, Starday SLP 186); *Inspirational Songs Sung by the Crossroads Quartet* (1965, Metro MS 528); *Singing on the Mountain* (1965, Dot DL 25642).

AZUSA STREET REVIVAL

1906–1909

The seeds of revival were planted in the hearts of many in several locations around the country— South, North, and East—before a movement would take root and flourish thousands of miles away on the West Coast by 1906. William Joseph Seymour, considered the father of the modern Pentecostal movement, was born May 22, 1870, of African American parentage in Centerville, Louisiana.

At about age twenty-five, Seymour moved from Centerville to Indianapolis, Indiana. There, he joined a black Methodist congregation. By 1900, he moved on to Cincinnati, Ohio and became affiliated with a Methodist church led by Euro-American the Reverend Martin W. Knapp, a trained clergyman who preached holiness and divine healing in integrated settings. Not long thereafter, Seymour began attending a congregation called the Evening Light Saints, which later became the Church of God (Anderson, Indiana). What Seymour had been searching for, he believed he had found. In one of the services, he approached the altar, "prayed through," and went back to the altar a second time, remaining until he

was wholly sanctified, as he later testified. While with the Evening Light Saints, he was ordained as an evangelist. In 1903, he moved to Houston, Texas, and on to Jackson, Mississippi, two years later, where he met Charles P. Jones, the founder of the Church of Christ (Holiness) USA.

One more person Joseph Seymour would meet later during Summer 1905 was Reverend Mrs. Lucy F. Farrow, a black holiness pastor from Houston. Reverend Farrow, who had attended the services of Texas revivalist Charles F. Parham, was invited to return with him and his family to Kansas as their governess. Parham, a Euro-American minister, ran a Bible school in Topeka, Kansas, where Agnes M. Ozman was baptized with the Holy Ghost, which was evidenced by her speaking in other tongues on New Year's Day 1901. The whites-only school was the first known American location where several individuals received the Holy Ghost. Parham enforced a whites-only policy at the altar. Blacks could engage in prayer and seek salvation from a segregated back room. In 1905, Seymour attended Parham's Bible Training School, which opened at 503 Rusk Street in Houston, but he too was forced to learn from a separate rear room.

By January 1906, Seymour had quit the Bible school and received a letter from Mrs. Neely Terry from Los Angeles inviting him to pastor the congregation of Reverend Mrs. Julia W. Hutchins. On the strength of Mrs. Terry's recommendation (based on her acquaintance with Seymour in Houston), Reverend Seymour was invited to pastor the twenty or so people who initially worshipped in the home of Mr. and Mrs. Richard Asbery, 214 North Bonnie Brae Street. Within a short period, the congregation outgrew the house and Reverend Mrs. Hutchins found new larger quarters at 9th and Santa Fe. When Seymour arrived in Los Angeles in late February or early March 1906, he preached holiness and divine healing as well as the baptism of the Holy Ghost with the initial evidence of speaking in other tongues. The doctrine became a hotly divisive issue with the burgeoning congregation.

One April Sunday evening when Seymour arrived at the church, he found the door padlocked, per Hutchins's orders. Mr. and Mrs. Edward S. Lee, an African American family under Hutchins, welcomed him to stay in their home, whereas the Asbery couple invited Seymour to conduct church meetings in their home. On April 9, 1906, Seymour went to Lee's home to pray for him for healing. While there, Seymour prayed for Lee to receive the Holy Ghost. Within minutes, Lee received the Holy Ghost and began to speak in other tongues. Two hours later they arrived together at the Asbery home, where the church meeting was scheduled. During the service, Brother Lee made testimony about his experience. During the course of the service, seven more people experienced what Brother Lee had. During this time, Seymour had preached to others the baptism in the Holy Ghost but had not himself experienced the infilling, until April 12, 1906. His quest for spiritual fulfillment and a deeper life in Christ was now accomplished.

In the meantime, the Asbery residence overflowed as more friends and neighbors came, were baptized with the Holy Ghost, and began to testify about the wonderful works of God (Acts 2:11). The group learned that a building located at 312 Azusa Street was available and immediately rented it. The First African Methodist Episcopal (AME) Church had owned the two-story wooden forty- by sixty-foot frame structure until 1903. In the interim, it had been used for storage and as a livery stable. Volunteers and church members cleaned and prepared the church, which at capacity would seat about seven hundred fifty worshippers. Similar to the circumstances of Jesus's birth, the revisitation of the Holy Spirit upon mankind included a stable

From these humble beginnings in 1906 until 1909, no one knows how many thousands of people came, were engulfed by the Holy Ghost, and departed to inform others and to plant or contribute to the birth of Pentecostal churches and missionary work. People from nearly every country, every tongue, race, and ethnic group found their way to the Azusa Street Revival. A *Los Angeles Times* reporter, unfamiliar with the biblical account of Acts 2, on April 18, 1906, wrote the front-page headline "Weird Babel of Tongues . . . New Sect of Fanatics Is Breaking Loose ... Wild Scene Last Night on Azusa Street ...

Gurgle Wordless Talk by a Sister." In September 1906, William Seymour penned the following headline in the first issue of his church newspaper, *The Apostolic Faith*: "Pentecost Has Come: Los Angeles Being Visited by a Revival of Bible Salvation and Pentecost as Recorded in the Book of Acts." Five thousand copies were printed. By 1907, fifty thousand copies were being printed regularly for worldwide distribution. In issue after issue of *The Apostolic Faith*, first-hand accounts by individuals representing more than fifty nations attributed their salvation experience directly to the Azusa Street Revival that had lasted about a thousand days, led by African American evangelist William Joseph Seymour.

EVELYN M. E. TAYLOR

Reference and Further Reading

du Plessis, David J. "Golden Jubilee of Twentieth-Century Pentecostal Movements." In *Azusa Street and Beyond: Pentecostal Missions and Church Growth in the Twentieth Century*, edited by L. Grant McClung, Jr. South Plainfield, NJ: Bridge Publishing, 1986.

McKinney, George D. "The Azusa Street Revival Revisited." Lecture presented at Beeson Divinity School, Sanford University, Birmingham, AL, October 3, 2001. San Diego, CA: American Urban University Press, 2001.

Noble, E. Myron, ed. *Like As of Fire: Newspapers from the Azusa Street World Wide Revival*. Los Angeles: Apostolic Faith Gospel Mission, originally published, 1906. Collected by Fred T. Corum and Rachel A. Harper Sizelove and republished, Washington, DC: Middle Atlantic Regional Press, 1994.

Noble, E. Myron, ed. "William Joseph Seymour, May 2, 1870–September 28, 1922." *MAR (Middle Atlantic Regional) Gospel Ministries Newsletter* 1, no. 1 (Spring–Summer 1990).

B

BAGWELL, WENDY

(b. May 16, 1925, Chamblee, GA; d. June 13, 1996)

Wendell Lee "Wendy" Bagwell was equally adept at singing a gospel song or spinning an amusing tale, and he did both to great acclaim as the longtime leader of Wendy Bagwell and the Sunliters.

Bagwell attended West Fulton High in Atlanta and was twice decorated for bravery as a combat Marine at Saipan and Iwo Jima. Returning home to Georgia, he won custody of an abused eight-year-old nephew, Ronnie Buckner (although Wendy was not quite 21), and he soon married Melba Louise Hogue of Simsville, Georgia. In church, Bagwell met two young singers, Geraldine Terry and Georgia Jones, and he formed an amateur gospel trio with them. Soon they had radio sponsors (a local supermarket, Mary Carter Paint) and were touring in the area as much as Wendy's full-time jobs allowed. They made $35 a week as regulars at the Georgia Jubilee in East Point (near Atlanta), where young Jerry Reed, Joe South, and others joined them as "underpaid talent." Geraldine Terry stayed with the group, marrying James Morrison and becoming known professionally as Jerri Morrison; Georgia Jones was succeeded by Dot Pressley, Virginia Williams, and then, about 1960, by "Little" Jan Buckner, who married Bagwell's adopted nephew Ronnie and became a longtime member of Bagwell's Sunliters.

Syndicated television helped make Wendy Bagwell and the Sunliters regionally popular (*America Sings, Guy Mobile Home Show, The Bob Poole Show, The Wally Fowler Show*), and they made their first recordings for Hilltop in the early 1960s, featuring then and always a mix of traditional gospel favorites with the sort of story songs Bagwell loved to write ("Pearl Buttons," "Willie McNeil," "Aunt Kate," "Uncle George"), presaging the spoken humor of later years. With great promotion, they became the first Southern gospel group to play Carnegie Hall (1962) and the first to tour Europe (1965). In 1968, they released their first of four albums for RCA Victor, then in 1970, began a long association with Canaan Records, for whom Bagwell released the million-selling monologue that established him as a top-flight comedian: "Here Come The Rattlesnakes" (sometimes titled "Rattlesnake Song"). Like much of his later humor, this was the true story of an on-the-road experience—the memorable night in which a Kentucky congregation brought out six rattlesnakes to handle after a concert. As Bagwell recounted the story, "If God ever told me to handle a rattlesnake, I would. But he didn't, and so I ain't." Soon he was gospel's version of Andy Griffith, Brother Dave Gardner, and Jerry Clower, and in 1975, he released his first all-comedy album, *Bust Out Laffin'* (Canaan CAS-9765). Bagwell's liner notes to this album won him his only Dove Award. Music, however, remained first and foremost, as Bagwell turned down repeated advice to leave the gospel field for full-time comedy.

In addition to making recordings and averaging one hundred and fifty road shows a year with the Sunliters, Bagwell, along with his daughter Wendy Lea and nephew Ronnie Buckner, operated a furniture business out of his Hiram, Georgia, home. Bagwell died in Atlanta after surgery on a ruptured brain aneurysm on June 13, 1996. Posthumously, he has been honored by induction in 1997 into the Southern Gospel Music Hall of Fame and (as Wendy Bagwell & the Sunliters) in 2001 into GMA's Gospel Music Hall of Fame.

RONNIE PUGH

Reference and Further Reading

Gentry, Linnell. *History & Encyclopedia of Country, Western and Gospel Music.* Nashville, TN: Clairmont, 1969.
"Wendy Bagwell: The Only Thing I'm Afraid of Is Melba." *The Singing News* (May 1989): 32.

BAILES BROTHERS, THE

Kyle O. Bailes (b. May 7, 1915; d. March 3, 1996)
John J. Bailes (b. June 24, 1918; d. December 21, 1989)
Walter Butler Bailes (b. January 17, 1920; d. November 27, 2000)
Homer Vernon Bailes (b. May 8, 1922)

The four Bailes Brothers constituted a country music duet (they usually worked in twos) that recorded a high proportion of gospel material and created numerous original songs, most notably the classic number "Dust on the Bible." The brothers were Kyle O., John Jacob, Walter Butler, and Homer Vernon. Natives of Kanawha County, West Virginia, the brothers were reared in poverty by their widowed mother after their father died in 1925. They worked to forge careers in country music from the mid-1930s, largely inspired by radio singers they heard via WCHS Charleston; they appeared on that station and other West Virginia broadcast outlets.

Generally speaking, the various combinations of brothers found little commercial success in depression-racked West Virginia, but, after World War II brought some return of prosperity, John and Walter achieved prosperity at WSAZ Huntington. In 1944, with the help of Roy Acuff, they secured a spot at WSM and the Grand Ole Opry. They began recording for Columbia in February 1945, waxing their classic "Dust on the Bible" and several other sacred and heart songs, most notably "I've Got My One Way Ticket to the Sky" and "Ashamed to Own the Blessed Savior." In all, they recorded twenty-eight sides for Columbia through 1947, with half of them being original religious songs. In the fall of 1946, the Bailes Brothers had a session for King, recording twenty-four songs, half of them gospel, including such classics as "An Empty Mansion," "Something Got Hold of Me," and "Daniel Prayed." The mandolin of Ernest Ferguson and steel guitar of Shot Jackson helped define their instrumental sound.

Late in 1946, the brothers moved to KWKH Shreveport, where they helped start the *Louisiana Hayride* in April 1948. In the meantime, Walter left to enter the ministry, and Homer, who had joined them at WSM after his release from the army, became Johnnie's duet partner. Kyle also worked with them periodically as bass player and handled their booking. The act broke up in 1949 but periodically reformed, most notably in 1953, when Johnnie and Walter recorded another dozen songs—all sacred—at three different sessions. In addition to several originals, these efforts included two songs written by others, "Muddy Sea of Sin" and "Avenue of Prayer."

Walter Bailes, who had been the group's principal songwriter, continued as such in addition to his ministerial efforts. His best-known later composition, "Give Mother My Crown," became one of the better-known Flatt and Scruggs songs of the later 1950s. Along the way, he received the title "Chaplain of Music Row" and had Sunday evening programs on WSM. In addition to numerous solo recordings, he cut several duets with Kyle and an album with Homer in 1968, who by this time had also entered the ministry. Many of these discs were on Walter's Loyal label. His later efforts were on a newer label, White Dove. Johnnie and Homer also cut a gospel album for Starday in 1972, and all four brothers did a reunion album in 1977 for Old Homestead. It even included sister Minnie helping out on a few numbers and Ernest Ferguson again playing mandolin. Walter, Kyle, and Ernest played numerous churches and a few bluegrass festivals in the later 1970s. Johnnie and Homer also played a few festivals in this era, but Homer, who regularly pastored a church, did little traveling. Homer did cut a pair of albums for Old Homestead in the 1980s. As the twenty-first century dawned, only Homer remained active, largely retired from his Methodist ministry but still preaching and singing on occasion.

Overall, the Bailes Brothers—with their sacred and heart songs—had a great deal of impact with their radio work in the 1944–1949 era, and to a lesser degree with their recordings. Commercially, they had periods of intense success, but their overall impact and sustained prosperity was hampered by periodic internal dissension. In 2002, Bear Family Records of Germany reissued all of their Columbia recordings on compact disc, an indication of continuing interest in their music. In addition, the impact of their original songs—largely composed by Walter—continues to be felt in country gospel music circles.

IVAN M. TRIBE

References and Further Reading

Saunders, Walt. "Walter Bailes" [obituary]. *Bluegrass Unlimited* 35, no. 7 (January 2001): 19.
Tribe, Ivan M. "The Bailes Brothers." *Bluegrass Unlimited* 9, no. 8 (February 1975): 8–13.
———. "West Virginia Home Folks: The Bailes Brothers." *Old Time Music* 19 (Winter 1975–1976): 17–22.

Discography

The Bailes Brothers. *Oh So Many Years* (2002, Bear Family BCD 15973).

BANJO

The banjo came to gospel music through its association with country, bluegrass, and popular music styles. Although there is not a "gospel banjo" style, the banjo played an important role as an accompaniment instrument for gospel performers.

The American banjo has its roots in African American stringed instruments brought to this country by the slaves. Although we do not know the specific model for the banjo, instruments with gourd bodies, four to eight strings, and guitar-like necks were known in Africa and were noted in the Southern colonies in the eighteenth century. Slaves with musical talent were often encouraged to play European instruments such as violins and guitars for dances and parties; the American banjo combines elements of these European instruments with its African predecessors.

Despite slavery and segregation, there was a good deal of interplay between black and white musicians in the South during the late eighteenth and early nineteenth centuries. One of the first white musicians to take up the banjo was Joel Walker Sweeney, who was performing in Virginia as early as the 1830s. White musicians turned to woodworkers to make their instruments; these sometimes featured gourd bodies, but they increasingly featured a hoop-shaped body with a skin head stretched across the top (like a modern tambourine). Sweeney is credited with adding the short, drone string to the banjo, or at least had instruments made with this feature for his own use. Sweeney originally performed with circuses and eventually joined the growing minstrel show circuit, where white musicians and performers imitated black musical styles. The banjo became a favorite of minstrel players because of its close association with plantation life. Specialty banjo makers such as William Boucher in Baltimore (and others) were in business by the mid-nineteenth century, showing the demand for the instrument. By this time, most instruments had either five or six strings (including the short drone string), with five strings increasingly becoming the norm. The traditional style of playing was known by various names (e.g., frailing, knocking, clawhammer, etc.), and it involved brushing across the strings with the back of the index or third fingernail while "catching" the fifth or drone string with the thumb to create a regular rhythmic pattern.

By the turn of the twentieth century, banjos were very much a part of American musical life. Makers such as S. S. Stewart of Philadelphia and Fairbanks (later Vega) of Boston promoted the instrument heavily, and college banjo clubs were established in major Ivy League schools, while performers worked the vaudeville circuit. Meanwhile, the need for dance bands to have a louder chord instrument than the guitar led to the development of hybrid instruments such as the banjo guitar (a banjo with a six-string guitar neck) and then the "tango," or tenor banjo (a four-string banjo). These instruments were more suited to being played with a flat pick (like a guitar) for playing either melodies or chords.

Early country five-string banjo players such as famed Grand Ole Opry star Uncle Dave Macon featured gospel music as part of their repertoire, although they were not primarily gospel performers. Macon recorded many gospel songs, along with songs with religious themes ("Jordan Am a Hard Road to Travel") commenting on the lack of religion in contemporary life. When bluegrass music became popular after World War II, gospel songs became an integral part of many bands' performances, although initially the banjo was not used on gospel numbers because of its association with secular dance music.

Bill Monroe, known as the "father of bluegrass music," recorded beautiful gospel quartet numbers, but they were accompanied only by guitar, mandolin, and bass. The Stanley Brothers, another early bluegrass group, similarly usually did not feature banjo on their gospel recordings. However, by the early 1950s a few bluegrass groups began specializing in gospel music proudly featuring the banjo. Notable among them was the Lewis Family, featuring the banjo playing of "Little Roy" Lewis on their bluegrass gospel television show, broadcast out of Augusta, Georgia, as early as 1954. In the 1960s and 1970s, more bluegrass groups began specializing in gospel music, notably Doyle Lawson with his group Quicksilver (originally using banjo player Terry Baucom), whereas old-timers such as Ralph Stanley (now leading the Clinch Mountain Boys on his own since the death in 1966 of his brother Carter) began using full band instrumentation—including the banjo—on their gospel recordings.

Outside of bluegrass, gospel country harmony groups were popular on local radio throughout the

South. Photos of these groups show that they often used tenor, banjo guitar, or even banjo ukulele (a hybrid featuring a small banjo head attached to a ukulele neck) as accompanying instruments. Although not many of these groups recorded, judging from recorded evidence and reminiscences of musicians, the style of performance on these instruments would have been similar to that of secular bands, who used them for rhythmic accompaniment and occasional lead melody work.

RICHARD CARLIN

Reference and Further Reading

Carlin, Bob. *Joel Walker Sweeney: Minstrel Banjo Player.* Unpublished manuscript.

Gura, Philip F.; James F. Bollman. *America's Instrument: The Banjo in the Nineteenth Century.* Chapel Hill, NC: University of North Carolina Press, 1999.

Webb, Robert Lloyd. *Ring the Banjar: The History of the Banjo, the Banjo in America from Folklore to Factory,* 2nd ed. Milwaukee, WI: Hal Leonard, 1997.

Discography

Gospel Collection, Vol. 1 (1993, Sugar Hill). Anthology of Doyle Lawson and Quicksilver's more popular material from the late 1980s through the early 1990s.

Go Long Mule (1998, County). 1926–1934 recordings by Uncle Dave Macon, including some religious-themed material.

Just Over in Heaven (2000, Sugar Hill). *A cappella* and accompanied gospel material, by Doyle Lawson and Quicksilver.

16 Greatest Hits (n.d., Hollywood). Compilation of recordings by the Lewis Family originally made for Starday in the late 1950s–early 1960s.

BARBERSHOP QUARTETS

Overview

Barbershop is a type of four-part (TTBB) vernacular vocal music generally performed with the melody in the second tenor, supported homophonically by major, minor, and major-minor seventh chords that tend to follow the circle-of-fifths progression. Although the earliest known use of the word "barbershop" to describe this style of music appears in 1900, its origins extend back at least to the mid-nineteenth century. It saw its heyday in the decades surrounding the turn of the twentieth century and is still practiced

worldwide by a relatively small but avid group of enthusiasts.

Origins

The origins of barbershop harmony are impossible to trace with any certainty. Some historians have attempted to connect it with the practice of amateur music making in the barbershops of seventeenth-century England. While they may share a common association with regard to setting, Elizabethan "barber's music" and barbershop harmony bear no significant musical relationship with one another. Barbershop is an American musical idiom, a conflation of the diverse musical and cultural sensibilities that pervaded the United States during the 1800s. Begun as a social activity enjoyed largely by amateurs, it was born out of improvisation and the nineteenth-century interest in vocal harmonizing. Strong evidence suggests that African Americans—particularly those in the South—were chiefly responsible for forging the early "close harmony" style that would later be called *barbershop*. In casual settings such as barbershops, barrooms, and street corners, African Americans that were denied access to many other venues used singing as one of their primary forms of recreation.

Almost from the beginning, these amateur excursions into close harmony singing have enjoyed a symbiotic relationship with the professional groups that played a large part in popularizing the style. Blackface quartets were a staple of minstrel shows. Their repertoire, including songs about the South and "days gone by" (for example, Stephen Foster's "Old Folks at Home"), may have established the association of barbershop with nostalgia that continues to this day. Quartet features were carried over from the minstrel shows into the vaudeville circuit and the recording studio. Amateur quartets also performed to some notoriety, representing businesses, police departments, churches, and the like. Several hundred amateur quartets and choruses continue to sing under the auspices of the various barbershop organizations.

Barbershop enjoyed the height of its popularity around the turn of the twentieth century as the recording industry was coming into its own. In the 1890s black foursomes such as the Unique Quartette and the Standard Quartette and white groups such as the Manhansett Quartet were some of the first recording artists. Well into the 1920s, close harmony foursomes—led by the Haydn Quartet, the American Quartet, and the Peerless Quartet—were the dominant forces in popular music.

Musical Elements Associated with Barbershop

It is impossible to list the musical elements of barbershop in any definitive way or to describe an authentic performance practice. It has no known point of origin, nor did it receive any scholarly attention during its formative years. Nonetheless, certain core elements do seem to have become identified with the barbershop style.

Barbershop historically is identified as a male quartet style. The four parts are identified as tenor (specifically first tenor), lead (which is in the second tenor range), baritone, and bass. Idiomatic to barbershop is the practice of placing the melody in the second tenor part while the first tenor harmonizes in a relatively lighter voice above it. The bass tends to sing the roots and fifths of the chords, and the baritone fills in the chord sometimes below the lead, sometimes above. The association of barbershop with male singing is so strong that even women who today sing in barbershop quartets still use the tenor, lead, baritone, and bass voice designations. Barbershop is now considered a form of *a cappella* music, although early documentation and recordings reveal that it was sometimes accompanied by any number of instrumental combinations.

The hallmarks that have come to represent the barbershop style speak to its character as an improvised vernacular music. One of barbershop's most iconic elements is its use of call and response. In one type, the lead will sing a lyric that is repeated verbatim by the harmony parts. Several songs in the standard barbershop lexicon employ this technique and were referred to by some early chroniclers as "echo songs." "You're the Flower of My Heart, Sweet Adeline"— which some consider the icon of barbershop music— is a classic echo song. As it is traditionally performed, every line except the last is offered first by the lead singing alone, and then the lyric is repeated by the other parts, who harmonize with the final note of the lead line, as follows:

Sweet Adeline (sweet Adeline)
My Adeline (my Adeline)
At night, dear heart (at night, dear heart)
For you I pine (for you I pine)

Perhaps because of its *a cappella* nature and its connection with African American musical tradition, the barbershop style has a strong metrical foundation, even in its *rubato* passages. This metrical foundation is manifested by means of a class of devices—called *rhythmic propellants* by later barbershop theorists— that are designed to maintain the pulse, especially when the melody is holding a note or resting between notes. Rhythmic propellants take many forms. The examples of call-and-response patterns cited earlier are but one technique that groups use in part to maintain the sense of meter.

Related to call-and-response are "echoes," a loose designation that applies to a situation in which the harmony parts sing a few words to fill a gap left by the melody line as it holds a note or rests between notes. The term "echo" no doubt refers to its use in early practice when the harmony parts would simply repeat the last few words of the melody. It is sometimes the case, however, that the echo parts—rather than repeat the melody's lyric verbatim—sing a short phrase with different words that relates directly to the words of the melody. A 1924 recording by the Shannon Quartet of "Sweet Rosie O'Grady" illustrates a classic example of echo (see Example 1).

Other common rhythmic propellants include "bass pickups" and "fills" (using either words or nonsense syllables), the "tiddlies," and "swipes." A tiddly is a brief embellishment effected by one or two voices over a static chord. It can resemble standard nonchord tones (especially neighboring and suspension tones), but the primary purpose of a tiddly is to maintain the quick rhythmic drive. Tiddlies seem to spring from the improvisational nature of vocal lines in the black musical tradition. A swipe occurs when one or more parts move to a different tone while the other part(s) maintain a steady pitch. The effect of a swipe is key to the barbershop sound. It not only keeps the rhythm going but also adds harmonic changes and fills out

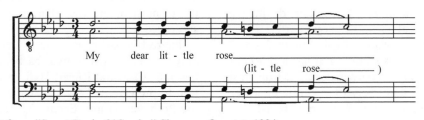

Example 1. Excerpt from "Sweet Rosie O'Grady." Shannon Quartet, 1924.

chords (for example, the bass and baritone might move from the root and fifth of a triad up to the fifth and seventh; this changes the triad with a doubled root to a complete seventh chord).

Barbershop utilizes a rich harmonic scheme. Again, owing to its improvisatory nature and its connection with African American idioms, the chord changes are rapid and often employ progressions uncommon to the classical standard practice. Barbershop leans toward consonant chords and features seventh chords for their ability to accommodate each singer on a distinct chord tone. Major-minor seventh chords are a particular staple of the barbershop style. In barbershop the major-minor seventh chord is found in two contexts. First, it acts in the traditional dominant seventh sense, resolving down a perfect fifth but with several secondary dominants strung together to effect a circle-of-fifths progression. Such a harmonic progression is found in Western classical music, often used as a modulatory device. It is rare in common practice music, however, to find entire songs based on the circle-of-fifths progression. The practice thrived, however, among popular-music composers of the late 1800s and early 1900s, particularly among ragtime and Tin Pan Alley composers.

Just as common to barbershop, however, are major-minor seventh chords that do not serve a dominant or secondary dominant function. Such cases suggest that in barbershop, as in other music linked to the African American tradition, the dominant seventh sound often arises as a result of a blues scale coloration on an otherwise major chord. In these instances, the harmony may not progress according to a dominant function but according to its function as a simple diatonic triad. Such nondominant major-minor seventh chords are the result of a heterophony— a horizontal rather than a vertical approach to music—and again speak to the improvisational nature of barbershop. When a blue third or blue seventh scale degree is added to the subdominant or tonic chords, respectively, the effect will resemble major-minor seventh chords. But because they are not conceived as dominant chords, they will resolve as if they were simple triads to whatever chord the melody dictates. It is this pervasiveness of—and freedom with—the major-minor seventh chord that is at the heart of barbershop harmony.

Barbershop is also known for certain distinctive vocal traits. Most amateur barbershop quartets incorporate a falsetto (literally a head voice quality) tenor. While rooted in the black tradition, it has a practical purpose for its existence in barbershop. The brilliance of a full-voice tenor can easily overpower the lower lead voice. Because the style is melody based, the falsetto tenor is used to support the lead without drawing attention to itself. Even tenors who sing in full voice generally do so with a softer, lighter quality that recalls falsetto singing. Barbershop singers today strive for what they call "expanded sound." This is literally a quality that is marked by strong overtones and is a result of several things, including a robust tone, justly tuned chords, matched vowels, and a balance that favors the lower voice parts and the most consonant intervals. Whereas earlier quartets used a great deal of *portamento* from note to note, modern quartets tend to sing cleaner intervals, reserving *portamento* for key places in the song in which they want to add *portamento* as a dramatic effect.

Barbershop's Influence

Although barbershop music has enjoyed only limited scholarly attention, its impact on vocal music in general and subsequent groups was enormous. Many prominent black musicians, such as Louis Armstrong, W. C. Handy, and Jelly Roll Morton, claimed barbershop singing as among their earliest musical experiences. Groups that would figure prominently in jazz and gospel began as barbershop quartets or claimed strong roots in barbershop music. The Mills Brothers' father, John Mills, Sr., sang in a quartet for many years, and it was in his barbershop in Piqua, Ohio, that the brothers began singing together. The popular gospel group the Golden Gate Jubilee Quartette also began as a barbershop quartet and started singing together in a barbershop. One of the early recording quartets, the Shannon Four, reinvented themselves as a jazz group called the Revelers. That incarnation was the prototype for the famous German quartet, the Comedian Harmonists. Even later popular ensembles, both male and female, had strong roots in barbershop singing. These include the Four Freshmen, the Hi-Lo's, and the Chordettes. Barbershop's influence is felt particularly in white and black gospel quartets from the early 1900s to the present, many of which use all of the standard barbershop idioms, including a voicing with melody in the second tenor. Thus, in spite of its unassuming image, barbershop was seminal to most of the vocal harmony genres that have succeeded it.

Interest in barbershop music had waned considerably by 1938, when two barbershop enthusiasts, Owen C. Cash and Rupert Hall, formed an organization to preserve it. Given the name "The Society for the Preservation and Encouragement of Barbershop

Quartets Singing in America"—whose lengthy initials (SPEBSQSA) were meant as a parody of President Roosevelt's New Deal agencies—the organization gained some popularity nationwide. This organization inspired a female barbershop organization called Sweet Adelines International. From these two groups have come several more male and female organizations worldwide. These organizations also fostered organized choruses that sing in the barbershop quartet style.

JAMES E. HENRY

Reference and Further Reading

Abbott, Lynn. " 'Play That Barber Shop Chord': A Case for the African-American Origin of Barbershop Harmony." *American Music* 10 (Fall 1992): 289–326.

Averill, Gage. *Four Parts, No Waiting: A Social History of American Barbershop Harmony.* New York: Oxford University Press, 2003.

Brooks, Tilford. "A Historical Study of Black Music and Selected Twentieth Century Black Composers and Their Role in American Society: A Source Book for Teachers." Ed.D. dissertation, Washington University, 1972.

———. *America's Black Musical Heritage.* (Based on his Ed.D. dissertation.) Englewood Cliffs, NJ: Prentice-Hall, 1984.

Cockrell, Dale. "Of Gospel Hymns, Minstrel Shows, and Jubilee Singers: Toward Some Black South African Musics." *American Music* 5, no. 4 (1987): 417–432.

Henry, James E. "The Origins of Barbershop Harmony: A Study of Barbershop's Musical Link to Other African American Musics as Evidenced Through Recordings and Arrangements of Early Black and White Quartets." Ph.D. dissertation, Washington University, 2000.

Mahar, William J. *Behind the Burnt Cork Mask: Early Blackface Minstrelsy and Antebellum American Popular Culture.* Urbana and Chicago: University of Illinois Press, 1999.

Nathan, Hans. *Dan Emmett and the Rise of Early Negro Minstrelsy.* Norman, OK: University of Oklahoma Press, 1962.

SPEBSQSA. *Contest and Judging Manual.* Kenosha, WI: SPEBSQSA, 1993.

Spaeth, Sigmund. *Barber Shop Ballads: A Book of Close Harmony.* New York: Simon & Schuster, 1925.

———. *Barber Shop Ballads and How to Sing Them.* New York: Prentice-Hall, 1940.

Stebbins, Robert A. *The Barbershop Singer: Inside the Social World of a Musical Hobby.* Toronto: University of Toronto Press, 1996.

Toll, Robert C. *Blacking Up: The Minstrel Show in Nineteenth-Century America.* New York: Oxford University Press, 1974.

"Tom the Tattler." *Freeman* [Indianapolis, IN] (December 8, 1900).

Wright, David. "History of Barbershop." Lecture notes for annual SPEBSQSA Harmony College, St. Joseph, MO.

Selected Discography

Bessemer Sunset Four. *Bessemer Sunset Four: Complete Recorded Works in Chronological Order* (Document Records DOCD-5379).

Flat Foot Four. *Barber Shop Melodies* (Columbia Records C-35).

Golden Gate Quartet. *Golden Gate Quartet: Gospel 1937–1941* (Frémeaux & Associés S.A. FA 002); *Travlin' Shoes* (Bluebird 66063-2).

Harmonizers. "Darktown Quartette Rehearsal" (Vocalion 14306).

Haydn Quartet. "My Wild Irish Rose" (Victor 16741-B).

Livingstone College Male Quartet. "Good Old Songs—Medley"/"Quartette Rehearsal" (Victor 20824).

"Way Down Yonder in the Cornfield" (Silvertone 714; unidentified quartet).

Compilations

Best of Barbershop: 25 Years of Champions (Decca; out of print).

Black Vocal Groups, Vol. 1: 1924–1930 (Document Records DOCD-5340).

The Earliest Negro Vocal Quartets: 1894–1928 (Document Records DOCD-5061).

The Earliest Negro Vocal Quartets: Volume 3 1921–1924 (Document Records DOCD-5355).

The Heritage Hall Museum of Barbershop Harmony Presents Close-Harmony Pioneers (SPEBSQSA HHM 1000).

I Hear Music in the Air: A Treasury of Gospel Music (RCA 2099-2-R).

BARREN CROSS

Jim LaVerde (b. May 1964)
Mike Lee (b. May 1964)
Ray Parris (b. March 29, 1964)
Steve Whitaker (b. July 10, 1963)

Barren Cross (BC) was born in November 1983, after nearly three years of gestation. The quartet was composed of bassist Jim LaVerde, singer Mike Lee, guitarist Ray Parris, and drummer Steve Whitaker, who were all natives of the Los Angeles area. Initially, Parris met Whitaker through a newspaper ad in early 1981. They both shared a vision for a Christian heavy metal band but were lacking a lead singer and bass player. Their communication was minimal for the next couple of years. In the spring of 1983, Whitaker met Lee through another newspaper ad and introduced him to Parris as their voice. The trio began rehearsing, writing songs, and looking for a bass player. By Fall 1983, LaVerde filled the void and completed the foursome. They named themselves BC because it symbolized the resurrection.

The new group was based in Inglewood, California. They played their first show in January 1984 at a girls' detention center. By early 1985, they met with Dino Elephante of the rock group Kansas. Elephante produced a six-song EP for them titled *Believe.* After making up press kits that included the EP, BC sent them out to a dozen record labels and landed a recording contract with Star Song records. In January 1986, Star Song released "Rock for the King,." composed of the six songs from the EP, remastered, along with three additional new tunes.

Touring tightened BC's performance as well as its cohesiveness. Live shows displayed the same incendiary guitar work found on the album. In some ways the band resembled a Christian version of Van Halen, with Paris's guitar work, while Lee's powerful singing style was reminiscent of Bruce Dickinson from Iron Maiden. Their songs were metallic and melodic at the same time. They contained killer hooks and had an overtly strong Christian message. When compared to their "Christian metal" counterpart Stryper, both groups' lyrics were both overtly Christian, but some considered BC's sound as being heavier.

In 1987, Barren Cross signed a contract with Enigma, a secular record label. *Atomic Arena* was released in 1988 and, after being marketed to both Christian and secular audiences, received some airplay on MTV and secular radio stations. During this time, they recorded *Hotter than Hell*, their live album, which was not released until 1990. It was also during this time that they collaborated with secular guitarist Ronnie Montrose for a remix of "Rock for the King."

During this period, the band was at its peak and recorded *State of Control,* which was once again engineered by the Elephante brothers. By August 1989 BC's cohesiveness began to unravel, with Whitaker and Lee leaving the band to return to school, raise families, and pursue other musical directions. Replacements were used temporarily for some touring, but that ended by 1990. The band temporarily reunited to record their fourth studio album, *Rattle Your Cage,* in 1994. Although the band has never officially disbanded, little has been heard from them since 1994, other than reuniting for an occasional concert.

BOB GERSZTYN

See also Rock Gospel; Stryper

Reference and Further Reading

Arnold, Christy; Rocker, Randy. "Barren Cross Interview." *Take a Stand* 4, no. 1 (July 1990).
Heaven's Metal homepage. http://heavensmetal.com/ (accessed March 30, 2003).
Paris, Ray. "Barren Cross Homepage." http://www.barren-cross.com/ (accessed March 30, 2003).

Whitaker, Beth. *The Calling of a Rock Star.* Hawthorne Publishing Company, 1988.

Discography

Believe (1985, EP Packaderm).
Rock for the King (1986, Star Song CD02679).
Atomic Arena (1988, Enigma D2-73311).
State of Control (1989, Enigma CD02540).
Hotter than Hell (1990, Medusa CD02684).
Rattle Your Cage (1994, Rugged).

BARRETT SISTERS

Widely considered the best documentary on gospel music—and considered one of the best documentaries ever—*Say Amen, Somebody* is ostensibly about two gospel legends, Thomas A. Dorsey and Willie Mae Ford Smith. However, the documentary's most electrifying performances are by DeLois Barrett (b. December 3, 1926) and the Barrett Sisters.

Three of ten children born in poverty on Chicago's South Side, sisters DeLois, Billie, and Rodessa drew widespread attention in Chicago's crowded gospel music field first by harmonizing in the homes of friends and neighbors and then by singing for the Morning Star Church in the mid-1940s. Lead vocalist DeLois was tapped to join the Roberta Martin Singers while still a teenager. Despite the presence of such luminaries as Eugene Smith, Norsalus McKissick, Myrtle Scott, Robert Anderson, Willie Webb, and Martin herself, Delois's operatic soprano and animated, emotional stage presence attracted attention wherever the group performed, especially in their trademark song, "Yield Not to Temptation."

While DeLois remained with the Roberta Martin Singers for eighteen years, sister Rodessa became a choral director, and Billie studied at the American Music Conservatory before becoming a church soloist. When DeLois married the Reverend Frank Campbell in the 1950s, she generally restricted her travel to the Chicago area. The sisters reformed their trio in 1961, began recording two years later, and have performed continuously since, generally in smaller venues and churches. The Barrett Sisters, like their friend the late Mahalia Jackson, have also remained active in social justice issues and Democratic Party politics.

The Barrett Sisters, lovingly called "the Sweet Sisters of Zion," were finally thrust into the national spotlight with the award-winning documentary *Say Amen, Somebody.* The subsequent acclaim finally enabled DeLois to fill a long-held dream (memorably voiced in *Say Amen, Somebody*) to perform throughout the world, and the Barrett Sisters have given concerts from Paris to the Fiji Islands.

After nearly sixty years of performing, the Barrett Sisters are one of the few remaining direct links to the original gospel sound of the 1930s and 1940s. DeLois's powerful voice and physical presence have made her the voice of choice for the funerals of some of gospel's most beloved artists, including Mahalia Jackson, Dorsey, Smith, even faith healer Kathryn Kuhlman.

ROBERT DARDEN

See also Dorsey, Thomas; Jackson, Mahalia; Smith, Willie Mae Ford

Reference and Further Reading

Erlewine, Michael; Vladimir Bogdanov; Chris Woodstra; Cub Koda, eds. *All Music Guide to the Blues*. 2nd ed. San Francisco: Miller Freeman Books, 1999.

Heilbut, Anthony. *The Gospel Sound: Good News and Bad Times*. New York: Limelight Editions, 1997.

Kael, Pauline. "Saved!" *The New Yorker* (April 4 1983): 125.

Nierenberg, George T. *Say Amen, Somebody*. Pacific Arts Video Records PAVR-547, 1980.

Reed, James. "Barrett Sisters Enjoy Singing Gospel Truth," *Boston Globe* (January 1, 2004): C1.

Reich, Howard. "Present at the Creation: Remember the Early Days of Gospel Music in Chicago." *Chicago Tribune* (May 27, 1990): 14.

Discography

With the Roberta Martin Singers

The Best of the Roberta Martin Singers (Savoy).
Old Ship of Zion (Kenwood).

With the Barrett Sisters

The Best of the Barrett Sisters (Intersound).
The Best of Delois Barrett Campbell (Nashboro).
Nobody Does It Better (Word).
Say Amen, Somebody (DRG).
What a Wonderful World (I AM).
What Shall I Render unto God (Sony Special Product).

BARROWS, CLIFF

(b. April 6, 1923)

Clifford "Cliff" Burton Barrows was for more than fifty years one of the most familiar personalities associated with gospel music during the second half of the twentieth century. As song leader, choir director, and master of ceremonies for the Billy Graham Crusade Association, beginning in 1945, Barrows exerted a significant influence on gospel music.

The son of Charles and Harriet Barrows, young Clifford was converted during a Sunday school meeting after hearing a message on John 3:16. He felt called to Christian ministry while in high school and later entered Bob Jones College for training, majoring in sacred music. While in school Barrows was influenced by Homer Rodeheaver, who had been evangelist Billy Sunday's song leader during the early decades of the century. Rodeheaver, as a charismatic soloist, song leader, and publisher, was then the leading figure in gospel music.

Upon Barrows's college graduation in 1944, he became an evangelist and song leader for Youth for Christ before joining Billy Graham. Barrows helped shape an approach to the Graham crusade meetings based on the model developed by Moody and Sankey during the 1870s and later continued by the Sunday/Rodeheaver team, wherein congregational song remained a conspicuous and important component of the revival meetings.

Unlike the earlier models, however, the music of the Graham crusades was characterized by a more conservative approach as Barrows and the "team" of musicians—including vocal soloist George Beverly Shea and pianist Tedd Smith—relied upon traditional hymns and older gospel songs as the core of their music. In fact, the song most identified with the Graham crusades, "Just As I Am," was a gospel hymn from a century earlier.

The impact of a revival "crusade," which involved a series of highly publicized and widely broadcast services that might last for many weeks, was to popularize whatever music Barrows chose for his crusade choirs to sing. As a result, some of the late twentieth century's best loved gospel songs were those made popular by their inclusion as a crusade "theme" song. Examples included "Great Is Thy Faithfulness," "To God Be the Glory," and "How Great Thou Art"—gospel songs no publisher could afford to leave out of a new hymnal after they gained fame in a Graham meeting.

Barrows also carried on the tradition of song leader as master of ceremonies, following in the footsteps of Ira Sankey, Homer Rodeheaver, and Charlie Alexander. In this role, Barrows reflected an energetic, smiling spokesman who smoothly tied together the disparate parts of a revival service. Unlike his former models, Barrows was not involved in composing or publishing music.

His efforts were directed toward other aspects of the Graham Association, however. These included being program director and host for the weekly *Hour of Power* radio program from its inception in 1950. From 1965 to 1970, Barrows was also president of World Wide Pictures, the film arm of the ministry known for its use of more contemporary music.

In 1966, Barrows and Donald Hustad compiled and edited *Crusader Hymns*, a volume of songs for use in the revival meetings. Barrows also assisted in compiling *Crusader Hymn Stories,* with biographical and anecdotal stories related to the hymns and gospel songs popular in the meetings.

Although the music of the Graham crusades tended to reflect a conservative bent, Barrows did feature new gospel writers as they began to emerge. These included John Peterson and the Gaithers, reflecting traditional gospel hymnody, and Andrae Crouch, reflecting the growing popularity of black gospel music. Also included were representatives of the folk music movement, such as Johnny Cash, and the newer leaders of contemporary Christian music.

With the Graham crusades being such an influential factor in evangelical life, Barrows did much to popularize the performance practice of gospel hymnody as congregational song led by an arm-waving conductor, accompanied by a piano and/or organ, assisted by a choir and sung in a fairly straightforward, nonimprovisatory manner.

Over his long career, Barrows may well have led more people in singing gospel and religious music than any other human being. For his contributions, he was inducted into the Gospel Music Hall of Fame in Nashville in 1988.

MEL R. WILHOIT

See also Crouch, Andrae; Rodeheaver, Homer Alvan

Reference and Further Reading

Graham, Billy. *Just As I Am: The Autobiography of Billy Graham.* New York: Harper Collins, 1997.

BARTLETT, EUGENE MONROE

(b. December 24, 1885; d. January 25, 1941)

Singer, songwriter, editor, and publisher Eugene Monroe Bartlett was born the day before Christmas in Waynesville, Missouri. His education came at the Hall-Moody Institute in Martin, Tennessee. Early in life he developed an interest in music that he manifested by teaching singing schools. In later years his schools brought together such well-known teachers as James Rowe and Homer Rodeheaver.

In 1918 Bartlett joined forces with John A. McClung and David Moore to form the Hartford Music Company in Hartford, Arkansas, thirty miles south of Fort Smith. Moore had been partners with Will M. Ramsey in the Central Music Company until Ramsey moved to Little Rock, Arkansas. He then threw in his lot with McClung and Bartlett to form a company that would have a significant influence on the development of the Southern gospel music industry. During the 1920s this company achieved some success with Bartlett's songs "Victory in Jesus" and "Everybody Will Be Happy Over There." Bartlett was president of the Hartford Music Company from 1918 to 1935, during which time it expanded to include branch offices in Nacogdoches, Texas, and Hartshorne, Oklahoma. This growth was accomplished in much the same way James D. Vaughan built up his Lawrenceburg, Tennessee, company.

In 1921, the Hartford Musical Institute—a shape-note school with sessions twice a year, in January and June—was established. By the early 1930s approximately four hundred students were attending this school. Bartlett also published *The Herald of Song,* a monthly magazine promoting shape-note singing and advertising quartets sponsored by Hartford to promote the company's products. These activities notwithstanding, Hartford's greatest claim to fame was Albert E. Brumley, who attended the Hartford school in 1926 and went on to become the best-known southern gospel songwriter of all time. Arriving in Hartford without sufficient money to pay the school's tuition, Brumley was enabled to enroll by Bartlett, who also put the youth up in his own house, an act of kindness Brumley never forgot.

Brumley attended music classes, earning his keep by working for the Hartford company and writing songs in his spare time. While in Hartford, he published his first song, "I Can Hear Them Singing Over There," with Bartlett's help. Brumley later described this 1927 effort as "not one of my better tunes." Brumley also was bass singer for the Hartford Quartet, which featured, in addition to gospel numbers, comedy songs such as Bartlett's "Take an Old Old Tater and Wait." The latter piece became a country hit when later recorded by the West Virginia singer Little Jimmy Dickens.

After leaving the Hartford Music Company, Bartlett worked briefly for the Stamps–Baxter Music Company and the James D. Vaughan Music Company. He remained active conducting singing schools throughout Arkansas, Oklahoma, Texas, Alabama, and Tennessee. Besides those already mentioned, his best-known songs are "I Heard My Mother Call My Name in Prayer" and "He Will Remember."

W. K. McNEIL

Reference and Further Reading

Goff, James R., Jr. *Close Harmony: A History of Southern Gospel.* Chapel Hill: University of North Carolina Press, 2002.

Hively, Kay; Albert E. Brumley, Jr. *I'll Fly Away: The Life Story of Albert E. Brumley.* Branson, MO: Mountaineer Books, 1990.

Reynolds, William J. *Companion to Baptist Hymnal,* Nashville, TN: Broadman Press, 1976.

BASS, MARTHA

Martha Carter Bass Peaston (b. 1921, Arkansas; d. September 21, 1998, Saint Louis, MO)

Martha Bass's family moved to Saint Louis, Missouri, when she was two years old, and Martha joined the Pleasant Green Baptist Church at an early age, under the leadership of Pastor Reverend G. H. Pruitt. Influenced by the National Baptist Conventions, she started to read the Bible and to sing in the choir with a dark, powerful contralto and, from the beginning, was outstandingly good, like her own mother, Nevada Carter.

She was chosen by Willie Mae Ford Smith to perform in her backup group, and of all of Smith's female pupils, Bass came closest to duplicating her vocal power and resonance, even if Martha's idol was Mahalia Jackson. Trained and obviously inspired by her mentor, she was known as a "house shouter," with bluesy accents, because of her ability to rouse a church into pandemonium. That is how she had a short stay of about three or four years with Clara Ward and the Ward Singers; she recorded with them for Savoy in 1950, and her version of "Wasn't It a Pity How They Punished My Lord" was a huge hit.

At about the same time, her family and entourage organized a private recording session, and two songs were issued on the Bass label. Then she got married, and, with two sons and a baby girl—later to be the famous soul singer Fontella Bass, married to Lester Bowie, the leader of the Chicago Art Ensemble— Martha chose to raise her family, staying at home and returning to the Pleasant Green Choir. However, she stayed in touch with the Ward Singers, and, in 1963, she was hired as sales manager of a music store the Wards opened to sell printed music, songbooks, records, and greeting cards.

The shop was closed two years later, and, in 1966, with plenty of free time again and eager to testify her faith and her love of God, Bass thought it was time to make new records under her own name. She "advertised" herself and was well received in Chicago by Checker Records. Her first album in March 1966 was entitled *I'm So Grateful,* with strong tracks such as "I Do, Don't You" and "What Manner of Man Is This." (Her daughter Fontella claimed she was playing piano and singing in the backing group.) It was a

sizeable hit in the Middle East, and it led to new albums on Checker, including *Rescue Me* in 1968, with, among other great songs, "In Times Like These" and "Now That I Found the Lord." In 1969, a tribute to her idol, *Martha Sings Mahalia Jackson,* her own favorite, a tribute that was not a servile copy of the model but a personal testimony to the greatest of the gospel singers ever.

In 1972, she recorded her last album for Checker, *It's Another Day's Journey,* and, after that, Martha, who sang only church songs—toured for some time with her mother Nevada and daughter Fontella, billed in Europe in the 1980s as "From the Roots to the Source." But from the late 1980s until her death in 1998, she was satisfied to be her daughter's best supporter, and she helped Fontella's career any way she could until Selah Records gave the whole family— Martha, Nevada, and Fontella—an opportunity to make a record altogether in 1990, with Fontella's brother and special guest David Peaston (*A Family Portrait of Faith*).

With Willie Mae Ford Smith and Cleophus Robinson, Martha Bass will remain one of the best gospel singers ever to come out of Saint Louis, Missouri. Unfortunately, she was sadly underrecorded.

ROBERT SACRÉ

See also Jackson, Mahalia; Smith, Willie Mae Ford; Ward Trio (Ward Singers)

Reference and Further Reading

Boyer, Horace Clarence. *How Sweet the Sound: The Golden Age of Gospel.* Washington, DC: Elliott & Clark, 1995.

Hayes, J. Cedric; Robert Laughton. *Gospel Records 1943–1969. A Black Music Discography*, 2 vols. London, UK: Record Information Services, 1992.

Heilbut, Tony. *The Gospel Sound: Good News and Bad Times.* New York: Limelight, 1985.

Reagon, Bernice Johnson, ed. *We'll Understand It Better By and By. Pioneering African American Gospel Composers.* Washington, DC: Smithsonian Institution Press, 1992.

Ward-Royster, Willa; Toni Rose. *How I Got Over. Clara Ward and the World-Famous Ward Singers.* Philadelphia: Temple University Press, 1997.

Wilmer, Val. "Martha Bass interview." *The Wire* (UK), 1985.

Discography

From the Root to the Source (1980, Soul Note LP SN1006).

Mother Smith and Her Children (1989, Spirit Feel CD1010).

A Family Portrait of Faith (1990, Selah Records SLD7506).

None But the Righteous: Chess Gospel Greats (1992, Chess CHD 9336).

Gospel Sisters and Divas 1943–51 (2002, Frémeaux et Associés FA5053; 2-CD box).

BAXTER, J. R., JR.

Jesse Randall Baxter, Jr. (b. 1887; d. January 1960)

J. R. Baxter, Jr., sometimes known as "Pap" or "Pa," was a singing schoolteacher whose partnership with Virgil O. Stamps ultimately resulted in the Stamps–Baxter Music & Printing Company, the leader in the field of gospel song publishing. A native of DeKalb County, Alabama, Baxter had briefly been a country schoolteacher, but his interest in gospel songs led him to study with such early practitioners of the trade as Thomas B. Mosley and Anthony J. Showalter.

In 1918, he married Clarice Howard. Working for Showalter, Baxter gained an acquaintance with Virgil Stamps and bought into his company in 1926. Initially, he ran the Stamps–Baxter office in Chattanooga, Tennessee, until Stamps died in August 1940, after which time the Baxters moved to Dallas, Texas, and took over the main office. By that time, Stamps–Baxter had moved ahead of its chief rival, the James D. Vaughn Music Publishing Company of Lawrenceburg, Tennessee.

Baxter continued to run Stamps–Baxter and maintain the company's position in the field throughout his lifetime. A composer of some note himself, the publisher's own credits as author or coauthor included "Try Jesus," "Travel the Sunlit Way," "Something Happens (When You Give Your Heart to God)," "I Have Peace in My Soul," "Living Grace," and "I Want to Help Some Weary Pilgrim." According to a November 7, 1949, article in *Time*, the company had fifty employees, did $300,000 worth of business yearly, and had four traveling quartets and "a school in Dallas to train itinerant song leaders." In addition to its Dallas premises, the firm still maintained an office in Chattanooga and another one in Pangburn, Arkansas, which was run by one of their key writers, Luther Presley.

Following J. R. Baxter's demise, Clarice "Ma" Baxter took charge of the firm and operated it until her own death, after which it was sold to Zondervan Publishing House of Grand Rapids, Michigan. Of J. R. Baxter, one friend was quoted at the time of his death as saying, "He never bruised a heart, nor made one bleed."

IVAN M. TRIBE

Reference and Further Reading

Baxter, Mrs. J. R.; Videt Polk. *Gospel Song Writers Biography*, 2–3, 8–9. Dallas, TX: Stamps–Baxter Music and Printing Company, 1971.

Goff, James R., Jr. *Close Harmony, A History of Southern Gospel*, 81–96. Chapel Hill: University of North Carolina Press.

BAYLOR, HELEN

(b. ca. 1950, Tulsa, OK)

Helen Baylor grew up in Los Angeles and was involved with popular music from an early age. At seventeen she became the youngest cast member in the road company of the Broadway musical *Hair*. She went on to work with Chaka Khan, Aretha Franklin, and Stevie Wonder but would ultimately testify to a life of degradation from which she had to be redeemed. Baylor began recording Christian music in 1990.

In 1992 she became affiliated with the Fellowship of Inner-City Word of Faith Ministries and on January 10, 1993, she was ordained a minister within that fellowship at Crenshaw Christian Center in Los Angeles. A year later, she received Dove Awards for Contemporary Gospel Album (*Start All Over*) and Contemporary Gospel Song ("Sold Out"). On February 18, 1995, Baylor was awarded an honorary doctorate in sacred music from Friends International Christian University (Merced, California). She later moved to Jonesboro, Georgia, where she became a member of Divine Faith Ministries, International, and she became involved in that church's ministries of music, healing, and deliverance. Baylor has also served on the boards of two facilities for unwed mothers: St. Domenic's in Tulsa, Oklahoma, and the Elizabeth Home in Ft. Worth, Texas. She is married to James Baylor and the mother of four children.

Baylor's husky voice has generally endeared her to critics, and her roots in rhythm and blues have given her music popular appeal. Her first album *Highly Recommended* featured several dance tracks and included two songs ("There Is No Greater Love" and "Victory") that became top-forty hits on Christian radio charts; in the mid-1990s she added light jazz influences to her repertoire. Baylor has often been described as a gospel artist with crossover appeal, and this may be owed in part to her penchant for recording duets with mainstays of both gospel and Christian pop: her various albums pair her with Andrae Crouch, Bob Carlisle, Phil Driscoll, Billy Preston, and Marvin Winans. She has also sometimes chosen to rework secular soul songs into gospel tunes, recording slightly rewritten versions of "Love Brought Me Back" (originally a hit by D. J. Rogers) and "How Sweet It Is" (a hit for Marvin Gaye and James Taylor).

Baylor's greatest success in the world of gospel came with *The Live Experience*, a recording of a 1994 benefit concert she gave to support a children's ministry. The album appealed to Christian pop fans but also brought Baylor to the attention of a more traditional gospel audience. Notably, the track that received the most attention was a spoken-word account of her conversion titled "My Testimony." Here, the artist credits her salvation from a life of promiscuity and drug addiction to the faithful prayers of her grandmother and the inexhaustible mercy of God. In 1999, Baylor released a second live album that evinced a more distinct worship focus.

MARK ALLAN POWELL

Reference and Further Reading

Baylor, Helen. *No Greater Love: The Helen Baylor Story.* Vision Publishing, 2005.

Discography

Highly Recommended (1990, Sony 47763).
Look a Little Closer (1991, Sony 48781).
Start All Over (1993, Sony 57463).
The Live Experience (1994, Sony 66443).
Love Brought Me Back (1996, Sony 67803).
Helen Baylor . . . Live (1999, Verity 43124).
Greatest Hits (1999, Sony 69793).
Super Hits (2000, Sony 85180).
My Everything (2002, Diadem 10682).

BECK, ELDER CHARLES D.

(b. ca. 1900, Mobile, AL [?]; d. ca. 1972, Ghana, West Africa)

Called "the Singing Evangelist," Elder Charles David Beck was born around 1900, probably in Mobile, Alabama (he is also listed with two other birthplaces: Georgia and Ghana, West Africa). Considered one of the formative artists during the prewar gospel blues and Southern gospel eras, Beck's work, by comparison, went largely unrecognized while writing and performing in the shadow of Thomas A. Dorsey and others from the 1930s through the 1950s.

Despite his prolific repertoire of more than sixty recordings during his lifetime under almost every available label, details about his life, work, and travels are scant. The first entry in the literature is from December 16 and 18, 1930, when he performed concerts at the King Edward Hotel in Jackson, Mississippi (OKeh label). With Beck on "full tilt barrelhouse piano," he accompanied popular singing preacher Elder Curry and his congregation. One of the songs performed was "Memphis Flu." The lyrics described the 1918–1919 influenza epidemic that killed nearly one million Americans. Fire-and-brimstone

delivery of sermons and songs, accompanied by rollicking hand-clapping, foot-stomping, and call and response, characterized the 1930 event and Elder Beck's lifelong career.

Many of Elder Beck's sermons and songs also dealt with object lessons and humorous, dramatic descriptions of "the wages of sin" from which he had been liberated. Following World War II, Elder Beck seized the opportunity afforded by a proliferation of label companies. He recorded with several, including Eagle, Gotham, King, Chart, and others, rerecording "There's a Dead Cat on the Line" (first released by Reverend F. W. McGee) and recording "Jesus, I Love You," "Winehead Willie Put That Bottle Down," "Dry Bones," "Delilah," "You Better Watch Your Close Friends," and "Don't Ride That Hell-Bound Train," among others.

Very few of his travels throughout the United States are described in the literature. He toured among Holiness and Baptist groups all over the country, including Charles Town, West Virginia, and Washington, D.C. Elder Beck's last concert was recorded in Buffalo, New York, at a Church of God in Christ, where his six-year-old son gave his personal testimony (Folkways, 1957). While the lively congregation sang "Walk in the Light," Elder Beck delivered a prayer and broke into his sermon based on Psalms 150, after which he returned to singing "Don't You See," accompanying himself on an electric xylophone. Elder Beck is thought to have become engaged in missionary work in Ghana in late 1960, and he died in Ghana circa 1972.

EVELYN M. E. TAYLOR

Reference and Further Reading

Brown, Florence Newman. Interview by Evelyn M. E. Taylor, Charles Town, WV, November 11, 2004.
"Elder Charles Beck Postwar Recordings." Blues Heritage Showcase, www.bluesbeforesunrise.com (accessed February 16, 2003).
Lewis, Uncle Dave. "Elder Charles D. Beck: Biography." www.djangomusic.com/artist_bio, www.boltmusic.com. All Music Guide (n.d.).
Noble, E. Myron. Interview with Evelyn M. E. Taylor, Washington, DC, December 15, 2004.
Tallmadge, W. H., ed. "Urban Holiness Service." Excerpts from a service at the Church of God in Christ, Buffalo, NY, December 30–31, 1956. Folkways 8901 (side 1, band 1; side 2, bands 1, 2, 3), 1957.

Discography

"Memphis Flu" (1930, OKeh; with Elder Curry); "Urban Holiness Service" (1957, Folkways); various recordings 1930–1947 on Eagle, Gotham, King, Chart, and other labels.

1946–1947

"Delilah"; "Didn't It Rain"; "Don't Ride That Hellbound Train, Pt. 1 and Pt. 2"; "Dry Bones"; "Handwriting on the Wall, Pt. 1 and Pt. 2"; "He Is Able"; "He Knows How Much I Can Bear"; "I Got a Home in That Rock"; "I'm Going to Live the Life I Talk About in My Song"; "I'm Gonna Tell God"; "Jesus, I Love You"; "Lord, I've Tried"; "O Jesus Let Me Ride"; "Rock and Roll Sermon, Pt. 1 and Pt. 2"; "Sermon, Hallelujah, Amen"; "Shouting with Elder Beck"; "There's a Dead Cat on the Line"; "Walk in the Light"; "What Do You Think About Jesus"; "When I Can Read My Title Clear"; "Why Should I Worry?"; "Winehead Willie Put That Bottle Down"; "You'd Better Watch Your Close Friends"; "You've Got to Move."

BENNARD, GEORGE

(b. February 4, 1873; d. October 9, 1958)

Author and composer of "The Old Rugged Cross," one of the most popular gospel songs, George Bennard was born in Youngstown, Ohio, but grew up in Iowa, where his family moved in the late 1870s. While attending a Salvation Army meeting in Lucas, Iowa, he was converted to Christianity. Thereafter, he wanted to be a minister and planned to continue his formal education with that goal in mind. But in 1889, his father, a coal miner, died, leaving the sixteen-year-old boy the sole support of his mother and four sisters. This situation made further schooling impossible, leaving him to his own means to gain theological knowledge. Through personal contact with numerous ministers and individual reading and study, Bennard became well versed in religious matters.

About 1890, Bennard moved his family to Illinois, where he later married. He and his wife joined the Salvation Army, Bennard eventually becoming a brigade leader of the corps. After several years, he resigned his position and joined the Methodist Episcopal Church, spending the last several years of his career as an evangelist in the United States and Canada. At some point prior to his retirement he moved to Reed City, Michigan, where he spent the remainder of his life.

Although he wrote more than three hundred gospel songs, he is remembered only for "The Old Rugged Cross." Even in his lifetime it was his only composition that achieved considerable acclaim. In Reed City, a twelve-foot-high wooden cross was erected bearing the words "Old Rugged Cross" and the notice "Home of Living Author, Rev. George Bennard." After his death this cross was replaced with another one located in a local museum. In 1990 a museum in honor of Bennard and his song was opened in Reed City's Rambardt Park.

"The Old Rugged Cross" was written in 1913, the composer-lyricist receiving his inspiration in Albion, Michigan, while praying for a full understanding of the cross and its plan in Christianity. The melody came first and then the theme of the words. Yet it was several weeks before he completed the lyrics. Shortly afterward, Bennard sang his new song in Pokagon, Michigan, and he then introduced it at a convention in Chicago. Apparently, the hymn was well received, but it did not make its first appearance in print until nearly two years later. Its earliest known publication is in *Heart and Life Songs, for the Church, Sunday School, Home and Campmeeting* (1915), a book compiled by George and Iva Durham Bennard and Joseph H. Smith.

The song was purchased by Homer A. Rodeheaver, who played a large role in its success. Rodeheaver, primarily remembered as the musical leader of William A. "Billy" Sunday's evangelistic crusades, published Bennard's song in forty-one different collections and also recorded the song ten times on Columbia, OKeh, and Victor in addition to his own Rainbow Records. Rodeheaver's January 1921 rendition on the Rainbow label (1015) with Virginia Asher—another member of Sunday's evangelistic team—may well be the first commercial recording of Bennard's song. In 1926 C. A. Tindley's Bible Class Singers made what is probably the first commercial recording of Bennard's song by a black group, for Paramount. On February 10, 1927, Ford and Glenn recorded "The Old Rugged Cross," and their rendition sold several thousand copies, which was very good for a gospel song at the time.

Since the 1920s the number has been often recorded by a variety of artists too numerous to list. Certainly these releases added to the song's popularity, and they are also indicative of its already existing popularity. According to a recent poll conducted by *The Christian Herald*, it is the most popular Protestant hymn, being chosen by Protestant churchgoers as their favorite of 1,666 hymns and songs.

W. K. MᶜNᴇɪʟ

Reference and Further Reading

McNeil, W. K. "The Old Rugged Cross." *Rejoice* iii, no. 1 (1990): 22–23.
Reynolds, William J. *Companion to the Baptist Hymnal.* Nashville, TN: Broadman Press, 1976.

BETHLEHEM

Danny Daniels (b. Unknown)
John Falcone (b. Unknown)
Dom Franco (b. Unknown)
Dan McCleery (b. Unknown)
Randy Rigby (b. Unknown)

Bethlehem was a Christian country rock band whose one album on the Maranatha label garnered sustained critical acclaim. The group featured the pairing of Danny Daniels on vocals and guitar with Dom Franco on pedal steel, along with Randy Rigby on keyboards, John Falcone on bass, and Day McCleery on drums. Bethlehem was associated with the 1970s Jesus movement revival and, in particular, with the Southern California manifestation of that movement, which centered around Calvary Chapel in Costa Mesa, California. Their sound was often likened to that of such general market groups as Poco or the Eagles.

Bethlehem formed as a Christian band in 1974, but the band members had all known each other and played together prior to that. They had been friends and bandmates prior to becoming Christians and, after going their separate ways, all experienced separate but similar conversions to the faith. When each discovered what had happened to the others, they were determined to reform as a Christian band. The group initially called itself Bethlehem Steel to highlight the pedal steel guitar that gave them their trademark sound but later shortened this to avoid allegations of trademark infringement. Bethlehem often played at the Palomino Club in North Hollywood, but they eventually directed their ministry to more rural areas, focusing on small towns that other Christian artists did not typically include in their tour schedules. By 1979, they had relocated to Boulder, Colorado.

Bethlehem's one album is praised by critics for evincing a laid-back country vibe that evokes humility and tenderness. The songs are melodic and the group performs them with vocal harmonies typical of the Southern California sound that was popular at that time. The album was produced by Al Perkins and Tom Stipe, both of whom were noted musicians and recording artists in their own right. Standout songs include the worshipful "Bright and Shining Son" and the loping "Desert Song," which likens the journey of life to Israel's divinely guided trek through the wilderness to a promised land. The songs "Night Rider" and "Dead Reckoning" have a harder edge to them.

After Bethlehem, Danny Daniels released a solo album for Maranatha and worked with John Wimber to form the Vineyard Church Fellowship. He became a staff pastor and worship leader at a Vineyard church in Aurora, Colorado. He also continued to write worship songs with Randy Rigby, and he released several albums of worship music. The song "Heart of Love" by Daniels and Rigby became especially well known in many settings. As of 2005, Daniels was still touring widely, performing concerts and conducting worship seminars and music workshops. Dom Franco became worship leader at Calvary Chapel in Portland, Oregon.

MARK ALLAN POWELL

See also Calvary Chapel, Costa Mesa; Maranatha! Music

Reference and Further Reading

Baker, Paul. *Contemporary Christian Music: Where It Came From, Where It Is Going*, 107. Westchester, IL: Crossway Books, 1985.
Di Sabatino, David. "Bethlehem." In *The Jesus People Movement: An Annotated Bibliography and General Resource*, 160. Westport, CT: Greenwood Press, 1999.
Powell, Mark Allan. "Bethlehem." In *Encyclopedia of Contemporary Christian Music*, 80–81. Peabody, MA: Hendrickson Publishers, 2002.

Discography

Bethlehem (1978, Maranatha 77-040).

Danny Daniels (solo)

Sons of Thunder (1982, Maranatha); *Hearts on Fire* (1991, Bluestone); *Praise Collection* (1994, Bluestone); *Another Shade of Blue* (1995, Vineyard); *Northern Light* (2001, Third Day); *Leavin' on the Special* (2004, independent).

BLACK GOSPEL MUSICALS

Capturing the Spirit on Broadway

Despite the inherent theatricality of black gospel, Broadway does not have a particularly good track record when it comes to incorporating America's most dynamic musical style. The early "ragtime musicals," based in minstrelsy, sometimes incorporated spirituals or quasi-spirituals, and black musical adaptations of popular Broadway shows such as *The Mikado* and *Carmen* in the 1930s and 1940s sometimes featured spiritual-like numbers. Even the legendary "Old Man River" from *Showboat* is performed in the manner of a Fisk Jubilee Singers spiritual.

Among the first major musicals to feature spirituals and early gospel numbers were Langston

Hughes (1902–1967) and Zora Neale Hurston's *Mule Bone* (1930), Marc Connelly's *Green Pastures* (1930), Hall Johnson's *Run, Little Chillun* (1933), and Owen Dodson's little-seen *Divine Comedy* (1938). However, the first generally successful musical to make significant use of gospel music was Hughes's *Black Nativity,* which premiered off Broadway in 1961. Hughes and producer Gary Kramer were inspired, in part, by a Christmas album recorded by Marion Williams and cast both Williams and Alex Bradford. Reviews were strong, but the production enjoyed greater success abroad and helped make stars out of both Williams and Bradford Specials singer Madeline Bell. *Black Nativity* was also the direct source of later rock gospel shows, such as *Jesus Christ Superstar* and *Godspell.*

Hughes then collaborated with Jobe Huntley to produce *Tambourines to Glory,* which is credited as the first gospel production to play Broadway, in 1963. Despite the presence of Clara Ward, the production received poor reviews and ran only three weeks. It has, however, enjoyed an enduring appeal in small and regional theaters through the years. Hughes's next gospel production, *The Gospel Glow* (1962), an African American Passion play, drew little attention. His *Jerico-Jim Crow,* while receiving better reviews, never made it to Broadway proper in 1964.

The year 1964 saw the introduction of perhaps the most significant artist in the history of black gospel on the legitimate stage, Vinnette Carroll (1922–2002). Carroll, a talented director/writer, adapted James Weldon Johnson's *Trumpets of the Lord* that year. Despite the presence of Cicely Tyson and a long run off Broadway, *Trumpets of the Lord* ran for only seven performances on Broadway in 1969. Carroll's revisualization of *Alice in Wonderland* in 1969, called *But Never Jam Today,* featured Bradford's music and universal kudos for its originality, but it too never clicked with Broadway audiences.

One of the big hits of the New York stage in 1970 was *Purlie,* a gospel version of Ossie Davis's earlier comedy, *Purlie Victorious.* Starring Cleavon Little and Melba Moore, *Purlie* ran for two years and continues to be popular in university and community theaters.

Bradford and Carroll reunited for Carroll's *Don't Bother Me, I Can't Cope.* The original production in 1972 made Carroll the first African American woman to direct on Broadway, and the production ran for nearly three years. Carroll struck gold with another gospel musical in 1976, *Your Arms Too Short to Box with God*—a gospel-styled reworking of the New Testament book of St. Matthew—with music by Bradford. *Arms* ran for two productions. A revival in 1982 with the Reverend Al Green and Patti LaBelle also did well at the box office. Bradford, just 51, suffered a stroke while working on still another musical, *Don't Cry, Mary,* in 1978 and died a few weeks later.

It would be several years before black gospel returned as the featured music on Broadway, although productions of *The Wiz, Bubbling Brown Sugar,* and *Timbuktu* and a revival of *Porgy and Bess* all featured spiritual overtones and the occasional outright gospel number. Two more overtly gospel-themed productions, including *Comin' Uptown* (1979) and an African American version of Dickens's *A Christmas Carol* (1979), both flopped after brief runs.

Off Broadway, *Jazzbo Brown,* a remake of *The Jazz Singer,* played for two months at the City Lights Theatre in 1981. Also off Broadway, *Mama, I Want to Sing* ran for many years in two separate productions in 1980 and 1983, at the East Harlem Cultural Arts Center. The mostly free-form gospel musical spawned *Mama, I Want to Sing II* and *Mama, I Want to Sing III* in the years that followed. On Broadway, both *Sophisticated Ladies* (1981) and *Dreamgirls* (1981) featured songs with a definite gospel flair.

Perhaps the most creative melding of black gospel and the legitimate stage was—of all things—a retelling of Sophocles's *Oedipus Rex. The Gospel at Colonus* featured the Blind Boys of Alabama, along with Morgan Freeman, and it won numerous awards during its long run off Broadway in 1983–1984. A PBS *Great Performances* production and smash tour of France followed, but *Colonus* closed after only 61 performances when it was transferred to Broadway in early 1988.

Gospel returned—briefly—to Broadway with a musical version to James Baldwin's *Amen Corner* in 1983, but it closed after a month of bad reviews. Superior performances and numerous high-octane gospel songs could not save either *Sing, Mahalia, Sing* (1986) or *Truly Blessed* (1990), and both closed after short stints on Broadway, although *Sing, Mahalia, Sing* has enjoyed numerous revivals elsewhere. Another gospel musical, *Don't Get God Started,* despite fine songs by Marvin Winans, closed after three months in late 1987. *Don't Get God Started,* however, has also continued to be performed by regional theaters and even large urban churches. The South African musical *Serafina!,* which also featured several musical numbers that would be familiar to black gospel music fans, was a smash hit both on Broadway and at the Lincoln Center in 1987.

While no overtly black gospel production has found success on Broadway for some time, the legacy of the earliest hits can still be heard in such disparate productions as *The Lion King, Rent, Bring In 'Da Noise, Bring In 'Da Funk, It Ain't Nothin' But the Blues,* and even the revival of *Jesus Christ Superstar.*

ROBERT DARDEN

See also Bradford, Alex; Fisk Jubilee Singers; Five Blind Boys of Alabama; Green, Al; Ward Trio (Ward Singers); Williams, Marion; Winans, The

Reference and Further Reading

Burdine, Warren, Jr. "The Gospel Musical and Its Place in the Black American Theater." In *A Sourcebook of African-American Performance: Plays, People, Movements,* edited by Annemarie Bean. London: Routledge Press, 1999.
Gussow, Mel. "Stage: Back on Broadway, *Your Arms Too Short.*" *New York Times* (June 3, 1980): C7.
Hamlin, Jesse. "What Blind Boys See in 'Gospel': Legendary Group Molded Play's Sanctified Sound." *San Francisco Chronicle* (November 8, 1990): E1.
Hill, Errol, ed. *The Theater of Black Americans, Vol. 1: A Collection of Critical Essays.* Englewood Cliffs, NJ: Prentice-Hall, 1980.
Hill, Errol G.; James V. *A History of African American Theatre.* Cambridge, UK: Cambridge University Press, 2003.
Jones, John Bush. *Our Musicals, Ourselves: A Social History of the American Musical Theatre.* Hanover, NH: Brandeis University Press, 2003.
Kroll, Jack. "Gospel Truth." *Newsweek* (January 10, 1977): 66.
Shepherd, Richard F. "*But Never Jam Today* Follows Recipe." *New York Times,* April 24, 1969): 40.
Trescott, Jacqueline. "As the Spirit Moves Him: *Black Nativity* Producer Mike Malones' Light-Footed Gospel." *Washington Post* (December 24, 1994): Style B1.

Discography

Black Nativity (Collectables).
Gospel at Colonus (Nonesuch).
Purlie (RCA).

BLACKWOOD BROTHERS

Roy Blackwood (b. December 24, 1900, Fentress, MS; d. March 21, 1971)
Doyle Blackwood (b. August 22, 1911, Ackerman, MS)
James Blackwood (b. August 4, 1919, Ackerman, MS; d. February 3, 2002)
Ronald Winston (R. W.) Blackwood (b. October 23, 1921; d. June 24, 1954, Alabama)
Cecil Blackwood (b. October 26, 1934, Ackerman, MS; d. November 13, 2000, Florida)
James Blackwood, Jr. (b. July 31, 1943, San Diego, CA)

During the 1950s, the Blackwood Brothers—a quartet of young men from Memphis, Tennessee—changed the face of American gospel music. With their superb musical skills and revolutionary promotional techniques, they brought the excitement and passion of gospel to millions of fans who had thought of it as a stodgy, formal church music and sanctimonious funeral hymns. They took what had been a niche music for working-class Southerners and broke it out to a huge national audience, and although they were by no means the first classic gospel quartet—"four men and a piano"— they were certainly the most colorful and the most famous. Young Elvis Presley had his heart set on joining them, and he was a regular backstage visitor to their concerts at Municipal Auditorium in downtown Memphis. All the major gospel songwriters, both white and black, sent their songs to them. Major record companies, which had largely ignored gospel music, courted them with contracts, and even national network television shows sought them as guests. By the end of the decade, as country singer Barbara Mandrell has said, it was impossible to think of gospel music without thinking of them.

For the first fifteen years of their career, the Blackwood Brothers were not all that different from the hundreds of other well-mannered happy little gospel groups that populated the South in those days. They traveled to small-town church concerts, got up early for local radio shows, and sold songbooks out of the trunk of their car. Then, in 1950, they moved from their conservative Iowa base to the bustling musical mélange of Memphis, and suddenly things began to change. Their music was injected with a new energy, and the Memphis scene of blues, jazz, rhythm and blues, and black gospel had the effect of supercharging the group and blasting it off into a territory where few quartets had gone before.

In their peak years (the early 1950s), the Blackwoods could boast the highest tenor, and, especially after J. D. Sumner joined the group, the lowest bass in gospel. They took songs at the fastest tempo and always had the hottest piano player. They had the most colorful and animated stage act, jumping around, bending over backward, and throwing the microphone and its stand back and forth, all like a military drill team. They used the most daring and complex vocal arrangements, often ending on breathtakingly high sustained harmonies.

The genesis of the Blackwood Brothers goes back to 1900 to a sharecropper's shack on the Mississippi delta belonging to William Emmett Blackwood and Carrie Prewitt Blackwood, with the birth of a first son, Roy. Though not musicians themselves, William and Carrie often attended church meetings and brush arbor meetings. The family quickly grew: Lena, a daughter, in 1905; a second boy, Doyle, in 1911; and then a third son, James, in 1919.

Roy was the first to develop an interest in singing; he had married in 1919 and soon started his own family with the birth of two sons, R. W. in 1921 and Cecil in 1934. Doyle emerged as the most interested in the new professional gospel quartets that companies such as Vaughan were sending out, and he decided to becomes a professional singer himself. He began learning the songs of two of the South's most popular acts, the Delmore Brothers and Jimmie Rodgers. By 1926 Doyle and his kid brother James began singing informally at local church suppers and even on local station WTJS. They managed to attend a singing school under the direction of Vardaman Ray, leader of the nationally known string band the Ray Brothers. Inspired also by the records of Frank Stamps and his All-Star Quartet, the brothers soon joined in the group.

Gradually, the radio shows and concerts grew more and more frequent. By 1938 the brothers began to dress alike, in sharp but conservative suits and then later in special concert suits of white linen. By the end of 1938, they had moved to a major radio station, KWKH in Shreveport, and were employed by Stamps–Baxter, one of the South's leading publishers. V. O. Stamps believed that quartet music should be done with a piano rather than a guitar, and be assigned them a piano player, Marion Snider. In 1940, Stamps asked them to make a daring move out of the South, to Shenandoah, Iowa, to work at the powerhouse KMA station owned by the huge mail-order Henry Field Seed Company. World War II disrupted their plans considerably as different members were drafted, but by the war's end, they were back at Shenandoah and were embarking on new promotional techniques.

One was recordings. The group decided to start their own record company, with masters recorded by a company in Kansas City. Their first release was "The Old Rugged Cross," backed with "When He Calls I'll Fly Away," featuring Roy, James, R. W., and Bill Lyles on bass. By 1950 the group had issued more than fifty Blackwood Brothers label records, selling them through the mail and at personal appearances. This increasing visibility won them an offer to go to Memphis, where they were offered a large chunk of air time over WMPS.

In the meantime, Roy and Doyle decided to retire from active performing to help manage the business. Aldon Toney stepped in as tenor and Jackie Marshall came on board as pianist. The group signed with a major label, RCA Victor, in 1951 and on January 4, 1952, they went into the RCA studios in Nashville and recorded their first four songs. The big hit was their energetic version of "Rock-A-My-Soul," which they had learned from the Golden Gate Quartet, but other standards were born as well, such as "I Won't Have to Cross Jordan Alone." In the next few

months, they recorded soon-to-be standards such as "Angels Watches Over Me," "My Journey to the Sky," "Peace in the Valley," "Wanna Rest," "Mansion Over the Hilltop," "Peace Like a River," and "Have You Talked to the Man Upstairs."

By 1954 the Blackwoods were winning a national reputation and even appeared in June on Arthur Godfrey's national television show. But then tragedy struck; two weeks after the show, R. W. and Lyles were killed in a plane crash. At first, the surviving brothers vowed never to sing again, but gradually they overcame their shock and regrouped. Bass singer J. D. Sumner was brought in to replace Lyles, and soon the Blackwoods were on the road again.

Throughout the 1950s and 1960s, the group did a long series of albums for RCA and later for Skylite. For a time they joined forces with another popular quartet, the Statesmen, to form Stateswood Music and to buy out several of the older songbook publishers (including James D. Vaughan). The association also led to the founding of the National Quartet Convention in 1956. James Blackwood emerged as the central figure in all this—he was being referred to as "Mr. Gospel Singer of America"—and dozens of new young singers made their way in and out of the organization. These include the great tenor Bill Shaw, pianist Hylton Griswald, and pianist Wally Varner.

They began winning the first of dozens of various Dove Awards. By the start of the new millennium, Ron and R. W., along with Steve Warren, were still performing as the Blackwood Brothers.

CHARLES K. WOLFE

Reference and Further Reading

Davis, Paul. *Legacy of the Blackwood Brothers.* London, n. d.

Wolfe, Charles. Booklet of liner notes accompanying *Rock A My Soul: Complete RCA Recordings of the Blackwood Brothers 1952–60.* Bremen, Germany: Bear Family Records, 2002.

Discography

Rock A My Soul: Complete RCA Recordings of the Blackwood Brothers 1952–60. Bremen, Germany: Bear Family Records, 2002.

BLISS, PHILIP PAUL

(b. July 9, 1838; d. December 29, 1876)

This native of Clearfield County, Pennsylvania, wrote a number of still-popular hymns during his brief lifetime, including "Hold the Fort," "Let the Lower

Lights Be Burning," "Wonderful Words of Life," and "Almost Persuaded." A self-trained musician, Bliss developed an interest in religious music at an early age. By the time he was a young adult he so impressed George Root—one of the leading songwriters and publishers of the second half of the nineteenth century—that Root hired him to conduct music conventions and training institutes throughout the Midwest.

While working for Root, Bliss received great attention as a song leader, singer, and writer of religious songs. In 1869, Bliss met Dwight L. Moody and soon thereafter began singing in the evangelist's meetings. His singing strengthened Moody's belief that music was important to an evangelistic ministry. In 1874, at Moody's urging, Bliss joined Daniel W. Whittle to do evangelistic work, a relationship that lasted until Bliss's death two years later. During this time, he continued to write songs prolifically, often receiving inspiration while listening to a sermon. Eventually, he wrote 303 religious numbers, producing both words and music for many of them. Although they are less well known than his sacred pieces, Bliss also wrote ninety-five secular songs.

Most of Bliss's published works appeared in seven books that he edited either alone or with Ira D. Sankey. His *Gospel Songs* (1874) contained the first use of the term "gospel song," and "gospel hymn" initially appeared in *Gospel Hymns* (1875), which he edited with Sankey. The two collaborated on a second volume, *Gospel Hymns No. 2* (1876). Sankey edited four more collections with James McGranahan and George Cole Stebbins; the last of these was issued in 1891. In 1894, the entire series was published as *Gospel Hymns Nos. 1–6 Complete*. These books became the main source of gospel hymns throughout the late nineteenth century and also provided the name by which all subsequent songs of this style became known. Thus, Bliss and Sankey are properly credited with being the founders of the American gospel song movement.

Bliss's life ended tragically but in a selfless manner that was characteristic of the man. While returning to Chicago from his childhood home in Pennsylvania during the Christmas season of 1876, a railroad bridge near Ashtabula, Ohio, collapsed, plunging the train into a sixty-foot ravine, where it caught fire. Bliss initially survived by escaping through a window. Unfortunately, in an effort to rescue his wife, he returned to the wreckage, and they both perished in the fire. Their bodies were never found, but in Bliss's trunk, which somehow escaped damage, the text of the hymn "My Redeemer" was located. James McGranahan, who succeeded Bliss as song leader of Whittle's evangelistic endeavors, provided music for the number, which became very popular in revivals.

W. K. MCNEIL

Reference and Further Reading

Kalis, Robert D. "The Poet of Gospel Song." *The Hymn* xxv (1974): 101–105; xxvi (1975): 46–50. Reprinted from *Bread of Life* (March 1964).
Osbeck, Kenneth W. *101 Hymn Stories*. Grand Rapids, MI: Kregel, 1982.
Whittle, Daniel W., ed. *Memoirs of Philip P. Bliss*. New York: A. S. Barnes & Co., 1877).

BLUE JAY SINGERS

Famous Blue Jay Singers of Birmingham, Alabama; Blue Jay Gospel Singers
Silas Steele (b. 1913, Brighton, AL) (lead)
Members: James "Jimmie" Hollingsworth (tenor); Charles Beal (baritone); Charles Bridges (lead vocals); Willie Rose (lead); Dave Davney (second tenor, lead); Clarence "Tooter" Parnell (bass); Nathaniel Edmonds (bass); Leandrew Woffard (or Wauford) (bass)

The group was formed by Silas Steele, ca. 1925–1926, in Jefferson County, Alabama, where the members developed their specific skills. It was a fertile territory for jubilee quartets, as they were called at that time.

Steele joined forces with Clarence Parnell, a former bass singer with the Pilgrim Singers (another local quartet) to form the Blue Jay Singers. Parnell had already gained local celebrity as a quartet singer, and Steele, a young baritone and the younger brother of James "Jimmie" Steele (leader of the Woodwards Big Four Quartet) was beginning to gain a reputation as an outstanding soloist in his church choir. Parnell and Steele "stole" James "Jimmie" Hollingsworth, tenor, and Charlie Beal, bass, from the Dunham Jubilee Singers—a tradition in gospel quartets—to form their group. Within a very short time, the Blue Jays—featuring young Silas as the lead (he was only thirteen when he joined the group)—were the biggest rivals of the Birmingham Jubilee Singers. Because Steele had extraordinary charisma and began to adopt the preaching style of singing introduced by the sanctified singers, the Jays usually "took the program" when they appeared on the same bill with the Birmingham Jubilee Singers.

Their style was one that would influence gospel quartets for the next fifty years. According to Horace Clarence Boyer, "they celebrated the beauty and character of the natural male voice with its low sounds and brassy but warm timbre"; they sang with the power of the African American Baptist and Pentecostal preachers. "They celebrated the African American tendency of gathering resonance from the fatty tissues of the mouth rather than placing the tone close to the bridge of the nose, and they were not afraid to celebrate the body in their rhythmic accompaniment to their singing." These are the qualities that they brought to their first recording in 1931, a Dorsey song, the first ever recorded by a quartet, "If You See My Saviour".

At the same time, the gospel quartet movement had spread to Dallas, Texas, and the Blue Jays began to divide their time between Dallas and Birmingham. On one of their trips home, they recruited Charles Bridges, former lead singer of the Birmingham Jubilee Singers. He agreed because his group had become inactive since the death of Dave Ausbrooks, their baritone singer. Bridges felt that they would find no suitable replacement to revive the group and, with Bridges, the Jays became one of the most popular quartets of their time.

Their original double-lead swinging technique in their recordings of 1947, involving both Silas Steele and Charles Bridges, is a perfect example of the popular Jays' style of the time. While in Texas, the Jays became close friends and frequent performers with the Soul Stirrers, whom they had influenced in the early 1930s but had surpassed in popularity within a few years. They followed the Soul Stirrers to Chicago in the mid-1940s. After settling in Chicago and seeing the rise of dozens of gospel quartets, Steele adopted the sanctified preaching style of talking through a song, which later became known as the "sermonette," before or during a song performance. His preacher shouts became legendary and marked both a clear break with their original style of sweet singing in the jubilee style and a pronounced entry into gospel. They were one of the first quartets—outside of the Tidewater gospel quartets such as the Golden Gates, the Silver Leafs, the Harmonizing Four, and others—to employ the "clank-a-lank" response as a rhythmic and syllabic accompaniment to a solo lead.

The Blue Jays had success until the early 1950s, but by the late 1940s, other groups had surpassed them in innovation and popularity, causing Steele to seek more current and fertile ground for his talent. In 1948, Silas Steele decided to leave Chicago and dropped out of the Famous Blue Jays Singers to join the Spirit of Memphis Quartet and to start a new career. The Blue Jays were forced to go on without their number one soloist, and this of course was a hard blow to their fortunes. For several years the group continued to tour and to record—now with Charles Bridges and Willie Rose sharing the leads—for Blue Bonnet, Decca, and Trumpet before going out of the scene in the early 1950s. Nevertheless, the Blue Jay Singers will remain one of the most important and original gospel groups in the history of African American religious music.

ROBERT SACRÉ

Reference and Further Reading

Boyer, Horace Clarence. *How Sweet the Sound: The Golden Age of Gospel.* Washington, DC: Elliott & Clark, 1995.
Hayes, J. Cedric; Robert Laughton. *Gospel Records 1943–1969. A Black Music Discography.* 2 vols. London, UK: Record Information Services, 1992.
Heilbut, Tony. *The Gospel Sound: Good News and Bad Times.* New York: Limelight, 1985.
Reagon, Bernice Johnson, ed. *We'll Understand It Better By and By. Pioneering African American Gospel Composers.* Washington, DC: Smithsonian Institution Press, 1992.

Discography

Going on Home to Glory. Trumpet Gospel Anthology (1991, P-Vine Records, Japan, PCD-2187).
Vocal Quartets, Vol. 2 , 1929–32 (1997, Document Records, Austria, DOCD-5538).

BLUE RIDGE QUARTET

Elmo Fagg (b. June 28, 1919; d. Unknown)
Kenny Gates (b. November 3, 1930)
Ed Sprouse (b. September 20, 1923)
George Younce (b. February 22, 1930)
Laverne Tripp (b. April 11, 1944)
Donnie Seabolt (b. June 30, 1944)
Fred C. Daniel (b. March 29, 1925)
Burl Strevel (b. June 14, 1928; d. November 12, 1981)

The Blue Ridge Quartet from Spartanburg, South Carolina, was known for having the sweetest singing this side of heaven. They were a very popular group in gospel music for more than thirty years.

The group was formed in Dallas, Texas, in February 1946 as a part of the Stamps Music Company organization. They were originally known as the Stamps–Blue Ridge Quartet. Original members were Red Mathis, James Smith, Rosie Rosebury, Shaw Eiland, and William Cunningham. Soon after their formation, the quartet moved first to Raleigh, North Carolina, and later Burlington, North Carolina, before finally moving to Spartanburg, South Carolina, where they remained for the rest of their career.

In the early years, the personnel of the quartet changed frequently, until the team of Elmo Fagg (lead and manager), Ed Sprouse (tenor), and Kenny Gates (baritone and pianist) got together in the early 1950s. These three men remained a part of the Blue Ridge Quartet for many years. Several bass singers filled the slot, including Burl Strevel, Cecil Gholston, Norman Allman, and, later, George Younce. After a few years of traveling as a four-man group, the quartet hired Jim Hamill to sing baritone, and they later hired Bill Crowe to replace Hamill. Crowe remained with the group until they disbanded.

When George Younce joined forces with the Cathedral Trio, Burl Strevil returned to the Blue Ridge Quartet. Burl remained with the group until his death on November 12, 1981. Shortly after Strevil rejoined the group, Fred Daniel replaced Ed Sprouse as the tenor. Interestingly enough, Strevil and Daniel spent many years together in the Sunshine Boys. They brought several of the Sunshine Boys' hits to the Blue Ridge Quartet.

When Elmo Fagg retired in 1969, Laverne Tripp joined the group as lead singer. His songwriting skills and intense delivery brought a new appeal to the group. They experienced some of their finest moments with the personnel of Fred Daniel, Laverne Tripp, Bill Crowe, Burl Strevil, and Kenny Gates as the group adapted a more "country" sound.

A number of personnel changes occurred in the 1970s. The quartet added a band and began to sing country music in addition to their gospel songs. Although they were not as prominent on the gospel music circuit, they continued to perform into the 1980s.

They were the one of the first gospel groups to record for Decca records. They recorded for several major labels and were the first white gospel group to record on Gotham Records. They were also the first professional gospel quartet to perform in a Catholic church. They recorded for Sing and Skylite gospel labels in the 1960s, and they were a major artist for Canaan in the late 1960s and 1970s. The Blue Ridge Quartet released more than a hundred albums.

The Blue Ridge Quartet was also instrumental in forming the Gospel Singing Caravan with the Lefevres, Prophets, and Johnson Sisters. This aggregation of singers performed to sold-out audiences all over the nation.

JOHN CRENSHAW

Reference and Further Reading

The Blue Ridge Quartet. Liner notes (Bibletone BL-3503).
Gates, Kenny. Interview April 22, 1997.
"Remembering the Glory Days." *Escape* (Spartanburg, SC, April 16, 1997): D6.
Through the Years. Historical account of the quartet (Private LP-1110).

Selected Discography

The Blue Ridge Quartet (1958, Bibletone 3503); *Echoes from the Forties* (1958, Stateswood 451); *He Bought My Soul* (1960, Skylite 5975); *He's Life* (1960, SING 452); *On the Wings of a Dove* (1961, Sing 453); *Our Best to You* (1961, Sing 454); *A Session with the Blue Ridge* (1962, Sing 455); *By His Hand* (1963, Sing 456); *The Love of God* (1965, Canaan CA-4616-LP); *America's 12 Favorite Hymns* (1966, Canaan CAS-9637-LP); *Who Am I?* (1966, Canaan CA-4622-LP); *. . . And That's Enough* (1969, Canaan CAS-9667-LP); *Ride That Glory Train* (1969, Canaan CAS-9675-LP); *Rise and Shine* (1970, Canaan CAS-9685-LP); *There's a Great Day Coming* (1971, Canaan CAS-9698-LP); *On the Move* (1972, Canaan CAS-9713-LP).

BLUE SKY BOYS (BOLICK BROTHERS)

William A. Bolick (b. October 28, 1917, Hickory, NC)
Earl A. Bolick (b. November 16, 1919, Hickory, NC; d. April 19, 1998)

As the Blue Sky Boys, brothers William "Bill" and Earl Bolick left an indelible mark on country music with their uncanny, haunting duet harmonies. Yet with their song choices and humble, dignified stage presence, the Blue Sky Boys also wrote an oft-overlooked, pioneering chapter in the history of white country gospel.

The fourth and fifth of six children born in the North Carolina Piedmont, Bill picked up the guitar and banjo early and then switched to mandolin, while Earl mastered the guitar. As a teenager, Bill began his musical career on radio station bands in Asheville, North Carolina, and then Atlanta. By 1936, both brothers were working for fiddler Homer Sherrill and looking to advance their careers.

On June 16, 1936, in Charlotte, North Carolina, Bill and Earl auditioned for producer Eli Oberstein, who was making records for Victor's new Bluebird label, and Oberstein cut ten sides from the duo. At that session the brothers chose the name Blue Sky Boys, an amalgamation of their beloved Blue Ridge Mountains and Asheville's slogan, "The Land of the Sky," purposefully differentiating the Bolicks from the many other brother acts of the day.

Their initial recordings' success launched a demand for new recordings, radio shows, and concert appearances. Their musical careers were interrupted by military service in World War II, but the Blue Sky Boys returned to the studio in 1946 for another half decade, bringing their total recordings to nearly 124. In 1951, they dissolved the act to pursue other interests.

As the folk revival emerged in the early 1960s, Starday Records rereleased some Blue Sky Boys radio transcriptions, and Bill and Earl were coaxed back into performing. A few high-profile concerts followed, including UCLA's 1965 Folk Festival, which earned them a new generation of fans. This second chapter in their career was short-lived, leading to retirement in the early 1970s.

From their first recordings, the core of their sound was Earl singing lead and playing guitar and Bill adding high tenor harmony and mandolin. Their unique style was partly shaped by the bright prominence of Bill's tenor harmony lines in the recordings. Following the war, they supplemented their records with fiddle and bass, but the core vocals remained unchanged.

They often put that formula to use on the gospel songs they had learned as youths. Their earliest radio show theme song was "Keep on the Sunny Side," a gospel song from one of Bill's Sunday school hymn-books, which they rendered complete with gospel-style after-beat harmonies. While they offered their audiences plenty of secular fare, such as "Kentucky" or "I'm Just Here to Get My Baby out of Jail," a majority of their recordings were gospel hymns and songs of moral message.

Bill and Earl were adamant that their performance style remain traditional, eschewing the stylistic modernization of country music in the 1940s. With this attitude, the brothers best fused their home region's gospel music with a successful hillbilly career, and part of their golden legacy is the southern Appalachian gospel songs that they offered with such sweet musical honesty.

JOCELYN R. NEAL

Reference and Further Reading

Wolfe, Charles K. *Classic Country: Legends of Country Music*. New York: Routledge, 2001.

Discography

Together Again (1963, Starday SLP 257).
Blue Sky Boys (1964, RCA Camden CAL 797).
The Blue Sky Boys in Concert, 1964 (1989, Rounder 0236).
Blue Sky Boys on Radio, Vol. 1 (1996, Copper Creek CCCD-0120).
Blue Sky Boys on Radio, Vol. 2 (1996, Copper Creek CCCD-0121).
The Sunny Side of Life (2003, Bear Family Records BCD 15951; boxed set compilation with biographical notes by Bill C. Malone).

BLUEGRASS

Sometimes called "hillbilly music" and often known as "that high, lonesome sound," bluegrass music developed as a distinct genre in the rural upland South, particularly in the hills of Appalachia. The music itself grows out the traditions of the blues, country, gospel (especially the shape-note singing of the Southern hill country), and folk, and these musical traditions flow in and out of one another to form this distinctive bluegrass style.

Although bluegrass has always been popular in certain communities, it gained a broad hearing in 2001 when a movie called *O Brother, Where Art Thou?* hit the screens and featured the plaintive and lonesome sounds of Ralph Stanley and the Clinch Mountain Boys as well as newer bluegrass stars Alison Krauss and Union Station. In the 1960s and 1970s, a variety of rock musicians rediscovered bluegrass, incorporating it into their music. Gram Parsons, the Flying Burrito Brothers, the Byrds (some of whose members had been members of the Burrito Brothers), the early Eagles (whose guitarist Bernie Leadon had been a member of the Burrito Brothers), and the Grateful Dead, among others, included bluegrass motifs in their music. In the 1970s, Jerry Garcia of the Grateful Dead formed his own bluegrass band, Old and In the Way, with David Grisman and fiddler Vassar Clements, who had once played with Bill Monroe.

There is some argument over just when bluegrass was born, but most critics attribute its birth to Bill Monroe and his group the Blue Grass Boys in 1939. Monroe played a distinctive form of music that grew out of his own musical upbringing on his father's farm in western Kentucky. During his childhood, Monroe and his family would play music at night as a respite from their daily work on the farm. That little band included all stringed instruments: guitars, fiddles, and mandolins. As Monroe began playing in various groups around the country and finally on his own with backing musicians, he introduced bluegrass as a form of country music, and a number of musicians—including the Stanley Brothers, the Osborne Brothers, the Louvin Brothers, Wilma Lee and Stony Cooper, Hazel Dickens, and Flatt and Scruggs—began to carry the bluegrass banner, influencing a number of other musical styles.

Several musical traits characterize bluegrass. First, a typical bluegrass band is composed of five to seven musicians who sing and accompany themselves on acoustic instruments. More than any other musical form, traditional bluegrass emphasizes the purity of acoustic music and frowns upon the use of electric instruments. Such an emphasis caused a rift between traditionalists such as Monroe and so-called "new grass" musicians—such as the Dillards on their later records—who introduced electric instruments into their sets. Some instruments, such as guitar, banjo, and mandolin, were standard to most groups in the early days. In spite of what most have come to expect of bluegrass groups, fiddles were not a part of original bluegrass combos, and they became a central instrument only in the 1950s. Second, bluegrass involves complex harmonies that include parts for all voices (tenor, baritone, bass). Third, the meter in bluegrass music is duple, and thus tempos are much faster than in other forms of country music. Finally, the rhythm of the classic bluegrass song features a stress on the offbeat.

The traditional repertoire for a bluegrass group is much like older country music (1925–1955). Groups play traditional folk songs and songs that they have just written for a certain occasion. Bluegrass groups often include a number of traditional hymns in their repertoire. The themes of secular songs that bluegrass groups sing include memories of old home and family, love affairs, and problems of city life. Religious songs include old spirituals and newly composed gospel songs.

In the early days of bluegrass, most groups publicized themselves by playing live on the radio. During the 1940s, radio stations WIS, WBT, WSM, and WLS all broadcast barn dance shows that featured bluegrass musicians such as the Stanley Brothers, the Monroe Brothers, and Flatt and Scruggs. Most of these programs played over powerful "clear channel" stations that could reach most of the East Coast and thereby go into the homes of the communities out of which the music itself grew. By the 1950s, some of these groups were also recording albums, which enabled their musical styles to be broadcast even farther.

During the 1950s, many bluegrass musicians began to appear on television shows, sometimes losing their more traditional audiences as they adapted to a new medium. In the 1960s, bluegrass experienced something of a revival as folk music grew in popularity throughout the country. Alan Lomax, who traveled the country for the Library of Congress trying to capture traditional music on vinyl, played a key role in bringing some bluegrass musicians to Carnegie Hall during these years. Bluegrass went electric in the 1960s as both bluegrass groups such as the Dillards as well as rock groups such as the Byrds attempted both to preserve bluegrass styles and to introduce bluegrass to a new generation.

By the end of the twentieth century, bluegrass experienced a revival, in part because of the movie *O Brother, Where Art Thou?* The soundtrack for the movie remained at number one on the billboard country charts for six months. The movie's music spawned several collections, but new bluegrass fans also turned to contemporary bluegrass groups such as Nickel Creek, Alison Kraus and Union Station, and the Dixie Chicks (whose use of the Dobro has brought attention once again to the beautiful sounds of that instrument). In addition, a number of traditional country artists—notably Dolly Parton—recorded their own bluegrass albums in a tribute to the genre.

Because it grew out of rural communities in which religion provided a foundation for family, bluegrass has always been a key musical genre for gospel music. The purity of the musical style of traditional bluegrass matches the concern for purity that most gospel songs strive to achieve. Bluegrass musicians often end their sets by singing a traditional hymn and inviting audience participation since they assume that the audiences will be very familiar with these songs. Also, because bluegrass grows out of a rural environment where poverty is often a central feature, gospel songs—such as "I'll Fly Away"—offer an escape from the torment and misery of this world. All traditional bluegrass groups feature gospel, but perhaps the best-known bluegrass gospel group is Doyle Lawson and Quicksilver, which has always used bluegrass as a vehicle for religious themes. Wilma Lee and Stony Cooper and the Carter Family, as well as the Nitty Gritty Dirt Band (especially with their tribute album *Will the Circle Be Unbroken?*), also provide models of both traditional and contemporary bluegrass groups whose central themes are religious.

Gospel music, in the forms of older spirituals and newer hymns, continues to provide a foundation for much of bluegrass music in much the same way that bluegrass music provides a musical structure for gospel music.

HENRY L. CARRIGAN, JR.

See also Lawson, Doyle, and Quicksilver; Monroe, Bill

Reference and Further Reading

Artis, Bob. *Bluegrass*. New York: Hawthorn Books, 1975.
Cantwell, Robert. *Bluegrass Breakdown: The Making of the Old Southern Sound*. Urbana: University of Illinois Press, 1984.
Rosenberg, Neil V. "Bluegrass." In *Encyclopedia of Southern Culture*, edited by Charles Reagan Wilson and William Ferris, 993–995. Chapel Hill: University of North Carolina Press, 1989.
———. *Bluegrass: A History*. Urbana: University of Illinois Press, 1993.

Discography

Harris, Emmylou. *Roses in the Snow* (1980).
Lawson, Doyle, and Quicksilver. *Quicksilver* (1980).
Mainer, Wade. *Sacred Songs of Mother and Home* (1971).
Scruggs, Earl. *I Saw the Light with Some Help from My Friends* (1972).
Stanley, Ralph, and the Clinch Mountain Boys. *Cry from the Cross* (1971).
Story, Carl, and the Rambling Mountaineers. *Gospel Favorites* (1958); *Bluegrass Gospel Collection* (1976).
Sullivan Family, The. *Bluegrass Gospel* (1966).
White Spirituals (1960, compilation).
Wiseman, Mac. *Keep on the Sunny Side* (1960).

BLUES

Blues is a form of African American music that emerged around the dawn of the twentieth century. Like its contemporary forms—ragtime-, jazz-, and Pentecostal-influenced gospel music—blues (and the twelve-bar blues form) has influenced and helped to define American popular music since the early 1900s. Significantly, each of these genres also developed in the South, where the largest percentage of African Americans lived at the time.

Blues emerged in the deep South—probably in East Texas, Mississippi, or Louisiana—in the late nineteenth century. Rooted in field hollers, country dance tunes played on guitars, fiddles, and banjoes, and spirituals, the twelve-bar blues form gradually became more standardized and popular in the early twentieth century. W. C. Handy first recalled hearing blues in Clarksdale, Mississippi, in 1903. By the teens, blues songs were being published on sheet music. The blues was further disseminated throughout the country by musicians as diverse as Gertrude "Ma" Rainy and Jim Jackson touring with minstrel, medicine, and traveling tent shows as well as musicians migrating from the rural South to the urban North.

In 1920, black vaudeville singer Mamie Smith recorded "Crazy Blues" for OKeh records, which stimulated a greater interest among both blacks and whites in this genre. It was not until 1924, when Ed Andrews recorded "Barrelhouse Blues," that the down-home country blues began to be recorded by commercial record companies. Since then, thousands of blues recordings have been made by a wide variety of male and female singers accompanied by acoustic and amplified ensembles.

The continued interest in blues has resulted in the fragmentation of the genre into diverse styles. Many of them are geographical (Chicago, East Coast, or Texas), while others reflect the lyrics or connotations of the songs (dirty or juke joint). Blues has also shifted from its base of support in the African American community to encompass a more diverse audience. Many of the artists most recently associated with blues, such as Kenny Wayne Shepard and Eric Clapton, are white. Clapton's inclusion underscores the international interest in blues. Since the 1960s, the interest in blues has had its strongest support among white musicians, many of whom live in Europe. Since the 1980s, blues has been embraced by this new audience, which has formed blues societies, organized blues festivals, and lionized their blues heroes. Despite this move away from its black roots, the blues remains an African American musical form at heart.

KIP LORNELL

Reference and Further Reading

Cohen, Larry. *Nothing but the Blues: The Music and the Musicians.* New York: Abbeville Press, 1999.

Evans, David. *The NPR Curious Listener's Guide to Blues.* New York: Penguin/Perigee Books, 2004.

BOBBY JONES AND NEW LIFE

Bobby Jones (b. 1938, Henry County, TN)

Bobby Jones attended Tennessee State University in 1956, graduating with a B.S. degree in elementary education in 1959. He earned a master's degree in elementary education from the same institution and an Ed.D. in multiculturalism and curriculum leadership from Vanderbilt University in 1980.

Although his roots in gospel music reach back to the church and his college years, Dr. Jones began his professional entertainment career in gospel music in November of 1980 on the BET network with *Bobby Jones Gospel*—a show that Jones first piloted in 1976 in an effort to develop a Black Expo for the Nashville area (Black Expo is a fair held in certain cities across the United States that focuses on the contributions African Americans have made to their communities). The *Bobby Jones Gospel* show was created, produced, and hosted by Jones and aired in Nashville from 1976 until it was picked up by BET in 1980 to be nationally syndicated. Based in Nashville, Tennessee, Jones is also the host of the *Bobby Jones Radio Show* and the *Bobby Jones Gospel Countdown,* two network radio broadcasts aired from Nashville. Moreover, Jones has three network shows that are aired from his own television network, called The Word Television Network: *Bobby Jones Presents, Bobby Jones Gospel on Stage,* and *Bobby Jones Gospel New Artists Showcase.*

As one who has "revolutionized" the industry of gospel music, according to a proclamation written by President George W. Bush, Bobby Jones has exposed numerous gospel artists to the world. As Jones flourished on television with *Bobby Jones Gospel,* he saw the need for a group of singers who would accompany him on stage. This group of nine singers became known to the world as the New Life singers. Coincidentally, Bobby Jones and New Life recorded nine albums. In 1984, the group won a Grammy Award for the song "I'm So Glad I'm Standing Here Today," which was performed with country music star Barbara Mandrell. Prior to that honor, Bobby Jones and New Life were nominated for a Grammy Award for Best Performance by a Black

Contemporary Gospel Group for the album *Soul Set Free* in 1982.

One of Jones's most famous compositions is a song entitled "There Is Hope for This World," which was recorded with the group New Life in 1987–1988. As a group, New Life no longer exists. Jones now works with an aggregation called the Nashville Super Choir. Every Sunday, Jones, along with the Nashville Super Choir, performs contemporary gospel music and welcomes a display of upcoming and well-known gospel artists to his show.

Before his debut in the gospel industry, Jones taught elementary school in the school systems of Missouri and Tennessee. He also instructed at Tennessee State University for seventeen years, where he taught thought processing. He continues to lecture and facilitate seminars around the nation that are inclusive of much of his work in the music industry. Many of his seminars are based on a learning theory he developed while at Vanderbilt University.

Jones is a member of several professional organizations as well as the national spokesperson for several associations. He is a member of 100 Black Men of America, a NAACP, Phi Beta Sigma fraternity, and the National Black College Alumni Hall of Fame. He is also a national spokesperson for HIV/AIDS, the American Heart Association, and the National Diabetes Association. He is a faithful member of Temple Baptist Church in Nashville, where he is a layman.

In June 2003, Jones was honored with the Unsung Hero Award at the Juneteenth Celebration in Dallas, Texas, by Congressman Al Edwards. In July of 2003, the government of Tobago, British West Indies, and the government of the Turks and Caicos Islands honored Dr. Jones for outstanding contributions and service in the field of gospel music. Concurrently, the Full Gospel Baptist Convention honored Dr. Jones for outstanding service and presented him a Trailblazer Award in gospel music. Moreover, the board of directors of the National Black College Alumni Hall of Fame Foundation selected Dr. Jones for induction into the 2003 Hall of Fame, for outstanding achievements in the field of entertainment as an alumnus of Tennessee State University as well as for his exceptional support of his community and historically black colleges and universities.

ALPHONSO SIMPSON, JR.

Reference and Further Reading

Jones, Bobby. Telephone interview with Alphonso Simpson, Jr., June 2004.

BOONES, THE

Deborah Anne Boone (b. September 22, 1956)
Cherry Boone (b. July 7, 1954)
Lindy Boone (b. October 11, 1955)
Laury Boone (b. Unknown)

This quartet of gospel-singing sisters came by their musical interests naturally, being the daughters of Pat Boone and granddaughters of famed country singer Red Foley. Their grandmother, Foley's second wife, was also a one-time star on the National Barn Dance and the Grand Ole Opry.

The group performed occasionally with their parents as the Boone Family Singers, but as the Boones, they formed in 1969 and scored big the following year, 1970, with their initial recording "What the World Needs Now." This record not only was a hit but their live appearances—called by *Variety* "one of the most talked about shows of this or any other season"—were enormously successful. Their two albums, *The Boone Girls* and *First Class,* were well received in the gospel community. They went on to perform on the soundtrack of the movie *Born Again.*

About this time Debby went solo, performing a mixture of religious and secular music. Her recording of the title song from the film *You Light Up My Life* sold four million copies, earning her a Grammy as best new artist, and the song garnered an Oscar as best original song. Her album of the same title sold two million copies. The recording also reached number four in the country charts. In 1978, she had two top forty country hits, "God Knows" and "Baby I'm Yours," and in 1979, she had success with a revival of Connie Francis's pop song "My Heart Has a Mind of Its Own." The following year, she had her biggest country hit, reaching number one with "Are You on the Road to Loving Me Again."

At this point she became the daughter-in-law of actor Jose Ferrer and singer Rosemary Clooney when she married their son Gabriel Ferrer. Shortly after her marriage she had a few more minor hits, then opted to pursue an acting career. At the same time, she let it be known that she had no intention of continuing in the country field, noting that it was not honest of her to seek success in that genre when it was not her first musical preference. When she returned to singing it was in religious music, with a series of albums for CCM/Benson Records.

W. K. MCNEIL

Reference and Further Reading

Boone, Debby; Dennis Baker. *Debby Boone So Far.* Nashville, TN: Thomas Nelson, 1981.

Discography

The Boone Girls (1970s, Lamb/Lion).
Born Again Soundtrack (1970s, Lamb/Lion).
First Class (1970s, Lamb/Lion).
Glass Castles (1970s, Lamb/Lion)

Debby Boone

You Light Up My Life (1977, Warner).
Friends for Life (1987, Benson).
Reflections (1987, Benson).

BOSTIC, JOE

(b. March 21, 1909, Mount Holly, NJ; d. May 29, 1988, Southampton, NY)

Considered the "Dean of Gospel Disk Jockeys," Joe William Bostic helped introduce gospel music, born in church sanctuaries, to radio audiences and the formal concert stage. As one of black radio's earliest personalities, Bostic presented the excitement of gospel music to millions of Americans who were not members of Baptist or Pentecostal churches and who were unfamiliar with the new religious music and its celebrities. In addition to his broadcasting career, Bostic was a concert promoter, record distributor, label owner, and civic leader.

Born March 21, 1909, in Mount Holly, New Jersey, Bostic graduated with a bachelor's degree from Morgan State College in 1929 and secured his first broadcasting job in Baltimore, where he also worked as a correspondent for the *Afro-American*. He moved to New York City around 1937, and until 1939, he hosted the weekly black music program *Tales from Harlem* on radio station WMCA (one of the first stations to offer a black religious quartet, the Southernaires, a live broadcast).

In 1939, Bostic moved to WLIB, then known as WCNW, the "Voice of the Negro Community" (the station changed its call letters to WLIB in 1942). Ninety percent of the thousand-watt station's programming was aimed at African Americans. It was during his tenure with WLIB that Bostic began hosting live weekly talent showcases as well as a Sunday morning gospel music radio show, *The Gospel Train*, which became one of the East Coast's most popular gospel broadcasts.

In addition to his precise and measured vocal delivery, resonant voice, and learned vocabulary, Bostic cut a striking figure. He was distinguished, well-groomed and -attired. Like many of his black radio contemporaries, Bostic was college-educated and represented the middle-class values that poorer African Americans sought to emulate.

Just as the sounds of rhythm and blues were introduced to black and white Americans via the radio, so gospel music was introduced to a much wider audience via programs such as Bostic's. Certainly many devoted members of Baptist and Pentecostal churches tuned in every Sunday to hear their favorite performers and recordings, but so did African Americans and whites who were not brought up in the church yet were nevertheless mesmerized by the raw emotion expressed in the performances. Thanks to pioneer announcers such as Bostic, radio remains a significant force for spreading gospel music from coast to coast.

Bostic is perhaps best known as one of the country's most powerful gospel promoters during the genre's golden age, staging popular multiple-act shows in New York City and on the East Coast. With Buddy Franklin, he produced the first Negro Gospel and Religious Music Festival at the austere Carnegie Hall in 1950. The show's success was due largely to Bostic's persuading rising star Mahalia Jackson to serve as its headliner. Based on the triumph of the first program, the Second Annual Negro Gospel and Religious Music Festival took place the following year, featuring Jackson as well as emerging gospel stars James Cleveland and Norsalus McKissick. In 1959, the show moved to Madison Square Garden where—billed as the First Annual Gospel, Spiritual and Folk Music Festival—it drew an audience of eleven thousand who came to see and hear their favorite gospel performers.

Bostic promoted gospel shows throughout the 1950s and 1960s in venues large and small. In July 1957, for example, Bostic introduced the Ward Singers, Jeff and Charles Banks's Back Home Choir, and the Drinkard Singers to a largely white audience at the popular Newport Folk Festival in Newport, Rhode Island. A more typical Bostic program was held at the Rockland Palace in New York City on October 31, 1965. The "carnival of major quartettes" featured the Swan Silvertones, the Mighty Clouds of Joy, the Davis Sisters, the Soul Stirrers, the Swanee Quintet, and the Five Blind Boys of Alabama. Local talent opening for the headliners were the Garden of Prayer Choir and Madame Lucille Harley.

Many professional and amateur gospel groups were booked on Joe Bostic programs at one time or another. It was widely acknowledged that getting his attention could make a group's career, so an invitation from Bostic to perform, even if it was not always economically satisfying, was worth the exposure it provided.

Bostic continued working in radio until 1973. To supplement his broadcasting and promotion incomes, he founded the Holy Hour record label and owned a gospel record distribution business in New York City.

In addition to his work in gospel music, Bostic was also active civically and socially. He died in Southampton, New York, on May 29, 1988, at the age of seventy-nine.

ROBERT MAROVICH

See also Jackson, Mahalia; New York, Gospel in

Reference and Further Reading

Boyer, Horace Clarence. *How Sweet the Sound: The Golden Age of Gospel.* Washington, DC: Elliot & Clark Publishing, 1995.
Goreau, Laurraine. *Just Mahalia, Baby.* Waco, TX: Word Books, 1975.
Heilbut, Anthony. *The Gospel Sound.* New York: Limelight Editions, 1992.
"New York City AM Radio History." http://www.radio-history.com.
Southern, Eileen. *Biographical Dictionary of Afro-American and African Musicians.* Westport, CT: Greenwood Press, 1982.

Discography

Gospel Singing at Newport (1957, Verve MGV-8245). On this LP, Bostic can be heard introducing Newark's Back Home Choir and the Drinkard Singers.

BOYER BROTHERS, THE

James B. Boyer (b. 1934)
Horace Clarence Boyer (b. 1935)

James B. and Horace Clarence Boyer are natives of Winter Park, Florida, a small town north of Orlando. Their parents were both religious leaders in the Church of God in Christ, an African American Holiness Pentecostal church, known as a "sanctified church." James began playing the piano at four years of age and was playing for the church choir at eleven. Horace was eight years old when he began singing in the children's choir. James and Horace left Winter Park to live in Panama City, Florida. James studied gospel piano with his aunt, who played hymns and sanctified music that was jubilant. James and Horace moved back to Winter Park and became the Boyer Brothers near the end of the golden era of gospel music (1945–1955). They sang spirituals, hymns, and gospel songs on church programs while they attended high school. They earned the reputation as "Those Sanctified Boys." They began producing records at fifteen and sixteen years of age on Nashboro and Savoy labels. Horace wrote their first and greatest hit, "Step by Step":

Step by step, I am nearing the kingdom
Step by step, I am going home
Jesus will welcome me in His kingdom
Step by step, around the throne

This dynamic duo was well known in the 1960s for their pantomime as they sang. They would step forward and the audience would relate to the music and movements of the singers.

To put themselves through college, they continued to perform at various churches in Florida and southern Georgia. The brothers have made more than five hundred appearances singing such hits as "Thank God for That" and "I Heard from Heaven." They both play several musical instruments, and they have been billed with Mahalia Jackson, Clara Ward, and many others. Both graduated from Bethune-Cookman College in Daytona Beach, Florida. James majored in education to become a teacher, and Horace studied music.

The brothers married and moved to different locations. Their singing careers became less prominent. James and Horace earned their doctoral degrees. James became a professor in education at Kansas State University. Horace became a professor of music at the University of Massachusetts. James became pastor of a Church of God in Christ congregation in Manhattan, Kansas. Horace has engaged in research, publishing, and performances while receiving many awards in the history and sharing of musical styles.

Since both brothers have retired as professors, they can be heard on special occasions. James often sings at the church he pastors. In 1983 and 1984 they were featured in concert at the Smithsonian Institution in Washington, D.C. On Christmas in 1997, they gave a performance at their home church in Winter Park; it was fantastic. The crowds were traditional gospel fans from the 1950s and 1960s and contemporaries who had not seen them perform live. On March 31, 2000, they gave a concert as part of the Colby Concert Series. For Black History Month in 2004, Horace came to Orlando to perform slavery, spiritual, jubilee, hymn, gospel, and other songs that expressed the Civil Rights Movement. The mayor of Orlando recognized him for remembering his Florida roots.

SHERRY SHERROD DUPREE

Reference and Further Reading

Boyer, Horace, Dr. "Church of God in Church." Amherst, Massachusetts. Interview by Sherry Sherrod DuPree via telephone, December 27, 2004.
Boyer, Horace Clarence. *How Sweet the Sound: The Golden Age of Gospel.* Washington, DC: Elliott & Clark, 1995.
Boyer, James, Dr. "Church of God in Church." Manhattan, Kansas. Interview by Sherry Sherrod DuPree via telephone, January 29, 2004.

DuPree, Sherry Sherrod; Herbert C. DuPree. *African-American Good News (Gospel) Music.* Washington, DC: Middle Atlantic Regional Press, 1993.

Stanley, Sadie; George Grove. *The New Grove Dictionary of Music and Musicians.* 20 vols, New York: Groves Dictionaries, 1995.

Discography

Le Gospel 1939–1952 (2003, AMG, France; compilation, CD). Separated into three discs, one of spirituals and preachers, one focusing on the modern quartet sound, and the third dealing with female gospel groups during the music's golden era. Includes "Step by Step" by the Boyer Brothers.

BRADBURY, WILLIAM BATCHELDER

(b. October 6, 1816; d. January 7, 1868)

This student of Lowell Mason was a prolific writer of hymn tunes, producing more than nine hundred in his fifty-one years. He was also a teacher, organist, publisher, and piano manufacturer.

A native of York, Maine, Bradbury demonstrated considerable musical talent at an early age, learning to play every instrument that came his way. After the family moved to Boston in 1830, he studied music with Sumner Hill, who gave him his first lessons in harmony. Soon he met Lowell Mason and entered his school, the Boston Academy of Music; he also joined Mason's choir at the Bowdoin Street Church and for three months was their organist. In 1836, he moved to Machias, Maine, where he taught music classes and gave private piano lessons. Then, in 1838, he became a singing schoolteacher in St. John's, New Brunswick. Two years later, in 1840, he moved to New York as choir leader of the First Baptist Church, Brooklyn; in 1841, he became organist at New York's Baptist Tabernacle. He soon established singing classes for children that became so popular that they led to the introduction of music in New York's public schools.

His first song collection, *The Young Choir,* which was compiled in collaboration with Charles Walden Sanders, was issued in 1841. It was followed in the next twenty-six years by fifty eight other compilations of religious music and eight books of secular songs. From 1847 to 1849 Bradbury was in Europe, where he studied piano, harmony, and composition and met several important classical musicians, such as Franz Liszt and Robert Schumann.

After returning to the United States, Bradbury busied himself teaching music to children, composing, compiling music collections, and conducting at several music conventions (the first held in 1851 at Somerville, New Jersey). For four years, he was choir director at Broadway Tabernacle, and later taught harmony in musical institutes held by Mason, Thomas Hastings, and George F. Root.

In 1854, he began manufacturing pianos with his brother, Edward, and F. C. Lighte. With endorsements from prominent musicians such as Louis M. Gottschalk, Bradbury pianos became well known; winning first prize at several state fairs in 1863 added to their popularity. After Bradbury's death, the firm was taken over by the Knabe Piano Company. In 1861, Bradbury established Bradbury Publishers in New York, which primarily printed his own tunebooks but also issued a few compilations by other composers. After his death, the company was acquired by Lucius Biglow and Sylvester Main and became known as Biglow and Main. Bradbury's works designed for Sunday school use were enormously popular; *The Golden Chain* (1861), *The Golden Shower* (1862), and *The Golden Censer* (1864) sold more than three million copies each, and *Fresh Laurels* (1867) sold more than one million copies.

This multitalented man's death at a relatively early age was brought on by a lung disease believed to be a result of overwork. Many of Bradbury's melodies, particularly "Jesus Loves Me" (at one time considered the favorite hymn of Chinese children) and "He Leadeth Me" (1864) (a slight reworking of a Joseph H. Gilmore text in which Bradbury added two lines to the refrain), are akin to those of songs that, in the 1870s, became known as gospel hymns. Other melodies by Bradbury that are still well known include "Just As I Am" (1849) (a setting for Charlotte Elliott's 1834 hymn) and "Sweet Hour of Prayer" (1861) (the most popular melody for a text of uncertain authorship). Bradbury's 1860 hymn "Angel Band" remains popular with folksingers and country performers. As one of the most prolific early gospel hymn composers, William B. Bradbury did much to popularize the style that came to be named in the 1870s.

W. K. MCNEIL

Reference and Further Reading

Metcalf, Frank J. *American Writers and Compilers of Sacred Music.* New York: Russell & Russell, 1967 [1925].

Reynolds, William J. *Companion to Baptist Hymnal.* Nashville, TN: Broadman Press, 1976).

BRADFORD, ALEX

(b. January 1, 1926; d. February 15, 1978)
Gospel's Great Restless Innovator

Child prodigy Alex Bradford is an important link between the golden age of gospel and contemporary black gospel music. He is also a pivotal figure in the history of the Broadway musical.

Bradford was born in the gospel music hotbed of Bessemer, Alabama, during the Great Depression, though his parents managed to scrape up money for piano and dance lessons. Before turning to gospel full time, he briefly taught school, earning the sobriquet "Professor." He was "discovered" by Roberta Martin during a tour with her singers through Bessemer. While in the Army in World War II, Bradford formed and toured with several musical troupes. After the war, he joined the Roberta Martin Singers in Chicago, composing such hits as "Since I Met Jesus" and "Let God Abide." He eventually joined first Mahalia Jackson and then Martin Singers alumnus Willie Webb. It was with Webb that Bradford scored his first gospel hit, an arrangement of "Every Day and Every Hour."

Bradford's multioctave voice—along with his composition, arranging, and performance skills—prompted a contract with Specialty Records as part of the "Bradford Specials." One of Bradford's first releases for Specialty, "Too Close to Heaven," noted for its still-fresh arrangement and breathtaking vocal swoops, became his signature song. The Specials also featured countertenor Charles Campbell, and the group's distinctive sound produced a series of hits through the 1960s, fueled by new (for gospel) instrumentation and Bradford's outlandish sense of choreography and costuming.

Bradford's need for experimentation took him through a number of gospel labels through the 1960s, each release featuring more and more elaborate instrumental backing and arrangements. By now, the Specials included big-voiced contralto Madeline Bell, and Bradford wrote and arranged for a variety of mainstream artists, including LaVerne Baker. Ray Charles openly acknowledged his debt to Bradford.

In mid-career, he became minister of music for the well-known Abyssinian Baptist Church in Newark, New Jersey. At the urge of legendary talent scout John Hammond, Columbia recorded a lived album with the 120-voice choir (although contractual arrangements prevented Bradford himself from singing), *Shakin' the Rafters*, which continues to be a popular item in the label's catalog and features the classic performance of "Ride That Glory Train."

Bradford became increasingly interested in the legitimate stage in the 1960s as well. His first foray was with long-time associate Marion Williams in *Black Nativity,* Langston Hughes's retelling of the Christmas story in a gospel setting. While warmly received in New York, *Black Nativity* found its greatest success overseas and made Bell a star in London. In 1969, Bradford served as arranger for Vinnette Carroll's adaptation of *Alice in Wonderland,* called *But Never Jam Today.* Later, he toured for two years with Carroll's *Don't Bother Me, I Can't Cope.* Even as his gospel career began to wane in the 1970s, Bradford continued to find success on Broadway. In 1976, he wrote the songs for Carroll's *Your Arms Too Short to Box with God,* another gospel-flavored revue with a decidedly religious message.

However, in 1978, while working on the musical *Don't Cry, Mary,* Bradford suffered a stroke. He died a few weeks later at the age of fifty-two. While Bradford was a prolific composer (three hundred songs) and arranger, his legacy also includes the many artists whose careers he helped support. In addition to Williams and Bell, Bradford was influential in the lives of Cissy Houston, Dionne Warwick, and Billy Preston (who, while only ten, played organ on one of Bradford's studio sessions).

ROBERT DARDEN

See also Houston, Cissy; Jackson, Mahalia; Martin, Roberta; Williams, Marion

Reference and Further Reading

Boyer, Horace Clarence. *How Sweet the Sound: The Golden Age of Gospel.* Washington DC: Elliott & Clark Publishing, 1995.

Burdine, Warren, Jr. "The Gospel Musical and Its Place in the Black American Theatre (1998)." In *A Sourcebook of African American Performance: Places, People, Movements,* edited by Annemarie Bean. London: Routledge Press, 1999.

Erlewine, Michael; Vladimir Bogdanov; Chris Woodstra; Cub Koba, eds. *All Music Guide to the Blues,* 2nd ed. San Francisco: Miller Freeman Books, 1999.

Heilbut, Anthony. *The Gospel Sound: Good News and Bad Times.* New York: Limelight Editions, 1997.

Reagon, Bernice Johnson, "Conversations: Roberta Martin Singers Roundtable." In *We'll Understand It Better By and By: Pioneering African American Gospel Composers,* edited by Pearl Williams-Jones and Bernice Johnson Reagon. Washington DC: Smithsonian Institution Press, 1992.

Discography

The Abyssinian Baptist Choir. *Shakin' the Rafters* (Columbia 47335).

A Lifetime of Believing/Black Man's Lament (Collectables COL 6812).

One Step/Angel on Vacation (Collectables COL 7235).

Pop Gospel from London/The Soul of Alex Bradford (Collectables COL 7211).

Rainbow in the Sky (Specialty SPCD 7015-2).

Too Close (Specialty SPCD 7042-2).

BRADLEY, JOHN ROBERT

(b. September 10, 1920, Memphis, TN)

John Robert Bradley was the eldest son of John and Lela Ellis Bradley; his younger sibling was a brother, Van. He attended Grant Elementary School in north Memphis, Tennessee, and demonstrated a singing ability at an early age. He used this talent to earn small amounts of money to help support his mother and brother after his father left the family. Bradley lost his right eye due to an infection while a young boy, and did not graduate from high school. At age thirteen, he met gospel songwriter Lucie Eddie Campbell, who introduced him to the National Baptist Convention, USA, in 1933. He became her protégé and began singing at churches around Memphis and in Birmingham, Alabama.

In addition to Campbell, he was nurtured as a singer by his pastor, songwriter and religious playwright Reverend W. Herbert Brewster of Pilgrim Baptist Church, and Thomas Shelby, gospel pianist and music director at the church. In 1939, Bradley and Shelby joined a team of six talented singers and preachers called the Goodwill Singers. They toured the country advertising the religious literature of the convention and the Sunday School Congress, and encouraged churches to remain loyal to the convention after the 1915 split. Their repertoire included Campbell's songs, and she visited them frequently during their travels. For more than a decade, the Goodwill Singers were heard at all meetings of the National Baptist Convention and the Sunday School Congress.

Bradley's stirring bass-baritone voice was now being recognized as an exceptional one. Although he had been influenced by a wide variety of singers of his era, such as Ma Rainey and Bessie Smith, it was the great contralto Marian Anderson whom he desired to emulate. He wanted to be considered a "dignified gospel singer" as well as a classically trained musician.

With the financial backing of friends, he began serious vocal training in the late 1940s with such luminaries as the Wagnerian soprano Edyth Walker in New York, and studied music theory at Trinity College of Music in London. He gave his first European recital at the famous Royal Festival Hall in London, and performed widely in Scandinavia, Latin America, and the United States.

Called "the Voice of the National Baptist Convention, USA," Bradley received excellent critical reviews both at home and abroad. He was the first acclaimed artist to take gospel music to the concert stage, always ending his recitals with the music of Campbell and other gospel songwriters, such as Roberta Martin. He received a signal honor in 1974 when he was knighted by the Liberian government after being heard by its president at a meeting of the National Baptist Convention.

When not touring, he continued to work with the convention, and he was made director of music promotion for the Sunday School Publishing Board of the convention in 1957. He served as Campbell's assistant for nearly thirty years, and, upon her death in 1963, he took her place as music director of the National Baptist Congress of Christian Education, USA. Now retired, J. Robert Bradley maintains his singular position in the history of African American musicians as "The National Baptist Singing Ambassador."

LUVENIA A. GEORGE

See also National Baptist Convention

Reference and Further Reading

Jones, Amos, Jr. *I Have Always Been in the Hands of God: An Autobiography of the Life of Dr. J. Robert Bradley.* Nashville, TN: Townsend Press, 1993.
Walker, Charles. *Miss Lucie.* Nashville, TN: Townsend Press, 1993.

BREWSTER, WILLIAM HERBERT

(b. July 2, 1897, near Somerville, TN; d. October 15, 1987)

Noted editor, publisher, poet, preacher, theologian, dramatist, teacher, organizer, civil rights leader, and administrator who was also one of the most prolific lyricists/composers of gospel music. Born on a farm near Somerville, Tennessee, on July 2, 1897, William Herbert Brewster entered the world as the first of eight children to sharecroppers William and Carrie Polk Brewster. The grandson of two Baptist preachers, Brewster received his early education in between agricultural seasons. At age sixteen and with the blessing of his father, Brewster accepted his call to the ministry, beginning a tremendous journey committed to education, civil rights, and spreading the gospel message by any means available.

Gospel's Elder Statesman

Brewster's attendance at Memphis's Howe Collegiate Institute under the tutelage of Reverend T. O. Fuller and Reverend Sutton Griggs exemplified his commitment to education. Brewster continued his study as a student at the American Baptist Theological Seminary in Nashville, Tennessee, enrolling as one of the first black students in 1919. Brewster accomplished course work in theology, Shakespearean literature, theory of law, Greek, Latin, and Hebrew, among other subjects. He even sought out the assistance of a Jewish rabbi in Forest City, Arkansas, for additional study in Hebrew. By 1920 Brewster enrolled at Roger Williams University in Nashville, graduating in 1922 with a Bachelor of Arts degree. Brewster relocated to Memphis in expectation of taking the helm as dean of a newly planned seminary catering to black ministers, but the racial challenges of the era prevented the opening.

In 1925, Brewster was called to pastor the East Trigg Baptist Church, a post he would hold until his death some fifty years later. Brewster utilized East Trigg to implement numerous initiatives, including the creation of the Brewster Theological Clinic in 1926, which aimed to train ministers, missionaries, and Christian workers in leadership and the Bible. At the time of his death, the clinic had satellites in more than twenty-five cities across the United States. Brewster later added a medical clinic in the basement of the church. Brewster's leadership and innovative thinking earned him the positions of dean of the Shelby County General Baptist Association as well as corresponding executive secretary of the Education Board of the National Baptist Convention.

Brewster edited the *Forest City Beacon of Light*, the only black newspaper in circulation in the Memphis/Little Rock area. During the late 1940s, he hosted a weekly radio show live from his church, *Camp Meeting on Air,* on WDIA, the United States' first radio station featuring all-black programming. By the late 1940s and 1950s, Brewster led numerous civil rights protests and rallies, and subsequently he sponsored many of Reverend Dr. Martin Luther King's visits to Memphis.

A Sermon Set to Music

Greatly influenced by noted "Father of the Blues" William Christopher Handy, whose compositions and business acumen had been the talk of Memphis since his arrival in 1909, Brewster quickly arose as Handy's equivalent specializing in religious music. Brewster in time became one of Tennessee's greatest gospel composers, along with fellow native Lucie Campbell. Brewster's style of composition was much different from Campbell's and Thomas Dorsey's, whom many claim as Brewster's competition.

Brewster's lyrics boast a refined and eloquent nature, often using poetry from the Bible and drawing on his study of Greek and Hebrew language and syntax. Primarily a lyricist, Brewster also captured the rhythms of the burgeoning holiness movement taking shape in Memphis under the leadership of Reverend (later Bishop) Charles Harrison Mason, the founder of the Church of God in Christ denomination. Often based on his own testimonies and desire to teach the Bible through music, Brewster's songs have rich content and strong Biblical context, making them some of the most captivating, memorable, and popular songs of the golden age of gospel.

During the years 1945 through 1960, numerous gospel soloists, groups, and quartets recorded more than fifty of Brewster's compositions. He composed songs for church services, gospel drama pageants, and his group, the Brewster Ensemble, yet it was the recordings of these songs that would make him one of the most revered gospel composers of the time. Although his first composition, "I'm Leaning and Depending on the Lord" (1939), was a hit, "Move On Up a Little Higher" (1941), recorded first by Mahalia Jackson, and "Surely God Is Able" (1947), recorded first by Clara Ward and the Ward Singers, were actually the first black gospel recordings to sell more than a million copies each.

Brewster composed more than fifteen gospel music dramas, including *From Auction Block to Glory* (1941), the first nationally staged black religious drama featuring gospel songs; prior dramas used hymns and spirituals. This drama was performed at an annual National Baptist Convention, earning Brewster the position of head of the Drama Department. *From Auction Block to Glory* eventually made it to Broadway.

His Legacy

In 1918, Brewster married Julianna Nelson. Two children were born to the union: Juanita and William Herbert T. Brewster. Brewster's son, William, Jr., also established himself as a capable composer, penning songs for Clara Ward and the Ward Singers, Albertina Walker and the Caravans, Marion Williams, and a host of other notable singers.

In addition to his son, Brewster mentored numerous singers and musicians, including a young vocalist, T. C. Anderson, who auditioned for one of his choirs in the 1930s. Brewster renamed her Queen C. Anderson after Queen Candice of Ethiopia in the Bible. Queen C. would become one of his featured soloists as well as one of the most popular and in-demand soloists of the South. Brewster also mentored Clara Ward, who in turn published many of his compositions through her Philadelphia-based Ward's House of Music. However, after 1958, Brewster published all of his material himself.

During the 1950s, Brewster opened his church to whites, who would often come to admire the singing and his preaching. One of Brewster's most famous white congregants was Elvis Presley, a young Memphis-based truck driver. In addition to an honorary doctorate from Bennett College in Greensboro, North Carolina, Brewster was honored by the Smithsonian Institute. William Herbert Brewster died on October 15, 1987, at age ninety.

EMMETT G. PRICE III

See also Campbell, Lucie; Caravans; Church of God in Christ (COGIC); Dorsey, Thomas; Jackson, Mahalia; National Baptist Convention; Presley, Elvis; Walker, Albertina; Ward Trio (Ward Singers); Williams, Marion

Reference and Further Reading

Boyer, Horace Clarence. *The Golden Age of Gospel.* Urbana and Chicago, IL: University of Illinois Press, 2000 [1995].
———. "William Herbert Brewster: The Eloquent Poet." In *We'll Understand It Better By and By: Pioneering African American Gospel Composers*, edited by Bernice Johnson Reagon, 211–231. Washington, DC: Smithsonian Institute Press, 1992.
Broughton, Viv. *Black Gospel: An Illustrated History of the Gospel Sound.* Dorset, UK: Blandford Press, 1985.
Cadden, Jerry. "Brewster, W(illiam) Herbert, Sr." In *Center for Black Music Research International Dictionary of Black Composers, Vol. 1,* edited by Samuel A. Floyd, Jr., 167–173. Chicago & London: Fitzroy Dearborn Publishers, 1999.
Heilbut, Anthony. "If I Fail, You Tell the World I Tried." In *We'll Understand It Better By and By: Pioneering African American Gospel Composers*, edited by Bernice Johnson Reagon, 233–244. Washington, DC: Smithsonian Institute Press, 1992.
———. *The Gospel Sound: Good News and Bad Times.* New York: Limelight Editions, 1997 [1971, 1975, 1985].
Reagon, Bernice Johnson. "William Herbert Brewster: Rememberings." In *We'll Understand It Better By and By: Pioneering African American Gospel Composers*, edited by Bernice Johnson Reagon, 185–209. Washington, DC: Smithsonian Institute Press, 1992.
Tribute: The Life of Dr. William Herbert Brewster. Memphis: The Brewster House of Sermon Songs, Christian Literature and Dramatic Arts, ca. 1982.
Wiggins, William H., Jr. "William Herbert Brewster: Pioneer of the Sacred Pageant." In *We'll Understand It Better By and By: Pioneering African American Gospel Composers*, edited by Bernice Johnson Reagon, 245–251. Washington, DC: Smithsonian Institute Press, 1992.

Selected Discography

The Brewster Ensemble. "I'll Go" (1950, Gotham 644).
Clara Ward and the Ward Singers. "Surely, God Is Able" (1950, Savoy 4017).
Jackson, Mahalia. "Move On Up A Little Higher" (1947, Apollo 164).
Soul Stirrers. "Lord I've Tried" (1946, Aladdin 203).

BROOKLYN TABERNACLE CHOIR

Resident choir at the Brooklyn Tabernacle, a nondenominational church founded in 1966 by the late evangelist Clair D. Hutchins. Originally called the Brooklyn Gospel Tabernacle, the church was first located at 88 Hanson Place in Brooklyn, New York; the congregation moved shortly thereafter to 453 Atlantic Avenue. In the autumn of 1971, Hutchins decided to turn his attention to missionary work abroad. He thus asked his daughter and son-in-law, Carol and Jim Cymbala, to take over the leadership of the struggling church, whose membership had dwindled to fewer than twenty members. At the time, Jim was working as an administrator at American Airlines and Carol was the receptionist at a pharmaceutical company. Although neither had received formal seminary training, the Cymbalas nevertheless felt compelled to take over the church. Jim Cymbala became the pastor of the Brooklyn Gospel Tabernacle, and he and his wife set their sights on saving the church by building its membership.

The Cymbalas succeeded in attracting enough new members that, by 1977, the Brooklyn Gospel Tabernacle had outgrown its home on Atlantic Avenue. The church began holding Sunday services at a nearby YWCA auditorium. In 1978, the church sold the Atlantic Avenue property, along with an adjacent lot it had purchased, and bought facilities at 290 Flatbush Avenue in Brooklyn, which it renovated and occupied in 1979. In 1984, the church changed its name to the Brooklyn Tabernacle. By 1996, the church had grown so significantly that Jim Cymbala and the associate pastors were compelled to begin providing four worship services every Sunday to accommodate all of its members. In May 1998, the Brooklyn Tabernacle purchased the abandoned and dilapidated Loew's Metropolitan Theatre, built in 1918 and located on Smith Street between Fulton and Livingston streets in downtown Brooklyn, for $6.3 million. The architectural firm of Kostow and Greenwood was commissioned to commence renovations. The newly refurbished building can accommodate five thousand worshippers at a given service. The Flatbush facility was sold in 2003.

The Brooklyn Tabernacle, which remains nondenominational, currently boasts a membership of roughly ten thousand congregants from a wide variety of racial, ethnic, and economic backgrounds. Jim Cymbala continues to serve as pastor; the church employs ten associate pastors, as well. Services are held on Sundays at 9:00 a.m., 12:00 noon, and 4:00 p.m. and on Tuesday evenings at 7:00 p.m.

The church's success is due in large part to its renowned choir, which was formed in 1973 by Carol Cymbala and eight other congregants. Despite her lack of formal musical training, Cymbala—who cannot read music—led rehearsals and conducted performances, selected traditional gospel songs and wrote original ones for the choir to sing, and provided keyboard accompaniment. Under Cymbala's direction, the Brooklyn Tabernacle Choir thrived. By 1981, it had grown to approximately sixty members; membership currently hovers around 275, and Cymbala continues to act as choir director. Originally open to any church member willing to show up for rehearsals, the choir now accepts new members on an audition basis only.

The Brooklyn Tabernacle Choir currently performs at two of the church's three Sunday services. While the size of the choir prohibits frequent appearances outside the New York metropolitan area, the choir appears regularly in and around the city and has performed at venues including Carnegie Hall, Radio City Music Hall, the Paramount Theatre at Madison Square Garden, and the Madison Square Garden arena.

In the early 1980s, Carol Cymbala made a tape of the choir singing a mix of traditional and original gospel songs to circulate among church members. A copy of the tape was brought to the attention of executives at Word Records, a Christian recording company now subsumed under the Word Entertainment division of the Warner Music Group and based in Nashville, Tennessee. The Brooklyn Tabernacle Choir was signed to the Word label and has since recorded three videos and more than twenty albums.

In the years since it began its recording career, the Brooklyn Tabernacle Choir has won a number of important awards, including five Grammy Awards in the category of Best Gospel Choir or Chorus Album (for *Live: We Come Rejoicing* in 1993, *Praise Him . . . Live!* in 1995, *High and Lifted Up* in 1999, *Live—God Is Working* in 2000, and *Be Glad* in 2002) and three Dove Awards in the category of choral collection of the year (for *Praise Him . . . Live!, High and Lifted Up,* and *Live—God Is Working*).

ELIZABETH L. WOLLMAN

Reference and Further Reading

Archibold, Randal C. "Brooklyn Choir Wins Praise by Singing the Lord's Praises." *The New York Times*, February 28, 2000.
The Brooklyn Tabernacle. http://www.brooklyntabernacle.org/ (accessed June 30, 2004).

Discography

Live: We Come Rejoicing (1993, Word Entertainment CD 45237).
Praise Him . . . Live! (1995, Word Entertainment CD 45928).
High and Lifted Up (1999, Word Entertainment CD 83182).
Be Glad (2002, Word Entertainment CD 886186).
Live—God Is Working (2002, Word Entertainment CD 886031).

BROWN'S FERRY FOUR

Alton Delmore (b. December 25, 1908; d. June 9, 1969)
Rabon Delmore (b. December 3, 1916; d. December 4, 1952)
Merle Travis (b. November 29, 1917; d. October 20, 1983)
Louis Marshall "Grandpa" Jones (b. October 20, 1913; d. February 19, 1998)

One of the most popular early country gospel quartets, the Brown's Ferry Four—like the Chuck Wagon Gang—featured quartet harmonies backed by acoustic guitar. The group was formed at WLW in Cincinnati in 1943, when George C. Biggar of that station, noting the popularity of gospel music with his listeners, searched the station's talent roster to form a regularly featured quartet. His original and most famous Brown's Ferry Four was composed of Merle Travis (bass and guitar), Grandpa Jones (baritone), and the Delmore brothers, Alton and Rabon, singing the two highest parts (and sometimes playing their inimitable tenor guitars for accompaniment). All had great careers in country music, and in fact, all have since been elected to the Country Music Hall of Fame. But all loved and grew up on the gospel harmonies, shape note and otherwise, from their childhoods in Kentucky (Travis and Jones) and Alabama (the Delmores). The group took its name, at Travis's suggestion, from the community in Northern Alabama near the Delmores' birthplace, immortalized in their 1933 classic "Brown's Ferry Blues."

In his autobiography *Truth Is Stranger than Publicity,* Alton Delmore recalls teaching some of his cohorts how to read music for this experiment, since for their broadcasts and later recording sessions they would be working from the published paperback songsters that Stamps Baxter, Vaughan, and other firms distributed. Existing gospel records, by white and black artists, provided another rich vein the group tapped for song material. Gratified by the huge mail response to the new quartet, WLW (which owned the group name) kept the Brown's Ferry Four on the air for many years, long after Merle Travis and Alton Delmore had to leave for World War II military service, with Cincinnati locals such as Rome Johnson, Roy Lanham, and even Dollie Good (half of the famous sister group, the Girls of the Golden West).

After the war, the original group reunited and made its first recordings for Cincinnati's King Records label, although Travis had left WLW for California by then, Jones would soon head to Nashville and Washington, DC, and the Delmores would go to Memphis. As a recording act, they sold well enough to justify cutting some forty-two sides between 1946 and 1952, although the quartet's personnel shifted over those years to include Clyde Moody, Red Foley, Louis Innis, and the Turner Brothers (known professionally as Zeke and Zeb). Rabon Delmore died in 1952, and the group never again recorded, although WLW kept the broadcast group alive with varied ensembles for several more years.

The group's recorded repertory, most of which has been reissued on compact disc, includes such songs as "Rockin' on the Waves, " "I'll Fly Away," "I've Got That Old Time Religion in My Heart," "Keep On the Firing Line," "Jesus Hold My Hand," and "I've Made a Covenant with My Lord." Not surprisingly, their repertory and style was very much reflected by a much later broadcast quartet that also included Grandpa Jones as a founding member, television's popular Hee Haw Gospel Quartet.

RONNIE PUGH

See also Hee Haw Gospel Quartet; King Records

Reference and Further Reading

Delmore, Alton. *Truth Is Stranger than Publicity.* Nashville: Country Music Foundation Press, 1977.
Jones, Louis M. "Grandpa"; with Charles K. Wolfe. *Everybody's Grandpa: Fifty Years Behind the Mike.* Knoxville: University of Tennessee Press, 1984.
Wolfe, Charles K. "Brown's Ferry Four." In *The Country Music Encyclopedia.* New York: Oxford University Press and Country Music Foundation Press, 1998.

Discography

78s

"Heaven Eternal for Me"/"I Am a Weary Pilgrim" (King 1032).
"His Boundless Love"/"I've Got That Old Time Religion in My Heart" (King 760).

"I'll Meet You in the Morning"/"Jesus Hold My Hand" (King 854).
"On the Jericho Road"/"I'm Naturalized for Heaven" (King 832).
"Rock of Ages Hide Thou Me"/"Keep On the Firing Line" (King 700).
"There's a Page in The Bible"/"We Should Walk Together" (King 1059).

CD Reissue

Brown's Ferry Four (SKU D-3506; 2 CD set, 44 songs).

BRUMLEY, ALBERT EDWARD

(b. October 29, 1905; d. November 15, 1977)

The man who wrote some of the most popular gospel songs of the twentieth century was born in Spiro, Oklahoma. Like many small-town and rural youths of his era, he attended singing schools and music normal schools, developing such an interest in music that for five years (1926–1931) he attended the Hartford Music Institute in Hartford, Arkansas. Here he met and studied under some of America's best-known writers of gospel music, such as Virgil O. Stamps, Eugene M. Bartlett, and Will M. Ramsey. He also wrote his first song while at Hartford.

Brumley's intention was to be a music teacher, but after marrying Goldie Schell in 1931, he decided to devote his energies to writing and settled down in Powell, Missouri. In 1932, Brumley wrote "I'll Fly Away," one of the most recorded gospel songs of all time. He had been ruminating on it for three years before actually completing the number. His original inspiration to write the piece came while picking cotton on his father's farm and humming a ballad, "The Prisoner's Song," which has the lines "If I had the wings of an angel, over these prison walls I would fly." Then it dawned on him that this secular plot might work well for a gospel song. He paraphrased one line from "The Prisoner's Song"—"Like a bird from prison bars have flown"—and, of course, the title "I'll Fly Away" was heavily influenced by the secular lyrics. Otherwise, everything about the classic originated with Brumley.

During the next 45 years, Brumley wrote approximately seven hundred songs, many of which became long-lasting favorites. These include "Turn Your Radio On," "I'll Meet You in the Morning," "Rank Strangers," "Jesus Hold My Hand," "If We Never Meet Again," "I'd Rather Be an Old-Time Christian," "He Set Me Free," "I've Found a Hiding Place," "Did You Ever Go Sailin'?," "Her Mansion Is Higher than Mine," "There's a Little Pine Log Cabin," and "Nobody Answered Me."

Being a shy person, Brumley preferred to avoid the limelight, and let others perform the numbers he wrote. He also shunned big cities, preferring to live in a small village, where he could indulge in his passions for baseball, checkers, and crossword puzzles. Considering how prolific a songwriter he was, Brumley was, surprisingly, not very well organized, and had what many people considered sloppy work habits. Apparently, though, he also had a good sense of humor and was able to laugh at himself. Indeed, he even told jokes about himself and his work habits. He also made fun of his absentmindedness, which evidently was notorious in Powell. At the same time, he was a good businessman who knew where—and how—to make deals and bring in orders.

Beginning in 1943, Brumley established what was essentially a family business in the strictest sense and made it profitable almost immediately. In 1948 he bought Hartford Music Company, the firm that originally published "I'll Fly Away" and several other Brumley songs. It ceased publishing in 1978. In 1970, Brumley was one of the first songwriters inducted into the Nashville Songwriters Hall of Fame. Appropriately, in 1972 he was elected to the Gospel Music Hall of Fame.

Most people refer to his songs as country music, but Brumley himself disliked the appellation because he thought it inaccurate for the numbers he and other gospel songwriters produced. Still, he accepted it because he considered it more correct than any other term commonly used during his lifetime. Certainly, there can be no argument that country performers have found his songs eminently recordable.

In 1990, a biography titled *I'll Fly Away: The Life Story of Albert E. Brumley,* written by Kay Hively and Albert E. Brumley, Jr., appeared. This volume relied largely on a series of interviews Al Jr. conducted with his father a few months before his death as well as on taped interviews with several neighbors and Goldie, Albert's wife. None of his six children followed their father into songwriting, but all are involved in some phase of the music business. Bill, Bob, and Betty run the family publishing company. Jackson is a manager and publisher, while Al (singer and guitarist) and Tom (steel guitarist) are both performers.

W. K. McNeil

Reference and Further Reading

Hively, Kay; Albert E. Brumley, Jr. *I'll Fly Away: The Life Story of Albert E. Brumley.* Branson, MO: Mountaineer Books, 1990.

BURNETT, REVEREND J. C.

(b. Unknown, probably Kansas City, MO; d. Unknown)

Reverend J. C. Burnett was one of the most commercially successful preachers on race records, alongside Reverend J. M. Gates and Reverend A. W. Nix. After making his debut for Winston Holmes's tiny Kansas City label, Meritt, with a sermon titled "The Downfall of Nebuchadnezzar," Burnett, a Baptist, settled in New York City, where from 1926 to 1929 he recorded thirty-two sides (four unissued) for Columbia. Among them was a remake of his first recording, which is known to have sold unexpectedly well.

Most of Burnett's sermons for Columbia—where he was often accompanied by Sisters Ethel Grainger and Odette Jackson on vocals and by Porter Grainger on organ or piano—were drawn from popular Biblical stories (especially the Revelation), as in "The Great Day of His Wrath Has Come," and occasionally also from other sources, as seems the case with "The Gambler's Doom," apparently the first recording of the "Deck of Cards" theme.

In 1938, Burnett returned to a New York City recording studio and cut eight sermons with singing for Decca, including another version of his Columbia hit. In 1945, thanks to Grainger's recommendation, he recorded eight more titles (two of which remain undiscovered) for the Joe Davis label. Nothing is known of Burnett's later life, but he very likely "returned to his ministry, and if he had indeed been preaching for 40 years in 1945, as he testified on 'I'm Not Ashamed of the Gospel of Christ,' it seems certain that he is now dead" (Smith 1997).

Luigi Monge

See also Nix, Reverend A. W.

Reference and Further Reading

Oliver, Paul. *Songsters and Saints: Vocal Traditions on Race Records.* Cambridge, MA: Cambridge University Press, 1984.

Discography

Smith, Chris. *Rev. J. C. Burnett: Complete Recorded Works in Chronological Order, Vol. 1 (1926–1927) and Vol. 2 (1927–1945)* (1997, Document Records DOCD-5557-8).

C

CAESAR, SHIRLEY

(b. October 13, 1938, Durham, NC)

From "Baby Shirley" to "the Electrifying Evangelist" to the "First Lady of Gospel Music," Shirley Caesar has climbed the ranks as one of the leading ladies of gospel music. The singer, pastor, and civic/community leader is one of gospel music's most passionate, charismatic, and revered leaders of all time.

The Voice of an Angel

Born on October 13, 1938, in Durham, North Carolina, to the union of James and Hallie Martin Caesar, Shirley was one of thirteen children. By the age of eight, Shirley was singing with siblings Joyce, Anne, and Solomon as the Caesar Singers. Her passion for gospel music, her big voice, and her electrifying and energetic style of presentation were inherited from her father, who sang with the Just Come Four Quartet and passed away in the same year she began singing. By the age of twelve, in addition to singing with the Mt. Calvary Holy Church Choir, Shirely sang with the Durham-based Charity Singers, traveled with the evangelist Rev. Leroy Johnson, and sang solo. By thirteen, she was a member of the very popular gospel group Thelma Bumpass and the Royalettes. Her desire to sing fulfilled her passion and supported her siblings as well as her disabled, widowed mother.

Traveling all around the Carolinas and into the Virginia/Maryland/Washington, DC, area, Shirley was known as "Baby Shirley," particularly due to her young age and her small physical stature, yet she had a huge, powerful voice. Upon completing high school Caesar enrolled at North Carolina College, yet departed after completing one year to join the Caravans, an immensely popular group led by Albertina Walker. Caesar remained under the tutelage of Walker and the Caravans for eight years (1958–1966) and, through numerous personnel changes, she evolved from "Baby Shirley" into the lead vocalist and featured soloist of the group. Upon leaving the group, Caesar ventured forth as a singing evangelist. In 1968, two years after leaving the Caravans, Caesar formed her own group, the Shirley Caesar Singers, with Linda Martin, Donna Jones, Anne Caesar (Price), and Johnny "Rainey" Griffin on piano. In 1972 when "queen of gospel" Mahalia Jackson died, she left critics, journalists, and gospel fans looking to install a new queen; many turned to Caesar, who in turn thought her mentor, Albertina Walker, was more worthy of the honor.

Although Caesar was called "queen" by some, her 1977 debut record with Roadshow Records, *First Lady,* gained her the title "First Lady of Gospel," a title backed by more than thirty albums and numerous awards, including eleven Grammy Awards, eighteen Dove Awards, fifteen Stellar Awards, three RIAA Gold certifications, an SESAC Lifetime Achievement Award, and an NAACP Image Award, among others. With an expansive career spanning more than five decades, Caesar has performed in three Broadway musicals (*Mama I Want to Sing, Sing: Mama 2,* and *Born to Sing: Mama 3*); appeared in commercials for MCI Communications; made cameo appearances in a motion picture (*Why Do Fools Fall in Love*) and a television sitcom (*Good News*); and authored an autobiography (*The Lady, the Melody and the Word*). In 2000, Caesar was inducted into the Gospel Music Hall of Fame for her lifelong contribution and dedication to gospel music.

The Electrifying Evangelist

Caesar's songs have changed the lives of many. Songs such as "Don't Drive Your Mama Away," "No Charge," and "I Remember Mama" offer testimony and appreciation for her relationship with her own mother while encouraging others not to take such relationships for granted. Other hallmark songs such as "He's Working It Out for You," or "Hold My Mule" attest to Caesar's strong passion for ministering to those in need.

In 1970, the year before Caesar won her first Grammy Award (she was the first black female gospel singer to do so), she initiated Shirley Caesar Outreach Ministries, Inc., providing food, clothing, shelter, and emergency relief to underprivileged and needy people. Caesar Ministries also hosts seminars about AIDS prevention, teenage pregnancy prevention, alcohol and narcotics recovery, educational assistance, as well as guidance in family relationships. As part of her ministry, she began an annual conference that has drawn a national and international audience since its inception. In 1990, Caesar was called to pastor the Mount Calvary Word of Faith Church in Raleigh, North Carolina. Caesar's popularity as an evangelist and minister of the gospel matched that of her singing, as she was heralded as one of the most prominent evangelists of the 1990s.

Civic/Community Service

Dedicated to the importance of education, Caesar returned to college in 1981, earning a BS degree in business administration from Shaw University with the distinction of magna cum laude in May 1984. Caesar has since been awarded honorary doctorates from Shaw University and Southeastern University. In the late 1990s, Caesar found time to begin graduate studies at Duke University. Married for over twenty years to Bishop Harold Ivory Williams, Caesar continued to shock followers when her dedication to issues of justice, equality, and civil rights led her to campaign for an at-large seat on the Durham, North

Carolina, city council in 1987, a seat that she won and served for a complete four-year term. The gospel living legend has made two appearances at the White House, at the invitation of President and Mrs. Jimmy Carter (1979) and of President and Mrs. George Bush (1992). In addition, she has performed twice for President Bill Clinton. The gospel singer, who prides herself on her scripturally based ministry through music, preaching, and service, has lived the words that she sings.

EMMETT G. PRICE III

See also Caravans; Dove Awards; Jackson, Mahalia; Walker, Albertina

Reference and Further Reading

Broughton, Viv. *Black Gospel: An Illustrated History of the Gospel Sound.* Dorset, UK: Blandford Press, 1985.

Caesar, Shirley. *The Lady, The Melody, & The Word: An Autobiography.* Nashville, TN: Thomas Nelson Publishers, 1998.

Cusic, Don. *The Sound of Light: A History of Gospel and Christian Music.* Milwaukee, WI: Hal Leonard, 2002 (1990).

Heilbut, Anthony. *The Gospel Sound: Good News and Bad Times.* New York: Limelight Editions, [1971, 1975, 1985] 1997.

Jones, Bobby; with Lesley Sussman. "Shirley Caesar." In *Touched by God: Black Gospel Greats Share Their Stories of Finding God,* 130–145. New York: Pocket Books, 1998.

Selected Discography

Rejoice (1980, Myrrh Records WR-8106).

Sailin' (1984, Myrrh Records WR-8109).

Live . . . in Chicago (1988, Word Records 47743).

He's Working It Out for You (1991, Word Records EX-48785).

Stand Still (1993, Word Records EK-57464).

Shirley Caesar Live . . . He Will Come (1995, Word Records 67301).

Shirley Caesar and Friends (2003, Word Entertainment 886008).

CALVARY CHAPEL, COSTA MESA

In 1965, Calvary Chapel, Costa Mesa had twenty-five members. By the end of the 1970s, more than twenty-five *thousand* people attended services each week. By the end of the twentieth century, there were hundreds of individual Calvary Chapel congregations in the United States and the rest of the world. Its influence extended well beyond its own walls by establishing a new paradigm for churches, which ultimately influenced the direction of church growth in general. Other examples of new paradigm churches that emanated from Calvary Chapel's influence are the Vineyard and Hope Chapel. The question that arises from this phenomenal growth is why and how did it happen? The answer to this can be found in the vision and work of one man: Chuck Smith (b. 1927).

Smith graduated from LIFE Bible College and was ordained a Foursquare Gospel minister in the late 1940s. After successfully serving in Foursquare churches in California and Arizona, Smith became disillusioned with the then existing Protestant church paradigm, which was highly structured and stressed denominational loyalty. In the early 1960s, Smith established an independent church called Corona Christian Center, where he experimented with verse-by-verse home Bible studies that were easily understood and applicable to people's needs in everyday life. In 1965, Smith accepted an invitation to become the pastor of Calvary Chapel.

At the same time that Smith began his new pastorate, the country was going through a cultural youth revolution. One of the revolution's epicenters was in California. Nearby beaches with names like Huntington, Newport, and Venice were hangouts for the hippies and surfers that made up the Southern California counterculture. Drug use was rampant, and music was the primary tool for communicating new ideas. Smith had three teenage children who developed friendships with some of the hippie converts of the early Jesus movement. They were called "Jesus freaks." Pastor Smith and his wife Kay decided to open up their home to the new converts. One of them was a charismatic young man named Lonnie Frisbee. Frisbee would canvas the beaches during the day, wearing a robe and carrying a Bible. Later in the day he would bring the fruits of his labor to Pastor Chuck at Calvary Chapel. Some of these converts were musicians, who began writing songs of worship and praise.

As the number of young people attending Calvary Chapel increased exponentially, the original building, with a capacity of three hundred, proved inadequate. Eventually, a circus tent was erected to contain the expanding congregation while a new building was being built on eleven acres of land. Services were held nightly, and included worship using converted hippie musicians such as Chuck Girard, Oden Fong, and Tom Stipe. Soon the musicians formed groups, some of which were Children of the Day, Country Faith, Love Song, and Mustard Seed Faith. Next, a record label named Maranatha was formed to market the new Christian music and book the groups for concerts. Eventually, churches throughout Southern California began coffeehouse ministries and folk worship services, which featured many of the new Maranatha groups. Sometimes speakers such as Mike Macintosh or Lonnie Frisbee would accompany the groups to do a Bible study.

A service at Calvary Chapel resembled a rock concert more than it did the traditional liturgy of that period. The pastoral staff was often indistinguishable from the congregation because of their casual attire. The worship service was led by guitar-playing young musicians wearing T-shirts and bell-bottom trousers, rather than a robed choir accompanied by a pipe organ. The new songs had contemporary melodies that expressed a relevant message, reflective of the authors' spiritual experiences and pertimer to the congregation. Oftentimes there would be a musical performance by one of the newly formed groups or solo artists on the Maranatha label. The message given by Pastor Chuck or another member of the pastoral staff would consist of a line-by-line exposition of Bible passages. The speaking technique used in the delivery was conversational in tone. Sermons in evangelical churches prior to the 1970s had been, for the most part, topical in nature, and had been presented in the formal elocutionary delivery style.

Calvary Chapel's theology is essentially conservative in nature, with a plenary verbal inspiration approach to Biblical hermeneutics and exegesis. It is charismatic (Pentecostal) in its approach to spiritual gifts, as they pertain to I Corinthians 12: 8–10. At the same time, the exercise of spiritual gifts is reserved for an afterglow service, rather than being incorporated into the main service as is common in mainline Pentecostal churches, such as Foursquare or Assembly of God.

BOB GERSZTYN

See also Fong, Oden; Girard, Chuck; Love Song; Maranatha! Music; Rock Gospel

Reference and Further Reading

Balmer, Randall Herbert. *Mine Eyes Have Seen the Glory: A Journey into the Evangelical Subculture in America.* New York: Oxford University Press, 1993.

Calvary Chapel home page, http://www.calvarychapel.com (accessed April 5, 2003).

"History of the Jesus Movement." http://www.calvarymusic. org/ (accessed April 5, 2003).

Miller, Donald E. *Reinventing American Protestantism: Christianity in the New Millennium.* Berkley: University of California Press, 1997.

CAMPBELL, LUCIE

(b. April 30, 1885, Duck Hill, MS; d. January 3, 1963, Nashville, TN)

Lucie Eddie Campbell was the youngest of nine children, and her parents, Burrell and Isabella Wilkerson Campbell, were former slaves. Following emancipation, the father secured work as an Illinois Central brakeman, and died shortly after his daughter's birth in a work-related incident. In 1886, Campbell's her mother moved the family to Memphis, Tennessee, where the children received their education. An exceptionally bright youngster, Campbell taught herself to play the piano by listening in on her older sister's lessons, as her mother could not afford lessons for both.

Campbell graduated from Kortrecht High School at age fourteen as valedictorian of her class, and immediately began teaching at Carnes Grammar School, as teachers were not required to have degrees at that time. In 1911, she was assigned to the high school from which she graduated (renamed Booker T. Washington) and taught algebra, ancient history, English, vocal music, physiology, and physical education during her forty-three–year tenure there. In 1927, Campbell received an A.B. degree from Rust College in Holly Springs, Mississippi, as a liberal arts major, by which time she was already considered an excellent teacher, stern and exacting, with strict rules about behavior and acceptable dress in her classroom.

The Campbell family were members of Metropolitan Baptist Church, and it was there that Lucie Campbell developed her musical talents. She possessed an outstanding contralto voice that she and combined with her skills as a pianist as she began teaching young people's choirs in Baptist churches and became active in musical circles in Memphis.

Since its organization in 1895, most prominent Baptist churches across the country were members of the National Baptist Convention of the United States of America (NBC), the largest African American organization in the world. In 1896, the convention established the National Baptist Publishing Board (NBPB), which produced Sunday School and other religious and denominational literature. In 1915 there was a split in the NBC, based primarily on a dispute of ownership of the NBPB, which by now was a thriving financial enterprise. Dr. R. H. Boyd, corresponding secretary and founder of the NBPB, had legal ownership; he and his followers left the original convention, taking with them the publishing board and the Sunday School and Baptist Young People Union (BYPU) Congress. At a reorganization the following year in Memphis, Lucie Campbell became one of the nine founders of a new congress and was appointed music director.

Campbell's job was multifaceted: she organized and presented pre-Congress musicals, which entailed going early to the cities where the congress would meet to train choirs; select soloists, songs, and singing groups for performance; direct the huge choirs and congregational singing; and, in general, construct the agenda for music during the congress, where thousands of delegates from across the country would be in attendance at the annual gathering. In addition, she joined with the Reverend E. W. S. Isaac to produce and publish songbooks that would be used throughout the denomination, such as *Gospel Pearls* (1921), the first songbook for African American churches with the word "gospel" in the title, the *Baptist Standard Hymnal* (1924), and *Spirituals Triumphant Old and New* (1927).

Lucie Campbell was music director of the Sunday School and BYPU Congress of the National Baptist Convention, USA, for forty-seven years, serving from 1916 until her death in 1963. She was not a particularly prolific composer, and many of her early songs were the property of the Congress. Her total output consisted of approximately fifty-five songs, three of which are titled anthems. She regularly introduced and sold new songs at the annual meetings of the Congress, an unprecedented venue of dissemination. Campbell's early songs were gospel hymns, heavily influenced by the style of the Reverend C. A. Tindley. They were in the familiar four-part, homophonic hymn format with features from Negro spirituals, suitable for use in the hymnbooks of the Baptist denomination. Her lyrics were the strongest aspect of her songs, reflecting her religious beliefs and trust in God that appealed to her vast audiences. "Something Within" (1919), "Heavenly Sunshine" (1928), and her most popular and best-loved, "He'll Understand, He'll Say, 'Well Done'" (1933) are outstanding examples of the gospel hymn style.

The decade of the 1940s was her most prolific; she changed her style to meet the competition of the "Chicago group" of gospel songwriters such as Thomas A. Dorsey and Sallie Martin. "Just to Behold His Face" (1941), "In the Upper Room with Jesus" (1946), and "Jesus Gave Me Water" (1946) were among the seventeen Library of Congress deposits that included several collections titled *Lucie Campbell's Soul-Stirring Songs*.

The 1950s were her second most productive period: twelve works were copyrighted between 1951 and 1959. Many of her lyrics became introspective, based on scripture and sermons. Such titles include "God's Long Reach of Salvation" (1954) and "His Grace Is Sufficient for Me" (1956). The influence of Lucie Campbell on music and worship in the black church was considerable, and her encouragement of young singers such as Robert J. Bradley and composers was legendary. She approved the appearance of the then-considered-flamboyant Clara Ward Singers at the Congress over some objections and embraced Thomas A. Dorsey at a time when gospel music was not universally accepted in the churches of some prominent ministers.

A masterful organizer, she used her position as music director to set the standard for music in church services. She composed new arrangements of spirituals to complement the traditional spirituals, hymns, and anthems that had been the standard repertoire for church choirs, and her acceptance and use of the "Chicago style" of gospel songs encouraged the sprouting of gospel choruses everywhere. A new format began to emerge during the Sunday morning service: the gospel chorus alternated with the senior choir in providing music for worship; this was a major change in the black Baptist church, which gradually affected the other mainline denominations.

She became Mrs. Lucie Eddie Campbell Williams when she married Reverend C. R. Williams in 1960 at the age of seventy-five, six years after her retirement from public school teaching and nearly three years before her death. Her religious fervor, expressed eloquently in her songs, and her dedication to service in the black Baptist Church, produced a legacy of love and nurturing that remain unmatched in the history of gospel music.

LUVENIA A. GEORGE

See also National Baptist Convention

Reference and Further Reading

Boyer, Horace Clarence. "Lucie E. Campbell: Composer for the National Baptist Convention." In *We'll Understand It Better By and By,* edited by Bernice Johnson Reagon. Washington, DC: Smithsonian Institution Press, 1992.

Bradley, J. Robert. "Miss Lucie: The Legacy of the Woman and Her Music." *National Baptist Voice* 30–31 (1979): 1–10.

Dinkins, Charles L. "The Saga of the National Baptist Congress/Christian Education in the National Baptist Convention: Historical, the Present Situation, Projections." In *Utilizing Resources for Christian Education: 1980 Emphasis,* edited by Maynard P. Turner, Jr. Nashville, TN: Townsend Press, 1980.

George, Luvenia A. "Lucie Campbell." In *We'll Understand It Better By and By,* edited by Bernice Johnson Reagon. Washington, DC: Smithsonian Institution Press, 1992.

———. "Lucie E. Campbell: Baptist Composer and Educator." *Black Perspective in Music* 15, no. 1 (Spring 1987).

———. "Lucie Campbell." In *International Dictionary of Black Composers,* edited by Samuel A. Floyd, Jr., 2 vols. Chicago: Fitzroy Dearborn Publishers, 1999.

Walker, Charles. *Miss Lucie.* Nashville, TN: Townsend Press, 1993.

CANAAN RECORDS

Canaan Records was established as a subsidiary of Word Records in 1964 by label founder Jarrell McCracken. He wanted to create a new label as a home for Southern gospel quartets and other artists in the genre. Marvin Norcoss was appointed to head the newly formed division that became a home to many of Southern gospels most successful groups.

The first group signed to the label was the Florida Boys, headed by founder Les Beasly. McCracken had seen the popular quartet perform on television and wanted to sign them to Canaan Records. Les Beasly accepted the invitation and their debut album for the label, *Florida Boys in Nashville*, was released in 1965.

Canaan Records attracted many of the major Southern gospel groups, and released albums the same year by the LeFevres, the Blue Ridge Quartet, and the Plainsmen Quartet and a collection titled *Gospel Singing Jubilee 1* that included selections from the Florida Boys, Couriers, the Goodman Family, and the Dixie Echoes.

Originally signed to Canaan as the Goodman Family and later known as the Happy Goodmans, the famous group released the album *The Best of the Happy Goodmans* in 1966, which included their signature song, "I Wouldn't Take Nothing for My Journey Now." The Happy Goodmans recorded dozens of albums for Canaan, and their most popular songs included "Who Am I," "John the Revelator" and "What a Lovely Name."

The Cathedral Quartet began a long affiliation with Canaan in 1970 with their debut release *A Little Bit of Everything*. Also joining the roster that year were the bluegrass-based Lewis Family with *The Lewis Family Sings in Gospel Country*, the Thraser Brothers with *Turning It On,* and Wendy Bagwell and the Sunliters with *Talk About the Good Times*.

Another important group that began a long association with Canaan in the 1970s was the North Carolina–based Inspirations. In the fall of 1973, their recording of the Harold Lane composition "Touring That City" rose to number one on *Singing News* magazine's top-forty chart and held the top spot for twenty-two months, as well as picking up the *Singing News* Fan Award for favorite song the following year. In 1974, the Inspirations also dominated the Southern gospel radio charts when the single "When I Wake Up (To Sleep No More)," composed by Marion W. Easterling, spent eight months at number one. Canaan Records ruled the year when the Thrasher Brothers recording of "One Day at a Time" rose to number one and held the spot for three months. The Marijohn Wilkin and Kris Kristofferson composition was named the Gospel Music Association Song of the Year in 1975.

Ken Harding joined Canaan Records as a director of A&R in 1976. Harding convinced the Waco, Texas–based label to let him open an office in Nashville to be closer to the artists and the recording studios. Harding oversaw the careers of the Cathedrals, the Thrasher Brothers, and Teddy Huffman & the Gems. According to Harding, Canaan was selling hundreds of thousands of albums, with groups such as the Cathedrals and the Inspirations often selling more than a hundred thousand albums per release at a time when most country music albums were selling about twenty thousand units.

When the Gospel Music Association introduced the new category "Southern Gospel Album of the Year" in the mid-1970s, Canaan Records picked up the Dove Award five times between 1977 and 1985. *Then and Now* by the Cathedrals (produced by Ken Harding) took the honor in 1977, and from 1982 to 1985, the Dove Award went to albums by the Rex Nelon Singers, all produced by Ken Harding. The Rex Nelon Singers were also radio favorites. One of their most popular songs was "We Shall Wear a Robe and Crown." The song was written by namesake Rex Nelon, and though it rose only to number two, it remained on the *Singing News* top-forty chart for nearly two years.

The Kingsmen were a popular group who joined the Canaan family of artists in the mid-1970s, releasing the album *1968 Pounds of Gospel*, the combined weight of the oversized singers. Other noteworthy releases included *Flatt Gospel*, by Lester Flatt with Nashville Grass, in 1975; *Just in Time*, by the Kingsmen, in 1976; and *This One's for You*, by former Louisiana Governor Jimmie Davis, in 1983. Throughout the 1980s, Canaan released additional albums by the Inspirations, the Rex Nelon Singers, the Lewis Family, the Florida Boys, the Talleys, Newsong, and Lulu Roman Smith (of *Hee Haw* fame).

JAMES I. ELLIOTT

See also Florida Boys, The; Thrasher Brothers, The

Reference and Further Reading

Callahan, Mike; David Edwards; Patrice Eyries. "Canaan Records Discography." http://www.bsnpubs.com/word/canaan/html.

Cusic, Don. *The Sound of Light: A History of Gospel Music.* Bowling Green, OH: Bowling State University Popular Press, 1990.

Dove Awards. http://www.doveawards.com/history.

Harding, Ken. Personal interview, December 14, 2004.

Heil, Paul. Liner notes. *Southern Gospel's Top 20 Songs of the Century, Vol. One* (2000, New Haven Records CD 28010).

Heil, Paul. Liner notes. *Southern Gospel's Top 20 Songs of the Century, Vol. Two* (2002, New Haven Records CD 28024).

CARAVANS

The Caravans are known for ballads and nonmetered hymns. They produced more gospel vocal stars than any other gospel group. In 1952, Albertina Walker, Ora Lee Hopkins, Elyse Yancey, and Nellie Grace Daniels were members of Robert Anderson's ensemble called the Gospel Caravans, which was organized in 1947. Anderson established a publishing house called Robert Anderson's Good Shepherd Music House in Gary, Indiana, in 1942.

Albertina "Tina" Walker was born August 29, 1930. A Chicago native, she formed the Caravans in 1952. Walker became the leader and founder of the Caravans, dropping the word "gospel." The women recorded "Think of His Goodness to You," "Blessed Assurance," and the Negro spiritual "All Night, All Day." In time, other individuals were added. In 1953, Bessie Griffin (1927–1990) joined the ensemble. Shirley Caesar (b. 1938), Dorothy Norwood (b. 1930), Inez Andrews (b. 1929), Casietta George (1928–1995), Eddie Williams, James Cleveland (1931–1991), Imogene Green, and Loleatta Holloway were at one time members of the Caravans in the 1950s.

A famous recording of the Caravans in 1953 was "Tell the Angels." In 1954, Casietta George composed more than twenty-five songs, including "To Whom Shall I Turn?" and "I Believe in Thee." In 1955, at the request of gospel music audiences, many of the songs became household favorites. Recorded and published in the book entitled *Martin & Morris Gospel Songbook of the "Singing Caravans" No. 23* were many great hits, such as "Going Back to My God" by James Boyer of the Boyer Brothers Duet. Many of the songs were arranged by Kenneth Morris for the Church of Deliverance (led by Reverend Clarence H. Cobb) Others were dedicated to Mt. Pizgah Radio Choir (Bessie Folk, director) "Jesus Heard My Earnest Plea," and "Lord, I Want to Thank You" were both written by Albertina Walker. Louise McDonald wrote "There Is Rest for the Weary," sung by the Caravans.

Until 1956, the Caravans with Griffin, Norwood, and Cleveland as members recorded for the States label. In 1958, the group moved to the Savoy Record label with Caesar and Andrews. In 1958, "I'm Not Tired Yet" and "I'm Willing to Wait" were written by Andrews and included in the *Caravan Specials No. 3* book. Two other songs included in this book, "I Cried Lord Please, Move These Things That's Worrying Me" and "Come to Jesus," were written and composed by Dorothy Norwood. At that time, the Caravans were the most popular female group in gospel music.

In the 1960s James Herndon wrote several compositions, among them "I Won't Be Back No More," "No Coward Soldier," and "He Sits High and Looks Low." In the early 1960s, Andrews left the Caravans to organize her own group, the Andrewettes. In 1966, Caesar left the group to pursue evangelism and a solo recording career. The Caravans were on *TV Gospel Time* in the 1960s. Others who performed with the Caravans or contributed are Imogene Green (a contralto). Cleveland's Gospel Chimes, and the Davis Sisters. In 1980, the song "Please Be Patient with Me," a duet with James Cleveland and Walker, was a great hit.

Few gospel or quartet groups can say they have not staged with the great Caravans. Those inducted into the International Gospel Music Hall of Fame and Museum in Detroit in 1997 who were associated with the Caravans are as follows: Shirley Caesar, who won nine Grammy awards, including for her album *Put Your Hand in the Hands of the Man from Galilee*; the late Reverend James Cleveland, founder of the Gospel Workshop of America; Dorothy Norwood, the famous gospel storyteller; and Albertina Walker, the founder of the famous Caravans.

The Chicago style of gospel music continued after the golden era of gospel music from 1945–1955. Its heyday lasted longer in Chicago, since the city was the home of Mahalia Jackson and the Martin & Morris Music Studio for sheet music and books printed for choirs. *The Chicago Defender* newspaper advertised gospel performances every week in local high school auditoriums, featuring "The Weekly Battle of the Quartets." Walker organized several editions of the Caravans, with each arrangement lasting a few years. Walker is a faithful pioneer who is "the Queen of Gospel."

In April 2003, at Detroit's National Association for the Advancement of Colored People (NAACP) Freedom Weekend Gospel Luncheon, Albertina Walker and Inez Andrews were featured speakers to several hundred guests. Andrews stated that "gospel music has been her only income." Andrews, who is also a poet, said the Lord keeps blessing her with favors from songs she wrote. Both thanked the Lord for blessing them and keeping them on the straight and narrow path of righteousness. Each year the Albertina Walker Scholarship Fund is awarded to a deserving student.

In 2004, Walker's seventy-fifth birthday celebration was a two-day gala banquet and benefit concert honoring the Caravans and the legacy of gospel music. Their legacy started in the heyday of gospel music, the golden era of gospel in the 1950s. They have traveled to many countries, performing at concert halls, churches, revivals, battles of the bands, conventions, and political activities. They have kept the traditional gospel flavor with little reference to contemporary gospel. The group is composed of "seasoned women" and "saints of Christ"; they promote the "Chicago gospel style"—the traditional Hammond organ sounds, soloist, a quartet-type female group, bright clothes and colors, and singing from their hearts. This historical traditional gospel group still sings each year at the Albertina Walker Birthday Celebration and on other special occasions.

SHERRY SHERROD DUPREE

Reference and Further Reading

Boyer, Horace Clarence. *How Sweet the Sound: The Golden Age of Gospel.* Washington, DC: Elliott & Clark, 1995.
The Caravans. *Let's Break Bread Together* (Exodus LP 51).
DuPree, Sherry Sherrod. *African-American Holiness Pentecostal Movement: An Annotated Bibliography.* Religious Information Systems Vol. 4; Garland Reference Library of Social Science Vol. 526. New York: Garland Publishing, 1996.
DuPree, Sherry Sherrod; Herbert C. DuPree. *African-American Good News (Gospel) Music.* Washington, DC: Middle Atlantic Regional Press, 1993.
International Gospel Music Hall of Fame and Museum. http://www.gmhf.org (accessed August 28, 2004).
Martin and Morris Gospel Star Song Book No. 3: Caravan Specials. Chicago: Martin and Morris Music, ca. 1958.
Shaffer, Nash Reverend. "Sunday Morning Golden Gospel Radio," Chicago. Interview by Sherry Sherrod DuPree via telephone, May 20, 2004.
Walker, Albertina; Inez Andrews; David Gough. National Association for the Advancement of Colored People (NAACP), Freedom Weekend, Gospel Luncheon, Detroit. Interview by Sherry Sherrod DuPree, April 18, 2003.

CARMAN

(b. January 19, 1956, Trenton, NJ)

Born Carmen Dominic Licciardello, the singer known simply as "Carman" would become one of the most successful performers of contemporary Christian music in the last two decades of the twentieth century. Nine of his albums were certified gold by the Recording Industry Association of America in recognition of sales of more than five hundred thousand, and two of these (*The Standard* and *The Absolute Best*) went platinum with sales exceeding one million. *Billboard* magazine twice named him Contemporary Christian Artist of the Year (1990 and 1992), and in 1994, he made national news for breaking box office records with a concert in Dallas, Texas that sold 71,132 tickets.

Carman grew up in New Jersey, where he played drums in his mother's band and formed a teenage group called the Broken Hearts. Around the age of twenty, he moved to California and decided to pursue a career in Christian music after accepting Christ at a Disneyland concert by Andrae Crouch in 1976. He subsequently moved to Las Vegas but, once he began recording, operated out of Tulsa, Oklahoma, and then Franklin, Tennessee. In 1981, after making one custom album, he was invited by Bill Gaither to tour with the Bill Gaither Trio—a turn of events that he would later maintain was "the biggest influence on my ministry."

Carman's first few records presented him as a singer with a style similar to that of Elvis Presley, but he would branch out to explore many types of music over the years. His diverse hits include samples of 1950s style rock 'n' roll ("Temptation Boogie"), energetic rhythm and blues ("I Got the Joy"), hip-hop ("Who's in the House?"), melodic pop ("Faith Enough"), and easy-listening ballads ("We Are Not Ashamed"). His trademark style, however, would become a sort of "talking song" in which he preaches or tells a story to musical accompaniment with occasional verses or choruses sung for emphasis: "Sunday's on the Way" recounts deliberations in hell on the three days leading up to Easter; "The Champion" presents the apocalyptic contest between Jesus and Satan as a boxing match. The artist also attempted to infuse his recordings and live performances with a good deal of humor, offering satirical or silly songs such as "Spirit-Filled Pizza" and "Soap Song" (which proclaims a gospel message with reference to numerous television soap operas).

Carman eventually became known as an unusually visual performer who crafted stage shows for which his recordings served mainly as soundtracks or souvenirs. His concerts evinced a flamboyance unusual for gospel music, complete with dancers, costume changes, and special theatrical effects. Each tour was styled as a crusade, supported by books, films, and various promotional programs designed around the particular theme. The *Radically Saved* tour was structured around a call for Christian service and its promotion included a contest among church youth groups invited to submit plans for service to their local communities. *The Champion* tour was supported by a novel and full-length motion picture.

Carman also recorded two albums of children's songs, both of which won the Dove Award for Children's Album of the Year (1993, 1995). He likewise won the Dove Award for Rap/Hip Hop Song of the Year in 1997 for his hit "R. I. O. T." (which stands for "righteous invasion of truth"). Toward the end of the twentieth century, he began recording classic hymns and other praise songs on albums that received high accolades from critics.

MARK ALLAN POWELL

Reference and Further Reading

Alfonso, Barry. "Carman." In *The Billboard Guide to Contemporary Christian Music*, 134–135. New York: Billboard Books, 2002.

Balmer, Randall. "Carman." In *Encyclopedia of Evangelicalism*, 111–112. Louisville: KY: Westminster John Knox Press, 2002.

Powell, Mark Allan. "Carman." In *Encyclopedia of Contemporary Christian Music*, 140–144. Peabody, MA: Hendrickson Publishers, 2002.

Discography

God's Not Finished with Me (1980, Klesis); *Carman* (1982, Priority; aka *Some O'Dat*); *Sunday's on the Way* (1983, Priority); *Comin' on Strong* (1984, Myrrh 701 6807 061); *The Champion* (1985, Myrrh); *His Name Is Life* (1986, Word); *A Long Time Ago in a Place Called Bethlehem* (1986, Benson); *Carman Live . . . Radically Saved!* (1988, Benson); *Revival in the Land* (1989, Benson); *Addicted to Jesus* (1991, Benson); *High Praises I* (1991, Benson); *High Praises II* (1991, Benson); *Shakin' the House . . . Live* (1991, Benson; with Commissioned and the Christ Church Choir); *Yo! Kidz: Heroes, Stories, and Songs from the Bible* (1992, Word 701 9356 605); *The Absolute Best* (1993, Sparrow SPD 1339); *Lord of All: Songs of Carman* (1993, Word); *The Standard* (1993, Sparrow SPD 1387); *Yo! Kidz! 2: The Armor of God* (1994, Word); *Christmas with Carman* (1995, EMI Special Markets 18247); *Lo Mejor* (1995, Sparrow); *R. I. O. T. (Righteous Invasion of Truth)* (1995, Sparrow SPD 1422); *I Surrender All: 30 Classic Hymns* (1996, Sparrow); *Yo Kidz! The Hitz* (1996, Sparrow); *The Best of the Early Years* (1997, Sony HYD-7900-2); *The Best of the Early Years 2* (1998, Sony); *Mission 3:16* (1998, Sparrow SPD 1640); *Passion for Praise, Vol. One* (1999, Sparrow SPD 1704); *Heart of a Champion* (2000, Sparrow SPD 1766).

CARMICHAEL, RALPH

(b. May 27, 1927, Quincy, IL)

Ralph Carmichael was born in Quincy, Illinois. By the early 1930s, his father, who was a pastor, moved the family to North Dakota. The elder Carmichael played the trombone and enrolled young Ralph in violin lessons before his fourth birthday. Soon afterward the piano, trumpet, and vocal studies were added to his repertoire. By the late 1930s, the family moved to Southern California. Carmichael's interest in music during this period included gospel, classical, and pop.

In 1944 Carmichael became born again and enrolled in Southern California Bible College (Vanguard University). His interest in pop, which he called "the music of the people," led him to experimentation, where he fused secular styles with sacred themes. He was especially interested in the big band styles of artists such as Tommy Dorsey, Cab Calloway, and

Glenn Miller. Carmichael put together a number of vocal groups and orchestras during his college years. One of his bands, made up of seminary students, began spreading the word by playing big band renditions of gospel standards and landed a position on a local television show called *The Campus Christian Hour.* The show won an Emmy in 1949.

After graduation, Carmichael served as the music minister at a Los Angeles–area Baptist church. It was during this time that he composed the popular hymn "The Savior Is Waiting." This in turn led to an opportunity to work with Billy Graham's film organization, World Wide Pictures. The popular standard "He's Everything to Me" was but one composition from more than twenty movie scores that he produced for Graham.

World Wide film scores were recorded at Capitol Records, in Hollywood, during the 1950s. Because of this, Carmichael began working with some of the label's pop artists. He was arranging, composing, and conducting orchestras and choruses for people such as Pat Boone, Rosemary Clooney, Nat King Cole, Perry Como, Bing Crosby, Ella Fitzgerald, Stan Freberg, Jack Jones, Stan Kenton, Peggy Lee, Debbie Reynolds, Tex Ritter, and Roger Williams. More than twenty albums were produced for Williams, including a gold record for *Born Free.* All of this exposure spotlighted Carmichael's musical talent and opened doors into the television industry. During its final years, he became the musical director for the *I Love Lucy* show, as well as a composer for *Bonanza, The Danny Kaye Show,* and *The Dinah Shore Show.* At the same time he continued his work with Christian artists. He arranged and conducted for Georgia Lee, Redd Harper, Anne Criswell, Charles Turner, Bob Daniels, Sue Raney, Jimmy Durante, the Good Twins, John Gustafson, Beth Farnum, Bill Carle, Thurl Ravenscroft, and Roy Rogers and Dale Evans.

He has written, arranged, and recorded songs for groups from a myriad of musical genres, including rock bands, big bands, jazz bands, string orchestras, choirs, and *a cappella* groups. Carmichael's writing repertoire includes carols, chorales, hymns, songs, suites, and symphonies. A number of pop singers, including Elvis Presley, have recorded his compositions. His Christian folk rock musicals, during the late 1960s, played a major part in the acceptance of pop music into the church. He helped create a receptive audience for the new music that was being produced by the youthful Jesus movement.

Many consider Carmichael to be the father of contemporary Christian music. In the late 1960s, after a discussion with Jarrell McCracken, president and founder of Word Records, about the need for a new Christian record label to showcase the new music,

Carmichael founded Light Records and Lexicon Music in a joint venture with Word Records. One of the first albums released on the new label was Andrae Crouch's "Gonna Keep On Singing." Carmichael signed and recorded dozens of Christian artists on the label, including Dino, Bryan Duncan, the Rez Band, and the Winans.

Carmichael's genius, influence, and contribution to the Christian music genre are considered comparable to Duke Ellington's in jazz. His ability to move in and around different musical styles defied the stereotype that defined the difference between secular and sacred music. He has served as president of the Gospel Music Association and was inducted into its Hall of Fame. He won a Dove Award and has been nominated for Grammy Awards numerous times. During the 1990s, Carmichael was the musical director of the hugely successful touring Christian musical *Young Messiah.* During that same period, big band music made a resurgence in the secular world, which prompted Carmichael to release a number of contributions. Carmichael's career has been responsible for the production of more than two hundred record albums, as well as more than seventy five television and motion picture scores.

BOB GERSZTYN

See also Calvary Chapel, Costa Mesa; Crouch, Andrae; McCracken, Jarrell; Rock Gospel

Reference and Further Reading

Brasher, Joan. "Leader of the Band." http://www.ccmmagazine.com/features/fullstory.asp?Id=991 (accessed April 21, 2003).

Carmichael, Ralph. *He's Everything to Me.* Word Publishing, May 1986.

Linzey, Jim. "Ralph Carmichael Interview." *Today's Pentecostal Evangel* (December 15, 2002).

"My Music Way." http://www.mymusicway.com/artists/rcarmcl.html (accessed March 30, 2003).

"Space Age Pop." http://www.spaceagepop.com/carmicha.htm (accessed March 27, 2003).

Discography

102 Strings (1958, Sacred Records 4027); *Man with a Load of Music* (1968, Kapp KL-1518); *I Looked for Love* (1969, Light LS-5510-LP); *Electric Symphony* (1970, Light LS-5541-LP); *Sometimes I Just Feel It This Way* (1970, Light LS-5542-LP); *Tell It Like It Is: A Folk Musical About God* (1970, Light LS-5512-LP); *Cross and the Switchblade* (1971, Light LS-5550-LP); *Centurion* (1971, Light LS-5534-LP); *My Little World* (1971, Light LS-5555-LP); *Natural High* (1971, Light LS-5558-LP); *Have a Nice Day* (1972, Light LS-5583-LP); *The Savior Is Waiting* (1975, Light LS-5674-LP); *Rhapsody in Sacred Music* (1976, Light WST-8673-LP); *102 Strings, Vol. 1* (1976, Light WST-8688-LP); *Portrait* (1977,

Light LS-5726); *The Best of Ralph Carmichael* (1981, Light LS-5798); *Big Band Christmas* (1998, Platinum Entertainment); *Big Band Gospel Classics* (1999, Intersound Records).

CARSON, JAMES AND MARTHA

James Carson (James William Roberts) (b. February 10, 1918)
Martha Carson (Irene Amburgey) (b. March 19, 1921; d. December 16, 2004)

During the 1940s, James and Martha Carson probably ranked as the country's leading gospel music duet. Headquartered at powerful WSB radio in Atlanta, Georgia, and heard first on White Church and then Capitol Records, their duet arrangements of quartet numbers, backed by their mandolin–guitar accompaniment, found a wide audience. Unfortunately, they split both maritally and musically in 1951 and brought their joint career to a sudden and bitter end. Martha continued as a solo act thereafter and James also continued in music for a time as a part of other groups.

James was born James William Roberts near Richmond, Kentucky. His father, Phillip "Fiddlin' Doc" Roberts, was a well-known old-timer who recorded widely in the 1925 to 1934 period for Gennett, Paramount, and the American Record Corporation. James, along with guitarist Asa Martin, played on many of those recordings from 1928 and later on radio in Iowa with his father. After a stint in the U.S. Navy, he joined Martin on radio at WLAP Lexington, where he met Irene Amburgey, a native of Neon, Kentucky, who also performed on the station with her sisters, Bertha and Opal. The two married on June 8, 1939, and soon struck out on their own at WHIS in Bluefield, West Virginia, and thence to the *Renfro Valley Barn Dance* and finally to WSB Atlanta, where James and Irene soon became James and Martha Carson, the Barn Dance Sweethearts. They remained at the station until 1949, when they relocated to WNOX in Knoxville, Tennessee.

Their first recordings appeared on White Church in 1947 and consisted of eight sides, seven of them sacred and the secular one being the sentimental J. B. Coats composition "The Sweetest Gift (A Mother's Smile)." Others included such originals by James as "The Man of Galilee," "There's an Open Door Waiting for Me," and "Budded on Earth to Bloom in Heaven." They signed with Capitol in 1949, where "Looking for a City" became the best known of the twenty-two numbers on that label, but they also did well with "I Ain't Got Time," "Sing, Sing, Sing," "When I Reach that City on the Hill," "I'll Shout and Shine," and the perennial Albert Brumley favorite "I'll Fly Away."

James Carson's later career included stints with Wilma Lee and Stoney Cooper's Clinch Mountain Clan; a staff band member at WWVA Wheeling, West Virginia; with the Masters Family; and as a featured performer on the *Cas Walker Farm and Home Hour* on radio and television in Knoxville. When he recorded with the Masters Family in the mid-1950s, he sang lead on several of his original songs such as "Everlasting Joy" and "I Wasn't There (But I Wish I Could Have Been)." After 1960, he retired from music and worked primarily at other jobs but still performed on a part-time basis, including a tour of the Netherlands and another sojourn at Renfro Valley. Martha Carson had an extensive career as a solo artist, primarily in Nashville. Both have been inducted into the Atlanta Music Hall of Fame. James lives in retirement in Lexington and Martha is retired in the Nashville area. Unfortunately, their recordings are no longer available.

IVAN M. TRIBE

See also Carson, Martha; Masters Family, The

Reference and Further Reading

Tribe, Ivan M. "Remembering . . . James and Martha Carson." *Precious Memories: Journal of Gospel Music* 1, no. 1 (May–June 1988): 16–24.

CARSON, MARTHA

Irene Amburgey (b. March 19, 1921; d. December 16, 2004)

Martha Carson, with her spiritual-styled country-gospel songs, made a major impact in sacred music circles during the 1950s. Earlier she had worked as a duet with her first husband, James Roberts (aka James Carson), and also with her sisters Bertha ("Minnie") and Opal ("Mattie"). Martha's career extended into the 1960s and 1970s with her brand of "happy spirituals."

Martha had been born Irene Amburgey in Neon, Kentucky. She and her older and younger sisters had formed an all-girl string band somewhat in the style of the Coon Creek Girls, that was known alternately as the Hoot Owl Holler Girls and Mattie, Martha, and Minnie prior to her marriage. After her divorce she worked briefly with the Carlisles before going solo.

Continuing to record for Capitol, she scored a major success with her song "Satisfied" in 1951, which was eventually covered by artists ranging from the Blackwood Brothers to Elvis Presley. She soon moved from Knoxville to Nashville and joined the Grand Ole Opry. Other popular numbers for her included "I'm Gonna Walk and Talk with My Lord" and "Old Blind Barnabus." During this period she also recorded secular material, again with her siblings, as the Amber Sisters.

A second marriage in 1953, to Xavier Cosse, resulted in a 1955 switch to RCA Victor and for a time a move to New York, where she managed to take her music (not all of it sacred) to major nightclubs and network television, appearing on such programs as *The Steve Allen Show*. Returning to Nashville, she spent many years touring with country acts and playing to audiences with whom she felt more comfortable and recording for such companies as Sims and Starday. Widowed in 1993, she then retired except for an occasional appearance. Of her many recordings, the only one currently in print is the Starday material initially released in the mid-1970s.

IVAN M. TRIBE

See also Carson, James and Martha

Reference and Further Reading

Wolfe, Charles K. "Martha Carson." In *Classic Country: Legends of Country Music,* 236–238. New York: Routledge, 2001.

Discography

Martha Carson: Gospel Hits (1999, Federal 6557).

CARTER FAMILY, THE

A. P. Carter (b. December 15, 1891; d. November 7, 1960)
Sara Dougherty Carter (b. July 21, 1899; d. January 8, 1979)
Maybelle Addington Carter (b. May 10, 1909; d. October 23, 1978)

Often referred to as "the Original Carter Family" to distinguish them from various later incarnations created by individual members and their families, the Carter Family started out as an unassuming trio from remote Southwestern Virginia under the shadow of Clinch Mountain. From 1927 to 1943, they created a type of music that would forge the link between the old mountain ballad styles and the newer country music and define the idea of country harmony singing. They created dozens of classic songs and arrangements that have become archetypes in country and especially country gospel music.

Their legacy consists of 292 songs issued on early 78s, three widely distributed songbooks, a shelf of radio transcriptions, and large numbers of LP and CD reissues. Though not known expressly as a gospel group, a large number of their songs—probably as much as thirty percent—were arrangements of old gospel songs, and in their early days, their initial best-selling numbers were often gospel tunes.

The leader, manager, song finder, promoter, and bass singer of the trio was Alvin Pleasant Delaney Carter, born in the hamlet of Maces Spring, Virginia, and called "Doc" by his friends and family. A tall, intense, introspective and moody man, he was born into a family that had been pioneers in the rugged Poor Valley since Revolutionary War times. He was one of eight children, and family legend tells that two months before he was born, a bolt of lightning struck very close to his mother, causing him to be afflicted with a mild palsy.

As a child he heard the ballads his mother sang and attended church regularly, singing from the shape-note gospel songbooks. By 1909 A. P. was enrolled in a singing school conducted by Flanders Bays, and later his uncle, Leigh Carter, taught shape-note schools himself. A. P. grew up with the small paper-backed songbooks of the time, and he became interested in arranging the songs—which were routinely sung *a cappella*—to be accompanied by a guitar. About 1914 A. P. met a young woman named Sara Dougherty from a nearby settlement called Copper Creek; fascinated with music, Sara had learned to play the banjo, the guitar, and a new, odd instrument called the autoharp that she had ordered from the Sears catalog. A. P. and Sara began courting and singing together at local church events; they were married on June 15, 1915. They became good enough that in 1926 they auditioned for the Brunswick Record Company, singing "Anchored in Love," but the company wanted Doc to record only as a fiddler. This he refused to do, partly out of religious conviction.

Returning home, the two added to their group a young teenage cousin named Maybelle Addington; though only in grade school when A. P. and Sara married, she was turning into a good singer and guitar player. (The guitar, at this early date, was just beginning to become popular in the Southern mountains.) In March 1927, A. P. met with another record scout, Ralph Peer, of the Victor Talking Machine Company. Peer was planning a recording session in Bristol, Virginia, that summer, and invited the trio to come in and make records. This they did, driving to Bristol on July 31 and recording in a makeshift studio with blankets hung around the walls for baffles. Among the six titles they recorded that day and on August 1 were two gospel songs from the old songbooks, "The Poor Orphan Child" and "Little Log Cabin by the Sea." The former became one side of the very first Carter record released, on November 4, 1927. In the Atlanta area alone, the disc sold two thousand copies during its first week of release—an astounding figure in an age when not many Southern homes had Victrolas.

Peer wasted no time in getting the Carters back into the studio, and paid their expenses to Camden, New Jersey, home of the Victor pressing plant and main studio, to record twelve more songs on May 9 and 10, 1928. Among these was the one that would be forever associated with the Carter Family style of music and that they used as their theme song, "Keep on the Sunny Side." The song had been published and copyrighted in 1899 by two well-known writers, Ada Blenklorn and Howard Entwhistle, and had been published first in *The Young People's Hymnal No. 2* (1912), though A. P. had learned it from Flanders Bays, his father's brother, a singing schoolteacher. The song became one of the Carters' best-selling records. The other classic from the session was "Anchored in Love," often published in shape note books as "Anchored in Love Divine." This had been sung in the Mt. Vernon Methodist Church that the family attended and was probably taken from a James D. Vaughan book called *Crowning Praises* (1911). The music was written by Vaughan himself, the words by his company wordsmith, James Rowe.

More gospel best-sellers soon followed: "God Gave Noah the Rainbow Sign" (1929), a song of uncertain provenance but which Sara recalled as coming from a black source; "Little Moses" (1929), a traditional song Sara had learned orally from a neighbor; "Motherless Children" (1929), a 1904 song the family learned from bluesman Lesley Riddle, who often accompanied A. P. on song-hunting trips; "On My Way to Canaan's Land" (1930), which the Carters described as "a Holiness song"; and "On the Rock Where Moses Stood" (1930), another black spiritual that the Carters adapted to their mountain singing style. By then, most of the singing was being handled by Sara and Maybelle, accented by Maybelle's innovative guitar picking style.

As the depression hit in late 1929, the Carter record sales and bookings began to slack off. This was reflected in songs such as "Sunshine in the Shadows" (1931), "Will the Roses Bloom in Heaven" (1932), and "No Depression in Heaven" (1936). In 1936 the group signed a new contract with the American Recording Company, and in the first session for them did their final great gospel standard, "Can the Circle Be Unbroken." It represents the greatest accomplishment of A. P.'s rewriting of older songs. The original was titled "Will the Circle Be Unbroken" and was a popular 1907 piece by Ada R. Habershon and Charles Gabriel; little is known about lyricist Habershon, but Gabriel, a Chicago resident associated with Homer Rodeheaver, was in the habit of buying song poems for as little as one dollar apiece, and this well might have been one. This original song appeared in numerous songbooks and was recorded by artists such as Frank Luther, the McCravy Brothers, and others. A. P. stripped away the Victorian verses, retaining the melody and chorus, and added new verses that were more modern and dramatic. It became one of the Carters' best-known songs and one that emerged as a country standard throughout the rest of the century.

The Carters had trouble capitalizing on their record hits, though; the women were busy raising their young families, and for a time Maybelle and her husband lived in Washington, DC, making it hard for the three to play concert dates. A. P. and Sara began having marital problems, and by 1933, Sara had separated from A. P. and was living across the mountain from him and the children. In 1936 this resulted in a divorce, though it was kept quiet in deference to the group's fans.

In 1938 Ralph Peer, who had been acting as their manager, negotiated a contract between the Carters and the Consolidated Royal Chemical Corporation, which made products such as Peruna (a tonic) and Kolorback (a hair dye). For a regular salary, the family would relocate to Del Rio, Texas, and broadcast over XERA, a Mexican border station that blasted its hundred thousand watts of power across the United States. The Carters stayed there for two winter seasons, returning home in the summer; the station dramatically increased their popularity and record sails soared, as did fan mail. They were on the verge of a national reputation when World War II intervened; Sara had remarried in 1939, and Maybelle was wanting to start her own group with her children, June, Anita, and Helen. A. P. returned to Poor Valley, where he occasionally did local radio and opened a general store. One of his last products was a tract he had written called *100 Bible Questions and Answers*.

CHARLES K. WOLFE

Reference and Further Reading

Atkins, John. "The Carter Family." In *Stars of Country Music,* edited by Judith McCulloh and Bill C. Malone. Urbana: University of Illinois Press, 1973.

———, ed. *The Carter Family. Old Time Music Booklet.* London: Old Time Music, 1973.

Kahn, Ed. "The Carter Family: A Reflection of Changes in Society." Ph.D. dissertation, UCLA, 1970.

Wolfe, Charles. *The Carter Family: In the Shadow of Clinch Mountain.* Book accompanying Bear Family box set of the complete commercial recordings of the Carter Family.

CASH, JOHNNY

(b. February 26, 1932; d. September 12, 2003)

Even though his era was one in which country singers routinely acknowledged their gospel roots by making a "sacred" album or two, country music superstar Johnny Cash was notable for his many gospel recordings and films and for an outspoken and very public Christianity that contrasted starkly with his occasional wild and troubled behavior.

The Cashes were Arkansas sharecroppers struggling with the Great Depression when J. R. (Johnny's given full name) was born in 1932. In the WPA's Dyess Colony in Northwestern Arkansas where Johnny was raised, the family attended Baptist services, and Johnny always cited his mother Carrie Cash as his inspiration and guide to the faith. Emotionally scarred by the accidental death in 1944 of his older brother Jack, Johnny served in the U.S. Air Force, and was stationed in Germany during the early 1950s.

Upon discharge from the Air Force, Cash was selling electrical appliances in Memphis when he and his friends Luther Perkins (electric guitar) and Marshall Grant (bass) started their rockabilly trio as Johnny Cash and the Tennessee Two. Sam Phillips of Memphis's Sun Records (the man and the label that had just discovered Elvis Presley) liked their sound, and their first Sun release (1955) of "Cry, Cry, Cry" and "Hey Porter" became a hit. The simple and spare "boom-chicka-boom" rhythm of his early Sun hits became a Cash trademark, as did, of course his, low and instantly recognizable singing voice.

He wrote many of his best-known hits, which for years routinely topped country and pop playlists: "I Walk The Line" (a million-seller), "Folsom Prison Blues" (based on an earlier Gordon Jenkins recording—a hit for Cash twice, in 1956 and 1968), "There You Go," "Big River," "Guess Things Happen That Way," and "Don't Take Your Guns to Town." As years passed, his songs displayed a growing social consciousness: "The Ballad of Ira Hayes" in 1964 (about an American Indian hero of World War II who faced discrimination back in the United States), "What Is Truth" in 1970 (echoing some questions of the young in the Vietnam era), and "Man in Black" the next year (about himself and his concern for the poor; this became Cash's best-known handle). By then, Cash was an international superstar and host of his own weekly prime-time musical variety show on ABC-TV, *The Johnny Cash Show* (1969–1971).

Though the hits came with regularity throughout the 1960s, it was just before those peak years of national television stardom that Cash emerged from the dark trough of drug abuse with the help of his faith, his second wife June Carter, a physician and musician named Nat Vincent, and other devoted friends and family members. Almost from the beginning of his career (and often over the objections of record producers, who were mindful of his tough guy persona), Cash had recorded gospel songs. There were two early albums of hymns: *Hymns By Johnny Cash* (1959) and *Hymns from the Heart* (1962). "Daddy Sang Bass," Cash's huge 1968 hit about a family quartet, had "He Turned the Water into Wine" on its flip side; then, in 1969, came a third gospel album, *The Holy Land.*

It was to that Holy Land in 1972 and 1973 that Cash went and, with more than a million dollars of his own money, financed and produced a film about the life of Jesus entitled *The Gospel Road,* which also generated a well-received soundtrack album (1973). Cash and his wife, during these peak years, were very publicly associated with the Reverend Billy Graham, often singing for his various crusades. Cash's last major-label gospel LP (all on Columbia, for whom he recorded between 1958 and 1984) was 1975's *Precious Memories,* but he recorded more gospel material for various small labels thereafter, stressing (as the titles indicate) the virtue of belief: *A Believer Sings the Truth* for Cachet Records in 1979; *I Believe* (Arrival, 1984); and *Believe in Him* (a 1986 production by Cash's then son-in-law and bandsman Marty Stuart, for Word).

Cash recorded a massive fourteen-cassette *The Spoken Word New Testament* in 1990 for Thomas Nelson, the Nashville-based Bible publishers, and six years later spoke *The Eye of the Prophet,* a cassette reading from Kahlil Gibran's works. Reader's Digest Records reissued all of Cash's gospel recordings (1958–1986)—sixty-two songs on three CDs—as *Timeless Inspiration.* His final major new gospel recording was "In The Garden" for the soundtrack to the Robert Duvall film *The Apostle.*

An inspiration to generations of folk and rock artists (Bob Dylan and Kris Kristofferson preeminently), Cash was elected to the Country Music Hall of Fame in 1980 and to the Rock and Roll Hall of Fame in 1992, making him one of the few performers elected to both. Despite failing health and limited personal appearances, he found a whole new audience and a career renaissance on Rick Rubin's California-based American Recordings, winning a Grammy for his 1998 album *Unchained,* a 2003 Grammy for a remake of "Give My Love to Rose" (his eleventh to date) and even an MTV Music Video Award (Best Cinematography) in 2003 for his cover of "Hurt," a song popularized by the rock group Nine Inch Nails. His wife June Carter Cash died in May 2003 from complications after heart surgery, and Cash, already very sick from diabetes and associated woes, lived only four more months, dying at Nashville's Baptist Hospital on September 12, 2003.

RONNIE PUGH

Reference and Further Reading

Cash, Johnny. *Man in Black*. Grand Rapids, MI: Zondervan Press, 1975.
Cash, Johnny; with Patrick Carr. *Cash: The Autobiography*. San Francisco: HarperSanFrancisco, 1997.
Streissguth, Michael, ed. *Ring of Fire: The Johnny Cash Reader*. New York: Da Capo Press, 2002.
Wren, Christopher. *Winners Got Scars Too: The Life and Legends of Johnny Cash*. New York: Dial Press, 1971.

Selected Discography

Hymns by Johnny Cash (1959, Columbia Records).
Hymns from the Heart (1962, Columbia Records).
The Holy Land (1969, Columbia Records).
Precious Memories (1975, Columbia Records).
A Believer Sings the Truth (1979, Cachet Records).
I Believe (1984, Arrival).
Believe in Him (1986, Word Records).

CATHEDRAL QUARTET

George Younce (b. February 22, 1930)
Glen Payne (b. October 20, 1926; d. October 15, 1999)

The Cathedral Quartet set the benchmark for Southern gospel quartets for nearly four decades. They set the standard by which all other quartets were judged. They embodied a smooth style and rich harmonies all woven around the voices of their leaders, Glen Payne and George Younce.

The roots of the Cathedral Quartet trace back to Rex Humbard's ministry at the Cathedral of Tomorrow. The Weatherford Quartet was the staff quartet at the Cathedral of Tomorrow. This quartet consisted of Bobby Clark, Glen Payne, Earl Weatherford, Armond Morales, and Danny Koker. The group had tremendous success as a church quartet and also traveled the gospel music circuit as time would allow. They were an exceptional quartet bathed in close harmony with stellar arrangements.

Glen Payne was a longtime member of this quartet, having joined the group in the mid-1950s. Glen had been in the Stamps organization prior to joining the Weatherfords. In the spring of 1963, Earl Weatherford decided to leave Ohio and the Cathedral of Tomorrow to relocate their ministry headquarters in California. They invited the other members of the quartet to go with them, but only Armond Morales took them up on the offer.

The remaining members of the Weatherford Quartet—Bobby Clark, Glen Payne, and Danny Koker—were left without a quartet and essentially without a job. Rex Humbard suggested that they continue as a trio, with the possibility of becoming staff members at the Cathedral of Tomorrow if things panned out for them.

It was a long spring and summer for the Cathedral Trio as they sought to find venues to display their considerable talent. Their main work was in small church settings in the Ohio area, and the financial burdens mounted for the group. However, vocally the Cathedral Trio flourished, and was indeed hired by the Cathedral of Tomorrow in September 1963 as the staff vocal group.

The blend of the Cathedral Trio was outstanding, and Danny Koker provided great arrangements for the trio. However, they all longed for the sound of four male voices blending in quartet harmony. In November 1964, bass singer George Younce left the Blue Ridge Quartet and joined forces with Clark, Payne, and Koker to give birth to the Cathedral Quartet.

Younce had been a member of the Blue Ridge Quartet for several years, and had established himself as one of the finest in the industry. His smooth voice blended with the trio from the first note. Not only did he blend vocally, but the personalities also meshed together perfectly. The early Cathedral Quartet embodied a sound that has never been duplicated in gospel music.

They continued their association with the Cathedral of Tomorrow for several years, doing some concert venues but mainly focusing on their church work. The group prospered, and their sound continued to improve. However, as in any gospel quartet, change is inevitable. First, Bobby Clark left in 1968; he had a beautiful lyric tenor voice that had no rival. Next to leave was Danny Koker; not only was Danny the baritone singer, but he was a wonderful master of ceremonies and one of the finest pianists in gospel music. The Cathedral Quartet built their sound around Koker's arrangements.

This would be the first in a series of changes that Glen and George would face through the years. They hired Mack Tauton to sing tenor, and George Amon Webster became the baritone and pianist. George and Glen then added responsibilities to their plate. George had traveled with Elmo Fagg, considered one of the finest emcees in the business. He picked up on Elmo's techniques and soon became known as one of the greatest masters of ceremonies himself. Glen's musical background with the Stamps organization proved invaluable as he started arranging the music for the quartet.

Not only did the quartet face changes in personnel, but they left Rex Humbard and the Cathedral of Tomorrow in 1968 to travel full time on the gospel music circuit. It took the quartet quite a few years to generate the bookings and contacts necessary to keep the wolves away from the door.

Canaan Records realized that the group was coming into its own vocally and offered them a recording contract in 1970. George Amon Webster and George Younce were both coming into their own as songwriters, so the material being offered by the Cathedral Quartet was fresh. The Cathedral Quartet was slowly making its way to the top echelon of the gospel quartet field. They began to appear on the *Gospel Singing Jubilee,* where they gained national exposure. They appeared on more and more of the large concert venues. By the late 1970s, the Cathedral Quartet was known to be one of the finest quartets in gospel music. They won many awards and had a steady stream of top gospel hits.

The winds of change blew through the quartet quite frequently. However, Glen Payne and George Younce were the two pillars around which the quartet had molded its signature sound. At one point, three members of the Cathedral Quartet (Roy Tremble, George Amon Webster, and Lorne Matthews) left the quartet abruptly to venture out on their own as a trio. However, George and Glen pulled themselves up by their bootstraps and quickly hired two young talents: Steve Lee and Kirk Talley. Soon thereafter they added pianist Roger Bennett to the mix and the Cathedrals were quickly at the top of their game again.

More changes occurred in the quartet, but the sound woven around Younce and Payne continued to thrill the gospel music audiences. Musicians such as Gerald Wolfe, Mark Trammell, and Danny Funderburk all perfected their skills under the watchful eye of Glen Payne and George Younce.

Age and health concerns finally took their toll on the Cathedral Quartet as they began a farewell tour in 1999. Fans flocked to see this great quartet one last time. By now the group consisted of Ernie Haase, Glen Payne, Scott Fowler, George Younce, and Roger Bennett. Unfortunately, this group was unable to complete the tour with the current personnel intact, as Glen Payne succumbed to cancer on October 15, 1999.

The Cathedral Quartet continues to live via its impressive alumni. Greater Vision, Signature Sound, and Legacy V—three of the top Southern gospel acts in 2005—all have former members of the Cathedral Quartet leading them. The legacy that George Younce and Glen Payne left for gospel music remains strong today.

JOHN CRENSHAW

Reference and Further Reading

Clark, Bobby. Various interviews, 1998 and 2001.
Crenshaw, John; Charlie Waller. "Well Glory!!! Glen Payne." *Gospel Singing World* 2, no. 4: 4–5. Published by GRC, Greer, SC.
Payne, Glen. Interview, June 1997.
Payne, Glen; George Younce; with Ace Collins. *The Cathedrals: The Story of America's Best-Loved Gospel Quartet.* Grand Rapids, MI: Zondervan, 2000.

Selected Discography

25th Anniversary (Riversong Hd-8912); *Albert E. Brumley Classics* (Eternal 760635); *Alive Deep in the Heart of Texas* (Homeland Hd-9707); *An Old Convention Song* (Riversong 150); *Better than Ever* (Canaan 9857); *Beyond the Sunset* (Eternal 700103); *Cathedral Qt. Hits* (Eternal 1002); *Cherish That Name* (Eternal 811215); *Classics* (Heartwarming 3886); *Climbing Higher and Higher* (Homeland Hd-9018); *Colors of His Love* (Canaan 9872); *Distinctively* (Eternal 840117); *Easy on the Ears* (Canaan 9791); *Especially for You* (Riversong 5407); *Everything's Alright* (Canaan 9697); *Faithful* (Homeland Hd-9801); *Favorites Old and New* (Canaan 9909); *Focus on Glenn Payne* (Hymntone 7220); *For Keeps* (Canaan 9776); *Greater* (Eternal 810550); *Greatest Gospel Hits* (Scripture 118); *I Saw the Light* (Eternal 998); *I'm Nearer Home* (Eternal 999); *Individually* (Eternal 830581); *Interwoven* (Eternal 800519); *It's Music Time* (Eternal 1001); *It's Music Time* (Eternal 761125); *Jesus Is Coming Soon* (Eternal 1000); *Keep on Singing* (Eternal 791006); *Land of Living* (Riversong 2389); *Land of the Bible* (Hymntone 2042); *The Last Sunday* (Canaan 9733); *A Little Bit of Everything* (Canaan 9688); *Live* (Eternal 791051); *Live in Atlanta* (Riversong 38632); *Live in Concert* (Eternal 740541); *Master Builder* (Riversong 8501); *Oh Happy Day* (Eternal 820606); *Oh What a Love* (Eternal 780303); *One at a Time* (Eternal 780302); *Plain Ole Gospel* (Eternal 751132); *Prestigious* (Riversong 8405); *Radio Days* (Homeland Hd-9633); *A Reunion* (Canaan 1995); *Right On* (Eternal 710853); *Seniors in Session* (Eternal 730634); *Smooth as Silk* (Eternal 791214); *Somebody Loves Me* (Eternal 721147); *Something Special* (Canaan 9890); *Statue of Liberty* (Canaan 9761); *Sunshine and Roses* (Canaan 9821); *Symphony of Praise* (Riversong 2402); *Taller than Trees* (Do Vi Ne 14029); *Telling the World About His Love* (Eternal 801027); *Then and Now* (Canaan 9807); *Then I Found Jesus* (Eternal 790250); *Town and Country* (Eternal 730651); *Travelin' Live* (Riversong 2324); *Two Record Set* (Eternal 8010227); *Voices in Praise* (Riversong 8308); *Welcome to Our World* (Canaan 9715); *With Brass* (Heartwarming 1909); *With Strings* (Heartwarming 1852); *You Ain't Heard Nothin' Yet* (Canaan 9842).

CATHOLIC CHURCH, GOSPEL IN

Gospel music is a musical style that originated from the grass roots of black society, a social setting markedly different from the stereotypical black middle-class Catholic community of the early twentieth century. While black Catholics chose to identify with European cultural values in their worship and life-style, individuals responsible for the development of gospel maintained an identity distinctly black and in many ways closely akin to traditional African culture.

Because of the historical development of gospel in Baptist and Pentecostal churches and its association with black folk traditions, when religious groups such as black Catholics adopt gospel, they are making a social statement. With the upsurge of movements to affirm black identity in the 1960s and 1970s, the Catholic church realized the benefits of a truly indigenous form of spiritual expression for its congregations of predominantly black cultural background. However, only in the 1970s did cities in various parts of the United States begin to see the effects of this quiet but spirited revolution in the church's musical offerings.

Black Conversion to Catholicism: Rise and Decline

The Roman Catholic Church in the United States had large numbers of African American converts and baptisms in the early twentieth century. While there are many reasons blacks were attracted to Catholicism, among the most prominent were: (1) the social status and education that came with the religion; (2) the church's position on social issues and involvement in civil rights; (3) the restrained and unemotional worship style identified with the Catholic church; and (4) family tradition.

In the 1920s and 1930s, blacks who had attained a high socioeconomic status sought some manner to display their new identity and believed that removing themselves from the traditional black church was one way of achieving this end. Similarly, when black parents wanted the very best education they could afford for their children, many sent them to Catholic schools. Once the child attended, the family was expected to join the church.

The Catholics' position on social issues and involvement in civil rights motivated blacks to become converts. Although the Catholic church did not begin to deal with the problem of discrimination against blacks until the 1940s, this activism occurred much earlier than in some black Protestant churches. In the South, the Catholic church attempted to desegregate schools and colleges. Blacks in some parts of the United States could attend white churches, yet most white Catholics preferred that blacks attend all-black churches. Catholic charity should not be overlooked. Poorer blacks often turned to the Catholics for food and shelter. Between the 1940s and 1960s, the number

of lower-class blacks converting to the Catholic Church stemmed from the aid provided to them during the depression years.

As some blacks became more upwardly mobile, many began to appreciate the music and religious behavior identified with European churches. Instead of the plantation hymns performed unaccompanied or with percussion, some black churchgoers wanted a more refined music supported by piano, organ, and other instruments. Rather than listening to ministers who tried to cover all subjects in their sermons, upwardly mobile blacks preferred someone who was prepared to preach to the point at hand. Instead of the dress parade that often occurred when collecting the offering, they believed that the raising of church funds should be reduced to a business transaction conducted without ostentation. Many blacks were truly inspired by the beauty of the liturgy and spiritual fulfillment attained through worshipping in the faith. Finally, many accepted Catholicism because "being Catholic" was part of their family heritage.

Membership in the Catholic Church and parish attendance decreased substantially during the 1970s. With the rise of the civil rights era in the mid-twentieth century, many black Catholics not only reevaluated their spiritual needs but questioned the role of religion in their lives. Some found themselves in such a state of disillusionment and discontent that they left the church completely or joined Protestant denominations. Another group remained in the Catholic Church but only if they could initiate changes to make the worship experience more relevant to their needs. They realized that, whereas other ethnic groups were able to integrate cultural traditions into the Catholic faith—for example, the practice of Catholicism among people in Africa or Latin America differed markedly from the church in Rome—black Americans had not taken or been given the opportunity to do likewise.

Changes in Worship

Early efforts by blacks to make changes in the Catholic church began during the mid-twentieth century. Father Clarence Joseph Rivers, the "grandfather" of black liturgy, is one of the first to work on a synthesis of African American and Euro-American traditions. His work *An American Mass Program* (1964, SP 1002) was based on spirituals and is the first recording of African American music developed specifically for black Catholics. The prominent use of spirituals by black Catholics began to decline through the 1970s, and this can be attributed to several factors. Although appreciated as an art form, especially when performed in a European art music concert style, the text and affective emotions of spirituals are symbolic of a Southern slave existence. Although some spirituals can be categorized as songs of hope, faith, protest, and revolt, a large number concern despair and reflect the inability of blacks to change their position in society. Catholicism in the United States has been most attractive to urban blacks. Like other blacks who migrated to cities, black Catholics may have found that the spiritual did not uplift them or satisfy their needs.

When trying to establish an identity, some will conform to the behavioral patterns of others who, in their mind, have successfully attained a certain level of consciousness or cultural awareness. This essentially was the reason many blacks between the 1920s and 1970s converted to Catholicism. In the mid-1970s, just the opposite occurred. Black Catholics began to imitate the music, mannerisms, and emotionalism associated with Baptist worship. Since gospel, by the mid-1970s, had become an integral part of most black churches, this was the music that black Catholics decided to include in their masses.

Introduction of Gospel

The leaders of Catholic churches with black congregants had different attitudes about the role of gospel. Some wholeheartedly embraced the music. Father William Norvel, a member of the Society of Saint Joseph of the Sacred Heart who was pastor of churches in Washington, DC, and Los Angeles, became nationally known for his efforts in adapting gospel for the Catholic church. While other leaders moderately adopted certain aspects of the gospel tradition, many questioned gospel's value and appropriateness in the worship experience. For churches that decided to incorporate change, the pastors took several courses of action: (1) actively encouraged the congregation to move in a particular direction; (2) allowed subordinates to initiate and implement changes so that the leader could be a neutral observer and mediator; or (3) did nothing and allowed members of the church to decide the direction that should be taken.

When the decision was made to adopt gospel, black Catholics used several methods to introduce the music in the church: (1) invited outside guests (for example, consultants affiliated with the National Office for Black Catholics) to conduct workshops or present special programs; (2) invited choir directors of other black Catholic churches to conduct gospel

workshops and give instruction in singing gospel used in Catholic liturgy; and (3) organized concerts by other Catholic church choirs. If these efforts were successful, gospel choirs were established. In some cases, membership in choirs grew immediately, with numbers increasing from a handful to more than a hundred in a few months. One of the first Catholic churches to incorporate gospel was Saint Francis de Sales Catholic Church in New Orleans, Louisiana.

By the late 1970s, Catholic churches in black communities in several cities in the United States (for example, Washington, DC, Baltimore, Maryland, and Los Angeles) had developed gospel choirs. In some instances, the churches implemented gospel masses. In so doing, several masses were held to satisfy the needs of the parishioners: a traditional mass, a gospel mass, and a Spanish mass, particularly if Spanish speakers constituted a large portion of the membership.

One of the first musicians to experiment with the use of gospel in Catholic liturgy was Grayson Brown (a Presbyterian who converted to Catholicism), who set the entire mass to newly created music in the gospel style. The first evidence of his efforts were realized in the recording *I Will Rejoice* (1979). Growing up in a church that used a liturgy helped him to capture through music the proper mood and feeling for certain portions of the mass. His handling of the material can be viewed as a synthesis of gospel and spirituals. Choir directors at churches also began to compose or arrange music for the liturgy.

Since the initial change, the acceptance of gospel has been widespread and uplifting among black Catholics throughout the United States. In addition to the publication of a hymnal including music that reflects both the African American heritage and Catholic faith, *Lead Me, Guide Me: The African American Catholic Hymnal* (1987), a wealth of new music material has been published by composers and arrangers.

JACQUELINE COGDELL DJEDJE

Reference and Further Reading

DjeDje, Jacqueline Cogdell. "An Expression of Black Identity: The Use of Gospel Music in a Los Angeles Catholic Church." *The Western Journal of Black Studies* 7 (Fall 1983): 148–160.
———. "Change and Differentiation: The Adoption of Black American Gospel Music in the Catholic Church." *Ethnomusicology* 30 (Spring/Summer 1986): 223–252.
Hovda, Robert W., ed. *This Far by Faith: American Black Worship and Its African Roots.* Washington, DC: National Office for Black Catholics, 1977.
Lead Me, Guide Me: The African American Catholic Hymnal. Chicago: G.I.A. Publications, 1987

CHAPMAN, GARY

(b. August 19, 1957)

Gary Chapman is best known as a songwriter, penning "My Father's Eyes" and "Tennessee Christmas" for Amy Grant, "Finally" for T. G. Sheppard, and songs recorded by Vanessa Williams, Alabama, Lee Greenwood, Kenny Rogers, Steve Wariner, Barbara Mandrell, Kathy Troccoli, and Russ Taff. Chapman has won six Dove Awards, including Male Vocalist of the Year and Songwriter of the Year; he was awarded a Dove for the Inspirational Recorded Song of the Year for "Man After Your Own Heart" and Special Event Album of the Year for "My Utmost for His Highest." Chapman has also received three Grammy nominations.

Chapman was raised in DeLeon, Texas, where his father was a minister. He attended Southwestern Assemblies of God College in Waxahachie, Texas, but dropped out to join the Downings, a Southern gospel group, as a guitar player. After the Downings, Chapman joined the band of Buck and Dottie Rambo; while playing guitar for the Rambos, Gary was influenced by Dottie's songwriting, which inspired him to try his hand at writing songs.

In 1980, Chapman was the opening act for Amy Grant on a tour. The two began dating and because of a rule imposed by Grant's manager, he had to leave the concert package. However, the two later married (1982) and toured together; later they divorced.

Gary Chapman served as host of TNN's *Prime Time Country* after Ralph Emery left, and was a founder of *Sam's Place,* a Sunday evening gospel show at the Ryman Auditorium. He also served as host of *CCM Countdown with Gary Chapman,* which was broadcast on two hundred radio stations.

In 2005, Chapman began his involvement in TV production with several CMT shows, including specials on *The Music Mafia,* and a concert featuring Big and Rich, Gretchen Wilson, Hank Williams, Jr., and Kid Rock.

DON CUSIC

Reference and Further Reading

Cusic, Don. *The Sound of Light: A History of Gospel and Christian Music.* New York: Hal Leonard, 2002.

Selected Discography

Everyday Man (1987).
The Light Inside (1994).
Shelter (1996).
This Gift (1997).
Outside (1999).
After God's Own Heart (2001).
Circles and Seasons (2002).

CHARIOTEERS, THE

Wilfred "Billy" Williams (b. December 28, 1910; d. October 17, 1972)
Edward Jackson
Ira Williams
Howard Daniels

This group, popular mainly in the 1940s, was formed in 1930 by Howard Daniels, a teacher at Wilberforce University in Ohio. They were originally called the Harmony Four but later became to the Charioteers, taking their new name from the song "Swing Low, Sweet Chariot," one of the most popular numbers in their repertoire. Initially they just sang spirituals but soon expanded their repertoire to include pop tunes.

In 1931 or 1934 (sources disagree) they won the Ohio State Quartet contest, which brought them a two-record recording contract with Decca and a radio show on WLW Cincinnati. Their stint at WLW lasted more than two years, after which they got a radio show in New York. Between 1935 and 1939 they recorded for V-Disc, Vocalion, Brunswick, and Decca. A large number of religious songs, such as "Little David Play on Your Harp," "My Lord, What a Morning," "Don't Dally with the Devil," "Steal Away to Jesus," and "Sometimes I Feel Like a Motherless Child," as well as pop fare such as "My Gal Sal," "Way Down Yonder in New Orleans," and "Who," were among the songs they recorded. There was not a hit among them, but the Charioteers became increasingly popular because of their radio and live performances. A long run as guests on Bing Crosby's radio show helped make their reputation.

When the group moved to Columbia Records, where they spent more than ten years, their new label changed them to a pop group. They soon scored with "So Long," and later hits included "On the Boardwalk in Atlantic City" and "Open the Door, Richard." In 1950, shortly after their Columbia contract expired, Williams left the Charioteers to form his own quartet; he was replaced by Herbert Dickerson. After recording "The Candles" and "I Didn't Mean to Be Mean to You" in 1957 for MGM, the Charioteers disbanded. Like the Delta Rhythm Boys, the Deep River Boys, and other similar groups, the Charioteers mingled religious and pop repertoires but gained their greatest commercial success with pop material. Even so, they represent a significant part of the story of gospel music in America.

W. K. MCNEIL

Reference and Further Reading

Warner, Jay. *The Billboard Book of American Singing Groups: A History 1940–1990*. New York: Billboard Books, 1992.

Discography

Jesus Is a Rock in a Weary Land (1991, Gospel Jubilee).

CHARLES E. FULLER AND THE OLD FASHIONED REVIVAL HOUR

Charles Edward Fuller (b. April 25, 1887, Los Angeles, CA; d. March 1968)

Charles Edward Fuller was born to Henry and Helen Day Fuller. A child of successful pioneers to the Northwest, he became a pioneer of gospel radio. Henry Fuller was an entrepreneur in Los Angeles and an orange grower in Redlands, where Charles went to high school. Henry and Helen Fuller were members of the Methodist church in Redlands, very evangelical in their faith, and known for their commitment to supporting mission work. When Henry traveled, he visited Christian missions and brought back stories and artifacts to share with the Christian community in Redla, Charles showed great commitment to Christianity, although later in his life he was ambivalent about whether this was "true conversion." On his 1919 application to the Bible Institute of Los Angeles (BIOLA), he wrote that he had accepted Jesus as the Lord and Savior of his life in 1903, the year he first began to show an interest in missions, but after he graduated from BIOLA he traced his conversion to evangelistic meetings he attended in 1916. Of this era, Fuller said he remembers being a Young Men's Christian Association cadet and marching "on all great civic occasions."

Retrospective analysis of his personal conversion aside, all the elements that led to Fuller's history-changing call to radio evangelism were present in his life by the time he was a teenager. As a sophomore in high school he discussed becoming a missionary with some of his close friends, including the young woman who would one day become his wife, Grace Payton. At sixteen Charles Fuller asked Grace Payton if she would ever consider marrying a missionary. She suggested that they were too young to speak of marriage and that both of them should attend college. Fuller also showed a prescient interest in emerging radio technology two years later when he bought his own telegraph with money he had saved from working in his father's orange groves. He taught himself Morse code and entered the world of telegraphic communication by the age of eighteen.

Charles E. Fuller attended Pomona College from 1906 to 1910, where despite of his previous shyness, he excelled in debate and football, and became president of his senior class. At Pomona, his biographers say, the teaching of evolution in biology class "worked up a havoc" in his faith, and the "dark cloud of unbelief settled in his heart." In his preaching ministry, which began to blossom a few years later, Fuller was numbered among the twentieth-century evangelicals who associated the theory of evolution with apostasy. For one year after graduating from college, Fuller worked as an overseer at an unsuccessful gold mine owned by his father, just north of Sacramento. At the mining camp Fuller lived among working men who drank, gambled, swore, and whored in their daily lives, although it is unclear whether he dabbled much in these activities himself. He found the whole mining lifestyle very sad and lonely, and when he began his evangelistic ministry, he went out to mining camps and other rural areas to preach the good news of the grace and mercy he had found in Jesus Christ.

After his year in the mining camp, Fuller returned to Redlands, went to work as a supervisor in one of his father's orange packing plants, and asked Grace Payton to marry him. Grace and Charles married October 21, 1911, and soon moved to Placentia, California, where they became members of the Placentia Presbyterian Church. Grace attended home Bible study classes taught by Dr. H. A. Johnson, but Charles claimed that he had little interest in spiritual matters during this time. During these years, (1912–1918), Charles worked as manager of the Southern California Citrus Packing Association. Around this time, Grace was deeply moved by reading *The Mysteries of the Kingdom of Heaven* by F. W. Grant, a Plymouth Brethren minister, and she persuaded Charles to read it also.

Charles traced his true spiritual awakening to an evangelistic crusade he attended at the Church of the Open Door in Los Angeles on Saturday, July 29, 1916. In an afternoon service he heard Paul Rader, an amateur wrestler and boxer, preach from Ephesians 1:18, "The eyes of your understanding being enlightened, that you may know what is the hope of his calling, and what the riches of glory of his inheritance in the saints." That text reached his heart, and between the afternoon and evening service, while sitting in his car, Charles E. Fuller turned his life over to God.

After this conversion experience Fuller was hungry to study the Bible and work in full-time Christian ministry. In 1919, he resigned his work in the orange packing industry and, financed by money provided by oil drilling on his father's orange grove property, he enrolled in BIOLA. He left BIOLA in 1921 to teach a Bible study class in his home church, Placentia Presbyterian. His Bible study grew so large that he moved it from the church to the town hall, and later broke with the Presbyterian denomination altogether. Fuller became an ordained Baptist minister in 1925, and organized a new church in Placentia called Calvary.

At Calvary Church he held evangelistic meetings and began a radio broadcast of his Sunday evening services. He felt the power of radio to carry the message of the gospel far beyond the walls of the church. To finance his emerging radio ministry, Fuller took on speaking engagements at conferences and evangelistic campaigns. Fuller's first evangelistic campaigns were held in Ocean Beach, California, in January and February of 1927. He also became a faculty member at Los Angeles Baptist Seminary and the chairman of the board of directors at BIOLA from 1927–1934. Calvary Church in Placentia voted in a new minister in 1933, and Fuller left to take on full-time radio evangelism.

In 1933 Charles E. Fuller helped establish the Gospel Broadcasting Association, and in October 1934 his most renowned ministry began: the *Old Fashioned Revival Hour* radio program. *The Old Fashioned Revival Hour* holds a special place in gospel music history because of its enormous global impact in spreading the melodies and spiritual songs of Western Christianity around the world. More than half of each hour-long broadcast was dedicated to the traditional hymns of Protestant evangelicalism. Youth groups around the United States, and listeners around the world, gathered around the radio to hear classic hymns such as "Just a Closer Walk with Thee," "Rock of Ages," "Jesus, Lover of My Soul," "No One Understands Like Jesus," and "Precious Lord, Take My Hand."

The musicians of *The Old Fashioned Revival Hour* freely blended the music of black evangelical Christians with the music of white evangelicalism, although the program did not feature African American participants. While segregation was still the de facto law of nations, the radio brought these hymns to listeners of every race and culture. The chorus "Heavenly Sunshine" became an anthem for the show, which by 1951 was carried by ABC radio and could be heard around the world on 650 stations. Fuller received letters of gratitude from listeners in Africa, China, India, Australia, and elsewhere. Missionaries wrote of whole villages converting to personal Christianity, and ministers wrote of the

unchurched being drawn to the gospel. Rudolph Atwood was a regular pianist for the program, and musicians such as Bill Shaw, H. Leland Green, Joseph Barclay, George Broadbent, and hundreds of others participated. The Cleveland Colored Quintet often sang in the preprogram service at the Long Beach Municipal Auditorium, where a majority of the broadcasts were recorded.

Charles E. Fuller went on to found the Fuller Evangelistic Association in 1943 and Fuller Seminary in 1947. He was also a significant mover in the founding of the National Association of Evangelicals (NAE) in the early 1940s—so much so that the first meetings of the NAE were scheduled around services at which Charles Fuller preached. He died of cancer in March 1968. The last prerecorded program of *The Old Fashioned Revival Hour* was broadcast in December of 1968. After Fuller's death, his son Daniel Fuller continued a gospel music–based radio ministry under the name *The Joyful Sound*. Artifacts of Fuller's life and ministry are housed in collections at Fuller Seminary in Pasadena, California, and at Wheaton College in Wheaton, Illinois.

TAMARA J. JAFFE-NOTIER

Reference and Further Reading

Billy Graham Center Archives, Wheaton College. "Research in the Archives: Sri Lanka, Youth Movements, and Radio Preachers." http://www.wheaton.edu/bgc/archives/NEWSLETT/199/wit199.htm.

Brown, Reverend Richard. E-mail correspondence, January 21, 2005.

Fuller, Charles E.; compiled by H. Leland Green and William MacDougall. *Old Fashioned Revival Hour Songs*. Winona Lake, IN: Rodeheaver Co., 1950.

Fuller, Daniel P. E-mail correspondence, January 20, 2005.

———. *Give the Winds a Mighty Voice: The Story of Charles E. Fuller*. Waco, TX: Word Books, 1972.

Fuller, Grace Payton. *Heavenly Sunshine: Letters to the Old Fashioned Revival Hour*. Westwood, NJ: Revell, 1956.

Goff, Philip. Telephone interview, January 20, 2005.

Smith, Wilber M. *A Voice for God: The Life of Charles E. Fuller,* 1949.

Wright, J. Elwin. *The Old Fashioned Revival Hour and The Broadcasters*. Boston, MA: Fellowship Press, 1940.

CHARLES FOLD SINGERS

Charles Fold (b. June 4, 1942, Atlanta, GA)

Charles Fold is a trailblazer in traditional gospel music, having created a significant record of achievement with the Charles Fold Singers and having collaborated with the Reverend James Cleveland on several of the genre's most celebrated albums. Inducted into the International Gospel Music Hall of Fame in 2002, Charles Fold and the Charles Fold Singers have left an enduring imprint on gospel music.

Four years old when his family moved from Atlanta, Georgia, to Cincinnati, Ohio, Fold began playing the piano in his local church. His musical acumen was nurtured and influenced through exposure to an array of musical styles. As a young musician, his favorite group was Dorothy Love Coates and the Gospel Harmonettes. He became familiar with their music through the Sunday night radio broadcasts from WLAC AM Nashville. In fact, he followed the Harmonettes from city to city, whenever they performed within a four-hour radius. He became such a fixture that Coates began to introduce young Fold and his friends at concerts whenever she would spot them sitting on the front row.

Fold was a high school classmate of the Isley brothers and was influenced by their burgeoning soulful sounds. As well, he once played piano on a session with R&B/blues singer Arthur Prysock at Cincinnati-based King Records. He later became a fan of the unique precontemporary gospel stylings of Savoy labelmate Reverend Charles Watkins. Perhaps his greatest influence took root, however, while attending college in Detroit. Fold met gospel legend James Cleveland and began playing piano for the Meditation Singers, which at that time boasted Della Reese and Laura Lee among its membership. This early association with Cleveland foreshadowed what would later become one of gospel music's most prolific duos.

After returning to Cincinnati, Fold formed the Gospel Messengers. Quite popular in churches throughout the region, they eventually recorded two sides for Peacock Records, "He'll Fight Your Battles" and "Meet Me at the River of Jordan," in 1962. However, in 1970 fold left the Gospel Messengers, with the intent to return to the music of his home church. That was shelved when six additional members of the Messengers also left the group. After discussions with the six, the Charles Fold Singers were born in 1971.

The Charles Fold Singers, a citywide group of Cincinnati's finest voices, became a popular local group, and their reputation grew in the gospel music community. In 1971, the group was invited to back up Reverend Cleveland in an Indianapolis concert featuring the Staple Singers and the Spinners. Afterward, Cleveland told Fold he wanted to record with the group. Six weeks later they were recording with Isaac Douglas, then with Cleveland on the Savoy Records label. Fold went on to collaborate on six albums with Cleveland. From them were birthed such well-known songs as "Jesus Is the Best Thing That Ever Happened to Me," "This Too Will Pass," "Thank You Lord For One More Day," "Can't

Nobody Do Me Like Jesus," "Touch Me," and the Grammy Award–winning "Lord, Let Me Be an Instrument."

The Charles Fold Singers have recorded fourteen albums on the Savoy, Muscle Shoals Gospel, and MCG labels. They have received four Grammy nominations for their work and have performed with the Cincinnati Symphony Orchestra. Dr. Fold is a longtime member of the Gospel Music Workshop of America and is on the group's board of directors. He became national chair for chapter representatives after the death of his friend Reverend Charles Nicks in 1988.

Timothy J. Moore

See also Cleveland, James; Gospel Music Workshop of America; International Gospel Music Hall of Fame and Museum, Inc.; Watkins, Charles; WLAC AM

Charles Fold Singers Personnel

Sopranos

Christine Brown, Martha Hill, Gladys Reynolds, Vicki Jones, Joyce Mack-Robinson, Rosetta Davis, Barbara Pinkston, Doretha Williams

Altos

Carol Taylor, Vertine Jones, Vera Whitfield, Yvette Jackson, Remeco Lattimore, Donald Morman

Tenors

Ronald Logan, Otis Spriggs, Phillip Calloway, Joshua Feltha, Phillip Gray, Greg Lattimore, Reverend Anthony Collier

Musicians

Bryan Phillips, Rashawn Matthews, Ernie Byrd, Donté Collier, Morris Mingo.

Reference and Further Reading

Fold, Charles. Founder, Charles Fold Singers. Interview February 9, 2005.

Gospel Music Workshop of America hme page, http://www.gmwa.org (accessed January 19, 2005).

Marovich, Bob. "Peacock Records: Discography of Gospel Singles." http://www.island.net/~blues/peacock.htm.

National Academy of Recording Arts & Sciences Inc. website, http://www.grammy.com (accessed February 2, 2005).

Stevens, Kathy. Director of Media, International Gospel Music Hall of Fame. "Inductee Biography." http://www.igmhfm.org (accessed January 21, 2005).

Selected Discography

He'll Fight Your Battles/Meet Me at the River of Jordan (1962, Peacock Records 1853); *Jesus Is the Best Thing That Ever Happened to Me* (1971, Savoy Records 7005); *Touch Me* (1976, Savoy Records 7009); *Tomorrow* (1978,

Savoy Records 7020); *Lord Let Me Be an Instrument* (1979, Savoy Records 7038); *You Don't Know How Good God's Been to Me* (1981, Savoy Records 7061); *This Too Will Pass* (1983, Savoy Records 62783); *Yes* (1988, Muscle Shoals Sound Gospel 8006); *I'll Be with You Always* (1993, Savoy Records 14813); *Live in Cincinnati* (1996, Savoy Records 7121); *One More Day* (1997, MCG Records).

CHEEKS, JULIUS

(b. August 7, 1929, Spartansburg, SC; d. January 27, 1981)

An electrifying singer with a larger than life stage persona, Julius "June" Cheeks—"the Reverend"—revolutionized gospel, becoming one of its great innovators. Cheeks is credited both as an innovative singer and as the first significant gospel artist to employ "clowning"—audience-grabbing (and pleasing) stage theatrics, later adopted by most rhythm and blues acts.

Born in Spartansburg, South Carolina, on August 7, 1929, one of thirteen children of an impoverished and widowed mother, Cheeks left school after the second grade and remained virtually illiterate throughout his life. He was working in the cotton fields and singing with a local gospel group when he was discovered by Barney Parks. Parks, formerly of the Dixie Hummingbirds, was crafting a new "supergroup" around guitarist Howard Carroll and Jo Jo Wallace and needed a powerful, hoarse-voiced shouter to complete his new Nightingales. With the addition of Cheeks, he changed the name to the Sensational Nightingales.

Fueled by Cheeks's staggering array of roars, falsetto, and growls, the group's first recordings for Peacock, "A Soldier Not in Uniform" and "Will He Welcome Me There," were immediate hits. Cheeks's ferocious baritone would often "over drive" the studio microphones, distorting the sound, a style soon imitated by a raft of R&B and soul singers. In a few years, the 'Gales were among gospel's most popular acts, even appearing on the first "Gospel Caravan" in December 1955 at the Apollo Theatre in New York City.

A deeply religious man, Cheeks periodically left the Sensational Nightingales, but generally returned. He joined the Soul Stirrers in 1954 where, according to long-time Soul Stirrer S. R. Crain, Cheeks "inspired" the flat-footed Sam Cooke to move with the music and once even bumped him off stage. His onstage theatrics were such that even the Blind Boys of Mississippi's Archie Brownlee, a legendary showman himself, once said, "Don't nobody ever give me trouble but June Cheeks."

Other 'Gales hits with Cheeks include "See How They Done My Lord," "Somewhere to Lay My Head," "To the End," "Burying Ground," and "Standing in Judgment." Cheeks's no-holds-barred performances, however, eventually shredded his powerful baritone, though he continued to appear with various groups, including his own Sensational Knights and the Mighty Clouds of Joy, who openly emulated him. When Cheeks died in on January 27, 1981, he was called "the hardest-singing lead in gospel."

ROBERT DARDEN

See also Dixie Hummingbirds; Five Blind Boys of Mississippi; Mighty Clouds of Joy; Sensational Nightingales; Soul Stirrers

Reference and Further Reading

Boyer, Horace. *How Sweet the Sound: The Golden Age of Gospel.* Washington DC: Elliott & Clark, 1995.
Funk, Ray. "The Soul Stirrers: A Look at the Early Years of One of the Most Influential Black Gospel Quartets," *Rejoice!* (Winter 1987).
Heilbut, Anthony. *The Gospel Sound: Good News and Bad Times.* New York: Limelight Editions, 1997.
"The Sensational Nightingales." In *All Music Guide of the Blues,* 2nd ed., edited by Michael Erlewine, Vladimir Bogdanov, Christ Woodstra, and Cub Koda. San Francisco: Miller Freeman Books,
Wolff, Daniel; with S. R. Crain, Clifton White, and G. David Tenenbaum. *You Send Me: The Life and Times of Sam Cooke.* New York: William Morrow and Company, 1995.
Zolten, Jerry. *Great God A'Mighty! The Dixie Hummingbirds: Celebrating the Rise of Soul Gospel Music.* Oxford, UK: Oxford University Press.

Discography

The Reverend Julius Cheeks. *Somebody Left on the Morning Train* (Savoy).
The Reverend Julius Cheeks and the Four Knights. *The Rev. Julius Cheeks and the Four Knights* (Savoy).
The Reverend Julius Cheeks and the Young Adult Choir. *We'll Lay Down Our Lives* (Savoy).
The Sensational Nightingales. *Best of the Sensational Nightingales* (MCA Special Products MCAD 22044); *Seek Ye First the Kingdom of God* (Malaco); *Sensational Nightingales' Greatest Hits* (Malaco).

CHERÉ, TAMI (TAMI CHERÉ GUNDEN)

Tami Cheré Gunden left two distinct marks in the world of contemporary gospel music, recording first as teenage pop star Tami Cheré and later as adult songstress Tami Gunden. Growing up on a chicken farm in Michigan, she made her singing debut at the age of three and began recording at the age of ten. This early start in the music business was owed both to natural talent—a remarkably powerful voice—and to the support of family and friends who were already involved in gospel music. Her uncle, Danny Lee, was leader of the pioneering Christian rock group Danny Lee & the Children of Truth.

After making one custom album, Tami Cheré came to the attention of Ralph Carmichael, who signed her as the youngest artist on his Light Records label. Her second album for Light, *He's Everything to Me*, featured as its title track an early rendition of what would become one of Carmichael's signature songs. The album also included teen-pop versions of Andrae Crouch classics "Just Like He Said He Would" and "Polynesian Praise Song." In 1978, Cheré moved to Charlotte, North Carolina, where she later attended Central Piedmont Community College.

With the album *Celebration* the singer, who now recorded as Tami Gunden, demonstrated maturity as a purveyor of adult pop similar in style to Amy Grant. In a review of the album, *CCM* magazine described Gunden's raspy voice as a cross between rock singer Bonnie Tyler and country star Emmylou Harris. The project paired Gunden effectively with producer Joe Huffman; Michael W. Smith contributed songs and also provided keyboards and background vocals. A second album by Tami Gunden would earn the singer a Christian radio hit with its title track "Written on My Heart." A third project, *Behind the Cover,* presented her as a power-pop singer in the mold of Belinda Carlisle or the Bangles, belting out previously unrecorded compositions by Smith and Phil Keaggy.

Gunden continued to perform into the first decade of the new millennium, often singing at conventions for Christian organizations and for such corporations as IBM and Amway. She also continued to record various projects on independent labels, applying her voice to classic hymns, patriotic material, and children's songs. Her album *Power of the Dream* includes a cover of the pop song "Walking on Sunshine" (originally a general market hit by Katrina and the Waves). Gunden garnered some renewed attention in the Christian music scene for the song "Shine On" from *The Songs I Love*. On the latter album she also revisited her teenage roots by recording Christian songs that had been popular in the 1970s (Keith Green's "You Put This Song in My Heart" and 2nd Chapter of Acts's "Easter Song").

MARK ALLAN POWELL

See also Crouch, Andrae; Grant, Amy; Light Records; Smith, Michael W.

Reference and Further Reading

Powell, Mark Allan. "Tami (Cheré) Gunden." In *Encyclopedia of Contemporary Christian Music*, 395–396. Peabody, MA: Hendrickson Publishers, 2002.

Discography

Tami Cheré. *Little Flowers* (1976, custom); *Keep Singin' That Love Song* (1977, Light); *He's Everything to Me* (1979, Light LP LS574).
Tami Gunden. *Celebration* (1983 Light); *Written on My Heart* (1987, Home Sweet Home); *Behind the Cover* (1992, Drexion); *The Songs I Love* (2002, Small Globe); *Redemption* (2003, independent); *Best of Tami Gunden* (date unknown, Small Globe); *Love Can Move Mountains* (date unknown, independent); *Power of the Dream* (date unknown, independent).

CHESTNUT GROVE QUARTET

The Chestnut Grove Quartet of Abingdon, Virginia, is credited with sparking the revival of *a cappella* group singing in the Appalachian region. While another group, the Hardin Brothers, started doing it earlier, the Chestnut Grove foursome began recording earlier. Over a period of more than thirty years on a half-hour weekly radio program and at appearances in local churches, this group sold some fifty thousand long-play albums in an eighteen-month period, and inspired professional bluegrass bands led by such musicians as Ralph Stanley and Doyle Lawson to take up the practice, which soon gained a wider popularity.

The original members of the Chestnut Grove Quartet—Bill and James Nunley, their uncle Archie Reynolds, and Gale Webb—came of age during the era of the Great Depression, and all but Webb played in a local string band favoring songs by popular radio acts of the time. The four also attended the rural Chestnut Grove Methodist Church, formed a quartet, and sang there. However, they did not get really serious about their singing until after World War II. About 1956, they initiated their radio programs at WBBI and, from the early 1960s, recorded long-play albums containing old songs found in paper-backed hymnals. Archie Reynolds died on September 25, 1962. After several months Ray G. Roe of Chilhowie, Virginia, took his place for the next twenty-four years, until his own death in 1987. After that, Bill Nunley's wife Ann sang the fourth part until in the early 1990s, when advancing age led them to retire. As of 2002, all members of the Chestnut Grove Quartet are deceased, except Bill Nunley, who is eighty-seven.

IVAN M. TRIBE

Reference and Further Reading

Wilson, Joe. "'We Come from a Place: The Chestnut Grove Quartet," *Bluegrass Unlimited* 30, no. 1 (July 1995): 50–54.

Discography

The Legendary Chestnut Grove Quartet (1995, County CO CD 2709).

CHUCK WAGON GANG, THE

David Parker Carter (b. September 25, 1889; d. April 28, 1963)

Ernest "Jim" Carter (b. August 10, 1910; d. February 2, 1971)

Rosa "Rose" Lola Carter (b. December 31, 1915; d. May 13, 1997)

Effie "Anna"; Carter (b. February 15, 1917)

The Chuck Wagon Gang, known exclusively as a gospel group throughout most of their sixty-plus–year career, originally performed a wide variety of songs as the Carter Quartet. The quartet consisted of members of the family of David Parker "Dad" Carter and his wife, Carrie Brooks Carter (b. February 7, 1891; d. 1984).

Born in Milltown, Kentucky, Dad Carter moved west as a child with his family. He met Carrie Brooks, who was two years his junior, while attending a singing school in Clay County, Texas, and married her in 1909. The couple had eight children, which Dad supported by working as a brakeman on the Rock Island Railroad. In 1927, the family began working in cotton fields. They performed music locally, but it was not until 1935, when one of their children became ill, that the Carters gave any thought to working as professional musicians. Because he could not afford medical treatment for the child, Dad Carter talked the people at radio station KYFO in Lubbock, Texas, into hiring the family quartet for a daily program. They began working for a total salary of $2.50 a week, which was soon raised to $15.

The Carter Quartet was made up of Dad, who sang tenor, his daughters Rosa "Rose" Lola, soprano, and Effie "Anna," alto, plus his son Ernest "Jim," who sang bass and doubled as a guitarist. They performed western songs such as "At the Rainbow's End," typical country fare such as "Take Me Back to Renfro Valley," pop songs such as "My Wild Irish Rose," and gospel songs.

In 1936, the Carter Quartet moved to WBAP Fort Worth, where they did shows sponsored by Bewley's Best Flour and changed their name to the Chuck Wagon Gang. The group was still singing more secular than sacred songs, a trend that lasted through their first two recording sessions on November 25 and 26, 1936, and June 25, 1937, for the American Record Corporation; but by their third recording session on April 25, 1940, they had become a solely gospel group. The Gang worked for a few months at KVOO Tulsa in 1942, after which they disbanded for the duration of World War II.

The Chuck Wagon Gang reunited after the war and returned to WBAP in Fort Worth, once again sponsored by Bewley Mills. They also went back to the American Record Corporation, which had become Columbia Records. The Gang was popular, but their success was mainly due to radio performances and recordings, because they made few personal appearances. Then, in 1950, Wally Fowler booked them on one of his *All Night Singing Conventions* in Augusta, Georgia; the success of this performance convinced them to perform in public more often. The following year, they gave up radio work to tour full time. Their fame spread nationally as, later in the 1950s, radio evangelist J. Bazzell Mull started featuring and selling their records on his widely syndicated *Mull's Singing Convention*.

The distinctive sound of the Chuck Wagon Gang played a part in their popularity. Their four-part harmony was strongly influenced by the style of quartets sponsored by the gospel publishing houses. Their vocals were usually underscored by a single chorded guitar, although they used a mandolin during their early years and added a piano during their later years. The public enjoyed their seemingly simple, predictable, down-home sound.

Membership in the group remained the same until Jim Carter quit in 1953. His sister Anna's husband, Howard Gordon, took over Jim's instrumental role, while brother Roy Carter handled the bass singing. Dad Carter died on April 28, 1963. Gordon died in 1967 and was replaced by his son, Greg, until a non-family member, Pat McKeehan, joined the Gang as a guitarist. Rose and Anna sang on all 408 recordings the group had made by 1975, but they did not always tour. (Anna was often unavailable after she married Jimmie Davis in 1969.) Rose retired, and she and Anna were replaced by their younger sisters Bettye and Ruth Ellen. While all these changes were taking place, the Chuck Wagon Gang quit working full time. Roy Carter earned his living as a schoolteacher, and for several years the group toured only during his vacations. The Gang returned to the studios in 1978 after a three-year break in recording, but they did not work full time again until 1987, with a new version of the group consisting of Roy Carter (now retired from teaching) his sister Ruth Ellen Yates, Pat McKeehan,

Debby Trusty, and Harold Timmons. McKeehan had worked for the Gang off and on since 1957, and Timmons, a pianist, was a long-time fan of the group.

Dad Carter was elected posthumously to the Gospel Music Hall of Fame in 1984. In 1986, the Selected Editions of Standard American Catalogues (SESAC) presented the Gang with a gold record commemorating fifty years of recording gospel music. The following year, SESAC gave them a Lifetime Achievement Award. For six years in a row (1988–1993), the Chuck Wagon Gang was named Gospel Artist or Group of the Year by *Music City News*. In 1990, Bob Terrell wrote its authorized history, *The Chuck Wagon Gang: A Legend Lives On*. Five years later, in December, 1995, the revived group broke up.

For a short time after Roy Carter's death on August 4, 1997, Harold Timmons led an authorized Chuck Wagon Gang that featured none of the Carter family. That group made some recordings and appeared at several venues until it finally disbanded. A short time later, a new version of the Gang was established. Shaye Truax, alto and granddaughter of Anna Carter Davis; Melissa Cavness, soprano; Rick Karnes, tenor and son of Rose Carter Karnes; and Darrell Morris, bass and guitarist, make up the current group, which is headquartered in Fort Worth.

W. K. McNEIL

Reference and Further Reading

Terrell, Bob. *The Chuck Wagon Gang: A Legend Lives On.* Asheville, NC: Bob Terrell, 1990.

Discography

Homecoming (1964, Copperfield); *Jubilee* (1971, Copperfield; CD 1994, MCA); *Family Tradition* (1973, CWG & Copperfield); *Looking Away to Heaven* (1976, Columbia); *Heaven Will Surely Be Worth It All* (1981); *Lord Lead Me On* (1985); *American Tradition* (1986, Copperfield; CD 1992, MCA); *Old Time Hymns, Vols. 1 & 2* (1991, Copperfield; CD 1994, MCA); *Amazing Grace* (1992, MCA); *Celebration* (1992); *Christmas with the Chuck Wagon Gang* (1993, Sony; 1995, Columbia); *Keep on Keepin' On* (1993, Copperfield); *In Harmony* (1994, Copperfield; CD 1994, MCA); *Headed for the Promised Land* (1995, Sony Special Products); *Songs of Inspiration* (1995; CD 1995, MCA Special Products); *Back to the Roots: The Acoustic Sound of the Chuck Wagon Gang* (2003); *Live in Renfro Valley* (2003); *Memories Made New, Vols., 1 & 2* (Associated Artists).

Compilations

The Chuck Wagon Gang Greatest Hits (1990, Columbia); *Columbia Historic Edition* (1990, Columbia); *20 Golden Gospel Greats* (1992, Copperfield); *16 Country Gospel Favorites* (1994, Copperfield); *Golden Legacy* (1994, Copperfield).

CHURCH OF GOD IN CHRIST (COGIC)

The Church of God in Christ (COGIC) is the largest African American Holiness Pentecostal church in North America, with more than 5.5 million members as reported in the 1993 *Yearbook of American and Canadian Churches*. The church was founded in 1896 by Charles Harrison Mason (1866–1961) and Charles Price Jones (1865–1949). Both were Baptist ministers who met in 1895 in Jackson, Mississippi. They were rejected by their Baptist church in 1896 for insisting on the deeper spiritual experience of entire sanctification as a second work of grace. This is the basic experience of the Holiness movement.

In 1896, Mason and Jones conducted a successful Holiness revival in Lexington, Mississippi, and formed the Church of God. In March 1897, Mason was walking the streets of Little Rock, Arkansas, when the Lord revealed to him the name "the Church of God in Christ" (1 Thess 1:1 and 2:14). That same year the Church of God in Christ was chartered, and the church headquarters moved to Memphis, Tennessee. The church continued to grow, with members from several Southern states. After Mason's first wife died, he married Lelia Mason in 1903, who was the mother of his eight children. She died in 1936.

Mason and Jones learned, in 1906, of the Azusa Street Revival in Los Angeles, California, led by Reverend William Joseph Seymour (1870–1922). In March of 1907, Mason, J. D. Young, and J. A. Jeter traveled to Los Angeles to learn and experience the baptism of the Holy Ghost at the Azusa Street Revival. Mason and Young experienced the baptism, all three returned to Memphis. When they arrived, the church was already divided over the doctrine of the baptism in the Holy Spirit.

In August 1907, the general assembly of COGIC met in Jackson, Mississippi, to discuss the future of the church. The assembly lasted for three days and nights. The right hand of fellowship was withdrawn from Mason and all who promulgated the Pentecostal doctrine of speaking in tongues. Jones kept half of the ministers, and the remainder went with Mason. For two years, Mason and Jones were in court over the name of the church and control of properties. In 1909, the courts allowed Mason and his followers to keep the charter and the name COGIC. The date of the church's founding became 1907, and the articles were changed to include the belief in the Holy Spirit, who proceeds from the Father and Son. In 1910, Jones and his followers became the Church of Christ (Holiness) U.S.A. They continued the Holiness tradition with an Episcopal structure. The Jones organization made its headquarters in Jackson,

Mississippi, and founded an industrial school in Pearl, Mississippi, a suburb of Jackson.

COGIC established an industrial school entitled the Saints Industrial School and Academy in Lexington, Mississippi, in 1918. The founders were Pinkie Duncan and James Courts (d. 1919). Arenia C. Mallory (1905–1977) was director following Courts's death. In 2000 the Arenia C. Mallory Health Clinic was opened in Holmes County, Mississippi, by Dr. Davis and others who had attended Saints Academy. By 1934, COGIC had 345 churches in twenty-one states and membership of more than twenty-five thousand; five bishops: I. S. Stafford of Detroit, E. M. Page of Dallas, W. M. Roberts of Chicago, O. T. Jones of Philadelphia, and R. F. Williams of Cleveland; plus ten overseers of states. The growth was phenomenal; membership increased tenfold during the next three decades.

In 1943, Mason married Elsie Washington, an educator in the Memphis city schools. She became editor-in-chief of *The Whole Truth Newspaper*. She is living in Memphis. In 1962, the membership was 382,679. Bishop O. T. Jones, Sr. church (1891–1972), was the second leader of COGIC, and Bishop J. O. Patterson (1912–1989) of Memphis, son-in-law of Mason, followed him. The membership became 3,709,661 in 1982. Bishop Louis H. Ford (1914–1994) of Chicago was the fourth leader; Bishop Chandler Owens of Atlanta was fifth. He retired because of health problems. The present leader is Bishop Gilbert Earl Patterson (b. 1939) of Memphis. Patterson was voted leader in November 2004 for his second term. COGIC membership has grown to 5.5 million, with churches in fifty-eight countries.

The church's first women's work leader was Mother Lizzie Woods Roberson (Robinson) (1860–1945); she established the Prayer and Bible Bands and the church's first savings account around 1911. Other women's leaders were Mother Lillian Brooks Coffey (1945–1964); Mother Annie L. Bailey from Detroit (1964–1976); Mother Mattie Carter McGlothen from Richmond, California (1976–1995); and Mother Emma Crouch from Dallas (1995–1997). Mother Willie Mae Rivers from Goose Creek, South Carolina (a suburb of Charleston) took up the position in 1997. The women's convention is held each year in May in various states.

The International Sunday School is the largest activity in the church. Elder F. C. Christmas (1865–1955) was the founder. Following him were L. C. Patrick, C. W. Williams, and Jerry Mackins, who recently retired. COCIC has established C. H. Mason Bible Colleges in all jurisdictions to enhance the church's teachings and train pastors. The C. H.

Mason Seminary, founded in 1970, is part of the International Theological College (ITC) in Atlanta. On April 3, 1968, Dr. Martin Luther King, Jr. (1929–1968), delivered his last speech at the Mason Temple, the church headquarters built in 1945. King's sermon was entitled "I Have Been to the Mountaintop."

Many gospel singers got their start in COGIC. Bishop Samuel Kelsey (1906–1993), overseer of Washington, D.C., was a pioneer who recorded traditional gospel songs and officiated at the wedding of gospel singer Rosetta Tharpe (1915–1973). Andrae Crouch, the Winans and the Clarks from Detroit, the Hawkins family from California, the Pace Singers, and Reverend James Moore (1956–2000) became gospel greats.

The C. H. Mason headquarters building in Memphis opened in 1945. It was listed in 1995 on the National Register of Historic Places, directed by Dr. Odie H. Tolbert, chairperson of the Historical Archives. The annual Holy Convocation is held in Memphis in each November. The church publication is the *Whole Truth*. COGIC has a publishing house that publishes all church materials, including those for its Sunday school. The hymnal is *Yes Lord!*

SHERRY SHERROD DUPREE

Reference and Further Reading

Banks, Adella M. "Presiding Bishop of Church of God in Christ Re-elected." Ethics Daily. http://www.ethicsdaily.com/article_detail.cfm?AID=502 (accessed November 24, 2004).

Burgess, Stanley M.; Eduard M. Van Der Mass. *The New Dictionary of Pentecostal and Charismatic Movements.* Grand Rapids, MI: Zondervan, 2002.

DuPree, Sherry Sherrod. *African-American Holiness Pentecostal Movement: An Annotated Bibliography.* Religious Information Systems Vol. 4; Garland Reference Library of Social Science Vol. 526. New York: Garland Publishing, 1996.

———. *Biographical Dictionary of African-American Holiness-Pentecostals 1880–1990.* Washington, DC: Middle Atlantic Regional Press, 1989.

———; Herbert C. DuPree. *African-American Good News (Gospel) Music.* Washington, DC: Middle Atlantic Regional Press, 1993.

Mason, Elise Washington. *From the Beginning of Bishop C. H. Mason and the Early Pioneers of the Church of God in Christ.* Memphis, TN: 1991.

Salzman, Jack; David Lionel Smith; Cornel West. "The Church of God in Christ." In *Encyclopedia of African American Culture and History. Library Reference USA*, vol. 1. New York: Simon and Schuster Macmillan, 1996.

Smith, Raynard D., Reverend. Director, Church of God in Christ Scholar's Group, Edison, New Jersey. Interview by Sherry Sherrod DuPree, via telephone, November, 10 2004.

CLARK, ELBERNITA

(b. November 15, 1954, Detroit, MI)

Known lovingly by her fans and all of the gospel music industry as "Twinkie," Elbernita Clark has become an icon of the gospel music industry. She has become a legend in her own right in gospel music history. Gospel music as it is known today has been heavily influenced by her contributions to the genre. Since the age of thirteen, she has traveled throughout the United States ministering and training choirs in various denominations on the three-part vocal harmony phenomenon that was initially introduced to gospel music by her mother, the late Dr. Mattie Moss Clark.

Elbernita Clark, who happens to be a member of the world renowned Clark Sisters (Jacky, Dorinda, Karen, and Elbernita), is considered to be the heart and soul of the group by many of their fans. The Clark Sisters have been the premiere female group in gospel music for more than three decades. It was Elbernita's music writing and arrangements that gave the group the unique and contemporary sound that has become its hallmark.

Elbernita received her formal music training from Howard University in Washington, DC Since then, she has been considered by many fans of gospel music to be the genre's greatest organist. Appearing in many live concerts and workshops, Elbernita has toured the United States and the United Kingdom, producing albums and writing for many gospel artists, including her sisters and many other contemporary artists of today. As a songwriter, Elbernita is best known for penned compositions such as "You Brought the Sunshine," "Is My Living in Vain," "Pray for the U.S.A.," and "I'm Looking for a Miracle."

As a musician, Elbernita serves as the leader of the music department at Holy Trinity Institutional Church of God in Christ in Muskegon, Michigan. Even in this capacity, she still travels across the country and overseas, evangelizing and teaching the good news of gospel music through song at workshops and clinics. In addition to her ministerial duties at Holy Trinity and her extensive traveling, Elbernita has produced six solo projects: *Praise Belongs to God* (1979), *Ye Shall Receive Power* (1981), *Comin' Home* (1982), *Masterpiece* (1996), *Live in Charlotte* (2002), and *Home Once Again* (2004).

Some of Elbernita's musical influences include Stevie Wonder, Walter and Edwin Hawkins, Andrae Crouch, Charles Nicks, and of course her mother, the late Dr. Mattie Moss Clark.

ALPHONSO SIMPSON

Reference and Further Reading

Mayer, Stephanie. E-mail to Alphonso Simpson, July 13, 2004.
Gospel Flava. http://www.gospelflava.com/reviews/twinkie clark.html website, (accessed June 21, 2004).
Simpson, Alphonso. Telephone correspondence with Stephanie Mayer, July 2004.
Sincerely . . . The Official Clark Sisters Fan Club website, http://www.theclarksisters.com/flash.html (accessed June 21, 2004).
Total Man Ministry website, http://www.totalmanministry.org/music.htm (accessed July 29, 2004).

CLAWSON, CYNTHIA

(b. October 11, 1948)

Cynthia Clawson was born and raised in Houston, Texas. She was the daughter of a Southern Baptist minister and began singing devotional music in her father's church services at the age of three. She graduated from Howard Payne University in Brownwood, Texas, with a major in vocal performance and a minor in piano. During her senior year in college, she won the Arthur Godfrey Talent Show and was discovered by a CBS television producer. He signed her as a headlining summer replacement for *The Carol Burnett Show*. As a result, record producer Red Buryl signed her to a recording contract. Two of Clawson's earliest musical influences were Julie London and Julie Andrews.

By the end of the 1970s she was an established artist on the Triangle label, after releasing three solo albums. She released a number of solo and collaboration albums during the 1980s. In 1995 she made a live *a cappella* video recording, "Prayer & Plainsong." It showcased her voice and creative spirit and was recorded at the three-hundred-year-old Spanish Mission San Jose in San Antonio, Texas. One of her favorite songs is "Jesus Wept," from the 1999 Civic release *Broken: Healing the Heart,* because John 11:35 "practically summarizes the entire gospel record for me. God understands."

Billboard magazine has called Cynthia Clawson "the most awesome voice in gospel music." A four-octave range combined with exceptional power and versatility make her singing voice the equivalent of a vocal orchestra. With a voice that transcends all musical barriers, she has the ability to melodically—and emotionally—interpret lyrics that touch the core of all who hear her.

During her fifty-year career, Clawson has mastered a number of musical styles, from traditional gospel to adult contemporary; and in the process, has recorded dozens of solo and compilation albums. During that time, she has been nominated for fifteen Dove Awards and has won five. She also won a Grammy Award and sang the title song "Softly and Tenderly" for the 1985 Academy Award–winning film *The Trip to Bountiful.*

Clawson has played in venues as diverse as Karla Faye Tucker's death row prison cell in Texas, at Billy Graham crusades, and has Wembly Stadium in England. She's been a guest on both the *PTL* and the *700 Club* as well as the Southern Baptist series *At Home with the Bible.* She has appeared on television and on radio jingles and station announcements for the Southern Baptist Convention, has been a frequent guest on Robert Schuller's *Hour of Power,* and has worked with James Robinson and other evangelist preachers.

After Cynthia married writer/actor Ragan Courtney, they began collaborating on songs together and became part of the ministerial staff at Tarrytown Baptist Church in Austin, Texas.

She has worked with Bill Gaither in his efforts to capture and present the gospel music of the Deep South, and appeared on the cast album of the revival of the musical *Smoke on the Mountain,* which opened in 1998 at the Lambs Theater in New York City.

BOB GERSZTYN

Reference and Further Reading

Clawson, Virginia. *The Family Symphony.* Baptist Sunday School Board, June 1984.
Connection Magazine. http://www.connectionmagazine. org/archives_old/2001_05/cynthiaclawson.htm (accessed May 18, 2003).
Talafuse, Judy; Marylynn Wolf. "Cynthia Clawson discography." http://www.geocities.com/heartland/flats/9846/discography.html (accessed May 17, 2003).

Discography

In the Garden (1974, Triangle TR101LP).
The Way I Feel (1976, Triangle TR112LP).
It Was His Love (1979, Triangle TR116LP).
Forever (1983, Triangle).
Immortal (1986, Triangle).
Hymnsinger (1987, Triangle).
Words Will Never Do (1990, Dayspring).
Prayer & Plainsong (1995, Civic Records Group).
Broken: Healing the Heart (1999, Civic Records Group)

CLEVELAND, JAMES

(b. December 5, 1932, Chicago, IL; d. February 9, 1991)

James Cleveland was the son of Ben Cleveland, a Works Progress Administration (WPA) worker. He was educated in the Chicago area and first sang solo at the age of eight in the choir of the Pilgrim Baptist Church. There he was influenced by Reverend Thomas A. Dorsey, its choir director, who was known as the father of gospel music. Dorsey had recorded blues under the name of Georgia Tom, and later became one of the most influential developers of the modern gospel choir tradition. Additionally during this period, he was influenced by Roberta Martin, another of Dorsey's protégés. Her group, the Roberta Martin Singers, was a source of inspiration to Cleveland, and she urged him to begin writing as well as performing. In 1948, Cleveland wrote "Grace Is Sufficient" for a Baptist convention, and Martin began publishing his work.

Cleveland joined a trio known as the Gospelaires in 1951; with Cleveland, they cut several sides for the Apollo label, including "Oh What a Time." Cleveland also wrote "Saved" and "Stand By Me" for Martin at this time, and performed with other groups during this period, including the Caravans. Cleveland arranged and performed two hits with the Caravans, "The Solid Rock" and an up-tempo "Old Time Religion," a traditional standard.

In 1959, Cleveland formed his first group, called the Gospel Chimes. During the next few years, he recorded many of his compositions with several groups and performed with the Gospel All Stars, Mahalia Jackson, the Meditation Singers, and the Thorn Gospel Singers.

The Cleveland Singers were formed by Cleveland in 1960 and were joined by a young organist named Billy Preston, who later gained fame with the Victory Baptist Church and Mahalia Jackson and as a regular guest performer on tour with the Beatles. Cleveland's 1962 album *Peace Be Still* was recorded with the Angelic Choir of Nutley, New Jersey, and is still regarded as the major founding effort of the modern black gospel chorus sound.

During the 1960s, Cleveland became a minister and founded the Cornerstone Institutional Baptist Church of Los Angeles. The church was his home base for the next thirty years of his prolific career. Cleveland recorded with dozens of talented individuals and groups; his work during this period led to a popular title, "Crown Prince of Gospel."

In 1968, Cleveland was influential in the founding of the Gospel Music Workshop of America in Philadelphia, Pennsylvania. His efforts influenced and inspired generations of gospel performers. The workshop had more than thirty thousand members in 150 chapters throughout the world. Kirk Franklin and John P. Kee were members of workshop chapters.

Cleveland was reunited with Aretha Franklin, a former piano understudy, as a guest performer on

James Cleveland and the Cleveland Singers. Photo courtesy Frank Driggs Collection

her album *Amazing Grace* in 1972. The album was hugely successful, becoming one of the largest selling gospel albums of all time. It was during this period that Cleveland received the NAACP Image Award and an honorary degree from Temple Baptist College.

Cleveland suffered from severe respiratory ailments in his later years, and limited his releases and performances greatly, though he was active in the Gospel Music Workshop of America and performed as a guest soloist on a limited basis.

Reverend Cleveland preached to his congregation on the last Sunday of his life; he was too ill to sing but was able to inspire his flock one last time. He died of a heart attack in Culver City, California, on

February 9, 1991, and his body is interred at Alta Mesa Garden Mausoleum in Inglewood, California. He was survived by a daughter, LaShone.

TOM FISHER

Reference and Further Reading

Broughton, Viv. *Black Gospel: An Illustrated History of the Gospel Sound.* Poole, England: Blandford Press, 1985.
Heilbut, Tony. *The Gospel Sound: Good News and Bad Times.* New York: Simon & Schuster, 1971.

Discography

Peace Be Still (1962/1995, Savoy 14076); *Jesus Is the Best Thing That Ever Happened to Me* (1975, Savoy 7005); *Live at Carnegie Hall* (1977, Savoy 7014); *World's Greatest Choirs* (1980, Savoy 7059); *I Stood on the Banks of Jordan* (1985/1995, Savoy 14096); *Having Church* (1990, Savoy 7099); *I Don't Feel Noways Tired* (1990, Savoy 7024); *And the Los Angeles Gospel Messengers* (1991, Savoy 7103); *Merry Christmas* (1991, Savoy 14195); *Victory Shall Be Mine* (1991, Savoy 14541); *This Too Will Pass* (1992, Savoy 7072); *The Best of Rev. James Cleveland* (1993, Savoy 7111); *Great Day: James Cleveland Sings with the World's Greatest Choirs—25th Anniversary Album* (1995, Savoy 7089); *I Don't Feel Noways Tired* (1998, Savoy 7024); *The Very Best of James Cleveland* (1998, Savoy 6102); *God Can Do Anything but Fail* (2003, Savoy 12083).

COATES, DOROTHY LOVE

(b. January 30, 1928, Birmingham, AL; d. April 9, 2002, Birmingham, AL)

A compelling, energetic performer, Dorothy Love Coates is also remembered today as one of the first gospel artists to become actively involved in the Civil Rights Movement in the 1950s. Born Dorothy McGriff, She was a childhood friend of Alex Bradford. She joined several regional gospel groups while still a teenager and married Willie Love of the Fairfield Four at age sixteen. After recovering from a serious illness, she joined the Gospel Harmonettes and even appeared on Arthur Godfrey's *Talent Scouts* radio program. A few sides for RCA in the late 1940s flopped.

After a brief hiatus, Dorothy (now divorced from Love) rejoined the Harmonettes in 1951. Together with organist Herbert "Pee Wee" Pickard, the group recorded some of their greatest songs for Specialty Records: "I'm Sealed," "Get Away, Jordan," "(You Can't Hurry God) He's Right on Time," "Strange Man," "I Wouldn't Mind Dying," "Come On in the House," "Jesus Knows It All," "These Are They," "Everyday Will Be Sunday," "There's a God

Somewhere," "Just to Behold His Face," "Am I a Soldier," and others.

Dorothy married Carl Coates of the Sensational Nightingales; Coates both wrote original material, and adapted older songs and spirituals, giving them contemporary lyrics. She was greatly influenced by W. Herbert Brewster. She favored loosely arranged, heavily rhythmic arrangements that allowed her room to improvise and "preach." But Coates's raspy, impassioned contralto was at its best when she sang about burning issues of the day, such as justice and racial discrimination. She courageously addressed injustice in a number of powerful tracks for Specialty, Nashboro, and Vee Jay, including "That's Enough," "The Hymn," and "How Much More of Life's Burdens Must We Bear?"

Coates marched with Dr. Martin Luther King, Jr., was arrested on more than one occasion for championing civil rights, worked voter registration drives, and was caught in the nightmarish Newark riots, barely escaping with her life.

After the civil rights era, Coates—now revered in the black gospel community—continued to record for various labels, sometimes as a solo performs and sometimes with the Dorothy Love Coates Singers. Her songs were recorded by artists ranging from Johnny Cash to Andrae Crouch to the Blackwood Brothers. In her later years, she appeared at the Newport Jazz Festival and in two motion pictures, *The Long Walk Home* (1990) and *Beloved* (1998). When she died in Birmingham on April 9, 2002, lavish tributes appeared in publications as diverse as *The Times* (London) and the folk magazine *Dirty Linen*.

ROBERT DARDEN

See also Bradford, Alex; Brewster, William Herbert; Crouch, Andrae; Fairfield Four; Nashboro Records; Sensational Nightingales; Specialty Records Company

Reference and Further Reading

Boyer, Horace Clarence. *How Sweet the Sound: The Golden Age of Gospel.* Washington DC: Elliott & Clark, 1995.
Carpenter, Bill. "Obituaries: Dorothy Love Coates." *Goldmine* (28 June 2002): 41.
Erlewine, Michael; Vladimir Bogdanov; Chris Woodstra; Cub Koda, eds. *All Music Guide to the Blues,* 2nd ed. San Francisco: Miller Freeman Books, 1999.
"Dorothy Love Coates, Singer of Gospel Music, Dies at 74." *New York Times* (April 12, 2002): B7.
Heilbut, Anthony. *The Gospel Sound: Good News and Bad Times.* New York: Limelight Editions, 1997.
Still Holding On: The Music of Dorothy Love Coates and the Original Gospel Harmonettes, produced by Dwight Cammeron. University of Alabama Center for Public Television and Radio, 2000.

Werner, Craig. *A Change is Gonna Come: Music, Race & the Soul of America*. New York: Plume/Penguin Group, 1998.

Young, Alan. *Woke Me Up This Morning: Black Gospel Singers and the Gospel Life*. Jackson: University of Mississippi Press, 1997.

Discography

The Best of Dorothy Love Coates and the Original Gospel Harmonettes Vol. 1 (Specialty).

Camp Meeting/God Is Here (Collectables 7231).

A City Built Four-Square (Savoy).

Get on Board (Specialty SPCD 7017-2).

The Soul of the Gospel Harmonettes/Peace in the Valley (Collectables 7229).

COATS, J. B.

(b. April 6, 1901; d. December 15, 1961)

James B. Coats is remembered as one of the principal gospel composers of the 1930s and 1940s. A native of Summerland, Mississippi, Coats became a lover of sacred music at an early age and joined the Baptist Church at the age of twelve. At fourteen he began teaching music, and it was said that he became one of the great music teachers of his day. He pursued a college education at Mississippi Southern and later at Louisiana State University. He taught in the public schools for some twenty years, served as a church deacon, and eventually became a minister until retiring because of ill health in 1959.

Although he is believed to be the leader of the group that recorded under the name "Coates Sacred Quartet" for the American Record Corporation in Jackson, Mississippi, in 1937, his claim to fame rests on his reputation as a songwriter for Stamps–Baxter beginning in 1933. By far his most noted composition was "Where Could I Go (But to the Lord)?" in 1940. Other Coats classics include "My Soul Shall Live On," "I'm Winging My Way Back Home," "Tomorrow May Mean Goodby," "A Wonderful Place," and "I'll Shout and Shine" (cowritten with Eugene Wright). He also wrote the sentimental favorite "The Sweetest Gift (A Mother's Smile)," which became a duet classic recorded by such artists as James and Martha Carson, the Blue Sky Boys, the Judds, and Linda Ronstadt and Emmylou Harris. In failing health for the last two years of his life, Coats died in 1961. Thirty years after his death, he was inducted into the Gospel Music Hall of Fame.

IVAN M. TRIBE

Reference and Further Reading

Baxter, J. R., Mrs.; Videt Polk. *Gospel Song Writers Biography,* 28–30. Dallas: Stamps-Baxter Music & Printing Co., 1971.

CONSOLERS

Sullivan Pugh (b. 1925)

Iola Lewis Pugh (b. 1926; d. 1993)

The Consoler Singers of Miami are Sullivan Pugh and Iola Lewis Pugh, a husband and wife duo from Miami, Florida, who began their repertoire based on traditional spirituals and songs of the Holiness Church.

Sullivan Pugh became noted for his composing abilities. It was this gift as well as his plaintive guitar playing and the couple's appealing vocal blend that made them unique. Pugh plays guitar in a way that most experts cannot understand. Pugh developed his own style; he said his gift came from God. He plays extended passages on a single string and uses legato, double-stops, and endings incorporating artificial harmonics. He has a distinct African American flavor. He uses percussive, rhythmic chords to accent the backbeat. He imitates the vocal style with his guitar, or slurs multinote phrases.

Sullivan was adopted by James and Virginia Pugh and was raised in Punta Gorda, Florida, where he attended school. Pugh's mother, along with hundreds of other people, lost her life in the destructive hurricane that struck Lake Okeechobee in the late 1920s. As an adult Pugh moved to Miami to find work.

Iola Lewis Pugh was the third oldest of four daughters, she was born in Cottonton, Alabama. Her mother died when she was three years old, she was raised by her maternal grandmother. She moved to Columbus, Georgia, where she completed high school. Then she attended Claflin College in Orangeburg, South Carolina. Later she moved to Miami and met Sullivan in 1949. They were married on March 11, 1950. The duo began singing in 1953 as the Consolers.

Sister Pugh always wore a natural Afro hair style, no makeup or jewelry. The Pughs performed in robes or clothes that did not promote worldliness. They were called Brother and Sister Pugh because men are brothers and women sisters in a tradition of the Holiness church. The Pughs were members of the First Born Church of the Living God in Miami. They had a Consolers Progressive Charity Club to help the needy with food, clothes, and some cash donations.

Their first recording was with Henry Stone, owner of T. K. Productions and Hialeah Gospel Roots Records in Miami. Ernie Young, the founder of Nashboro Records in Nashville, Tennessee, signed them in 1954. Singing for more than forty years together, this dynamic couple's greatest hits were "Waiting for My Child to Come Home," "May the Work I Have Done Speak for Me," "Give Me My Flowers While I Can Smell Them," "Lord If I Am

Too High Bring Me Down," and "Thank God, Things Are as Well as They Are." In 1963, *Waiting for My Child to Come Home* became a gold album, selling more than a million copies.

Family life conditions were very hard in the South. Most African American families were still sharecropping on the farm. The civil rights struggle worried parents, because their youth were leaving home to become involved. These youth were put in jail in the South. Sullivan Pugh stated that as the Consolers traveled, people would ask if they had seen their children. This inspired him to write the song "Waiting for My Child to Come Home," along with more than ninety other great-selling gospel songs.

> I was talking to a lady a few days ago,
> And these are the words she said.
> If you see my child somewhere as you travel here and there,
> Tell him I am waiting for my child to come home.
> Lord my child may be somewhere in some lonely jail,
> Is there someone to pay his bail?
> Lord my child may be somewhere lost in sick bed,
> It is someone to rub his aching head?
> I am waiting and waiting for my child to come,
> I am waiting and waiting for my child to come.
> If you can't come home will you please send me a letter?
> A letter would mean so much to me.
> If I only knew which town my child is in,
> I would be there on the early morning train,
> And no matter what the crime,
> Lord you know this child is mine,
> Lord I am waiting for my child to come home.

The Pughs traveled to the Virgin Islands, singing the praises of God. Sister Iola Pugh's alto voice was forceful, with shouts and moans. Brother Pugh's second wife, Margie, was a teacher in the Miami-Dade Public Schools.

In 2002, Brother Pugh received the Florida Folk Heritage Award in Tallahassee for his down-home music and composing. His was also recognized for the Consolers, who supported traditional gospel music. In October 2003, the Consolers were inducted into the International Gospel Music Hall of Fame and Museum in Detroit, Michigan. Master of Ceremonies Dr. Bobby Jones, from Black Entertainment Television (BET) and the program *The Bobby Jones Gospel,* stated that Sullivan Pugh is a pioneer who made the way for all contemporary gospel singers. Living and sleeping in their car and not allowed to eat in restaurants, still the Pughs carried the word of God with joy in their hearts. The audience sang "May the Work I Have Done Speak for Me." The Pugh's pastor, Bishop Watson from the First Born Church in Miami, came to support this prestigious award.

In August 2004, Malaco Records invited old traditional gospel groups to Jackson, Mississippi, to record a live video. Pugh said, "It was a reunion of Shirley Caesar, Ira Tucker from the Dixie Hummingbirds, Dorothy Norwood, Margaret Wells Allison from the Angelic Gospel Singers, Albertina Walker from the Caravans, and many others who performed for two days singing and talking about the golden era of gospel music and other historical events."

SHERRY SHERROD DUPREE

Reference and Further Reading

Boyer, Horace Clarence. *How Sweet the Sound: The Golden Age of Gospel.* Washington, DC: Elliott & Clark, 1995.
DuPree, Sherry Sherrod. *African-American Holiness Pentecostal Movement: An Annotated Bibliography.* Religious Information Systems Vol. 4; Garland Reference Library of Social Science Vol. 526. New York: Garland Publishing, 1996.
———. *Biographical Dictionary of African-American Holiness-Pentecostals 1880–1990.* Washington, DC: Middle Atlantic Regional Press, 1989.
———; Herbert C. DuPree. *African-American Good News (Gospel) Music.* Washington, DC: Middle Atlantic Regional Press, 1993.
Give Me My Flowers (1955, Nashboro Record Co. LP7004).
International Gospel Music Hall of Fame and Museum website http://www.gmhf.org (accessed August 28, 2004).
Pugh, Sullivan. Interview by Sherry Sherrod DuPree via telephone, August 30, 2004.
Shaffer, Nash Reverend. "Sunday Morning Golden Gospel Radio," Chicago. Interview by Sherry Sherrod DuPree via telephone, May 20, 2004.

COOKE, EDNA GALLMON

(b. 1918, Columbia, SC; d. September 4, 1967)

With the beginning of the golden age of gospel music in 1945, Madame Edna Gallmon Cooke born to Reverend and Mrs. Eddie J. Gallmon, became one of the outstanding female gospel mezzo-soprano singers using youth choirs as backup. Her father was a Baptist preacher. The family moved to Washington, DC during the Depression. She lived and studied in Washington and Philadelphia, attended Temple University, and taught in the elementary schools. Cooke was well educated and musically trained. She wanted to sing semiclassics and show tunes.

Cooke kept the name of her first husband, who passed away at an early age. Then she married Barney Parks, Jr., a former member of the Dixie Hummingbirds and founder of the Sensational Nightingales. Parks's tutelage and management made Cooke a household name in gospel music. The changes she implement were to moan and to give a short sermon. quartets were used as her backup. This was from her husband Parks' use of quartet singing. In 1938 in Washington, DC she heard the famous contralto gospel singer Mother Willie Mae Ford Smith (1906–1994), who was from St. Louis.

Mother Smith, a female minister in the Apostolic Church, was the pivotal figure in Cooke's life. Mother Smith was not an entertainer but a servant of the Lord. In 1937, Smith set a new standard for solo singing and arranging with her radical "If You Just Keep Still," delivered at the National Baptist Convention with Thomas A. Dorsey as director of music. She was one of the first to bring a lengthy sermon mixed with songs. This changed Cooke's perspective on music; she quickly wanted to learn the gospel style of Mother Smith's arranging and reinterpretations of hymns. With the support of Smith, Cooke began singing hymns at Baptist, Holiness, and Pentecostal churches. She toured the Southeast billed as the "Sweetheart of the Potomac," a name given to her from her association with the Holiness Church and Mother Smith. The title of "Madame" came from Mother Smith; it showed that she was devoted, poised, and dignified in her delivery of songs.

Cooke began recording in 1949 on the Nashboro Record label in Nashville, Tennessee, accompanied by the Young People's Choir of the Springfield Baptist Church, her father's choir. In the early 1950s, her style became more pronounced. In 1951, Cooke toured with Madame Marie Roach Knight (b. 1918) and the Nightingales Quartet. She continued to used sermonettes and spirituals that her father, Reverend Gallmon, and Mother Smith had used in the 1920s and 1930s. Cooke and Smith recorded together "There's Not a Friend," "Higher Ground," "Come by Here," and "Here is One." These songs were preaching as well as singing about Jesus. She is best remembered for her recordings of "Stop Gambler," "Amen," and "Heavy Load." One can see the connection to lifestyle and the need for Christ. In "Stop Gambler," the audience relates to gambling and playing cards. She recounts the crucifixion of Christ and the gambling for his red robe by the Roman soldiers. The song begins with counting the cards up from the deuce to the ace. Cooke talked about each card in the deck.

> I can see the first gambler as he throws down the deuce, the two spot,
> Representing Paul and Silas bound in jail.
> They didn't do any wrong, God delivered them.
> The next gambler throws down the trey, the three spot,
> Representing Shadrach, Meshach, and Abednego.
> God delivered them from a fiery furnace.

By the time she reached the ace, the Father, Son, and Holy Ghost, the audience would be jumping and shouting in the Spirit. Many people would not attend a church service, yet they would buy a ticket to a gospel show. Cooke would sing and explain the role of Christ and how he delivered his people from gambling. The background was soft organ music. This song was played on gospel and rhythm and blues stations, converting sinners to saints. They were listening to laugh but were converted to serve the Lord.

In November 1953, "Evening Sun" by Edna Gallmon Cooke and the Radio Four Quartet was released on the Republic label, a subsidiary of the Tennessee label located in Nashville. Cooke was a message singer. She was vibrant and exciting. Cooke became ill and died in 1967 in Philadelphia at the age of forty-nine. In 1989, *Mother Smith and Her Children* was recorded on the Nashboro label. Included were Brother Joe May (1912–1972), Martha Bass, and Cooke.

SHERRY SHERROD DUPREE

Reference and Further Reading

Boyer, Horace Clarence. *How Sweet the Sound: The Golden Age of Gospel.* Washington, DC: Elliott & Clark, 1995.

DuPree, Sherry Sherrod. *African-American Holiness Pentecostal Movement: An Annotated Bibliography.* Religious Information Systems Vol. 4; Garland Reference Library of Social Science Vol. 526. New York: Garland Publishing, 1996.

———. *Biographical Dictionary of African-American Holiness-Pentecostals 1880–1990.* Washington, DC: Middle Atlantic Regional Press, 1989.

———; Herbert C. DuPree. *African-American Good News (Gospel) Music.* Washington, DC: Middle Atlantic Regional Press, 1993.

International Gospel Music Hall of Fame and Museum website, http://www.gmhf.org (accessed August 28, 2004).

Discography

Madame Edna Gallmon Cook 21 Greatest Hits (1979, Nashboro Record 27218; two-record set).

COOKE, SAM

(b. January 22, 1931 Clarksdale, MS; d. December 11, 1964)

Although Sam Cooke was internationally known as a pop singer, songwriter, and producer, he found considerable early success in gospel music. Samuel Cook was one of eight children of Reverend Charles and Annie Mae Cook. At the age of nine, Cooke performed with two of his sisters as a gospel trio, the Singing Children.

A few years later, Cooke and his brother, L. C. Cook, were members of the famous Highway QC's. Until his later departure to secular music, Cooke used the "Cook" spelling of his family name. The Highway QC's dramatically expanded Cooke's exposure to the world of commercial gospel music, and it was at this time that he met J. W. Alexander of the Pilgrim Travelers.

Alexander formed a new group called the Soul Stirrers and brought this group to Specialty in 1949. In 1950, the lead singer, R. B. Robinson, quit the group and Alexander asked Cooke to join as lead vocalist. He performed with the group until he ventured into pop music with "Loveable" under the pseudonym of Dale Cook. Two more successful Dale Cook releases followed and Cooke signed with Specialty's Keen Records. In 1957, Cooke's release of "You Send Me" became a number one hit and sold almost two million copies.

After a contractual disagreement, Cooke went to RCA in 1959, where he cut several moderately successful sides, including "Wonderful World," "Chain Gang," and "Cupid." He finally had a real hit with "Twistin' the Night Away" in 1962. He sang duet with Lou Rawls on "Bring It on Back to Me" later that year, and those singles propelled his LP into the top thirty.

He was celebrating his success in Los Angeles on December 11, 1964, when he was shot and killed at the Hacienda Hotel. The shooting was ruled a justifiable homicide. Cooke is interred at Forest Lawn Cemetery in Glendale, California.

Cooke was inducted into the Rock and Roll Hall of Fame in 1986.

TOM FISHER

Reference and Further Reading

Wolff, Daniel. *You Send Me: The Life and Times of Sam Cooke.* Quill Publications, 1996.

Discography

The Soul Stirrers Featuring Sam Cooke (1959, Specialty SPS2106); *The Gospel Soul of Sam Cooke with the Soul Stirrers, Vol. 1* (1969, Specialty SPS2116); *That's Heaven to Me* (1970, Specialty SPS-2146); *Two Sides of Sam Cooke* (1970, Specialty SPS2119); *The Gospel Soul of Sam Cooke with the Soul Stirrers, Vol. 2* (1971, Specialty SPS2128); *Forever* (1974, Specialty SPS2164); *In the Beginning* (1989, Ace Records CDCHD-280); *Jesus Gave Me Water* (1992, Specialty SPCD-7031-2); *The Last Mile of the Way* (1994, Specialty SPCD-7052-2); *Sam Cooke with the Soul Stirrers: The Complete Specialty Recordings* (1994, Specialty 38PCD-4437-2); *Sam Cooke with the Soul Stirrers* (1999, Specialty SPCD-7009-2).

COOPER, WILMA LEE AND STONEY

Dale Troy "Stoney" Cooper (b. October 16, 1918; d. March 22, 1977)
Wilma Leigh Leary Cooper (b. February 7, 1921)

The country music husband–wife duet team of Wilma Lee and Stoney Cooper rank among the most significant of the 1940–1970 era for the high proportion of sacred songs—some highly influential—in their repertoire. Three numbers in particular—"Thirty Pieces of Silver," "The Legend of the Dogwood Tree," and "Walking My Lord Up Calvary Hill," sometimes termed the "crucifiction trilogy"—have gained the status of classics. Following her husband's death, Wilma continued her career for another generation with the brand of traditional music that became their trademark.

Dale Troy "Stoney" Cooper and Wilma Leigh Leary hailed from opposite ends of mountainous Randolph County, West Virginia. Wilma was part of the Leary Family Singers, and Stoney joined their group as a fiddler at WSVA radio in Harrisonburg, Virginia. The couple married in 1941 and soon struck out on their own, working at a series of radio stations in such diverse locales as Blytheville, Arkansas; Grand Island, Nebraska; Fairmont, West Virginia; and Asheville, North Carolina. In 1947, they came to WWVA Wheeling, West Virginia, where they remained for a decade. Ten years later they moved on to WSM Nashville and the Grand Ole Opry, where they remained until Stoney's death and Wilma Lee's retirement for health reasons in 2000. They began recording for Rich-R-Tone Records in 1947, Columbia in 1949, and Hickory in 1955, and their most memorable songs appeared on the latter two labels.

In addition to the aforementioned sacred country classics, their notable gospel recordings included Cap, Andy, and Flip's "I'm Taking My Audition to Sing up in the Sky," "Mother's Prayer," "He Will Save Your Soul," and "He Taught Them How" and Hank Williams's "Are You Walking and Talking for the Lord." Wilma Lee also did successful covers of several sacred songs introduced by Molly O'Day, such as "Tramp on the Street," "Matthew 24," and "When My Time Comes to Go." In 1963, 1972, and 1973, they waxed gospel albums for Hickory, Skylite, and Gusto Records, respectively.

The Coopers usually recorded with acoustical instrumentation—calling their band the Clinch Mountain Clan—that included resonator guitar, mandolin, fiddle, and sometimes five-string banjo. After Stoney's death, the band almost always had a bluegrass banjo, and they worked frequently at bluegrass festivals. Wilma Lee Cooper suffered a stroke in 2000 and virtually retired from music. Daughter Carol Lee

Cooper worked with her parents for a time in the mid-1950s and, after her marriage to Jimmie Rodgers Snow, recorded several albums for Heartwarming prior to their split. Afterward, she led the Carol Lee Singers, a vocal support group at the Opry. A recent reissue on Varese includes many of their best Hickory numbers, including several sacred songs.

IVAN M. TRIBE

Reference and Further Reading

Cogswell, Robert. "'We Made Our Name in the Days of Radio': A Look at the Careers of Wilma Lee and Stoney Cooper." *JEMF Quarterly* 11, no. 2 (Summer 1975): 67–79.
Tribe, Ivan. "Wilma Lee & Stoney Cooper," *Precious Memories* 2, no. 6 (March–April 1990): 15–22.

Discography

Walking My Lord Up Calvary's Hill (1973, Power Pak 242; recuts of earlier recordings).
The Very Best of Wilma Lee and Stoney Cooper (2002, Varese 302 066 323 2).

COX FAMILY, THE

Willard Cox (b. June 9, 1937)
Evelyn Cox (b. June 20, 1959)
Sidney Cox (b. July 21, 1965)
Suzanne Cox (b. June 5, 1967)

The Cox Family is a family bluegrass group that, like many such bands, prominently features gospel songs. Willard, an oilfield worker from Cotton Valley, Louisiana, listened to country, bluegrass, and gospel music for much of his life. His wife, Marie, sang country music, and from both parents their four children inherited a love of music. At an early age each of Willard and Marie's offspring learned to play an instrument: Lynn, the bass; Evelyn, guitar; Suzanne, mandolin; and Sidney, Dobro, banjo, and guitar. They also developed a distinctive vocal style, and by 1972 they were ready to start performing in public.

This initial group included Lynn and mother Marie as well, but they dropped out early on. Until 1974, the family played only local dates; that changed in 1974 when Willard produced a demo tape to help with promotion. This brought them so many additional bookings that Willard was soon able to quit his regular job. They got an additional boost in 1989 when Alison Krauss heard one of their tapes and was greatly impressed by the band's sound and Sidney's songwriting. Thereafter, Krauss became their champion, reportedly saying of their singing: "When you reach the Pearly Gates, they'll be playing the Cox Family."

Through Krauss, they were able to sing backup for Randy Travis and Emmylou Harris, and Suzanne Cox and Krauss appeared on Dolly Parton's live album *Heartsongs*. Krauss produced their albums on Rounder, including their Grammy-winning gospel disc *I Know Who Holds Tomorrow*. They signed with Asylum, and Krauss produced their album *Just When We're Thinking It Over*. Their first single was of Del Shannon's "Runaway."

W. K. MCNEIL

Discography

I Know Who Holds Tomorrow (1994, Rounder).

CROSBY, FANNY JANE

(b. March 24, 1820; d. February 12, 1915)

At six weeks old, the infant Frances "Franny" Jane (Van Alstyne) Crosby was rendered permanently blind by the medical malpractice of a self-proclaimed physician treating her for an eye inflammation. In Despite that, Fanny developed into a precocious young girl with great powers of memorization, enabling her to recite large portions of Scripture and literature.

In 1835 she entered the newly founded New York Institution for the Blind, mastering not only all of her studies but also developing a reputation as "the blind poetess." She became an instructor at the school in 1847, and enjoyed a growing reputation as a published poet. Part of her literary collaboration was with George F. Root, composer of highly successful Sunday school hymns, Civil War melodies, and popular secular songs of the day. For Root, Crosby supplied numerous lyrics.

It was during revival services held at New York City's Methodist Broadway Tabernacle in 1850 that Crosby, a staunch Calvinist, underwent a "born again" conversion experience. That changed her life and contributed to the belief that her mission was henceforth to write hymns. She submitted an early effort to William B. Bradbury, the composer–publisher of popular Sunday school songs, and he was impressed, launching her hymn-writing career.

Crosby left the Institute in 1858 upon her marriage to Alexander Van Alsteine, Jr., another blind teacher at the school. She retained her maiden name, however, resorting to "Van Alstyne" (Crosby's preferred spelling) only as a poetic pseudonym in later years. After the death of the couple's only child during infancy, they apparently lived separate lives until Van Alsteine's death in 1902.

Even though Crosby had wealthy friends who would have supported her financially, she chose to live in crowded tenement houses, giving away all money that was not needed for essentials. She considered herself a social worker, not a poet or hymn writer. Living under such conditions, Crosby was able to speak in a powerful language that addressed the hopes and needs of the masses who readily sang her hymns. Overall, Crosby is credited with nearly nine thousand hymn texts, with her most famous being originally written as Sunday school songs. However, with the rise of urban revivalism in the 1870s—as epitomized by the revival team of Dwight Moody and Ira Sankey—Crosby's Sunday school songs became the quintessential expressions of revivalism, with its emphasis on salvation from sin as provided by the work of Jesus Christ on the cross.

Crosby's texts about a Savior's love and the hope of heaven were successfully paired with attractive melodies from the best composers of Sunday school and revival music, principally William H. Doane and William J. Kirkpatrick. These were then published and widely distributed in the *Gospel Hymns* series (six volumes, 1875–1894) published by Biglow and Main of New York City as edited by Philip Bliss and Ira D. Sankey. (In England, similar material was published by Morgan Scott with Sankey as its editor in *Sacred Songs and Solos*.) Crosby's hymns soon became paradigmatic of all revival music, and were eventually carried around the world by English-speaking missionaries.

Her texts reflect a wide variety of styles and moods, including praise, testimony, prayer, meditation, and instruction. Her most popular contributions have been "Jesus, Keep Me Near the Cross" (1869), "Praise Him, Praise Him" (1869), "Safe in the Arms of Jesus" (1869), "Pass Me Not, O Gentle Savior" (1870), "Rescue the Perishing" (1870), "Blessed Assurance" (1873), "All the Way My Savior Leads Me" (1875), "Draw Me Nearer" (1875), and "To God Be the Glory" (1875). With the possible exceptions of Isaac Watts and Charles Wesley, Crosby has generally been represented by the largest number of hymns of any writer during the twentieth century in nonliturgical hymnals.

Fanny Crosby never felt her blindness was a handicap but actually saw it as a gift from God that allowed her to accomplish things a sighted person could not. Although few songs produced during her later years were widely sung, she became recognized as one of the most prominent figures in American evangelical life, remaining highly active in revival meetings until her final years.

MEL R. WILHOIT

See also Bradbury, William Batchelder; Doane, William Howard; Kirkpatrick, William James; Sankey, Ira David

Reference and Further Reading

Crosby, Fanny J. *Memories of Eighty Years.* Boston: James H. Earle & Co., 1906.

Neptune, Darlene. *Fanny Crosby Still Lives.* Gretna, LA: Pelican Publishing Company, 2001.

Ruffin, Bernard. *Fanny Crosby.* Philadelphia: United Church Press, 1976; reprinted by Barbour and Co., 1996.

Wilhoit, Mel R. "Crosby, Fanny." In *American National Biography,* vol. 5, edited by John A. Garraty and Mark C. Carnes. New York: Oxford University Press, 1999.

CROUCH, ANDRAE

(b. July 1, 1942, Los Angeles, CA)

Andrae Crouch and his twin sister Sandra were born in Los Angeles, California, on July 1, 1942. His father Benjamin owned and operated Crouch Cleaners in central Los Angeles. Some of Andrae's earliest memories were of hearing his father asking his customers if they had ever met Jesus Christ. Eventually the elder Crouch founded Christ Memorial Church, where young Andrae began to sing and play the piano at the church services.

He wrote his first song, "The Blood Will Never Lose Its Power," when he was fourteen. After Manna music took over the copyright, the song became very popular and was recorded by both black and white groups. While attending Campus Crusade for Christ (CCFC)–sponsored Campus Life meetings after school during the early 1960s, he met Perry Morgan and Billy Thedford and led them to the Lord. Before their Bible studies they worshiped in song. This trio became the core of the Disciples. Their first public appearance was at a CCFC youth rally at a Nazarene church in Pasadena, California. Soon they were playing for church audiences, youth meetings, and even special events, such as Disneyland's Night of Joy, on a regular basis.

During the late 1960s, Ralph Carmichael formed Light records to record the new Christian music that was emerging. In 1968, Crouch recorded his first album, *Take The Message Everywhere,* on the Light label. His influences were varied, since his father did noapos;t restrict his children's listening, except if it spoke against the Kingdom of God. Blues, jazz, pop, and gospel music were all part of the mix. Some of the people who inspired Crouch's musical development were the Caravans, James Cleveland, the Davis Sisters, Thomas A. Dorsey, Duke Ellington, Mahalia Jackson, Carole King, Paul Simon, and James Taylor. Some of his most memorable songs have been "Just Like He Said He Would," "Perfect Peace," "This Is Another Day," "Jesus Is the Answer," "It Won't Be Long," and "Through It All."

The 1970s brought Crouch even greater success and recognition, after he won the first of nine Grammy awards. His songs were translated into more than twenty different languages, and he continued to play to sold-out concerts around the world. His songs have been recorded and admired by pop royalty as varied as Bob Dylan, Elton John, Barbara Mandrell, Little Richard Penniman, Elvis Presley, and Paul Simon. He has launched the careers of numerous artists, including Tramaine Hawkins and the Winans.

Crouch's work with music impresario Quincy Jones expanded his musical sphere into the movie industry. In 1984 he and Jones collaborated on Steven Spielberg's film *The Color Purple.* Crouch served as the film's gospel music historian and arranged all the choir segments of the soundtrack. He also cowrote the film's rousing "Maybe God Is Trying to Tell You Something." His writing, producing, and arranging were used in a number of other film projects as well, including *Once upon a Forest, The Lion King, Free Willy,* and the title theme from the television comedy *Amen.*

Crouch worked with Michael Jackson as a vocal arranger on his *History, Bad, Dangerous,* and Grammy-nominated *Man in the Mirror* albums. His fame as a gospel music songwriter reached a new level when in 1997, the album *Tribute: The Songs of Andrae Crouch* won a Grammy. The songs were performed by a variety of gospel superstars, including the Brooklyn Tabernacle Choir, Michael W. Smith, Take 6, and the Winans.

The joy of accomplishment and recognition during the 1990s was tempered by personal tragedy and addition of an overpowering new responsibility. Within a short period of time his father, mother, and elder brother all passed away, leaving the pastoral mantle in the hands of the junior Crouch. Somehow, through it all, he managed to assume the responsibilities of being the senior pastor of The New Christ Memorial Church of God in Christ, located in San Fernando, California, along with his sister Sandra.

Crouch has continued to record and tour, releasing albums that reflect his current dependency on the grace of God. The 1996 release "Pray" is a case in point. In 2002 after having been on some of the largest secular and sacred record labels for four decades, Crouch formed his own record label, Slave. The basis of the name is found in Romans 6:18, which states ". . . and having been freed from sin, you became slaves of righteousness" (NASB). Through it, the Gospel Music Hall of Fame member and five-time Dove Award recipient continues the ministry that he began more than fifty years ago.

BOB GERSZTYN

See also Hawkins, Tramaine; Light Records; Winans, The

Reference and Further Reading

Ball, Nina; Andrae Crouch *Through It All.* Waco, TX: Word Books, 1974.

Boyer, Horace Clarence. *How Sweet the Sound: The Golden Age of Gospel.* Washington, DC: Elliott & Clark, 1995.

"The Exhaustive Christian Discography." http://ccmdiscography.150m.com/C-WebSite.html (accessed May 11, 2003).

"Jaspella." http://www.jaspella.com/music/artists/crouch_andrae (accessed May 10, 2003).

"Richard De LaFont Agency, Inc." http://www.delafont.com/music_acts/andrae-crouch.htm (accessed May 10, 2003).

Discography

Take the Message Everywhere (1968, Light); *Keep on Singin'* (1971, Light); *Live at Carnegie Hall* (1973, Light); *This Is Another Day* (1976, Light); *I'll Be Thinking of You* (1979, Light); *Don't Give Up* (1981, Warner Brothers); *Finally* (1982, Light); *No Time to Lose* (1984, Light); *Autograph* (1986, Light); *Mercy* (1994, Warner Alliance); *Pray* (1997, Warner Alliance).

D

DAVIS SISTERS

Thelma Davis (b. 1930; d. 1963)
Ruth Davis (b. 1928; d. 1970)
Audrey Davis (b. 1931; d. 1982)
Alfreda Davis (b. 1935; d. 1989)
Imogene Green (b. 1930; d. 1986)
Curtis Dublin, piano (b. 1928; d. 1965)

The family group the Davis Sisters was organized in 1945 and quickly became one of the most famous and most outstanding group of gospel singers in existence. Hailing from Philadelphia, the group was led by Ruth Davis (aka "the Big Maybelle of Gospel Music" and "Baby Sister"), whose contralto was deep, powerful, almost manly, and moving. She was idolized by many singers such as Aretha Franklin and Mavis Staples. Thelma and Audrey sang soprano, and Alfreda second contralto. Thelma also helped with the sermonettes (spoken narratives conveying the Bible's messages), and pianist Curtis Dublin—a cousin of the Davises—served occasionally as colead in the group; after his death in 1965, he was replaced by Eddie Brown, evangelist Rosie Wallace's husband.

The Davis Sisters were members of a Pentecostal sect called Fire Baptized, founded in 1908 in Atlanta, Georgia, and the Davis family were among the first members of the Mount Zion Fire Baptized Holiness Church in Philadelphia, Pennsylvania, after its founding in the late 1910s. Of course, the young women sang in their church, inspired by their parents' practice of down-home countrified Southern church singing. A young Ruth Davis served as a WAC during World War II, and in 1945 she organized her group; she was only seventeen at that time, Thelma was fifteen, Audrey was fourteen, and Alfreda was only ten! After establishing a reputation as "house rockers" in their area, they made their official debut in 1946 at their parents' home in Port Deposit, Maryland, and then, with parental blessing, they followed the Pentecostal circuit, performing in churches and schools.

Gospel talents were plentiful in Philadelphia during the late 1940s and the 1950s, with the Angelic Gospel Singers, the Ward Singers, and many more. Gertrude Ward, Clara's mother, took the Davis Sisters under her wing, guided them, taught them courage, and instilled performance skills. During the spring of 1949, she also introduced the group to Ivin Ballen of Gotham Records, and he signed them to a three-year contract. But the Davis Sisters' first two known records were issued on Ballen's Apex subsidiary label in 1949. They were accompanied by their cousin, Curtis Dublin, whose piano style was between the sanctified church and the nightclub, with occasional jazz riffs.

The following session, in 1950, took place in the Gotham studios in Philadelphia, and alto singer Imogene Green, an outsider from Chicago, joined the group to add depth and excitement to the group's performance. She was reluctant, however, to assume lead in the Gotham studios until the summer of 1952, when she headed up "Bye and Bye," which became the group's first hit record.

Before that, in 1951 the Gay Sisters had organized a concert package at the Atlanta Auditorium to promote their own hit ("God Will Take Care of You"), and the Davis Sisters, who were a part of the program, tore up the place and stole the show. They did it again in New York in 1953, when they appeared before a full-capacity audience on Joe Bostic's Fourth Annual Negro Gospel and Religious Musical Festival at Carnegie Hall.

All in all, some thirty sides were issued on Gotham between 1950 and 1953, some with organist Herman Stevens. Many songs of the Davis Sisters were taken directly from the church services they attended and experienced while growing up, but they were familiar with other music (Ruth was inspired by Dinah Washington) and with famous gospel composers such as Lucie Campbell and Kenneth Morris and gospel artists such as Ira Tucker and Alex Bradford, whose "Too Close to Heaven" was the Davis Sisters' second big hit in 1953.

With "Baby Sister" in the lead, the Davis Sisters emerged as the first female group to sing the "hard" gospel that appeared in the early 1950s and was totally different from the Baptist style of singing, which emphasized beauty of tone, precise rhythm, and occasional ornamentation; hard gospel was characterized by straining the voice during periods of spiritual ecstasy, singing at the extremes of ranges, repeating words or syllables, adding lots of interjections, and "acting out" songs with motions, stoops, and movements.

In 1955 the group moved to Savoy Records, adding Jackie Verdell to the crew to replace Imogene Green, who came back later, in 1960. From their first recording for Savoy ("Twelve Gates to the City") to the 1970s, they added hits to hits, and the group became a force in gospel music, performing exclusively in churches and auditoriums; their combination was devastating and for years they were "the Queens of the Gospel Highway." Unhappily, they were ill-fated: Thelma died in 1956, removing the group's spiritual center; Dublin died in 1965, Ruth in 1970, Imogene in 1986, and Alfreda three years later. Their deaths were considered tragic losses in the African American church community.

ROBERT SACRÉ

Reference and Further Reading

Boyer, Horace Clarence. *How Sweet the Sound: The Golden Age of Gospel*. Washington, DC: Elliott & Clark, 1995.
Hayes, J. Cedric; Robert Laughton. *Gospel Records 1943–1969. A Black Music Discography*, 2 vols. London: Record Information Services, 1992.
Heilbut, Tony. *The Gospel Sound: Good News and Bad Times*. New York: Limelight, 1985.
Reagon, Bernice Johnson, ed. *We'll Understand It Better By and By. Pioneering African American Gospel Composers*. Washington, DC: Smithsonian Institution Press, 1992.

Discography

Davis Sisters 1949–52 (2003, Heritage [UK] HTCD47).

DAVIS, JAMES HOUSTON "JIMMIE"

(b. September 11, 1899, Beech Springs, LA; d. November 5, 2000, Baton Rouge, LA)

James Houston "Jimmie" Davis enjoyed several extremely successful careers, as a country and gospel singer, songwriter, music publisher, and politician. Born into poverty in rural Louisiana, Davis was the son of sharecroppers Sam and Sarah Davis. He learned to sing from his family, particularly his grandfather Henry Davis, and at local singing conventions. Davis's first recognition as a singer came at a Baptist church–sponsored singing school.

Davis attended Louisiana College, earning a BA in history (1924), and Louisiana State University, from which he earned an MA in education (1927). That year he took a position teaching history at Dodd College in Shreveport, Louisiana. In 1928, Davis began singing on KWKH and recorded his first records, a mixture of popular tunes and Jimmie Rodgers covers, for the local Doggone label. He also began a successful political career, first serving as clerk of the Shreveport criminal court.

Davis steadily advanced up the Louisiana political ladder, winning election as Shreveport police commissioner (1938–1942), public service commissioner (1942–1944), and governor of the state of Louisiana (1944–1948, 1960–1964). A moderate Democrat in Louisiana state politics, Davis presided over numerous accomplishments as governor. Davis remained a popular politician and was noted for his unique campaigning style, which included use of a country band and performances of country and gospel music.

Coinciding with his political activity, Davis gained great popularity as a singer and songwriter. He recorded extensively for Victor (1929–1933), Decca (1934–1972), Capitol (1950), and Word–Canaan (1970s). A devoted follower of Jimmie Rodgers early in his career, Davis's repertoire spanned the range of Southern styles. He gained notice as a singer of risqué blues songs and Western swing. He recorded with a wide variety of backup bands, including African American blues and jazz musicians. But Davis found his niche with sentimental country and honky-tonk songs such as "Nobody's Darling but Mine," "Shackles and Chains," and his most famous song, "You Are My Sunshine."

During the 1930s and 1940s, Davis did not record any gospel music, though he did perform gospel live and in his political rallies, where he used "Blessed Be the Tie that Binds" as a song of unification across political tines. His "When It's Roundup Time in Heaven," however, gained a reputation as a religious song and was performed in some Southern churches. During the 1940s Davis acted in several B-grade Westerns starring Charles Starrett. In 1947 he starred in *Louisiana,* a biopic of his own life that documented his rise from poverty to the governor's mansion.

During the early 1950s, Davis returned to KWKH with a regular radio program. Numerous requests for gospel numbers led him to record Southern gospel music. His popularity as a gospel singer was cemented with the hit "Suppertime" in 1953. Though he never stopped recording country music, Davis focused his talents on gospel music for the next four decades. He enjoyed success with such songs as "I Wouldn't Take Nothing for My Journey Now," "One More Valley," "The Three Nails," "Taller Than the Trees," and the classic "Someone to Care," which he wrote.

Davis's contribution to Southern gospel extended beyond performance and recording. He became a major publisher of gospel music and helped to foster the careers of many young performers, such as Rusty Goodman and Dottie Rambo. With his prominence as a politician and established country star, Davis brought prestige and respect to the growing Southern gospel field in the 1950s. Many country artists (such as Red Foley and Ernest Tubb) recorded gospel songs, but Davis was the only major country star to make the genre his primary recording interest. Davis was actively involved in the Gospel Music Association, serving as its second president.

Davis married Alvern Adams in 1936. Two years after the death of his first wife, he married Anna Carter Gordon of the Chuck Wagon Gang (1968). They performed and recorded together for the rest of Davis's life. From the 1960s until the late 1970s, Davis toured widely and was a regular at bluegrass and gospel festivals. He built the Jimmie Davis Tabernacle near his birthplace, and it became a center for gospel singing in north Louisiana.

Davis's later years saw him win recognition for his achievements in many fields. He was elected to the Country Music Hall of Fame, the Gospel Music Hall of Fame, the Songwriters Hall of Fame, and the Louisiana Political Hall of Fame. "You Are My Sunshine" was named an official song of Louisiana. Davis died in his sleep at the age of 101 and was buried at the Jimmie Davis Tabernacle in Beech Springs, Louisiana.

KEVIN S. FONTENOT

Reference and Further Reading

Davis, Jimmie. Interviews by Kevin S. Fontenot, 1992–1999.
Weill, Gus. *You Are My Sunshine: The Jimmie Davis Story.* Waco, TX: Word Books, 1977.

Selected Discography

Country Music Hall of Fame (MCA MCAD 10087).
Gospel Favorites (Ernest Tubb Record Shops ETRS 1003).
Nobody's Darling but Mine (Bear Family BCD 15943 EI).
You Are My Sunshine (Bear Family BCD 16216 EI).

DAVIS, REVEREND GARY (BLIND GARY DAVIS)

(b. April 30, 1896; d. May 5, 1972)

Reverend Gary Davis found a solid niche in the 1950s and 1960s revival of American blues music, and he recorded and performed regularly with success until his death in 1972. His innovative fret techniques and vibrant performances were first captured many years earlier, but interest in his music waned during the post–World War II years. His repertoire comprised both secular folk and religious material, and he drew deeply from his scandalous vagabond life during his early career.

During his early middle age, Davis became religious, and his releases were almost entirely gospel in the blues style. His guitar virtuosity was legendary; Dave Van Ronk was quoted as saying "He was the most fantastic guitarist I'd ever seen." Bob Weir of the Grateful Dead said "Rev. Davis taught me, by example, to completely throw out my preconceptions of what can or can't be done on the guitar."

Davis, the son of John and Evelina Davis, was born in 1896 in Laurens, South Carolina, and was raised by his grandmother on a farm near Greenville, South Carolina. He was influenced by the music of the churches and local musicians who entertained at dances and small performances. Davis first sang at the Center Raven Baptist Church in Gray Court, South Carolina, and later in a string band in Greenville. An accident in Spartanburg at the Cedar Springs School for the Blind severely injured Davis's wrist and led to his unique guitar style; he went on to influence hundreds of young guitarists as a result of this incident.

In 1931, Davis moved to Durham, North Carolina, where he met Blind Boy Fuller and honed his craft with many other early blues performers. Davis became an ordained minister of the Free Baptist Connection Church in Washington, North Carolina, in 1933. In 1935, Davis and Fuller traveled to New York to record for the American Record Company. During his first sessions, he cut fifteen tracks of gospel music.

Davis married his second wife, Annie Wright, and relocated to Mamaroneck, New York, in 1937. During this period, he performed regularly as a street singer in New York City and recorded on several labels, including Folkways and Prestige. In 1940, Davis and his wife moved to Harlem, and he became a minister at the Missionary Baptist Connection Church.

During the 1950s and 1960s folk/blues revival, Davis toured college campuses and performed in several of Manhattan's Greenwich Village clubs. Many young musicians, including Taj Mahal and Bob Dylan, flocked to see him perform, and hundreds were influenced by his forceful style and delivery. Davis's expertise can be experienced in his later works on *Say No to the Devil*. It is the work of an inspired, talented artist with a lifetime of experience on which to draw. Davis continued to work diligently throughout his long career and enjoyed the acclaim that his music produced in his later years. Davis performed at folk festivals throughout the United States and Europe, and his performance at the Newport Folk Festival was recorded. He also released a live album for the Vanguard label and was the subject of two television documentaries in 1967 and 1970.

On May 5, 1972, Davis suffered a fatal heart attack on the way to a performance. He is interred in Rockville Cemetery in Lynbrook, New York.

TOM FISHER

Reference and Further Reading

Bastin, Bruce. *Red River Blues*. Urbana and Chicago: University of Illinois Press, 1995.
Grossman, Stefan. *Rev. Gary Davis/Blues Guitar*. New York: Oak Publications, 1974.
———. *Rev. Gary Davis/The Holy Blues*. New York: Robbins Music Corporation, 1970.
———. *Stefan Grossman's Masters of the Country Blues Guitar*. Miami, FL: CPP Belwin, 1991.
Mann, Woody. *Six Early Blues Guitarists*. New York: Oak Publications, 1978.
Tilling, Robert. *Oh, What a Beautiful City: A Tribute to Rev. Gary Davis 1896–1972*. Jersey, UK: Paul Mill Press, 1992.

Discography

Blind Gary Davis Harlem Street Singer (1960, Prestige Bluesville BV-1015; 1992, Original Blues Classics OBCCD-547-2).
A Little More Faith (1961, Prestige Bluesville BV 1032).
Reverend Gary Davis and Pink Anderson/Gospel, Blues and Street Songs (1961, Riverside RLP-148; 1987 Original Blues Classic OBCCD-542-2).
Say No to the Devil (1961, Prestige Bluesville BVLP 1049).
Rev. Gary Davis at Newport (1967, Vanguard Records 73008-2).

Pure Religion and Bad Company (1991, Smithsonian/ Folkways CD SF 40035).
Reverend Blind Gary Davis Complete Recorded Works 1935–1949 (1991, Document Records DOCD-5060).

DC TALK

Toby McKeehan (b. October 22, 1964)
Michael Dewayne Tait (b. May 18, 1966)
Kevin Max Smith (b. August 17, 1967)

The name "DC Talk" was the moniker that white rapper Toby McKeehan, who was born in Falls Church, Virginia, acquired because of being from the Washington, DC, area. While attending Liberty University in Lynchburg, Virginia, during the mid-1980s, he met and became friends with Michael Dewayne Tait, a native of Washington, DC. The two began to perform music together and were soon joined by Kevin Max Smith, a native of Michigan. Some of their musical influences included the Clash, Nat King Cole, Kool and the Gang, the Steve Miller Band, Run DMC, and U2. The trio called themselves "DC Talk and the One Way Crew." They produced and marketed a demo tape in the Washington, DC, area, which led to a recording contract with ForeFront Records.

Their name was shortened to "DC Talk," which now meant "decent Christian talk." In 1989, DC Talk released its first, self-titled rap album on ForeFront. More than a hundred thousand copies were sold using traditional Christian marketing channels. When the group released *Nu Thang* in 1990, they began to expand their market. Part of that expansion involved touring as the opening act for Michael W. Smith. By 1991 *Nu Thang* had hit the two hundred thousand mark and had won a Dove Award. In 1992 they appeared on *The Arsenio Hall Show, Nu Thang* crossed the three hundred thousand mark, and they won two more Dove awards.

In 1993 *Free at Last* was released; it went platinum, stayed at number one on *Billboard*'s contemporary Christian music chart for thirty-four weeks, and won a Dove Award. In 1994, *Free at Last* won a Grammy for Best Rock Gospel album, which led to *People* magazine doing a feature article on DC Talk. The band headlined their *Free at Last* tour, with Audio Adrenaline. *Free at Last* crossed the seven hundred thousand mark, and DC Talk cohosted America's Christian Music Awards and performed live on a televised Billy Graham Crusade.

The year 1995 resulted in the release of the group's fourth album, *Jesus Freak,* and then *Free at Last* went platinum. They changed the uppercase "DC Talk" initials to the lowercase "dc talk." This change in the band's literary identification was a reflection of internal changes that were taking place in their style. This transition took them from rap to rock/alternative, with a focus on more personal lyrics. *Jesus Freak* broke the first-week sales record for Christian music and eventually went platinum, and dc talk won another Dove Award.

In 1996, dc talk toured the United States and Europe. In November, the group signed with Virgin Records to handle the secular distribution of their music. Signing with Virgin allowed the group to market itself to a mainstream secular audience. "Just Between You and Me" was released and reached number twelve on the top forty chart, while the song's video was added to the rotation on MTV, MTV2, and VH1.

A live concert video titled *Welcome to the Freak Show* was released by dc talk in 1997. A live album would follow, which included some additional cuts and resulted in a Best Rock Gospel Album Grammy Award for *Jesus Freak*, as well as three Dove awards. "Colored People" was released to top forty radio in February.

The band released its fifth studio album, *Supernatural,* in September 1998. It differed from their previous efforts in two ways. First, the band discarded any remaining vestiges of rap and completely embraced the pop/rock genre through which it had gained its mass acceptance through. Second, it was the group's first collaborative writing effort. *Supernatural* debuted at number four on the *Billboard* chart. This was the highest entry position that any Christian rock album had achieved thus far. At the same time, it broke previous first-week sales records for the best-selling Christian album and went gold six months later.

The year 2000 brought rumors of dc talk breaking up. The band denied the rumors and released a greatest hits album, titled *Intermission.* In April 2001 dc talk released *Solo,* which contained two songs from each of its three members. The EP also contained some of the band's favorite live tracks. They won a Dove Award for it. Next, Kevin Max, Toby McKeehan, and Michael Tait each released solo albums. The members continued to tour as dc talk, but also played solo. *Solo* won a Grammy in 2002, while dc talk's three members continued to pursue individual projects. In 2002 Tobymac won three Dove awards for his solo album *Momentum*, the Tait band toured with Third Day, and Kevin Max toured Europe.

BOB GERSZTYN

See also Jars of Clay; Rock Gospel; Smith, Michael W.

Reference and Further Reading

Ardent-Enthusiast home page, http://www.ardent-enthusiast.com (accessed May 23, 2003).

DC Talk home page, http://www.dctalk.com (accessed May 25, 2003).
Max, Kevin. *Unfinished Work*. Nashville, TN: Thomas Nelson Publishing, 2001.
Rumburg, Gary. "The Rockford Files." *CCM Magazine* (October 1995).

Discography

DC Talk (1989, ForeFront).
Nu Thang (1990, ForeFront).
Free at Last (1992, ForeFront).
Jesus Freak (1995, ForeFront, 1996, Virgin).
Welcome to the Freak Show (1997, ForeFront).
Supernatural (1998, ForeFront).
Intermission (2000, ForeFront D136975).
Solo (2001, ForeFront).

DEAL FAMILY, THE

Philmore Deal (b. March 6, 1881; d. May 24, 1968)
John Deal (b. January 21, 1909; d. January 9, 1968)
Melvin Deal (b. April 16, 1903; d. 1967)
Vadia Deal Lail (b. Unknown; d. May 31, 1972)
George Deal (b. June 6, 1908; d. April 16, 1979)

The Deal Family ranks as the first traditional sacred singing group to make recordings from the tradition-rich state of North Carolina. Philmore Deal hailed from Connelly Springs in Burke County, where he earned his living as a music teacher and also ran singing schools. A devout Baptist and "Mountain Republican," he also worked at times as a deputy sheriff and revenue agent. However, gospel music was his avocation, and he taught the vocal parts to his children. The entire family sang as a quintet, with sons John as tenor, Melvin as baritone, and George as bass and daughter Vadia as alto. Philmore sang lead and played pump organ.

Between April 1927 and April 1929, the Deals journeyed to Atlanta, where they placed some twenty numbers on Columbia records. In September 1927, they recorded four additional songs on the Okeh label at a session in Winston–Salem under the pseudonym Valdese Quartet. Perhaps the most notable song recorded by the family was one of the first waxings of the multipart harmony "Rocking on the Waves," a recent composition by Arthur B. Sebren of the Vaughn Happy Two.

With the onset of the Great Depression, the Deal Family career as a recording unit ended. Thereafter, they sang only in their local region. By the time old-time music scholar Clarence H. Greene learned their story in 1969, all members of the family that made the discs were deceased.

IVAN M. TRIBE

Reference and Further Reading

Greene, Clarence H. "The Deal Family: Carolina Gospel Singers," *JEMF Quarterly* 19, no. 1 (1969): 8–11.

DERRICKS, CLEAVANT

(b. May 13, 1910, Chattanooga, TN; d. April 14, 1977)

Cleavant Derricks was a composer, preacher, music arranger, choir director, and performer and a member of the Gospel Music Hall of Fame. He worked at the Stamps–Baxter office in Chattanooga, Tennessee, and began to study music formally when he attended the Cadek Conservatory at Knoxville, Tennessee. He later studied at Tennessee A & I college (now Tennessee State University) and the American Baptist Theological Seminary in Nashville. In 1931 he traveled to Washington, DC, to direct a choir of more than a hundred voices at the Vermont Avenue Baptist Church. In later life, he would be pastor and direct choirs at churches at Dayton, Knoxville, and Jackson (all in Tennessee) and Beloit, Wisconsin. For thirteen years he was pastor of the Pleasant Grove Baptist Church in Washington, DC, then moved to Knoxville in the late 1940s, where he built the Ebenezer Baptist Church. He was living in Knoxville when he died.

In the early 1930s, Derricks began to publish songs with Stamps–Baxter, making him one of the few African American composers to write for traditional seven-shape note convention songbooks. His first well-known song was "We'll Soon Be Done with Troubles and Trials" (1934), which he dedicated to his parents, Mr. and Mrs. J. T. Derricks. In 1934 Stamps–Baxter thought highly enough of his work that it issued a separate collection of his songs, *Pearls of Paradise* (Stamps–Baxter, Dallas, 1934). In 1937, Derricks sent to Stamps–Baxter what would be his best-known song, "Just a Little Talk with Jesus," which first appeared in *Harbor Bells No. 6* and which has become a quartet standard since then. A third key song was "When God Dips His Love in My Heart," written in 1944 or 1947 and published in a book by the Tennessee Music and Printing Company of Cleveland.

During the late 1930s, Derricks also began working as a music editor and arranger for Sally Bowles's songbook company in Chicago. He occasionally contributed a song to the Bowles books as well. In about 1951, Derricks organized a singing group, comprised of relatives and church members, and entered the Nashville studios of Tennessee Records, where they did four sides under the name "The Derricks Singers." These sides included arrangements of "Stand By Me" and "Do You Know Him."

In the late 1960s, Derricks rather casually dropped in at the offices of Word/Canaan Records in Nashville and inquired about making an album. When he told the skeptical manager he was the author of "Just a Little Talk with Jesus," he was laughed at and dismissed. Later he returned with proof, and the amazed company quickly signed him to an LP contract. Two albums resulted: *Just a Little Talk with Jesus* and *Satisfaction Guaranteed*. They were to be Derricks's last testimony as a singer.

CHARLES K. WOLFE

Discography

Just a Little Talk with Jesus.
Satisfaction Guaranteed.

DIXIE HUMMINGBIRDS

The Dixie Hummingbirds have had a long career and greatly influenced other popular African American gospel vocal groups, as well as mainstream pop vocal groups from Motown, and soul singers such as Jackie Wilson.

The group was formed by lead vocalist James B. Davis in Greenville, South Carolina, in the late 1920s when he was still a high school student, to perform locally in churches. In the later 1930s, Davis recruited two singers from another gospel group, the Heavenly Gospel Singers to form a trio: baritone Ira Tucker (who was only thirteen years old when he came on board in 1938) and bass Willie Bobo. In 1939, they made their first recordings for Decca Records. In 1942, the group moved to Philadelphia, Pennsylvania, where their powerful stage show—including Tucker's dynamic performances running up and down the aisles and jumping from the stage into the crowd—made them an immediate sensation. At this time, tenor singer Paul Owens rounded out the lineup to form a full quartet.

The Hummingbirds performed regularly on local radio, sometimes using the names the Jericho Boys or the Swanee Quartet. Famed producer John Hammond heard them sing, and this led to a booking at New York's Café Society in 1942, which was then a center for a wide range of African American performers (including Billie Holiday and Josh White) who appealed to a liberal, white audience. After a period out of the studio, the quartet resumed recording for smaller New York–based labels in 1946.

The year 1952 marks a key time in the group's history, because it was then that the "classic" lineup

The Dixie Hummingbirds. Photo courtesy Frank Driggs Collection.

was formed that would last more or less intact for the next quarter-century. This consisted of original members Davis, Tucker, and Bobo, who were joined by James Walker (taking Paul Owens's tenor spot) and additional vocalist Beachery Thompson.

Pop-styled guitarist Howard Carroll became the group's accompanist and was prominently featured in their stage show and on record. This group signed with the Houston-based Peacock label, owned by African American entrepreneur Don Robey, and had an immediate hit in 1952 with "Trouble in My Way," continuing through the decade's end with several more popular releases.

The 1960s saw the Hummingbirds build on their fan base beyond the traditional gospel circuit. They even recorded secular material, including blues, jazz, and some rock songs, during this time. In 1966, a landmark appearance at the Newport Folk Festival was captured on a live recording, which built their reputation among urban listeners. The group gained further fame in 1973, when Paul Simon hired them to sing backup on his gospel-influenced song "Love Me Like A Rock."

The group's classic lineup came to an end in 1976 with the death of Willie Bobo. Nonetheless, they soldiered on under Tucker's determined leadership. Tucker retired in 1984, and Walker and Thompson died in 1992 and 1994, respectively. New recruits filled out the ranks. Most recently, Bob Dylan featured the group in the soundtrack of his film, *Masked & Anonymous*. Seventieth and seventy-fifth anniversary recordings were issued in 1999 and 2004, respectively.

RICHARD CARLIN

Reference and Further Reading

Zolten, Jerry. *Great God A'Mighty: The Dixie Hummingbirds*. NY: Oxford University Press, 2003.

Discography

Gospel at Newport (1995, Vanguard Records; reissue of 1966 live performances at the Newport Folk Festival).
Diamond Jubilation (2004, Rounder Records; seventy-fifth anniversary album by the latest version of the group includes pop material as well as gospel).

DIXIE MELODY BOYS

Ed O'Neal (b. May 28, 1936)
Dustin Sweatman (b. June 16, 1983)
Dan Keeton (b. ca. 1968)
Andrew King (b. ca. 1983)

The Dixie Melody Boys of Kinston, North Carolina, have four and a half decades of experience as one of the top groups among Southern gospel quartets. They first organized in 1960 under the leadership of Avis Adkins. Ed O'Neal became their bass singer in 1961 after brief experience with the Serenaders and the Gospel Harmony Quartet, and later became manager and owner. As a long-time major figure in Southern gospel, O'Neal was chosen for the Southern Gospel Music Hall of Fame in 2004, having earlier (in 2000) been a recipient of the Marvin Norcross Award.

Numerous musicians and vocalists have been associated with the Dixie Melody Boys at one time or another. Some have called their training and experience gained with the group an education at "E. O. U." (Ed O'Neal University). In this sense, the Dixie Melody Boys have played a role not unlike that of the Weatherfords a few years earlier. As O'Neal himself explained, he has typically taken younger musicians and developed them under his tutelage. Many have gone on to become quartet leaders in their own right.

The most outstanding example of this training has been McCray Dove, who worked with the Dixie Melody Boys for eleven years and then went on to make the Dove Brothers group one of the outstanding quartets in southern gospel today. Other veterans of the foursome include Devin McGlamery, Derrick Selph, Harold Reed, Henry Daniels, and David Kimbrell. Former pianists include Greg Simpkins and Eric Ollis, the latter spending most of the 1990s with the Boys. In addition to bass vocalist Ed O'Neal and lead vocalist Dustin Sweatman, the other quartet members, as of February 2005, include tenor Dan Keeton and baritone Andrew King. Sweatman doubles on piano whenever the group uses that instrument.

Over the years the Dixie Melody Boys have had more than twenty numbers in Southern gospel's top forty and eight in the top ten. Some of their more recent popular numbers include "Antioch Church Choir," "I'll Be Living That Way," "Don't Point a Finger," and "When the Son of My Life Goes Down." They have made numerous long-play albums and compact discs over their years in music, and one live video.

IVAN M. TRIBE

Reference and Further Reading

Dixie Melody Boys website, www.dixiemelodyboys.com.

Discography

The Dixie Melody Boys Live in Music City USA (CD).
The Dixie Melody Boys Vintage (CD).
Quartet Classics (CD).
Request Time (CD).

DIXON, JESSY

(b. March 12, 1938, San Antonio, TX)

Reverend Jessy Dixon was born March 12, 1938, in San Antonio, Texas. Dixon studied piano at St. Mary's College. His is a blend of black gospel from the golden era (1945–1955) and contemporary

Christian music. As a lover of gospel music he became pianist for Clara Ward and the Ward Singers from Philadelphia and Dorothy Love Coates and the Original Gospel Harmonettes from Birmingham, Alabama. He was pianist for "the Thunderbolt of the Midwest," Brother Joe May (d. 1972), after being recommended by the talent scout for Specialty Records, James "Woodie" Alexander, director of the Pilgrim Travelers.

Dixon is known for his progressive harmonies on the piano. He joined "the Crown Prince of Gospel" James Cleveland's (d. 1991) Gospel Chimes in 1960. In 1965, Dixon became director and lead singer of the Thompson Community Singers, recording with them under the name Chicago Community Choir. In the late 1960s, he organized the Jessy Dixon Singers and the J. D. Singers, and he also founded the Omega Singers. He was minister of music at the Omega Baptist Church. In 1971, he appeared in films and at the Newport Jazz Festival. In June 1980, he was selected to represent contemporary gospel at the Golden Jubilee Year Celebration of Gospel Music held in Chicago.

His best-known song compositions are "The Failure's Not in God," "Bring the Sun Out," and "Satisfied." His style of gospel music has changed to contemporary gospel. As a result of his hundreds of concerts worldwide—appearing in concert halls from New York's Carnegie Hall to England's Royal Albert Hall, and throughout Africa, Europe, Scandinavia, and the Caribbean—he has earned himself the title "the King of Gospel." In November and December 1999, he was on tour with the Chicago Community Choir in Germany, Italy, Switzerland, Austria and France, culminating in a concert on Christmas Eve at Euro Disney Paris.

He has made more than two dozen albums, including three gold, and he also has a handful of Grammy nominations to his credit. Dixon has been nominated for induction into the International Gospel Music Hall of Fame and Museum in Detroit. He has released four albums of music made during his association with the Gaithers: *My Brand New Home, Jessy Dixon Sings Homecoming Classics, Heavenly News,* and *I Saw The Light.* Bill and Gloria Gaither's audiences' style of music is a "Southern country" gospel style. Dixon is a crossover artist; he appeals to all age groups and sings a wide range of material, including ballads, hymns, and gospel music.

SHERRY SHERROD DUPREE

Reference and Further Reading

Boyer, Horace Clarence. *How Sweet the Sound: The Golden Age of Gospel.* Washington, DC: Elliott & Clark, 1995.

DuPree, Sherry Sherrod. *Biographical Dictionary of African-American Holiness-Pentecostals 1880–1990.* Washington, DC: Middle Atlantic Regional Press, 1989.

———; Herbert C. DuPree. *African-American Good News (Gospel) Music.* Washington, DC: Middle Atlantic Regional Press, 1993.

International Gospel Music Hall of Fame and Museum. http://www.gmhf.org (accessed August 28, 2004).

Jessy Dixon Biography website, http://www.jessydixon.com (accessed September 30, 2004).

Discography

Get Away Jordan—Jessy Dixon (2003, Gaither Gospel Series CD 1788424582).

DOANE, WILLIAM HOWARD

(b. February 3, 1832; d. December 24, 1915)

Although he was a well-trained musician who conducted the Norwich, Connecticut, Harmonic Society for two years, who composed well over two thousand gospel melodies and compiled hymnbooks, Doane did all of this as a sideline. He was a very successful manufacturer of woodworking machinery, the president of several businesses, and an inventor with more than seventy patents to his credit.

His avocation of setting religious texts to music began after he suffered a near-fatal heart attack at age thirty. Eventually, he composed melodies for more than a thousand songs by Fanny Crosby alone. These include "Pass Me Not," "Rescue the Perishing," Jesus, Keep Me Near the Cross," and "I Am Thine, O Lord." With others he wrote "Take the Name of Jesus with You" and "More Love to Thee." About twenty-five numbers from his enormous output are still in common use.

Doane's several hymnals, including *Songs of Devotion* (1870), *Pure Gold* (1871), *Brightest and Best* (1875), and *The Baptist Hymnal* (1883), were mostly compiled in collaboration with Robert Lowry. Among Doane's other accomplishments, he helped popularize the Christmas or "Santa Claus" cantatas. All of his music shows the influence of nineteenth-century popular music; perhaps that is one reason why his songs were so successful in their day and why several of them are still in use. They represented a mode of music that was accessible to most audiences.

In addition to his music and business ventures, Doane was active as a philanthropist, generously donating to the YMCA, Denison University, and the Cincinnati Art Museum, where his collection of musical instruments is housed. At his death he left a large fortune in trust, which has been used to fund a variety of projects, including the construction of the Doane Memorial Music Building at the Moody Bible Institute in Chicago.

W. K. McNEIL

Reference and Further Reading

"Doane, William Howard." *The National Cyclopedia of American Biography,* Vol. Xli, p. 95. New York: 1956 [1971].

Hall, J. H. *Biography of Gospel Song and Hymn Writers.* New York: 1914 [1971].

Osbeck, Kenneth H. *101 More Hymn Stories.* Grand Rapids, MI: Kregel Publications 1985.

DON AND EARL

Don Williams (b. June 18, 1924; d. March 5, 1985)
Earl Mays (b. May 14, 1935)

The team of Don and Earl treated late-night radio listeners to transcribed quarter-hour programs for many years with their gospel songs and mail order offers. They were heard on Mexican border stations and stations that specialized in P. I. advertising, such as KXEL in Waterloo, Iowa, and WCKY in Cincinnati, Ohio. Based in Knoxville, Tennessee, the duo also turned out numerous songbooks and recordings while playing at many revivals throughout the South, especially East Tennessee, until the mid-1980s. Don retired in 1984, having experienced serious health problems. Earl then continued on by himself for a time.

Don Williams was a native of Briceville, Tennessee, while Earl Mays hailed from Knoxville. They usually sang accompanied by their own guitars. Don also whistled on a few numbers. Their early recordings appeared on Starday, but they soon started their own Gospel Light label and issued a series of albums, sold via mail order and in plain covers, which enabled them to be priced at $1.25 each. They also sold songbooks, usually published by Albert E. Brumley and Sons, with their own covers attached.

IVAN M. TRIBE

Reference and Further Reading

Gentry, Linnell. *A History and Encyclopedia of Country, Western, and Gospel Music*, 2nd ed., 483, 585. Nashville, TN: Clairmont Corp., 1969.

Discography

Old Camp Meetin' Days (Gospel Light LP 00194).
Turn Your Radio On (Gospel Light LP 00186).

DON RENO AND RED SMILEY (AND THE TENNESSEE CUT-UPS)

Donald Wesley Reno (b. February 21, 1926; d. October 16, 1984)
Arthur Lee "Red" Smiley, Jr. (b. May 17, 1925; d. January 2, 1972)

Don Reno and Red Smiley led one of the most important bluegrass bands through the 1950s into the mid-1960s. With a daily television show that ran for several years at WDBJ in Roanoke, Virginia, they had a steady if unspectacular income during the rock 'n' roll era. Like the other pioneer bluegrass artists—Flatt and Scruggs, Bill Monroe, and the Stanley Brothers—their repertoire contained a generous number of sacred songs. After Reno and Smiley each went their separate ways, they continued to create tasteful mixtures of gospel and secular music.

Arthur "Red" Smiley was born in Asheville, North Carolina, where he was exposed to and played with several of the musicians at WWNC radio. While in military service during World War II, he suffered serious injuries in Sicily that ultimately resulted in the removal of one lung, but he managed to recover. When he worked as part of a band called Tommy Magness and the Tennessee Buddies, he met and first recorded with banjo picker Don Reno.

Reno, born in Spartanburg, South Carolina, took to the banjo at an early age and soon came under the influence of radio musician DeWitt "Snuffy" Jenkins, who picked the instrument in a three-finger style. At age thirteen, Don was playing on the radio with the Morris Brothers. Although he was offered a job with Bill Monroe in 1943, he opted for military service instead, serving a stint with the unit known as Merrill's Marauders. In 1948, he did work with Monroe for a time and then with Tommy Magness and finally with Toby Stroud. The Magness and Stroud groups also included Red Smiley.

Don and Red first led their band into a studio for King Records at Cincinnati in January 1952, where they recorded sixteen numbers, ten of which were sacred. The latter included their signature song, "I'm Using My Bible for a Roadmap," as well as some of their other better-known offerings such as "A Rose on God's Shore," "The Lord's Last Supper," "I Want to Live Like Christ My Savior," and "Let in the Guiding Light." A session the next year yielded "He's Coming Back to Earth Again" and "I Can Hear the Angels Singing." A 1954 session resulted in the first bluegrass recitation number, "Someone Will Love Me in Heaven" and one of the few gospel "answer" songs, "Since I've Used My Bible for a Roadmap."

Ironically, while they were recording these and numerous other secular songs and instrumentals, Reno and Smiley were not a full-time musical group, but primarily a studio act. Don Reno was actually a regular member of Arthur Smith's group at WBT Charlotte, while Red Smiley worked in a nonmusical job. Finally, early in 1955, they assembled a full-time band, the Tennessee Cut-Ups, adding John Palmer on bass and Mack Magaha on fiddle. Later additions to the band included Ronnie Reno on mandolin, Steve Chapman on lead guitar, and Sid Campbell on rhythm guitar. They became regulars on the "Old Dominion Barndance" at WRVA in Richmond, Virginia. Not long afterward, they began their daily television show (*Top O' the Morning*) in Roanoke, which lasted until February 1965. They had an additional evening weekly television program at WSVA in Harrisonburg, Virginia.

With the exception of a short time with Dot Records in 1957, Reno and Smiley spent the remainder of their performing years back with King, where their recording focus became more oriented toward long-play albums. They waxed three sacred ones in the late 1950s and early 1960s in addition to an occasional gospel song on their more numerous secular offerings. These three albums were *Sacred Songs, Hymns and Sacred Gospel Songs,* and *The World's 15 Greatest Hymns.* Two additional albums were made up of compilations of their earlier singles: *Sacred Songs by Don Reno and Red Smiley* and *Someone Will Love Me in Heaven.*

After their February 1965 split, Smiley continued with the television show at WDBJ Roanoke until 1969, when the program ended and he retired. With his band restyled as the Bluegrass Cutups, Red cut four studio albums, with one being an all-gospel effort on the Rimrock label in 1966. John Palmer, from the old band, remained with Red. Other regulars included David Deese, followed by Billy Edwards on banjo, Clarence "Tater" Tate on fiddle, and Gene Burrows and later Udell McPeak (who both sang tenor) on mandolin or rhythm guitar. During 1970 and 1971, Red Smiley made several reunion appearances at bluegrass festivals with Don Reno. He passed away early the next year from diabetes complications.

Don Reno kept the band name Tennessee Cut-Ups and had a brief partnership with Benny Martin, which resulted in a gospel album on Cabin Creek. He had a longer teaming with Bill Harrell (1966–1976) that included two gospel albums on King, one of which was *I'm Using My Bible for a Roadmap.* Buck Ryan and Ed Ferris were band members during the Reno and Harrell era. After dissolving his partnership with Harrell, Reno built his last version of the Tennessee Cut-Ups around sons Ronnie, Dale, and Don Wayne

Reno, and they worked the bluegrass festival circuit as long as Don's slowly deteriorating health permitted.

DEANNA L. TRIBE AND IVAN M. TRIBE

Reference and Further Reading

Reid, Gary B. *Don Reno & Red Smiley and the Tennessee Cut-Ups, 1951–1959.* Dearborn, MI: Highland Music, 1993.

Discography

The World's 15 Greatest Hymns (1963, King LP 853).
Don Reno & Red Smiley, 1951–1959 (1993, King KBSCD-7001; boxed set of four compact discs containing the Tommy Magness recordings and all other material recorded through mid-October 1959, including that from the first three gospel albums).
Red Smiley Most Requested Gospel Songs (1999, Old Homestead OHCD-4120; from 1966 Rimrock masters).

DORSEY, THOMAS ANDREW

(b. July 1, 1899, Villa Rica, GA; d. January 23, 1993, Chicago, IL)

Acknowledged as the father of gospel music, Thomas Dorsey was a composer, music publisher, performer, educator, choir director, and organizer of some of the most important conventions in the genre. He worked tirelessly for the acceptance of gospel into Baptist churches, and revolutionized gospel music publishing. Dorsey, known as "Georgia Tom" and "Barrelhouse Tom," was a noted blues artist and composer during the 1920s and early 1930s. Dorsey composed sacred music on the side, but continued to work in the jazz and blues field as it provided him a good living. In 1932, he dedicated the remainder of his life to composing, performing, and promoting gospel music exclusively.

The oldest of three children, Thomas Dorsey was born in Villa Rica, Georgia, to Thomas Madison and Etta Plant Dorsey. His father, who graduated from what is now Morehouse College, was a farmer and itinerant revivalist preacher. Dorsey's mother was an organist who accompanied her husband on a portable pump organ. The Dorsey family moved to Atlanta while Thomas was a youth. He began playing a portable pump organ and soon was playing at his father's services.

Life in Atlanta took a toll on the rural Dorsey family, and religion ceased to be the focal point of the home. Thomas's father no longer preached with any regularity, and his mother stopped playing the organ. Thomas dropped out of school in Atlanta at age eleven and began to focus on his music. Thomas still had an organ at home, and he also practiced on his uncle's piano.

Dorsey became influenced by local Atlanta blues pianists and jazz artists, as well as by the hymns of Isaac Watts. He attended performances by stars such as Ma Rainey and Bessie Smith at the Eighty-One Theater in Atlanta, and he learned by watching the pianists there. Dorsey eventually obtained a job at the Eighty-One Theater selling drinks and popcorn during intermissions, which enabled him to further his contact with musicians. Ed Butler, the Eighty-One's main pianist, showed Dorsey how to play songs. Soon Thomas began playing "house parties," dances, and bordellos. After short-lived formal piano lessons, Dorsey learned to sight-read well enough to provide live music for theater shows. He was well known as a party pianist in Atlanta from 1911 to 1916.

Dorsey left Atlanta in 1916, heading to Philadelphia via Chicago for a job; he never made it past Chicago, where many of his father's relatives lived. Chicago was a hotbed of music industry activities, with numerous performing, recording, publishing, and educational opportunities. For two years, Dorsey worked odd jobs and played house parties during the summer months and traveled back to Atlanta for the mild winters. He made his permanent move to Chicago in 1919.

Because the desirable piano jobs required excellent sight-reading skills, Dorsey enrolled in the Chicago School of Composition and Arranging to improve his sight-reading abilities and learn to arrange. By October 1920, he registered his first composition with the U.S. Copyright Office, *If You Don't Believe I'm Leaving, You Can Count the Days I'm Gone.* Dorsey began to garner respect as a blues pianist in Chicago around 1920.

Dorsey suffered the first of two "nervous breakdowns" during the fall of 1920. The situation was serious enough that his mother traveled to Chicago from Atlanta. She brought him back to Atlanta, where he regained his health. He returned to Chicago the following year.

In 1921, Dorsey reluctantly attended the National Baptist Convention in Chicago. There he heard W. M. Nix sing and was immediately drawn to his charisma and style of sacred music. Nix was promoting *Sacred Pearls*, the first official collection of songs by the National Baptist Committee. Dorsey wanted to inspire people as he was inspired by Nix. Dorsey wrote his first gospel song, *If I Don't Get There,* for the second edition of *Gospel Pearls*, which was released in late 1921.

Soon after hearing W. M. Nix, Dorsey became the music director at New Hope Baptist Church on Chicago's South Side. This tenure at New Hope was short-lived, as Dorsey soon left the position to join Will Walker's band The Whispering Syncopators in 1923. This group, which played jazz and blues, worked for clubs, theaters, and dances and performed on the road. Dorsey served as pianist, composer, and arranger for the group, and made a good living. Dorsey also gained work as an arranger for Vocalion, Brunswick, and Paramount records. In 1923, his composition "Riverside Blues" was recorded by Joe "King" Oliver's Creole Jazz Band. The tune became a hit. In 1924, Dorsey became the accompanist to Paramount recording artist Gertrude "Ma" Rainey and leader of her "Wild Cats Jazz Band." He wrote her theme song, "The Stormy Sea Blues," and toured with Rainey through 1926.

Despite Dorsey's success as a blues and jazz artist, he continued to write gospel songs. Dorsey's "We Will Meet Him in the Sweet By and By" was published in the *National Baptist Hymnal* in 1924. His first attempt at self-publishing occurred around 1925, when he published "Someday, Somewhere." Dorsey printed the song and sent it out to two hundred fifty churches, using addresses obtained from a magazine of the National Baptist Convention. He did not receive any orders for more than a year and was discouraged with the possibility of self-publication.

Dorsey married Nettie Harper in August 1925. Nettie traveled with Thomas on the road with Ma Rainey, working as Rainey's wardrobe mistress. In 1926, Dorsey suffered another breakdown that resulted in two years of severe depression. The debilitating depression was brought to an abrupt end after a spiritual experience at Sunday services with Bishop H. H. Haley. Dorsey once again composed both sacred and secular music, performed blues, and promoted his gospel songs.

Dorsey began working with slide guitarist Tampa Red (Hudson Whittaker) in 1928. Dorsey cowrote and recorded the double entendre tune "It's Tight Like That" and released it under Tampa Red's name. The song became one of the best-selling blues records of the time and launched the "hokum" craze. The duo also recorded under the name "Famous Hokum Boys" and made more than sixty recordings between 1928 and 1932.

Despite making his living from blues music through 1932, Dorsey's gospel and publishing endeavors enjoyed a boost when in 1930, the National Baptist Convention allowed two Dorsey compositions— "How About You" and "Did You See My Savior"— to be performed at their annual meeting. The songs' reception was overwhelmingly positive, and the musical directors of the event, Lucie Campbell and

E. W. Isaac, allowed Dorsey to sell his sheet music at the meeting. Dorsey claims to have sold more than four thousand copies of his music that weekend; this was an indication of the success he would have selling his sacred music.

In 1931, Dorsey and Theodore Frye organized one of the first gospel choirs at the Ebenezer Baptist Church in Chicago. One year later, Dorsey became the choral director for Chicago's Pilgrim Baptist Church. Dorsey held this post for more than 40 years and was able to write and experiment for the church's choirs. To promote gospel choirs, he cofounded—with gospel singer Sallie Martin—the National Convention of Gospel Choirs and Choruses, Inc. The convention, which still meets today, convenes annually and provides workshops and showcases for gospel singers, and helps promote gospel choir music. Dorsey also began the Dorsey House of Music, which was the first music company created to sell black gospel compositions.

Thomas Dorsey experienced tragedy in 1932, which produced one of his most famous compositions. Dorsey traveled to St. Louis from his Chicago home to participate in a revival at a Baptist church. Once in St. Louis, Dorsey received a telegraph stating that his wife Nettie had died during childbirth. Although the baby boy was born healthy, he died the next day. Overcome with emotion, Dorsey retreated to his music room and composed "Precious Lord, Take My Hand." The melody is loosely based on the Protestant hymn "Must Jesus Bear the Cross Alone," and it became one of his most popular compositions. The song became a best-seller for Elvis Presley.

Dorsey struggled to have his gospel music accepted in Baptist churches. Numerous preachers were proponents of restrained worship and felt that his blues-tinged gospel music did not have a place in their churches. Dorsey accompanied singers who sang his songs in order to gain acceptance in the churches and to sell sheet music. Sallie Martin was one of the first to do this with him, and this partnership lasted until 1940. Dorsey also traveled with New Orleans native Mahalia Jackson from 1939 to 1944, with Willie May Ford Smith, and Roberta Martin.

Dorsey toured throughout the United States between 1932 and 1944 performing and promoting gospel music. The concerts, entitled "Evenings with Dorsey," were the first to feature gospel music in a concert setting. Participating vocalists included Mahalia Jackson, Sallie Martin, and Theodore Frye. Admission to the concerts was minimal, with Dorsey using the opportunity to sell sheet music. Unlike sacred sheet music of the past that only contained lyrics, Dorsey printed sheets of his music that had both lyrics and notation. By selling directly to churches, vocalists, and accompanists, Dorsey offered an alternative to buying a book of songs. His prominence during the 1940s and 1950s is evident from the fact that gospel songs were frequently referred to as "Dorseys."

Dorsey's gospel style was influenced by Charles Albert Tindley, Sanctified church vocalist and pianist Arizona Dranes, as well as his blues experiences. Dorsey integrated harmonic and melodic elements of blues into his pieces, along with a definite beat and a simple form that allowed for personal interpretation. He also introduced improvisation—a key feature of blues and jazz—to gospel. Dorsey established the traditional black gospel piano playing style and influenced numerous pianists, including Clara Ward and Roberta Martin. The lyrics of Dorsey's songs captured the feelings of African Americans while speaking to all peoples.

It is estimated that Thomas Dorsey composed around eight hundred songs. His gospel songs were performed and recorded by many white performers, including Eddy Arnold, Tennessee Ernie Ford, Elvis Presley, Guy Lombardo, Morton Downey, and Red Foley. His most famous compositions include "We Shall Walk Through the Valley in Peace," "I Surely Know There's Been a Change in Me," "It's My Desire," "Peace in the Valley," "If I Don't Get There," "Singing in My Soul," "Remember Me," "The Lord Will Make a Way Somehow," "I'm Going to Live the Life I Sing About in My Song," "When I've Done My Best," "I Will Trust in the Lord," and "Precious Lord Take My Hand." "Precious Lord Take My Hand" is published in more than forty languages. It was sung at the funeral of Lyndon Baines Johnson and was requested by Martin Luther King, Jr., for the rally on the day of his assassination.

Thomas Dorsey was featured in George Nierenberg's 1982 documentary *Say Amen, Somebody!*, and was elected to the Georgia Music Hall of Fame, the Nashville Songwriter's Association International Hall of Fame, and the Gospel Music Association's Hall of Fame. The Thomas A. Dorsey Archives opened in August of 1982 at Fisk University, and Dorsey received an honorary doctorate degree from Simmons Institute in Charleston, South Carolina. Dorsey influenced many of the top gospel vocalists as vocal coach and accompanist, including Mahalia Jackson, Sallie Martin, Roberta Martin, and Clara Ward. Dorsey served as the president of the National Convention of Gospel Choirs and Choruses, Inc., from its first convention year in 1933 until 1982.

JOE C. CLARK

107

See also Campbell, Lucie; Dranes, Arizona Juanita; Foley, Red; Frye, Theodore R.; Gospel Music Association; Jackson, Mahalia; Martin, Roberta; Martin, Sallie; National Baptist Convention; Presley, Elvis; Tindley, Charles Albert

Reference and Further Reading

Boyer, Horace Clarence. "Take My Hand, Precious Lord, Lead Me On." In *We'll Understand It Better By and By*, edited by Bernice Johnson Reagon. 165–182. Washington, DC: Smithsonian Institution, 1992.
———. *How Sweet the Sound: The Golden Age of Gospel*. Washington, DC: Elliott & Clark, 1995.
Cusic, Don. *The Sound of Light: A History of Gospel Music*. Bowling Green, OH: Bowling Green State University Popular Press, 1990.
Darden, Robert. *People Get Ready! A New History of Black Gospel Music*. New York: Continuum, 2004.
Harris, Michael W. *The Rise of Gospel Blues: The Music of Thomas Andrew Dorsey in the Urban Church*. New York: Oxford University Press, 1992.
———. "Conflict and Resolution in the Life of Thomas Andrew Dorsey." In *We'll Understand It Better By and By*, edited by Bernice Johnson Reagon, 165–182. Washington, DC: Smithsonian Institution, 1992.
Heilbut, Anthony. *The Gospel Sound: Good News and Bad Times*. 5th ed. New York: Limelight Editions, 1997.
Jackson, Jerma A. *Singing in My Soul: Black Gospel Music in a Secular Age*. Chapel Hill, NC: The University of North Carolina Press, 2004.
Kalil, Timothy M. "Thomas A. Dorsey and the Development and Diffusion of Traditional Black Gospel Piano." In *Perspectives on American Music, 1900–1950*, edited by Michael Saffle, 171–191. New York: Garland, 2000.

Discography

Precious Lord: The Great Gospel Songs of Thomas A. Dorsey (1994, Sony CD 57164).

DOVE AWARDS

In 1969, the Gospel Musical Association (GMA) hosted its first awards show, *The Dove Awards*, at a banquet during GMA Week. A year earlier, Bill Gaither helped to name the show and design the Dove Award itself. In 2000, the GMA signed an exclusive long-term agreement with Dick Clark Productions, Inc., to produce the Dove Awards for television, beginning with the 2001 show, though the Thirty-fifth Annual Dove Award broadcast was produced by Nashville-based NorthStar Studios.

Over the years, the Dove Awards changed to reflect the growing trends in gospel music. In 1973, there were fourteen categories of awards, a number that has since grown to forty-three categories. The year 1978 marked the last time that the Best Television Program and the Best DJ were honored, and the Songwriter of the Year award was discontinued in 2004. Christian Music Industry, Praise, and Worship was introduced as a category in 1981, and 1987 saw the addition of the Best Short Form Music Video and the Best Long Form Video categories. Hard music was introduced to the Dove Awards in 1989, while the Rap/Hip Hop category was added in 1991. In 1996, dc talk's rocker "Jesus Freak" won the Dove Award for Song of the Year, making them the first hip-hop performers to take the prize. A Worship Song of the Year category was added in 2003.

The forty-three categories awarded at the Thirty-fifth Annual Dove Awards on April 28, 2004, at the Municipal Auditorium in Nashville, were as follows:

Song of the Year
Songwriter of the Year
Female Vocalist of the Year
Group of the Year
Artist of the Year
New Artist of the Year
Producer of the Year
Rap/Hip Hop Recorded Song of the Year
Modern Rock Recorded Song of the Year
Rock Recorded Song of the Year
Rock/Contemporary Recorded Song of the Year
Pop/Contemporary Recorded Song of the Year
Inspirational Recorded Song of the Year
Southern Gospel Recorded Song of the Year
Bluegrass Recorded Song of the Year
Country Recorded Song of the Year
Urban Recorded Song of the Year
Traditional Gospel Recorded Song of the Year
Contemporary Gospel Recorded Song of the Year
Rap/Hip Hop Album of the Year
Modern Rock Album of the Year
Rock Album of the Year
Rock/Contemporary Album of the Year
Pop/Contemporary Album of the Year
Inspirational Album of the Year
Southern Gospel Album of the Year
Bluegrass Album of the Year
Country Album of the Year
Urban Album of the Year
Traditional Gospel Album of the Year
Contemporary Gospel Album of the Year
Praise & Worship Album of the Year
Instrumental Album of the Year
Children's Music Album of the Year
Spanish Language Album of the Year
Special Event Album of the Year
Musical of the Year
Youth/Children's Musical of the Year
Choral Collection of the Year
Worship Song of the Year

Recorded Music Packaging of the Year
Short Form Music Video of the Year
Long Form Music Video of the Year

To date, Steven Curtis Chapman has been the recipient of more Dove Awards than any artist in GMA history. In 2004, Word Records and the GMA released *Dove Hits 2004,* a compilation of Christian music's eighteen biggest songs of the year. Other Dove products include the Dove Awards DVD, Dove Songs for Kids, and various educational, inspirational, and children's books.

Currently, the Dove Awards are broadcast on PAX-TV. In previous years, the show has aired through syndication or on cable networks, including TNN and the Family Channel. Past shows have been hosted by celebrities such as Kathie Lee Gifford, John Tesh, Naomi Judd, Barbara Mandrell, Michael W. Smith, and Glen Campbell and have included performances by notable artists, including Bono, Amy Grant, Whitney Houston, Dolly Parton, and Third Day.

BECKY GARRISON

See also Gospel Music Association; Smith, Michael W.

Reference and Further Reading

Gospel Music Association website, http://www.gmamusic awards.com/.
"History of the Dove Awards." http://christianmusic.about. com/library/04/bldovehistory03.htm

DOVE BROTHERS, THE

The Dove Brothers Quartet was formed in 1998 as the dreams of McCray Dove came to fruition. Although McCray Dove is young in age, his experience in gospel music made him a quartet veteran. He spent many years perfecting his craft through his work with the Countrymen Quartet (formerly the Serenaders) and the Dixie Melody Boys.

After spending many exciting years with the Dixie Melody Boys, McCray realized his dream of forming his own quartet. He enlisted the services of his brother Eric to sing baritone. Close friend Burman Porter was chosen to sing bass. John Rulapaugh, a recent graduate of the Stamps School of Music with a strong and soulful voice, was chosen to sing tenor with the group. Richard Simmons was the pianist for this early version of the Dove Brothers.

The Dove Brothers made their first big concert appearance at the 1998 Grand Ole Gospel Reunion, and they continue to thrill audiences all around the country. The Dove Brothers present a very exciting

program combining songs of today with songs of yesteryear in an upbeat style that keeps the audiences entertained and blessed. McCray is a gifted songwriter, and his compositions have been mainstays of the group's repertoire.

The quartet has undergone several personnel changes, and only Eric and McCray remain from the original quartet. Each vocalist in the current group grew up within just a few miles of each other in eastern North Carolina. The current group consists of Jerry Martin, McCray Dove, Eric Dove, David Hester, and Andrew Smith.

The Dove Brothers have garnered many awards, including Male Quartet of the Year by both the SGMA and the *Singing News.* They have been featured performers on *America's Gospel Favorites,* and presented a gospel song on each broadcast of the PBS series *Carolina's Calling.* They have been the host group at the Grand Ole Gospel Reunion. They are also the featured performers on the Quartet Legacy Tour.

The quartet embodies class and dignity from the stage. They pride themselves as five men dressed in matching suits, singing quartet-style music with complex arrangements and exciting choreography and providing great entertainment with a true spiritual emphasis.

JOHN CRENSHAW

Reference and Further Reading

Dove, McCray. Interview, June 2004, Conover, NC.

Discography

Pure Tradition (1998, Homeland).
On the Wings of a Dove (1999, Homeland).
Singing the Quartet Way (1999, Homeland).
Flying High (2000, Homeland,).
Every Time I Feel the Spirit (2001, Landmark).
Old Country Church (2001, Landmark).
You Can't Stop God from Blessing Me (2002, Crossroads).
Born Again (2003, Crossroads).
Quartet Legacy Tour (2004, Private).
A Tribute to Mosie Lister (2004, Sonlight).

DOVE RECORDS

Dove Records, an independent Christian record label based in Charleston, South Carolina, was formed in 2003 by Dr. Darrell A. Boone. His first project was to create original songs and tracks specifically for the debut album in 2002 of Stanisha Brown, the Christian "diva." Other artists represented on this label include Jerome Batiste and the Real Zyde Ko Players, Tracy,

Bezzle Boys, Bezzle Ballers, Burn Out Boys, Mega Bucks, and Patrick Williams.

In the mid-1970s, Dr. Boone played trombone for a jazz and R&B group from Dallas, Texas, called Larry "T-Bird" Gordon and the T-Birds. Boone worked with the Texas hip-hop record label Sucka Free Records in the production of the label's first project, "Lil' Flip and Hustlaz Stackin' Endz," in 1988 at the suggestion of Humpty Hump. Boone is a concert promoter and manager of several groups in different music genres and continues to have a business relationship with Sucka Free Records. He has a BA degree from Wiley College and a master of divinity/counseling degree from Southern Methodist University in Dallas, Texas.

BECKY GARRISON

Reference and Further Reading

All Record Labels website, http://www.allrecordlabels.com/db/7/4457.html.
Dove Records website, http://www.doverecords.20m.com.

DRANES, ARIZONA JUANITA

(b. 1905; d. 1957)

Believed to be of partial Mexican ancestry, this member of the Church of God in Christ (COGIC) was popular in the 1920s for her intense, high-pitched vocals backed by her solid barrelhouse-style piano. At age twenty-one, the blind singer was discovered by musician and talent scout Richard M. Jones performing in a church in Fort Worth, Texas, for the Reverend Samuel Crouch. Jones invited her to Chicago to record for the Okeh label, and her initial 1926 effort made her the first COGIC singer–musician to make a record.

She debuted with a rendition of "My Soul Is a Witness for the Lord." Her thin, effective soprano voice combined with her pronounced use of *ostinato* was impressive but was hardly as much of a revelation as her piano playing. Dranes's driving rhythmic mix of ragtime and barrelhouse techniques was totally unlike the piano work on earlier religious recordings.

Dranes's recordings were very popular and led to subsequent sessions over the next two years, and had she not been subject to recurrent bouts of influenza, she would have probably done more. These sessions also enabled her to perform in churches throughout Texas and Tennessee and in Chicago. On her last recordings, in 1928, she was backed by her own piano, a mandolin player, and several exuberant female singers. On "Just Look" and other songs waxed at this session, Dranes demonstrated a rousing call-and-response style. She shouted short lines calling for quick, loud responses that she slightly anticipated, giving a greater ragtime feeling to the number.

Dranes was popular with the Okeh executives, as shown not only by her subsequent recording sessions but by their use of her to accompany blues singer Sara Martin and other singers. Dranes used her success to enable other gospel artists to record. One of the most important was the Reverend Ford Washington McGee, a friend Dranes had helped to build up his congregation in Oklahoma City. He came to Chicago in November 1926 with his COGIC Jubilee Singers to wax four titles with Dranes, including "Bye and Bye We're Going to See the King" and "Lamb's Blood Has Washed Me Clean." He later recorded under his own name "Lion in the Tribe of Judah," on which he was backed by the spirited piano playing of Dranes. He subsequently went on to record approximately forty sides for the Victor label.

All of the tracks that Dranes recorded were issued except for "God's Got a Crown," which was considered not appropriate for release. Those selections that were issued made Dranes an important influence on many other singers, including Jessie Mae Hill and Laura Henton. Her recording career ended either because of the Great Depression, which greatly curtailed the making of records, her own fragile health, most likely, a combination of both. Still, she remained active as a performer in Holiness churches throughout the 1930s. After that she generally faded from public view. Her last years were spent in Los Angeles, California.

W. K. McNEIL

Reference and Further Reading

Boyer, James B.; Odie Tolbert. "Gospel Music in the Cogic Tradition: A Historical Perspective." *Rejoice* 2, no. 2 (Fall 1989): 15–19.
Oliver, Paul. *Songsters and Saints: Vocal Traditions on Race Records.* Cambridge, England: Cambridge University Press, 1984.

Discography

Barrelhouse Piano with Sanctified Singing 1926–1928 (1976, Herwin 210).
Songsters and Saints Vol. Two (1984, Matchbox MSEX 2003/2004).
Complete Recorded Works 1926–29 (1993).

DRINKARDS, THE

The Drinkard family hailed from Newark, New Jersey. "Nitch" Drinkard, a factory worker and devout

Baptist, and his wife Delia raised eight children there. Nitch encouraged them to sing gospel music from an early age, to serve, in his daughter Emily's words, "as junior ambassadors—not just sowing the gospel but also reaping the blessing of singing God's word in our own lives." Four of the siblings—Anne, Emily ("Cissy"), Larry, and Nicholas—began performing gospel music together in the late 1930s, when they were young children. Their eldest sister, Lee, was initially their manager, but eventually she too joined the group. The group became a popular attraction at Newark's New Hope Baptist Church and soon established a strong following in the Newark area.

By the early 1950s, nonfamily members Marie Epps and Judy Guions (later known as Judy Clay) joined the group, which was then known as the Drinkard Singers. Clay was only fourteen years old when she joined in 1952, and she was soon adopted by Lee Drinkard as a daughter. At this time, the group recorded a few singles for a local jazz label, Savoy, as well as Chess and Verve. The Drinkards' popularity was increased when they were booked to perform at the 1957 Newport Jazz Festival, introducing them to a broader audience and leading to a recording contract with RCA; they were the first gospel group to be signed to this pop label. Following this appearance, famed gospel star Mahalia Jackson invited them to accompany her at the prestigious National Baptist Convention. However, by the end of the decade the group broke up, with the individual Drinkards pursuing various careers in the gospel and pop industries.

Ann Drinkard, known by her married name of Ann Moss, retired from the group to become choir director at New Hope Baptist; her long career as an inspiration to dozens of young singers inspired Alex Bradford's play *Your Arm's Too Short to Box with God*. Judy Clay left to pursue a career in pop music, going solo in 1960; she had a spotty pop career through the late 1970s, when she was slowed by an operation for a brain tumor. Following this procedure, she returned to performing gospel music.

Emily "Cissy" Drinkard later became well known under her married name of Cissy Houston. By the early 1960s, Cissy was working with her nieces, Dionne and Delia "Dee Dee" Warwick (daughters of Cissy's elder sister, Lee, whose married named was actually Warrick), along with nonfamily member Myrna Smith, in the vocal group the Gospelaires. The group broke up when the two Warwicks began pursuing solo careers; Dionne was the most successful, working with the songwriting team of Burt Bacharach and Hal David and achieving a series of pop hits in the mid-1960s.

Cissy and Myrna formed a new group, the Sweet Inspirations, with Estelle Brown (formerly with the Gospel Wonders) and Sylvia Shemwell (Judy Clay's sister); they became popular backup singers for R&B singers such as Aretha Franklin and Wilson Pickett from the mid-1960s through the mid-1970s. The group also had hits on their own, notably with "Sweet Inspiration." Cissy also recorded both pop and gospel material on her own. In 2004, Cissy was honored for her fifty-year service at the New Hope Baptist Church, where she remains an active member. Cissy's daughter, Whitney Houston, achieved considerable success from the mid-1980s through the 1990s as a pop singer.

The Drinkards had a lasting effect on pop and soul music. Their energetic singing and strong harmonizations transferred easily from the gospel setting to pop material. When Aretha Franklin—herself the daughter of a minister, Reverend C. L. Franklin—combined gospel and R&B to help create soul music in the 1960s, it was natural for her to use the Sweet Inspirations (with Cissy prominently featured) as her backup singers.

RICHARD CARLIN

Reference and Further Reading

Houston, Cissy; with Jonathan Singer. *How Sweet the Sound: My Life with God and Gospel*. New York: Doubleday, 1998.

Discography

A Joyful Noise (1958, RCA; out of print LP of gospel material by the Drinkard Singers).
The Best of the Sweet Inspirations (1994, Ichiban Soul Classics; 1967–1970 Atlantic recordings, mostly of pop material).
Soul and Inspiration (2002, Rhino; two-CD set features one track by the Drinkard Singers and one by Cissy Houston with the Sweet Inspirations).

DUCK CREEK QUARTET, THE

Dewey Hurley (b. ca. 1920; d. 1984)
Calvin Hurley (b. ca. 1926; d. February 2001)
Ralph Hurley (b. November 21, 1929)
Hubert Wilder (b. ca. 1919)
Kyle Wilder (b. ca. 1918; d. 1982)

The Duck Creek Quartet exemplified the type of tightly knit quality singing groups that once flourished in the mountains of East Tennessee. Initially inspired by the Vaughn-sponsored singing schools, the pupils learned singing by the shape note method and formed quartets. The Duck Creek Quartet formed in 1941 at the Duck Creek Baptist Church of Sneedville, Tennessee, and flourished for nearly fifty-five years before death and age took their toll.

The original members were two sets of brothers, Calvin, Dewey, and Ralph Hurley and their cousins Kyle and Hubert Wilder. Ralph Hurley played guitar accompaniment and could fill in when needed on any vocal part. Some churches frowned on the use of instruments, so they sometimes sang *a cappella* and nearly always sang in that manner at neighborhood funerals. The group performed mostly at church gatherings of all denominations that asked them, sometimes in auditoriums and, when requested, at funerals—a number estimated to be somewhere between fifteen hundred and two thousand—during five decades.

In 1968 and 1970, the original quartet recorded albums. In 1982, Kyle Wilder died and Ralph Hurley continued on guitar and replaced him on the bass vocals. After Dewey Hurley died in 1984, Tim Wilder (son of Kyle) joined the quartet. From 1984 through 1988, the group made six additional albums (the last four on cassette only). In 1986, they appeared at the Smithsonian Festival of American Folklife, and they sang several times at John Rice Irwin's Museum of Appalachia near Norris, Tennessee. In 1991, they celebrated their fiftieth anniversary as a vocal unit. Time eventually stilled their powerful voices in around 1994, and as of 2005, only Hubert Wilder and Ralph Hurley of the five original Duck Creek Quartet members remained alive.

IVAN M. TRIBE

Reference and Further Reading

Powell, Wayde. "The Duck Creek Quartet: A Half Century of Traditional Quartet Singing." *Precious Memories: Journal of Gospel Music* 2, no. 6 (March–April 1990): 3–7.

Discography

Just Got to Heaven (1968, Tri-State).
That's the Reason (1970, Tri-State).

E

EASTER BROTHERS, THE

Russell Lee Easter (b. April 22, 1930)
James Madison Easter (b. April 24, 1932)
Edward Franklin Easter (b. March 28, 1934)

The Mount Airy, North Carolina–based Easter Brothers have long been a significant bluegrass group since their formation in 1953. They have been turning out quality recordings featuring their original songs since 1960. Through television appearances on the evangelistic programs of Reverend Leonard Repass, their music received wide distribution throughout the Appalachian region. While most of their accompaniment is pure bluegrass, pedal steel guitar can be heard on some of their efforts.

Russell, James, and Edd Easter all were born and grew up in the musically rich area of Carroll and Grayson counties in Virginia and Surrey County, North Carolina, which gave the world such noted figures as Andy Griffith, Tommy Jarrell, Emmett Lundy, and the Stoneman Family, as well as numerous gospel musicians. Russell Easter took up music first and, as his younger brothers matured, they too began to play; the family formed a team in 1953. Taking on a fourth person, they became the Green Valley Quartet in 1955. Other musicians—including some of their own children—worked with them from time to time.

The earliest Easter recordings were made for King in 1960 and 1961 as the Green Valley Quartet. Afterward they recorded numerous albums for such labels as Commandment, County, Rebel, Old Homestead, Life Line, Morningstar, Thoroughbred, and others.

Original songs form the heart of their vocal sound, with such numbers as "They're Holding Up the Ladder" and "Thank You Lord, for Your Blessings on Me" having been recorded by other groups. Other outstanding Easter originals include "He's the Rock I'm Leaning On," "Peter Was a Fireball," "A Heart that Will Never Break Again," and "I Want My Light to Shine."

While the brothers have played concerts as far afield as Texas and Oklahoma, their area of greatest popularity remains that part of Appalachia extending from Pennsylvania to Georgia and the Virginia–Carolina Piedmont. In late July they hold an annual gospel sing in Mount Airy that has attracted large audiences. Among the Easter offspring, Steve "Rabbitt" Easter gained considerable renown as an acoustic instrumentalist, while Jeff Easter with his wife Sheri have done well as a separate entity. Grandson Jason Easter, however, has probably played more with the original Easter Brothers.

IVAN M. TRIBE

See also Easter, Jeff and Sheri

Reference and Further Reading

Hutchins, Doug. "The Easter Brothers." *Bluegrass Unlimited* 18, no. 5 (November 1983): 42–45.
Tribe, Ivan M. "The Easter Brothers." In *Definitive Country: The Ultimate Encyclopedia of Country Music and Its Performers.* 262–263. New York: Perigee Books, 1995.

Discography

The Sun's Still Shining (1996, Lifeline CD 412696).

Favorites (1998, Lifeline CD 495698).
By Request: Their Greatest Hits (Thoroughbred THB 2038).
Heart and Soul (Thoroughbred THB 2036).

EASTER, JEFF AND SHERI

Jeff Easter (b. March 18, 1960)
Sheri Williamson Easter (b. October 27, 1963)

Jeff and Sheri Easter have become major players in the Southern gospel music field during the past two decades. As the offspring of important figures in bluegrass, country, and gospel music, the Easters come by their musical talents honestly and genetically. Jeff was reared in Mount Airy, North Carolina, the son of James Easter of the Easter Brothers. Sheri grew up in Lincolnton, Georgia, where the Easters now reside. She is the daughter of Elzie and Polly Lewis Williamson, Polly being of the Lewis Family, which is often called the "first family of bluegrass gospel music."

Both Jeff and Sheri come from families in which sacred singing formed not only a significant part of their cultural and religious heritage but also their livelihoods. Following their parents into gospel music, Jeff took a job playing bass for the Singing Americans and also performed with the Easter Brothers and the Gold City Quartet. Sheri had filled in with the Lewis Family at various times, beginning in 1980. The two met at the annual Albert E. Brumley Gospel Sing in Arkansas in the summer of 1984. Their wedding took place in Sheri's hometown of Lincolnton on June 18, 1985, shortly after her graduation from the University of Georgia with a B.A. in marketing. Initially, they worked with the Lewis Family and had two albums released during this era, *A New Tradition* and *Home Folks* on the Benson Company's Riversong label. The success of their first album and the success of the Lewis Family as a gospel group provided great encouragement for their own music careers in which they initially tried "to cover the bluegrass field with live performances and have chart singles in gospel music."

In 1988, the Easters struck out on their own and quickly became favorites on the Southern gospel circuit. They continued with Benson until 1993, and then affiliated with Spring Hill. Over the years, some of their most popular songs have been "Roses Will Bloom Again," "Goin' Away Party," "Praise His Name," and "Thread of Hope." When choosing songs for their projects, variety is a strong consideration—in style and in message, with songs about heaven and love (for God and between husband and wife) being important to the Easters. They have received multiple *Singing News* fan awards. They have been nominated for Dove awards, receiving two, and Sheri has been named *Singing News* Favorite Alto eight times.

In addition to Jeff and Sheri, Greg and Charlotte Ritchie form a part of their touring entourage and teenage son Madison (b. November 26, 1988) has recently joined them, making them an intergenerational act. Daughter Morgan (b. September 30, 1993) frequently performs with the group. Jeff plays keyboard and bass; Madison plays guitar; and Greg has been the group's drummer for the past ten years. While Jeff and Sheri Easter make frequent appearances on the Gaither Homecoming tours and videos, they maintain an active touring schedule themselves and particularly enjoy their live performances, where they "create and perform music that is uplifting, life-changing, and God-honoring."

DEANNA L. TRIBE AND IVAN M. TRIBE

See also Easter Brothers; Lewis Family, The

References and Further Reading

Jeff and Sheri Easter website, http://www.jeffandsherieaster.com.
Powell, Wayne. "Home Folks: Jeff and Sheri Easter." *Precious Memories* (May–June 1988): 5–7.

Selected Discography

Thread of Hope (1994, Chapel CMD3300).
By Request: A Collection of Favorites (1995, Benson CD-84418-4181-2).
Ever Faithful to You Love Songs: A 10 Year Celebration (1995, Chapel CMD5310).

EASY INSTRUCTOR, THE

The full name of this shape-note tunebook published in 1801 was *The Easy Instructor, or a New Method of Teaching Sacred Harmony*. It used a four syllable or *fasola solmization*, the first shape-note system to gain acceptance.

This book was the work of two men about whom very little is known. William Little, a printer, is known to have lived in Philadelphia from 1798 to 1805. Apparently, he intended to bring the book out in 1798, because he filed for copyright protection for it in that year, but no printing prior to 1801 has been located. Perhaps the typographical novelty of the project and the difficulty of preparing suitable plates accounts for the three-year gap between manuscript and book. Little's collaborator was William Smith (1761–1808); he replaced Edward Stammers, who died sometime between 1798 and 1801. Originally Little and Smith worked well together, gathering about three thousand subscriptions for *The Easy Instructor* by 1801. This happy association did not last and Smith brought out a second edition of the book on his own in 1803.

In the next twenty-eight years the book underwent thirty-five editions, sold several thousand copies, and became very influential. Neither compiler, however, had any connection with the volume after 1803. *The Easy Instructor* was unusual among early songbooks in that it was made up mainly of American pieces; only five of its 105 numbers were not. Little contributed four works, Smith only one. This new world orientation was one factor in the book's success. Of course, another reason for its popularity is that it made music more accessible. Although theirs was not the only four-shape shape-note system available, Little and Smith's was by far the most successful and was the one used by most Southern singing-school teachers.

W. K. McNeil

Reference and Further Reading

Hatchett, Marion J. *A Companion to The New Harp of Columbia.* Knoxville: University of Tennessee Press, 2003.

Lowens, Irving; Alan P. Britton. *Music and Musicians in Early America.* New York: Norton, 1964.

EDWIN HAWKINS SINGERS

The Edwin Hawkins Singers, a gospel group founded and led by Edwin Hawkins, is best known for the 1969 gospel hit "Oh Happy Day." Hawkins was born in Oakland, California, in 1943, where he was raised. He grew up in the Pentecostal church and sang in the youth choir. By age five he was playing the piano in church and regularly participating in church programs. At an early age, he was the accompanist for his family when they sang together in community concerts. In his teens, Hawkins served as pianist for several male and female gospel groups in the San Francisco Bay area.

When Hawkins and his family worshiped at Berkeley, California's Ephesians Church of God in Christ (COGIC)—an important center for gospel during the 1960s (founded by Bishop Elmer Elijah Cleveland)—he initially served as organist of the church's inspirational choir under Ola Jean Andrews, a well-known Bay Area performer and arranger of gospel who was director of the choir from 1958 to 1965. After Andrews left Ephesians, Hawkins took over the choir and became minister of music.

In 1967, Hawkins formed a forty-member group from members of Pentecostal churches in Berkeley, San Francisco, Oakland, San Jose, and Richmond,

California, for the Annual Youth Congress of COGIC. In 1968, it was this group—then known as the Northern California State Youth Choir—that first recorded the legendary LP, *Let Us Go into the House of the Lord,* which included the song "Oh Happy Day" with Dorothy Combs Morrison as lead vocalist.

Based on a nineteenth-century white hymn, the gospel arrangement of "Oh Happy Day" was successful because the jazz and popular music harmonies, rhythms, and instruments included in the song produced a sound not often identified with gospel at that time. When interest in the song grew on radio playlists in San Francisco, the album was rerecorded by Hawkins, his family, and friends under the name the Edwin Hawkins Singers. Later, the single began earning airplay on mainstream rhythm and blues and pop radio broadcasts across the United States. Eventually selling seven million copies, "Oh Happy Day" reached the top five in the United States and earned a Grammy Award. Because "Oh Happy Day" is regarded as the springboard for the development of contemporary gospel, Hawkins is often acknowledged as the "father of contemporary gospel," and artists such as Andrae Crouch in California are considered the most important innovators in this style.

The Edwin Hawkins Singers remained popular through the 1980s and won several other Grammy awards, for *Every Man Wants to Be Free* (1972), *Wonderful* (1980), and *If You Love Me* (1983). In 1982, Hawkins established the Edwin Hawkins Music and Arts Seminar, an annual week-long convention that offers workshops on all aspects of gospel music and culminates in a live performance by a mass choir of those in attendance. Although he does not record as much he did earlier in his career, Hawkins continues to tour within the United States and abroad. Also, the group has performed with major symphony orchestras (for example, the National Symphony Orchestra in Washington, DC, and the Oakland Symphony Orchestra) in the United States.

Other members of the Edwin Hawkins Singers have become noted gospel artists. Walter Hawkins, Edwin's younger brother, founded and became pastor of the Love Center Church in 1973. Using original compositions by Walter, the Love Center choir made several live recordings during the 1970s and 1980s that became hit albums. Tramaine Hawkins (Walter's former wife) became a sought-after gospel artist during the 1970s and 1980s after singing the lead on songs recorded by the Love Center choir. Since the 1980s, Tramaine has recorded several albums and been involved with numerous concert tours in the United States and abroad. Probably her best-selling song among churchgoers is "What Shall I Do" by Los Angeles gospel composer Quincy Fielding.

Lynnette Hawkins, a younger sister, has established a solo career as a gospel singer; she often tours, conducts workshops, and performs in concerts in different parts of the United States. Daniel, a brother, plays the organ and is a song arranger. Two sisters, Feddie and Carolyn, and a cousin, Shirley Miller, sing with Walter and Edwin. Joel, a nephew, plays drums. Brenda Roy and Yvette Flunder are not members of the family but are part of the Edwin Hawkins Singers.

JACQUELINE COGDELL DJEDJE

See also Crouch, Andrae; Hawkins, Tramaine; Hawkins, Walter

Reference and Further Reading

Broughton, Viv. *Too Close to Heaven: The Illustrated History of Gospel Music*. London: Midnight Books, 1996.
DjeDje, Jacqueline Cogdell. "The California Black Gospel Music Tradition: A Confluence of Musical Styles and Cultures." In *California Soul: Music of African Americans in the West*, edited by Jacqueline Cogdell DjeDje and Eddie S. Meadows, 124–175. Berkeley: University of California Press, 1998.
———. "Hawkins, Tramaine." In *Black Women in America: An Historical Encyclopedia*, edited by Darlene Clark Hine, 503–504. Brooklyn, NY: Carlson Publishing, 1993.

ELY, BROTHER CLAUDE

(b. July 21, 1922; d. May 7, 1978)

In his relatively short lifetime, Ely—"the Gospel Ranger," as he was sometimes known—put on records some of the most powerful country gospel songs ever made.

Born in a home near Pennington Gap, Virginia, at age twelve he was diagnosed with tuberculosis, which was believed to be terminal. Ely, however, recovered, and his illness served him well in one way; during his recuperation he started playing musical instruments, even though he had shown no earlier interest in them. A few years later he started working in the coal mines, but he left to join the U.S. Army during World War II. After the war's end he returned to the mines, but in 1949 he had a conversion experience and became a preacher. This was when he acquired the title "brother," a common fundamentalist Pentecostal designation for ministers.

Ely spent most of the next two decades holding revivals and pastoring churches in the central Appalachian regions of eastern Kentucky, eastern Tennessee, and southwestern Virginia. While pastoring the Free Pentecostal Church of God in Cumberland, Kentucky, he made two recordings for King Records.

He was reluctant to make recordings in a commercial studio but was finally persuaded to allow cutting of the material in a live service and putting it on disc. Therefore, the first session was taken from an October 12, 1953, remote broadcast in his church to a radio station in Whitesburg, Kentucky; the second was taken from a June 1954 recording of a revival held in the courthouse in Letcher County, Kentucky.

Fifteen numbers were recorded at these two sessions, only eight of which were released as singles. Evidently they were successful enough commercially to justify future recordings. They also met with critical success, for they have long been prized by folklorists and other students of Appalachian religious traditions. Most of the numbers are outstanding, but three stand out: "Holy, Holy, Holy," "There's a Leak in This Old Building," and "There Ain't No Grave Gonna Hold My Body Down." The latter two songs have become standards in gospel music.

By the 1960s Ely was agreeable to working in a recording studio and did so twice for the King label, in 1962 and 1968. In the meantime he had moved to Newport, Kentucky—an Appalachian migrant community in the suburbs of Cincinnati, Ohio—to pastor the Charity Tabernacle. It was his last move, for he spent the rest of his life with this church. Shortly after the 1968 session for King, Ely did an album, *Child of the King*, that he released on his own Gold Star label. In September 1977, Brother Claude suffered a heart attack but apparently recovered. Perhaps his health problems motivated him to tape many of his own unrecorded compositions so that they would be preserved. If so, it was a fortuitous move, because while conducting a service at his church in May 1978 he suffered a fatal heart attack. His daughter, Claudette, compiled an album and a sermon from her father's home recordings and they appeared in 1979 on the Jordan label.

Ely exerted an influence on several other Appalachian gospel singers, of whom the most notable is probably J. D. Jarvis, the composer of "Take Your Shoes Off, Moses" and "Six Hours on the Cross," both bluegrass gospel standards. Furthermore, there is still an interest in his music, not only in the United States but in England as well. In 1993 Ace, a British label, released a compact disc of all of Ely's numbers from 1953 and 1954 as well as a few numbers from 1962.

W. K. MCNEIL

Discography

The Gospel Ranger (1962, King).
At Home and At Church (1968, King).
Child of the King (1969, Gold Star).
Where Could I Go but to the Lord (1979, Jordan).
Satan Get Back (1993, Ace).

F

FAIRFIELD FOUR

The Fairfield Four was formed as a child group in 1921 at the Nashville, Tennessee, Fairfield Baptist Church. The group was formed by J. R. Statton. The early members included John Battle, Samuel McCrary, Willie Love, and bass Rufus Caruthers. Samuel McCrary, tenor and lead singer, became pastor of the Mark Baptist Church in Nashville. Willie Love sang with the Fairfield Four; he married Dorothy Love Coates, the leader of the Original Gospel Harmonettes of Birmingham. The harmony and rich blend of traditional gospel meshed with sharing the message of God's love describes this historical quartet.

They began their radio broadcasting in the late 1930s. This quartet helped to bring in the golden era of gospel music (1945–1955) by singing on the radio for fifteen minutes each Sunday morning. From 1939 to 1951, WLAC in Nashville, Tennessee, served as the radio home of the Fairfield Four. Disc jockey Bill "Hoss" Allen ("the Hossman") stated that "radio was the most important media to black gospel artists and their listeners." These radio gospel programs were exposed to several regions in the United States, Canada, and the Caribbean, and by shortwave radio to New Zealand, Europe, and North Africa.

The Fairfield Four were the first nationally popular black gospel quartet. Some of their recordings that became national hits include "Don't Let Nobody Turn You Around," "Let Me Tell You About Jesus," "I'll Be Satisfied," "Stand by Me," "I've Got Good Religion," and "Don't Want to Join That Number." Their songs transcend color and class, giving a vibrant message of hope, faith, and joy. Ray Funk, an attorney and gospel music researcher, produced a half-hour feature about the Fairfield Four for National Public Radio (NPR) on the history of gospel music, sponsored by the Tennessee Endowment for the Humanities.

This traditional historical gospel quartet was inducted in 1998 in Detroit, Michigan, into the International Gospel Music Hall of Fame and Museum by "the Mayor of Gospel," David Gough. This gospel quartet is of legendary status, with the distinction of being one of the few African American gospel quartets to bring gospel music to the mainstream population by radio. This group is yet performing on special occasions; it is one of the oldest and best-known gospel quartets in the country.

SHERRY SHERROD DuPREE

Reference and Further Reading

Boyer, Horace Clarence. *How Sweet the Sound: The Golden Age of Gospel*. Washington, DC: Elliott & Clark, 1995.

DuPree, Sherry Sherrod; Herbert C. DuPree. *African-American Good News (Gospel) Music*. Washington, DC: Middle Atlantic Regional Press, 1993.

International Gospel Music Hall of Fame and Museum home page, http://www.gmhf.org (accessed August 28, 2004).

Landes, John L. "WLAC, the Hossman, and Their Influence on Black Gospel." *Black Music Research Journal* 7 (1987): 67–82.

Reagon, Bernice Johnson, ed. *We'll Understand It Better By and By. Pioneering African American Gospel Composers*. Washington, DC: Smithsonian Institution Press, 1992.

The Fairfield Four. Photo courtesy Frank Driggs Collection.

Discography

One World, One People, One God, One Religion (1980, Nashboro Records).
Angels Watching Over (1981, AVI Records).

FAVORS, MALACHI

Later, Malachi Favors Maghostut
(b. August 22, 1937, Chicago, IL; d. February 2, 2004, Chicago, IL)

Malachi Favors was best known as the bass player with the Art Ensemble of Chicago. Although he did not perform in conventional gospel contexts, church music played a key part in his musical development, as it did in the overall conception of "Great Black Music" that drove the Art Ensemble's creative redefinition of their sources.

Although born in Chicago, his family roots lay in Mississippi. He was the eldest of ten children. His father, Dr. Isaac Favors, was a pastor, and other relatives were preachers. His early musical and

spiritual influence came through the Church of God in Christ, founded in 1897 by Bishop Charles Harrison Mason. Music and singing were integral to worship in the church, and the bassist acknowledged its deep influence on him, although he did not become involved in playing until his late teenage years.

He began learning double bass with jazz bassist Wilbur Ware and played jazz with pianist Andrew Hill and other young musicians in Chicago. He was a member of pianist Richard Muhal Abram's Experimental Band in 1961, which marked the beginning of a lifelong involvement with the extended group of musicians who formed the radical Association for the Advancement of Creative Musicians (AACM) in 1965. He began working with saxophonist Roscoe Mitchell in 1963.

The Art Ensemble of Chicago existed prior to adopting that name in 1969, when Favors, Mitchell, saxophonist Joseph Jarman, and trumpeter Lester Bowie moved to Paris. They were joined there by drummer Don Moye. They returned to the United States in 1971. The Art Ensemble attempted a new creative synthesis under the banner "Great Black

Music—Ancient to Modern," drawing on jazz, blues, gospel, spirituals, African music, reggae, and many other styles in their often very abstract and freely structured music. They collaborated with gospel singer Fontella Bass, who later married Bowie.

They utilized all manner of unconventional techniques, sonic experiments, and unusual instruments (Favors contributions included zither, melodica, harmonica, banjo, whistles, and diverse percussion instruments), and their performances were notably theatrical, although less so in later years. Both the bassist and drummer painted their faces in homage to the spirit of the music and a stylized acknowledgment of their African heritage. Favors adopted the additional surname of Maghostut (or sometimes Magoustous, derived from an African word meaning "I'm your host") in the mid-1970s. The group achieved an international reputation over three decades.

Favors remained with the band until his death from a stomach cancer that he had kept from his fellow musicians, and is firmly identified with them. He recorded a solo album, *Natural and the Spiritual*, in 1977, and led his own quintet in the early 1980s. He recorded with groups led by Mitchell and Bowie and was also a member of Chicago-based percussionist Kahil El'Zabar's Ritual, later known as the Ritual Trio. He worked with free-jazz luminaries Archie Shepp, Sunny Murray, and Dewey Redman in Paris in 1969, and later collaborated with Richard Muhal Abrams (1975), Tosuke Yamashita (1979), Charles Brackeen (1987), Dennis Gonzalez (1988), and Tatsu Aoki (1998).

KENNY MATHIESON

Reference and Further Reading

Beauchamp, Lincoln T. *Art Ensemble of Chicago: Great Black Music, Ancient to the Future*. Chicago: Art Ensemble Publishing, 1998.

Litweiler, John. *The Freedom Principle: Jazz After 1958*. New York: William Morrow, 1984.

Wilmer, Val. *As Serious as Your Life*. London: Allison & Busby, 1977.

Selected Discography

Art Ensemble of Chicago. *A Jackson in Your House* (1969, BYG 529302); *With Fontella Bass* (1970, America 6117); *Bap-tizum* (1972, Atlantic 1639); *Fanfare for the Warriors* (1974, Atlantic 1651); *Urban Bushmen* (1980, ECM 1211); *Soweto* (1990, DIW 837); *Coming Home Jamaica* (1996, Atlantic 83149); *Tribute to Lester* (2003, ECM 1808).

Muhal Richard Abrams. *Sightsong* (1974, Black Saint BS003).

Lester Bowie. *Numbers 1&2* (1967, Nessa 1).

Charles Brackeen. *Bannar* (1987, Silkheart 105).

Malachi Favors. *Natural and the Spiritual* (1977, AECO 003).

Roscoe Mitchell. *Sound* (1966, Delmark 408); *Hey Donald* (1994, Delmark 475).

Sunny Murray. *Live at Moers Festival* (1979, Moers 01054).

FISCHER, JOHN

(b. May 17, 1947, Pasadena, CA)

John Fischer entered gospel music as an early performer of contemporary Christian folksongs and then transcended stardom to become a senior statesmen of the guild. Although he was a pioneer of pop styles that would become standard for contemporary Christian music, his greatest influence on the gospel music scene probably came through his pastoral counsel and writings.

Fischer graduated from Wheaton College in 1969 and toured as a musician with evangelist Leighton Ford. That same year, he released the first of two albums that seemed to preview the music of the Jesus movement revival that would come to the fore in Southern California in 1971. *The Cold Cathedral* and its follow-up *Have You Seen Jesus My Lord?* contain spiritual songs with a pop sound similar to that associated with the Kingston Trio or the New Christy Minstrels. "Look All Around You" from the first album and the title song from Fischer's sophomore project became classic "youth group songs" sung at churches and summer camps across America. He would repeat this success later with "All Day Song" from *Still Life*, and he would garner Christian radio hits with "Johnny's Café" in 1979 and "Dark Horse" in 1983.

In general, however, Fischer moved out of the spotlight to make albums that were often critics' favorites in spite of achieving only moderate commercial success. He came to be regarded as a thoughtful lyricist whose albums evinced mature folk stylings comparable to those of Gordon Lightfoot or John B. Sebastian. The album *Wide Angle* was produced by Mark Heard and features guest vocals by Julie Miller; despite acclaim, it was not widely distributed, and Fischer would later reissue an expanded version of the project retitled *Some Folks World* on his own Silent Planet label.

During the 1970s, Fischer settled in Palo Alto, California, where he formed the Discovery Arts Guild as a ministry of Peninsula Bible Church, committed to promoting new Christian talent. He later served as artist in residence at Gordon College in

Massachusetts, where he lived for much of the 1980s before moving again to Laguna Beach, California. Throughout this time, he turned increasingly to writing, producing a number of devotional books and theological studies in addition to a handful of novels. Although many of these writings were popular with gospel music fans (and artists), his most direct influence on the gospel music scene came via a monthly column that he wrote for *CCM* magazine. Some of these pieces were collected for publication in the books *Real Christians 'Don't Dance* and *True Believers 'Don't Ask Why*. A sought-after speaker, Fischer has also hosted the *Wide Angle Radio Show*.

MARK ALLAN POWELL

Reference and Further Reading

Fiction

Dark Horse (Multnomah, 1983); *Saint Ben* (Minneapolis: Bethany House, 1993); *The Saints' and Angels' Song* (Minneapolis: Bethany House, 1994); *Ashes on the Wind* (Minneapolis: Bethany House, 1998).

Nonfiction

Real Christians 'Don't Dance (Minneapolis: Bethany House, 1988); *True Believers 'Don't Ask Why* (Minneapolis: Bethany House, 1989); *Making Real What I Already Believe* (Minneapolis: Bethany House, 1991); *On a Hill Too Far Away* (Servant, 1994); *Be Thou My Vision* (Servant, 1995); *What On Earth Are We Doing?* (Servant, 1997); *12 Steps for the Recovering Pharisee (Like Me)* (Minneapolis: Bethany House, 2000); *Fearless Faith* (Minneapolis: Bethany House, 2002).

Discography

The Cold Cathedral (1969, FEL 362); *Have You Seen Jesus My Lord?* (1970, FEL 542); *Still Life* (1974, Light LS-5645); *The New Covenant* (1975, Light LS5658); *Naphtali* (1976, Light LS 5693); *Inside* (1978, Light LS 5711); *Johnny's Café* (1979, Light LS 5757); *Dark Horse* (1982, Myrrh MSB 6713); *Between the Answers* (1985, Myrrh); *Casual Crimes* (1987, Myrrh); *Wide Angle* (1992, Urgent); *Some Folk's World* (1999, Silent Planet SPR 0601).

FISK JUBILEE SINGERS

On October 6, 1871, George White and nine black singers set out to raise funds for the nearly bankrupt Fisk University. The singers ranged in age from fifteen to twenty-five years old and were all ex-slaves or children of ex-slaves.

One of the many black schools established after the Civil War to teach reading and writing to tens of thousands of emancipated slaves, the Fisk Free Colored School was founded in 1866 by the Congregational Church's American Missionary Association, the Western Freedmen's Aid Commission, and former Union Army General Clinton B. Fisk of the Freedmen's Bureau. The group's manager and Fisk University's treasurer, George White, although not formally trained, was a fine singer. He also had the special gift of inspiring this group of young people to the highest musical standards. Withstanding hardships and indignities, this nameless and almost penniless group persevered against all odds to save their school from bankruptcy and closure.

The original repertoire of the Jubilee Singers included classical literature, popular ballads, and patriotic anthems. Offstage, the singers continued to perform the music that was dear to their hearts: the spiritual. Because they were financially unsuccessful at first, White convinced the singers that they should add one or two spirituals to their concert repertoire. This decision changed the course of music history. Audiences were moved to tears by their stirring interpretations of this repertoire. White adapted the unaccompanied, improvised folk spirituals into a standard four-part choral format. The harmonies were rich and evoked the incredible beauty and rich heritage of African Americans in this country.

At a time when most black music was being performed by white minstrel musicians in blackface and vulgar caricature, the Jubilee Singers were able to reintroduce a sense of authenticity into the music and to elevate this important American music form to a place of respect and dignity.

After the repertoire of the ensemble was firmly established, George White introduced a new name, the Fisk Jubilee Singers. The name is derived from Old Testament history, where each fiftieth Pentecost was followed by a "year of jubilee"—a year in which Hebrew law required that all slaves be set free. Organized in the dark shadow of slavery, this name seemed to be most appropriate. With their performances, the Jubilee Singers were able to reveal the emotions and strong faith of the African American slave.

Infusing the spiritual with more European choral characteristics and deliberately minimizing the more African characteristics (such as improvisation and call and response) could not erase the distinctive black character. The influence of the spiritual can clearly be heard in the works of other composers. Czech composer Anton Dvorak, for example, incorporated elements of spirituals into his symphonies. Spirituals also became the cornerstone of the blues and gospel music. The influence can be heard particularly in the works of great gospel composers such as Thomas Dorsey and Charles Tindley.

Fisk Jubilee Singers, circa 1880. Photo courtesy Frank Driggs Collection.

The Jubilee Singers introduced scores of spirituals, from "Steal Away" to "Swing Low, Sweet Chariot" to the world, and spawned landmark musical collections that are still highly revered. Their ingenuity helped to create a crucial musical link between the past and future with their fusion of African and European musical characteristics. But their contribution extended well beyond their music and the salvation of their educational institution. Forced to do battle with American racism in the dark, chaotic era following the Civil War, they bravely denounced segregation from choir lofts and concert stages. In their wake, Northern hotels, railroads, and schools opened their doors to blacks. Ejected from hotels and railroad cars, the bedraggled singers continued to perform from one end of the country to the other, often following the old Underground Railway. They caused such a sensation that soon they were raising thousands of dollars a week performing to overflow audiences up and down the Eastern seaboard.

Unfortunately, their success came at great personal cost. Benjamin Holmes, who had taught himself to read as a slave, died of tuberculosis. Julia Jackson, who as a small girl had helped her relatives escape from bondage, suffered a paralytic stroke. Ella Sheppard, the matriarch of the Jubilee Singers, nearly died

of pneumonia after struggling with the malaise for seven years. As they sought to overcome exploitation and prejudice, the Jubilee Singers transformed American music forever, foreshadowing the triumphs and travails of thousands of black performers.

Between 1871 and 1881, the group toured most of the northern states, performed at the White House, toured England and much of Europe, and sang for Queen Victoria. After several tours throughout the United States and Europe, the Jubilee Singers eventually raised $150,000, thus securing the school's future. Their diligence purchased the campus on which the university sits today in north Nashville. They also built Jubilee Hall, the first permanent building in America for the education of blacks (now designated as a national historic landmark). Each October 6, Fisk University celebrates Jubilee Day, commemorating the original Jubilee Singers, who sang before kings, queens, and heads of state; who captured the hearts of all who heard their music; who introduced to the world the beauty and tradition of the Negro spiritual; and who, with steadfastness and commitment, virtually saved their university.

The Fisk Jubilee Singers, whose legacy continues in a present-day iteration of the ensemble, did more than simply save a university that has since had an illustrious history. Their efforts made it possible for Fisk to grow into one of the nation's preeminent African American institutions of higher learning. Each year the university honors the 1871 concert tour that bailed the failing institution out of financial trouble with a pilgrimage to the gravesite of the four original singers. More broadly, the Jubilee Singers reflected a tradition relevant to African American life as a whole: using black culture as a means of support in times of adversity. The Jubilee Singers were inducted into the Gospel Music Hall of Fame in 2000.

DONNA M. COX

Reference and Further Reading

Ward, Andrew, ed. *Dark Midnight When I Rise: The Story of the Jubilee Singers, Who Introduced the World to the Music of Black America.* New York: Farrar, Straus and Giroux, 2000.

FIVE BLIND BOYS OF ALABAMA

The group was formed at the Talladega (Alabama) Institute for the Deaf and Blind in 1937. Like many such institutions spread throughout the South, this school encouraged its handicapped students to study music as a means of supporting themselves. Founder/ lead vocalist Clarence Fountain was inspired to form the group after hearing the popular gospel group the Dixie Hummingbirds on the radio.

The group went professional by the early 1940s, sometimes billing themselves as the Happyland Gospel Singers, sometimes simply as the Blind Boys. Their recording debut came in 1948 with "I Can See Everybody's Mother But Mine" released on the jazz label Savoy. Around 1950, the group finally settled on the name the Blind Boys of Alabama, because their blindness was a large part of their appeal to the gospel audience. The group recorded for various small labels through the 1950s (including the pop label Specialty) and 1960s (notably for Chicago-based Vee-Jay). Fountain left the group to pursue a solo career on the gospel circuit in 1969, and the group remained inactive until he decided to gather the original members for a reunion about a decade later.

The group continued to work the gospel circuit without gaining much recognition in the wider musical world before reaching a new level of fame when they were invited in 1984 to appear as the choir on Broadway in the *Gospel at Colonus,* a reworking of the Oedipus legend. This led to engagements in larger halls beyond the gospel circuit, as well as European

tours. In 1994, they were awarded a National Heritage Award by the U.S. government. In 2001, pop star Peter Gabriel signed them to his Real World label, and a series of highly produced albums followed, melding their traditional harmony style with pop instrumentation. Although many of its original members are gone, Fountain continues to lead the group in its traditional style.

RICHARD CARLIN

Reference and Further Reading

Heilbut, Anthony. *The Gospel Sound: Good News and Bad Times, Updated and Revised.* New York: Limelight, 1997.

Discography

The Sermon (1993, Specialty CD). Reissue of a 1953 recording by the group, re-creating a traditional church service.
Have Faith: The Very Best of the Five Blind Boys of Alabama (1998, Collectables). One of many "best of" selections available on CD, collecting 1950s- and 1960s-era recordings.
Higher Ground (2002, Real World). Recent Grammy-winning recording with the Boys' vocals set among a slick pop production.

FIVE BLIND BOYS OF MISSISSIPPI

The group was formed in the mid-1930s by students at the Piney Woods School, located outside Jackson, Mississippi, one of many Southern schools for poor, handicapped children. Like most of these schools, Piney Woods emphasized music as part of its curriculum, with the idea that a musical career was one way for a blind person to make a living in the South.

The group's leader was vocalist Archie Brownlee (sometimes spelled Brownley), who enlisted his fellow students Joseph Ford, Lawrence Abrams, and Lloyd Woodward to make up the original lineup. Initially known as the Cotton Blossom Singers, they performed at the school and for local functions; folklorist Alan Lomax, when visiting the school in 1937, made the group's first (noncommercial) recordings for the Library of Congress. After graduating from school, the group "went professional," continuing as the Cotton Blossom Singers for secular performances and taking the name the Jackson Harmoneers for gospel work.

In the mid-1940s, the group's first nonblind member, Percell Perkins, joined the ranks both as its manager and as a fifth voice. They made their recording debut in 1946, but it was not until they signed with Houston-based Peacock Records in 1950, owned by black entrepreneur Don Robey, that they achieved broad success, with their R&B hit "Our Father." Brownlee's lead vocals featured impassioned growls and yells that became a hallmark of postwar gospel (and greatly influenced the developing soul style, which wed gospel's fervor with R&B's pop instrumentation and subject matter).

The group enjoyed a long, productive relationship with Robey, producing more hit singles and albums through 1960, when Brownlee died at the young age of 35 of complications from pneumonia. He was replaced by two singers, Roscoe Robinson (who had sung and recorded with the Five Trumpets and the Highway QCs, among others, and later had a major R&B hit with "That's Enough" in 1966) and lead tenor Willmer (sometimes known as Wilmer, Wilbur, and Willie "Little Ax") Broadnax, who began singing gospel in 1950 with the Spirit of Memphis. Broadnax was known for his "ringing tenor" and was a favorite wherever he appeared.

With various lineups, the Blind Boys continued to tour and occasionally record from the 1960s through the early twenty-first century, with occasional periods of inactivity as old members passed and new members were enlisted. Lead singer Sandy Foster has led the latest version of the group since the mid-1990s. Their style is little changed, and their repertoire is based on their early hits and gospel standards.

RICHARD CARLIN

Reference and Further Reading

Heilbut, Anthony. *The Gospel Sound: Good News and Bad Times.* Updated and revised ed. New York: Limelight, 1997.

Discography

I Never Heard A Man/I'll Make It Right (1996, Jewel). Two separate CDs reissuing their 1950s-era recordings.

FLATT, LESTER, AND EARL SCRUGGS

Lester Raymond Flatt (b. June 19, 1914, Duncan's Chapel, TN; d. May 11, 1979)
Earl Eugene Scruggs (b. January 6, 1924, Flint Hill, NC)

The famous tandem of Lester Flatt & Earl Scruggs did much to create and popularize bluegrass music in America from the time both men were in Bill Monroe's Blue Grass Boys (1945–1948) right through and beyond their twenty-one years together (1948–1969) on Mercury and Columbia Records.

Flatt's rapid-fire guitar runs and his warm, drawling singing voice seemed perfectly paired with Scruggs's original and universally imitated three-finger banjo playing. *New York Times* critic Robert Shelton famously described their style as "folk music in overdrive," a big part of which was their Foggy Mountain Boys band: over the years it included such long-time members and venerable legends as fiddler Paul Warren, Dobroist Burkett "Uncle Josh" Graves, and mandolinist Curly Seckler.

Popular from the Grand Ole Opry to Carnegie Hall and college campuses, Flatt and Scruggs were semiregulars on the popular CBS-TV show *The Beverly Hillbillies* after scoring a major hit in 1962 with its theme song, "The Ballad of Jed Clampett." This was their breakthrough national hit (after fourteen years together), but a loyal body of devoted fans already loved them for such classic instrumentals as "Foggy Mountain Breakdown" (Earl's defining banjo performance), "Randy Lyn Rag," "Flint Hill Special," and "Earl's Breakdown" and for such vocal favorites as "I'm Gonna Sleep with One Eye Open," "Dim Lights, Thick Smoke, and Loud, Loud Music," "You're Not a Drop in the Bucket," and "Over the Hills to the Poorhouse."

Their fondness for gospel or inspirational songs, typically arranged for four vocal parts and introduced on broadcasts or concerts as being by the Foggy Mountain Quartet (Flatt singing lead, Scruggs singing baritone, Seckler high tenor, and Paul Warren or others on bass), helped create the genre now recognized as bluegrass gospel. Banjo virtuoso that he was, Earl Scruggs often laid that instrument down on gospel songs and played instead a wonderful and captivating Maybelle Carter–style acoustic guitar on the instrumental breaks.

It is significant that their very first record release for Mercury (issued in January 1949) paired two original sacred songs, "God Loves His Children"/ "I'm Going to Make Heaven My Home." In fact, of the twenty-eight total recordings they made for Mercury during those first two years, nine were inspirational. Perhaps the best known of these was Frank Southern's "Take Me in a Lifeboat." Joining Columbia Records in 1951, gospel remained a staple of their 1950s repertory. Of the single releases, "Get in Line Brother" (1951), "Be Ready for Tomorrow May Never Come" (1953), "You Can Feel It in Your Soul" (1955), "Old Fashioned Preacher" (1955), "Bubbling in My Soul" (1955), and "Joy Bells" (1956), all written or cowritten by Flatt or Scruggs, became classics of their type and were later gathered in reissue packages.

While they did not often record gospel material by other writers, the results when they did were usually superb, as with Onie Wheeler's "Mother Prays Loud in Her Sleep" (1953), Walter Bailes's "Give Mother My Crown" (1956), or Bill Carlisle's "Gone Home" (1955). When the studio LP became popular in the late 1950s, the boys wasted no time in cutting a new gospel package (some of them remakes of their earlier records), *Songs of Glory* (Columbia CL-1424, issued in April 1960).

The folk revival brought renewed popularity for bluegrass acts in the 1960s after the lean years of rock 'n' roll, and not surprisingly, the recorded repertory of Flatt & Scruggs in that decade shows a lot more folk music (both traditional and new urban) and a good deal less gospel. They enjoyed a chart hit with another Onie Wheeler song in 1961, "Go Home," in which a redeemed alcoholic converts an entire barroom crowd. For a 1964 Columbia single, Flatt performed his first gospel recitation, "Father's Table Grace" (to Earl's accompaniment on a twelve-string guitar). It was so well received that when they cut a second all-gospel LP, "When the Saints Go Marching In" (1966), Lester included another recitation, "Call Me On Home Too." The bulk of that LP was new material written by Flatt, but interestingly there is a song written by young Tom T. Hall, "A Stone the Builders Refused."

After recording for the last time in August 1969, the great Flatt & Scruggs team split apart rather acrimoniously over stylistic differences and career direction. Scruggs, increasingly attuned to music that his sons were listening to and playing, had pushed them toward country covers of pop and rock and MOA favorites ("Blowin' in the Wind," "The Times They Are A-Changin'"), while Flatt preferred their traditional bluegrass material. These opposing directions were apparent after the split, as Flatt hired most of their bluegrass pickers for his new RCA band, Lester Flatt & The Nashville Grass (even adding a very young Marty Stuart in 1972), and stayed on the Grand Ole Opry until his death in 1979. Scruggs and his sons, meanwhile, formed the rock-flavored Earl Scruggs Revue and dropped out of country radio in favor of the college and university circuit. The historic team was elected to the Country Music Hall of Fame in 1985.

RONNIE PUGH

Reference and Further Reading

"Flatt & Scruggs & The Foggy Mountain Boys." *The Encyclopedia of Country Music: The Ultimate Guide to the Music*. New York: Oxford University Press, 1998. Liner note booklets to Bear Family CD box sets (see Discography).

Rosenberg, Neil V. "The Flatt & Scruggs Discography." In five parts. *The Journal of Country Music* 12, no. 3, through 14, no. 1 (1989–1991).

Selected Discography

78s

"Get in Line Brother"/"Brother I'm Getting Ready to Go" (Columbia 20915).
"God Loves His Children"/"I'm Going to Make Heaven My Home" (Mercury 6161).
"Mother Prays Loud in Her Sleep"/"Be Ready for Tomorrow May Never Come" (Columbia 21209).
"Reunion in Heaven"/"Pray for the Boys" (Okeh 18004).

45s

"Gone Home"/"Bubbling in My Soul" (Columbia 4-21460).
"Joy Bells"/"Give Mother My Crown" (Columbia 4-21536).
"You Can Feel It in Your Soul"/"Old Fashioned Preacher" (Columbia 4-21370).

LPs

Songs of Glory (Columbia CL-1424).
When the Saints Go Marching In (Columbia CL-2513).

CD Reissues

Flatt & Scruggs 1948–1959 (1992, Bear Family BCD 15472).
Flatt & Scruggs 1959–1963 (1992, Bear Family BCD 15559).
Flatt & Scruggs 1964–1969 (1993, Bear Family BCD 15879).

FLORIDA BOYS, THE

J. G. Whitfield (b. September 8, 1915)
Glen Allred (b. June 19, 1934)
Les Beasley (b. August 16, 1928)
Derrell Stewart (b. October 6, 1934)

The Florida Boys have been one of the most important and influential groups in the history of Southern gospel music. Their roots go back to the Happy Hitters, a group that J. G. Whitfield sang with in Pensacola, Florida, before World War II.

After serving in the armed forces during World War II, Whitfield returned to Pensacola and formed the Gospel Melody Quartet in 1947 with himself singing bass, Guy Dodd on tenor, Edward Singletary on baritone, Roy Howard singing lead, and Tiny Merrell on piano. Roy Howard died suddenly of a heart attack in 1951 but the group continued to perform, adding Glen Allred in 1952 and Les Beasley in 1953; Allred played guitar and sang baritone, while Beasley sang lead.

The group's name changed to the Florida Boys around 1954, because concert promoter Wally Fowler did not believe that the name "Gospel Melody Boys" was distinctive and began billing them as "The Boys from Florida." Whitfield agreed and renamed the group the Florida Boys. At this point their lineup consisted of Beasley, Allred, Whitfield, Buddy Mears on tenor, and Emory Parker on piano.

In 1958, J. G. Whitfield left the group to pursue his business interests; he eventually owned a chain of food stores, three drug stores, a department store, a trading stamp company, a mail order merchandise house, and a concert promotion company that promoted gospel concerts. Because of Whitfield's success in business, he could put money into his first love: promoting Southern gospel music.

When Whitfield left the group, Beasley, Allred, and Derrell Stewart, who had joined as the piano player, took over ownership of the Florida Boys.

In 1959 the group began taping a thirty-minute television show, *The Gospel Songshop,* which acquired the Chattanooga Medicine Company as a sponsor and went into national syndication. After several years, the sponsor dropped out of this arrangement and Noble Dury and Associates, an advertising agency in Nashville, began marketing the company. Beasley and Jan Doughten, vice president of Noble Dury, developed and coproduced the television show *Gospel Singing Jubilee,* an hour-long television program hosted by the Florida Boys that featured a number of other Southern gospel groups as guests. Later, the show was produced by Show Biz, headed by Bill Graham.

The Gospel Singing Jubilee, which became the most watched gospel program on television, began in 1964 on a Sunday morning and at one time was on in virtually every major television market in the United States. The show ran for twenty-five years and won a number of Dove Awards (for Best Television Program).

The Florida Boys first recorded for their own label, which was a subsidiary of King Records, headed by Syd Nathan in Cincinnati. They sold these records (78s) on their radio show and at personal appearances. Bill Beasley (no relation to Les) in Cincinnati had a label that recorded "sound-a-likes" (records that copied the hits of the day), and he hired the Florida Boys to record. In 1959, Bill Beasley formed Faith, a gospel label, and offered the Florida Boys a thousand-dollar advance per album to record. The group recorded several albums on Faith.

The first hit for the Florida Boys was "There's a Leak in This Old Building" in 1954, which received additional attention when Elvis Presley sang it in his debut movie, *Love Me Tender.* The first album by the Florida Boys, *The Eleventh Anniversary,* was released in 1958. This was the first release on LP for the group; previously, all of their releases had been on single 78s.

In 1963 Jarrell McCracken, founder and president of Word Records, called Les Beasley to ask if the group would consider recording for Word. McCracken had seen the group on television and wanted to start a Southern gospel division. Also, Marvin Norcross, a partner with McCracken in Word, wanted Word to begin a Southern gospel label. The Florida Boys agreed and became the first act on Canaan Records, the southern gospel label for Word.

Les Beasley was elected to the Gospel Music Hall of Fame in 1989, and the Florida Boys were elected in 1999. The core members of the Florida Boys—Les Beasley, Glen Allred, and Derrell Stewart—have all been inducted into the Southern Gospel Music Hall of Fame. Beasley, who began his singing career with the McManus Trio in 1946, served in the Marines during the Korean War before joining the group; he was inducted in 1997. Allred, who performed with the Dixie Drifters, Happy Rhythm Quartet, the Spirit of Dixie Trio, and Oak Ridge Boys before joining the Florida Boys, was inducted in 2001. Derrell Stewart began his professional career with the Dixie Rhythm Quartet; he was inducted to the Southern Gospel Music Hall of Fame in 2004.

DON CUSIC

Reference and Further Reading

Goff, James R., Jr. *Close Harmony: A History of Southern Gospel.* Chapel Hill: University of North Carolina Press, 2002.

Cusic, Don. *The Sound of Light: A History of Gospel and Christian Music.* New York: Hal Leonard, 2002.

Selected Discography

Greatest Hits (1994).
Home Once Again (1994).
I've Got a Feeling (1994).
Brand New Feeling (1995).
A Taste of Heaven (1996).
Vintage Gospel (1998).
He Shall Return (2002).
I'm Gonna Rise (2002).

FOLEY, RED

(b. June 17, 1910, Blue Lick, KY)

Country Music Hall of Fame member Clyde Julian "Red" Foley did much to popularize gospel music with his classic early 1950s hit recordings of "Peace in the Valley" and "Just a Closer Walk with Thee."

Foley was "Clydie" to his parents Ben and Kate Foley (who ran their small town's general store) but "Red" (for his hair, of course) to his friends and fans.

Trained in voice at Kentucky's Georgetown College, Foley in 1931 found regular radio singing work at $60 per week at WLS Chicago, home of the *National Barn Dance*. There, Red joined John Lair's old-time vocal and string ensemble, the Cumberland Ridge Runners, but he also sang duets with popular comedienne Lulu Belle and soloed on novelty and sentimental songs, including his self-penned favorite "Old Shep." He cofounded the *Renfro Valley Barn Dance* in 1937 and worked in radio with another Red—Skelton—on a variety show called *Avalon Time*, but returned to the *National Barn Dance* in 1940.

After recording for the American Record Corporation in the 1930s, he signed with Decca Records in 1941 and worked for them for the rest of his life, also making a few singing Hollywood Westerns in the 1940s. He came to Nashville in 1946 to replace Roy Acuff as host of the half-hour NBC network segment of the *Grand Ole Opry*, a lucrative assignment that took his voice into some ten million homes every Saturday night. The exposure no doubt also boosted record sales of such late 1940s Decca releases as "Tennessee Saturday Night," "Sugarfoot Rag," and the huge 1950 crossover hit—number one on both country and pop charts—"Chattanoogie Shoe Shine Boy."

In 1951 Foley, who had always included some gospel recordings in his repertoire (such as his 1946 recording of Lee Roy Abernathy's "Gospel Boogie"), recorded the Reverend Thomas A. Dorsey's great song of consolation, "Peace in the Valley." With quartet vocal backing and Grady Martin's stunning electric guitar riffs, the record's simultaneous sales on three of Decca's numerical series (14573–Faith, 27856–Pop, and 4631–Country) made it reportedly the first million-selling gospel recording ever. Almost as popular had been his 1949 recording (Decca 14505) of the traditional "Just a Closer Walk with Thee." Foley brought both songs into the white gospel mainstream. Backed by Martin's acoustic guitar and producer Owen Bradley's organ, Foley cut the best country rendition of Cleavant Derricks's great song, "When God Dips His Love in My Heart." The smooth, versatile, and trained Foley voice was soon blending well on duet releases with Decca's great spiritual star, Sister Rosetta Tharpe.

Recitations and hymns became staples of Foley's album repertoire in later years, as he left the Opry and radio stardom for the new medium of television with Springfield, Missouri's *Ozark Jubilee* (1954–1960) and later a regular role in ABC's Fess Parker series, *Mr. Smith Goes to Washington*. Through it all, Foley had a certain level of discomfort with his gospel notoriety, because he was not a particularly religious man. He was the target of a 1952 alienation of affections lawsuit and IRS tax fraud suits, and he suffered frequent bouts with alcoholism. His personal life, which was well-publicized, held no exemplary standard for believers.

Though he seemed much older at the time, "the Old Master" was only fifty-eight when he died on September 19, 1968, in a Fort Wayne hotel room following a personal appearance in that city. Both of his parents, his second wife Sally Sweet, and his four daughters (including Shirley, who is Mrs. Pat Boone) survived him, but Red lived long enough to have old friend Ernest Tubb welcome him into the Country Music Hall of Fame the year before.

RONNIE PUGH

Reference and Further Reading

Rumble, John. "Red Foley." *The Encyclopedia of Country Music: The Ultimate Guide to the Music*. New York: Oxford University Press, 1998.

FOLKWAYS RECORDS

Folkways Record was founded by Moses "Moe" Asch (1905–1986) and Marian Distler (1919–1964) in New York City in 1948. The principal focus of the label's activities lay in a broad range of folk musics, but they documented a remarkably broad spectrum of music in many genres and international styles, as well as a series of spoken word, documentary, and instructional recordings (one of the label's most successful recordings was an "audio documentary" of the Civil Rights march to the Lincoln Memorial in 1963). Although it remained a small-scale and permanently cash-strapped independent operation, the label released a total of 2,168 recordings between its founding and the death of Moe Asch in 1986.

Asch began the label by signing "genre" artists dropped by bigger companies. The success of blues recordings by Huddie Ledbetter (Leadbelly) established the label nationally, and he is one of Folkways's best-known names, alongside Big Bill Broonzy, Pete Seeger, and Woody Guthrie.

Gospel inevitably played its part in the evolution of Folkways, and although it was never an area in which the label specialized heavily, they did issue significant recordings. A section of gospel music was featured within the historic and subsequently very influential *Anthology of American Folk Music*, edited by Harry Smith and first issued in LP form by Folkways in 1952 (a CD reissue followed in 1997). It included music by Reverend J. M. Gates, the Alabama Sacred Harp Singers, the Middle Georgia Singing Convention No. 1, Sister Mary Nelson, the Memphis Sanctified Singers, Elders McIntosh and Edwards's Sanctified Singers, Reverend Moses Mason, Bascom Lamar

Lunsford, Blind Willie Johnson, the Carter Family, Ernest Phipps and His Holiness Singers, Reverend F. W. McGee, and Reverend D. C. Rice and His Sanctified Congregation, much of it unknown to the wider American audience at that time.

The Folkways catalog also featured a number of individual gospel albums by artists that included Brother John Sellers, Little Brother Montgomery, Harry and Jeannie West, the Fisk Jubilee Singers, the Moving Star Hall Singers, the Missionary Quintet, Artus Moser, Guy Carawan, Elder Charles D Beck, and the Porter Singers Second Canaan Baptist Church, as well as numerous compilation albums (Mahalia Jackson was added to the list with *I Sing Because I'm Happy* in 1992).

Moses Asch was born in Poland but immigrated to New York with his family at the age of eight. A lifelong socialist, he worked against the grain of the American recording industry by refusing to make commercial prospects the basis of his decision making, and by ignoring the conventional wisdom that particular types of recordings must be marketed only to specific social or racial groups. He believed that the music he was releasing was of equal potential interest and value to everyone and wanted toward disseminate the huge range of interests reflected in his catalog as widely as possible. Asch's disregard for commercial imperatives was also reflected in his attitude toward paying royalties to his artists, and while many of them were willing to forgo their due reward in the light of his obvious commitment to the label and the music, it did lead to friction with some of his artists over the years.

Nonetheless, the recorded legacy he left is an invaluable and literally unique resource. The Smithsonian Institution Center for Folklife and Cultural Heritage in Washington, DC, acquired the Folkways label and its archives as part of the Moses and Frances Asch collection in 1987. The holdings are part of the Ralph Rinzler Folklife Archives and Collections and consist of original recordings, business records, correspondence, and photographic material that came with the purchase of Folkways Records. The label forms the core of Smithsonian Folkways Recordings, although other labels and newer recordings have been added to that imprint. They have pledged to keep all of the Folkways catalog of recordings permanently available through a system of custom ordering.

The tradition of never deleting anything on the label was inherited from Asch's own unwavering practice. His reply to questions about the commercial acumen of this policy solicited his frequently cited response: "Do you delete the letter Q from the alphabet just because you don't use it as much as the others?" His professional expertise was as a recording engineer, but his mission with Folkways Records was nothing less than preserving and presenting the cultural heritage of as many different peoples and groups as he possibly could. That aim is reflected not only in the breadth and scope of the Folkways catalog, but also in its attractive but rather eccentric eclecticism.

KENNY MATHIESON

Reference and Further Reading

Goldsmith, Peter D. *Making People's Music: Moe Asch and Folkways Records.* Washington, DC: Smithsonian Institution Press, 1998.

Olmsted, Anthony. *Folkways Records: Moses Asch and His Encyclopedia of Sound.* New York: Routledge, 2003.

Smithsonian Institution Center for Folklife and Cultural Heritage, Moses and Frances Asch Collection home page, http://www.si.edu/folkways.

FONG, ODEN

(b. February 27, 1950, Hollywood, CA)

Oden Fong was born in Hollywood, California, to movie actor parents. His musical influences included the Beach Boys, the Beatles, blues musicians, Jimi Hendrix, the Grateful Dead, Jefferson Airplane, Joni Mitchell, the Rolling Stones, and surf music. During the late 1960s Fong was involved with a group led by ex-Harvard professor and psychedelic drug guru Timothy Leary. During an LSD trip, Fong encountered Jesus Christ for the first time. He started telling his old friends about Jesus and soon afterward began performing with Pedro Buford and Wade Link, who had a group called Mustard Seed.

In 1971, the group changed their name to Mustard Seed Faith and became part of the coterie of Christian rock bands that emanated from Calvary Chapel in Costa Mesa, California. They appeared on *Maranatha Three* and *Four* before producing their own classic Jesus rock album *Sail on Sailor.* Prior to recording the album Link left the band, and three new members were added: Lewis McVay, Steve Berchtold, and Darrel Cook. They released a second album, titled *Limited Edition,* and disbanded in 1977, after averaging sixty thousand miles a year touring by car and trailer.

Fong began to perform as a solo artist, releasing *Come for the Children* in 1978. After the album's release he began to tour again, but in 1982 he left the Christian music industry and went to work managing his father's Chinese restaurant chain. Three years later he returned to Calvary Chapel and worked closely with Pastor Chuck Smith. He became the overseer of nearly five hundred affiliate churches, conducted pastors' conferences, managed the music ministry, and began a musicians' fellowship, which grew into a Bible study attended by fifteen hundred people.

In 1995 Fong left Calvary Chapel to plant a church in Huntington Beach. In 2000 he moved to Hollywood to begin a ministry, and in 2003 moved back to Orange county to begin Poiema Chapel. At the same time he began overseeing Covering Wings, a homeless ministry, and serving as a chaplain for the Huntington Beach Police Department. He has not completely closed the door to the possibility of making another album sometime in the future.

BOB GERSZTYN

See also Calvary Chapel, Costa Mesa; Girard, Chuck; Love Song; Maranatha! Music; Rock Gospel

Reference and Further Reading

Balmer, Randall Herbert. *Mine Eyes Have Seen the Glory: A Journey into the Evangelical Subculture in America.* New York, Oxford University Press, 1993.
"History of the Jesus Movement." http://www.calvarymusic.org (accessed April 5, 2003).
"Interview with Oden Fong." November 1998. http://www.one-way.org/jesusmusic/index.html (accessed May 5, 2003).

Discography

Maranatha Three (1973, Maranatha Music HS 777/5).
Maranatha Four (1974, Maranatha Music HS 777/10).
Sail On Sailor (1975, Maranatha Music HS 777/18).
Come for the Children (1978, Asaph Records).
Limited Edition (1980, Road Records).
Invisible Man (1985, Frontline Music Group).

FORD, TENNESSEE ERNIE

Ernest Jennings Ford (b. February 19, 1919, Fordtown, TN; d. October 17, 1991, Reston, VA)

With his strong, clear baritone and folksy good humor, Tennessee Ernie Ford enjoyed a career on several fronts from the 1950s to the 1990s: he was a leading country singer, a television show star, a familiar commercial spokesman, and the creator of some of the most popular gospel albums ever produced.

Ford was raised in Bristol, Tennessee, the mountain city that had been the site where greats such as the Carter Family and Jimmie Rodgers were discovered. He attended church there, sang in the choir, and completed high school; he began his show business career by working as an announcer over the town's radio station, WOPI. He also briefly attended the

Cincinnati Conservatory of Music to get what formal voice training he received. With the outbreak of World War II, he joined the Army Air Corps and became a bombardier instructor. After the war, he decided to move to the West Coast.

Soon he had another announcing job, at KFXM in San Bernardino, California, where he began adopting his "down-home" persona, replete with country phrases and a slight Southern accent; he also began calling himself "Tennessee Ernie." He soon moved up to a larger station in Pasadena, where he attracted more attention through his habit of singing along to the records he played. One day he was heard by singer and promoter Cliffie Stone, who decided to groom him as a singer and began to invite him to guest on his radio show. Stone was a singer who was in the middle of the California country music scene, which featured Western swing–style backup, with electric guitars, drums, and other instruments. Ford's popularity soon won him a contract with the recently formed Capitol records in 1949; before the year was out, he had produced five chart hits, including titles such as "Smoky Mountain Boogie," "Tennessee Border," and his first number one hit, "Mule Train."

During the next five years, his fondness for jazzy, up-tempo boogie songs such as "Shotgun Boogie" and "Blackberry Boogie" won him show dates in Las Vegas and even at the London Palladium. By 1954 he had moved to television, first as the host of *College of Musical Knowledge* and then in 1956 on his own prime-time network show, *The Ford Show.* He also continued to have major hits with "The Ballad of Davy Crockett" and his biggest of all, "Sixteen Tons."

On his television shows, Ford was fond of ending the program with a hymn or gospel song, and this soon began drawing bags of viewer mail. Capitol, meanwhile, was starting to produce the new long-play albums and saw Ford as a natural for it. In October 1956, for his second LP, they released an entire album of Ford doing sacred songs, *Hymns* (T-756); these were straightforward readings of classic hymns such as "Rock of Ages," "Softly and Tenderly," "Sweet Hour of Prayer," "The Old Rugged Cross," and "The Ninety and Nine." Buoyed by the popularity of Ford's television show, the album became an instant best-seller and stayed on the *Billboard* charts for an unprecedented 277 consecutive weeks. Some music observers give it credit for ushering in a new popularity for gospel music, as all the major labels rushed out to start building their sacred catalogs. By 1963, *Hymns* was honored as being the most successful LP ever produced by a Capitol artist.

Capitol wasted no time in releasing a follow-up album; on April 1, 1957, they issued *Spirituals,* a collection of songs associated with the African American gospel songs; these included pieces such as Thomas Dorsey's "Peace in the Valley" and "Take My Hand, Precious Lord," as well as Cleavant Derricks's "When God Dips His Love in My Heart." It too was a huge seller, and Ford and Capitol determined that gospel would henceforth be a major part of his album release schedule, leading to *Nearer the Cross* (1959); *What a Friend We Have in Jesus,* with the Jordanaires (1959); *Sing a Hymn with Me,* designed to exploit the "Sing along with Mitch" fad of the time (1960); and *Sing a Spiritual with Me* (1960). One of Ford's personal favorites was *Hymns at Home* (1961), recorded in Bristol at the Anderson Street Methodist Church where Ford had sung as a child and featuring a special choir of Ford's relatives recruited for the album. By 1976, Ford had released some forty-eight LPs on Capitol, roughly half of which were gospel. During the following years, these sides were reissued and repackaged numerous times, testifying to the continuing popularity of Ford's booming voice and honest, straightforward style.

CHARLES K. WOLFE

Reference and Further Reading

Tennessee Ernie Ford website, http://www.ErnieFord.com.

FOREHAND, BLIND MAMIE

Blind Mamie Forehand was a Memphis street singer who worked with her husband, A. C. Forehand. Both recorded some songs under their own names, but they are primarily known for their records together. He played guitar and harmonium while she played hand-held bell cymbals. Their voices indicate that the couple were of advanced age; their vocals are not in the tradition of most other sanctified singers of the 1920s. Her delivery is deliberate and measured, her voice thin and quavery. A. C. Forehand's vocals are also weak and quavery, like those of an old man. He alternated verses with instrumental breaks.

The Forehands' two best efforts for posterity are their February 1927 recordings of "Wouldn't Mind Dying If Dying Was All" and "Honey in the Rock." On the latter number he played slide guitar in a manner similar to that later displayed by Blind Willie Johnson.

W. K. McNEIL

Reference and Further Reading

Boyer, Horace Clarence. *The Golden Age of Gospel.* Urbana and Chicago: University of Illinois Press, 2000 [1995].

Oliver, Paul. *Songsters & Saints: Vocal Traditions on Race Records.* Cambridge, UK: Cambridge University Press, 1984.

FOWLER, WALLY

Wally Fowler (1917–1994) served gospel music as a singer, songwriter, music publisher, promoter, and controversial spokesman for the industry as it moved out of the churches and onto the modern concert stage. During the era of the 1940s and 1950s, key transition years for Southern gospel music, Fowler was perhaps the best known and most effective promoter in the business. He formed one of the first independent publishing companies in Nashville, created a new system of distributing records, established the concert venue called "The All-Night Sing," wrote dozens of good songs, both secular and sacred, and formed the legendary group the Oak Ridge Quartet.

John Wallace "Wally" Fowler came from a background of singing conventions, quartets, and rural poverty; born the youngest son of a sharecropper near Adairsville, Georgia, he began singing with professional quartets as early as age eighteen. By 1936 he had started singing baritone for the John Daniel Quartet, one of the most popular and high-profile groups to come out of Alabama. Working with Daniel, Fowler was exposed to the grueling round of one-night stands and local singing conventions, all sandwiched in between radio programs. But in 1940 the Daniel Quartet landed a job on WSM's Grand Ole Opry; this was about the time that portions of the show were broadcast on a network, and the Daniel group soon had themselves a huge national audience. They began to diversify, and by 1944 Fowler began to write new, nongospel songs such as "Propaganda Papa" and "Mother's Prayer."

In 1944, Fowler decided to form his own band and try to make it as a full-time country singer—a trend that would be repeated in later years by the likes of the Louvin Brothers, Martha Carson, and the Oak Ridge Boys. With a new string band called the Georgia Clophoppers, Fowler moved to Knoxville, Tennessee, where he became a major figure in booking, promoting, and writing. One of his songs, "That's How Much I Love You," was to be recorded widely by singers such as Eddy Arnold, Bing Crosby, and even Frank Sinatra. While in Knoxville, he began to give regular free concerts to the children in the nearby town of Oak Ridge, many of whose parents worked at the top secret government atomic research facility there. The concerts were so successful that Fowler began to call his group the Oak Ridge Quartet and began to consider going back into gospel full time.

The opportunity came in 1945, when WSM rehired him and the Oak Ridge Quartet, first for a series of early morning (5:30 a.m.) broadcasts and then for a portion of the Opry broadcast over NBC. The quartet also signed a contract with Capitol and produced one of the most attractive and successful record sets in 1948. By this time the members of the quartet, almost as popular with fans as Wally, included Curly Kinsy, Johnny New, and "Deacon" Freeman, in addition to Fowler.

Drawing from his own experience as a country singer and publisher, Fowler now began to apply some of his promotional techniques to gospel. He founded Wallace Fowler Publications in December 1945; next to Acuff–Rose, it was the earliest country publishing house to be established in Nashville. Soon the company was releasing sheet music for Opry stars, but also song folios (often containing twenty songs) for figures such as Johnnie and Jack, Eddy Arnold, Milton Estes, Cliff Carlisle, and Fowler's own Oak Ridge Quartet. He also negotiated distribution rights for a collection of Albert E. Brumley's popular songs. In 1946 Fowler also began to work as a talent scout and representative for the New York publisher Edwin H. Morris. His own group had, on his own label, a substantial end-of-the-war hit in "Pray, Pray, Pray for the USA."

Fowler's greatest forte during these postwar years was new promotional devices. In 1948 he fused two earlier traditions in gospel, the "all-night singing" that had for years been a feature of the old Stamps–Baxter singing schools and the "battle of the quartets," an idea created by Le Roy Abernathy in Atlanta in 1946. But instead of just having two name quartets compete, Fowler decided to book six, seven, or even a dozen groups—a sort of a gospel version of the country "package show" or jazz's "Jazz at the Philharmonic" series. He tried his idea first in Nashville, at the Ryman Auditorium on November 5, 1948; advertisements promised that "25 quartets" would sing nonstop from 8:30 p.m. to 4:00 a.m. The result was dramatic: letters poured in, and soon Fowler was taking his new style of show on the road. By 1955, the formula was so successful that a national magazine, *Collier's,* reported that the show was playing in two hundred towns each season and attracting audiences of as many as fifteen thousand.

Fowler continued to promote gospel music throughout the rest of his life, though he sold his interest in the Oak Ridge Quartet and watched them become Nashville superstars as the Oak Ridge Boys. He was elected to the Gospel Music Hall of Fame in 1988, but he continued to be active in the business. He released a number of LPs during the 1960s and 1970s, including the popular *A Tribute to Mother* (Nashwood), *16*

Greatest Hits (Gusto), and *All Nite Singing Gospel* (Starday). For a time, he set up theaters in Nashville and then in Branson, Missouri. He died in a boating accident near Nashville in 1994.

CHARLES K. WOLFE

FRANCISCO, DON

(b. February 28, 1946, Louisville, KY)

Christian folksinger Don Francisco made his greatest impact on gospel music by writing and recording story songs that relate or reflect upon biblical narratives. The best known of these, "He's Alive," relates the dramatic discovery of Jesus's resurrection from the point of view of Peter. The song won the Dove Award for Song of the Year in 1980, and Francisco was named Songwriter of the Year by the Gospel Music Association. *Cashbox* magazine called "He's Alive" one of the "best folk gospel ballads of all time," and more than twenty years after its debut, *CCM* magazine selected it for the top ten on their list of the best songs in the history of contemporary Christian music. As of 2005, "I'm Alive" was still tied with Dallas Holm's "Rise Again" as the most popular song ever to appear on Christian radio charts.

The son of a Baptist minister and seminary professor, Francisco rebelled briefly against his upbringing to pursue a life in the hippie culture of the early 1970s. His life was turned around in 1974 after what he would describe as a miraculous experience of hearing God speak to him in an audible voice. He went on to study music business at Belmont College and connected with producer Gary Paxton to make Christian albums for NewPax. In 1982, Francisco moved to Colorado, where he would eventually form Rocky Mountain Ministries.

Musically, the records that Francisco made for NewPax display a country flair, with doses of Dobro, mandolin, banjo, and guitars accompanying a vocal style reminiscent of Jim Croce. Following quickly on the success of "He's Alive" (from *Forgiven*), Francisco had a second radio hit with "Got to Tell Somebody," an ode to witnessing that remained number one on the Christian radio charts for eighteen weeks in 1980. Beginning with *Holiness* in 1984, Francisco's style shifted to emphasize more worship songs and meditative pieces, and this new format would remain in evidence on most of the projects that he recorded for StarSong (1987–1994). After that, he devoted himself to independent projects. Rocky Mountain Ministries has released a number of projects by both Don Francisco and his wife, Wendy Francisco.

MARK ALLAN POWELL

Reference and Further Reading

Alfonso, Barry. "Don Francisco." In *The Billboard Guide to Contemporary Christian Music*, 166–167. New York: Billboard Books, 2002.

Baker, Paul. *Contemporary Christian Music: Where It Came From, Where It Is Going*. 124–124, 166–167. Westchester, IL: Crossway Books, 1985.

Powell, Mark Allan. "Don Francisco." In *Encyclopedia of Contemporary Christian Music*, 340–341. Peabody, MA: Hendrickson Publishers, 2002.

Discography

Brother of the Son (1976, NewPax NP33010); *Forgiven* (1977, New Pax NP33042); *Got to Tell Somebody* (1979, New Pax NP33071); *The Traveler* (1981, New Pax 33106); *The Live Concert* (1982, New Pax 33128); *Holiness* (1984, New Pax 33144); *The Poet: A Collection of the Best* (1984, New Pax NWP03916); *One Heart at a Time* (1985, Myrrh NWR 681506-4); *The Power* (1987, StarSong SSD 8097); *High Praise* (1988, StarSong SSD 8100); *Live in the U.K.* (1989, Window 7101); *The Early Works* (1991, Benson INC/CD02769); *Vision of the Valley* (1991, StarSong SSD 8187); *Come Away* (1992, StarSong SSD 8262); *Songs of the Spirit, Vol. 1: Genesis and Job* (1994, StarSong SSD 8803); *He's Alive, Collection Vol. 1* (1997, Progressive); *Beautiful to Me, Collection Vol. 2* (1998, Shelf Life); *Grace on Grace* (1998, Shelf Life); *Only Love Is Spoken Here* (2001, Airlift); *The Package, Collection Vol. 3* (date unknown, independent).

FRANKLIN, ARETHA

(b. March 25, 1942)

In addition to her well-deserved title "Queen of Soul," Aretha Franklin also has a page or two in the book of American gospel. Franklin was born in Memphis, Tennessee, to the Reverend C. L. Franklin and his wife, Barbara Siggers Franklin. Reverend Franklin was an outstanding gospel orator and minister of the Salem Baptist Church at the time. The family relocated to Detroit in 1946, and Reverend Franklin built a strong congregation at the New Bethel Baptist Church; his sermons were widely broadcast on the radio in Detroit and later issued as LP albums by Chess Records.

Aretha Franklin's formative musical education came from her early years in the choir at New Bethel, where she began singing. By the time she was twelve, Franklin was a featured soloist in the choir and began recording two years later for Checker and JVB Records. By the time she was eighteen, Franklin had released several gospel albums.

In 1960, Franklin signed with John Hammond of Columbia Records and began her legendary pop/soul career. After twelve releases by Columbia, she moved to Atlantic Records, where she soared to fame with the release of "I Never Loved a Man," in 1967, produced by Jerry Wexler. Her subsequent releases on Atlantic brought a great deal of success, and her musical fame was assured by her success with "Respect," "Chain of Fools," "Think," and others. Aretha Franklin had twenty number one R&B hits and won seventeen Grammys during her career.

In 1970, Franklin returned to gospel briefly with the release of the double album *Amazing Grace*, recorded with James Cleveland and the Southern California Community Choir. The double LP was a tour de force and made the top ten nationally. This placed the album as one of the largest selling gospel LPs of all time. During this period, her covers became major hits for Franklin. "Bridge over Troubled Waters," "Day Dreaming," and Ben E. King's "Spanish Harlem" were hits on both pop and R&B charts.

In 1980, Franklin's appearance in the film *The Blues Brothers* led to new interest in her career and she moved to Arista Records. She paired with Luther Vandross on the R&B number one hit "Jump to It." They teamed again the following year with the single "Get It Right." The 1985 album *Who's Zoomin' Who* featured the hit single "Freeway of Love" that hit both pop and R&B charts. She had hits with Annie Lennox ("Sisters Are Doin' It for Themselves") and George Michaels ("I Knew You Were Waiting for Me," which charted at number one in 1987).

Franklin returned to the gospel genre again in 1987 with the Arista Records release *One Lord One Faith One Baptism*. Franklin was inducted into the Rock and Roll Hall of Fame in 1987.

TOM FISHER

See also Franklin, Reverend C. L.

Reference and Further Reading

Bego, Mark. *Aretha Franklin: The Queen of Soul*. Cambridge, MA: Da Capo Press, 2001.

Franklin, Aretha; David Ritz. *Aretha from These Roots*. New York: VillardBooks, 1999.

Nathan, David; Luther Vandross. *The Soulful Divas*. New York: Watson-Guptill Publications, 2002.

Discography

Aretha Arrives (1967, Atlantic SD-8150); *I Never Loved a Man* (1967, Atlantic SD-8139); *Aretha Franklin in Paris* (1968, Atlantic SD-8207); *Lady Soul* (1968, Atlantic SD-8176); *Now* (1968, Atlantic SD-8186); *Aretha's Gold* (1969, Atlantic SD-8227); *Greatest Hits* (1971, Atlantic SD-8295); *Live at Fillmore West* (1971, Atlantic SD-7205); *Amazing Grace* (1972, Atlantic SD2-906); *Ten Years of Gold* (1976, Atlantic SD-18204); *Who's Zoomin' Who* (1985, Arista AAL8-8286); *One Lord One Faith One Baptism* (1987, Arista AL-8497).

FRANKLIN, KIRK

(b. January 26, 1970, Fort Worth, TX)

Kirk Franklin was born in Fort Worth, Texas. After his young mother abandoned him, he was raised by his elderly aunt and uncle. He began playing piano by the age of four and was offered a recording contract at the age of seven, but his guardians declined it. His aunt raised him in the Baptist church, which gave him a strong Christian foundation. At the same time, she encouraged his musical development by collecting bottles and cans to pay for his piano and voice lessons. By the age of eleven he was earning a hundred dollars a month as the "Minister of Music" at the Mt. Rose Baptist Church in Dallas.

Acceptance in the church, however, did not endear Franklin to his peers, who derided him with the name "church boy." He left the church and immersed himself in a life of street crime, which included theft and violence. Then when he was fifteen years old, one of his close friends was shot and killed. The event sobered his thinking and became the catalyst for his repentance and return to the church.

Upon returning to the church he concentrated on his music, composing and recording new songs. His music was influenced by the gospel music of Andrae Crouch and James Cleveland, as well as by R&B, pop, and rock, which included artists such as George Clinton, Rick James, Depeche Mode, INXS, and U2. In 1991 Franklin put together a band and gospel choir called the Family. The Family was composed of seventeen members, most of whom were neighborhood friends and associates. In 1992 he signed with an up-and-coming label called Gospo Centric Records.

In 1993, *Kirk Franklin and The Family* was released on Gospo Centric. It was recorded in 1992 and stayed on *Billboard's* gospel music chart for nearly two years. In 1994 the song "Why We Sing" was released as a single. It reached number one on the Christian music chart and, by December, R&B music stations all over the United States began to play it. The single crossed over to the R&B side and became the first gospel music album to ever go platinum and sell more than one million units.

In 1995, Kirk Franklin and the Family released *Christmas.* It was on *Billboard's* gospel music chart for eight weeks. In 1996 *Watcha Lookin' 4* was released on B-Rite Records, a division of Interscope Records. The album was originally recorded in 1994 and went to the number twenty-three spot on *Billboard's* contemporary Christian album chart for nineteen weeks. At the same time, it stayed on the gospel album chart for thirty weeks and eventually went platinum in the United States. In February 1997,

Watcha Lookin' 4 won a Grammy Award for Best Contemporary Soul Gospel Album, and Franklin won a *Billboard* Music Award for Gospel Artist of the Year.

The year 1997 was a transitional one for Franklin, as he took over the production of God's Property, a fifty-voice inner-city choir and five-piece band composed of at-risk young people of various ages, ranging from sixteen to twenty-six. The group was originally formed by Linda Searlight in 1992 and was directed by Robert Searlight. *God's Property from Kirk Franklin's Nu Nation* was an innovative masterpiece. The album produced the hit single "Stomp," which became a gospel hit. The video featured a guest appearance by Cheryl "Salt" James and became the first gospel video ever played on MTV. The album and single dominated both Christian and R&B charts; it eventually went triple platinum in the United States and won a Grammy for being the Best Gospel Choir or Chorus Album in 1998. It also won two *Billboard* Music Awards and two Dove Awards.

Franklin produced his own solo album, *New Nation Project,* in 1998. The first single off it was "Lean on Me," which included help from Mary J. Blige, Bono of U2, and R. Kelly, among others. Proceeds from the single went toward helping Southern churches victimized by arson. "Lean on Me" won two NAACP Image Awards, for Best Song and Outstanding Gospel Artist. The album won a Grammy in 1999 for being the Best Contemporary Soul Gospel Album. "Lean on Me" received a Grammy nomination for Song of the Year, which made Franklin the first gospel artist ever nominated for it. The album also won two Dove awards and eventually went double platinum.

The song "Thank You"—from the *Kingdom Come* motion picture soundtrack that Franklin wrote, scored, and produced in 2001—won a Dove Award in 2002. The year 2002 also saw the release of a new solo album titled *The Rebirth of Kirk Franklin.* The effort was the result of collaborations between Franklin and some of the biggest names in gospel, including Pastor Shirley Caesar, Bishop T. D. Jakes, Crystal Lewis, Donnie McClurkin, tobymac, and Jackie Valesquez. The album won the Soul Train Music Award for Best Gospel Album in March 2003 and went platinum in May. Writing, arranging, producing, and recording gospel music continue to be Franklin's driving passions as he spreads the "good news" in the twenty-first century.

BOB GERSZTYN

See also Caesar, Shirley; Cleveland, James; Crouch, Andrae; DC Talk; Lewis Family, The; McClurkin, Donnie

Reference and Further Reading

Franklin, Kirk. "The Rebirth of Kirk Franklin." http://www.nunation.com/bio.html (accessed May 28, 2003).
Franklin, Kirk; Jim Nelson Black (contributor). *Church Boy*. Word Publishing, 1998.
"God's Property." http://www.hiponline.com/artist/music/g/gods_property/ (accessed June 14, 2003).
"Richard De LaFont Agency, Inc." http://www.delafont.com/music_acts/kirk-franklin.htm (accessed May 20, 2003).
Rimmer, Mike. "Kirk Franklin, 'Church Boy'!" http://www.premieronline.co.uk/pages/feature/feature_kirkf.htm (accessed June 8, 2003).

Discography

Kirk Franklin & The Family (1993, Gospo Centric).
Christmas (1995, Gospo Centric).
Watcha Lookin' 4 (1996, Gospo Centric).
God's Property from Kirk Franklin's Nu Nation (1997, B'Rite Music).
New Nation Project (1998, Gospo Centric).
Kingdom Come Soundtrack (2002, Gospo Centric).
The Rebirth of Kirk Franklin (2002, Gospo Centric).

FRANKLIN, REVEREND C. L.

Clarence LeVaughn Franklin (b. January 15, 1922; d. July 27, 1984)

Clarence LeVaughn Franklin was born in rural Sunflower County, Mississippi, to sharecroppers. The family moved to Cleveland, Mississippi, where he was educated. Franklin was ordained and began preaching at the age of sixteen. Franklin later met and married his first wife, Barbara Siggers, who was a church pianist. Mrs. Franklin died after giving birth to five children throughout their marriage.

Franklin was an outstanding speaker and, later in his career, was thought to be one of the twentieth century's finest orators. His ministry and fame grew during this period and he began touring the United States, delivering sermons to thousands of worshipers. Franklin served briefly as pastor of the Salem Baptist Church in Memphis, Tennessee, before accepting the post as founding pastor of the New Bethel Baptist Church in Detroit, Michigan, in 1946. His calling was extremely successful, and in 1961 the church moved from its original location to a converted twenty-two-hundred seat theater at 8430 Linwood in Detroit.

In the early 1960s, Franklin became active in politics and was an active participant in the Civil Rights Movement. He was a coorganizer of the Walk Toward Freedom March with his friend, Dr. Martin L. King, Jr. He also strongly supported the NAACP, the Urban League, and the Southern Christian Leadership Conference (SCLC).

Much of the strength of the Franklin ministry was in the spoken word; his regular sermons were broadcast on the radio. During his lifetime, Franklin recorded seventy-six albums of sermons and gospel songs on the Chess label; they represent a significant body of work.

Franklin was severely injured in an armed robbery at his residence in Detroit on June 10, 1979, and died following five years in a comatose state on July 27, 1984, in Detroit. He was eulogized by the Reverend Jasper Williams, Sr., as "a good soldier," and the Reverend Jesse Jackson also spoke at the four-hour service attended by almost ten thousand supporters and members of his congregation. Reverend C. L. Franklin is interred at the main mausoleum of Woodlawn Cemetery in Detroit.

TOM FISHER

See also Franklin, Aretha

Reference and Further Reading

Titon, Jeff Todd. *Give Me This Mountain: Life, History and Selected Sermons*. Foreword by Reverend Jesse L. Jackson. Urbana and Chicago: University of Illinois Press, 1989.

Discography

Except I Shall See in His Hands the Print of the Nails and Thrust My Hand into His Side (Chess LP-54).
I Heard It Through the Grapevine (Chess LP-73).
My Kingdom Is Not of This World (Chess LP-68).
Nothing Shall Separate Me from the Love of God (Chess LP-16).
Two Fishes and Five Loaves of Bread (Chess LP-28).
Ye Must Be Born Again (Chess LP-17).

FRYE, THEODORE R.

(b. September 10, 1899, Fayette, MO; d. August 26, 1963)

Theodore R. Frye moved to Chicago in 1927, looking for an opportunity to serve as a church musician. He was a trained composer, songwriter, and pianist, and he played the piano for "the Father of Gospel Music," Thomas A. Dorsey (1899–1993). Dorsey learned that Frye had a beautiful high baritone voice, so Dorsey played piano so that Frye could sing spirituals. The two became close friends, serving as codirectors of the junior choir at Ebenezer Baptist Church.

Frye and Dorsey were called "Professor" by church members because of their musical abilities. In 1932,

Frye became director of the Ebenezer Junior Choir. In 1933, the National Convention of Gospel Choirs and Choruses, Inc. (NCGCC) was formed by Dorsey along with Sallie Martin (1896–1988), Magnolia Lewis Butts (ca. 1880–1949), Frye, and Beatrice Brown. Each year the NCGCC convention was held in a different city. New songs were introduced and performed to allow choir directors to teach them to their local choirs. To help promote sales and give performances of the new "Chicago style" of gospel music, Martin and Frye formed the Martin–Frye Quartet of young men from Pilgrim Baptist Junior Choir.

In 1939, Kenneth Morris (1917–1988) transcribed Frye's song, "I'm Sending My Timber Up to Heaven," under the Morris and Bowles banner. It was a big success in the 1940s and again in the 1980s. In the 1940s, Frye became associated with "the Queen of Gospel," Mahalia Jackson (1911–1972), and Reverend Eugene D. Smallwood, a gospel musician and choir leader who owned his own music publishing company from 1931 to 1945. Smallwood was a composer/arranger of much of Dorsey and Frye's music, thereby allowing Frye and Dorsey time to train choirs.

Frye was the cofounder, with Dorsey, of the National Baptist Music Convention in 1948. The purpose was to train Baptist church musicians. Frye was a partner with Lillian Bowles and Dorsey in their publishing firms. In 1948, Frye founded Frye's Publishing. He is a pioneer who helped create the golden era of gospel music (1945–1955). The Smithsonian Institution has Frye's publishing collection as part of the American Music Collection.

SHERRY SHERROD DUPREE

Reference and Further Reading

Boyer, Horace Clarence. *How Sweet the Sound: The Golden Age of Gospel.* Washington, DC: Elliott & Clark, 1995.

DuPree, Sherry Sherrod; Herbert C. DuPree. *African-American Good News (Gospel) Music.* Washington, DC: Middle Atlantic Regional Press, 1993.

Reagon, Bernice Johnson. *We'll Understand It Better By and By.* Washington, DC: Smithsonian Institution, 1992.

Richardson, Deborra. *Eugene D. Smallwood Gospel Music Collection, 1931–1945.* Number 456. Washington, DC: Smithsonian Institution, 1992.

Discography

"Song Books." *Martin & Morris Music Company Records 1930–1985.* Number 492. Box 3, Folder 1, Frye Publishers; Box 4, Folder 7–8, Frye Publishers. Washington, DC: Smithsonian Institution.

FUNK, JOSEPH

(b. April 6, 1778, Berks County, PA; d. December 24, 1862, Singers Glen, VA)

Patriarch of a family of shape-note music teachers, composers, and publishers who were active in Virginia's Shenandoah Valley from at least 1816 until the 1940s, Joseph Funk was an active and influential singing teacher best known historically for publishing four-shape-note and, later, seven-shape-note tunebooks for the Shenandoah Valley's German- and English-speaking populations. He also published one of the South's first music periodicals. His sales and influence eventually extended far beyond the valley. Under the leadership of his grandson, Aldine S. Kieffer, who adhered to many of his grandfather's precepts, the family business became the clear leader in the growth and dissemination of shape-note and Southern gospel music.

Joseph was born to John and Barbara Showalter Funk, German-speaking Mennonites who, toward the end of the eighteenth century, moved from Eastern Pennsylvania into Virginia's Shenandoah Valley, settling near Harrisonburg. Joseph married Elizabeth Rhodes (anglicized from Roth) and built a homestead in an area he named Mountain Valley. When a post office was established there in 1860, the name was changed to Singers Glen in honor of Funk's successful music business. Although there is no evidence that Funk was formally educated, his publications and letters prove that he was facile with both the German and English languages, as well as with music. In 1816, at age thirty-eight, Funk compiled and published his first tunebook, a German-language, four-shape-note book entitled *Die allgemein nützliche Choral-Music* (printed in Harrisonburg by Laurentz Wartmann). In the standard oblong format, *Choral-Music* comprised mainly chorales taken from Mennonite and Lutheran sources. Also included, however, were four Anglo-American folk hymns from Ananias Davisson's *Kentucky Harmony* (Harrisonburg, 1816), published just a few months earlier. The tunes had two parts, bass and tenor only. *Choral-Music* apparently had no second edition.

In 1832 Funk published *A Compilation of Genuine Church Music*, a four-shape-note tunebook in English containing comparatively traditional, mostly Anglo-American tunes in three parts. This work was followed by multiple editions (ten by 1860). The first two editions were printed in Winchester; the third, in Harrisonburg. The fourth edition (1847) Funk published in his shop in Mountain Valley. His company, Joseph Funk & Sons, had two sons, Solomon and Benjamin, doing the printing, while Benjamin and another son, Timothy, bound the books. According to Jackson, sales of the first four editions totaled twenty-eight thousand copies.

For the fifth edition (1851), Funk changed the title to *Harmonia sacra, being a Compilation of Genuine Church Music* and the notation to a seven-shape system of his own design, though it was similar to those of Jesse Aikin (appeared in 1846) and Alexander Auld (appeared in 1847). This book was successful: as of 2004, *Harmonia sacra* was in its twenty-fifth edition (Intercourse, Pennsylvania: Good Books, 1993) and still in use, especially among the Mennonites of the Shenandoah Valley. Funk also established a monthly magazine, *The Southern Musical Advocate and Singer's Friend,* to advertise his music books and singing schools. He and his heirs claimed it was the first of its kind in the South. The periodical ran from July 1859 to April 1861, when it folded due to the outbreak of the Civil War. Funk also published *A Map or General Scale of Music* (printed in Philadelphia, 1847), a pedagogical aid for his singing schools.

Funk believed strongly that music should be sung by all members of a congregation as a participatory form of worship and consequently was opposed to paid or select choirs (and likely, to quartets). He understood congregational singing as a kind of musical democracy. Because he believed that shape notes were easier for the average citizen to learn to read and thus contributed to congregational singing; he preferred them to standard notation. Funk also appreciated the use of instruments in sacred music, contrary to his Mennonite background. He bequeathed these ideas to his grandson, Aldine Kieffer, who promoted them passionately as editor of *The Musical Million,* bequeathing them in turn to the Southern gospel tradition.

In honor of Funk's accomplishments, Alice Parker wrote an opera, *Singers Glen* (1978), based on his life.

STEPHEN SHEARON

See also Gospel Periodicals; Shape-Note Singing; Singing Schools

Reference and Further Reading

Eskew, Harry. "Joseph Funk's *Allgemein nützliche Choral-Music* (1816)." *Report of the Society for the History of the Germans in Maryland*, 32 (1966): 38–46.
———. "Shape-Note Hymnody in the Shenandoah Valley, 1816–1860." Ph.D. dissertation, Tulane University, 1966.
Goff, James R., Jr. *Close Harmony: A History of Southern Gospel.* Chapel Hill & London: University of North Carolina Press, 2002.
Horst, Irvin B. "Joseph Funk, Early Mennonite Printer and Publisher." *Mennonite Quarterly Review* 31 (1957): 260–280.
———. "Singers Glen, Virginia, Imprints, 1847–1878, a Checklist." *Eastern Mennonite College Bulletin* 44, no. 2 (1965): 6–14.
Jackson, George Pullen. *White Spirituals in the Southern Uplands.* Chapel Hill: University of North Carolina Press, 1933.
Wayland, John W. "Joseph Funk, Father of Song in Northern Virginia." *The Pennsylvania German* 12 (October 1911).

G

GAY SISTERS

Evelyn Gay (b. 1924; d. 1984)
Mildred "Millie" Gay-Chison (b. 1926; d. February 28, 2003)
Geraldine Gay-Hambric (b. 1931)

The Gay family hailed from Georgia. They moved to Chicago just after World War I. Jerry Gay, the father, ran two second-hand furniture stores and Fanny Parthenia Barnes, the mother, directed a choir at Elder Lucy Smith's All Nations Pentecostal Church on West 30th Street. Fanny was a major influence on her children: soon after World War II, she organized her three daughters into a singing group and had them schooled in harmony until they were ready to perform in public. Evelyn (alto, contralto) and Geraldine (tenor) had studied piano at an early age, and for all her talent, Geraldine became known later as "the Erroll Garner of gospel."

Evelyn and Mildred (tenor) began singing as a duet, with Evelyn also playing piano. One of their first engagements was in New York, where they befriended Professor James Earl Hines from Cleveland, who was directing a choir out of the Trinity Baptist Church in Brooklyn when they met. He encouraged the Gay Sisters to seek their fortunes out on the West Coast.

In 1948, the Gay Sisters, with Fanny serving both as manager and chaperone, traveled out to Los Angeles and attended both the Baptist Alliance and Ministerial Alliance meetings, where ministers could choose artists to feature on their church music programs. The Gays were regularly chosen, and that is how they were introduced to John Dolphin of Recorded-in-Hollywood Records. They recorded their first record in late 1949, but it was not successful, and by the summer of 1950 the Gays were back in Chicago, seeking a label to record them.

They tried Apollo Records in New York and then Gotham Records in Philadelphia, without success. But three months later, their luck changed: they were playing a church in Brooklyn and were introduced to Herman Lubinsky of Savoy Records in Newark, New Jersey. They signed a contract in March 1951 and recorded four songs with Herman Stevens on organ; the first single broke into the charts, and the Gay Sisters started to appear at major venues. At that time, the Gays had built a repertoire of intense Baptist and Dr. Watts hymns and sanctified shouts "right out of the 1920s" (Heilbut, 1985).

Evelyn wrote most of the scores, and the group played it straight and refused to let gimmicks and fancy showmanship get in the way of their act; they accepted, however, wearing colorful robes and sporting fancy hairdos. More Savoy sessions followed in May and July 1951, and the Gays played Carnegie Hall and toured Texas and California.

In early 1955, Evelyn was introduced to Decca Records, and the sisters, with their mother Fanny Parthenia and brother Preacher Gregory Donald, recorded a long session in the Decca studios, but only one single was released, in March. Poorly promoted, it did not get attention.

Throughout the mid-1950s, a lot of people tried to lure Evelyn away from her sisters and she was encouraged to lead her own group, but it was not successful, even if she became a regular on radio programs. In the early 1960s, the reunited Gay Sisters recorded vanity recordings on Evelyn's own P.E.A. label and toured occasionally. Then Evelyn formed a group called the Pilgrim Outlets and recorded a single for Faith. In 1966, Geraldine and Gregory Donald, labelled as the Gay Singers, recorded for Chess Records in Chicago, but only one single ever surfaced. The Gay Sisters' last major gig was an appearance at the 1976 Bicentennial celebration at the Smithsonian Institute in Washington, DC.

After Evelyn's death, Mildred stayed in show business, fronting a Dixieland band in the early 1990s and recording gospel songs for Tony Heilbut and Spirit Feel Records in 1993. In June and July 2004, Geraldine Gay, the last of the Gay Sisters still alive, recorded for The Sirens Records in Chicago; she played her jazz-influenced piano to accompany her singing brother Pastor Donald and her nephew Gregory, Jr.

ROBERT SACRÉ

Reference and Further Reading

Boyer, Horace Clarence. *How Sweet the Sound: The Golden Age of Gospel*. Washington, DC: Elliott & Clark, 1995.
Hayes, J. Cedric; Robert Laughton. *Gospel Records 1943–1969. A Black Music Discography*. 2 vols. London: Record Information Services, 1992.
Heilbut, Tony. *The Gospel Sound: Good News and Bad Times*. New York: Limelight, 1985.
Nations, Opal Louis. "The Gay Sisters." *Blues Gazette* (Belgium) 3 (Summer 1996): 18–19.
Sacré, Robert. "The Gay Sisters." *Blues Gazette* (Belgium) 3 (Summer 1996): 22.

Discography

The Soul of Chicago (1993, Shanachie/Spirit Feel CD 6008).
In the Right Hands: Chicago Gospel Keyboard Pioneers (2004, The Sirens Records SR-5010).

GIRARD, CHUCK

(b. August 27, 1943, Los Angeles, CA)

Chuck Girard became one of the architects of contemporary Christian music. He formed Love Song with Tommy Coomes, Jay Truax, and Fred Fields in 1970. Their self-titled debut album was an instant hit, attracting national media attention and propelling the group as one of the musical leaders of the emerging 1970s religious revival that was known as the Jesus Movement.

Prior to launching a career in Christian music, Girard experienced success as a member of several popular music groups while still a teenager, including the Casteels, who scored the top-twenty hits "Sacred" and "So I Love." He also worked as a studio musician in Hollywood and later joined the group the Hondells, providing lead vocals on their radio hit "Little Honda."

Success had a downside for Girard, and he found himself abusing alcohol and drugs. He spent some time in Las Vegas, performing in various groups on the famous Vegas strip, but returned to Orange County, California, and got a regular gig at a club called Gold Street as a member of the band Bigfoot. While living in Laguna Beach, he was invited to attend a small church called Calvary Chapel, led by Pastor Chuck Smith. Girard was drawn to the message of faith presented by Smith and was converted to Christianity.

Girard immediately turned his musical gifts to expressing his newfound faith. Soon he teamed with three friends to form Love Song, and their first performances were at Calvary Chapel Bible studies. "From the beginning, our idea was to compose and perform music that would be uncompromising in its content, yet contemporary in style," Girard recalls of his early writing for the group.

Love Song added guitarist Bob Wall to the group and recorded its first album for Good News Records. The 1972 self-titled debut *Love Song* was distributed by United Artist Records and included the popular songs written or cowritten by Chuck Girard, "A Love Song," "Two Hands," and "Little Country Church." The album spent more than a year as the nation's best-selling gospel album and Love Song performed that summer for a hundred thousand people in Dallas, Texas, at Campus Crusade's Explo '72 in the Cotton Bowl.

Following the release of their sophomore album in 1974, *Final Touch*, Love Song broke up and Chuck Girard pursued a solo career. He continued to record for Good News Records and his self-titled debut *Chuck Girard* was released in 1975. The album was well received and included the autobiographical "Rock 'n' Roll Preacher" and what became Girard's most popular song, "Sometimes Alleluia."

Girard followed his solo debut with *Glow in the Dark* (1976), *Written on the Wind* (1977), and *Take It Easy* (1979). Girard continued to release albums in the 1980s and 1990s, including *Name Above All Names*, *Fire and Light*, and *Voice of the Wind*. In 2004, Chuck Girard moved from Southern California to Nashville, Tennessee, with his wife Karen.

JAMES I. ELLIOTT

See also Love Song

Reference and Further Reading

Chuck Girard website, http://www.chuck.org.
Cusic, Don. *The Sound of Light: A History of Gospel Music.* Bowling Green, OH: Bowling Green State University Popular Press, 1990.
"History of Love Song." http://www.one-way.org/lovesong/history1.html.
Joseph, Mark. *The Rock & Roll Rebellion.* Nashville, TN: Broadman & Hollman, 1999.

Discography

Love Song

Love Song (1972, Ocean Records LP 701816698); *Final Touch* (1974, Ocean Records LP 701816694); *Feel the Love* (1977, Ocean Records Live LP 701817696); *Love Song Reunion* (2005, J&B Media WWMD1171; Legacy Series).

Chuck Girard

Chuck Girard (1975, Good News Records LP); *Glow in the Dark* (1976, Good News Records LP); *Written on the Wind* (1977, Good News Records LP); *Take It Easy* (1979, Good News Records LP); *The Stand* (1980 Good News Records LP); *All Those Years* (1983, Good News Records); *Name Above All Names* (1983, Seven Thunders Records CGCD-7001); *Fire & Light* (1991, Seven Thunders Records CGCD-7002); *Voice of the Wind* (1996, Seven Thunders Records CGCD-7003); *Chuck Girard Legacy Series: A Heart on Fire* (2005, J&B Media WWMD1170).

GLOBALIZATION OF GOSPEL

Spirituals and Traditional Gospel Spreads Around the World

Ever since the Fisk Jubilee Singers left Nashville to spread the concert spiritual across the globe, American sacred music has attracted a worldwide audience. The Fisk Singers departed for Europe in 1873, the same year that evangelist Dwight Moody and his song leader, Ira D. Sankey, began traveling throughout England spreading the Christian message through sermon and song (Cusic, 1990, 62; Boyer, 1995, 253). These two developments in the late nineteenth century mark the onset of the globalization of American gospel, which would continue throughout the twentieth and early twenty-first centuries.

The Fisk Jubilee Singers were led by George L. White, a music teacher and treasurer at Fisk University who formed the group as a means of raising funds for the newly founded institution. The ensemble toured through Europe, Africa, and Asia for seven years before returning to the United States. From 1884 to 1890, a restructured version of the Fisk Singers made another trip, this time under the leadership of Frederick Loudin. This tour included stops in India and Australia, as well as parts of East Asia (Erlmann, 1991, 24–26).

Within two months of the troupe's return to the United States, Orpheus McAdoo, a member of the ensemble, formed the Virginia Jubilee Singers, who subsequently set sail for England and spent most of the 1890s abroad, further introducing American sacred music to foreign listeners. Although the group struggled in Europe, their popularity soared during a three-year stay in Australia, as well as in South Africa, where they spent nearly five years (ibid, 26–35). Like other jubilee groups of that era, the Virginia Jubilee Singers incorporated classic minstrel tunes into their repertoire of spirituals (ibid, 27).

During the 1920s, jubilee quartets inspired by the Fisk Singers continued to travel abroad (Boyer, 1995, 253). By the 1930s, the seeds planted by these African American troupes began to yield noticeable fruit in South Africa, and Columbia Records captured four spirituals sung by the Wilberforce Institute vocal ensemble led by Dr. Francis Herman Gow in Johannesburg. Although these recorded performances were very similar in style to those of university-affiliated black vocal groups in the United States, they helped to launch a distinctly South African brand of quartet singing, exemplified by the Fort Hare–based Wesley House Quartette, and impacted the early creators of the Zulu vocal genre that came to be known as *isicathamiya* (Erlmann, 1991, 52–53).

After World War II, North American missionaries stepped up their worldwide proselytizing efforts. Just as Dwight Moody had teamed up with Ira Sankey in the late nineteenth century, evangelist Billy Graham joined forces with gospel singer George Beverly Shea, who became internationally renowned through his performances on radio and television, as well as through globally distributed recordings and appearances in Graham's overseas crusades (Cusic, 1990, 182).

In the 1950s, traditional gospel music began to have its deepest impact outside of the United States. The year 1953 was a watershed, as Mahalia Jackson embarked on a tour of Europe and the Golden Gate Quartet relocated there permanently. Both Jackson and Golden Gates experienced enormous success before European audiences, many of whom had grown to appreciate gospel sounds through radio, television, and records imported from the United States (Boyer, 1995, 253). During this time,

Jackson experienced her first huge international hit recording when "Silent Night" became a top seller in Norway (Cusic, 1990, 206).

The 1960s saw the further spread of American gospel music abroad. In 1962, a production of Langston Hughes's song-play, *Black Nativity*, featuring Marion Williams, Princess Stewart, and Alex Bradford, toured Europe. Clara Ward and the Ward Singers traveled to Europe and Asia during the same year (Heilbut, 1989, 110; Boyer, 1995, 253). Gospel music in Europe received a boost from two German concert promoters, Horst Lipmann and Fritz Rau, who organized a series of events known as the American Spirituals and Gospel Festival, beginning in 1965. Through broadcasts of these festivals on television and radio, American gospel artists such as Inez Andrews, the Five Blind Boys of Mississippi, Dorothy Norwood, and Cleophus Robinson were presented to German audiences (Grimmel, 1997).

As this decade came to a close, American gospel artists and their recordings had circulated the globe, impacting numerous musical landscapes and influencing an array of popular artists. For example, the recordings of Sam Cooke and the Soul Stirrers were featured on Caribbean radio stations and helped to shape the sound of popular Jamaican vocalist Toots Hibbert of the Maytals (Bilby, 1995, 171). Jamaican gospel artists such as the Grace Thrillers, Gloria Bailey, and Claudelle Clark were also strongly influenced by gospel music stemming from the United States.

Gospel's Ongoing Global Impact, 1970–Present

In the late 1960s and early 1970s, as Edwin Hawkins and Andrae Crouch burst onto the gospel music scene with their smoother, R&B-inflected style, they made waves that went beyond the boundaries of North America. Crouch has performed in Norway on numerous occasions, working with local choirs such as the Oslo Gospel Choir and the Reflex Choir (Aanestad, 1997). Hawkins, along with artists such as Richard Smallwood, Walt Whitman, and Daryl Coley, has been featured in Norway's Seaside Gospel Choir Festival. Modeled after the Gospel Music Workshop of America since the late 1980s, this annual event continues to draw prominent gospel performers from the United States.

Scandinavian countries remained among the most popular European destinations for contemporary gospel artists in the late twentieth century. The Oak Ridge Boys toured Sweden in 1970 (Cusic, 1990, 260), and Danniebelle Hall recorded an album with Swedish gospel choir Choralern for the gospel label Sparrow in 1977. Several choirs have emerged in Sweden since the 1980s. The sixty-member Stockholm-based ensemble Source of Joy was founded in 1993 and has gained esteem through its recordings and travels to Norway, England, and the United States during the late 1990s and early 2000s (Wickberg and Hagen, 1997).

Contemporary North American gospel artists continue to have a global reach, both through widely disseminated recordings and also through appearances at gospel festivals held around the world. Many have appeared throughout the Caribbean at venues such as Jamaica's Fun in the Son Festival and Barbados's Gospelfest. The latter festival, which was first held in 1993, has featured singers such as Yolanda Adams, Alvin Slaughter, Kurt Carr, Donnie McClurkin, and Trin-i-tee 5:7, along with a host of popular Caribbean-based gospel artists. In the early 2000s, the Brooklyn Tabernacle Choir began performing in Jamaica before enthusiastic audiences who were well familiar with their music through radio.

In Australia, gospel music remains very popular, and a number of choirs have worked to incorporate American gospel sounds into localized musical expressions of the Christian message. Australian-based record labels such as Maranatha! Music produce some of the world's most successful contemporary Christian artists, whose songs are heard in churches throughout North America. Formed in 1986, the Café of the Gate of Salvation has become one of Australia's most successful gospel choirs (Johnson, 2002, 101). In 1999, this choir traveled to the United States and performed in black churches in Birmingham, New Orleans, and New York City (ibid, 115).

When the black gospel musical *Mama I Want to Sing* came to Japan in the 1980s, it marked the beginning of a gospel boom in this predominantly Buddhist country (Haranoh, 1997). With advances in technology and the globalization of Hollywood films, such as *Sister Act* and *The Preacher's Wife,* gospel music made huge inroads in Japan during the 1990s. Edwin Hawkins, Daryl Coley, Take 6, and the Mississippi Mass Choir are among the many artists who have performed there. African American musicians often travel or relocate to Japan, where they have been instrumental in the rising popularity of black gospel music. For example, Ronald Rucker and Alexander Easely migrated to Japan in the late 1970s and have worked steadily by conducting gospel workshops and directing Japanese gospel choirs such as the Bright Lights Gospel Choir, which performs throughout the country (Barrager, 1999).

As American gospel music migrates from the United States to various countries throughout the world, local practitioners often do more than simply imitate the stylings of foreign performers. Rather, gospel music often takes on the flavor of the sociomusical community in which it becomes situated. For example, the South Africa–based Soweto Gospel Choir emerged in 2002 and has since begun recording and touring extensively around the world. The group, which earned the prize for Best Gospel Choir at the 2003 American Gospel Music Awards, sings with a distinctly South African flavor that nonetheless draws from the Western spiritual tradition. In the United States, gospel artist Dickson Guillaume formed the Haitian Interdenominational Mass Choir in the early 1990s. This ensemble, which has been featured at Cornell University's annual Festival of Black Gospel, has a diverse repertoire of songs in English and Haitian Creole.

It is also true that contemporary American gospel artists have increasingly begun to explicitly incorporate foreign styles into their compositions and arrangements, often featuring diverse sounds on their recordings to appeal to a wide array of listeners. For example, Kirk Franklin's debut CD features the song "Speak to Me, Lord Jesus," which draws on Caribbean rhythms and accents. The "Caribbean Medley" on Donnie McClurkin's recording *Live in London and More* (2000) uses Jamaican reggae and dance hall rhythms throughout. The globalization of gospel thus involves not only the worldwide spread of this music but also its localization by musicians and audiences situated around the globe and the steady appropriation of global sounds by North America–based gospel musicians.

MELVIN L. BUTLER

See also Adams, Yolanda; Andrews, Inez; Bradford, Alex; Brooklyn Tabernacle Choir; Cooke, Sam; Crouch, Andrae; Fisk Jubilee Singers; Five Blind Boys of Mississippi; Golden Gate Quartet, The; Gospel Music Workshop of America; Hall, Danniebelle; Jackson, Mahalia; McClurkin, Donnie; Norwood, Dorothy; Oak Ridge Boys; Robinson, Cleophus; Sankey, Ira David; Shea, George Beverly; Soul Stirrers; Take 6; Ward Trio (Ward Singers); Williams, Marion

Reference and Further Reading

Aanestad, Ragnhild Hiis. "Gospel Around the World: Norway." 1997. http://www.gospelflava.com/articles/gospelaroundtheworld-norway.html (accessed December 4, 2004).
Barrager, Davis. "Spreading the Gospel of Gospel in Japan." *Japan Times* (1999). http://www.ronruck.com/e/index.html.
Bilby, Kenneth. "Jamaica." In *Caribbean Currents: Caribbean Music from Rumba to Reggae*, edited by Peter Manuel, 143–182. Philadelphia, PA: Temple University Press, 1995.
Boyer, Horace Clarence. *How Sweet the Sound: The Golden Age of Gospel*. Washington, DC: Elliott & Clark, 1995.
Cusic, Don. *The Sound of Light: A History of Gospel Music*. Bowling Green, OH: Bowling Green State University Popular Press, 1990.
Erlmann, Veit. *African Stars: Studies in Black South African Performance*. Chicago: University of Chicago Press, 1991.
Grimmel, Bernd. "Gospel Around the World: Germany (Part I: History)." 1997. http://www.gospelflava.com/articles/gospelaroundtheworld-germany1.html (accessed December 4, 2004).
———. Sebastian Hentsch. "Gospel Around the World: Germany (Part II: Influences)." 1997. http://www.gospelflava.com/articles/gospelaroundtheworld-germany2.html (accessed December 4, 2004).
Haranoh, Nobuko. "The Rising Popularity of Gospel." Translated by Manami Oshima with Ronald Rucker. *Weekly Aera*. 1997. http://www.ronruck.com/e/index.html (accessed December 4, 2004).
Heilbut, Anthony. *The Gospel Sound: Good News and Bad Times*. Third Limelight Edition. New York: Proscenium Publishers, 1989.
Johnson, E. Patrick. "Performing Blackness Down Under: The Café of the Gate of Salvation." *Text and Performance Quarterly* 22, no. 2 (April 2002): 99.
Taylor, Timothy D. *Global Pop: World Music, World Markets*. New York: Routledge, 1997.
Wickberg, Lena; Marie Hagen. "Gospel Around the World: Sweden." 1997. http://www.gospelflava.com/articles/gospelaroundtheworld-sweden.html (accessed December 4, 2004).

GOLDEN GATE QUARTET, THE

The Great Jubilee Innovators

Jubilee music in the late 1920s was little different than it had been in the 1880s. In the 1930s, two quartets changed everything: the Mills Brothers and the Golden Gate Jubilee Quartet. The Mills Brothers paved the way for all the great doo-wop, R&B, and gospel quartets to come by introducing jazzier, "swing"-style arrangements, a New Orleans–influenced "pump bass," and an uncanny ear for vocally imitating not just jazz instruments, but also jazz solos. The Golden Gate Quartet (the group dropped the word "Jubilee" from their name in 1940) took the Mills Brothers' innovations a step further and—along with Sister Rosetta Tharpe—were the "face" of gospel music to the public until the advent of Mahalia Jackson.

The Golden Gate Jubilee Quartet was founded in a Norfolk, Virginia, barbershop in around 1930 and quickly became popular by adding a soulful gospel intensity to the Mills Brothers' vocal harmonies. The Gates achieved acclaim from both white and black audiences up and down the East Coast when they began broadcasting on Charlotte, North Carolina's clear-channel WBT. In the beginning, the group

The Golden Gate Quartet. Photo courtesy Frank Driggs Collection.

wrapped its rich, complex harmonies—which often incorporated ad-libs, improvisations, and the occasional falsetto—around familiar spirituals and hymns. The ever-enterprising Gates quickly became one of the first groups to add the new gospel songs of Thomas Dorsey, Lucie Campbell, and W. Herbert Brewster to their repertoire; it is believed that they may have been one of the first full-time professional groups in gospel.

The group was signed to Victor Records' race imprint Bluebird in 1937, and their first session produced an unexpected—but quickly imitated—hit, a comic, rhythmic retelling of the story of Jonah. From there, the Gates produced a steady stream of hits for Bluebird, which culminated in a performance on NBC's *Magic Key Hour* later that year—one of the first appearances by an African American group on national radio. The Gates soon became the idol—then the model—for innumerable African American quartets, even as hits such as "Noah," "Shadrack," "Samson," and others followed.

Talent scout extraordinaire John Hammond personally selected them to sing in the second of his influential "From Spirituals to Swing" concerts in New York in 1939. They also became one of the first African American groups to perform before racially mixed audiences in New York's Café Society, often accompanied by Lester Young's group. Shortly after Eleanor Roosevelt's famous encounter with the Daughters of the American Revolution over Marian Anderson's proposed appearance in Constitution Hall, Roosevelt was instrumental in scheduling the Golden Gate Quartet to appear at her husband Franklin Delano Roosevelt's inaugural gala in 1941, also at Constitution Hall. The group also recorded several sides with folk singer Leadbelly, which were released later that year on the Victor label.

During the war, the Gates recorded V-Discs for the Armed Forces Radio Services and sang regularly for "The AFRS Jubilee," as well as continuing to release hits in both the gospel and popular marketplaces—including "Coming In on a Wing and a Prayer" and "Stalin Wasn't Stallin'." The group also appeared in several motion pictures during this period, including *Star-Spangled Rhythm* (1943) and *Hollywood Canteen* (1944).

But public tastes changed in the years following World War II, and the Golden Gate Quartet eventually moved to France in 1959, where they enjoyed a two-year run at the Casino de Paris. The Gates continued to perform in Europe before packed houses for another thirty years, recording more than fifty albums for EMI-UK, Pathe-Marconi in France, and EMI-Germany. The State Department also continued to book the Gates as "goodwill ambassadors" for the United States, sending them on long tours throughout Africa and Asia.

The Golden Gate Quartet's legacy as the most popular jubilee group in the United States remains unchallenged, and their innovations in storytelling, rhythm, improvisation, and harmony were an important step in the founding of modern gospel music.

ROBERT DARDEN

See also Brewster, William Herbert; Campbell, Lucie; Dorsey, Thomas; Jackson, Mahalia; Tharpe, Sister Rosetta

Reference and Further Reading

Boyer, Horace. *How Sweet the Sound: The Golden Age of Gospel*, Washington DC: Elliott & Clark Publishing, 1995.
Buchanan, Samuel Carroll. "A Critical Analysis of Style in Four Black Jubilee Quartets in the United States." Ph.D. dissertation, New York University, 1987.
Dent, Cedric. "The Harmonic Development of the Black Religious Quartet Singing Tradition." Ph.D. dissertation, University of Maryland at College Park, 1997.
Heilbut, Anthony. *The Gospel Sound: Good News and Bad Times*. New York: Limelight Editions, 1997.
Lornell, Kip. *Happy in the Service of the Lord: Afro-American Gospel Quartets in Memphis*. Urbana: University of Illinois Press, 1988.
"Obituaries: Orlandus Wilson." *Times* (London) (January 29, 1999): Sec. 1F, 27.
Rubman, Kerill. "From 'Jubilee' to 'Gospel' in Black Male Quartet Singing." MA thesis, University of North Carolina at Chapel Hill, 1980.
Shaw, Arnold. *Black Popular Music in America: From the Spirituals, Minstrels and Ragtime to Soul, Disco and Hip-Hop*. New York: Schirmer Books, 1986.
Warner, Jay. *The Billboard Book of American Singing Groups: A History 1940–1990*. New York: Billboard Books, 1992.

Discography

Golden Gate Jubilee Quartet: Complete Recorded Works in Chronological Order, Vol. 1, 1937–1938 (Document).
Golden Gate Jubilee Quartet: Complete Recorded Works in Chronological Order, Vol. 2, 1938–1939 (Document).
Golden Gate Jubilee Quartet: Complete Recorded Works in Chronological Order, Vol. 3, 1939–1940 (Document).
Golden Gate Quartet: Complete Recorded Works in Chronological Order, Vol. 4, 1941–1944 (Document).
Golden Gate Quartet: Complete Recorded Works in Chronological Order, Vol. 5, 1945–1949 (Document).

With Josh White

Freedom: The Golden Gate Quartet and Josh White in Concert (Great Performances from the Library of Congress, Vol. 14).

GOOD SHEPHERD QUARTET, THE

David M. Fannon (b. October 30, 1946)
Michael Mooney (b. October 2, 1944)
James Clark (b. July 4, 1950)
James Hartsock (b. November 30, 1955)

The Good Shepherd Quartet of Pennington Gap, Virginia, with their brand of archaic mountain quartet singing with guitar accompaniment (or sometimes *a cappella*), have won considerable recognition over the years with their traditional vocal harmonies. As one member observed, "We sing the old style that was sung here in these mountains back fifty or sixty years . . . . We sing shape notes which is sort of a dying thing." Originally singing *a cappella,* they did eventually add a regular and a bass guitar when they had their first personnel change. However, about a third of their recordings are done with no instrumentation. Although they have a few original songs in their repertoire, most of their material comes from the old quartet hymnals, such as those of Vaughn and especially of Stamps–Baxter.

The original members of the Good Shepherd Quartet as formed in 1982 were David Fannon, lead vocal; Michael Mooney, bass vocal and bass guitar; Millard Fannon; and Betty Kirk. After Millard Fannon and Betty Kirk dropped out in 1984, they were replaced by James Hartsock, tenor vocal and guitar, and James Clark, baritone vocal. David Fannon has been described as the quartet's "diehard traditionalist" and the driving force behind their devotion to the older style. Because all the members hold regular jobs, they play only about two weekends per month.

Beginning in 1985, they started making a series of recordings at Maggard Studios in Big Stone Gap, Virginia, which now number twenty-one. Their first recordings were issued on cassettes, but they soon added compact discs. They have also done three videos. One of the older numbers they sang, "Hiding from the Storm Outside," was picked and recorded by Doyle Lawson. They have appeared twice on the Grand Ole Opry, in 1995 and 1998. Michael Mooney handled the business chores for the Good Shepherds for several years, but in 1999, David Fannon took over those chores.

IVAN M. TRIBE

Reference and Further Reading

Powell, Wayde. "Singing for the Good Shepherd." *Precious Memories: Journal of Gospel Music* 1, no. 5 (January–February 1989): 30–32.

Tribe, Ivan M. "The Good Shepherd Quartet: They Like the Old-Time Way." *Bluegrass Unlimited* (forthcoming).

Discography

Past and Present I (1991, MS 32091).
Past and Present II (1992, MS 32092).
Keepin' It Simple (1993, MS 32093).
Heaven Is My Home (2001, MS 01472).
Sacred Tones of Yesteryear (2001, MS 01332).
Whisper My Name in Prayer (2003, MS 03042).

"GOSPEL BOOGIE"

"Gospel Boogie" was one of the first modern gospel compositions to break from the traditional seven-shape-note songbook style and to utilize elements of pop and rhythm and blues. Recorded by numerous singers in the early 1950s, it became one of the best-selling gospel records of all time and won even greater fame in 1958, when pop singer Pat Boone recorded it under the name "A Wonderful Time up There" and took it into the top ten of the *Billboard* charts. Though controversial when it first emerged in the late 1940s, the song today has acquired the status of a Southern gospel classic.

The song originated with a popular Atlanta-area group, the Homeland Harmony Quartet; in 1945 they were joined by Lee Roy Abernathy, a pianist and composer, and a shrewd promoter who saw gospel quartet singing as show business. Abernathy soon became their manager and attracted attention for them first when, in 1947, he wrote and had the group record a topical song about a tragic fire in Atlanta's Winecoff Hotel.

Breaking from the older gospel songbook publishers such as Stamps–Baxter and Vaughan, Abernathy began publishing his new songs in sheet music form. In November 1947 he copyrighted "Gospel Boogie," and the Homeland Harmony Quartet recorded it for the independent White Church label a few months later. It came out at a time when country music was being swamped with various up-tempo songs such as "Cherokee Boogie" and quickly became a best-seller; though advertisements in *Billboard* were to claim sales of more than two million, members of the quartet say the actual sales were closer to two hundred thousand—still remarkable by gospel standards of the day. Soon major stars such as Red Foley, Sister Rosetta Tharpe, Wally Fowler, and the Pilgrim Travelers were rushing out cover versions.

To traditional gospel fans who were upset at the jazz and blues connotations of the word "boogie," Abernathy replied that "boogie" was just another word for "rhythm" and that he was "inspired to write it. I felt it was one way of reaching distant places where no ministers go."

CHARLES K. WOLFE

Reference and Further Reading

Wolfe, Charles K. "'Gospel Boogie': White Southern Gospel Music in Transition, 1945–55." In *Popular Music I: Folk or Popular? Distinctions, Influences, Continuities*, edited by Richard Middleton and David Horn. Cambridge, UK: Cambridge University Press, 1981.

GOSPEL CHOIRS

Origins and Early Development

Although the Fisk Jubilee Singers toured internationally as an eleven-member group in the late nineteenth century, they, along with many other college-affiliated vocal groups, had reduced their numbers by the early 1900s to become one of several sacred quartets in the United States. The newly founded National Baptist Convention played a highly significant role in the ongoing formation of larger vocal ensembles dedicated to musical articulation of the gospel message. By 1916, composer and educator Lucie Campbell had begun to take on leadership responsibilities at the annual convention, working as music director for mass choirs of up to one thousand members and writing songs for various pageants and musicals (Darden, 2004, 163). Campbell had a major influence on the style and repertory of songs used not only at the Convention, but also in churches around the United States, where choirs often sought to learn pieces that Campbell had recently introduced (Boyer, 1995, 139).

During the 1900s and 1910s, many African American church leaders in the North sought trained music directors to organize choirs that would add prestige and social respectability to their ministries. Achieving the goal of cultural advancement meant leaving behind the vestiges of slavery and the folk spiritual in favor of the more refined, "sophisticated" music from the European classical tradition. Hence, many Baptist choirs eschewed the highly demonstrative expressions of the Sanctified black church, choosing instead to perform works by composers such as Handel, Bach, and Mendelssohn. Church leaders began to recognize that music rivaled preaching as

The Abyssinian Baptist Choir, Newark, New Jersey, 1961. Photo courtesy Frank Driggs Collection.

a tool for attracting members, and some even hired orchestras to accompany the singing as part of their efforts to compete with area churches (Harris, 1992, 106).

Unlike many of his predecessors in the church music arena, who tended to favor a European classical aesthetic, Thomas Dorsey inflected his choral compositions with a blues flavor that was highly controversial, yet extremely appealing to the increasing numbers of Pentecostal and Baptist churchgoers, many of whom had migrated to northern cities from the deep South. After Dorsey moved to Chicago in 1921, he had a profound impact on the evolution of church choirs in the United States, writing songs that became nationally known and emblematic of a more modern gospel sound.

During the 1930s, Dorsey formed choirs that sometimes grew alongside the existing "senior" church choirs, which continued to sing in the traditional styles preferred by more conservative Baptists. Such was the case at Ebenezer Baptist Church in Chicago, where Dorsey organized a gospel choir in 1931. The following year, Pilgrim Baptist Church featured a similar choir, which Dorsey also had formed. In 1932, Dorsey was also elected president of the National Convention of Gospel Choirs and Choruses. During the 1930s and early 1940s, he toured with Sallie Martin, the convention's secretary, who helped to form dozens of choirs across the United States and increase the popularity of Dorsey's compositions (Darden, 2004, 170–173).

While amateur church choirs proliferated throughout the United States during the Great Depression and in the years preceding the Second World War, a few ensembles managed to achieve professional status. Wings Over Jordan was formed by Glenn Settle at Cleveland's Gethsemane Baptist Church and earned a reputation as a refined choir capable of singing in a variety of styles ranging from Negro spirituals to classic hymns. With as many as forty members, the choir began singing on local radio, eventually garnering national attention through a ten-year stint (1937–1947) on the CBS network's *Wings Over Jordan* weekly radio broadcast (Boyer, 1995, 182). Under the direction of J. Earle Hines, the St. Paul Baptist Church Choir—also known as Echoes of Eden—became one of the first professional choirs to make commercial records during the 1940s, and they had a successful radio show in Los Angeles (Darden, 2004, 271; Boyer, 1995, 206).

With greater participation in choir conventions, more widespread access to technologies such as the phonograph and radio, and the onset of the Civil Rights Movement, community choirs became increasingly popular after World War II (Jackson, 1995, 193). In the late 1940s, an eighteen-year-old Milton Brunson first organized the Chicago-based Thompson Community Singers (also known as the Tommies), which would become one of the oldest and most respected professional choirs of the twentieth century. As the bass guitar became more frequently used as an accompanying instrument, some choral arrangers found the bass vocal part redundant and chose to use three harmony parts (soprano, alto, tenor) instead of four. One of the earliest professional choirs to embrace this three-part texture was the Voices of Hope Choir, organized in 1957 by Thurston Gilbert Frazier (Boyer, 1995, 182).

Change and Continuity: 1960–Present

As the Civil Rights Movement heated up, professional "freedom choirs" were formed and organized in various parts of the United States by members of the Student Nonviolent Coordinating Committee (SNCC). One such group, the nationally known Freedom Singers, was founded in 1962 and eventually performed with vocalists Mahalia Jackson and Marian Anderson. Freedom choirs such as the Selma Freedom Choir and Carlton Reese's Gospel Freedom Choir of the Alabama Christian Movement (also known as the Birmingham Choir) performed mostly on black college campuses during the 1960s and were devoted to increasing awareness of the civil rights struggle.

By the 1960s, "Professor" Alex Bradford had become the director of Newark's Abyssinian Baptist Church choir, with whom he recorded the album *Shakin' the Rafters* (Darden, 2004, 267). Bradford's influence on the religious choral music was widespread; however, James Cleveland, his most renowned protégé, had an even more profound impact on the development of mass gospel choirs in the United States. The 1950s and 1960s saw Cleveland begin a steady rise to gospel stardom. He composed hundreds of songs, such as his 1960 hit "The Love of God," which he recorded with the Detroit-based choir Voices of Tabernacle (Heilbut, 1971, 211).

Cleveland worked with an array of established gospel soloists and groups, including the Caravans, before moving from Chicago to Southern California in 1962. He continued to achieve nationwide recognition through Savoy Records, which featured him with mass choirs from around the country. During the 1960s, he recorded his well-known song "God Has Smiled on Me" with Detroit's Prayer Tabernacle Choir. The New Jersey–based First Baptist Church Choir sang with Cleveland on his 1963 release, *Peace Be Still*, which sold over one million copies (Heilbut, 1971, 270–271).

Cleveland helped sustain interest in the mass choir movement through the Gospel Music Workshop of America, which he founded in 1968 (Darden, 2004, 272). Along with his Southern California Community Choir, Cleveland influenced generations of gospel singers, composers, and choir directors, such as Mattie Moss Clark, who recorded with both the Southwest Michigan State Choir and also the Church of God in Christ (COGIC) Convocation Choir during the 1960s (Boyer, 1995, 126–127).

As the 1970s brought newer, more contemporary vocal styles, COGIC singers and songwriters continued to play a major role in the ongoing evolution of gospel choirs in the United States. One of the most famous COGIC groups to emerge from this period was the Love Center Choir, directed by Walter Hawkins. The choir's 1975 debut album, *Love Alive I*, which featured "Going Up Yonder," led by Tramaine Hawkins, became one of the top-selling gospel recordings of the 1970s. The Hawkins family set the stage for the ensuing decades, during which a number of regionally based choirs were formed, such as the Georgia Mass Choir, which performed with Whitney Houston in the 1996 film *The Preacher's Wife*, and the world-renowned Mississippi Mass Choir, which earned increased recognition during the 1990s through their work with Rev. James Moore.

Some choirs gained popularity largely through charismatic leaders, such as Memphis-based O'Landa Draper, who organized the Associates in 1986, and James Hall, who founded Worship and Praise the following year in New York City. Both of these choirs experienced their greatest commercial successes during the 1990s. Draper and the Associates were often referred to as "the choir of the 90s," and they appeared with singer Billy Joel during the 1994 Grammy Awards (Collins, 1998, 4). Both Hezekiah Walker's Love Fellowship Crusade Choir and the New Life Community Choir, under the direction of eminent singer–songwriter Reverend John P. Kee, became well known during this time.

One of the most prolific singers, composers, and choir leaders of the 1980s and early 1990s was Thomas Whitfield, who directed and composed more than two hundred songs for his choir, the Whitfield Company. Many contemporary gospel artists, such as Yolanda Adams, Kirk Franklin, and Fred Hammond, acknowledge the creative influence of Whitfield, also known as "The Maestro," on their musical growth and professional careers. The 1990s saw the development of more state- and city-based choirs such as the Colorado Mass Choir, led by Joe Pace, and the multiethnic Brooklyn Tabernacle Choir, directed by Carol Cymbala. Milton Brunson's years of hard work reaped dividends, as his Thompson Community Choir won numerous accolades during the decade and helped popularize the use of jazzy horn arrangements.

Whitfield's legacy of musical refinement and heartfelt worship was continued by his ensemble members and by gifted musicians such as Richard Smallwood. As a student at Howard University in the late 1960s, Smallwood had played an instrumental role in the emergence of what became the first campus-organized college gospel choir in the United States. A classically trained pianist and arranger, Smallwood became internationally known in the 1990s as he showcased his exceptional compositional prowess through his choir, Vision. One of his best-known choral compositions, "Total Praise," was featured on his 1996 recording, *Adoration: Richard Smallwood, Live in Atlanta*, which received widespread acclaim among gospel music enthusiasts.

Gospel choirs continued to perform and record during the late 1990s and at the turn of the century. However, the popularity of smaller gospel ensembles, such as those led by contemporary artists such as Kurt Carr and Donnie McClurkin, began to surpass that of the larger mass choirs that dominated previous decades.

MEL R. WILHOIT

See also Angelic Gospel Singers; Brooklyn Tabernacle Choir; Gospel Music Workshop of America; Gospel Quartets; Malaco Records; Mississippi Mass Choir; National Convention of Gospel Choirs and Choruses; Southern California Community Choir; St. Paul Baptist Church Choir of Los Angeles

Reference and Further Reading

Boyer, Horace Clarence. *How Sweet the Sound: The Golden Age of Gospel*. Washington, DC: Elliott & Clark, 1995.

Collins, Lisa. "Gospel Choir Stalwart O'Landa Draper Dies." *Billboard*, 110/31 (August 1, 1998).

Cusic, Don. *The Sound of Light: A History of Gospel Music*. Bowling Green, OH: Bowling Green State University Popular Press, 1990.

Davis, Danny K. "Tribute to Rev. Milton Brunson." House of Representatives (Extension of Remarks, April 24, 1997). http://thomas.loc.gov/cgi-bin/query/z?r105: E24AP7-221 (accessed February 18, 2005).

Darden, Robert. *People Get Ready!: A New History of Black Gospel Music*. New York: Continuum Press, 2004.

Harris, Michael W. *The Rise of the Gospel Blues: The Music of Thomas Andrew Dorsey in the Urban Church*. New York: Oxford University Press, 1992.

Heilbut, Anthony. *The Gospel Sound: Good News and Bad Times*. New York: Limelight Editions, 1971.

Jackson, Joyce Marie. "The Changing Nature of Gospel Music: A Southern Case Study." *The African American Review* 29, no. 2 (1995): 185.

"Lest We Forget: Legends of Detroit Gospel, A Virtual Exhibit. Minister Thomas Anthony Whitfield." http://www.museum.msu.edu/museum/tes/gospel/whitfield.htm (accessed February 17, 2005).

Love Center Ministries, Inc. "About Us." http://www.lovecenter.org/ (accessed February 17, 2005).

Selected Discography

The Abyssinian Baptist Choir under the Direction of Professor Alex Bradford. *Shakin' the Rafters* (1991, Sony 47335; originally released 1960).

Milton Brunson and the Thompson Community Choir. *Available to You* (1991, Sony 47761; originally released 1988).

New Life Community Choir featuring John P. Kee. *Wash Me* (1994, Jive 43004).

O'Landa Draper and the Associates. *Above and Beyond* (1991, Sony 48687).

Reverend James Cleveland and the Angelic Choir, Vol. 3. *Peace Be Still* (1995, Savoy 14076; recorded in 1962).

Richard Smallwood with Vision. *Adoration: Richard Smallwood, Live in Atlanta* (1996, Jive 43015).

Walter Hawkins and the Love Center Choir. *Love Alive, Vol. 1* (1993, Platinum Ent. 161012; originally released 1975).

Thomas Whitfield. *Alive and Satisfied* (1992, Platinum Ent. 8533).

Compilations

Chicago Mass Choir. *The Best of the Chicago Mass Choir*. (1995, Platinum Ent. 16116).

Georgia Mass Choir. *Greatest Hits* (1996, Savoy 7123); *Gospel's Heavenly Choirs* (1999, K-Tel 4319).

Mississippi Mass Choir. *Greatest Hits* (1995, Malaco 6021); *The World's Greatest Choirs. Vol. II* (1995, HOB Records HBD3537).

GOSPEL HARMONY BOYS

Original Members:
Leonard Adams (b. January 8, 1922; d. May 30, 2002)
Harold Lane
John Embry
J. B. Short

This Southern gospel quartet spent half a century (1952–2002) ministering in song to audiences primarily east of the Mississippi River in the United States as well as giving occasional performances in Canada and the Bahamas.

Huntington, West Virginia, natives Leonard Adams and Harold Lane, who would later perform with the Homeland Harmony Quartet and the Speer Family, founded this quartet in 1952 so they could explore different styles of harmony in praising God. Lane sang lead; Adams served as first tenor. John Embry and J. B. Short completed this quartet as the baritone and bass.

The Gospel Harmony Boys earned a pair of distinctions in the history of televised Southern gospel music. They were the first Southern gospel group to perform on a live network television broadcast. They achieved this milestone when Dave Garroway invited them to perform on NBC's *Today Show* in the early 1950s. Additionally, they were the first Southern gospel group to host a weekly television show, *Gospel Harmony Time* (1954–1971).

Television was not the only venue through which the quartet expressed their message. They released records under their own label, Gospel Harmony Records. They issued their first single, "Mercy, Lord," in 1953 and their first album, *I'm Redeemed,* in 1961. Another album of note is 1965's *Presenting The Cathedral Quartet, Mariner's Quartet, Gospel Harmony Boys,* a record consisting of four songs sung by each group.

Membership in the quartet changed as the years progressed, yet individuals such as Homer Fry and Clacy Williams performed with the group for more than a quarter of a century. In 2002, the last members of the Gospel Harmony Boys—Will Adkins, Rusty Phillips, Rod Taylor, and Greg Tingler—decided to disband the quartet because of other demands upon the members' daily lives.

The Gospel Harmony Boys issued their last album, *Live in Mississippi,* in 2001 and their last radio release, "He's in the House," in 2002. The group reorganized in 2004 under the leadership of Clacy Williams.

WILLIAM E. PLANTS

See also Cathedral Quartet; Homeland Harmony Quartet; Speer Family, The

Reference and Further Reading

Adams, Oleta. Widow of Leonard Adams. Telephone interview with author, March 27, 2003.
Fry, Homer. Former member of the Gospel Harmony Boys. Telephone interview with author, March 25, 2003.
Lane, Harold. Founder of the Gospel Harmony Boys. Telephone interview with author, March 24, 2003.
Tingler, Greg. Later leader of the Gospel Harmony Boys. Telephone interview with author, March 24, 26, and 31, 2003.
Williams, Clacy. Former member of Gospel Harmony Boys. Telephone interview with author, March 29 and April 1, 2003.

Discography

"Mercy, Lord"/"His Hand in Mine" (1953, Gospel Harmony Records; originally issued as a 78 and later reissued as a 45).

I'm Redeemed (1961, Gospel Harmony Records LP 6101).
Presenting The Cathedral Quartet, Mariner's Quartet, Gospel Harmony Boys (1965, Gospel Harmony Records SELP 6502).
Live in Mississippi (2001, Gospel Harmony Boys 5689 Cassette/CD).

GOSPEL MOVIES

As a particularly visual musical form, gospel music has intrigued filmmakers since the early days of cinema, but successful films featuring spirituals, black gospel, or Southern gospel music have been few and far between.

Spirituals and Black Gospel

Unfortunately, because both genres have always been composed of predominantly African American audiences and artists, white filmmakers have generally avoided the topic. As for the flourishing black cinema of the 1930s to 1950s—the obvious home for African American religious music—only a small percentage of the known titles have survived. Among those that do, *The Blood of Jesus* (1941) contains numerous renditions of spirituals by "The Heavenly Choir," including "Go Down, Moses" and "Steal Away to Jesus." Also featuring spirituals and gospel music are *Going to Glory, Come to Jesus* (1947), *Sunday Sinners* (1940), and the short film *Broken Earth* (1939).

Still, some early Hollywood films do include at least some religious music, including King Vidor's *Hallelujah!* (1929), *The Song of Freedom* (1936), *The Green Pastures* (1936), and the famed *Cabin in the Sky* (1943), director Vincente Minnelli's first film. *The Green Pastures* and several other early films feature music by the Hall Johnson Choir. The jubilee-singing Golden Gate Quartet have featured performances in *Star-Spangled Rhythm* (1943), *Hollywood Canteen* (1944), and *A Song Is Born* (1948). But perhaps the most curious gospel appearance of all is by Clara Ward, who appears as the mysterious singing angel who "redeems" Hank Williams, Jr., in *A Time to Sing* (1968).

Among the later Hollywood films with gospel music in a prominent role, Steve Martin's *Leap of Faith* (1992) boasts an all-star gospel choir, while Robert Duvall's *Apostle* (1998) features an authentic look at small African American choirs. Also spotlighting gospel music are *Sister Act* (1992), *Sister Act II*

(1993), *The Preacher's Wife* (1996), *The Fighting Temptations* (2003), and *Ladykillers* (2004).

Perhaps a better venue to see gospel music has been in the form of the film documentary. The Academy Award–winning documentary *Say Amen, Somebody* (1980) has repeatedly been named to lists of the best documentaries in cinema history. Director George Nierenberg's extraordinary film focuses on the lives of gospel legends the Reverend Thomas Dorsey and Willie Mae Ford Smith in their final years and somehow manages to tell the entire history of gospel music in the process. The film is highlighted by numerous performances by Dorsey, Smith, the Barrett Sisters, and the O'Neal Twins and contains some of the last known footage of Dorsey.

On a smaller scale, Tom Davenport's documentary *A Singing Stream: A Black Family Chronicle* (1987) traces the history of the Landis family of Granville County, North Carolina, through the lives of eighty-six-year-old Bertha M. Landis and her sons' gospel quartet, the Golden Echoes. As in *Say Amen, Somebody,* Davenport wisely allows the camera to record a number of electrifying performances.

A good overview of the history of gospel music, from Africa through the spirituals to modern black gospel, is given by a three-part documentary from Great Britain, *Too Close to Heaven: The Story of Gospel Music* (1998). It is notable for hundreds of snippets of various gospel artists, engaging commentaries by Dr. Horace Boyer and Albertina Walker, and an instructional section that ties black religious music with the Civil Rights Movement. (It is also available commercially under the title *The Story of Gospel Music: The Power in the Voice.*)

There are several collections that feature gospel's greatest artist, Mahalia Jackson, including *Mahalia Jackson* (rereleased in 1998), which chronicles her final European tours, and *Mahalia Jackson: The Power and the Glory—The Life and Music of the World's Greatest Gospel Singer* (1997).

Among the most recent productions of note are *The Jubilee Singers: Sacrifice and Glory,* produced by the PBS series *The American Experience* (2000), *Trying to Get Home: A History of African American Song* (1994), and Bill Moyers's interview with historian/musician Bernice Johnson Reagon, *The Songs Are Free* (1997).

Southern Gospel

Southern gospel has been the subject of even fewer films, although some fine performances have been captured on celluloid. The Sunshine Boys Quartet (often featuring J. D. Sumner) appeared in a host of Western films and serials, beginning in 1945, singing hymns, spirituals, old time gospel, and Southern gospel. Other movies featuring some Southern gospel include the Statesmen Quartet in *A Man Called Peter* (1955) and *God Is My Partner* (1957) and the Gold City Quartet in *Midnight Cry* (1988). Still more performances by different groups can be found in *Stars in My Crown* (1950), *Tender Mercies* (1983), *Matewan* (1987), *O Brother, Where Art Thou?* (2000) and *Ladykillers* (2004).

However, the most notable proponent of gospel music—black and Southern—was Elvis Presley, who continually featured the Jordanaires, the Statesmen Quartet, the Stamps Quartet, the Imperials, and other groups in his various movies. The best film on Presley's life-long love affair with gospel is *He Touched Me—The Gospel Music of Elvis Presley* (1999).

ROBERT DARDEN

See also Barrett Sisters; Dorsey, Thomas; Golden Gate Quartet, The; Jordanaires, The; Jackson, Mahalia; Presley, Elvis; Smith, Willie Mae Ford; Stamps Quartet; Sunshine Boys Quartet; Walker, Albertina; Ward Trio (Ward Singers)

Reference and Further Reading

Elert, Nicolet V., ed. *International Dictionary of Films and Filmmakers: Actors and Actresses, Vols. I–IV.* Detroit: St. James Press, 1997.

Lopez, Daniel. *Films by Genre: 775 Categories, Styles Trends and Movements Defined, with a Filmography for Each.* Jefferson, NC: McCarland & Company, 1993.

Magill, Frank, ed. *Magill's Survey of Cinema: English Language Films, Vols. I–VI.* Englewood Cliff, NJ: 1981.

GOSPEL MUSIC ASSOCIATION

The Gospel Music Association (GMA) was founded in 1964 with Tennessee Ernie Ford as its first president and J. D. Sumner, Charlie Lamb, and Vestal Goodman serving as some of its founding members. From its inception the GMA has represented all styles of gospel music, including contemporary pop, rock, urban gospel, inspirational, hip-hop, Southern gospel, Latin, country, and children's.

The GMA's sister organization, the GMA Foundation, operates the Gospel Music Hall of Fame. The foundation's mission is "to recognize and preserve the history and legacy of all forms of gospel music and to provide educational resources that encourage participation and appreciation by the general public." In 1971, the Gospel Music Hall of Fame inducted its first members, G. T. "Dad" Speer and "Pappy" Jim

Waites. In March 1982, Thomas A. Dorsey became the first black elected to the GMA Hall of Fame.

Among the more than 140 inductees into the GMA Hall of Fame are Lee Roy Abernathy (1973), Bentley Deforest Ackley (1991), Doris Akers (2001), Charles McCallum Alexander (1991),Wendy Bagwell (2001), Cliff Barrows (1988), E. M. Bartlett, Sr. (1973), J. R. Baxter, Jr. (1973), the Benson Company (1981, 1982, and 1991), George Bernard (1976), the Blackwood Brothers (1998), the Blind Boys of Alabama (2003), Philip Paul Bliss (1989), Albert E. Brumley (1972), Shirley Caesar (2000), Ralph Carmichael (1985), the Cathedral Quartet (1999), the Chuck Wagon Gang (1998), James Cleveland (1984), J. B. Coates (1992), Fanny Jane Crosby (1975), Andrae Crouch (1998), Jimmie Davis (1994), Cleavant Derricks (1984), the Fairfield Four (1999), Fisk Jubilee Singers (2000), Florida Boys (1999), Tennessee Ernie Ford (1994), Wally Fowler (1984), Bill Gaither (1983), Gloria Gaither (1997), the Reverend Billy Graham (1999), Amy Grant (2003), Keith Green (2001), Stuart Hamblen (1994), the Happy Goodman Family (1999), Al Green (2004), Mahalia Jackson (1978), the Jordanaires (1998), Kurt Kaiser (2001), the Kingsmen (2000), the LeFevres (1998), Haldor Lillenas (1982), Mosie Lister (1976), Sallie Martin (1991), Dr. Lowell Mason (1982), Jarrell McCracken (1993), Mighty Clouds of Joy (1999), Marvin Norcross (1983), the Oak Ridge Boys (2000), Adger M. Pace (1973), Sandi Patti (2004), John W. Peterson (1986), Petra (2000), Elvis Presley (2001), Will M. Ramsey (1991), Homer Rodeheaver (1973), Ira D. Sankey (1979), George Beverly Shea (1978), Speer Family (1972, 1975, 1995, and 1998), Frank Stamps (1973), Virgil Oliver Stamps (1973), Ira F. Stanphill (1981), J. D. Sumner (1984), Charles Albert Tindley (1993), Glenn Kieffer Vaughan (1974), James D. Vaughn (1972), Albertina Walker (2001), Clara Ward (1984), Ethel Waters (1984), James S. "Big Chief" Wetherington (1977), Charles Wesley (1995), Robert E. Winsett (1973), and P. J. Pat Zondervan (1984), as well as other noteworthy and notable individuals, groups, and organizations.

Every April the GMA sponsors GMA Week, a weeklong event held around Nashville, Tennessee, that attracts more than three thousand participants. The culmination of GMA Week is the annual GMA Awards ceremony, where its members vote on the Dove Awards, a ceremony that recognizes achievement in all genres of gospel music.

Another event sponsored by the GMA is GMA Music in the Rockies (formerly Seminar in the Rockies), a competition, gathering, and educational event in Christian music launched in 1984 by Cam Floria and purchased by the GMA in 2003. Artists

such as Stacie Orrico, Rachael Lampa, Babbie Mason, Point of Grace, and Mark Lowry began their careers at Music in the Rockies. The GMA launched the GMA Academy, a regional talent competition and seminar, in 1995. A song-critiquing service that provides unsigned songwriters with an opportunity for their songs to be heard and evaluated by gospel music professionals was added as an extension of the GMA Academy in 2004.

In 2004, the GMA, under the direction of a CMTA Anti-Piracy Task Force, launched Millions of Wrongs Don't Make It Right. This is a grass roots, industry-wide campaign to educate and inform Christian music consumers about illegal downloading, file sharing, and CD burning.

On January 11, 2005, the GMA announced the establishment of Project Restore, an Asian tsunami awareness, prayer, and fund-raising effort in coordination with World Vision, an international Christian disaster relief agency. Also, the GMA worked with World Vision after September 11, 2001, when artists, writers, musicians, and executives in the gospel music industry contacted the GMA wanting to be a part of the healing response for that tragic event.

Presently, the GMA has more than five thousand members, who are involved in the gospel music ministry and business in a variety of capacities, including record company professionals, aspiring and established artists/writers/musicians, concert promoters, radio professionals, retailers, publishers, producers, booking agents, artist managers, and more.

BECKY GARRISON

Reference and Further Reading

Gospel Music Association website, http://www.gospelmusic. org.

GOSPEL MUSIC WORKSHOP OF AMERICA

Reverend James Cleveland developed and built the Gospel Music Workshop of America, Inc., where the perpetuation and promotion of gospel music has been and remains a primary purpose of the organization.

The Gospel Music Workshop of America is a Christian organization convening annually, where national performers, recording artists, new and aspiring songwriters, educators, liturgical dancers, the young and the old, pastors, and others minister to each other and to the needs and directions within the African American religious experience. Although the Gospel Music Workshop of America is a predominantly African American assembly, it has opened its doors to welcome and receive people of different colors, influences, and cultures.

The development and skills of African American sacred music are a primary focus at the Gospel Music Workshop of America. This includes an understanding of the major characteristics of the African influence: dynamics, improvisations (vocal and instrumental), and the use of instruments and interpretation. At the Gospel Music Workshop of America, the students are able to realize their potential by building on experiences, as well as present interests and needs, through options for study as well as a variety of resources and learning experiences that emphasize the development of mature self-directions.

The Gospel Music Workshop of America is an annual assembly of interdenominational musicians from throughout the country. Its enrolled membership is above thirty thousand. Its purposes are to enhance the Christian music ministry of the enrolled membership; to perpetuate, promote, and advance Christian ideals through the medium of music; to provide scholarships for the perpetuation and continued development of African American sacred musicianship at the national level; to open new areas where talent (large or small) can perform in some of the largest and finest theatres and arenas in the country before vast audiences; and to promote the purposes of the Gospel Music Workshop of America, via a national convention to be held each year.

Reverend James Cleveland (1932–1991), in March 1967, called together musicians from across the United States in an effort to brainstorm his idea of producing a venue for gospel music presentations. The selection of people he called together was chosen due to individual contributions in gospel music, their visibility in gospel music, and the high prominence of gospel music in their respective areas of residency. This association formed the Gospel Music Workshop of America Association with a national convention motto of "Where Everybody Is Somebody."

The object of the association at that time was to perpetuate, promote, and advance the Christian ideal through the medium of music by joining together gospel choirs, choruses, and analogous entities and people affiliated therewith throughout the United States in a voluntary association for education, cooperation, promotion, and the communication of ideas and ideals. The Gospel Music Workshop of America Association was incorporated in Detroit, Michigan, with its home office at 3908 West Warren Avenue. This location is still considered the central office of the Gospel Music Workshop of America and houses the director of operations and the convention manager, who are responsible for the day-to-day operations of the organization.

People are attracted to the Gospel Music Workshop of America because of its unique and structured program format. The program format is made up of divisions and auxiliaries, with each having separate and distinct functions. Auxiliaries are formed out of the divisions. The divisions in the program format include the following:

Academic
Chapter Representatives
Gospel Announcers
Men
Youth and Young Adults
Ministry
Quartet
Transportation
Security
Nurses
Ushers
Debutante/Fashion Show
Business and Professional

The constitution, by-laws, and operations manual of the organization describe fully the operations of the divisions and auxiliaries. Other printed literature made available by the dean of the Academic Division also describes operations and program formats of the organization.

Other Workshop Highlights

Communion/Consecration Service

This service always signals the beginning of the convention session and is arranged and planned by the Ministry Division and director of planning. Upon entering the service, delegates and others receive the sacraments (bread and wine) from members of the Evangelistic Board (consumption is during the service). The Grand Processional, which includes the board of directors, youth/young adult board of directors, faculty, chapter representatives, evangelistic board, and gospel announcers' guild and is led by the dean of the Academic Division, precedes the service. Academic protocol is employed in the grand processional as members of the board of directors and faculty are robed in white gowns and the cap and hood (of their discipline) of the school from which they graduated.

Nightly Musicals

Each night during the convention week, a musical is held. The musicals include CHAPTER Choirs of the organization, soloists, groups, ensembles, and national recording artists.

Gospel Music Excellence Awards

The lack of comprehensive recognition given to all categories in the field of gospel music by various award selection committees gave impetus to the development of the Gospel Music Excellence Awards. The program recognizes the efforts of gospel singers, groups, musicians, and instrumentalists who have achieved levels of national visibility and excellence in gospel music. The program gives awards in various categories.

New Artist Showcase

The New Artist Showcase gives aspiring gospel artists who are not currently signed with a record company the opportunity to perform in a concert-type setting before officials from record and recording companies. It also allows smaller independent record companies the opportunity to showcase their rosters of artists.

GMWA Programs

The Academic, Performance and Recording, Chapter Representatives, and Gospel Announcers divisions account for more than seventy-five percent of program operations at the Gospel Music Workshop of America. The other program operations are important to the overall success of the organization but play a lesser role in developments for people coming to convention sessions. A legal team oversees contract negotiations and other business affairs of the organization.

The need to extend, promote, and advance the Gospel Music Workshop of America outside the scope and boundaries of the continental United States gave rise to the Expansion, Research, Visibility, and Accountability divisions of the organization. The African-American Sacred Music Network, a program within the Academic Division, was established to help meet these needs. This program brings together people, systems, and institutions in need of the offerings of the Gospel Music Workshop of America. The African-American Sacred Music Network proposes that there are major differences in worldviews between African Americans and European Americans that are foundational to perspectives of worship, music, energy in worship, modes of thinking at all

levels, and other barriers that could possibly lead to misunderstandings and an assumption of superiority/inferiority. Research in specialized areas within academia to keep abreast of changes and current technological trends in music, and visibility of the numerous unique program offerings within the organization, were and still are apparent to show the world that the Gospel Music Workshop of America is a leader in both African American sacred music and other forms of music.

The legacy left by Reverend James Cleveland continues today and is alive in the program operations of the Gospel Music Workshop of America.

CHARLES F. REESE

Reference and Further Reading

Gospel Music Workshop of America website, http://www.gmwa.org.

GOSPEL PEARLS

Published by the National Baptist Convention (the largest African American Christian organization in the United States) and introduced at their forty-first annual convention in September 1921, *Gospel Pearls* was the first collection of songs published by a black group that used the term "gospel" to refer to the new kind of music that was becoming popular in religious circles. The chief editor was Willa A. Townsend, a professor of church worship, music, and pageantry at Nashville's Roger Williams University, but she had lots of help. Lucie E. Campbell, E. W. D. Isaac, Sr., and L. K. Williams all played significant roles in compiling the collection.

The songs relied heavily on the lining hymn tradition of singing, in which each piece was done at a slow tempo and every syllable was elaborated with three to five embellishment tones. The goal was to capture the feeling of the Holiness church singers minus excesses such as singing very loudly at the extremes of the register, putting additional words into the text, hand clapping, and shouting.

There were 163 songs in the book; all but twenty were standard Protestant hymns by such writers as Isaac Watts, Charles Wesley, and Fanny Crosby, revival songs by writers such as Ira D. Sankey, or patriotic numbers such as "Battle Hymn of the Republic." A section was reserved for spirituals that featured numbers by Charles A. Tindley, John W. Work, and Lucie Campbell, among others.

This collection soon became popular in the black church and brought about two styles of gospel music. One stressed embellishment, volume, and improvisation as dictated by the spirit; the other, while emphasizing the spirit, modified renditions to suit the musical tastes of individual congregations. This latter style inspired the development of gospel groups, such as Tindley's Gospel Singers. So popular was *Gospel Pearls* that the National Baptist Convention used the original plates when publishing its second edition in late 1921. They then used them for all subsequent editions through the 1990s.

W. K. McNeil

Reference and Further Reading

Boyer, Horace Clarence. *The Golden Age of Gospel*. Urbana and Chicago: University of Illinois Press, 2000 (1995).

Darden, Robert. *People Get Ready: A New History of Black Gospel Music*. New York: Continuum International Publishing Group, 2004.

GOSPEL PERIODICALS

Introduction: In the Past . . .

Times have changed but, until recently, there was a noticeable dearth of magazine publications devoted entirely or broadly to African American and/or white American religious music. In the past, notable exceptions, among others, have been *The Gospel Messenger* in the 1970s (more a fanzine than a periodical and very short-lived) and, most of all, *Rejoice!*, published by the University of Mississippi (and for one year jointly with Baylor University) between 1986 and 1994.

Other great sources of information not to be neglected are the many nonscholarly magazines published in the United States, Europe, Australia, and Asia, mostly since the end of World War II, that specialized in jazz, blues, R&B, soul, and associated styles and occasionally or regularly featured gospel artists, gospel history, record reviews, discographies, and so on. Some of them are still in print, and many have been indexed (see below).

In the early and mid-1990s, contemporary songs of praise and stars have made gospel music a multimillion-dollar business, and that led to a lot of specialized publications, some local (such as *Gospel Chicago Style*, *The Chicago Gospel*, *Positive Connections*, *Kingdom Insight Magazine*, *The Spiritual Perspective Inc.*, *The Salem Chronicle*, *Trumpet*, *Christian Happenings*, and *Saints—A Christian Lifestyle Publication*, in Chicago alone, the battlefield of Thomas A. Dorsey), and some national, such as *Score: America's Gospel Music Magazine* in Nashville, *Gospel Music*

Exclusive in California, and too many more elsewhere to be listed here.

. . . and Today!

More recently, urban contemporary and hip-hop–flavored gospel and Christian music have become more and more popular, with the Holy Hip Hop Music Awards, Stellar Awards, and Soul Train Music Awards challenging the Dove Awards and the prizes awarded during gospel conventions such as the Gospel Music Workshop of America. The magazine *Billboard* added an *In the Spirit* column to its *Record Reviews* and *Charts* sections.

Many magazines devoted to gospel music are now available on a monthly, bimonthly, quarterly, or annual basis, such as *Gospel Today*, *Gospel Industry Today*, *The Gospel Times*, *CCM Magazine*, *Gospel Synergy*, *Gospel Flava Magazine*, *Gospel Source*, *Gospel USA Magazine*, *The Gospel Truth*, *IMANI Magazine*, *Jazzspel Journal Magazine*, *The National Black Christian Resource Directory*, and, to end this far from exhaustive listing, *The Gospel Music Industry Round-Up*, which may today be the main reference for black gospel music. Some publications deal strictly with black gospel music, others with white Christian music, and a few cover both. Last but not least, there are currently many gospel e-zines and journals.

In addition to these sources, scholarly journals such as *The Black Perspective in Music* (United States, published between 1973 and 1990), *Ethnomusicology: Journal of the Society for Ethnomusicology*, *MAWA Review*, *MELUS: The Journal of the Society for the Study of the Multi-Ethnic Literature of the United States*, *The Journal of Musicology*, *Jazz Forschung/Jazz Research* (Austria), *American Music* (University of Illinois Press), *Black Music Research Journal*, *Lenox Avenue—A Journal of Interarts Inquiry* (Center for Black Music Research, Chicago), and more include important articles about black religious music in America and elsewhere.

Main Sources Available

Scholarly Journals

Since the demise of *The Black Perspective in Music* in 1990, *Black Music Research Journal*, published by the Center for Black Music Research (Columbia College, 600 S. Michigan Avenue, Chicago IL 60605-1996), is the main source for in-depth essays and articles about black religious music; a special issue was entirely devoted to *Negro Spirituals and Gospel Songs: Indexes to Selected Periodicals* (Sacré, 1995).

Black Gospel Magazines

As mentioned in the introduction, there are new generations of gospel music lovers, and the success of religious and Christian music since the mid-1990s has led to the publication of a lot of commercial magazines devoted chiefly to contemporary gospel; most of them have active websites asking readers to contact them and giving lots of information such as new releases, artist information, photo galleries, partners, and links. It must be said that the musical content of the paper magazines is usually weak, with lots of advertisements and family-oriented issues, health and fashion tips, and so forth.

A number of publications come out on a monthly basis. *Gospel Today* (http://www.gospeltoday.com), which advertises itself as "the best magazine this side of heaven," focuses on high-profile Christians, family-oriented issues, black gospel music, urban ministry, relationship issues, self-improvement, book and CD reviews, travel, and much more.

Gospel Industry Today provides information regarding the gospel music industry, including current news, new records, and related legal advice and producer's tips; it also includes a gospel radio chart. *The Gospel Times* (Richmond, Virginia) covers similar material.

Other magazines are published on a bimonthly basis. *Gospel Flava Magazine* advertises itself as "the first urban gospel music magazine targeting urban inner city youth." Each issue features contemporary artist and industry executive interviews, as well as fashion, health, and sports articles (http://afgen.com/gospel.html). This paper magazine is not to be confused with an e-zine on-line at http://www.gospel flava.com, which also interviews established and new artists and provides a list of upcoming new releases, archives, articles, news, reviews, live music on video, and interactive resources.

Gospel USA Magazine (http://www.gospelusama gazine.com), whose goal is "to help you keep up-to-date with America's growing music industry," provides interviews, playlists, a gospel television broadcast guide, and another very useful website, http://www. GospelEventsonline.com. *The Gospel Truth* (http:;// www.gospeltruthmagazine.com) features interviews, new releases, GTM awards, and other information.

IMANI Magazine (http://www.imanimag.com) is "the magazine of faith, family, and empowerment," and its musical content is tenuous. *Gospel Synergy* (Chicago), *Gospel Source* (Pittsburgh), and *Trumpet* (Trinity United Church of Christ, Chicago; http://www.tucc.org) are also worth a look.

There are also quarterly magazines such as *IN YA EAR! Magazine* (Brooklyn, New York) and *Jazzspel Journal Magazine* (http://www.jazzspel.com), a national jazz and gospel periodical featuring stories about black religious–related artists but also R&B artists, smooth jazz artists, and entertainers.

Once a year are published *The National Black Christian Resource Directory* (Plantation, Florida) and *The Gospel Music Industry Round-Up* (http://www.gospelroundup.com).

There are no magazines in print, distributed on a national or international basis, that deal exclusively with the history of traditional gospel music and gospel styles, the golden age of gospel, and the reviewing of biographies of gospel artists from the past. It must be said, though, that there are currently plenty of books dealing with these topics.

The most important of all the periodicals listed is probably *The Gospel Music Industry Round-Up*. It is what it says it is: "the bible of the gospel music business." Once a year, it looks back at the previous years; all the gospel record companies are listed, as well as the African American religious organizations, gospel radio stations and television programming, Christian bookstores, and the like. Another section deals with the most influential people in gospel, the top choirs, the quartet scene, and so on. "Gospel and the Internet" is one of the most useful features, giving access to the best gospel websites on the Internet (gospel network, gospel artists, churches and ministries, gospel stores, radio, gospel industry resources, record companies, television, and more).

White Southern Gospel Magazines

U.S. Gospel News, "the monthly magazine delivered right to your mailbox," is a paper magazine but also has a website (http://www.usgospelnews.com). It must be said that white Christian music colonized the World Wide Web and can be found chiefly in on-line e-zines and journals. *Renown Magazine* (http://www.renownmagazine.com) covers Christian music with interviews, photos, CD reviews, mission and human interest stories, and much more.

The Southern Gospel News Magazine has recently been changed to *SGN SCOOPS Magazine* (http://sgscoops.com). *So Gospel News* is another on-line source for Southern gospel news (http://www.sogospel-news.com), like *Singing News* (http://www.singingnews.com). *Southern News* (http://www.inu.net/sthrnws) bills itself as "your source for Southern news in East Texas and the world." Other sources are *Gospel Wire* (http://www.gospelwire.com) and *Gospel Music Associates* (http://www.gospelmusic.org).

Black and White Gospel Music

CCM Magazine (Nashville, Tennessee) is a monthly publication with a weekly contemporary Christian music update. It offers book and music reviews, interviews, and articles (http://www.ccmmagazine.com). *The Shepherd's Guide (The Christian's Choice of Yellow Pages)—Greater Memphis and Surrounding Areas* (http://www.shepherdsguide.com) lists all of the black and white churches of the area.

Nonmusical Commercial Newspapers and Magazines

It would be fastidious and purposeless to give details at length, but gospel music and artists are occasionally featured in daily newspapers such as *The New York Times, Chicago Tribune, Chicago Sun Times, Dallas Morning News, Detroit Free Press, LA Focus on the Word, Los Angeles Times, New York Daily News, Kingdom Gospel Music Newspaper, Philadelphia Inquirer,* and *Washington Post* in the United States, *Le Monde* (France), and *Voice* and *Melody Maker* (United Kingdom) as well as in mainstream publications such as *Entertainment Weekly, USA Today, Vibe Magazine, Ebony, Jet,* all of the publications of the Johnson Publishing Company, *Time Magazine, American Visions,* and more.

Musical Commercial Magazines in Print

As expected, most musical magazines everywhere in the world have "gospel corners" or feature, more or less regularly, articles about gospel music. Those in boldface type in the selection that follows are especially noteworthy:

Back to the Roots (Belgium), http://www.backtotheroots.be
Best of New Orleans (U.S.), http://www.bestofneworleans.com
Big City Blues (U.S.), http://BcityBlues@aol.com
Block (Netherlands), http://block.magazine@wxs.nl
Blues and Rhythm: The Gospel Truth (U.K.), http://www.bluesandrhythm.co.uk
Blues Revue (U.S.), http://www.bluesrevue.com
Blues & Soul Records (Japan), http://brs@bls-act.co.jp

Jazz Around (Belgium), c/o Muzakasbl BP 134, B-4020 Liege 2, Belgium
Jazz Hot (France), http://www.jazzhot.net
Jazz Magazine (France), http://www.jazzmagazine.com
Jazzman (France), http://jazzman.redaction@wanadoo.fr
Jefferson (Sweden), SBA, Box 40230, S 102-61 Stockholm, Sweden
Juke Blues (U.K.), c/o Juke@jukeblues.com
Living Blues (U.S.), http://www.livingblues.com
Offbeat (U.S.), http://www.offbeat.com
Rollin' and Tumblin' (Luxemburg), c/o rotrie@pt.lu
Real Blues (Canada), http://www.realbluesmagazine.com
78 Quarterly (U.S.), http://seventyeightquar@hotmail.com
Soul Bag (France), http://www.soulbag.presse.fr

Out-of-Print Periodicals

A lot of out-of-print magazines and publications are worth a search because they covered important fields of black gospel and white Christian music (boldface items in the selection that follows); public and university libraries sometimes have whole collections, either on paper or microfilm.

American Folk Music Occasional (U.S.), 1964–1970
Black Stars (U.S.) Johnson Publications, early–mid-1960s
Bleu Banane (Belgium), 1997–2000
Blue Flame (U.S.), 1969–1972
Blue Notes (Belgium), 1990–1993
Blues: Bimestriel International Blues Jazz (Belgium), 1970–1971
Blues Access (U.S.), 1990–2002
Blues Gazette (Belgium), 1995–1996
Blues Link (U.K.), 1973–1975
Blues Power Magazine (Denmark), 1992–1994
Blues Unlimited (U.K.), 1963–1987
Blues Unlimited Collectors Classics (U.K.), 1964–1966
Blues World (U.K.), 1965–1974
Les Cahiers du Jazz (France), 1961
Crazy Music: The Journal of the Australian Blues Society, 1974–1977
Hot Buttered Soul (U.K.), 1971–1974
Jazz, Blues & Co (France), 1976–1986
Jazz in Time (Belgium), 1989–1995
Jazz: Unterhaltungs- und Informationszeitschrijf für Jazz, Blues, Gospel and Spirituals, R&B, Soul Country and Western (Switzerland), 1974–1978
Le Jazzophone (France), 1978–1984

Keskidee: A Journal of Black Musical Traditions
(U.K.), 1986–1993

Musical Traditions (U.K.), mid-1980s–1993

New Kommotion (U.K.)

Old Time Country (U.K.) 1971–1989

Old Time Music (U.K.), 1971–1989

The Original Chicago Blues Annual (U.S.),
1989–1994

Pickin' the Blues (U.K.), 1982–1984

Le Point du Jazz (Belgium), 1969–1986

Prologue: Opera Musique (Belgium), 1969–1992

Record Research (U.S.)

Rejoice! The Gospel Music Magazine (U.S.),
1988–1994)

Rhythm & Blues Panorama (Belgium), 1960–1965

Sailor's Delight (U.K.), 1978–1984

Shout (U.K.)

Talking Blues (U.K.), 1976–1979

Wavelength: New Orleans Music Magazine (U.S.),
mid-1970s–1991

Whiskey, Women and . . . (U.S.), 1971–1989

In this series, the best reference is *Rejoice!*, which deserved a longer life but did not get the support it should have received from collectors and fans. A whole collection may be read and studied at the Blues Archives Department of the University of Mississippi in Oxford. Most of the other magazines are in private collections or libraries around the world.

ROBERT SACRÉ

Reference and Further Reading

Floyd, A. Samuel; J. Marsha Reisser. *Black Music in the United States—An Annotated Bibliography of Selected Reference and Research Materials*. White Plains, NY: Kraus International Publications, 1983.

Sacré, Robert. *Les Négro Spirituals et les Gospel Songs*. Paris: Presses Universitaires de France, Que Sais-Je? no. 2791, 1993.

———. "Negro Spirituals and Gospel Songs: Indexes to Selected Periodicals." *Black Music Research Journal* 15, no. 2 (Fall 1995).

Vann, R. Kimberley. *Black Music in* Ebony: *An Annotated Guide to the Articles on Music in* Ebony *Magazine, 1945–1985*. Chicago: Center for Black Music Research, CBMR Monographs, no. 2, 1990.

GOSPEL QUARTETS

Nineteenth-Century Foundations

Several parallel singing traditions were born in the United States during the period of slavery, allowing blacks and whites to engage in four-part singing and draw from a shared vernacular culture (Averill, 2003, 11). As blackface minstrelsy became increasingly popular in the 1850s and 1860s, black and white performers sometimes sang spirituals in quartet fashion.

Throughout the period of Reconstruction, financially strapped black institutions often formed vocal ensembles, the most famous of which was the Fisk Jubilee Singers, an eleven-member ensemble established in 1871, five years after Fisk University welcomed its first students. During the 1890s, many university jubilee ensembles began to shrink in size, performing and recording both sacred and secular material in four-part harmony. Recording for Columbia in 1895 and Victor in 1902, respectively, the Standard Negro Quartette from Chicago and the Dinwiddie Colored Quartet, comprised of students from the John A. Dix Industrial School in Dinwiddie, Virginia, made the earliest known recordings by African American quartets (Lornell, 1995, 19).

In African American communities, close harmony singing became associated with recreational spaces such as the barbershop (Averill, 2003, 39), and some blacks participated in shape-note singing societies through the South during the late nineteenth century (ibid, 22). White quartets were more strongly influenced by shape-note singing as this genre became more widely disseminated at the turn of the twentieth century. It was largely through the work of James David Vaughan, a white shape-note teacher from Southern Tennessee, that gospel quartet music was made commercially available. In 1910, Vaughan financed a tour for his family group, which he called the Original Vaughan Quartet, and they became the first of sixteen quartets Vaughan sponsored under that name to travel and advertise his close-harmony songs. The establishment and growth of the professional gospel quartet tradition in the rural South were facilitated by Vaughan's success (Goff, 2002, 63).

Evolution of the Jubilee Style

In the 1910s and 1920s, a confluence of several phenomena contributed profoundly to the ongoing development of a modern gospel quartet sound. The 1906 Azusa Street Revival in Los Angeles had precipitated a global Pentecostal movement. This movement spawned multiple congregations across the country as pastors who attended the revival returned home to launch—or to transform—ministries in their hometowns. Unlike the Baptist congregations from which many gospel quartets sprang, the Pentecostals embraced a lively, "sanctified" form of sacred music and allowed energetic use of the body during praise and worship.

The growing influence of Pentecostal faith coincided with the migration of over more than one million Southern blacks to the North in search of jobs and better economic opportunities. These black migrants arrived in cities such as Chicago, Detroit, Cleveland, and Philadelphia, and they brought with them a set of expectations and preferences concerning ideal forms of church music. When Thomas Dorsey moved from Georgia to Chicago in 1921, his style of blues-inflected gospel music had a major impact on the evolving quartet tradition.

The first two decades of the twentieth century thus saw the gradual transformation of university-affiliated jubilee quartets. By 1905, the Fisk Jubilee Quartet had gained popularity, and it eventually became the model for numerous African American jubilee quartets throughout the Southern United States. Black vocal quartets sprang up in several Southern states, often near black colleges. In Bessemer, Alabama, R. C. Foster formed one of the earliest jubilee quartets in 1915.

Throughout the 1920s, several amateur and professional quartets formed in and around Jefferson County. The Foster Singers inspired a generation of early jubilee groups in Alabama, such as the Famous Blue Jay Singers and the Birmingham Jubilee Singers, which were founded in 1926 and were among the first professional black quartets to emerge (Boyer, 1995, 33). During this time, other Southern states also boasted successful black jubilee quartets. The Tidewater area of Virginia proved fertile ground for an array of popular groups such as the Norfolk-based Silver Leaf Quartet and the Norfolk Jubilee Singers, both of which became prominent after World War I. In 1927, the Harmonizing Four was formed in Richmond.

Although these early gospel quartets naturally maintained distinctive sounds according to their geographical location and personnel, they were unified by certain features characteristic of the jubilee style of singing. Most jubilee quartets featured four male voices singing in close harmonies very similar to those of barbershop quartets. Since the Baptist churches in which many quartets performed often did not allow musical instruments such as drums, pianos, or guitars, quartets typically sang without any instrumental accompaniment.

Whereas older groups, such as the Fisk Jubilee Quartet, had attempted to constrain the emotional affect of their performances, emphasizing proper diction and melodic precision over smooth ornamentation and danceable grooves, post-World War I quartets began to sing hymns and spirituals with a stronger rhythmic emphasis, accenting the pulse with vocal inflections and through subtle body movements from side to side (Lornell, 2005, 12). Furthermore, the newer jubilee singers increasingly produced sound from the back, rather than the front, of their mouths to create a full-bodied, earthy tone. They also employed an arsenal of vocal techniques, bending notes and ending them with a humming sound for greater emotional impact. The lyrics of jubilee songs were often narrative in character, relating biblical parables or recounting the experiences of Old Testament figures such as Noah, Moses, Jonah, and Job (Lornell, 2005, 23).

While black jubilee quartets flourished throughout the 1920s, white quartets also grew in popularity, especially throughout the South. Many white quartets became professional ensembles on their own, breaking away from their dependence on publisher-sponsored tours and singing conventions (Cusic, 1990, 95). In 1926, J. R. Baxter and Virgil O. Stamps joined forces to create the Stamps–Baxter Company. A Texas native, Stamps also formed a vocal ensemble, the Stamps Quartet, which recorded for Victor in 1927. He eventually sponsored several other quartets that used the Stamps name while touring extensively throughout the Southwest. The Stamps Quartets were influenced by popular jazz pianists and featured songs with rhythmic syncopation in addition to classic hymns in the shape-note tradition.

As the 1920s came to a close, the Great Depression hindered gospel quartet touring and recording. Nevertheless, the 1930s saw the rise of African American groups such as the Virginia-based Golden Gate Quartet. Influenced by the Silver Leaf Quartet, the Golden Gate Quartet was founded by Willie Johnson, who put together a group of students attending Booker T. Washington High School in Norfolk. The Golden Gates are considered by many to be emblematic of the classic jubilee quartet, and they perfected a hard-driving style characterized by the use of jazz-influenced rhythmic syncopation and vocal imitations of musical instruments.

Radio became a crucial media through which gospel quartets were popularized outside of local churches. After the Southernaires began broadcasting live performances on New York City radio stations in 1933, many quartets—such as the Swan Silvertones, the Golden Gate Quartet, and the Soul Stirrers, which were based in other cities—quickly followed suit (Boyer, 1995, 52).

As the Pentecostal movement continued to spread and Dorsey's music became increasingly popular, many jubilee quartets felt pressure to modify their performance styles to satisfy the changing demands of their listeners. The alternative was to hold fast to the more conservative jubilee tradition and risk losing much of their audience support. The Golden Gate Quartet continued to sing in the jubilee style popularized during the 1920s and 1930s, and facing a diminishing American audience, they relocated to Europe in the 1950s (Boyer, 1995, 253).

Hard Gospel Quartet Singing After World War II

The late 1940s and 1950s was a period during which many sacred quartets began attracting larger audiences by using a screaming, shouting, or preaching style associated with Pentecostal churches. The newer "hard gospel" genre of quartet singing differed in significant ways from the "sweet" style of vocalizing popularized by prewar jubilee ensembles. Gospel quartets increasingly began using musical instruments, which Pentecostal churches were more likely to embrace. The piano, bass guitar, and drums comprised a typical rhythm section and provided a more driving accompaniment to the singing. Hard gospel soloists began to use more demonstrative approaches to gospel performance, sometimes walking or running across the stage or through the aisles during a selection.

Several African American quartets migrated from the South and established home bases in New York City, where they procured recording contracts and participated in radio broadcasts. A number of white quartets achieved professional status during this era, including the Statesmen, the Blackwood Brothers, the Oak Ridge Boys, and the Jordanaires. In 1956, the Statesmen and the Blackwoods collaborated to establish the National Quartet Convention, which held annual meetings in Memphis. The Jordanaires became well known for their performances with Elvis Presley (Cusic, 1990, 116 and 222).

By the early 1940s, the role of the solo singer had become much more prominent than it was in the older-style jubilee quartets, which continued to utilize a full harmonic texture in which all voices were given equal weight. Many of these individuals, such as Ira Tucker of the Dixie Hummingbirds and Julius Cheeks of the Sensational Nightingales, became famous in their own right and had a profound influence on gospel soloists such as Sister Rosetta Tharpe and Mahalia Jackson (Lornell, 2005, 28). Women's groups, such as the Gospel Harmonettes (led by Dorothy Love Coates) and the Caravans (founded by Albertina Walker) were highly influential. Rebert "R. H." Harris, leader of the Soul Stirrers, developed a smooth, yet powerful, brand of gospel singing that made him one of the most popular quartet soloists during the 1940s.

The Soul Stirrers increased in popularity during the 1950s, when Harris was replaced by Sam Cooke, who left the Highway QCs and gained fame. To maintain a rich vocal background while increasing the emotional range and flexibility of solo parts, quartets began to employ an additional lead vocalist. This modification, known as the "swing lead" technique, featured two or more soloists, each of whom would give way to the next soloist after singing a verse or chorus (Boyer, 1995, 97). Thus, it was quite common for "enlarged" quartets of this era to contain from five to seven members. The "quartet" designation was nevertheless used, as the term came to denote an approach to singing rather than the number of members in a group. Enlarged quartets such as the Five Blind Boys of Mississippi and the Five Blind Boys of Alabama, both of which were founded in the 1930s, experienced much success during the postwar period with their hard gospel style (Boyer, 1995, 199–202).

Although many quartets rose to stardom during the 1950s, the subsequent decade brought a decline in quartet popularity, as the secular influences of rhythm and blues and the Motown sound were felt nationwide. During the 1960s and 1970s, many of the white quartets that stayed afloat, such as the Happy Goodman Family and the Florida Boys, used television as a means of spreading the gospel through song. The Blackwood Brothers remained very popular, but found new competition in the mid-1960s from white groups such as the Cathedral Quartet and the many black quartets that continued to perform by adjusting, often with changes in membership, to audience tastes and the demands of the fast-changing music industry (Malone and Strickland, 2003, 121–122).

Organized in 1959 by Willie Joe Ligon, the Mighty Clouds of Joy became one of the most well-known hard gospel quartets of the 1960s. They maintained their success through the 1970s and 1980s by employing a smoother, more contemporary style, popularized by artists such as Edwin Hawkins and Andrae Crouch (Boyer, 1995, 239).

Gospel Quartets 1980–2005

As the gospel music industry evolved in the late twentieth century, the popularity of traditional quartet singing continued to decline in the United States. Groups such as the Winans and Take 6, which emerged during the 1980s, were influenced by older quartets but also incorporated newer styles that appealed to younger audiences. While drawing from more contemporary sounds, recording artists such as Keith "Wonderboy" Johnson remain particularly committed to the gospel quartet tradition. Chosen Few, a white quartet, continues to perform throughout the South and Midwest, especially near Branson, Missouri.

Although first established in the 1940s, the Canton Spirituals experienced their greatest success in the 1990s and earned a reputation as solid performers in the quartet tradition. However, other groups, such as Men of Standard and the female quartet Witness, employ an urban gospel sound more influenced by the hip-hop styles of the late twentieth and early twenty-first centuries. While professional gospel quartet singing as typified by the post–World War II ensembles has become increasingly rare, amateur quartet singing maintains a steady following in a wide variety of churches across the United States. Moreover, the Gospel Music Workshop of America founded a quartet division in the early 1990s that continues to thrive in the early twenty-first century. Like other genres of gospel music, quartet singing evolves with newer audiences while sustaining links to its treasured past.

MELVIN L. BUTLER

See also Azusa Street Revival; Blue Jay Singers; Caravans; Cathedral Quartet; Coates, Dorothy Love; Crouch, Andrae; Dixie Hummingbirds; Dorsey, Thomas; Fisk Jubilee Singers; Five Blind Boys of Alabama; Five Blind Boys of Mississippi; Florida Boys, The; Golden Gate Quartet, The; Gospel Music Workshop of America; Harmonizing Four; Highway QCs, The; Jackson, Mahalia; Jordanaires, The; Mighty Clouds of Joy; National Quartet Convention; Norfolk Jubilee Singers; Oak Ridge Boys; Sensational Nightingales; Silver Leaf Quartet; Soul Stirrers; Stamps Quartet; Swan Silvertones; Take 6; Tharpe, Sister Rosetta; Vaughan Quartet; Walker, Albertina; Winans, The

Reference and Further Reading

Allen, Ray. *Singing in the Spirit: African-American Sacred Quartets in New York City*. Philadelphia: University of Pennsylvania Press, 1991.
Averill, Gage. *Four Parts, No Waiting: A Social History of American Barbershop Harmony*. New York: Oxford University Press, 2003.
Boyer, Horace Clarence. *How Sweet the Sound: The Golden Age of Gospel*. Washington, DC: Elliott & Clark, 1995.
Cusic, Don. *The Sound of Light: A History of Gospel Music*. Bowling Green, OH: Bowling Green State University Popular Press, 1990.
Goff, James R. *Close Harmony: A History of Southern Gospel*. Chapel Hill: University of North Carolina Press, 2002.
Jackson, Joyce Marie. "Cultural Evolution of the African American Quartet." In *Saints and Sinners: Religion, Blues and (D)evil in African-American Music and Literature*, edited by Robert Sacre. 97–112. Liege, Belgium: Societe Liegeoise de Musicologie, 1996.
———. "The Performing Black Sacred Quartet: An Expression of Cultural Values and Aesthetics." Ph.D. dissertation, Indiana University, 1988.
Lornell, Kip. *Happy in the Service of the Lord: African-American Sacred Vocal Harmony Quartets in Memphis*. Knoxville: University of Tennessee Press, 1995.
Malone, Bill C.; David Strickland. *Southern Music/American Music*. Revised Edition. Lexington: University Press of Kentucky, 2003.

Discography

Blind Boys of Alabama. *Oh Lord, Stand by Me/Marching Up to Zion* (1991, Specialty 7203).
Blind Boys of Mississippi and Various Artists. *Lord Will Make a Way: Early Recordings 1947–1951* (P-Vine Japan 5837).
The Caravans. *The Best of the Caravans*. (1998, Savoy 7012; originally released 1977).
Cathedral Quartet. *Signature Songs, Vol. 1* (2000, Homeland Records 63).
Sam Cooke. *Complete Recordings of Sam Cooke with the Soul Stirrers* (2002, Specialty 4437).
The Dixie Hummingbirds. *Journey to the Sky* (2002, P-Vine Japan 5818).
Dorothy Love Coates & the Original Gospel Harmonettes. *The Best of Dorothy Love Coates & the Original Gospel Harmonettes, Vols. 1&2* (1991, Specialty 7205).
Golden Gate Quartet. *Golden Gate Quartet, Complete Recorded Works in Chronological Order, Vol. 1: 1937–1938* (2000, Document 5472); *Golden Gate Quartet, Complete Recorded Works in Chronological Order, Vol. 2: 1938–1939* (2000, Document 5473); *Golden Gate Quartet, Complete Recorded Works in Chronological Order, Vol. 3: 1939* (2000, Document 5474); *Golden Gate Quartet, Complete Recorded Works in Chronological Order, Vol. 4: 1939–1943* (2000, Document 5475); *Golden Gate Quartet, Complete Recorded Works in Chronological Order, Vol. 5: 1945–1949* (2000, Document 5638).
Happy Goodman Family. *Southern Gospel Treasury: The Goodman Family* (2002, Word Entertainment 886106).
J. D. Sumner and Stamps. *Hall of Fame Series* (2000, Benson 2426).
Keith "Wonderboy" Johnson & Spiritual Voices. *Tribute to Quartet Legends, Vol. 1* (2001, Verity 3000).
Men of Standard. *Men of Standard* (1996, Muscle Shoals 8013).
Mighty Clouds of Joy. *The Best of the Mighty Clouds of Joy* (1995, MCA Special Products 22045; originally released 1973); *The Best of the Mighty Clouds of Joy, Vol. 2* (1995, MCA Special Products 22050).
The Sensational Nightingales. *The Best of the Sensational Nightingales* (1995, MCA Special Products 22044; originally released 1978).
Silver Leaf Quartette of Norfolk. *Complete Recorded Work*. (1995, Document 5352).

The Statesmen. *Gospel Classics Series* (2001, BMG Special
   Products 45912).
The Winans. *Introducing the Winans* (1981, Platinum Ent.
   161069).
Witness. *The Best of Witness* (1999, CGI Records 5348).

Compilations

Golden Age Gospel Quartets, Vol. 1 (1947–1954) (1997,
   Specialty 7069).
Golden Age Gospel Quartets, Vol. 2 (1954–1963) (1997,
   Specialty 7070).

GOSPEL SINGING JUBILEE

The *Gospel Singing Jubilee* was instrumental in bringing gospel music into the homes of America during
the 1960s and 1970s. This program, coproduced by
Les Beasley of the Florida Boys and Jane Dowden of
Showbiz, Inc., was one of the longest running gospel
music television programs in history.

In 1961, the Florida Boys produced a thirty-minute
black-and-white television program called *Gospel
Song Shop*. The program achieved great success and
became the catalyst for the *Gospel Singing Jubilee*.
The *Gospel Singing Jubilee* was one hour in length
and soon began production in living color. During
the first year of production, the show featured the
Florida Boys, the Happy Goodman Family, the
Dixie Echoes, and the Couriers Quartet.

The popularity of the program continued to spread.
It quickly became the largest syndicated program in
the history of gospel music. Every Sunday, the *Gospel
Singing Jubilee* would feature guest groups drawn
from some of the biggest names in gospel music.
Well-known groups appearing on the program included the Statesmen Quartet, the Blackwood
Brothers, the Inspirations, the Speer Family, the
Cathedral Quartet, Wendy Bagwell and the Sunliters,
the Rambos, the Oak Ridge Boys, J. D. Sumner, and
the Stamps Quartet, among many others.

Major markets throughout the country began to
feature the *Gospel Singing Jubilee* in their Sunday
morning lineup. Soon all of America was able to
prepare for church while listening to the strains of
"Jubilee Jubilee!" The program was produced quite
simply with a minimum of props and stage effects.
The backdrops were eye appealing, and the talking
was minimal. On this syndicated series, gospel music
was the star.

Produced for more than a decade, the program
at one point was available in all the major television
markets across the country. During its heyday, the
Gospel Singing Jubilee was shown in more than
ninety markets. The program made media stars
of its anchor groups, most notably the Happy Goodman Family and the Florida Boys. The world of
gospel music is indebted to the *Gospel Singing
Jubilee* for distributing gospel music throughout the
nation.

JOHN CRENSHAW

Reference and Further Reading

Beasley, Les. Interview August 2004, Greenville, SC.
Goff, James R. *Close Harmony: A History of Southern
   Gospel.* 228–229. Chapel Hill: University of North
   Carolina Press, 2002.
Les Beasley Presents Jubilee Favorites. Liner notes to CD.

GOUGH, DAVID

(b. August 14, 1949)

David L. Gough, son of William and Ruth Gough, is
the oldest of three children raised in Detroit. He is
husband to Carolyn Gough; they have three adult
children, Damon, David DoRohn, and Devin.
Gough is an entrepreneur, artist, songwriter, producer, and founder of the International Gospel Music
Hall of Fame and Museum (IGMHFM).

Edward Smith (January 19, 1935–March 28, 1994),
a businessman from Detroit and secretary of James
Cleveland's (1931–1991) Gospel Music Workshop of
America, approached Gough to preserve black gospel
history. The 1994 vision to establish something for
gospel music came to Gough at a video recording
session called the "Coming Home Series," recorded
at the Bill Gaither Studios in Alexandria, Indiana.
The session was recorded but never released.

Adding to the desire to establish a lasting memorial
for gospel music was Gough's traveling incident.
While riding the bus from the recording studio there
was an ice storm; the roads were slippery and a car
ran into the bus. This sparked memories of old; he
began to reflect on how rough it must have been for
those trailblazing gospel musicians as they continued
to deliver the message of God in song through the
tribulations of racism and discrimination. African
Americans had to travel the back roads and were
only able to eat at certain restaurants and to stay at
certain hotels. Most of the singers were forced to sleep
in their vehicles and prepare their own meals.

When Gough returned home to Detroit, sitting in
his office, he asked God, "What is my purpose?" God
confirmed the vision to start a Gospel Music Hall of
Fame and Museum to honor pioneers. God told
Gough to protect the history so that it is never forgotten what our foreparents contributed to the fibers
of American history. Gough called friends and told
them about the vision. In 1995, a board of directors
was formed and the name was trademarked as the

Gospel Music Hall of Fame and Museum. In 2002, the organization voted to add "international" to its name so as to include gospel singers from other countries.

Gough is known as the "Mayor of Gospel" because of his commitment to introducing gospel music and entertainment to mainstream audiences. He was the first gospel artist to perform at the Festival of Arts in Kunming, China.

Gough began his serious pursuit of music by performing while in the Navy during the Vietnam War. Gough and four friends formed Five Way, a self-contained top-forty band representing five members from different nationalities. He strongly believes in creative music that features a diversity of styles and points of view. He launched DoRohn Entertainment in 1978 to promote his first album and to launch the careers of other gospel artists. Gough is promoting a new form of gospel music, a gospel hip-hop choir; the Emmanuels, a quartet with an old-school rhythm and blues flavor; Esther Smith, a traditional gospel singer; RXG, the radical X generation; Michael Van Tull, an urban American poet; J'Nettle, a songstress; and Pam Jones Burleigh, a vocal jewel from Memphis.

Gough has released six albums including *Heart-fixer, Masterpiece, Picture This, Living Out His Love,* and *No Walls.* He is a frequent guest on national and international television shows and a world traveler, visiting South Africa for a gospel festival in 2004. David Gough albums include *Good News* and *This Christmas.* Gough is a pioneer, with two music videos, *Hold On* and *Good Feeling,* being the first gospel music videos with animation. He is one of the defining voices in gospel music and entertainment.

SHERRY SHERROD DuPREE

Reference and Further Reading

"Biography of Evangelist Esther Smith." http://www.gospelcity.com/dynamic/artist-articles/artists/38 (accessed February 13, 2005).

Crosby, Keith. International Gospel Music Hall of Fame & Museum, 8th Annual Induction Awards Banquet. http://www.detroitgospel.com/IGMHFM.htm.

DoRohn Records Entertainment website, http://www.dorohn.com (accessed February 20, 2005).

International Gospel Music Hall of Fame and Museum website, http://www.gmhf.org (accessed February 18, 2005).

Stevens, Kathy A. "God, the Man and the Vision for International Gospel Music Hall of Fame and Museum, Detroit." February 11, 2005.

Discography

David Gough. *Living Out His Love* (2000).
David Gough and Valdez Brantley. *No Walls* (1993, DoRohn Records).

GRANT, AMY

(b. November 25, 1960 in Augusta Georgia)

In the 1980s, Amy Grant was the darling of contemporary Christian music. Her way into the scene had been prepared by the soaring voices, jazzy rhythms, and true-to-the-gospel stylings of Sandi Patti and Cynthia Clawson. Her musical style—a combination of country, jazz, and pop—grew out of the movement among Christian musicians of the late 1960s and 1970s—such as Andrae Crouch and Mylon LeFevre—to present the Christian message in a form that was appealing to a generation raised on rock and folk music. Grant's own music, in turn, paved the way for popular singers such as Cindy Morgan and Jaci Velasquez and groups such as Point of Grace.

In the early 1990s, Grant moved away from the Christian music scene and began recording pop music albums. Although her fans viewed her movement into the pop music scene as a defection, Grant never thought of herself as a "Christian musician," often refusing to recognize "Christian music" as a distinct genre.

Born in 1960 in Augusta, Georgia, during her father's medical residency, Grant is the youngest of four sisters. Shortly after her birth, the family moved to Nashville, and she quickly became a child of Music City. Although she attended a fundamentalist church that prohibited dancing and musical instruments in worship, Grant soon began to attend a Bible study class at a local church where music played a significant part in creating an intimate spiritual environment. While she had always been a musical child, she now began writing some of her own songs and performing them for her classmates in chapel.

When she was fifteen, she was sweeping floors and demagnetizing tapes at a Nashville studio. She asked a family friend, producer Brown Bannister, at the studio if she could make a tape of her own songs as a gift to her parents. Hearing Grant's tape, a producer at Word Records sensed he had discovered a major new talent and convinced his company to sign her immediately. By seventeen, then, Grant had her first recording contract. Her first album, released while she was still a junior in high school, sold fifty thousand copies and she was on her way to becoming one of the most influential musical artists—Christian or otherwise—of the last two decades of the twentieth century.

Although she began to tour and record almost immediately, Grant continued to try to complete her studies. She postponed her work at Furman University and at Vanderbilt University to pursue her career as her fame grew.

In the early days of her career, Grant remained naïve about the ways of the recording industry.

When a promoter told her that she could do a concert for three hundred dollars, she replied that she had only five hundred and wanted to save it. She had not yet learned that she would be paid for singing the music she had written and that she loved.

Her first album, the self-titled *Amy Grant* (1977), introduced this marvelous new talent to the world. Produced by Brown Bannister, her high school youth group leader, the songs on the album were influenced by the reigning pop music of the late 1970s that emanated from the pens and music of singer–songwriters such as Carole King and James Taylor. Grant's album marked a new direction in gospel music and, in some ways, spearheaded the movement toward what is now called contemporary Christian music, a combination of pop rhythms and stylings and lyrics about salvation, heaven, and other traditionally Christian topics. Some of the songs, such as "Mountain Top" and "What a Difference You've Made in My Life," became popular hits on Christian radio stations.

In 1979, she recorded her second album, *My Father's Eyes*. The title song was written by Gary Chapman, a singer–songwriter with whom Grant had been touring. In 1982, Grant and Chapman married. Their marital ups and downs provided fodder for the tabloids for much of their married life. Various magazines presented them as the perfect model of the wholesome Christian married couple. Yet all was not well in paradise, and stories of marital discord soon surfaced and dogged them through most of their marriage. Chapman descended into substance abuse, and their careers were often at odds.

Throughout these struggles, the couple did express a belief in the sustaining power of God in their marriage and honestly professed to the media their struggles and their attempts to overcome them through counseling. In the late 1990s, rumors surfaced that Grant was involved with her friend and golf partner, country music singer–songwriter Vince Gill, who was recently divorced. While Grant acknowledged her emotional involvement with Gill, she disavowed any sexual relationship with him. Nevertheless, Grant's marriage to Chapman ended in 1999, and she married Gill a few months later.

Grant also collaborated with Chapman on her third album, *Never Alone* (1980). While her first two albums had shown the influence of folk, country, and pop, as well as the musical strains of more traditional gospel music, her third album began to move her in a new direction toward a harder-edged rock and jazz sound. During these years, Grant recorded the duet "Nobody Loves Me Like You" with the Christian rockers DeGarmo and Key, with whom she also recorded two live albums in 1981. She also debuted

some of her own compositions on this third album. *Never Alone* signaled the emergence of Grant from a young artist to a more mature talent. *Contemporary Christian Music (CCM)* magazine named *Never Alone* one of the top ten albums of 1980.

By most accounts, Grant's *Age to Age* (1982) came to be regarded as her breakthrough album and her signature album. *CCM* called it "a stunning collection of direct, mature, and inspiring material, delivered with emotion and skill." The two most recognized songs from the album—"Sing Your Praise to the Lord" and "El Shaddai"—quickly became classics of contemporary Christian music and were included in hymnbooks in many Christian traditions. Grant won her first Dove Award when the album won the 1983 award for Pop/Contemporary Album. In that same award ceremony, Grant was named Artist of the Year. In 1998, a group of critics from *CCM* chose Grant's recording of "El Shaddai" as the second-best contemporary Christian song of all time. The album also garnered the Grammy for the year's Best Gospel Performance. In addition, *Age to Age* was the first Christian music album ever to sell a million copies and go platinum. With the phenomenal success of this album, Grant was calling attention to the Christian music industry as well as to her tremendous talent as an artist.

Her next album, *Straight Ahead* (1984), builds on the success of *Age to Age*. Still collaborating with popular Christian singer–songwriters such as Michael W. Smith and Gary Chapman, Grant took her music to the next level by using straightforward rock 'n' roll rhythms and phrasing to make her points. She earned yet another Dove Award for the Best Pop/Contemporary Album for *Straight Ahead*. She performed the song "Angels" from the album on the Grammy Awards national broadcast, a first for a contemporary Christian music artist. The songs most recognized from this album are the title track, "Straight Ahead," and "It's Not a Song," "The Now and the Not Yet," and "Thy Word," a meditation on Psalm 119:105 that has also made it into hymnbooks.

Unguarded (1985) took Grant to even greater heights and was the first of her albums that broke the *Billboard* top one hundred charts when the song "Find a Way" debuted at #29 on the list. This song has a music video that showed on MTV, and soon Grant found herself making the rounds of national television talk shows and hosting her own special on CBS. Grant's debut with Peter Cetera of the rock group Chicago, "The Next Time I Fall in Love (It Will Be with You)," debuted at number one on the *Billboard* charts. Grant's album became the first contemporary Christian music album recorded on a Christian record label (Myrrh) to break through to a secular audience. Once again Grant garnered top honors at both the Dove Awards and the Grammy Awards, winning the Dove for Artist of the Year and the Grammy for Best Gospel Performance. Grant also shifted from recording for Myrrh to recording for the pop label A&M after this album. Although many of her fans accused Grant of "selling out" to the pop music world, she used her new popularity as a platform both for the Christian message and for her own proclamations that being human was an essential part of being Christian. *Unguarded* was Grant's breakthrough album and her popularity and her music simply continued to flourish in the following years.

Although *Lead Me On* (1988) became Grant's first gold album, the music and lyrics represent a departure from her earlier albums. While some critics consider it the greatest Christian album of all time, Grant reveals in her songs the pain of her life at the time—a miscarriage, marital woes with Chapman, a difficult pregnancy. Grant gives voice to this pain and darkness in the poignant lyrics of songs such as "Faithless Heart" and "Shadows." The album won a Dove Award and a Grammy for Best Gospel Performance, Female.

If *Lead Me On* was Grant's paean to human suffering, she rebounded three years later with a joyous album that celebrated love and life. *Heart in Motion* (1991) made Grant a household name on contemporary radio with hits such as "Baby, Baby" and "Every Heartbeat." The album sold six million copies, and "Baby, Baby" debuted at number one. While her Christian radio fans disdained the romantic video produced for the song (which was actually about her own six-week-old daughter), a close listen to the song's lyrics reveals that Grant has not abandoned her views of the power of Christian love.

In the years between *Heart in Motion* and her next major album, *House of Love* (1994), she recorded a Christmas album and an album with various other artists. *House of Love* sold around three million copies and featured the same joyous approach to life Grant expressed on *Heart in Motion*. The best-known songs from the album are "Lucky One" and "Heart in Motion," a duet with her soon-to-be husband Vince Gill included in the soundtrack for the movie *Speechless*.

Behind the Eyes (1997) forsakes for a moment the celebration of life on *Heart in Motion* and *House of Love* and reenters the territory of *Lead Me On*. With her marriage to Chapman breaking apart and the death of her close friend and songwriting collaborator Rich Mullins, Grant once again ponders the nature of marital fidelity, the sadness of broken relationships, and the pain of death. Although the album did not score well in the mainstream pop market, Christian radio and Christian music critics acclaimed the power

of Grant's music on the album. She won a Dove for the best Pop/Contemporary Album in 1998 for *Behind the Eyes*.

In 1999, Grant married Vince Gill and the two often tour together. She has been a spokesperson for Habitat for Humanity and for cancer research. In 2004, she released a greatest hits album simply entitled *Greatest Hits: 1986–2004*.

Throughout the many changes that Grant has undergone, she has remained faithful to her Christian roots and shown in her music that Christian themes can be expressed with vivacity and life through the medium of pop music. Without Amy Grant, contemporary Christian music would never have attained the popularity or status that it has.

HENRY L. CARRIGAN, JR.

Reference and Further Reading

Amy Grant website, http://www.amygrant.com.
Millard, Bob. *Amy Grant: A Biography*. New York: Doubleday, 1986.
Powell, Mark Allan. "Amy Grant." In *Encyclopedia of Contemporary Christian Music*, 373–379. Peabody, MA: Hendrickson, 2002.

Discography

Amy Grant (1977); *My Father's Eyes* (1979); *Never Alone* (1980); *In Concert; In Concert 2* (1981); *Age to Age* (1982); *A Christmas Album* (1983); *Straight Ahead* (1984); *Unguarded* (1985); *The Collection* (1986); *Lead Me On* (1988); *Heart in Motion* (1991); *Home for Christmas* (1992); *Songs from the Loft* (1993); *House of Love* (1994); *Behind the Eyes* (1997); *A Christmas to Remember* (1999); *Greatest Hits: 1986–2004* (2004).

GREATER VISION

Greater Vision was organized in 1990 by Gerald Wolfe, the group's lead vocalist. Rodney Griffin sings baritone for the group, and Jason Waldroup was added later to sing tenor. Together, these three men put an unusual twist on their music that draws audiences to their shows. There is no doubt that this dynamic group with its catchy comedy routines, powerful melodies, and well-crafted lyrics (usually written by Rodney Griffin) are all a part of a music ministry that encourages the message of salvation.

Over the years, Greater Vision has achieved much success. They have been named Trio of the Year and achieved the Song of the Year award. Each member of the group has been recognized individually. Rodney Griffin has been named Songwriter of the Year five times. Gerald Wolfe has been named Male Vocalist of the Year four times. Jason Waldroup has been named gospel music's Favorite Young Artist and is one of gospel music's favorite tenors.

In addition to personal achievements, the group has released numerous hits. Such songs include "My Name Is Lazarus," "Just One More Soul," "God Wants to Hear You Sing," "With All the Many Miracles," "They Should Have Cried Holy," "Soon We Will See," and "Just Ask." Greater Vision has produced many projects. They have recorded with the Budapest Philharmonic Orchestra, Hungarian Radio Symphony, and Atlantic Festival Orchestra. They recorded a live project (on the Daywind Music Group label) called *Live at First Baptist Atlanta,* which received Album of the Year and Video of the Year. With much success, Greater Vision has become the most awarded trio in gospel music history.

In 2004, Greater Vision combined talents with popular producers Lari Goss and Wayne Haun to coproduce the group's new project, *Faces.* The album has twelve songs, six of which were written by Rodney Griffin.

The group always makes it a point to express that they sing for the work of the Lord. They choose songs that minister to them first. When sincerity is portrayed, they feel that the audience will be blessed. They do not measure success by the awards and hit songs, but by the people they encourage and the lost souls led to Christ.

ANDREA GANNAWAY

Reference and Further Reading

Huffman, Barbara. "Greater Vision: Something Special's in the Making." *Singing News* (January 2002): 58–61.
Greater Vision website, http://www.greatervisionmusic.com.

Selected Discography

Take Him at His Word (1995, Riversong).
Far Beyond This Place (1999, Daywind Records).
A Greater Vision Christmas (1999, Daywind Records).
Perfect Candidate (2000, Daywind Records).
Live at First Baptist Atlanta (2002, Daywind Records).
Quartets (2003, Word Entertainment).
Faces (2004, Word Entertainment).

GREEN, AL

(b. April 13, 1946, Dansby, AR)

Born in Dansby, Arkansas, Al Green was the sixth of ten children born to sharecropper parents. He performed on the gospel circuit with the Green brothers until the family moved to Grand Rapids, Michigan. His father banished him to the street for listening to Jackie Wilson records. In the early 1960s he formed an R&B group called the Creations, which later evolved into Al Green & the Soulmates. In 1967, *Back Up Train* was released and peaked at number five on the R&B charts.

Green eventually became a solo act and joined forces with producer Willie Mitchell. He began recording with the legendary Memphis Horns and the Hi Records Rhythm section. His voice contrasted with the raw and gritty vocals that dominated the genre by offering a sweeter sound, not unlike that of the late Sam Cooke. The 1970s saw Green come into his own as a pop star, with a string of successful albums that produced hit singles, including "Green Is Blues, "Al Green Gets Next to You," "Let's Stay Together," "Call Me," and "I'm Still in Love with You."

In 1977 Green started American Music Studios, where he produced *Belle* and *Truth and Time.* In 1979 an accidental fall from a Cincinnati stage became the catalyst for his shift from pop to gospel music for the next fifteen years. His first all-gospel album, *The Lord Will Make a Way,* was released in 1980, and in 1981 it garnered Green his first Grammy Award. In 1982, *Precious Lord* earned both a Grammy and a Dove award. By 1989, Green had accumulated a total of eight Grammy awards for his gospel music.

In 1994, he recorded "Funny How Time Slips Away" with Lyle Lovett on the multiplatinum album *Rhythm, Country and Blues.* In 1995 the album won a Grammy, and he was inducted into the Rock and Roll Hall of Fame. At the same time he continued to pastor the Full Gospel Tabernacle in Memphis, Tennessee, which he founded in 1976. The twenty-first century saw Green finally at peace with performing both the secular and sacred sides of his musical career.

BOB GERSZTYN

See also Soul Gospel

Reference and Further Reading

Al Green website, http://www.algreen.com (accessed June 26, 2003).
Green, Al; Davin Seay. "Take Me to the River." Edinburgh, Scotland: Payback Press, 2000.
Hunter, James. "Green Is Blues." *Rolling Stone* 917 (March 6, 2003).
Rolling Stone website, http://www.rollingstone.com/artists/bio (accessed May 23, 2003).

Discography

Green Is Blues (1969, Hi-Records); *Al Green Gets Next to You* (1971, Hi-Records); *Let's Stay Together* (1972, Hi-Records); *I'm Still in Love with You* (1972, Hi-Records); *Call Me* (1973, Hi-Records); *The Lord Will Make a Way*

(1981, Hi-Myrrh/Word); *Higher Plane* (1982, Myrrh/Word); *Precious Lord* (1982, Myrrh/Word); *I'll Rise Again* (1983, Myrrh/Word); *Sailin' on the Sea of Your Love* (1984, Myrrh/Word); *Soul Survivor* (1987, A&M); *Greatest Gospel Hits* (2000, The Right Stuff, EGD-25262).

GREEN, KEITH

(b. October 21, 1953; d. July 28, 1982)

A child prodigy who was referred to by many members of his generation as "the prophet," Green was for several years after his death one of the most popular contemporary Christian artists.

His family on his mother's side had considerable show business experience. Green's grandfather was a successful composer and screenplay writer who worked for Warner Brothers and wrote for Eddie Cantor. He also put together the Ritz Brothers act and owned an early rhythm and blues record company. His mother was an excellent singer who was offered a contract to perform with Benny Goodman but turned it down to marry Keith's father. So it was not too surprising that the young boy manifested interest in music.

At age two and a half, Green won a kids' talent show singing "Love and Marriage," and six months later he was strumming the ukulele. Then at age eight he made his theatrical debut in a summer stock presentation of Arthur Laurent's comedy *The Time of the Cuckoo.* Later that year (1962) he wrote his first song, and during the next three years he produced thirty-nine more. In 1964, when he was ten, Keith garnered rave reviews for his role as Kurt Von Trapp opposite Janet Blair's Maria in *The Sound of Music.* The following year, his first record was released and he signed a five-year recording contract with Decca Records. At the time he was billed as a "prepubescent dreamboat who croons in a voice trembling with conviction." Yet despite this promising beginning, Green never really made it as a secular music star.

Throughout the late 1960s and early 1970s Green pursued his musical dream and experimented with drugs, "free love," and Eastern and metaphysical philosophies. Then in the early 1970s, he became a self-proclaimed "follower of Jesus," although according to his own account, true conversion did not happen until 1975. After that time his music career really took off, so well in fact that he became one of the best-selling Christian artists of all time.

In 1980 he hit upon a novel idea to make his music available even to those who were unable to pay. He offered copies of his third album, *So You Wanna Go Back to Egypt,* for whatever one could afford. This became his policy for subsequent albums and for all ministry materials offered by Last Days Ministries, an organization established by Green and his wife, Melody.

During the last seven years of his life Keith was totally uncompromising in his faith, setting strong spiritual standards for himself and others, and often struggling to live up to them. Never one to take the easy way out of any situation, Green's enthusiasm sometimes offended those he met. Still, his career was in high gear when his fifth album, *Songs for the Shepherd,* was released on April 12, 1982. Three and a half months later, on July 28, 1982, he and two of his children, along with nine other people, were killed in a plane crash. In 1989 his wife collaborated with writer David Hazard on a biography, appropriately titled after his second album, *No Compromise: The Life Story of Keith Green.*

The release of five posthumous albums indicates that Green's Christian protest songs based on nineteenth-century evangelistic literature were popular after his death. Green influenced a number of contemporary Christian artists, the most notable being Amy Grant. Had he not died at such an early age, his name would be better known today.

W. K. McNeil

Reference and Further Reading

Green, Melody; David Hazard. *No Compromise: The Life Story of Keith Green.* Chatsworth, CA: 1989.

Discography

For Him Who Has Ears to Hear (1977, Sparrow).
No Compromise (1978, Sparrow).
So You Wanna Go Back to Egypt (1980, Pretty Good).
The Keith Green Collection (1981, Sparrow).
Songs for the Shepherd (1982, Pretty Good).
I Only Want to See You There (1983, Sparrow).
The Prodigal Son (1983, Pretty Good).
Jesus Commands Us to Go (1984, Pretty Good).
The Ministry Years 1977–1979 Vol. 1 (1987, Sparrow).
The Ministry Years 1980–1982 Vol. 2 (1988, Sparrow).

GREENES, THE

Tim Greene (b. March 31, 1964)
TaRanda Kiser Greene (b. April 6, 1979)
Tony Greene (b. October 17, 1968)

The Greenes, a Southern gospel trio from Boone, North Carolina, have gained wide popularity in the past decade. Consisting of the husband and wife duo of Tony and TaRanda Greene on respective baritone and soprano, augmented by older brother Tim Greene on tenor, they have won a large following.

As a group, the Greenes originated in 1978, with Tony, Tim, and sister Kim as the trio and their father Everette accompanying on piano. They had their first charted hit with "Gloryland" in 1983, but Kim departed in 1989 to marry Dean Hopper of the Hoppers. Thereafter, the third part in the trio was taken first by Amy Lambert, from 1989 until 1994, and then by Milena Parks until 1999. TaRanda Kiser joined the Greenes in 1999, and with her marriage to Tony Greene on February 1, 2001, the trio became an all-family unit again.

Over the years, some of the best-known Greene songs have been "They Shall Never Crucify Him Again," "Glorious City of God," "The Blood Covered It All," "Miracle in Me," "When I Knelt, the Blood Fell," and "I'm So Happy." However, they also throw a few old standards into their repertoire, such as "The Old Account Settled." Many of their songs are originals by Tim Greene. Their offerings have appeared on the ACA and New Haven labels. As of 2005, the trio has fifteen compact discs in print; TaRanda and Tim each have solo vocal projects, and Tony has a compact disc of Christian comedy.

In August the Greenes play host to the Gospel Singing Jubilee, which has grown to be the largest outdoor gospel music event in the Tarheel state and features many leading Southern gospel groups in addition to the Greenes. Groups featured in 2004 included the Hoppers, the Perrys, the Lewis Family, and the Talley Trio. A full biography of the trio is entitled *Hold On,* and Tim Greene has authored an inspirational book, *His Healing Touch.*

IVAN M. TRIBE

Reference and Further Reading

The Greenes website, http://www.thegreenesgospel.com.

Discography

The Greenes: Testimony/Greatest Hits, Vol. One (1990, ACA CD).
So Happy (2000, New Haven CD 8016-2).

GUITAR

The guitar came to gospel music through American folk and popular music. With a minimum amount of skill or training, basic chord accompaniments can be easily played on the guitar; more skillful players are capable of much more, making it one of the most popular of all instruments. Its portability, reasonably low price, and adaptability to a wide range of music have made the guitar the most popular of musical instruments, and naturally, gospel musicians have eagerly adopted it.

The history of the guitar in America reflects changes in the way the instrument was designed and built, which in turn influenced how it was used and played. The common "Spanish" or so-called "classical" guitar features a wide fingerboard, gut strings, a slotted peghead, and a fan-shaped bracing system under the instrument's wooden top, giving it a sweet sound. However, the American guitar has its roots in a group of talented Viennese instrument builders who developed a new way of building guitars. Most notably, a German immigrant named Christian Friedrich Martin began making instruments in 1833 in New York City, moving six years later to Nazareth, Pennsylvania, where the company is still located.

Martin either developed or perfected a new form of bracing called an X-brace. This allowed for greater volume and eventually the introduction of steel strings. He also redesigned the guitar's body shape, exaggerating the lower bout (or half) of the instrument's body so that it was no longer symmetrical in appearance. By the late 1800s, the Martin style had been copied by mass producers, and guitars were made by the hundreds and were available inexpensively through mail-order catalogs. To produce an even louder instrument, around the mid-1910s Martin developed a new body style called the "Dreadnought." This squarer and larger-bodied instrument was an immediate success among folk and country musicians. Again other makers followed suit, making larger guitars, sometimes with arched tops, specifically for use in jazz and dance bands.

Electrically amplified guitars were developed in the 1930s. Initially, lap steels—guitars that were tuned to open tunings and played with a metal bar or glass slide while being held, face up, on the player's lap— were the most popular electric guitars. After World War II, solid-body, electrified "standard" guitars were introduced and became popular, notably the Fender Telecaster (and later Stratocaster) designs and Gibson's Les Paul model. Electric instruments had the advantage of being much louder and could be played through portable PA systems, which are commonly found in many churches.

The guitar is found in many different styles of gospel music. From the mid-1920s, recording blues artists often doubled as gospel performers, sometimes performing under a different name when recording religious material. However, the typical finger-style blues accompaniment was maintained even for gospel material. Some performers specialized in blues material, including the popular recording artist Blind Willie

Johnson, whose intense, growling vocals and powerful guitar work were highly influential on a group of followers, notably Reverend Gary Davis. Johnson would often alternate a sung chorus with a half-recited, half-shouted sermon, based on a biblical story.

Davis had a long career, first recording in ragtime-blues style with Blind Boy Fuller in the mid-1930s, then settling in Harlem in New York City in the late 1940s. Davis recorded gospel-blues prolifically through the 1950s, 1960s, and early 1970s and was a popular performer on the folk-blues circuit. His version of "Twelve Gates to the City" became a pop hit in the early 1960s, when the folk vocal trio Peter, Paul, and Mary recorded it.

The revival of interest in acoustic guitar playing that occurred during the folk revival years of the 1960s brought on new interest in arranging hymns, gospel music, and classical music with religious themes for finger-picked guitar. John Fahey, a popular acoustic guitar soloist who began recording in the early 1960s, helped popularize an arrangement of "In Christ There Is No East or West," which was widely copied. Many other players have followed with their own arrangements of gospel music. While not specifically played for religious purposes, the fact that this music draws on the gospel tradition is certainly one reason for its popularity.

During the post–World War II period, most gospel vocal groups featured at least simplified guitar accompaniment. Many were influenced by the success of the pop vocal group the Mills Brothers, featuring John Mills, Jr., as their guitarist (until his untimely death in 1935; he was initially replaced by jazz guitarist Bernard Addison). Mills's and Addison's work drew on jazz harmonies with tasteful lead work; this became the model for other pop and gospel vocal groups. Most notably, Howard Carroll's pop-jazz–styled guitar accompaniments for the Dixie Hummingbirds in the 1950s were highly influential on a generation of gospel guitarists who drew on popular styles in their playing.

In the 1930s, the steel guitar became a popular instrument in Holiness churches in the South. Steel guitar—in which the player used a metal or glass slide to note the strings—became popular when Hawaiian musicians, such as master steel guitarist Sol Hoopi, toured and recorded in the 1910s and 1920s. Hoopi played a National Steel Guitar, featuring an all-metal body and a special system of resonating cones that made it much louder than a standard guitar.

When amplified (electric) steel guitars became available in the early 1930s, the instrument became popular in the House of God and other fundamentalist churches because of its ability to project over the sound of large choirs and often enthusiastic vocal response from the congregations. Troman and Willie Eason were early exponents of the instrument. Troman played a National Steel Guitar like Sol Hoopi's and, from the mid-1930s, toured with J. R. Lockley, a bishop in the House of God church whose Gospel Feast Party performed at tent revivals all up and down the Eastern seaboard. Younger brother Willie took up the amplified steel guitar and also toured with Lockley in the early 1940s. His work in the church and some postwar recordings for various small labels helped popularize the style.

Henry Nelson was the next great steel player. When he was twelve years old, his sister married Willie Eason, and Nelson quickly learned Eason's style. Nelson built on Eason's technique, developing an ability to play vocal lines on the treble strings while playing complex rhythmic accompaniments in the bass; his accompanists played a single, unchanging chord, giving the music an unusually strong rhythmic pulse. Nelson lived in Queens, New York, from 1959 until his death in 1994 and was quite influential among younger players. His son, Aubrey Ghent, has continued his father's tradition while also incorporating more modern influences from blues and rock.

Meanwhile, a separate sacred steel tradition was developing in Detroit, with more emphasis on traditional chord harmonies than is found in Nelson's work. Notable players included Lorenzo Harrison of the Jewell Dominion church and his followers Calvin Cooke and Maurice Ted Beard, Jr. (who both moved to the House of God church in the mid-1950s). Both Cooke and Beard took up the steel guitar in the 1970s, and have been active as teachers and performers both in the gospel community and on the folk and rock club circuits, with Cooke often opening for popular young steel guitarist Robert Randolph.

Cooke also mentored Charles T. "Chuck" Campbell, noted as one of the first sacred steel players to take up the more complicated pedal steel guitar. Chuck formed a group with his brothers Darick (who plays regular lap steel) and Phil (who plays conventional guitar), along with their nephew Carlton on drums, to form the popular Campbell Brothers group in the late 1990s. They have been very successful in the folk-revival community, recording several highly praised albums for the Arhoolie label.

Out of the rich Holiness communities in Florida comes one of the most popular of the current groups, the Lee Boys. They were led by talented guitarist Glenn Lee, who, until his untimely death from cancer in 2000 at age 32, inspired many others with his unique repertoire of melodic licks. The group is now led by his brother Alvin on guitar, with Glenn's student (and family cousin) Roosevelt Collier manning the steel.

From the mid-1990s, Robert Randolph has achieved great popularity, combining traditional sacred steel stylings with more modern techniques influenced by rock guitarists such as Jimi Hendrix and Eric Clapton. Randolph comes from suburban Maplewood, New Jersey, and was encouraged to take up the lap steel by Chuck Campbell, who gave him his first instrument. He formed a group with his cousins, Danyel Morgan (bass, vocals) and Marcus Randolph (drums). Their recordings have garnered Grammy nominations and attracted listeners among blues, rock, and pop fans, as well as among the traditional audience for sacred steel.

RICHARD CARLIN

Reference and Further Reading

Gura, Philip F. *C. F. Martin and His Guitars, 1796–1873*. Chapel Hill, NC: University of North Carolina Press, 2003.
Ruymar, Lorene. *Hawaiian Steel Guitar*. Milwaukee, WI: Hal Leonard, 1996.
Stone, Robert L. "Sacred Steel: From Hula to Hallelujah." *Sing Out!* (Spring 2004).
Wheeler, Tom. *American Guitars: An Illustrated History*. New York: Harper Collins, 1992.

Discography

Best of John Fahey, 1959–1977 (1977, Takoma). Collection of Fahey's most popular instrumentals, including several gospel arrangements.
Harlem Street Singer (1960, Prestige Bluesville). Great album by Reverend Gary Davis featuring many of his finest songs, including "Samson and Delilah," "12 Gates to the City," and "Death Don't Have No Mercy."
Sacred Steel: Traditional Sacred African-American Steel Guitar Music in Florida (1997, Arhoolie). Anthology featuring Willie Eason, Sonny Treadway, Glenn Lee, Henry Nelson, and Aubrey Ghent.
Sacred Steel Instrumentals (2004, Arhoolie). Selections from a variety of players demonstrating the style's many different aspects.
Sacred Steel on Tour (2002, Arhoolie). The Campbell Brothers in a live performance.

H

HALL, CONNOR

(b. January 25, 1916, Brunville, SC; d. July 19, 1992, Cleveland, TN)

A singer, composer, and publisher, Connor B. Hall was best known for his work with the nationally popular Homeland Harmony Quartet and as an editor for the Tennessee Music and Printing Company, one of the major shape-note convention book sources from the 1930s to the present.

Hall grew up around the Greenville, South Carolina, area, singing old sentimental country songs; as a young man, he served as a singing school teacher. In 1942 he joined with two other employees of the Tennessee Music and Printing Company, Otis and James McCoy, along with B. C. Robinson and pianist Hovie Lister to form the Homeland Harmony Quartet. By 1945 Lee Roy Abernathy had replaced Lister, and his aggressive promotion and marketing of the group pushed it fully into the commercial music arena. Soon they were full-time staff musicians on Atlanta radio WAGA and had a syndicated program heard on fifty Southern stations. They recorded for several of the independent record labels specializing in gospel music, including White Church and Bibletone, and later on their own custom label.

In early 1948 they recorded one of Abernathy's new songs, "Gospel Boogie," and watched it become a nationwide hit. Soon major stars such as Red Foley, Sister Rosetta Tharpe, the Pilgrim Travelers, and Wally Fowler were covering it, and a few years later it became an even bigger hit when pop star Pat Boone recorded it under the title "A Wonderful Time Up There." In many ways, it was a cornerstone for the hot new dynamic quartet style of the 1950s.

Hall also worked as an editor for the Church of God Publishing Company and the Tennessee Music and Printing Company (TMPCo) and became a leader among Southern publishers in the 1940s. Among his innovations was an alliance between the publishers that would facilitate the trading of songs from one publisher's book to another; each song would be engraved on a separate plate, replete with composer credits and original songbook source. If, for example, Stamps–Baxter wanted to include a TMPCo song in one of their books, TMPCo would simply mail them the plate. Hall also became editor of the Vaughan company when it was acquired by TMPCo and for some years kept alive the venerable Vaughan magazine *The Vaughan Family Visitor*.

CHARLES K. WOLFE

HALL, DANNIEBELLE

(b. October 6, 1938, Pittsburgh, PA; d. December 28, 2000, Fremont, CA)

Born Danniebelle Jones, she was the fourth of eight children of William and Danniebell Jones, who taught Sunday school at a Larimer Avenue storefront (Dyer, 2001). She graduated from Peabody High School and attended Mount Mercy College (now Carlow). Her musical career began with the piano at age three and culminated in an international award-winning life's work of singing and songwriting.

Her first musical venture was with her two younger sisters, Paula and Cynthia, in a trio called the Jones Sisters in Pittsburgh. In 1958, she married the late Charles Hall, who encouraged her to follow her passion and dream—evangelizing in a worldwide music ministry context. By 1969, Danniebelle formed the quartet the Danniebelles in the San Francisco Bay area. The group produced an album and toured with World Crusade Ministries, inspiring and encouraging U.S. armed forces stationed in Vietnam with the gospel in song.

In 1974, she launched two solo albums, *Danniebelle* and *He Is King* (both on Light Records). Two popular selections therefrom were "Great Is Thy Faithfulness" and the Christmas rendition "Go Tell It on the Mountain." That was America's introduction to that unforgettable, gutsy yet intimate alto reminiscent of Roberta Flack, according to one reviewer (Danniebelle.com website). In 1969, four years after the group's formation, Danniebelle joined Andrae Crouch and the Disciples and, in the words of Crouch, "She made many of the songs she recorded work because of her talent more than the song itself." America got the message: from the coasts and valleys to the plains, urban and rural communities were listening to *Soon and Very Soon* (1977, Light), *Take Me Back* (1978, Light), *Tell Them* (1978, Light), and *Quiet Times* (1977, A&M, Light; platinum).

When not recording and concertizing, Danniebelle wrote songs for other high-profile artists: "Hymn of Love" for Eartha Kitt; "Ordinary People" for James Cleveland (and later Delores Winans), and "Keep Holding On" for Pat Boone. In 1977, she released *Danniebelle Live in Sweden* (Sparrow), a project with Choralerna—a singing aggregation from Stockholm—blending her rollicking gospel roots on "I Go the Rock" with a Scandinavian backup choir. This album also featured "My Tribute," written and arranged by the friend who made her famous, Andrae Crouch. The album entitled *Designers Original* (1994, CGI) with "O Se' BaBa," a Nigerian praise, and *The Best Gets Better* (1995, CGI) were her last published efforts before succumbing to diabetes and renal failure.

Danniebelle died on December 28, 2000, in Fremont, California. Her vision became reality when her daughter, Cynthia Philpot, with the help of industry friends and associates, released two pending companion CD retrospectives as a double collector's set—*Danniebelle.com Collectors Release* and *Remembering the Times* (2001, EMI). Finally, the Danniebelle Hall Diabetes Foundation was created following her death

to educate the church community about the ravages of diabetes.

EVELYN M. E. TAYLOR

Reference and Further Reading

"Andrae Crouch." Jaspella Gospel Guide website, http://www.Jaspella.com (2002–2004).

Crouch, Andrae. Interview by Evelyn M. E. Taylor, January 12, 2005.

Dyer, Ervin, "Danniebelle Hall: Stylish Gospel Singer, Songwriter for Recording Stars." *Pittsburgh Post-Gazette* (January 6, 2001).

Philpot, Cynthia Hall. Preliminary draft of obituary for funeral program. Forever Danniebelle Ministries, http://www.Danniebelle.com (accessed January 5, 2001).

Discography

Danniebelle (1974, Light).
He Is King (1974, Light).
This Moment (1975, Light).
Let Me Have a Dream (1976, Sparrow).
Danniebelle Live in Sweden with Choralerna (1977, Sparrow).
Unmistakably Danniebelle (1978, Onyx).
Song of the Angels (1983, Onyx).
Designers Original (1994, CGI).
Danniebelle.com Collectors Release (2001; released with permission from EMI)
Let Me Have a Dream/Live in Sweden with Choralerna (two-disc set).

HALL, VERA

(b. ca. 1902 [1906?], Livingston, AL; d. January 29, 1964, Tuscaloosa, AL)

Christened Adell Hall, the youngest of three sisters born to rural farmer Ephron "Zully" Hall and his wife Agnes was known almost immediately by the nickname "Vera." Agnes was a talented amateur singer, often singing spirituals, and both she and her husband encouraged Vera to sing from an early age, although her mother disapproved of secular music, particularly the blues. Nonetheless, Vera was inspired to learn blues songs from a traveling musician, Rich Amerson, who spent a good deal of time around the Hall farm when he was not on the road.

As a young teenager, Vera "got religion" and began singing in the church choir, which became an important source of religious songs for her. Hall also began working as a nanny for a local white family who summered in Tuscaloosa, Alabama. There, Hall met her future husband, Nels Riddle, and the couple married when she was about sixteen years old (or around 1920). Sadly, the marriage lasted only six years before her husband was shot and killed. By the beginning of the Depression, Hall was back in her hometown of Livingston, living in near poverty.

In 1935, a local white woman named Ruby Pickens Tartt applied to work for the WPA documenting local traditions. Tartt was close to many local blacks, enjoying their songs and stories; a particularly close acquaintance was farmer Dock Reed, who happened to be Vera Hall's cousin. Reed probably introduced Hall to Tartt, who in turn introduced the singer to folklorist John Lomax, who came to Livingston in 1937. Lomax made four trips to the area, in 1937, 1939, 1940, and 1941. On his first trip, he recorded Hall and Reed singing unaccompanied spirituals; Reed was deeply religious, and Hall was unwilling to perform "sinful" (secular) music when he was present. On his second and third trips, Lomax recorded Hall on her own, including her haunting version of the blues song "Another Man Done Gone."

Hall and Reed remained in contact with Lomax through Ruby Tartt. In 1947, Vera moved with her mother back to Tuscaloosa, and a year later Lomax's son, Alan, contacted the singer about coming to perform at Columbia University in New York City. She was one of the performers at a folk festival that Lomax arranged at the university, and she came in May to stay with him and his wife. Lomax recorded an extensive oral history with the singer, as well as many songs, which became the basis for his book about her and Dock Reed, *The Rainbow Sign* (published in 1959). Hall returned to Tuscaloosa, where folklorist Harold Courlander visited her and recorded Reed, Hall, and other local musicians in 1950; several albums of this material were released by Folkways Records in 1956. Alan Lomax himself returned in 1959 with stereo recording equipment and again recorded Reed and Hall for his *Sounds of the South* series for Atlantic Records. Hall did not record again, and died on January 29, 1964, in Tuscaloosa.

Hall had a striking voice, marked by a pronounced vibrato. Her recorded material ranges from her deeply moving solos, including half-chanted moans and prayers, to her more formal duet singing with her cousin Dock Reed. Her performance of "Trouble So Hard" is perhaps her most famous recording, thanks to its sampling by pop singer Moby on his album *Play* in 1999 for his own song, "Natural Blues."

Hall and Dock Reed can be heard on several Library of Congress anthology albums, including *Negro Religious Songs and Services; Afro-American Spirituals, Work Songs, and Ballads;* and *Afro-American Blues and Game Songs.* Harold Courlander's 1950 recordings of Hall, Reed, and others from Livingston appear on several albums of the series *Negro Folk Music of Alabama,* originally released by Folkways Records in 1956.

RICHARD CARLIN

Reference and Further Reading

Courlander, Harold. *Negro Folk Music, U.S.A.* New York: Columbia University Press, 1963.
Greenberg, Gabriel. "Like a Spirit on the Water: The Life and Music of Vera Hall." Vera Hall Project website, http://www.verahallproject.com/spirit/index.html (accessed January 28, 2005).
Lomax, Alan. *The Rainbow Sign: A Southern Documentary.* New York: Duell, Solan and Pearce, 1959.

Discography

Deep River of Song: Alabama (2001, Rounder; 1959-era recordings by Alan Lomax of Vera Hall).

HAMBLEN, STUART

Carl Stuart Hamblen (b. October 20, 1908; d. March 8, 1989)

Stuart Hamblen had a lengthy career in both country and gospel music. In both fields, he is probably best known for his compositions, which include "It Is No Secret (What God Can Do)," "Open Up Your Heart (and Let the Sunshine In)," and the spiritual-flavored "This Ole House." He also hosted a long-time syndicated program, *Cowboy Church of the Air.*

Hamblen was born in Kellyville, Texas, the son of a country preacher. He attended McMurray College in Abilene, training to be a teacher, but ultimately opted for a career as a radio cowboy. He had sung on the air in both Dallas and Fort Worth as a teenager and had his first Victor session in their Camden, New Jersey studios in June 1929. Moving to California, he had brief experience with the singing group the Beverly Hillbillies before landing his own programs on KFI and then from 1932 for about twenty years at KFWB. He continued with Victor in the early 1930s and then had Decca sessions in 1934 and 1935.

As a composer, his songs from this period included "My Brown Eyed Texas Rose," "My Mary," "Golden River," and "Texas Plains." During World War II Hamblen wrote a militantly patriotic song, "They're Gonna Kill Ya." Later 1940s songs include "I Won't Go Huntin' with You Jake" and "Remember Me (I'm the One Who Loves You)." Hamblen did a few bit parts in Western films, usually as a villain, and gained

171

some renown as a trainer of race horses. He also acquired a reputation as a rowdy character when drinking.

Stuart Hamblen turned his life around in 1949 as a result of attending a Billy Graham Crusade revival. He began to channel his singing and writing skills toward sacred music. His best-known sacred song, "It Is No Secret (What God Can Do)," allegedly grew out of a conversation with actor John Wayne. When Wayne asked if the rumor were true that Hamblen had got saved, Hamblen replied, "It's no secret what God can do." Wayne is reported to have commented, "That sounds like a song title." Hamblen composed a number of other notable sacred songs, such as "Until Then," "I Believe," "He Bought My Soul at Calvary," "King of All Kings," and "I've Got So Many Million Years."

After discontinuing his regular radio show, Stuart Hamblen had a Sunday program, *Cowboy Church*, which ran well into the 1970s. An offshoot of this program, the Cowboy Church Sunday School Choir, recorded several Hamblen compositions on Decca, most notably the 1954 children's gospel classic "Open Up Your Heart (and Let the Sunshine In)". Hamblen also appeared frequently as a featured vocalist at Billy Graham revivals in this period.

Ironically, Hamblen's best-known song, "This Ole House," from 1954 had been inspired by an experience he had of finding the body of an old prospector in a cabin in the mountains. The scene provided the idea for what became his biggest hit. Written as a sad, sensitive song with an inner meaning, it was turned into a number one pop hit by Rosemary Clooney and into a hand-clapping spiritual by such cover versions as those of Martha Carson and the Statesmen Quartet. According to reports, Hamblen used his royalties from "This Ole House" to purchase the mansion that formerly belonged to the late swashbuckling film star, Errol Flynn.

Two unusual sidelights in the life of Stuart Hamblen date from the 1950s. In 1952, he accepted the nomination of the Prohibition Party as their presidential candidate. He came in a distant third behind Eisenhower and Stevenson. Around the same time, his sister authored an inspirational biography entitled *My Brother, Stuart Hamblen*.

Hamblen slowed down in the 1960s and 1970s, playing rarely except for the *Cowboy Church of the Air* and cutting albums for Word and also Lamb & Lion. He also served on the advisory board of the John Edwards Memorial Foundation and received several honors for his songwriting. He passed away during a brain tumor operation at age eighty.

DEANNA L. TRIBE AND IVAN M. TRIBE

Reference and Further Reading

Griffis, Ken. "I've Got So Many Million Years: The Story of Stuart Hamblen." *JEMF Quarterly* XIV (1978): 4–22.

Selected Discography

Hymns Sung by Stuart Hamblen (1957, Harmony HL 7009).
Stuart Hamblen: In the Garden (1966, RCA Camden CAL/CAS 973).
Cowboy Church (n.d., Word WST 8509).

HAMMOND, FRED

Fred Hammond's sphere of influence has been ever increasing since he began singing with the church choir at the age of twelve in his native Detroit. He played bass and sang with the Winans before founding the soulful men's ensemble Commissioned in 1984. (The Winans made their debut in 1981 and are considered the most important group in the past thirty years. They are credited with pushing the crossover of gospel into both soul and pop radio.)

Hammond recorded eight albums with Commissioned before leaving the group in 1995. The world grew to appreciate Hammond's superb arranging, production, and songwriting skills as well as his soaring vocals as Commissioned took the gospel music industry by storm. Hammond began to pursue a solo career with the release of his debut *I Am Persuaded* (1991) while still a member of Commissioned. In 1995, at the height of the group's popularity and after a decade as lead singer, Hammond made the difficult decision to turn his full attention to a variety of other projects.

Hammond began writing songs while still in high school, and throughout his tenure with the Winans and Commissioned, he honed those skills. Studying the writing of legends in gospel music such as Marvin Winans, Hammonds developed a sensitivity to vocal line and harmonies that has made him one of the most successful writers and producers in the gospel industry.

Already established as a multi-instrumentalist, producer, and vocalist, Fred Hammond became one of the most popular praise and worship leaders in the field. He made it his personal quest to deliver praise and worship music with an urban flair, and utilized funk grooves, gospel vamps, and other techniques to rework many of the emerging standards in worship repertoire. In the late 1990s he formed Radical for Christ and recorded *The Inner Court* (1995) and *Spirit of David* (1996), albums of fresh praise and worship. These recordings built upon the tradition of West

Angeles Church of God in Christ (COGIC) in introducing this genre into the black community. West Angeles COGIC is recognized for introducing the praise and worship repertoire to the black church with the release of *Saints in Praise Vol. 1* in 1999.

Pages of Life, Chapters 1 & 2 (1998), a sweeping double album, was a definitive personal statement built on Hammond's praise-oriented and modern gospel style. *Pages* went platinum and garnered 1999 Stellar Awards for Artist, Song, Male Vocalist, and Album of the Year. Hammond was inducted into the Gospel Music Hall of Fame in 2001, with an impressive record of recording more than fifteen albums and producing more than forty-eight other projects.

DONNA M. COX

Discography

I Am Persuaded (1991, Benson Records); *Deliverance* (1993, Benson Records); *The Inner Court* (1995, Benson Records); *Shakin' the House . . . Live in L.A.* (1996, Benson Records; with Yolanda Adams and Hezekiah Walker); *Spirit of David* (1996, Benson Records); *Pages of Life, Chapters 1 & 2* (1998, Face to Face/Verity Records); *Purpose by Design* (2000, Verity Records); *Christmas: Just Remember* (2001, Verity Records); *In Case You Missed It . . . And Then Some* (2001, Verity Records); *Speak Those Things: POL Chapter 3* (2002, Verity Records); *Something 'bout Love* (2004, Verity/Jive Records).

HAPPY GOODMAN FAMILY

Howard "Happy" Goodman (b. November 7, 1921; d. November 30, 2002)

A singing group active from the late 1940s to the 1990s, the Happy Goodman Family demonstrated the popularity of Southern gospel through their television and personal appearances.

The group was formed in the 1940s by Alabama native Howard "Happy" Goodman. Initially a duo with his sister Gussie Mae, the group expanded under Howard's leadership to a vocal quartet with various family members providing musical backup. At various times siblings Stella, Eloise, Ruth, and Bob also performed with the group. In 1949 Howard married Vestal Freeman (b. December 13, 1929; d. December 27, 2003). The addition of Vestal created the basic quartet, along with brothers Sam and Charles "Rusty" Goodman (1933–1990).

Membership often changed, especially as Rusty struck out on his own and performed with artists Jimmie Davis and Martha Carson and with the groups the Rangers and the Plainsmen. Rusty also honed his skills as a writer, eventually contributing some of the Goodmans' most enduring songs, including "I Wouldn't Take Nothing for My Journey Now," "Wait 'Til You See My Brand New Home," "Who Am I," and "Had It Not Been." In 1973 tenor Johnny Cook joined the group.

The group of Howard, Vestal, Sam, and Rusty experienced great success during the 1960s and 1970s. That success was based on a series of popular recordings on Canaan and exposure on *The Gospel Singing Jubilee,* which they cohosted. The group received numerous awards, including a Best Gospel Album Grammy for *The Happy Gospel of the Happy Goodmans* in 1968. Among the Dove Awards garnered by members of the group were Vestal's Female Vocalist (1969), Rusty's Best Male and Favorite Bass Singer, and Sam's 1974 Favorite Baritone. A second Grammy was awarded to the family for their album *Refreshing* (Best Gospel Performance, Traditional, 1978).

The Goodmans combined their singing careers with long-time evangelism and church ministries. Their success grew through the exposure they received on television, including performances on such shows as *The Dinah Shore Show* and on various Oral Roberts broadcasts. The Goodmans hosted their own program, *The Happy Goodman Hour,* for a time. They also sang at the White House for President Jimmy Carter in 1979. In 1998, the Happy Goodman Family was elected to the Gospel Music Hall of Fame. Rusty Goodman had been elected the previous year in recognition of his talents as a songwriter and solo performer.

The 1990s were a time of adjustment for the group, as Rusty died in 1990 and the other members aged. Howard and Vestal enjoyed a surge of recognition late in the decade as a result of their appearances on Bill Gaither's various Homecoming projects. Howard died in Nashville in 2002, and Vestal died the following year in Florida. Members of the Goodman family continue to be active in the gospel music industry, especially Rusty's daughter, Tanya Goodman Sykes.

KEVIN S. FONTENOT

Reference and Further Reading

Buckingham, Jamie. *O Happy Day.* Waco, TX: Waco Books, 1973.
Goff, James R. *Close Harmony.* Chapel Hill: University of North Carolina Press, 2002.
Goodman, Vestal. *Vestal!* Colorado Springs, CO: Waterbrook Press, 1998.

Discography

The Best of the Happy Goodmans (Canaan CAS 9614).
Good 'n' Happy (Canaan CAS 9636).
Good Times with the Happy Goodmans (Canaan CAS 9682).
Happy Goodman Hour (Canaan CAS 9755).
The Happy Gospel of the Happy Goodmans (Canaan CAS 9644).
In Concert . . . Live (Canaan CAX 9816).
Refreshing (Canaan CAS 9828).
What a Happy Time (Canaan CAS 9628).

HARMONIZING FOUR

The quartet was formed by four students at the Dunbar Elementary School in south Richmond, Virginia, in September 1927; they rehearsed at the home of John T. Scott, first and tenor singer, with Joe Curby, second tenor, Lawrence Hatcher, baritone, and Willie Peyton, bass, all of whom were already singing in local churches choirs. Music teacher Lawrence Langhorne, a friend of Scott's, became the group's first manager.

After much practice, the name of the group was chosen, and they sang regularly at Dunbar, especially at the start of each school day. By 1930, Curby had left the group to join the Heavenly Choir, and he was replaced by Leon Gibson, who left in 1932 and was replaced himself by Thomas "Tommy" ("Goat") Johnson. Joseph "Gospel Joe" Williams (baritone/alto soloist; b.1916, Richmond, Virginia) joined the group in 1933, and by the mid-1930s, Peyton had been replaced by Levi Hansley.

The group specialized in close harmony singing, Negro spirituals, and hymns with precise attack and releases and a smooth sound that gained considerable attention in their area. For sixteen years they sang hymns and spirituals *a cappella,* always impeccably dressed and conservative in style and image, and they won the trust and respect of church folk.

"Gospel Joe" Williams, who claimed his main influence was Glen T. Settle (Wings Over Jordan choir), became the new manager and the leader of the group. John T. Scott, the last founder–member, left and was replaced by guitarist–pianist–arranger Lonnie Smith before the group's first recording session, which took place in New York in June 1943 for Decca. They were billed as Richmond's Harmonizing Four and cut eight smooth, polished songs. Then they headed to Richmond, where they obtained a regular radio slot on WRNL, drawing more listeners to the station.

The quartet continued touring, appearing at the National Baptist Convention in Atlanta in 1944 and singing to an audience of forty thousand souls. They then spent several weeks in San Antonio, Texas. Their notoriety went higher and higher, and the quartet was invited to the White House to sing at the funeral ceremony following President Franklin Roosevelt's death in April 1945.

Vance Joyner quit the group in 1946, but soon after, the group was recording again: four sides for Religious Recording in Chicago (1947) as the Richmond Harmonizers of Richmond (sic), four sides for Coleman (1948), and two sides for MGM (1949), with moderate success. In July 1951 the wedding ceremony of Sister Rosetta Tharpe to Russell Morrison at the Griffith Stadium in Washington, DC, was recorded live and issued on an album; the Harmonizing Four had been invited and rendered four songs.

At the same time, the group had been signed by Gotham Records in Philadelphia, and more than forty songs were recorded and issued between 1950 and 1956, with new changes in the composition of the group: Levi Hansley quit in 1953 and was replaced first by James Walker (tenor) for a few months only—he joined the Dixie Hummingbirds—and then by Clarence Ross (bass); Tommy Ellison also came in 1955 and settled with the group, but briefly, like Jimmy Jones (bass), who came to replace Ross but left after a couple of memorable recordings, and Ross came back.

In 1957 the group (with Johnny Jones again) signed with Vee-Jay Records in Chicago and definitively went up to stardom, with their spiritual and hymn singing gaining global acclaim. All of their Vee-Jay singles and albums (some 60 songs) sold very well from 1957 to 1967, despite more changes of personnel and new trends in the tastes of their public. By 1962 Smith had to hang up his acoustic guitar, and was replaced by a long series of young male electric players (Sterling Holloman, Jesse Pryor, Clement Burnett, and others); at that time they switched to Atlantic Records (1967–1968) and then to King Records (1969), Chess Records (1972), Jewel (late 1970s), and a variety of labels. The 1990s lineup, its older participants engaged in semiretirement or dead (Jimmy Jones died in 1991), consisted of Tommy Johnson, Lonnie Smith, Ellis Ellison, Eddie Green, and Calvin Meekins, but the group, as such, has been inactive since the mid-1990s.

ROBERT SACRÉ

Reference and Further Reading

Boyer, Horace Clarence. *How Sweet the Sound: The Golden Age of Gospel.* Washington, DC: Elliott & Clark, 1995.

Hayes, J. Cedric; Robert Laughton. *Gospel Records 1943–1969. A Black Music Discography*. 2 vols. London, UK: Record Information Services, 1992.
Heilbut, Tony. *The Gospel Sound: Good News and Bad Times*. New York: Limelight, 1985.
Reagon, Bernice Johnson, ed. *We'll Understand It Better By and By. Pioneering African American Gospel Composers*. Washington, DC: Smithsonian Institution Press, 1992.

Discography

Harmonizing Four 1950–55 (1995, Heritage, UK HTCD 29).
The Harmonizing Four, 1957 (1993, Vee-Jay NVG2-604).

HARP OF ZION, THE

This collection, which appeared in 1893, was the work of William Henry Sherwood, about whom little biographical information is known. He lived his entire life in Petersburg, Virginia, where he owned an orphanage for black children. Sherwood was a composer with several songs to his credit, of which the most famous is "The Church Is Moving On," which appeared in a songbook as late as 1927. He was also a choir director and band leader but is significant in the history of gospel music as one of the first to draw on the return to the roots movement of the ex-slaves who formed the Azusa Street Revival.

Sherwood's book included many of his own songs as well as those of several other composers. More important, he was the first African American to publish numbers in the pregospel mode. Melodically, harmonically, and rhythmically, these songs foreshadowed what would later be called gospel. Lyrically, Sherwood's numbers are spare, making great use of call-and-response; their melodies are simple and catchy, and the harmonies generally consist of three or four chords, while the rhythms are relatively uncomplicated. These features made Sherwood's songs easy to remember and, hence, appealing to a large number of people. This is perhaps the reason why *The Harp of Zion* was adopted by the all-black National Baptist Convention and republished in an unaltered edition under the title *The National Harp of Zion and Baptist Young People's Union Hymnal*, and was widely used by black Baptists until the end of World War I.

W. K. McNeil

Reference and Further Reading

Boyer, Horace Clarence. *The Golden Age of Gospel*, 26–27. Urbana and Chicago: University of Illinois Press, 2000 (1995).

HARPER, REDD

Milburn C. "Redd" Harper (b. September 29, 1903; d. Unknown)

Redd Harper, a one-time actor and member of a variety of Western and dance bands, became known after his 1951 conversion as a sacred singer, evangelist, and star of inspirational films. A native of Nocona, Texas, Harper grew up in Oklahoma and attended the University of Oklahoma in the mid-1920s. He appeared on radio at WKY Oklahoma City and also at KSO and KRNT in Des Moines, Iowa. Around 1936, he moved to Hollywood, where he married Laura Kinks in 1941. During World War II, he served in the Coast Guard as a motor machinist mate, and also in entertainment. Much of his acting work tended to be in network radio drama. He also had small parts in such films as *The Strawberry Roan*, a Western that starred Gene Autry.

Early in 1951, at the behest of Tim Spencer, a former member of Sons of the Pioneers, Redd began attending meetings of Hollywood Christian groups and in May was converted. He subsequently starred in such Billy Graham–produced films as *Mr. Texas* and *Oil Town, U.S.A.* He also did a program for the Armed Forces Radio Service.

Perhaps most important, Harper did evangelistic work and recorded gospel albums for companies such as Sacred and Christian Faith. In 1957, the Fleming H. Revell Company published his inspirational life story *I Walk the Glory Road*, and Christian Faith released his album of the same name. In 1988, he was living in Hollywood. According to Marilyn Tuttle, widow of another noted cowboy singer–evangelist, Harper has been deceased for several years.

Ivan M. Tribe

Reference and Further Reading

Gentry, Linnell. *A History and Encyclopedia of Country, Western, and Gospel Music*. 438. Nashville, TN: Clairmont Corp., 1969.
Harper, Redd. *I Walk the Glory Road*. Woodlawn, NJ: Fleming H. Revell Co., 1957.

Discography

I Walk the Glory Road (1957, Christian Faith RH-1253).

HARRINGTON, BOB

Evangelist known as the "Chaplain of Bourbon Street" (b. 1927, Sweetwater, AL)

Bob Harrington was born in 1927 to Robert and Ludie Harrington. He grew up in the Methodist church. At the age of nine he joined the church through the influence of his grandmother. Harrington became a successful insurance salesman and demonstrated a unique ability to sell himself and a message. At the age of thirty, he was saved at a Baptist revival in Alabama and soon felt the call to enter the ministry.

Harrington moved to New Orleans and began to evangelize in the heart of the French Quarter, an area of the city known for it bars and strip clubs. He soon gained a reputation as the "Chaplain of Bourbon Street," a title acknowledged by Mayor Victor Schiro. Harrington cultivated an image of a hard-hitting evangelist in one of the best known American "good time" districts. He preached outside strip joints on Bourbon Street, with gospel music blaring out of loudspeakers.

Harrington's fame expanded to the national stage, and he exhibited an uncanny ability to use the media (especially television, where he hosted a syndicated talk show) to his advantage. He debated noted atheist Madalyn Murray O'Hair and was covered in *Hustler* magazine. Larry Flynt, *Hustler's* publisher, even allowed the evangelist to use the company airplane for travel. During the height of his fame, Harrington wrote several books (including a memoir) and recorded numerous sermon albums released on his own label. In 1973 he released an album on Canaan.

In the late 1970s Harrington's ministry and life began to fall apart. He divorced his wife in 1979 and left the ministry shortly thereafter. Harrington moved to Florida, where he became a motivational speaker. Trouble haunted him; a second marriage ended in divorce, and he filed for bankruptcy. He became mired in debt. In 1995 Harrington returned to New Orleans and started preaching again. He married a third time and moved to Mansfield, Texas, where he and his wife own a miniature horse farm. Harrington continues to preach, though his activities are far more low key than in the past.

Bob Harrington's career typified the flamboyant style of evangelism during the 1960s and 1970s. He experienced both joyful success and dire trouble, and he survived both.

KEVIN S. FONTENOT

Reference and Further Reading

Harrington, Bob; compiled by Steve Callahan. *The Wit and Wisdom of the Famous Chaplain of Bourbon Street.* Nashville: Impact Books, 1970.
———; with Walter Wagner. *The Chaplain of Bourbon Street.* New Orleans: Chaplain Productions, 1971.

Discography

Bob the Baptist (Record 6).
Holy Happy Hour (Canaan CAS 9744).
It's Fun Being Saved (Record 8).
Laughter, Truth, and Music (Record 1).
My Life Story (Record 4).
Old Time Religion (Record 7).
Preaching in Viet Nam (Record 2).
Sho-Bar (Record 3).
Talking with Teens (Record 5).

HARRIS, LARNELLE

(b. 1947, Danville, KY)

A singer of what is often called "inspirational music," Larnelle Harris rose to prominence in the last two decades of the twentieth century, as a commercially successful performer of gospel music that tends toward the easy listening end of the adult contemporary spectrum. His mellifluous vocal style is sometimes compared to that of mainstream artists such as Johnny Mathis.

His repertoire has favored hymns and ballads, though he has also recorded a sampling of more upbeat pop songs and dance tracks. Harris majored in voice at Western Kentucky University and toured as a drummer with the Spurlows. Before embarking on his solo career, he also recorded two albums with a Christian rock band called First Gear and, from 1984 to 1987, sang with Bill Gaither and Gary McSpadden in the Gaither Vocal Band.

As a mainstay of inspirational radio stations, Harris has recorded numerous hit songs, including "I Miss My Time with You," "Beyond All the Limits," and "Take the Time." Lyrically, he consistently selects or composes songs that have explicit evangelical messages. Praise and worship are a common theme, along with songs that commend Christian virtues or values. "Blessing and Honor" opens *First Love* as a ready-made choir anthem with full orchestration and choral accompaniment. "The Other Woman" from *Beyond All the Limits* is a sentimental ode to the singer's now-grown daughter.

Early in his career, Harris recorded a number of duets with Sandi Patti, two of which won Grammy awards ("More than Wonderful" in 1983 and "I've Just Seen Jesus" in 1985). He would win three more Grammys as a solo artist, in addition to eleven Dove awards. The Gospel Music Association named Harris Male Vocalist of the Year three times (1983, 1986, and 1988) and Songwriter of the Year once (1988). In 1988, his album *The Father Hath Provided* had the unusual distinction of receiving the Grammy, Dove, and Stellar awards for Album of the Year in the category for which it was nominated, and a year later his song "I Can Begin Again" was named Contemporary Gospel Single of the Year by *Cashbox* magazine.

In the mid-1990s Harris's song "Mighty Spirit" was featured as part of a public service announcement for the Points of Light Foundation and, as a result, Harris received a Silver Bell Award for Distinguished Public Service and was invited to the White House to perform for President George H. W. Bush. In 1999, Harris was awarded an honorary doctorate of music from Campbellsville University in Campbellsville, Kentucky.

As an African American artist with widespread appeal to white audiences, Harris has sometimes played a significant role in furthering racial integration within the gospel music world. In his early years, especially, he spoke out in interviews concerning what he called "a legacy of intentional segregation" in the field, and he sought to remedy this situation by performing in settings where African Americans had rarely been featured. The song "Teach Me to Love" on *Beyond All the Limits"* deals specifically with racial prejudice.

MARK ALLAN POWELL

Reference and Further Reading

Powell, Mark Allan. "Larnelle Harris." In *Encyclopedia of Contemporary Christian Music.* 401–402. Peabody, MA: Hendrickson Publishers, 2002.

Discography

First Gear. *First Gear* (1972, Myrrh); *Caution! Steep Hill Use* (1974, Myrrh).
New Gaither Vocal Band. *New Point of View* (1984, Dayspring 701 4127 012).
Gaither Vocal Band. *One X 1* (1986, Word).
Larnelle Harris. *Tell It to Jesus* (1975, Word); *Larnelle . . . More* (1977, Word 7-01-873110-0); *Free* (1978, Word 7-01-879510-9); *Give Me More Love in My Heart* (1981, Benson CO3713); *Best of Larnelle* (1982, Word 7-01-887110-7); *Touch Me, Lord* (1982, Impact CO3779); *I've Just Seen Jesus* (1985, Impact RO3732); *From a Servant's Heart* (1986, Benson RO3956); *The Father Hath Provided* (1987, Benson 2370); *Larnelle . . . Christmas* (1988, Benson); *I Can Begin Again* (1989, Benson); *Larnelle Live . . . Psalms, Hymns, and Spiritual Songs* (1990, Benson); *The Best of Ten Years, Vols. 1 & 2* (1991, Benson); *I Choose Joy* (1992, Benson); *Beyond All the Limits* (1994, Benson); *Unbelievable Love* (1995, Benson CD 4195); *Collector's Series* (1998, Benson 84418-2242-2); *First Love* (1998, Brentwood); *A Story to Tell: Hymns and Praises* (2000, Reunion 83061-0512-2); *Forgiven* (date and label unknown).

HARTFORD MUSIC COMPANY

Established in 1918 in Hartford, Arkansas, by Eugene M. Bartlett and David Moore, the Hartford Music Company became a major Southern gospel songbook publisher, with annual songbook sales, even during the Depression, approaching a hundred thousand. Gospel music singing conventions from the mid-1920s through the early 1940s, especially in Arkansas, often featured Hartford songbooks, of which two or more were published each year. Like other, similar large Southern publishers, it also supported a musical institute, traveling "normal" schools, touring quartets, and itinerant singing school teachers that trained many hundreds of future music teachers, singers, and songwriters.

The musical institute began in 1921, and in the next twelve years the student body grew from seventy-five pupils to close to four hundred. During the 1930s, the institute—with classes in subjects such as voice, harmony, poetry, and piano—organized three-week sessions in January and June during which students generally boarded with local families. Its teachers included J. B. Herbert, head of the institute, and other major gospel music luminaries such as Albert E. Brumley, Frank Stamps, James Rowe, the Ruebush brothers, and Homer Rodeheaver.

John A. McClung replaced Bartlett as head of the company in 1931, and he bought the company in 1936. Both of these charismatic leaders died in the early 1940s, leading to a turbulent period for the company. In 1943, only one songbook was published. In 1944, the company moved to Hot Springs, Arkansas, and published three books, one of which featured "radio" songs sung by Odis Echols and the Hartford Melody Boys. In 1947, the company, run by individuals with little connection to the earlier Hartford Music Company, moved back to Hartford and published only one book.

A resurgence began in 1948 when Albert E. Brumley bought the company, in part to keep the rights to his song "I'll Fly Away." In the early 1950s he moved the company to Powell, Missouri, and, except for a period in the mid-1950s, Brumley—with the help of family—continued to publish Hartford songbooks there until a year before his death in 1977. These songbooks were often published in conjunction with National Music Company, based in Jefferson, Texas.

The Hartford Music Company became an arm of Albert E. Brumley and Sons, and this relationship was formalized during incorporation proceedings in the mid-1980s. Robert Brumley became head of the company after his father died. The name Hartford Music Company is rarely used now, except to handle the legal matters related to the vast amount of music published under that name. Albert E. Brumley and Sons continues the legacy of the Hartford Music Company by publishing reprints of selected gospel and "pioneer" songbooks as well as cassettes and CDs featuring the music of the Brumley family.

DREW BEISSWENGER

Reference and Further Reading

Deller, David C. "Sing Me Home to Gloryland: Arkansas Songbook Gospel Music in the Twentieth Century." Ph.D. dissertation, University of Arkansas, Fayetteville, 1999.

Hively, Kay; Albert E. Brumley, Jr. *I'll Fly Away: The Life of Albert E. Brumley*. Branson, MO: Mountaineer Books, 1990.

HAVEN OF REST QUARTET

Founded by Paul Meyers in 1934 as the musical arm of the *Haven of Rest* radio program, the quartet—which took its name from the gospel song of the same name (beginning "My soul in sad exile was out on life's sea") with words by Henry Gilmour and music by George Moore—broadcast live, five days a week, from station KFI in Los Angeles. During the next seventy years, the group exemplified mainline gospel hymnody, reflecting the Northern, urban revivalism stemming from the days of Dwight Moody and his musical associate Ira Sankey in the 1870s.

The quartet's popularity and its radio program grew quickly and by the 1950s was heard nationwide and in Canada. In addition to the quartet singing four or five songs each program, either *a cappella* or accompanied by the organ, the program included poetry, instrumental music, and preaching. Throughout much of its history, the quartet toured nationally and produced around fifty albums.

The quartet employed a nautical theme—inspired by hearing the morning watch bells from a ship anchored in San Diego harbor—in its promotions and Hollywood recording studio set, complete with portholes and decks. Original, longtime members included Ken Nelson (first tenor), Ernie Payne (bass), and Bob Bowman. From 1934 until 1985 the group had only two organists, Lorin Whitney and Dean McNichols.

When McNichols retired, the musical approach of the group shifted somewhat, updating its arrangements to reflect a more contemporary approach and employing electronic keyboards and other instruments. Although younger members came in to replace older ones over the years, the audience for the quartet's traditional gospel hymnody aged, and it ultimately could not compete with contemporary

Christian music, despite a name change to Haven Quartet in the late 1980s. By 2003, the radio program no longer boasted a live, in-house group and relied on guest artists or recordings.

Both practically and symbolically, the Haven of Rest Quartet represented mainline gospel hymnody, which dominated much of evangelical church music during most of the twentieth century.

MEL R. WILHOIT

Reference and Further Reading

Haven Today website, http://www.HavenToday.org.

Discography

Haven: Best of Vol. I (Haven Ministries).
Haven: Best of Vol. II (Haven Ministries).

HAWKINS, TRAMAINE

(b. October 11, 1957, San Francisco, CA)

Tramaine Davis, born and raised in Northern California, is the granddaughter of Bishop E. E. Cleveland, one of the founders of the Church of God in Christ. She got her start at a young age singing with Andrae Crouch and the Disciples and then with the Edwin Hawkins Singers. With this group she sang lead vocal in a recording session that produced "Oh Happy Day," a song that changed gospel music forever and remains popular to this day in its recorded form and in published choral arrangements.

Tramaine married Walter Hawkins, Edwin's younger brother. He later led the choir at the Berkeley Love Center Church of Christ church; Tramaine sang lead soprano. In the 1970s, they produced two *Love Alive* albums that became best-sellers. Each featured Walter's sermons, Edwin on piano, and Tramaine on lead vocals. In 1998, they produced a twenty-five year anniversary album of the first *Love Alive* album.

Hawkins began her solo recording career in the mid-1980s. Her songs were derived from traditional gospel, blues, soul, jazz, and occasionally hard-driving funk, thus blending the sacred with the secular. Her music crossed over but her faith-based lyrics did not. In many respects, gospel and jazz share common roots. In a 1990 concert, Tramaine affirmed the common roots of gospel and jazz by inviting two jazz greats to participate: organist Jimmy McGriff and tenor saxophonist Stanley Turrentine. Also participating was the great rock guitarist Carlos Santana. This blending of genres in the late 1980s and early 1990s undoubtedly helped shape the style of contemporary gospel.

Tramaine Hawkins Live earned her one of her two Grammys. It was awarded at the Thirty-Third Annual Grammy Awards (1990) for Best Traditional Soul Gospel Performance. She earned another Grammy at the Twenty-Third Annual Grammy Awards (1980). It was awarded for a compilation album, *The Lord's Prayer*, for Best Gospel Performance, Contemporary or Inspirational. This recording featured, among others, Walter Hawkins and Andrae Crouch.

Hawkins also earned two Dove Awards from the Gospel Music Association, both in 1991: one for *Live*—Traditional Gospel Album of the Year—the other, with Walter Hawkins and V. Michael McKay, for "The Potter's House"—Traditional Gospel Song of the Year.

DAVID WILLOUGHBY

Reference and Further Reading

Christianity Today website, http://www.christianitytoday.com/music/reviews/2001/stilltramaine.html.
Dove Awards website, http://www.doveawards.com.
Gospel Music Association website, http://www.gospelmusic.com.
Richard De La Font Agency website, http://www.delafont.com/music_acts/tramaine-hawkins.htm
"Walter Hawkins biography." Love Center Ministries website, http://www.lovecenter.org/.

Selected Discography

Live (1992 [1990], Sparrow/Emd CD 51426).
Love Alive (1993 [1973], Light Records CD 1012).
Love Alive II (1993 [1978], CGI Records 1011).
All My Best to You (1994, Sparrow/Emd CD 51429).
To a Higher Place (1994, Sony CD 57876).
All My Best to You, Vol. 2 (2001, Chordant CD 20315).
Love Alive V: 25th Anniversary Reunion (2001 [1998], Gospo Centric Records CD).
Still Tramaine (2001, Gospo Centric CD 70036).
Mega Collection (2002, Compendia Music Group CD 5400).

HAWKINS, WALTER

Walter Hawkins is one of the most beloved figures in contemporary gospel music. In the more than thirty years of his music career, Hawkins has created one of the most prolific and outstanding catalogs of hit gospel recordings and published songs.

Walter's musical debut actually came anonymously when he sang in the youth choir at Ephesians Church of God in Christ (COGIC) in Berkeley, California, his hometown. The choir, under the direction of Walter's older brother, Edwin (who has had a rich career in gospel music since 1968 and has been a tremendous influence in the development of contemporary gospel choral music), recorded an album, *Let Us Go into the House of the Lord*, in 1968 to raise money to attend a convention in Washington, DC. The intent was to sell the album locally. However, to everyone's surprise, a song from that album, "Oh Happy Day," became a national success, selling more than a million copies. For the next few years, Walter toured nationally and internationally with the Edwin Hawkins Singers before leaving in the early 1970s to concentrate on his music and ministry.

After earning a master of divinity degree from the University of California at Berkeley, Walter founded the Love Center Church in Oakland in 1973, where he remains the pastor. Under Walter's direction and with eighteen hundred dollars borrowed from his mother-in-law, the Love Center Choir returned to Ephesians COGIC to record *Going Up Yonder* (1975). This debut album became one of the best-selling gospel albums in the 1970s. For several months it rode the gospel charts, became a mainstay on *Billboard's* gospel top-forty chart for three consecutive years, and set the pattern for Hawkins's future success.

Marvelous

Not only is Bishop Walter Hawkins one of gospel's most successful performers, but he has launched or inspired the careers of many of today's biggest gospel stars through his work as a songwriter, producer, singer, and musician and as cofounder and spiritual leader of the Edwin Hawkins & Walter Hawkins Music and Arts Seminar/Love Fellowship. These include Tramaine Hawkins, Mary Mary, Kirk Franklin, John P. Kee, Richard Smallwood, Donny McClurkin, LaShaun Pace, Kurt Carr, Yolanda Adams, Lynette Hawkins-Stephens, Shirley Miller, Daryl Coley, Byron Cage, and many more.

Special Gift

Walter has appeared on the covers of *BRE* (*Black Radio Exclusive*) and numerous other gospel magazines during his career, and he was prevailed upon to give an unprecedented command performance to the Announcer's Guild of the Gospel Music Workshop of America after the release of his last album project, the Grammy-nominated *Love Alive V—The 25th Anniversary Reunion* in June 1998.

Walter Hawkins. Photo courtesy Frank Driggs Collection.

Come Live With Me

Walter is the recipient of many awards, including a Grammy Award, more than eight Grammy nominations, three Dove awards, the San Francisco Chapter of the Recording Academy's 2003 Governors Award for Creative Excellence and Outstanding Achievement, *Billboard* #1 awards (the *Love Alive IV* album project spent an unparalleled thirty-nine weeks at number one atop the *Billboard* gospel charts), Gospel Music Workshop of America awards, Gospel Music's Lifetime Heritage Award, Gospel Music Hall of Fame and Museum Award, and many others.

So We Learn

Walter Hawkins's last album release was the fifth in a series of live recordings, *Love Alive V—The 25th Reunion,* on Gospo Centric Records. The long-awaited double CD reunited Hawkins with gospel greats such as Grammy Award winners Edwin Hawkins and Tramaine Hawkins, Lynette Hawkins Stephens, Pastor Yvette Flunder, and Shirley Miller.

Dear Jesus I Love You

Recorded at Oakland's Historic Paramount Theatre, the collection featured Hawkins's World Renowned Love Center Choir. The concert celebrated the twenty-fifth anniversary of Hawkins's ordination as a pastor and recording artist. *Love Alive V—The 25th Reunion* embraces a central theme—giving praise and thanks to God. Excitement surrounding this self-produced LP was high in gospel music circles, and it was heralded as the most anticipated gospel album of that year. For the occasion Hawkins wrote six of the eleven original pieces on disc one and gathered his all-time favorite past recordings for disc two. "This was a reunion album," he notes. "I got to work again with people I've always enjoyed working with,

Tramaine, my sister Lynette, my brother Edwin, my cousin Shirley, and Yvette."

Changed (Reprise)

Young and old, traditional and contemporary gospel fans all enjoy *Love Alive V—The 25th Reunion*. R&B/pop-friendly tracks such as the heart-wrenching ballad "Cry On," featuring Tony Timmons and Flunder, have strong crossover appeal. *Love Alive V—The 25th Reunion* leads off with the rousing "Thankful," then eases into the soul-stirring "Marvelous," a song that superbly showcases Hawkins's dynamic voice. "Safe in His Arms," written by Kevin Bond, carries an up-tempo, hip-hop flavor, while the jazzy "Nick of Time" broaches a subject we all can relate to: "There have been times when I've been so close to death and then been pulled to safety, it makes you think about how God always arrives just in the nick of time," explains Hawkins.

The delicate "He Made a Way" is another of Hawkins's favorites. The performers raise the roof with the rock 'n' rolling "God Is Standing By." "All things work together for good to them that love God, to them who are the called according to His purpose" (Romans 8:28) was the scripture that inspired Hawkins to write "It's Right and Good," a true showstopper performed with customary verve by Tramaine. The deeply inspirational "For My Good" was a contribution from Rusty Watson, who solos on the track.

Thank You

Disc two continues the central theme with "God Is Standing By," originally done with Lynette in 1976; "I'm Not the Same"; "Thank You"; "I Must Go On," performed with Miller; and "He Brought Me," featuring Tramaine. "When I reached back, I took songs that involved giving gratitude," says Hawkins.

Solid Rock

With great expectations by the industry and fans alike, Hawkins says he is glad to be part of contemporary gospel music's worldwide growth. "There's always been controversy around modern versus traditional gospel. What is tradition anyway? Gospel music doesn't have a particular style. Gospel's got to

progress," says Hawkins. "We [the Edwin Hawkins Singers] had probably one of the major crossover gospel songs of all time with 'Oh Happy Day,' and it brought in a whole new generation of listeners." That song did more than break gospel music barriers; it helped launch Hawkins's career.

Be Grateful

In 1978 Hawkins released *Love Alive II*. It sold 290,000 copies, won two Dove Awards from the Gospel Music Association, was nominated for a Grammy Award, and garnered awards from *Billboard, Record World,* and *Cash Box* music trade publications. It was not until 1985 that *Love Alive III* was finished. It earned a Dove Award nomination and sold more than a million copies. Four years later came *Love Alive IV*, which was nominated for a Grammy and remained on top of *Billboard's* gospel chart for more than thirty-nine weeks.

Changed

Besides his own recordings, Hawkins has collaborated with a number of other artists. With the Love Center Choir he appeared on Edwin Hawkins's *Live with the Oakland Symphony* LP and on recordings by Celt rocker Van Morrison and Lee Oskar. Hawkins himself has worked with Diahann Carroll, Jennifer Holliday, Earth, Wind and Fire, the late house music king Sylvester, and R&B star Jeffrey Osborne, as well as gospel artists Yolanda Adams, Donald Lawrence, Richard Smallwood, John P. Key, Vanessa Bell Armstrong, the Williams Brothers, and the Gospel Music Workshop of America.

In 1985, he wrote and produced "Everybody Ought to Know," featured on Tramaine Hawkins's album, *The Search Is Over*. Bishop Hawkins also wrote and produced three songs for the Williams Brothers' LP *Hand in Hand* that same year. He wrote and coproduced *I Must Go On*, Shirley Miller's 1986 album. The next year, Hawkins wrote and produced a debut album for his youngest sister, Lynette, called *Baby Sis*. In 1988, *Special Gift*, an album produced and written by Bishop Hawkins and performed by the Hawkins Family, was released on Birthright/Capitol Records. Hawkins also coproduced, musically directed, and arranged the Grammy-winning *Tramaine Live* for his former wife, Tramaine Hawkins, in 1991.

When the Battle Is Over

When looking back at his musical endeavors, Hawkins understands their place in his ministry. "Early on I thought my ministry and my music were apart from each other. But now I see they work hand in hand," he observes. "I can go a lot of places with my music that I can't go as a pastor and vice versa. The purpose of both is getting the message out to people. I've had some material blessings and it's okay to have them, but to be blessed with peace of mind and joy in your life, that's when you will be truly fulfilled."

DONNA M. COX

HEARN, BILLY RAY

(b. April 26, 1929)

Through the sheer force of ability and creative imagination, Billy Ray Hearn has gone from serving as minister of music at small Southern churches to being chair of the EMI Christian Music Group (EMI CMG), the world's largest religious music label.

Hearn was reared in an active Southern Baptist family and went into various music ministries after two stints in the U.S. Navy. A talented composer and arranger, he was involved in some of the earliest church youth choir "musicals" of the 1960s. Through the musicals, he was hired by Word Records in Waco, Texas, where he joined an enormously creative team that included founder Jarrell McCracken, composer Kurt Kaiser, and, a few years later, composer Ralph Carmichael.

With the advent of the Jesus Movement in the late 1960s and early 1970s, McCracken tabbed Hearn to develop Word's contemporary Christian music (CCM) label, Myrrh, in 1972. Hearn's better-known signees with Myrrh included Randy Matthews, Ray Hildebrand, Dust, Crimson Bridge, the Sparrows, First Gear (with a drummer named Larnelle Harris), the 2nd Chapter of Acts, Barry McGuire, Gene Cotton, and David Meece.

Hearn left Word and Myrrh in 1975 and, after a series of business ventures, joined the fledgling Sparrow label. (He would buy out his remaining partners and become sole owner of Sparrow in 1981.) As with Myrrh, Hearn displayed an astute eye for talent in a variety of musical styles. The first additions to the new label were John Michael and Terry Talbot, followed by Janny Grine, the Agapeland children's music troupe, and the late Keith Green. Several former Myrrh acts eventually followed Hearn to Sparrow as well.

While Green remains a towering figure in the history of CCM, Hearn would later sign numerous other significant artists, including Phil Keaggy, Steve Taylor, Steve Camp, Sheila Walsh, Whiteheart, Carman, Tramaine Hawkins, Steven Curtis Chapman, and Bebe and CeCe Winans. Sparrow also distributed a number of other Christian labels, including Star Song and Fore Front.

In 1992, Hearn sold Sparrow—then second only to Word in total sales—to EMI Music, an international music conglomerate, forming EMI CMG. At the time, Hearn was named chairman and CEO. The label would eventually grow to include more than fifty artists, including Avalon, Andy Griffith, Delirious, Jump5, the Newsboys, and Zoegirl. The label, along with its sister label EMI Gospel (Potter's House Mass Choir, Smoke Norful, Donald Lawrence, and others) began its domination of the Christian music charts in the late 1990s. Hearn continued composing and arranging, including the best-selling collections of sacred hymns with Tom Fetke, *The Majesty and the Glory* and *The Majesty and the Glory of Christmas.*

Hearn was elected to the Gospel Music Hall of Fame in 1997, and in 1999 both Hearn and Sparrow were awarded Lifetime Achievement awards by the Gospel Music Association (GMA). He is past chairman of the GMA and past president of the Church Music Publishers Association. While Hearn stepped down as CEO of EMI CMG and Sparrow in 2001, turning over the day-to-day operations to his son Bill, he continues active in the Christian music industry. He is the founder and sponsor of the biannual Hearn Symposium on Christian Music—a series of events that bring together choir directors, working Christian musicians, producers, and academicians at Baylor University in Waco, Texas—and director of the Sparrow Foundation, which contributes to numerous music education institutions, needy students, and young artists each year.

ROBERT DARDEN

See also Carman; Carmichael, Ralph; Gospel Music Association; Green, Keith; Harris, Larnelle; Hawkins, Tramaine; Kaiser, Kurt; McCracken, Jarrell; Myrrh Records; Newsboys; Talbot, John Michael; Taylor, Steve; Winans, The

Reference and Further Reading

Alfonso, Barry. *Billboard Guide to Contemporary Christian Music.* New York: Billboard Books, 2002.

Baker, Paul. *Contemporary Christian Music: Where It Came From, Where It Is Going.* Westchester, IL: Crossway Books, 1985.

Cusic, Don. *The Sound of Light: A History of Gospel Music.* Bowling Green, OH: Bowling Green State University Popular Press, 1990.

Darden, Robert. "Billy Ray Hearn: His Eye Is on Sparrow." *Rejoice!* (December 1991–January 1992): 19–22.
———; with P. J. Richardson. *Corporate Giants: Personal Stories of Faith and Finance.* Grand Rapids, MI: Fleming H. Revell, 2002.
"Year in Music & Touring." *Billboard* (December 25, 2004): YE-76.

HEART WARMING RECORDS

Heart Warming Records was initiated in 1962 as a subsidiary of the John Benson Publishing Company of Nashville, Tennessee, with, according to James R. Goff, Jr., "an emphasis on quality recordings for gospel music quartets." To quote Goff again, "by the end of the decade it was a resounding success." It remained a major force in Southern gospel recording for some two decades and added three additional labels to its conglomerate, Impact in 1968, Greentree in 1976, and Vista.

During the 1960s the company signed a number of well-known artists and groups in the field and began turning out albums on a regular basis in well-produced, attractive covers. The company made use of producers who knew the music and also the record business, such as Bob Benson, Don Light, and Bob McKenzie. Because many of their sessions were held in the RCA Victor studios, they had the advantage of good sound engineers, such as Charles Seitz who had helped create the "Nashville sound."

The Heart Warming "stable" of artists soon came to include figures such as the Speer Family, the Singing Rambos, the Hemphills, the Oak Ridge Boys, the Tennesseeans, Henry and Hazel Slaughter, the Kingsmen, and the Sego Brothers and Naomi. Lesser figures included country recitation expert Buddy Starcher and hardcore bluegrass traditionalist J. D. Jarvis, repackaged for a broader audience. To get some idea of the impact that Heart Warming had, in the Southern gospel album of the year category, a Heart Warming album took the Dove Award nine times from 1969 through 1986. A Canaan album won the prize six times, an RCA Victor once, and in two years no award was given.

Impact Records was designed for the more "uptown" gospel or inspirational groups and artist. The Bill Gaither Trio proved to be the most significant act on this label, but several others also made their mark. These included Doug Oldham, the Imperials (post–Jake Hess era), the Archers, the Lanny Wolfe Trio, and Bill Gaither's younger brother Danny Gaither. Greentree signed young "contemporary artists" that included Reba Rambo, the interracial Andrus, Blackwood & Co, Phil Johnson, Sharalee Lucas, Tim Sheppard, and the Wall Brothers.

After 1986, the Benson Company changed their names, and while they remained a major force in recording, their labels bore such names as Riversong and Benson.

IVAN M. TRIBE

Reference and Further Reading

Goff, James R. Jr. *Close Harmony: A History of Southern Gospel.* 231–233, 242–243. Chapel Hill: University of North Carolina Press, 2002.

HEAVENLY GOSPEL SINGERS

Founded in Detroit in the late 1920s when the Whitmore Family formed the Masonic Glee Club, the Heavenly Gospel Singers' longevity and success can be largely attributed to their leader and great bass singer, Jimmy Bryant, who steered the group during the middle 1930s.

By the early 1930s only Fred Whitmore remained from the original ensemble, and the key person he recruited was bass singer Jimmy Bryant, whose strong personality and emotional singing galvanized the group. The other new members included lead singer Roosevelt Fenoy from the gospel center of Bessemer, Alabama, as well as Spartanburg, South Carolina–based baritone Henderson Massey, who also took over as manager. In 1933 the group was renamed the Heavenly Gospel Singers by an Akron, Ohio, preacher, "Daddy" Smith, and they became a semi-professional group that initially sang throughout Southern Michigan and Northern Ohio.

During the next few years, the quartet's home base shifted many times, from Akron and Columbus, Ohio, to Spartanburg, and then to nearby Charlotte. They often traveled northwest to the coalfields of Southwestern Virginia, where the economy remained relatively strong because the demand for coal did not diminish during the Depression. The coal camps also attracted many black workers in search of steady employment during these difficult times.

Charlotte also hosted many recording sessions for Victor and their Bluebird subsidiary beginning in 1935. The popularity of the Heavenly Gospel Singers and their Charlotte base soon led to their first recordings for Bluebird in 1935; they attracted attention due to their innovative style, which relied upon the emerging sound of jubilee groups such as the Golden Gate Quartet along with style that emphasized emotional lead singing. For the next four years their close association with the Golden Gate Quartet, which was also based in Charlotte during the middle 1930s, led to a "quartet contest" that drew hundreds of enthusiastic fans who crowded churches throughout the Carolinas.

For the next three years, Victor called the group into the studios once or twice a year to record eight or ten tracks, making them one of the most often recorded black gospel quartets of the 1930s. In fact, during their career on record, the Heavenly Gospel Singers cut 102 titles for Bluebird, ninety-four of which were issued on that label, many also seeing release on Victor's cheaper Montgomery Ward subsidiary. Although the charismatic and talented Jimmy Bryant left the group in late 1938, the group quickly replaced him with another strong bass singer, Willie Bobo. Bobo remained with the group for about three years before departing the Heavenly Gospel Singers to join the Dixie Hummingbirds, where he remained until the early 1970s. Between Bryant's departure and the outbreak of World War II (two members—Henderson Massey and Bob Beatty—were drafted into the Army), the group began to lose its momentum.

After the war, the quartet reformed under the leadership of Henderson Massey, who acquired the group's name, but they never returned to their previous popularity and finally disbanded in the early 1950s. Various members of the Heavenly Gospel Singers went on to sing with important groups. Bob Beatty, for example, extended his career singing with the Sensational Nightingales, the Violinaires, the Gospel Knights, and the Soul Lifters, while Bryant when on to sing with the Gospel Light Jubilee Singers and the Detroiters.

KIP LORNELL

Reference and Further Reading

Briggs, Keith. Liner notes to *Heavenly Gospel Singers Vol. 14* (Document Records 5452-5455).
Zoltan, Jerry. *"Great God A' Mighty!" The Dixie Hummingbirds Celebrating the Rise of Soul Gospel Music.* Oxford, UK: Oxford University Press, 2003.

Discography

Heavenly Gospel Singers, Vol. 1 (1997, Document 5452).
Heavenly Gospel Singers, Vol. 2 (1997, Document 5453).
Heavenly Gospel Singers, Vol. 3 (1997, Document 5454).
Heavenly Gospel Singers, Vol. 4 (1997, Document 5455).

HEE HAW GOSPEL QUARTET

Kenny Price (b. May 27, 1931; d. August 4, 1987)
Louis Marshall "Grandpa" Jones (b. October 20, 1913; d. February 19, 1998)
Roy Clark (b. April 15, 1933)
Alvis Edgar "Buck" Owens, Jr. (b. August 12, 1929)

Named for and featured on the long-running country music television show that created them, the Hee Haw Gospel Quartet was a 1970s–1980s throwback to the Brown's Ferry Four of thirty years before, with one man, Country Music Hall of Fame member Grandpa Jones, a regular member of both.

Published reminiscences by Jones and by the show's producer, Sam Lovullo, agree on the main details of how the group came to be. Early in *Hee Haw's* CBS-TV run (1969–1971), cast members Roy Clark, Buck Owens, Kenny Price, Archie Campbell, and Grandpa Jones were harmonizing on old-time gospel favorites in one of the dressing rooms with guests Merle Travis (like Jones, a one-time member of the Brown's Ferry Four) and Tennessee Ernie Ford when producer Lovullo passed by. He liked the sound so much he rushed them into the studio to get videotape before the impromptu group lost its verve and close harmony.

Viewer response to the gospel songs was good (in spite of the hesitance of some of the show's executives, who thought the quartet slowed the pace of the show too much), so after a few months a regular cast quartet of Buck Owens (lead), Roy Clark (high tenor), Grandpa Jones (tenor), and Kenny Price (bass) began tapings. All had long and successful country music careers, with Jones a veteran of the Brown's Ferry Four. Similar to that earlier group, the quarter's only accompaniment was a single acoustic guitar, played by Clark. The popularity of this Hee Haw Gospel Quartet led the show to form various instrumental quartets (banjo, fiddle, harmonica) and rotate them in a regular sequence. Most weeks the quartet song closed the broadcast, bringing what many considered a healthy, family-value balance to the image of the *Hee Haw* beauties with their low necklines and miniskirts.

The group mostly performed songs from the shape-note era (for example, "The Unclouded Day," "The Old Country Church") and from such early twentieth-century Southern writers as Albert E. Brumley ("I'll Fly Away") and E. M. Bartlett ("Everybody Will Be Happy Over There"). Its few albums made for a custom Hee Haw label and, marketed by television ads, took performances straight off the show, though sometimes extra musicians were overdubbed onto the tracks, outraging purists. Some of these have been reissued in CD format. The quartet won the Best Gospel Group Award from *Music City News,* a Nashville country music publication (later merged as an awards organization with TNN, the Nashville Network, as TNN/Music City News Awards) for seven straight years in the 1980s.

Buck Owens's decision in 1986 to leave the show after some seventeen years as cohost and Kenny Price's death the next year deprived the quartet of half of its original membership. Lovullo has said that these departures cost the group its unique sound. Joe Babcock from the Nashville Edition replaced Owens on lead, and Tennessee Ernie Ford often took the bass part until his own death in 1991. The show ended new production in 1993, which closed the long career of one of country gospel's most visible and popular quartets, a television and recording act that never made a single personal appearance.

RONNIE PUGH

Reference and Further Reading

Jones, Louis M. "Grandpa"; with Charles K. Wolfe. *Everybody's Grandpa: Fifty Years Behind the Mike*. Knoxville: University of Tennessee Press, 1984.
Lovullo, Sam; Marc Eliot. *Life in the Kornfield: My 25 Years at Hee Haw*. New York: Boulevard Books, 1996.

HEIRLOOM

Tanya Goodman-Sykes (b. October 21, 1957)
Candy Hemphill Christmas (b. ca. 1961)
Sheri Easter (b. October 27, 1963)
Barbra Fairchild (b. November 1950)

Heirloom was a trio of country-oriented gospel singers whose collaboration seemed to mirror the recently successful trio of Linda Ronstadt, Dolly Parton, and Emmylou Harris in the world of mainstream country. The initial lineup featured Tanya Goodman-Sykes, who had sung with the Happy Goodman Family, Candy Hemphill Christmas from the Singing Hemphills, and Sheri Easter, who often recorded with her husband Jeff. Easter departed after Heirloom released one self-titled album; she was replaced by Barbra Fairchild, who had charted a number one hit on general market country stations in 1973 ("Teddy Bear Song"). Heirloom recorded two more albums with this new lineup and then Easter returned, making Heirloom a female quartet for a one-album collection of hymns released in 1995.

The first Heirloom album won the Dove Award for 1990 Country Album of the Year, and one single from the project ("There's Still Power in the Blood") did especially well on Southern gospel charts. The group, however, did not attract much of a crossover audience from the contemporary Christian market. They only performed a few select dates in public and were viewed as an on-and-off studio project rather than as a full-time touring group. All members continued to record and perform separately and had successful careers in gospel music independent of the Heirloom projects.

MARK ALLAN POWELL

See also Easter, Jeff and Sheri; Happy Goodman Family

Reference and Further Reading

Powell, Mark Allan. "Heirloom." In *Encyclopedia of Contemporary Christian Music*. 410. Peabody, MA: Hendrickson Publishers, 2002.

Discography

Heirloom (1989, Benson).
Apples of Gold (1990, Benson).
Uncommon Love (1991, Benson).
The Best of Heirloom (1993, Benson).
Hymns That Last Forever (1995, Benson).
20 Favorites (2000, Budget).

HIBBARD, BRUCE

(b. June 2, 1953)

Christian pop singer Bruce Hibbard became involved with contemporary gospel music during the early years of the Jesus Movement revival and later made contributions as both a solo performer and as a songwriter. Hibbard was a member of the early Christian rock band Amplified Version, which had a sound indebted to such secular outfits as Ides of March or Blood, Sweat, & Tears. He was also associated with the group Sonlight, which served as an instrumental backing band for Andrae Crouch and the Disciples and later morphed into the jazz-fusion band Koinonia. Hibbard wrote the Christian radio hit "I'm Forgiven" for the Imperials (number one on the Christian music chart for thirteen weeks in 1980) and contributed songs to albums by Andrus, Blackwood & Company, Roby Duke, Fireworks, First Call, Amy Grant, and Lisa Welchel. He also sang as a background vocalist on projects by Phil Keaggy and Kelly Willard.

Hibbard's two solo albums present smooth arrangements of somewhat jazzy pop songs, with Willard and some of Hibbard's Sonlight/Koinonia friends assisting. Hibbard was a self-confessed protégé of Christian musician Paul Clark, and his albums are similar to that artist's work in style and content. Clark coproduced the album *A Light Within*, which includes the songs "All That I Want to Be" and "Givin' Myself Over." Hadley Hockensmith of Sonlight/Koinonia produced *Never Turnin' Back* and cowrote most of the songs for that sophomore project. The title track for the latter album would give Hibbard his only radio hit as a performer, reaching number fourteen on the Christian music charts in 1980.

MARK ALLAN POWELL

Reference and Further Reading

Powell, Mark Allan. "Bruce Hibbard." In *Encyclopedia of Contemporary Christian Music*, 413. Peabody, MA: Hendrickson Publishers, 2002.

Discography

A Light Within (1977, Seed PSR 006).
Never Turnin' Back (1980, Myrrh).
Time Waits (2001, Vizor).

HIGHER VISION

Rob Morgan (b. January 29, 1962)
Dedria Baker Morgan (b. February 9, 1961)
Kelly Caldwell (b. October 3, 1973)
Ronnie Merrill (b. June 3, 1963)
Dale Thomas (b. June 23, 1987)

Higher Vision is a bluegrass gospel group characterized by three strong lead singers who can also blend into an excellent vocal trio. Four of the five members had worked for several years as part of a band called Dean Osborne and Eastbound, but in 2002 they decided to go their own way, with Osborne forming a new group. The remaining four renamed themselves Higher Vision and became an almost total gospel group with the addition of a new banjo player. Their work has been performed both in churches and outdoor festivals ranging from Prince Edward Island to Mississippi, but with a heavy concentration of appearances in Kentucky and Ohio.

Rob Morgan, a native of Cincinnati, married Dedria Baker, a native of Owsley County, Kentucky, in 1981. Rob was an experienced mandolin player and bluegrass vocalist who played with different groups and also performed as a gospel duet. In 1992, first Rob and then Dedria joined Eastbound, whose membership had included guitarist Ronnie Merrill since 1990. Kelly Caldwell joined them on electric bass in 1996. While part of Eastbound, they recorded a sacred album titled *Roads of Faith,* and in 1999 Kelly made a bluegrass gospel album titled *That's Where I'm Bound.*

Following the summer season of 2002, Rob, Dedria, Kelly, and Ronnie founded Higher Vision. At this time, Dedria took up the electric bass and Kelly switched to fiddle. They took in Chris Hill on banjo to replace the departed Osborne. Hill remained their banjo player through August 2003, when Jimmy Smith joined the band. Smith departed in May 2004 and was replaced by teenage banjo picker Dale Thomas of Irvine, Kentucky. To date, Higher Vision

has one compact disc release on MasterShield Records and another scheduled for release.

IVAN M. TRIBE

Reference and Further Reading

Higher Vision website, http://www.highervisionband.com.
Tribe, Ivan M. "Higher Vision: A Calling to Play and Sing Bluegrass Gospel." *Bluegrass Unlimited* 39, no. 4 (October 2004): 66–69.

Selected Discography

Higher Vision. *Lifetime Guarantee* (2004, MasterShield).
Kelly Caldwell. *That's Where I'm Bound.*

HIGHWAY QCS, THE

The Highway QCs were one of the most important postwar black gospel vocal groups, not only because of their contribution to gospel music but also because the group nurtured several important singers who would become major pop stars, notably Sam Cooke and Lou Rawls. The Highway QCs performed in a style similar to that of many of the other popular 1950s-era gospel vocal groups. Inspired by pop groups such as the Ink Spots and the Mills Brothers, they incorporated pop and jazz-flavored harmonies into their repertoire of hymns and newly composed religious songs. One of their major hits was a cover of the traditional spiritual "Rock My Soul." The focus of the group was always on the dynamic lead singer, but their tight vocal harmonies were also a major attraction.

The group was formed in 1945 by members of Chicago's Highway Baptist Church and students at the local Quincy College High School; their name, the Teenage Highway QCs, memorialized both institutions. The original membership was somewhat fluid, but eventually settled around two sets of siblings—Marvin and Charles Jones and Curtis and Lee Richardson—along with Cooke as lead vocalist and Creadall Copeland. Cooke's talent was apparent from the start, and he soon was attracting national attention. In 1951, the well-established gospel group the Soul Stirrers lured him away for more prestigious bookings and recording opportunities. Luckily, another local group, the Holy Wonders, had an equally talented lead vocalist—Lou Rawls—who ably filled Cooke's shoes in the QCs. Rawls sang with the group for two years before joining the Chosen Gospel Singers out of Los Angeles, and was replaced by another talented singer, Johnnie Taylor. Taylor was befriended by Sam Cooke in 1953 when the two met on the gospel circuit, and he would later follow Cooke into secular music, scoring a number one R&B hit in 1968 with "Who's Making Love" and later scoring in the 1970s with "Disco Lady." In 1955, the QCs were signed to the local Vee-Jay label, making their first recordings.

In 1956, Johnnie Taylor left to go to the Soul Stirrers, replacing Cooke, who was enjoying his first major R&B hit with the secularized gospel song "You Send Me." Spencer Taylor—no relation to Johnnie—was enlisted to replace him. Spencer was another ex-member of the Holy Wonders, and he would become the driving force behind the QCs during the following decades. After recording for the Houston-based Peacock label in the 1960s, the group primarily performed on the road, occasionally recording for smaller gospel labels. In 2004, a live performance was released by the group on DVD, *He Said!*, still featuring Spencer Taylor as its leader.

RICHARD CARLIN

Reference and Further Reading

Heilbut, Anthony. *The Gospel Sound: Good News and Bad Times*. Updated and revised ed. New York: Limelight, 1997.

Discography

The Lord Is Sweet (1965, Peacock). Early to mid-1960s recordings made for Don Robey's Peacock and related labels.
Spencer Taylor and the Highway QCs (1959, Vee-Jay). Compilation of 1950s-era recordings actually featuring both Johnnie Taylor and Spencer Taylor as lead vocalists.

HILL, JAMES VAUGHN "JIM"

James Vaughn Hill (b. November 2, 1930)

With a name like James Vaughn Hill, one would seem like a natural for a career in gospel music. A native of Portsmouth, Ohio, which might be described as at the northern edge of the Bible Belt, Jim spent several years each with both the Stamps Quartet and the Statesmen. As middle age approached he ultimately chose a business career, but retained close ties with the sacred music world so dear to his heart.

After completing high school in 1948, Hill attended the local Interstate Business College and later went to Ohio University in Athens and worked in the office of the Norfolk and Western Railway. Together with Harold Patrick, he organized a part-time quartet, the Golden Keys, whose membership included Bill Gaither's younger brother Danny. They sang on weekends and recorded an album for Skylite, *The*

Ninety & Nine. The group attracted wider attention and sang as the Sunday morning opener at the National Quartet Convention. Jim's original composition "What a Day That Will Be" impressed Ben Speer, and the Homeland Harmony Quartet, the Speer Family, the Blackwood Brothers, the Statesmen, and the Oak Ridge Boys, among others, helped make it a standard.

Jim Hill joined the Stamps Quartet in 1962, remaining with them until the end of 1968. Hill sang tenor on several Skylite albums in that period, including one on which he was featured. He also sang on one with J. D. Sumner on Heart Warming and another with Jake Hess on RCA Victor. At the end of 1968, he left the Stamps and joined the Statesmen Quartet, changing his vocal part from tenor to lead.

Hill sang lead with the Statesmen for four years, during which time he sang on six of their albums for the Skylite label. Other members of the quartet in this period included Sherrill Neilson, Doy Ott, and James "Big Chief" Wetherington. Hill left the band in 1973, some months prior to the death of Wetherington, to become a sales representative for a shoe manufacturer. He also became a church choir director and did a few solo concerts from time to time. In recent years, the man J. D. Sumner described as "quite an operator" is retired in Middletown, Ohio, has done additional recording projects, and has appeared on videos in the Gaither Homecoming series.

IVAN M. TRIBE

Reference and Further Reading

Gentry, Linnell. *A History and Encyclopedia of Country, Western, and Gospel Music*, 2nd ed, 445–446. Nashville: Clairmont Corp., 1969.
Taylor, David L. *Happy Rhythm: A Biography of Hovie Lister & the Statesmen Quartet*, 130–132, 139–140. Lexington, IN: LexingtonHaus, 1998.
Terrell, Bob. *The Life and Times of J. D. Sumner*, 137, 203–204. Nashville: J. D. Sumner, 1994.

HOFFMAN, ELISHA ALBRIGHT

(b. May 7, 1839; d. November 25, 1929)

Although untrained musically, Elisha Hoffman produced more than two thousand gospel songs and compiled and edited fifty songbooks. A native of Orwigsburg, Pennsylvania, he was a pastor and mission worker for the Congregational and Presbyterian churches and the Evangelical Association. With his son, Ira, he opened a small publishing company that issued many of his own songs. He also worked for other companies; as the Hope Publishing Company's first music editor, he co-edited the series Pentecostal Hymns. For two years (1869–1871) he edited the periodical *Living Epistle*, and for several years produced *Hoffman's Musical Monthly: A Journal of Song*.

Hoffman's songs show a marked influence of secular song styles of the late nineteenth century. This is particularly true of his 1878 "Are You Washed in the Blood of the Lamb," which became a marching song for the Salvation Army. Indeed, it is often printed without listing Hoffman as lyricist or composer, as a "Salvation Army hymn." Vachel Lindsay used it as the basis for his poem *General William Booth Enters into Heaven*, which was later set to music by Charles Ives. This song first appeared in *Spiritual Songs for Gospel Meetings and the Sunday School*, a book edited by Hoffman and J. H. Tenney. In 1881 it was published in England in Ira D. Sankey's *Sacred Songs and Solos* but, interestingly, it did not appear in any of the four editions of *Gospel Hymns* that were issued after 1878.

Hoffman's other songs that are still in common use include "Down at the Cross" and "Leaning on the Everlasting Arms," the latter written in conjunction with A. J. Showalter. Both of these songs originally appeared in collections not edited by Hoffman.

W. K. McNEIL

Reference and Further Reading

Hall, J. H. *Biography of Gospel Song and Hymn Writer*. New York: AMS Press, 1971 (1914).

Osbeck, Kenneth W. *101 More Hymn Stories*. Grand Rapids, MI: Kregel Publications, 1985.

Reynolds, William J. *Hymns of Our Faith*. Nashville, TN: Broadman Press, 1967.

Wilhoit, Mel R.; Robert S. Wilson. "Elisha Albright Hoffman." *The Hymn* xxxv (1984): 35–39.

HOMELAND HARMONY QUARTET

The Homeland Harmony Quartet earned the reputation of being the first gospel group to start the trend toward making Atlanta a major center of sacred music. From 1942 until 1958 they sang regularly on WAGA, earning regular weekly salaries of seventy-five dollars for three daily radio programs. With later ventures into television, they were at one time heard on fifty stations.

The foursome had originated back in the 1930s, when Otis Leon McCoy (b. February 17, 1897) used the name for a quartet at the Church of God Bible Training School at Cleveland, Tennessee. *Homeland Harmony* had been the name of a popular songbook they had published in 1936. By 1942, its members included Otis and James McCoy, B. C. Robinson,

and Connor Brandon Hall (b. January 25, 1916). Reorganized under Hall's leadership in Atlanta during 1945, the group entered into a period of widespread popularity and influence, with such changing personnel at various times as James P. "Big Jim" Waits, Hovie Lister, Rex Nelon, Paul Stringfelow, Shorty Bradford, Lee Roy Abernathy, Aycel Soward, and, for a brief time, Eva Mae LeFevre.

The quartet made recordings for RCA Victor and Bibletone. After thirteen years at the helm, Connor Hall had developed other interests, so he disbanded the Homeland Harmony Quartet and went to work for Sing Records. He later worked for James D. Vaughn Music Company as editor of the *Vaughn Family Visitor*.

IVAN M. TRIBE

Reference and Further Reading

Blackwell, Lois S. *The Wings of the Dove: The Story of Gospel Music in America*. 65, 69–73. Norfolk, VA: Donning Co., 1978.

Goff, James R., Jr. *Close Harmony: A History of Southern Gospel*. 176–177. Chapel Hill: University of North Carolina Press, 2002.

HOMELAND RECORDS

Homeland Records was started in 1987 and became the home of some of Southern gospel's most popular artists, including the Cathedrals, the Florida Boys, the Hemphills, the Speer Family, Walt Mills, the Hoppers, and the Bishops.

Homeland Records was started by longtime music executive Bill Traylor. After working in radio promotions for the Benson Company, he eventually rose to label executive, directing the Heart Warming and Impact labels. Traylor exited the company in 1982 to start Riversong Records and released albums by the Cathedrals and other groups. The Benson Company acquired Riversong in 1985 and hired Traylor to run the label. After two years running the large company, Traylor left a second time to start Homeland Recording and Publishing.

The Cathedrals followed Traylor to his new venture, releasing *Goin' in Style* in 1988. Produced by Lari Goss, the album earned the Gospel Music Association's Dove Award for Southern Gospel Album of the Year in 1989. Homeland Records and the Cathedrals earned the Dove Award in the same category in 1990 with *I Just Started Living* and in 1991 with *Climbing Higher and Higher*. The latter recording's multiple producers included the Cathedrals, Bill Gaither, Mark Trammel, and Lari Goss. The group also earned a Dove for Southern Gospel Recorded

Song of the Year in 2000 for the Roger Bennett composition "Healing" from the Homeland album *Faithful.*

Another popular recording by the Cathedrals was a live album recorded at the Roy Acuff Theater in Nashville, titled *Reunion.* The concert featured group stalwarts Glenn Payne and George Younce and many of the famous alumni, including Bobby Strickland, Kirk Talley, and Gerald Wolfe. The accompanying video was even more successful than the album, eventually selling a hundred thousand copies.

The Dove Award–winning family group the Hemphills joined the Homeland roster in the late 1980s, releasing an album titled *Celebration.* It was one of the last recordings on which parents Joel and LaBreeska Hemphill were joined by children Joey, Trent, and Candy. The album produced the radio hit "Let's Have a Revival."

In the early 1990s, Homeland signed another family group, the Hoppers. Lead by father Claude Hopper, the group scored a big radio hit with the title song of their *Shouting Time in Heaven* album. The success of the song led to an invitation to appear on the popular Bill Gaither Homecoming concert series.

Homeland Records added the Florida Boys, the Bishops, and the Dove Brothers to the roster in the mid-1990s. The label also signed the legendary Speer Family, releasing a *75th Anniversary* album recorded live at the Roy Acuff Theater.

In addition to the many groups on the label, Homeland signed several solo artists, including Texan Walt Mills, who released more than a dozen albums. His most successful album was *I've Got a Feeling,* with the title track spending three months at number one on the Southern gospel radio charts. Popular TBN television soloist Vern Jackson also released several albums on Homeland.

One of the marketing tools that Homeland employed to sell records was a weekly television show they produced called *Homeland Harmony.* Hosted by Bill Traylor and Bill Gaither, the show featured artists signed to the label. When the program began in 1990, it was seen on four networks, INSP, TBN, ACTS-TV, and CTN. Eventually, Gaither left his hosting duties to start his own successful television productions. Traylor continued to host *Homeland Harmony* until it ceased production in 1997. In 2005 reruns of the program could be seen on the INSP network.

Homeland Records was an innovator of accompaniment tapes that were popular with Southern gospel music fans. Calling the product line EZ Key Soundtracks, the cassettes featured six different versions of one song. In addition to the original recording, the tapes featured the music in high and low keys to accommodate a wider range of amateur singers who could use the tapes to perform in their local churches. The best-sellers in the series were classic songs such as "Amazing Grace" and "Because He Lives."

Facing mounting financial concerns, Homeland Records began downsizing in 2000 and 2001, but the efforts were not enough and Bill Traylor decided to close the doors in 2003. He then launched Landmark Entertainment to sell a variety of music products, including the EZ Key Soundtracks. Traylor released series collections on Landmark that included selections from many of the artists who had released albums on Homeland Records.

JAMES I. ELLIOTT

Reference and Further Reading

Dove Awards website, http://www.doveawards.com/history.
Traylor, Bill. Personal interview, February 12, 2005.
The Hemphills website, http://www.thehemphills.com/biography.html.
Walt Mills Ministry website, http://www.waltmillsministry.org/bio/html.

HOPPERS, THE

Claude Hopper (b. October 8, 1937)
Connie Shelton Hopper (b. July 14, 1940)
Dean Hopper (b. October 24, 1962)
Kim Hopper (b. May 25, 1967)
Mike Hopper (b. September 5, 1969)
Denice Hopper (b. February 9, 1974)

The contemporary Southern gospel group known as the Hoppers—styled as "America's favorite family of gospel music"—have evolved over a period of forty-five years. Initially a quartet composed of four brothers from Madison, North Carolina, they began as a part-time act consisting of Claude, Steve, Will, and Monroe Hopper. A year later Connie Shelton, who became Claude's wife in April 1961, joined as a pianist, and they took the name Hopper Brothers and Connie. In 1971 they became full-time professionals, and gradually, by 1984, all the brothers but Claude had dropped out and his and Connie's children and in-laws had joined, at which time they became simply the Hoppers. At times nonfamily members have been part of the aggregation, including Janet Paschal, Little Rex Foster, Sharon Watts, Shannon Briggs, Roger, and Kirk and Debra Talley.

The Hopper Brothers and Connie cut their first record album *Gospel Favorites* in 1962, but their first number one hit on the gospel charts, "Here I Am," came in 1990. Since then, the Hoppers have had many more hit songs, such as "From Disgrace to His Grace,"

"Heavenly Sunrise," "Anchor to the Power," and "Walk Right Out of This Valley." Numerous honors have come to them, including being chosen as the Favorite Mixed Group Award for 1997–2002. Connie Hopper won the Marvin Norcross Award in 1998. In 1981, the group represented Southern gospel music at the Reagan presidential inaugural.

As of mid-2003, the six Hoppers consisted of Claude and Connie, their sons Mike and Dean, and their respective wives Denice and Kim. Their recent recordings have been on the Spring Hill label. Over the years, Claude Hopper has been involved in music publishing and other business ventures in the Southern gospel industry. Connie has written two inspirational books and does a column, "Connie's Corner," for *The Singing News*.

IVAN M. TRIBE

Reference and Further Reading

"The Hoppers." *Gospel Music Profiles* (Fall 2002): 22–23.
The Hoppers website, http://www.thehoppers.com.

Discography

Shoutin' Time (2001, Spring Hill).
A Legacy of Sonshine (2002, Farm House).
Steppin' Out (2002, Spring Hill).

HOUSTON, CISSY

(b. September 30, 1933, Newark, NJ)

Although primarily known as the mother of the famed vocalist Whitney Houston, Cissy Houston (born Emily Drinkard) has made her own lasting impact on American gospel as well as on other genres of contemporary music, from rhythm and blues to disco. Her vocal style, while rooted in traditional African American gospel, frequently reveals a gritty, authentic edge that has made her a powerful performer of both sacred and secular songs.

Houston's musical career began at the age of five, when at the instigation of her father she joined her family's gospel group, the Drinkards. The group, which at one point also included Houston's nieces Dee Dee and Dionne Warwick, performed extensively throughout the 1940s and 1950s, sharing the stage at Carnegie Hall in 1952 with such gospel luminaries as Mahalia Jackson and the Ward Singers. As one of the first gospel groups invited to perform at the Newport Folk Festival in 1957, the Drinkards began to draw a wider audience, and they were the first gospel group signed by RCA in 1958, which released the first Drinkards album, *A Joyful Noise,* in 1958.

By 1961, Houston had begun doing session work as a background singer for a number of notable recording groups and solo acts, including the Drifters, Dionne Warwick, Solomon Burke, Wilson Pickett, Gene Pitney, and others. As a "first-call" singer, she joined an elite—though anonymous—group of background vocalists (which included the late Doris Troy and Dee Dee Warwick) whose talents were much in demand. In 1963 alone, Houston sang on six top-twenty hit recordings.

In 1967, she formed the singing group the Sweet Inspirations with Sylvia Shemwell, Myrna Smith, and Estelle Brown. As a group, the Sweet Inspirations created much of the infectious, gospel-flavored backup vocal stylings for soul artist Aretha Franklin, and she can be heard on a number of her hits, including "Respect" and "Chain of Fools." The group had its own hit single, "Sweet Inspiration," in 1968, which received a Grammy, and consequently released a gospel album, *Songs of Faith and Inspiration* (Atlantic), that same year. The Sweet Inspirations also provided backup vocals for Elvis Presley in 1968 during his historic comeback concerts in Las Vegas.

Houston left the Sweet Inspirations in 1969 and issued her first solo album of gospel-flavored pop, *Presenting Cissy Houston* (Commonwealth United), in 1970. While continuing to record throughout the early 1970s, Houston also continued to do vocal session work with such artists as Roberta Flack, Herbie Mann, Bette Midler, and Paul Simon. Working with producer Michael Zager, Houston enjoyed a major hit with the disco single "Think It Over" and two subsequent disco albums, *Think It Over* (Private Stock) and *Warning—Danger* (Columbia).

However, by the 1980s, Houston had withdrawn from popular music and instead concentrated on her role as the director of music at the New Hope Baptist Church in Newark, New Jersey, where she had first begun directing choirs at the age of nineteen. Houston returned to recording in 1996 with the album *Face to Face* (House of Blues), for which she received a 1997 Grammy Award in the Traditional Soul Gospel category. A follow-up album, *He Leadeth Me* (House of Blues), appeared in 1997.

DAVID BEAUDOUIN

See also Drinkards, The

Reference and Further Reading

"Cissy Houston." AMG All Music website, http://www.allmusic.com/cg/amg.dll.
"Cissy Houston." Disco Museum website, http://www.discomuseum.com/CissyHouston.html.

Houston, Cissy; with Jonathan Singer. *How Sweet the Sound—My Life with God and Gospel*. New York: Doubleday Books, 1998.
"Mom Can Carry a Pretty Mean Tune." *Los Angeles Times* (February 28, 1995).

Selected Recordings

Presenting Cissy Houston (1970, Commonwealth United LP).
Face to Face (1996, House of Blues CD 161275).
He Leadeth Me (1997, House of Blues CD 161312).

HOVIE LISTER AND THE STATESMEN QUARTET

Hovie Franklin Lister (b. September 17, 1926; d. December 28, 2001)
W. J. "Jake" Hess (b. December 24, 1927)
Denver Crumpler (b. 1913; d. March 21, 1957)
Doy Willis Ott (b. April 28, 1919; d. November 6, 1986)
James Stephen Wetherington (b. October 22, 1922; d. October 3, 1973)
Roland Dwayne "Rosie" Rozell (b. August 28, 1928; d. February 28, 1995)
James Vaughn "Jim" Hill (b. November 2, 1930)

Hovie Lister and the Statesmen rank near the top among the all-time greats of Southern gospel quartets. Lister was primarily a piano player who sang on occasion, but he assembled some of the best gospel singers in the business, and with his group spending two years on Capitol Records and fifteen on RCA Victor, they reached more audiences than most gospel acts, probably exceeded only by the Blackwood Brothers and, more recently, the Gaithers. For more than fifty years, Lister and his associates proved themselves major forces and innovators within the industry.

Hovie Lister was born in Greenville, South Carolina, and fell in love with both the piano and quartet singing as a child. After high school and a stint at the Stamps–Baxter School of Music, he came to Atlanta, where he gained brief but valuable experience as pianist for the Rangers Quartet, the Homeland Harmony Quartet, and the LeFevre Trio. Desiring to lead his own group, Lister formed the Statesmen in Fall 1948, taking their name from the Talmadge newspaper of the same name.

After some early fluctuation in personnel that included figures such as Bobby Strickland, Mosie Lister, Aycel Soward, and Claris "Cat" Freeman, Lister assembled what many people termed the "perfect" quartet, with Jake Hess, lead, Denver Crumpler, tenor, Doy Ott, baritone, and James "Big Chief" Wetherington, bass. After Crumpler's death, Roland "Rosie" Rozell took his place. This foursome remained together until late 1963 when Hess left; he was replaced by Jack Toney. The latter was in turn replaced by James Hill.

The Statesmen had radio programs in Atlanta for some years, had one of the first television shows, and became the first Southern gospel quartet to have a nationally syndicated TV program, *Singing Time in Dixie*, sponsored by Nabisco. In 1949 they began recording for Capitol Records, making some thirty-six sides by 1953. In August 1954 they began a fifteen-year stint with RCA Victor, during which time they had more than thirty albums released. The Statesmen were guests on several network television programs and did the soundtrack for the motion pictures *A Man Called Peter* in 1955 and *God Is My Partner* in 1957. After their contract with RCA expired in 1968, they recorded for Skylite, a label the Statesmen and the Blackwood Brothers had founded earlier but had sold in 1966. An extremely energetic individual, Lister became an ordained Southern Baptist minister and pastored the Mount Zion Baptist Church in Cobb County, Georgia, from 1951 to 1963.

Lister disbanded the Statesmen Quartet in 1980 and then helped form the all-star group the Masters V with James Blackwood, J. D. Sumner, Jake Hess, and Rosie Rozell. After eight years this group dissolved, and a restless Hovie worked for politicians Zell Miller and Wyche Fowler for a time, and even played piano for the South Carolina–based Palmetto State Quartet. Ultimately, he revived the Statesmen, and even had Toney, Hess, and Rozell back in it at times. Other, newer members included Doug Young, bass, Wallace Nelms, tenor, and Mike LoPrinzi and Rick Fair, baritones.

Numerous honors came to Lister, including a 1984 induction into the Gospel Music Hall of Fame and in 1986 being named to the Georgia Music Hall of Fame. Battling cancer in his later days, he managed to complete one final album less than three weeks before his passing. It was aptly titled from the Albert Brumley song, *If We Never Meet Again*.

IVAN M. TRIBE

See also Hill, James Vaughn "Jim"; Jake Hess and the Imperials; Wetherington, James S. "Big Chief"

Reference and Further Reading

Taylor, David L. *Happy Rhythm: A Biography of Hovie Lister & the Statesmen Quartet*. Alexandria, IN: LexingtonHaus, 1998.

Tribe, Ivan M. "Brother Hovie Franklin Lister, 32°: A Legend in Southern Gospel Music." *The Scottish Rite Journal* CX, no. 10 (October 2002): 45–49.

Discography

Gospel Classics, The Statesmen with Hovie Lister (1993, BMG 75517 45912 2).
Hovie Lister and the Grand Ole Gospel Quartet: If We Never Meet Again (2002, BRG Music 01142 2).

HOWARD HUNT AND THE SUPREME ANGELS

Howard Hunt (b. December 13, 1934)

The Reverend Elder Howard "Slim" Hunt and the Supreme Angels comprise a noted African American quartet. Hunt is a gospel veteran who is still very active and popular in the quartet scene. The group was formed near the end of the golden era of gospel (1945–1955). They were known for slow ballads with beautiful harmony.

This group has performed for more than fifty years, with their early recordings on the Nashboro label in the late 1950s. They were first known as the Supreme Angels of Milwaukee, and then moved to Texas. *I'll Rise Again* was one of their first albums and became a classic hit. One of their classic songs is "Stay Under the Blood." In 1993, this group's picture was featured on the front cover of *African-American Good News (Gospel) Music.* Hunt was happy to have his group recognized. He said, "This picture is the only picture I have of my brother, who is deceased, performing with our early group."

They became a legendary classical quartet, and now they are a live recording contemporary quartet. Hunt, with his distinctive nasal-patterned tones, is the lead vocal; Robert "Sugar" Hightower plays the lead guitar and does vocals; Michael "Big Mike" Kimpson plays the bass guitar and does vocals; Maurice Robinson is drummer and does vocals; Quincy King is on keyboard and background vocals; and Hunt's son Lorenzo Timmons does background vocals.

In July 1998, they released *Howard "Slim" Hunt and the Supreme Angels Live in Atlanta.* The Supreme Angels preformed at Gospel Fest 2000 on October 7, 2000, in Atmore, Alabama. A video released on September 18, 2001, *Slim & the Supreme Angels By and By,* features gospel greats such as "Lord Bring Me Down," Calvary," and "Precious Memories." Another well-known video, *Blind Man Live,* was produced live in Danville, Virginia, in the summer of 1999. It was an outstanding hit. "Sugar" Hightower, a legend in his own right, gave a splendid performance on "Saved and Sanctified." Some songs are stories, such as "Blind Man." Most of their gospel songs were written by Hunt.

Elder Hunt is pastor of Deliverance Temple Church of God in Christ in Dillon, South Carolina. Hunt and his wife and family live in Goldsboro, North Carolina. The motto of the group is "Take Jesus for Your Partner and All Your Journeys Will Be Safe."

SHERRY SHERROD DuPREE

Reference and Further Reading

Boyer, Horace Clarence. *How Sweet the Sound: The Golden Age of Gospel.* Washington, DC: Elliott & Clark, 1995.
DuPree, Sherry Sherrod; Herbert C. DuPree. *African-American Good News (Gospel) Music.* Washington, DC: Middle Atlantic Regional Press, 1993.
Hunt, Howard, Elder. "Church of God in Church." Dillon, South Carolina. Interview by Sherry Sherrod DuPree, Goldsboro, North Carolina, December 27, 1992.
———. "Church of God in Church." Goldsboro, North Carolina. Interview by Sherry Sherrod DuPree, via telephone, December 29, 2004.

Discography

The Best of Howard "Slim" Hunt & The Supreme Angels (1995, Nashboro Records #4236).
Shame on You (1996, Nashboro Records #4258).
Over Yonder: Recorded Live in Atlanta, GA (1998, Majestic [Soh] #7005).

I

INGALLS, JEREMIAH

(b. March 1, 1764; d. April 6, 1828)

Important for providing, in his *The Christian Harmony, or Songster's Companion* (1805), the first publication of the spiritual folksong—a religious text set to a secular or folk melody. Born in Andover, Massachusetts, Ingalls moved to Newbury, Vermont, in the 1780s, where he ran a tavern for more than ten years. He later earned his living as a farmer, cooper, and singing master. Ingalls was well qualified for the latter role because he had an excellent voice, could easily read music, and was an expert player of the bass viol. He was also a composer; "New Jerusalem" and "Northfield" are generally regarded as his two best tunes. These were introduced by the choir that he conducted at the Newbury Congregational Church; at this initial performance they used manuscript copies.

Ingalls frequently composed and wrote lyrics for songs for special occasions, such as "Election Hymn" and the funeral piece "An Acrostic on Judith Brock." In 1819 Ingalls moved to Rochester, Vermont, and then to Hancock, where he died nine years later. While still in Newbury he published his 144-page book containing 137 tunes. Much of *The Christian Harmony's* contents are typical of Northern tunebooks issued before 1820, but several selections show great similarity to later Southern compilations. In addition to spiritual folksongs, there are rhythmic and scalar influences from folk and secular music, repeated phrases, three-voice settings, melodies with added choruses, revivalist poetry, the use of complete texts, and tunes named after the texts to which they are set, all traits more characteristic of Southern than Northern compilations.

Several of Ingalls's songs enjoyed long-term popularity, including "Lavonia," "Pennsylvania," "Filmore," "Kentucky," and "Come, Ye Sinners." An anonymous song Ingalls included in his compilation, "I Love Thee," was the last hymn included in the 1956 edition of the *Baptist Hymnal*.

W. K. McNeil

Reference and Further Reading

Metcalf, Frank J. *American Writers and Compilers of Sacred Music*. New York: Russell and Russell, 1967 (1925).
Reynolds, William J. *Hymns of Our Faith: A Handbook for the Baptist Hymnal*. Nashville, TN: Broadman Press, 1967.

INTERNATIONAL GOSPEL MUSIC HALL OF FAME AND MUSEUM, INC.

Born of Negro field and work songs, spirituals, the blues, and church songs, gospel music has its origins in the black soul.

Two composers who copyrighted songs in the early 1900s were Reverend Charles Albert Tindley (ca. 1856–1933) and Reverend Charles Price Jones (1865–1949). Reverend Thomas A. Dorsey (1899–1993), "the Father of Gospel," coined the phrase "gospel music," with altered scale degrees and intricate rhythm being what separates this music from all other styles. Dorsey was a prolific writer; he composed more than fifteen hundred gospel tunes and is best known for "Precious Lord, Take My Hand," which he wrote in 1932 after his wife and son's death.

Many of the groups and singers inducted into the International Gospel Music Hall of Fame and Museum started in the heyday of gospel music—the golden era from 1945 to 1955—with radio, LP records, and gospel promoters. Contemporary gospel started in 1970 with "Oh Happy Day." The contemporary music reflects the Mississippi Mass Choirs.

Businessman Edward Smith (b. January 19, 1935; d. March 28, 1994) from Detroit was the manager of Reverend James Cleveland (1932–1991), who was founder of the Gospel Music Workshop of America (GMWA). Smith approached David L. Gough (b. August 14, 1949) about how to preserve black gospel history. Smith told Gough the GMWA decided to bring gospel artists together for three days of recording in hopes of producing a video. Gough, along with three hundred artists, went to the recording session. The 1994 vision of establishing the Gospel Music Hall of Fame and Museum (GMHFM) came to Gough at the three-day video recording session, called the Coming Home Series, which was recorded at the Bill Gaither Studios in Alexandria, Indiana. The session was recorded in January 1994 but never released.

Adding to the impetus to establish the GMHFM was Gough riding the bus in from the recording studio. There was an ice storm; the roads were slippery and a car ran into the bus. This sparked memories of old; he began to reflect on how rough it must have been for those trailblazing gospel musicians as they continued to deliver the message of God in song through the tribulations of racism and discrimination. Most of the singers were forced to sleep in their vehicles and prepare their own meals. Yet they pressed on. When Gough returned to Detroit from Indiana, he asked God, "What is my purpose?" God confirmed the vision to start a GMHFM to honor pioneers. God told Gough to protect the history so that what his foreparents had contributed to the fibers of American history would not be forgotten.

Gough called friends and told them the vision. In 1995, a board of directors was formed with David Gough and wife Carolyn, Johnny Stewart, Phyllis Siders, Sherry DuPree, Jean Anderson, Thomas Willis, and Ida B. Tomlin. They started meeting and setting guidelines for potential inductees and gathering items for the museum. An advisory board was formed with members from all walks of life as it related to gospel music. As of 2005, thirty members were on the advisory board. The name was to be the Gospel Music Hall of Fame and Museum.

The museum opened in March 1995. Its goal was to establish a repository for gospel music annuals, where people could come to share, learn, and enjoy the legacy of gospel music. The museum has vintage album covers, original recordings, documents, sheet music, photographs, and other memorabilia. Biographies, photos, and songs of the inductees can be seen and heard on computer touch screens. An electronic panel called the Wall of Time covers gospel music history from 1865 to present. Nominees to the International Gospel Music Hall of Fame and Museum must have been involved in gospel music activities for at least twenty-five years. Individuals, groups, choirs, quartets, broadcast personalities, and promoters are represented among past years' inductees.

In October 2003, the GMHFM went global to include gospel singers from other countries. The official name became the International Gospel Music Hall of Fame and Museum (IGMHFM), dedicated to the preservation of and education about gospel music and entertainment. Every year, in October, the IGMHFM holds its annual induction celebration honoring legends in gospel music. All of the inductees are legends in their own right for their many contributions to gospel music over the years as singers, songwriters, musicians, producers, or radio/television personalities. IGMHFM has kept the traditional gospel flavor with some contemporary gospel. The induction dinner is a black-tie affair that provides an evening of elegance, class, and outstanding gospel entertainment. The inductees come to receive a beautiful trophy. Some will entertain the audience; others will bring their fan clubs. The Phyllis Siders Award of Merit recognizes those in the corporate, civic, and ecumenical communities for their support of the furthering of gospel music. Ford Motor Company has been a recipient.

The list of inductees is approaching one hundred. Among the inductees are the Rance Allen Group, Dottie Peoples, and Dr. Bobby Jones, who were inducted in 1998; Jimmy Dowell in 2003; and the Mighty Clouds of Joy and Andrae Crouch. Performers have been the Eastern Michigan Gospel Choir and One Luv. Guest artists for 2004 were Sheryl Swope DuPree from Chicago, tap dancer Floyd Griffin Walton III, and Same Seed, male twins from Lexington, Kentucky.

The first inductees in 1997 include the late Mahalia Jackson, the late Thomas A. Dorsey, the late James Cleveland, the late Reverend Charles Nicks and the Young Adult Choir of St. James Missionary Baptist Church in Detroit, and the late Mattie Moss Clark of Detroit. Gospel event coordinator Edward Smith was inducted posthumously for his vision for gospel music. Several inducted in 1997 had been associated with the Caravans from Chicago: Shirley Caesar (b. 1938), who won nine Grammy awards, including for her album *Put Your Hand in the Hands of the Man from Galilee;* the late Reverend James Cleveland; Dorothy Norwood (b. 1930), the famous gospel story-teller; and Albertina Walker (b. 1930), the founder of the famous Caravans. The Caravans were known for ballads and nonmetered hymns. Martha Jean ("the Queen") Steinberg, a Detroit gospel radio personality, and Dan Underwood, a Detroit gospel music promoter, were included in 1997. The Sensational Nightingales were inducted in 1977. In 1998 they became the first African American group inducted into the American Gospel Quartet Hall of Fame.

The traditional historical gospel quartet the Fairfield Four was inducted in 1998. This gospel quartet is of legendary status, with the distinction of being one of the few African American gospel quartets to bring gospel music to the mainstream population by radio. Reverend James Moore (b. February 1, 1956; d. June 7, 2000) was inducted in 1998. Moore sang in his baritone voice "It Ain't Over." He talked about his performances at home in Detroit as a "hotbed" of gospel music.

In 1999, the Williams Brothers were inducted. A Williams Brothers Road was named in their honor in Smithdale, Mississippi. Brother Joe May (1912–1972) was inducted October 2000; two of his songs, "Search Me Lord," and "I'm Gonna Live the Life I Sing About," were played as background music during the ceremony. In 2001, special guest Reverend Nash Shaffer, radio personality, musician, and singer from Chicago, had the audience spellbound with his historical rendition of "Chicago Gospel" featuring Mahalia Jackson, the Caravans, Theodore Frye, Thomas A. Dorsey, and the late Dr. Ralph Goodpasteur from the Deliverance Church.

Bill Gaither was a 2002 inductee. Reverend Cleophus Robinson, Sr. (1932–1998) was inducted in October 2002. Robinson was unique in that his gospel music style was cultured for the Civil Rights Movement in the 1960s. In 2003, Brother Sullivan S. Pugh (b. 1925) was recognized for his down-home music and composing. He was also inducted for the Consolers, his husband-and-wife team with Iola Pugh (1926–1994), who supported traditional gospel music. Master of Ceremonies Dr. Bobby Jones from Black Entertainment Television (BET), with the network's longest running program (twenty-five years), *The Bobby Jones Gospel,* stated that "Sullivan Pugh and his deceased wife were pioneers who made the way for all contemporary gospel singers. Living and sleeping in their car, not allowed to eat in restaurants,

yet they carried the 'word of God with joy in their hearts.'" The audience sang "May the Work I Have Done Speak for Me."

The Swans Silvertones were inducted in 2003, with background music "Trouble in My Way." Inductees for 2004 were the late Anna Crockett Ford, Dr. Albert Lewis, Jr., Donnie McClurkin, Bill Moss and the Celestials, the O'Neal Twins, and CeCe Winans. Joseph Niles was the first inductee from the Bahamas. Aretha Franklin, Reverend F. C. Barnes, Luther Barnes & the Sunset Jubilaires, John P. Kee, Reverend Timothy Wright, Bishop Paul S. Morton, Reverend Dr. Lawrence C. Roberts, and Dr. Myles Munroe were 2005 inductees to the IGMHFM.

One of the great accomplishments that the IGMHFM participated in was the U.S. Postal Service's release of gospel music commemorative stamps. On July 15, 1998, David Gough attended the ceremony in New Orleans for the Legends of American Music, Series 12. The thirty-two–cent gospel singers stamps included Mahalia Jackson, Roberta Martin, Clara Ward, and Sister Rosetta Tharpe.

A special project that the IGMHFM supports is the "Della Reese: Stronger Than Diabetes" campaign to help people with type 2 diabetes. Reese was a 2001 inductee. The IGMHFM is helping to educate others by making diabetes information available with news releases, media prints to visitors, and on its website.

The IGMHFM conducted its first webcast panel on June 21, 2004, moderated by Gough. The panelists were Horace Boyer, retired professor of music, University of Massachusetts, Amherst; James Abbington, professor of music at Morgan State University and the executive editor of the African American Church Music Series published by GIA Publications, Inc., of Chicago; Sherry Sherrod DuPree, archivist of the IGMHFM; and Gayle Wald, associate professor of English at Georgetown University, who is working on a biography of Sister Rosetta Tharpe. The webcast was part of the educational outreach, designed to make stories of gospel music accessible to people of every nation and generation. Participants could submit questions for the panelists during the ninety-minute presentation. The induction dinner was televised by TCT, The Word Network, MBC, CTN, and BET. Currently, the IGMHFM is conducting a building fund for a new museum in downtown Detroit.

SHERRY SHERROD DUPREE

Reference and Further Reading

Banks, Adele M. "First Group of Gospel Greats for Hall of Fame Unveiled." Religion News Service, Washington, DC, October 1977.

Crosby, Keith. "International Gospel Music Hall of Fame & Museum 8th Annual Induction Awards Banquet." http://www.detroitgospel.com/IGMHFM.htm.

Hewitt, Marylynn G. "Gospel Music Hall of Fame and Museum with Sing Praises." *The Oakland Press* (December 13, 1998): gospel section.

International Gospel Music Hall of Fame and Museum website, http://www.gmhf.org (accessed August 28, 2004).

Lackey, Dana. "Gospel Music Hall of Fame and Museum." *African American Family* (June 2004).

Shaffer, Nash, Reverend. "Sunday Morning Golden Gospel Radio," Chicago. Interview by Sherry Sherrod DuPree, via telephone, May 20, 2004.

Stevens, Kathy A. "God, the Man and the Vision for International Gospel Music Hall of Fame and Museum, Detroit." February 11, 2005.

Walker, Albertina; Inez Andrews; David Gough. "National Association for the Advancement of Colored People (NAACP) Freedom Weekend Gospel Luncheon." Detroit. Interview by Sherry Sherrod DuPree, April 18, 2003.

ISAACS, THE

Joe Isaacs (b. January 24, 1947)
Lily Fishman Isaacs (b. Unknown)
Ben Isaacs (b. 1972)
Sonya Isaacs (b. 1974)
Rebecca Isaacs (b. 1975)

In the past two decades the Isaacs have become one of the most talented and appealing groups on the Southern gospel scene. Founded in 1971 by Joe and Lily Isaacs as a bluegrass band, they added their three children to their act as they grew older. They also moved to a smoother sound in the late 1980s and then moved back toward a more traditional flavor. Joe left the Isaacs in 1999, but the others carried on with their popularity unabated.

Joe Isaacs came from the large family of a mountain preacher in Jackson County, Kentucky. Like many Appalachian youth, he moved to Ohio after high school to find work. He also developed a serious interest in bluegrass music and developed expertise on the banjo, working with local bands and also in New York with the Greenbriar Boys. In New York he met and married Lily Fishman, whose parents were holocaust survivors. Returning to Ohio, Joe played banjo with Larry Sparks.

Following the tragic death of Joe's brother in December 1970, both Isaacs had a conversion experience and thereafter sang only bluegrass gospel. First calling their group the Calvary Mountain Boys and then the Sacred Bluegrass, they recorded albums for such labels as Pine Tree and Old Homestead. In 1988, they became known simply as "the Isaacs" and broadened their "musical perimeters" to encompass more styles. With son Ben (b. July 1971) on bass, daughter Sonya (b. July 1974) on mandolin, and daughter Rebecca (b. August 1975) on guitar and piano, they became primarily a family. As the girls acquired fiancés and husbands (Tim Surrett and John Bowman), they too became part the band. After the children completed high school, the Isaacs relocated in 1992, from Morrow, Ohio to LaFollette, Tennessee.

The Isaacs found their first real recording success on the Morningside and Horizon labels, and their songs began to appear on the national gospel charts. Sonya developed into a real whiz on the mandolin, and also cut a solo album for Lyric Street Records, produced by Vince Gill, with whom she toured on occasion. Joe Isaacs left the band in 1999, being replaced on banjo by his son-in-law John Bowman. In spite of his departure, the Isaacs continue as one of the top groups in Southern gospel.

IVAN M. TRIBE

Reference and Further Reading

"The Isaacs: A Conversation with Lily Isaacs." *Bluegrass Music Profiles* 1 (March–April 2003): 22–23.

Powell, Wayde. "The Isaacs: Bold New Traditionalists." *Precious Memories: Journal of Gospel Music* 2, no. 2 (July–August 1989).

McHaney, Kathleen. "The Isaacs: The Spirit of Bluegrass." *Bluegrass Now* 6, no. 5 (September–October 1996): 4–10.

Discography

Our Style (1993, Morningside MSCD 4175).
Increase My Faith (1996, Horizon HR 07042).
Mountain Praise (1996, Horizon HR 05742).
Bridges (1997, Horizon HR 05622).

J

J. T. ADAMS AND THE MEN OF TEXAS

James Taylor Adams (b. July 17, 1926)

J. T. Adams had a pleasing tenor voice and a talent not only for singing but also for choir directing and music instruction. A native of Sulphur Springs, Texas, Adams served in the Army during the latter part of World War II and then attended East Texas State University, where he graduated and subsequently taught. In 1952, he began recording with the Republic label of Nashville, where he cut some twenty sides over the next three years, about half of them with choral support from the Men of Texas, which one record company described as "a male glee club made up of outstanding voices from every section of the state." "My God Is Real" constituted the most notable of their early recordings.

Adams also served as Director of Music and Youth at the First Baptist Church of Sulphur Springs. With support from the Men of Texas, he recorded albums on both the Word and Wrangler labels. His repertoire varied from old spirituals such as "Dry Bones" and nineteenth century standards such as "Softly and Tenderly" to newer songs such as "What a Day that Will Be" and his own compositions, typified by "Chapel Bells" and "Every Man Has a Price."

IVAN M. TRIBE

Reference and Further Reading

Gentry, Linnell. *A History and Encyclopedia of Country, Western, and Gospel Music*, 2nd ed., 359–360. Nashville, TN: Clairmont Corp., 1969.

McCloud, Barry, *Definitive Country: The Ultimate Encyclopedia of Country Music and Its Performers*, p 5. New York: Perigee Books, 1995.

Hawkins, Martin; Colin Escott. *A Shot in the Dark*. 139–142. Hamburg, Germany: Bear Family Records, 2000.

Discography

In Times Like These (Word WST 8113 LP).
With Hearts Aflame (Word WST 8017 LP).

JACKSON SOUTHERNAIRES

The Jackson Southernaires were formed in Jackson, Mississippi, in 1940 by Frank Crisler, a local music producer, following the same music tradition of the Mississippi Blind Boys. The group members—Roger Bryant, Jr., Maurice Surrell, James Burks, Huey Williams, and Luther Jennings—built their own style, being the first gospel group to use guitar, bass, and drums in their stage performances. Their upbeat, charismatic performances won them acclaim.

Although the group performed together many years, it was not until 1963 that they first recorded an album. Their debut, *Too Late*, was a success for them as well as for their Duke/Peacock's Songbird label, becoming one of its top-selling albums.

In addition to their recordings and performances, the Jackson Southernaires became part of the localand national fiber through their regular performances on radio and television. Their weekly radio show was one of the longest-running radio shows in the United States, with Sunday morning performances for forty-three years. With their notoriety, they were brought to more national attention and secured a five-year television program called *Gospel Unlimited*.

The Jackson Southernaires, in addition to being a top-charted recording and performing gospel group, also produced many of the industry's most noted acts, including the Sensational Nightingales, the Original Soul Stirrers, the Williams Family, the Truthettes, the Evereadys, the Angelic Gospel Singers, and the Fantastic Violinaires.

During the more than forty-five years of its duration, the group released works on Duke/Peacock, ABC/Dunhill, and Malaco. The Jackson Southernaires had an incredible and lengthy streak of popular gospel tunes, with nineteen top ten albums, out of which four reached number one.

The accolades for the Jackson Southernaires were not limited to chart rankings; the group was nominated and won many awards. In 1985, they were nominated for the Stellar Awards and the Gospel Music Workshop of America Award as the Traditional Male Group of the Year. In 1989, they won the Stellar Award for Traditional Male Group of the Year.

MARGARET B. FISHER

See also Angelic Gospel Singers, The; Malaco Records

Reference and Further Reading

Ankeny, Jason. "The Jackson Southernaires." All Music Guide website, http://www.allmusic.com (accessed 2003).

Callahan, Mike; David Edwards. "Songbird Album Discography," http://www.bsnpubs.com/songbird.htm (accessed November 24, 2003).

McIver, Robert H. "The Jackson Southernaires," http://afgen.com/jackson_southernairs.html (accessed April 2003).

Discography

Too Late (1963, Duke/Peacock SBLP-212); *Thank You Mama* (1971, Malaco); *Lord You've Been Good to Me* (1973, Universal); *Down Home* (1975, Malaco); *Legendary Gentlemen* (1979, Malaco); *Touch of Class* (1981, Malaco); *It Started at Home* (1982, Malaco); *Jackson Southernaires* (1982, Malaco); *Hear Our Prayers O Lord* (1990, Malaco); *Oh Lord I'm Still Waiting* (1990, MCA); *Lord, We Need Your Blessings* (1991, Malaco); *Love and Anointed* (1992, Malaco); *Presenting Joy, Peace, Happiness & Love* (1992, Universal); *No Failure* (1995, Redemption); *Word in Song* (1995, Malaco); *How Far Is Heaven* (1997, 601 Records); *Warrior* (1998, Malaco); *Hymns* (2000, Malaco); *Made in Mississippi* (2000, Malaco); *Power Packed* (2000, Malaco).

JACKSON, GEORGE PULLEN

(b. August 20, 1874; d. January 19, 1953)

This folksong scholar and teacher was born in Monson, Maine, and educated at the Royal Conservatory of Music in Dresden, Germany, Vanderbilt University, the universities of Munich and Bonn, and the University of Chicago, from which he received a doctorate in 1911, writing a dissertation on romantic literature.

In 1918 he joined the German department of Vanderbilt University and shortly afterward learned by "pure accident" about country singing. The occasion was a chance conversation with Dr. John W. Barton of Ward-Belmont School in Nashville. Dr. Barton talked about "singin'-all-day-and-dinner-on-the-grounds" conventions he witnessed in Texas, of the strange notation they used, with a music theory, singing schools, teachers, and songbooks exclusively their own. This information fascinated Jackson so much that he spent the rest of his career studying the "lost tonal tribe," as he once referred to these rural musicians.

Jackson was not the first collector to notice white religious folksongs but he became their foremost student. In addition, he was unusual among folklorists of his time in gathering material from shape-note hymnbooks and for paying attention to the music of the songs. His several volumes, *White Spirituals in the Southern Uplands* (1933), *Spiritual Folk-Songs of Early America* (1937), *Down-East Spirituals* (1943), *White and Negro Spirituals* (1943), and *Another Sheaf of White Spirituals* (1952) constitute a virtual history of the singing-school movement, the compilers and composers, and the camp-meeting compositions.

He initially started his work with hopes of studying a cultural survival but soon changed his thinking. He had fortuitously discovered a thriving, creative folk tradition with an impressive body of song. Through his examination of rural hymnbooks Jackson concluded that they were significant repositories of orally transmitted religious songs, numbers that consisted of religious verses set to secular folk melodies by traditional composers. Moreover, he determined that merely because an item was credited to someone was often meaningless. It may have meant that the person wrote the piece, or it may merely have indicated that he arranged it or was the person from whom the compiler learned the song.

Jackson also found that the tunes were what he called "Southernized," that is, specifically altered to fit the style of the Southern singers. He found three chief differences between the vocal styles of the South and the North. In the former region, singers used a more rapid tempo, relied on repetition of notes for successive text syllables and words, and had a greater inclination for melodic ornamentation.

The most controversial aspect of Jackson's studies concerns his contention that Negro religious songs were developed from white spirituals. First in *White Spirituals in the Southern Uplands*, and later—and more thoroughly—in *White and Negro Spirituals,* he investigated, both analytically and genetically, white and Negro spirituals, finding significant genetic relationships in 116 out of 892 Negro tunes and 555 white spirituals. Seventy-five were found to be in the folk tradition of the British Isles or of white North America, seventeen were by known nineteenth-century composers, and fifteen were what Jackson called "general melodizing," while the exact source of the remaining nine was unknown.

The rest of Negro songs were made by blacks in exactly the same way whites made their songs, "by endless singing of heard tunes and by endless, inevitable, and concomitant singing differentiation." Jackson concluded that black singers usually borrowed pentatonic tunes and in singing refined their tonal content. Blacks preferred more major sequences than whites but seldom altered modes, preferring to sing the songs as they heard them. Although other writers maintained that the call and response, repetition, and syncopation common to black singing were African, Jackson contended these features were adapted from white spirituals of the camp-meeting period and were intensified by the Negro's racial emphasis. While this emphasis might be akin to a similar one in Africa, it was not necessarily African. Even the surge songs (that is, hymns performed in slow tempo and highly ornamented style), the most "African sounding" of black songs were merely a survival of the traditional country style of singing eighteenth-century psalm tunes.

Jackson may not have been prepared for the attacks—some of them irrational and personal—that resulted when he published his views on the sources of black song, but they came. So many, in fact, that he wrote a chapter called "Farewell to Africa" in *White and Negro Spirituals*. Most of the attackers did not contradict Jackson's evidence but merely repeated older arguments for the "Africanness" of black song. Despite the heavy criticism, Jackson never wavered from his views, convinced that he was right based on the evidence. In his first book, *White Spirituals in the Southern Uplands,* he succinctly stated the problem with the "Africanist" argument. He said there were "two unfortunate elements." One was "the romantic zeal of those who wish to believe that the Negro's songs are exclusively his own creation." The second was "the scarcity of evidence already presented in proof that the romancers are either correct or mistaken in their assumptions." Through his research he sought to correct the latter situation.

Jackson was not just a bookish academic. In 1920 he founded and directed an orchestra in Nashville, and over the years he established several other organizations. Considering his career, the most important of these is the Tennessee State Sacred Harp Singing Association formed in 1939.

W. K. McNeil

Reference and Further Reading

Jackson, George Pullen. *Another Sheaf of White Spirituals*. Gainesville: University of Florida Press, 1952.
———. *Down-East Spirituals*. New York: Augustin, 1953 (1943).
———. *Spiritual Folk-Songs of Early America*. Locust Valley, NY: Augustin, 1965 (1937).
———. *White and Negro Spirituals*. New York, Augustin, 1943.
———. *White Spirituals in the Southern Uplands*. Chapel Hill: University of North Carolina Press, 1965 (1933).
Wilgus, D. K. *Anglo-American Folksong Scholarship Since 1898*. New Brunswick, NJ: Rutgers University Press, 1959.

JACKSON, MAHALIA

(b. October 11, 1911; d. January 27, 1972)

Mahalia Jackson was among the best-known and celebrated solo gospel vocalists of the twentieth century. Jackson broke down several barriers through her career: she blended the vocal styles of blues singers such as Bessie Smith and Ma Rainey with her gospel repertoire; her recordings and performances appealed equally to black and white audiences; and she made gospel music truly "popular," something that could be heard on national radio and televised variety programs such as *The Ed Sullivan Show*. For many listeners, she embodied gospel music.

Jackson was born into an impoverished New Orleans family in 1911. Her father worked on the docks loading freight during the daytime hours and freelanced as a barber at night; on Sundays, he preached at a Holiness church. From the age of four, Mahalia was singing in Holiness Church choirs. Unable to raise his son and daughter, Mahalia's father passed her on to his wife's sister, "Aunt Duke," who raised her. Her aunt encouraged Mahalia to sing gospel music but disapproved of the blues; nonetheless, Mahalia heard the recordings of early blues singers such as Bessie Smith on record and was greatly moved by them.

In 1927, Mahalia left school and New Orleans to travel north to Chicago. There she began working as a maid–laundress while continuing to sing in local choirs. A local gospel group, the Johnson Brothers, heard her sing at the Greater Salem Baptist Church and invited her to join their successful vocal group. They performed locally, with Mahalia's powerful blues-inspired vocals winning them a strong following. The group broke up by the mid-1930s, and Mahalia began pursuing a solo career. In 1937, she made her first recordings for Decca Records, but these initial recordings were not commercially successful. That same year, prominent gospel songwriter Thomas A. Dorsey took her under his wing and included her in his touring shows. She made major successes out of his songs "Precious Lord" and "If You See My Savior."

In 1946, Jackson signed to the small Apollo label. Again, her first release was not successful, but her second single—1948's "Move On Up a Little Higher"—was a major hit, becoming the best-selling gospel release to that date. This record made Jackson an immediate sensation. In Chicago, radio personality Studs Terkel featured her on his program, introducing her to a white audience. In 1954, she was invited by CBS radio's Chicago affiliate to broadcast a gospel program, the first such program of its kind on network radio; she was also signed to the company's Columbia record label, scoring an immediate hit with "Rusty Old Halo." Two years later, she made her network TV debut on CBS's *Ed Sullivan Show*. Her appearance at the 1958 Newport Jazz Festival furthered her appeal across both racial and musical genre lines. So great was her success that she was invited to sign at John F. Kennedy's inauguration in 1961. Through the 1960s, Jackson performed around the world, while also becoming a champion in the Civil Rights Movement and a close supporter and associate of Reverend Martin Luther King, Jr. Jackson died in a suburb of Chicago on January 27, 1972.

Jackson's melding of blues-influenced vocal stylings with the deep feeling of traditional gospel singing made her both tremendously popular and somewhat of a lightning rod in the gospel community. Considered too "secular" by some, she lost her original audience in the 1950s and 1960s when she became more of a "pop star." Many of her later recordings featured full orchestral accompaniments and background vocals in the style of the mainstream pop of the day, further dismaying her original fans. Nonetheless, Jackson's prominence and success helped legitimize gospel music and also pointed the way to the success of soul music, the R&B/gospel hybrid style developed by stars such as Aretha Franklin in the 1960s.

RICHARD CARLIN

Reference and Further Reading

Burnim, Melonie. "Voices of Women in Gospel Music: Resisting Representation." In *African-American Music: An Introduction*, edited by Portia Maultsby and Melonie Burnim. New York: Routledge, 2005.

Jackson, Mahalia; with Evan McLeod Wylie. *Movin' On Up*. New York: Hawthorne Books, 1966.

Discography

Live at Newport 1958 (1958, Columbia; a stunning live performance).

Live in Europe (1961, Columbia; live performances from a European tour with simple, piano accompaniment).

JACKSON, WANDA LAVONNE

(b. October 20, 1937)

This gospel singer, who at one time was considered by many to be the queen of rock 'n' roll and has been called by some critics the greatest rock 'n' roll singer the world has ever known, was born in Maud, Oklahoma, to Tom and Nellie Jackson. As a youth her father played piano with small bands around Oklahoma, but in 1937 he was having difficulty earning a living. In 1941 he took his family to Los Angeles, where he became a barber. Evidently, this profession did not bring in enough money quickly for, after three months, he moved his family to Bakersfield.

Besides providing her with a peripatetic lifestyle, Tom Jackson had a profound influence on his daughter in other ways. First, he bought her a guitar when she was six and taught her how to play it. Second, he saw to it that she got piano lessons and learned to read music. Third, her parents took her to the Baptist church, where she got her first taste of religious music. Fourth, her parents encouraged her in writing songs, and she produced several before she was in her teens.

Of all these activities, the young girl took most readily to the guitar. Nellie Jackson was quoted as saying "Wanda wasn't like other children after the guitar came into her life." Her mother was right, because in 1950, a year after the family moved from California to Oklahoma City, thirteen-year-old Wanda had a fifteen-minute radio show on KLPR (later expanded to thirty minutes), where she came into contact with Hank Thompson, who at the time had one of the most popular country acts. Impressed with her singing, he asked her to join his band, the Brazos Valley Boys, as a featured vocalist.

Although it has often been reported that Jackson toured with Thompson, this seems unlikely because she was performing in high school musicals at the time, an activity that would have been very difficult if she had been touring. Thompson urged Capitol to sign her to a recording contract, which, because of her age, they refused. Billy Gray, a former sideman for Thompson's band, did persuade his label, Decca, to sign her in March 1954. Of her fifteen recordings for Decca, only "You Can't Have My Love," a duet with Gray, made it to the charts.

After graduating from high school, Jackson joined the first important country music television program, *The Ozark Jubilee,* in August 1955 and stayed for a couple of years. In 1955 and 1956, she toured with Elvis Presley, who encouraged her to sing rock 'n' roll, but she decided to try her luck at country for a while longer. In 1956, she signed with Capitol and soon recorded "I Gotta Know," which made the top twenty on country charts. It also earned her *Cashbox* magazine's acclaim as "Most Promising Female Vocalist." Two years later, in 1958, Wanda scored her first major rock hit, "Fujiyama Mama." At that same session she recorded what many critics consider her best rock effort, a version of Elvis Presley's "Let's Have a Party," which became a top-forty pop hit for her in 1960.

Over the next several years Wanda became a fixture in Las Vegas, recorded several chart-making songs, and had a highly successful television show, *Music Village.* Despite her great popularity, she and her husband were increasingly unhappy with their personal lives. In an effort to find a new life for themselves, they reentered the church. In 1971 she announced that she was a born-again Christian and henceforth was not going to record anything but religious material, a promise she kept for about ten years. In 1972 Capitol released her first gospel album, *Praise the Lord.* This was followed by three albums for Myrrh: *When It's Time to Fall in Love, Now I Have Everything,* and *Make Me a Child Again.* After moving to Word Records, she recorded *Country Gospel* and *Closer to Jesus.* In 1980 and 1981 Jackson toured Europe doing secular songs, recording an album of rock 'n' roll in Sweden at the same time. In 1995, she teamed up with Rosie Flores on her *Rockabilly Filly* album. Wanda has decided to abandon neither gospel nor rock 'n' roll, and she does both religious and secular songs very well.

W. K. McNeil

Reference and Further Reading

Garbutt, Bob. *Rockabilly Queens.* Toronto: Ducktail Press, 1979.

Tosches, Nick. *Unsung Heroes of Rock 'n' Roll.* New York: Da Capo Press, 1984.

JAKE HESS AND THE IMPERIALS

W. J. "Jake" Hess (b. December 24, 1927; d. January 4, 2004)

During a period of five decades, W. J. "Jake" Hess was a major figure in Southern gospel music circles as a lead vocalist in quartets. Hess spent many years with other groups—most notably the Statesmen Quartet—prior to organizing the Imperials, which he then led from late 1963 through 1967. Recurring health problems caused him to take periodic rest periods, but he resumed his career several times, including two later stints with the Statesmen and seven years with the all-star quartet known as the Masters V. Among other accolades, Hess was reputed to have been Elvis Presley's favorite vocalist.

Hess was born near Athens, Alabama, the son of a sharecropper who was a shape-note singing-school teacher. He became an experienced quartet vocalist and served brief stints with such noted groups as the Sunny South Quartet (1946), the John Daniel Quartet (1946–1947), and the Melody Masters (1947–1948) before joining the Statesmen in the Fall 1948. He spent most of the next fifteen years with this group, except for brief periods in 1957 and 1962, singing on most of their Capitol and RCA Victor sessions in this period. However, by the early 1960s, he aspired to found his own group, and he departed in December 1963.

The Imperials' personnel came from other groups and met with rapid success. Veteran pianist Henry Slaughter had been with the Weatherfords (among others), as had bass-voiced Armond Morales. Gary McSpadden had worked with the Statesmen during Hess's 1962 illness, and young Sherrill Neilson had worked with the Speer Family. Hess based the Imperials in Nashville, and they recorded first for Skylite and then Heart Warming. During that time, the group, according to historian David L. Taylor, "pioneered new directions into contemporary vocal arrangements." Adopting a more casual look on stage, they also added electric guitars and drums to their instrumentation in 1965. However, Hess had to leave the Imperials at the end of 1967 because of health problems, after which Armand Morales continued as leader.

After recovering from a heart attack, Jake Hess did not long remain idle. He soon became host of a daily television show at WLAC Nashville, recorded as a solo artist for RCA Victor, and led a group called the Music City Singers and later the Jake Hess Sound, which included his teenage children. After a stint in Los Angeles, he rejoined the Statesmen again from 1977 to 1979, and then early in 1981 joined with

Hovie Lister, James Blackwood, J. D. Sumner, and Rosie Rozell to form the Masters V. Hess remained with the Masters for seven years, then in 1988 got back with Lister as part of a reformed edition of the Statesmen Quartet, remaining for another five years.

Again plagued with heart ailments, Jake Hess retired to Columbus, Georgia, in 1993. After that, he made occasional public appearances, most often at Bill Gaither concerts, and worked on his autobiography. In 1997, he was inducted into the Southern Gospel Music Hall of Fame. His persistent health problems ultimately ended his life.

IVAN M. TRIBE

See also Armand Morales and the Imperials; Hovie Lister and the Statesmen Quartet

References and Further Reading

Hess, Jake; with Richard Hyatt. *Nothin' but Fine: The Music and the Gospel According to Jake Hess.* Columbus, GA: Buckland Press, 1995.
Taylor, David L. *Happy Rhythm: A Biography of Hovie Lister & The Statesmen Quartet.* 22–27, 113–115, 169. Lexington, IN: Lexington Haus, 1998.
Terrell, Bob, "Jake Hess: A True Singer's Singer." *The Singing News* 35, no. 11 (March 2004): 40–43.

Selected Discography

Jake Hess may be heard to best advantage on those recordings he made with such groups as the Statesmen Quarter and the Imperials. However, he also made solo recordings under his own name:
Everything Is Beautiful (1970, RCA Victor LSP 4400).

JARS OF CLAY

Dan Haseltine (b. January 12, 1973)
Charlie Lowel (b. October 21, 1973)
Matt Odmark (b. January 25, 1974)
Steve Mason (b. July 18, 1975)

Dan Haseltine, lead vocals, Charlie Lowel, keyboards/background vocals, Matt Odmark, guitars/background vocals, and Steve Mason, guitar/background vocals, formed Jars of Clay in 1993. Their name was adopted from II Corinthians 4:7, which states that ". . . we have this treasure in earthen vessels, ..." (KJV). At the time, they were all majors in contemporary Christian music at Greenville College in Greenville, Illinois. The band was influenced by grunge and alternative groups such as Nirvana and Toad the Wet Sprocket.

Jars entered a class project, a demo tape, for a Gospel Music Association band competition in 1994.

They won the competition, moved to Nashville, Tennessee, and signed a recording contract with Essential records. Their debut album, *Jars of Clay,* was released in May 1995 and was nominated for a Grammy. Four Christian radio hits, including "Liquid" and "Flood," which MTV regularly played, came from the album, causing it to go double platinum by 1997. Endless touring also helped to increase their exposure, especially as guests of Billy Graham, Matchbox Twenty, Michael W. Smith, and Sting.

The band's ability to transcend genres also manifested itself in the film and television industries. Film examples include *The Chamber, Crossroads, Jack Frost, The Prince of Egypt,* and *We Were Soldiers.* Their songs were used on a variety of television shows, from *Felicity* to *Roswell,* and they made appearances on talk shows, ranging from David Letterman's and Conan O'Brien's to CBS's *Early Show* and CNN's *Worldbeat.* Press covering Jars of Clay included *Rolling Stone, Billboard, Entertainment Weekly, People,* and *CCM Magazine.*

Much Afraid, the Jars' sophomore album, was released in September 1997. With it they began touring in Europe, Australia, and Asia. The album went gold in less than five weeks, was eventually certified platinum, and won a Grammy in 1998. In November 1999 they released *If I Left The Zoo,* which won a Grammy in 2001 and was certified platinum. *The Eleventh Hour,* their fourth album, was released in March 2002 and won a Grammy in 2003. They have also received twenty-two Dove Award nominations, out of which they claimed six. Their fifth album, *Furthermore,* was released in February 2003.

BOB GERSZTYN

See also DC Talk; Franklin, Kirk; Rock Gospel; Smith, Michael W.

Reference and Further Reading

Angelini, Fabio. "Jars of Clay." *Music Biz* 4 (July/August 2002): 4.
"Jars of Clay." Richard De LaFont Agency website, http://www.delafont.com/music_acts/jars-of-clay.htm (accessed July 1, 2003).
Jars World website, http://www.jarsworld.com (accessed July 1, 2003).
Price, Deborah Evans. "Artists & Music." *Billboard* (March 2, 2002).

Discography

Jars of Clay (1995, Essential).
Much Afraid (1997, Essential).
I Left the Zoo (1999, Essential).
The Eleventh Hour (2002, Essential/Silvertone).
Furthermore (2003, Essential).

JARVIS, J. D.

John Dill Jarvis (b. April 21, 1924)

For more than four decades, John Dill "J. D." Jarvis has been a major figure in bluegrass gospel and country music, recording numerous albums and composing songs that have become standards in the field, such as "Take Your Shoes Off Moses" and "Six Hours on the Cross."

A native of Clay County, Kentucky, Jarvis grew up in a mountainous area steeped in traditional music, and after spending time in the Civilian Conservation Corps and the U.S. Army—suffering serious combat wounds—he joined the flood of Appalachian migrants to the city. J. D. eventually settled in Hamilton, Ohio, and operated a paint contracting business.

After a self-confessed rowdy lifestyle in early adulthood, Jarvis converted and began devoting his surplus energy to sacred music. He sang in churches for years and began a recording career in around 1960. While he made many albums in the 1960s and 1970s, many of them on Rusty York's Jewel label, those with the most widespread distribution appeared on Rural Rhythm, and he did a country-oriented sacred album for Heart Warming. In addition to the aforementioned standards, some of his other well-known songs include "My Lord Will Send a Moses," "Life of Ransom," and the patriotic "Thank God for Old Glory."

Despite his numerous long-play albums, Jarvis remained a part-time performer, maintaining his business until turning it over to his son. In recent years, he has continued singing in the local area around his home in Hamilton. Two compact disc compilations of his best sides appeared in the 1990s.

IVAN M. TRIBE

Reference and Further Reading

Tribe, Ivan M. "J. D. Jarvis: The Voice of Bluegrass Gospel." *Bluegrass Unlimited* 31, no. 6 (December 1996): 56–59.

Discography

Bluegrass Gospel at Its Finest (ca. 1997, Down Home DH 501029).
Mother Needs No Marker (1999, Old Homestead OHCD 4018).

JAZZ

The birth of jazz in the brothels of Storyville, the red light district of New Orleans, and its early incubation in the speakeasies of Prohibition did not exactly produce a style of music embraced by the church. But jazz nevertheless did impact religious, and particularly gospel, music in various ways.

Even before jazz coalesced into a recognizable genre in the 1920s and 1930s, some of its basic components were already shaping popular church music. One of these was ragtime, a style of primarily piano music in which the left hand provides a steady two-beat pattern underneath a right-hand part performing syncopated (described as "ragged") melodies characterized by short–long–short rhythms. While Scott Joplin was the style's most popular practitioner, the influence of ragtime-inspired music—usually in diluted form—can be seen in Irving Berlin's "Alexander's Ragtime Band," the dance craze "Charleston," and in gospel song melodies such as "Since Jesus Came into My Heart."

Jazz per se influenced gospel music more in its performance practices than it did in its formal design or harmonic structures. One of the earliest of these was in vocal delivery. From Ira Sankey in the 1870s to the present, most untrained gospel singers imitated the popular styles of the day. With the advent of radio and phonograph records in the 1920s and 1930s, Bing Crosby's crooning and Louis Armstrong's jazz vibrato influenced many a gospel song delivery. Overall, however, the most successful soloists in this tradition—such as George Beverly Shea—sang with a more "legitimate" approach to vocal production.

Jazz also influenced the role of the piano in gospel music, especially in the practice of improvisation, which is at the heart of jazz. The piano accomplished this role best when the performer was not limited to the four-part choral arrangement of a song as printed in a hymnal but, rather, filled out the texture to six notes per chord, adding various runs, arpeggios, and other improvisatory devices to enliven and support gospel singing. The earliest exponent of this approach was Robert Harkness, who in 1902 changed the musical landscape. Harkness's method developed into a wide-ranging style that became the standard way of playing gospel piano, stretching from evangelist Billy Sunday to the Billy Graham Association evangelistic team, as epitomized by pianist Rudy Atwood.

A different approach to piano known as "Southern gospel" became popular in much of the South. This style resulted from the a technique known as stride piano, which borrowed ragtime's steady left-hand technique but vastly expanded the role of the right hand melodically. Its application to Southern gospel quartets, beginning around 1927, is associated with performers Dwight M. Brock ("Stomp Beat") and Hovie Lister, the latter being known for his showy style of playing ("Gospel Boogie"), which reflected jazz emphases on rhythm and pianistic virtuosity.

At the same time, blind pianist Arizona Juanita Dranes employed a style called barrelhouse piano—associated with honky-tonks—to accompany congregational and solo performances in the black "Sanctified" tradition associated with the fledgling charismatic movement. Although she made a few recordings, it is unclear to what degree her "worldly" style of playing influenced others.

While the rhythmic aspects of jazz strongly influenced gospel music to one degree or another, jazz harmonies had a more limited impact because gospel hymnody was characterized by simple harmonies. However, as gospel song arrangements for piano—to be used as solos for preludes, offertories, or special music—became popular, arrangers turned to a wide variety of styles, including jazz. By the 1940s bebop and cool or progressive jazz of the 1950s had radically expanded the harmonic vocabulary available to jazz musicians. Harmonies with ninth, eleventh, and thirteenth chords, complex chromatic harmonies, modality, and the resultant progressions also became available to arrangers of gospel piano solos. However, most jazz harmonies were incorporated more as an element of novelty than as part of a basic characteristic of gospel music.

Although the piano became the instrument of choice for gospel music, the organ in its electronic incarnation was also adapted for gospel music. In 1935, the Hammond Organ Company developed an electronic keyboard instrument designed for churches that could not afford a pipe organ, and it was quickly adapted to gospel music in both white and black churches. It was in black churches, however, that the Hammond developed its most characteristic jazz-like application, with its unique percussive attack and conspicuous vibrato.

The influence of jazz on black gospel music is somewhat deceptive, for in the early part of the twentieth century, secular influences such as the blues and jazz were considered sinful by the black religious community. For years, gospel composer Thomas A. Dorsey, who had been a blues musician, vacillated between the worlds of blues and gospel, for the two were clearly separate. Eventually he sided with gospel music, but subsequently he brought some of his blues experience (such as "swing eighths") into his religious music.

Developing as both solo and choral music in the 1940s and 1950s, this stream of black religious music included a powerful emotional intensity, animated vocal delivery, and call-and-response features. Although much of the style found roots in the black Sanctified church, it also had an affinity to blues shouting. Important exponents of what later became known as black gospel music included Roberta Martin, William Brewster, and James Cleveland.

When soul music became popular in the 1960s, it reflected much of the same style as gospel music but with a secular message.

While jazz composers such as Duke Ellington and Dave Brubeck have mixed jazz and religious music, their contributions have been limited to shaping gospel music overall. During the late twentieth century, gospel choirs—such as the Brooklyn Tabernacle Choir—employing a distinctly black aesthetic became very popular. While the accompaniments to their choral arrangements often featured jazz influences, the choral parts themselves reflected the Sanctified style of syncopation and high-intensity delivery.

Jazz itself has developed into such a vast universe of styles and techniques—one of these being fusion—that the influence on other genres has become nearly impossible to trace at times. However, it is clear that during the twentieth century, a fertile cross-pollination was going on between jazz and gospel music that has immeasurably enriched both.

MEL R. WILHOIT

Reference and Further Reading

Cusic, Don. *The Sound of Light: A History of Gospel Music.* Bowling Green, OH: Bowling Green State University Popular Press, 1990

Goff, James R. *Close Harmony: The History of Southern Gospel.* Chapel Hill and London: University of North Carolina Press, 2002.

Reagon, Bernice Johnson, ed. *We'll Understand It Better By and By: Pioneering African American Gospel Composers.* Washington and London: Smithsonian Institution Press, 1992.

JENKINS, BLIND ANDY

(b. November 26, 1885; d. ca. 1956 or 1957)

The man who was one of the most important country composers of the 1920s was born sighted in Jenkinsburg, Georgia, a community on the outskirts of Atlanta. A faulty medication prescribed for him as an infant left him virtually sightless, and in 1939 what limited vision he had was lost. During his early adulthood, Jenkins made his living selling newspapers, but at age twenty one he became a preacher and thereafter was addressed as the Reverend Jenkins. Those who knew him well were not surprised by the move. After converting to Methodism at age nine, he began to preach to playmates from stumps and porches. He was also known for being able to play virtually any instrument placed in his hands.

As a youngster, Andrew also began to write songs, an activity at which he excelled. Still, it was only after he married his second wife, Francis Jane Walden Eskew, in 1919 that Jenkins's abilities gained a wide audience. With his wife's three children—Irene, Mary Lee, and T. P.—he formed the Jenkins Family, a band that debuted on Atlanta radio station WSB. This family group became very popular during the 1920s, receiving fan mail from throughout the United States, Canada, and Mexico. Their demonstrated talent led to their initial recording session on August 29, 1924, when they recorded "Church in the Wildwood" and "If I Could Hear My Mother Pray Again," neither of them Jenkins originals. This made them probably country music's first family group, because they preceded the now better-remembered Carter Family into the studio by three years.

Their first records sold well enough that they were brought back for a second session, at which they recorded Jenkins's own "Sing It and Tell It" and hymns such as "Jesus Is Calling" and "The Old Rugged Cross." During the next several years, members of the Jenkins Family recorded in various combinations and under several names: Jenkins Sacred Singers, the Irene Spain Family, Blind Andy, Gooby Jenkins, and Andrew Jenkins and Carson Robison.

Despite his extensive recording career, Jenkins is best remembered as a songwriter who produced religious songs, tragedy and disaster ballads, and outlaw songs. Of his five hundred gospel songs, only "God Put a Rainbow in the Clouds," once a frequent radio quartet number, is well known today. His approximately three hundred tragedy and disaster songs, which his stepdaughter said he turned out like a mill grinding wheat, include "Little Marian Parker," "Wreck of the Royal Palm," and "The Death of Floyd Collins." The two best-known of his several outlaw ballads are "Kinnie Wagner" and "Billy the Kid." Even in these nonsacred numbers, Jenkins added a touch of religion with a moral ending. Thus, in "The Death of Floyd Collins," about a Kentucky spelunker who died in a sand cave, he concluded with lines about getting "right with your maker, before it is too late" because "at the bar of judgment, we, too, must meet our doom."

Although he wrote approximately eight hundred songs, some of which were very popular, Jenkins made little money from them. Usually he sold them outright for a fee, as, for example, "The Death of Floyd Collins," which Jenkins reportedly sold for twenty-five dollars. Evangelistic work was his main source of income; these efforts were aided by weekly radio broadcasts on WSB until 1931, and by appearances on other regional radio stations until Jenkins's death in a car wreck in the late 1950s.

W. K. McNeil

Reference and Further Reading

Wolfe, Charles K. "Frank Smith, Andrew Jenkins, and Early Commercial Gospel Music." *American Music* 1, no. i (1987): 49–59.

JOHN DANIEL QUARTET

John Daniel (b. 1903, Boaz, AL; d. 1961)

Singer, composer, publisher, and quartet leader John Tyra Daniel is best known for organizing the John Daniel Quartet, one of the most popular gospel groups of the 1940s. For a number of years, it was the most widely heard Southern gospel group through its regular NBC network appearances on *The Grand Ole Opry* and through its popular syndicated radio show heard over a hundred and twenty stations. It was the most important transitional group between the older, song-publisher–sponsored quartets and the newer, flashy independent groups such as the Blackwood Brothers and the Statesmen.

Daniel came from the Sand Mountain area in Northeast Alabama, which was a center for classic quartet singing, and he began singing with his family in informal settings and organized his first group as a family quartet with his brother Troy and sisters Mary and Orna in the early 1920s. Soon he began working for publishers A. J. Showalter and then James D. Vaughan, and for a time the group was known as the Vaughan–Daniel Quartet. By 1937, the group had recruited Carl Rains to sing bass and E. C. Littlejohn to sing tenor. After a stint with Stamps–Baxter, Daniel decided to strike out on his own and become fully independent. The group moved to Nashville in 1940, singing first over WLAC and then on WSM; by then, Wally Fowler had replaced Littlejohn, with Troy still singing lead. Throughout the years, the Daniel Quartet served as a training ground for a number of key singers, including Jake Hess, Tommy Fairchild, Gordon Stoker (later of the Jordanaires), Jim Waits, and Bill Lyles (later of the Blackwood Brothers).

The group recorded prolifically for several labels, including Bama, Bullet (some thirty-two sides in 1946–1948), Daniel (owned by John Daniel himself), Liberty, and Columbia (some twelve sides as the Daniel Family). Among their best-known songs were "Beautiful Star of Bethlehem" (later to become a bluegrass standard), as well as "Visions of Rainbow," "My Mother's Song," "City Built Foursquare," "Good News," and "Just a Rose Will Do." His Columbia sides, which were widely circulated, were done under the name Daniel Family, possibly in deference to Columbia's other successful group, the Johnson Family.

While in Nashville, Daniel also began publishing his own songbooks, eventually issuing ten titles during the 1940s. His radio transcriptions were the first in the long-running SESAC gospel music series.

CHARLES K. WOLFE

JOHNSON, BLIND WILLIE

(b. ca. 1902; d. 1950)

The man who made some of the grittiest, most dramatic religious songs on records was born sighted to a farm family near Marlin, Texas. Johnson was blinded at age seven when his stepmother, in a jealous rage, threw lye water in his face to get even with his father for a beating. This tragic incident forced him to find some means other than farming to earn his living. He turned to music and began singing gospel songs on the streets of the small cotton towns in south central Texas.

In 1927, Johnson traveled into Dallas, where he met his future wife, Angeline, at a Columbia field recording unit. There, on December 3, he made his first records, six sides that included a retelling of the Samson and Delilah story, "If I Had My Way I'd Tear the Building Down," a harsh, shouted "It's Nobody's Fault But Mine," and a rendition of a gospel classic, "Motherless Children Have a Hard Time." These releases were lauded for Johnson's "violent, tortured, and abysmal shouts and groans and his inspired guitar."

Evidently they were also successful commercially, because the following year he recorded four more sides in Dallas on December 5, 1928, including "Jesus Is Coming Soon" and "Keep Your Lamp Trimmed and Burning." On December 11, 1929, Columbia brought him from Beaumont, Texas, to New Orleans to record six more songs, including "Take Your Burden to the Lord and Leave It There," a version of Charles A. Tindley's "Leave It There," and "God Moves on the Water." By this time the Depression was in full swing; even so, Columbia brought him to Atlanta on April 20, 1930, where he recorded ten final selections, including a version of "John the Revelator." With his recording career over, Johnson returned to Beaumont, where he eked out a living as a street singer, his main means of support all along. His death came from pneumonia in the winter of 1949–1950, reportedly after being refused admission to a local hospital.

Johnson was one of the most intense singers who ever made records. Although possessing a strong, clear voice, he usually performed pieces in a rasping, false bass. On some numbers, such as "If I Had My Way," he sings so intensely that the lyrics are virtually unintelligible, while on "Lord I Can't Keep from Crying," he seems to cry, skillfully wrenching every bit of honest emotion from the piece. But he was not important just because of his vocals; he also was one of the finest country guitarists on record. He weaves the instrument in and out of his vocals, ending a sung phrase on the guitar or letting the voice end a melodic phrase started on the guitar. He demonstrated his abilities in this regard at his very first recording session, when he waxed "Dark Was the Night." This moaning masterpiece is a wordless chant used in Baptist church services in East Texas. With this number from his own folk tradition, Johnson provided an excellent example of the kind of effective performance he could produce simply by making the guitar more than just an accompanying instrument. The feeling of melancholy is sustained as the melody line travels from voice to guitar and back. On his records Johnson played with finger picks, as on "Trouble Will Soon Be Over," or with a knife, as on "Jesus Make Up My Dying Bed"; thus, he was able to produce a steady, percussive sound or a complex interplay between the voice and guitar.

It would be impossible to list every musician influenced by Blind Willie Johnson, because it would require mentioning almost everyone who ever listened to one of his records. Reverend Gary Davis, another blind singer, found Johnson's songs of great interest, while Fred McDowell and others were more indebted to his instrumental work. He was without question the most famous and influential early gospel musician as far as blues performers are concerned.

W. K. MCNEIL

Reference and Further Reading

Oliver, Paul. *Songsters & Saints: Vocal Traditions on Race Records.* Cambridge, UK: Cambridge University Press, 1984.

Discography

Blind Willie Johnson 1927–1930 (1965, RBF).
Praise God I'm Satisfied (1976, Yazoo).
Songsters and Saints, Vol. Two (1984, Matchbox MSEX 2004).
Sweeter As the Years Go By (1990, Yazoo).
Dark Was the Night: The Essential Recordings (1995, Indigo).
Let Your Light Shine On Me 1927–1930 (Earl BD 607).

JONES, ABSALOM

(b. November 6, 1746, Sussex, DE; d. February 13, 1818, Philadelphia, PA)

African American religious leader, founder of St. Thomas African Episcopal Church, and the first black

Columbia *"New Process"* Records
REG. U. S. PAT. OFF.

BLIND WILLIE JOHNSON

THIS Race artist's singing of Sacred Songs and Hymns is remarkable for its simplicity and melody. It's the sort of singing that grips you and holds you, having a strain of the spiritual in it. Blind Willie Johnson usually plays his own accompaniments on a guitar.

The demand for his recordings, places him in the front rank of Race artists. He is of course, an exclusive Columbia artist.

MOTHER'S CHILDREN HAVE A HARD TIME . . . . IF I HAD MY WAY I'D TEAR THE BUILDING DOWN	14343-D	75c
IT'S NOBODY'S FAULT BUT MINE . . . DARK WAS THE NIGHT—COLD WAS THE GROUND	14303-D	75c
I KNOW HIS BLOOD CAN MAKE ME WHOLE . . . . JESUS MAKE UP MY DYING BED	14276-D	75c

REV. T. E. WEEMS

IF I HAD MY WAY I'D TEAR THE BUILDING DOWN—*Singing Sermons* . . . . IF I HAVE A TICKET LORD CAN I RIDE?	14254-D	75c
THE DEVIL IS A FISHERMAN—*Sermons with* GOD IS MAD WITH MAN— *Singing*	14221-D	75c

MADE THE NEW WAY—ELECTRICALLY
[22]

Columbia Records announcement for recordings by Blind Willie Johnson, 1928. Photo courtesy Frank Driggs Collection.

priest in the Episcopal Church, Absalom Jones was instrumental in helping to establish one of the first free black communities in the United States.

Jones was born a slave in Sussex, Delaware, on November 6, 1746. At sixteen he was taken to Philadelphia, where he worked as a shopkeeper and attended a night school for blacks under the auspices of his master. In 1770, Jones married a fellow slave and eventually saved enough money to purchase their independence in 1784.

Thereafter, Jones became a lay minister at St. George's Methodist Episcopal Church and one of the first black men to receive a preaching license from the Methodist Church. One Sunday morning in 1787, while worshipping at the altar, Jones was pulled from his knees and asked to pray elsewhere, to which he responded by leading the remainder of the black congregation from the church building. Following this incident, he and the minister Richard Allen led the separatist movement and formed the Free

African Society of Philadelphia. By 1794 a new building had been constructed, and the first African Episcopal Church of St. Thomas was formed, ordaining Jones as a deacon in 1795 and as a priest in 1804. Jones died on February 13, 1818.

Similar to many clergymen in the nineteenth century, Jones was an activist for the abolition of slavery and coauthored "A Narrative of the Proceedings of the Black People During the Late Awful Calamity in Philadelphia," a defense of black contributions to the yellow fever plague in 1793, with Richard Allen. Jones also served as a teacher in schools established by the Pennsylvania Abolition Society, where he used music and the singing of hymns to train local black youth.

SARAH ARTHUR

See also Allen, Richard

Reference and Further Reading

Handy, James A. *Scraps of African Methodist Episcopal History*. Philadelphia: A.M.E. Book Concern, 1902. http://docsouth.unc.edu/church/handy/handy.html.
Payne, Daniel A. *History of the African Methodist Episcopal Church*. Nashville, TN: Publishing House of the A.M.E. Sunday-School Union, 1968 (1891).
Wright, Richard R., Jr. *Centennial Encyclopaedia of the African Methodist Episcopal.*
———. *The Encyclopaedia of the African Methodist Episcopal Church* [microform], 2nd ed., Philadelphia: Book Concern of the A.M.E. Church, 1947.

JONES, BESSIE

(b. February 8, 1902; d. September 4, 1984)

Bessie Jones was born in Smithville, Georgia, on the Georgia Sea Islands, in 1902. Originally a large plantation, the Sea Islands were captured by Union troops in the early years of the Civil War, and the remaining slave population remained there afterward as free farmers. Much of the African culture, including the Gullah language, was maintained there, and a rich tradition of harmony singing also survived.

Jones was a key practitioner of this style, first recorded in the 1950s by visiting folklorists, including Alan Lomax. She formed the Georgia Sea Island Singers in the early 1960s, who traveled widely, performing at folk festivals, clubs, and on college campuses, spreading this unique unaccompanied singing style around the country. Many of her most popular albums were aimed at children, as the traditional singing games and dances from the Sea Islands were uniquely suited to young listeners. The group also performed the traditional ring shouts of the islands, the primary musical form of religious expression. In 1972,

Jones published a collection of her songs, stories, and children's games called *Step It Down*, which was coauthored by folklorist/song collector Bess Lomax Hawes. Jones died in Brunswick, Georgia, on her beloved Sea Islands, in 1984.

RICHARD CARLIN

Reference and Further Reading

Jones, Bessie; Bess Lomax Hawes. *Step It Down*. New York: Harper & Row, 1972.
Parrish, Lydia. *Slave Songs of the Georgia Sea Islands*. Athens: University of Georgia Press, 1992 (1942).

Discography

Been in the Storm So Long (1967, Folkways; excellent collection of recordings by Jones and the Sea Island Singers).
Step It Down (1981, Rounder; issued in conjunction with the paperback edition of the book of the same name featuring Jones performing some of her best-loved songs).

JORDANAIRES, THE

Although they began their career as a traditional Southern gospel male quartet, the Jordanaires emerged in the 1950s as one of the most popular and most recorded quartets in gospel, country, pop, and even rock 'n' roll. After July 1956, when young sensation Elvis Presley asked them to sing backup on what would become his classic rock 'n' roll recording "Don't Be Cruel," the Jordanaires became part of the Nashville studio "A team," and they began to appear on dozens of hit singles in addition to touring with Presley. They became one of the most successful artists to adapt a gospel tradition to various forms of popular music and continued to work up through the turn of the twentieth century.

The Jordanaires originated in Springfield, Missouri in about 1948, when two brothers named Bill and Monty Matthews decided to organize a quartet. Both men were ministers and had learned to sing by traveling with their father, who was a traveling evangelist. After winning some fame as part of a juvenile quartet called the Matthews Brothers, Bill and Monty decided to organize their own group; they hired as bass Culley Holt from McAlester, Oklahoma, and as baritone Missourian Bob Hubbard. In 1949, when their original pianist Bob Money was drafted, they hired Gordon Stoker to replace him. Stoker was a veteran of the gospel scene who had previously played with the famed WSM group the John Daniel Quartet. Stoker soon graduated to singing lead and began to play a pivotal role in the group's development.

The Jordanaires. Photo courtesy Frank Driggs Collection.

In 1953, the original Matthews brothers left the group and returned to Missouri, and Stoker asked young tenor Neal Matthews, Jr., to join up. Matthews was the son of Neal Matthews, Sr., who had sung for years on the Grand Ole Opry with the Crook Brothers band. Neal, Jr., had also joined the show, playing guitar with Wally Fowler's Oak Ridge Quartet. By now baritone Hoyt Hawkins signed on, fresh from a stint with a family singing group that worked out of Nashville: the Hawkins Family. The Jordanaires located in Nashville, and with their talent and varied experience, started exploring new roles for harmony singing in the 1950s.

By 1949, even before the Matthews brothers had left, the Jordanaires had signed a record contract with Decca; they transferred to RCA Victor during 1951–1953, and then to Capitol. In an age when most country and gospel was still issued on singles, the Jordanaires crafted a number of major hits, most of which became standards. They included "Mansion Over the Hilltop" (1951), "On the Jericho Road" (1953), "Gonna Walk Those Golden Stairs" (1951), and "Tattler's Wagon" (1953). Their singles soon won them the reputation of specializing in what the music business at that time called "spirituals"—not the classic nineteenth-century spirituals but the code word for any black-derived gospel. The Jordanaires did cover versions of songs by African American groups such as the Golden Gate Quartet, such as "Noah." Soon they were appearing on Eddy Arnold's summer TV show and backing up singers such as Hank Snow, Elton Britt, Stuart Hamblen, and Red Foley. They were also doing a lucrative sideline in nationally known singing commercials.

After their initial success with Presley, the Jordanaires began appearing on almost every one of his sessions for the next fifteen years, as well as touring with him. With what little time was left, they managed to maintain their own recording career, and, in 1965, they were voted one of the top five singing groups in the world. Their press releases were announcing that they had "initiated a new type of vocalizing by providing a background of vocal harmonizing for a lead singer"—a claim not far from the truth. Through their extensive Nashville studio work, they also perfected a shorthand musical notation system for work in studio sessions—a way of jotting down chord changes that later became known as "the Nashville number system."

CHARLES K. WOLFE

See also Presley, Elvis

K

KAISER, KURT

(b. December 17, 1934)

Kurt Kaiser was born in Chicago, Illinois, and studied at the American Conservatory of Music there prior to attending Northwestern University's School of Music in Evanston, Illinois. In 1959, after graduate school, Kaiser joined Word Records in Waco, Texas. His first position with the company was director of artists and repertoire, but he eventually became Word's vice president and director of music. During the next four decades Kaiser arranged and produced albums for many gospel artists, including Kathleen Battle, Ernie Ford, Larnelle Harris, Burl Ives, Ken Medema, Christopher Parkening, George Beverly Shea, Joni Eareckson Tada, Ethel Waters, and Anne Martindale Williams.

Kaiser has recorded sixteen piano solo albums of his own and even won a Dove Award for one on the Sparrow label, titled *Psalms, Hymns, and Spiritual Songs,* in 1994. For more than thirty years he has accompanied George Beverly Shea in concert on the piano. His musical influence has been instrumental in the transformation of contemporary church music. In the 1960s, he collaborated with Ralph Carmichael to write musicals such as "Tell It Like It Is," "Natural High," and "I'm Here, God's Here, Now We Can Start." Nearly five hundred thousand copies of the musical "Tell It Like It Is" were sold worldwide, which spawned church youth choirs and provided a place for young people in the church once again. The simplicity of choruses such as "Pass It On," and "Oh How He Loves You and Me" made them a dominant part of church worship services.

Kaiser has written and copyrighted more than two hundred songs, and in 1992 he was presented with a Lifetime Achievement Award from the American Society of Composers, Authors and Publishers (ASCAP) for his contributions. He has received two honorary doctorates, one in humane letters from Baylor University in Waco, Texas, and the other in sacred music from Trinity College in Illinois. In 2001, he was inducted into the Gospel Music Hall of Fame. Although his musical taste favors classical and traditional church music, he continues to work with churches, choirs, and musicians, showing them how to stretch musically, improve their skills, and reach their full potential in performance.

BOB GERSZTYN

See also Carmichael, Ralph; McCracken, Jarrell; Shea, George Beverly

Reference and Further Reading

Callahan, Mike; David Edwards; Patrice Eyries. "Word Album Discographies," http://www.bsnpubs.com/word/word8000.html (accessed September 5, 2003).

Gospel Music Association website, http://www.gospelmusic.org/news/article.cfm?ArticleID=37 (accessed September 2, 2003).

Hall John. "The Baptist Standard." http://www.baptiststandard.com/2002/1_7/print/kaiser.html (accessed September 2, 2003).

Kurt Kaiser website, http://www.kurtkaiser.com (accessed September 1, 2003).

Smith Creek Music website, http://www.smithcreekmusic. com/Hymnology/PraiseAndWorship/praiseandworship. roots.html (accessed September 1, 2003).

Word Label Group website, http://www.wordlabelgroup.com (accessed September 1, 2003).

Discography

Kurt Kaiser Piano (1959, Word W 3093-LP/WST 8035-LP); *Preludes to Faith* (1962, Word W-3157-LP/WST 8095-LP); *Hymntime Sing-Along* (1963, Word W-3176LP/WST 8110-LP); *From London . . . Kurt Kaiser's Sweeping Strings* (1965, Word W-3301-LP/WST-8301-LP); *Master Designer* (1965, Word W 3322-LP/WST 8322-LP); *Hymns of Prayer* (1966, Word W-3327/WST-8327-LP); *Kaiser, Kurt: Pass It On* (1972, Word WST 8562 LP); *An Offering* (1975, Word WST-8679-LP); *Alone with the Music* (1987, Word 701-9046-106-CD); *The Lost Art of Listening* (1991, Word 701-9239-609-CD); *Psalms, Hymns, and Spiritual Songs* (1994, Sparrow).

KAREN PECK AND NEW RIVER

Karen Peck Gooch (b. March 12, 1960)
Susan Peck Jackson (b. February 4, 1957)
Devin McGlamery (b. June 9, 1982)

Over the past fourteen years, the vocal trio known as Karen Peck and New River has established itself as a major force on the Southern gospel music scene. Karen's soprano voice has won her a large following that has resulted in eleven fan awards from *The Singing News*. A native of North Georgia, her love for gospel music dates back to her childhood, when her parents often took her to all-night sings in Atlanta, where she became particularly inspired by the sounds of the now legendary LeFevres. In 1980, one of her aspirations was fulfilled when she became a member of the LeFevres briefly and then for ten years with their successor group, the Rex Nelon Singers. After a decade of experience with the Nelons, she left to form her own vocal trio.

In 1991, with the aid of her older sister Susan and a third vocalist, David White, Karen Peck and New River came into being. Karen's husband Rickey Gooch has served as the band's road manager and sound technician from the beginning. In later years John Darin Rowsey sang the third part in the trio, and most recently Devin McGlamery, a veteran of five years as lead vocalist for Ed O'Neal's Dixie Melody Boys, has filled this role. Through January 2005, Karen Peck and New River have placed twenty-five songs on the gospel charts, including five at number one: "Four Days Late," "God Likes to Work," "When Jesus Passes By," "I Wanna Know How It Feels," and "That's Why They Call It Grace." In addition, "Four Days Late" took the Southern Gospel Music Association's Song of the Year Award in 2001. Karen took home the SGMA Female Vocalist of the Year Award in 2002, and the trio has received numerous nominations in other categories.

IVAN M. TRIBE

Reference and Further Reading

Karen Peck and New River website, http://www.karenpeck andnewriver.com.

Discography

Triumph (2001, Spring Hill CD).
For His Glory (2003, Spring Hill CD).

KARNES, ALFRED GRANT

(b. February 2, 1891; d. May 18, 1958)

Gospel singer, songwriter, minister in both the Baptist and Methodist churches, and evangelist Alfred Grant Karnes was born in Bedford, Virginia, but he spent most of his adult life in Kentucky and always considered himself a Kentuckian. From the time he was a small boy, Karnes had two major desires: preaching and music. He would often go into a large field near his house with his cigar box fiddle, where he would play and then practice stump preaching.

After serving in the U.S. Navy during World War I, he moved to Jellico, Tennessee, where he became a barber. When a short time later he married Flora Etta Harris, he moved to her home state, Kentucky. It was in the Bluegrass state that Karnes's musical skills received their first public exposure. His rich vocals and his skills on the violin and banjo made him in demand at local gatherings. He was so fond of singing "Red Wing" that the song's title became his nickname. By 1925, Karnes had graduated as a Methodist minister from the Clear Creek Mountain Minister's Bible School. One of his teachers, a firm Baptist, converted him to that denomination.

Karnes was a hard-working minister, frequently pastoring as many as four rural churches at a time. He also kept busy with his music, and, in July 1927, he heard about the recording sessions in Bristol being held by the Victor Talking Machine Company; there, on July 29, he cut six sides backed by his own harpguitar. Five of the six selections, including his own composition and most popular song, "Called to the Foreign Field," were released by Victor. In October

1928, Karnes returned to Bristol for another Victor recording session, waxing four sides on October 28 and three on October 29, but only three of the seven were released. With that, the recording career of Alfred Karnes ended.

Karnes continued his ministerial duties and established at least two churches, one in Kentucky and another in Ohio. He kept up his musical activities by forming a family band made up of himself, his four sons, and his daughter. They gave four "courthouse steps" concerts every Sunday, covering a rather extensive area from Mount Vernon to Stanford, Kentucky, always attracting a large crowd. One of their most requested numbers was "This Is My Day, My Happy Day." Although most of his music was religious in nature, Karnes did play such fiddle tunes as "Eighth of January" and "Wednesday Night Waltz" and, unlike many ministers, was not averse to dancing. In fact, he loved doing the Charleston.

Karnes engaged in a strenuous program of gymnastics to keep himself physically fit. Even so, after his second wife died in 1944, his health went gradually downhill. Early in 1957 he suffered a stroke that left him partially paralyzed, and a second stroke, on May 18, 1958, ended his life. Although only four records by Karnes were ever released, they were so powerful that they have kept his memory alive to the present day.

W. K. McNeil

Reference and Further Reading

Nelson, Donald Lee. "The Life of Alfred G. Karnes." *John Edwards Memorial Foundation Quarterly* VIII, Part 1, no. 25 (Spring 1972): 31–36.

Discography

Goodbye Babylon (2003, Dust-to-Digital Records; has "Called to the Foreign Field" on disc five).

KARTSONAKIS, DINO

(b. New York City)

Dino Kartsonakis was born to John and Helen Kartsonakis, who were both of German ancestry. Kartsonakis's father was a chef, and his mother was a homemaker who took care of young Kartsonakis and his older sister, Christine. Before his birth, Kartsonakis's mother and grandmother were extremely diligent in praying when they learned that the young Kartsonakis was to be a stillborn baby. His mother

and grandmother would not accept that as fact, and they dedicated his life to the Lord before he was born. His grandmother owned an old upright piano that had been in their family for two generations; however, no one in his family knew how to play it. One day, when Kartsonakis was three years old, he sat down at that piano and began to pick out the hymn "At the Cross" one finger at the time. Two years later, his mother enrolled him in piano lessons. His talent began to flourish as he became an accompanist at Glad Tidings Tabernacle in New York City, where he accepted Christ at the age of seven.

After completing high school, Kartsonakis trained formally in music at King's College, Julliard School of Music, and conservatories of music in Germany and France. Initially, Kartsonakis considered becoming an architect; however, when he was seventeen years old, a solo performance at an Assembly of God convention in Springfield, Missouri, opened the door for him and confirmed his dream of finding out exactly how the Lord desired to use him. Kartsonakis knew that the Lord desired to use him and his music to touch lives.

In the 1970s, Dino was brought into the public eye as he launched a solo career that took him to the outtermost parts of the world with performances before millions of people. To his credit, he was presented several awards, including a Religion in Media Award, several Dove Awards for Instrumentalist of the Year, a 1983 Grammy nomination for his instrumental album *Chariots of Fire,* and a Grammy Award for his artistry on the soundtrack for the 1997 movie *The Apostle.*

With his wife Cheryl and daughters Christina and Cherie as his biggest fans, Dino Kartsonakis is a man with a drive to serve the Lord while ministering through song. He is indeed one of the top performers of our time and in every respect "America's Piano Showman."

ALPHONSO SIMPSON, JR.

Reference and Further Reading

"Dino Kartsonakis." http://www.onlinetalent.com/khgtjDino. htm (accessed July 29, 2004).
"Dino Kartsonakis." http://www.dinoplayspiano.com/bio. htm (accessed July 29, 2004).
Spicer, Tammi. Telephone interview by Alphonso Simpson, Jr., July 2004.

Selected Discography

Majestic Peace (1991).
Peace in the Midst of the Storm (1993).
Quiet Inspiration (2000).

KELSEY, SAMUEL

(b. April 27, 1897, Sandville, GA; d. January 8, 1993, Washington, DC)

Bishop Samuel Kelsey, Jr., began preaching in the U.S. Army at Camp Hancock in Augusta, Georgia. With a Holiness–Pentecostal evangelistic crusade, he left Philadelphia and moved to Washington, DC, in 1923. Kelsey's Church of God in Christ church started very humbly, in a tent. Kelsey was known as a singing minister; he would sing on street corners, for tent revivals, and in his church. His songs are folk heritage with the long and short meters, some are *a cappella,* and others are solos with little musical background. His voice is sweet, very humble, and yet forceful and sincere. He sang, prayed, preached, taught, praised, and worshipped in many areas.

In 1936, he established a radio ministry that lasted for forty years without interruption. In early 1941 he started his weekly radio broadcasts. Kelsey's broadcast was heard by two white men in 1946; these two men encouraged him to record his traditional gospel songs. Thirty songs were recorded and distributed in the United States, Canada, and England. Kelsey said he did not receive any royalties as contracted. In 1950, Kelsey went to London and in 1965 to Frankfurt, Germany, to preach and sing his songs. Kelsey said, "My records were all over there." He was never bitter about what happened; he stated that this happened to many African American gospel musicians. He knew that the Lord would provide for him, and he felt that many were saved by hearing his songs.

Kelsey said that most of his songs were from the Old Testament in the Bible, and he loved to sing jubilees, spirituals, and Southern Negro work songs. Kelsey said that "he made up songs to encourage people as the needs presented themselves, especially for prisoners who were on death row." He said that his most famous song was "Little Boy." He also mentioned "The Old Ship of Zion," "Hide My Soul," "I'm a Witness for My Lord," "Where Is the Lion in the Tribe of Judah?," "Low Down the Chariot," "Shine for Jesus," and "I'm a Royal Child."

In 1950, Kelsey's title changed to bishop. He was appointed by Bishop Charles Harrison Mason, the founder of the Church of God in Christ, headquartered in Memphis, Tennessee. In 1972, a housing complex was named in his honor. The February 17, 1976, issue of the *Congressional Record* published a "Bicentennial Salute to Kelsey." He was a beacon of light who served people with his music. In Washington, there is a Kelsey Housing Project and a Kelsey Bible College named in his honor. His music was reissued on September 7, 2000, on an album entitled *Popular*

Music: Rev. Kelsey: 1947–1951. This release includes a wedding ceremony. Kelsey has been nominated for induction into the International Gospel Music Hall of Fame and Museum in Detroit.

SHERRY SHERROD DuPREE

Reference and Further Reading

"Bicentennial Salute to Kelsey." *Congressional Record* (February 17, 1976).

DuPree, Sherry Sherrod. *African-American Holiness Pentecostal Movement: An Annotated Bibliography.* Religious Information Systems Vol. 4; Garland Reference Library of Social Science Vol. 526. New York: Garland Publishing, 1996.

———. *Biographical Dictionary of African-American Holiness–Pentecostals 1880–1990.* Washington, DC: Middle Atlantic Regional Press, 1989.

———; Herbert C. DuPree. *African-American Good News (Gospel) Music.* Washington, DC: Middle Atlantic Regional Press, 1993.

International Gospel Music Hall of Fame and Museum website, http://www.gmhf.org (accessed August 28, 2004).

Kelsey, Samuel, Jr. Interview by Sherry Sherrod DuPree, Washington, DC, October 4, 1983.

Salzman, Jack; David Lionel Smith; Cornel West. "The Church of God in Christ." *Encyclopedia of African American Culture and History.* Library Reference USA. Vol. 1. New York: Simon and Schuster Macmillan, 1996.

Discography

Rev. Kelsey & His Congregation 1947–1951. Complete Recorded Works in Chronological Order (2000, Document Records DOCD-5478). Kelsey preaches and sings with the congregation of the Temple Church of God in Christ. The wedding ceremony of gospel singer Sister Rosetta Tharpe is on the CD.

KENNY PARKER TRIO

The Kenny Parker Trio was formed in 1971 by founding members Kenny Parker, his wife Peggy, and their friend Elmer Cole. They had a unique sound and a successful albeit brief career in gospel music.

Kenny Parker got his first taste of gospel music as the talented pianist for the Singing Rambos. Through his association with the Rambos, he learned the tricks of the trade in the gospel music industry. His piano technique was excellent, and he filled the role of accompanist for this fine family trio in a superb manner. His harmonic stylings fit the unusual sound of Dottie, Buck, and Reba quite well.

In the early 1970s, the Rambos decided to curtail some of their touring. The allure of having his own group soon drew Kenny to form his own trio. The Rambos had already signed Kenny's wife Peggy to an exclusive songwriting contract, so her potential was quickly noticed in the industry.

Parker sought to form a trio that was different from the norm. One of the things that established the unique sound of the Kenny Parker Trio was a Wurlitzer electric piano. They were one of the first groups in gospel music to stray away from the standard acoustic piano and use a keyboard in their concert settings. This gave a very commercial sound to the Kenny Parker Trio. They were soon signed to an exclusive recording contract with Heart Warming Records.

Elmer Cole, the third member of the Kenny Parker Trio, soon began to establish himself as a major songwriter in the gospel music field. His talents were not wasted in the trio as they featured several of his songs in their repertoire, including the gospel music classic "Ten Thousand Years."

Peggy and Kenny Parker were quite impressive songwriters. The Kenny Parker Trio always featured their own compositions in their recordings and live performances. When the Kenny Parker Trio arrived on the stage, they did not rely on loud flashy presentations. Instead, they were very harmonious and mellow, relying on smooth, lush harmony and inspiring words to enthrall their audience.

JOHN CRENSHAW

Reference and Further Reading

Liner notes. *Afterglow* (Heart Warming 3220).
———. *Reach Out . . . And Touch Him* (Heart Warming 3248).
———. *Ten Thousand Years* (Heart Warming 3234).

Discography

Afterglow (Heart Warming 3220).
Reach Out . . . And Touch Him (Heart Warming 3248).
Ten Thousand Years (Heart Warming 3234).

KENTUCKY HARMONY

This, the first shape-note tunebook published in the South, was the work of composer, printer, and tunebook compiler Ananias Davisson (b. February 2, 1780; d. October 21, 1857). *Kentucky Harmony* appeared in 1816 and was the first of thirteen shape-note tunebooks printed before 1860 in the Shenandoah Valley. Nothing is known of Davisson's activities before 1816. Evidently, he had worked as a printer's apprentice, because he printed his own book and fourteen others during the next ten years. Thereafter, owing to wise investment of the profits from his tunebooks in land, he was able to retire from printing and teaching music and live as a "gentleman farmer."

Kentucky Harmony, which went through five editions from 1816 to 1826, and the *Supplement to the Kentucky Harmony,* of which three editions appeared between 1820 and 1826, were the two most important tunebooks published by Davisson. There is no evidence Davisson was ever in Kentucky or that any of the melodies in his books originated there. It is thought that use of "Kentucky" in the titles was designed to appeal to people migrating to the state; his home town in Virginia was a major stopover and supply point along the way.

In its first edition, *Kentucky Harmony* had melodies taken primarily from John Wyeth's *Repository of Sacred Music* (1810) and several other Northern tunebooks. Subsequent editions were made up less of Northern materials and included more folk-like melodies that were popular in the South. The *Supplement* had an even greater orientation to the South and abounded in folk elements; it is generally considered Davisson's most innovative work. Both *Kentucky Harmony* and the *Supplement* were two of the most popular Southern tunebooks compiled in the nineteenth century.

W. K. MCNEIL

Reference and Further Reading

Hatchett, Marion J. *A Companion to The New Harp of Columbia*. Knoxville: University of Tennessee Press, 2003.
Music, David W. "Ananias Davisson, Robert Boyd, Reubin Monday, John Martin, and Archibald Rhea in East Tennessee, 1816–26." *American Music* I, no. 3 (1983): 72–84.

KIEFFER, ALDINE S.

(b. August 1, 1840, Saline County, MO; d. November 30, 1904, Dayton, VA)

The primary creative force behind the success of the Ruebush–Kieffer Company, Aldine S. Kieffer was perhaps the single most important figure in the birth of Southern gospel music. He was active as a singing teacher, composer, poet, and editor. His supporters called him "the apostle of musical democracy" and "the defender of popular notation and mass singing"; his detractors knew him as "The Don Quixote of Buckwheat Notes."

Kieffer was born to John and Mary Funk Kieffer, both natives of the Shenandoah Valley. His father, a farmer and singing-school teacher, died in 1847. His mother subsequently returned with him and his siblings (sources differ on the number) to Mountain Valley (later Singers Glen), Virginia, where he was raised by his maternal grandparents. He was influenced particularly by his grandfather, Joseph Funk, who oversaw the boy's education. At the age of nine, Kieffer began working in the family business, Joseph Funk & Sons publishers. Showing real ability, he taught his first singing-school class at the age of sixteen.

In 1859, Kieffer and his friend and associate Ephraim Ruebush, a Funk employee, began to build a reputation as a singing-school teaching team. These efforts were interrupted by the Civil War. Kieffer joined the Tenth Virginia Volunteer Infantry and left for duty on April 19, 1861, shortly after Ruebush had married his sister. He expected to serve three months, but his soldierly duties ended when he was captured at the Battle of Spotsylvania Court House in May 1864 and imprisoned at Fort Delaware. Even during the war, Kieffer continued his activities as a singing teacher, musician, and student.

Upon his release in April 1865, Kieffer returned to Singers Glen to continue with the family business. Although his grandfather had passed away in 1862, he joined with other family members to rebuild the business (then in disarray) as Joseph Funk's Sons. Initially (1865), he and William S. Rohr revived Funk's periodical *The Southern Musical Advocate and Singer's Friend* as *The Musical Advocate and Fireside Friend*, but it folded in 1869. In November 1865, Kieffer married Elizabeth Josephine Hammon, a union which produced five sons. Joseph Funk's Sons' first postwar tunebook, which used Funk's seven-shape notation, was published in 1866 with the Ruebush & Kieffer imprint added. Gospel characteristics are already evident in the songs of that publication.

In 1870, Kieffer, his brother Rollin, and two uncles, Solomon and Timothy Funk, formed the Patent Note Publishing Company ("patent note" being synonymous with shape note) and launched a new periodical, *The Musical Million and Fireside Friend* (later shortened to *The Musical Million*). Under Kieffer's editorial and creative leadership, it became very successful, eventually attracting ten thousand subscribers. In 1872, Kieffer, Ruebush, and John W. Howe reorganized the company under the name Ruebush, Kieffer & Company (later the Ruebush–Kieffer Company), with Ruebush as the senior partner and business manager, and in 1878, they moved the business to nearby Dayton.

This manifestation of the Funk family business became known to shape-note teachers and singers throughout North America for its fervent promotion of shape notes (especially via *The Musical Million*), its numerous and popular seven-shape-note songbooks, and its highly influential educational enterprises, including schools for both singers and singing teachers.

Among the many songbooks they produced, *The Temple Star* (first edition, 1877) was their most popular, selling more than five hundred thousand copies.

Although the partners always offered singing schools, in 1874 they opened the South's first normal music school (a school for music teachers) with the respected Benjamin C. Unseld as principal. (This institution, the Virginia Normal Music School, eventually became part of Shenandoah University, now in Winchester, Virginia.) The normal school educated many who later became well-known teachers and who promoted the fame and songbooks of the Ruebush–Kieffer Company. Many of them and their students also became Southern gospel publishers (A. J. Showalter and James D. Vaughan being prime examples), as well as composers, poets, and quartet singers. Perhaps the company's last major innovation was the adoption in 1876 of Jesse Aiken's system of seven-shape notation. This led the entire seven-shape-note industry to embrace one system, boosting its fortunes: one system meant greater ease for everyone involved. In 1892, the company also began to publish music in standard notation; this is probably evidence of shape notes' declining popularity.

Toward the end of century, Kieffer's activities declined. After years of effort on behalf of his company, shape notes, and Southern music, he retired from the business in 1901 (some sources indicate that he was pushed or bought out); the Ruebush family inherited it. In 1903, he published a new periodical, *Our Musical Advocate and Singer's Friend*, under the A. S. Kieffer Company imprint. That periodical died with him. His most popular works were "My Mountain Home," "Old Schoolhouse," "Twilight Is Falling," and "Grave on the Green Hillside."

STEPHEN SHEARON

See also Funk, Joseph; Gospel Periodicals; Ruebush, Ephraim; Showalter, Anthony Johnson; Singers Glen, Virginia; Singing Schools; Unseld, Benjamin Carl; Vaughan, James David

Reference and Further Reading

Cusic, Don. *The Sound of Light: A History of Gospel and Christian Music.* 1st Hal Leonard ed. Milwaukee, WI: Hal Leonard, 2002.

Eskew, Harry Lee. "Shape-Note Hymnody in the Shenandoah Valley, 1816–1860." Ph.D. dissertation, Tulane University, 1966.

Gabriel Shank and Aldine Kieffer Collection. Available from http://www.rootsweb.com/%7Evarockin/shank/Shank_Kieffer.htm (accessed September 8, 2004). [Contains letters from Aldine Kieffer and newspaper articles about him dating from 1860 until at least 1935.]

Goff, James R., Jr. *Close Harmony: A History of Southern Gospel.* Chapel Hill & London: University of North Carolina Press, 2002.

Hall, Paul M. *"The Musical Million:* A Study and Analysis of the Periodical Promoting Music Reading Through Shape-Notes in North American from 1870 to 1914." D.M.A. dissertation, Catholic University of America, 1970.

Jackson, George Pullen. *White Spirituals in the Southern Uplands.* Chapel Hill: University of North Carolina Press, 1933.

Morrison, Charles Edwin. "Aldine S. Kieffer and Ephraim Ruebush: Ideals Reflected in Post–Civil War Ruebush–Keiffer Company Publications." Ed.D. dissertation, Arizona State University, 1992.

Showalter, Grace I. *The Music Books of Ruebush & Kieffer, 1866–1942: A Bibliography.* Richmond: Virginia State Library, 1975.

KING RECORDS

King Records was an independent record label that thrived between 1944 and 1968. Based in Cincinnati, Ohio, the company specialized in African American and country and western music. However, the firm also managed to record and issue a sizable amount of both black and white gospel music in both genres during their years in business, much of it influential.

King Records as a corporation was the brainchild of a Jewish entrepreneur named Sydney Nathan (b. April 27, 1904; d. March 5, 1968). Nathan, who suffered from asthma and poor eyesight, had a used record store in Cincinnati and, noting that hillbilly discs sold well, decided to start his own company. Another King executive, Henry Glover (b. ca. 1922; d. April 7, 1991) ranks as the second African American to hold a high position in a record company. At its peak, King had four hundred regular employees and a multiracial workforce. Initially, King was the label for white artists, and Queen was for the rhythm and blues market. However, in 1947, Nathan discontinued Queen and added a 4000-number series for African American music and the 500-number series for country.

Among the significant black gospel groups on King were the Wings Over Jordan choir, the Swan Silvertone Singers, the Harmoneers, the Spirit of Memphis Quartet, the Four Internes, the Galatian Singers, the Trumpeteers, and the Patterson Singers. The only all-gospel white groups were Buford Abner's Atlanta-based quartet the Swanee River Boys, the rural Ohio all-female Trace Family Trio, the all-star country quartet Brown's Ferry Four, Brother Claude Ely, and such other single-session conglomerates as the King Sacred Quartet and the Harlan County Four. The Bailes Brothers and Cowboy Copas also recorded many gospel songs. However, such bluegrass groups as those led by Don Reno and Red Smiley, the Stanley Brothers, Don Reno and Bill Harrell, Ralph Stanley, and Charlie Moore and Bill Napier all recorded numerous sacred songs. The Reno and Smiley song "I'm Using My Bible for a Roadmap," first recorded in January 1952, ranks as one of the most significant and original bluegrass gospel numbers ever written.

In the later 1950s, King began to decline somewhat as an influential force in the record industry, but it continued to record influential rhythm and blues artists such as James Brown and bluegrass groups typified by the Stanleys and Reno and Smiley and issued long-play albums from former King artists such as Cowboy Copas, Hawkshaw Hawkins, Freddy King, and Earl Bostic. After Nathan's death the King catalog was purchased by Starday in October 1968 and the company became Starday–King and later Gusto. Their material continues to be issued from time to time by such firms as Hollywood and Westside.

IVAN M. TRIBE

Reference and Further Reading

Tracy, Steven C. *Going to Cincinnati: A History of the Blues in the Queen City.* 114–153. Urbana: University of Illinois Press, 1993.

Ruppli, Michel. *The King Labels: A Discography*, 2 vols. Westport, CT: Greenwood Press, 1985.

KING SACRED QUARTET

Jack Anglin (b. May 13, 1916; d. March 7, 1963)
Johnnie Wright (b. May 13, 1914)
Raymond "Duck" Atkins (b. February 19, 1927; d. February 1, 1997)
Clyde Moody (b. September 19, 1915; d. April 7, 1989)

Although the King Sacred Quartet was only a recording unit, the six sides the group made for the King label on August 8, 1947, proved to be quite popular and significant within the ranks of country gospel music. Quartet members consisted of Jack Anglin, Johnnie Wright, and Raymond "Duck" Atkins—all of whom were then part of the Tennessee Mountain Boys—as well as Clyde Moody. Moody's guitar and Ernest Ferguson (b. July 16, 1918) on mandolin supplied the instrumentation. Their songs included "I'll Be Listening," "The Old Country Church," "My Main Trial Is Yet to Come," "He Will Set Your Fields on Fire," and two Albert Brumley compositions, "Turn Your Radio On" and "I Heard My Name on the Radio."

Johnnie and Jack had a lengthy career, as did Wright's wife, Kitty Wells. Their repertoires contained a generous amount of sacred songs. Anglin's death in 1963 ended their duo, but Wright continued as a solo performer along with Wells. Moody, a veteran of both Mainer's Mountaineers bands and Bill Monroe's Blue Grass Boys, also sustained a lengthy solo career in country music. After working as a band member with various groups, Atkins eventually went into radio station management. Their recordings, after being out of print for decades, came out in 1993 as part of a *Johnnie & Jack* boxed set from Bear Family Records.

IVAN M. TRIBE

Reference and Further Reading

Stubbs, Eddie; Walt Trott. Liner notes to *Johnnie & Jack*. 12–13 (Bear Family Records, Hamburg, Germany, BCD 15553, 1993).

Discography

Johnnie & Jack (1993, Bear Family BCD 15553; six compact disc boxed set).

KINGDOM HEIRS, THE

Jeffrey Chapman (b. July 17, 1969)
Kreis French (b. March 13, 1961)
Steve Curtis French (b. September 24, 1959)
Adam David Harman (b. November 8, 1977)
Jodi Hesterman (b. December 8, 1968)
Dennis Murphy (b. October 24, 1967)
Arthur Rice (b. December 27, 1962)

The Kingdom Heirs have become one of the nation's best-known gospel groups through their regular appearances at the Dollywood theme park at Pigeon Forge, Tennessee. The group dates back to 1981, when baritone vocalist Steve French and his brother, bass guitarist Kreis French, formed a quartet to play at churches and gospel sings in East Tennessee, including visits to Silver Dollar City. When the park was renamed Dollywood in 1986, the Kingdom Heirs became the gospel group in residence and have remained so for nearly two decades. Being located adjacent to the Southern Gospel Music Hall of Fame and Museum has undoubtedly also been an asset to their career success.

Personnel have changed over the years, with the Frenches being the only constant members, but they have experienced more stability than many groups, partly because their concerts are in a fixed location for nine months of the year. Among current members, drummer Dennis Murphy, a native of Oceana, West Virginia, has been with the group since 1990, and lead vocalist Arthur Rice, from Asheville, North Carolina,

has been a member since 1995. Tenor Jodi Hesterman, bass vocalist Jeff Chapman, and pianist Adam Harman each have three years of experience with the Kingdom Heirs. Earlier personnel included tenor David Sutton, bassist Eric Bennett, and pianist Jamie Graves.

Over the years, the Kingdom Heirs have been nominated for numerous Dove and *Singing News* Fan awards. They took the Band of the Year Award in both 2002 and 2004. Having had numerous songs on the gospel charts, their best-known numbers include "I Know I'm Going There," "I've Been Rescued," "City of Light," and "He Lifted Me."

DEANNA L. TRIBE AND IVAN M. TRIBE

Reference and Further Reading

Kingdom Heirs website, http://www.kingdomheirs.com/bio.

Discography

City of Light (Sonlite CD).
Gonna Keep Telling (Sonlite CD).
Shadows of the Past (Sonlite CD).

KINGSMEN, THE

The Kingsmen were an immensely popular group in Southern gospel throughout the 1970–2000 period, led by Eldridge Fox and Jim Hamill. Hamill described the group as "three chords and a cloud of dust" and the image fit; the Kingsmen were known as rock-solid fundamentalists who performed basic, straight-ahead Southern gospel music with uncomplicated melodies and uncompromising lyrics.

The original Kingsmen were formed in Asheville, North Carolina, by three McKinney brothers—Lewis (lead), Raymond (baritone) and Reece (bass)—with tenor singer Charles Colyer and with Charles Mathews as pianist. Mathews, who gave the group its name, died and was replaced by Martin Cook.

In 1957 Charles Cutshall, who had been a member of the Silvertones (a high school group in Ashville), returned home from the service and joined the Kingsmen, replacing Louis McKinney, who had been killed in an automobile accident. Eldridge Fox (b. July 10, 1936; d. November 21, 2002), also a native of Ashville, had joined the Ambassadors, singing lead and playing the piano in 1955 and 1956 before serving in the Army during 1956 and 1957. Fox was stationed in Atlanta and, after his tour of service duty, he returned to Ashville and joined the Kingsmen, replacing Martin Cook as pianist.

Eldridge Fox soon became the driving force behind the group, which had played primarily on weekends before Fox joined. Fox wanted to be in gospel music full time, so he bought out the other members and retained the name Kingsmen.

Fox hired Jim Hamill (b. August 10, 1934) in 1971 to sing lead. Hamill, the son of a preacher, was born in Big Stone Gap, Virginia. The family moved to Memphis, where Hamill's father pastored the First Assembly of God Church, the church that members of the Blackwoods singing group attended. In high school, Hamill and Cecil Blackwood formed the Songfellows, a quartet that later became famous as the quartet for which Elvis Presley auditioned but was turned down.

In 1954, the Blackwoods suffered the loss of two members, R. W. Blackwood and Bill Lyles, in an airplane crash; Cecil Blackwood then joined the Blackwoods, while Hamill attended Bible college. Hamill was offered a job with a group, also called the Songfellows, in Shenandoah, Iowa, and he went to work for them, dropping out of Bible college.

After the Songfellows, Hamill joined the Melody-men and then the Weatherford Quartet before singing with the Foggy River Boys on Red Foley's *Ozark Jubilee*. After this, Hamill sang with the Blue Ridge Quartet, the Rebels, the Oak Ridge Boys, and the Rebels again until he joined the Kingsmen. Hamill remained with the Kingsmen for twenty-eight years, until he retired in 1999.

Jim Hamill joined a lineup that included Jerry Redd, tenor; Ray Dean Reese (b. May 16, 1939), bass; and Charles Abee, who sang baritone and played piano. Eldridge Fox was the manager of the group but soon found that managing was a full-time job, so he moved out of the spotlight, concentrating on the business side, and he let Jim Hamill take over the songs and stage shows of the group. Hamill elected to mold the quartet into an emotional, rough-edged group with a strong backbone of fundamentalism.

By the late 1970s, the lineup for the Kingsmen included Hamill on lead, Johnny Parrack on tenor, Ray Dean Reese on bass, and Eldridge Fox on bari-tone when he joined the group from time to time.

In September 2001, Eldridge Fox and his son sold the name Kingsmen to a group of investors; Ray Dean Reese formed the Carolina Boys Quartet. In June 2004, the owners of the name Kingsmen allowed it to be used by a group led by Ray Dean Reese. In 2005, the lineup for the Kingsmen was Ray Dean Reese, bass, Jeremy Peace, first tenor, Philip Hughes, lead, and Tim Surratt, baritone and guitar, with band members Brandon Reese, drums, Jason Self, bass, and Nick Succi, piano.

The Kingsmen were elected to the Gospel Music Association Hall of Fame in 2000. Eldridge Fox was elected to the Southern Gospel Music Hall of Fame in 1998; he died in 2002. Jim Hamill was elected to the Southern Gospel Music Hall of Fame in 2004.

DON CUSIC

Reference and Further Reading

Cusic, Don. *The Sound of Light: A History of Gospel and Christian Music*. New York: Hal Leonard, 2002.
Goff, James R., Jr. *Close Harmony: A History of Southern Gospel*. Chapel Hill: University of North Carolina Press, 2002.

Selected Discography

Georgia Live (1995).
Live from the Alabama Theater (1995).
Revival Time (1995).
Ridin' High (1995).
Big & Live (1998).
Gospel Legacy Series: All Time Favorites (2004).

KIRK FRANKLIN & THE FAMILY

Kirk Franklin (b. January 26, 1970)

Kirk Franklin took the gospel music world by storm in 1993 with the release of his debut album, *Kirk Franklin & The Family*. The album quickly rose to number one on *Billboard* magazine's gospel album chart and crossed over to the R&B charts as well, propelled by the popular single "Why We Sing." The song became a radio hit in multiple formats, and the album sold more than a million copies.

Abandoned by his mother, Kirk was raised by a devout Christian aunt who took him to church every time the doors were open. He displayed musical talent at an early age and was playing piano by four years old. Recognizing Kirk's musical ability, his sixty-four-year-old Aunt Gertrude collected and sold aluminum cans to get the money for piano lessons. By the time Kirk was eleven, the pastor at Mount Rose Baptist Church invited him to lead the choir. Franklin began writing and recording his songs, and he formed a gospel group with some friends, called Humble Hearts, while he was a teen-ager. Kirk honed his musical skills at a performing arts high school on the campus of Texas Wesleyan University and continued leading music at various Fort Worth churches.

The first major step in Franklin's career came as the result of gospel music executive Milton Biggham listening to a tape of some songs he had composed and recorded. Biggham invited Franklin to perform his composition "Every Day with Jesus" with the Dallas/Fort Worth Mass Choir. The performance went well and led to an invitation to direct the song for the National Mass Choir in Washington, DC, at the annual convention of the Gospel Music Workshop of America. Franklin eventually recorded the song with the Georgia Mass Choir, and the song was included on the soundtrack of the movie *The Preacher's Wife,* starring Whitney Houston and Denzel Washington.

While Franklin enjoyed his work with various choirs, he wanted to put together his own group that would have elements of gospel but also incorporate elements of R&B, pop, and his other musical influences. In 1992, he turned to a group of close friends and they began rehearsing at the apartment complex where Kirk was living. He dubbed the group the Family and soon they began recording Franklin's compositions.

In late 1992, Kirk Franklin came to the attention of a new label in Los Angeles, called GospoCentric. Label president Vicki Lataillade had started the label with a six-thousand-dollar loan, and she offered Kirk five thousand for the album he had produced and that became his million-selling debut, *Kirk Franklin & The Family.* The success of the album brought Franklin multiple Dove, Stellar, and Gospel Workshop of America awards in 1994.

Franklin's sophomore release, *Whatcha Lookin' 4,* quickly rose to number one on the contemporary Christian charts and to number five on the *Billboard* R&B album chart, eventually being certified platinum with sales of one million records. Franklin's next album, *God's Property,* became his first multiplatinum release, propelled by the song "Stomp," which became a favorite on MTV and pop radio. The album went on to sell three million copies. He repeated his multiplatinum sales with his next release, the Grammy Award–winning *The Nu Nation Project.* The album featured the popular single "Lean On Me," with guest vocalists Bono, Mary J. Blige, R. Kelly, and Crystal Lewis.

On *The Rebirth of Kirk Franklin* in 2002, Franklin continued his tradition of including guests, with guest vocals from friends Donnie McClurkin and the legendary Shirley Caesar. The project also featured the famous preacher Bishop T. D. Jakes on a unique dialog song titled "911."

JAMES I. ELLIOTT

Reference and Further Reading

Franklin, Kirk; Jim Nelson Black. *Church Boy.* Nashville, TN: Word Publishing, 1998.
Grammy Awards website, http://www.grammy.com/awards/.
Joseph, Mark. *The Rock & Roll Rebellion.* Nashville, TN: Broadman & Holman, 1999.
"Kirk Franklin." Nu Nation website, http://www.nunation.com/bio.html.
Recording Association Industry of America website, http://www.riaa.com/gp/database/.

Discography

Kirk Franklin & The Family (1993, GospoCentric 72219).
Whatcha Lookin' 4 (1995, GospoCentric).
God's Property from Kirk Franklin's Nu Nation (1997, GospoCentric 70007).
Nu Nation Project (1998, GospoCentric 70013).
God's Property: The Rebirth of Kirk Franklin (2002, GospoCentric 70037).

KIRKPATRICK, WILLIAM JAMES

(b. February 27, 1838; d. September 20, 1921)

Gospel music pioneer William James Kirkpatrick was noted as a composer, teacher, and compiler of Sunday school and gospel hymnbooks. After studying with a number of music instructors, he started teaching music in the Philadelphia area. He also became music director of several Methodist churches, at the same time earning his living as the manager of a furniture business.

Kirkpatrick's output as a composer began modestly with transcriptions of tunes heard at camp meetings near Philadelphia. Thereafter, he published numerous melodies, several of them reflecting camp meeting and brass band influences. In 1878, he established, in collaboration with John R. Sweney, the Praise Publishing Company. These two men compiled fifty songbooks that sold several million copies. After Sweney's death in 1899, Kirkpatrick published fifty more collections. In addition, the two men collaborated with the leading gospel songwriters of the day, publishing almost a thousand of Fanny Crosby's songs alone.

Kirkpatrick's songbooks were very popular at revivals and camp meetings, and they helped to establish and popularize the gospel style that developed in the late nineteenth and early twentieth centuries. Of Kirkpatrick's prolific output, "Jesus Saves" and "'Tis So Sweet to Trust in Jesus" (both 1882) are the best known today. Appropriately, he died doing something he loved, expiring from a heart attack while in Germantown, Pennsylvania, working on a new hymn.

W. K. McNEIL

Reference and Further Reading

Hall, J. H. *Biography of Gospel Song and Hymn Writers.* New York: Fleming H. Revell, 1971 (1914).
Osbeck, Kenneth W. *101 More Hymn Stories.* Grand Rapids, MI: Kregel, 1985.

KLAUDT INDIAN FAMILY, THE

Reinhold "Pop" Klaudt (b. December 21, 1908; d. July 5, 2001)

Lillian Little Soldier "Mom" Klaudt (b. June 29, 1906; d. March 3, 2001)

Vernon Klaudt (b. July 5, 1930)

Melvin Klaudt (b. June 5, 1933)

Raymond Klaudt (b. May 15, 1936)

Kenneth Klaudt (b. May 10, 1943)

The Klaudt Indian Family—certainly one of the most atypical groups in the annals of Southern gospel music—was formed when a young German farmer, Reinhold Klaudt, received a call into the ministry during his late teens in northwest North Dakota. Upon beginning his ministry at the Fort Berthold Indian Reservation, he met a young Arikara maiden named Lillian Little Soldier. She had learned piano and organ from the missionary's daughter, Dora Hall, at the local mission school. Reinhold and Lillian soon fell in love and were married on September 13, 1929. Their ministry began on the evening of their wedding day. Musically, Reinhold played the banjo.

During the next fourteen years, while the Klaudts worked as traveling evangelists, their family increased to include five children, who joined the musical group as they became old enough. Vernon emceed, sang bass in the quartet and lead in the trios and duets, and played upright bass. After his marriage, his wife, the former Betty Lauer, played piano. Melvin, the second son, who sang first tenor and baritone, played trombone. He married Margie Terrell in 1953, and of their two children, son Michael played drums in the group for several years. Raymond sang second tenor and also played tenor saxophone. Kenneth, the youngest son, played alto saxophone and did most of the vocal solos. In addition, daughter Ramona (b. May 5, 1932) sang alto and played trumpet. She married Charles Carpenter, and both traveled with the family for two years before going into their own evangelistic work.

The Klaudts conducted their evangelistic and musical endeavors largely in the West until 1946, when the parents relocated to Cleveland, Tennessee, so that the children could receive an education at the Church of God Bible Training School. They subsequently settled in the Atlanta area and traveled the nation with their concerts through the 1950s, 1960s, and 1970s. Pop Klaudt left the musical group but continued to manage the Klaudt Indian Family. After Betty stopped traveling, Ralph Seibel worked as the family's piano player. As James Goff stated in his authoritative work *Close Harmony,* "sometimes appearing in full Indian regalia, the family drew attention within an industry replete with traditional Southern quartets and trios." They appeared frequently on the syndicated gospel music television programs and recorded a series of well-received albums on their own Family Tone label.

The Klaudt Indian Family retired from full-time gospel music at the end of the 1970s. With the exception of the parents, who passed away in their mid-nineties in 2001, all live with their families in suburban Atlanta, where they also engage in church, school, and business endeavors. Over the years, they have received numerous awards from Native American groups across North America, and they have a place in the Historic Section of the Southern Gospel Music Association at Dollywood in Pigeon Forge, Tennessee. Unfortunately, their many recordings from the 1960s and 1970s are all out of print.

MELVIN KLAUDT, WITH IVAN M. TRIBE

Reference and Further Reading

Goff, James R., Jr. *Close Harmony: A History of Southern Gospel*, 204–205. Chapel Hill: University of North Carolina Press, 2002.

Discography

Gospel Favorites (Family Tone 902).
Traveling On (Family Tone 901).
Whispering Hope (Family Tone 903).

KNIGHT, MADAME MARIE

(b. 1918, Sanford, FL)

As a child, Marie Knight lived in Newark, New Jersey. Her parents were members of the Old Tabernacle Church of God in Christ (COGIC), and Marie started to sing in their sanctified choir when the was five; she attended the COGIC conventions in Memphis and even served as secretary of the Ministerial Alliance.

When she was twenty, thanks to her beautiful contralto, Knight was already a well-known soloist in the COGIC circles, performing their theme song, "Doing All the Good We Can," and other songs such as Thomas Dorsey's "Today." In the early 1940s, she joined the revival team of Frances Robinson, a Philadelphia evangelist. Around this time, in Texas, she married a COGIC minister and started to sing at revival meetings across the country, and she also worked with male quartets. She made her first recordings in 1946 for Haven Records with *a cappella* jubilee groups such as the Sunset Four.

Madame Marie Knight. Photo courtesy Frank Driggs Collection.

Knight formed the first female duo in the history of gospel music with Rosetta Tharpe in 1947, and this association was incredibly popular during the nine following years. They recorded some twenty songs for Decca Records with the swinging Sammy Price Trio. Most were hits, such as "Didn't It Rain," "Beams of Heaven," and "Precious Memories." At the same time, she underwent personal tragedies: a fire killed her mother and her two children, and she was on the verge of quitting singing when she got a moral rescue from prophetess Dolly Lewis, and she perked up.

However, the times were changing. During the 1950s, the popularity of black gospel music went down, and many artists crossed over to the much more lucrative R&B market. Marie Knight did it too, in 1954 singing a duet with heavyweight boxing champion Jersey J. Walcott. It was, at best, poor R&B, and at the same time she recorded a couple of gospel records. When her contract with Decca ran out in 1955, she was signed by Mercury Records and made better records, with one foot in R&B and one foot in gospel, such as "Songs of the Gospel" with backup singers and guitarist Mickey Baker.

From 1956 until the mid-1970s, she was a pop singer with occasional hits that lead to international tours (Europe and Australia, among others). At the same time, she went on performing gospel at churches, with her friend Ernestine Washington in New York, for instance. In 1973 she was ordained an evangelist. Her comeback album for Blue Labor, with Louisiana Red on guitar, was excellent; on it, she sang duets with her sister, Bernice Roach Henry, on a couple of songs (such as "Florida Storm"), and the session was reissued on CD in 1996. At the end of the 1970s, Knight came back into the Savoy recording studios, producing a strong gospel album.

During the 1980s and 1990s, Marie Knight worked as an evangelist in her church, The Gates of Prayer in New York. She went on writing songs, ready to record again and to tour extensively, everywhere in the world, if there was an opportunity.

ROBERT SACRÉ

See also Tharpe, Sister Rosetta; Washington, Ernestine B.

Reference and Further Reading

Boyer, Horace Clarence. *How Sweet the Sound: The Golden Age of Gospel*. Washington, DC: Elliott & Clark, 1995.
Hayes, J. Cedric; Robert Laughton. *Gospel Records 1943–1969: A Black Music Discography*, 2 vols. London, UK: Record Information Services, 1992.
Heilbut, Tony. *The Gospel Sound: Good News and Bad Times*. New York: Limelight, 1985.
Kochakian, Dan. "The Legacy of Sam Price." *Whiskey, Women, and ...* 12/13 (December 1983): 10–26.
Reagon, Bernice Johnson, ed. *We'll Understand It Better By and By. Pioneering African American Gospel Composers*. Washington, DC: Smithsonian Institution Press, 1992.

Discography

Today (1975) (1996, the Blues Alliance TBA-13006).
Marie Knight, Hallelujah What a Song (1947–1951) (2002, Gospel Friend Records PN 1500; Sweden).

L

LANE, CRISTY

(b. January 8, 1940)

The woman best known for singing Marijohn Wilkin and Kris Kristofferson's "One Day at a Time" was born in Peoria, Illinois, as Eleanor Johnston. One of a poor family of twelve, the girl early displayed a love of and talent for singing but, being shy, she was too timid to perform in public. She would probably never have become a professional entertainer had she not met Lee Stoller when she was seventeen. The couple soon married and in seven years had three children. More important for her career, Stoller made a demo tape of his wife's singing and carried it around wherever he went. A singer in a Peoria nightclub called Wayne's Club invited Lee to bring his wife in and see how she went over with the public. Singing some country standards, she was a big hit with the crowd and Lee pushed her to get further experience, which she did by performing in dance halls.

Stoller's persistence paid off when he was able to get her a guest performance on the venerable *National Barn Dance,* which resulted in her first paid live performance; she made eighty-seven dollars. Soon she changed her name to Cristy Lane, taking the stage name from a flyer containing the name of a disc jockey, Chris Lane. He gave Cristy permission to use his name and invited her to perform on his popular television show *Swing Around.*

Not all of Lee's machinations were successful. Wanting Cristy to adopt the "Nashville sound" and look, he persuaded her to go blonde and took her to Nashville in 1966. A tape he made of her singing got no takers. Only slightly more successful was a record he paid to have distributed to three hundred country music stations. In 1969 the couple toured Vietnam, an experience that made such an indelible impact on Cristy that once she returned home, she tried to commit suicide.

In 1972, Cristy and Lee were living in the Nashville suburb of Madison. After several more disappointments, she finally scored big with "Let Me Down Easy," which reached the top ten on country charts in the late 1970s, followed by the Christmas tearjerker "Shake Me I Rattle!" In 1979, she received the Academy of Country Music New Vocalist of the Year award and made appearances on several national television shows. During this time, her husband Lee was jailed for financial irregularities.

In many ways, 1980 was the most important year in Cristy's career, because that was when she recorded the gospel number that made her famous. Perhaps because other artists had recorded "One Day at a Time," the record label United Artists was reluctant to release Cristy's single of the song. When they did, it was an instant success, going to number one on country charts. In 1986, Lee was out of jail and, inspired by Slim Whitman's television marketing success, telemarketed Cristy's album *One Day at a Time.* It became one of the biggest-selling albums of all time and the only gospel disc to be given an Ampex Golden Reel Award.

In 1987, Lane's last chart entry was also of a religious song, "He's Got the Whole World in His

Hands." In 1993, Lee Stoller and Pete Chaney produced Cristy's biography, appropriately titled *One Day at a Time*. During the same decade, she and her husband led the exodus from Nashville to Branson, Missouri. They own a theater in the Ozark town where she regularly performs.

W. K. McNEIL

Reference and Further Reading

Stoller, Lee; Pete Chaney. *One Day at a Time*. New York: St. Martin's Press, 1993.

Discography

Amazing Grace (1982, United Artists).
Christmas Is the Man from Galilee (1983, United Artists).
Footprints in the Sand (1983, United Artists).
Amazing Grace Vol. 2 (1986, Arrival).
One Day at a Time (1986, LS Records).
All in His Hands (1989, Heart Warming).
My Best to You (1992, Arrival).

LANNY WOLFE TRIO

Lanny Wolfe (b. Unknown)
Marietta Wolfe (b. Unknown)
Dave Peterson (b. Unknown)

The Jackson, Mississippi–based Lanny Wolfe Trio has been a stalwart in gospel music for many decades. During the 1970s, the group recorded numerous albums for the Benson Company's Heart Warming and Impact labels. Lanny Wolfe, a prolific songwriter, composed many of their numbers, some with the help of his wife Marietta. Wolfe also taught music at the Jackson College of Ministries. Some of their best-known originals include "Come On, Let's Praise Him," "Greater Is He," "God's Wonderful People," and "A Brand New Touch." In 1976, the Wolfes' daughter, Lanna-Marie, joined them on recordings for the first time. The trio was still musically active at last report.

IVAN M. TRIBE

Reference and Further Reading

Anderson, Robert; Gail North. *Gospel Music Encyclopedia*. 187–188, 313. New York: Sterling Publishing 1999.

Discography

Shout It ... Jesus Is Coming! (1975, Heart Warming LP R 3356).

A Brand New Touch (1976, Impact LP R 3407).
Have a Nice Day (1978, Impact LP R 3482).

LAWSON, DOYLE, AND QUICKSILVER

Doyle Wayne Lawson (b. April 20, 1944)

Doyle Lawson is one bluegrass performer who has attained a level of fan appreciation and influence roughly equal to that of the founding father of the music. He also has demonstrated a commitment to sacred song in his repertoire that approaches and perhaps surpasses that of the Stanley Brothers/Ralph Stanley. Lawson and his group Quicksilver have also displayed a flair for high quality *a cappella* quartet performance. They have become regulars on Southern gospel chart listings as well. They are known for their "tight singing, precise playing and thoughtful songs." Ron Vigue, an Ohio University Public Radio bluegrass host, contends that Doyle Lawson and Quicksilver have no signature song because everything they do is good.

Doyle Lawson was born in Ford Town near Kingsport, Tennessee, and reared in Sneedsville from the age of ten, where his father was a devotee of old-time quartet singing. Doyle not only learned to love that style of music but also developed skill on such acoustical instruments as guitar, banjo, and especially mandolin. At age fourteen, he met Jimmy Martin and became determined to make music his career. His early professional experiences consisted of two short stints with Jimmy Martin's Sunny Mountain Boys, longer ones with J. D. Crowe's Kentucky Mountain Boys, and about eight years with the Country Gentlemen. In 1979, Lawson left the latter band to form his own group with "his sound." The band, first called Foxfire, soon changed its name to Quicksilver.

The first version of Quicksilver included Terry Baucom on banjo, Jimmy Haley on guitar, and Lou Reid on bass, all of whom were heard on the first two albums on Sugar Hill, the second of which was the gospel *Rock My Soul*. By the second sacred album, *Heavenly Treasures*, in 1983, Randy Graham had replaced Reid. Graham, Baucom, and Haley soon left to form a short-lived New Quicksilver. Lawson assembled a new set of musicians consisting of Russell Moore on guitar, Scott Vestal on banjo, and initially Curtis Vestal followed by Ray Deaton on bass. Quicksilver's fourth sacred effort, *Heaven's Joy Awaits*, included a dozen *a cappella* quartets sung by Lawson, Moore, Vestal, and Deaton. By 1989, Jim Mills had replaced Vestal in the band.

Throughout the 1990s and afterward, Doyle Lawson and Quicksilver found continued success with the pattern that served them well in their first decade, with at least every other album being gospel, recording for Brentwood as well as Sugar Hill. Band personnel continued to change, but musical standards remained both high and consistent, with a recognizable style. Doyle himself has referred to his band's being a farm club for bluegrass because of the personnel changes. Perhaps his most noted effort for the decade was *Gospel Radio Gems*, a project that emulated those quartets of an earlier generation that had performed with only the accompaniment of a single guitar, played by Doyle himself in this case. Already the band had been using a single microphone since 1995. Quicksilver had become among the most acclaimed acts in bluegrass. They have also hosted a successful bluegrass festival in Denton, North Carolina, for more than twenty years. A few years ago, Doyle added a golf tournament, another of his interests.

In 1998, Doyle Lawson and Quicksilver became the first bluegrass aggregation invited to the National Quartet Convention in Louisville. In 2000, their compact disc, *Winding Through Life*, took the International Bluegrass Music Association's (IBMA's) Gospel Recorded Performance Award. They were named IBMA's Vocal Group of the Year in 2001, 2002, and 2003. The 2004 aggregation of the band included Terry Baucom, banjo; Jamie Dailey, guitar; Barry Scott, bass; Jesse Stockman, fiddle; and Doyle on mandolin.

In April 2004, the twenty-fifth anniversary of Doyle Lawson and Quicksilver was celebrated with all but two of the twenty-some band members returning for the reunion show at the War Memorial Auditorium in Nashville. A two-disc CD on Crossroads, *A School of Bluegrass*, was released in 2004, composed of rehearsals and live performances (not studio recordings) as a musical trip through those twenty-five years.

DEANNA L. TRIBE AND IVAN M. TRIBE

Reference and Further Reading

McIntyre, Les. "Doyle Lawson and Quicksilver: The First 20 Years." *Bluegrass Unlimited* 34, no. 12 (June 2000): 36–40.
Doyle Lawson website, http://www.doylelawson.com.

Selected Discography

Rocky My Soul (1981, Sugar Hill SH 3717).
Heaven's Joy Awaits (1988, Sugar SH 3760).
Gospel Radio Gems (1998, Sugar Hill SH 3879).
Thank God (2003, Crossroads CR 004972).

LEAVITT, JOSHUA

(b. September 8, 1794; d. January 16, 1873)

Compiler of *The Christian Lyre* (1831), the most imitated revival collection before the Civil War, Joshua Leavitt was born in Heath, Massachusetts. He graduated from Yale in 1814 and was later ordained. In 1828 he moved to New York state, where he edited several religious and abolitionist journals, the most important of which was *The Evangelist*, established in 1830. It was not only a significant voice for a new style of revivalism, represented by such preachers as Charles G. Finney, but it also included revival hymns that later appeared in *The Christian Lyre*.

Leavitt published a *Supplement to the Christian Lyre* (1831), a collection of traditional psalm tunes, and a *Companion to the Christian Lyre* (1833), a compilation of texts without tunes. *The Christian Lyre* contained spirituals, traditional hymns, and newly composed religious poems set to popular melodies from Europe and the United States. Leavitt claimed little musical ability and chose pieces for his book due to their popularity and "good influence." This reflected his belief that, for revivals, melodies already known or that could be easily learned were more suitable than church hymns.

Leavitt's method of selection explains why *The Christian Lyre* was both influential and controversial. It had twenty-six editions within eleven years, with nine appearing during the first six months after its initial publication. Printing full texts and melody and bass lines together in a pocket-size format and including several up-tempo secular melodies, traditional spirituals, and camp meeting hymns with choruses represents Leavitt's main innovations. Due to the wide-ranging choice of selections, Leavitt's book, which appeared in both round- and shape-note editions, represents a compromise between the "respectable" hymn style of composers such as Lowell Mason, George Root, and Thomas Hastings and the enthusiastic camp-meeting spirituals. Later editions of Leavitt's book expanded the title to *The Christian Lyre: A Collection of Hymns and Tunes, Adapted for Social Worship, Prayer Meetings, and Revivals of Religion*.

W. K. MCNEIL

Reference and Further Reading

Coburn, F. W. "Leavitt, Joshua." *Dictionary of American Biography*.
Cole, C. G., Jr. *The Social Ideas of the Northern Evangelists*. New York: Columbia University Press, 1954.
Hatchett, Marion J. *A Companion to The New Harp of Columbia*. Knoxville: University of Tennessee Press, 2003.

LEFEVRES, THE

Urias LeFevre (b. 1910; d. 1979)
Alphus LeFevre (b. 1912; d. 1988)
Maude LeFevre
Eva Mae Whittington (b. 1917)

The LeFevres were pioneering Southern gospel performers. From the 1920s to the mid-1970s, they were an influential force in the development of gospel music and more specifically Southern gospel music. Like many Southern gospel acts, the LeFevres were based in Pentecostal and Church of God churches. As such, they grew out of what is known as the shape note singing tradition.

From 1939 to the group's demise in the mid-1970s, they were based in Atlanta. In the early years, they performed in and around Atlanta and toured throughout the Southeast. In 1921, the group began as a trio featuring the brothers Urias (1910–1979) and Alphus LeFevre (1912–1988) and their sister Maude. This version of the group lasted until 1934, when Urias married Eva Mae Whittington (b. 1917), who is the daughter of a Church of God pastor, where the trio frequently performed. Eva Mae joined the group, singing alto and playing the piano in the place of Maude.

As a mixed group, the Lefevres were unique among Southern gospel groups and were especially controversial among many of their Church of God brethren. Despite this, the group's instrumental and vocal virtuosity won them many fans. It was Eva Mae's organ and piano playing that helped create the group's signature sound. With the addition of Urias and Eva Mae's oldest son Pierce LeFevre in 1959, the group became more focused on performing instrumentals. Over the years, the LeFevres' repertoire of songs featured accordion, violin, trumpet, bass, guitar, piano, and organ.

With their relocation to Atlanta in 1939, the trio began performing on the WGST radio station as the LeFevre Trio. As the group added other family members and professional musicians and singers, they began performing as the LeFevres. They would perform as a trio, a quartet, a quintet, and like many gospel groups, the LeFevres parlayed radio play into fame and to help book concerts. It was at WGST that the group recorded its first 78 rpm. These early records were released by the Bibletone label. The group would later record for Word Records as well as Sing Records.

Following their early appearances on Atlanta-based television as well as others in the Southeast, the LeFevres created the first gospel-music–focused syndicated television program, *The Gospel Singing Caravan*. Included in the *Caravan* were the Blue Ridge Quartet, the Johnson Sisters, and the Prophets Quartet. At its height, *The Gospel Singing Caravan* appeared on fifty-seven television stations. *The LeFevre Family Show* took over after *The Gospel Singing Caravan* dissolved. *The LeFevre Family Show* is notable for being the first gospel television show to be broadcast in color.

In addition to embracing the use of television to market their music, the LeFevres were among the first groups to own their own recording studios. This mingling of music and business was a well-established practice among gospel singers and songwriters, as evidenced by the existence of the various Vaughn Quartets and Stamps Quartets; however, the LeFevres were among the first to move beyond merely owing songbook publishing houses or singing schools. Urias, Alphus, and Eva Mae are all individual members of the Gospel Music Association's Hall of Fame as well as being members through the LeFevres.

Throughout the late 1950s and early 1960s, the group often performed as a trio with the instrumental backing of the other members. The trio featuring Rex Nelon, Pierce LeFevre, and Jimmy Jones on vocals was one of the most popular versions of the group. In 1961, the group recorded one of its most popular songs, "Without Him." Written by the young Mylon LeFevre, it soon became a regular part of their performances. Following Elvis Presley's recording of the song in 1966, more than 120 other artists and groups recorded it as well. The song quickly became a staple of gospel music performances.

Throughout the years, the lineup of the LeFevres changed considerably, with the core always being Urias, Alphus, and Eva Mae. Other members of the group included Pierce LeFevre, Mylon LeFevre, Jimmy Jones, Hovie Lister, Jim Waits, Jimmy Kirby, Connor Hall, Troy Lumpkin, Johnny Atkinson, Bob Prather, Bob Robinson, Bill Huie, Earl Terry, Ron and Barbara Daily, Sharon and Teresa McNeill, Rex Foster, Ronnie Hutchens, Barbara Hodge, Rodney Swain, Janet Pascal, Kelly Nelon, and Doug Prater. Long-time bass singer Rex Nelon, who joined the group in 1957, purchased the group and much of the LeFevres' business interests in the mid-1970s and subsequently changed the group's name to the Rex Nelon Singers after Eva Mae retired in 1977.

SCOTT BANVILLE

See also Blue Ridge Quartet; Canaan Records; Gospel Music Association; Homeland Records; Prophets Quartet; Rex Nelon Singers, The; Shape-Note Singing; Stamps Quartets; Vaughan Quartet

Reference and Further Reading

Blackwell, Lois S. *The Wings of the Dove: The Story of Gospel Music in America.* Norfolk, VA: Donning, 1978.

Goff, James R., Jr. *Close Harmony: A History of Southern Gospel.* Chapel Hill: University of North Carolina Press, 2002.

Jackson, George Pullen. *White Spirituals in the Southern Uplands.* Chapel Hill: University of North Carolina Press, 1933.

"The LeFevres." Grand Ole Gospel Reunion website, http://www.grandolegospelreunion.com/sg-101/lefevres.htm.

"The LeFevres." *The New Georgia Encyclopedia.* http://www.georgiaencyclopedia.org/nge/Article.jsp?path=/TheArts/Music/Religious/SouthernGospel&id=h-885.

Terrell, Bob. *The Music Men: The Story of Professional Gospel Quartet Singing.* Asheville, NC: Bob Terrell, 1990.

Discography

Sing the Gospel (1965, Sing Records MFLP-3212); *You Need the Lord* (1965, Sing Records MFLP-3216); *The Best Is Yet to Come* (1969, Canaan Records CAS-9661-LP); *The New Sounds of The LeFevres* (1972, Canaan Records CAS-9721-LP); *Now and Always* (1972, Canaan Records); *Happiness Is Gospel* (1973, Canaan Records CAS-9742-LP); *Stepping on the Clouds* (1974, CAS-9757-LP); *Experience* (1975 Canaan Records CAS-9777-LP); *The LeFevres* (1975, Power Pak PG-721); *Gospel Music USA* (1976, Canaan Records CAS-9790); *Whispering Hope* (1976, Pickwick JS 6192); *Singing 'Til He Comes* (1977, Canaan Records CAS-9805); *16 All Time Favorites* (1977, Starday/Gusto Records 3006); *The Old Rugged Cross* (1985, Golden Circle Records GC57528); *The Best of the LeFevres* (Sing Records LP-3220); *The LeFevres, Vol. 1* (Bibletone Records); *The LeFevres, Vol. 2* (Bibletone Records); *The LeFevres with Jimmy Jones* (Sing Records LP-3204); *Lord It's Me Again* (Sing Records MFLP-3211); *A Man Who Is Wise* (Sing Records MFLP-3219); *Moving Up* (Canaan Records CAS 9684); *Play Gospel Music; Rainbow of Love* (Sing Records LPS-327); *Sing* (Sing Records MFLP-3209); *Sing and Be Happy* (Sing Records LP-320); *A Visit with The LeFevres* (Sing Records MSLP-3217); *Without Him* (Sing Records MLSP 3210).

LEWIS FAMILY, THE

Roy "Pop" Lewis, Sr. (b. September 22, 1905; d. March 24, 2004)
Nannie Omega "Miggie" Lewis (b. May 22, 1926)
Wallace Lewis (b. July 6, 1928)
Talmadge Lewis (b. December 31, 1934)
Polly Lewis Williamson Copsey (b. January 23, 1937)
Janis Lewis Phillips (b. February 13, 1939)
Roy "Little Roy" Lewis, Jr. (b. February 24, 1942)
Travis Lewis (b. December 26, 1958)
Lewis Phillips (b. April 5, 1972)

Lincolnton, Georgia's Lewis Family has earned much respect in both bluegrass and gospel, having become known as the "First Family of Bluegrass Gospel Music." Their musical skills augmented by their strength as entertainers have made them one of the few groups to win wide acceptance in both fields. In addition, the comedy antics of Little Roy Lewis have charmed audiences all over America for some thirty-five years. The Lewis Family as a gospel group have a history that extends well over half a century, with their recordings ranging from 78-rpm records to compact discs and videotapes.

The Lewises' appreciation for quality traditional music dates back into the 1930s. One of Pop's favorite stories is about the time the Monroe Brothers came to their community and the family had Charlie and Bill at their house for supper. In the later 1940s Esley (a brother who dropped out of the group early), Talmadge, and Wallace Lewis began performing for local entertainments as the Lewis Brothers. In 1951, Esley entered military service, and nine-year-old Little Roy took his place playing the five-string banjo. Meanwhile, Pop and the three sisters began singing songs with them, and the Lewis Family became a full-fledged singing group.

In 1954, their careers took another forward leap when they secured a weekly television spot at WJBF in Augusta, Georgia. They continued to do this program for some thirty-eight years, and at times it was syndicated on other stations extending from North Dakota to Arkansas. They also began making records about this time, first for the small Sullivan and Hollywood labels, but they eventually began to record for Starday, where they turned out several four-song extended-play releases, which were eventually followed by fourteen albums (not including those that were repackaged). For some years, most family members held down jobs in textile mills, but by 1967 all had become full-time musicians.

When Starday Records went into hiatus in the late 1960s, the Family did a custom album for a company called Solid Rock and then in 1969 began a seventeen-year association with Canaan Records that resulted in an even greater number of albums. In 1970, the Lewis Family played their first bluegrass festival in Hugo, Oklahoma, and thereafter they gained as much if not more popularity on those circuits than they had at gospel concerts. Throughout this era, their personnel remained stable, with the only change occurring when Talmadge Lewis, who alternately played fiddle and mandolin, left in 1972 to devote full time to his business endeavors.

Other changes took place in later years, nearly all within the family context. In 1974, Travis Lewis, the sixteen-year-old son of Wallace, replaced Pop on bass fiddle. Pop, however, continued to help with the singing until 2002, when advancing age forced him to stop traveling. Meanwhile, the son of Janis, Lewis Phillips, slowly worked his way into the group, taking on an ever more significant role as Parkinson's disease finally led rhythm guitarist Wallace Lewis to retire. Polly's daughter Sheri and son-in-law Jeff Easter worked with them from 1985 until 1988, when the Easters went on their own. Not long after Pop's death in 2004, Travis Lewis chose to retire from the group, causing them to hire their first nonfamily member to play bass fiddle, Scott Yarbrough. Although not a musician, Pauline "Mom" Lewis (b. 1908 or 1910; d. 2003) traveled with the family and looked after their record table as long as her health permitted.

Over the years, the Lewis Family always managed to have a good mixed repertoire of older and newer songs consisting of old standards, numbers drawn from country gospel, and bluegrass tunes and lyrics. Little Roy recorded a number of five-string banjo albums, but on stage he proved equally adept at acoustical lead guitar, autoharp, and mandolin. By the 1970s, writers such as Paul Craft and Randall Hylton began writings songs designed to fit the Lewis Family style. Their 2004 CD, *Angels Gathering Flowers*, includes two songs written by Tom T. and Dixie Hall. Little Roy proved a perennial showstopper with his comic version of "Honey in the Rock," which they frequently used to close their concerts. Pop included some recitations such as "Just a Rose Will Do" and "Someone Will Love Me in Heaven." Lewis Phillips made "God's Little People" virtually his own, while the whole family shone on songs such as "Hallelujah Turnpike," "Slippers with Wings," and "Walkin' and Talkin'."

In 1986, the Lewis Family began recording for Benson's Riversong label and more recently for Thoroughbred and Daywind. Throughout their careers their recordings—sometimes augmented by studio musicians—have maintained a high standard. However, recreating their stage performance on a sound recording is always difficult, and they always go over best when seen in person. They average about two hundred personal appearances a year. The Lewis Family began their own Homecoming and Bluegrass Festival, held in Lincolnton, the first weekend in May; this has been an annual event since 1988. Appreciation for the Lewis Family shows up in their having won several Dove and Society for the Preservation of Bluegrass Music of America awards. They were also inducted into the Georgia Music Hall of Fame in 1992; several of their items are on display at the Southern Gospel Music Hall of Fame at Dollywood, where Pop Lewis was inducted into its Hall of Fame in 2000.

DEANNA L. TRIBE AND IVAN M. TRIBE

Reference and Further Reading

LeRoy, Lance. *The Lewis Family History/Picture Book—45 Years on the Stages of America: A Retrospective.* 1996.
Rhodes, Don. "The Lewis Family Has Left an Imprint on Country Gospel." *Augusta Chronicle*, Ramblin' Rhodes Column, http://chronicle.augusta.com/stories/100600/app_142-5393.000.shtml (web posted October 6, 2000).

Selected Discography

The Lewis Family, Better Than Ever/Good and Plenty (1988 and 1989, Riversong CD02587).
Bluegrass Country Club (1995, Thoroughbred Records THB2027D).
Time (1997, Thoroughbred Records THB2039D).
50th Anniversary (2000, Thoroughbred Daywind 2041D).
Angels Gathering Flowers (2004, Thoroughbred Records THB2045D).

LIGHT RECORDS

One of the seminal labels in the early days of contemporary Christian music (CCM), Light Records evolved into a black gospel powerhouse during the 1970s and 1980s. It continues releasing stirring gospel music—both old and new—as part of the Compendia Music Group.

Light was founded by the multitalented Ralph Carmichael (b. May 27, 1927). Carmichael was a pioneering musician in the early days of television, writing, producing, and arranging for such artists as Nat King Cole, Peggy Lee, Bing Crosby, and Ella Fitzgerald. He even served as musical director of *The Lucy Show*. Carmichael, who had grown up in a Christian home, became acquainted with World Wide Pictures, the motion picture division of Billy Graham Ministries, and he eventually scored more than twenty films for World Wide. He also continued working with a wide variety of popular musicians, including Stan Kenton and Roger Williams.

Carmichael's involvement in church music deepened with the dawning of "Jesus music" in the late 1960s. He wrote and recorded a number of youth musicals, often in conjunction with Kurt Kaiser. The best-known of these, *Tell It Like It Is* and *Natural High,* spawned two of the best-known contemporary Christian songs, "He's Everything to Me" and "The Savior is Waiting."

Although Carmichael's heart was in big band swing and jazz, he founded Light Records and Lexicon Publishing as a joint venture with Jarrell McCracken's Word Records in 1966, which provided the distribution and promotion of his ventures. Light's early releases included Richard and Patti Roberts, 102 Strings, the Continental Singers, Cliff Richard, the Archers, Children of the Day, Jessy Dixon, the Jeremiah People,

Jamie Owens-Collins, and even an album of actor/comedian Jimmy Durante singing hymns.

But Carmichael's biggest signing was Andrae Crouch and the Disciples in 1968. Crouch had been working with a ministry to drug addicts called Teen Challenge when Carmichael heard of him through an engineer at RCA. Carmichael signed the group almost immediately, and the Disciples revolutionized CCM. Crouch provided Light with many of its first hits, with groundbreaking albums such as *Keep On Singin'* (1971) and *Soulfully* (1972). During the late 1970s, Light also ventured into CCM, releasing albums by such popular acts as Allies, Bryan Duncan, the Resurrection Band, Dino, and the Sweet Comfort Band.

In 1974, Word Records was sold to ABC. Carmichael struggled to raise funding but eventually bought Word's half of Light/Lexicon from ABC/Capitol Cities in 1980. Light switched to Elektra for distribution in 1982. During this period, few albums in any genre outsold the Walter Hawkins and Love Alive Choir series. Between 1975 and 1989, the four releases sold more than two million units. *Love Alive IV* remained atop the *Billboard* charts for more than thirty-nine weeks in 1989. Despite an array of strong black gospel artists, Light continued to financially founder, coming close to bankruptcy in 1982. Carmichael eventually sold Light to CGI in the late 1980s.

In 1993, CGI/Light was purchased by Platinum Entertainment, Inc., which actively began rereleasing classic albums by Light mainstays Walter Hawkins, Vickie Winans, Danniebelle Hall, the New Jersey Mass Choir, and the Winans. In 1997, Platinum Entertainment also acquired rival gospel label Intersound Inc. for twenty-nine million dollars and established a distribution agreement through Polygram. Among Platinum Entertainment's innovations (through its now wholly owned subsidiary CGI Records) was the first exclusive contract with a major religious denomination, the National Baptist Convention USA, Inc., to record live gospel music for the denomination for wide distribution.

Despite record sales in 1997, a series of other acquisitions in the following years taxed Platinum Entertainment/CGI's resources, and the company filed for Chapter 11 reorganization in 2001. From the reorganization emerged the Compendia Music Group, operated by the financial firm Dominion Resources. Compendia, a group of full-service labels along with a distribution arm, retained the name Light for its still-potent roster of black gospel artists, including Rizen, Bishop Paul S. Morton, Earl Bynum, the Mighty Clouds of Joy, and a series of reissues titled "Light Records Classic Gold Series," featuring earlier Light Records releases by Sandra Crouch, Commissioned, Tramaine Hawkins, and others.

In December 2004, Compendia was purchased from Dominion by Sheridan Square Entertainment, a New York–based holding company controlled by Redux Records.

In early 2005, Light scored one of its biggest coups, signing Shirley Caesar away from her long-time home with Word Records.

ROBERT DARDEN

See also Caesar, Shirley; Carmichael, Ralph; Crouch, Andrae; Hawkins, Tramaine; Hawkins, Walter; Kaiser, Kurt; McCracken, Jarrell; Mighty Clouds of Joy; National Baptist Convention; Winans, The

Reference and Further Reading

Anderson, Robert; Gail North. *Gospel Music Encyclopedia*. New York: Sterling Publishing Co., 1979.
Carmichael, Ralph. *He's Everything to Me*. Waco, TX: Word Books, 1986.
Collins, Lisa. "In the Spirit." *Billboard* (December 7, 1996): 37.
———. "In the Spirit." *Billboard* (December 29, 2001): 28.
———; Gail Mitchell. "Gospel Catalog: A Wealth of Reissued Oldies Testifies to the Market's Enduring Value." *Billboard* (June 7, 2003): 30.
Crouch, Andrae; Nina Ball. *Through It All*. Waco, TX: Word Books, 1974.
Jones, Bobby; Lesley Sussman. *Touched By God: Black Gospel Greats Share Their Stories of Finding God*. New York: Pocket Books, 1998.

LILLENAS PUBLISHING COMPANY

In 1922, Haldor Lillenas founded the Lillenas Publishing Company. Born on November 19, 1885, in Norway, he was brought to the United States as a child by his parents and was confirmed in the Lutheran Church at the age of fifteen. He entered Deets Pacific Bible College in Los Angeles (later known as Pasadena College) and married Bertha Mae Wilson. Together, the couple traveled as evangelists, penning more than four thousand hymns, including "Wonderful Grace of Jesus." After leaving evangelistic work, Haldor Lillenas pastored First Church of the Nazarene churches from 1914 through 1922.

Originally, Lillenas Publishing Company published songbooks and accumulated copyright in Indianapolis, Indiana, until 1930, when the Nazarene Publishing House in Kansas City, Missouri, purchased the company. Haldor Lillenas moved to Kansas City and became manager of the Nazarene Publishing House's newly organized music department. He remained in that role until his retirement in 1950 and then served in an advisory capacity until his death on August 18,

1959. In 1982, Haldor Lillenas was inducted into the Gospel Music Association Hall of Fame.

In the 1940s, Lillenas Publishing Company expanded its program offerings by producing program builders, which were collections of recitations and scripts for special seasons and occasions in the church. In 1984, this venture blossomed into Lillenas Drama Resources, led by its founder, Paul Miller. Currently, its drama collection features more than seventy sketch collections, forty plays and play collections, fifteen how-to books, more than sixty program builders, and hundreds of scripts that can be downloaded via its website. Among the best-selling authors who contributed resources to Lillenas are Martha Bolton, Jim Custer & Bob Hoose, Chuck Neighbors, and Jeff Smith. The annual Lillenas Music and Drama Worship Conference offers workshops, speakers, and other programs geared toward worship leaders and others involved in creating church drama.

In 1995, two new imprints were added to Lillenas's line of product: Easy 2 Excel, offering choral music designed for smaller choirs, and Allegis, featuring materials for larger, more progressive music ministries. In the fall of 2000, Lillenas premiered *Called to Worship,* a quarterly newsletter with new congregational songs, service outlines, and other performance and programming that helps enrich local church worship.

Currently, Lillenas is one of the largest church music publishers in the world, owning more than twenty thousand song copyrights. Each year, they publish a dozen or more new musicals and choral collections, forty choral octavos, and numerous collections for vocal and instrumental solos and ensembles. The imprints handled by Lillenas Publishing Company include Allegis Publications, Beacon Hill Music, Crystal Sea Recordings, Faith Music, J. M. Henson, Mosie Lister Songs, Pilot Point Music, and PsalmSinger Music.

Today, Lillenas Publishing Company is guided by the leadership of a management group headed by Nazarene Publishing House president Dr. Hardy C. Weathers, aided by a panel of consultants that includes such well-known arrangers and church musicians as Marty Parks, Mike Speck, Pam Andrews, Lloyd Larson, and Ed Hogan.

BECKY GARRISON

See also Gospel Music Association

Reference and Further Reading

Christian History Institute website, http://chi.gospelcom.net/DAILYF/2002/11/daily-11-19-2002.shtml.

Gospel Music Association Hall of Fame website, http://www.gmahalloffame.org/inductee_bio.cfm?ID=292.

(Note: The statistics offered here differ from those stated by Lillenas.)

"Haldor Lillenas Biography." Cyber Hymnal website, http://www.cyberhymnal.org/bio/l/i/lillenas_h.htm.

Lillenas Publishing Co. website, http://www.lillenas.com.

LISTER, MOSIE

Thomas Mosie Lister (b. September 8, 1921)

Mosie Lister ranked as one of the major gospel songwriters of the second half of the twentieth century. While he had some experience as a member of various gospel quartets, Lister's real mark came as a composer. These talents were sufficient that, in 1976, he was chosen as the sixth living member of the Gospel Music Hall of Fame.

Lister was born in Cochran, Georgia. As a youth he attended singing schools taught by such gospel pioneers as Adger Pace and G. T. "Dad" Speer, which helped him to overcome a problem of tone deafness. It has been alleged that Speer predicted that he would "make a name for himself." He also spent time at the Vaughn School of Music in Lawrenceburg, Tennessee and attended Middle Georgia College in his hometown. He later worked with such groups as the Sunny South Quartet and the Melody Masters. When Hovie Lister (no relation) was organizing the Statesmen Quartet, Mosie was working as a piano tuner for Rich's Department Store. Mosie did not wish to travel but agreed to sing lead with the Statesman until a replacement could be found. A few months later, Mosie was replaced by Jake Hess, who, coincidentally, had replaced him in both of his earlier quartet jobs. Lister also dropped out of singing work because he had experienced voice problems and because he wished to concentrate on song composition.

Ironically, one of Lister's earliest songs to gain attention was "Happy Rhythm," which the Statesmen would use as a theme. As a writer, Lister pioneered such techniques as crafting songs designed to utilize the talents of a particular vocalist or singing group. Another up-tempo Lister composition recorded by the Statesmen, "I'm Feelin' Fine," proved to be a popular showstopper. Many of his compositions were designed to fit the lead voice of Jake Hess. Over the years, some of the best-known groups and vocalists recorded his songs, including the Blackwood Brothers, the Statesmen Quartet, the LeFevres, and Jimmie Davis. In 1953, he started his own publishing firm, Mosie Lister Publications.

Some of the better-known Lister compositions include "Then I Met the Master," "Till the Storm Passes By," "Where No One Stands Alone," and "He Knows

Just What I Need." His composition "His Hand in Mine" became the title song for Elvis Presley's acclaimed first sacred album. Otherwise, his best-known original is "How Long Has It Been." As early as August 1955, an article in *Gospel Singing World* stated "It would be hard to find a known quartet not singing one of Mosie's compositions among their best-loved numbers." Remaining relevant in later years, his "Still Feelin' Fine," a sequel to "I'm Feelin' Fine," has been a gospel hit for the Booth Brothers.

As the gospel music industry became better organized, Mosie Lister was among the first people to serve on the board of directors of the Gospel Music Association. For many years, Lister has made his home in the Tampa, Florida, area, where he served as conductor of the Men's Chorus at Riverside Baptist Church. Although he never enjoyed traveling, fans report that he is a regular at the annual Grand Old Gospel Reunions in Greenville, South Carolina. Now past eighty, he is among the great living writers of sacred song.

IVAN M. TRIBE

Reference and Further Reading

Baxter, Mrs. J. R.; Videt Polk. *Gospel Song Writers Biography*, 95–96. Dallas: Stamps–Baxter Music & Printing Co., 1971.
Goff, James R. *Close Harmony: A History of Southern Gospel*, 215–217. Chapel Hill: University of North Carolina Press, 2002.
Wolfe, Charles. *The Blackwood Brothers: Rock-a-My-Soul*, 30–31. Hamburg, Germany: Bear Family, 2002.

LOS ANGELES, GOSPEL IN

The history of gospel music in Los Angeles can be divided into several periods: beginnings (1930–1943), expansion and growth (1943–1955), emergence as a national center (1955–1970), and global prominence (1970–present).

Beginnings (1930–1943)

During the 1930s, gospel was not wholeheartedly accepted by the Los Angeles black populace, although from 1906 to 1909 the city had been home to the Azusa Street Revival that scholars believe to be the genesis of Pentecostalism. Most gospel performances during the early period occurred when traveling musicians from the Midwest and South visited the city. After gospel pioneers from Chicago—Sallie Martin (1896–1988)

and Thomas Dorsey (1899–1993)—frequented churches in both black and white neighborhoods, other Chicago-based artists appeared in concert and spent time in the city.

One of the primary reasons for the growth of Los Angeles gospel during the 1930s and 1940s can be attributed to the support it received from churches and the media. People's Independent Church of Christ, founded in Los Angeles in 1915 by Reverend N. P. Greggs, was one of the first churches to organize a gospel choir (the N. P. Greggs Gospel Choir). Gospel singing groups were also formed at Phillips Temple Colored Methodist Episcopal; Zion Hill Baptist; Bethel Church of Christ, Holiness; Progressive Baptist; and Emmanuel Church of God in Christ (COGIC).

Another trend was the growing professionalism among local performers. Although groups such as the Sons of Thunder (Arthur Atlas Peters, Eugene Douglass Smallwood, Earl Amos Pleasant, and Nathan John Kirkpatrick), the E-Flat Gospel Singers, the Radio Four Gospel Singers, the Cornerstone Quartet, and the Carter Sisters never received national acclaim, they were considered "stars" because of performances in churches and on radio. In 1939, a radio (KGFJ) program known as *The Gold Hour* was instituted on Wednesdays at 6:30 p.m. as part of a weekly series. Gospel performed by Los Angeles artists during this early period did not include much rhythmic or melodic variation. Part of the reason for this is that most were formally trained in Western art music.

Expansion and Growth (1943–1955)

During the mid-1940s and early 1950s, new religious institutions that supported gospel were organized, and several churches founded during the early 1900s installed leaders who were more responsive to the needs and desires of Southern blacks migrating into the city as a result of the wartime industry. Men such as Peters (formed Victory Baptist in 1943), Pleasant (formed Mount Moriah Baptist in 1945), Smallwood (formed Opportunity Baptist in 1946), William Jack Taylor (installed as pastor of Grace Memorial COGIC in 1941), and John L. Branham (became pastor of Saint Paul Baptist in 1946) introduced innovations that made their churches models for others.

Coming from Chicago, Branham knew much about gospel. Therefore, when he hired Atlanta-born James Earle Hines (1916–1960), a nationally known gospel singer and choir director, and Gwendolyn Cooper Lightner (1925–1999), a gospel pianist who had lived in Chicago and performed with established gospel musicians in that city, to develop his gospel program, major changes occurred. What resulted was the Echoes of Eden Choir, a group organized in 1946 by Hines and Lightner that grew to more than one hundred voices. The choir made its radio debut in February 1947 on KFWB, the Warner Brothers Station, with Joe Adams as producer and radio announcer. The program was broadcast from 10:30 to 11:30 p.m. and was heard in seventeen states, with a listening audience of one million people, the largest on the West Coast. Not only was the church packed each Sunday night, with people arriving at 8 p.m. to get a good seat, but Hollywood celebrities often visited the church to hear the music.

Echoes of Eden became one of the first church choirs in the United States to popularize gospel and make commercial recordings—"I'm So Glad Jesus Lifted Me" (April 1947, Capitol 40018) and "What Could I Do If It Wasn't for the Lord?" (June 1947, Capitol 40076). In the 1950s, an album, *Revival Day: The Saint Paul Church Choir of Los Angeles* (Capitol T791), was released. Saint Paul's notoriety inspired other churches in Los Angeles and the state to establish choirs, radio programs, and even television broadcasts. Performances by the Voices of Victory Choir under the direction of Thurston Gilbert Frazier (1930–1974) on a weekly television program (KTTV, channel 11) during the 1950s and various church recordings gave Victory Baptist enormous visibility.

In addition to the increase in the number of churches that performed gospel, other indicators demonstrate that the tradition expanded. Not only were there visiting artists (the Original Gospel Harmonettes, the Pilgrim Travelers, and the Sallie Martin Singers) who often resided in the city for long periods of time, but groups that originated elsewhere permanently settled in Los Angeles. Also, many small groups were organized in Los Angeles: the Caravans of Los Angeles, the Chosen Gospel Singers, the Dave Weston Singers, the Ebony Echoes, the Golden Jubilee Singers, the Gospel Pearls, the Macedonians, the Simmons–Akers Singers, the Spiritual Five, the Victory Trio, the West Coast Jubilees, and the Zion Travelers. Following in the tradition of earlier performers, several large community choirs were established. The Venerable–Smallwood Gospel Singers were formed through Smallwood's collaboration with E.B. Venerable during the late 1940s, and the Hines Goodwill Choir, with Frazier serving as Hines's assistant, was started in the 1950s.

The publishing and recording of gospel became profitable. Not only were a number of black Angelenos composers who established their own publishing companies, but Specialty Records, along with other black- and white-owned record companies, recorded Los Angeles artists and performers who traveled to the city. National conventions normally held on the East Coast and in the Midwest took place in Los Angeles. The performance of gospel outside the church setting also began to occur more frequently, such as Dorsey's concert at Wrigley Stadium in 1946 and Herald Attractions' Gospelcade at the Embassy Auditorium in 1953.

A distinctive gospel style became associated with Los Angeles because of the background of performers. Similar to their counterparts from the 1930s and 1940s, both Hines and Lightner had attended music schools and knew much about Western art music. Songs recorded by the Echoes of Eden Choir ("God Be with You," "Yield Not to Temptation," "I'm So Glad Jesus Lifted Me") had a swinging rhythm, with piano and organ accompaniment and some melodic variation. However, there was not a lot of emphasis on rhythm or improvisation as one would hear in Pentecostal churches. The Simmons–Akers Singers, formed in 1948 by Dorothy Simmons (1910–1996) and Doris Akers (1923–1995), had a lyrical, smooth sound with emphasis on the melody. Most small male groups, however, performed with a hard and driving rhythm, similar to quartets in Southern states.

Emergence as a National Center (1955–1970)

The increased socioeconomic opportunities that became available in Los Angeles during the 1950s and 1960s caused more gospel artists to migrate to the city. As the gospel industry grew and Los Angeles emerged as a national center, artists no longer depended on religious institutions for support; many began to perform in secular venues. Although many gospel artists who migrated had already attained some renown, the Los Angeles environment helped them achieve even greater recognition. Among these were Margaret Aikens-Jenkins (b. 1925), James Cleveland (1931–1991), Cassietta George (1928–1995), Bessie Griffin (1922–1989), Isaiah Jones (b. 1940), Raymond Rasberry (1932–1995), and Clara Ward (1924–1973) and the Ward Singers. More important, Los Angeles natives such as Albert A. Goodson (b. 1933), Margaret Pleasant Douroux (b. 1941), and Andrae Crouch (b. 1942) became nationally known for their compositions and recordings.

Community choirs and small groups continued to be popular. In 1956, Harrison A. Johnson, who worked closely with James Cleveland and the Southern California Community Choir during the 1960s, formed the Los Angeles Community Choir, which grew to more than two hundred voices and led to several recordings and television appearances.

Originally formed by Frazier and Lightner in 1957 as a campaign to raise funds for the March of Dimes, the Voices of Hope was another large choir that became nationally known. In addition to releasing two recordings with Capitol Records ("We've Come This Far by Faith" and "Walk On by Faith"), the choir made local and national appearances in churches and auditoriums, on television, and at amusement parks. Because of Lightner's and Frazier's influence at national conventions, signature songs by the Voices of Hope—"We've Come This Far by Faith," "The Beautiful Garden of Prayer," and "Jesus"—were performed by church choirs nationally. As with the music of the Echoes of Eden Choir and the Simmons–Akers Singers, the Voices of Hope placed more emphasis on melody without extensive variation or intense rhythms.

Of the small groups organized in Los Angeles during the 1950s and 1960s (the COGICs, the Golden Jubilee Singers, the Gospel Consolaters, the Ladies of Song, the Los Angeles Gospel Chimes, the Melody Kings, and the Sweet Singing Cavaliers), the Mighty Clouds of Joy, formed in 1960, is one of the few to attain international fame and perform in secular venues.

Global Prominence (1970–Present)

Several factors helped gospel in Los Angeles to reach global prominence. When the city became more ethnically and culturally diverse and the media capital of the world, this caused gospel to move into new arenas. The emergence of contemporary gospel on the West Coast, with contributions by the Edwin Hawkins Singers, Crouch, and other performers, gave the music a crossover appeal that made it more widespread and popular among the youth.

In addition to catapulting some churches (such as West Angeles COGIC) to national prominence, gospel could be heard in practically all black churches in the city, including African American and mainline European denominations that initially thought the music was unacceptable (for example, African Methodist Episcopal, Catholic, Lutheran, Methodist Episcopal, Presbyterian). Gospel continued to be popular among whites, but it also became a mainstay among other ethnic groups (for example, Asians and Latinos).

Established stars in other parts of the world continued to visit Los Angeles to perform and take advantage of opportunities in the entertainment and music industries. Also, Los Angeles artists regularly toured countries in Africa, Asia, Europe, and Latin America. With all types of musical backgrounds, gospel performers in Los Angeles were not afraid to experiment with global sounds. Therefore, it was not uncommon to hear popular music, jazz, blues, art music, and African and Caribbean sounds in performances.

JACQUELINE COGDELL DJEDJE

See also Akers, Doris; Azusa Street Revival; Cleveland, James; Crouch, Andrae; Dorsey, Thomas; Edwin Hawkins Singers; Martin, Sallie; Specialty Records Company

Reference and Further Reading

DjeDje, Jacqueline Cogdell. "Akers, Doris." In *Black Women in America: An Historical Encyclopedia,* edited by Darlene Clark Hine, 16. Brooklyn, NY: Carlson Publishing, 1993.
———. "The California Black Gospel Music Tradition: A Confluence of Musical Styles and Cultures." In *California Soul: Music of African Americans in the West,* edited by Jacqueline Cogdell DjeDje and Eddie S. Meadows, 124–175. Berkeley: University of California Press, 1998.
———. "Douroux, Margaret Pleasant." In *Black Women in America: An Historical Encyclopedia,* edited by Darlene Clark Hine, 353–354. Brooklyn, NY: Carlson Publishing, 1993.
———. "Gospel Music in the Los Angeles Black Community." *Black Music Research Journal* 9 (Spring 1989): 35–79.
———. "Griffin, Bessie." In *Black Women in America: An Historical Encyclopedia,* edited by Darlene Clark Hine. 503–504. Brooklyn, NY: Carlson Publishing, 1993.
———. "A Historical Overview of Black Gospel Music in Los Angeles." *Black Music Research Bulletin* 10 (Spring 1988): 1–5.
———. "Lightner, Gwendolyn." In *Black Women in America: An Historical Encyclopedia,* edited by Darlene Clark Hine, 720–721. Brooklyn, NY: Carlson Publishing, 1993.
———. "Los Angeles Composers of African American Gospel Music: The First Generations." *American Music: A Quarterly Journal Devoted to All Aspects of American Music and Music in America* 11 (Winter 1993): 412–457.
———. "Martin-Moore, Cora." In *Black Women in America: An Historical Encyclopedia,* edited by Darlene Clark Hine, 751–752. Brooklyn, NY: Carlson Publishing, 1993.
———. "Simmons, Dorothy Vernell." In *Black Women in America: An Historical Encyclopedia,* edited by Darlene Clark Hine, 1035–1036. Brooklyn, NY: Carlson Publishing, 1993.
Kidula, Jean. "The Gospel of Andraé Crouch: A Black Angeleno." In *California Soul: Music of African Americans in the West,* edited by Jacqueline Cogdell DjeDje and Eddie S. Meadows, 294–320. Berkeley: University of California Press, 1998.

LOUVIN BROTHERS, THE

Ira Lonnie Loudermilk (b. April 21, 1924, Section, Sand Mountain, AL; d. 1963)
Charles Elzer Loudermilk (b. July 7, 1927, Section, Sand Mountain, AL)

The Louvin Brothers are best known today as one of the greatest modern harmony duets in country music, originating classics such as "When I Stop Dreaming" and "The Knoxville Girl" and singing in a high, piercing lonesome harmony that made them Grand Ole Opry stars and best-selling recording artists. However, the Louvins also had a strong interest in gospel music; they started out recording gospel songs exclusively for Capitol records and continued to do gospel albums throughout their career.

The Louvins grew up in an area of remote Sand Mountain, where the old Sacred Harp singing still flourished; in fact, their mother's side of the family, the Wootens, were known for their Sacred Harp writing and editing. The brothers also heard at an early age such acts as the Delmore Brothers and Roy Acuff and began their career singing secular duet songs such as "Take the News to Mother." They began their professional career playing with Bob Douglas's Foggy Mountain Boys over radio WDOD in Chattanooga.

By 1946, the brothers had joined forces with Eddie Hill and were singing as the Lonesome Valley Trio over WMPS. Most of their repertoire at this time was gospel, and soon the brothers—primarily Ira—were writing their own gospel songs. Pieces such as "God Bless Her Cause She's My Mother," "Robe of White," "I'll Live with God (To Die No More)," and "No One to Sing for Me" soon became favorites with fans.

In 1949, the brothers signed a songwriting contract with Acuff–Rose in Nashville and got a contract with MGM records. Their first release was "The Weapon of Prayer," and the Memphis songs soon were released as well. "They've Got the Church Outnumbered" and "Insured Beyond the Grave" reflected the unsettled paranoia of the early 1950s, as did their most popular early song, "Great Atomic Power" (1951). Gospel singles continued after the duo got onto the bigger label Capitol, though they started resenting the fact that their bosses thought of them only as "sacred" artists. Finally, when they persuaded producer Ken Nelson to listen to "When I Stop Dreaming," they were allowed to do secular songs as well as gospel. In 1958 they did their most controversial gospel set, *Satan Is Real,* with its dramatic cover shot of a giant Satan rising from the flames of hell.

By 1963, the brothers had decided to go their separate ways, but after a couple of years of separate careers, Ira was killed in a car crash in Missouri. Charlie continued on as a solo artist.

CHARLES K. WOLFE

Reference and Further Reading

Wolfe, Charles. *In Close Harmony: The Story of the Louvin Brothers.* Jackson: University of Mississippi Press, 1996.

LOVE SONG

Tom Coomes (b. May 19, 1946)
Chuck Girard (b. August 27, 1943, Santa Rosa, CA)
John Mehler (b. Long Beach, CA)
Jay Truax (b. September 24, 1947)
Bob Wall (b. Burbank, California)

Love Song was a band of the Jesus movement revival of the early 1970s whose popularity and influence would far exceed their output. They made only two albums (plus a live set and, decades later, a reunion package) but were dubbed "the Christian Beatles" by critics and historians, who thought their transforming effect on gospel music was analogous to the role played by the Beatles in mainstream pop. The popularity and commercial viability of Love Song's albums paved the way for the development of a new genre that would be called contemporary Christian music. Lyrically, their music was similar to hymns and other gospel songs, but stylistically it sounded completely secular, more like top-forty radio than traditional gospel or church music. In particular, the music of Love Song would be a harbinger of modern worship music, especially that represented by a series of praise albums released by Maranatha! Music in the 1970s and 1980s.

Love Song came together as a group in Southern California in 1970. The band was fronted by Chuck Girard (keyboards, vocals) and Tom Coomes (guitar, vocals), with Jay Truax and John Mehler on bass and drums, respectively. Fred Field and Phil Keaggy played lead guitar in some incarnations of the band, but that spot was filled by Bob Wall on the main recordings. Girard and Keaggy would go on to have highly successful solo careers in Christian music, and Coomes became an executive at Maranatha! Music.

The lives and music of the Love Song members reflected the spirit of the Jesus movement revival itself. Spirituality was pushed to the fore, with an emphasis on emotion. Eschewing message songs for the most part, the group presented the love of Christ and communion with the Holy Spirit as experiential realities that one could *feel*, and their concerts were often described as sacramental events at which such connections were realized. The song "Little Country Church" describes the phenomenon of hippie Christians finding a welcome among traditional worshipers. "Let Us Be One" and "Two Hands" likewise present worship as a unifying force for individuals with diverse or competing interests. Musically, Love Song was sometimes compared with pop bands such as America or Bread. Their songs featured catchy melodies and vocal harmonies comparable to the songs of Paul McCartney or Brian Wilson.

Love Song was closely connected with Calvary Chapel in Costa Mesa, California, and the group often performed at Knott's Berry Farm amusement park, where they drew crowds that set new box office records for the venue. Internationally, they scored a number one hit on general market radio in the Philippines ("Love Song") and sold out a fifty-thousand-seat arena for a concert in Manila in 1973.

MARK ALLAN POWELL

See also Calvary Chapel, Costa Mesa; Girard, Chuck; Maranatha! Music

Reference and Further Reading

Alfonso, Barry. "Love Song." In *The Billboard Guide to Contemporary Christian Music*, 192–194. New York: Billboard Books, 2002.

Baker, Paul. *Contemporary Christian Music: Where It Came From, Where It Is Going*, 30–33, 53–54. Westchester, IL: Crossway Books, 1985.

Powell, Mark Allan. "Love Song." In *Encyclopedia of Contemporary Christian Music*, 543–547. Peabody, MA: Hendrickson Publishers, 2002.

Discography

Love Song (1972, Good News GNR-08100).
Final Touch (1974, Good News GNR-08101).
Feel the Love (1977, Good News GNX-8104).
Welcome Back (1995, Word 701 628 4840).

LOWRY, ROBERT

(b. March 12, 1826; d. November 25, 1899)

This important figure in early gospel music was born in Philadelphia and, for more than forty years, pastored several Baptist churches in Pennsylvania, New York, and New Jersey. He attended the University of Lewisburg (now Bucknell University) and was a professor of belles lettres at his alma mater from 1869 to 1875. He was very well suited for the position because he was a spellbinding orator with considerable administrative ability.

As a sideline from his other duties, Lowry began to write gospel hymns and tunes. Lacking formal training in music, he leaned toward writing religious songs that indicated the strong influence of popular music of the day. This feature made his songs appealing to a wider audience than was usual for religious numbers. Indeed, one of his best remembered numbers, "Where Is My Wandering Boy Tonight," which Lowry originally titled "The Absent Child," was sung in a great variety of venues, including revivals, music halls, and temperance meetings. It is thought that the song was suggested to Lowry by a question addressed to him by a parishioner on one of the composer's pastoral visits.

This was typical of his methodology, which he said was dictated by his moods. Whenever anything caught his attention he wrote it down, often on the margin of a newspaper or the back of an envelope. In 1868, upon the death of William Bradbury, Lowry became the editor of Sunday school music at Biglow & Main, where he compiled several popular collections of hymns, many in collaboration with William Doane.

For a large number of his songs he supplied both words and music, and he was one of the first gospel songwriters to do so. This practice soon became a distinctive feature of the then developing gospel song movement. Another characteristic of his style was to add a refrain from the last line of the lyrics or to provide a chorus. This was particularly true when he was creating musical settings for words by other authors. With other lyricists, Lowry produced "I Need Thee Every Hour" (Annie S. Hawks), "All the Way My Savior Leads Me" (Fanny J. Crosby), and "We're Marching to Zion" (Isaac Watts), to cite just a few.

He composed both words and music to "Christ Arose," which first appeared in the collection *Brightest and Best* (1875), edited by Doane and Lowry; "Nothing but the Blood," which was first published in another Doane–Lowry collection, *Gospel Music* (1876); and his most famous number, "Shall We Gather at the River," which initially appeared in *Happy Voices* 1865), another Doane–Lowry compilation. This song, which has sometimes been mistakenly called a Southern folk song, was included by Aaron Copland in a collection called *Old American Songs, Second Set* (1954) that was performed on a national telecast in 1962 by William Warfield backed up by the Philadelphia Orchestra, Eugene Ormandy conducting.

The number is said to have been inspired by events that occurred in New York City during the summer of 1864. Lowry had just become minister of a Baptist congregation there when a heat wave hit the city. This was soon followed by an epidemic of some sort. These twin catastrophes were claiming hundreds of lives, and Lowry busied himself visiting the homes of the sick and bereaved. Frequently, he was asked by people he saw if they would meet those who died at the river of life. Using a figure of speech from Revelations 22:1, he assured them that their broken family circles would be complete again "at the river of life that flows by the throne of God." Then, late one afternoon in his living room while seated at the organ, the words and music came to him as if by inspiration.

Although music and hymnology were always an avocation for him, Lowry produced more than twenty songbooks, several of them considered to be the finest published in their day. One of them, *Pure Gold for the Sunday School* (1871), sold more than a million copies. He thought a hymn should be easily apprehended, come from the writer's experience, and be written with strong, inspiring words. He followed this dictum consistently, which may explain the continuing popularity of several of his songs.

W. K. McNeil

Reference and Further Reading

Emurian, Ernest K. *Living Stories of Famous Hymns.* Grand Rapids, MI: Baker, 1955.

Hall, J. H. *Biography of Gospel Song and Hymn Writers.* New York: Fleming H. Revell, 1971 (1914).

Osbeck, Kenneth W. *101 More Hymn Stories.* Grand Rapids, MI: Kregel, 1985.

Reynolds, William J. *Companion to the Baptist Hymnal.* Nashville, TN: Broadman Press, 1976.

Wells, Amos R. *A Treasury of Hymn Stories: Brief Biographies of 120 Hymnwriters with Their Best Hymns.* Grand Rapids, MI: Baker, 1992 (1945).

Zellner, John F., III. "Robert Lowry: Early American Hymn Writer." *The Hymn* xxvi (1975): 117–124; xxvii (1976): 15–21. [Originally in *The Bucknell World.*]

M

MALACO RECORDS

Malaco Records was started in 1962 by University of Mississippi students Tommy Couch and Wolf Stevenson to promote concerts in the Jackson, Mississippi, area. After graduation, they joined with Couch's brother-in-law, Mitchell Malouf, to form the promotion company Malaco. The name comes from a combination of the names Malouf and Couch.

Malaco Records became a major force in the U.S. gospel, rhythm and blues, and soul production market during the last two decades of the twentieth century. Originally, Malaco promoted pop concerts in the Jackson area; it then expanded during the late 1960s to include production as well as promotion.

In 1967, Malaco opened a recording studio and began releasing masters through other licensed companies. At that time, they aligned themselves with ABC, Mercury, and Bang Records. They also found success with several Capitol releases by Mississippi Fred McDowell and received a Grammy nomination in the process.

Concert promotion continued to be the major source of revenue for Malaco until 1970, when the company released recordings by famous New Orleans performers including Fats Domino and Professor Longhair. King Floyd's "Groove Me" and Jean Knight's "Mr. Big Stuff," produced by Wardell Quezergue, improved the firm's position dramatically when they were released as the first sides on the Chimneyville label created by Malaco. Distribution of these singles and subsequent Chimneyville hits was done by Stax and Atlantic Records. "Mr. Big Stuff" went on to sell more than two million copies and made it to number one on *Billboard*'s R&B chart and number two on the pop chart.

Rhythm and blues artists on Malaco included Bobby Blue Bland, Shirley Brown, Tyrone Davis, King Floyd, Z. Z. Hill, Fern Kinney, Denise LaSalle, Latimore, Little Milton, Dorothy Moore, Johnnie Taylor, Tonya, and Anita Ward.

Consistent success in the rhythm and blues field led Malaco to test the gospel market in 1975 with the formation of a gospel division, led by Frank Williams of the Jackson Southernaires as director. In addition to Williams's group, other early artists on the Malaco gospel label were the Soul Stirrers, the Sensational Nightingales, the Williams Brothers, the Truthettes, the Georgia Mass Choir, the Florida Mass Choir, and the Angelic Gospel Singers. Williams continued on as director, producing every release until his death in 1993.

In 1985, Malaco acquired the Muscle Shoals Sound Studios, along with the talents of David Hood and Roger Hawkins, which gave the growing soul label a fertile garden to develop young songwriters and performers.

In 1986, Malaco purchased the huge catalog of Savoy Records and further established its presence in the marketplace. The division was headed by Jerry Mannery of Malaco and Milton Biggham of Savoy. The catalog included recordings by Shirley Caesar, Reverend James Cleveland, Albertina Walker, the Caravans, and Inez Andrews.

Billboard number one artists during this period were Reverend James Cleveland, Reverend Clay Evans,

Walter Hawkins, the Mississippi Mass Choir, Reverend James Moore, Dorothy Norwood, and Keith Pringle. In addition, Malaco's gospel division also issued recordings by Mahalia Jackson and the Jackson Southernaires.

Freedom Records, a contemporary Christian division, was formed to capitalize on the growing Christian music movement during the late 1980s. Initially signed artists included the Kry and Hokus Pick.

Malaco Records' catalog includes many artists from several genres of contemporary music. The gospel list features Shirley Caesar, Reverend James Cleveland, the Florida Mass Choir, Walter Hawkins, Mahalia Jackson, the Jackson Southernaires, the Mississippi Mass Choir, Reverend James Moore, Dorothy Norwood, Keith Pringle, and Albertina Walker. On the soul roster are Bobby Blue Bland, Shirley Brown, Tyrone Davis, King Floyd, Z. Z. Hill, Fern Kinney, Denise LaSalle, Latimore, Little Milton, Dorothy Moore, Johnnie Taylor, Tonya, and Anita Ward. Performing jazz classics are Cannonball Adderly, Louis Armstrong, Count Basie, Duke Ellington, Dizzy Gillespie, Thelonious Monk, and Oscar Peterson.

In addition, Malaco continues publishing operations in Jackson and in Nashville, Tennessee, with more than thirty catalogs comprising more than ten thousand songs. Licensing agreements administered by Malaco place their material in hundreds of film, video, television, radio, and theatrical efforts produced around the world. Distribution of Malaco products to customers total more than thirty million copies per year, and Malaco also operates jointly owned outlets under the name Select-O-Hits, which supplies product to retailers, chain stores, and wholesalers.

TOM FISHER

Reference and Further Reading

Bowman, Rob. *The Last Soul Company: Malaco, A Thirty Year Retrospective*. Jackson, MS, and Nashville: Malaco Records, 1999.

MARANATHA! MUSIC

Maranatha! Music was a record company that was started at Calvary Chapel in Costa Mesa, California. The small church begun by Chuck Smith became a gathering place for "hippies" seeking truth and, within a few years, it was attracting thousands of young converts. Many of those who joined the church were musicians, and they began to compose music expressing their newfound faith. Smith recalls that many of his new members were high school students who started forming bands. The church and the music grew, and at one point there were about seventeen different groups who called Calvary Chapel home. They played their music at weekly services and other special concerts. The religious revival was known as the "Jesus movement" and the emerging music was dubbed "Jesus music," the forerunner of contemporary Christian music.

Maranatha! Music was started in a Sunday school classroom at Calvary Chapel in 1971 by Tommy Coomes (Love Song) and Chuck Smith's nephew, Chuck Fromm. The first album was recorded with a loan from Smith. Maranatha!'s first release was a collection of various artists titled *The Everlastin' Living Jesus Concert*. The album, produced by Chuck Girard for about two thousand dollars, included Girard & Love Song, Selah, Gentle Faith, Debby Kerner, the Way, and Children of the Day. The second album released by the new label was titled *Come to the Waters* from the group Children of the Day, who had been singing at Calvary Chapel since 1969.

With no formal distribution or marketing, the first two releases from Maranatha! Music sold a combined total of more than twenty-five thousand copies. The label had a unique approach with the many groups in the church who wanted to record albums. The profits from one recording were used to finance the next, and dozens of artists recorded and released albums in the 1970s, including Country Faith, the Way, Blessed Hope, Good News, Mustard Seed Faith, Karen Lafferty, Ernie Rettino & Debbie Kerner, Kenn Gulliksen, Daniel Amos, Kelly Willard, and the Sweet Comfort Band. Maranatha! also released more that a dozen collections in the 1970s featuring various artists signed to the label.

Other notable releases in the 1970s include two albums from the comedy sketch team of Isaac Air Freight, *Fun in the Sun* (1978) and *In the Air/On the Air* (1979). The 1979 album *First Things First* from singer/songwriter Bob Bennett drew critical praise, and *Dance Children Dance* from former Santana keyboard player and vocalist Leon Patillo also drew media attention.

In 1974, Maranatha! released an album containing the popular choruses being sung weekly at Calvary Chapel. *The Praise Album* was the first of what would become a twenty-volume *Praise* series. *Praise II* was released two years later, and the label also introduced an instrumental version titled *Praise Strings* in 1976. Maranatha! also developed another instrumental series they dubbed *Colours,* presenting their popular songs along with original versions of traditional hymns. Another part of the *Praise* franchise is guitar-driven worship music called *The Praise Band Series*.

As the 1970s came to a close, Maranatha! decided to focus exclusively on providing music for the church. The leaders of the label wanted to provide quality worship music that would facilitate churches in the United States and around the world. Reflecting back on the early days of the label, President Chuck Fromm said, "Our vision at Maranatha! Music is to make every car, every home, every church, every heart a sanctuary. As providers of worship resources, it is up to us to continually focus on the power and purposes of God and not on the instruments of worship."

In 1980, Maranatha! began producing recordings designed for children. *The Kids' Praise Album!* by the Kids' Praise Singers was the first of many popular recordings. The album was warmly embraced by Christian parents, giving Maranatha! their first gold album with sales of five hundred thousand. In addition to subsequent releases in the series, the label also released a series of very successful corresponding videos, earning gold and platinum video awards for *Kids' Praise IV* and *Kids' Praise V*.

Other product lines developed by the label include the *Top 25* series, with the *Top 25 Praise Songs* earning Maranatha! another gold album award in 2001. Maranatha! launched a book publishing division in 1999, partnering with Zondervan to create the *NIV Worship Bible*.

In recognition of its contribution and leadership in Christian music, Maranatha! was honored with the prestigious National Religious Broadcasters' President's Award in 1990. The label was also honored by the Gospel Music Association in 1991 with their Lifetime Achievement Award.

JAMES I. ELLIOTT

See also Calvary Chapel; Costa Mesa

Reference and Further Reading

Callahan, Mike; David Edwards; Patrice Eyries. "Maranatha! Album Discography." Both Sides Now Publications website, http://www.bsnpubs.com/word/maranatha.html.
Cusic, Don. *The Sound of Light: A History of Gospel Music*. Bowling Green, OH: Bowling Green State University Popular Press, 1990.
"History of Maranatha!" Yahoo website, http://store.yahoo.com/maranathaweb/history.html.
Joseph, Mark. *The Rock & Roll Rebellion*. Nashville, TN: Broadman & Holman, 1999.
Recording Industry Association of America website, http://www.riaa.com/gp/database/.

MARKSMEN, THE

Earle Wheeler (b. February 5, 1940)
Mark Wheeler
Keith Chambers
Rob Gillentine
Nicky Powell

The Marksmen of Murraysville, Georgia, combine the four-part harmony of gospel quartet singing with guitar and mandolin accompaniment. Founded and led by Earle Wheeler, the group has made a positive impression in bluegrass circles despite the absence of a banjo in their sound. Initially, at the time of their founding in 1967, the Marksmen used piano accompaniment but switched to the string-backed format about 1977 with success.

Earle Wheeler reports that he fell deeply in love with gospel music when he attended a concert in Gainesville as a child and heard such now legendary figures as the Blackwoods, the Statesmen, the Chuck Wagon Gang, and the Speer Family. He sang in numerous local groups before forming his own. The original Marksmen, in addition to Wheeler, consisted of Sonny Seabolt, Frank Grindle, Bobby Barnes, and pianist Roy Abee, Jr. Changes took place over the years as Jerry Phillips, Swain Brown, Darrell Bagwell, and Doug Freeman came and went. But the principal alteration came when Keith Chambers joined the quartet. With the group having trouble keeping a pianist, Chambers played mandolin and Earle's son Mark joined as guitarist. With Rob Gillentine and then Darrin Chambers on bass, they became an all-string group. For a time they had a fifth member named Randy Franks who played fiddle. Eventually Keith Chambers retired for health reasons, and Nicky Powell took his place on mandolin.

Over the years, the Marksmen played churches, gospel sings, and bluegrass festivals over a wide area ranging as far north as Ohio and Michigan but primarily in the Southern Appalachian region. Three times they were honored by SPGMA as the bluegrass gospel group of the year. During that time, they made numerous recordings, with an old spiritual, "Get Away Jordan," being their most requested number. Although many of their recordings were custom made, some on labels such as Old Homestead and K-Tel had a broader distribution. Their first compact disc offering bore the title *Sacred Sounds of the Marksmen* in 1990. Earle Wheeler reports that, as of December 2002, they had about ten CDs in print.

IVAN M. TRIBE

Reference and Further Reading

Powell, Wayde. "Earle Wheeler and the Marksmen: Twenty-One Years of Bluegrass Gospel." *Precious Memories: Journal of Gospel Music* 1, no. 3 (September–October 1988): 6–11.

———. "The Marksmen—Bluegrass Gospel." *Bluegrass Unlimited* 30, no. 5 (November 1995): 34–36.

Discography

Sacred Sounds of the Marksmen (1989, Arrival).

MARTIN, ROBERTA

(b. February 12, 1907, Helena, AR; d. January 18, 1969, Chicago, IL)

A singer, pianist, composer, arranger, organizer of groups and choirs, and operator of one of Chicago's largest gospel music publishing houses, Roberta Martin was one of the innovators of the dominant sound during the golden age of gospel music (1945–1960) as well as a progenitor of the new sounds of gospel music immediately after.

Born Roberta Evelyn Winston on February 12, 1907, in Helena, Arkansas, to William and Anna Winston, Roberta began the study of piano at age six. When the family (including six children) moved to Chicago in 1917, Roberta continued studying the piano while also venturing out to play for various church Sunday school departments and choirs with a repertoire of hymns, spirituals, anthems, and choral/choir arrangements. While attending Wendell Phillips High School, she met Mildred Bryant Jones, the school's choral director, who began to instruct Roberta in piano and choral directing. Under Jones's tutelage, Roberta aimed to study classical music and aspired to a career as a concert pianist.

Influenced by the blind pianist Arizona Dranes and the teaching of Jones, Roberta met her newest influences in 1932 when she auditioned for Thomas Dorsey's and Theodore Frye's Young People's Choir at the Ebenezer Baptist Church, touted as one of the first gospel choirs. Roberta was hired as the choir's pianist due to her versatile skills as a singer, accompanist, arranger, and director. While at Ebenezer, she heard the Bertha Wise Quartet during a 1933 concert and was impressed by the style of gospel music they sang. She quickly adopted a new style based on her rich musical training and the sounds of Dranes, Dorsey, Frye, Sallie Martin, and Wise.

In 1933, Roberta Martin and Theodore Frye organized a male quartet featuring Norsalus McKissick, Robert Anderson, Willie Webb, and Eugene Smith, with Martin as the accompanist and occasional soloist.

By 1936, the group was known as the Roberta Martin Singers. By the 1940s, the group had become one of the first groups featuring male and female voices. Strong females such as Bessie Folk, Delois Barrett Campbell, Myrtle Scott, and Lucy "Little Lucy" Smith Collier joined the group, adding a new flare. Other members at various times included Myrtle Jackson, Gloria Griffin, Romance Watson, Archie Dennis, and Louise McCord.

The group developed the "Roberta Martin sound" that boasted musical accompaniment of rich harmonies and fluid runs and arpeggios along with falling melodic lines and innovative use of dissonance. The vocal arrangements boasted no bass part, instead using a baritone voice to complement Roberta's deep, dark, rich contralto voice. The group recorded more than a hundred compositions over forty years, many of which were composed by Roberta as well as by James Cleveland and Alex Bradford, both of whom she took a special interest in for nurturing and developing their talents.

During the 1940s and 1950s, the Roberta Martin Singers were the most popular recorded gospel group, and the most sought after, of the period. They toured extensively in the United States and Europe. Recordings on the Apollo (1940s) and Savoy (mid-1950s through mid-1960s) labels attest to the group's popularity and earned them three gold records. In 1963, Roberta Martin was featured at Gian-Carlo Menotti's Spoleto Festival of Two Worlds in Italy.

Martin's influence expanded into the business realm when she opened Roberta Martin's Studio of Music in 1939, one of the largest of the Chicago gospel publishing houses. She published more than 280 songs, many of which were her own compositions, including "He Knows How Much We Can Bear" (1941), "Try Jesus, He Satisfies" (1943), "Only a Look" (1948), "Certainly Lord" (1958), "God Is Still on the Throne" (1959), and "No Other Help I Know" (1961). Martin's publishing house served as a home for many of James Cleveland's and Alex Bradford's early compositions as well.

Known as a very spiritual person who taught Bible classes and traveled the country training musicians, singers, and choirs, often at storefront churches, Roberta Martin died on January 18, 1969, in Chicago, Illinois. She was posthumously honored with a conference in her name in 1981 at the Smithsonian Institute as well as by a U.S. Postal Service commemorative postage stamp issued on July 15, 1998.

EMMETT G. PRICE III

See also Anderson, Robert; Barrett Sisters; Bradford, Alex; Cleveland, James; Dorsey, Thomas; Dranes, Arizona Juanita; Frye, Theodore R.; Martin, Sallie

Reference and Further Reading

Boyer, Horace Clarence. *The Golden Age of Gospel*. Urbana and Chicago, IL: University of Illinois Press, 2000 (1995).
———. "Roberta Martin: Innovator of Modern Gospel Music." In *We'll Understand It Better By and By: Pioneering African American Gospel Composers*, edited by Bernice Johnson Reagon. 275–286. Washington, DC: Smithsonian Institute Press, 1992.
Broughton, Viv. *Black Gospel: An Illustrated History of the Gospel Sound*. Dorset, UK: Blandford Press, 1985.
Heilbut, Anthony. *The Gospel Sound: Good News and Bad Times*. New York: Limelight Editions, 1997 (1971, 1975, 1985).
Hine, Darlene Clark, ed. *Black Women in America*. Brooklyn, NY: Carlson Publishing, 1993.
Southern, Eileen, ed. *Biographical Dictionary of Afro-American and African Musicians*. Westport, CT: Greenwood Press, 1982.
Williams-Jones, Pearl. "Roberta Martin: Spirit of an Era." In *We'll Understand It Better By and By: Pioneering African American Gospel Composers*, edited by Bernice Johnson Reagon, 255–274. Washington, DC: Smithsonian Institute Press, 1992.
———; Bernice Johnson Reagon, eds. "Conversations: Roberta Martin Singers Roundtable." In *We'll Understand It Better By and By: Pioneering African American Gospel Composers*, edited by Bernice Johnson Reagon, 287–306. Washington, DC: Smithsonian Institute Press, 1992.

Selected Discography

What a Friend We Have in Jesus (1950, Apollo 238).
Grace (1958, Savoy 14022).
The Unforgettable Voice of Roberta Martin (1958, Savoy MG 14221).
Prayer (1964, Kenwood LP 480).
The Best of the Roberta Martin Singers (Savoy SGL 7018).
Old Ship of Zion (Kenwood 507).
Try Jesus (Savoy 14039).

MARTIN, SALLIE

(b. November 20, 1896, Pittfield, GA; d. June 18, 1988, Chicago, IL)

Singer, entrepreneur, civil rights activist, and philanthropist Sallie Martin was the first to travel the country as a gospel soloist. She organized the first all-female gospel group and was named the "Mother of Gospel" by the National Convention of Gospel Choirs and Choruses, an organization she cofounded.

Martin was born in Pittfield, Georgia, on November 20, 1896, and she was raised by her mother and grandparents; her father died early on during her childhood. During the eighth grade, she left Pittfield for Atlanta, where she worked as a babysitter, domestic, and launderer. In 1916, seeking a more emotional and charismatic worship experience, Martin joined the Fire Baptized Holiness Church. The former Baptist quickly rose as a spirit-filled song leader and soloist, singing the sanctified songs of the new Holiness movement.

In 1917, Martin moved to Cleveland, Ohio, where she and her husband remained for a few years before relocating to Chicago, Illinois, during the 1920s (the couple divorced in 1929). In Chicago, Martin worked at a local hospital while pursuing her gospel singing. Although her singing style was described as rough and unrefined, she was able to connect with her audience, making her an extremely popular soloist.

In 1932, Martin joined the new gospel chorus organized by Thomas Dorsey and Theodore Frye at the Pilgrim Baptist Church. Martin heard of Dorsey and even bought some of his music back in 1929, and she was now determined to work with him as his soloist. Not impressed by her singing but touched by her compassion for ministry, Dorsey committed to working with Martin, and he offered her a solo in 1933.

Although Martin served as a featured soloist for Dorsey's compositions, her greatest contributions were her business skills and her ability to quickly turn Dorsey's publishing company into an extremely profitable and influential business. She marketed his sheet music, negotiated cheaper printing costs, organized his music store, hired assistants to run the counter, and kept records on inventory. She also kept diligent watch over all expenses and income. Martin also assisted in founding the National Convention of Gospel Choirs and Choruses, serving as the vice president (1932–1988). Although she was one of the original organizers, her greatest contribution was traveling the country establishing affiliate choruses and selling Dorsey's music in various cities, from New York to California.

In 1937, Martin sang with Dorsey's University Gospel Singers, along with Bertha Armstrong, Dettie Gray, and Mattie Wilson. The group served as a broadcast choir on Chicago's WLFL radio station, singing Dorsey's compositions, which were also known as "Dorseys." With the addition of Mahalia Jackson that same year as Dorsey's featured soloist and tour companion, Martin continued to focus on the business of running the Dorsey House of Music until her departure in 1940.

In 1940, after eight years, Martin moved forward in search of greater opportunity. Now attending the First Church of Deliverance, Martin began to confide in Pastor Clarence H. Cobb regarding her desire to open her own publishing company. Reverend Cobb urged Martin to pursue her desires by investing in the formation of the company and insisting that she partner with gospel composer, musician, and arranger Kenneth Morris, who served as choir director at the First Church of Deliverance, the choir with which

Martin often sang. Martin teamed up with the Morris, who had spent the past six years working with the Lillian M. Bowles House of Music. The two opened Martin and Morris Music Company, with financing from Reverend Cobb.

The new publishing company utilized Morris's skills at composing and arranging and Martin's business savvy and talent at organizing groups. Martin put together a group to travel the country performing and selling the compositions and arrangements published by Martin and Morris Music Company. The group Martin assembled—Dorothy Simmons, Sarah Daniels, Julie Mae Smith, and Melva Williams, with Ruth Jones (later known as Dinah Washington) on piano—were known as the Sallie Martin Singers as well as the Sallie Martin Colored Ladies Quartet, the first all-female group to sing gospel songs.

During the 1950s, they changed the company's name to Martin and Morris Studio of Music, adding music lessons to their slate of offerings; they were one of the largest Chicago gospel music publishing houses, with a catalog of compositions by William H. Brewster, Dorothy Love Coates, Lucie Campbell, Alex Bradford, Sam Cooke, and Raymond Rasberry, among other notables. During the 1960s, Martin was a generous supporter of Reverend Dr. Martin Luther King, Jr., and the Civil Rights Movement. Martin represented Dr. King at a 1960 ceremony marking the independence of Nigeria, where a state office building was subsequently named in her honor.

Martin retired from the publishing business in 1970, selling her share of the business to Morris three years later. After years of intermittent touring around the United States and Europe, Martin disbanded the Sallie Martin Singers in 1975. In 1985, Martin was honored as an African American Living Legend by the Los Angeles County Public Library. Sallie Martin died on June 18, 1988 in Chicago, at age ninety-two.

EMMETT G. PRICE III

See also Bradford, Alex; Brewster, William Herbert; Campbell, Lucie; Coates, Dorothy Love; Cooke, Sam; Dorsey, Thomas; Frye, Theodore R.; Jackson, Mahalia; Morris, Kenneth; National Convention of Gospel Choirs and Choruses

Reference and Further Reading

Boyer, Horace Clarence. *The Golden Age of Gospel*. Urbana and Chicago: University of Illinois Press, 2000 [1995].
———. "Kenneth Morris: Composer and Dean of Black Gospel Music Publishers." In *We'll Understand It Better By and By: Pioneering African American Gospel Composers*, edited by Bernice Johnson Reagon, 309–328. Washington, DC: Smithsonian Institute Press, 1992.
Broughton, Viv. *Black Gospel: An Illustrated History of the Gospel Sound*. Dorset, UK: Blandford Press, 1985.
Harris, Michael W. *The Rise of Gospel Blues: The Music of Thomas Andrew Dorsey in the Urban Church*. New York and Oxford: Oxford University Press, 1992.
Heilbut, Anthony. *The Gospel Sound: Good News and Bad Times*. New York: Limelight Editions, 1997 (1971, 1975, 1985).
Nierenberg, George T. *Say Amen, Somebody*. United Artists Classics, 1982.
Reagon, Bernice Johnson. "Kenneth Morris: 'I'll be a Servant for the Lord'." In *We'll Understand It Better By and By: Pioneering African American Gospel Composers*, edited by Bernice Johnson Reagon, 329–341. Washington, DC: Smithsonian Institute Press, 1992.

Select Discography

Eyes Hath Not Seen (Specialty 808).
Precious Lord (Trip TLP 7021).
Sallie Martin (Savoy MG-14242).
Throw Out the Lifeline (Specialty SPCD 7043-2).

MASON, LOWELL

(b. January 8, 1792; d. August 11, 1872)

The father of American church and school music was born in Medfield, Massachusetts. At an early age he displayed an aptitude for music, becoming leader of the local church choir while still in his teens. He also learned to play numerous musical instruments and at age eighteen led the Medfield band. In 1812, he moved to Savannah, Georgia, to work in a dry goods store; five years later he became a partner in the firm. When his partner died two years later, Mason started working in a bank. During this time he was an organist at the Presbyterian Church, and he was a founder and active member of the Savannah Missionary Society, established in 1818.

Mason also studied harmony and composition under Frederick Abel and began composing hymn tunes and anthems. At the same time, Mason began compiling a large manuscript of hymns set to tunes arranged from European composers, such as Mozart and Haydn. This anthology was published in 1822 by the Boston Handel and Haydn Society but without Mason's name, at his request, because he did not want to be known as a professional musician. Later editions, however, listed him as editor.

After the success of his tunebook Mason received invitations to lead music in three Boston churches for the then grand sum of two thousand dollars per year. In 1829, he compiled the *Juvenile Psalmist,* or *The Child's Introduction to Sacred Music,* believed to be the first Sunday school collection with music published in America. This was followed the next year by the *Juvenile Lyre,* a school music collection. In 1833, he headed the Boston Academy of Music to promote mass music education and elevate the standards of church music. As a result of his efforts, music was adopted as one of the regular school studies in 1838.

For the next thirteen years that he taught, seven of those years were spent as superintendent of music in the Boston schools. From 1845 to 1855, he was a staff member of the Massachusetts State Board of Education's teachers' institutes. During this time, he was active in musical conventions and normal institutes, where he trained numerous public school music teachers. After a trip to Europe in 1851, Mason moved to New York, where his sons, Daniel and Lowell, Jr., had started a music business. In 1855, New York University gave him an honorary doctorate in music, the second such degree given by an American university.

Mason composed and arranged about sixteen hundred hymn tunes, although because many were published without attribution, it is difficult to determine the exact number. Among his best-remembered melodies are "From Greenland's Icy Mountains," for which Reginald Heber supplied the text; "Nearer My God to Thee," with Sarah Flower Adams's famous lyrics, said to have been President William McKinley's favorite hymn; "When I Survey the Wondrous Cross," said to have been arranged from a Gregorian chant that Mason provided for the Isaac Watts text; "A Charge to Keep I Have," for a text by Charles Wesley; and "My Faith Looks Up to Thee," for a text by Ray Palmer. Mason also provided the best-known arrangement of "Joy to the World."

He opposed the secular style represented by such works as *The Christian Lyre* and sought to counteract such influences in his compilations. Even so, some of his own tunes reflect secular style, such as repeated dotted eighth and sixteenth notes and extended repeated notes in the tenor and bass voices, which were commonly encountered in late-nineteenth century gospel music.

W. K. McNEIL

Reference and Further Reading

Emurian, Ernest K. *Living Stories of Famous Hymns.* Grand Rapids, MI: Baker, 1955.

Metcalf, Frank J. *American Writers and Compilers of Sacred Music.* New York: Russell and Russell, 1967 (1925).

Osbeck, Kenneth W. *101 Hymn Stories.* Grand Rapids, MI: Kregel, 1982.

———. *101 More Hymn Stories.* Grand Rapids, MI: Kregel, 1985.

Rich, Arthur L. *Lowell Mason: The Father of Singing Among School Children.* Chapel Hill: University of North Carolina Press, 1946.

Wells, Amos R. *A Treasury of Hymn Stories.* Grand Rapids, MI: Baker, 1992 (1945).

MASTERS FAMILY, THE

John Masters (originally Purdom) (b. May 27, 1913; d. January 21, 1980)
Lucille Ferdon Masters (b. September 13, 1917)
Johnnie Owen Masters (b. February 3, 1935; d. March 1, 1997)

The Masters Family achieved widespread popularity during the late 1940s and early 1950s and then, after a few years of relative inactivity, renewed their efforts briefly again in the early 1960s before retiring. The group consisted of Johnnie Masters, his wife Lucille, and son Johnnie Owen. In addition to contributing several classic songs to the gospel field, such as "Gloryland March" and "Cry from the Cross," the Masters Family is also memorable for being the first gospel group to record with standard country and western instrumentation. Until then, gospel groups generally had used only a piano or, in some cases, a guitar.

Johnnie Masters (his original family name was Purdom) was born in Jacksonville, Florida, and he began playing both country and gospel music on local radio in that locale. In about 1941, Lucille joined him, and they began performing as the Dixie Sweethearts and cut a single record under that name in about 1946. When son Owen joined them, they became known as the Masters Family, played gospel music almost exclusively, and recorded eight songs for Mercury in the late 1940s with mandolin and guitar accompaniment. Their best-known song from these sessions, "Little Old Country Church House," became something of a bluegrass gospel standard.

In 1950, they moved to Knoxville and station WROL. They signed with Columbia Records and did another thirty-four sides, all but four of them sacred. These included the aforementioned classics and such other notable lyrics as "This Old World Is Rocking in Sin," "Stop Kicking God's Children Around," and "They Made a New Bible," which might be considered a protest song in opposition to the Revised Standard Version. On their two final Columbia sessions in 1954 and 1956, James Carson joined them and contributed several of his originals, including "Everlasting Joy" and "I Wasn't There But I Wish I Could Have Been."

Owen Masters suffered serious injuries in an auto accident in 1955, which curtailed the group's activities. They did albums for Decca in 1961 and Starday in 1963 but had pretty much lost their momentum. Johnnie had hopes for a comeback in the late 1970s, but his death prevented it. As of August 2002, Lucille was confined to a nursing home, but daughter Evelyn reports that Owen's son, known as Johnnie Masters

III, is active as a gospel singer in Mississippi. Columbia released three vinyl albums of Masters Family recordings in the early 1960s, but all of their material is currently out of print.

IVAN M. TRIBE

Reference and Further Reading

Tribe, Ivan. "The Masters Family: Pioneers in Country Gospel Music." *Precious Memories* 3, no. 5 (January–February 1991): 21–27.

Discography

Everlasting Joy (Harmony HL 7295).
The Masters Family (Harmony HL 7197).
Spiritual Wings (Harmony HL 7298).

MATTIE MOSS CLARK AND THE SOUTHWEST MICHIGAN STATE CHOIR

Mattie Moss Clark (b. March 26, 1925, Selma, AL; d. September 22, 1994, Southfield, MI)

The Southwest Michigan State Choir of the Church of God in Christ (COGIC)—led by director, pianist, vocalist, arranger, and composer Mattie Juliet Moss Clark—helped inspire the mass choir movement. Thanks to Clark's pioneering effort and uncompromising musical standards, there is hardly a state or major city in the United States today that does not have a mass choir. Indeed, many cities worldwide now have mass choirs.

Clark was born in Selma, Alabama, on March 26, 1925, as one of eight children to Edward and Mattie Moss. The Mosses were a musical family: the elder Mattie played piano and guitar, the younger Mattie began taking piano lessons at age six, and other Moss children also sang and played instruments. Clark's brother Bill would later form the highly successful Bill Moss and the Celestials.

The seeds of the Southwest Michigan State Choir were planted during the 1959 Church of God in Christ State Music Convention when Clark—by then a Detroit resident—successfully demonstrated how to teach a gospel song to an aggregation of choristers from various churches and, in a short period of time, have them sing the composition confidently. The State Choir was organized officially soon afterward, with Clark as director and Cleveland Cole as chairman.

The Southwest Michigan State Choir was not the first multivoiced gospel choir from Detroit to gain national reputation. Two that came earlier were Reverend James Lofton's five-hundred-voice chorale from the Church of Our Prayer and the Voices of Tabernacle, led by Charles Craig and James Cleveland. These ensembles, however, were associated with specific churches. The two hundred or more members of the Southwest Michigan State Choir heralded from many COGIC churches throughout the denomination's Southwest Michigan jurisdiction.

The choir's debut recording was released on Kapp Records around 1961. The first single, "Going to Heaven to Meet the King" (K436), which was credited to the State Choir of Southwestern Michigan Church of God in Christ, filled both sides of the 45-rpm disc. The performance contained much of what would become the choir's musical trademarks: a Clark-penned composition rendered with percussive vocal phrasing and soulful lead singing; an infectious rhythm propelled by piano and organ; hand clapping; and a live church service feeling.

The group's Kapp output, however, received little attention. It was not until the choir signed with Savoy Records in 1963, recording the single "Saved Hallelujah" (another Clark composition) and the LP *Wonderful, Wonderful,* that the nation took notice. On this LP, which was recorded on Saturday, September 21, 1963, in Detroit's Bailey Temple COGIC, the choir captured the essence of the Pentecostal service, complete with a shouting audience, hand clapping, extended codas, musical improvisation, a ringing tambourine, and instrumental prowess from organist Ronald Kersey and pianists Janet Cole and Bobbie Slappy.

During this session, the choir became one of the first to record "Yes Lord," a spontaneous praise-chant that, for the COGIC, signifies the entry of the Holy Ghost into the religious service.

Clark wrote more than a hundred songs and recorded more than thirty-five albums during her lifetime. She was among the first gospel artists to earn a gold record. However, her influence on gospel music is not limited to the achievements of the Southwest Michigan State Choir. She also directed the COGIC Convocation Choir and was named president of the Music Department of COGIC, a position she held for more than twenty-five years. She founded the Mattie Moss Clark Conservatory of Music in Detroit and, through her "Midnight Musicals" and many other activities, introduced artists such as Douglas Miller and Vanessa Bell Armstrong to national gospel audiences.

Clark parlayed her family into a gospel music dynasty. Her daughters—Dorinda, Jackie, Denise, Karen, and Elbernita "Twinkie"—pursued gospel music careers individually and as the Clark Sisters. The group's "You Brought the Sunshine" (1983) became a crossover hit and dance floor classic. Karen's daughter Kierra "KiKi" and Denise's sons Lorenzo, Larry, and Derrick (as the Clark Brothers) and cousin James Moss (the J Moss Project) represent the newest generation of Clark Family artists.

Shortly before Clark's death from diabetes in Southfield, Michigan, on September 22, 1994, the Bailey Cathedral COGIC in Detroit witnessed a reunion of original members of the Southwest Michigan State Choir. Performing its most popular gospel hits led by the original soloists such as Ora Watkins ("Climbing up the Mountain"), Rose Marie Rimson ("I Thank You Lord"), and Clark herself ("Salvation Is Free"), the choir sounded as fresh and vibrant as it did in the 1960s. Clark was inducted posthumously into the Gospel Music Hall of Fame in 1997.

ROBERT MAROVICH

See also Church of God in Christ (COGIC); Clark, Elbernita; Cleveland, James; Gospel Choirs

Reference and Further Reading

Boyer, Horace Clarence. *How Sweet the Sound: The Golden Age of Gospel*. Washington, DC: Elliott & Clark, 1995.
Hayes, Cedric; Robert Laughton. *Gospel Records 1943–1969: A Black Music Discography*. London: Record Information Services, 1993.
Heilbut, Anthony. *The Gospel Sound*. New York: Limelight Editions, 1992.
Mason, Mack C. *Saints in the Land of Lincoln*. Hazel Crest, IL: Faithday Press, 2004.
"Mattie Moss Clark." All Music website, http://www.allmusic.com.
McCoy, Eugene B. *Climbing up the Mountain: The Musical Life and Times of Dr. Mattie Moss Clark*. Nashville, TN: Sparrow Press, 1994.

Discography

Wonderful, Wonderful (1963, Savoy LP MG-14077).
The Southwest Michigan State Choir of the Church of God in Christ (1964, Savoy LP MG-14099).
Salvation Is Free (1965, Savoy LP MG-14120).
Dr. Mattie Moss Clark Presents a Reunion of the Southwest Michigan State Choir (Live) (1995, Sparrow CD SPD 1463).

MAY, JOSEPH "BROTHER JOE"

(b. November 9, 1912, Macon, MS; d. May 14, 1972, Thomasville, GA)

Brother Joe May was born on a small farm in Macon, Mississippi. May was raised by his mother, Aslean May, who was very active in the Church of God. May began singing at age nine. He later joined the senior choir at the Church out on the Hills and the Church of God Quartet. May graduated high school and then began working as a laborer in Macon. He soon developed a reputation in Mississippi and Alabama as a soloist. The name "Brother" was given to him in Mississippi, because men are referred to as "brother" and women as "sister" in the Church of God.

May met Mother Willie Mae Ford Smith (1904–1994), who ran a musical revival at May's church in Macon. Mother Smith was a minister in the Church of God Apostolic, a Holiness Pentecostal organization. She was well known in gospel music circles for her preaching and arrangements of hymns. Smith encouraged May to sing and mentioned opportunities for his family to receive an education and a better paying job for him. Brother May, his wife Viola, and their two children, Annette and Charles, moved from Macon to St. Louis, Missouri, to establish his singing career with the famous Mother Smith. He worked as a laborer for the Monsanto Chemicals plant. May worked all day and received mentoring from Smith in the evening.

Because of Brother May's earth-shattering voice and rich harmony, Mother Smith gave him his stage name, "the Thunderbolt of the Middle West." Mother Smith performed each year at the National Baptist Convention at the request of "the Father of Gospel Music," Thomas A. Dorsey (1899–1993). Smith took May to the convention in Los Angeles for an audition and he was accepted. May impressed Joseph W. Alexander, a talent scout for Specialty Records, who signed him to a recording contract. His first recording was in 1959: "Search Me Lord," written by Thomas A. Dorsey.

May learned to moan on hymns, along with his powerful tenor voice, making him a great success on gospel quartet billboards. He often performed on the same bill with Mahalia Jackson (1911–1972), bringing standing room only crowds. Brother May traveled with Mother Smith for several years. He also toured and recorded with many singers from the golden era of gospel, namely Sallie Martin, the Pilgrim Travelers, and Sister Wynona Carr (1924–1976), who left gospel to sing rhythm and blues.

In 1964, May recorded "To Run," "I'm Gonna Live the Life I Sing About," and "What Is This?" All were gospel hits recorded on the Nashboro label in Nashville. As May's popularity waned in the West, North, and Midwest, he supported his family with his low-cost music books. One title was *Martin & Morris Joe May's Special*; these books had pictures of his wife and children, and they contained songs made popular by May. His books were easily accessible in major cities, at a cost of five dollars per dozen. Thus, soloists and choirs continued to sing his songs in areas other than the South.

White audiences in the 1950s and 1960s did not accept him as a crossover artist. It was believed that his strong voice was too "churchy" and not refined for crossover audiences. Many gospel music scholars strongly believe that May was the greatest male soloist in gospel music history; he was the male counterpart of Mahalia Jackson. May usually wore a long white robe with a long roped cross. He was the key male solo gospel leader in the golden era of gospel. "Do You Know Him?" and "Search Me Lord" sold more than a million copies, giving him gold records. He had forty 45-rpm records, and they sold very well.

Three of his favorite songs were duets with Mother Smith: "The Old Account," "God Leads Us Along," and "Search Me Lord." Brother May had several long-playing albums: *Don't Let the Devil Ride, In Church with Brother Joe May,* and *The Brother Joe May Story.* In May 1972, Brother Joe May visited Major James Hollis (1910–1996), a gospel promoter in Gainesville, Florida, and they took time to go fishing. May was ill, yet he performed in Florida. He traveled to Thomasville, Georgia, for another concert and died of a stroke on May 14, 1972.

Brother May's daughter Annette and son Charles are contemporary gospel singers, thereby continuing the family gospel roots. In October 2000, May was inducted into the International Gospel Music Hall of Fame and Museum in Detroit. The ceremony played two songs, "Search Me Lord" and "I'm Gonna Live the Life I Sing About," as background music.

SHERRY SHERROD DUPREE

Reference and Further Reading

Boyer, Horace Clarence. *How Sweet the Sound: The Golden Age of Gospel.* Washington, DC: Elliott & Clark, 1995.
DuPree, Sherry Sherrod. *African-American Holiness Pentecostal Movement: An Annotated Bibliography.* Religious Information Systems Vol. 4; Garland Reference Library of Social Science Vol. 526. New York: Garland Publishing, 1996.
———. *Biographical Dictionary of African-American Holiness-Pentecostals 1880–1990.* Washington, DC: Middle Atlantic Regional Press, 1989.
———; Herbert C. DuPree. *African-American Good News (Gospel) Music.* Washington, DC: Middle Atlantic Regional Press, 1993.
Hildebran, Ike; Opal Nations. "Brother Joe May." Liner notes, *Thunderbolt of the Mid-West* (1992, Specialty SPCD 7033-2).
Hollis, Major James. Gainesville, Florida. Interview by Sherry Sherrod DuPree via telephone, April 26, 1992.
International Gospel Music Hall of Fame and Museum website, http://www.gmhf.org (accessed August 28, 2004).

Discography

In Church with Brother Joe May (Nashboro LP 7093).
The Master on Our Side (Nashboro LP 7001).

McCLURKIN, DONNIE

(b. November 9, 1959, Amityville, NY)

Tragic Childhood

Donnie McClurkin was one of Francis and Donald McClurkin's ten children. He showed an early talent for music and sang his first solo in church when he was three years old. Church was the centerpiece of the McClurkin family, and their home was filled with gospel music. Patriarch Donald provided for the family by working construction but also relied on government assistance to feed his large family.

Tragedy struck the McClurkin family when Donnie was eight years old. He was playing with his baby brother when a ball went out into the street. Donnie watched in horror as his brother chased the ball and was struck by a car and killed. The death devastated the family and began a downward spiral that led to a disintegration of the McClurkin household. Domestic violence, drug addictions, and sexual abuse all plagued the family. On the day of his young brother's funeral, Donnie was molested by an uncle. He was later abused by a cousin and kept the crime a secret. McClurkin recounts his difficult childhood in his 2001 autobiography, *Eternal Victim/Eternal Victor.*

Salvation and Healing

The loss of Donnie's brother propelled his mother into manic depression. Donnie went to live with his grandmother and found a safe haven at church. When he was nine, he made a commitment to Christ at the Bethel Gospel Tabernacle in his hometown. Two years later he met Andrae Crouch following a concert at the Bethel Gospel Tabernacle in New York City. Donnie was a big fan of Andrae and was thrilled when his hero prayed for him. McClurkin credits that prayer with giving him the ability to play piano. He dedicated his time to playing, and he found acceptance and accolades because of his musical talent.

The Music World Discovers Donnie McClurkin

In 1979, Donnie put together his first group, called the McClurkin Singers, with his sisters and a few friends. By 1982, McClurkin had become a member of the Kings Temple Choir with Benny Cummings. It was also during this time that he met Marvin Winans, who was impressed with his musical talent. Winans was recruiting for the gospel Broadway musical *Don't Get God Started*. Donnie was hired as the understudy for the lead, and he spent four months on Broadway and eighteen months in the touring production.

Following the end of the musical, Donnie spent some time in Detroit, helping Marvin Winans start a church. He later returned to New York to start the New York Restoration Choir and signed a recording contract with Savoy, releasing the album *I See a World* in 1990. The choir received national attention when they performed at the Democratic National Convention in Madison Square Garden.

During the mid-1990s, Donnie McClurkin turned his attention to a solo career, releasing his self-titled debut on the Warner–Alliance label in 1996. The album featured the hit singles "Stand" and "Speak to My Heart." The industry took notice, awarding McClurkin two Stellar Awards and nominating the project for both Grammy and Dove awards.

Donnie's album also became a favorite of Oprah Winfrey, who invited him onto her television show to sing his signature song, "Stand." While he was on the show, Oprah asked him if the record was gold yet (selling five hundred thousand copies). When Donnie told her it had not, Oprah held up the CD and told her audience of millions that it was her favorite CD and that everyone should go out and buy it. Within two weeks the album passed the half-million sales mark.

In 1999, Donnie McClurkin recorded his *Live from London and More* album at Fairfield Hall in Croydon, England. When the album was released on Verity Records in 2001, it spawned the surprise radio hit "We Fall Down." Although Donnie writes most of his material, he discovered the song when he was in the audience at a Dove Awards ceremony, where it was performed by composer Kyle Matthews. The message of hope connected with McClurkin, and he began performing the song in his concerts. When "We Fall Down" was released, it rose to number one on the gospel charts and also became popular on R&B radio, rising into the top twenty. The song earned McClurkin the Traditional Gospel Recorded Song of the Year Dove Award in 2001. *Live from London and More* sold more than a million copies, and the accompanying video was a best-seller, too.

In 2003, Donnie McClurkin followed up his successful live album with the studio release *Again*. The new collection included a duet with friend Yolanda Adams, titled "The Prayer." The Carol Bayer/David Foster composition was produced by award-winning producer Foster. Donnie also included the Walter Hawkins gospel standard "Special Gift." Walter's sister, Lynette, joined McClurkin for the studio recording. The success of the album brought Donnie the 2004 NAACP Image Award for Outstanding Gospel Artist. Another highlight of the year was the release of the DVD *The Donnie McClurkin Story: From Darkness . . . to Light*. The Stephanie A. Frederick film provides candid interviews with Donnie and his family as well as friends Andrae Crouch, Beyonce Knowles, CeCe Winans, T. D. Jakes, Kirk Franklin, Magic Johnson, and others. The film was named Best Feature Documentary at the Sabaoth International Film Festival in Italy.

McClurkin has made cameo appearances on the UPN television sitcoms *Girlfriends* and *The Parkers*. He also appeared in the motion picture *The Fighting Temptations*, which starred Cuba Gooding, Jr., and Beyonce Knowles.

For most of his career as a gospel artist, Donnie McClurkin has also served as a pastor, first as associate pastor at Marvin Winan's Perfecting Church in Detroit. In 2003, he started Perfecting Faith Church in Long Island, New York. He told *Jet* magazine in 2003 that "Preaching is my passion, and music is a byproduct of that." Even when on tour, McClurkin always returned home to preach on Sundays. He told *Gospel Today* magazine in 2005 that he was planning to leave his career in gospel music to focus his energies on working as a pastor and establishing new churches.

JAMES I. ELLIOTT

Reference and Further Reading

Donnie McClurkin website, http://www.donniemcclurkin.com/bio2.html.

Frederick, Stephanie. *The Donnie McClurkin Story: From Darkness . . . to Light, a Stephanie Frederick Film* (Image Entertainment 2656FGDVD).

Grammy Awards website, http://www.grammy.com/awards/search/index.

Recording Industry Association of America website, http://www.riaa.com/gp/database.search.

"The Phenomenal Pastor Donnie McClurkin." *Gospel Today* (January 2005): 38–41.

Waldron, Clarence. "Donnie McClurkin: Gospel Music's Hidden Treasure." *Jett* (January 6, 2003): 57–61.

Discography

Stand (1996, Warner Alliance 46297-2).

Live from London and More (2000, Verity/Zomba 01241-43150-2).
Again (2003, Verity/Zomba 01241-43199-2).
Psalms, Hymns, and Spiritual Songs (2005).

McCRACKEN, JARRELL

(b. November 18, 1927)

Jarrell McCracken grew up the son of a Baptist minister in Dodge City, Kansas. He graduated from Baylor University in Waco, Texas, where in 1950 he earned a BA degree in speech and religion. In 1953, he earned an MA in religion and history. The young entrepreneur supported himself while attending Baylor by working at local radio station KWTX as a deejay and radio announcer. He was the play-by-play voice for Pittsburgh's Class B farm team, the Waco Pirates. Since he had to rely on sparse wire service reports when the team went on the road, he devised a way to add more life to the broadcasts. He interjected previously recorded sounds from home games, such as the bat cracking against the ball, or the crowd cheering after a home run. He and the studio engineer got so good at coordinating the prerecorded sound effects with the reports that most people thought he was really at the game.

One day in 1950, a Baptist youth minister in Hearne, Texas, located sixty miles south of Waco, asked McCracken to address his group on the subject of Christianity and football. Inspired by an article he had read by Jimmy Allen about a football game between the forces of good and evil, the young sports announcer came up with a sermon that he titled "The Game of Life." It was an allegory about a football game in which the teams were coached by Jesus and Satan. He recorded it on tape, using some of the same sound effects that he used for his radio announcing. It was a play-by-play broadcast from the "stadium of life" of a cosmic football game over a fictional radio station called "WORD." He sent it with the youth minister to play for his group. It was a huge success, and soon other youth ministers began asking for copies. Since the 78-rpm record was the industry standard at the time, McCracken found a studio in California that agreed to produce one hundred discs for him. When the recording engineer asked what name to put on the label, the twenty-three-year-old announcer used the call letters of the imaginary radio station that the "Game of Life" was broadcast from. With this, Word Records began; the year was 1951.

During the next two decades, Word established itself as the major Christian music label. During the 1950s, the label carried black spirituals, classical oratorios, pipe organ music, and traditional hymns. During the late 1960s and early 1970s, the musical direction changed as successful country, folk, and rock musicians began undergoing religious conversions. Their music began to reflect their religious experiences in a style that was consistent with their secular sound. "Rock gospel" soon began to flood the Christian marketplace. Soon Christian radio stations began to pop up in cities throughout the country to play the new genre.

Although McCracken himself could not stand listening to rock music, he understood that the only way to reach young people was by using it. Listeners would accidentally tune into a Christian radio station and hear lyrics singing about Jesus and salvation for ten minutes before they realized it. To ensure that Word and its subsidiaries produced a quality product that was comparable with the secular market, it used excellent production. Word used the same Los Angeles and Nashville studios, along with the same engineers and session musicians, that produced the top-forty radio hits for secular artists.

In 1974, McCracken and his partner, Marvin Norcross, sold Word to the American Broadcasting Company (ABC) for seven million dollars. McCracken stayed with Word as president until 1987. During the interim, hundreds of new rock acts were signed to the label. In 1984, McCracken pioneered a deal with A&M Records for the secular distribution of Word products, which included records, religious books, and printed music.

McCracken invested some of his profits from Word to breed and market Egyptian Arabian horses at Bentwood Farms. The enterprise he began in the late 1960s eventually flourished, as he provided oilmen and professional athletes with the most sought after equine that the world offered. However, the collapse of oil, real estate, and banking during the late 1980s plummeted the value of the steeds by two-thirds, forcing Bentwood Farms to file chapter 11 bankruptcy. McCracken continued developing projects in the Christian recording industry until he retired from public life at the dawn of the twenty-first century because of failing health due to Alzheimer's disease. In 2000, McCracken won the Evangelical Christian Publishers Association's Gold Medallion Lifetime Achievement Award.

BOB GERSZTYN

See also Grant, Amy; Maranatha! Music; Myrrh Records; Rock Gospel

Reference and Further Reading

Callahan, Mike; David Edwards; Patrice Eyries. "Word Records Story." Both Sides Now Publishers website, http://www.bsnpubs.com/word/wordstory.html (accessed July 20, 2003).

Gangl, Bert; Zik Jackson. "Word Gold: Five Decades of Hits." Phantom Tollbooth website, http://www.toll booth.org/2001/reviews/wowgold5.html (accessed August 31, 2003).

Granger, Thom. "Word Gold: The Music." Jamsline website, http://www.jamsline.com/wdgold.htm (accessed July 21, 2003).

Imperial Egyptian Stud website, http://www.imperialegyptianstud.com/our_story3.htm (accessed September 19, 2003).

Pierce, John. "Baptists Remember Word Entertainment's Humble Roots in Texas." Baptist Standard website, http://www.baptiststandard.com/2001/12_17/print/wordrecords.html (accessed July 19, 2003).

Sheehy, Sandy. *Texas Big Rich*. New York: William Morrow and Company, 1990.

McCRAVEY, FRANK AND JAMES

The McCravey Brothers, Frank and James, were among the most commercially successful singers of the late 1920s, spreading their influence far beyond the South via network radio and best-selling Victrola records.

Frank Edwin (1889–1939) and his brother James Boyd (ca. 1898–1938) came from a large, well-connected family in Laurens County, South Carolina; their grandmother had been the first music graduate of the old Salem College in 1856, and their father was a long-time sheriff of the county. In about 1910, Frank met a Baptist preacher named DeGarmo from Mississippi, who was holding revivals in the area; the preacher encouraged Frank to develop his talent for church singing. He soon attended the Moody Institute in Chicago, one of the country's leading church music centers. Upon returning, Frank began to work with his younger brother, and by the time of World War I, they were singing regularly and traveling widely on the revival circuit.

In early 1925, while visiting an aunt in New Jersey, the brothers went into New York and recorded several sides for the General Phonograph Company (OKeh Records). One of these was "We'll Understand It Better Bye and Bye," an old camp meeting song that had even made its way into the repertoire of New Orleans jazz bands. It became wildly popular and was the first of a line of McCravey Brothers hits on record. Indeed, the following years (1925–1932) saw the duo release more than sixty songs on as many as twelve different labels, including OKeh, Brunswick, Victor, Edison, and the American Recording Company (a conglomerate specializing in cheap dime-store labels). The McCraveys also used several pseudonyms so that they could record the same song for different companies; these included Al and Joe Blackburn, the Southern Twins, the Gospel Pair, and others.

Friends recall that the brothers sold "piles" of their records at concerts and revivals throughout the South and Midwest. However, the records appealed to the general public as well; several became bona fide hits, recorded again and again to meet demand, including "Jacob's Ladder," "These Bones Gwine Rise Again," "Dip Me in the Golden Sea," "Ring Them Heavenly Bells," "Sister Lucy (No Hiding Place Down Here)," and Frank's own masterpiece, "Six Feet of Earth Makes Us All One Size." Many of these songs were of black origin and were learned by the brothers from their Uncle Charlie McCravey, who had a country store in Laurens and who remembered dozens of songs he had heard from ex-slaves in the region.

One of the songs they learned from an old hymnal became their most enduring success, "Will the Circle Be Unbroken." A 1929 Brunswick catalog bragged that this record "is one of the most popular of all the sacred records available in America." This version is related to the Carter Family version (introduced some years later in 1935), called "Can the Circle Be Unbroken"; both share a common refrain, though the Carter version begins with a secular verse about the death of a mother. The original text comes from 1907, written by well-known writers Ada B. Habersham and Charles R. Gabriel (music). The McCraveys' was the first version to be recorded, and it became the model for later versions by the Blue Sky Boys and the Monroe Brothers.

Although both could play instruments, for most recordings the McCraveys were backed by a small studio orchestra: a couple of violins, a cello, perhaps a banjo, trumpet, piano, or guitar. It was not traditional as such, but the band complemented the McCraveys' soft, precise, cultured voices. This helped win them a radio show called *Fireside Songs* over the NBC network in 1933. Generations before the Blackwood Brothers and the Statesmen achieved fame by popularizing black spirituals, the McCraveys blazed the trail. They made available to millions of Americans the rich fruits of Southern gospel music.

CHARLES K. WOLFE

McGRANAHAN, JAMES

(b. July 4, 1840; d. July 7, 1907)

James McGranahan displayed early musical ability and pursued training that allowed him to team up with music educator and songwriter George Root, assisting him in numerous normal institutes—the first types of concentrated instruction for music teachers. After years of playing, teaching, composing, and conducting music in the Chicago area, McGranahan

251

joined evangelist Dwight Moody's network of revival preachers and musicians. He was paired with Daniel Whittle in 1877, and they spent the next decade conducting revival services in the United States and Great Britain.

During this period and after his retirement from travel, McGranahan set about a hundred and fifty melodies to the hymns of nearly a dozen hymn writers, the most successful collaboration being with his partner, Daniel Whittle. His most successful tunes were set to the gospel songs "I Know Whom I Have Believed," "I Will Sing of My Redeemer" (words by Bliss), "The Banner of the Cross," and "There Shall Be Showers of Blessing."

Of perhaps greater influence was his role as an editor for the famous *Gospel Hymns* series, created by Ira Sankey and Philip P. Bliss in 1875. With the sudden death of Bliss in 1876, McGranahan was asked to join the team of Sankey and George C. Stebbins to continue the work. The result was *Gospel Hymns No. 3* (1878), *No. 4* (1883), *No. 5* (1887), *No. 6* (1891), and *Gospel Hymns Nos. 1–6 Combined* (1894). In addition, McGranahan coedited numerous additional song collections such as *Christian Endeavor Edition of Sacred Songs No. 1* (1897). He also pioneered the use of men's choral arrangements in gospel music, and some of his most popular tunes were introduced in that context, with "Christ Receiveth Sinful Men" ("Sinners Jesus Will Receive") appearing *The Gospel Male Choir, No. 2*.

MEL R. WILHOIT

See also Bliss, Philip Paul; Root, George Frederick; Sankey, Ira David; Whittle, Daniel Webster

Reference and Further Reading

Hall, J. H. *Biography of Gospel Song and Hymn Writers.* New York: Fleming Revell, 1971 (1914).
Wingate, Mary. *James McGranahan.* Published ca. 1907.

McGUIRE, BARRY

(b. October 15, 1935, Oklahoma City, OK)

After his parents divorced, Barry McGuire moved to California with his mother. His teenage years were spent working on fishing boats and in the Navy. He enjoyed the folk music of Woody Guthrie, Leadbelly, and Pete Seeger, and in 1960 he purchased his first guitar. He began to play at some of the local bars in Santa Monica, where he was discovered by Peggy Lee and her producer, Fred Briskin. In 1961, he recorded his first 45-rpm single, titled "The Tree," on Mosaic Records. In 1962, when Art Podell started a folk group called the New Christy Minstrels, McGuire became the group's lead singer. The Christys appeared on the Vic Damone and Andy Williams television shows, as well as at Los Angeles' Greek Theater.

In 1963, McGuire wrote the New Christy Minstrels' biggest hit single, "Green, Green," which appeared on their fourth album, *Ramblin'.* The album stayed on the charts for seventy-seven weeks, eventually hit number fifteen, and was declared gold. By the summer of 1964, the Christys were invited to play at the White House for President Lyndon Baines Johnson and had their own summer replacement television show. Earlier that year, the Beatles made their debut in America, signaling the end of the folk era.

McGuire left the New Christy Minstrels in January 1965, and in the spring of that year he met producer Lou Adler, who started Dunhill Records, and introduced him to Phil Sloan. Sloan was writing songs that contained serious social commentary, reflecting the upheaval of that era. One such song was "Eve of Destruction," which had a prophetic message of impending apocalyptic doom. After it was released in July, it took over the radio airwaves like wildfire. In August, *Barry McGuire Featuring Eve of Destruction* was released.

The same week of September that the album reached number thirty-seven on the *Billboard* charts, "Eve of Destruction" became the number one record in the United States, on both the *Cashbox* and *Billboard* charts. Despite the song's popularity and McGuire's appearances on TV shows such as *Hullabaloo,* the song drew adverse reactions from both the left and the right. During the next few years, McGuire recorded a couple of albums that received critical acclaim but did not sell. He began to work in the movie industry and appeared in *The President's Analyst,* which led to an opportunity to star in the original cast of the rock musical *Hair* in New York City for a year.

By 1971, McGuire was in poor health due to drug use, and his career was on the skids. His last film role was in Michel Levesque's avant-garde horror film, *Werewolves on Wheels.* That same year, he converted to Christianity and moved from Hollywood to Fresno, California, where he worked with a Christian ministry called Agape Force. During this time, he met a Christian recording engineer named Buck Herring and recorded his first Christian album, *Seeds,* in 1973 on Myrrh Records. Herring's wife Annie sang in a gospel trio with her younger sister and brother, called the 2nd Chapter of Acts, which sang backup on *Seeds* and toured with McGuire for the next three years. In 1975 they released a live album together, titled *To the Bride.* In the mid-1970s, when Billy Ray Hearn left

Myrrh Records to start Sparrow Records, McGuire and the 2nd Chapter of Acts were among the first to join him.

McGuire released more than a dozen Christian albums, including *Cosmic Cowboy, Bullfrogs and Butterflies, Polka Dot Bear,* and *Exaltation,* and he toured incessantly. During the early 1980s, he moved to his wife's native country of New Zealand, where he worked with World Vision, which was the world's largest children's relief organization at that time. In the early 1990s, he moved back to the United States and began to record albums again, which included two children's albums, on the Gospel Light label, titled *Adventures on Son Mountain* and *Journey to Bible Times.*

During the mid-1990s, McGuire began to perform with another Christian folksinger named Terry Talbot. Together they formed a duo called Terry and Barry, and in 1996, after touring together for a couple of years, they released *When Dinosaurs Walked the Earth.* The money generated by the collaboration helped to fund Mercy Corps, a Catholic relief organization. By the time McGuire began to perform as a solo act again, the duo had released four albums together. In 2004, McGuire and his wife Mari once again moved back to her native New Zealand, where he continues to occasionally perform and tour.

BOB GERSZTYN

See also 2nd Chapter of Acts

Reference and Further Reading

Barry McGuire website, http://www.barrymcguire.com/bio02/ (accessed January 1, 2004).
Bennett, David. "The Barry McGuire Album Page." http://barrymcguire.byrdsnet.com/ (accessed January 7, 2004).
Donaldson, Devlin. "Rewind." http://www.peoplejustlikeus.org/Music/BARRY_McGUIRE.html (accessed January 7, 2004).
Iceberg Radio.com website, http://www.theiceberg.com/artist/9686/barry_mcguire.html (accessed January 2, 2004).
Music Voyager website, http://music.ruv.net/Bands_and_Artists/M/McGuire,_Barry/ (accessed February 2, 2004).
Prato, Greg. "Barry McGuire Biography." MSN Music website, http://entertainment.msn.com/artist/?artist= 105536 (accessed January 3, 2004).
Ruhlmann, William. "All Music Guide." http://www.rollingstone.com/artists/bio.asp?oid=1361218 (accessed January 2, 2004).
Scaruffi, Piero. "The History of Rock Music." http://www.scaruffi.com/vol1/mcguire.html (accessed January 2, 2004).
Untenberger, Richie. "Barry McGuire Interview." http://www.icebergradio.com/artist.asp?artist=9686 (accessed February 2, 2004).
———. *Turn, Turn, Turn: The '60s Folk–Rock Revolution.* San Francisco, CA: Backbeat Books, 2002.
White, Logan; Barry McGuire. *In the Midst of Wolves.* Wheaton, IL: Crossway Books, 1990.

Discography

The Barry McGuire Album (1963, Horizon WP1636); *The New Christy Minstrels in Person* (1963, Columbia 8741); *The New Christy Minstrels Tell Tall Tales! Legends & Nonsense* (1963, Columbia 8817); *Merry Christmas* (1963, Columbia 8896); *Ramblin' Featuring Green, Green* (1963, Columbia 8855); *Land of Giants* (1964, Columbia 8987); *Today* (1964, Columbia 8959); *Barry McGuire, Featuring Eve of Destruction* (1965, Dunhill 50003); *Chim Chim Cheree* (1965, Columbia 9169); *Cowboys and Indians* (1965, Columbia 9103); *Star Folk with Barry McGuire* (1965, Surrey SS1003); *This Precious Time* (1965, Dunhill 50005); *Greatest Hits* (1966, Columbia 9279); *Star Folk Vol. 2 with Barry McGuire* (1966, Mira 3000); *The World's Last Private Citizen* (1967, Dunhill 50033); *Barry McGuire and the Doctor* (1971, Ode 77004); *Seeds* (1973, Myrrh A-6519); *Lighten Up* (1974, Myrrh A-6531); *Jubilation* (1975, Myrrh A-6555); *To the Bride* (1975, Myrrh A-6548); *C'mon Along* (1976, Sparrow); *Firewind* (1976, Sparrow); *Jubilation Too* (1976, Myrrh A-6568); *Have You Heard* (1977, Sparrow); *Bullfrogs and Butterflies* (1978, Birdwing); *Cosmic Cowboy* (1978, Sparrow); *The Witness* (1978, Light); *Inside Out* (1979, Sparrow); *Best of Barry McGuire* (1980, Sparrow); *Polka Dot Bear* (1980, Sparrow); *Exaltation* (1981, Paragon); *Finer than Gold* (1981, Sparrow); *Pilgrim* (1989, Word); *El Dorado* (1990, CBS-German Import); *Let's Tend God's Earth* (1991, Maranatha); *Adventures on Son Mountain* (1993, Gospel Light); *Journey to Bible Times* (1994, Gospel Light); *When Dinosaurs Walked the Earth* (1996, Custom TM1001); *Ancient Garden* (1997, Custom TM 1002); *Frost and Fire* (1999, Custom TM 1003); *Live* (2000, Custom TM 1004).

McKAMEYS, THE

Begun as a singing trio of sisters—Dora, Peg, and Carol McKamey—in 1954 from their home in Clinton, Tennessee, the McKameys have entertained and inspired fans of their style of Southern gospel music now for a full fifty years. The family trio had no plans initially to sing outside their home church, but when other churches extended invitations to sing, they came, and venues for their 150-plus concerts per year now include auditoriums, festivals, and singing conventions.

Ruben Bean, the guitarist who joined to accompany them in 1957, married Peg McKamey, and their daughters Connie and Sheryl later filled parts in the trio as Dora and Carol retired in 1971. When Sheryl left the group to be a full-time minister's wife in the mid-1980s (she still writes much of the group's music), her Aunt Carol returned, and at their golden anniversary the McKameys consisted of originals Peg and Carol McKamey, Peg's husband Ruben Bean, and their daughter Connie. Roger Fortner plays bass guitar, with Randall Hunley on piano, but like many

Southern gospel groups, digital accompaniment tracks are also used at personal appearances.

New albums (and in recent years CDs) have appeared annually since the early 1980s for Morning Star Records (through 1991) and Horizon Records (since 1992), and eleven of their single tracks have topped the *Singing News* Southern gospel charts over almost a twenty-year period, including "Who Put the Tears" (1984), "Getting Used to the Dark" (1987), "God on the Mountain" (1989), "God Will Make This Trial a Blessing" (1991), "A Borrowed Tomb" and "Do You Know How It Feels" (both 1993), "Arise" (1994), "Right on Time" (1997), "Roll That Burden on Me" (1999), and "I've Won" (2001). Of their many videos produced since 1988, *McKameys Hometown Live* in 2003 was voted Video of the Year at the *Singing News* Fan Awards.

RONNIE PUGH

Reference and Further Reading

The McKameys website, http://www.mckameys.com.

Discography

He Didn't Let Us Down (1981, Morning Star); *By Faith* (1982, Morning Star); *Keepsake* (1983, Morning Star); *Tennessee Live* (1984, Morning Star); *Fruitful* (1985, Morning Star); *Unique* (1986, Morning Star); *More than Music* (1987, Morning Star); *Covered by Love* (1988, Morning Star); *Gone to Meetin'* (1988, Morning Star); *Sing Praises* (1989, Morning Star); *Purpose* (1990, Morning Star); *Just Thinking* (1991, Morning Star); *With Feeling* (1992, Horizon); *With His Power* (1993, Horizon); *It's Real* (1994, Horizon); *Sheltered* (1995, Horizon); *Still Have a Song* (1996, Horizon); *Remembrance* (1997, Horizon); *Always* (1998, Horizon); *Waiting* (1999, Horizon); *I've Won* (2001, Horizon); *Trophy of Grace* (2002, Horizon); *An Acoustic Journey* (2003, Horizon); *Fresh Manna* (2004, Horizon).

MEDITATION SINGERS

The Meditations were organized by Earnestine Rundless in 1947 in Detroit out of the Voices of Meditation Choir at the New Liberty Baptist Church. The group quickly became the Motor City's most famous female gospel group, with Lillian Mitchell, soprano, Carrie M. Williams, lead, Loraine Vincent, soprano, Delloreese Patricia Early (Della Reese; b. 1932), lead, and Marie Waters (Della's sister), contralto/alto, accompanied by Emory Radford, piano, and James Cleveland, piano. When Della Reese quit in 1954 to sing popular music, she was replaced by Earnestine's daughter, Laura Lee Rundless, a teenager then, who was also bound to pursue a successful career in popular music and soul singing from 1965 on.

Between 1953 and 1959, the group personified the gospel sound in Detroit and the surrounding area, introducing instrumental accompaniment where an *a cappella* quartet style had been dominant before them.

Earnestine Rundless was born in Mound Bayou, Mississippi, but was reared in Chicago. When she went to see the Soul Stirrers, she met E. A. Rundless, one of the singers, whom she married; soon after, her husband quit the quartet to enter the ministry and they moved to Detroit in March 1945, where Reverend Rundless was called to pastor the New Liberty Baptist Church. Having grown up singing in choirs, Earnestine had a rough, emotional, and strong voice, and she leaned more and more toward the sanctified style of singing.

Della Reese was born in Detroit, attended high school there, and studied at Wayne State University before being recruited by Rundless; she had been singing in church choirs since she was six years old and was an accomplished and experienced singer when she joined the Meditations in 1947. She left in 1954 and went into secular music, beginning a very fruitful recording career in 1955 as a pop singer and actress, showing the influence of Dinah Washington (herself an ex-gospel singer).

In September 1953, the Meditation Singers made their first single in Detroit for De Luxe Records in Joe Von Battle's studios, with James Cleveland on piano. In 1954, they were signed to Specialty Records, making the recordings in Chicago; the sales were poor, and Specialty dropped the group until 1959, when Alex Bradford urged the company to sign them again. At that time, Laura Lee was lead/alto singer and James Cleveland was back with the group (baritone and piano); he was already known as one of the best gospel composers of his time. Specialty complied, and a recording session was held in July 1959; unhappily, the company was getting out of gospel in the early 1960s, and that was the end of the association.

The Meditations went to Hob Records and recorded three albums (1960–1962), and then Cleveland went his own way to glory and fame as a composer and choir leader, while the Meditations recorded a gospel album with ex-member Della Reese for Jubilee Records and appeared on Reese's television shows. In 1962, Reese took the Meditations on a tour of colleges, auditoriums, night clubs, and casinos. They traveled to Europe for a jazz festival in the late 1960s and recorded for a series of labels, including SAR, Gospel (Savoy), D-Town, Chess/Checker, and Jewel. The group disbanded in the early 1980s.

ROBERT SACRÉ

Reference and Further Reading

Boyer, Horace Clarence. *How Sweet the Sound: The Golden Age of Gospel*. Washington, DC: Elliott & Clark, 1995.

Hayes, J. Cedric; Robert Laughton. *Gospel Records 1943–1969. A Black Music Discography*, 2 vols. London, UK: Record Information Services, 1992.

Heilbut, Tony. *The Gospel Sound: Good News and Bad Times*. New York: Limelight, 1985.

Reagon, Bernice Johnson, ed. *We'll Understand It Better By and By. Pioneering African American Gospel Composers*. Washington, DC: Smithsonian Institution Press, 1992.

Discography

The Meditation Singers—Good News (1993, Specialty/Ace [UK] CDCHD465).

The Best of Jubilee Gospel. Heaven Belongs to You (1999, Westside [UK] WESM 588).

MEMPHIS, GOSPEL IN

Pentecostalism

The most important aspect of modern gospel music in Memphis—Pentecostalism—can be traced to the establishment of the Church of God in Christ (COGIC) during the late 1890s. The church relocated its headquarters to Memphis from Northern Mississippi in the 1910s and built its first National Tabernacle at 958 South Fifth Street in 1925. During World War II, the church built Mason's Temple, an auditorium with more than four thousand seats used for large church gatherings as well as other sacred and civic events.

From its inception, the church was particularly strong in the mid-South immediately outside of Memphis, and many black Memphians were quite familiar with its tenets, practices, and music. During its often highly emotional worship services, members often feel the presence of the Holy Ghost, speak in tongues, and break into improvised songs and testimonials. The music and the spontaneous nature of the service helped to set the stage for local and national gospel music performance practices.

Quartets

In addition to the energetic gospel music performed by the congregations and ensembles of the Church of God in Christ, quartets began singing in Memphis churches as early as the 1910s. All of these early quartets were either community based (the Orange Mound Specials, for example, were named after a section of the city) or affiliated with a particular church, such as the Middle Baptist Quartet. They sang at churches throughout the city and often for relatives who had remained in rural areas surrounding Memphis. One important early group, the I. C. Glee Club Quartet, began recording their mixture of traditional material, some of it based on spirituals, and newly written gospel songs during the late 1920s. But the Spirit of Memphis Quartette best exemplifies gospel quartet singing in the city.

The Spirit (their unofficial local moniker) began as a community-based group in the late 1920s; the group was named after the famous airplane flown across the Atlantic by aviator Charles Lindbergh. They sang throughout the mid-South for two decades before making their first commercial recordings and turning professional. For the next ten years the Spirit of Memphis traveled across the United States, recorded extensively for King and Peacock Records, and appeared alongside such nationally recognized groups as the Pilgrim Travelers, the Soul Stirrers, and Mighty Clouds of Joy. The group stepped down as a full professional group in the early 1960s but continues to sing in Memphis.

Composers

Composers represent another important aspect of twentieth-century African American gospel music in Memphis. Reverend Herbert W. Brewster and Lucie Campbell are the two most notable gospel composers associated with Memphis; both were born—Brewster in Fayette County, Tennessee (ca. 1897), and Campbell in Duck Hill, Mississippi (1885)—just as gospel music emerged. That neither was born in Memphis underscores the fact that many Memphians were born elsewhere in the mid-South and moved to the city.

Campbell began composing gospel songs during the 1910s. Her first composition ("The Lord Is My Shepherd") came out in 1919 and marked the beginning of a long and distinguished writing career that ended with her death in 1963. She was particularly prolific in the 1920s, when she composed standards such as "Something Within" (1919), "Heavenly Sunshine" (1923), and "The King's Highway" (1923). Although Campbell continued writing until her death, by the early 1930s she had stepped forward to spend more time teaching others, leading her local choir and teaching "colored children" in the Memphis public schools. Not surprisingly, Campbell helped to organize the burgeoning gospel scene, and she was a dedicated member of the National Baptist Convention.

Herbert Walker Brewster gained recognition as a composer in the early 1940s and helped to shape the sound of gospel music during its public emergence following the close of World War II. Brewster, who for many years preached at the Trigg Avenue Baptist Church, published more than two hundred songs, most of them between 1940 and 1960. During these two decades, Brewster wrote songs such as "I'm Leaning and Depending on the Lord" (1941), "Move On Up a Little Higher" (1946), "Let Us Go to the Old Land Mark" (1949), and "Faith That Moves Mountains" (1954), which remain standards. His compositions have been recorded by dozens of gospel groups, including Sister Rosetta Tharpe, Mahalia Jackson, and the Ward Singers, and his reputation as a composer of popular, well-crafted, highly spiritual gospel songs is matched only by Reverend Thomas A. Dorsey.

Singing works written by these local composers as well as by others, such as Kenneth Morris, large choirs and choruses began to gain popular acceptance in Memphis during the 1960s. Smaller ensembles, consisting of perhaps a dozen or fifteen voices, had been part of African American AME and Baptist worship services for decades. Along with quartets, church choirs not only provided an outlet for spiritual expression but served as the musical ministry for churches throughout the city. But in the 1960s, choirs grew not only in size but also in importance.

Recent Developments

More recently, gospel music in Memphis has further emphasized the relationships between the secular (including hip-hop) and sacred styles as well as the continuing importance of the COGIC. Radio WBBP (1480 AM), owned by Gilbert E. Patterson, a major local force in the Church of God in Christ, plays a wide range of commercially potent gospel music as well as emphasizing the spiritual and musical elements of COGIC beliefs. Both news talk/gospel WLOK (1340 AM) and "Hallelujah FM" (WHAL 95.7) feature contemporary African American gospel music.

Al Green is perhaps the most well-known contemporary Memphis-based gospel singer. He turned his back on a highly successful career as a soul singer in 1976 to found and lead the Full Gospel Tabernacle in the Memphis suburb of Whitehaven. In the summer of 2003, Green decided that he could mediate the

sacred and secular worlds, and he returned to the Hi Studios under the direction of his former collaborator, Willie Mitchell, to record soul songs for the highly acclaimed *I Can't Stop* release. Despite the release of these new soul recordings, Green remains the pastor of the Full Gospel Tabernacle.

KIP LORNELL

Reference and Further Reading

Lornell, Kip. *Happy in the Service of the Lord: African American Sacred Vocal Harmony Quartets in Memphis.* Knoxville: University of Tennessee Press, 1995.

Reagon, Bernice Johnson, ed. *We'll Understand It Better By and By. Pioneering African American Gospel Composers.* Washington, DC: Smithsonian Institution Press, 1992.

MICHAUX, ELDER LIGHTFOOT SOLOMON

(b. November 7, 1884; d. October 20, 1968)

Lightfoot Solomon Michaux was born in Newport News, Virginia. His parents were John and May Blanch Lightfoot. His ancestry was African, Indian and French-Jewish. He attended the Twenty-Second Street School in Virginia.

In 1906, Michaux married Mary Eliza Pauline, a mulatto orphan. The couple had no children but helped raise Michaux's two younger sisters. His wife was a singer who developed her own revival hymnal booklet for camp meetings. Michaux, an entrepreneur, moved his fish peddler and grocer business to Hopewell, Virginia, in 1917. In 1918, he was ordained in the Church of Christ (Holiness) U.S.A. under the leadership of Bishop Charles Price Jones (1865–1949). The headquarters of the church were located in Jackson, Mississippi.

In 1921, Michaux established an independent church called the Church of God. This church was incorporated as the Gospel Spreading Tabernacle Association. Most of its members were immigrants from the South seeking work during the postwar recession following World War I. In 1922, segregationists put Michaux on trial for conducting integrated church meetings, but he was acquitted. He was the leader of the Radio Church of God Choir. In 1929, he began his radio ministry at station WSJV in Washington, DC. The call letters WSJV stood for "Willingly Suffered Jesus for Victory over the Grave." His famous radio broadcast moved to the Columbia Broadcasting System (CBS) in 1932, the eve of radio's golden era.

From 1933 to 1936, Michaux recorded his thirty-minute sermons on the radio; the Happy Am I Choir sang with his congregation on the Savoy Label. Two of Michaux's best-known songs were "We've Got the Devil on the Run" and "Happy Am I." Michaux was known as the "Happy Am I" radio preacher. His choir was composed of 156 members. They accompanied special guests such as Mahalia Jackson (1911–1972), "the Queen of Gospel Music" and Clara Ward, a renowned soloist.

Around 1945, Michaux made a motion picture entitled *We Have Come a Long Way*. It was produced by Jack Goldberg of Herald Pictures, Inc., in New York. It ran in "colored" segregated theaters and educational institutions. Mary McLeod Bethune (1875–1955), founder of Bethune–Cookman College in Daytona Beach, Florida, was featured in the film. On September 24, 1951, at the anniversary program celebrating twenty years of broadcasting, Michaux was commended by John S. Hayes, president and general manger of WTOP, for his series of broadcasts, *Radio Church of God*. He also received congratulatory telegrams from General D. Eisenhower and many other Washington leaders.

For more than thirty years, Michaux's broadcast was carried on WTOP. He became internationally known because his message was carried over the British Broadcasting Corp. From 1937 until the Griffith Baseball Stadium was demolished, Michaux performed his annual baptism on a Sunday night at the stadium. The water in the rubber pool came from the Jordan River. More than eight hundred Bibles would be given to teenagers, and more than twenty-five thousand people watched. He attracted prominent white supporters.

In 1946, Michaux built and founded the Mayflower Housing Development. Presently, his church operates under the name Gospel Spreading Association. In 1970, Louis Michaux, the brother of Solomon Michaux and owner of the National Memorial African Bookstore in Harlem, New York, discussed the importance of black religion and literature. He talked about his brother Solomon, who had published the local *Happy Am I* newspaper and opened the Happy News Cafe in the 1940s.

SHERRY SHERROD DUPREE

Reference and Further Reading

DuPree, Sherry Sherrod. *African-American Holiness Pentecostal Movement: An Annotated Bibliography*. Religious Information Systems Vol. 4; Garland Reference Library of Social Science Vol. 526. New York: Garland Publishing, 1996.

———. *Biographical Dictionary of African-American Holiness-Pentecostals 1880–1990*. Washington, DC: Middle Atlantic Regional Press, 1989.

———; Herbert C. DuPree. *Exposed!!! Federal Bureau of Investigation (FBI) Unclassified Reports on Churches and Church Leaders*. Washington, DC: Middle Atlantic Regional Press, 1993.

Michaux, Louis. Oral Interview with Robert White, New York, 1970. Ralph J. Bunche Oral History Collection, Moorland–Spingarn Collection, Howard University, Washington, DC.

Payne, Wardell J., ed. *Directory of African-American Religious Bodies*, 2nd ed. Washington, DC: Howard University Press. 1995.

Webb, Lillian Ashcraft. *About My Father's Business: The Life of Elder Michaux*. Westport, CT: Greenwood Press, 1981.

Discography

Lightfoot Solomon Michaux. "Happy Am I" (recorded Washington, D.C., June 24, 1961).

Compilation, *Singin' the Gospel 1933–1936* (Document, CD 5326).

MIGHTY CLOUDS OF JOY

Willie Joe Ligon (b. September 11, 1942)
Johnny Martin (b. Unknown)
Richard Wallace (b. June 6, 1940)
Elmo Franklin (b. October 8, 1936)

Willie Joe Ligon grew up in Troy, Alabama. He was too shy to perform in public until his mother coerced him into singing in a group with his cousins. At the age of fourteen he relocated to Los Angeles, California, where he lived with his uncle and continued his schooling.

There Ligon met some other boys who shared his passion for music, and in 1955 they formed a quartet. Ligon sang lead vocals, dominating with his powerfully rich and raspy voice. Johnny Martin, a Los Angeles native, sang alternate lead, balancing Ligon's rough vocals with his smooth tenor falsetto. Richard Wallace, from Georgia, sang bass, and Elmo Franklin, a native of Louisiana, completed the foursome by singing baritone. They were inspired by Reverend Julius Cheeks of the Sensational Nightingales. After being tutored by a musically gifted neighbor, they began performing in local churches in the Los Angeles area. During the next four years, they traveled around California and the Southwest, performing on the gospel circuit.

By the end of the 1950s, the Mighty Clouds of Joy had polished their act to the point of impressing a local gospel deejay. Brother Henderson made a rudimentary recording of the group and sent it in to Peacock Records in 1959. Peacock was already home for many gospel groups, including the Blind

Boys of Alabama, the Nightingales, and the Dixie Hummingbirds. The demo impressed Don Robey, owner of Peacock, who quickly signed the Clouds to the label. They released their first single, "Steal Away to Jesus," in 1960, which was followed in 1961 by their debut album, titled *Family Circle*. They became the top black quartet in the second wave of gospel.

The group became one of the most innovative in the gospel field. One of the aspects unique to the Clouds, at this time, was the sermonette. This was a morality tale that acted as a bridge between preaching and singing and was spoken by the lead singer while the rest of the group hummed or sang softly in the background. They were the first to incorporate a full backup band composed of bass, drums, and keyboards, along with the customary accompaniment of an electric guitar. They included showmanship in their ministry through dress and choreography. They wore bright, color-coordinated outfits and became known as the "Temptations of Gospel." However, many of the group's numerous innovations caused controversy at the time of their initial adoption.

Over the years band personnel were added or replaced and included Paul Beasley, Michael Cook, Orrick Ewing, Dwight Gordon, Michael McGowan, Leon Polk, Ron Staples, Johnny Valentine, David Walker, and Tim Woodson. The Mighty Clouds of Joy produced more than thirty albums during their career. They stayed with the Peacock label throughout the 1960s, where they were influenced by sources as diverse as the legendary Chicago blues artist Willie Dixon and soul superstars Curtis Mayfield and the Impressions. By the 1970s, they switched to ABC Records and produced *Time,* with the help of producers Gamble and Huff. In 1976, the album's song "Mighty High" became their highest-charting single and brought them pop stardom, when they became the first gospel group to ever appear on *Soul Train.* They became an established soul and R&B group but held to their initial religious beliefs. In 1980, they changed record labels again, this time to Word Records. Their first album on Word, *Cloudburst,* was produced by Earth, Wind, and Fire member Al McKay.

They have shared the stage with dozens of artists, including B. B. King, the Blind Boys of Alabama, Shirley Caesar, Reverend James Cleveland, Andrae Crouch, the Dixie Hummingbirds, Aretha Franklin, Marvin Gaye, Al Green, Smokey Robinson, Richard Pryor, the Rolling Stones, Paul Simon, the Soul Stirrers, the Temptations, and Stevie Wonder. They have appeared before two U.S. presidents, Richard M. Nixon and Jimmy Carter. Their act has appeared on numerous major television shows, including a CBS

network special: *The Johnny Cash Show, The Grammy Awards, The Merv Griffin Show, The Arsenio Hall Show,* a Jerry Lewis telethon, *Prime Time Country,* and *The Lou Rawls Parade of Stars.* They even starred in *Gospel,* a full-length feature movie. During their nearly five-decade-long career, they were nominated for eleven Grammy Awards. They brought home the honors three times in the Best Traditional Soul Gospel Album category, in 1978 for *Live and Direct,* 1979 for *Changing Times,* and in 1991 for *Pray for Me.* In 1999, they were inducted into the Gospel Music Hall of Fame.

BOB GERSZTYN

See also Blues; Caesar, Shirley; Caravans; Cleveland, James; Crouch, Andrae; Dixie Hummingbirds; Five Blind Boys of Alabama; Green, Al; Soul Stirrers

Reference and Further Reading

Boyer, Horace Clarence. *How Sweet the Sound: The Golden Age of Gospel.* Washington, DC: Elliott & Clark, 1995.

Europe Jazz Network website, http://www.ejn.it/mus/mighty. htm (accessed July 21, 2003).

Mighty Clouds of Joy website, http://www.mightycloudsof-joy.com/ (accessed August 2, 2003).

Richard De LaFont Agency website, http://www.delafont. com/music_acts/mighty-clouds.htm (accessed August 1, 2003).

Discography

A Bright Side (1960, Peacock); *Family Circle* (1960, Peacock); *The Best of the Mighty Clouds of Joy, Vol. I* (1973, MCA); *The Best of the Mighty Clouds of Joy, Vol. II* (1973, MCA); *It's Time* (1974, ABC); *Kickin'* (1976, ABC); *God Is Not Dead* (1978, ABC); *Live and Direct* (1978, ABC); *Changing Times* (1979, Epic); *Cloudburst* (1980, Word); *The Mighty Clouds Above* (1982, Word); *Miracle Man* (1982, Word); *Request Line* (1982, ABC); *Pray for Me* (1990, Word); *Power* (1995, Intersound); *It Was You* (1999, CGI Records).

MISSISSIPPI MASS CHOIR

Frank Williams (b. June 25, 1947; d. March 22, 1993)

The Mississippi Mass Choir, considered one of the most influential gospel groups of the late twentieth century, with its vitality and style revitalizing the American gospel choir tradition, is also one of gospel history's most successful choirs. The choir was founded by Frank Williams, long-time member of the Jackson Southernaires gospel quartet. In 1988, as an executive of Malaco's gospel music division, he decided to put into action a dream he had long held: bringing together the best gospel voices in

Mississippi. He wanted it to be a mass choir (as compared with a church choir) consisting of singers from across denominational lines. He teamed with David R. Curry to hold open auditions. From hundreds of applicants, they chose one hundred of the greatest singers in a state known for its musical talent pool and dubbed them the Mississippi Mass Choir.

The choir's first album paired the sound of those voices with the Jackson Southernaires' rhythm section on a variety of hymns and traditional gospel songs from the genre's golden age. The result, *The Mississippi Mass Choir Live,* remained number one for forty-five consecutive weeks on the *Billboard* charts, an all-time record for a gospel recording. More than four hundred thousand copies were sold. The choir's next album, recorded with Reverend James Moore, topped the charts again, and the story was the same with each new collection.

What followed was a flurry of awards unparalleled for a gospel choir, including Grammy, Stellar, Soul Train, Dove, Indie, and 3M Corporation Innovation awards. Since its inception, the choir has been an almost constant presence on *Billboard*'s gospel charts. The choir's sound has been aptly described as a blend of "tight, modern arrangements and old-time churchy passion," and that sound has been heard around the world. The choir has sung for Pope John Paul II, and it has performed in Spain, Japan, the Bahamas, and at the Umbria Jazz Festival. It became the first gospel choir to perform at the Acropolis. Its fame and influence inspired inclusion in PBS's *The Mississippi: River of Song* project. "From teenagers to grandparents," stated the PBS documentary, "these are the deepest, soulfulest singers in America."

LINDA RUTLEDGE STEPHENSON

Reference and Further Reading

Alexanian, Nubar. "Where the Music Comes From: The Mississippi Mass Choir." Nubar Alexanian website, http://www.nubar.com/booksprints/wheremusic/MMCPAGE.HTM.

——. *Where the Music Comes From.* Stockport, England: Dewi Lewis Publishing, 1996.

Darden, Robert. *People Get Ready! A New History of Black Gospel Music.* New York: Continuum, 2004.

Harris, Craig. "The Mississippi Mass Choir." All Music Guide website, http://www.allmusic.com.

Heilbut, Anthony. *The Gospel Sound: Good News and Bad Times.* 336. New York: Limelight Books, 1997.

"Mississippi Mass Choir." In *The Mississippi: River of Song.* Smithsonian Institution series for PBS (aired January 6, 1999), http://www.pbs.org/riverofsong/project.

Mississippi Mass Choir website, http://www.themississippimasschoir.com.

Discography

The Mississippi Mass Choir, Live (1989, Malaco).
God Gets the Glory (1991, Malaco).
It Remains to Be Seen (1993, Malaco).
Greatest Hits (1995, Malaco).
I'll See You in the Rapture (1996, Malaco).
The Mississippi: River of Song (1998, Smithsonian Folkways Recordings).
Emmanuel (1999, Malaco).
Praise the Lord (1999, Malaco).
Amazing Love (2002, Malaco).
Not by Might Nor by Power (2005, Malaco).

MISSOURI HARMONY, THE

The Missouri Harmony was the most popular tune-book published in America prior to the Civil War. It was first issued in 1820 and went through twenty-two editions by 1857. It was compiled by Allen D. Carden (b. October 13, 1792; d. October 18, 1859), a native of eastern Tennessee. His family migrated from Virginia to Tennessee, eventually settling in Franklin.

Nothing is known about Carden's early training or activities, but by the second decade of the nineteenth century, he was working as a music teacher in Tennessee, Kentucky, and Virginia, because in *The Kentucky Harmony* Ananias Davisson lists him as one of the "gentlemen teachers" in those states who was helpful to him. Simultaneously with the publication of *The Missouri Harmony,* Carden advertised a singing school, but whether the latter was successful is not known. Carden published two more tunebooks, *The Western Harmony* (1824) and *The United States Harmony* (1829), neither of which were as successful as his first effort. Thereafter, he became more interested in nonmusical activities, getting involved in property transactions in several Tennessee counties.

Undoubtedly, one reason for the great popularity of *The Missouri Harmony* was its use of folk tunes with which purchasers were already familiar. Among the book's 185 selections are found religious texts set to the melodies of traditional ballads, such as "Captain Kidd" and "Lord Thomas and Fair Elenor." Such familiar tunes made the book appealing to many, including a young Abraham Lincoln, who reportedly sang from *The Missouri Harmony* in New Salem.

Despite his book's huge success, Carden had no editorial role or financial interest in his collection after 1824. A *Supplement* (1835) was by an unknown compiler identified only as "an amateur." Its twenty-nine additional selections were in marked contrast with the rest of the book's contents; they seem more representative of the emerging "respectable" style of hymnody than the more folk-like offerings of the original. This supplement appeared in every subsequent edition of the tunebook.

The last significant edition of *The Missouri Harmony* appeared in 1850 and was the work of a trained musician named Charles Warren (b. January 1808; d. November 24, 1884). The tunes remained basically the same, with the biggest change being in harmonization. Several errors found in earlier printings were corrected, the settings being arranged so that the accompanying parts did not rival the tune for melodiousness. This was obviously an attempt on the publisher's part to bring the popular tunebook into line with "proper" scientific taste.

W. K. McNeil

Reference and Further Reading

Carden, Allen D. *The Missouri Harmony, or A Collection of Psalm and Hymn Tunes, and Anthems*, 9th edition. Lincoln: University of Nebraska Press, 1994 (1840).

Krohn, Ernst C. *Missouri Music*. New York: Da Capo, 1971.

MOLLY O'DAY AND LYNN DAVIS

Lois LaVerne Williamson Davis (b. July 9, 1923; d. December 5, 1987)

Leonard "Lynn" Davis (b. December 15, 1914; d. December 18, 2000)

In her time, many people considered Molly O'Day the greatest female country singer. Born Lois Laverne "Dixie Lee" Williamson and reared in Pike County, Kentucky, she learned to play guitar and sing while brother Cecil "Skeets" played fiddle and brother Duke played the banjo. She emulated the popular radio singers of the day, such as Lulubelle Wiseman and Lily May Ledford.

In 1939, Skeets and Dixie (as she called herself then) went to Charleston, West Virginia, where they played on WCHS radio. Later, she worked at WHIS in Bluefield, West Virginia, where she met and in April 1941 married Lynn Davis, a native of Floyd County, Kentucky, and they became a team. During the next several years, they worked at WJLS in Beckley, West Virginia, at WAPI in Birmingham, Alabama, at WHAS in Louisville, Kentucky (where she took the new stage name of Molly O'Day in 1942), and at KRLD in Dallas, Texas. In mid-1945, they moved to WNOX in Knoxville, Tennessee, where they attained their highest popularity. During those years their repertoire was a mixture of sacred and secular songs, as well as solos featuring Molly and harmony duets.

The following year, Fred Rose signed the pair to a Columbia contract, where Molly's recording of "Tramp on the Street" became very popular. Many of her other sacred songs also earned her wide recognition, such as "Matthew Twenty-Four," "Coming Down from God," "When God Comes and Gathers His Jewels," and "Don't Forget the Family Prayer." In 1947, Molly and Lynn left radio for a time, but they later worked for brief periods at WBIG in Greensboro, North Carolina, WROL in Knoxville, and WVLK in Versailles, Kentucky.

According to Molly's own account, every time she heard one of her own gospel songs on radio, she "sang herself under conviction" and finally yielded and surrendered to God in February 1950, as did Lynn. Thereafter, they only did evangelistic work for the Church of God (Cleveland, Tennessee), and they fulfilled their Columbia contract by doing only sacred material, such as "If You See My Savior," "It's Different Now," "Traveling the Highway Home," and the temperance ballad "Don't Sell Daddy Anymore Whiskey." During the 1960s, they made two gospel albums, *Molly O'Day Sings Again* for REM and *The Heart and Soul of Molly O'Day* for GRS (both currently on CD from Old Homestead).

In 1973, Molly and Lynn initiated a gospel record radio show, *Hymns from the Hills,* from their home and broadcast through WEMM in Huntington, West Virginia. The program, which always began with Molly's rendition of "Living the Right Life Now," became quite popular with gospel music fans and won them much favor throughout the area, including adjacent parts of Ohio and Kentucky. Plagued with ill health during her later years, Molly "went home to be with the Lord" in 1987. Lynn continued the program by himself until the day of his own death.

Abby Gail Goodnite-Ehman

Reference and Further Reading

Goodnite, Abby Gail; Ivan M. Tribe. "Lynn Davis & Molly O'Day: 'Living the Right Life Now.'" In *Mountains of Music: West Virginia Traditional Music from Goldenseal,* edited by John Lilly, 188–195. Urbana: University of Illinois Press, 1999.

Selected Discography

Molly O'Day & the Cumberland Mountain Folks (1992, Bear Family BCD 15565; complete Columbia recordings).

The Soul of Molly O'Day Vol. 1 (1998, Old Homestead OH CD 312).

The Soul of Molly O'Day Vol. 2 (1998, Old Homestead OH CD 313).

MONROE, BILL

(b. September 13, 1911, Jerusalem Ridge, KY; d. September 9, 1996, Springfield, TN)

Known as the "Father of Bluegrass," Monroe influenced more bluegrass musicians than any other musician of his generation. He fashioned the plaintive high lonesome sound for which he and his groups became famous. Monroe invented a style—a five-piece string band playing rapidly and with precision—that gave bluegrass its distinctive style and that others have forever tried to imitate. The word "bluegrass," in fact, comes from the name of his first group, the Blue Grass Boys. He fronted several groups during his career, and many well-known bluegrass musicians began their careers in one of Monroe's bands and went on to fame. Among the most notable are Lester Flatt, Earl Scruggs, and Vassar Clements.

Born on a farm in western Kentucky, Monroe was the youngest of six children. His father owned 655 acres on which he cut timber, grew crops, and mined coal. Each member of the family pitched in to help with the mining and farming. As a respite from their work, his parents would play music and dance. His father was an excellent dancer, and his mother played harmonica, button accordion, and fiddle. Monroe's uncle was a fine fiddle player and often played at dances in their community. Monroe's brothers and sisters each excelled at certain instruments. His brother Birch played the fiddle, and brother Charlie and sister Bertha played the guitar. Although Monroe wanted to learn the fiddle or guitar, his brothers and sisters vetoed him and assigned him the mandolin instead. They instructed him to play on only four of the eight strings so that he would not make such noise in the family band.

Monroe's poor vision prevented him from playing the baseball that he so loved with his friends. This disability, combined with his place in the family band, gave Monroe the drive he needed to become the most accomplished mandolin player he could be. When Monroe was sixteen, his father died (his mother had died six years earlier); he went to live with his Uncle Pen, a fiddler, and he soon accompanied his uncle at local dances, playing the guitar. A local blues musician, Arnold Schultz, influenced Monroe during these years.

In 1929, when he was almost eighteen, Monroe left western Kentucky to join his brothers in East Chicago, Indiana, where he worked with them in the Sinclair Oil refinery. He worked there through most of the depression, even supporting them when his brother Charlie was fired from the job. Although he once complained that all he got out of his hard work was a mandolin and a couple of suits of clothes, he never forsook his job because it would not have been right not to support his family.

The brothers kept playing music as they had at home. For a few years, Charlie, Birch, and Bill played dances and then for four or five months played on WAE in Hammond, Indiana. They soon started doing a weekly show on WJKS in Gary, Indiana. Their big break came when an owner of a square dance team from the *National Barn Dance* discovered them playing at a dance in Hammond. Playing at the *National Barn Dance* gave the brothers an opportunity to play for a large national crowd, as the *Dance* was broadcast on WLS in Chicago, the most powerful radio station at the time. The brothers played on the *National Barn Dance* between 1932 and 1934.

In 1934, Texas Crystals, a laxative company, offered to sponsor Charlie on a program in Iowa. Charlie did not want to perform alone, so he took Bill with him, and the Monroe Brothers were born. The Monroe Brothers played a variety of hillbilly standards as well as a number of hymns. When the Monroe Brothers were transferred to another station in Omaha, they took a former announcer, Byron Parker, into their act. Parker, who had been singing gospel hymns, sang bass on the Brothers' songs. In 1935, Bill and Charlie left for Columbia, South Carolina, where they worked on WIS and went out to stations in the Appalachians. They moved from Columbia to WBT in Charlotte, North Carolina, where they broadcast from their own *Tennessee Dance Barn*.

In 1936, the Monroe Brothers participated in their first recording session for RCA Victor's Bluebird label, producing their first record, "What Would You Give in Exchange?" In April 1936, RCA declared the Monroe Brothers' version of the gospel standard "This World Is Not My Home" to be a "Great Country Hill Hit." Many of their songs were religious, and their versions of several songs became the standard versions of them: "My Long Journey Home," "Roll in My Sweet Baby's Arms," "He Will Set Your Fields on Fire."

The Monroe Brothers broke up in 1938, and Bill started perfecting the style of music for which he and his groups were to become known. Bill first formed the short-lived Kentuckians in Little Rock, and he then moved to Atlanta, where he formed the Blue Grass Boys. In October 1939, Monroe appeared on the Grand Ole Opry, where he sang "New Muleskinner Blues," the song that secured his reputation for his plaintive voice and fast-driving mandolin playing. Many music historians declare this moment to be the beginning of bluegrass music.

Lester Flatt and Earl Scruggs (most famous for their theme song for *The Beverly Hillbillies* television show) joined the band in the mid-1940s, but they left by the late 1940s to develop their own style. Although Monroe and his group flourished during the 1940s, the competition for an audience heated up when a number of imitators—most notably the Stanley Brothers—appeared on the scene.

In 1951, Monroe opened a country music park in Bean Blossom, Indiana, where the Bill Monroe Bean Blossom is still an annual tradition. An automobile accident in 1953 kept him off the stage for several months, but he was soon back on the road touring in his ruthless fashion. Monroe released his first album, *Knee Deep in Bluegrass*, in 1958, and Elvis Presley performed a rocking arrangement of Monroe's "Blue Moon of Kentucky" on the Grand Ole Opry. Monroe spent much of the 1950s competing with a number of imitators, including his legendary feud with Flatt and Scruggs. The folk revival of the 1960s brought Monroe back to the spotlight.

Monroe was inducted into the Country Music Hall of Fame in 1970 and into the Nashville Songwriters Association International Hall of Fame in 1971. For many years, he introduced and presided over a weekly segment of the Grand Ole Opry. He was diagnosed with cancer in 1981 and underwent coronary bypass surgery in 1991. With his usual stubbornness, he recovered from these ailments and continued to tour and host the Opry. He received a Lifetime Achievement Award from the Grammys in 1993. In 1996, he suffered a stroke and died a few days later.

HENRY L. CARRIGAN, JR.

See also Bluegrass; Flatt, Lester, and Earl Scruggs

Reference and Further Reading

Rosenberg. Neil V. *Bluegrass: A History.* Urbana: University of Illinois Press, 1993.
Smith, Richard D. *Can't You Hear Me Callin': The Life of Bill Monroe, The Father of Bluegrass.* Boston: Little, Brown and Co., ca. 2000.

Discography

Bill Monroe and His Blue Grass Boys (1956); *Bluegrass Rambles* (1962); *The Father of Bluegrass Music* (1962); *Songs with the Blue Grass Boys* (1964); *Bluegrass Instrumentals* (1965); *The High, Lonesome Sound* (1966); *Bill Monroe's Greatest Hits* (1968); *A Voice from On High* (1969); *Kentucky Blue Grass* (1970); *Sixteen All-Time Greatest Hits* (1970); *Bill Monroe's Country Music Hall of Fame* (1971); *Bill Monroe's Uncle Pen* (1972); *Bean Blossom* (1973); *The Best of Bill Monroe* (1975); *Bill Monroe and His Blue Grass Boys, Vol. 2, 1950–1972* (1976); *Bill Monroe with Lester Flatt and Earl Scruggs* (1978); *Bean Blossom '79* (1980); *Bluegrass Classics: Radio Shows, 1946–1948* (1980); *The Classic Bluegrass Recordings, Vols. 1 and 2* (1980).

MOORE, REVEREND ARNOLD DWIGHT "GATEMOUTH"

(b. November 8, 1913, Topeka, KS; d. May 19, 2004, Yazoo City, MS)

Blues shouter and gospel personality Gatemouth Moore was a living legend in his hometown of Yazoo City, Mississippi, where a street is named after him. Moore started his secular career in Kansas City in the late 1920s, singing in several jazz and blues bands and itinerant shows, such as Ida Cox's "Darktown Scandals Revue," throughout the 1930s and learning from some of the most popular blues singers of the time, such as Ma Rainey and Bertha "Chippie" Hill.

In the 1930s, Moore made his debut as a gospel singer on WIBW, a radio station in his hometown. Then he joined the Walter Barnes band, miraculously escaping death in the 1940 Natchez Rhythm Club fire. In the 1940s, Moore cut the first two versions of "I Ain't Mad at You Pretty Baby" and "Did You Ever Love a Woman?" for Gilmore's Chez Paree label. In 1945, "Gatemouth" (so nicknamed by a drunk woman in the audience) remade his two warhorses and other titles for National, and two years later he recorded extensively for King.

After temporarily losing his voice during a show while at the top of his success, Moore stopped singing secular songs and devoted himself to sacred music. He worked again as a religious deejay (mostly in Chicago, Birmingham, Alabama, and Memphis) and performer, and he recorded gospel singles for Aristocrat/Chess, Artists, and Coral. Two religious albums by Moore were released by Audio Fidelity (1960) and BluesWay (1973). In the former, Reverend Moore and His Gospel Singers' repertoire is mainly traditional ("Jesus on the Main Line," "Down by the Riverside"), whereas in the latter he adopts a more modern approach to gospel music and recounts the moment he was saved ("The Conversion of Gatemouth Moore").

During the late 1970s and all through the 1980s, Moore tried to reconcile sacred and secular music, recording an R&B album for Blues Spectrum (1977). Reverend Moore was a featured character in the film *Saturday Night, Sunday Morning* (1996), and he appeared in the Bertrand Tavernier–directed feature film *Mississippi Blues* (1986) and the Richard Pierce–directed film *The Road to Memphis* (2003).

LUIGI MONGE

See also King Records

Reference and Further Reading

Lee, Peter; David Nelson. "Bishop Arnold Dwight 'Gatemouth' Moore: From Shoutin' the Blues to Preachin' the Word." *Living Blues* 86 (May/June 1989): 8–19.
Lisle, Andria; Mike Evans. *Waking Up in Memphis*. London: Sanctuary Publishing, 2003.

Discography

Reverend Gatemouth Moore. *After Twenty-One Years* (1973, Bluesway BLS 6704).
Reverend Gatemouth Moore and His Gospel Singers. *Revival!* (1960, Audio Fidelity AFLP 1921).

MOORE, REVEREND JAMES

(b. February 1, 1956, Detroit, MI; d. June 7, 2000, Memphis, TN)

Evangelist James Moore, a contemporary Pentecostal gospel performer, gave his first performance at the age of seven. In 1974, at the James Cleveland Gospel Music Workshop of America (GMWA) held in Chicago, Moore received his professional break by winning the Thurston Frazier Scholarship Award. He recorded his first album, *I Thank You Master,* on Savoy Records and three others: *I'll Be Praying for You* on Luminar-Light Records, *God Can Do Anything* on Secret Records, and *Something Old, Something New* on Sound of Gospel Records. In the fall of 1990, Moore was featured at the John Fitzgerald Kennedy Memorial Stadium in Washington, DC. The Mississippi Mass Choir and the Florida Mass Choir performed.

Moore has produced several *Billboard* gospel hits on Malaco Records in Jackson, Mississippi. The one recorded in March 1991, *Live with the Mississippi Mass Choir,* includes songs such as "Joy," "We Worship Christ the Lord," and "God Will Take Care of You." This album became the number one album on the *Billboard* magazine chart; it received four Stellar Awards, three GMWA Excellence Awards, three Dove nominations, and one Soul Train Award nomination. Moore's other album hits were *Live in Detroit, I Will Trust in the Lord,* and *Live at Jackson State University with the Mississippi Mass Choir.*

Moore credits the Church of God in Christ for his musical success, especially the late Mattie Moss Clark (1924–1994), a gospel songwriter and choir director from Detroit. Moore acknowledged the influence of the late "Crown Prince of Gospel," Reverend James Cleveland (1932–1991); Reverend Richard White, known as "Mr. Clean," from Atlanta; and the late Frank Williams, director of the Mississippi Mass Choir.

Moore was inducted into the International Gospel Music Hall of Fame and Museum (IGMHFM) in Detroit, Michigan, in 1998. Moore sang in his baritone voice "It Ain't Over." He talked about his performances at home in Detroit as a "hotbed" of gospel music and musicians. Moore and David Gough, founder and director of IGMHFM, shared the history of gospel music in Detroit. Blind and on dialysis, Moore encouraged the audience to continue singing God's praises. Moore's legacy will continue to live.

SHERRY SHERROD DuPREE

Reference and Further Reading

DuPree, Sherry Sherrod; Herbert C. DuPree. *African-American Good News (Gospel) Music*. Washington, DC: Middle Atlantic Regional Press, 1993.
International Gospel Music Hall of Fame and Museum website, http://www.gmhf.org (accessed August 28, 2004).
"Reverend James Moore." http://afgen.com/james_moore.html (accessed August 27, 2004).
Shaffer, Nash, Reverend. "Sunday Morning Golden Gospel Radio," Chicago. Interview by Sherry Sherrod DuPree via telephone, May 20, 2004.
Walker, Albertina; Inez Andrews; David Gough. National Association for the Advancement of Colored People (NAACP), Freedom Weekend, Gospel Luncheon, Detroit. Interview by Sherry Sherrod DuPree, April 18, 2003.

MORRIS, HOMER FRANKLIN

(b. March 4, 1875; d. January 25, 1955)

Prolific gospel composer, editor, and music company owner Homer Franklin Morris was born in Draketown, Georgia. Displaying an early interest in music, he began singing at ten years of age, and by sixteen he was teaching. Along the way he studied under A. J. Showalter, J. Henry Showalter, and Dr. J. B. Herbert, among others.

In 1910, he became associated with the Southern Music Plate Company in Atlanta. A few years later he and J. M. Henson formed the Morris–Henson Company and Southern Music Plate Company, Inc., with Morris as president and manager. The company, which had offices in Atlanta, Little Rock, and Oklahoma City, published books for churches and Sunday schools, revivals, and singing conventions. One of the company's songbooks, *Complete Church Hymnal,* sold more than a million copies, and all of their more than fifty songbooks sold well.

According to some accounts, Morris performed on commercial recordings, although the exact date of these is unknown. He also was one of the most prolific gospel song composers, having produced between one thousand and two thousand numbers (sources vary); several of his efforts became popular. His most successful was "Won't It Be Wonderful There," written in collaboration with prolific gospel lyricist James Rowe. According to an obituary in the *Atlanta Constitution,* it sold four million copies.

With his business partner, J. M. Henson, he wrote "Anywhere Is Home." "O Love Divine," "What a Glory Day," "When the Glory Morning Comes," "Love Enough for Me," "Have You Invited Him Back?" "His Love Is Mine," "Over in Glory," and "When My Dreams Come True" were the most popular of his other songs. In 1937, Morris sold his interest in the Morris–Henson Company and moved to Dallas, where he worked for the Stamps–Baxter Music and Printing Company. In 1952 he retired, and three years later, just a few weeks shy of his eightieth birthday, he died in a Dallas hospital. He was buried in Atlanta's Westview Cemetery.

W. K. McNeil

Reference and Further Reading

Baxter, Mrs. J. R. "Ma" (Clarice Howard); Videt Polk. *Gospel Song Writers Biography.* 257–258. Dallas Stamps–Baxter Music & Printing Company, 1971.

"Homer Franklin Morris [obituary]." *Atlanta Journal* (1955).

"Homer Franklin Morris [obituary]." *Atlanta Constitution* (1955).

Knippers, Ottis J. *Who's Who Among Southern Singers and Composers*, 99–100. Hot Springs National Park, Arkansas: Knippers Brothers, 1937.

MORRIS, KENNETH

(b. August 28, 1917, Jamaica, NY; d. February 1, 1989, Chicago, IL)

If he had not been a prolific songwriter and one-half of gospel music's most successful publishing team, Kenneth Morris would still have secured his place in gospel music history for introducing the Hammond organ to the genre and for finding, arranging, and publishing the universally popular song "Just a Closer Walk with Thee."

Kenneth Morris was born on August 28, 1917, in Jamaica, New York, to Ettuila (White) and John Morris. Growing up in the 1920s, Morris's earliest

musical interest was jazz. Although he studied classical music at the Manhattan Conservatory of Music, he also learned to play jazz piano and organized the Kenneth Morris Jazz Band.

The ensemble's big break came when it was invited in 1934 to perform at the Century of Progress Exposition in Chicago. During the fair, Morris became weakened by tuberculosis and was unable to complete his performing responsibilities. Rather than return home, he remained in Chicago to recuperate. Around this time, Charles Henry Pace (1886–1963) exited the Lillian M. Bowles House of Music, leaving proprietor Lillian Bowles (ca. 1884–1949) without an arranger. She learned about Morris's arranging skills and hired him to replace Pace.

In 1937, Morris was invited by Reverend Clarence Cobb (1907–1979) of the Spiritualist First Church of Deliverance to serve as choir director and organist. Two years later, First Church needed a new organ, and Morris persuaded Cobb to purchase the novel Hammond organ because of its versatility of sound. No church had had a Hammond organ prior to this, and people came from everywhere to hear First Church's revolutionary new instrument. The Hammond organ would become the organ of choice for African American churches throughout the country, and it is now one of the most recognized sounds in gospel music.

By the late 1930s, Morris was becoming dissatisfied with his work at Bowles House of Music. At the same time, the business partnership between Thomas A. Dorsey (1899–1993) and Sallie Martin (1896–1988) was unraveling. Reverend Cobb encouraged Martin and Morris to enter into business together and helped finance their new enterprise, the Martin and Morris Music Studio Teaching School.

For more than fifty years, Martin and Morris Music was the largest, most financially successful, and oldest continuously operating gospel music publishing and distribution firm in the United States. The store was located at 43rd Street and Indiana Avenue in Chicago's south side Bronzeville neighborhood. Many a gospel artist—superstar to amateur—made the journey to the store that boasted, "If it's in music, we have it!"

Unlike Dorsey's studio, which published only his songs, or Roberta Martin's studio, which published only material sung by the Roberta Martin Singers, Martin and Morris published the compositions of a variety of well-known and emerging composers, such as Lucie Campbell, W. Herbert Brewster, Alex Bradford, Sam Cooke, James Cleveland, and Dorothy Love Coates. Sallie Martin organized the Sallie Martin Singers to perform the Martin and Morris catalog on the road and on recordings, while Morris managed the store and arranged music. In 1948, Martin moved to the West Coast and established a Martin and Morris outpost there.

During the 1940s, Morris continued to pursue his own songwriting, eventually composing a portfolio of more than three hundred songs. Among them are some of gospel music's best-known works, such as "Christ Is All," "Does Jesus Care," "My God Is Real," and "Jesus Steps Right In." Martin's songs are characterized by a poetic lyricism, expressing the earthly trials and frustrations of the poor and working-class African American while concluding confidently that Jesus will never let His people down.

While "My God Is Real" is arguably Morris's most popular gospel composition, he is best known for arranging and publishing "Just a Closer Walk with Thee" because of its widespread popularity in the sacred and secular (jazz) music arenas. Morris first heard the song performed by a Kansas City choir directed by William R. Hurse. Hurse was unfamiliar with the song's origins, so Morris arranged and presented it at the 1944 National Baptist Convention, where it became an instant hit.

Sallie Martin sold her part of the publishing and distribution business to Morris in 1973. Later, Morris bought out the catalogs of Roberta Martin, Theodore Frye, and former employer Lillian Bowles, becoming one of the last surviving gospel music distributors from gospel's golden age. Morris died in Chicago on February 1, 1989, at age seventy-one. His widow Necie kept the business together until 1993, when the remaining contents of Martin and Morris Music were distributed to the Chicago Public Library and other archives.

ROBERT MAROVICH

See also Martin, Sallie; Pace, Reverend Charles, and the Pace Jubilee Singers

Reference and Further Reading

Boyer, Horace Clarence. *How Sweet The Sound: The Golden Age of Gospel*. Washington, DC: Elliot & Clark Publishing, 1995.
———. "I'll Be a Servant for the Lord." In *We'll Understand It Better By and By: Pioneering African American Gospel Composers*, edited by Bernice Johnson Reagon. Washington, DC: Smithsonian Institution Press, 1992.
———. "Kenneth Morris: Composer and Dean of Black Gospel Music Publishers." In *We'll Understand It Better By and By: Pioneering African American Gospel Composers*, edited by Bernice Johnson Reagon. Washington, DC: Smithsonian Institution Press, 1992.
Reagon, Bernice Johnson. "The Chicago School of Gospel: The Music of Roberta Martin and Kenneth Morris." In *Wade in the Water: African-American Sacred Music Traditions* [26-part radio program]. Broadcast May 26, 1994.

Discography

Morris compositions on recordings are as follows:
"How Sweet It Is." St. Paul Baptist Church Choir of Los Angeles (1948, Capitol 70002).
"Yes! God Is Real." Prof. J. Earle Hines and His Goodwill Singers (1948, Sacred 108).
"Does Jesus Care?" Fairfield Four (1950, Dot 1040).
"Christ is All," Soul Stirrers (1951, Specialty 928).
"Jesus Steps Right In." Famous Davis Sisters (1952, Gotham G736).

MORTON, PAUL

(b. July 30, 1950, Windsor, Ontario, Canada)

Paul Sylvester Morton, Sr. was raised by religious parents. His father, the late Bishop C. L. Morton, noticed that his young son had the gift of singing at around six years of age. "My father used to stand me on a chair, telling me that I was going to sing." Morton's father and Aretha Franklin's father, Reverend C. L. Franklin, were well-known pastors in the 1950s; they hosted the two most popular ministry radio shows in the Detroit area. Morton's favorite passage of scripture was Isaiah 1:17 "Learn to do well . . . ."

In 1972, he moved to New Orleans, Louisiana. He was installed as pastor of the Greater St. Stephen Missionary Baptist Church in 1975. His copastor is his wife Debra B. Morton, and they have four children. Morton began the Full Gospel Baptist Church Fellowship as a movement with the purpose of helping Baptist parishioners operate in the fullness of the Holy Spirit. In 1992, the church's name was changed to Greater St. Stephen Full Gospel Baptist Church. The church has more than twenty thousand members. In 1997, the ministry purchased a decommissioned naval base and renamed it St. Stephen City. This development gives affordable housing to more than seventy-five families.

Morton is president of the Paul S. Morton Bible College and School of Ministry. In 1997 the ministry purchased an office building for its corporate headquarters. Morton has daily radio and weekly television broadcasts. The ministry "spreads the word" with the slogan "Changing a Generation." Morton is the author of several books; some of his best-sellers are *Why Kingdoms Fall* and *It's Time for the Outpouring*. Morton is also a world-renowned singer. In 1999, he released his solo CD entitled *Crescent City Fire*.

Aretha Franklin invited Morton to perform a duet in 2001 at a benefit concert in New Orleans. The song they performed was the gospel version of the hymn entitled "Precious Memories," written by Roberta Martin (1907–1969) and Georgia Jones. The original version of the hymn was written by J. B. F. Wright. Morton is featured on the all-star recording of a tribute to Rosa Parks, *Something Inside So Strong*. For three years Morton was off the music scene. Morton and his church's latest project, *Let It Rain*, are on Morton's new church-based label, Tehillah Music Group.

At the Twentieth Annual Stellar Awards on January 15, 2005, at the George R. Brown Convention Center in Houston, Morton and the Full Gospel Baptist Church Fellowship's Mass Choir of three hundred won in the categories Traditional Male Vocalist of the Year, Music Video of the Year, and Traditional Choir of the Year for *Let It Rain*. Morton and the Full Gospel Baptist Church Fellowship's Mass Choir are 2005 inductees into the International Gospel Music Hall of Fame and Museum in Detroit.

SHERRY SHERROD DUPREE

Reference and Further Reading

"Bishop Paul S. Morton and Aretha Franklin Perform Live!" (New Orleans, LA, April 04, 2001). Gospel City website, http://www.gospelcity.com/dynamic/industry-articles/ industry_news/174 (accessed February 28, 2005).
Bishop Paul S. Morton Ministries website, http://www. paulmorton.org/index.html (accessed February 28, 2005).
International Gospel Music Hall of Fame and Museum website, http://www.gmhf.org (accessed February 28, 2005).
Payne, Wardell J., ed. *Directory of African American Religious Bodies*, 2nd edition. Washington, DC: Howard University Press, 1995.

Discography

Crescent City Fire (2003, Universal IMS CD).
Louisiana State Mass Choir (2004, Light Records CD).

MYRRH RECORDS

Myrrh Records was launched in 1972 as a division of Word Records, under the direction of Billy Ray Hearn. Myrrh Records was one of the driving forces in bringing the emerging contemporary Christian music to prominence, launching the careers of CCM pioneers Randy Matthews, 2nd Chapter of Acts, Honeytree, and Barry McGuire. It also launched the career of superstar Amy Grant, who went on to sell twenty-five million albums.

Billy Ray Hearn was a Texas native who was working as the minister of music at the First Baptist Church in Thomasville, Georgia, when he came to the attention of Word Records. He was hired to help promote musicals that the label was developing because of his work with the popular musical *Good News*.

Once at Word, Hearn saw the increasing potential of blending the message of the gospel with contemporary music. As the driving force creating the new division, Hearn went to work signing Ray Hildebrand and Randy Matthews, who both released albums in 1972. Matthews followed his Myrrh debut, *All I Am Is What You See ... I Pray You See the Truth in Me*, with *Son of Dust* (1973) and *Wish We'd All Been Ready* the following year, with the title song written by Christian music pioneer Larry Norman.

Barry McGuire had experienced popular music success as a member of the New Christy Minstrels and as a solo artist with the radio hit "Eve of Destruction." After his conversion to Christianity, he began to write songs about his newfound faith and signed with Myrrh, releasing the album *Seeds* in 1973. Also that year, Indiana-based folk singer Honeytree signed with the label, releasing a self-titled debut.

Billy Ray Hearn heard about a family trio who took their name from a chapter in the New Testament. The night he went to a small coffee house to hear sisters Annie and Nelly Herring and brother Matthew perform, he was impressed. "There was one piano, Annie played and the three of them singing. I have never been so impressed with music in my life, chills and crying and everything else went all over me and I said, 'I've got to sign this group.'" The 2nd Chapter of Acts 1974 Myrrh debut titled *With Footnotes* included the popular songs "Which Way the Wind Blows" and "Easter Song." Hearn would exit Myrrh in 1976 to start his own Sparrow Records, and 2nd Chapter of Acts and Barry McGuire eventually followed him there.

Other notable releases in the 1970s included the self-titled debut *Petra* by Christian rock band Petra, *In the Volume of the Book* by 2nd Chapter of Acts, *White Horse* by Michael Omartian, *Home Where I Belong* by B. J. Thomas, *God Gave Rock & Roll to You* by Petra, *Behold* by Billy Preston, and the three-album set *How the West Was One* by 2nd Chapter of Acts and Phil Keaggy.

Myrrh discovered their most commercially successful artist when they signed Nashville teenager Amy Grant. Her albums released in the late 1970s were well received, but her major breakthrough came with her 1982 album *Age to Age*. Within a year it sold five hundred thousand copies, earning Grant her first of many gold albums and becoming Word's fastest seller. Grant was named Artist of the Year in 1983 by the Gospel Music Association, and "El Shaddai" (written by Michael Card and John Thompson) earned a Dove Award as Song of the

Year. Within two years, the album passed the one million sales mark, earning Grant and Myrrh their first platinum album award.

Grant continued her dominance in the 1980s with six additional albums receiving gold or platinum certification by the Recording Industry Association of America. Myrrh took an interesting marketing approach with her 1985 *Unguarded* album by issuing four different album covers for the release, with different poses of Amy Grant in a leopard print jacket. Within a year, the album sold more than one million copies.

Myrrh Records signed CCM pioneer Randy Stonehill in the 1980s, releasing *Between the Glory and the Flame.* The label also released *Seasons of Change* by Richie Furay, who came to fame as a member of the seminal country rock groups Buffalo Springfield and Poco. Other noteworthy albums were issued by Myrrh in the 1980s and 1990s by Bruce Cockburn,

Cliff Richards, Don Francisco, the Imperials, Joe English, Russ Taff, Benny Hester, Leon Patillo, Phil Keaggy, John Fisher, and Carman. Word discontinued the Myrrh label in 2000, moving the current roster to the Word label.

JAMES I. ELLIOTT

See also Grant, Amy; Hearn, Billy Ray

Reference and Further Reading

Callahan, Mike; David Edwards; Patrice Eyries. "Myrrh Album Discography." Both Sides Now Publications website, http://www.bsnpubs.com/word/myrrh.html.

Collins, Dan. *First Love, Vol. 1.* Video, NewPort Records, 1998.

Cusic, Don. *The Sound of Light: A History of Gospel Music.* Bowling Green, OH: Bowling Green State University Popular Press, 1990.

Recording Industry Association of America website, http://www.riaa.com/gp/database/.

N

NASHBORO RECORDS

Nashville's *Other* Sound

During the great boom of indie labels in the years following World War II, one of gospel's most enduring—and endearing—underdogs began in a record store in Nashville. Ernie's Record Mart had generated a bustling business for years through its sponsorship of *Ernie's Record Parade,* hosted by the legendary deejay John R. (Richbourg) on WLAC and by heavily advertising records to rural America on the great clear-channel stations of Memphis and Nashville.

In 1951, Ernie Lafayette Young (b. December 2, 1892; d. June 8, 1977), who was white, had a revelation. Instead of serving as the middleman for this steady market for gospel and R&B product, why not *create* it—and preserve a greater share of the profits for himself? The same year that his fiercest competitor—Randy Wood of Randy Record Store—started Dot Records, Young founded the gospel label Nashboro. A year later, Young created Excello Records, which featured rockabilly, R&B, swamp rock, blues, and country—in every weird combination imaginable.

Because his advertising was focused on the South, Nashboro quickly became known for its thriving roster of Southern-oriented gospel artists: Brother Joe May, the Consolers, the Fairfield Four, the Dixie Nightingales, the Swanee Quintet, a seventeen-year-old Candi Staton, and others. Later, when some of this gospel competitors began failing in the 1960s, Young added their artists, including the Angelic Gospel Singers.

Like Excello, Nashboro releases generally featured sparse instrumentation, tiny budgets, and often generic album covers. But the artists and their producers were given great leeway in the studio, often producing achingly honest, refreshingly raw performances, sometimes produced by stellar backing musicians, including the Muscle Shoals rhythm section.

In 1966, Young sold Excello, which enjoyed several regional and R&B chart hits, usually by Slim Harpo and almost always recorded in Louisiana producer Jay Miller's funky Crowley studio. Though Young died in 1977, the publishing and marketing empire he created continued.

By the 1970s, Nashboro was issuing fewer and fewer new releases, instead repackaging or simply reprinting gospel albums from its deep vaults. In time, even the reissues dried to a trickle. The label was sold to AVI Entertainment Group in 1994, which announced plans to remaster and rerelease the best of Nashboro's catalog, beginning with the Fairfield Four's *Standing on the Rock* and two compilations, *The Best of Nashboro Gospel* and *It's Jesus, Y'all.*

But AVI eventually only released a few CDs and sold the catalog to MCA/Universal. MCA/Universal had also recently completed the purchase of the long-dormant Peacock, Chess, ABC, and Decca labels, and it too announced an ambitious reissue release schedule. By the year 2000, a sluggish economy had slowed the release schedule for MCA/Universal as well. Eventually, MCA/Universal assigned release rights to the Hip-O label, which has concentrated on Excello reissues, with the occasional Nashboro release. A more vigorous release schedule has since been maintained by the Ace label in the United Kingdom.

ROBERT DARDEN

See also Angelic Gospel Singers; Consolers; Fairfield Four; May, Joseph "Brother Joe"; Swanee Quintet

Reference and Further Reading

Collins, Deborah. "Black Music Month. Gospel Catalog: A Wealth of Reissued Oldies Testifies to the Market's Enduring Value." *Billboard* (June 7, 2003): 27.

Evans, Deborah Price. "MCA Bows Peacock Imprint for Gospel Releases." *Billboard* (October 3, 1998): 18.

Floyd, John. "Southern Fried Soul." *Miami News Times* (July 15, 1999): Music, 1.

George, Nelson. *The Death of Rhythm & Blues.* New York: Pantheon Books, 1988.

Heilbut, Anthony. *The Gospel Sound: Good News and Bad Times.* New York: Limelight Editions, 1997.

Meyerowitz, Robert. "The Good Foot: A Survey of Recent Blues, Soul, R&B, and Roots Releases." *Phoenix New Times* (October 10, 1996): Music, 1.

Reynolds, R. J. "AVI Expands into Reissue Biz with Nashboro, Excello Titles." *Billboard* (December 10, 1994): 18.

Smith, Wes. *Pied Pipers of Rock 'n' Roll.* Athens, GA: Longstreet Press, 1989.

Discography

Compilations. *The Best of Excello Gospel* (Ace); *The Best of Nashboro Gospel* (Nashboro); *The Excello Story* (Hip-O); *The Heart of Southern Soul: From Nashville to Memphis to Muscle Shoals Vol. 1* (Nashboro/Excello); *The Heart of Southern Soul: From Nashville to Memphis to Muscle Shoals Vol. 2* (Nashboro/Excello); *It's Jesus, Y'all* (Nashboro).

The Consolers. *The Best of the Consolers* (Nashboro).

The Fairfield Four. *Standing on the Rock* (Nashboro).

Willie Neal Johnson. *The Best of Willie Neal Johnson* (Nashboro).

The Savannah Community Choir. *Alive Forever* (Nashboro).

NATIONAL BAPTIST CONVENTION

The National Baptist Convention, USA, Inc., was founded in 1895 through the merger of the Baptist Foreign Mission Convention, the American National Baptist Convention, and the Baptist National Educational Convention. The Reverend E. C. Morris was elected the first president of the convention and served in that capacity for twenty-seven years.

Shortly thereafter, the National Baptist Publishing Board (NBPB) was founded in Nashville, Tennessee, with the Reverend Richard Henry Boyd as corresponding secretary, so that black churches could publish their own religious educational materials. The convention organized the Baptist Young People's Union (BYPU) in 1899, and the following year they formed the Women's National Auxiliary Convention and established an alliance with the Southern Baptist Convention for home mission work.

In 1897, a group of National Baptist pastors left to form the Lott Carey Foreign Mission Convention over concerns regarding the complete break from the use of literature by the white American Baptist Publication Society as well as the move of the Foreign Mission Board's headquarters from Richmond, Virginia, to Louisville, Kentucky. Later, under Dr. Boyd, the Home Mission Board and the NBPB split from the convention in 1915.

By 1916, Lucie E. Campbell had been named as music director of the National Baptist Convention's Sunday school and BYPU, where she organized thousand-voice choirs to sing at the annual conventions and wrote songs, elaborate musicals, and pageants. She served on the selection committee for the convention's series of new hymnbooks and songbooks, including *Golden Gems, Inspirational Melodies, Spirituals Triumphant,* and *Gospel Pearls,* all of which include her compositions. The songs she penned for the National Convention were copyrighted and dedicated to the National BYPU Board until the late 1930s and early 1940s, when she began copyrighting songs in her own name.

The August 1930 National Baptist Convention in Chicago launched the gospel career of Thomas A. Dorsey. His song "If You See My Savior" was performed at the morning session of the annual meeting and was an immediate hit, selling four thousand copies at the convention alone. Also, at the 1943 Baptist National Convention, the Consecrated Gospel Singers sang four songs, including Dorsey's "If We Never Needed the Lord Before." They created a sensation at the convention, thus enabling them to move from semipro to professional singers, touring the country.

During Joseph H. Jackson's tenure as president from 1953 to 1982, he purchased the National Baptist Freedom Farm and set up an unrestricted scholarship at Roosevelt University. Under his reign, a third split occurred in the convention over the issues of tenure and the lack of support of the Civil Rights Movement.

Currently, the National Baptist Convention represents the nation's oldest and largest African American religious convention, with an estimated membership of seven and a half million. A board of directors, led by a president who is elected by the member churches every five years, governs the convention. To date, there are sixty-two state Baptist conventions, and 341 district associations have registered with the convention. Both the state Baptist conventions and the district associations are autonomous organizations, supported by the voluntary membership of churches and individuals. In addition, there are ten recognized auxiliaries/subsidiary bodies that work with the convention.

BECKY GARRISON

See also Campbell, Lucie; Dorsey, Thomas; Gospel Music Association

Reference and Further Reading

Darden, Robert. *People Get Ready*. New York: Continuum Publishing Company, 2004.

National Baptist Convention website, http://www.national-baptist.com.

Reagon, Bernice Johnson. *We'll Understand it Better By and By: Pioneering African American Gospel Composers*. Washington, DC: Smithsonian Institution Press, 1992.

NATIONAL BARN DANCE, THE

The most important of the radio barn dances during the first half of the twentieth century was the *National Barn Dance*, broadcast out of WLS in Chicago. When the show started in April 1924, it was called the *WLS Barn Dance*, but the name was later expanded to the *WLS National Barn Dance*. WLS was an abbreviation of "World's Largest Store," a reference to Sears Roebuck, owner of the station.

The program was designed to attract rural audiences, with a variety of music that they would likely find appealing. Thus, featured performers were as varied as pioneer recording artist Henry Burr, banjo player Chubby Parker, harmonica soloist Walter Peterson, singer Grace Wilson, the blind vocal duo of Mac and Bob (Lester McFarland and Robert Gardner), yodeler Swiss Miss Christine (Holden), singing cowboy Gene Autry, and ballad singer Bradley Kincaid, the program's first real star.

Initially, shows were conducted in front of live audiences in a theater in the Sherman Hotel that seated only a hundred. In March 1932 the program moved to the twelve-thousand–seat Eighth Street Theater, where it remained for the next twenty-five years. During this period, the NBC network started carrying a half hour of the program. By the late 1940s, the program had lost some of its prestige but was still important enough to be one of the first country music shows on television. For thirty-nine weeks in 1949, the ABC-TV network carried a half hour of the show. Not even the loss of its Eighth Street Theater in 1957 ended the program. It lingered on until March 1960, when WLS changed formats; the show then went into television syndication, finally ending in 1969.

Straight gospel acts were a rarity on the *Barn Dance*, although WLS used elsewhere on the station the Little Brown Church Quartet, Bill O'Connor, and Adele Brandt, among others. Furthermore, many performers included some religious numbers in their repertoire. Hymns were, in fact, among the favorite songs performed by Mac and Bob. Clyde Julian "Red" Foley later became known as much for his gospel material as for his secular items. In 1950, he scored big on country charts with "Just a Closer Walk with Thee," and his 1951 waxing of Thomas Dorsey's "Peace in the Valley" became the first million-selling gospel record. Even balladeer Bradley Kincaid occasionally performed such numbers as "How Beautiful Heaven Must Be" and "Beautiful Isle of Somewhere."

More involved in gospel were such acts as Gene (Carroll) and Glenn (Rowell), who performed such self-penned items as "Next Door to Jesus," "Market Day," "What's the Difference Brother?" "Tune Jesus In to Your Heart," and "If You Will Work for Jesus" and such semireligious poems as "My Mother's Bible." On the *National Barn Dance*, gospel was seen as only one of many parts essential to the program's goal of appealing to rural audiences.

W. K. MCNEIL

Reference and Further Reading

Evans, James F. *Prairie Farmer and WLS: The Burridge D. Butler Years*. Urbana, University of Illinois Press, 1969.

Gene and Glenn. *Our Songs and Poems*. New York: 1937.

Jones, Loyal. *Radio's "Kentucky Mountain Boy," Bradley Kincaid*. Berea, KY: Appalachian Center: Berea College, 1988 (1980).

WLS Family Albums. Chicago: WLS, 1930–1957.

Discography

Saturday Night at the Old Barn Dance (ca. 1965, Kapp).

NATIONAL CONVENTION OF GOSPEL CHOIRS AND CHORUSES

Formed on August 17, 1932, the Gospel Choral Union at Pilgrim Baptist Church in Chicago, Illinois, was the first of a series of burgeoning gospel music unions developing around the country. Thomas Andrew Dorsey was elected the union's first president. As he traveled throughout the United States and gospel music began to spread in popularity, the need to organize emergent unions into a single organization became apparent. The following year, on August 30, 1933, the National Convention of Gospel Choirs and Choruses and Smaller Musical Groups, Inc., was born at Pilgrim Baptist Church. This was the first annual session of the convention, and the aggregation was the first of its kind anywhere.

Five gospel music personalities were involved in its formation: Professor Dorsey, Theodore Frye, Magnolia Butts, Sallie Martin, and Henry J. Carruthers. The mission of the convention was to benefit the Christian singer, instrumentalist, and music educator or leader in the following areas: growth, enablement, and motivation toward excellence in all areas of Christian music. Further, members were expected to live the Christian life.

Each year, new developments for the benefit of the convention and its membership were instituted. Bylaws were adopted, and Professor Thomas Dorsey was elected president of the convention during its 1933 session. A year later at its St. Louis convention, an advisory board was created, and Dorsey Day was instituted. Magnolia Butts, one of the convention co-organizers, established the convention's Scholarship Department in 1935, and the following year, in 1936, Professor Butts instituted artists' night.

Worship continued to have an emphasis in the convention's annual program. The Indianapolis convention held its first vesper service, led by Dr. Theodore Frye, in 1937. A consecration service by Magnolia Butts followed in 1938 at the Dayton convention. The 1939 convention was hosted in East St. Louis, Illinois. That year, the Youth Department was established and staffed by Theodore Frye, Ruth Hutchins, and Roberta Martin, who worked with young people such as Della Reese, Dinah Washington, and Aretha Franklin. Willa Mae Ford founded the Soloist Council, the name of which was later changed to the Soloist Bureau, which featured Mahalia Jackson, Delores Barrett, the O'Neal Twins, Joe May, and Geneva Gentry.

The 1950 Cincinnati convention instituted the Leadership Training School (Artelia Hutchins, founder). In 1956, James Cleveland and the O'Neal Twins became Youth Department directors. At the 1971 convention in Los Angeles, arrangements were made to open a home for singers, which was purchased and built in Chicago. No area of the United States was excluded in hosting annual conventions through the decades. Because of Professor Dorsey's illness, Joshua Gentry assumed the presidency at the 1983 convention in Orlando, Florida, and *Say Amen, Somebody* was recorded there. In 1990, Joshua Gentry died, and Reverend Kenneth Moales became interim president, becoming president in 1993.

Training through the National Convention's departments encompasses all ages and interest levels. The Carol E. Hays Pre-Teen Department trains youths between the ages of three and twelve to direct a choir, sing solos, and present a play featuring their talents. The Youth and Young Adult Department, for ages thirteen through sixteen, trains and encourages young songwriters, directors, musicians, and vocalists to glorify God with their talents. The department awards trophies for Song of the Year and Director of the Year and renders an evening concert of original compositions. The Supervisor's Guild and Soloist Bureau further encourage and challenge members toward excellence in character and use of their gifts. The Alumni Chorale, for ages twenty-six through fifty, continues to stimulate and train members of the convention's parent body. The Heritage Voices are for the seasoned and senior members who want to sing Dr. Dorsey's music exclusively, and the Thomas A. Dorsey Mass Choir represents all segments of the National Convention in a grand finale concert. Finally, the Artelia Hutchins Training Institute is the academic arm of the convention, with course offerings in piano, organ, and various phases of gospel music and music ministry.

The National Convention of Gospel Choirs and Choruses now has forty-eight unions that are divided into regions across the United States. It continues its goal "to foster an appreciation of gospel music and to develop the spiritual growth of our membership." Among its distinguished alumni are James Cleveland, Hezekiah Walker, Donald Lawrence, and Eddie Robinson, to name a few.

EVELYN M. E. TAYLOR

See also Cleveland, James; Dorsey, Thomas; Frye, Theodore R.; Gospel Choirs; O'Neal Twins; Smith, Willie Mae Ford

Reference and Further Reading

Boone, Dan S. National Chairman of Finance, NCG CC. Interview and email correspondence, January 7 and 24, 2005.

National Convention of Gospel Choirs and Choruses website, http://www.ncgcc.org.

NATIONAL GUITARS (NATIONAL MUSIC COMPANY)

The metal-bodied National guitar has achieved an iconic status in guitar circles. In addition to the highly finished metal construction (the source of Paul Simon's evocative simile "The Mississippi Delta was shining/Like a National guitar" in his song "Graceland," 1986), the instrument differs from a conventional acoustic guitar by employing a resonator system rather than the hollow body of the instrument to generate sound. Because the body itself was not required to produce volume, that also meant that the instrument could be physically smaller than a conventional guitar. It was designed to allow a much greater level of volume than was possible with an unamplified acoustic guitar, a function which was rendered partly redundant by the development of the electric guitar in the 1930s.

The history of the company that made the instruments is complex, and some details remain in dispute. It began when George Beauchamp, a Vaudeville performer, approached John Dopyera to build a guitar with an added horn-like device for amplification (something similar had been achieved with a violin). The prototype was little more than a novelty, and Beauchamp quickly abandoned it, but Dopyera then came up with the idea of his first resonator guitar and applied for a patent in 1927.

The resonator guitar works by mounting the bridge of the instrument directly to a conical resonator. The first model designed by Dopyera used three of these cones (tricone) connected by a metal T-bar in a metal body shell. They set up the National String Instrument Company in Los Angeles in early 1928 to begin manufacture, with Beauchamp as general manager and Dopyera as factory superintendent (the National brand name was initially registered and used on banjos made by Dopyera and his five brothers). The body of the instrument was made from an alloy of copper, zinc, and nickel known as "German silver" or "nickel silver." Beauchamp favored a single cone version of the instrument. The tricone had a mellower sound and was the favored model for the professional market, but the single was louder and could be made more cheaply.

The two principals quarreled when Beauchamp applied for his own patent for the single cone. Dopyera resigned in February 1929 and set up the rival Dobro Manufacturing Company with some of his brothers, making guitars built on a single cone resonator principle but using a wooden body rather than metal. Louis Dopyera gained control of National in 1932, and the two companies merged as National–Dobro and relocated to Chicago in 1936. They continued manufacturing instruments in a wide range of models until 1941, in both single-cone and tricone versions. In addition to the various versions of their guitars, the company also manufactured mandolins, ukuleles, a four-string tenor guitar, a Hawaiian guitar, and other models.

The company was incorporated as Valco in 1942 and continued to manufacture guitars under many brand names until the mid-1960s, but the focus had shifted to electric rather than resonator instruments under the National brand name, and instruments of the 1928 to 1941 era became valuable items. Manufacture of National resonator guitars resumed when Don Young and MacGregor Gaines, two former employees of the Original Musical Instrument Company (formed in 1967), formed National Reso-Phonic Guitars in San Luis Obispo, California, in 1988. The company continues to manufacture a range of metal-bodied resonator instruments.

The instrument found niches in several musical genres, notably blues and Hawaiian music, whereas the Dobro was taken up in country music. During the initial heyday of the guitar (roughly from 1928 until the mid-1930s), it produced an unrivaled level of volume ideal for performances in noisy tents and juke joints, advantages that would have been equally pertinent in noisy revival meetings or church services, where guitar was already well established as an accompanying instrument in gospel music.

One of the earliest major proponents of the National guitar was blues player Tampa Red, who formed a duet with Georgia Tom Dorsey, subsequently better know as gospel artist Thomas A. Dorsey. They made a substantial number of recordings under such names as Tampa Red's Hokum Jug Band and the Hokum Boys before Dorsey gave up secular music in 1932. Other major exponents of the instrument include Reverend Gary Davis, who recorded with a National guitar in the 1930s, Son House, Bukka White, Bo Carter, and Blind Boy Fuller. Bob Brozman is a leading contemporary practitioner on the instrument and is the author of a highly regarded book on the subject, *The History and Artistry of National Resonator Instruments*.

KENNY MATHIESON

Reference and Further Reading

Brozman, Bob. *The History and Artistry of National Resonator Instruments.* Fullerton, CA: Centerstream Publishing, 1993.

Gruhn, George; Walker Carter. *Acoustic Guitars and Other Fretted Instruments: A Photographic History.* San Francisco: Miller Freeman, 1993.

Handa, Al. "The National Steel Guitar Series." 1998. National Steel Guitar website, http://www.nationalguitars.com/history.html.

NATIONAL QUARTET CONVENTION

The National Quartet Convention was first held in Memphis in 1957. J. D. Sumner had the idea to bring together all of the professional quartets in gospel music for a convention full of singing and fellowship. J. D. had considered this venture for several years before he was able to convince James Blackwood and the Blackwood Brothers to underwrite the convention. He envisioned a homecoming atmosphere

273

where all of those who blazed the quartet trails could gather for a few nights of fun.

The first two National Quartet Conventions were held in Memphis, Tennessee. This was the home of the Blackwood Brothers and offered a central location for the gospel singing faithful. Ellis Auditorium was the chosen venue, offering a great facility for the convention. Ellis Auditorium was no stranger to gospel music, for the Blackwood Brothers promoted many concerts in that auditorium.

The first convention was a two-day event featuring a talent contest in the afternoon and singing by all the major gospel groups in the evening. The Blackwood Brothers were the consummate hosts for the event, and it was a rousing success. Through the years, the National Quartet Convention was the chosen place to honor gospel singers of the past and to propel the careers of gospel singers of the future.

Memphis hosted the convention for two years, and then it was decided to try other gospel music hotbeds around the South. The National Quartet Convention moved to Birmingham, Alabama, in 1959 and to Atlanta, Georgia, in 1960. The results of the move were not successful, so by 1961 it was back in its original home in Memphis.

There is a current misconception that the early conventions featured only male quartets. Most of the performers were indeed quartets, but that was the makeup of gospel music during the infancy of the National Quartet Convention. In fact, the early conventions featured soloists, trios, and mixed groups in addition to the stereotypical male quartet. Performers who did not fit this mold included the Speer Family, the Chuck Wagon Gang, Sons of Song, Big Jim Waits, and the Johnson Sisters.

The National Quartet Convention was relocated to Nashville, Tennessee, in 1971. Nashville was becoming a more central location for the music business, and the facilities in Nashville were better for handling the large number of people who were attending. Soon, the National Quartet Convention became a place for making contacts, selling product, and booking dates. Professional and semiprofessional quartets would often fill their entire date books at the National Quartet Convention.

It has often been said that the National Quartet Convention was the finest thing that ever happened to the gospel music industry. Quartets that appeared on the main stage of the convention became "in the loop," so to speak, and gained prestige throughout the industry. Their bookings increased, their fee schedules rose, and their chance at major recording contracts increased significantly. Many fledgling groups received their first major break from the stage of the National Quartet Convention.

Through the years, the National Quartet Convention has grown from a two-day event to a week-long gathering of fans, promoters, and musicians. The convention moved from its longtime home in Nashville to Louisville, Kentucky, in 1994. Freedom Hall has a seating capacity of more than twenty thousand. The increased capacity was necessary to handle the influx of crowds to this gathering of faithful gospel music followers. J. D. Sumner ran it single-handedly for several years before eventually selling it to *Singing News* owner and concert promoter J. G. Whitfield. Whitfield sold the ownership in 1982 to eight men who became the board of directors.

Although the ownership in the National Quartet Convention has changed through the years, it remains the most anticipated yearly event in gospel music. Currently, the exhibit hall is nearly as busy as the auditorium. Groups, both professional and amateur, showcase their wares in the spacious exhibit hall. All types of gospel-music–related memorabilia are available to the fans. As the convention has grown, so too has the number of groups desiring to appear on the program. Afternoon "showcases" have been the norm in recent years, giving a place for groups that have not been granted a time slot on the main stage to appear. Currently, the National Quartet Convention is run much differently than it was during the days when J. D. Sumner ruled with an iron fist. There is a board of directors that determines which groups will appear on the evening program and the time allotted to those groups; they have some difficult decisions to make.

When J. D. Sumner first had the idea for the National Quartet Convention, little did he know the ramifications it would have throughout the world of gospel music. The National Quartet Convention has grown by leaps and bounds, affecting the livelihood of many of the groups that sing gospel music. It continues to be a stellar event in gospel music.

JOHN CRENSHAW

Reference and Further Reading

Goff, James R., Jr. *Close Harmony: A History of Southern Gospel*, 173–174. Chapel Hill: University of North Carolina Press, 2002.

Special Convention Issue. *Gospel Singing World* 4, no. 10 (October 1957).

Terrell, Bob, *The Music Men: The Story of Professional Gospel Quartet Singing*, 161–164. Alexander, NC: Mountain Church, 2000.

NEW YORK, GOSPEL IN

The term "gospel" was not commonly used in New York until the 1940s, but its musical and social precursors had a firm presence in the city for several decades before that. Although New York's black population dated back to the 1700s, it was the mass arrival of Southern black migrants before World War I that brought the musical and spiritual tenets of gospel performance to the city. Attempting to escape economic hardship and brutal racial oppression, migrants settled in and expanded New York's preexisting black enclaves in Harlem, the Bronx, and Queens. Already deprived and overcrowded, these were filled to a bursting point, offering conditions often little better than those in the South.

New York's first independent black church, the African Methodist Episcopal Church, was founded by ex-slave Peter Williams in 1876. Despite this, New York's black population retained the restrained, static, and noninteractive approach to worship that characterized white services. This was reflected in their musical activities. Jubilee quartets and choirs were the most common form of black religious music in the decades before and after the turn of the century. These groups performed a range of repertoire from popular songs through spirituals to jubilee songs. Their style emphasized close harmony, smooth timbres, and precise delivery, unspoiled by excessive physical movement. As such, they appealed to both the black and white middle classes. The importance of the jubilee or spiritual quartets is indicated by the presence of sixty-three groups performing and competing at a momentous festival of black music held in New York in 1894.

With the arrival of large swathes of Southern migrants, New York's independent black churches were unable to satisfy the sheer numbers of newcomers, and most Southerners were Pentecostal or Holiness, whereas the native New Yorkers were Methodist and Baptist. Further, due to the far more segregated nature of the South, the migrants had retained their affinity with African modes of worship and musical performance. Storefront churches were set up in the 1920s and 1930s by Southern families, community leaders, preachers, and entrepreneurs to enable the unrestrained, interactive, and community-bound worship to which they were accustomed.

The music in these churches, normally called "sanctified music" or Holy-roller hymns, contained the essence of early gospel style. These quartets and choral groups sang with rougher-edged timbres. Precision of ensemble was generally sacrificed for unfettered expression. Solo roles were built within the group context, enabling call-and-response. Repetition of key phrases was used extensively to engulf the performers and congregation in ever-deepening fervor. Performers were more physically expressive, and the congregation would intensify the emotional extremities of the performance by moving, clapping, and verbalizing their approval and empathy.

By the 1940s, the gospel sound and style of the Southern congregations had eased its way into the public realm. An important event that marked this process in New York was John Hammond's From Spirituals to Swing concert held in Carnegie Hall in December 1938. The concert featured the young Sister Rosetta Tharpe, who had recently moved to New York from Chicago, and Mitchell's Christian Singers, artists who were firmly entrenched in the Southern gospel or "Holy roller" tradition. Yet the popularization of gospel within secular spaces was problematic to both the Southern and Northern communities. The former viewed the development as a threat to their way of life, the latter as a threat to their own conservative religious expression.

Both jubilee and gospel styles could be heard in the city's black churches by the late 1930s. Jubilee groups native to New York include the Golden Crown, the Selah Jubilee Singers, and the Sunset Jubilees. Other quartets moved to the city, drawn by record deals and possibilities of radio broadcasts. The Utica Jubilee Quartet moved to New York in 1926, and in 1927 they became the first African American quartet to broadcast on nationally syndicated radio. The Golden Gate Quartet made New York their home in the mid-1940s. The Norfolk Jubilee Singers signed a deal with Decca and settled in New York in 1937. The Southernaires were also based there, as were the all-female, Harlem-raised White Rose, Galilee Sisters, and Nazareth Singers. There were also many jubilee choirs with formal musical training singing a repertoire of spirituals and folk songs. The most famous of these, founded in 1920s Harlem, were the Hall Johnson Singers and the Eva Jessye Choir.

By the 1940s and 1950s, New York had become a major center for recording, broadcasting, and performing gospel music. With a further mass migration from the South during the war and the growing influence of Thomas A. Dorsey's Chicago-based sound, New York was finally overcome by the "hard" gospel style. Home-grown gospel groups such as the Brooklyn All Stars, the Mighty Gospel Giants (also of Brooklyn), and the Skylight Singers (of Harlem) were joined by visiting stars, such as the Dixie Hummingbirds, the Soul Stirrers, the Deep River Boys, and the Charioteers. Soloist James Cleveland also came to base his concert and tour activities around New York in the late 1950s.

The first ever gospel radio show, Joe Bostic's Gospel Train, began broadcasting from New York every Sunday morning during the mid-1940s. Bostic was also a concert promoter, responsible for bringing Mahalia Jackson to Carnegie Hall in 1950 and for establishing the Negro Gospel and Religious Musical Festival, also in Carnegie Hall. Several white entrepreneurs, including Johnny Myers and Ronny Williams, began to exploit gospel's commercial possibilities by organizing star-studded concerts and selling thousands of tickets at the box office. Many venues around New York opened themselves to gospel, breaking down the resistance to its popularization. The Apollo theatre became a popular gospel venue, hosting many of the major performers through the 1950s.

Bostic also discovered and broadcast Edwin Hawkins's smash hit "Oh, Happy Day" on his radio show in 1969. This hit provoked a flurry of renewed gospel activity and enthusiasm in New York through the 1970s, including the formation of the Institutional Radio Choir of Brooklyn, whose performances were broadcast every Sunday night. With New York's black population ever growing—with bases in Harlem, the South Bronx, significant areas of central Brooklyn, and Southeast and Northern Queens—the gospel scene continues to thrive, particularly through the competition circuit.

HILARY MOORE

See also Bostic, Joe; Charioteers, The; Cleveland, James; Dorsey, Thomas; Edwin Hawkins Singers; Golden Gate Quartet, The; Jackson, Mahalia; Norfolk Jubilee Singers; Selah Jubilee Singers; Soul Stirrers; Tharpe, Sister Rosetta

Reference and Further Reading

Allen, Ray. *Singing in the Spirit: African-American Sacred Quartets in New York City.* Philadelphia: University of Pennsylvania Press, 1991.

Allgood, B. Dexter. "Black Gospel in New York City and Joe William Bostic, Sr." *The Black Perspective in Music* 18 (1990): 101–116.

Boyer, Horace Clarence. *How Sweet the Sound: The Golden Age of Gospel.* Washington, DC: Elliott & Clark, 1995.

Heilbut, Anthony. *The Gospel Sound: Good News and Bad Times.* New York: Simon & Schuster, 1971.

Wald, Gayle. "From Spirituals to Swing: Sister Rosetta Tharpe and Gospel Crossover." *American Quarterly* 55 (September 2003): 387–417.

NEWSBOYS

Jody Brian Davis (b. September 26, 1967)
Jeffrey Ryan Frankenstein (b. June 26, 1974)
Peter Andrew Furler (b. September 8, 1966)
John James (April 27, 1964)
Duncan Phillips (b. March 3, 1964)
Sean Taylor (b. November 4, 1966)
Phillip Joel Urry (b. January 5, 1973)

The Newsboys began as an Australian garage band in Queensland during the early 1980s and were originally called the News. Initially, the group was made up of John James (lead vocals), Corey Pryor (keyboards), Peter Furler (drums), and Sean Taylor (bass). Their early influences included the Cure, Keith Green, the Police, the Rolling Stones, and Jimmy Swaggart. The rowdy patrons of local clubs and pubs made up the group's first audiences.

Contemporary Christian music was nearly unknown in Australia until the late 1980s, when major Christian bands from the United States began touring there. By this time, the Newsboys' popularity in Australia made them the obvious choice to open for Christian artists such as Phil Keaggy, David Meece, Petra, and White Heart. The experience stretched the young band and encouraged them to expand their vision beyond their own back yard.

In early 1988, the Newsboys arrived in Los Angeles, California. They got their first break after they played at the Atlanta Christian Music Festival. Soon afterward they released their first album, *Read All About It,* on Refuge Records and began playing for youth groups on the church circuit. Within a year their dynamic live show garnered them a recording contract with Star Song Records, and they released *Boys Will Be Boyz.* The band's stage antics, such as playing drums in an inverted position, garnered them a reputation as amazing live performers.

The Newsboys had a number of personnel changes during the 1990s. By the time John James left the band in 1997, Pete Furler was the only original Newsboy remaining. Some of the other former members were Vernon Bishop, Jonathan Geange, Kevin Mills, George Perdikis, and Phil Yates. The constant personnel changes resulted in a continual evolution of their sound and musical direction.

With their fourth album, *Not Ashamed,* Steve Taylor became a collaborator as well as a coproducer and sometime band member. The album generated both Grammy and Dove Award nominations. Their first number one hit, "Shine," came from their second Star Song album with Steve Taylor, in 1994, titled *Going Public.* Once again they were nominated for a Grammy for Best Rock Album, and they won Dove Awards for Song of the Year and Rock Album of the Year in 1995.

In 1996, the Newsboys continued working with Steve Taylor, who once again coproduced *Take Me to Your Leader,* with Pete Furler. Taylor wrote the lyrics to the title song, which was released as a single on Virgin Records. In 1998 they released *Step Up to the Microphone,* which was produced by Furler without Taylor's help, although he cowrote lyrics for two songs. It was released on both Star Song and Virgin Records, and it was the first album that Furler took over singing lead full time. The Newsboys' popularity continued to increase as they were featured in periodicals such as *Newsweek, USA Today, Teen People, ESPN2, Guitar Player, Motocross Journal,* and *Entertainment Weekly.* They performed at Pope John Paul II's World Youth Day and live on the nationally televised Dove Awards.

Love Liberty Disco was the Newsboys' first release on the Sparrow Records label in 1999, followed by *Shine: The Hits* in 2000. By 2001, the multiplatinum-selling group had earned more than three million dollars from all their album sales. With their popularity at an all-time high, the group masterminded one of the most successful traveling festivals to date. Using secular predecessors such as Lollapalooza and Ozzfest as examples, they kicked off the first annual Festival Con Dios on May 18, 2001. With the Newsboys headlining, each stop included performances by a dozen other Christian bands—such as Audio Adrenaline, Pillar, the O C Supertones, Skillet, Earthsuit, Plus One, Kutless, and Thousand Foot Crutch—performing on multiple stages. Also included were extreme sports demonstrations, a village area to purchase artist merchandise, and interactive activities, including a rock-climbing wall and bungee jumping. The festival's attendance for its first year was almost two hundred thousand, which was successfully repeated during the following years.

The year 2002 saw the release of two albums on Sparrow, *Thrive* and *The Newsboys Remixed. Thrive* produced the single "It Is You" and a Steve Taylor composition titled "John Woo," inspired by the film director of the same name. The *Remix* album gave new life to old favorites, with a techno-sounding dance beat. In spring 2003, the band released its first worship album, on Sparrow, titled *Adoration.* Compositions such as "He Reigns," "In Christ Alone," and "Hallelujah" demonstrated that the Newsboys could write reverent gospel music as well as entertaining pop rock.

BOB GERSZTYN

See also Petra; Rock Gospel; Swaggart, Jimmy; Taylor, Steve

Reference and Further Reading

Ali, Lorraine. "The Glorious Rise of Christian Pop." *Newsweek* (July 16, 2001).
Finelli, Lana. "Newsboys Biography." *Rolling Stone* website, http://www.rollingstone.com/reviews/cd/review.asp?aid=38316 (accessed September 12, 2003).
Krause, Anya. " Boys, Oh Boys." *CCM Magazine* website, http://www.ccmmagazine.com/features/fullstory_cont2.asp?Id=79 (accessed August 13, 2003).
Newsboys. *Shine: Make Them Wonder What You've Got.* Whitaker House, 2002.
Shine: The Newsboys Archive website, http://www.shinemedia.de/newsboys/ (accessed September 14, 2003).

Discography

Read All About It (1988, Refuge/Star Song); *Hell Is for Wimps* (1990, Star Song); *Boys Will Be Boyz* (1991, Star Song); *Not Ashamed* (1992, Star Song); *Going Public* (1994, Star Song); *Take Me to Your Leader* (1996, Star Song); *Step Up to the Microphone* (1998, Star Song); *Love Liberty Disco* (1999, Sparrow); *Shine: The Hits* (2000, Sparrow); *Thrive* (2002, Sparrow); *Newsboys Remixed* (2002, Sparrow); *Adoration: The Worship Album* (2003, Sparrow).

NIX, REVEREND A. W.

(b. probably Birmingham, Alabama; d. Unknown)

Reverend A. W. Nix recorded fifty-seven sermons (three unissued) in Chicago for Vocalion between 1927 and 1931. Information about Nix's life is scarce, but from his recordings it is reasonable to assume that he was a Baptist or Methodist. Among his most popular sermons, which mainly dealt with Biblical topics, are "Black Diamond Express to Hell" (of which Nix recorded six versions), "The White Flyer to Heaven," "It Was Tight Like That," and "The Dirty Dozen."

LUIGI MONGE

Discography

Rev. A. W. Nix: Complete Recorded Works in Chronological Order, Vol. 1 (1927–1928) (1994, Document Records DOCD-5328).
Rev. A. W. Nix & Rev. Emmett Dickinson: In Chronological Order, Vol. 2 (1928–1930) (1996, Document Records DOCD-5490).

NORCROSS, MARVIN

(b. March 15, 1929, Fort Worth, TX; d. June 18, 1980)

Marvin Norcross joined Word Records as an investor and partner in 1952, helping the founder of the fledgling label, Jarrell McCracken, with his accounting and financial skills. Norcross had attended Texas Christian University and then served in the Korean War as part of the Air National Guard before joining Word. In 1957, Norcross, who loved Southern gospel music, wanted to start a Southern gospel division at Word, but he was premature. However, in 1964, the label got under way; the first signing was the Florida Boys, who hosted the successful TV show *Gospel Singing Jubilee.*

Canaan Records and Canaanland Publishing, both led by Aaron Brown, thrived, becoming the leading record label and publishing company for Southern gospel music during the 1960s and 1970s. Norcross headed Canaan Records, handling the daily operations, and under his guidance the label signed acts such as the Happy Goodman Family, the Dixie Echoes, Teddy Huffam and the Gems, the Blue Ridge Boys, Steve Sanders, and the Lewis Family.

Norcross was active in the Gospel Music Association and served as president of that organization in 1974 and 1975. In addition to his activities in gospel music, Norcross was active in the Rotary Club, achieving a perfect attendance record for twenty-five years. Norcross was also active in Little League baseball, serving as district administrator and as Texas State Tournament committee chairman for that organization; there is a Little League stadium in Waco, Texas, named after him.

In 1980, Marvin Norcross died at the age of fifty-one; a year later, *The Singing News* magazine instituted the Marvin Norcross Award, which is given annually "in honor of a Southern gospel music figure who has made an outstanding contribution to the industry." In 1983, Norcross was elected to the Gospel Music Hall of Fame; in 1997, he was elected to the Southern Gospel Music Hall of Fame.

DON CUSIC

Reference and Further Reading

Cusic, Don. *The Sound of Light: A History of Gospel and Christian Music*. New York: Hal Leonard, 2002.

Goff, James R. Jr. *Close Harmony: A History of Southern Gospel*. Chapel Hill: University of North Carolina Press, 2002.

NORFOLK JUBILEE SINGERS

Formed during World War I, the Norfolk Jazz/Jubilee Singers emerged as one of the most popular and prolific of the early gospel quartets in Tidewater, Virginia. The group, which originally consisted of bass singer Len Williams, tenor singers Buddy Butts and Otto Tutson, and baritone singer Delrose Hollins, stayed together for approximately twenty-five years. During these two and a half decades, the Norfolk Jazz/Jubilee Singers shifted from their roots as a community-based ensemble to become a semiprofessional group that appeared not only on local vaudeville stages but on numerous phonograph records.

The group began singing in local churches, but by the early 1920s they had become popular enough to travel the vaudeville circuit from Chicago as far north as New York City. In the spring of 1921, the Norfolk Jazz Quartet (the jubilee name was attached to their sacred recordings, while the jazz moniker appears on their secular selections) made their initial recordings for the OKeh Company. Their records apparently sold well enough that the group was quickly called back to the studio two times in rapid succession, and by September of 1921 they had recorded twenty selections—all of them secular—in three sessions.

In 1923, the ensemble switched to the Paramount Company, with whom they stayed for six years. The group was successful enough that they continued not only to record but to perform throughout the Mid-Atlantic States and into New England. Their recording output for Paramount included many religious sides and apparently ended only when the company began to sink under the weight of the Depression.

Shortly before they stopped recording for Paramount, the Norfolk Jazz/Jubilee Singers added Norman "Crip" Harris to their group. This move signaled the first major shift in their personnel, and by the time the group returned to the Decca studios in 1937, it consisted of tenor singer Raymond Smith, baritone singer Melvin Colden, and bass singer Len Williams, along with Harris. The group had also made New York City their second home during the 1930s, spending as much time there as in Tidewater, and appearing on programs with such noteworthy contemporaries as the Golden Gate Quartet and the Deep River Boys (who first formed at Hampton Institute).

The Norfolk Jazz/Jubilee Singers remained active until late 1940. They fell apart within months of Len Williams's sudden and dramatic death following his collapse on stage. His death left the group leaderless, and the restrictions imposed by World War II rationing made travel much more difficult. Two of the group's members, Harris and Colden, moved on to other New York City–oriented groups and continued to sing for another ten years.

KIP LORNELL

Reference and Further Reading

Lornell, Kip. *Virginia's Blues, Country, & Gospel Records 1902–1943: An Annotated Discography*. Lexington: University Press of Kentucky, 1989.

NORMAN, LARRY

(b. April 8, 1947)

Larry Norman was born in San Francisco, California, and he began singing when he was two years old. He learned to play the piano at the age of four. When he was nine, he started composing and performing his songs in public. By the time he was eighteen, he had written more than five hundred songs. Some of his musical influences were Mahalia Jackson, Django Reinhardt, Paul Robeson, and Bert Williams. In 1965 he formed a band called People, and in 1966 they signed a recording contract with Capitol Records. After a disagreement over the album title and other differences, Norman left the band in 1968.

Norman recorded and released *Upon This Rock* in 1969, after Capitol signed him as a solo artist. The album produced one of his most memorable songs, "I Wish We'd All Been Ready," but it failed to make an impact on the record charts, so Capitol terminated his contract. He began his own record label, One Way Records, and put out two albums, *Street Level* and *Bootleg*. In 1972, he began recording with MGM/Verve Records and released two landmark—and controversial—albums, *Only Visiting This Planet* and *So Long Ago in the Garden*. It was during this time that he worked with legendary Beatles producer George Martin. In 1974, he left MGM and signed with ABC, which soon afterward purchased Word Records. The same year he began his own record label, Solid Rock Records, and released *In Another Land*. All of Norman's music was now being distributed by Word Records.

Norman was considered by many to be the father of what is today known as rock gospel. With the formation of Solid Rock Records, Norman established himself as one of the primary leaders of the new genre of Christian rock music. He began recording, producing, and in some cases even distributing new artists. *Horrendous Disc* by Daniel Amos, *Appalachian Melody* by Mark Heard, and *Welcome to Paradise* and *The Sky Is Falling* by Randy Stonehill were some of the landmark albums released on Solid Rock.

By the end of the 1970s, Norman was negotiating a contract with Warner Brothers when he incurred a head injury during a commercial airline flight. Soon afterward he dismantled Solid Rock, and in 1980 he moved to Europe, where he started Phydeaux (pronounced "Fido") Records. He continued to record and tour but with less intensity than before. In 1991, he released *Stranded In Babylon,* which was considered by many European journalists to be the best gospel album produced that year. The album was never officially released in the United States, because Norman suffered a heart attack in February 1992.

Heart problems slowed down his touring and recording intensity during the 1990s. In 2001 he released *Tourniquet,* his first studio album of new material in ten years. Regular touring resumed, which produced a live album, titled *Larry Norman Live at Cornerstone, Mainstage, July 7, 2001.* It was released

on Solid Rock in 2003. In November 2001, Norman was inducted into the Gospel Music Hall of Fame.

BOB GERSZTYN

See also Calvary Chapel, Costa Mesa; Rock Gospel

Reference and Further Reading

Callahan, Mike; David Edwards; Patrice Eyries. "Solid Rock Album Discography." Both Sides Now website, http://www.bsnpubs.com/word/solidrock.html (accessed July 7, 2003).
Gospel Music Association website, http://www.gospelmusic.org/news/article.cfm?ArticleID=37 (accessed September 2, 2003).
Hagestedt, André. "Larry Norman—(Sub)Urban Hymns." Yahoo GeoCities website, http://www.geocities.com/TheTropics/Resort/8891/norman.html (accessed September 22, 2003).
Larry Norman website, http://www.larrynorman.com (accessed July 19, 2003).
Nelson, Torrey. "People." Ape Camp website, http://www.apecamp.com/music/people/ (accessed October 6, 2003).
O'Neill, Dan. *Signatures: The Story of John Michael Talbot. Troubadour for the Lord*, 2003.
Spencer, Michael. "So Long Ago, When CCM Wasn't wful." Internet Monk website, http://www.internetmonk.com/larry.html (accessed October 6, 2003).
Thompson, John J. *Raised by Wolves*. Toronto, Canada: ECW Press, 2001.
———. "The Saga of Norman, Stonehill, Jesus Music and Grace." *Christian Music* 8, no. 3 (May/June 2003).

Discography

Upon This Rock (1969, Capitol); *Only Visiting This Planet* (1972, Verve, V6-5092); *So Long Ago in the Garden* (1973, MGM, SE-4942); *In Another Land* (1976, Solid Rock, SRA-2001); *Streams of White Light into Darkened Corners* (1977, Solid Rock, SRD-028); *Something New under the Son* (1981, Solid Rock, SRA-2007); *Home at Last* (1989, Benson/Solid Rock, CD-02304); *White Blossoms from Black Roots* (1989, Solid Rock, SRD-030); *Children of Sorrow* (1994, Street Level, SLD-023); *Stranded in Babylon* (1994, Solid Rock, SRD-016); *Down Under—But Not Out* (1996, Phydeaux, PRD-017); *Tourniquet* (2001, Solid Rock); *Live at Cornerstone* (2003, Solid Rock, PDX-207).

NORWOOD, DOROTHY

(b. 1930, Atlanta, Georgia)

An evangelist, Dorothy Norwood began singing and touring with her family at eight years old. She grew up in the Baptist Church singing in choirs and groups in Atlanta. In 1956 she moved to Chicago. There she began to sing with "the Queen of Gospel," Mahalia Jackson (1911–1972); the Caravans; and "the Crown Prince of Gospel," Reverend James Cleveland (1932–1991).

Norwood began her solo career in 1964, recording her first album, *Johnny and Jesus*, on Savoy Records. She then recorded *The Stirring Denied Mother*. Both records became gold, selling more than a million copies and earning her the title of "World's Greatest Storyteller." In Chicago, Reverend Nash Shaffer spoke on his Sunday morning *Golden Gospel* radio program about Norwood, "You can't move, only cry; Dorothy has your mind, body, and soul wrapped up in a gospel truth."

Norwood has many talents: she is a vocalist, a songwriter, and a producer. She functions with choirs, on her own as a soloist, with her own group, as a storyteller, and as an evangelist. She has traveled the world singing gospel music, performing in Germany, France, Sweden, Denmark, The Netherlands, and England. In 1972, Norwood toured thirty states with Mick Jagger and the Rolling Stones. During the 1970s, Norwood moved to New Jersey, but she later moved back to Georgia.

Norwood signed with Malaco Records in Jackson, Mississippi, in February 1991. She recorded *Live with the Northern California Gospel Music Workshop of America Mass Choir,* which reached number one on *Billboard*'s top forty after only seven weeks; her reward was a Stellar and Grammy Award nomination. In 1997, Dorothy Norwood was inducted into the International Gospel Music Hall of Fame and Museum, Detroit, Michigan.

Some of the forty albums recorded by Norwood are *Live at Home* (recorded live in Atlanta), *Ol Rickety Bridge, The Lord Is a Wonder,* her famous *Hattie B's Daughter, Shake the Devil Off, Lord Keep Me Day by Day, Better Days Ahead, Up Where We Belong, Look What They've Done to My Child, Answer Me Dear Jesus,* and the famous *I Don't Feel No Ways Tired.* Norwood often appears on Black Entertainment Television's *Bobby Jones Gospel* show that airs every Sunday morning.

SHERRY SHERROD DUPREE

Reference and Further Reading

Boyer, Horace Clarence. *How Sweet the Sound: The Golden Age of Gospel.* Washington, DC: Elliott & Clark, 1995.

DuPree, Sherry Sherrod; Herbert C. DuPree. *African-American Good News (Gospel) Music.* Washington, DC: Middle Atlantic Regional Press, 1993.

Gospel Music Catalog. Jackson, MS: Malaco/Savoy Records, n. d.

International Gospel Music Hall of Fame and Museum website, http://www.gmhf.org (accessed August 28, 2004).

Ruppli, Michael. *The Savoy Label: A Discography.* Vol. 2: Westport, CT: Greenwood Press, 1980.

Shaffer, Nash, Reverend. "Sunday Morning Golden Gospel Radio," Chicago. Interview by Sherry Sherrod DuPree via telephone, May 20, 2004.

Walker, Albertina; Inez Andrews; David Gough. National Association for the Advancement of Colored People (NAACP) Freedom Weekend Gospel Luncheon, Detroit. Interview by Sherry Sherrod DuPree, April 18, 2003.

Selected Discography

Stand on the Word (2004, Malaco Records CD 4533).
Dorothy Norwood (2005, Fuel2000 CD 06145; remastered).

NUTT, GRADY

(b. September 2, 1934, Amarillo, TX; d. November 23, 1982, Vinemont, AL)

"The Prime Minister of Humor," Grady L. Nutt was an ordained Baptist minister, comedian, author, singer, and television personality. Nutt was the oldest child of Grady C. Nutt, a dairy salesman and dry cleaner. Young Grady did not go to church until he was eleven but was licensed as a Baptist minister by age thirteen, and the next year his family moved from the Texas panhandle to Jacksonville in East Texas, where his father took ministerial training and where Nutt later completed high school. He enrolled at Wayland Baptist College in Plainview, Texas, and he then transferred to Baylor University at Waco, where he earned his BA in 1957.

Nutt served as minister of youth at churches in Waco and Dallas, and then, in 1960, he moved to Louisville, Kentucky, to enroll for graduate studies at Southern Theological Seminary. In 1964, Nutt received his bachelor of divinity degree, and the coursework there inspired his first book, *Being Me: Self, You Bug Me,* published in 1971 by Broadman Press in Nashville. Nutt had entered the entertainment world two years before this publication and had for years in church circles entertained youthful audiences with true-life church stories and his versions of well-known Biblical events.

He gained a national reputation as a humorous speaker when television's Ralph Edwards "discovered" Nutt and arranged some twelve appearances on the syndicated *Mike Douglas Show.* Soon Nutt was averaging some twenty speaking engagements per month. *People* magazine profiled Nutt in May 1977, as he continued to speak and write, producing books closer to his comic vein: *The Gospel According to Norton* (1974), *Agaperos,* and *Family Time* (both 1977).

In 1979, Nutt was hired as a regular comedian on the nationally syndicated *Hee Haw* TV show, introduced before each of his vignettes of church humor as "The Prime Minister of Humor," which had been the title of his first comedy LP for Waco's Word Records in 1976. For Triune Records in 1979, he recorded *The Grady Nutt Parables,* and the next year he showed his talents as a gospel singer on *All Day Singin' and Dinner on the Ground* (Heart Warming Records, 1979). His recordings of "Turn Your Radio On," "Give The World a Smile" (with the Kingsmen), and two Christmas songs, "Silver Bells" and "Angels We Have Heard On High," were later anthologized on reissues. Impact Books published his 1979 autobiography, *So Good So Far.*

Nutt was returning home to his wife and two sons in Louisville after a speaking engagement in Cullman, Alabama, on November 23, 1982, when his privately chartered plane crashed shortly after takeoff from the airport in Vinemont, Alabama, killing him and the two crew members. He was forty-eight years old. Honoring his memory, the Gospel Music Association annually bestows the Grady Nutt Humor Award to the best gospel humorist. Nutt's widow, Eleanor Nutt Maddox, and her second husband, Louisville businessman Robert Maddox, have established the Grady Nutt Endowment Fund through the University of Louisville, which annually awards the four-hundred-dollar Grady Nutt Prize "for the most creative project in humanities and civic leadership."

RONNIE PUGH

Reference and Further Reading

Anderson, H. Allen. "Nutt, Grady Lee." The Handbook of Texas Online website, http://http://www.tsha.utexas.edu/handbook/online/articles/view/NN/fnu7.html.

Nutt, Grady. *So Good So Far*. Nashville, TN: Impact Books, 1979.

Discography

All Day Singin' and Dinner on the Ground (Heart Warming Records R-3720).

Grady Nutt Parables (Triune TR 125).

Prime Minister of Humor (Word WST-8699).

O

OAK RIDGE BOYS

Duane David Allen (b. April 29, 1943, Taylortown, TX)
Joseph Sloan Bonsall (b. May 18, 1948, Philadelphia, PA)
William Lee Golden (b. January 12, 1939, Brewton, AL)
Richard Anthony Sterban (b. April 24, 1943, Camden, NJ)
Steve Sanders (b. September 17, 1952, Richland, GA; d. June 10, 1998)

As one of the foremost vocal ensembles in country music, the Oak Ridge Boys have woven together gospel and country music making for more than half a century, with more than forty different members and dozens of hits on the gospel, country, and pop charts. In spite of their deep gospel roots, the quartet's greatest commercial success appeared with their secular country recordings. Yet their rich four-part harmonies, emphasis on lively stage performances, and preference for "message" music have allowed the Oak Ridge Boys to infuse mainstream country with a substantial dose of Southern gospel.

The gospel group known as the Oak Ridge Quartet first emerged during World War II, singing with Wally Fowler's Georgia Clodhoppers around Knoxville, Tennessee. The ensemble took their name from the nearby town of Oak Ridge, where they performed frequently. Under Fowler's leadership and with members Curly Kinsey, Johnny New, and Lon "Deacon" Freeman, the quartet joined the Grand Ole Opry in 1945.

In 1948, the Oaks helped launch all-night gospel concerts at Nashville's Ryman Auditorium, events that simultaneously promoted gospel music to a wider public and earned the group a larger following.

Membership in the quartet was always in flux, but the early 1950s found the Oaks touring and performing with notable success, favoring crowds with their renditions of such hits as "Go Out to the Program" and "Tearing Down the Kingdom."

In 1956, group member E. Smith "Smitty" Gatlin took over leadership from Fowler. The group formally changed their name to the Oak Ridge Boys and began to incorporate more commercial country sounds. The most popular personnel lineup began to take shape in 1964, when Gatlin hired baritone William Lee Golden. Gatlin left in 1966 to pursue full-time ministry, and Duane Allen, who had sung with the Prophets, replaced him as lead vocalist. Richard Sterban, whose resume included backing Elvis Presley while in the Stamps Quartet, was hired to sing bass in 1972, and tenor Joe Bonsall, who had sung with Sterban in the Keystone Quartet, joined in 1973.

With these four vocalists, the Oak Ridge Boys reached the pinnacle of success in the gospel music arena. They received two Gospel Music Association Dove Awards for Album of the Year with *It's Happening* (1969) and *Street Gospel* (1973), and their 1969 recording of "Jesus Is Coming Soon" won top honors as Song of the Year.

Meanwhile, the group's sound was borrowing more heavily from mainstream country. Within the competitive gospel music world, alarm was voiced about the Oaks' rowdy lifestyles possibly not aligning with their gospel message. In 1975, the group effectively finalized their separation from the Southern gospel industry and began to work toward country music recognition.

The quartet hired Jim Halsey, who was a manager for major country acts, including Roy Clark. Under Halsey's guidance, the struggling country ensemble's first chart-topping country hit finally materialized in 1977 with "Y'All Come Back Saloon." Their first number one hit on *Billboard*'s Hot Country Singles chart, "I'll Be True to You," followed soon after. The Oak Ridge Boys successfully crossed into mainstream pop with their 1981 version of "Elvira," and they then continued with a long string of country hits in the early 1980s, including "American Made" and "Touch a Hand, Make a Friend." Sterban's resonant bass and vocal arrangements that featured all four singers prominently became hallmarks of their sound.

Both the Academy of Country Music and the Country Music Association honored them with Top Vocal Group and Vocal Group of the Year awards in 1978, unseating their longtime rivals, the Statler Brothers, who also claimed roots as a gospel quartet.

For nearly a decade and a half, the group's membership remained constant, but by 1986, Golden had embraced both the lifestyle and image of a mountain man, which was too far from the clean-cut representation the Oak Ridge Boys sought in the midst of that era's pop-country and urban-cowboy trends. The band fired Golden, citing continuing musical and personal differences, and Steve Sanders, their longtime guitarist, replaced him.

The Oak Ridge Boys enjoyed a few country hits during this time, notably "No Matter How High," but when Sanders left in 1995, the band reconciled with Golden and brought him back into the group for that year's New Year's Eve concert. In the late 1990s, Branson, Missouri's entertainment business exploded as an alternative to Nashville with its specialization in traditional country music. The Oak Ridge Boys found a sustaining audience there, where they perform most of the year.

JOCELYN R. NEAL

See also Dove Awards; Gospel Music Association; Presley, Elvis; Prophets Quartet; Stamps Quartet

Reference and Further Reading

Goff, James R., Jr. *Close Harmony: A History of Southern Gospel*. Chapel Hill and London: University of North Carolina Press, 2002.
Widner, Ellis; Walter Carter. *The Oak Ridge Boys: Our Story*. Chicago and New York: Contemporary Books, 1987.

Selected Discography

It's Happening (1969, Heartwarming 3012).
The Oak Ridge Boys (1973; Columbia Records KC 32742).
Y'All Come Back Saloon (1977, ABC/Dot Records DO-2093; rereleased 1979, MCA Records DO-2093).
Greatest Hits, Vol. 1 (1980, MCA Nashville 5150).
20th Century Masters—The Millennium Collection: The Best of the Oak Ridge Boys (2000, MCA Nashville 170150).
From the Heart (2001, Spring Hill WEA 406 21017).

O'NEAL TWINS

Edward O'Neal (b. August 17, 1937, St. Louis, MO; d. December 9, 1990, St. Louis, MO)
Edgar O'Neal (b. August 17, 1937, St. Louis, MO)

Edward and Edgar were twin sons born to Edward O'Neal and Rowena Taylor O'Neal. Their father was a professional cook and their mother was a government employee.

The twins demonstrated their musical gift early in the choirs of the God in Christ Church in St. Louis, and they became students of Willie Mae Ford Smith and Professor P. C. Smith while quite young. Willie Mae Ford Smith was a very influential force in the Midwest gospel movement. Edward and Edgar quickly became the center of attention because of their forceful talent, poise, and youth.

They first signed with Peacock Records in Houston, and their early hits ensured that they would be a vibrant part of the industry throughout their musical ministry. During the mid-1970s, they moved to Savoy Records, where they produced more than twenty albums. At Savoy, they became a benchmark of the traditional gospel market and produced many hits for the label over the years.

The O'Neal Twins found another success in 1983 with the release of a motion picture. They became famous with the release of *Say Amen, Somebody*, a profile of American gospel music pioneers Willie Mae Ford Smith and the Reverend Thomas A. Dorsey, who were both founders of the modern gospel choir movement in America during the middle of the last century. Edward and Edgar were interviewed and performed in this moving documentary by producer/director George T. Nierenberg. They found new secular and religious audiences with this film.

In the 1990s, the O'Neal Twins signed with Atlanta International and produced several hits, including *20th Year Reunion Celebration—Live from St. Louis*. Their last hit for Atlanta International was a single written by Edward entitled, "I Can't Let a Day Go By." It was a fitting tribute to a great artist.

Edward passed away after suffering a heart attack on December 9, 1990, and is buried in St. Louis, his lifetime home.

On October 24, 2004, the O'Neal Twins were inducted into the Gospel Music Hall of Fame in Detroit for their outstanding contribution to this art form. They were stirring performers who understood their craft and performed with power, conviction, and dedication.

TOM FISHER

Reference and Further Reading

O'Neal, Edgar. Interview by Tom Fisher, St. Louis. MO, January 15, 2005.

Discography

O'Neal Twins. *Best of the O'Neal Twins* (1990, MCA 2545); *He Chose Me* (1990, Savoy SAV 7074); *I Won't Be Silent Anymore* (1990, Atlanta International 14846); *Saved by His Love* (1990, Savoy SAV 7065); *O'Neal Twins and Interfaith Choir of St. Louis, Missouri: 20th Reunion Celebration—Live from St. Louis* (1997, Atlanta International 7441).
O'Neal Twins: Selected Films. *Say Amen, Somebody* (1983, Xenon Pictures; directed by George T. Nierenberg).
Edgar O'Neal. *Edgar O'Neal Live in St. Louis* (1995, Word).

ORIGINAL GOSPEL HARMONETTES

Evelyn Starks Hardy (b. 1922)
Mildred Madison Miller Howard (b. 1923)
Odessa Glasgow Edwards (b. July 18, 1921, Birmingham, AL; d. February 22, 2004, Birmingham, AL)
Vera Conner Kolb (b. 1924)
Willie Mae Brooks Newberry (b. 1923)
Starks Hardy (b. 1922)

During the 1940 National Baptist Convention held in Birmingham, Alabama, Evelyn Starks Hardy—a local pianist, composer, and arranger who played for the convention—decided to form a group with second soprano Mildred Madison Miller Howard, second alto Odessa Glasgow Edwards, first soprano Vera Conner Kolb, and first alto Willie Mae Brooks Newberry. They named themselves the Gospel Harmoneers, a name that was changed to the Lee Harmoneers when they started to tour with Georgia Lee Stafford; it was again changed to the Gospel Harmonettes when, approached to sing for a half-hour weekly radio program on station WSGN, they sang on the program for a year and became regional stars, touring Alabama and several eastern and western states.

In the spring of 1949, they appeared on Arthur Godfrey's *Talent Scouts* program and won a recording contract with RCA Victor. Eight songs were recorded and issued but yielded little results; however, the group continued to travel and to gather large audiences, drawing the attention of gospel talent scouts working with Specialty Records, such as Alex Bradford and J. W. Alexander. They were signed to Specialty in 1951. At that time, Dorothy McGriff Love (b. 1928), who had sung with the group on several occasions in the 1940s and who was a disciple of Reverend Brewster, became a regular member of the group, now renamed the Original Gospel Harmonettes.

The first releases were hugely successful and were followed with a string of hits spanning a five-year period, with Love starring from the beginning as an extraordinary soloist, a gifted songwriter, and a hard gospel singer with a sanctified timbre and a preacher's delivery; Miller proved to be another formidable singer, matching Love nuance for nuance. Their shouting style brought in a whole new era in gospel music, and their influence is still heard everywhere today. In 1953, they appeared at Carnegie Hall, and in 1954, Love, who by this time had married Carl Coates of the Nightingales, recorded perhaps her finest composition, "You Must Be Born Again," with Herbert "Pee Wee" Pickard on piano (he was also the studio organist).

The Harmonettes appeared at the Apollo Theatre, Madison Square Garden, and concert halls all over the United States and the Bahamas. They recorded briefly for Andex in 1958, followed by a four-year stint with Savoy Records (1959–1962), a single cut for Motown (1962), and a longer association with Vee Jay Records in Chicago (1963–1966); they then followed with an album each for Hob and OKeh (1968) before signing with Nashboro in 1968. At that time, the group included Dorothy Love Coates, lead, Mildred Miller Howard, lead, Lillian McGriff (Dorothy's sister), Cleo Kennedy, and Willie Mae Newberry Garth; they were accompanied by Reverend Charles Kemp on piano. The group disbanded in 1971, and Coates organized the Dorothy Love Coates Singers, who made several tours in Europe and appeared in concert at Harvard University.

Throughout their days, the Harmonettes brought a new intensity to gospel that could only be matched by the frenzy of a sanctified shout, with dignity and elegance.

ROBERT SACRÉ

See also Bradford, Alex

Dorothy Love Coates and the Gospel Harmonettes. Photo courtesy Frank Driggs Collection.

Reference and Further Reading

Boyer, Horace Clarence. *How Sweet the Sound: The Golden Age of Gospel*. Washington, DC: Elliott & Clark, 1995.

Hayes, J. Cedric; Robert Laughton. *Gospel Records 1943–1969. A Black Music Discography*, 2 vols. London, UK: Record Information Services, 1992.

Heilbut, Tony. *The Gospel Sound: Good News and Bad Times*. New York: Limelight, 1985.

Reagon, Bernice Johnson, ed. *We'll Understand It Better By and By: Pioneering African American Gospel Composers*. Washington, DC: Smithsonian Institution Press, 1992.

Discography

The Best of Dorothy Love Coates and the Original Gospel Harmonettes (1991, Specialty/Ace [UK] CDHD 343).

Get on Board (1992, Specialty/Ace [UK] CDCHD412).

The Original Gospel Harmonettes Featuring Dorothy Love Coates: Camp Meeting & God Is Here (1993, Vee Jay CD NVG2-607).

The Best of Dorothy Love Coates & the Gospel Harmonettes (1995, Nashboro NASH4508-2).

P

PACE, REVEREND CHARLES, AND THE PACE JUBILEE SINGERS

Charles Henry Pace (b. August 4, 1886; d. December 16, 1963)

The Bridge Between Old and New Jubilee Styles

The Reverend Charles Pace and the Pace Jubilee Singers are an important bridge between the nineteenth century "jubilee" style of singing spirituals and the first wave of quartets and groups that sang a livelier brand of jubilee—one that emphasized the close harmonies of barbershop, rhythm, and the longer, often comic, story songs.

The Fisk Jubilee Singers spun off smaller, less-expensive aggregations as the jubilee craze began to wane in the early years of the twentieth century, most notably the Fisk Jubilee Quartet, led by John Wesley Work, Jr. Among the groups to spring up singing the newer, more rhythmic style were the Pace Jubilee Singers, founded by Charles Henry Pace, from the Senior Choir of the Beth Eden Church of Chicago in 1925. Pace was a noted composer, musician, publisher, and conductor, first in Chicago and then in Pittsburgh, where he moved in 1936.

The Pace Jubilee Singers, which ranged from six to nine members, included his wife, Arlene Pace, and his primary soloist, Hattie Parker. It was Parker who began to infuse a more expressive, rhythmically progressive foundation into the music. Thomas A. Dorsey also briefly served as the Jubilee Singers' pianist, which may have influenced both Parker and Pace. The group began recording within two years of its founding, primarily for the Victor, Paramount, Brunswick, and Black Patti labels, and it was among the first to record songs by Charles Albert Tindley.

Pace composed more than a hundred "spiritual anthems," "spiritual medleys," and even "gospel songs." His best known songs—"Bread of Life," "We Will Shout Hallelujah, Afterwhile," "Amen," "Nobody but You Lord," "Rockin' in My Jesus' Arms," and "Hide My Soul"—would later be rerecorded by top gospel artists. He also wrote more than two dozen popular songs, including the lovely "The Rose That Made Me Happy Is the Rose That Made Me Sad."

The Pace Jubilee Singers were also significant for being among the first religious artists to broadcast their music on radio, particularly Chicago stations WLS and WGN. Pace organized a second group, the Pace Gospel Choral Union, which ranged in size from twenty-five to three hundred members, depending on the occasion.

After leaving Chicago, Pace built a publishing empire in Pittsburgh. At their peak, his Ole Ship of Zion Music and Charles H. Pace Music Publishers employed more than three hundred sales agents. Pace continued to write prolifically into the 1950s. He died in his beloved Pittsburgh in 1963.

ROBERT DARDEN

See also Dorsey, Thomas; Fisk Jubilee Singers; Tindley, Charles Albert

Reference and Further Reading

Boyer, Horace. *How Sweet the Sound: The Golden Age of Gospel*. Washington DC: Elliott & Clark Publishing, 1995.

Buchanan, Samuel Carroll. "A Critical Analysis of Style in Four Black Jubilee Quartets in the United States." Ph.D. dissertation, State University of New York, 1987.

Oliver, Paul. *Songsters and Saints: Vocal Traditions on Race Records*. Cambridge, UK: Cambridge University Press, 1984.

Reagon, Bernice Johnson, ed. *We'll Understand It Better By and By: Pioneering African American Gospel Composers*. Washington DC: Smithsonian Institution Press, 1992.

Rubman, Kerill Leslie. "From 'Jubilee' to 'Gospel' in Black Male Quartet Singing." MA thesis, University of North Carolina at Chapel Hill, 1980.

Turner, Patricia. *Dictionary of Afro-American Performers: 78 rpm and Cylinder Recordings of Opera, Choral Music and Song, c. 1900–1949*. New York: Garland Publishing, 1990.

Tyler, Mary Ann L. "The Music of Charles Henry Pace and Its Relationship to the Afro-American Church Experience." Ph.D. dissertation, University of Pittsburgh, 1980.

Discography

Pace Jubilee Singers Vol. 1, 1926–1927 (Document).
Pace Jubilee Singers Vol. 2, 1927–1928 (Document).

PARIS, TWILA

(b. December 28, year unknown)

Twila Paris, a praise and worship artist, is a singer and songwriter who considers herself a "musical minister." She has been a successful presence in contemporary Christian music circles for more than two decades. All of her recorded songs were written or cowritten by her; many have become hymns and anthems used in worship services.

The Gospel Music Association has to date honored her with ten Dove Awards, including three Female Vocalist of the Year awards (1993, 1994, 1995), Song of the Year for "God Is in Control" (1995), and Praise and Worship Album of the Year for *Sanctuary* (1992). Collaborative CD projects involved Paris with such artists as Amy Grant, Michael W. Smith, Steven Curtis Chapman, and Sandi Patti. These projects included *My Utmost for His Highest* (1996), *Tribute— The Songs of Andrae Crouch* (1997), and *God with Us—A Celebration of Christmas Carols and Classics* (1998).

Twila Paris has been remarkably productive and successful, recording eighteen CDs, conducting successful tours, and having thirty-three songs reaching number one on Christian radio charts. Among her most popular songs are "God Is in Control," "He Is Exalted," "Lamb of God," "Warrior Is a Child," "We Bow Down," and "We Will Glorify."

DAVID WILLOUGHBY

Reference and Further Reading

Dove Awards website, http://www.doveawards.com.
Gospel Music Association website, http://www.gospelmusic.org.
Twila Paris website, http://www.twilaparis.com.

Selected Discography

Beyond a Dream (1994, Star Song Communications CD 20006). Includes "God Is in Control."
Sanctuary (1995, Star Song Communications CD 20011). Includes "He Is Exalted" ("Ele E Exaltado"), "Lamb of God" (instrumental), "We Bow Down" (instrumental), and "We Will Glorify."
Bedtime Prayers: Lullabies & Peaceful Worship (2001, Sparrow Records CD 51782).
Greatest Hits, Time and Again (2001, Sparrow Records CD 51825). Includes "God Is in Control," "He Is Exalted," "Lamb of God" (instrumental), "Warrior Is a Child," "We Bow Down," and "We Will Glorify."
House of Worship (2003, Sparrow Records CD 39799). Includes new recordings of "We Bow Down" and "We Will Glorify."

PARKER FAMILY, THE (REX AND ELEANOR PARKER)

Charles E. "Rex" Parker (b. September 30, 1921; d. June 2, 1999)
Eleanor Neira Parker (b. February 28, 1922)

Rex and Eleanor Parker, who sometimes performed with their daughters as the Parker Family, spent their entire career doing radio, television, and appearances in southern West Virginia and environs. They did gain some wider exposure through recordings on the King label. As age began to slow them down, their activity became increasingly confined to their *Songs for Salvation* radio program in Princeton, West Virginia, and local church gatherings.

Charles "Rex" Parker was born in Maplewood, West Virginia, while Eleanor Neira, a child of Spanish immigrants, was born in neighboring Beard's Fork. Rex played country music on various local radio stations, and after Eleanor returned from New York City, where she went to high school, they married on August 31, 1941, as part of a stage show in Beckley.

They worked as a live country act on radio and later television, mostly at WHIS in Bluefield and later on a long-running television program at WOAY in Oak Hill, both in West Virginia. They recorded sparingly on the Cozy and Coral labels, and when their daughters Conizene and Rexana became old enough, they joined the act, and it became the Parker Family. Rex was a strong instrumentalist on banjo, mandolin, and electric lead guitar, which gave the Parkers musical versatility.

In 1959, the Parkers had a conversion experience and thereafter did only sacred music. They began recording for King Records shortly after and did four albums, two of them released on King's Audio Lab subsidiary. Their best original song, "Build Your Treasures in Heaven," could best be described as an underrated classic of country gospel. Another excellent patriotic–inspirational number, "Moonlight on West Virginia," had earlier been recorded for Cozy and covered by Wilma Lee and Stoney Cooper on Columbia. Several of their songs were based on their own religious experiences.

They did another album for Joyful Sound Records in 1971, and they also recorded a few singles. Their television program continued into the late 1970s, after which their broadcasts were confined to WAEY radio in Princeton, West Virginia. Rex's death in the spring of 1999 found Eleanor carrying on the program alone with some help from Conizene, who had returned to West Virginia after working for many years as a nurse in Indiana.

IVAN M. TRIBE

Reference and Further Reading

Dorgan, Howard. *The Airwaves of Zion: Radio and Religion in Appalachia*, Chapter 3, 73–112. Knoxville: University of Tennessee Press, 1993.

Tribe, Ivan M. "Rex and Eleanor Parker: The West Virginia Sweethearts." *Bluegrass Unlimited* 10, no. 10 (April 1976): 18–25.

Discography

Songs for Salvation (1960, Audio Lab AL 1548).
Songs for Salvation II (1962, Audio Lab AL 1574).
A Real Nice American Family (King SLP 923).

PARSONS, SQUIRE

Squire Enos Parsons, Jr. (b. April 4, 1948, Newton, WV)

Squire Parsons is one of Southern gospel music's most prolific songwriters and popular baritone singers. His best-known composition, "Sweet Beulah Land," has become a Southern gospel standard recorded by dozens of artists. Before establishing himself as a solo artist, Squire had a distinguished career as a member of several popular groups.

Squire developed a love of gospel at an early age. His home in the mountains of West Virginia was filled with the sound of the 78-rpm recordings of the Chuck Wagon Gang, the Statesmen, and the Blackwood Brothers. Squire's father was the music leader at church, and he passed on his love of gospel songs and taught Squire to sing from the shape-note songbooks.

Following graduation from high school, Squire attended West Virginia Institute of Technology, earning a BS degree in music education. Squire began his musical career in 1969 with the Calvarymen. He also worked as an elementary school music teacher and band director at Hannah High School in Macon County, West Virginia, from 1971 until 1975.

Squire Parsons came to national attention in 1975 when he was invited to become the baritone singer for the popular Southern gospel group the Kingsmen Quartet of Ashville, North Carolina. His work with the well-known recording and touring artists provided a natural outlet for his songwriting. The Kingsmen recorded many of Squire's songs, including "I Stand Upon the Rock" and "You're Not Alone." Parsons became an integral part of the group's success, and the accolades from fans began coming when, in 1978, he received the first of many nominations in the annual poll by the *Singing News* magazine in the categories of Favorite Baritone, Favorite Gospel Songwriter, and Favorite Gospel Singer.

Deciding to step out on his own, Parsons left the Kingsmen in 1979 to launch a solo career. His debut recording released in 1979 included "Sweet Beulah Land," which was voted Song of the Year by the fans in the 1981 *Singing News* poll. Parsons went on to record twenty-five albums, and accolades from both the fans and the industry followed. The readers of *Singing News* voted him Favorite Baritone Singer in both 1986 and 1987. The fans showed their appreciation for his composing skills, naming him Favorite Gospel Songwriter in 1986, 1992, 1994, and 1995. He was also named Favorite Southern Gospel Male Singer in 1986 in the annual poll. Industry recognition came to Parsons in the form of multiple Dove Award nominations. In 1990, Parsons received the prestigious Marvin Norcross Award recognizing service to the church and community and contributions to the gospel music industry.

Squire Parsons's most popular songs include "The Broken Rose," "I Sing Because," "He Came to Me," and "I Call It Home." Other groups who have recorded his songs include Gold City ("I'm Not Giving Up," "If God Be for Us") and the Kingdom Heirs ("I Go to the Rock").

JAMES I. ELLIOTT

Reference and Further Reading

Herald-Dispatch website, http://www.hdonline.com/2004/July/16/LFlist2.html.
Squire Parsons website, http://www.squireparsons.com/biography.php.

Discography

He Found Me (1999, Parable 85).
Silver Anniversary Collection (1999, Parable 7132).
Southern Gospel Soloist (1999, Crossroads 70).
We Shall Get Home (2000, Horizon 850).

PATTI, SANDI

(b. July 12, 1956)

During the early part of her career, Sandi Patti established herself as the preeminent female vocalist in the contemporary Christian music field, a singer who connected to the church world by recording songs for the church. By 2004, she had won thirty-one Dove Awards and five Grammys and had sold eleven million albums, including three platinum and five gold.

Born in Oklahoma City, Oklahoma, to parents who were touring with the Christian Brothers Quartet (her father was singing while her mother played the piano), Patti's family moved to Phoenix, Arizona, when she was two and a half, where her father was a minister of music at a Church of God. After ten years in Arizona, the Patty family moved to San Diego, California, where her father again worked with a church and formed a family group, the Ron Patty Family. Heavily influenced by Karen Carpenter and Barbra Streisand, Patti entered Anderson College in Anderson, Indiana, the alma mater of her parents. There she became active in a student singing group, New Nature, where she met her first husband, John Helvering; they were married on November 17, 1978.

Before her marriage, Sandi had recorded a custom album, *For My Friends*, and the printer had misspelled her last name as "Patti." Rather than send the albums back, she went under the name Sandi Patti during the first decade of her professional career.

In 1979, she was signed to the Benson Company in Nashville and released *Sandi's Songs*. That same year,

she worked as a studio singer in nearby Alexandria, Indiana, in Bill Gaither's studio, Pinebrook. In 1981, she began touring with the Bill Gaither Trio as a backup singer. That same year she released her second album, *Love Overflowing*, which yielded the song, "We Shall Behold Him," which was written by Dottie Rambo. Because of the popularity of this song and her tours with Gaither, Sandi Patti won Dove Awards for Artist of the Year and Female Vocalist in 1982. In 1983, she released the album *Lift Up the Lord*, which contained the song "How Majestic Is Your Name," written by Michael W. Smith, which led to her second Dove Award for Female Vocalist as well as the Dove Award for Inspirational Album of the Year.

In 1986, Sandi's recording of "The Star Spangled Banner" was heard on ABC television during a Fourth of July broadcast; this led to a number of patriotic appearances, where she sang the national anthem as well as "God Bless America." Patti's career continued in an upward spiral until 1993, when she divorced her husband; in 1995, it became public knowledge that she had had an extramarital affair with one of her backup singers, Don Peslis. In August 1995, she married Peslis, and they blended their families (she had four children, he had three, and they adopted one after their marriage). The controversy over her affair erupted into a scandal that caused a number of Christian radio stations to stop playing her recordings, a number of Christian retailers to pull her recordings from their shelves, and a number of Christian buyers to quit purchasing her albums. She cut back on her public appearances, although she continued to appear with symphonies and in patriotic concerts.

After her divorce and remarriage, Sandi let her professional name revert to "Patty" and continued releasing albums, but the big sales were no longer there. Still, she remains a force in the Christian music world, and her legacy is secure as the most awarded female artist in the history of the Dove Awards.

DON CUSIC

Reference and Further Reading

Cusic, Don. *Sandi Patti: The Voice of Gospel.* New York: Doubleday, 1988.
———. *The Sound of Light: A History of Gospel and Christian Music.* New York: Hal Leonard, 2002.

Discography

Sandi's Song (1979); *Love Overflowing* (1981); *Lift Up the Lord* (1982); *The Gift Goes On* (1983); *Live: More Than Wonderful* (1983); *Songs from the Heart* (1984); *Hymns Just for You* (1985); *Morning Like This* (1986); *Make His*

Praise Glorious (1988); *A Symphony of Praise* (1988); *The Finest Moments* (1989); *Sandy Patty and The Friendship Company* (1989); *Another Time, Another Place* (1990); *The Friendship Company: Open For Business* (1991); *Hallmark Christmas Album: Celebrate Christmas* (1992); *Le Voyage* (1993); *Find It on the Wings* (1994); *An American Songbook* (1996); *Hallmark Christmas Album: It's Christmas* (1996; with Peabo Bryson); *O Holy Night* (1996); *Artist of My Soul* (1997); *Libertad Me Das* (1998; Spanish language album); *Sandi Patty & Kathy Troccoli, Together* (1999); *These Days* (2000); *All the Best . . . Live!* (2001); *Take Hold of Christ* (2003); *Hymns of Faith . . . Songs of Inspiration* (2004).

PERFORMANCE STYLES

The value of any musical genre is reflected, in part, in its ability to generate new forms and directions as it develops stylistically over time and in various places. With more than a century and a quarter of history behind it, gospel music has manifested itself in an amazing array of styles. Variety notwithstanding, by the end of the twentieth century there were three main streams of gospel music stylistically, each with various subsets. The oldest is usually called gospel song or gospel hymnody. By the twenty-first century, it might be called traditional gospel or, more properly, historic gospel, for from it flow the other two streams of black gospel and Southern gospel.

Traditional gospel grew out of the Northern, urban revival tradition of evangelist Dwight L. Moody and his song leader/soloist Ira D. Sankey in the 1870s, and it remained the dominant musical style in revivalist-oriented churches for more than a century. Its rhythmic, melodic, and harmonic structures were rooted in the European tradition of music composition and performance. Its best-known contributors were the blind poet Fanny Crosby and poet/songwriter Philip P. Bliss. Although the poetry of gospel hymnody spoke in simple words and employed limited rhetorical devices, it was rooted in biblical language, metaphor, and allusion.

The music was melodically tuneful, employing eighth notes more often than the slower-feeling quarters. Compound meters, particularly 6/8, were characteristic, producing a lilting quality for which gospel hymnody became famous (as in, for example, "Blessed Assurance, Jesus Is Mine"). The melodic range was designed for congregational song and was therefore limited to that of the untrained voice from about middle C to top-line F. Harmonies were generally primary triads, although secondary triads, borrowed minor chords, and secondary dominants became part of the harmonic vocabulary. The often-published characterization of gospel music employing "barbershop" harmonies is inaccurate, however.

Most characteristic of the gospel song was a contagious chorus or refrain that summed up the text's meaning in a succinct and memorable manner. The opening words of the refrain were usually the name of the song, unlike older hymns that were identified by their opening words. The precedent for these choruses was the secular "household" or "parlor" song, composed by Stephen Foster and others. In fact, many of the first generation of gospel hymnists such as George F. Root were successful composers of secular music in the verse/chorus mode.

Traditional gospel song was popularized in practice and publication via the major revivalists of the century, stretching from Moody through Billy Sunday to Billy Graham. This style—in its various guises—remained fairly consistent throughout the twentieth century, with Bill and Gloria Gaither being its last significant contributors.

Developing later—but operating on a parallel track—was gospel music in the African American tradition, often called black gospel. During the early decades of the twentieth century, black churches often emulated their neighboring white churches, singing the same gospel songs of Crosby and Bliss. However, with the development of the modern Pentecostal movement growing out of revivals in the early 1900s, an amorphous movement (sometimes called the "sanctified church") began to take shape. Unhampered by traditional concepts of worship, the movement was quick to adopt more secular influences into its services and music-making. These influences included ragtime, blues, and jazz, as well as black spirituals.

For the most part, the basic difference between early black and white gospel music was more in its performance practice than in its content. One important difference was a sense of rhythm, specifically the "gospel meter," wherein songs written in 4/4 were performed in the compound meter of 12/8, as popularized by former bluesman Thomas A. Dorsey—the "father" of black gospel. Closely related to rhythm was a freedom and intensity of expression related to the "filling" of the Holy Spirit, resulting in performances characterized by high intensity, conspicuous physical responses, and a sense of improvisation—especially by soloists interpolating runs or groans—as popularized by singers such as James Cleveland.

It was not until the 1950s, however, that this style achieved a conscious sense of self-identity as significantly different from traditional gospel, becoming popular outside the black community with the recordings of singers such as Mahalia Jackson. This style eventually became known as "black gospel" and finally as just "gospel," virtually leaving traditional gospel music without any identifying name. During the 1980s, R&B exerted a strong influence, producing a more contemporary sound from exponents such as Andrae Crouch, reflecting influences of secular pop music, and becoming an important component of contemporary Christian music (CCM). In this style, solo and ensemble performance displaced the congregation as the dominant medium. While traditional gospel was closely aligned with published music, black gospel was much closer to the aural traditions of blues or jazz.

Southern gospel also took shape in the early twentieth century with the merger of traditional gospel and shape-note hymnody prominent in the South. It was popularized by male quartets formed by publishing companies such as James D. Vaughan or Stamps–Baxter to sell their paperback collections of shape-note music. Texts generally focused more on subjects with strong emotional connections (mother, home, heaven) than on theological concerns (for example, A. E. Brumley's "I'll Fly Away").

Musically, songs had a strong rhythmic component resulting from a "walking bass," stride piano techniques, or the "gospel meter" frequent in black gospel. Added to those components was a harmonic vocabulary that employed more augmented sixth-chords of barbershop fame, parallel tenths in the accompaniment, melodic call-and-response passages, and conspicuous syncopation—all delivered with a vocal technique closer to straight-toned, nasal country music than European-inspired vocalisms. Southern gospel continually absorbed diverse influences, first adopting the piano and then drums and guitars as it also reflected the influences of secular pop music and CCM as well as bluegrass. When notated, it employed the shape-note system.

A survey of the ever-fluctuating gospel-related Dove or Grammy Award categories reveals the dominance of these three basic styles, despite their myriad offspring. Much like the blues, which are based on fairly modest resources, gospel music has absorbed and cross-pollinated with a great variety of secular and sacred musics, producing a rich tapestry of styles stretching from traditional to hip-hop.

MEL R. WILHOIT

See also Bliss, Philip Paul; Cleveland, James; Crosby, Fanny Jane; Crouch, Andrae; Jackson, Mahalia; Root, George Frederick; Sankey, Ira David

Reference and Further Reading:

Cusic, Don. *The Sound of Light: A History of Gospel Music.* Bowling Green, OH: Bowling Green State University Popular Press, 1990.

Goff, James R. *Close Harmony: The History of Southern Gospel.* Chapel Hill and London: University of North Carolina Press, 2002.

Reagon, Bernice Johnson, ed. *We'll Understand It Better By and By: Pioneering African American Gospel Composers.* Washington, DC: Smithsonian Institution Press, 1992.

Discography

Brighten the Corner Where You Are: Black and White Hymnody (New World Records 224).

Close Harmony: A History of Southern Gospel Music, Vol. I, 1920–1955 (Dualtone).

PERRY SISTERS

Diana Perry Gillette (b. December 18, 1954)
Tammy Belcher Underwood (b. January 16, 1971)
Carol Perry Markin (b. Unknown)
Bonnie Perry Belcher (b. Unknown)

The Perry Sisters began their singing career in 1974 in Huntington, West Virginia. The group was made up of three sisters: Diana, Carol, and Bonnie. In 1984, the girls signed with the Eddie Crook Agency and began singing professionally; never before had Southern gospel music experienced a ladies' trio singing in this capacity. They soon became known as "the First Ladies of Gospel Music." The sisters created such a beautiful harmony together that they began to spread their music ministry successfully. Such songs include "There'll Be a Payday," which was the highest chart topper for the girls in the *Singing News,* and "Resurrection Morn," which went to number one on the *Billboard* charts.

In 1990, Carol Perry Markin and Bonnie Perry Belcher retired from the road. This left Diana Perry Gillette as the remaining member. Diana's daughter, Angela Gillette, and niece, Tammy Belcher Underwood, joined the group shortly after her sisters left. In 1992, the girls changed recording labels and signed with Sunlight Records. The ladies sang together until 1996. Diana's daughter left the group and was replaced by Karen Akeman. Karen sang with the group for only three years. When Karen left, Jada Hite began singing alto for the Perry Sisters. When Jada and her husband were called into another ministry for the Lord, she left the group in February 2003. Diana Gillette and her niece Tammy are the only members left singing.

The success of the Perry Sisters is a true family effort. Diana's husband Bob was the former drummer for the group and is now driving the group's bus. Diana's other daughter, Nicole Mathews, fills in for the group on an occasional basis. Tammy's husband, Rodney, plays keyboards and bass guitar and is the sound technician. Tammy's sister, Tina, has helped to write songs for the Perry Sisters.

Diana is truly gifted with her songwriting abilities. Songs she wrote for the group are "I Wonder How Mary Felt," That Wonderful Name," "More Like You," and "Resurrection Morn." The Perry Sisters have been nominated for Favorite Trio, Favorite Soprano, Horizon Award, and Favorite Video. Other popular Perry Sister songs include "Lean on the Rock," "We Need a Helping Hand," "More Than Just a Hill," and "If It Had Not Been."

ANDREA GANNAWAY

Reference and Further Reading

Gillette, Diana. Interview, June 25, 2004.
Perry Sisters website, http://www.perrysisters.com.

Discography

Diamond Forever. Includes "Then Came the Dawning" and "Clap Your Hands."
The Evening Shades. Includes "I Just Want to Thank You Lord."
A Family Portrait. Includes "I Am Coming Out of This Valley" and "They Can't Take the Blood."
Reminisce. Includes "Lean On the Rock," "We Need a Helping Hand," "There'll Be a Payday, " "More Than Just a Hill," and "Resurrection Morn."
The Still of the Night. Has a Christmas theme.
This Kind of Love. Includes "More Like You" and "That Wonderful Name."

PETRA

Bob Hartman (b. December 26, 1949)
Greg Hough (b. September 22, 1949)
John DeGroff (b. September 3, 1953)
Bill Glover (b. November 22, 1952)

Petra, whose name means "rock" in Greek, was founded by Bob Hartman in 1972 while he was attending the Christian Training Center in Ft. Wayne, Indiana. Hartman recruited Greg Hough (guitar and vocals), John DeGroff (bass guitar), and Bill Glover (drums) to form the group. There was early opposition to using the rock 'n' roll genre for Christian music, but the trail had already been blazed by artists such as Love Song and Larry Norman.

In 1973 the band was signed to Myrrh Records, a subsidiary of Word Records. They released a self-titled debut album in 1974 that was more akin to country rock than the hard rock sound for which they earned their reputation. It was not until 1977 that they released their sophomore effort, *Come and Join Us.* Greg Volz contributed lead vocals, and the sound evolved into a harder rock.

Band personnel changed, but the group kept developing under Hartman's continuing leadership and songwriting. When *Washes Whiter Than* was released in 1979, it produced "Why Should the Father Bother," which became a Christian radio hit. By 1980, the new Petra was headed by Hartman and Volz, with John Slick (keyboards), Mark Kelly (bass guitar), and Louie Weaver (drums). They released three albums in the early 1980s, and in 1985 John Lawry took over on keyboards, while lead vocals were assumed by John Schlitt. The band made a transition in their sound, going from slick and polished to bare boned and raw. By 1988, Ronny Cates joined Petra to help create a heavier guitar sound, which was influenced by the then-popular "hair metal" bands such as Stryper. In 1995, Jim Cooper took over on keyboards, and David J. Lichens replaced Hartman on guitar.

By the beginning of the twenty-first century, Petra had sold more than seven million records, won four Grammy Awards and ten Dove Awards, and were inducted into the Gospel Music Hall of Fame. In 2001, the band signed with Inpop Records and released *Revival.* In 2002, Bob Hartman rejoined the group as its lead guitarist, and the band recorded *Jekyll & Hyde,* which was produced by Pete Furler on Inpop.

BOB GERSZTYN

See also Calvary Chapel, Costa Mesa; Myrrh Records; Love Song; Newsboys; Norman, Larry; Rock Gospel; Stryper

Reference and Further Reading

Huey, Steve. "Back Sliding Blues by Petra." Extended Hand Ministries website, http://extendedhandchapel.org/backslidingblues.html (accessed October 27, 2003).
Jones, Michael; Cathy Jones. A Guide to Petra website, http://www.guidetopetra.com/bios.html (accessed October 27, 2003).
One-Way.org website, http://one-way.org/ (accessed October 27, 2003).
Petra Means Rock website, http://www.petrameansrock.com/ (accessed October 27, 2003).
Renaud, Josh. Petra Rocks My World website, http://www.petrarocksmyworld.com/band.html (accessed October 27, 2003).
Sheahan, Bernie. "Petra Biography." Christian Music Online website, http://www.cmo.com/cmo/cmo/data/petra.htm (accessed October 25, 2003).

Discography

Petra (1974, Myrrh); *Come and Join Us* (1977, Myrrh); *Washes Whiter Than* (1979, Star Song); *Never Say Die* (1982, Star Song); *More Power to Ya* (1983, Star Song); *Not of This World* (1983, Star Song); *Beat the System* (1985, Star Song); *Back to the Street* (1986, Star Song);

Captured in Time and Space (1986, Star Song); *This Means War* (1987, Star Song); *On Fire* (1988, Star Song); *Petra Praise: The Rock Cries Out* (1989, Dayspring); *Beyond Belief* (1990, Dayspring); *Unseen Power* (1992 Word/Epic); *Wake-Up Call* (1993, Word); *No Doubt* (1995, Word/Epic); *Petra Power Praise* (1995, Star Song); *Petraphonics* (1995, Star Song); *The Rock Block* (1995, Star Song); *The Early Years, Vol. I* (1996, Sparrow); *Petra Praise 2* (1997, Word/Epic); *Beat the System* (1998, Star Song); *God Fixation* (1998, Word); *Not of This World* (1998, Star Song); *On Fire* (1998, Star Song); *This Means War* (1998, Star Song); *Unseen Power* (1998, Word); *Double Take* (2000, Word); *Revival* (2002, Inpop); *Still Means War* (2002, Word); *Jekyll & Hyde* (2003, Inpop); *The Power of Praise* (2003, Word/Curb/ Warner Bros.); *Till Everything I Do* (2003, Inpop).

PHILLIPS, PHILIP

(b. August 13, 1834; d. June 25, 1895)

Known as the "Singing Pilgrim" (a reference to *Pilgrim's Progress*), Philip Phillips gained fame, beginning around 1866, from his worldwide tours of sacred solo concerts. This brought him to the attention of evangelist Dwight Moody, who requested that Phillips accompany him on his first evangelistic tour to England in 1873, but Phillips was already engaged. Moody eventually chose Ira Sankey, a pairing that turned out to be the most important in gospel music history.

Phillips was apparently one of the first to popularize sacred music as solo song during that era. His style of singing, in which he accompanied himself on a melodeon or portable organ, reflected one he considered halfway between popular, frivolous songs and a more classical approach. Particularly novel in a church service was his habit of singing an appropriate solo at the close of a sermon. Phillips's concerts usually lasted about ninety minutes, and he often interspersed Bible readings between the songs. Although Phillips pioneered a new approach to sacred music, the songs he sang tended toward the older style of purely strophic song, without the presence of the popular new chorus.

In January 1865, Phillips sang "Your Mission" for a meeting of the U.S. Christian Commission. President Lincoln was present and was so moved that he requested Phillips repeat the song at the conclusion of the service.

In addition to his singing, Phillips was an active publisher, turning out *Early Blossoms* (1861), *Musical Leaves* (1862), *Hallowed Songs* (1863), and *American Sacred Songster* (1868), selling more than a million copies. *Hallowed Songs* was the collection that Sankey was using on his first evangelistic foray to England in

1873. When this collection proved unsatisfactory for his purposes, Sankey tried to get the publisher to print a new edition to include the Sunday school songs he was employing so successfully. Meeting with no success from the publisher, Sankey produced his own collection, going on to become one of the major publishers of gospel hymnody. As Phillips produced little of the new type of gospel song, his contributions to gospel hymnody were soon eclipsed by the newer, more prolific gospel songwriters.

MEL R. WILHOIT

Reference and Further Reading

Eskew, Harry. "Phillips, Philip." In *New Grove Dictionary of American Music*. New York: Macmillan Press, 1986.

Hall, J. H. *Biography of Gospel Song and Hymn Writers.* New York: Fleming Revell, 1971 (1914).

Phillips, Philip. *Song Pilgrimage Around the World.* Chicago: Fairbanks, Palmer, 1880.

PHILLIPS, WASHINGTON

(b. ca. 1891; d. December 31, 1938)

Washington Phillips, who was probably born in Freestone County, Texas, was a farmer and a "jack-leg" preacher. That meant that he had no ministerial training or a regular church, but he did have a strong call to preach. He was also the only artist, gospel or otherwise, to record with the dulceola, a rare instrument invented in 1902 during a time when a large number of "easy-to-play" instruments were manufactured. Apparently it did not catch on, because only about a hundred dulceolas were produced. As played by Phillips, the instrument, which was a zither equipped with a piano-like keyboard, sounded like a lightly hammered dulcimer. So rare was the dulceola that the record company merely listed it as "novelty accompaniment" on four of Phillips's five sessions. Only on his last session, December 2, 1929, in Dallas, did they state "accompanied by own dulceola."

At his first session in Dallas on December 2, 1927, Phillips recorded four numbers, including a biblical story, "Paul and Silas in Jail," as well as a version of Charles A. Tindley's "Leave It There," under the title "Take Your Burden to the Lord and Leave It There." Three days later, on December 5, 1927, he recorded his classic "Denomination Blues," a two-part piece decrying, among other things, the squabbling of black Christian sects. For this number, he borrowed the secular melody "Hesitation Blues."

On December 4, 1928, Phillips recorded two songs, one of which—"I Am Born to Preach the

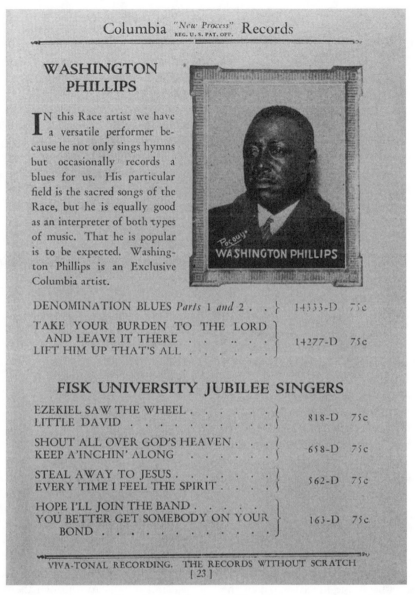

Columbia Records announcement for recordings by Washington Phillips. Photo courtesy Frank Driggs Collection.

Gospel"—gave some biographical details of his life and affirmed his commitment to his calling. He noted that he had little formal education but "Jesus Christ sure didn't leave me no fool." The next day (December 5, 1928), he recorded two songs, including one of his "lectures," "Jesus Is My Friend." Another lecture, "Train Your Child," was the second piece recorded a day earlier.

Phillips's last session, in Dallas, on December 2, 1929, was his most prolific, with eight sides being cut; one of these, a two-part "You Can't Stop a Tattler," was considered unsuitable for issue at the time. Phillips's last recording session took place after the Great Depression was under way, and its effect on the recording industry may explain why the Texas dulceola player had no further sessions.

W. K. McNeil

Reference and Further Reading

Oliver, Paul. *Songsters and Saints: Vocal Traditions on Race Records*. Cambridge, England: Cambridge University Press, 1984.

Discography

Denomination Blues (1980, Agram AB2006).
Songsters and Saints Vol. One (1984, Matchbox MSEX 2001/2002).
I Am Born to Preach the Gospel (1992, Yazoo).

PHIPPS FAMILY, THE

Arthur Leroy Phipps (b. August 12, 1916; d. August 30, 1995)

Kathleen Norris Helton Phipps (b. April 22, 1924; d. November 4, 1992)

The Phipps Family performed hymns and ballads in a style reminiscent of the Carter Family. Indeed, so clearly identified were they with the Virginia family's sound that they were sometimes criticized as being nothing more than Carter clones.

This Knox County, Kentucky, group had its beginnings when Arthur (A. L.) Phipps and Kathleen Helton were married on September 6, 1937. Because the couple were drawn together by their love of the old hymns and ballads of their native region, it is hardly surprising that all of their thirteen children displayed some musical abilities, five of them eventually appearing on record with the Phipps Family. At first, A. L.'s niece, Hester Anderson, sang the third part in trio numbers, but she was later replaced by various Phipps children, most notably their daughter Trueleen Helen, who is heard on most of the family's records.

Although the Phipps Family started playing regularly in 1943, their radio career did not begin until 1950, when they landed a job at WCTT Corbin, Kentucky. They later had a program on WYWY Barbourville and also appeared on a continuing basis on WNOX Knoxville's *Mid-Day Merry-Go-Round*. They even made occasional appearances on WWVA Wheeling. Originally, they sang secular songs in a Western style, but they got so many requests for Carter Family songs that they finally adopted the Carter manner. Later, they met A. P. Carter and recorded several live shows with him and his family. They also made their first records for the same Acme label for which the A. P. Carter Family made their last.

In 1960 the Phipps Family made three records for Starday, the first and third of Carter Family songs, including one of the Carters' religious songs, while the second was devoted to rarer old-time numbers. With their old-time sound, the Phippses appealed to the folk revival audience of the 1960s, and in 1964 they appeared at the Newport Folk Festival; shortly thereafter they recorded an album for Folkways. Such activities made their music available to urban audiences. Soon after the Folkways effort, A. L. started his own Pine Mountain Records and later added a second label, Mountain Eagle.

For a decade (1962–1972), they taped fifteen-minute radio programs for broadcast on stations ranging from WCKY in Cincinnati, Ohio, to XEG in Monterrey, Mexico, where they sold records via mail order. They also traveled frequently, eventually performing in thirty-two states. In addition to Carter Family songs and traditional ballads, their numerous recordings include thematic albums of Christmas and Easter numbers and one of *a cappella* mountain hymns.

The Phipps Family's career ended in 1991 when Kathleen was diagnosed with cancer. She lingered on until November 4, 1992, the last seven months in a coma. A. L.'s end was more grisly; he was murdered by one of his renters, John Mills, during a robbery at his house.

W. K. McNeil

Discography

Most Requested Sacred Songs of the Carter Family (1960, Starday).
Greatest Old Time Gospel Hymns (1966, Pine Mountain).
Christmas with the Phipps Family (Pine Mountain).
In the Sweet Bye and Bye (Pine Mountain).
Just a Few More Days (Pine Mountain).
Suffering, Crucifixion, and Resurrection of Christ (Pine Mountain).

PHIPPS, ERNEST

(b. May 4, 1900, Knox Country, KY; d. April 17, 1963, Gray, KY)

Ernest Phipps was a popular preacher and singer in the Holiness churches in Eastern Kentucky. He won national acclaim by taking members of his congregation into Bristol, Tennessee, in 1927 and 1928 to record a series of fevered up-tempo gospel performances that were distributed nationwide by the Victor/Bluebird company and that gained a second wave of popularity through their inclusion in Harry Smith's 1950s *Anthology of American Folk Music*.

Not to be confused with the other gospel singer, A. L. Phipps, Ernest Phipps recorded some of the few examples of the exuberant Holiness-Pentecostal style, replete with instruments, hand clapping, jangling tambourines, fiddles, and a piano. He made what is probably the first recording of the popular "Do Lord Remember Me" as well as "Bright Tomorrow," "Shine on Me," and "The Firing Line."

In later years, Phipps sought to record no more (unfortunately so for those interested in the development of the Holiness singing style) but did a lot of preaching and singing in the Corbin, Kentucky, area. His marriage fell apart in the 1930s, and for a time he moved to Knoxville, Tennessee, and he was actually drafted into the Army during World War II (at the age of forty-three), where he served in a hospital unit.

Later he remarried and had a successful business trucking coal. He remained active in the ministry and, before his death, he was pastoring a church in Gray, Kentucky.

CHARLES K. WOLFE

Reference and Further Reading

Story, Brandon. "The Music and the Memory of the Ernest Phipps Story." In *The Bristol Sessions*, edited by Charles Wolfe and Ted Olson, 96–118. Jefferson, NC: McFarland, 2005.

PHIPPS, WINTLEY

(b. January 7, 1955 in Trinidad, West Indies)

Heal our land.
Please grant us peace today,
And strengthen all who lack the faith
To call on Thee each day.
Heal our land,
And keep us safe and free.
Watch over all who understand
The need for liberty.

These poignant and spirit-filled lyrics from the first stanza of a song by Senator Orrin Hatch were rendered by Wintley Phipps at the preinaugural ceremonies for President George W. Bush. This song, arranged by Greg Hansen Phipps and set to music by Janice Kapp Perry, was presented by a gifted artist and performer. Phipps, a two-time Grammy nominee, has inspired audiences with his gift of music for the past twenty-five years in churches and the community and for celebrities, presidents, and national and international leaders. In addition to his appearance at the White House, he has performed at the Vatican and on numerous television programs, including *The Oprah Winfrey Show*.

Presently a resident of Florida, Wintley Augustus Phipps was born in Trinidad, West Indies, on January 7, 1955. Phipps, an internationally known gospel singer, was raised in Montreal, Quebec. His degrees include a BA degree and a master of divinity degree.

Early in his life, Phipps had dreams. He stated that he and his mother would have conversations about his dreams on their infrequent visits, and she referred to him as her "dreamer boy." Phipps noted that she believed that God had something special for her elder son. He added that she always encouraged him and nurtured his dreams. Phipps, who has founded two recording companies—Songs of Freedom and Coral Records—is also the author of the book *Power of a Dream*.

In 1998, Phipps founded the U.S. Dream Academy, a nationally recognized youth program that works to break the cycle of intergenerational incarceration and academic underachievement for children of prisoners and children falling behind in school. The Dream Academy provides after-school programs for youth, offering academic enrichment, one-on-one mentoring, values education, and computer technology training. The academy's national programs utilize e-classroom platforms that offer a web-deployable, self-paced instructional curriculum to increase reading, math, and English comprehension and proficiency. Intensive mentoring and life skills coaching are hallmarks of the academy's approach, which Phipps believes helps to create safe learning environments and build strong foundations for youth who are at risk of incarceration, school failure, future unemployment, or becoming involved in gang activity or who are already involved in the criminal justice system.

Phipps's contributions to gospel music have been monumental. His music transcends and speaks to individuals from numerous cultures. In an article in a 1984 issue of *Spectrum: Journal of the Association of Adventist Forums,* Phipps is described as the "singer of the rainbow." In San Francisco, he was the mystery singer at the Democratic National Convention. "But at his song's end, he had a rainbow of blacks, whites, Hispanics, and Native Americans holding hands and swaying back and forth like a forest caught up in a forceful but calm tropical storm. Tears flowed freely. Many of those in the crowd were disarmed and numbed by the moment."

Wintley A. Phipps's vocal artistry cascades across a huge spectrum. His style, universal and rich in spirit, touches individuals across a multidimensional nation. His songs express his love for people and God. These sentiments are expressed in his song "I Give You My Life."

SIMMONA E. SIMMONS-HODO

Reference and Further Reading

Aubespin, Eriska. "Palm Bay Pastor Shares His Dream." *Southern Tidings* 97 (January 2003): 22.
August, Mark. "Wintley Phipps: Man on a Mission." *Message* 76 (July/August 2001): 14–15, 17, 44.
Goldstein, Clifford R. "Wintley Phipps Setting the Standard." *Listen* 44 (August 1991): 4–7.
Goode, Stephen. "Phipps Helps Youth Hum a Different Tune." *Insight on the News* 17 (June 18, 2001): 36.
Humphrey, Patricia L. "Wintley Phipps: Musician Extraordinaire!" *Message* 54 (July/August 1988): 26–29.
Parkinson, Lester A. "Wintley Phipps: From a Dream to an Academy." *Message 70* (January/February 2004): 12–14.
Phipps, Wintley. "Wintley Phipps: Dreamer." *Review and Herald Publication* 26 (May 27, 1995): 8–11.

————; Goldie Down. *The Power of a Dream: The Inspiring Story of a Young Man's Audacious Faith*. Grand Rapids, MI: Zondervan Publishing House, 1994.

Sargent, Edward D. "Adventist Baritone Sings at Democratic Convention." *Adventist Review* 161 (September 20, 1984): 26.

———— "Singer of the Rainbow." *Spectrum: Journal of the Association of Adventist Forums* 15 (1984): 61–62.

"Wintley A. Phipps." U.S. Dream Academy website, http://www.usdreamacademy.com/2002/uda_phipps.html (accessed February 15, 2005).

Discography

Favorite Hymns; Favorite Spirituals; Great Controversy; Heal Our Land; Out of the Night; I Choose You Again; I Give You My Life; It's Christmas Time; Lord, You Are My Music; A Love Like This; The Power of a Dream; Saviour: The Story of God's Passion for His People; Songs of Christmas; Spirituals: A Symphonic Celebration; The Sun Will Shine Again; We Are One; Wintley Phipps; Wintley Phipps Live!

PIANO

Although Cristofori is credited with inventing the piano around 1700, it took nearly a century for it to replace the popular harpsichord of Bach's day. Even during the nineteenth century, after the piano had became central to both the concert hall and the family parlor, it was still not considered a "church" instrument, for that was clearly the organ, of either the mighty pipe or the lowly pump variety.

By 1900, the piano had had an impact on religious life, primarily in the Sunday schools and popular revival meetings. Although Ira Sankey, the father of gospel song, became famous in the 1870s for singing from a pump organ, he was employing the piano for accompaniments on his Edison cylinder recordings by 1898. About the same time, ballplayer-turned-evangelist Billy Sunday began holding large-scale meetings and using pianists to accompany the gospel solos and congregational songs.

The most important development in gospel piano came from Australia, where in 1902 Charlie Alexander led singing for the revival meetings of Reuben A. Torrey. In the dusty town of Bendigo, a local pianist named Robert Harkness halfheartedly volunteered to act as accompanist for the local meetings. When Harkness found the simple four-part harmony of the gospel songs boring, he began to improvise. Instead of the expected reprimand from Alexander, he encouraged Harkness to pursue his unusual musical approach and invited the Australian to join the revival team.

That began a twelve-year partnership of global revival meetings that saw the piano and an improvisatory approach to accompanying gospel music become the new paradigm for musical revivalism.

Harkness's style of playing was eventually disseminated through *The Harkness Piano Method of Evangelistic Hymn Playing* (1941), and it influenced generations of gospel pianists.

By 1900, it had already become evident that the piano—with its more percussive quality and lilting possibilities—proved a much better instrument than the organ for accompanying gospel music. Soon, gospel piano correspondence courses proliferated, and formal instruction in gospel piano was offered at institutions such as Moody Bible Institute—where George Schuler produced *Evangelistic Piano Playing* (1925)—and later at Bob Jones University.

This style, referred to as "evangelistic piano," was generally associated with the white, urban, Northern revivalism originating with Moody/Sankey (1870–1890) and extending to Billy Graham/Cliff Barrows (1950–2000). Gospel pianists in this tradition included B. D. Ackley, Henry Barraclough, Leonard Voke, H. C. Hamilton, George Schuler, Lance Latham, Merrill Dunlop, Virgil Brock, Herbert Buffum, Bert H. Wilhoit, and Rudy Atwood. Musically, the style was rooted in the European tradition of classical pianism. In addition, expansion of the original four-voice hymn texture and improvisation by means of arpeggiation, broken chords, and chord extensions provided more rhythmic impetus.

Another style, "(black) gospel piano," developed from the ragtime/blues tradition as filtered through the lens of the "sanctified" style of music associated with the early Pentecostal/charismatic tradition. Its origins are traced to revivals in Azusa, California, beginning in 1906, in which worshipers were often overcome with the power of the Holy Spirit, spoke in "tongues" (glossolalia), and experienced physical healings. Juanita Arizona Dranes was the first influential practitioner of a style called barrelhouse, which was essentially a pianistic approach to blues-based music. She combined this with the intensity and spontaneity of the "sanctified" church, playing for various revival preachers and recording sixteen sides for OKeh records between 1926 and 1928. While numerous holiness groups accepted this new style, mainstream black churches opposed any music that smacked of "worldly" influences such as the blues.

Nowhere was that opposition more clear than in the life of Thomas A. Dorsey, whose successful blues career as Georgia Tom was considered antithetical to religious life. Years of waffling between the two disparate worlds finally found him abandoning the blues for religious music but bringing his earlier experience as accompanist to blues singer Ma Rainey with him into the church. This was especially evident in his popularizing the "gospel meter" style by performing songs written in 4/4 in the compound meter of 12/8. This stylistic approach soon came to be one of the most characteristic features of black gospel music.

While ragtime influences produced the stride style of playing and blues expanded the expressive aspects, rhythm and blues influenced performers from the 1940s onward. These included Roberta Martin, Clara Ward, Mildred Falls (whose "vamp" style as accompanist to Mahalia Jackson became popular), and James Cleveland, who often employed a rolling bass contrasted with accented upper notes over a thick middle register—resulting in another classic gospel style.

Southern gospel quartets began life, as did their black counterparts, as *a cappella* groups. But in 1927, the Frank Stamps Quartet added a "fifth man" on piano and permanently changed Southern gospel. That was Dwight Brock, who pioneered a strong rhythmic approach via stride piano ("Stomp Beat"), providing variety with his "turnaround," a short improvised interlude between vocal verses that reflected the piano's growing role. During the 1950s, Lee Roy Abernathy and Hovie Lister added wild showmanship and a boogie-woogie style that garnered much praise and criticism. The use of parallel tenths in the left hand soon became another characteristic feature.

For most of the twentieth century, gospel music of all styles recognized the piano as *the* instrument of choice for congregational, ensemble, or solo playing. A large body of solo gospel piano literature also developed, focusing on the solo performer, of whom Dino Kartsonakis was the most conspicuous. It is significant that, during the twentieth century, the piano slowly usurped the prominent role held by the organ and became the preferred instrument in churches of all types in which gospel music was held dear.

With the popularity of contemporary Christian music in the 1970s, with its guitar and drum-based approach, the piano was forced to share the spotlight and develop a style reflecting the secular influences of Elton John and Billy Joel.

Considering the diverse styles of gospel music and the varying requirements for accompanying congregational song, choirs, and soloists, as well as the vast body of solo literature available, the piano has clearly demonstrated itself to be one of the most important constants in the history of gospel music.

MEL R. WILHOIT

Reference and Further Reading

Cusic, Don. *The Sound of Light: A History of Gospel Music.* Bowling Green, OH: Bowling Green State University Popular Press, 1990.

Gentry, Ted. "The Origins of Gospel Pianism." *American Music* 11 (Spring 1993): 90.

Goff, James R. *Close Harmony: The History of Southern Gospel.* Chapel Hill and London: University of North Carolina Press, 2002.

Reagon, Bernice Johnson, ed. *We'll Understand It Better By and By: Pioneering African American Gospel Composers.* Washington, DC: Smithsonian Institution Press, 1992.

PILGRIM TRAVELERS

One of the early professional African American gospel quartets, the close-harmony group Pilgrim Travelers, was formed in 1936 in Houston, Texas. The group, which initially consisted of Joe Johnson, Kylo Turner, Keith Barber, and Rayfield Taylor, began around 1934 as a community-based group affiliated with the Pleasant Grove Baptist Church. For nearly a decade they sang around the Houston metropolitan area, gradually expanding their performance territory to include more of Southeastern Texas and Southern Louisiana. The Pilgrim Travelers were greatly influenced by the Golden Gate Quartet, whose Blue Bird recordings and CBS radio broadcast informed many gospel quartets across the United States. They were popular enough by the outbreak of World War II that the group had attained semiprofessional status before the war halted all but vital travel.

In 1942 the Pilgrim Travelers entered and won a local talent contest, the prize for which was a national tour with the Soul Stirrers, another quartet that began in Houston around 1937. After the tour the group relocated to Los Angeles, California, adding J. W. Alexander as tenor and Jessie Whitaker as baritone, which broadened their sound and added more voices that could also serve as lead singers. By this time, their highly choreographed and emotional performances were drawing large crowds wherever they appeared.

After brief spells with Big Town and Swing Time in 1947, the Pilgrim Travelers moved directly to Specialty Records. This aggressive label quickly issued six selections, and within two years Specialty Records had issued sixteen sides, all of them *a cappella*. Two of these early selections, "Jesus Met the Woman at the Well" and "Mother Bowed," sold very well. A 1950 automobile accident left founding member Keith Barber incapacitated and barely able to sing. This tragic incident, plus the rise to prominence of the Soul Stirrers (who were propelled by Sam Cooke's smooth but emotional singing), signaled the end of the Pilgrim Travelers' national prominence.

For the next seven years, the group retained a strong core of support in Southern California and continued to record for Specialty. By 1957, longtime members Kylo Turner and Keith Barber had left and were replaced by Ernest Booker and Lou Rawls (formerly with the Teenage Kings of Harmony and Holy Wonders). With Rawls, Whitaker, and Booker alternating leads, the group, now known simply as the Travelers, released a string of singles for Andex Records in the late 1950s, with Sam Cooke appearing on some recording sessions and a few touring dates. The group disbanded two years later, with Rawls continuing with a successful R&B career while Alexander partnered Sam Cooke in the formation of SAR Records before dying of an alcohol-related illness in the middle 1960s.

KIP LORNELL

Reference and Further Reading

"Pilgrim Travelers." Information and Entertainment Center website, http://afgen.com/pilgrim.html.

Discography

Walking Rhythm (1992, Specialty 7030).
Better than That (1994, Specialty 7053).
Did You Pray This Morning? (2004, Liquid 8).

PLAINSMEN QUARTET

Howard Welborn, tenor
Bill Randall, baritone
Jack Mainord, lead
Joe B. Davis, bass
Easmon Napier, pianist

Active from 1956, the Plainsmen crossed stylistic and genre boundaries in the 1960s, becoming one of the best-known gospel groups in America. In the process, they helped define modern gospel quartet sound with unusually tight and high harmonies.

In August 1956, Howard Welborn (tenor), Bill Randall (baritone), Jack Mainord (lead), Joe B. Davis (bass), and Easmon Napier (pianist) left the Stamps Music Company family and established the Plainsmen in Dallas, Texas. They maintained a "Stamps sound" until the addition of Rusty Goodman the following year. In 1959, Ermon and Thurman Bunch joined the Plainsmen, completing the most famous lineup of the group.

Goodman's bass and the Bunch brothers' range combined for a unique and tight harmony. This particular Plainsmen group recorded one album, *Songs and Hymns by the Plainsmen Quartet,* an important recording that became highly prized among fans. Ermon Bunch left shortly thereafter, replaced by a returning Howard Welborn. This version of the Plainsmen developed an unusual high harmony sound, and

the vocalists constantly pushed the limits of their abilities.

In 1958, Jimmie Davis approached the group to sing with him in his second campaign for the governorship of Louisiana. Davis won the election, and the group moved its base of operations to Baton Rouge, where they regularly performed with Davis. During the early 1960s, the Plainsmen also sang secular music and backed Johnny Horton on his hit recording "North to Alaska." In 1963, Rusty Goodman joined his family's group and Seals Hilton replaced him in the Plainsmen. During the 1960s, there were numerous personnel changes in the group, with some of the better-known members being Larry Denim, Jay Simmons, David Reece, and Eddie Crook. Some members formed the Marksmen with Eason Napier. This group included country music in their repertoire and operated out of Wichita, Kansas.

The Plainsmen were extremely popular and opened many venues for gospel music performers. They played the Landmark Hotel in Las Vegas and regularly performed with noted country acts.

KEVIN S. FONTENOT

Reference and Further Reading

Buckingham, Jamie. *O Happy Day*. Waco, TX: Waco Books, 1973.
Goff, James R., Jr. *Close Harmony: A History of Southern Gospel*. Chapel Hill: University of North Carolina Press, 2002.

Discography

Both Sides of the Plainsmen (Hickory 4513).
Jimmie Davis with the Plainsmen. Someone Watching Over You (Decca DL 4186).
Plainsmen Quartet Vol. One (Canaan CA 4611).
Plainsmen Quartet Vol. Two (Canaan CA 4612).
Softly and Tenderly (Modern MS 811).
Wonderful Time Up There (Canaan CA 4600).

POINT OF GRACE

Shelly Phillips Breen (b. May 1, 1969, Belleville, IL)
Denise Jones (b. March 22, 1969, Norman, OK)
Terry Lang Jones (b. May 17, 1970, Marin County, CA)
Heather Floyd Payne (b. January 18, 1970, Abilene, TX)

Point of Grace became one of the most popular examples of what was called "adult contemporary" Christian music in the 1990s. The all-female vocal quartet charted twenty-four consecutive number one songs on adult contemporary Christian radio; five of their albums were certified gold for sales of more than five hundred thousand, and two were certified platinum for sales exceeding one million. Their music evinced contagious melodies and tight harmonies, with lyrics that portrayed a typically happy, bright outlook on life.

The combo formed in the early 1990s at Ouachita Baptist University in Arkadelphia, Arkansas, where the four original members were students. Heather Floyd, Denise Jones, and Terry Lang had been members of the same church in Norman, Oklahoma. Joined by Shelly Phillips, they formed a Christian vocal group called Say-So and later adopted the name Point of Grace (from the writings of C. S. Lewis) after winning the grand prize at the Christian Artist Seminar in Estes Park, Colorado, in 1992. Their sound was often compared to that of general market act Wilson Phillips, in that all members had distinctive voices and would trade off singing lead. Leigh Cappillino replaced Terry Jones in 2004.

The first Point of Grace album featured the rhythm-and-blues–inflected "I'll Be Believing" and won the group the Dove Award for Best New Artist of 1994. Future albums would deliver the rock-tinged "Gather at the River" and buoyant "Circle of Friends" as the group forged a style that seemed to lay Andrews Sisters–style harmonies over a strong undercurrent of black gospel. The formula worked with radio programmers, critics, and fans alike, and Point of Grace won more Dove Awards for 1996 Group of the Year, 1996 Pop/Contemporary Album of the Year (*The Whole Truth*), 1996 Pop/Contemporary Song ("The Great Divide"), and 1999 Group of the Year.

Point of Grace has endorsed and supported the charitable organization Mercy Ministries, which builds homes for unwed teenage mothers. In 2002, they also launched the organization Girls of Grace, which sponsors conferences for young Christian women. The original group members coauthored a book with Davin Seay that relates anecdotes from their daily lives and offers advice to teenage girls about such matters as dating and sexual purity.

MARK ALLAN POWELL

Reference and Further Reading

Point of Grace; with Davin Seay. *Life, Love, and Other Mysteries*. New York: Simon & Schuster, 1996.

Discography

Point of Grace (1993, Word 701 9426 603); *The Whole Truth* (1995, Word WD2-883073); *Life, Love, and Other Mysteries* (1996, Word WD2-884420); *Steady On* (1998, Word WD2-885444); *Free to Fly* (2001, Word

WD2-886112); *Christmas Story* (2002, Word WD2-885993); *24* (2003, Word WD2-886251); *I Choose You* (2004, Word).

PRESLEY, ELVIS ARON

(b. January 8, 1935; d. August 16, 1977)

A singer and actor known worldwide for his hard-driving rock 'n' roll and for his integration of African American music with Southern country music, Elvis Presley actually performed a wide variety of American music during his twenty-three–year recording and film career. One of the most pervasive and enduring of these other musics was gospel, including classic Southern gospel, black spirituals and quartet music, and modern praise music. Presley devoted several albums to such music and routinely used gospel groups on stage with him during concerts. His Grammy awards came not from rock 'n' roll collections but for his albums *How Great Thou Art* (1967) and *He Touched Me* (1972). He repeatedly told interviewers that his singing style was modeled on that of Jake Hess, former lead singer of the Statesmen and the Imperials. He carried with him on his tour bus tapes of every sort of gospel, from 1940s singles to modern songs by Bill Gaither.

Growing up in his birthplace of Tupelo, Mississippi, he started singing in his local First Assembly of God Church (according to one account) when he was five years old. His mother, Gladys, was fond of the country gospel of the 1940s: early sides by the Bailes Brothers, the Louvin Brothers, James and Martha Carson, and Bill Monroe's Blue Grass Quartet. Elvis later told Carl Story that his mother had "all" of Story's Mercury and Columbia records, and Northeast Mississippi was in those days full of local stations that broadcast live performances of everything from sacred harp singing to Pentecostal shouters.

In November 1948, when Elvis was thirteen, his family moved to Memphis. Since the 1920s, Memphis had been a center for gospel music recording and radio; by 1950 this scene was revving into high gear. Stations WDIA and KWAM fed large doses of black gospel to the city; disc jockeys played records by nationally known groups such as the Trumpeteers, the Golden Gate Quartet, the Dixie Hummingbirds, and the Jubilaires. They also featured live music by local groups such as the Spirit of Memphis Quartet, the Brewsteraires, and the Dixie Nightingales. Young Elvis heard this on the air, but he also found his way to the East Trigg Baptist Church, with its preacher Reverend Herbert W. Brewster and his leading soloist, Queen C. Anderson. Brewster was considered second only to Thomas A. Dorsey as the country's leading black gospel composer; Queen Anderson was thought by many to be the country's greatest gospel singer, largely on the strength of Brewster songs such as "Move On Up a Little Higher."

The River City was also home of important white gospel and country gospel groups. The Delmore Brothers, famed for their "Blues Stay Away from Me," were working gospel shows and recordings with their friend Wayne Rainey out of West Memphis, Arkansas. The hard-edged, Pentecostal style of the Louvin Brothers had a regular radio show with Eddie Hill. In 1950 the famed Blackwood Brothers decided to relocate to Memphis from their home base in Shenandoah, Iowa, winning a spot on WMOS radio and promoting regular concerts at the big downtown Ellis Auditorium. Elvis began attending these when he was sixteen, and he absorbed not only the music of the Blackwoods but also the Statesmen (Atlanta), the Harmoneers (Knoxville, Tennessee), and the Crusaders (Birmingham, Alabama).

Friends such as J. D. Sumner used to sneak Elvis into the backstage area, where he played his guitar and informally jammed with the groups. Sumner recalls that Elvis "really dug bass singers" and worshipped Big Chief Weatherington and Sumner. "I think if he had had a choice, he would have been a bass singer," recalled Sumner. He, unfortunately, did not have a deep bass voice, nor could he hear harmony well. A few years later, an offshoot of the Blackwoods, the Songfellows, invited Elvis to audition for them, but they had to turn him down because he could sing only lead and was unable to fill in on harmony.

Elvis listened to the group, improved, and a few months later passed a second audition, but by then he had signed his Sun contract and was either unwilling or unable to break it. Starting in 1954, he became a rock 'n' roll singer on the strength of rhythm and blues standards such as "That's All Right, Baby" and "Mystery Train." Though he recorded only one gospel song while with Sun (an unreleased version of Martha Carson's "Satisfied"), in December 1956 he returned to Memphis for Christmas and gathered in the Sun studio for an informal jam session with fellow Sun artists Johnny Cash, Carl Perkins, and Jerry Lewis. Unaware that the tape was running, the four formed an ad hoc gospel quartet and did a set of gospel classics such as "Just a Little Talk with Jesus" and "Mansion on the Hilltop." For years, the tape was rumored to have been lost, but in the 1980s it surfaced and was eventually released to the public.

Elvis's rise to fame on RCA Victor corresponded with a wave of popularity for other Southern gospel quartets, and soon the Blackwoods, the Harmoneers, the Jordanaires, and the Statesmen had themselves all signed contracts with major labels. This made it easier for Elvis to start insisting on having such groups sing on his new RCA records. For his first two RCA sessions in early 1956, he used on secular sides a trio made up of the Speer Family along with Jordanaire Gordon Stoker. By July 1956, when he recorded "Don't Be Cruel," Elvis for the first time used the full Jordanaires to back him up, starting a trend that would last fifteen years.

In the meantime, in an attempt to repair the image he was getting for his twisting and dancing on stage, Elvis used *The Ed Sullivan Show* to sing the vintage gospel classic from Thomas A. Dorsey, "Peace in the Valley." Dealers were swamped with requests for the disc, and RCA rushed into print a four-song EP album with "Peace" and three other gospel favorites, "Take My Hand, Precious Lord" "It Is No Secret What God Will Do," and "I Believe." The liner notes asserted that Elvis had in his collection most of the records by the major quartets.

It was not until he had returned from army service and completed two films that Elvis was able to follow up on his little 1957 EP. In 1960, he produced his first full-length gospel LP, *His Hand in Mine*. Recorded in Nashville with the Jordanaires and soloist Millie Kirkham, the set included a driving version of "Milky White Way," based on a 1947 hit by the black group the Trumpeteers. No fewer than seven other songs came from the Statesmen; some, such as "I Believe in the Man in the Sky," were copied directly from the Statesmen's own personal label, sold only at concerts. "I Believe" featured Jake Hess on solo, and Elvis tried his best to emulate him. The album itself sold well enough to eventually win a gold record, but a cut from it, "Cryin' in the Chapel," was later issued as a single and became a top-ten hit. It was enough to start Elvis and his producers thinking of another gospel set.

Thus it came to be that, in May 1966, after doing nothing but movie soundtracks for three years, Elvis returned to Nashville and recorded the tracks that would form his next sacred album, *How Great Thou Art*. This set featured a new "supergroup" that Jake Hess had just organized, the Imperials Quartet. Among its members were some of the stars of the modern gospel movement developing then in Nashville: pianist Henry Slaughter and singers Sherill Nelson, Gary McSpadden, and Armond Morales, in addition to Hess.

For the title song and a couple of others, Elvis wanted a large choir effect and added to the group the Jordanaires and four additional female studio singers. The set included traditional Southern and black gospel numbers, such as "Further Along," "Where Could I Go but to the Lord," and Charles

Tindley's "Stand By Me," but this time Elvis also added some songs from the contemporary Christian music scene: "If the Lord Wasn't Walking by My Side" and "Without Him." When *How Great Thou Art* was released in March 1967, it was well received and Elvis won his first Grammy Award—for Best Sacred Performance.

Though he made occasional gospel tracks during his studio sessions, Elvis did not devote his time to another full-gospel set until 1971, when he had made his spectacular comeback and resumed touring. This time he more fully embraced the "praise music" and "California sound" of Bill Gaither, Andrae Crouch, and Ralph Carmichael. "He Touched Me," by Gaither, became the set's title, and it too won a Grammy in 1972.

During his later years, Elvis became close friends with the man he introduced as "the world's deepest bass singer," J. D. Sumner. He began using Sumner and his group, the Stamps, in most of his live shows, and he enjoyed jamming with them backstage, singing old quartet favorites. Elvis always tried to sing bass, though, as he complained in a documentary, "J. D. always covered me up." During the last two years of his life, Elvis became interested in raising money for a Gospel Music Hall of Fame, to be located on a plot of land near the original Country Music Hall of Fame. His friends feel he was moving more and more into gospel music, but the plans and his movement were cut short by his sudden death in 1977.

CHARLES K. WOLFE

See also Jordanaires, The

Reference and Further Reading

Guralnick, Peter. *Last Train to Memphis: The Rise of Elvis Presley*. Boston: Little, Brown, 1994.
———. *Careless Love: The Unmaking of Elvis Presley*. Boston: Little, Brown, 1999.
Wolfe, Charles. Liner notes to *Amazing Grace: His Greatest Sacred Performances* (1994, RCA/BMG CD set).

Selected Discography

His Hand in Mine (1960, RCA).
How Great Thou Art (1967, RCA).
He Touched Me (1972, RCA).
Amazing Grace: His Greatest Sacred Performances (1994, RCA/BMG CD set).

PRESLEY, LUTHER

(b. March 6, 1887; d. December 6, 1974)

Luther G. Presley was born in Beckett Mountain, Arkansas, in 1887. He was raised in the Southern gospel music tradition of his local Free Will Baptist Church. Shortly after attending his first music school, Presley began directing his church choir at the young age of fourteen. Presley's first song, "Gladly Sing," was written when he was just seventeen. In the early 1900s, Presley attended the Clay Graded School, a primary and teacher training school, where he also taught music to students in the lower grades.

A prolific poet, lyricist, and composer, Luther Presley wrote either the lyrics, music, or both to well over one thousand hymns and gospel songs. According to his family, Presley composed the music and lyrics of at least 649 songs, the lyrics for more than four hundred others, and the music for twenty-five others. Some of his more famous works include "I'd Rather Have Jesus," "I Know the Lord Is with Me," "I'll Have a New Life," and "He Wills It So." He also helped edit the Reverend Guy Smith's "The Great Speckled Bird," a song made popular by Roy Acuff and also recorded by Johnny Cash.

Presley is perhaps best known for having penned the lyrics to a melody that Virgil Stamps composed, "When the Saints Go Marching In" (1937). This song later became a Dixieland ragtime standard and was once even the theme song of the New Orleans Saints professional football team. Although Presley worked for a number of small publishing companies early on, he spent much of his career (from 1930 on) working for Stamps–Baxter Company, the famous publishing/radio/talent agency that defined the sound of Southern gospel music for several decades. Presley was a consistent contributor to their ever-expanding catalog, with several of his songs included in their semiannual songbooks.

Luther Presley drew on a number of personal tragedies as he composed his songs, including the birthing death of his first wife and child. Presley's two sons, Leister and Clarence, both served overseas during World War II, during which time he wrote "Give Them Red Roses (The Boys Will Be Coming Home)." Presley's second wife, Rena Henderson Presley, was herself a singer and songwriter, and the two would frequently collaborate by performing his songs in public; she also handled his business affairs for Stamps–Baxter, which was later bought up by Zondervan Company, well after his death. Presley died in 1974 and was buried in Rose Bud, Arkansas, a small town within five miles of his birthplace. The Torreyson Library at the University of Central Arkansas holds a number of Presley's lyrics and compositions in their archives and special collections, which were donated primarily by Presley's son Leister.

BEN MCCORKLE

See also Acuff, Roy; Cash, Johnny; Zondervan Publishing Company

Reference and Further Reading

Sallee, Bob. "He Wrote 'When the Saints Go Marching In' for $5." *Arkansas Democrat-Gazette* (April 21, 1998).

PRIMITIVE QUARTET, THE

Reagan Riddle (b. July 30, 1946)
Larry Riddle (b. April 15, 1952)
Michael Riddle (b. May 1, 1957)
Norman Wilson (b. July 2, 1944)
Randy Fox (b. June 26, 196?)

From modest beginnings in the spring of 1973, the Primitive Quartet of Candler, North Carolina have established themselves as a major force in the gospel music world. Somewhat remarkably, they managed this achievement by eschewing ever-increasing trends toward modernization in sound and using stringed-instrument accompaniment. While members of the Primitive Quartet would not call themselves a bluegrass gospel band, there is considerable similarity in their sound, which they describe as "just mountain music, mountain singing."

The original Primitive Quartet consisted of a pair of brothers, Reagan and Larry Riddle, and Furman and Norman Wilson. Somewhat early—1977—in the group's development, Furman Wilson received the "call" to preach, and Michael Riddle replaced him. Randy Fox, who became Reagan Riddle's son-in-law in May 1988, also sings in many of their four-part harmonies. Several additional musicians have worked with the Primitives over the years, with Tim Chandler, Roger Fortner, Bruce Penland, Charlie Chandler (fifteen years), and Jeff Tolbert (seven years and counting) among the more significant.

Until 1977, the Primitive Quartet sang mostly at local functions, but they began doing some concerts with the Inspirations, and after about a year and a half, they made the decision to go on the road full-time. In 1981, they also began their annual outdoor Hominy Valley Singing, which has been quite successful and has continued to be gathering place for thousands of fans who love traditional gospel music. The Primitives began cutting records almost as soon as they were formed in 1973, and they have turned out a large volume of recorded music, all of high quality and under their own control. As of 2002, the Primitive Quartet have at least ten compact discs and an additional twenty cassettes in their catalog, and they continue to have a heavy touring schedule.

IVAN M. TRIBE

Reference and Further Reading

Powell, Wayde. "The Primitive Quartet." *Precious Memories: Journal of Gospel Music* 1, no. 2 (July–August 1988): 25–31.

Discography

The Best of the Primitive Quartet (1992, Crystal 81692).
Smoky Mountain Songs of Faith by the Primitive Quartet (1994, Mountain Heritage 3010).
Everlasting Joy (1999, Mountain Heritage 3035).

PRINCIPLES, THE

Ronnie Slagle (b. April 4, 1947)
Linda Shelton Slagle (b. Unknown)
Lloyd Shelton (b. Unknown)
Ashley Slagle (b. Unknown)

The Principles of Johnson City, Tennessee, have been described by Michael Kelley as "polished southern gospel singers whose arrangements tend toward a blend of country and bluegrass and whose voices artfully interweave with one another." In fact, they sometimes seem like a newer version of the legendary Carter Family. A constant throughout their twenty-plus year history has been the strong lead voice of Linda Shelton Slagle, assisted by her brother Lloyd Shelton.

The origins of the Principles date back to the late 1970s, when Reverend Winfield Shelton, his wife, Madonna, and their children, Linda and Lloyd, formed a singing group for their own and neighboring churches. Although the elder Sheltons dropped out relatively early, the others persisted, as did Linda's husband Kyle English and Ronnie Holland. These four were heard most often on their early recordings, which were released on cassette only. After Kyle's death, Linda then married Ronnie Slagle, who sings tenor, plays mandolin, and manages the group. They received two Dove Award nominations in 2000 and have been on the charts several times.

Later Principles recordings have been on Dawn, Laurel, Thoroughbred, Freeland (who reissued on compact disc some of their earlier cassettes), and more recently Reformation. Judy and Randy Rice played on some of their later recordings. The most recent foursome on their vocals is comprised of Linda, Ronnie, Lloyd, and Brenda Vaughn. Ronald White plays either lead guitar or banjo. Young Ashley Slagle has become a featured lead on special numbers.

IVAN M. TRIBE

Reference and Further Reading

Kelley, Michael. Liner notes to *The Best of the Principles, I* (1996, Freeland FRC CD 644), *I Don't Like the Devil* (1997, Freeland FRC CD 651), *The Best of the Principles, II* (1998, Freeland FRC CD 656), and *Home to Heaven* (Freeland FRC CD 664).
The Principles website, http://www.theprinciplesgospelmusic.com.

Discography

I Wouldn't Miss It Would You?/ Old-Time Bluegrass Hymns (1994, Thoroughbred).
The Best of the Principles, I (1996, Freeland FRC CD 644).
I Don't Like the Devil (1997, Freeland FRC CD 651).
The Best of the Principles, II (1998, Freeland FRC CD 656).
Home to Heaven (Freeland FRC CD 664).

PROPHETS QUARTET

Ed Hill (b. February 23, 1935)
Duane Allen (b. April 29, 1943)
Donnie Seabolt (b. June 30, 1944)
Joe Moscheo (b. August 11, 1937)

"The most unique sound in gospel music" was the trademark of the Prophets Quartet. With the soaring first tenor voice of "Big Lew" Garrison and the solid baritone of Ed Hill as the anchors of the group, the unique sound of the Prophets thrilled audiences for nearly fifteen years.

Big Lew had a great tenor voice that was complemented by some of the finest lead singers in gospel music history. All of the Prophets' lead singers possessed an upper range as high as many first tenors. With the added sound of several excellent bass singers and pianists, the unique sound of the Prophets continued throughout the many personnel changes that beset the group through the years.

The Prophets can trace their lineage to the Kings Men Quartet from St. Louis, Missouri. Ed Hill and Jerry "Jay" Berry were founding members of the Kings Men Quartet. The quartet was invited to the 1958 National Quartet Convention, where Hill and Berry realized their desire to sing on a full-time basis. They moved to Knoxville, Tennessee, and formed the Prophets in March 1959. They joined forces with Lewis Garrison, Rancell Taylor, and Gary Trusler, and they recorded their first album on the predominately pop label Coral.

Their early sound was molded by noted gospel music writer, teacher, and pianist Joe Roper; the group developed their style under his leadership. In the short time that he was with the quartet, Roper taught the group new songs and unusual arrangements and expanded their musical capabilities.

The world of gospel music saw the potential in this fine group, and they soon became members of the Gospel Singing Caravan. Joe Moscheo replaced Joe Roper as pianist for the group, and the group continued to prosper. Innovative arrangements, likable personalities, and great stage presence made the group quite popular with the fans. Big Lew and Ed Hill had a wonderful stage rapport and always made their programs entertaining.

The Prophets Quartet continued to blaze trails in gospel music until their retirement in 1973. Many famous names in gospel music have taken the stage as a Prophet, including current Oak Ridge Boy Duane Allen, Roy McNeil, Jay Simmons, Dean Brown, Donnie Seabolt, Jim Boatman, and Dave Rogers.

JOHN CRENSHAW

Reference and Further Reading

Wonderful World of Gospel Music, 8. Nashville Talent Research, 1971.

Discography

Again (BMC 4352); *Beauty Power & Peace* (Canaan 9642); *Best Yet* (Sumar 4323); *Camp Meeting Time* (BMC 4335); *Featuring Roy McNeal* (BMC 4354); *Glory Glory Amen* (Skylite 5985); *Gospel Rhythm* (Sing 3005); *The Gospel Songs* (Coral 57330); *I Know* (QCA 1339); *I've Gotta Tell It* (Sing 3006); *If We Never Meet Again* (QCA 90983); *A Joyful Sound* (Heart Warming 1934); *Just a Rose Will Do* (Heart Warming 1889); *Love like the Sun* (Heart Warming 1889); *A New Day* (BMC 4362); *No Disappointments* (Sing 3002); *On the Right Track* (BMC 4381); *Packin' Up* (Sing 3001); *Peace in the Valley* (QCA 443); *Piano Artistry of Joe Moscheo* (Sing 3004); *Relax* (Sing 3003); *Sing a Song* (BMC 4370); *Sweeter as the Days Go By* (QCA 90807); *Upward and Onward* (Heart Warming 1964); *Vital and Vibrant* (Heart Warming 1873); *Why Should I Worry* (Sumar 4309).

R

RAINBOW RECORDS

Rainbow Records was one of the two earliest record labels featuring Anglo American gospel music. An earlier attempt to start a religious label had occurred around 1915 when a company called Angelophone released hymns by popular singer Henry Burr; the company soon failed, due in part to the fact that they issued all their sides on a seven-inch format (as opposed to the standard ten). Shortly before Rainbow was started, the James D. Vaughan Publishing Company started its own all-gospel label, Vaughan. By the early 1920s, gospel—like other forms of American music—was quickly gaining a foothold in the new mass media.

Rainbow was the brainchild of Homer Rodeheaver (1880–1955), at the time the most famous song leader in the nation. The son of a Tennessee sawmill operator, he went on to college at Ohio Wesleyan, fought in the Spanish-American war, and began to work as a song leader for local evangelists. He was a rugged, handsome young man with a robust style of conducting that often included leading the singing with his trombone. By 1909, he was asked to join up with the nation's most colorful evangelist, Billy Sunday. Rodeheaver moved Sunday's stately crusade music from the more classic hymns of Ira Sankey and others to the livelier strains of E. O. Excell and newer songs such as "Brighten the Corner."

Though Rodeheaver had been recording on his own with big commercial labels (such as Victor) since 1913, in late 1921 he began to record some of his own published songs on his newly formed Rainbow Records label. Advertised in Rodeheaver songbooks and sold on his tours, the new label became an instant success. By 1925, its catalog included more than a hundred releases, including Rodeheaver's favorites, as well as black spirituals, sentimental songs, and occasional piano solos. William G. McLoughlin, Jr., Sunday's biographer, has written that, in a matter of months, Rodeheaver's "gospel hymns were making more money from record sales than from sheet music." Many of the discs also featured Rodeheaver performing duets with Mrs. William Asher, Sunday's "director of extension work." Most of the music on the label was very formal and very European, often with orchestral accompaniment. A few exceptions were by a team named Perry Kim and Einer Nyland, Texas singers who used guitar and mandolin accompaniment to produce favorites such as "I Will Sing of My Redeemer."

The depression curtailed the first Rainbow incarnation, but the label was resurrected about 1941, when Mrs. Asher and Rodeheaver rerecorded some of their favorite pieces. The company this time survived into the 1950s, releasing its last sides on the new 45-rpm format.

CHARLES K. WOLFE

Reference and Further Reading

McLoughlin, William Gerald. *Billy Sunday Was His Real Name*. Chicago: University of Chicago Press, 1955.

RANGERS QUARTET

Arnold Hyles (b. 1917; d. 1979)
Vernon Hyles (b. Unknown)
George Hughes (b. Unknown)
Walter Leverette (b. Unknown)

A singing group active from 1936 to 1956, the Rangers helped forge the commercial quartet style through their repertoire and stage performance. The Rangers Quartet was formed at the time of the Texas centennial by brothers Vernon and Arnold Hyles, George Hughes, and Walter Leverette, and it was originally known as the Texas Rangers Quartet. The group quickly gained a reputation in Texas for their tight harmony and Arnold Hyles's low bass, which became their trademark.

The Rangers expanded their reputation nationwide when they announced that they would ride bicycles from Texas to New York to perform on *Major Bowes' Amateur Hour*. The group donned cowboy outfits for the trip and deftly utilized newspaper and radio publicity for exposure. In Louisville, Kentucky, the quartet accepted an offer to perform regularly on WHAS. By the late 1930s, the group was one of the best-known gospel quartets in the nation. They added secular material to their repertoire and recorded for Decca and Columbia. One of their best recordings, featuring Hyles's bass, was "I've Found a Hiding Place."

As with most quartets, personnel and broadcast locations changed regularly. In 1939, they began broadcasting on Charlotte, North Carolina's WBT. The program was carried nationally by CBS. During the next seventeen years the quartet had regular programs in Wheeling, West Virginia; Atlanta, Georgia; Topeka, Kansas; Raleigh, North Carolina; and Shreveport, Louisiana. The Hyles brothers remained the backbone of the group throughout its history. Other important members included Denver Crumpler, whose Irish tenor formed a natural counterpoint to Hyles's bass, pianists Marion Snyder, David Reece, Lee Roy Abernathy, and Hovie Lister, Doy Ott, and Ermon Slater. In many ways, the Rangers were an important training ground for singers who later played major roles as members of the Swanee River Boys, the Statesmen, and other groups.

The end of World War II marked the gradual decline of the Rangers as accidents and ill health took their toll. In 1949 Walter Leverette died, and in early 1951 an automobile accident killed Slater and severely injured Arnold Hyles. Despite the tragedies, the group continued to perform live and on radio via the Liberty Broadcasting System, which gave them a national presence. They recorded for the White Church label and their own Ranger label during the postwar years. In 1956, the Hyles brothers decided to disband the Rangers due to ill health. David Reece reformed the group as the Rangers Trio and broadcast successfully for several years out of Charlotte.

The Rangers Quartet left a lasting impression on the quartet tradition as a result of their performance styles, good humor on stage, and savvy business skills. They also represent a link to the secular tradition that many gospel acts would continue to forge over time.

KEVIN S. FONTENOT

Reference and Further Reading

Goff, James R., Jr. *Close Harmony: The History of Southern Gospel*. Chapel Hill: University of North Carolina Press, 2002.
Russell, Tony. *Country Music Records: A Discography 1921–1942*. New York: Oxford University Press, 2004.
Terrell, Bob. *The Music Men*. Alexander, NC: Mountain Church, 2001.

Discography

"I've Found a Hiding Place," on *Close Harmony: A History of Southern Gospel Music Vol. 1, 1920–1955* (2003, Crossroads CR04242; compilation).

REBELS QUARTET

John Mathews (b. Unknown)
Lee Kitchens (b. Unknown)
Horace Parrish (b. Unknown)
James Park "Big Jim" Waits (b. 1899; d. 1973)
Jimmy Taylor (b. Unknown)
Jim Hamill (b. 1934)
Conley "London" Parris (b. 1931; d. 1992)

First organized in 1949, the Rebels Quartet became one of the best-known gospel groups of the 1950s and 1960s. From their home base at WFLA radio and later television in Tampa, Florida, the Rebels toured widely through the South and later appeared on many syndicated programs as well.

While their personnel fluctuated over the years, John Mathews, who sang baritone, and Horace Parrish, who sang tenor, were the most constant members. The other original founders were lead vocalist Lee Kitchens, a veteran of the Sunny South Quartet, and "Big Jim" Waits, whose bass vocals had already made him a virtual legend as a member of several early foursomes. When Waits and Kitchens departed in the middle and late 1950s, they were replaced by Jim Hamill (formerly of the Weatherford Quartet) and London Parris (formerly of the Homeland Harmony Quartet), respectively. Jimmy Taylor played piano with the quartet and also worked as lead vocalist after Hamill departed from the Rebels.

The earliest recordings by the Rebels were singles on the Bibletone label. Later, they recorded albums for Sing and then for Skylite. Some of their better-known recordings include "I'm Bound for that City," "The Highest Hill," "I'll Meet You by the River," and James Vaughn Hill's classic composition "What a Day That Will Be."

From the later 1960s, the Rebels experienced numerous personnel changes. Newer members included Charles and Ron Booth, John Gresham, and Kenny Hicks. By 1971, all of the older veterans were gone from the group, although Jimmy Taylor and Lee Kitchens returned in 1973. By the end of the decade, the group had virtually disbanded. Jim Hamill became best known as lead vocalist for the Kingsmen. John Mathews later led a family group, and London Parris led a combination known as the Apostles. Except for Waits and Parris, various other members of the group remain alive and well and have been enthusiastically received at the annual Grand Ole Gospel Reunions in Greenville, South Carolina.

IVAN M. TRIBE

Reference and Further Reading

Anderson, Robert; Gail North. *Gospel Music Encyclopedia.* 149. New York: Sterling Publishing, 1979.
Goff, James R., Jr. *Close Harmony: A History of Southern Gospel*, Chapel Hill: University of North Carolina Press, 2002. 182–183.

Discography

The Angels Must Have Cried (SRLP 6017).
Rebels Quartet Family Album (Sing LP 8004).
When I Stand with God (Skylite SRLP 5977).

REED, BLIND ALFRED

(b. June 15, 1880; d. January 17, 1956)

Accomplished as a singer, songwriter, fiddler, guitarist, mandolinist, and banjo player, Alfred Reed was born blind in Floyd, Virginia, but he spent most of his life near Princeton, West Virginia. He learned to play several instruments to accompany his excellent singing voice. Reed was at his most interesting when backing his singing with an archaic-sounding fiddle style.

His musical skills proved very useful, because in the pre-welfare state era, they enabled him to earn a living by playing on the streets in Princeton, Hinton, and Bluefield, West Virginia, and at any other venues, such as dances, available locally. Reed sang traditional numbers as well as songs of his own creation. His lyrics abounded with social commentary, humor, irony, and satire, and they often reflected his deep religious views. He was especially critical of what he considered excessive materialism, hypocrisy, and the lifestyles of modern women.

After a train wreck on May 24, 1927, killed a noted local engineer, P. C. Aldrich, Reed wrote a ballad about the incident. He then contacted the Victor Talking Machine Company, and they scheduled a session for him at Bristol, Tennessee, on July 28, 1927. Accompanying himself on guitar and fiddle, he recorded his new ballad, "The Wreck of the Virginian," and three religious songs, "I Mean to Live for Jesus," "You Must Unload," and "Walking in the Way with Jesus." These sides apparently sold fairly well, because Reed was invited to do a second session, this one in Camden, New Jersey, on December 19, 1927. On these recordings, he was accompanied by his own fiddle and by his guitar-playing son, Arville (who was incorrectly identified by the record label as Orville). Among the numbers recorded here was a tearjerker, "The Prayer of the Drunkard's Little Girl," and one of Reed's best-remembered songs, a critique of flapper hair styles titled "Why Do You Bob Your Hair Girls?" At the same session, Arville recorded both as a solo artist and with fiddler Fred Pendleton as the West Virginia Night Owls.

Reed's final session, on December 3 and 4, 1929, in New York City, yielded "Why Do You Bob Your Hair, Girls? No. 2," which was in a lighter vein than the original; "Money-Cravin' Folks"; and "There'll Be No Distinction There," for which Arville supplied the vocal. At the time these records were made the Great Depression was on, and it ended Reed's recording career and that of many other artists. It did not, however, curtail his music, for he continued to play in and around Princeton, both alone and with Pendleton and Arville or another local blind musician, Richard Harold.

In later years, local laws made it more difficult for street musicians to ply their trade, so Reed's public performances became rare. In 1972, Rounder Records released an entire album of Blind Alfred Reed songs, making them available to urban audiences. Most of his other recordings appeared on several anthology LPs. With his rich vocals, multi-instrumental talent, and fine songwriting, Blind Alfred Reed was an excellent representative of the emerging commercial country music industry of the 1920s. As with most country performers of that era, gospel played a significant part in his repertoire.

W. K. MCNEIL

Reference and Further Reading

Tribe, Ivan M. *Mountaineer Jamboree: Country Music in West Virginia*. Lexington: University of Kentucky Press, 1984.

Discography

Blind Alfred Reed: How Can a Poor Man Stand Such Times and Live? (1972, Rounder).

RELIGIOUS FOLK SONGS OF THE NEGRO

There are three primary types of songs typically included in the corpus of religious folk music of the African American: shouts, jubilees, and spirituals.

The shout grew out of West African religious practices, and this influence can be readily observed in the fusion of counterclockwise movements, call-and-response singing, percussive hand clapping, and a stick beating a rhythmic pulse on a wooden floor. As in West Africa, the ring shout affirms oneness with the Spirit and ancestors as well as community cohesiveness.

The form of the shout is clear and easy to follow. The "songster" will "set" or begin a song, slowly at first, and then accelerate to an appropriate tempo. These lines are answered by a group of singers called "basers" in call-and-response fashion. The stick-man, sitting next to the leader, beats a simple rhythm with a broom or other wood stick, and the basers contribute to the rhythmic mélange with hand clapping and foot patting.

The songs performed during the ring shout were called "running spirituals." Typically, they form a separate repertoire from spirituals, jubilees, and later gospel songs. Ranging from light-spirited to apocalyptic, they often carried coded references to slavery in song and pantomime. The Southeastern ring shout is probably the oldest surviving African American performance tradition on the North American continent. It was first described in detail during the Civil War by outside observers in coastal regions of South Carolina and Georgia, where communities were able to maintain strong cultural ties to Africa. The practice continued in those areas well into the twentieth century, and its influence can be observed in later musical forms such as gospel and jazz. By the last quarter of the twentieth century, however, the ring shout itself was presumed to have died out until its rediscovery in 1980 in McIntosh County, Georgia, and the McIntosh County Shouters were established.

It is much more difficult to distinguish between spirituals and jubilees. In a broad sense, jubilees were often considered to be the more exuberant of the two forms; however, any distinction between the two has long been blurred, as the terms have come to be used interchangeably. For the purposes of this essay, the collective corpus that is referred to as spirituals will be used.

When enslaved Africans were brought to the United States, they had no material possessions. However, they carried in their minds and hearts a rich cultural and musical heritage. This tradition included verbal responses, singing, dancing, and shouting. It also included a heavy reliance on percussion that was translated into clapping, chest and thigh thumping, and foot tapping when the drums were banned because they were tools for communication.

Forbidden to continue certain religious practices, the enslaved Africans met in "invisible churches" in ravines, forests, fields, slave quarters, and anywhere else that they could get away from the critical eyes and ears of the oppressor. It was in these illegal gatherings that they were able to worship with total freedom and thus preserved elements of African culture. It was out of this fertile ground that the spiritual as we know it today was born.

The origin of the spiritual has been the cause of much debate among scholars. Those represented by writers such as George Pullen Jackson argued that the spiritual had its roots in the camp meeting songs sung by Southern whites. While there is solid evidence that the black and white spirituals coexisted, there is no proof of the preexistence of the white spiritual. In fact, the camp meeting tradition that produced the white spiritual did not get started until the beginning of the nineteenth century, while the black spiritual was established by the end of the seventeenth century. Contentions that black spirituals were simply reinventions of white melodies were greatly contested and refuted by scholars such as Alain Locke and John Lovell, Jr., who were able to trace the roots to West Africa.

There are several broad characteristics of the folk spiritual. At the heart is the call-and-response pattern of singing, a cultural trait that has flourished everywhere the people of Western and Central African countries have gone. It represents a two-part style of singing, with the first part being that of the leader and the second that of the group. Other variations of this pattern include solo answered by solo or group answered by group. It is an important cultural characteristic that actually finds expression throughout the black community in religious services (where the congregation responds to the call of the preacher), in conversation, and in other forms of black music. Inherent in the spiritual was a strong reliance on rhythmic, melodic, and textual improvisation.

Another characteristic lies in the picturesque language used. Many of the spirituals were based on biblical passages, particularly those that dealt with liberation. Old Testament stories such as Daniel's deliverance from the lion's den and Moses's command to tell Pharaoh to release the Israelites were favored texts. There were also frequent references to modes of transportation, such as chariots and trains.

In the spirituals, the enslaved Africans encouraged each other and affirmed their God-given humanity in the face of a system that treated them as chattel. The spirituals, although sometimes referred to as sorrow songs, clearly reveal the strength of spirit of the creators. Intrinsic to most of these seemed to be a sense of hope and belief in ultimate deliverance in the face of the sheer reality of the situation. It was this that allowed people to sing "I got a shoes and when I get to heaven gonna put on my shoes and walk all over God's heaven," even though the singer might be barefoot.

Unlike European Americans who made clear distinctions between sacred and secular musics, Africans did not. Africans used song to recite history and express feelings about each other, and it was tied to all aspects of life. Influenced by traditions of Africa, spirituals were created by individual and group contribution. This translated into the infusion into the spiritual of coded messages about impending escape attempts, directions for how to head north on the Underground Railroad, or which houses were safe havens while traveling. Although the texts, on the surface, might be about Moses leading the Hebrews out of exile, the message frequently revealed plans for secret meetings or imminent escape. They also were used as social commentary about their lot in life. Lines such as "everybody talkin' about heaven ain't goin' there" spoke volumes about the singer's disregard for the espoused Christianity of the slaveholder.

After the Civil War, the prevalence of spirituals waned since many former slaves did not want to be reminded of the past. However, it was in 1871 that a group of students known as the Fisk University Jubilee Singers revived spirituals when they set out to raise money for the university. For the first time, white people, non-Southerners, and others were able to hear the significance of slave songs. Even today, spirituals provide a way to comprehend the joys, sorrows, and lives of slaves.

DONNA M. COX

Reference and Further Reading

Jackson, George Pullen. *White and Negro Spirituals*. New York: J. J. Augustin, 1943.

Lovell, John, Jr. *Black Song: The Forge and the Flame*. New York: Macmillan, 1972.
Parrish, Lydia. *Slave Songs of the Georgia Sea Islands*. Athens: University of Georgia Press, 1992 (1942).

REVEREND JOHN P. KEE AND THE NEW LIFE COMMUNITY CHOIR

John Prince Kee (b. 1962)

John Prince Kee, the fifteenth of sixteen children, exhibited extraordinary talent at an early age, both vocally and instrumentally. As a result, John had the benefit of an excellent music education, starting when, as a small child, he was placed in a special school for the musically gifted. John went on to study voice and classical music at the North Carolina School of the Arts in Winston–Salem and later at the Yuba College Conservatory School of Music in Marysville, California. Off campus, John was given the opportunity to perform with jazz and popular music greats such as Donald Byrd & the Blackbirds and Cameo. In his late teens, John drifted into a street lifestyle that took him to Charlotte, North Carolina. It is the combination of the years spent on the streets of Charlotte as a hard-core drug dealer, his formative years spent in church, and his formal music training that combine to make John P. Kee's music powerful and effective.

Considered to be the successor of James Cleveland as the "Crown Prince of Gospel Music," Kee is clearly a student of Cleveland's powerful stage persona and charismatic style. It was, in fact, the Gospel Music Workshop of America that propelled Kee into national prominence when, in 1975, he became the first artist to record lead vocals on two selections for the Gospel Music Workshop of America's annual mass choir recording. In the mid-1980s, he started a community choir in Charlotte that eventually grew to become the New Life Community Choir.

Kee achieved rapid success with albums titled *Wash Me* (1991) and *We Walk by Faith* (1992). In early 1995, Kee released his gold award-winning *Show Up* CD that further cemented his popularity in the gospel music industry. Between 1987 and 2004, Kee recorded twelve albums and garnered more than twenty-five awards, nominations, and gold album sales. His style is characterized by his ability to reach a wide range of listeners, from the grandmother to the person on the streets. The church founded by John Kee, New Life Fellowship Church, is planted in the same community where he lived his life of crime.

DONNA M. COX

See also Cleveland, James

Discography

John P. Kee. *Walk by Faith* (1992, Tyscot Records); *Color Blind* (1994, Jive Records); *Surrender* (1994, Jive Records); *Wait on Him* (1994, Jive Records); *Wash Me* (1994, Jive Records); *Yes Lord* (1994, Jive Records); *Show Up!* (1995, Jive Records); *Strength* (1997, Verity Records); *14 Karat Dreams* (2000, Black N Brown); *Not Guilty . . . The Experience* (2000, Verity Records); *Mighty in the Spirit* (2001, Verity Records); *Blessed by Association* (2002, Verity Records); *Color of Music* (2004, Verity Records); *John P. Kee Presents: Lil' Rufus & The Melody Train* (2005, Verity Records).
John P. Kee & The VIP Music and Arts Seminar Mass Choir. *Stand* (1996, Jive Records).
The VIP Music and Arts Seminar Mass Choir. *Any Day* (1993, Verity Records).
The VIP Music and Arts Seminar Choir Featuring John P. Kee. *Lily in the Valley* (1993, Jive Records).

REVIVALS

If, as Paul Tillich's work suggests, religion is the soul of culture and culture is the form of religion, then revivals have shaped the soul of American culture from the beginning. Revivals begin and flourish in times of lost faith and hopelessness by holding out the possibility of immediate change and healing. The first European settlers to British North America came in the midst of a revival—the Puritan Awakening in England—and shortly began their own colonial revival, the Great Awakening. The Native American religious revival marked by the Ghost Dance came in the midst of genocide. Perhaps the recurring revivals across North America arose as a witness against the soul-destroying aspects of colonial imperialism, just as gospel music did.

As gospel music emerged from African American culture and spread throughout the United States, it became a natural partner for revivals, offering an immediate experience of heavenly joy and salvation as well as a direct iteration of the judgment that awaits the unjust. In African American religious life, revivals and gospel music were synonymous. For whites, revivals often introduced gospel music into otherwise segregated churches. Some historians still postulate that Protestant revivalism in the United States descended directly from German Pietism and English Methodism, but a clear detour through West Africa has affected African American and Caucasian American revival preaching and singing styles from the 1800s through the present. Whatever the source, U.S. revival evangelists of the nineteenth through the twenty-first centuries incorporate dramatically physical storytelling, rhythmic voice tics, hand clapping, and sing-preaching—all marks of African influences in gospel music.

Spiritual revivals are usually marked by public preaching to crowds, which may begin as small gatherings or prayer meetings but eventually grow to thousands of participants. All revivals create and sustain a unique emotional rendering of religion for the communities involved, often characterized by spontaneous healings, charismatic gifts, and an experience of freedom from bondage. Denominational boundaries tend to blur during periods of revival, because preaching focuses on the large spiritual issue of "getting right with God."

In the United States, religious revivals occurred among Catholics and Protestants alike. The four eras of Protestant revival in the United States are generally thought of as the 1730s through the 1760s; "the Great Awakening," during the 1800s through the 1830s; "the Second Awakening"; and the 1890s through the 1930s, although specific revival meetings have occurred from the early 1700s through the present. Some historians include the "youth revivals" of the 1960s as a fifth revival period.

Catholic revivals, or "focus on the parish mission," took place throughout the nineteenth century and continued into the early twentieth century. Some Catholic commentators viewed Protestant revival rituals as "weak in the mind" and "heathenish," but choral and congregational revival singing became a part of Catholic practice. Early Catholic revivals did not use the folk and gospel music familiar to African American and white Protestants, but during the youth revivals of the 1960s, Catholics sang gospel music in masses and revival services. Catholic "gospel masses" focusing on African American music and worship styles are still an important element of Catholic practice in some parishes in the United States today. Revivals were a source of the rapid dissemination and integration of spirituals—and eventually gospel music—into American culture, and also of racial strife.

In the early eighteenth century, African slaves met together in secret camp meetings, which were called "cultish" or "Christian," depending on the reporter, and these involved spiritual ministries, marriages, storytelling or preaching, and singing. These revivals of Christian or African religion were held in secret, because Southern colonies usually prohibited any gathering of slaves. When the Great Awakening reached the South, slaves were alternately encouraged or discouraged from attending revival meetings with their masters. Some argued that too much religion made slaves "uppity" and others that Africans needed Christianity in order to be "civilized."

The singing in the white-dominated revivals originally tended toward regular denominational hymns, but by the time that the Cane Ridge revival broke out in Kentucky, in August 1801, the music described sounds much more like up-tempo gospel. Moving choruses and simple songs with repeated refrains were syncopated with clapping and shouting—classic signs of African influence on American music. Gospel rhythms and melodies forged in the crucible of slavery rang true at the revivals on the western and southern frontiers, where life was often lonely, hard, bitter, and monotonous.

Almost a hundred years after the Cane Ridge revival in Kentucky, on the opposite side of the country, an African American preacher—Elder W. J. Seymour—led one of the most racially revolutionary revivals in American history. Seymour had received his training in the Apostolic Faith, the original name of the Pentecostal movement, in Houston, Texas, under the instruction of Charles F. Parham, a white man. At Parham's Bible school, Seymour, the only African American student, was forced to sit apart from the other students. Some historians attribute this to "strict Jim Crow laws," but it became clear later that Parham himself endorsed racial segregation.

Seymour accepted his first ministerial post in 1906 at the Azusa Street Apostolic Faith Mission in Los Angeles. There, while William J. Seymour preached and sang the gospel to a racially mixed assembly of Pentecostal believers, the Azusa Street Revival broke out. Gospel singing, shouting, speaking and praying in tongues, healing, and other powerful "signs" of the Holy Spirit marked this revival, but the most extraordinary feature was unifying love. Hundreds of African Americans, whites, Hispanics, and people of other ethnic origins worshiped together under Seymour's powerful preaching.

When Parham heard of the racially mixed revival at Seymour's church, he was so distressed that he traveled to Los Angeles to create a race-based rift in Seymour's ministry, and he established a separate white Apostolic Faith Church in Seymour's neighborhood. Seymour returned the favor by preventing whites from holding positions of authority in his church, and the racial boundaries once broken by a gospel revival were firmly reestablished by man.

One powerful result of the recurring racism in American religious practices was the establishment of hundreds of black denominations, in which gospel music has flourished as part of the liturgy. The most famous of these churches is probably the Church of God in Christ (COGIC), the founder of which—Charles Harrison Mason—received his baptism in the Holy Spirit during Seymour's Azusa Street Revival.

No matter how firmly revivalists of the nineteenth and twentieth centuries attempted to erect and maintain racial boundaries, gospel music broke these barriers in breathtaking moments of reconciliation. One of the most memorable of these was Billy Sunday's revival services in Atlanta, Georgia, in November and December of 1917—just ten years after a violent white mob had destroyed a large section of the Decatur Street neighborhood of black Atlanta, leaving at least ten dead and scores wounded.

Not a supporter of social equality or integration of races, Sunday held separate revival services for African Americans and whites in Atlanta, only to be so overcome by the spiritual power of black gospel music that he requested the black choirs to sing at the white services. A white Salvation Army worker present at one of these services testified, "Seldom have the very depths of my emotions been so stirred. I wanted that music to go on forever."

Few white revivalists condemned segregation; most followed Jim Crow in the South, but some began to incorporate African Americans musicians on their revival platforms. During the 1950s, white charismatic evangelist A. A. Allen publicly pledged himself to an interracial platform and held mixed services in Little Rock, Arkansas, and Atlanta. The convicting and convincing power of gospel music eventually led the way to that great revival known as the Civil Rights Movement of the 1960s.

TAMARA J. JAFFE-NOTIER

See also Azusa Street Revival; Church of God in Christ (COGIC)

Reference and Further Reading

Boles, John B. *The Great Revival, 1787–1805: The Origins of the Southern Evangelical Mind.* Lexington: University Press of Kentucky, 1972.

Bruns, Roger A. *Preacher: Billy Sunday & Big-Time American Evangelism.* New York: W. W. Norton & Company, 1992.

Darden, Robert. *People Get Ready! A New History of Black Gospel Music.* New York: Continuum International Publishing Group, 2004.

Dolan, Jay P. *Catholic Revivalism: The American Experience 1830–1900.* Notre Dame, IN: University of Notre Dame Press, 1978.

McGee, Gary B. "William J. Seymour and the Azusa Street Revival." *Enrichment Journal* (Fall 1999). Available at Assemblies of God USA website, http://www.ag.org/enrichmentjournal/199904/026_azusa.cfm.

McLoughlin, William G. *Revivals, Awakenings, and Reform.* Chicago: University of Chicago Press, 1978.

Sims, Patsy. *Can Somebody Shout Amen! Inside the Tents and Tabernacles of American Revivalists.* Lexington: University Press of Kentucky, 1996.

REX HUMBARD FAMILY SINGERS

The Rex Humbard Family Singers were the musical progeny of itinerant evangelists Alpha E. Humbard

(b. White County, Arkansas) and his wife, Martha Bell Childers Humbard (b. Chillicothe, Missouri). Mrs. Humbard played and sang at her husband's preaching services. Their first and best-known child, the future televangelist Rex Humbard (full name Alpha Rex Emmanuel Humbard), was born in Little Rock, Arkansas, on August 13, 1919. Of their five later children, the oldest three (Ruth, Clement, and Leona) joined Rex in the first and best-known musical Humbard Family. During the late 1930s, they became radio regulars on KTHS (Hot Springs, Arkansas) in addition to their church work. They turned down an offer to move to WLS in Chicago for four hundred dollars a week per person at the *National Barn Dance*, because they would not agree to add secular songs to their sacred music.

In January 1939, Virgil O. Stamps of Stamps–Baxter brought the group to Dallas for an appearance at the State Fair Auditorium. There they so impressed Stamps and Pastor Albert Ott of Bethel Temple Church (then the largest Assembly of God church in America) that the group made Dallas their home for almost two years, doing thirteen weekly radio broadcasts from the church and touring in a five-hundred–mile radius as school permitted.

The Humbard Family made their first and best-known commercial recordings for OKeh Records at Fort Worth, Texas, on April and 16 and 17, 1940, including "The Meeting in the Air," "I'll Fly Away," and "Christ Is Keeping My Soul." This early acoustic instrumentation featured Rex on guitar, Leona on string bass, Ruth playing accordion, and Clement playing everything else as needed (including mandolin, banjo, and steel guitar).

Rex Humbard married one of Pastor Ott's best young Dallas radio singers, Maude Aimee Jones, on August 2, 1942. Her voice was soon a staple of the Humbard Family sound on coast-to-coast radio broadcasts for Mutual and NBC and on their postwar recordings for Sacred Records and White Church Records. Traveling in their own plane as early as 1945, they lost fourteen thousand dollars' worth of instruments when the City Auditorium in Daytona Beach burned, by which time the family instrumentation included organ, piano, harp, vibraharp, cowbells, sleigh bells, accordion, bass, acoustic guitar, and electric guitars.

By 1950, the Humbards' three-week–long crusades in cities across America were held under a twenty-one–thousand dollar tent (purchased from Oral Roberts), seating some six thousand people. In 1952, they used an even larger, circus-sized tent, the Gospel Big Top, for the first time at a Houston crusade, but early the next year, Rex decided to put down roots and build a church in the Akron, Ohio, area, while his parents and most of his siblings stayed in itinerant evangelism. Humbard opened the Calvary Temple in Akron in February 1953 and five years later moved to the Cathedral of Tomorrow in nearby Cuyahoga Falls.

Worldwide television evangelism became Rex Humbard's focus for the rest of his ministry, while family music remained a staple of their services and television offerings for many years. His four children (Rex, Jr., Donnie, Elizabeth, and Charlie), extended family, and grandchildren took up the musical mantle and joined in on several albums for family labels HFG and Impact, the distribution of which came primarily through the ministry's radio and television offers. The Cathedral Quartet, who took their name from his building, were regular features of Humbard's broadcasts in the late 1960s.

At his ministry's peak in the late 1970s, Rex Humbard could be viewed weekly on more than six hundred and fifty television stations worldwide (more than two hundred in the United States), but controversy and mounting debt dogged him. In 1980, the Humbards and two of their sons bought a home and condominiums in Boynton Beach, Florida, for six hundred and fifty thousand dollars, shortly after publicly announcing that the ministry was more than three million dollars in debt. Humbard explained to the press that he was "not concerned about what members of his congregation or the public may think about the purchases," adding, "My people don't give a hoot what I spend that money for."

In February 1983, he turned the pastorate of the Cathedral of Tomorrow over to his brother-in-law and longtime associate Reverend Wayne Jones, and made the move to Florida permanent. For several years thereafter, the Humbards continued to record in a studio they built in Boynton Beach and to tape half-hour television programs in Callaway Gardens, Georgia.

RONNIE PUGH

See also Cathedral Quartet; Stamps–Baxter

Reference and Further Reading

Humbard, Rex. *Miracles in My Life: Rex Humbard's Own Story*. Old Tappan, NJ: Fleming H. Revell, 1971.

REX NELON SINGERS, THE

Rex Lloyd Nelon (b. January 19, 1932; d. January 23, 2000)

The Rex Nelon Singers were led by Rex Lloyd Nelon, who sang bass and played guitar for the LeFevres beginning in 1957 and until his retirement in 1997.

In the mid-1970s, Rex Nelon purchased the LeFevres name and many of their business ventures, including the LeFevres–Sing Music record label. After the retirement of Eva Mae LeFevre in 1977, Rex changed the name of the group to the Rex Nelon Singers and eventually to the Nelons.

Like many Southern gospel trios and quartets, the membership has changed over the years, but it has always retained strong family ties. In 1972, Rex's daughter Kelly joined the LeFevres for a summer tour and over the years became a fixture in the group. Jason Clark, Kelly's husband, joined the group in 1994, and Amber, Kelly's daughter, began singing with the group in 2002. With Rex's retirement in late 1997, Kelly took over managing the group.

As leader of the group, Rex Nelon always welcomed younger performers into the Southern gospel fold by giving them a spot in the Rex Nelon Singers' lineup. Many of these singers and musicians went on to have successful solo careers or to join other popular groups. Prominent members of the group included Russell Easter of the Easter Brothers, Rex Foster during the 1970s, Karen Peck Gooch during the 1980s and early 1990s, Todd Nelon, Janet Paschal in the late 1970s and early 1980s, Jeff Stice (who played piano for the group during much of the 1980s), Rodney Swain, and Jerry Thompson.

Stylistically, the Rex Nelon Singers are best known for blending traditional country music with gospel sounds. Like the LeFevres, the various manifestations of the Rex Nelon Singers are known for their stunning vocal harmonies mixed with virtuoso instrument playing and often combined with complex instrumental arrangements. The Rex Nelon Singers incorporated elements of jazz instrumental and vocal arrangements in many of their songs throughout the 1970s and early 1980s. Vocally, the group is known for its clear and light harmonic presentations.

Over the years, the Rex Nelon Singers became a prominent fixture on Southern gospel radio and the concert circuit. The group has received three Grammy nominations, one each in 1979 and 1982 for Best Gospel Performance (Traditional) and one in 1990 for Best Southern Gospel Album for *Let the Redeemed Say So*. They have also won numerous Gospel Music Association Dove Awards and *Singing News* fan awards, including Dove Awards for Southern Gospel Album of the Year from 1982 to 1985. The group was named by *Singing News* readers as the Best Mixed Group in 1981 and the Best Group in 1985.

Throughout the years, individuals in the group, including Rex Nelon, have won numerous *Singing News* fan awards, including Rex Nelon being named Mr. Gospel Music in 1982. Rex was also a two-time winner of the Favorite Bass Singer award. Kelly Nelon is also a two-time winner of the Favorite Vocalist of the Year Award, along with numerous other accolades from the readership of *Singing News*. Rex Nelon was inducted into the Southern Gospel Music Hall of Fame in 1999.

The group's first single, "The Sun's Coming Up," was a top-twenty hit in 1978, 1979, and 1980. "O For A Thousand Tongues" remains one of the group's most popular songs, being named *Singing News* readership's Song of the Year in 1984. Other popular songs include "Come Morning," "I'll Talk to the Father," "I'm Glad I Know Who Jesus Is," "I've Got a Right," "Let the Redeemed Say So," "Sweet Beulah Land," "That's Enough," "Thanks," and "We Shall Wear a Robe and Crown." Many of the group's songs have become standards on gospel radio playlists.

Throughout the 1970s and 1980s and into the early 1990s, the Rex Nelon Singers recorded with Caanan Records (a subsidiary of Word Records) and RNS Records. They then moved first to Homeland Records, then Daywind Records, and eventually to Seraphim Music Group in the late 1990s and early 2000s. Throughout most of their early career, the group worked with producer Ken Harding and later with Lari Goss, who also played piano on many of their recordings. It was Goss's arrangements and piano playing, along with Rex Nelon's signature bass voice, that for many years helped to define the Nelons' sound.

Scott Banville

See also Canaan Records; Easter Brothers; Gospel Quartets; Homeland Records; LeFevres, The

Reference and Further Reading

Blackwell, Lois S. *The Wings of the Dove: The Story of Gospel Music in America*. Norfolk, VA: Donning, 1978.

Goff, James R., Jr. *Close Harmony: A History of Southern Gospel*. Chapel Hill: University of North Carolina Press, 2002.

Goff, Jim. "Southern Gospel Mourns the Loss of Rex Nelon." *Singing News* (2000). Available at *Singing News* website, http://www.singingnews.com/news/features/archive/2000/rex_nelon.lasso?page=2.

Jackson, George Pullen. *White Spirituals in the Southern Uplands*. Chapel Hill: University of North Carolina Press, 1933.

"Rex Nelon Biography." Southern Gospel Music Association website, http://www.sgma.org/bios.lasso?id=61.

Rex Nelon website, http://www.rexnelon.com/.

Terrell, Bob. *The Music Men: The Story of Professional Gospel Quartet Singing*. Asheville, NC: Bob Terrell, 1990.

The Nelons website, http://www.thenelons.com.

Discography

The Sun's Coming Up (1977, Canaan Records); *I've Never Been This Homesick Before* (ca. 1978, RNS Records); *Live* (1978, Canaan Records); *Feelings* (1979, Canaan Records); *Expressions of Love* (1980, Canaan Records); *One More Song* (1981, RNS Records); *One Step Closer* (1981, Canaan Records); *Sing the Gospel* (1981, RNS Records); *Feeling at Home* (1982, Canaan Records); *We Shall Behold the King* (1983, Canaan Records); *The Best and a Whole Lot More* (1984, Canaan Records); *I've Got My Foot on the Rock* (1984, RNS Records); *Precious Story of Love* (1984, RNS Records); *In One Accord* (1985, Canaan Records); *Journeys* (1986, Canaan Records); *Thanks* (1987, Canaan Records); *Get Ready* (1988, Canaan Records); *Let the Redeemed Say So* (1989, Canaan Records); *The Best of Times* (1990, Canaan Records); *A New Generation* (1991, Canaan Records); *One Less Stone* (1991, RNS Records); *Right on Time* (1992, Canaan Records); *Kelly Nelon and the Nelons* (1993, Benson Records); *He's My Comfort* (1994, RNS Records); *A Promised Reunion* (1994, Benson Records); *Triumphant* (1994, Chapel Records); *Hallelujah Live* (1995, Chapel Records); *We're Glad You're Here* (1996, Chapel/Spring Hill Records); *All Rise* (1997, Nelons); *Live* (1997, Nelons); *A Timeless Collection* (1997, Spring Hill); *We've Got to Praise Him* (1997, Homeland Records); *The Collection* (1998, Homeland Records); *Expressions of Love* (1998, Homeland Records; reissue); *Peace Within the Walls* (1998, Daywind Records); *A Journey* (1999, Daywind Records); *Out Front* (1999, Homeland Records); *Following After* (2000, Daywind Records); *Seasons of Songs Vol. 1* (2001, Seraphim Music Group); *United for Christ* (2002, Seraphim Music Group); *Seasons of Songs Vol. 2* (2003, Seraphim Music Group); *The Light of Home* (2004, Seraphim Music Group).

ROBINSON, CLEOPHUS

(b. March 18, 1932, Canton, MS; d. July 2, 1998)

Reverend Cleophus Robinson, Sr., was born in Canton, Mississippi and moved with his family to Memphis when he was a teenager. He attended LeMoyne-Owen College for two years. Robinson established his career at the end of the golden era of gospel music (1945–1955). He was pastor of Bethlehem Missionary Baptist Church in St. Louis, Missouri.

Gospel music in the Baptist churches, especially in the Midwest, had not changed from the use of piano and organ as background music. Robinson would sing solos accompanied by choral singers; usually the songs were praise songs. In 1957, Robinson recorded with his sister Josephine James (b. 1934) "Pray for Me." Robinson was influenced by "the Queen of Gospel," Mahalia Jackson (1911–1972), from whom he learned deliberate phrasing. From Brother Joe May (1912–1972), he learned the technique of growling in the upper part of the tenor register. Reverend James Cleveland (1932–1991) and Reverend Robinson made several recordings together, including "Pray for Me" and "When I Cross Over." Robinson and Cleveland were outstanding Baptist ministers. In 1956 at the end of the Golden Era, Robinson's famous song "Pray for Me" was placed in *Sallie Martin's Gospelodiums No. 25.*

Robinson received the Humanitarian Award and the Professor of Humanities Award from Mississippi Valley State University in February 1957. He was the first gospel artist to receive the Jubilee Award from the Atlanta Branch of the National Association for the Advancement of Colored People (NAACP). He made appearances at the White House, Carnegie Hall, Constitution Hall, and the Apollo Theatre and on *The Merv Griffin Show, The Dinah Shore Show, The 700 Club,* and others. On the international side, he appeared on the French, Swiss, and Spanish television networks. Robinson performed at the Hebrew University of Jerusalem and he appeared at the Montreaux International Jazz Festival, where he was recorded live.

His famous recordings were "I Know Prayer Changes Things," recorded in 1963, "Know his Strength," recorded on September 2, 1964, and "How Sweet It Is to Be Loved by Jesus," recorded in 1965. In 1979, on Sonet Records in London, England, he was included in the album entitled *The Soul of Black Music, Vol. 1.* Many gospel groups were included: the Swanee Quintet, the Angelic Gospel Singers, the Gospel Keynotes, the Supreme Angels, the Fairfield Four, the Soul Searchers, the Original Gospel Harmonettes, the Bright Stars, the Consolers, the Pilgrim Jubilee Singers, and the Birmingham Community Choir. Robinson was the soloist on the album.

Many of Robinson's records were recorded on Malaco Records (Jackson, Mississippi), including *What You Need* and *Back Again.* Robinson recorded eighty-four songs, of which many were sermonettes (preaching with singing). On October 22, 1993, he recorded the following albums: *Back Again, Live; Someone to Care,* released March 25, 1994; *What You Need, Live,* released November 14, 1995; and *I Can See So Much,* released May 13, 1997. A praise album of Robinson from High Stacks Records entitled *A Tribute to Rev. Cleophus Robinson, Sr., The World's Most Famous Gospel Singer & Preacher* was released in 2002. Robinson's sons Reverend Cleophus Robinson, Jr. and Shadrach Robinson, and Brother Ray Magee, a longtime colleague of Robinson, Sr., performed on the album. Robinson's popular songs were performed on this album, including "Wrapped Up, Tied Up, Tangled Up" and "It Won't Hurt You to Speak."

He is known as one of the world's greatest gospel singers and preachers, second to Reverend James Cleveland. Reverend Cleophus Robinson, Sr., was inducted into the International Gospel Music Hall of Fame and Museum in Detroit, Michigan, in October 2002.

Robinson was unique in that his gospel music style was cultured for the Civil Rights Movement in the 1960s. His faith and identity with many gospel greats made him an important male singer. He was not a full-time gospel singer; he was a preacher first, a pastor who devoted a portion of his time to gospel music. Robinson traveled internationally as well as locally. He received more awards than most gospel singers. He was well known as a very capable businessman and spiritual leader.

Always the gospel of Christ prevailed with worship as Robinson popularized his sacred and gospel music among mainly middle-class Baptist and many Holiness Pentecostal fans. He was not a crossover artist. Robinson gave a message and witness in his songs, especially "Pray for Me" and "Wrapped Up, Tied Up, Tangled Up in Jesus." His songs stressed that a person living for Jesus cannot get out of the tangles of Jesus. These songs were both huge hits, earning him a national reputation.

SHERRY SHERROD DUPREE

Reference and Further Reading

Boyer, Horace Clarence. *How Sweet the Sound: The Golden Age of Gospel*. Washington, DC: Elliott & Clark, 1995.

DuPree, Sherry Sherrod. *African-American Holiness Pentecostal Movement: An Annotated Bibliography*. Religious Information Systems Vol. 4; Garland Reference Library of Social Science Vol. 526. New York: Garland Publishing, 1996.

———; Herbert C. DuPree *African-American Good News (Gospel) Music*. Washington, DC: Middle Atlantic Regional Press, 1993.

International Gospel Music Hall of Fame and Museum website, http://www.gmhf.org (accessed August 28, 2004).

Discography

The Soul of Black Music, Vol. I (1979, Sonet Records).

ROCK GOSPEL

Rock gospel has its roots in the black churches of the Southern United States. The same rhythms and melodies that found their way into the early work of rhythm and blues pioneers such as Fats Domino, Little Richard Penniman, Big Joe Turner, and Ike Turner originated from the developing blues, jazz, and gospel music of this same time period. The 1950s served as both the golden age of gospel and the genesis of rock 'n' roll. As newly emerging record labels such as Chess, Peacock, Stax, and Sun began recording and distributing the new music, a growing radio market across the country began to play it. Some lauded rock 'n' roll as a new form of creative expression, while others condemned it as "the devil's music."

Some of the earliest rock gospel pioneers could be found in black gospel groups such as the Dixie Hummingbirds, the Five Blind Boys of Alabama, the Mighty Clouds of Joy, the Soul Stirrers, and the Staple Singers. Light Records, founded by Ralph Carmichael in the 1960s as a joint venture with Word Records, recorded and distributed new artists such as Andrae Crouch and the Disciples to WASP churches.

By the end of the 1960s, rock music had matured to the point that it gained worldwide recognition as being a valid form of musical expression. That period was also rife with cultural, political, religious, and social revolution, which manifested itself in a subculture. The counterculture revolution's interest in these areas was reflected in its music, and it was natural that, as many counterculture musicians converted to Christianity, they should want to express their new-found faith through rock music. Secular artists such as Barry McGuire, Chuck Girard, Richie Furay, and Larry Norman became counterculture Christians—or Jesus freaks—who became pioneers of the first wave of white "Christian rock" artists.

The Jesus freaks did not fit in the traditional churches at the time, which necessitated the emergence of a new paradigm church. One of the first—, and ultimately the most successful—was Calvary Chapel in Costa Mesa, California. Its success spawned a number of other new paradigm churches across the country to provide places for the Jesus freaks to worship. These new houses of worship often had the ambiance of a rock concert, with one or more individuals leading worship with guitars rather than the traditional organ.

Some of the new paradigm churches began their own record labels to help market groups originating from their fellowship as part of an evangelistic outreach. Calvary Chapel's Maranatha! Music produced many early Christian rock groups, such as Children of the Day, Love Song, and Mustard Seed Faith. Producer Billy Ray Hearn started two new record labels. His first was Myrrh Records, as a subsidiary of Word Records, which produced Amy Grant, Al Green, and Petra, to name some. In 1976, Hearn started his own record label, Sparrow Records, which produced new artists such as Keith Green and John Michael Talbot, as well as some crossovers from Myrrh, such as the 2nd Chapter of Acts. By the end of the 1970s, rock gospel was a firmly established music genre. Word, the largest Christian record label, had been purchased by the American Broadcasting Company (ABC), and in 1984, A&M Records began its secular distribution.

The 1980s began the second wave of Christian rock groups with more musically radical genres, as secular rock continued to evolve and influence Christian rock. Heavy metal and punk rock were as offensive to some as hippie rock had been during the 1960s. Some of the bands from this time period were Barren Cross, the Newsboys, Steve Taylor, Stryper, and Undercover.

Musical styles continued to evolve such that the 1990s saw rap and alternative rock as the norm. Christian artists such as Audio Adrenaline, DC talk, Jars of Clay, and Kirk Franklin received airplay on both Christian and secular radio stations and, in some cases, even on MTV. Rock gospel was recognized by the Christian music industry in 1988, when Mylon LeFevre & Broken Heart won the first Best Rock Gospel Album Dove Award for *Crack the Sky*. In 1990, the secular recording industry began a new Grammy Award category for Best Rock/Contemporary Gospel Album, which Petra won for *Beyond Belief*.

By the turn of the millennium contemporary Christian music was as much an established musical genre as country and western. Annual Christian music festivals such as Alive, Con Dios, Cornerstone, and Creation showcased both newly emerging bands such as Earthsuit, Lifehouse, and P.O.D. as well as exposing younger crowds to pioneers such as Daniel Amos, Randy Stonehill, and Sweet Comfort.

BOB GERSZTYN

See also 2nd Chapter of Acts; Barren Cross; Calvary Chapel, Costa Mesa; Carmichael, Ralph; Crouch, Andrae; DC Talk; Dixie Hummingbirds; Five Blind Boys of Alabama; Franklin, Kirk; Girard, Chuck; Grant, Amy; Green, Al; Green, Keith; Hearn, Billy Ray; Jars of Clay; Light Records; Love Song; Maranatha! Music; Mighty Clouds of Joy; Myrrh Records; Newsboys; Norman, Larry; Petra; Soul Stirrers; Staple Singers; Stryper; Talbot, John Michael; Taylor, Steve

Reference and Further Reading

Ball, Nina; Andrae Crouch. *Through It All*. Waco, TX: Word Books, 1974.
Boyer, Horace Clarence. *How Sweet the Sound: The Golden Age of Gospel*. Washington, DC: Elliott & Clark, 1995.
Carmichael, Ralph. *He's Everything to Me*. Nashville, TN: Word Publishing, 1986.
Franklin, Kirk; Jim Nelson Black (contributor). *Church Boy*. Nashville, TN: Word Publishing, 1998.
Green, Al; Davin Seay. *Take Me to the River*. Edinburgh, Scotland: Payback Press, 2000.
"History of the Jesus Movement." Calvary Chapel website, http://www.calvarychapel.com (accessed April 5, 2003).
Max, Kevin. *Unfinished Work*. Nashville, TN: Thomas Nelson Publishing, 2001.
Miller, Donald E. *Reinventing American Protestantism: Christianity in the New Millennium*. Berkeley: University of California Press, 1997.
O'Neill, Dan. *Signatures: The Story of John Michael Talbot*. Franklin, TN: Troubadour for the Lord, 2003.
One-Way Christian Music website, http://www.one-way.org (accessed May 5, 2003).
Richard DeLaFont Agency website, http://www.delafont.com (accessed May 10, 2003).
Rolling Stone website, http://www.rollingstone.com (accessed November 10, 2003).
Thompson, John J. *Raised by Wolves*. Toronto, Canada: ECW Press, 2001.
Whitaker, Beth. *The Calling of a Rock Star*. Hawthorne Publishing Company, 1988.

RODEHEAVER, HOMER ALVAN

(b. October 4, 1880; d. December 18, 1955)

Homer Alvan Rodeheaver, the man who was Billy Sunday's music director during the height of the evangelist's fame, was born in Union Furnace, Ohio but grew up in Jellico, Tennessee. He showed some early interest in music and learned to play the cornet. In 1896, he started college at Ohio Wesleyan and, while there, changed over to the trombone, the instrument that is most often associated with him. The only one he ever owned was purchased used at this time for seven dollars. With a break during the Spanish–American War, Rodeheaver stayed at Ohio Wesleyan for eight years but never obtained a degree. He did, however, take several music courses and played in the college band, so he was involved in a lot of musical activities. Rodeheaver left college in 1904 to work for evangelist William E. Biederwolf, staying with him until 1909.

It was in 1910 that Rodeheaver began his twenty-year association with Billy Sunday. His attempts to make evangelistic music informal, congenial, and enjoyable brought gospel music much closer to pop music. He felt this approach was necessary because it was essential to entertain people to get their attention. It was also easy for him, because Rodeheaver was a consummate entertainer.

Rather than just sticking with old hymns, he often used light, optimistic, semireligious numbers, such as Charles H. Gabriel's "Brighten the Corner Where You Are." Some critics suggested that such a piece, with its ragtime syncopation and bass arpeggios, was inappropriate in a religious service. To these people

Homer Alvan Rodeheaver. Photo courtesy Frank Driggs Collection.

he responded, "It was never intended for a Sunday morning service, nor for a devotional meeting—its purpose was to bridge that gap between the popular song of the day and the great hymns and gospel songs, and to give men a simple, easy lilting melody which they could learn the first time they heard it, and which they could whistle and sing wherever they might be."

Rodeheaver employed more than just songs to win over his audiences. Frequently he told funny stories or resorted to magic tricks, producing various "noises" from his trombone, or he pulled practical jokes on other team members on the stage. But more than just his sense of humor helped him achieve his goals. He displayed a great deal of enthusiasm and expected his choirs to do the same. By encouraging competition among choirs, he sought to get the best from them. He also urged audiences to sing, thereby making them part of the music program. His thick

Southern accent and his ability to evaluate a crowd and capture its feeling proved invaluable for performing his job. One other factor needs to be considered, one that was unusual for evangelistic musicians of his time: namely, his sex appeal. Rodeheaver, a bachelor, was the first chorister to blatantly appeal to women.

In 1910, the same year he joined Sunday, Rodeheaver became associated with Bentley DeForrest Ackley to establish the Rodeheaver–Ackley publishing firm in Chicago. The following year, 1911, it became the Rodeheaver Company. After purchasing the Hall–Mack Company of Philadelphia in 1936, the name was changed again to the Rodeheaver–Hall–Mack Company. This firm became a leader in the field of gospel music, but it underwent a name change again, to the Rodeheaver Company, after moving to Winona Lake, Indiana, in 1941. Twenty-eight years later, in 1969, it became a division of Word, Inc., and was known as Rodeheaver–Word Music. After the American Broadcasting Company purchased Word in 1974, it became known as Word Music.

In addition to publishing, Rodeheaver also established Rainbow Records, one of the first labels solely devoted to gospel music. He took the name from the closing phrase of the song "If Your Heart Keeps Right," which said "Ev'ry cloud will wear a rainbow, if your heart keeps right." There is some uncertainty about when this company was founded, with estimates ranging from 1910 to 1920. Most authorities, however, suggest the latter date. Their is no dispute about Rodeheaver's reasons for starting the label; he saw it as an opportunity to counteract the influences of popular songs and jazz. Undoubtedly, he also saw it as an opportunity to introduce new songs. His greatest success in this regard was George Bennard's 1913 hymn "The Old Rugged Cross," which he recorded ten times.

Although technically Rodeheaver worked with Sunday until 1930, for all practical purposes their relationship ended in 1927. Dissatisfaction with the evangelist's platform manner, his refusal to help Rodeheaver plan the service's music, and Sunday's handling of finances led to the dissolution of the partnership. Rodeheaver's various interests kept him busy after leaving Sunday. In 1936, he undertook a tour of African missions with Arthur J. Moore, bishop of the Methodist Episcopal Church, specifically for the purpose of finding out the source of the black spirituals. During World War II, he toured Europe for the YMCA, reportedly giving three hundred and twenty concerts in one hundred and twenty days. Rodeheaver also kept busy with the Song Directors' Conferences that he established in 1920.

His nonmusical activities included the founding of Rainbow Ranch for underprivileged boys near Palatka, Florida. Rodeheaver compiled eighty collections of gospel songs but composed relatively few, possibly because of his limited abilities in music reading and notation. His two most popular originals were "Good Night and Good Morning" and "Then Jesus Came." He also wrote several secular songs, including "The Old Sun Dial" and "Goodbye, France! Hello, Miss Liberty?" Generally, however, he was content to promote the works of others.

W. K. McNEIL

Reference and Further Reading

Cusic, Don. "Homer Rodeheaver." *Rejoice* 2, no. 2 (Fall, 1989): 10–14.

McLoughlin, William G., Jr. *Billy Sunday Was His Real Name*. Chicago: University of Chicago Press, 1955.

Rodeheaver, Homer A. *Singing Black: Twenty Thousand Miles with a Music Missionary*. Chicago: Rodeheaver Co., 1936.

———. *Twenty Years with Billy Sunday*. Nashville, TN: Cokesbury Press, 1936.

ROGERS, ROY, AND DALE EVANS

Roy Rogers (Leonard Franklin Slye) (b. November 5, 1911, Cincinnati, OH; d. July 6, 1998, Victorville, CA).

Dale Evans (Frances Octavia Smith) (b. October 31, 1912, Ulvalde, TX; d. February 7, 2001, Apple Valley CA)

Known as the "King of Cowboys" and the "Queen of the West," respectively, Roy Rogers and Dale Evans were singers, television and film stars, and prolific songwriters of country-western and gospel music. Rogers starred in ninety-one feature films, 102 half-hour television films, touring rodeos, and radio programs; he made records in western and gospel music; and he developed business interests in real estate, music publishing, and fast-food restaurants. Evans costarred with Rogers in twenty-eight films, composed more than twenty-five songs, wrote more than twenty books, and made thirty children's records. The pair recorded a number of gospel records, and Evans wrote the enormously popular gospel song "The Bible Tells Me So," in 1955, which remains today an enduring standard of the gospel repertoire.

Rogers was brought up on a farm in Ohio, where he first performed in public at barn dances and often acted as a caller for square dances. He moved to California in 1931 with the intent of pursuing a career as a musician. There, he performed with several groups, including the O-Bar-O Cowboys, the Rocky Mountaineers, and the Pioneer Trio, a group Rogers founded in 1933. The Pioneer Trio changed their name to the Sons of the Pioneers a year later, and the group went on to become one of the best-known western groups of all time, known for hit singles such as "Tumbling Tumbleweeds" and "Cool Water." Rogers began his career as a movie actor in the mid-1930s, playing bit parts in Westerns, and he made his Republic Pictures debut—billed under his new name, Roy Rogers—in *Under Western Skies* in 1938. Rogers married Arlene Wilkins in 1936, only to become a widower when his wife died from complications during the birth of their son, Roy, Jr., in 1946.

Dale Evans was born Frances Octavia Smith in Uvalde, Texas, in 1912. She married at fourteen, gave birth to her first child, and found herself the following year a single parent living in Memphis, Tennessee. She spent the next several years working at small radio stations in the Midwest and as a vocalist for a number of bands. Spotted by a talent scout, by 1940 Evans had moved to Hollywood and embarked on a film career. After a number of bit parts, Evans had her first starring role in the 1944 film *The Cowboy and the Senorita*, which costarred Rogers. Rogers and Evans married on December 31, 1947, beginning a professional and personal partnership that continued until Rogers's death in 1998.

In 1950, Rogers and Evans developed their own production company and began producing a half-hour television series, *The Roy Rogers Show*, which ran from 1951 to 1957. Later incarnations of their television program included *The Roy Rogers and Dale Evans Show* (1962) and *Happy Trails Theatre* (1986–1989), which featured Rogers and Evans movies with added commentary provided by the pair. They also created several long-running radio series that featured their singing duets and dramatic sketches, and they regularly rode in parades and performed at rodeos throughout America. In 1951, Evans penned the song "Happy Trails," which became their theme song.

Shortly after their marriage, Evans had a religious awakening in the Christian faith. Rogers followed her example shortly thereafter, and the pair became charter members of the Hollywood Christian Group. Perhaps compelled by the national spiritual revival sweeping across America in the late 1940s and early 1950s or by a personal need to explain the tragic loss of three of their children, from the late 1940s on, Rogers and Evans increasingly incorporated their spiritual beliefs into their performances. In particular, Rogers and Evans's music, films, and television and radio appearances featured a particular type of spiritual enlightenment, one that linked religious devotion with patriotism and civic responsibility; with their extensive presence on radio, television, and film,

Rogers and Evans had numerous outlets through which to express their views. They concluded one of their 1951 radio programs with the patriotic religious song "What This Country Needs Is to Talk with the Lord," and in 1952 Rogers made a somewhat risky career decision to add a patriotic–religious segment to each of his public appearances and rodeo performances.

Throughout the 1950s, 1960s, and 1970s, Rogers and Evans released a number of gospel singles, many of which appeared on subsequent albums. In 1949 they recorded Roger's composition "May the Lord Take a Likin' to You," and in 1955 Evans wrote the gospel music standard "The Bible Tells Me So," with lyrics drawn from the New Testament's I Corinthians 13:13. They released their first spiritual album, *Peace in the Valley,* in 1950, which was followed by several other gospel albums, including *Hymns of Faith* (1954), *Jesus Loves Me* (1959, featuring the entire Rogers family), *Jesus Loves Me* (1960), *The Bible Tells Me So* (1962), *In the Sweet By and By* (1973), *The Good Life* (1977), and *Say Yes to Tomorrow* (1995).

Rogers and Evans earned numerous awards, including multiple stars on the Hollywood Walk of Fame for Rogers and Evans as well as Rogers's double inductions into the Country Music Hall of Fame—in 1980 as a member of the Sons of the Pioneers and in 1988 as a solo artist. They were known for their charitable works up to their deaths, in particular for the establishment of the Happy Trails Children's Foundation, which endeavored to improve the lives of abused and neglected children. They established the Roy Rogers–Dale Evans Museum in Victorville, California, in 1965.

ERIN STAPLETON-CORCORAN

Reference and Further Reading

Morris, Georgia; Mark Pollard, eds. *Roy Rogers: King of the Cowboys*. San Francisco: Collins, 1994.

Rogers, Roy; Dale Evans; with Jane and Michael Stern. *Happy Trails: Our Life Story*. New York: Simon and Schuster, 1994.

White, Raymond E. "Roy Rogers: An American Icon." *Back in the Saddle: Essays on Western Film and Television Actors,* edited by Gary A. Yoggy. Jefferson, NC: McFarland, 1998.

Discography

Roy Rogers and Dale Evans. *Peace in the Valley* (1950, Pair); *Hymns of Faith* (1954, RCA Victor); *Jesus Loves Me* (1960, RCA Camden); *The Bible Tells Me So* (1962, Capitol); *In the Sweet By and By* (1973, Word); *The Good Life* (1977, Word).

Roy Rogers, Dale Evans, and Dusty Rogers. *Say Yes to Tomorrow* (1995, Homeland Records).

ROMAN, LULU

(b. May 6, 1946)

From go-go dancing to gospel music—with *Hee Haw* comedy along the way—sums up the professional life of Lulu Roman. She was born Bertha Louise Habler about 1946 in a home for unwed mothers in Dallas, and she was soon placed in the Buckner Benevolent Orphanage, a Baptist institution. Suffering from birth with a thyroid dysfunction, she grew to be an overweight but agile and personable young lady, her humor hiding the pain of the teasing she endured as a girl.

Turning to show business as "Lulu Roman, the World's Biggest Go-Go Dancer," she performed in Dallas nightclubs owned by the notorious Jack Ruby. She impressed country music superstar Buck Owens with her comedic talents, and he brought her to the attention of those planning a CBS-TV series for the summer of 1969 in which Owens would costar: *Hee Haw*, a country music version of the wildly popular *Rowan & Martin's Laugh In*. Producer Sam Lovullo acted on Buck's recommendation and at first used Lulu in silent, background videos filmed for the show in California. Later she was given speaking roles in such popular *Hee Haw* comedy segments as "The Culhanes," "Truck Stop," and "The Jug Band." On March 19, 1971, she was arrested for drug possession (LSD, marijuana, hashish, and paraphernalia) in a raid on her Dallas apartment. Roman received a conviction and a four-year sentence in January 1972, but *Hee Haw*'s willingness to hire her back (without name billing for a while and removed from some of the group scenes) induced the leniency of a ten-year probation, which was later commuted by a pardon.

Lulu's emotional conversion to Christianity shortly after her arrest emboldened her to approach *Hee Haw* producers with a willingness to sing gospel songs; she auditioned with an *a cappella* "Blessed Assurance." Eventually her well-received songs, stylistically between traditional and contemporary gospel, became a regular feature of the show (which stayed in national syndication until the middle 1990s), and they have appeared on her dozen gospel albums since 1975: four for Rainbow (a Dallas label) in the 1970s, three for Word and two for Homeland in the 1980s, and albums for Benson and Silver Wing in the 1990s. Daywind, in 1997, released *Hymns, Promises and Praises* and, in 2003, *Intimate Expression,* a project seven years in the making. Some of her work was originally issued as being by Lulu Roman Smith, from her thirteen-year marriage to Woody Smith.

She won a Dove Award in 1985, when *You Were Loving Me* won Best Album by a Secular Artist, and she has had chart-topping singles with "King of Who I Am" (1985 duet with Russ Taff) and "Two More Hands" (with Ricky Skaggs and Sharon White in 1988). In addition to her years with *Hee Haw,* Lulu guested on *The Love Boat, The Mike Douglas Show, Sally Jesse Raphael, The 700 Club,* and other national programs, and she hosted the gospel portion of the *National Cerebral Palsy Telethon* each year from 1992 to 1995.

RONNIE PUGH

Reference and Further Reading

Lovullo, Sam; with Marc Eliot. *Life in the Kornfield: My 25 Years at Hee Haw.* New York: Boulevard Books, 1996.
"Lulu Roman Biography." Beckie Simmons Agency website, http://www.bsaworld.com/LuLuRoman.html.
Roman, Lulu. *Lulu/Lulu Roman.* Old Tappan, NJ: F. H. Revell, 1978.

Selected Discography

Love Coming Down (Rainbow).
No One's Child (Silver Wings).
One Day at a Time (Rainbow).
Take Me There (Word).

ROOT, GEORGE FREDERICK

(b. August 30, 1820; d. August 6, 1895)

One of the composers of "respectable" gospel music, George Frederick Root was unusual in that he was successful as a composer of both popular and gospel songs. His best-remembered pop numbers are "There's Music in the Air" (1854), written in conjunction with one of his students, Fanny J. Crosby; "The Vacant Chair" (1861); "The Battle Cry of Freedom" (1862); "Just Before the Battle, Mother" (1862); and "Tramp! Tramp! Tramp!" (1864). The latter melody was used for the still-popular Sunday school piece, "Jesus Loves the Little Children."

A native of Sheffield, Massachusetts, Root grew up in Reading, where his family moved when he was six. His maternal grandfather was a singing-school teacher, and his mother and her five sisters all sang and played the double bass. Root's father taught him to play the flute, and the young boy soon learned to perform on other instruments as well. His first formal music lessons came at age eighteen, when he became a piano student of Artemas Nixon Johnson in nearby Boston; he also took singing lessons from George James Webb and joined the Handel and Haydn Society. One day, one of his teachers asked the young man to learn some hymn tunes to play at prayer meetings. This incident launched Root's musical career, for he was soon given a student to teach, and he began to conduct singing schools. In 1841, he became associated with Lowell Mason's teacher's classes, becoming so popular that he shortly became an instructor in vocal technique.

In 1844, Root moved to New York to teach at Jacob Abbott's School for Young Ladies, later moving to a variety of other schools, including Rutgers Female Institution, Miss Haines's School for Young Ladies, Union Theological Seminary, the Spingler Institute, and the New York State Institution for the Blind. Fanny J. Crosby was one of his students at this latter school; in later years she would write several verses that Root set to music. During his time in New York, Root directed the Mercer Street Church choir and also formed a vocal quartet with his wife, a sister, and a brother.

In 1846, he published *The Young Ladies' Choir,* the first of seventy-five collections that appeared during his lifetime. Root spent eight months in Paris during 1850 and 1851, going there to study singing with Giulio Alary, an association that ended abruptly when Root declined, on religious grounds, to attend rehearsals of an opera by Alary. Subsequent lessons were with a tenor at the Paris Opera, Jacques Potharst. After returning to the United States, Root developed the idea of holding a three-month session of a Normal Musical Institute for instructing teachers, but he had to delay his plans for a year, because Lowell Mason, whom he wanted as one of its instructors, was unavailable. Once the institutes got started, they proved to be very popular, and for several years Root devoted most of his time to them.

His busy schedule did not keep him from writing music, and in 1852, to a text by Fanny Crosby, he composed the first secular cantata by an American, *The Flower Queen, or The Coronation of the Rose.* In all but name it was an opera, a term Root avoided on moralistic, antitheater principles. It was successful enough that he was inspired to produce several other cantatas, none of which enjoyed the popularity of his initial effort.

In 1859, Root moved to Chicago, where his brother, Ebenezer Tourner Root, had opened a music store with Chauncey Marvin Cady. The following year, Root became a partner in the firm, being placed in charge of publications. He urged songwriters to make their products accessible to the widest possible audience, and he conformed to these standards in his own works. For nine years (1863–1872), Root contributed songs and articles to the company's periodical, *The Song Messenger of the Northwest,* but after the Chicago

fire of 1871 almost ruined the firm, Root withdrew but remained active musically.

For his accomplishments, the University of Chicago later conferred upon Root the honorary degree of doctor of music. At the invitation of his British publisher, Root visited England in 1886; there he made contacts that led to several commissions for religious cantatas to texts by British authors. He later collaborated with his daughter, Clara, on a series of dramatic cantatas for children.

Throughout his life, however, Root's main interest was in writing songs that could be easily sung by anyone. His several gospel numbers include "Ring the Bells of Heaven," a melody originally written for a secular song; "When He Cometh," a tune adapted from a secular song; "Johnny Schmoker"; "The Lord Is in His Holy Temple"; and "Come to the Savior, Make No Delay." Only the first two have any current popularity.

W. K. MCNEIL

Reference and Further Reading

Epstein, Dena J. *Music Publishing in Chicago Before 1871: The Firm of Root & Cady, 1858–1871.* Detroit, MI: Information Coordinators, 1969.

Howard, John T. "Root, George Frederick." *Dictionary of American Biography.*

Osbeck, Kenneth W. *101 Hymn Stories.* Grand Rapids, MI: Kregel, 1982.

———. *101 More Hymn Stories.* Grand Rapids, MI: Kregel, 1985.

Root, George F. *The Story of a Musical Life.* New York: AMS Press, 1973 (1891).

RUEBUSH, EPHRAIM

(b. September 26, 1833, near Churchville, Augusta County, VA; d. November 18, 1924, Dayton, VA).

Ephraim Ruebush was an influential singing teacher, music publisher, and businessman in the Shenandoah Valley following the Civil War. He was best known for being the senior partner of the Ruebush–Kieffer Company, the earliest and most important publisher in the Southern gospel field.

The youngest of twelve children born to John and Mary Huffman Ruebush, Ephraim was raised in a family that valued education and that was strictly religious. They were members first of the German Reformed Church and then of the United Brethren Church. In 1853, Ruebush moved to Mountain Valley (later Singers Glen), Virginia, to learn music, bookbinding, and printing from Joseph Funk. There he met and became a close associate of Funk's grandson, Aldine S. Kieffer, who was seven years his junior and the single most important figure in the birth of Southern gospel.

In 1859, Ruebush and Kieffer began team-teaching singing schools throughout Virginia. On March 28, 1861, Ruebush married Kieffer's sister, Lucilla Virginia, a union that produced six children. Accounts differ regarding Ruebush's service in the Civil War. Kieffer himself, who fought for the Confederacy, wrote that Ruebush had been a captain in the Union Army and, at the end of the war, helped obtain his release from Fort Delaware. Morrison, however, quotes sources that report that Ruebush, opposing his state's secession from the Union, moved to Mineral and Grant counties (in present-day West Virginia), where he taught music until the end of the conflict, and that he refused a lieutenancy in the Union Army because he did not wish to fight against his family and friends. Of his three brothers who fought for the Confederacy, two were killed.

After the war, Ruebush joined Kieffer to establish Ruebush, Kieffer & Company. While Kieffer handled creative matters, Ruebush effectively managed the business operations. From 1866, their company published numerous popular gospel songbooks and, in 1874, established a highly influential music school for teachers. They also published *The Musical Million* (1870–1914), the most prominent nineteenth-century periodical championing shape notes and Southern music. Ruebush's superior business skills helped his company establish the foundation upon which Southern gospel grew.

STEPHEN SHEARON

See also Funk, Joseph; Kieffer, Aldine S.; Singers Glen, Virginia; Singing Schools

Reference and Further Reading

Cusic, Don. *The Sound of Light: A History of Gospel and Christian Music*, 1st Hal Leonard edition. Milwaukee: Hal Leonard Corporation, 2002.
Eskew, Harry Lee. "Shape-Note Hymnody in the Shenandoah Valley, 1816–1860." Ph.D. dissertation, Tulane University, 1966.
Goff, James R., Jr. *Close Harmony: A History of Southern Gospel*. Chapel Hill: University of North Carolina Press, 2002.
Hall, Paul M. "The 'Musical Million': A Study and Analysis of the Periodical Promoting Music Reading Through Shape-Notes in North America from 1870 to 1914." D.M.A. dissertation, Catholic University of America, 1970.
Jackson, George Pullen. *White Spirituals in the Southern Uplands*. Chapel Hill: University of North Carolina Press, 1933.
Morrison, Charles Edwin. "Aldine S. Kieffer and Ephraim Ruebush: Ideals Reflected in Post–Civil War Ruebush–

Keiffer Company Publications." Ed.D. dissertation, Arizona State University, 1992.
Showalter, Grace I. *The Music Books of Ruebush & Kieffer, 1866–1942: A Bibliography*. Richmond: Virginia State Library, 1975.

RURAL HARMONY, THE

This early tunebook, consisting of seventy-one pieces, was the work of Jacob Kimball (b. February 15, 1761; d. July 24, 1826) and was issued in Boston in 1793. Kimball later published *The Village Harmony* (1798) and *The Essex Harmony* (1800), all of them showing a compositional style far more sophisticated—from a European perspective—than those of most of Kimball's American contemporaries. *The Rural Harmony* is noteworthy for its treatment of fugal tunes.

Kimball demonstrated musical talent at an early age, playing fife and drum in the Massachusetts Militia at the Revolutionary War battles of Lexington and Bunker Hill in 1775, when he was only fourteen. In 1776, he entered Harvard College, graduating in 1780. Most of the next thirty-four years he spent as a schoolteacher in Ipswich, Massachusetts, and in his hometown of Topsfield, Massachusetts. Briefly he studied and practiced law but found the profession not to his liking. It was sacred music by which he made his name, first as a singing-school teacher working throughout New England and then as a singer. In 1798, he joined the Essex Musical Association, but it was as a composer that he made his chief mark.

Although Kimball's work was good musically, his tunes did not prove to be very popular, although "Invitation" was reprinted in several eighteenth- and nineteenth-century American tunebooks. *The Rural Harmony* contained only Kimball compositions, and forty-four of the forty-six pieces in *The Essex Harmony* were by Kimball; but *The Village Harmony*, which was very popular in Eastern Massachusetts (1795–1815), included fewer of the compiler's original works than his other two books. Kimball's lack of success as a businessman and alcoholism led him to a pauper's death in the almshouse of Topsfield, his hometown.

W. K. MCNEIL

Reference and Further Reading

Metcalf, Frank J. *American Writers and Compilers of Sacred Music*. New York: Russell & Russell, 1967 (1925).
Wilcox, G. C. "Jacob Kimball, a Pioneer American Musician." *Essex Institute Historical Collections* xciv (1958): 356.

S

SACRED HARP, THE

The Sacred Harp is a shape-note tunebook first published in Hamilton, Georgia, in 1844. It is considered exemplary in its resiliency, having remained in print since the first edition. As did other Southern tunebooks of its era, it contained musical and theological elements that would later influence gospel music. It derives from the eighteenth-century New England singing-school movement and is associated with singing conventions.

The songs compiled in *The Sacred Harp* preserve the style and repertoire of the shape-note tunebooks of the nineteenth century. Included are fugues and anthems from eighteenth-century New England composers, camp-meeting songs, strophic hymns, folk hymns, and nineteenth-century secular songs. The book employs the four-shape notation system introduced around 1800, the note names of which lend the term "fasola" to its musical style. It features the signature four-part polyphonic style called "dispersed harmony," with melodic involvement in all parts, parallel movement, open fifths, and gapped and diatonic scales.

The Sacred Harp was compiled by B. F. White and E. J. King. White, the principal compiler, had come to Georgia from South Carolina, where his brother-in-law, William Walker, had recently published *Southern Harmony* (1835). White established himself as editor of a local newspaper, *The Organ*, which prominently featured musical discourses, among other news. The first edition of *The Sacred Harp* followed established models of Southern tunebooks unremarkably, featuring typical arrangements of a familiar repertory of songs.

What distinguished *The Sacred Harp* were White's brilliant efforts to establish the book as a centerpiece of regional tradition. He solicited compositions from local singers for the book. When the stock of books was exhausted, he assembled a committee of prominent singers to revise the book—three times in his lifetime—adding regional compositions and better accommodating regional tastes. Most significant, he founded the Southern Musical Convention, an organization with bylaws and elected officers, its primary purpose being to host an annual singing convention. Together these innovations ensured that, unlike almost all other tunebooks, *The Sacred Harp* was embraced by a loyal following who would carry on its use after White was gone.

During the nineteenth century, shape notes declined in prominence, especially in the urban North, due to efforts to promote musical refinement in churches and schools. However, *The Sacred Harp* was affected more by the rise of gospel music in the South, which prevailed upon the tastes and loyalties of prominent singers and composers. After the turn of the twentieth century, the singing community was split into factions over the issue of gospel style, which was reflected by several competing revisions of the tunebook. The most enduring were those by W. M. Cooper of Dothan, Alabama, whose 1902 Cooper Revision was a modest accommodation to changing tastes, and those by J. L. James of Atlanta, whose 1911 James Revision was titled *The Original Sacred*

Harp to reflect its antiquarian stance. The 1936 Denson Revision, which followed the James Revision, introduced many new compositions and reflected the prominence of the Denson family of Northwest Alabama.

The discovery of Sacred Harp singing as folk music after 1920—particularly in the writings of folklorist George Pullen Jackson—reintroduced the music to the public as a form linked to antiquity. During the post–World War II years, this association drew new adherents to the style as a part of the folksong revival and spurred the spread of Sacred Harp to the urban North. Under the leadership of Hugh McGraw of Bremen, Georgia, some Southern singers encouraged this trend and traveled to new areas to help instill traditional style and values in the new singing community. The 1991 Revision, which replaced the Denson Revision, included songs by composers in both traditional and new areas and retained the commitment of its predecessors to pre-gospel style. Ultimately, this revision became the centerpiece of a new fellowship of harpers, whose broad and avid interest in the tunebook idiom was rekindled.

JOHN BEALLE

See also Jackson, George Pullen; Shape-Note Singing; Singing Schools; *Southern Harmony, The*

Reference and Further Reading

Bealle, John. *Public Worship, Private Faith: Sacred Harp and American Folksong.* Athens: University of Georgia Press, 1997.

Cobb, Buell E. *The Sacred Harp: A Tradition and Its Music.* Athens: University of Georgia Press, 1989.

Fasola website, http://fasola.org. Guide to recordings, tunebooks, and publications; schedule of singings with maps and directions; historical overview; and access to e-mail discussion lists (accessed July 17, 2004).

Jackson, George Pullen. *White Spirituals in the Southern Uplands: The Story of the Fasola Folk, Their Songs, Singings, and "Buckwheat Notes."* Chapel Hill: University of North Carolina Press, 1933.

Discography

In Sweetest Union Join (1999, Sacred Harp Musical Heritage Association; recording of the 1999 United Sacred Harp Convention; double CD).

Sacred Harp Singing (1997, Rounder Records CD #1503; recording of the 1942 Alabama State Convention).

Traditional Musics of Alabama, Vol. 3: 2002 National Sacred Harp Singing Convention (2002, Alabama Center for Traditional Culture; CD).

SACRED PAGEANTS

Definition

Sacred pageants—also called gospel dramas, gospel song plays, or biblical music dramas—are Christian theatricals using gospel music to advance the plot and/or as scene transitions. Just as medieval passion plays emerged from early religious ceremonies, sacred pageants, which were written to be performed for church congregations, were born from the union of the black gospel tradition and the theater. Gospel music removed the solemnity of the passion, replacing it with overcoming and victory. Themes are primarily biblical, dramatizing victorious motifs with the intent to "get the lost saved and the saved growing" and to unite and uplift. The pageants celebrate spiritual and political redemption, such as William H. Brewster's *Sowing in Tears, Reaping in Joy* and *From Auction Block to Glory*.

Chronology

During the 1920s, the Johnson Gospel Singers traveled the Midwest in three sacred pageants—*Hellbound, From Earth to Glory*, and *The Fatal Wedding*—written and directed by Robert Johnson. Johnson also played lead in the productions to female lead Mahalia Jackson. In 1924 at the General Conference of the African Methodist Episcopal Church, Reverend J. McCoo successfully debuted *Ethiopia at the Bar of Justice*, a sacred pageant featuring standard spirituals. The pageant became a staple of Negro History Week.

Other early versions of the form—for example, Nannie Helen Burroughs's *Slabtown Convention*—did not include original scores. Indeed, these plays were authored to suit the popular sacred music—hymns, gospels, and chants—of the 1930s. The most famous of this ilk was *Heaven Bound*, by Atlanta, Georgia, Sunday school teachers Lula B. Jones and Nellie L. Davis (copyrighted in 1971 by William Walker). Written to raise funds for their beloved Big Bethel African Methodist Episcopal Church, *Heaven Bound* is a portrait of good versus evil. As Christians attempt to enter heaven, they are confronted by Satan. The February 17, 1930, premier was largely ad-libbed except for the standard spirituals sung by the beleaguered travelers on the way to "higher ground." This successful sacred pageant portrayed a certain dignity, in that racially stereotyped language was not used. The production toured the Southeast during most of the 1930s, playing to integrated audiences. In 1937 and 1938, the Federal Theater Project of Atlanta produced *Heaven Bound* at the Atlanta Theatre.

In the 1940s, sacred pageants were widely popularized by Baptist minister and gospel music legend William H. Brewster (1897–1987), whose songs include "Peace Be Still," "How I Got Over," "I Am Leaning and Depending on the Lord," and "Let Us Go Back to the Old Landmark." Recognized as "Pioneer of the Sacred Pageant" (Wiggings, in Reagon, p. 245), Reverend Brewster authored more than fifteen pageants, including the complete scores. Hallmarks of his pageants were the original scores and the use of standard American English rather than Southern black vernacular. His historic production *From Auction Block to Glory* premiered in 1941 at the National Baptist Convention. The composition was the first black religious pageant produced on a national scale to have a score written expressly for the production. Single compositions he originally penned as parts of scores for the pageants often became hits for gospel music greats Mahalia Jackson, Marion Williams, and Clara Ward of the Ward Trio and Ward Singers.

Drawing on the black religious custom of creating folksy theatricals based on spirituals, Brewster converted sanctuaries to stages, often using surplus, donated, and adapted materials. He often opened and perfected his pageants at his home church, East Trigg Baptist in Memphis, before opening them on the road. In deference to audience size, performance venues ranged from sanctuaries to professional theaters. Some of Brewster's other sacred pageants include *Old Ship of Zion*, *These Our Children*, *Rejected Stone*, *Via Dolorosa*, and *Deep Dark Waters*. They were used as fundraisers, fellowship activities, celebrations, and for evangelism.

The Smithsonian Institution honored Brewster's musical talents in 1982 by presenting his sacred pageant *Sowing in Tears, Reaping in Joy*.

During the 1950s and 1960s, sacred pageants continued to attract wider audiences. Written by preachers, poets, and playwrights, the art form planted itself on the American cultural landscape. Langston Hughes wrote several pieces in this genre, most notably *Tambourines to Glory*, which played at the Second Canaan Baptist Church in Harlem as well as on Broadway, and *Black Nativity: A Gospel Song Play*. Ossie Davis's enduring comedy *Purlie Victorious* opened at New York's Cort Theater in 1961 and ran for seven months. In 1963, it was made into a motion picture, retitled *Gone Are the Days*. In 1970,

Purlie Victorious was back on Broadway as *Purlie*, starring Cleavon Little and Melba Moore, both of whom won Tony awards for their performances.

Though their primary intent is to entertain rather than evangelize, Andrew Lloyd Webber and Tim Rice's *Joseph and His Amazing Technicolor Dreamcoat* (1968) and *Jesus Christ Superstar* (1971), as well as *Godspell* by John-Michael Tebelak and Stephen Schwartz, might be considered variant forms of the sacred pageant in that the productions use original music to advance the sacred-themed stories.

SARAH E. CREST

See also Brewster, William Herbert; Jackson, Mahalia; Ward Trio (Ward Singers); Williams, Marion

Reference and Further Reading

Boyer, Horace Clarence. "Brewster, W(illiam) Herbert." In *Grove Music Online*. Oxford University Press, 2004, http://www.grovemusic.com.

Coleman, Gregory D. "Heaven Bound." In *New Georgia Encyclopedia*. Atlanta: Georgia Humanities Council and University of Georgia Press, 2004–2005, http://www.georgiaencyclopedia.org.

Morgan, Paula. "Gospel Music." In *New Grove Dictionary of American Music*, edited by H. Wiley Hitchcock and Stanley Sadie, vol. 2, 248–260. New York: Groves' Dictionaries of Music, 1986.

Moore, Allan, ed. *Cambridge Companion to Blues and Gospel Music*. Cambridge: Cambridge University Press, 2002.

Reagon, Bernice Johnson, ed. *We'll Understand It Better By and By. Pioneering African American Gospel Composers*. Washington, DC: Smithsonian Institution Press, 1992.

Wynn, Linda T. "William Herbert Brewster Sr." In *Tennessee Encyclopedia of History and Culture*, Online Edition. Knoxville: University of Tennessee Press, 2002. http://tennesseeencyclopedia.net/.

SANKEY, IRA DAVID

(b. August 28, 1840; d. August 13, 1908)

Singer, gospel hymn composer, and hymnbook compiler Ira Sankey, the man who played a major role in the gospel hymn emerging as a major force in American religious music, was born in Edinburgh, Pennsylvania. His parents, David and Mary Sankey, encouraged their son in his love of music, spending many evenings with him singing church hymns. By the time he was eight, he could read a little music and knew by heart the parts of several melodies, such as "St. Martin's," "Belmont," and "Coronation." The boy's musical interest drew him to church and Sunday school, but surprisingly, it was not his parents but a kindly neighbor named Frazer whom Sankey recalled as introducing him to Sunday school.

In 1856, while attending a revival meeting at the King's Chapel near his home, the youth was converted. In 1857, the Sankey family moved to the nearby town of New Castle, where Ira soon became Sunday school director and leader of the choir at the local Methodist Episcopal Church. This experience proved useful, for it helped him refine his musical abilities while at the same time learning how to apply them in effective ways. He attained further knowledge by attending a twelve-week musical convention led by William B. Bradbury in Farmington, Ohio. His father, however, feared that Ira would "never amount to anything, all he does is to run around the country with a hymnbook under his arm," but his mother's faith in her son remained strong, and she won over her husband.

Following a brief service of two terms during the Civil War, Sankey returned to New Castle. There he sang at Sunday school conventions and political gatherings in surrounding counties. In 1867 he took a job with the YMCA in New Castle and, as a representative of that organization, went to Indianapolis in 1870, where he met evangelist Dwight L. Moody. There his singing and song leading made such an impression on Moody that he offered Sankey a job, saying "I have been looking for you for the past eight years." Flabbergasted by the offer, Sankey returned to Pennsylvania to ponder the invitation. After six months, he moved to Chicago and began his long and fruitful association with the famed evangelist.

Sankey became famous as a result of a series of revivals held in England from 1873 to 1875, but ironically, he was not even Moody's first or second choice to provide the music. He turned to his assistant Sankey only after Philip Phillips, "the Singing Pilgrim," and Philip Paul Bliss were unavailable. Their tour of England started off poorly, primarily because the two men's presentations differed from that previously experienced by English audiences. Some British ministers were also skeptical of Moody and Sankey's theology and methods. Slowly, however, they won over crowds, with Sankey playing just as important a role as Moody.

With his small portable organ, Sankey performed the songs of such composers as Philip Phillips, Philip Paul Bliss, and William B. Bradbury. These offerings served as a simple means of getting the evangelistic message across and also helped establish gospel hymnody as an accepted form of evangelism. There was such a demand for the music used in their meetings that Sankey published a twenty-four–page pamphlet, *Sacred Songs and Solos* (1873), containing some of the more popular numbers. This booklet was later expanded into a volume with twelve hundred songs; it sold more than eighty million copies and is still selling, because it has remained in print to the present day. After returning to the United States, Sankey collaborated with Philip Paul Bliss to produce *Gospel Hymns and Sacred Songs* (1875).

After Bliss's tragic death at age thirty-eight, Sankey, assisted by George C. Stebbins and James McGranahan, edited five further volumes (1876–1891) and then issued the complete series as *Gospel Hymns Nos. 1–6 Complete* (1894). This series became the yardstick by which other gospel hymn collections were judged, and it also helped popularize the term "gospel song." In 1895, Sankey became president of Biglow & Main, the firm that published many of his works; he held the position until his death.

Although Sankey did write several songs, it was as a singer that he made his mark. Untrained vocally, he had the ability to move people with his voice, but his style bothered some listeners, who found it more like that of popular singers than "technically correct" in the European sense. He explained his method as lacking in art or conscious design. "Before I sing, I must feel, and the hymn must be of such kind that I know I can send home what I feel into the hearts of those who listen." His presentation, involving pauses at the ends of phrases to allow listeners to absorb the message and dramatic breaks—not to mention his clear, melodious, powerful voice that enunciated every word distinctly—definitely played a significant role in his impact.

Sankey wrote more than eighty gospel songs, some under the pseudonym Rian A. Dykes, including "The Ninety and Nine" (1874), "I'm Praying for You" (1875), "Trusting Jesus" (1876), "Hiding in Thee" (1877), "A Shelter in the Time of Storm" (1885), and "Faith in the Victory" (1891). Of these, "The Ninety and Nine" is by far the best remembered, and Sankey reportedly spent less time writing it than any of his other songs. He found Elizabeth Clephane's lyrics in a newspaper purchased at a train station in England and clipped them out. Then, a short time later, during a revival in Edinburgh when asked by Moody for a song appropriate for the evangelist's sermon "The Good Shepherd," he pulled out the poem and on the spot he sang the melody that has been used ever since.

In 1980 Ira Sankey was inducted into the Gospel Music Hall of Fame. Ten years later, in 1990, his home town of New Castle, Pennsylvania, celebrated the sesquicentennial of his birth with thirty choirs from across the United States combining to present a retrospective of Sankey's songs.

W. K. McNeil

Reference and Further Reading

Findlay, James F., Jr. *Dwight L. Moody: American Evangelist, 1837–1899.* Chicago: University of Chicago Press, 1969.
Ludwig, Charles. *Sankey Still Sings: The Life Story of Ira D. Sankey.* Anderson, IN: Warner Press, 1947.

Osbeck, Kenneth W. *101 Hymn Stories*. Grand Rapids, MI: Kregel, 1982.

———. *101 More Hymn Stories*. Grand Rapids, MI: Kregel, 1985.

Sankey, Ira D. *My Life and the Story of the Gospel Hymns and of Sacred Songs and Solos*. New York: AMS Press, 1974 (1907).

Wilhoit, Mel R. "Ira Sankey: Father of Gospel Music." *Rejoice* 3, no. iii (1991): 8–16.

SAXOPHONE

The saxophone is a single-reed instrument that is widely used in many forms of popular music but less so in classical music. The saxophone takes its name from its inventor, Adolphe Sax (1814–1894). The instrument is a hybrid of woodwind and brass, combining a reed and mouthpiece broadly similar to that of a clarinet with a metal tube of wide conical bore (plastic has also been used as a cheaper material for the body). It has from eighteen to twenty-one tone holes controlled by keys and supplemented by two small "octave" keys for use in producing notes in the high register through harmonics. The instrument's nominal range can be extended by the use of a technique known as "false fingering."

Adolphe Sax, a Belgian who also invented a valved instrument known as a Saxhorn, patented the saxophone in Paris in 1846. The instrument is most familiar in its soprano, alto, tenor, and baritone forms. The instruments commonly used are pitched alternately in E-flat and B-flat; in order of pitch from highest to lowest, they are sopranino (E-flat), soprano (B-flat), alto (E-flat), tenor (B-flat), baritone (E-flat), bass (B-flat), and contrabass (E-flat). Sax also patented a corresponding range of instruments in the alternate pitches of F and C. These did not find general favor, although the C-melody (tenor) saxophone, which avoided the need for transposition when playing from the written scale of C, was popular at one time, and a soprano in C is used in orchestral contexts.

The saxophone normally has an upward pointing bell and a curved neck, but the sopranino and soprano models are commonly found as straight horns without the characteristic curves (the soprano is available in both styles), and some instrument makers have also produced straight alto and tenor models. Other variants on the saxophone include the saxello, made by the King company in the 1920s, and a slide saxophone, made in France during the same era. Jazz saxophonist Rahsaan Roland Kirk adopted the "manzello," a modified saxello, and the "stritch," a modified straight alto saxophone, during the 1960s.

The saxophone is sometimes found in classical music, but it has never become an established component of the symphony orchestra. It was first adopted in military and marching bands, but it found its most familiar use in popular music, particularly in jazz. Vaudeville artist Rudy Wiedoft popularized the C-melody instrument from around 1916. Saxophones began to appear with increasing regularity in jazz and dance bands during the 1920s, and a saxophone section remains a staple element of the jazz big band. A series of distinguished saxophone soloists established and developed the saxophone as arguably the quintessential jazz instrument throughout the evolving history of jazz, including Lester Young, Coleman Hawkins, Ben Webster, Charlie Parker, John Coltrane, Sonny Rollins, and Ornette Coleman.

Gospel music has exercised an influence on jazz in all periods and was a significant element in the dominant forms of the 1950s: hard bop and soul jazz. Many jazz musicians adopted gospel songs and spirituals within their secular repertoire or were strongly influenced by them, notably Duke Ellington (including but not limited to his sacred concerts of the 1960s), Horace Silver, Charles Mingus, and John Coltrane, among many others (Mingus's "Wednesday Night Prayer Meeting" [1959] is a particularly vivid example and featured passionate contributions from saxophonists John Handy, Jackie McLean, Booker Ervin, and Pepper Adams). All of these artists made use of the saxophone's highly expressive voice-like qualities, tonal color, power, and flexibility, as did more commercial gospel-influenced singers such as Ray Charles, Aretha Franklin, and Al Green. The saxophone also had a powerful impact in various other forms of popular music, including blues, rhythm and blues, and soul.

Although keyboards and guitars were the primary accompanying instruments in gospel music, the spread of the saxophone through its secular use within the African American communities ensured that the instrument would have been represented in the local churches to some degree. The emergence of gospel music as a commercial entity greatly increased the scope for saxophones as accompanying instruments within the genre.

While gospel is still primarily regarded as a vocal medium, a more recent development has been the emergence of a number of saxophonists who have made instrumental gospel music their primary medium or who have produced gospel recordings within a wider body of work. They include Kirk Whalum's *Gospel According to Jazz* (1998) and *Unconditional* (2000), Mel Holder's *Now and Forever: The Continuation* (1999), Rob Maletick's *Walking the Path* (1999), and Greg Vail's *The Gospel Truth* (2001).

KENNY MATHIESON

Reference and Further Reading

Gelly, Dave, ed. *Masters of Jazz Saxophone*. San Francisco: Miller Freeman, 2000.

Ingham, Richard, ed. *The Cambridge Companion to the Saxophone*. Cambridge: Cambridge University Press, 1998.

Porter, Lewis. "Saxophone." In *The New Grove Dictionary of Jazz*, Second Edition, edited by Barry Kernfeld, vol. 3, 507–514. New York: Macmillan, 2002.

2ND CHAPTER OF ACTS

Annie Herring (b. September 22, 1945)
Matthew Ward (b. February 15, 1958)
Nelly Greisen (b. December 11, 1955)

The 2nd Chapter of Acts was formed in Los Angeles, California, in 1970, by three siblings after the deaths of both of their parents. Twelve-year-old Matthew Ward and his fourteen-year-old sister, Nelly, were taken in by their married sister Annie and her husband, Buck Herring. Singing together after school was a way to channel their pain; their intention was never to become a professional singing group.

Buck was a recording engineer, and in 1972, he played a recording of "Jesus Is" by Matthew, backed by his sisters, for Pat Boone. Soon afterward, the family was signed to a recording contract with MGM Records. They chose the name 2nd Chapter of Acts because it encapsulated the entire gospel message. Buck was producing an album for Barry McGuire, who had a successful secular recording career prior to his conversion to Christianity. The 2nd Chapter of Acts sang background vocals on it and toured with him for the next three years. During this time, Acts released a top-ten radio hit on MGM Records called "I'm So Happy." In 1973, they recorded their first album, *With Footnotes,* and released it on the newly formed Myrrh Records, a division of Word Records, which was led by Billy Ray Hearn. The album contained one of the group's most enduring compositions, "Easter Song," which even received airplay on secular radio stations.

In 1974, Acts began touring as a solo act, so they recruited a group of musicians from the Church on the Way, their home church in Van Nuys, California, called A Band Called David. The same year, Billy Ray Hearn left Myrrh Records to start his own label, Sparrow Records, and Acts was among the first to join him. They released *The Roar of Love* and *Mansion Builder,* as well as Annie and Matthew's first solo recordings.

The group's anticommercial attitude often ran counter to the record label's ideas for advertising and promotion. They considered themselves ministers who led the audience into a worship experience rather than entertainers. They felt that their ministry had a twofold purpose: evangelism and the edification of the body of Christ. In 1977, during an eighteen-city concert tour, guitar virtuoso Phil Keaggy joined their band, and a triple-live album entitled *How the West Was One* was produced. In 1978, when most Christian groups were selling tickets, Acts returned to offering only free concerts.

In 1981, the group moved from California to Texas, where they built their own recording studio. After recording and releasing *Singer Sower* in 1984, they went on the road once again. Their most enduring recordings were *Hymns* and *Hymns II. Hymns* won a Dove Award in 1987. In 1988, the group retired after playing its last concert in Houston, Texas. They performed more than fifteen hundred concerts during sixteen years of touring, and they recorded sixteen albums. After the group retired, Annie and Matthew continued to produce solo albums while Nelly raised her family and became involved in numerous ministry efforts.

BOB GERSZTYN

See also Boones, The; Calvary Chapel, Costa Mesa; Hearn, Billy Ray; Myrrh Records; Rock Gospel

Reference and Further Reading

"Exhaustive Christian Music Discography." http://ccmdiscography.150m.com/Collection/Num/2ndChapter/2ndChapter10-B-a.html (accessed October 26, 2003).

Greisen, Nelly. "Easter's Song, 2nd Chapter of Acts." http://www.2ndchapterofacts.com (accessed September 30, 2003).

Herring, Annie. *Glimpses: Seeing God in Everyday Life*. Bloomington, MN: Bethany House, July 1996.

Kieslin, Angela. "The 2nd Chapter of Acts: Closing the Book." *Charisma* (December 1988).

Mansfield, Brian. "2nd Chapter of Acts Biography." http://shopping.yahoo.com/p__1927036353?d=product&id=1927036353& (accessed September 30, 2003).

Redding, Tom. "Annie Herring." http://www.annieherring.com (accessed October 26, 2003).

Ward, Matthew. "Matthew Ward Ministries." http://www.matthewward.com (accessed September 30, 2003).

Discography

With Footnotes (1974, Myrrh); *In the Volume of the Book* (1975, Myrrh); *To the Bride* (1976, Myrrh); *How the West Was One* (1977, Myrrh); *Mansion Builder* (1978, Sparrow); *Roar of Love* (1980, Sparrow); *Rejoice* (1981, Sparrow); *Singer Sower* (1983, Sparrow); *Together Live* (1983, Sparrow); *Night Light* (1985, Live Oak); *Hymns, Vol. I* (1986, Live Oak); *Far Away Places* (1987, Live Oak); *Hymns, Vol. II* (1988, Live Oak); *Far Away Places* (1991, Sparrow, SPD1288).

SELAH JUBILEE SINGERS

Thermon (Thurmond) "T. Ruth" Ruth, lead (b. March 6, 1914, Pomaria, SC)
Nathaniel Townsley, tenor
Monroe Clark, baritone
John Ford, lead, tenor
Clifton Antley, bass
Andrew Antley, piano
Fred Baker, lead, guitar
J. B. Nelson, bass
John Kaiser, baritone
Melvin Coltden, baritone
Norman "Crip" Harris, tenor
Recorded secular music under the name the Larks

T. Ruth's family moved from South Carolina to Brooklyn, New York, around 1922. They joined St. Mark Holy Church (Pentecostal), under a lady pastor (Bishop Eva Lambert). By age twelve, Ruth organized the Selah Jubilee Six with members of the church choir. They sang every Sunday in their church for about ten years; the service was broadcast, and they sang on four radio stations. They started out as disciples of the Fisk Jubilee Quartet, but in 1937, Bishop Lambert took them down to Houston, where they met the Soul Stirrers, discovering a new style of religious singing; the groups exchanged songs.

Back in New York, they became part of a rapidly changing gospel quartet scene under the influence of the Golden Gate Quartet, whose popularity was prodigious. Ruth also acknowledged the Mills Brothers and the Charioteers as an influence on the "rhythmic spirituals" style he developed with his group. They recorded for Brunswick in 1931 (although the matrix numbers suggest that it was Columbia), but the seven tracks remained unissued.

By 1939, the group was called the Selah Jubilee Singers, and they came to the attention of J. Mayo Williams, who signed them to Decca and issued fourteen sides in the same year (some with Sam Price on piano). This led to no money but to plenty of appearances and show dates, including more sessions for Decca while still singing every Sunday night at their church. In 1941, Ruth decided to take the group on tour down South to North Carolina, but the Antley brothers and Monroe Clark, who were reluctant to travel, were replaced by Fred Baker, J. B. Nelson, and John Kaiser.

They did a little USO camp show work, and, stranded in Raleigh, North Carolina, they were hired by WPTF, a fifty-thousand–watt radio station, and they worked there in the mornings five days a week for a couple of years, with plenty of show dates filling the nights. They made frequent trips back to New York to perform and to record for Decca (until 1944), but their radio program became one of the most popular and influential black broadcasts of that era; their brand of jubilee quartet singing influenced a legion of young harmony singers on the East Coast.

In 1943, most members of the group quit, and Ruth hired baritone Melvin Coltden and legendary second tenor Norman "Crip" Harris (both formerly with the Norfolk Jubilee Quartet) to make a nationwide USO tour (1945–1946), with tenor Bill "Highpocket" Langford (formerly of the Golden Gate Quartet and the Southern Sons) playing guitar and with new members Theo Harris (baritone) and Jimmy Gorham (bass). The Selahs spent the late 1940s in Raleigh, broadcasting regularly on WPTF again and singing in churches and auditoriums; they also recorded as the Selah Singers for a series of labels, including Manor, Continental, Lenox, Arista, Mercury, Capitol, Cross (as the Sons of Heaven), and Jubilee.

The Selahs used to do jubilee songs, and Ruth wanted to do gospel or even secular music, but their audiences did not accept it, and Ruth decided to leave the group to lead another group in New York with guitarist Alden (Tarheel Slim) Bunn, Junius Parker, Gene Mumford, David McNeil, and Pee Wee Barnes. That group sang under many names, such as the Jubilators (Regal), the Four Barons (Regent), and the Southern Harmonaires (Apollo Records) in 1950, but they are best remembered today as the Larks (1950–1954, Apollo and Lloyds Records). However, the Selah Jubilee Singers still existed as a group, and they went back to New York, where Ruth joined them for a Savoy recording session in 1955. After that, everyone went his own way. Ruth stayed busy as a disc jockey, concert promoter, and emcee at the Apollo Theater in New York and then in Philadelphia, Raleigh and Durham, North Carolina, and New York again.

The Selahs were reunited for the last time in 1968 as the Jubilators for a recording session (Veep-Gospel Records). They will stay in gospel history as the only quartet to break through the Mecca of talent that was New York and to become a major force in gospel during the golden age.

ROBERT SACRÉ

See also Fisk Jubilee Singers; Golden Gate Quartet, The; Norfolk Jubilee Singers; Soul Stirrers

Reference and Further Reading

Boyer, Horace Clarence. *How Sweet the Sound: The Golden Age of Gospel*. Washington, DC: Elliott & Clark, 1995.
Hayes, J. Cedric; Robert Laughton. *Gospel Records 1943– 1969. A Black Music Discography*, 2 vols. London, UK: Record Information Services, 1992.

Heilbut, Tony. *The Gospel Sound: Good News and Bad Times.* New York, Limelight, 1985.

Horner, Charlie. "The Whole Truth about T. Ruth—The Larks, Part 2." *Whiskey, Women, and . . .* 10 (November 1982): 24–27.

Reagon, Bernice Johnson, ed. *We'll Understand It Better By and By. Pioneering African American Gospel Composers.* Washington, DC: Smithsonian Institution Press, 1992.

Seroff, Doug. "The Whole Truth about T. Ruth." *Whiskey, Women, and . . .* 9 (July 1982): 14–18.

———. "The Whole Truth about T. Ruth. Update & Discography." *Whiskey, Women, and . . .* 10 (November 1982): 28–33.

Discography

Complete Recorded Works in Chronological Order, 1939–1945, Vol. 1 (1996, Document Records [Austria] DOCD 5499).

Complete Recorded Works in Chronological Order, 1939–1945, Vol. 2 (1996, Document Records [Austria] DOCD 5500).

The Best of Jubilee Gospel: Heaven Belongs to You (1999, Westside [UK] WESM 588).

Selah Gospel Train, 1945–49 (1999, P-Vine Records [Japan] PCD-5547).

SENSATIONAL NIGHTINGALES

The Nightingales, or "the Gales," known as "the Gentlemen of Songs," were founded in 1942 by Barney L. Parks, Jr., a singer from the Dixie Hummingbirds of Philadelphia. Parks's wife was gospel soloist Madame Edna Gallmon Cooke (1917–1967). Other original members were Howard Carroll of the Hummingbirds, Paul Owens of the Swan Silvertones, Ben Joiner, and William Henry. Baritone Julius "June" Cheeks (1929–1981) joined at the request of Parks. Cheeks was a member of the Baronets from Spartanburg, South Carolina. Their first record with Cheeks was "Vacant Room in Glory."

In 1946, Parks changed the format of the group. Joseph "JoJo" Wallace, from Wilmington, North Carolina, who sang high falsetto, joined the Gales as guitarist. He was a member of the Silveraires in Pennsylvania. Carl Coates, who was living in Birmingham but who was from Washington, DC, also joined; his wife was the famous gospel singer Dorothy Love Coates (1928–2003), leader of the Original Gospel Harmonettes.

In 1947, the Nightingales recorded their first single, "Will You Welcome Me," on Peacock Records. Peacock was sold to ABC/Dunhill in California. The Nightingales became very famous and were called a sensational group; therefore, they added Sensational to their name. The group released twenty-five single records on various labels. They cut records on the Coleman label in 1949, more records on the King label in 1950, on Savoy Records in New Jersey, and on the Decca Records label.

Around 1950, Cheeks became instrumental in using new tempos in his arrangements, which allowed him to stretch out with improvisations as the lyrics progressed. Cheeks was known for his shouts, expressive singing, and quick movements. He had growls and preacher moans that stirred the audience. Cheeks was the originator of rock gospel, and he was one of the first singers to move into audiences to shake hands while singing. In 1952, the Gales recorded on Peacock Records. During those hard times, funds were low, and the group disbanded. The Gales quartet had been centered on Cheeks, who became a reverend in 1954. Cheeks went to the Soul Stirrers, and Paul Owens, baritone, left for the Dixie Hummingbirds.

In 1960, Cheeks continued to record for Peacock. Horace Thompson, bass guitarist and background singer for the Gales, joined in 1962. Thompson sang with Madame Edna Gallmon Cooke. From the mid-1960s through the mid-1970s, the Gales continued to sing, but they changed their style to hard gospel and regrouped. Gospel music had to reflect the Civil Rights Movement and have the beat of rock 'n' roll music. African American gospel fans wanted choirs moving to the beat while the lead singer was telling a story through song. In 1970, contemporary gospel was born with the Edwin Hawkins Singers and "Oh Happy Day."

During the early 1970s, the Gales were still famous for the songs "He Prayed Too Late," "The Love of Jesus," and "Wooden Church." In 1977, the group recorded on Crumco Records in Chicago. In 1979, the group signed with Malaco Records in Jackson, Mississippi. Calvert McNair replaced Charles Johnson, who left in 1983 to found his own gospel ensemble, McNair. In 1992, the Gales recorded *Stay on the Boat*; in 1993, *Seek Ye First the Kingdom of God*; in 1994, *Live So God Can Use You*; and in 1995, *Live! In the Spirit*. In 1996, they celebrated fifty years of singing with a golden anniversary concert in Durham, North Carolina. Accolades came from the governor of North Carolina and the mayor of Durham.

In 1983, the Gales traveled to Europe for the first time to the Bern and Villingen festivals. In 1984, they were at the American Spiritual & Gospel Festival. On the program were the Stars of Faith, the Barrett Sisters, and Reverend Robert Mayes. They have appeared in Montreux, Berlin, Vienna, and France. In 1984, they made a two-month tour of Africa and of Europe. From 1984 through 1985, the LP *I Surrender All* was on the *Billboard* Top Spirituals Albums.

This quartet always opens and ends with prayer. Many souls have been saved through their concerts

Sensational Nightingales. Photo courtesy Frank Driggs Collection.

and by listening to their music. They sing about their lifestyles. Bill Woodruff (d. 1993), baritone singer, was from Spartanburg, South Carolina. He was replaced after his death by Richard Luster. In 1997,

the Sensational Nightingales were nominated for induction into the International Gospel Music Hall of Fame and Museum in Detroit. In 1998, they became the first group inducted into the American Gospel

Quartet Hall of Fame. In 1998, Larry Moore from Norfolk, Virginia, joined the Gales. Darrell Luster was the fourth singer of the Gales. In 2003, on the Malaco record label, the Gales recorded *Songs to Edify*. The most popular albums by the Gales have been *The Best of the Sensational Nightingales* and *The Sensational Nightingales—Greatest Hits*.

This group was formed before the beginning of the golden era of gospel music (1945–1955). Renditions of their beautiful harmony and gospel flair during the 1940s gave them status in the music world. Because the Gales are nationally known, they have been able to continue singing gospel music. In 1992 they celebrated fifty years as one of the oldest quartet groups. The Gales are still strong, a true legacy of gospel music.

SHERRY SHERROD DuPREE

Reference and Further Reading

Bekker, Peter O. E., Jr. Liner notes to *Gospel: The Life, Time, and Music Series* (1993, Friedman/Fairfax Publishers, New York; CD).

Boyer, Horace Clarence. *How Sweet the Sound: The Golden Age of Gospel*. Washington, DC: Elliott & Clark, 1995.

DuPree, Sherry Sherrod. *Biographical Dictionary of African-American Holiness-Pentecostals 1880–1990*. Washington, DC: Middle Atlantic Regional Press, 1989.

———. Herbert C. DuPree. *African-American Good News (Gospel) Music*. Washington, DC: Middle Atlantic Regional Press, 1993.

Heilbut, Anthony. Liner notes to *Fathers and Sons* (2003, Spirit Feel CD 1001).

International Gospel Music Hall of Fame and Museum website, http://www.gmhf.org (accessed August 28, 2004).

The Sensational Nightingales. Liner notes to *My Sisters and Brothers* (1974, ABC Peacock PLP-59209).

SHAPE-NOTE SINGING

Shape-note singing refers to a method of teaching music to singers who were not musically literate; it was employed during the late eighteenth and early nineteenth centuries by traveling "singing masters." Originally in New England and then spreading to the South and West, these itinerant teachers came to towns, mostly at the invitation of the local church, to teach the local choirs how to sing.

In the shape-note system, the vocal parts were notated using different shapes for the various scale tones (triangles, squares, diamonds, and so on), and they were often limited to a five-note (pentatonic) scale (four scale notes and the octave), which was common to folk and hymn tunes. The system was known as "fasola" because of its use of vocal syllables to represent the different scale tones. Most of the tunes were drawn from common folk songs, which were likely to be familiar to the congregants, aiding the quick learning of new material. The harmonies were simplified, based on common intervals such as fourths and fifths, giving the music a distinct, archaic sound. By singing the tones associated with the shapes, the congregation could quickly learn new songs and new harmonies. The common Western scale of eight notes (seven notes and the octave) was also translated into the shape-note tradition by the early nineteenth century.

One of the first books to promote the shape-note system was William Little and William Smith's *The Easy Instructor*, published in 1795, which promoted the five-note system. A rival publication, *Choral-Music*, published in 1816 by Joseph Funk in Virginia, expanded shape notes to the full eight-note scale. Funk was a member of the German Mennonite religion, and his system became popular in Amish/Mennonite regions. Funk's grandson, Aldine S. Kieffer, formed a publishing partnership with James H. Ruebush after the Civil War, and the Ruebush–Kieffer publishing company became the first prolific Southern producer of shape-note hymnals; more important, they also established a network of singing schools to teach music to ordinary folk. From the 1870s to the turn of the twentieth century, numerous shape-note hymnals were published by a variety of firms.

Although shape-note singing soon died out in the cities, where more sophisticated congregations learned to read music "properly," it lingered in rural areas. Annual conventions were held with the purpose of singing an entire songbook in a single day and evening (this was accomplished by rapidly "reading" each hymn). This helped singers remember the repertoire and also encouraged them to broaden the number of songs they performed throughout the year. These events would also involve communal socializing, and often a large community-prepared meal would be served about halfway through the day.

Even in churches that did not employ shape-note singing, the harmonies from these hymnals could be heard, so an older style of singing was unintentionally preserved. When bluegrass groups began incorporating gospel music into their repertoires, they naturally drew on the rich shape-note singing tradition. Many bluegrass singers were raised performing in their local church choirs, so their vocal styles and harmonies often recall the tonalities of this earlier style. This is particularly true of the more traditionally oriented groups, such as the Stanley Brothers, although more modern bands ranging from the Red Clay Ramblers to the Nashville Bluegrass Band have made this style of singing a part of their performances.

The folk music revival also led to a renewed interest in shape-note singing. Although a few shape-note groups were recorded during the 1920s and 1930s on 78-rpm records, folklorist Alan Lomax was the first to record an "all-day" shape-note convention on modern stereo equipment in 1959; this was issued as part of his historic *Southern Journey* collection on Atlantic Records. During the 1970s, several of the classic shape-note hymnals were reprinted for use by shape-note clubs operating in urban areas and separate from the traditional church-based groups. Meanwhile, all-day singings continued in the South associated with church groups, and the tradition remains vibrant into the twenty-first century.

RICHARD CARLIN

Reference and Further Reading

Bealle, John. *Public Worship, Private Faith: Sacred Harp and American Folksong.* Athens, GA: University of Georgia Press, 1997.

Boyd, Joe Dan. *Judge Jackson and the Colored Sacred Harp.* Montgomery, AL: Alabama Folklife Association, 2002.

Cobb, Buell E. *The Sacred Harp: A Tradition and Its Music.* Athens, GA: University of Georgia Press, 1989 (1987).

Fasola.org—Sacred Harp and Shape Note Singing website, http://fasola.org/ (accessed January 31, 2005).

Discography

Fasola: All Day Singing (1970, Folkways; two-LP set recorded by Frederic and Amelia Ramsey at an all-day Sacred Harp singing at Houston, Mississippi).

The Social Harp: Early American Shape Note Songs (1990, Rounder).

SHEA, GEORGE BEVERLY

(b. February 1, 1909)

The man largely responsible for the current popularity of "How Great Thou Art" was born the son of a Wesleyan Methodist minister in Winchester, Ontario, Canada, and he grew up in parsonages in New York and New Jersey. Both parents encouraged his musical interests, and, as a youth, he frequently sang in his father's church and other local churches. After high school, he attended Houghton College in New York, but due to family financial problems he had to drop out. In 1956, the school awarded him an honorary doctorate. He spent the next several years after leaving college working as a clerk in the New York City offices of the Mutual of New York Life Insurance Company.

During this time, George continued his vocal training, singing in churches and for local religious broadcasts. A network director who heard him sing one day was so impressed with his voice that he arranged an audition for a national program with the Lynn Murray Singers. George passed the audition and was offered a job but, because he did not feel right about performing secular music, he reluctantly turned down the position.

In 1934, after marrying his childhood sweetheart, they moved to Chicago, where he became a member of the staff at radio station WMBI. Ten years later, in June 1944, the thirty-five-year-old singer achieved his longtime goal of singing gospel music on a nationally aired radio program. For eight years, Herbert J. Taylor, a Christian businessman who headed an aluminum firm, sponsored *Club Time*. This show brought Shea national recognition, as did his participation in large Youth for Christ rallies throughout the United States and Canada during the 1940s and 1950s.

In 1947, he joined the Billy Graham Evangelistic Association as a featured soloist on Graham's crusades. In fulfilling his duties, he had the opportunity to introduce several songs to Graham's audiences. By far the best known of these is "How Great Thou Art," which was written by the Reverend Stuart K. Hine in the 1920s but was based on an 1886 Swedish poem by the Reverend Carl Boberg, "O Store Gud." It was introduced into the United States by Dr. J. Edwin Orr in 1954. That same year a friend, Andrew Gray, gave George a four-page leaflet containing the song, which he quickly examined and immediately noted that it had lyrics in both English and Russian, and he found its worshipful title memorable. He later sang it at the Toronto, Canada, Crusade of 1955, the real start of the number becoming the most recorded gospel song. According to a poll conducted by *Christian Herald* magazine in 1974, it is the number one hymn in America.

George signed with RCA Victor in 1951, and fourteen years later, in 1965, he received a Grammy for Best Gospel or Other Religious Recording (Musical) for his album *Southland Favorites*. In addition to his other accomplishments, Shea is a talented songwriter whose best-known work is "I'd Rather Have Jesus," the first number he ever wrote. The lyrics were the work of Mrs. Rhea F. Miller and were brought to George's attention by his mother. She loved to share poetry and frequently left verses on the piano music rack for her son to peruse. He liked Mrs. Miller's words and immediately set them to music, and he sang the song that same day in his father's church service. The composer was only twenty years old.

Other songs penned by Shea include "The Wonder of It All" and "I Will Praise Him in the Morning." For his several accomplishments and above all for his rich, resonant singing, Shea was inducted into the Gospel Music Association Hall of Fame in 1978.

W. K. MCNEIL

George Beverly Shea. Photo courtesy Frank Driggs Collection.

Reference and Further Reading

Osbeck, Kenneth W. *101 More Hymn Stories*. Grand Rapids, MI: Kregel, 1985.
Shea, George Beverly; Fred Bauer. *Songs That Lift the Heart: A Personal Story*. Old Tappan, NJ: Fleming Revell, 1972.

SHERWOOD, WILLIAM HENRY

(flourished 1890s)

An enigmatic figure who spent his life in and near his Petersburg, Virginia, home, William Henry Sherwood was an evangelist and composer who led local choirs and bands and who was superintendent of Sherwood's Orphan School, an orphanage for black children. In 1891, he published *Soothing Songs Hymnal*, followed two years later by *Harp of Zion*. The latter features gospel songs and spirituals by Sherwood and other writers. This hymnal made him the first African American to publish songs in the Negro spiritual, pregospel style. His harmonic, melodic, and rhythmic structure all were precursors of the music that later came to be called gospel.

Sherwood's *Harp of Zion* was released in 1893 with a few changes as *Baptist Young People's Union National Harp of Zion* as their hymnal. Sherwood's lyrics are relatively sparse and make frequent use of call and response; the melodies are simple and catchy. These features help make the songs easy to remember. Some of his songs include "Happy Hosts of Zion," "Mountain Top Dwelling," "Take It to the Lord," and "The Church Is Moving On." The National Baptist Convention Publishing Board liked Sherwood's "lively arrangements" and recognized their power; for these reasons, they adopted *Harp of Zion* as their own hymnal. Thus, it might be said that they were aware of gospel's coming importance.

W. K. McNeil

Reference and Further Reading

Boyer, Horace Clarence. *The Golden Age of Gospel*. Urbana and Chicago: University of Illinois Press, 2000 (1995).

Darden, Robert. *People Get Ready: A New History of Black Gospel Music*. New York: Continuum International Publishing Group, 2004.

SHOUT (RING SHOUT)

The ring shout is a unique African American tradition that combines rhythmic movement with intense vocals to express deep religious feeling. There are many African traditions that include dances performed in a circular formation, and undoubtedly these served as the model for the African American ring shout. The ring shout survived primarily in areas in which large, independent African American communities developed, notably on the islands off the coast of South Carolina and Georgia, where ex-slaves lived with very little contact with more organized white or black religions. Even the Holiness churches tended to reject this tradition, because dancing was seen as a secular—if not sinful—activity.

Although there is some controversy about the direct derivation of the word "shout," it is clear from interviews with traditional performers that the word connotes a type of dance rather than a vocalization (even though the intense, tight-throat singing style might suggest shouting to some listeners). Some suggest an African root for the word itself, which would further the connection with traditional African dance.

The group is led by a songster, who first sings the song in a slow rhythm, gradually building up to speed; the group then takes up the song, accompanying it by slow stepping. The movement is highly ritualized, a kind of slow, walking shuffle, performed in unison either in a ring or line. Unlike secular dancers, the participants do not cross their feet—they believe that crossing the feet would be "unholy"—and there is very little upper body movement, although they often clap out complex rhythm patterns as they move. When performed in a circular formation, the

group always moves in a counterclockwise direction, again to distinguish these dances from secular ones. A separate "stick man" beats the rhythm on the floor using a broomstick or tree limb. Because the church did not approve of this tradition, it was often performed following the formal church service in a separate building or barn or out in the woods.

John and Alan Lomax were among the first folklorists to record traditional ring shout songs. "Shout Old Jeremiah" came from a field trip to Jennings, Louisiana, in 1934, where it was performed by Washington Brown and Austin Coleman, and it was released on an early LP by the Library of Congress. Lydia Parrish documented the shout tradition on the Georgia Sea Islands in the early 1940s, which inspired folklorist Art Rosenbaum to revisit the area in the 1970s. There, he discovered an active shout tradition in McIntosh County, led by songster Lawrence McKiver. Rosenbaum documented this group in an excellent book and CD. The group became known as the McIntosh County Shouters and were popular performers at folk festivals and on record. In 1993, they were awarded a National Heritage Fellowship from the National Endowment for the Arts.

Richard Carlin

Reference and Further Reading

Parrish, Lydia. *Slave Songs of the Georgia Sea Islands*. Athens: University of Georgia Press, 1992 (1942).

Rosenbaum, Art. *Shout Because You're Free: The African American Ring Shout Tradition in Coastal Georgia*. With photographs by Margo Newmark Rosenbaum. Athens: University of Georgia Press, 1998.

Discography

Afro-American Spirituals, Work Songs, and Ballads (1950, Library of Congress Archive of Folk Song; edited by Alan Lomax).

Been in the Storm So Long (1967, Folkways; excellent collection of recordings, including many shouts, made on the Georgia Sea Islands by Guy and Candie Carawan).

The McIntosh County Shouters: Slave Shout Songs from the Coast of Georgia (1983, Folkways; recorded and annotated by Art Rosenbaum).

Video

Down Yonder: The McIntosh County Shouters (Georgia Public Television; produced by Clate Sanders with Art Rosenbaum).

SHOWALTER, ANTHONY JOHNSON

(b. May 1, 1888; d. September 24, 1924)

This music educator, publisher, and composer was born in Rockingham County, Virginia, a section of the Shenandoah Valley with a rich singing and song-book tradition. He was a direct descendant of the first Mennonite bishop in the country, who was the progenitor of an important musical family. A. J.' s father, John, was a singing-school teacher and composer from whom his son received his first music training. He later sent the boy to the Virginia Normal Music School, where he studied under Benjamin C. Unseld. Later, Showalter studied with several other teachers in the United States and Europe.

As a young adult, Showalter started teaching and working for the local music publisher, the Ruebush–Kieffer Company. As an agent for this company, he was sent in 1884 to Dalton, Georgia, to open a branch office. He fell in love with the city, and it soon became his adopted home. In 1885, he opened his own company in Dalton, and it soon grew into the largest music publishing house south of Cincinnati. By the time it stopped publishing music in 1940, it had sold six million copies of Showalter's song and hymn collections and theory books.

Shortly after starting his publishing company, Showalter established the Southern Normal Conservatory, the most successful of all Southern schools of this type. His other activities included publishing the monthly *Music Teacher and Home Magazine* and writing books such as *The Best Gospel Songs and Their Composers* (1904). He also received acclaim as a singing leader, his crowning achievement in that regard being when he was chosen to lead thousands of singers at the 1905 Southeastern Fair in Atlanta, an exhibition that one critic called the outstanding "field day of all time for the shape-noters." For this effort, Showalter was paid the then princely sum of five hundred dollars for his day's work.

Of his varied activities, Showalter's main enthusiasm seems to have been for composing, an interest he pursued vigorously and on a daily regimen. Regularly he went into his office before breakfast, composed a couple of songs, and tried them out on the office piano. In this manner he turned out numbers faster than they could be published; at his death his company had hundreds of his songs in manuscript form, many of which they proceeded to publish during the subsequent sixteen years.

Showalter's music training inclined him to be antagonistic to shape notes, but realizing that they ruled the day in rural Georgia, he put aside his personal prejudices and bowed to demand. Still, he hedged his bets, publishing books with both round and shape notations. Throughout his company's music publishing career, the shape-note books far outsold the round-note ones.

Showalter edited more than a hundred collections and wrote more than a thousand gospel and secular songs, anthems, and hymns, yet all but one of his huge output is forgotten today. That one, "Leaning on the Everlasting Arms," was written for a text by Elisha A. Hoffman to express sympathy for two friends who had recently lost their wives. It initially appeared in *The Glad Evangel for Revival, Camp, and Evangelistic Meetings* (1887), a collection compiled by composer S. J. Perry.

W. K. McNeil

Reference and Further Reading

Jackson, George Pullen. *White Spirituals in the Southern Uplands: The Story of the Fasola Folk, Their Songs, Singings, and "Buckwheat Notes."* New York: Dover, 1965 (1933).

Reynolds, William J. *Companion to the Baptist Hymnal.* Nashville, TN: Broadman, 1976.

SILVER LEAF QUARTET

Founded around 1920, when quartet singing was very popular in the Hampton Roads area of Virginia, the Silver Leaf Quartet of Norfolk became one of the region's most respected and influential vocal harmony ensembles. From their beginnings as a community-based quartet in the Berkley section of Norfolk, the group soon began singing at Baptist and Methodist churches throughout Hampton Roads. The Silver Leafs (as they were often referred to) remained together for nearly sixty years with relatively few personnel changes.

In 1923, the group added eighteen-year-old Melvin Smith, who soon became the group's leader and remained with the group until it disbanded. Under Smith's leadership the Silver Leaf Quartet flourished, and in 1927 they began an annual Northern tour, which focused on churches in and around New York City but also included stops in Maryland, Pennsylvania, and New Jersey. The group also eyed the Southeast and began regular tours, with annual performances in Charlotte and Durham, North Carolina, and Atlanta, Augusta, and Savannah, Georgia.

Their popularity soared in the fall of 1928 following the release of their first commercial recordings on the widely distributed OKeh label. Their initial release—"I Can Tell the World" and "I Am a Pilgrim" (OKeh 8594)—featured Smith's lead and William Thatch's distinctive falsetto voice, and it sold well enough that OKeh invited the Silver Leafs back into their studios regularly until 1931, when the decimated recording industry all but shut down. During this three-year period, the Silver Leaf Quartet recorded memorable versions of traditional material such as "Will the Circle Be Unbroken," "My Soul Is a Witness for My Lord," and "Hope I'll Join the Band." Perhaps their strongest recording, however, was a stunning version of "Sleep On, Mother," which was echoed in later recordings by the Dixie Hummingbirds and Sister Rosetta Tharpe.

The group remained very popular in Hampton Roads, but they particularly looked forward to their Northern tours. The Silver Leaf Quartet was especially popular at Manhattan's Metropolitan Baptist Church; they attracted capacity crowds to the church for twenty-one consecutive nights in 1930. One night the crowd was so large that attendees were divided into two groups, one in the upstairs sanctuary and the other in the downstairs meeting hall. The quartet performed upstairs and then regrouped in the meeting hall during the upstairs intermission in order to accommodate the entire audience.

By 1937, the Silver Leaf Quartet had abandoned the extensive annual tours that had them singing as far north as Canada, west to the Dakotas, and south to Florida. They focused instead on Hampton Roads, singing over the radio as well as at local churches. In 1947, the Silver Leafs began an extended engagement at Virginia Beach's exclusive, all-white Cavalier Hotel. Performing as the Cavalier Singers, the group finally lost two of its original members: William Thatch and baritone singer William Bousch.

The Silver Leaf Quartet continued to be strong into the 1950s, mirroring the popular interest in gospel quartet singing. They sang weekly at local churches until the early 1960s, when the increasing age of group members, coupled with changing trends in African American gospel, shifted the focus away from quartets toward choirs and choruses. Performing became more sporadic, and the group disbanded around 1979, following the death of bass singer Luther Daniel. Melvin Smith, who provided most of the information about the group and who also trained local gospel quartets from the 1930s through the 1960s, died in 1985.

KIP LORNELL

Reference and Further Reading

Lornell, Kip. *Virginia's Blues, Country, & Gospel Records 1902–1943: An Annotated Discography*. Lexington: University Press of Kentucky, 1989.

Discography

Complete Recorded Works (1995, Document 5352).

SINGERS GLEN, VIRGINIA

A hamlet in the Shenandoah Valley about eight miles north–northwest of Harrisonburg, Singers Glen had originally been named Mountain Valley by its German-speaking Mennonite settler, Joseph Funk (1778–1862; buried in Singers Glen). It was renamed Singers Glen in 1860 when a post office was established there and after Funk's music business had become successful. Its significance is twofold: it was the original base of the music publishing business established by Funk (known variously as Joseph Funk & Sons, Joseph Funk's Sons, the Patent Note Publishing Company, Ruebush, Kieffer & Company, and the Ruebush–Kieffer Company) and cultivated by his familial and musical descendants, and it is a symbol of the Southern shape-note and singing traditions that emerged in the Shenandoah Valley during the second decade of the nineteenth century, developed into Southern gospel, spread throughout the Southern states by the late nineteenth century, and today constitute a significant part of the American sacred music industry. Singers Glen, in other words, may be thought of as the Old Homeplace of Southern shape-note and Southern gospel music.

The Shenandoah Valley, long having been part of the ancestral lands of various Eastern woodland Native American tribes, began to fill with European settlers from Pennsylvania—predominantly German-speaking evangelical Christians and Scots–Irish immigrants—around 1730, many from Eastern Pennsylvania. By 1810, the New England singing-school masters, with their tunebooks and their new four-shape notation, were, in part, following the same course, pushed by the declining popularity of that tradition in the Eastern cities and drawn by the receptive new market opening up on what was then the Western frontier. Singing schools were surely held there early on, but the first tunebook published in the valley was *Kentucky Harmony* (Harrisonburg, 1816), compiled by Ananias Davisson (1780–1857).

Aside from its commercial success, *Kentucky Harmony* is important historically, because it was the first tunebook to incorporate arrangements of the revival hymns that were being created within the oral tradition of the camp meetings of the Great Revival, which had caught fire in Kentucky and Tennessee in around 1800. Davisson's musical innovation proved highly popular among Southerners and still flourishes today in the Sacred Harp tradition. Funk's first publication, *Die allgemein nützliche Choral-Music* (1816; printed in Harrisonburg by Laurentz Wartmann), followed within months. *Choral-Music*, in the standard oblong format, was a German-language, four-shape-note compilation containing primarily chorales taken from Mennonite and Lutheran sources and intended for the German-speaking settlers of the valley. Also included, however, were four Anglo-American folk hymns from *Kentucky Harmony*. There apparently was no second edition.

During the next fifty years, numerous tunebooks, some with multiple editions, were printed in the vicinity of Harrisonburg and Winchester by compilers such as Davisson, Funk, and James P. Carrell (1787–1854; buried in "Old Cemetery" just outside Lebanon, Virginia). Perhaps the most prominent of them was Funk's *A Compilation of Genuine Church Music* (first edition, 1832), a conservative, four-shape-note publication in English. For its fifth edition (1851), Funk made two important changes: he changed the name to *Harmonia Sacra, Being a Compilation of Genuine Church Music*, and he switched to a seven-shape notation of his own design. This latter innovation placed him near the forefront of the move among Eastern singing teachers from the old four-syllable, English, fa-sol-la solfege system of eighteenth-century New England to the more European, seven-syllable do-re-mi system espoused by Lowell Mason and others.

Harmonia Sacra's success was such that the firm produced many new editions. The last prewar edition (tenth edition, 1860) contained one tune that displayed characteristics that were to become common in Southern gospel music (see Eskew, 1966, 144 ff.). As of 2004, it was in its twenty-fifth edition (Intercourse, Pennsylvania, Good Books, 1993), making it the oldest continually published tunebook in America.

As the business grew, Funk decided to initiate a periodical to promote singing, his business, and related activities. Thus, in July 1859, Joseph Funk & Sons began publishing a monthly periodical called *The Southern Musical Advocate and Singer's Friend*. After April 1861, however, publication was suspended because of the Civil War.

The musical heyday of Singers Glen followed the war, when leadership of the family business gradually was assumed by Funk's grandson, Aldine S. Kieffer (1840–1904), and Kieffer's brother-in-law and former Funk employee, Ephraim Ruebush (1833–1924). Kieffer and Ruebush had been friends since Ruebush arrived in Singers Glen in 1853, and, by 1859, they had begun to establish a reputation as a singing-school teaching team.

After the war, Kieffer returned to Singers Glen to continue with the family business. He joined with other family members to rebuild the business (then in disarray) as Joseph Funk's Sons. Initially (1865), he and William S. Rohr revived Funk's periodical, *The Southern Musical Advocate and Singer's Friend*, as *The Musical Advocate and Fireside Friend*, but it folded in 1869. Joseph Funk's Sons' first postwar tunebook, which used Funk's seven-shape notation, was published in 1866 with the Ruebush & Kieffer imprint added. Gospel characteristics were even more evident in the songs of that publication. In 1870, Kieffer, his brother L. Rollin Kieffer, and two uncles,

Solomon and Timothy Funk, formed the Patent Note Publishing Company and launched a new periodical, *The Musical Million and Singer's Advocate*. Under the passionate editorship of Kieffer, this periodical became the nation's primary vehicle for the promotion of seven-shape-note music.

In January 1872, the family business was reorganized to reflect the reunion of Kieffer and his old partner, Ephraim Ruebush, who assumed control of business matters. Kieffer continued as editor of the journal and the major artistic force behind the company. Together these two friends and partners built the most successful shape-note music-publishing house of the nineteenth century, simultaneously laying the foundations for Southern gospel music. The company instituted the practice of publishing new songbooks (in an upright octavo format) every year or two. They produced specialized books, such as separate books for Sunday schools, singing schools, congregational use, and so on. Both innovations increased the demand for their product. That demand was filled with the new gospel hymns coming out of the Northern cities as well as those written specifically for Ruebush–Kieffer publications, necessitating the cultivation of a stable of poets and songwriters. In short, the music became ever more commercial and popular. They also started a highly influential normal music school to train teachers, but that occurred outside Singers Glen.

In 1878, the company moved to nearby Dayton, probably to be near the railroad line and thus lower shipping costs. However, even today, the Ruebush–Kieffer Company is associated in the minds of many with Singers Glen. Southern gospel music exists in great part because of the work of Joseph Funk and his descendants, and Singers Glen was where it began. The legacy of the music business and music making in Singers Glen has been commemorated in Alice Parker's opera, *Singers Glen* (1978), which is based on Funk's life.

STEPHEN SHEARON

See also Funk, Joseph; Gospel Periodicals; *Kentucky Harmony*; Kieffer, Aldine S.; Ruebush, Ephraim; *Sacred Harp, The*; Shape-Note Singing; Singing Schools

Reference and Further Reading

Cusic, Don. *The Sound of Light: A History of Gospel and Christian Music*, 1st Hal Leonard edition. Milwaukee, WI: Hal Leonard Corporation, 2002.

Eskew, Harry. "Joseph Funk's *Allgemein nützliche Choral-Music* (1816)." *Report of the Society for the History of the Germans in Maryland* 32 (1966): 38–46.

Eskew, Harry Lee. "Shape-Note Hymnody in the Shenandoah Valley, 1816–1860." Ph.D. dissertation, Tulane University, 1966.

Goff, James R., Jr. *Close Harmony: A History of Southern Gospel*. Chapel Hill & London: University of North Carolina Press, 2002.

Hall, Paul M. "The 'Musical Million': A Study and Analysis of the Periodical Promoting Music Reading Through Shape-Notes in North America from 1870 to 1914." D. M.A. dissertation, Catholic University of America, 1970.

History of Virginia. New York and Chicago: American Historical Association, 1924.

Horst, Irvin B. "Joseph Funk, Early Mennonite Printer and Publisher." *Mennonite Quarterly Review* 31 (1957): 260–280.

———. "Singers Glen, Virginia, Imprints, 1847–1878, a Checklist." *Eastern Mennonite College Bulletin* 44, no. 2 (1965): 6–14.

Jackson, George Pullen. *White Spirituals in the Southern Uplands*. Chapel Hill: University of North Carolina Press, 1933.

Morrison, Charles Edwin. "Aldine S. Kieffer and Ephraim Ruebush: Ideals Reflected in Post–Civil War Ruebush–Keiffer Company Publications." Ed.D. dissertation, Arizona State University, 1992.

Showalter, Grace I. *The Music Books of Ruebush & Kieffer, 1866–1942: A Bibliography*. Richmond: Virginia State Library, 1975.

Wayland, John W. "Joseph Funk, Father of Song in Northern Virginia." *The Pennsylvania German* 12 (October 1911).

SINGING COOKES, THE

Hubert Cooke (b. March 16, year unknown)
Jeanette Cooke (b. February 16, year unknown)
James Cooke (b. January 11, year unknown)
Ronnie Cooke (b. December 5, year unknown)
Donnie Cooke (b. November 1, year unknown)

Initially known as the Cooke Duet, the husband-and-wife team of Hubert and Jeanette Cooke of Wise, Virginia embarked on a career in gospel music in May 1962. During the following four decades, they attained wide popularity and added their three sons: Donnie, James, and Ronnie. They became known first as the Cooke Duet and Sons and finally as the Singing Cookes. In recent years, they have subdivided into two groups, with the younger generation now known as the Cooke Brothers. The Cooke vocals have always retained more than a touch of the "mountain sound" that has produced such noted musical figures over the years as the Carter Family, the Stanley Brothers, and Brother Claude Ely.

Growing up in Wise, Virginia, which has been a center of the Appalachian coal industry as well as an area known for its traditional music, Hubert Cooke went to work in the mines until demand for his and Jeanette's music opened a new career opportunity for the couple. Son James began playing bass guitar for his parents and eventually started singing as well. By the time of their ninth album, they had become known (with Ronnie and Donnie on keyboard and drums) as the Cooke Duet and Sons and finally as the Singing Cookes. Their first song to gain national attention, "He Rows Us Over the Tide," was followed by "My Lord Will Send a Moses," "Earth's Loss and Heaven's Gain," and "Walk the Last Mile Together." By 1999, the Cookes had forty-four albums to their credit, and the Cooke Brothers had an additional thirteen. Among the more memorable numbers of the Brothers have been "Chiseled in Stone" and "Go Rest High on the Mountain." In recent years, the Cookes have varied their music somewhat with an album of mother songs and two featuring bluegrass instrumentation. The latter has long seemed a natural for the Cookes, because Hubert's brother Jack is a former bandmate of Bill Monroe's and he has spent some thirty-five years with Ralph Stanley's Clinch Mountain Boys. Early recordings by the Cookes often appeared on the Jewel label, but in recent years they have had their own Cooke Records.

IVAN M. TRIBE

Reference and Further Reading

The Singing Cookes website, http://www.singingcookes.com.

Discography

Best of the Cooke Duet (1995, Freeland FRC 641).
Cooke Duet and Son (1998, Freeland FRC 659).
Bluegrass Gospel (2000, Cooke SC-171600).
Songs About Mama (2001, Cooke SC-220401).

SINGING IN TONGUES

The practice of singing in tongues has existed within Christian communities since the Church was founded in the first century. The apostle Paul's reference to singing in, or with, the Spirit (I Corinthians 14:15) is understood by some scholars to indicate that the phenomenon was well established among early believers (Graves, 2001, 1; Spencer, 1990, 154). However, tongue-singing, along with the more common practice of tongue-speaking, remains a subject of considerable controversy in twenty-first–century Christendom. Most Pentecostals and charismatics contend that modern-day tongue-speaking is a continuation of the phenomenon that marked the birth of the New Testament church. Some also understand tongues as a significant physical manifestation or "initial evidence" of Holy Spirit infilling, but there is disagreement among Pentecostals over whether it is an essential aspect of the biblical new birth experience. Other Christians posit that divinely sanctioned tongue-speaking has ceased and that it occurred in the early church primarily for purposes of spreading the gospel effectively to every part of the world.

The phrase "speaking in tongues" generally denotes either glossolalia (talking in an unlearned foreign language, often for purposes of evangelization) or xenoglossy (speaking in a supernatural, heavenly language). According to the historical account written by Luke in Acts 2, the baptism of the Holy Spirit occurred on the Day of Pentecost, when one hundred and twenty of Jesus's followers assembled in an upper room to wait for the promised Holy Spirit. After suddenly hearing a sound "from heaven as of a rushing mighty wind," they "began to speak with other tongues, as the Spirit gave them utterance." In an epistle to the Corinthian church, Paul describes tongue-speaking as one of several "gifts" *(charismata)* that the Holy Spirit could bestow upon the baptized body of believers.

Tongue-speaking has remained popular within many religious communities since the apostolic age. In Italy, the Montanists and Waldensians practiced it during the second and thirteenth centuries, respectively, and in twelfth-century France, the Albigenses were known to sing in tongues. There is a greater amount of historical evidence supporting the survival of tongue-singing during the eighteenth and nineteenth centuries among the Mormons, Irvingites, Shakers, and various Holiness denominations in Europe and North America. The newly established Shaker communities of late–eighteenth-century New England rejected the hymns and anthems of the established churches in favor of "gift" and "vision" songs that were believed to be transmitted from the spiritual realm (Andrews, 1940, 23). These songs, which were often learned while in trance and rendered in an "unknown tongue," were thought to be given to individuals by the Savior, angelic entities, or deceased members of the Shaker community (ibid, 25).

The 1906 Azusa Street Revival sparked a twentieth-century explosion of Pentecostalism and a renewed emphasis on manifestations of the Holy Spirit in the United States and, in turn, around the world. Speaking or singing in tongues was, by this time, quickly becoming a well-defined component of the charismatic Christian experience, even as mainline denominational Protestants generally frowned upon the practice, denigrated it as meaningless babble, or condemned it as the work of Satan. During the Azusa Street services, *The Apostolic Faith* newsletter published eyewitness accounts of singing in tongues. Jennie Moore, a young African American woman, testified

that she "sang under the power of the Spirit in many languages," eventually being empowered by the Holy Spirit to play the piano, despite never having taken lessons (Moore, 1907, 3; cited in Spencer, 1990, 155).

Some missionaries claimed to have preached, prayed, and sung in foreign languages such as "Chinese," which were understood by others present (Johnson, 1907, 1; cited in Spencer, 1990, 156). In many cases, churchgoers who deemed tongue-speaking to be strange and unorthodox were more willing to embrace tongue-singing and could appreciate the beauty and emotional impact of the melodies (Spencer, 1990, 159). Those attending the revival sometimes sang English-language hymns for extended periods, after which the same melody would be sung using a foreign or unknown language. One congregant recalled receiving the baptism of the Holy Spirit during a three-hour rendition of the hymn "Jesus, Oh, How Sweet the Name." She testified, "I sang it until the Precious Holy Ghost took my tongue and spoke for Himself" (Neale, 1908, 4; cited in Spencer, 1990, 160).

Although musical glossolalia and xenolalia are less common among modern-day Pentecostals and charismatics in the United States, many regard the Old Testament instruction to "sing unto the Lord a new song" (Psalm 98:1) as a biblical validation for the ongoing practice of singing in tongues. During emotional musical praise and worship segments of charismatic church services, participants often sing in tongues or ecstatic utterances softly to the sustained chords played by instrumentalists. Such practices gained increased visibility during the late twentieth century, with the growth of televangelism and transnational music ministries.

MELVIN L. BUTLER

See also Azusa Street Revival

Reference and Further Reading

Andrews, Edward D. *The Gift to Be Simple: Songs, Dances and Rituals of the American Shakers*. New York: Dover Publications, 1940.

Graves, Robert. "Singing in the Spirit." *Pneuma Review* 4, no. 2 (Spring 2001). Available at http://www.pneuma foundation.com/resources/articles/rwgraves010.pdf.

Johnson, Andrew G. "In Sweden." *The Apostolic Faith* 1, no. 6 (February 1907).

Moore, Jennie. "Music from Heaven." *The Apostolic Faith* 1, no. 8 (May 1907).

Neale, Martha. "To a Friend." *The Apostolic Faith* 1, no. 11 (October 1908).

Spencer, Jon Michael. *Protest and Praise: Sacred Music of Black Religion*. Minneapolis, MN: Fortress Press, 1990.

SINGING NEWS, THE

The Singing News, which has long been the primary print publication for Southern gospel music, was formed by J. G. Whitfield (b. September 8, 1915) in 1969. The idea came from *Good News*, the publication of the Gospel Music Association, which had been launched in early 1969. Whitfield was a founding member of the Florida Boys who left the group in 1958 to concentrate on his business interests. One of these interests was promoting Southern gospel concerts, and he had been using bulk mail to reach potential consumers for his concerts. Whitfield quickly realized that he could create a publication that would contain all of the necessary concert promotion information and solve the problem of numerous bulk mailings.

In May 1969, Whitfield issued the first *Singing News*, which was sent free to everyone who had ordered songbooks from *Gospel Singing Jubilee*, the TV program hosted by the Florida Boys. That initial run of a hundred thousand copies published announcements of upcoming concert appearances, features about artists, and industry gossip.

Whitfield convinced Lloyd Orrell and W. B. Nowlin, who also promoted Southern gospel concerts, to mail copies of *The Singing News* to everyone on their mailing lists in exchange for advertisements in the publication. The three-dollar-per-year subscription fee covered some costs, but by the mid-1970s, only about ten percent of the three hundred thousand copies in the print run was sent to subscribers; the rest were sent to people on mailing lists in order to boost attendance at Southern gospel concerts.

The Singing News introduced a monthly chart, "Gospel Hit Parade," in the January 1970 issue. This chart was compiled from reports of airplay by more than two hundred gospel disc jockeys as well as sales reports from distributors and retailers. This brought about an important change in the Southern gospel industry. Prior to this time, it was the touring acts with the most longevity who were most popular; after the introduction of charts, it was hit singles that determined the most popular groups.

The Singing News was originally based in Pensacola, Florida, where Whitfield lived, but in 1986 Whitfield sold the publication to Maurice Templeton, who moved it to Boone, North Carolina. *The Singing News* had attempted to cover a wide variety of gospel news before the sale—including contemporary Christian music and black gospel—but after the sale, Templeton and long-time editor Jerry Kirksey decided to concentrate on Southern gospel.

Jesse Gillis (J. G.) Whitfield was inducted into the Gospel Music Hall of Fame in 1990 and the Southern Gospel Music Hall of Fame in 1997.

DON CUSIC

Reference and Further Reading

Cusic, Don. *The Sound of Light: A History of Gospel and Christian Music*. New York: Hal Leonard, 2002.

Goff, James R., Jr. *Close Harmony: A History of Southern Gospel*. Chapel Hill: University of North Carolina Press, 2002.

SINGING RAMBOS, THE

Buck Rambo (b. September 15, 1931)
Dottie Rambo (b. March 2, 1934)
Reba Rambo (b. October 17, 1951)

The Singing Rambos, who performed during the 1960s and 1970s, are a family group consisting of Buck, Dottie, and Reba Rambo. They actually evolved from the solo career of Dottie (Luttrell) Rambo, who started singing and writing songs at the age of eight. At age twelve, she left her home in Morganfield, Kentucky, to sing at church revivals throughout the Southern and Central United States. Governor Jimmie Davis of Louisiana was so impressed by Dottie's songwriting skills that he signed her to a writer's contract. In addition to Governor Davis, several artists began recording her songs, a trend that would continue throughout her life.

Dottie married Buck at the age of sixteen, and they formed the Singing Echoes in the 1950s. Although the Singing Echoes gained regional success, they changed their name to the Singing Rambos when their daughter Reba joined the group.

In 1964, the Singing Rambos signed a recording contract with the Benson Company to record on the Heart Warming Record label, and they started to receive national attention. At the time, Southern gospel music groups were dominated by male quartets with piano accompaniment, but the Singing Rambos were able to compete with these groups as a trio with guitar accompaniment. They toured with the Stamps Quartet and the Oak Ridge Boys as "Gospel Festival, U.S.A." and performed at the National Quartet Convention, even though they were a trio. They had a unique sound, which they referred to as "inverted harmony," an idea that they got from the male trio Sons of Song. Since the group only had three voices and lacked a bass, they would take turns singing the lead, tenor, baritone, and bass parts; therefore, the three voices would cover the four parts in a song. This vocal movement gave the group a full sound without a bass singer.

While the group had a distinct sound as a trio accompanied with guitars, they often added additional instrumentalists such as pianist Darius Spurgeon and accordionist Pat Green. The group's accompaniment was unique in that Dottie was one of the first women to play lead guitar in a Southern gospel group.

As the Singing Rambos, the group became one of the best-known families in Southern gospel music, with more than sixty recordings. Their popularity is reflected in their number one Southern gospel recordings, "Tiny" in May 1972 and "I've Never Been This Homesick Before" in November 1977. Although the family's sound was compelling, it was Dottie's songs that greatly contributed to the group's success.

Dottie has written more than twenty-five hundred songs, many of which have been recorded by other artists and appear in church hymnals. Her songs have been so popular that they have been recorded by many gospel and secular artists, including Elvis Presley, Sandy Patti, Dolly Parton, George Beverly Shea, Barbara Mandrell, Bill Monroe, Crystal Gayle, Johnny Cash, Vince Gill, Bill Gaither, Andrae Crouch, Steve Greene, and Larry Gatlin. Her most famous song is the 1970 hit "He Looked Beyond My Fault and Saw My Need." Although the melody is similar to "Oh, Danny Boy," the encouraging words were inspired by a deathbed conversation with her brother Eddie. "We Shall Behold Him," "I Will Glory in the Cross," "I Go to the Rock," and "Sheltered in the Arms of God" are among her other hit songs. Her children's musical "Down by the Creekbank" has become one of the most successful Christian musicals in history.

Dottie's solo career extends beyond her inspirational songs to her solo performances. In 1968, she won a Grammy for her solo album *It's the Soul of Me* and was named Trendsetter of the Year by *Billboard* magazine. The Christian Country Music Association honored her in 1994 as the Songwriter of the Century and, in 2002, they presented her with the Living Legend Award. In 1997, she was inducted into the Southern Gospel Music Association Hall of Fame, and she has been inducted into the Gospel Music Hall of Fame twice, as a soloist in 1991 and as part of the Singing Rambos in 2001.

The Singing Rambos stopped performing as a group during the late 1970s. Dottie continued performing, with six solo albums and her own Christian variety show on TBN called *The Dottie Rambo Magazine*. Despite this, Dottie stopped performing in the early 1980s due to health problems. Fortunately, she returned to performing in 2003 when she released the album *Stand by the River*, which included a duet of the title cut with Dolly Parton.

Buck and Dottie divorced in the early 1990s. Dottie continued to write music, but Buck switched his creative talent to oil painting. Their daughter, Reba, married Donny McGuire, and they became a successful songwriting team. All three members continued to sing in public through 2004.

THEODORE E. FULLER

Reference and Further Reading

More Than the Music website, http://www.morethanthemusic.net/.

Rambo, Mae. Personal correspondence, Rambom@comcast.net.

Terrell, Bob. *The Music Men: The Story of Professional Gospel Quartet Singing.*

———; Buck Rambo. *The Legacy of Buck and Dottie Rambo: The Inspiring Story of the Family that Changed the Direction of Gospel.* Nashville, TN: Star Song Publishing Group, 1992.

Discography

If That Isn't Love (1969, Vista LP R1228); *Soul Singing Rambos* (1969, Heart Warming LP HWS 1953); *An Evening with the Singing Rambos* (1970, Heart Warming LP HWS 1991); *Nashville Gospel* (1970, Heart Warming LP HWS R3076); *Best of the Rambos* (1972, Heart Warming LP R3187); *Soul in the Family* (1972, Heart Warming LP R3173); *Belief* (1973, Vista LP R1242); *Sing Me on Home* (1973, Vista LP R1719); *Too Much to Gain to Lose* (1973, Vista LP R1247); *Alive . . . And Live at Soul's Harbor* (1974, Heart Warming LP R3347); *Gospel Music Association's Top Ten for 1974* (1974, Heart Warming LP R328; song "Ten Thousand Years"); *Presenting the Singing Rambos* (1974, Heart Warming LP TC 1969); *Softly and Tenderly* (1974, World of Rambo LP WR 0050); *Gospel Music Association's Top Ten Songs for 1975* (1975, Canaan CAS 9785); *Gospel Music Association's Top Ten Songs for 1976* (1976, Heart Warming LP; song "Tears Will Never Stain the Streets of That City"); *Naturally* (1977, Heart Warming LP R3459); *Rambo Country* (1976, Heart Warming LP R3429); *Top Ten Songs of 1980* (1981, Heart Warming LP R3769; song "Behold the Lamb"); *Memories Made New* (1983, Heart Warming LP R3814); *Masters of Gospel* (1992, Benson CD 84418-2882-2; reissue of original from 1968); *20 Favorite Gospel Songs* (1994, Benson Records); *Dottie Rambo—Stand by the River* (2003, Spring Hill WEA 406. Cat. 421045); *Very Best of the Rambos* (2003, New Haven 28040); *Buck, Dottie, Reba, The Singing Rambos* (Vista LP R1232); *Come Spring* (Heart Warming LP HF-1885); *Gospel Ballads* (Heart Warming HWS 1919); *Queen of Paradise* (Heart Warming R3499); *Reunion* (1981, Heart Warming R3576); *The Singing Rambos . . . Live* (Heart Warming LP R3116); *The Son Is Shining* (Heart Warming R3398); *Songs of Love and Hope* (Vista LP R1222); *Soul Classics* (Heart Warming HWS LP R3100); *There Has to Be a Song* (Heart Warming R3359); *These Three Are One* (Heart Warming R3366); *This Is My Valley* (Heart Warming LP HWS R3032).

SINGING SCHOOLS

Singing schools were short-term classes designed to instruct beginners in the basics of singing and note reading, with a focus on religious music. Although singing schools came to fruition in New England during the eighteenth century, the first written evidence of one is in the South. In his diary entries for December 1710 and January 1711, William Byrd of Westover, Virginia, comments that local citizens were learning to sing psalms from a singing book under a singing teacher's instructions.

It was clergymen in and around Boston, however, who opposed the old way of singing and who are usually credited with starting the singing-school movement. They believed that congregations should sing the traditional psalm tunes as they were notated in metrical psalters, so beginning in 1714, schools for instruction in psalm singing were established in Boston and soon proliferated throughout much of New England, the mid-Atlantic region, and the South. Schools generally lasted no more than two or three months, often providing a source of recreation—particularly in rural areas—as well as musical instruction. They flourished among Protestant evangelicals, who were more comfortable leaving music making to the congregation rather than to professional musicians.

Singing schools made possible the first American musical profession—that of singing master—and facilitated the publication of music, mostly in the form of tunebooks (collections of religious music intended mainly for use in singing schools). By creating a market for their publications, singing schools encouraged American composers. William Billings, Daniel Read, Jacob Kimball, Jr., and Oliver Holden are but a few of the psalmodists who were active during the eighteenth century.

Initially, singing schools were organized by the singing master, who advertised a school, built up a clientele, and collected fees from each student. This remained the most popular means of running a school, but by the late eighteenth century, they were held at the behest of a congregation or even a town. One singing master collected subscriptions from community members, making it possible for students to attend his school free of charge; his interesting approach was, apparently, unique.

After vocal music became part of the New England public school curriculum, singing schools began to die out in the Northeast but continued to flourish in the South and the Ohio Valley. Several published tunebooks combined with musical conventions—such as the still active Chattahoochie Musical Association, established in 1852—helped keep the tradition alive there. Soon "normal schools" for the training of teachers arose, as did publishing companies that supplied inexpensive handbooks containing the rudiments of music and collections of religious songs in seven-shape notations. During the nineteenth century, there arose singing schools devoted to specific tunebooks, such as *The Sacred Harp* or *The Southern Harmony*, which continue to the present day. Other contemporary singing schools are sponsored by such churches as Primitive Baptists and Church of Christ, which ban instrumental music in their services.

More popular through the first half of the twentieth century were the singing schools promoted by seven-shape-note gospel publishing companies. Typically, these lasted one to two weeks and were held in a rural community's school or church house (often those were the same building) and were sponsored by local singing conventions or a publishing company. Usually, a representative of the company—generally a songwriter whose works were published by the company—would come through a community and see if he could stir up interest in a school. Gospel songwriters such as Eugene M. Bartlett and Thomas Jefferson Farris are just two of the many who worked in this way. If there was enough response, the school would be held immediately. Companies backed this practice, of course, because it was a relatively easy way to sell songbooks. After midcentury, this type of singing school began to decline, being replaced largely by quartet performances.

W. K. McNeil

Reference and Further Reading

Britton, Allen P. "The Singing-School Movement in the United States." In *International Musicological Society, Report of the 8th Congress*, New York, 1961.

Jackson, George Pullen. *White Spirituals in the Southern Uplands: The Story of the Fasola Folk, Their Songs, Singings, and "Buckwheat Notes."* New York: Dover, 1965 (1933).

Stevenson, Robert. *Protestant Church Music in America: A Short Survey of Men and Movements from 1564 to the Present.* New York: Norton, 1966.

SKYLITE RECORDING COMPANY

The Skylite Recording Company, formed in 1959, was a pioneering recording company established to record and promote Southern gospel music, especially Southern gospel quartets. Before this label, gospel groups either recorded for a major label, such as RCA Victor and Capitol, or released custom albums on independent labels, such as White Church. However, with the exception of Word Records in Waco, Texas, which recorded predominantly solo singers and preachers in 1959 (Word formed Canaan Records to record Southern gospel groups in 1963), and Vaughan Phonograph Records, none of these record labels were solely dedicated to Southern gospel music groups.

Given that the Blackwood Brothers and the Statesmen quartets had worked together since the early 1950s, the two successful quartets solidified their business ventures in 1959 with the formation of Blackwood–Statesmen Enterprises, which created the Skylite Recording Company. The inspiration for the Skylite Recording Company came from Jake Hess of the Statesmen Quartet and J. D. Sumner of the Blackwood Brothers Quartet. Through the success of their perspective quartets, Sumner and Hess had both become accomplished composers. To obtain financial freedom for their publishing rights, both singers created their own publishing companies. Sumner created the Gospel Quartet Music Company, and Hess created the Faith Music Company. With the rise of professional gospel quartets and the decline in sales for the big shape-note publishing companies during the 1950s, Hess also bought the Henson Publishing Company, and Sumner, along with the Blackwood Brothers, bought the famed Stamps Music Company. With a multitude of copyright holdings, the next logical step in promoting Southern gospel music was to create a record label. Therefore, the Blackwood Brothers and Statesmen quartets founded the Skylite Recording Company to record and support Southern gospel music.

Although the Blackwood Brothers were headquartered in Memphis and the Statesmen were in Atlanta, most of the Skylite projects were recorded in Nashville at the RCA and CBS studios. J. D. Sumner and, to some extent, Jake Hess were in charge of managing the Skylite Recording Company, which was named by Blackwood pianist Wally Varner. The Skylite recordings were distributed through the same network of stores as RCA's religious products due to James Blackwood's work as the first distributor of exclusively religious records for RCA.

Because the Blackwood Brothers and the Statesmen were still touring at the time, Sumner and Hess could not be present for most of the Nashville recording sessions. The first group to record for the Skylite Recording Company, the Speer Family, solved this problem. After the Speer Family recorded *Dad Speer's Golden Anniversary in Gospel Music* and *Songs You've Requested*, Brock Speer, who served as the producer on both albums, was put in charge of producing future projects for the label. This arrangement worked out well for the company geographically, because the Speer family was based in Nashville. In addition, Brock and his brother, Ben Speer, functioned as the Artist and Repertoire agents for the Skylite Recording Company. To keep recording costs down, Brock Speer played electric guitar and Ben Speer played bass on many of the sessions.

Among the notable groups to record for the label were the Speer Family, the Statesmen Quartet, the Harvesters, the Rangers (Quartet), the Blue Ridge Quartet, the Oak Ridge Quartet, the Florida Boys, the Harmoneers, the Stamps Quartet, the Masters V, Ken Turner, and the Blackwood Brothers Quartet.

Although the Blackwood Brothers and Statesmen quartets were under contract with RCA Victor, they were allowed to record on the Skylite label. With the permission of RCA Victor, the quartets could record on the Skylite label any song in the public domain that they had not previously recorded for RCA. Therefore, their early works on Skylite included many older songs, such as those from the Stamps songbooks, and existing recordings not previously released on RCA. These agreements allowed both groups to record on the Skylite label.

In addition to the Skylite Recording Company, Blackwood–Statesmen Enterprises formed a subsidiary label called StatesWood Records, which produced inexpensive albums of quartets and sermons.

The Skylite Recording Company produced several award-winning albums, such as the Blackwood Brothers' *Release Me (From My Sin)* (Skylite SLP 6124), which won both Grammy and Dove Awards in 1973. In 1979, the Blackwood Brothers Quartet won a Grammy for Best Gospel Performance, Traditional, for *Lift Up the Name of Jesus* (Skylite SLP 6128). In 1981, the Masters V won a Grammy for Best Gospel Performance, Traditional, for *The Masters V* (Skylite SLP 6256). Due to the success of the Skylite Recording Company, new record companies such as the Sing Recording Company (formed by the LeFevre family in 1963), Benson's Heart Warming Records, and Zondervan entered the gospel music industry.

With increasing competition from larger record labels and J. D. Sumner's move to the Stamps Quartet, the Skylite Record Company was sold to a group of independent investors from Cleveland, Tennessee, led by record producer Joel Gentry in 1966. Although the original owners—the Blackwood Brothers and the Statesmen—had sold the company, they continued to record on the label. The Blackwood Brothers Quartet released records on Skylite until 1989, and James Blackwood continued to record on the label until 1991.

The Skylite Recording Company merged with the Atlanta-based Sing Recording Company to form Skylite–Sing records during the 1970s. Also during the 1970s, "Little" Johnny Dempsey became a featured guitar player and producer for the label. Skylite–Sing Records continued to release recordings through the early 1990s.

THEODORE E. FULLER

Reference and Further Reading

Davis, Paul. *The Legacy of The Blackwood Brothers: Authorized Biographies of Cecil Blackwood and James Blackwood*. Greenville, SC: Blue Ridge Publishing, 2000.

Goff, James R., Jr., *Close Harmony: A History of Southern Gospel Music*. Chapel Hill: University of North Carolina Press, 2002.

Taylor, David L. *Happy Rhythm: A Biography of Hovie Lister and The Statesmen Quartet*. Lexington, IN: LexingtonHaus Publications, 1998.

Terrell, Bob. *The Music Men: The Story of Professional Gospel Quartet Singing*. Alexander, NC: Mountain Church, 2001.

SLAUGHTER, HENRY AND HAZEL

Henry T. Slaughter (b. January 9, 1927)
Hazel Myers Slaughter (b. May 29, 1935)
David Slaughter (b. December 17, 1953)
Michael Slaughter (b. September 25, 1958)
Amanda Joy Slaughter (b. August 25, 1961)

Henry Slaughter first made a name for himself in gospel music as a piano player. He went on to form a duet with his wife, Hazel, which eventually developed into a family group that included his sons, David and Michael, as well as daughter, Amanda Joy. Along the way, Henry picked up five consecutive Dove Awards (1973–1977) from the Gospel Music Association as Instrumentalist of the Year.

Henry T. Slaughter hailed from Roxboro, North Carolina. After army service at the end of World War II, he began his gospel music career with a now nearly forgotten group called the Ozark Quartet (one of many Stamps groups) that worked out of Siloam Springs, Arkansas, before moving to Wichita Falls, Texas. His entry into major group status came when he joined the Weatherford Quartet, then affiliated with Rex Humbard's Cathedral of Tomorrow in Akron, Ohio. In 1963, he became pianist for Jake Hess's new group, the Imperials, until he and Hazel—a native of Laurel, Mississippi, whom he had married in 1952—formed their duet in 1967.

In their earlier days, Henry and Hazel Slaughter had often worked in combination with the Bill Gaither Trio, but as their children grew, David joined as full-time bass player in 1971, Michael in 1976, and finally Amanda in 1978. The Slaughters made most of their many albums for the Benson Company's Heart Warming Records, but Henry later started his own company, Accord, and opened a studio. Over the years, some of their best-known songs included "Then the Answer Came," "I've Never Loved Him Better Than Today," "The Sweetest Hallelujah," and "What a Precious Friend Is He." They also found space on each album for one or two standards, such as "Blessed Assurance" and "Standing Somewhere in the Shadows."

In addition to his work as a gospel musician, Henry Slaughter started his own company, Harvest Time Publishing, in 1959. He wrote a pair of instruction books: *The Henry Slaughter Gospel Piano Course* in 1969 and *Gospel Organ Techniques* in 1972. He later developed his *Praise and Worship Piano Lessons* instructional booklets and teaching tapes. In 1980, Henry authored his informative autobiography, *In Search of the Pearl of Great Price*, with the help of Darryl E. Hicks. A perceptive observer of the gospel music scene, Henry authored a satirical essay about the conflicts and commonalities within the industry that appeared in two parts in *The Singing News* in 1984.

As time went by, the children went into other activities, knowing that their parents would eventually retire. Amanda Joy married in 1980, whereas the sons remained in music a few years longer. Henry and Hazel continued to work, although their concert schedule gradually wound down; their daughter Amanda reports that they now have only a few concerts a year, more often than not in Florida, where they spend part of each winter.

As of January 2005, Henry and Hazel were residing in Ashland City, Tennessee. Except for the occasional concert, they are retired, having sold their studio in about 2002. David and Michael also reside in the Nashville area. Daughter Amanda Joy maintains a website and keeps Harvest Time Publishers active from her home in northwest Ohio (Harvest Time Publishers, P.O. Box 324, Bryan, OH 43506), through which the instruction books, autobiography, and a limited selection of some of Henry and Hazel Slaughter's recordings may still be purchased.

IVAN M. TRIBE

Reference and Further Reading

Gentry, Linnell. *A History and Encyclopedia of Country, Western, and Gospel Music*, 2nd ed., 544. Nashville, TN: Clairmont, 1969.

Slaughter, Henry. "A Gospel Music Story." *The Singing News* (June and July 1984).

———. *In Search of the Pearl of Great Price*. Nashville, TN: Harvest Time, 1980.

Discography

Tribute to God Be the Glory (1973, Heart Warming R 3208).
Blessed Assurance (1974, Heart Warming 3255).
The Sweetest Hallelujah (1976, Heart Warming 3395).
Thanks . . . I Think I'll Play One (Harvest Time CD).
We've Come This Far by Faith (Harvest Time CD).

SLAVE SONGS OF THE UNITED STATES

This book, the first extensive collection of Negro folklore and an important early compilation of religious songs, was the combined effort of William Francis Allen (b. September 5, 1830; d. December 9, 1889), Charles Pickard Ware (b. June 11, 1840; d. 1921), and Lucy McKim Garrison (b. October 30, 1842; d. May 11, 1877). Of these three editors, the one who did the most work on the publication was Allen, the moving force behind getting the collection in print.

Like many nineteenth-century intellectuals, Allen was well versed in several areas, although he was primarily known as a classical scholar. Born in Northborough (this spelling, used in Allen's time, was later changed to Northboro), Massachusetts, he grew up in a musical atmosphere and, not surprisingly, showed a strong inclination for music. He even tried his hand at songwriting, producing at ten a political song for the campaign of William Henry Harrison. Eventually, Allen became a skilled pianist and flautist as well as an adept sight singer.

In addition to his musical accomplishments, Allen was a trained historian, who exerted a major influence on frontier historian Frederick Jackson Turner, and a philologist by instinct. His article on "The Negro Dialect" for the December 1865 issue of *The Nation* is considered the earliest scholarly investigation of nonmusical black traditions. Allen came to the South during the Civil War as a member of government organizations and spent two years at St. Helena Island, South Carolina, and Helena, Arkansas. A brief stint as superintendent of schools in Charleston, South Carolina, concluded his stay in the South.

In 1867, he became chair of ancient languages and history at the University of Wisconsin, remaining there until his death. During his stay in the South, Allen had collected songs from black informants. When Allen started his work in the South in November 1863, his first cousin, Charles Pickard Ware, had been in the region for a year and a half. After graduating from Harvard in 1862, Ware joined his sister Harriett in the Sea Islands, where she was working for the Educational Commission. Almost immediately he started collecting songs from blacks around Coffin Point, South Carolina, and he soon obtained enough material that he began thinking about compiling a book based on the collection. In a July 1862 letter to his sister, Ware stated he had "175 pages of Negro melodies," which was probably an exaggeration. He did, however, eventually amass a sizeable collection that was the largest single contribution to *Slave Songs of the United States*. After the book appeared in 1867, Ware maintained an interest in the songs of blacks,

but he was involved in no further publications. He worked briefly as a lawyer, teacher, and, from 1889 until his retirement, for American Bell Telephone Company.

Lucy McKim Garrison grew up in a strongly anti-slavery atmosphere, the daughter of a noted abolitionist. Her family was also very interested in music and saw to it that their daughter received considerable training in that area. She became proficient on the piano but, more important as far as her later work in folk music was concerned, she was able to appreciate and realize the significance of music alien to European classical music. At age nineteen, she spent three weeks collecting songs in the South Carolina Sea Islands. As a result of this experience, she wrote an oft-quoted letter to *Dwight's Journal of Music* that was the first printed description of black music style and technique.

In 1862 Garrison initiated a series of sheet music arrangements of black folk songs, but poor sales resulted in only two of the proposed eight titles being issued. The arrangements are significant because they present the songs on their own terms rather than "Europeanizing" them. It was also a pioneering attempt at notating black folk songs for the general public. Garrison contributed only three songs to *Slave Songs of the United States*, but without her the book probably would not have appeared. She interested her husband, Wendell Phillips Garrison, in the songs and their publication. Moreover, she knew many other collectors, and she and her husband contacted these potential contributors, got the songs, and saw the book through publication. Her primary motive—and that of her coeditors—was to preserve items they thought in danger of being lost forever, a desire common to many early folklore collectors.

Little else about the volume was common, though, for this pioneering effort set a high standard. Its virtues include providing musical settings for each of its 136 texts and variants, which is no small feat when one considers that the editors had no prior model to go by nor the benefit of tape recorders. Moreover, supplying melodies with words did not become standard practice among American folk song collectors until the second half of the twentieth century. The editors also considered regional characteristics of black folk music, a point that was overlooked by most of their successors, and they considered the contexts in which songs were performed.

Some of the book's most worthwhile portions are observations concerning black singing styles. Attention is called to the nonpart harmony of the singers that gave the music a sound totally foreign to anything these commentators had ever heard. The "irregularities," "slides," and "turns" used by the singers were also alien to the European tradition. Even so, the editors concluded that "the chief part of the Negro music is civilized in its character" and, although partly imitative of white music, it was "original in the best sense of the word." Allen thought the words of black songs were mostly derived from the Bible, church hymns, and adaptations of camp-meeting hymns, such as "The Old Ship of Zion" and "Jacob's Ladder." Other songs, such as "King Emanuel," sounded as though they were of white origin, but because the editors could not find them in any hymnbook, they included them as slave songs.

Most texts found only in hymnals were rejected, because the intent was to present items that truly belonged to the Negroes. An attempt to trace tune sources was very difficult because of the improvisatory nature of black folk singing, in which the same melody was rarely used twice for a specific set of lyrics. This, of course, made it impossible to say whether a tune was old or newly made up on the spot. What few tune analogs Allen found led him to conclude that most tunes were original products of "a race of remarkable musical capacity" and, although influenced by European music, still retained "a distinct tinge of their native Africa." This conclusion remained unchallenged for two decades.

Among the book's weaknesses are the insistence that slave songs were dying, but this was a common complaint of folklore collectors of that time and to be expected. The editors culled the "least interesting" songs without mentioning by what standard they were found to be so. Furthermore, they judged Negro music to be either civilized or barbaric rather than as a musical system with values different from those with which they were familiar. The book achieved mixed reviews, the most negative appearing in *Lippincott's Magazine* in 1868. The unsigned critic called the songs "trash, vulgarity, and profanity" totally unworthy of publication. Yet the book triumphed over such criticism by bringing black folk music to widespread public attention and by whetting the interest in collecting, studying, and performing black folk music that has not abated since 1867. Furthermore, *Slave Songs of the United States* provided a solid collection of black religious music during the years shortly before the gospel song movement got under way.

W. K. McNeil

Reference and Further Reading

Allen, William Francis; Charles Pickard Ware; Lucy McKim Garrison. *Slave Songs of the United States*. New York: Dover, 1992 (1867).

Epstein, Dena J. *Sinful Tunes and Spirituals: Black Folk Music to the Civil War*. Urbana: University of Illinois Press, 1977.

SMITH BROTHERS, THE (TENNESSEE AND SMITTY)

John Onvia "Tennessee" Smith (b. August 15, 1918)
Aubrey Lee "Smitty" Smith (b. March 13, 1916; d. August 27, 1989)

During the era from 1948 to 1965, the Smith Brothers boasted one of the finest gospel duets in the sacred music field. Known for the wide range of their musical background, John "Tennessee" and A. L. "Smitty" Smith, natives of Oneida, Tennessee, aspired to musical careers from childhood. At one time—in company with Milton "Ace" Richman, among others—they performed Western swing, barber shop, and country, eventually becoming best known, after Eddie Wallace joined them, as the Sunshine Boys, a gospel quartet. In addition to radio work in the Atlanta area, the foursome appeared in Western films with such cowboy stars as Eddie Dean, Lash LaRue, and Charles Starrett.

Leaving the Sunshine Boys to go on their own in mid-1949, the Smiths worked radio and television in Atlanta for twelve years, often in the company of such musical figures as Cotton Carrier, Pat Patterson, Paul Rice, and Boots Woodall. Recording for Mercury, they cut such titles as "Happy Birthday in Heaven" and "Getting Ready to Leave This World," and they did the vocals on Woodall's "They Locked God Outside the Iron Curtain." Moving to Capitol in 1953, some of their best-known songs included "I Have but One Goal" (with Bill Lowery lining-out the lyrics), "Child of the King," "I'm Gonna Shout," "The Sure Hand of God," and two songs steeped in the symbolism of technology, "Working in God's Factory" and "God's Rocket Ship."

In 1960, the Smiths left Atlanta and moved to Pittsburgh, where they did daily television with Slim Bryant and worked at the *World's Original Jamboree* on WWVA radio in Wheeling, West Virginia, on Saturday nights. After two years, they went to WMAZ-TV in Macon, Georgia, during which time (1964) they did an album for Sing Records of Atlanta titled *That's My Jesus*, which consisted of six new songs by Walter Bailes and other recently composed numbers. In 1965, they left the music world and returned to the Atlanta area, where Tennessee worked as a draftsman and Smitty worked in charge of rental property in shopping centers, until they both retired.

Ivan M. Tribe

See also Sunshine Boys Quartet

Reference and Further Reading

Tribe, Ivan M. "The Smith Brothers: Tennessee and Smitty." *Bluegrass Unlimited* 15, no. 1 (July 1980): 22–25.

SMITH, CONNIE

Constance June Meador (b. August 14, 1941)

Connie Smith, a major country music star of the 1960s, made her commitment to Christ and to sing more sacred music thereafter. Although this may have limited her commercial success in secular music, the mental and emotional satisfaction more than compensated. After four decades as a professional, Smith continues to sing both country and gospel and to appear regularly on the Grand Ole Opry with her ever-strong voice.

Born Constance June Meador in Elkhart, Indiana, the future songstress grew up relatively poor in West Virginia and Ohio, where she was graduated from Lower Salem High School in 1959. She sang locally and then on television jamboree shows in Huntington and Parkersburg, West Virginia, but a chance meeting with Bill Anderson led to a contract with RCA Victor in 1964 and a major hit, "Once a Day," with her first record. Other hits and numerous albums followed, including *Great Sacred Songs* in 1966 and *Come Along and Walk with Me* in 1970. Despite her success, she lacked inner satisfaction until her 1968 born-again experience.

Connie left RCA in 1972 and signed with Columbia, where she could record more sacred music. The latter included *God Is Abundant* in 1973 and the excellent *Connie Smith Sings Hank Williams Gospel* in 1975. During much of the 1970s and 1980s, she seldom sang except for in churches, at recording sessions, and on the Grand Ole Opry. Gradually, she began to perform a mixture of sacred and secular songs. Her most notable sacred offering is probably her inspiring four-minute rendition of "How Great Thou Art," which originally appeared on the otherwise secular album *Back in Baby's Arms* in 1969. Smith later recorded for Monument, Warner Brothers, and Laser Light, with her only recent sacred album being *Clinging to a Saving Hand* on the latter label.

As of 2004, Connie was married to her fourth husband, fellow Grand Ole Opry star Marty Stuart, and remains part of the Nashville scene.

DEANNA L. TRIBE AND IVAN M. TRIBE

Reference and Further Reading

Escott, Colin. *Connie Smith: Born to Sing*. Bremen, Germany: Bear Family Records, 2001.

Discography

Born to Sing (Bear Family BCD 16368; four-CD boxed set that includes great sacred songs).
Clinging to a Saving Hand (Laser Light).

SMITH, MICHAEL W.

(b. October 7, 1957, Kenova, WV)

Michael W. Smith is one of the most prolific and honored artists in contemporary Christian music (CCM). He attended college at Marshall University in West Virginia, but after one semester, he dropped out to move to Nashville and pursue a career in music. In 1992, Michael received an honorary doctorate of music degree from Alderson-Broaddus College in Philippi, West Virginia. He and his wife Debbie have five children

Michael enjoyed providing music at Billy Graham Crusades, and, in 1994 in Nashville, he founded a teen club called Rocketown in an effort to provide a place for teens to gather in a safe, loving environment. As founder of Rocketown Records, he influenced and mentored talented new artists. His career, spanning from 1981 to the present, includes work primarily as songwriter, singer, keyboardist, record producer, and author. He is also a devoted worship leader and creator of music to use in worship.

Smith was one of the first CCM artists to cross over and achieve success in the mainstream popular music market. In 1981, he signed to Meadowgreen Music as a staff writer, where, during the next few years, he provided gospel hits for such artists as Sandi Patti, Bill Gaither, and Amy Grant. He began touring as a keyboardist with Grant in 1982, and, the following year, he released his first album, *The Michael W. Smith Project*. This "project" became her opening act. Grant's managers, Mike Blanton and Dan Harrell, started their own record label, Reunion Records, which has produced all of Smith's recordings. In 1991, Reunion Records arranged for Geffen Records to distribute Smith's albums. They chose a two-pronged promotion campaign, with ads designed to appeal to both CCM audiences and to the mainstream pop audience. Some thought he was selling out to the more lucrative secular market, but he saw it differently, claiming that he was trying to reach a wider audience to help young people. Smith's style blends contemporary Christian, contemporary gospel, praise and worship, pop, and rock—thus appealing to both Christian and mainstream audiences. Combined, his work accounts for more than twelve million albums sold, thirteen gold and five platinum records, ten mainstream pop hits, twenty-eight number one Christian singles, and three DVD recordings His current creative output includes eighteen CDs, seven videos, and twelve books. His honors include forty Gospel Music Association Music Awards (Dove Awards), three Grammy Awards, and eight Grammy nominations. He was a performer and presenter at the Forty-fourth Annual Grammy Awards live telecast (2002).

DAVID WILLOUGHBY

Reference and Further Reading

Dove Awards website, http://www.doveawards.com.
Gospel Music Association website, http://www.gospelmusic.com.
Michael W. Smith website, http://www.michaelwsmith.com.
Reunion Records website, http://www.reunionrecords.com.
Rocketown Records website, http://www.rocketownrecords.com.
Rocketown website, http://www.rocketown.com.

Selected Discography

Christmas (1993, Reunion Records CD 49208; includes "All Is Well," "Gloria," and "Lux Venit").
The First Decade: 1983–1993 (1993, Reunion Records CD 49231; includes "Friends," "Great Is the Lord," and "I Will Be Here for You").
I'll Lead You Home (1995, Reunion Records CD 49253; includes "Cry for Love," "I'll Be Around," and "I'll Lead You Home").
Worship (2001, Reunion Records CD 10025; includes "Above All," "Agnus Dei," and "Awesome God").
Second Decade 1993–2003: (2003, Reunion Records CD 10080; includes "Above All," "Signs," and "This Is Your Time").

SMITH, WILLIE MAE FORD

(b. June 23, 1904, Rolling Rock, MS; d. February 2, 1994, St. Louis, MO)

An anointed soloist, passionate evangelist and renowned teacher, Willie Mae Ford Smith was the seventh of fourteen children to the union of Clarence and Mary Williams Ford. Clarence, a railroad brakeman, sought better opportunities and moved the family to Memphis, Tennessee, where Willie Mae spent her childhood.

In 1917, the Fords moved to St. Louis, Missouri. At the encouragement of their father, a devout Baptist deacon, four of the Ford daughters combined to form the Ford Sisters. Willie Mae, Mary, Emma, and Geneva modeled themselves after the popular male quartets of the day. The Ford Sisters traveled locally and regionally prior to their big debut at the 1922

National Baptist Convention, where they sang "Ezekiel Saw the Wheel" and "I'm in His Care." The successful engagement gained the sisters an even larger following, yet the group fell apart as the sisters married and took time off to give birth and raise children.

With the encouragement of her family, Willie Mae set out on a career as a soloist, journeying from church to church in concert. Her passion for ministry quickly matched her love for song as she journeyed out as one of the first black female traveling soloists, often giving little sermonettes prior to and during songs. In 1929, Willie Mae married James Peter Smith, a small-business owner from New Orleans. To their union were born Willie James and Jacquelyn.

After hearing Willie Mae sing in 1931, Thomas Dorsey invited her to help organize the National Convention of Gospel Choirs and Choruses the following year. Willie Mae soon established a St. Louis chapter of the convention. During the early 1930s, Willie Mae and James adopted Bertha, who would serve as Willie Mae's primary accompanist for the next twenty years. With all of the notoriety, Willie Mae's travels increased along with her responsibilities. In 1936, Dorsey asked if she would serve not only as the director of the soloist bureau for the National Convention of Gospel Choirs and Choruses but also as the principal voice instructor. By 1937, Willie Mae had set a very high standard for soloists as she sang an arrangement of her own composition, "If You Just Keep Still," at the 1937 National Baptist Convention. The 1940s witnessed the prime of her career as she sang all across the country in high demand. In 1950, when her husband James passed away, she returned to St. Louis, leaving all of the traveling and a blooming national career behind.

Willie Mae first accepted her call to ministry in the African Methodist Episcopal Zion Church in 1938, leaving the Baptist church of her childhood in exchange for a more spirit-filled and charismatic experience. She took part in the new rhythms and melodies of the fervent sanctified church, adding testifying and witnessing to her performances, which led to her joining the Church of God Apostolic a year later. Forbidden from preaching or even singing from the pulpit because she was a woman, she continued to sing with conviction and authority, not discouraged by tradition. By the 1950s, Willie Mae was known as an evangelist who was widely sought after. After the death of her husband, Willie Mae was ordained as a minister at the Lively Stone Apostolic Church, an affiliate of the Pentecostal Assemblies of the World (the largest of several Pentecostal–Apostolic denominations).

The widely known yet rarely recorded soloist was a mentor to many. Among her most notable protégées were Brother Joe May (who first called her "Mother

Smith"), Mahalia Jackson ("the Queen of Gospel"), Myrtle Scott, Edna Gallmon Cooke, Martha Bass, the O'Neal Twins, Fannie Foster, Fletcher and Elizabeth Higgins, Genesser Smith, Geneva Gentry, and Lucy Fletcher.

Although Willie Mae did record a few 78-rpm records during the height of her career during the 1940s, her major recordings did not occur until the 1970s, when she recorded a few albums for the Savoy label. Mother Smith was featured in the 1983 documentary *Say Amen, Somebody*, along with her mentor, Thomas Dorsey, and peer, Sallie Martin. In 1988, Willie Mae was awarded the Heritage Award from the National Endowment for the Arts for her longtime contributions as a performer and educator. Her role as an innovator of gospel music in St. Louis earned her a star on the St. Louis Walk of Fame in 1990 (at 6392 Delmar Boulevard). Mother Smith passed away on February 2, 1994, in St. Louis, Missouri, at age 89.

EMMETT G. PRICE III

See also Bass, Martha; Cooke, Edna Gallmon; Dorsey, Thomas; Jackson, Mahalia; Martin, Sallie; May, Joseph "Brother Joe"; National Baptist Convention; National Convention of Gospel Choirs and Choruses

Reference and Further Reading

Boyer, Horace Clarence. *The Golden Age of Gospel*. Urbana and Chicago: University of Illinois Press, 2000 (1995).

Broughton, Viv. *Black Gospel: An Illustrated History of the Gospel Sound*. Dorset, UK: Blandford Press, 1985.

Dargan, William Thomas; Kathy White Bullock. "Willie Mae Ford Smith of St. Louis: A Shaping Influence upon Black Gospel Singing Style." In *This Far by Faith: Readings in African-American Women's Religious Biography*, edited by Judith Weisenfeld and Richard Newman, 32–55. New York: Routledge, 1996.

Nierenberg, George T., director. *Say Amen, Somebody*. United Artists Classics, 1982.

Selected Discography

"Call Him"/"Jesus Is the Name" (1950, Gotham G667).

"Goin' on with the Spirit"/"Pilot, Take My Hand" (1950, Sacred 6015).

Going On with the Spirit (1975, Nashboro 7148).

Mother Smith and Her Children (1989, Spirit Feel LP 1010).

I Am Bound for Canaan Land (Savoy SL 14739).

SMITH'S SACRED SINGERS

Smith's Sacred Singers was a singing group from North Georgia that revolutionized commercial gospel music recording in the 1920s. Their long series of recordings for Columbia and RCA Victor Bluebird included some of the best-selling records of the 1920s—even outselling well-known fiddlers and singers of the age. Their success helped convince the major record companies that there was a large market for Southern gospel music recordings, and their most popular records made a good half-dozens songs into gospel standards.

The organizer of the group was J. Frank Smith (1885–1937), a barber by trade but an early and influential singing-school teacher who settled in Braselton, Georgia, at about the turn of the century. He himself attended singing schools taught by famed local composer John B. Vaughan (not to be confused with James D. Vaughan of Tennessee). By 1926, he had organized a quartet and was regularly traveling down to Atlanta to broadcast over WSB. This attracted the attention of Frank B. Walker, a talent scout for the large Columbia record company, who had arrived in Atlanta in April to begin a series of field recordings for his blues and "Old Familiar Tunes" series. On April 23, in a temporary studio, Walker recorded Smith and his singers.

At this time the group included Smith himself singing lead; the Reverend M. L. Thrasher singing bass; Clyde B. Smith (no relation) singing baritone; and Clarence Cronic, who had an amazingly high voice, doing tenor. A friend of Smith's, Mrs. T. C. Llewellyn, played piano. They sang directly from old shape-note songbooks. Smith chose as his first records "Pictures from Life's Other Side," a John B. Vaughan song dating from 1900, and "Where We'll Never Grow Old," by another Georgian, the Reverend James Cleveland Moore from Paulding County. This first record was released on Columbia (15090) on August 30, 1926; sales were sudden and spectacular. Within sixty days, the Atlanta office alone had sold fifteen thousand copies, and Columbia's publicity people were claiming in ads that Smith's "had made the largest sale since the release of any sacred record ever recorded by the company." Sales were eventually to top 277 thousand—at a time when an average record was selling around five thousand.

Columbia rushed the group back into the studios on November 2 and had them do ten more sides. The amazing run of hits continued; "Shouting on the Hills" and "The Eastern Gate" eventually would sell more than sixty-eight thousand copies, while "Going Down the Valley" would sell some seventy-five thousand copies. Smith himself was starting to get some idea of the effect his records were having; in Braselton, the post office was delivering sacks of fan mail to his house. The quartet itself underwent some important changes; Reverend Thrasher left in 1927 to start his own recording group, and singers Willie Fowler, W. A. Brewer, Charley Hall, and Bob Coker joined up with Smith, who by now had moved to Lawrenceburg. Smith would go on to record some sixty-six sides for

Columbia—more than any other single group. Later, between 1934 and 1936, he rerecorded some of these and others for the budget Bluebird label.

Somewhat like the Carter Family, Smith's role was not to write new songs but to choose old familiar songs, usually dating before the turn of the century, and arrange them in simple, unadorned rural singing styles. In doing so, he reinforced the importance of older Southern gospel songs and established gospel as a valid field for commercial phonograph records.

CHARLES K. WOLFE

SOUL GOSPEL

The term "soul gospel" is used with relative frequency but is rarely defined. Its most common appearances suggest that it is often regarded either as a gospel subgenre, as a cross between gospel and soul, or as a pseudonym for any gospel music that reverberates within the soul (thus encapsulating most of the gospel repertoire.) The ephemeral and unbounded nature of the term reflects the true fluidity within gospel styles and the close relationship between gospel and soul as genres.

Soul gospel, as a style or subgenre, is usually placed as developing a few years into the popularization of the "hard gospel" sound of the 1940s. Jerry Zolten (2003) suggests that soul gospel introduced a slightly more contemplative and lyrical soundscape, with fewer extremities of vocal timbre, a more flexible beat, and an increased subtlety of word placement in relationship to pulse. Up-tempo numbers may be a little less heavily driven, with less frenetic, physical energy, emphasizing instead a more uplifting lyricism. Slower numbers would prevail, however, introducing many of the vocal nuances and elastic expressiveness that would be adapted by Ray Charles to create soul. Despite these guidelines, however, soul gospel is not a subgenre with either the recognition or distinctive qualities attributed to bebop, for example, as a subgenre of jazz.

This is partly due to the ambivalence between music as subgenre or crossover. Since the "invention" of soul in the 1950s, gospel and soul have had a relationship of mutual musical enrichment, troubled by commercial and ideological disjuncture. While gospel has retained its sacred and uncommercialized rigor, its birth child, soul, has enjoyed massive commercial success due to its secular and popularized nature. The story of the gospel singer or group that "crosses over" in the pursuit of fame and economic accolade is painfully familiar within the gospel community and is commonly regarded as a betrayal to the ideals of the church. Numerous gospel/soul stars have experienced troubled relationships with the church for this reason. Aretha Franklin, Sam Cooke, Al Green, Solomon Burke, and Little Richard are among the most prominent. Al Green, at the height of his fame as a soul star in the 1970s, decided to give it up to become a preacher and devote himself to gospel. His final decision was made after falling off the stage at one of his soul concerts. He considered it a sign from God that he must return to the gospel fold.

The similarity between much soul and gospel music—and the constant flux of styles and artists crossing the border between the two—has compounded these ideological difficulties and has made the categorization of artists, styles, and songs a tricky and perhaps pointless task. The clearest distinction between the genres probably lies with the sacred or secular content of the lyrics. Even this, however, can be unclear, with many songs requiring minimal lyrical adaptation to cross from gospel to soul. The ordering of the "soul gospel" label, however, certainly implies that crossover influence is still subsumed within a gospel structure of religious song.

The Grammys display a shifting understanding of soul gospel. They have awarded various Soul Gospel Awards since 1969, but, although the award was initially presented alongside Gospel and Inspiration Gospel awards, there is now no straight Gospel Award, and Soul Gospel, divided into Traditional and Contemporary categories, appears to embrace the central gospel canon. Prominent winners include Edwin Hawkins ("Oh Happy Day," 1969); Shirley Caeser (1972, 1981, 1993, 1994, 1996, and 2000); Aretha Franklin ("Amazing Grace," 1973); Mahalia Jackson ("How I Got Over," 1977); James Cleveland (1975, 1978, and 1981); Al Green ("Precious Lord" and "Higher Plane," both 1982); and Andrae Crouch ("Take Me Back," 1975, 1979, and 1982.)

The later understanding of soul gospel as representative of the entire black gospel tradition is reflected by advertisements for the legendary *Gospel Train* radio show, which uses "soul gospel" synonymously with all black gospel music. It describes itself as a "Program that will endeavor to bring authentic soul gospel in the tradition of the black experience in North America . . . with a vast library from the beginning of the recording industry up to the present day" (*Gospel Train* website). *Gospel Train* highlights a further important element of the "soul" concept: that of a specifically black aesthetic, embedded within the black experience generally (within the blues), and the surviving inviolability of the gospel spirit. As implied by the use of the word "authentic," the *Gospel Train*, far from associating soul gospel with crossover, identifies the "soul" of black music as gospel's central tenet.

HILARY MOORE

See also Caesar, Shirley; Cleveland, James; Cooke, Sam; Crouch, Andrae; Franklin, Aretha; Franklin, Reverend C. L.; Green, Al; Jackson, Mahalia

Reference and Further Reading

Boyer, Horace C.; Lloyd Yearwood. *How Sweet the Sound: the Golden Age of Gospel.* Washington, DC: Elliot & Clark Publishing, 1995.
Grammy Awards website, http://www.grammy.com/awards/.
Headlam, David. "Appropriations of Blues and Gospel in Popular Music." In *Cambridge Companion to Blues and Gospel Music,* edited by Allan Moore. New York: Cambridge University Press, 2003
Robinson, Wally. *Gospel Train* website, http://www.gospel train.com/gospel.html.
Zolten, Jerry. *Great God A'Mighty! The Dixie Humming-birds: Celebrating the Rise of Soul Gospel.* New York: Oxford University Press, 2003.

SOUL STIRRERS

Silas Roy Crain (b. ca. 1911; d. 1996)

One of the most influential and longest-lived African American gospel quartets, the Soul Stirrers was founded in East Texas by Silas Roy Crain, and it enjoyed tremendous popularity during the 1940s and 1950s. Its many outstanding lead singers have included Rebert H. Harris (ca. 1916–2000), Sam Cooke (1931–1964), and Johnnie Taylor (1938–2000).

The "Original" Soul Stirrers

The origination of the Soul Stirrers came in stages through the convergence of multiple groups of gospel singers in East Texas. Silas Roy "Senior" Crain is credited with the foundation of the group. Crain sang with a teenage gospel quartet formed at the Mount Pilgrim Baptist Church in Trinity, Texas, around 1926; the quartet's other members were Reed Love, Bennie Albott (later replaced by El Connie Davis), and Lloyd Bailey. Told by an audience member at one performance that their music had "stirred his soul," the group took the name the Soul Stirrers. When Trinity's lumber mills shut down during the Great Depression, this incarnation of the Soul Stirrers dispersed in search of employment, and Crain moved to Houston around 1930.

Crain became the new baritone of a Houston-based quartet, formed in the late 1920s by Reverend Walter Lee LeBeaux, called the New Pleasant Green Gospel Singers, though only after insisting that they change their name to the Soul Stirrers. A second baritone was subsequently added, making the quartet a quintet: LeBeaux, Edward D. Rundless, Crain, A. L. Johnson, and O. W. Thomas. It is this aggregation that Crain referred to as "the first Soul Stirrers." This group was documented for the Library of Congress in 1936 by folklorist John Lomax.

The Soul Stirrers were influenced by the Birmingham, Alabama, quartet style that established its presence in Texas from the mid-1930s through the relocation of the Famous Blue Jay Singers and the Kings of Harmony to Dallas and Houston, respectively. The intersection of these three seminal groups in the late 1930s established Houston as a hotbed of quartet activity.

The Houston members of the Soul Stirrers were gradually replaced by singers Crain knew from the Trinity area, including bass Jesse Farley in 1936 and tenor Rebert H. Harris in 1937. Between around 1939 and 1948, the quartet made a substantial body of commercial recordings, all but a dozen or so for the Aladdin label in Chicago, where the group moved around 1937. It was during this period that the Stirrers settled on the fixed personnel of Harris, Crain, Farley, and baritones Thomas Bruster, James Medlock, and R. B. Robinson. They earned a reputation as one of the preeminent quartets in the country.

Early Recordings and Rise to Prominence

From early on in their history, the Stirrers employed the "switch lead," beginning a song with one lead singer and then passing off the lead mid-song to a new singer, thereby elevating the energy of the performance. This technique is among the most consequential performance practices popularized (though not necessarily initiated) by the group. Increasingly, the strategic use of contrasts in individual vocal timbre and singing styles became a defining feature of the group's arrangements, which regularly pit the more understated, playfully ambling approach of Medlock against Harris's exuberant high tenor. This can be heard to great effect on recordings such as "One Day" and "A Little Talk with Jesus." On their later recordings for Los Angeles's Specialty label, with whom they signed in 1950, Harris's setup man was hard gospel veteran Paul Foster (for example, on "I'm Gonna Move in the Room with the Lord"). The Stirrers were at the forefront of the transition from ensemble-dominated quartet performances to an emphasis on the lead singer as charismatic front man.

The Stirrers used the switch lead to exploit the verse–chorus form of the newer blues-tinged gospel compositions flooding out of Chicago during the

1930s and 1940s. These songs were already being pro-moted nationally by soloists such as Sallie Martin and Mahalia Jackson. But the Soul Stirrers were among the very first quartets to make these compositions—especially those by Thomas A. Dorsey and Kenneth Morris—a centerpiece of their live and studio reperto-ry. Though as late as the early 1940s the group still identified itself as "The Five Soul Stirrers of Houston, Texas," they had already become major contributors to the synergy of composers, performers, music publishers, and recording studios that comprised the influential Chicago school of gospel.

Even as the throng of quartets expanded after World War II, what continued to distinguish the Stir-rers from other top groups was the combination of their pristine harmony singing and their tenor lead, Harris. Harris's lithe melismas, soaring falsetto, rhyth-mically elastic rendering of the melody against the chanting background singers, and artful manipulation of a song's lyrics made him one of the earliest and most distinctive stylists among quartet leads. Among the outstanding recordings on which Harris is featured are "His Eye Is On the Sparrow" and "Does Jesus Care."

The Soul Stirrers achieved a string of extramusical accomplishments almost as impressive as their recor-ded output, becoming in 1940 the first gospel quartet to have its own weekly radio show and performing on the White House lawn for Franklin Delano Roosevelt and Winston Churchill. Back in Texas, the group had already become one of the earliest full-time profession-al, nationally touring gospel quartets; in Chicago they actively booked and promoted major gospel quartet programs. In the late 1940s the Stirrers cofounded the National Quartet Convention, which sought to pre-serve the religious function of gospel quartet singing but also helped working quartets develop musically and professionally.

The Sam Cooke Years

In September 1950, Harris, citing dismay over the growing secularization of the gospel world and a grueling touring schedule, left the Soul Stirrers while still in his mid-thirties. His chosen replacement was Sam Cooke, the nineteen-year-old lead singer of the Highway QCs, a young Chicago-based quartet that apprenticed under, performed with, and occasionally subbed for the Stirrers.

The Soul Stirrers achieved their greatest commer-cial success during Cooke's tenure. Recordings such as "Nearer to Thee" and "Jesus Gave Me Water" sold tens of thousands of copies, enormous at the

time for a gospel release. This was in no small part due to the boom in black gospel music's popularity in the mid-1950s; in addition to the vast increase in the number of labels recording gospel, Specialty estab-lished its own booking agency, Herald Attractions, which it used to showcase its impressive roster of gospel acts, including the Stirrers, sometimes in front of audiences of as large as ten thousand. But equally significant were Cooke's talents as a singer, songwrit-er, and charismatic stage presence. His youthful good looks and sensitivity to popular music trends helped gospel music extend its appeal to a new teenaged fan base.

Despite the different character of Cooke's and Harris's respective vocal instruments, the younger singer's phrasing and melodic vocabulary was pro-foundly indebted to—and at times clearly derivative from—Harris's. Over time, however, the Stirrers' repertory (arranged primarily by Crain) catered to Cooke's distinctive strengths as a singer. Although the group continued to regularly feature Foster, many of their switch-lead gospel blues tunes gradu-ally gave way to vehicles for Cooke, for example, narrative "story songs" such as "Touch the Hem of His Garment" or quasi-ballads such as "Jesus Wash Away My Troubles," marked by spacious, subtly pop-inflected melodic lines with gently unfolding melismas and supported by smooth, doo-wop–style backing vocals.

Recordings during these years reflect other chang-es in gospel quartet performance: The Stirrers' February 2, 1952, session was their first to use instru-mental accompaniment, and on subsequent record-ings they experimented with various combinations of bass and snare drums, piano, organ, upright bass, and guitar. Leroy Crume became the group's full-time guitar accompanist and baritone harmony singer in 1955. Just as the quartet drew on secular music styles, numerous popular music groups—including the Temptations, the Four Tops, and the O'Jays—claimed the Soul Stirrers as primary influences.

Recent History

Cooke quit the Soul Stirrers in 1957 to record popular music; Crain, the Stirrers' founder, left shortly there-after to become Cooke's road manager. As with Harris when he departed the group, Cooke's eventual replacement was a nineteen-year-old singer from the Highway QCs, Johnnie Taylor. Taylor sang with the group for two years, sharing lead duties with Foster. He departed the group in 1960 to become a full-time preacher, then in turn left the ministry a year later—at the coaxing of Cooke—to cross over to popular music.

With the exodus of many gospel singers to popular music, the postwar black gospel music industry's commercial heyday waned; this reality was emphatically confirmed when the Soul Stirrers were dropped by Specialty in 1959. The quartet was quickly signed by Cooke's new label, SAR Records, which recorded the group from 1959 to 1963. Arthur Crume took over as the Stirrers' guitarist and baritone when his brother Leroy left the group in 1965. Other notable Stirrers leads have been Jimmy Outler, Willie Rogers, and Martin Jacox.

The Soul Stirrers ultimately split into two groups: one managed by Arthur Crume and the other under the leadership of Rogers. Highlights in recent decades include participation in the 1983 premiere of *The Gospel at Colonus* and induction into the Rock and Roll (1989), International Gospel Music (2000), and Vocal Group (2000) halls of fame. The Soul Stirrers' recordings from the 1950s were featured in the Coen Brothers 2004 remake of the film *The Ladykillers*.

MARK BURFORD

See also Cooke, Sam; Dorsey, Thomas; Gospel Quartets; Highway QCs; Morris, Kenneth; Specialty Records Company

Reference and Further Reading

Crain, S. R. *The Changing Faces and Places of the Soul Stirrers, 1926–1956*, edited by Travis Kitchens. Lufkin, TX: Sempco Publishing Company, 1990.

Feathers, Amelia. "The Soul Stirrers: Anchoring Traditional Gospel Music." *Blues Access* 28 (Winter 2002): 26–28.

Funk, Ray. "The Soul Stirrers." *Rejoice* (Winter 1987): 12–20.

———. Liner notes to the Soul Stirrers, *Shine on Me* (1992, Specialty SPCD-7013-2).

Guralnick, Peter. Liner notes to *Sam Cooke's SAR Records Story* (1994, ABKO 2231).

Heilbut, Anthony. *The Gospel Sound: Good News and Bad Times*. New York: Limelight Editions, 1997.

Hildebrand, Lee; Opal Nations. Liner notes to the Soul Stirrers, *Heaven Is My Home* (1993, Specialty SPCD-7040-2).

Reich, Howard. "Inspired Gospel Beat." *Chicago Tribune* (January 8, 1997): 1, 3 (Entertainment section).

Seroff, Doug. "On the Battlefield: Gospel Quartets in Jefferson County, Alabama." In *Repercussions: A Celebration of African American Music*, edited by Geoffrey Haydon and Dennis Marks, 30–53. London: Century Publishing, 1985.

Wolff, Daniel; with S. R. Crain, Clifton White, and G. David Tenenbaum. *You Send Me: The Life and Times of Sam Cooke*. New York: William Morrow, 1995.

Discography

Resting Easy (1966, Checker LPS-10021).
Shine On Me (1992, Specialty SPCD-7013-2).
Heaven Is My Home (1993, Specialty SPCD-7040-2).
Sam Cooke's SAR Records Story (1994, ABKO 2231).
He's My Rock: Their Early Sides (2000, P-Vine PCD 5594/5).
Sam Cooke with the Soul Stirrers (2002, Specialty 3SPCD-4437-2).

SOUTHERN CALIFORNIA COMMUNITY CHOIR

James Cleveland (b. December 5, 1932; d. February 9, 1991)

The creation of gospel choir genius James Cleveland, the Southern California Community Choir is easily the world's most recognizable gospel choir as well as one its foremost gospel groups. If Cleveland single-handedly gave the world a picture of the modern black gospel choir, in the iconic "image of a choir in white robes swinging in unison around a hot rhythm section" as one scholar has suggested, then the Southern California Community Choir was that picture.

Founded in the early 1970s, the Southern California Community Choir has been called "James Cleveland personified." At the top of his profession during the late 1960s, Cleveland was restless and strangely unfulfilled, feeling he had done all there was to do in gospel music. He moved to California, "leaving gospel alone for awhile," as he told an interviewer. Instead, he kept remembering his childhood spent in the choirs of Thomas Dorsey. For several years, he worked with choirs across the country, reinventing the choir sound so recognizable today as a mass gospel choir.

He noticed a discipline in California choirs evolving out of the state's continual influx of influences and talent. It seemed to be rooted in a honed musicianship coming from a long-held tension between tradition and innovation. So he formed the Southern California Community Choir to perfectly match his own talent for tradition and innovation. Cleveland's Southern California Community Choir, along with his Gospel Music Workshop of America, soon became deeply influential on the entire emerging gospel choir tradition in California, especially in Los Angeles.

With its blend of Cleveland's famous pop–soul choir style with the California artistic and cultural fusion, the choir became beloved across music and even film boundaries. Beyond their gospel choir appearances, under Cleveland's leadership they became famous for partnering with such diverse musical performers as Elton John, Aretha Franklin, and Arlo Guthrie, as well as for memorable appearances in Hollywood films, most notably in *The Blues Brothers*. The choir was also the subject of a documentary video of its performance in Jerusalem, entitled *Gospel from the Holy Land*.

Possibly its most influential and timeless recording was the choir's 1972 collaboration with Aretha Franklin, entitled *Amazing Grace: The Complete Gospel Recordings*. The entire album was recorded during two live performances at the New Temple Missionary Baptist Church in Los Angeles. As soon as the album hit the airwaves, it reached most pop music charts' top ten, including *Billboard*'s; received unprecedented reviews in *Rolling Stone* magazine; and became one of the best-selling gospel–pop crossover albums of all time. The album's recording of "Amazing Grace" has become one of the most beloved renditions of the song, winning a 1999 induction into the Grammy Hall of Fame, which honors recordings of "qualitative or historical significance."

Cleveland, himself a recipient of five Grammy Awards, won several of them with the choir he created, most notably for his rendition of "In the Ghetto" in 1975 and, most poignantly, for his Southern California Community Choir's album *Having Church* after his death in 1991.

LYNDA RUTLEDGE STEPHENSON

See also Cleveland, James; Los Angeles, Gospel in

Reference and Further Reading

Ankeny, Jason. "Reverend James Cleveland and the Southern California Community Choir." Malaco Music Group website, http://www.malaco.com (accessed November 2004).

Brown, Mick. "Pastor Cleveland, Superstar." *Manchester Guardian Weekly* (January 11, 1981): 19.

California Soul: Music of African Americans in the West, edited by Jacqueline DjeDje and Eddie S. Meadows. Berkeley: University of California Press, 1998.

Collins, Lisa. "James Cleveland Dead at 59; He was Dubbed 'King' of Gospel Music." *Billboard* (February 23, 1991): 4.

Darden, Robert. *People Get Ready! A New History of Black Gospel Music*. New York: Continuum, 2004.

DjeDje, Jacqueline Cogdell "The California Black Gospel Music Tradition: A Confluence of Musical Styles and Cultures." In *California Soul: Music of African Americans in the West*, edited by Jacqueline Cogdell DjeDje and Eddie S. Meadows, 141–143. Berkeley: University of California Press, 1998.

"Grammy Awards: James Cleveland and the Southern California Community Choir." Grammy Awards website, http://www.grammys.com/awards.

"Grammy Hall of Fame Award." Grammy Awards website, http://www.grammy.com/awards/hall_fame.aspx#a.

Harris, Craig. "Southern California Community Choir: Biography." All Music website, http://www.allmusic.com (accessed December 2004).

Discography

Amazing Grace (1970, Savoy).

Aretha Franklin: Amazing Grace with James Cleveland and the Southern California Community Choir (Atlantic, 1972).

James Cleveland & the Southern California Community Choir (1978, Savoy, Arista).

Where Is Your Faith (1981, Savoy).

It's a New Day (1987, Savoy).

Breathe on Me (1989, Savoy).

Having Church (1990, Savoy).

Let Your Glory Be Revealed (1993, A&M).

SOUTHERN GOSPEL

The term "Southern gospel" describes the multifaceted genres of vernacular sacred music that have evolved among white Southerners since the late 1800s. Southern gospel has strong ties to its African American counterparts, most notably the spiritual tradition. Black and white Southern Christians also shared other characteristics, such as the use of shape notes to teach music and performances by quartets. Nonetheless, Southern gospel has evolved into its own distinctive genres, such as gospel bluegrass, which remain strong into the twenty-first century.

Although the roots of Southern gospel music clearly lie in the antebellum South, the genres and styles that are today identified as Southern gospel first emerged during Reconstruction. As early as 1879, itinerant teachers representing the A. J. Showalter Company of Dalton, Georgia, had traveled as far as East Texas to conduct singing schools that lasted up to several weeks. During the 1880s, important Southern gospel pioneers such as Tennessean James D. Vaughan attended singing schools, where they learned to sing using a seven-shape-note style of music notation. This "solfège" system used geometric shapes and names for each note in the scale.

Vaughan became enthralled with this music and sang locally for years, forming a quartet with his brothers in the 1890s. In 1902, he moved into publishing with the establishment of the James D. Vaughan Publishing Company. The songbooks he published sold more slowly than he had hoped, so in 1910 Vaughan came up with the idea of sponsoring an all-male gospel quartet to help boost the sales of songbooks. The sales of songbooks increased, but more significantly, the popularity of gospel quartets

Gospel radio program billboard in Georgia. Photo by Frederic Ramsey, Jr. Photo courtesy Frank Driggs Collection.

grew even more quickly. James Vaughan started the Vaughan School of Music in 1911, which further diversified his budding gospel empire.

During the first two decades of the twentieth century, Southern gospel music was largely the realm of nonprofessional and community-based singing by Christians, many of whom were Baptists. Local churches sponsored singing schools, which lasted from one long weekend to several weeks and which enabled ordinary citizens to sing using the solfège method that was fully developed in the Shenandoah Valley of Virginia during the 1870s. Rural communities often held singings on a monthly basis, but eventually the movement gained enough popularity that the smaller communities gathered into conventions.

Reconstruction also saw the rise of gospel composers, whose newly minted songs first gained currency among evangelical Christians. Many of these Northern-born composers, most notably Ira Sankey and Dwight Moody, published songs in compilations that were

printed and disseminated by fledgling companies eager to reach a nationwide audience. These hymn-books, led by Moody's *Gospel Hymns and Sacred Songs* (1875), found a particularly receptive audience in the South. This book not only sold well, it also helped to link the term "gospel" with the various forms of black and white sacred music that developed in the United States following the Civil War. Other songwriters, such as Fanny Crosby, James Rowe, and Robert Lowry, also composed and published many gospel hymns during this period.

The nascent Southern gospel movement received an important boost in the early twentieth century with the rise of Pentecostalism. Following a wave of revivals that swept the Midwest between 1901 and 1905, the Azusa Street Mission in Los Angeles, California, became the focal point for this spiritual movement, which cut across racial lines. This emotional style of sacred worship and singing found an audience in the South at about the same time that blues, gospel, and jazz were emerging as distinctive musical genres. Pentecostalism found a strong base of support in the South among both black and white Christians, and it continues to inform Southern gospel music to this day.

Although hymnals had brought newly composed gospel hymns to eager congregants, the emergence of radio and sound recordings in the 1920s brought about the commercialization of Southern gospel music. It also permitted quicker dissemination of music and musical genres. Entrepreneurs such as the Vaughans in Tennessee and the Texas-based Stamps–Baxter Publishing Company quickly realized that radio and recordings could bring their message and music to a wider audience much more quickly than hymnals and singing schools, and they eagerly embraced the new technology. By 1930, Southern gospel groups as diverse as the Stamps–Baxter Quartet, the Turkey Mountain Singers, and the Phipps Holiness Singers had been recorded by the RCA Victor Company. The power of radio is underscored by the fact that James Vaughan placed WOAN (Lawrenceburg, Tennessee), which featured live daily broadcasts by his gospel quartet, on the air early in 1923. Other early Southern radio stations, such as WSB in Atlanta and Nashville's WSM, also included Southern gospel music—performed live in the studio—as part of their daily broadcast schedules.

Southern gospel flourished during the 1930s and 1940s. Hundreds of family groups sang at local churches and monthly gatherings. Occasionally a group such as Bill & Charlie Monroe brought their tight harmony singing of songs such as "God Holds the Future in His Hands" and "What Would You Give in Exchange for Your Soul?" to a large audience via the mass media. Singing schools began to diminish in importance as radio and recordings disseminated Southern gospel to an ever more receptive audience, but the schools continued to be an important part of Southern rural life, especially in the Southeastern states.

The rise of quartets, the professionalism of Southern gospel music, and the development of gospel bluegrass continued during the years following the Depression. Quartets sponsored by the James D. Vaughan Music Publishing Company had begun touring as early as 1910. They not only brought sacred music to audiences across the South, they also helped to sell thousands of copies of Vaughan songbooks. Quartets became even more popular following their media exposure, and by the mid-1930s there were nearly a dozen Vaughan-affiliated groups, including the Vaughan Melody Girls, the Vaughan Office Quartet, and the Speer Family. Late in 1927, the Stamps Quartet, organized and led by Frank Stamps, recorded "Give the World a Smile" for RCA Victor. This recording not only launched what remains a Southern gospel standard (written only two years earlier by Otis Deaton and M. L. Yandell), it also helped to promote the quartet to the extent that they were soon able to eke out a full-time living from performing Southern gospel.

Some twenty years later, dozens of semiprofessional and professional gospel quartets, such as the John Daniel Quartet, the Blackwood Brothers Quartet, the Swanee River Boys, and the Statesmen Quartet, were regularly performing from Texas to Maryland. Many of these groups enjoyed more widespread popularity in Detroit, central Pennsylvania, and other sections of the United States to which white Southerners had migrated. By the early 1950s, quartets—both black and white—were in demand across the land. They recorded for the myriad of small independent labels that emerged following the end of World War II, and many broadcast over local and regional radio stations. In Texas, groups such as the Stamps–Baxter Quartet participated in "all-night sings," which began in 1938 and continued into the 1950s.

During the late 1940s, nascent bluegrass groups such as Bill Monroe and the Bluegrass Boys and the Stanley Brothers naturally incorporated gospel material into their repertoire. Having grown up in the South, Monroe (Western Kentucky) and Ralph and Carter Stanley (Southwestern Virginia) were raised on the gospel music that they absorbed through the Baptist Church. Steeped in shape-note singing as well as the quartet tradition, gospel bluegrass usually featured four-part harmony singing as well as the high tenor so commonly heard in secular bluegrass.

Within a decade, gospel bluegrass had developed into its own genre. A group such as the Lewis Family from North Georgia was billed as the "First Family of Gospel Bluegrass" and focused exclusively on performing sacred bluegrass music. There are currently dozens of bluegrass gospel bands across the United States as well as bluegrass bands, such as Doyle Lawson and Quicksilver, the Country Gentlemen, and Nickel Creek, which often feature gospel but that do not focus exclusively on the genre.

"Southern gospel" continues to encompass a wide variety of vernacular genres; artists as diverse as Billy Graham, the Kingsmen, and the LaFevres all come under its banner. Even a more obscure, older genre, such as Sacred Harp singing (which remains popular in Georgia and Alabama), is considered to be Southern gospel. Ironically, Southern gospel can now be heard throughout the United States, especially in areas such as Northeastern Ohio and Detroit, where Southerners have migrated since World War II.

KIP LORNELL

Reference and Further Reading

Cusic, Don. *The Sound of Light: A History of Gospel and Christian Music*. Milwaukee, WI: Hal Leonard Music, 2002.

Goff, James, R. *Close Harmony: A History of Southern Gospel*. Chapel Hill: University of North Carolina Press, 2002.

Johnson, Kenneth M. *The Johnson Family Singers: We Sang for Our Supper*. Lexington: University Press of Mississippi, 1997.

SOUTHERN HARMONY, THE

Probably the most popular tunebook published by a Southerner before the Civil War, this volume's full title was *The Southern Harmony, and Musical Companion: Containing a Choice Collection of Tunes, Hymns, Psalms, Odes, and Anthems, etc.* It was initially issued in New Haven, Connecticut, in 1835, and went through five editions during the next nineteen years. Its compiler was William Walker (b. May 6, 1809; d. September 24, 1875), a native of Cross Keys, South Carolina.

In about 1827, Walker's family moved to Spartanburg, South Carolina, by which time the eighteen-year-old had received his only formal education. He had also joined the Baptist church and determined that praising the Lord on stringed instruments and with the human voice was a necessity. Therefore, he took upon himself the task of perfecting "the vocal mode of praise" that led to his compiling *The Southern Harmony*. Walker's book sold more than six hundred thousand copies by 1866, and he chose to benefit from its popularity by adding the initials A. S. H. (author of *The Southern Harmony*) to his signature. This was also to distinguish him from other William Walkers in the region; there were two in Spartanburg at the time.

Walker opened a bookstore in his home town and participated in various church and religious organizations. In 1846, he brought out a second collection, *Southern and Western Pocket Harmonist*, which, like his first book, was in four-shape notation. This second volume was smaller and contained more revival spirituals than the earlier work. When he brought out his *Christian Harmony* in 1867, he bowed to the demands of "respectable" sacred song composers and used a seven-shape notation, but one of his own invention. He also included more European melodies and pieces by Lowell Mason and his followers. Walker produced one final collection, *Fruits and Flowers* (1873), and it was also in his unique seven-shape notation. *Christian Harmony* and *Southern Harmony* are both still in use; Benton, Kentucky, has had an annual "Big Singing" in the *Southern Harmony* tradition since 1884.

The initial edition of *The Southern Harmony* contained mostly American tunes, but, as subsequent editions appeared, European melodies and pieces by the "good music" American composers replaced them. Six European numbers and one tune from the "better music" school appeared in the 1835 edition of *The Southern Harmony*. These numbers increased to twelve and four out of thirty-nine melodies added to the first of two 1847 editions; two British tunes and two each by Lowell Mason and Thomas Hastings appeared in the second 1847 edition. The 1854 edition deleted twenty-four old tunes, mostly Southern or pre–Lowell Mason Northern tunes, replacing them with one British melody and eleven that were either arranged or composed by Lowell Mason.

Several melodies appearing in *The Southern Harmony* showed up in later collections that evidently borrowed from Walker's compilation. For example, fourteen items found in the Walker book appeared in W. H. Swan and M. L. Swan's *Harp of Columbia* (1848). This practice, which probably was a good indicator of popularity, was commonplace among songbook compilers, as evidenced by Walker's own use of melodies found in *Kentucky Harmony* (1816), Jeremiah Ingalls's *Christian Harmony* (1805), and others. Some of the borrowing he did is documented by the numbers for which he claimed composer credits. These include "Bruce's Address," which had earlier appeared in Joshua Leavitt's *The Christian Lyre* (1831), "Sweet Rivers," which was previously found in William Moore's *Columbian Harmony* (1825) and in Ananias Davisson's *A Supplement to the Kentucky Harmony* (1820), and "Parting Glass," which originally was published in Jeremiah Ingalls's *The Christian Harmony* (1805). These few examples sufficiently make the point that Walker was basically an arranger rather than a composer.

W. K. McNEIL

Reference and Further Reading

Hatchett, Marion J. *A Companion to The New Harp of Columbia*. Knoxville, TN: 2003.

Jackson, George Pullen. *White Spirituals in the Southern Uplands: The Story of the Fasola Folk, Their Songs, Singings, and "Buckwheat Notes."* Chapel Hill: University of North Carolina Press, 1933.

Reynolds, William J. *Companion to the Baptist Hymnal*. Nashville, TN: Broadman, 1976.

SPECIALTY RECORDS COMPANY

Specialty Records, a white-owned company based in Los Angeles, was established in 1946 by Art Rupe (born Arthur Goldberg in 1917 in Greensburg,

Pennsylvania). During his youth, Rupe often visited a local black Baptist church to listen to the music. This early interest in African American culture probably contributed to his career as a producer of both sacred and secular black music. After attending Miami University in Oxford, Ohio, Rupe moved to Hollywood in 1939 and was a student at UCLA for a short time before becoming involved in the entertainment industry.

In 1944, Rupe became a partner with Bob Scherman in Atlas Records. Although Atlas had several noted rhythm and blues artists under contract (for example, Nat "King" Cole and Charles Brown), the record company folded. This experience made Rupe realize that he could not compete with the major record companies on their own turf. Before starting a new label, Rupe analyzed the black music scene in Los Angeles by going to Central Avenue (the heart of the black community) and purchasing "race" records that were popular among blacks. As a result of doing this, Rupe decided to focus on ethnic and specialty music that major companies had abandoned because of the wartime shortage of shellac. The first artists he recorded on his new label, called Juke Box, performed rhythm and blues. Although the recordings did well, Rupe sold his interests in the label to his copartners (because of disagreements) and established Specialty Records.

When Rupe started Specialty, he continued to focus on secular music and did not begin recording gospel until 1948. After his first record—by the Pilgrim Travelers—sold well, Rupe started recording other gospel artists who were either based in Los Angeles or traveled to the city. Among these were Alex Bradford, Sister Wynona Carr, the Chosen Gospel Singers, the Detroiters, Bessie Griffin and the Consolaters, J. Earle Hines, Brother Joe May, the Original Gospel Harmonettes, the Soul Stirrers, and the Swan Silvertones. Specialty was also involved in the promotion of concert tours through Herald Attractions, with Lillian Cumber, a black female gospel booking-agency manager. Specialty used its subsidiary, Venice Music, to publish songs recorded and produced on its label. Generally, Kenneth Morris, of the publishing firm Martin and Morris Music Studio of Chicago, arranged and exclusively distributed the songs recorded by Venice.

Specialty's recordings of gospel ended in the late 1950s, but the company continued to record secular music. Starting in 1970, Rupe reactivated his catalog and occasionally released classic albums by sacred and secular artists. In 1990, the company was sold to Fantasy Records, which is based in the San Francisco Bay area.

JACQUELINE COGDELL DJEDJE

See also Bradford, Alex; May, Joseph "Brother Joe"; Morris, Kenneth; Original Gospel Harmonettes; Pilgrim Travelers; Soul Stirrers, Swan Silvertones

Reference and Further Reading

DjeDje, Jacqueline Cogdell "The California Black Gospel Music Tradition: A Confluence of Musical Styles and Cultures." In *California Soul: Music of African Americans in the West*, edited by Jacqueline Cogdell DjeDje and Eddie S. Meadows, 124–175. Berkeley: University of California Press, 1998.
———. "Gospel Music in the Los Angeles Black Community." *Black Music Research Journal* 9 (Spring 1989): 35–79.
———. "Los Angeles Composers of African American Gospel Music: The First Generations." *American Music: A Quarterly Journal Devoted to All Aspects of American Music and Music in America* 11 (Winter 1993): 412–457.
Goldberg, D. K. "Art Rupe's Specialty Records." History of Rock 'n' Roll website, http://www.history-of-rock.com/specialty.htm (accessed December 27, 2003).

SPEER FAMILY, THE

George Thomas "Dad" Speer (b. March 10, 1891; d. September 7, 1966)
Lena Brock Speer (b. November 4, 1899; d. October 6, 1967)
Pearl Speer Claborn (b. August 17, 1902; d. March 1979)
Logan Claborn (b. November 12, 1896; d. February 1981)

A truly bedrock group in the creation and popularity of Southern gospel music was the Speer Family, who for more than seven decades toured professionally in addition to making broadcasts and recordings.

The original group grew out of the marriage union of two singing families, the Speers and the Brocks. George Thomas "Dad" Speer (b. March 10, 1891; d. September 7, 1966) was born near Fayetteville, Georgia, and was raised in Southern Alabama, alongside siblings who, like him, could raise the rafters with their singing voices. He began studying music in 1908 and, by 1912, was himself a singing-school instructor and published songwriter. After military service took him to France in World War I, Tom Speer settled down on a farm in Winston County, Alabama, at Double Springs, at least when he was not teaching at singing schools throughout the South.

At one of these "singing conventions" in Lawrenceburg, Tennessee, he met Lena Brock (b. November 4, 1899; d. October 6, 1967) of Cullman County, Alabama. Her father, C. A. Brock, managed Athens

The Speer Family. Photo courtesy Frank Driggs Collection.

Music Co. in Athens, Alabama, and her brother, Dwight Brock, was later the pianist for the original Stamps All Star Quartet and much later the general manager of Stamps–Baxter Music.

Tom and Lena married, and in February 1921, weeks after the birth of their first child, Ben, they gave up on farming for good and followed the Lord's call into full-time gospel music work by launching the first family quartet, adding Tom's sister Pearl (b. August 17, 1902; d. March 1979) and her husband Logan Claborn (b. November 12, 1896; d. February 1981). One of the first gospel quartets to feature women, this group stayed together for about five years, at which time the Claborns, tired of the travel, dropped out, and one by one the young children of Tom and Lena Speer were brought in—son Brock (1920–1999), daughters Rosa Nell (b. 1922) and Mary Tom (b. 1925), and son Ben (b. 1930)—making the Speers basically a family sextet until 1948, when Rosa Nell married and left the group (Mary Tom did likewise in 1954). Various family members played accordion, guitar, and ukulele for accompaniment, and the roles of the children changed as they grew up: Brock became the bass and concert emcee, Mary Tom the alto, Ben the lead, and Rosa Nell the pianist.

The family moved its base of operations in 1930 to Lawrenceburg to work for the James D. Vaughan Publishing Co. In 1941, they moved to Montgomery, Alabama, where they worked twice daily radio programs on WSFA, their morning show following a program by an aspiring young local honky-tonk singer named Hank Williams. Their final base of operations was Nashville, where they moved in 1946.

Dad Speer handled the bookings as the Speer Family traveled upward of fifty thousand miles per year to auditoriums, schoolhouses, and churches across the Eastern United States. They first made records for Bullet, the famous Nashville independent, in 1947, and during their heyday had major label contracts with Columbia and RCA Victor. Brock and Ben even moonlighted with vocal background work on countless country and pop records made in Nashville, including some of Elvis Presley's earliest sessions.

The Speers began a long-running morning TV program on Nashville's WLAC-TV in 1954, making them pioneers in bringing Southern gospel music to television, and as before, they had transcribed radio programs to do. Brock Speer's wife Faye replaced Rosa Nell as pianist when she left, and Joyce Black joined at Mary Tom's departure. Dad Speer dropped out because of ill health in 1963, at which time Mom left to care for him, briefly returning between Dad's death in September 1966 and her own in October 1967. The female singing parts since then have been handled by a succession of talented ladies, whose tenures were usually brief because of marriage and the coming of children. Among them were Ann Sanders Downing, Sue Chenault Dodge (thrice the GMA Female Vocalist of the Year), Jeanne Johnson, and Karen Apple. Arranger Harold Lane was a twenty-year group member (mid-1960s to mid-1980s), and in the early 1990s the group included pianist Tim Parton and singer/songwriter Daryl Williams.

Ben Speer's interests turned from performing to audio engineering and music publishing. Like his uncle Dwight Brock, he was general manager of Stamps–Baxter Music Company, and he still promotes summer youth singing schools for Stamps–Baxter. Since 1946 he has operated Ben Speer Music Company, and in 1997 he returned to performing part-time when the reconstituted Speer Family became once again an all-family group, as Rosa Nell and Mary Tom, long widowed, returned to sing with their brothers and to run the family's Nashville offices. Brock Speer died in March 1999, and Ben, in addition to his other work, became at about that time musical director for the popular Bill Gaither Homecoming Video Series, on which the veteran Speer Family was prominently featured.

Small wonder the Speer Family can look back on a host of accomplishments. Besides the full group itself, four members have been elected individually to the Gospel Music Hall of Fame: Dad in 1970, Mom in 1971, Brock (a one-time GMA president) in 1974, and Ben in 1995. Among their Dove Awards received were Group of the Year each year from 1970 through 1978 and Album of the Year in 1976 and 1977.

RONNIE PUGH

Reference and Further Reading

Becker, Paula. *Let the Song Go On: Fifty Years of Gospel Singing with the Speer Family*. Nashville, TN: Impact Books, 1971.
Blackwell, Lois S. *The Wings of the Dove: The Story of Gospel Music in America*. Introduction By Brock Speer. Norfolk, VA: Donning, 1978.
Cusic, Don. *The Sound of Light: A History of Gospel and Christian Music*. Milwaukee, WI: Hal Leonard, 2002.

Selected Discography

75th Anniversary (K-Tel CD 022775960327).
He's Still in the Fire (Homeland CD 045371891123).
The Speer Family Collection (Homeland CD 9708).
Through All the Years (Homeland CD 701122994221).

SPIRIT OF MEMPHIS QUARTET

The Spirit of Memphis Quartette (as they were originally known) began in 1928 as the T. M. & S. Quartet, an amateur group based in South Memphis. The group soon changed its name to reflect the interest in Charles Lindburgh's solo crossing of the Atlantic ocean in his Spirit of St. Louis airplane. During its extended career, the Spirit of Memphis has emphasized change and innovation within the aesthetic limits of African American gospel quartet singing.

By the mid-1930s the Spirit (as they were locally known) began traveling outside the city, expanding their base of support to include churches within a hundred miles of Memphis. These churches, most of which were Baptist, invited them to bring their nicely blended *a cappella* style to rural areas, where they sometimes engaged local groups in contests. By the start of World War II, the Spirit of Memphis was a strong, semiprofessional vocal ensemble that featured such outstanding locally bred singers as James Darling and Earl Malone. Inspired by nationally recognized groups such as the Famous Blue Jay Singers of Birmingham and the Soul Stirrers, the Spirit was contemplating turning professional when World War II's travel limitations forced them to stay close to home.

By 1948, the Spirit of Memphis Quartet had all of the ingredients in place to become a fully professional group. The group then sported some of the best singers in all of gospel music, and its overall lineup was outstanding. Willmer "Little Axe" Broadnax alternated between tenor and lead; Robert Reed focused on tenor; Jethroe Bledsoe and Silas Steele sang both baritone and lead; James Darling managed the group and served as their solid baritone singer; and Earl Malone held forth on bass. The Spirit sang daily over WDIA, the nation's first all–black-oriented radio station. These broadcasts only served to reinforce the group's regional popularity, which was about to expand to a national audience.

The popularity of the Spirit of Memphis Quartet expanded greatly in 1950, when the first of their records for the Cincinnati-based King label helped to bring their talent to a much wider audience. These records, along with the general popularity of gospel music, helped to push the group members to quit their day jobs and become full-time gospel warriors.

Between 1950 and 1956, the Spirit of Memphis was at the top of their chosen field. They traveled an average of two hundred thousand miles annually, most of it in a large touring limo; between April and September 1952, the group's engagements included stops in San Antonio, El Paso, Phoenix, San Francisco, Topeka, Washington, DC, and New York City. The Spirit of Memphis appeared with the top groups in black gospel quartet singing, including the Pilgrim Travelers, the Dixie Hummingbirds, and the Fairfield Four. In 1952, they signed an even more lucrative contract with the mercurial Don Robey of Duke/Peacock Records. This Houston-based label had a strong roster of black artists, ranging from Bobby "Blue" Bland to the Five Blind Boys of Mississippi, and better distribution than King Records. As a result, strong performances such as "Surely, Surely, Amen"

reached a wider audience than they had touched on their previous label.

By this time the group had expanded to include instrumental accompaniment (usually a guitar and drums), which followed a larger trend among African American gospel quartets. Depending on the song, the Spirit of Memphis also featured three outstanding lead singers—Little Axe, Silas Steel, and Jet Bledsoe—who were among the best in all of gospel music. Like other similar groups, the Spirit of Memphis had expanded beyond their original four-voice format, now featuring six or seven singers. Most of these singers fulfilled more roles, both in a support role as well as in the capacity as a lead singer.

By the end of the 1950s, the Spirit of Memphis and most of their contemporaries had run their course as a fully professional vocal ensemble. Popular interest in quartet singing had waned, and the Spirit of Memphis returned to their home base. They have recorded sporadically since they stopped recording for Peacock in 1958 but have never stopped performing. Several of their prominent early members, most notably James Darling and Earl Malone, passed away in the 1980s. Nonetheless, the Spirit of Memphis remains a popular and historically significant group in the mid-South, still singing and praising God into the twenty-first century.

KIP LORNELL

Reference and Further Reading

Lornell, Kip. *Happy in the Service of the Lord: African American Sacred Vocal Harmony Quartets in Memphis.* Knoxville: University of Tennessee Press, 1995.

Discography

When Mother's Gone (1990, Gospel Jubilee Records RF-1404).
Travelin' On (1998, Hmg Records 6507).

SPIRITUALS

The most powerful influence on church music in the nineteenth, twentieth, and twenty-first centuries has been African American spirituals. Spirituals brought a new genre of music to the world, which has influenced gospel, big bands, jazz, blues, rock 'n' roll, hip-hop, and soul music.

Between 1609 and 1770, more than twelve million African slaves were captured and brought to the Southern states of America. The slaves worked under harsh conditions on plantations for white slave masters. They were stripped of their African identities, family ties, and religious rituals, but the slave masters allowed them to sing work songs. The messages of liberation and freedom in these work songs became very important to the slaves' mental stability. The songs allowed the work to be done at a faster pace, saving the white slave master money and forcing the slaves to do more work in a shorter span of time. Slave masters set a rhythm to do hard tasks. What was overlooked by the slave master was that fifty percent of the songs were about their lives and could not be interpreted by the slave master.

Many of these songs had prayer and praise that were Africanized versions of Christianity. The poetry and musicality of the prayers and praise songs are different from other styles of music. There are no identifiable authors. All of the spirituals are of Southern origin. This is music of rural roots; the repletion reveals the oral tradition of the South. Most of the songs are sung *a cappella* or with a handmade instrument such as a bottle to blow sounds or an object to give the beat of the music. The repetitive character found in spirituals serves as a memory device to help the singers remember the words and tones. West African music has this repetitive style of music.

Many of the songs have traveling, many use nature to give directions, and they are testimonial showing evidence of God's encounter with their lives. An example of a spiritual work song is the "Gandy Dancers" from Birmingham, Alabama, the name derived from the Gandy Manufacturing Company, a maker of railroad tools, equipment, and accessories. The term "dancers" applied to the dance-like movement the black men made while laying and readjusting the tracks. The men laid railroad tracks by whistles, chants, and work songs. They lifted, hammered, and moved rails to the rhythm. They would breathe, groan, and moan at the end of each line, as, for instance, in the song entitled "Toiling to See King Jesus":

I am toiling to see the Master, King Jesus [breathe with groans and moans]
I am toiling to see my family and friends [breathe with groans and moans]
I am toiling to see some kindness and rest [breathe with groans and moans]
I am toiling to see the river, over Jordan [breathe with groans and moans]

These spiritual work songs allow a pause to breathe. They learned the labor task by the beats, which were unique, giving them the ability to express deep emotions for their stress and experiences. Many of the early spirituals were healing songs, such as "Don't Drink Water that Is Standing Still." These Negro folk songs taught the children in the fields how to protect themselves. Neither the adult slaves nor the children could read.

Songs and rhythms from Africa, mixed with what the slaver owners allowed them to say, formed messages to prevent capture, since all assemblies were banned and drums could not be played because they could carry messages. The first Christian music was believed to have been sung by Negro house slave servants. They were hymns by John and Charles Wesley (brothers) and Isaac Watts. The hymns were brought to America during the Wesleyan Methodist Evangelical movement in 1766. Slaves mixed their work songs, feelings, interpretation of Christianity, and hymns, producing what became known as Negro spirituals.

The song "Tis the Old Ship of Zion, Get on Board," in the slave masters' thinking, was about taking slaves from life to death. Christianity taught the slave to feel safe in God's waters. To the slaves, this song expressed the desire to ride a boat or train that had landed many a thousand slaves to freedom; the trip would not be dangerous, because God would guide them to safety. The slave ships that had brought them to America were evil, but there would not be danger in God's waters as they traveled back to Africa, their homeland. The slave master, sometimes called the overseer, could not interpret moans and groans and many of the African dialects.

Many of the Negro spirituals were spontaneously put together in the fields as slaves worked. They sang about the work, the fields, and the hot sun beating down on them. The African musical scales were unknown to Europeans; therefore, the timing and poetry found in African American music was misinterpreted by whites. The spirituals were synchronized with rhythmic chanting. The arms, feet, and body moved with the words. This tradition of chants and dancing has continued in Holiness Pentecostal churches, known as the "holy dance." The term "overseer" is used in black churches to depict a leader of a region. The raising of the hand and pointing is used by blacks in Southern churches to denote permission to be excused; this sign was used in slavery to get permission from the overseer to move out of the field.

"Steal Away to Jesus" and "Swin' Low Sweet Chariot" were spirituals used by Harriet Tubman (ca. 1821–1913; known as "the Black Moses") to help slaves escape to freedom; the movement was known as the "underground railroad." Reverend Richard Allen (1760–1831), who organized the African Methodist Episcopal Church, compiled the first African American hymnal in 1801. It was a mixture of old English hymns and Negro spirituals.

After the Civil War many African traditions surfaced, particularly in the Deep South. In 1871, the Fisk Jubilee Singers from Fisk University in Nashville,

Tennessee, sang Negro spirituals "tailored" for a white audience. They traveled to England to sing for Queen Victoria. The Fisk Singers gave birth to the jubilee style of unaccompanied singing, introducing jubilee quartets without losing the moan and groan sounds of slavery.

Many educated African Americans felt spiritual songs would make them proud of their heritage of slavery. On the other hand, blacks believed that "swinging spirituals" were against their religious beliefs and demoted their African American heritage. During the 1930s, Thomas A. Dorsey (1899–1993), "the Father of Gospel Music," spoke out to keep and preserve spirituals and gospel songs from the dance bands. Rosetta Tharpe (1915–1973), a national gospel singer, and many others were told that they were "taking spirituals and offering them as a sacrifice to the god Money!" Mr. Alto Peeples from Florida appealed to Louis Armstrong (1901–1971) to stop rearranging spirituals and gospel music such as "When the Saints Go Marching In" to satisfy the emotions of a gang of jitterbugs.

Sanctified evangelists such as Reverend Utah Smith, singing "Two Wings," and church singers focused their efforts marketing spiritual music on black street corners and at neighborhood churches to preserve spiritual music. Race records for Negroes were marketed to black consumers regardless of religion; the promoters wanted the money. During the late 1930s, the sale of recordings was increased by the emergence of radio. In the 1940s, commercial entertainment and sheet music companies increased the sale of Negro spirituals. The golden era of gospel music from 1945 to 1955 made religious spirituals and gospel music a high-commodity item, with live performances presented at ball fields, tents, auditoriums, and large churches. African American male harmony quartet groups were billboard hits. These quartet groups harmonized songs and introduced the guitar into worship services. Women's groups became well known, such as the Clara Ward Singers, the Angelic Gospel Singers, and many others.

The Civil Rights Movement of the 1950s and 1960s allowed audiences to hear and buy more spirituals and gospel music commercially. African American artists such as Mahalia Jackson (1911–1972), the "Queen of Gospel Music," provided proof that talented musicians did not have to leave the church to be successful. Spirituals were appreciated with joy during the 1950s, with various rhythms, moans, and moods. Curtis Mayfield (d. 1999) wrote "People Get Ready." The Impressions, a black soul music group, recorded "People Get Ready." It made the *Billboard* charts on March 25, 1965. As a successful gospel song, it became a crossover hit on the *Billboard* charts. It is laced with spiritual and biblical language:

> People get ready
> There's a train a'comin'
> You don't need no baggage
> Just get on board
>
> People get ready
> For the train to Jordan
> Picking up passengers from coast to coast
> Faith is key . . . .

Mayfield's Chicago religious upbringing influenced the lyrics of "People Get Ready." The train image finds its roots in Negro spirituals from the black Methodist, Baptist, and Pentecostal movements that predate the 1960s Civil Rights Movement by generations. The gospel group the Blind Boys of Alabama, Al Green, soul queen Aretha Franklin, folksinger Bob Dylan, the Staple Singers, and many other artists have recorded Mayfield's spiritual anthem.

Spirituals have been in Broadway shows, with Alex Bradford (1927–1978) film music used for television background music. Singers would witness in song, talking about illness, disappointments, and pain as a part of the struggles of life. Singers such as Madame Edna Gallmon Cooke (1918–1967) and Brother Joe May (1912–1972) would encourage the audience to continue in the sun, the rain, or the storm. These singers were lively, with homey conversation, a sense of humor, and a commitment to God.

In contemporary gospel music, spirituals are still very popular. "Oh Happy Day," sung by the Edwin Hawkins Singers from California in 1970, ushered in contemporary gospel music with its use of a mass choir and musical beats. The lyrics are spiritual:

> Oh happy day
> Oh happy day
> Oh happy day
> When Jesus washed
> When Jesus washed
> When Jesus washed
> When Jesus washed
> He washed my sins away
> Oh happy day

Choirs are singing spirituals and gospel songs for Black History Month each February. The "Negro National Anthem" words were written by James Weldon Johnson (1871–1938), and his brother Rosamond Johnson wrote the music. Keeping the tradition of learning about black history was established by Carter G. Woodson (1875–1950), "the Father of Black History Month."

Spirituals are for the world to enjoy. England, Africa, and the Internet have continued to sell high volumes of black religious spiritual music. It is, therefore, of serious concern that this music continue for the express purpose of preserving such excellent harmony and poetic singing. The struggles, attainments, and aspirations of slave voices, their sorrows, and their joys are all wrapped up and tied up in these religious spiritual songs. Spirituals explain the slave's adaptability and survival under adverse circumstances in a civilization that is strange and hostile. From the field to the small towns to the cities and other countries, the word of God and freedom continue to travel in these songs.

Spirituals have a universal appeal in their message. They can adapt to any situation: to war, to peace, for love, for a new day. Above all, spirituals show that people are involved and hopeful for the coming of Jesus. Spiritual musical is uplifting; it is physical because the body moves to the beat of the music, with its moans and groans reviving the soul.

SHERRY SHERROD DuPREE

Reference and Further Reading

African American Heritage Hymnal. Chicago: GIA Publications, Inc., 2001.

DuPree, Sherry Sherrod. *African-American Holiness Pentecostal Movement: An Annotated Bibliography*. Religious Information Systems Vol. 4; Garland Reference Library of Social Science Vol. 526. New York: Garland Publishing, 1996.

———. *Biographical Dictionary of African-American Holiness-Pentecostals 1880–1990*. Washington, DC: Middle Atlantic Regional Press, 1989.

———; Herbert C. DuPree *African-American Good News (Gospel) Music*. Washington, DC: Middle Atlantic Regional Press, 1993.

Falsani, Cathleen. "Message of Civil Rights Anthem Remains Powerful." *Chicago Sun-Times* (August 28, 2003).

Jackson, Jerma A. *Singing in My Soul: Black Gospel Music in a Secular Age*. Chapel Hill: University of North Carolina Press, 2004.

Reitz. Liner notes to *Sincerely Sister Rosetta Tharpe*. Clipping File, Sister Rosetta Tharpe, "Paramount, NY," *Variety* (December 7, 1938). Billy Rose Theater Collection.

Songs and Spirituals of Negro Composition for Revivals and Congregational Singing: The Largest Manufacturing Enterprise in the United States Owned and Operated Exclusively by Colored People. Chicago: The Overton-Hygienic Co., Home of the High-Brown Toilet Preparations, n.d.

Walker, Wyatt Tee. *Spirits that Dwell in Deep Woods: The Prayer and Praise Hymns of the Black Religious Experience*. Chicago: GIA Publications, 1991.

ST. PAUL BAPTIST CHURCH CHOIR OF LOS ANGELES

The St. Paul Baptist Church Choir of Los Angeles, California, variously known as the St. Paul Church Choir of Los Angeles and the Echoes of Eden Choir, was one of the most popular gospel choruses of the 1940s. It is considered the first black gospel choir to have its own weekly radio broadcast and to have made commercial recordings.

St. Paul Baptist Church was founded in April 1907. Its famous choir was formed after Reverend John L. Branham was assigned to the church in 1946, succeeding Dr. Samuel Aaron Williams, who passed away. Branham wanted St. Paul's choir to sing gospel music with the verve of the Thomas A. Dorsey–tutored ensembles he encountered in his native Chicago. He hired J. Earle Hines (1916–1960) in 1946 and founded the Echoes of Eden Choir in 1947, with Hines as director and Gwendolyn Cooper Lightenr as pianist (Albert A. Goodson would serve as assistant pianist). Hines, like Branham, was a newcomer to the West Coast. Born in Atlanta, Hines was a successful performing and recording artist. His fame came as chief soloist for the Goodwill Singers, an ensemble that served as ambassadors of the National Baptist Convention.

In February 1947, the 150-voice Echoes of Eden inaugurated a regular Sunday evening radio broadcast on KFWB. The program reached seventeen states and eventually garnered an estimated one million listeners. Two months after launching its radio program, the choir began recording for Capitol Records. The ensemble's first disc was also its biggest hit: Dorsey's "God Be with You" (Capitol 40018) sold very well and introduced the choir to a national audience. The record's flip side, "I'm So Glad Jesus Lifted Me," written by Clarence H. Cobb of Chicago's First Church of Deliverance, became the choir's theme. Recordings were captured live during church services.

The Echoes of Eden Choir was patterned after the Chicago gospel choruses taught by Dorsey in the 1930s and 1940s, and its repertory was filled with songs by Chicago composers. In addition to compositions by Dorsey and Cobb, works by Kenneth Morris, Roberta Martin, and Lillian Bowles could also be heard on the choir's records and radio broadcasts and during church services.

In additon to Hines, Lightener, and Goodson, other musicians of distinction who sang with the Echoes of Eden Choir included Sallie Martin, her adopted daughter Cora Martin, and the Sallie Martin Singers. During the late 1950s, future pop star Darlene Love was among its members.

The choir's open-throated, *fortissimo* vocals, accompanied occasionally by hand clapping and expressive body movements, remains the paradigmatic style for amateur and professional gospel choirs alike.

The St. Paul Baptist Church Choir recorded thirty tracks for Capitol between 1947 and 1950. Hines, Cora Martin, Ruth Black, and Erie Gladney were featured soloists on these records.

By 1949, Hines had left St. Paul to serve as minister of music at Grace Memorial Church of God in Christ and for a short period led another acclaimed Los Angeles choir, the Voices of Victory of the Victory Baptist Church.

ROBERT MAROVICH

See also Gospel Choirs; Los Angeles, Gospel in; Martin, Roberta; Martin, Sallie; Morris, Kenneth

Reference and Further Reading

Boyer, Horace Clarence. *How Sweet the Sound: The Golden Age of Gospel*. Washington, DC: Elliott & Clark, 1995.

DjeDje, Jacqueline Cogdell. "Los Angeles Composers of African American Gospel Music: The First Generations." *American Music* (Winter 1993). Available at http://www.findarticles.com/p/articles/mi_m2298/is_n4_v11/ai_14758892.

Hayes, Cedric; Robert Laughton *Gospel Records 1943–1969: A Black Music Discography*. London: Record Information Services, 1993.

Heilbut, Anthony. *The Gospel Sound*. New York: Limelight Editions, 1992.

Discography

On Revival Day! (ca. mid-1950s, Capitol LP T 791).

STAMPS QUARTET

Like most of the other publishers of Southern gospel music in the 1920s and 1930s, the Stamps–Baxter company sponsored quartets to travel, record, and broadcast their songs and songbooks. During the late 1920s, there were at least two separate quartets touring and recording for major labels; one was led by V. O. Stamps (the cofounder of the Stamps–Baxter Company) and the other by his brother Frank. As the quartets developed, Frank Stamps gradually emerged as the cornerstone figure and as a popular figure in his own right.

The first Stamps Quartet recordings for a major label were done in Atlanta on October 20, 1927; these included what would be the signature song for many later quartets, "Give the World a Smile," an upbeat song that became so popular that later groups referred to this style of snappy singing as "give-the-world-a-smile" music. The recording also marked the first wide use of "afterbeats" or "backfire," a style of counterpoint singing that many classic quartets

adopted. The personnel on this first record—which sold very well—included Palmer Wheeler (tenor), Roy Wheeler (tenor), Frank Stamps (bass), and Odis Nichols (baritone). The pianist was a young jazz-oriented musician named Dwight Brock. Most of the 1928 Victor records used this personnel.

Although the Stamps Quartet continued to record through the early 1930s for OKeh, Brunswick, and Bluebird, the next major incarnation was the quartet that began working over KRLD in Dallas in 1936. Headed by V. O. Stamps, it became the quintessential quartet, remembered by generations of listeners. Its members included Walter Rippetoe (tenor), Jim Gaither (baritone), Bob Bacon (lead), and Marion Snider (piano). Popularizing songs such as "Further Along," "There's a Little Pine Log Cabin," and "Just a Little Talk with Jesus," the group won a recording contract with the huge American Recording Company and, by 1937, were drawing some twenty-five thousand letters a month.

In later years, this group (with Frank Stamps stepping in again) recorded for Bibletone, Mercury, Sellers, and Columbia. A completely different quartet, built around the tenor singing of Clyde Garner, began recording for Columbia in 1951.

CHARLES K. WOLFE

See also Stamps–Baxter

Reference and Further Reading

Russell, Tony. *Country Music Records 1921–42*. New York: Oxford, 2004.

Stamps, Mrs. Frank. *Give the World a Smile. A Compilation of Songs by Frank H. Stamps with a Story of His Life*. Wesson, MS: Lynwood Smith, 1969.

STAMPS–BAXTER

Virgil Oliver Stamps (b. September 18, 1892, Upshur County, TX; d. August 19, 1940, Dallas, TX)
J. R. (Jesse Randal) Baxter, Jr. (b. December 8, 1887, DeKalb County, AL; d. January 21, 1960, Dallas, TX)

The Stamps–Baxter Printing and Publishing Company emerged through much of the twentieth century as possibly the largest and best-known maker and promoter of seven-shape-note gospel songbooks. Their sales ran into the millions and reached into at least twenty-eight states from their central headquarters in Dallas, Texas. The company pioneered dozens of promotional techniques and attracted the talents of some of the South's leading songwriters. Like many other similar publishers, they promoted singing schools around the South, urged their quartets to make phonograph records and appear on radio, and encouraged the formation of singing conventions that attracted all the good singers in a church or even a county. Most of their publications were, in fact, "convention books," though they also produced several popular "church books" for use in formal church services.

The company's founders were Virgil Oliver Stamps and J. R. (Jesse Randal) Baxter, Jr. Stamps came from a rural area of East Texas. In this region, through the efforts of singing-school teachers such as A. J. Showalter and the influence of Ruebush–Kieffer songbooks, the seven-shape songbooks had pretty much replaced the older Sacred Harp or four-shape books, and young Stamps was fascinated with the new music—especially with the increasing use of male quartets to introduce the new songs.

In about 1907, Stamps attended his first singing school and began to learn the "rudiments" of reading, harmony, and composing. He wrote his first song in 1917, and having no contacts with book publishers, he printed it up on small song sheets, which he sold for a few cents. During his twenties, he worked for several publishing houses until he decided to open his own business, the V. O. Stamps Music Company, in 1926 in Jacksonville, Texas. In 1926, he issued his first book, *Silver Strains*.

In the meantime, J. R. "Pap" Baxter was serving a similar apprenticeship, studying under figures such as T. B. Mosley and the great A. J. Showalter himself. He began writing "song poems" and worked with James Rowe, the Englishman who was the leading lyricist for James D. Vaughan's company, and for the classic hymnist Charles Gabriel. In 1918, he married Clarice Howard, herself a literature teacher, and this encouraged his songwriting even more. Soon after his marriage, he began managing the branch office of the Showalter firm in Texarkana, Texas.

When Showalter died in 1924, Baxter and Stamps, who had known each other for eight years, decided to form a partnership and create a new business, the Stamps–Baxter Publishing Company. Three years earlier, in 1923, when he was working for a Showalter company, Baxter wrote to an eager young songwriter who wanted to publish his own books, "The great trouble with a great many is that they begin to think that they are the best musicians on the globe and want to get a book out themselves, not thinking that it takes money and experience and means to advertise before publishing can be made a success. I know of a great many young fellows who have been ruined by just such business." This practical, hard-headed advice was to become a cornerstone of the new company: it would be run on sound business principles, not on moral fervor or idealism.

The first songbook under the new imprint appeared in 1926 and was called *Harbor Bells*. During the next few years, new convention books followed each year: *Golden Harp* (1927), *Sparkling Gems* (1928), *Crystal Rays* (1929), and *Priceless Pearls* (1930). Starting in 1932, the company began issuing two books a year, often one a "special," such as *Modern Quartets for Men* and *Solos, Duets, and Special Songs*. The company was soon attracting a roster of well-known writers, including Luther G. Presley, Albert E. Brumley, Eugene Wright, J. B. Coats, William A. McKinney, V. O. Fosset, Marion Easterling, L. D. Huffstulter, Homer F. Morris, Emory Peck, Lonnie B. Crumbs, and others.

One of the songs in the original *Harbor Bells* was an effort by Otis Deaton and M. L. Yandell, "Give the World a Smile Each Day." This up-tempo song featuring "afterbeats" became the theme song for the new company; a Victor recording of the song established it as a standard, and in later years it gave its name to a whole genre of song: "that old give-the-world-a-smile music."

In addition to the songbooks, the company also published a monthly magazine to allow fans and customers to keep up with new books, the travels of quartets, upcoming conventions, and scheduled singing schools. At first this was called *The Southern Music News* but in 1940 was renamed *Gospel Singing News*. In 1936, the company leaders traveled to Cincinnati, where they bought the old printing presses of the Armstrong Printing Company, which had done the printing for most of the songbook companies, including James D. Vaughan. Relocating that to Dallas, the firm now changed its name to the Stamps–Baxter Printing and Publishing Company.

With its expanded location on Tyler Street in Dallas, the new firm became the nation's largest publisher devoted to gospel books. By 1940, the company was also printing books for more than a dozen leading denominational publishing houses in addition to their own books and was capable of turning out more than two million books a year. The company also began sponsoring gospel radio programs, and by 1940 there were at least a dozen Stamps Quartets on major radio stations throughout the South. Agents also visited mainstream radio singers, urging them to use Stamps–Baxter songs; artists who did include the Chuck Wagon Gang, the Blackwood Brothers, the Blue Sky Boys, Carl Story, Lonnie and Thelma Robertson, the Callahan Brothers, and numerous others. The company issued in the late 1930s a series of *Super Specials*, which were collections of songs chosen to appeal to radio fans.

With the death of Pap Baxter in 1960, his wife Clarice ("Ma" Baxter) ran the company for the next fifteen years, continuing to release new books and to sponsor singing conventions. Among her most useful publications was a 1960 book, *Biographies of Gospel Songwriters*.

CHARLES K. WOLFE

Reference and Further Reading

Beary, Shirley L. "The Stamps–Baxter Music and Printing Company: A Continuing American Tradition, 1926–1976." Ed.D. dissertation, 1977.

STANLEY BROTHERS, THE (RALPH STANLEY)

Carter Stanley (b. August 27, 1925; d. December 1, 1966)
Ralph Stanley (b. February 25, 1927)

Virginia brothers Carter and Ralph Stanley are universally recognized, along with Bill Monroe and Flatt and Scruggs, as comprising the "Holy Trinity" of bluegrass music. But the Stanley Brothers' two-decade—and Ralph's half-century-plus—careers mark and are marked by gospel music in ways that are much more vital than that happenstance theological labeling.

Like country music in general, bluegrass is inextricably rooted in the worship and churchgoing that afforded its Appalachian composers and performers their earliest opportunities to sing and make music. Dating from the 1930s, bluegrass melded elements of old-time string band music, the "hillbilly" songs popularized via early radio and recordings, and African American blues. Its hallmarks include rapid tempos, pure acoustic stringed instrumentation (predominantly the banjo, guitar, fiddle, mandolin, and Dobro), and sky-high-pitched tenor vocals. Lyrically, it typically reflects hardscrabble blue collar working worlds, a deep and often sentimentalized adoration of home and family, and devout religious faith.

Bluegrass music usually hinges on musical virtuosity. The Stanley Brothers, though musically able, were not virtuosos—at least not on the level of other luminaries. Their more striking contributions, beginning with their first recordings in 1947, were vocal and lyrical. Carter's earthy baritone was one of the most soulful voices in bluegrass. Ralph's keening tenor, providing harmonic lacings to Carter's vocal fabric, exemplified the "high lonesome" sound. The Brothers' repertoire included traditional gospel songs such as "Angel Band" and "Beautiful Star of Bethlehem," as well as Albert Brumley selections from paperback hymnals. They also waxed a classic, rollicking rendition of Cleavant Derricks's "Just a Little Talk with Jesus."

Carter, the elder sibling, was the more frequent composer. His enduring gospel-themed pieces include "Calling from Heaven" and "Let Me Walk, Lord, by Your Side." These songs carry the pining, bittersweet tinge of most Stanley Brothers' music, but that gothic tone prevails even more heavily in such Carter-penned classics as "The White Dove" and "Life of Sorrow." Such songs, while not strictly religious in theme, have their mournful, doleful strains abated only by the hope of heavenly reunion with deceased loved ones.

Sadness and unrequited longing were emotions tailored to Ralph's "high lonesome" tenor. Carter, a heavy drinker, succumbed to ill health when he was forty-one years old; Ralph was at the time just pressing forty. He would have a long life ahead of him, stamped musically by lingering grief over Carter's early death and the suitability of his own vocal instrument for haunting material. Accordingly, among the genuinely great gospel material of his solo career is his own original song, "The Darkest Hour Is Just Before Dawn."

The younger Stanley has continued performing and recording into his old age and has been a key figure in two national revivals of bluegrass and "roots" music. Appalachian music was first rediscovered outside its own tight circles in the folk music scene of the 1960s. Here the Stanley Brothers and Ralph as a solo artist garnered such admirers and promoters as Bob Dylan. The second rediscovery occurred in 2000, with the release of the Coen Brothers' film *O Brother, Where Art Thou?* Rock impressario T-Bone Burnett gathered a stellar lineup of tradition-steeped musicians for the movie's soundtrack, which itself became a best-seller and ignited a roots music craze. Among the soundtrack's standouts is Ralph Stanley's chilling, utterly compelling *a cappella* rendition of the gospel traditional "O Death."

There are other ways that the work of the Stanley Brothers and Ralph remains a living influence in gospel music. Songs made famous by them and other bluegrass performers have been incorporated into church services, especially in Baptist and Pentecostal traditions. Ralph pioneered the *a cappella* styling long before it was exploited to striking effect in *O Brother, Where Art Thou?* In Ralph's wake, bluegrass concerts now regularly include, in addition to other religious numbers, one *a cappella* gospel song.

Finally, during the course of Ralph's performing lifetime, summertime bluegrass festivals have become an annual fixture in the musical and religious life of the Southern United States. Held at parks and campgrounds, these events gather headline performers such as Ralph Stanley and thousands of families for multiday events. The fans camp on festival grounds for the duration. They are assured of a wholesome family atmosphere and plenty of hymnody and gospel sounds and perhaps even some "testifying" and preaching from the onstage performers. (Ralph Stanley is an eager and persistent evangelist.)

Thus, the bluegrass festival carries on a living embodiment of the campground revival meetings of the nineteenth and early twentieth centuries which were at the very heart and wellspring of American gospel music.

RODNEY CLAPP

Reference and Further Reading

Dawidoff, Nicholas. *In the Country of Country: People and Places in American Music.* New York: Pantheon, 1997.

Malone, Bill C. *Don't Get Above Your Raisin': Country Music and the Southern Working Class.* Urbana: University of Illinois Press, 2002.

Wright, John. *Traveling the High Way Home: Ralph Stanley and the World of Traditional Bluegrass Music.* Urbana: University of Illinois Press, 1993.

Discography

The Stanley Brothers, Angel Band: Classic Mercury Recordings (1995, Mercury 528191).

The Stanley Brothers, Complete Columbia (1996, Columbia/Sony 53798).

Ralph Stanley and Friends, Clinch Mountain Country (1998, Rebel 5001).

O Brother, Where Art Thou? (2000, Lost Highway 170069; soundtrack).

STANPHILL, IRA F.

(b. February 4, 1914; d. December 30, 1993)

The composer of more than five hundred gospel songs, Ira F. Stanphill was born in Bellview, New Mexico, where his schoolteacher parents were homesteaders, having traveled from Arkansas in a covered wagon. When Ira was eight years old, his family moved to Coffeyville, Kansas, where he remained for fourteen years. There he attended Coffeyville Junior College and also had a daily program on radio station KGGF from 1930 to 1934. Then, in 1936, he became an evangelist and pastored churches in West Palm Beach, Florida, and Lancaster, Pennsylvania. Beginning in 1966, he was pastor for several years of the Rockwood Park Assembly of God Church in Fort Worth, Texas.

Despite his extensive evangelical work, Stanphill is primarily remembered as a gospel songwriter. He wrote his first number at age seventeen and continued producing songs until shortly before his death. His best-known songs are "Room at the Cross," "Happiness Is the Lord," "Mansion over the Hilltop," "I Know Who Holds Tomorrow," and "Supper Time." The latter song was written in 1949 in Osceola, Missouri, where Stanphill was conducting a tent revival. Thought by some to be derived from the author's life experiences, the words were written at his five-year-old son's bedside while the boy was taking a nap. Actually, it was inspired by Revelations 19:9, which says: "Blessed are they who are called to the marriage supper of the Lamb."

In February 1993, Stanphill moved from his longtime home in Fort Worth to Overland Park, Kansas, where he died. Earlier he had been inducted into the Gospel Music Hall of Fame.

W. K. MCNEIL

Reference and Further Reading

Horstman, Dorothy L. *Sing Your Heart Out Country Boy.* New York: Dutton, 1975.

"Ira F. Stanphill." [Obituary.] *The Hymn* 45 (April 1994): 2.

Reynolds, William J. *Companion to Baptist Hymnal.* Nashville, TN: Broadman, 1976.

STAPLE SINGERS

Roebuck "Pop" Staples (b. December 28, 1915, Winona, MS; d. December 19, 2000)
Cleotha Staples (b. April 11, 1934)
Mavis Staples (b. July 10, 1939)
Pervis Staples (b. November 1935)
Yvonne Staples (b. October 23, 1938)

No other twentieth-century gospel music group was quite like the Staple Singers. Their blend of gospel, blues, and folk struck a chord that resounded across genres for decades, making them one of the most successful crossover artists ever to record. The group's career was a marvel of eclecticism. They have been called one of the most influential gospel groups in pop music. They even became one of the voices of America's Civil Rights Movement, with its spiritual mooring, its hope, and its pain, all wrapped up in their unique musical message of dignity, peace, and compassion.

A singing family, the Staple Singers consisted of Roebuck "Pops" Staples and his children, Mavis, Cleotus, Pervis, and later, upon Pervis' exit, Yvonne. They were a unique part of the American music scene for almost fifty years, continuing to both record and sing together up until Pop's death. Described as "God's great hitmakers," the Staple Singers charted fifteen hits on the *Billboard* Hot 100 during their long career, including two number one hits, such as "Respect Yourself," "I'll Take You There," "Touch a Hand, Make a Friend," "Be What You Are," "This World," and "If You're Ready (Come Go With Me)." In 1994, Pop Staples, the group's patriarch, won a Grammy for his solo performance, "Father, Father," a testament to his songwriting's enduring themes of hope, faith, and compassion.

Roebuck "Pops" Staples was born in 1915 on a plantation outside of Winona, Mississippi. The last of fourteen children, his first job was picking cotton. He grew up singing gospel at home with his big family and hearing Delta blues performed by legendary performers. In 1931, he joined a local gospel group called the Golden Trumpets. In 1936, he and his wife Osceola joined the throngs moving to Chicago for a better life. He worked in a meatpacking plant by day and played blues guitar in "joints" at night and gospel on Sunday, singing and playing guitar for the Chicago gospel group the Trumpet Jubilees. His early exposure to both the blues and gospel would also find its way into his original songs, which were somehow both haunting and hopeful.

When his wife suddenly died, Pop had to raise his children alone. He began setting his young children in a circle on their Chicago home's floor, teaching them to harmonize on gospel favorites. By 1948, they were performing in churches across the city. The youngest member, Mavis, who was only seven years old yet already a contralto, sang the bass parts. Soon they were offered a recording contract, and Pop ultimately dropped an "s" from their name, dubbing the group the Staple Singers. In 1956, they recorded their first gospel hit, "Uncloudy Day." In the years to come, they would have many revered gospel hits, including "Too Close," "Will the Circle Be Unbroken," and "This May Be the Last Time."

The Staple Singers, however, were destined to be more than just another gospel group. When Pops met Martin Luther King, Jr., in 1963, he told his children, "If he can preach this, we can sing it." They began traveling with Dr. King, writing songs for the Civil Rights Movement, all of them deeply rooted in the gospel message of God-given dignity, songs such as "March Up Freedom's Highway," "We'll Get Over," and "Why? (Am I Treated So Bad)." Their songs' blend of the anguish of the blues, the hope of gospel, and the social consciousness of protest folk was pitch-perfect for the moment in American history.

After the civil rights years, their music continued to find its way to a large, diverse audience. Pop saw that their message of love could build bridges between gospel and other music audiences and guided the group into its crossover fame, despite controversy from gospel purists. The Southern gospel style behind even their most roof-raising rhythm and blues renditions gave their work a joyful depth that reverberated across genres. Their sound was unmistakable. Pop's liquid tenor was as memorable as his guitar and songwriting gifts, especially mixed with Mavis's gifted contralto and the group's soul-stirring sibling harmonies. They were revered by such diverse figures as Bob Dylan, Jesse Jackson, Harry Belafonte, Aretha Franklin, and the Rolling Stones, and they influenced countless musicians for more than half a century.

Their contribution to the American music scene was honored numerous times, including the Rhythm & Blues Foundation's Pioneer Award in 1992, the National Endowment for the Arts' National Heritage Fellowship in 1998, Rock and Roll Hall of Fame induction in 1999, and a Grammy Lifetime Achievement Award in 2005.

LYNDA RUTLEDGE STEPHENSON

Reference and Further Reading

Bowman, Rob. "Staple Singers: Biography" All Music website, http://www.allmusic.com (accessed December 2004).

Calloway, John. "Chicago Stories: The Staple Singers." WTTW-11 Chicago website, http://www.wttw.com/chicagostories/staplesingers.html (accessed December 2004).

Carpenter, Bill. "Staple Singers: God's Greatest Hitmakers." *Goldmine* (August 30, 1996): 19.

Darden, Robert. *People Get Ready! A New History of Black Gospel Music*. New York: Continuum, 2004.

Heilbut, Anthony. *The Gospel Sound: Good News and Bad Times*. Garden City, NY: Anchor, 1975.

"Inductees: The Staple Singers." Rock and Roll Hall of Fame website, http://www.rockhall.com/hof/inductee.asp?id=195 (accessed March 1, 1999).

Janega, James. "'Pop' Staples, 85: Tried to Improve World With Music." *Chicago Tribune* (December 20, 2000).

"Press Room: January 4, 2005. Staple Singers to Receive the Recording Academy Lifetime Achievement Award." Grammy Award website, http://www.grammy.com/press/press_releases/2005/0104a.aspx.

"The Staple Singers." Richard De La Font Agency website, http://www.delafont.com/music_acts/staple-singers.htm (accessed December 2000).

Discography

"Sit Down Servant" (1953, United Records); *Uncloudy Day* (1959, Vee-Jay); *Swing Low Sweet Chariot* (1961, Vee-Jay), *The 25th Day of December* (1962, Riverside); *Hammer and Nails* (1962, Riverside); *Swing Low* (1962, Vee-Jay); *Gamblin' Man* (1963, Riverside); *This Little Light* (1964, Riverside); *Amen!* (1965, Epic); *Freedom Highway* (1965, SMM Columbia); *For What It's Worth* (1967, Epic); *Soul Folk in Action* (1968, Stax); *Will the Circle Be Unbroken* (1969, Buddah Vee-Jay); *Landlord* (1970,

United Artists); *We'll Get Over* (1970, Stax); *The Staple Swingers* (1971, Stax); *Be Altitude: Respect Yourself* (1972, Stax); *Be What You Are* (1973, Stax); *City in the Sky* (1974, Stax); *Let's Do It Again* (1975, Curtom); *Pass It On* (1976, Warner); *Family Tree* (1977, Warner); *Unlock Your Mind* (1978, Warner); *Hold On to Your Dream* (1981, 20th Century Fox); *Turning Point* (1984, Epic); *The Staple Singers* (1985, Private 1); *Sit Down Servant* (1991, Nashboro); *Swingline* (1991, Nashboro).

STARS OF FAITH, THE

Marion Williams (b. August 29, 1927, Miami, FL; d. July 2, 1994)

The group Stars of Faith was formed in 1958 when Marion Williams and Henrietta Waddy quit the Ward Singers after an argument about their fees and salary with the manager, Gertrude Ward. Williams contacted other members of the Ward Singers such as Kitty Parham, Frances Steadman, and Esther Ford, who agreed to become members of the group she was organizing, and the Stars of Faith were born. Ford was quickly replaced by Mattie Harper but would return on several occasions (1973).

Marion Williams was born in Miami, Florida, and brought up in a Pentecostal church. She developed her taste for shout songs at fast tempo and her unique talent to climb into the highest of the soprano register, stay easily, and then drop to the bottom of it and deliver growls like sanctified preachers. In 1947, she joined the Clara Ward Singers in Philadelphia and was a driving wheel for the group, who had hits, packed houses, and won a lot of money, partly thanks to Marion.

Henrietta Waddy (1902–1981) was born in South Carolina. She had a rough, unsophisticated alto that blended perfectly with her partners' voices in the Ward Singers and then in the Stars of Faith. Kitty Parham (b. 1931, Trenton, New Jersey; d. July 3, 2003) grew up in the Church of God in Christ (COGIC) and was a leading soprano soloist in that denomination. She was a welcome addition to the Stars. Esther Ford (b. 1925, Detroit, Michigan) was also a COGIC singer and an associate of Mattie Moss Clark before coming to the Stars. Her soprano and her multioctave range highlighted more than one song of the Stars. Mattie Dozier Harper (b. 1934) was a member of the Sallie Jenkins Singers and recorded with Alex Bradford before joining the Stars; her mezzo-soprano tones could change into growls and hollers on command. She did well with the Stars of Faith.

In 1961, the Stars had the honor to appear on Broadway in Langston Hughes's *Black Nativity*, and in 1962 this show toured Europe several times with the Stars, Alex Bradford, and Princess Steward and became a sensation.

Frances Steadman (b. 1915, Greensboro, North Carolina) lived in Baltimore and was brought up in both the Baptist and sanctified churches. She was—and remains—one of the most talented contraltos in gospel; she sang with the Waldo Singers, the Mary Johnson Davis Singers, the Clara Ward Specials, and the Ward Singers before joining the Stars, and she became the leader of the group when Marion Williams quit to start a solo career in the early 1970s. Frances's daughter, Sadie Frances Keys (b. 1933), is also a member of the group, like pianist and tenor Eddie Brown (formerly of the Famous Davis Sisters). They toured Europe on an annual basis, appearing at the Montreux Jazz Festival (1983), in churches and auditoriums, and recording for Black & Blue and Ebony Records.

In 1995, the surviving Ward Singers were reunited for one concert with Steadman, Parham, Ford, and Willa Ward. In the meantime, the Stars occasionally sang backup for Marion Williams, and they go on touring the United States and Europe regularly.

ROBERT SACRÉ

See also Ward Trio (Ward Singers); Williams, Marion

Reference and Further Reading

Boyer, Horace Clarence. *How Sweet the Sound: The Golden Age of Gospel*. Washington, DC: Elliott & Clark, 1995.

Hayes, J. Cedric; Robert Laughton *Gospel Records 1943–1969. A Black Music Discography*, 2 vols. London, UK: Record Information Services, 1992.

Heilbut, Tony. *The Gospel Sound: Good News and Bad Times*. New York: Limelight, 1985.

———. "Queens of Negro Spirituals and Gospel." *Jazz* (Switzerland) 75, no. 6 (December 1975): 15–18.

Reagon, Bernice Johnson, ed. *We'll Understand It Better By and By. Pioneering African American Gospel Composers*. Washington, DC: Smithsonian Institution Press, 1992.

Discography

Marion Williams *O Holy Night* (1993, Savoy SCD14032); *My Soul Looks Back* (1994, Shanachie/Spirit Feel 6011).

The Stars of Faith. *The Best of the Stars of Faith: In The Spirit* (1995, Nashboro NASH4519-2); *Live at the Montreux Jazz Festival: Glory Glory Hallelujah* (1990, Black & Blue [France] 59.186 2).

STATLER BROTHERS

The Statler Brothers, best known as a popular country group with hits from the mid-1960s through the

1990s, came out of the gospel music singing tradition of the Shenandoah Valley in Virginia. Harold Reid, one of the four members of the group, explained the influence of gospel music as follows: "We started out admiring all the gospel groups of the day, and that's . . . what we based our career sound/attitude on . . . . We took the gospel harmonies and put them over into country music" (*The News Leader*).

The group, from Staunton, Virginia, always maintained their connection to gospel music. Beginning with their third album, they included at least one gospel song on every album, in every concert, and on every television show. Several of their albums featured gospel music, from *Oh Happy Day* (1969) to *Amen* (2002). On their album *Thank You World* (1974), the group included, as a tribute to their favorite gospel group, the song "The Blackwood Brothers by the Statler Brothers."

Members of the future Statler Brothers first performed at the Methodist Church in Lyndhurst, near Staunton, in 1955 as teenagers in a group called the Four Star Quartet. The group consisted of bass singer Harold Reid (b. 1939), baritone Phil Balsley (b. 1939), tenor Lew DeWitt (b. 1938; d. 1990), and Joe McDorman, who later dropped out of the group. Around 1961, the group reformed, with new member Don Reid, under the name the Kingsmen. They changed their name to the Statler Brothers after another group called the Kingsmen released the hit "Louis, Louis." In 1964, the group was hired by Johnny Cash to open his show, and the Statler Brothers began their climb to success. Their first top-ten hit was the 1965 release "Flowers on the Wall."

The group had only one shift in personnel since 1961. Lew DeWitt left the group in 1982 because of health problems and was replaced by Jimmy Fortune. After a successful run that lasted more than forty years, the group played its last concert in Salem, Virginia, in October 2002. The group's awards include three Grammys, nine Country Music Association awards, eleven gold albums, and three platinum albums. The Statler Brothers found their success primarily in songs and performances about sentiment, nostalgia, and humor, but their link to gospel music was apparent in all of their music.

DREW BEISSWENGER

Reference and Further Reading

"Final Bow." *The News Leader* (Staunton, VA) (October 26, 2002).

Holtin, Alice Y. *The Statler Brothers Discography*. Westport, CT: Greenwood Press, 1997.

STEBBINS, GEORGE COLES

(b. February 26, 1846; d. October 6, 1945)

This important figure in gospel music history was born in East Carlton, New York. As a youth, George Coles Stebbins learned to play piano and attended singing schools, then, after moving to Rochester, New York, he studied singing and joined a church choir. He also studied in Buffalo, New York, but in 1869 he moved to Chicago to accept a position with the Lyon & Healy Music Company.

Stebbins stayed in the Windy City for five years, during which time he served as music director of the First Baptist Church. After moving to Boston in 1874, he became music director of the Clarendon Street Baptist Church. Then he returned to Chicago to work as an evangelistic singer with Dwight L. Moody's campaigns. This proved to be a long, successful association that lasted until 1901, two years after Moody's death. During this twenty-five–year span, Stebbins worked with Moody, Ira D. Sankey, and such other evangelists as George Needham, George Pentecost, and Daniel W. Whittle.

This era also saw Stebbins compiling several song collections—for which he often composed the tunes—for use in these evangelists' meetings. He wrote some of these songs under the pseudonym George Coles. Stebbins pioneered arrangements for men's voices when, at the insistence of George F. Root, he provided musical settings for several gospel song collections for male choruses. After the untimely death of Philip P. Bliss, he became joint editor, with Sankey and James McGranahan, of the important *Gospel Hymns and Sacred Songs* series, helping produce volumes three through six. In 1924, he wrote *Reminiscences and Gospel Hymn Stories*, one of the more interesting early gospel autobiographies.

Stebbins's best-remembered melodies include "There Is a Green Hill Far Away," which was provided for a text by Mrs. Cecil F. Alexander; it first appeared in *Gospel Hymns No. 1* (1878) and became one of the most widely used songs in Moody's evangelistic campaigns. Stebbins's theme for Adelaide A. Pollard's "Have Thine Own Way, Lord!" first appeared in *Northfield Hymnal with Alexander's Supplement* (1907), while Fanny Crosby's text "Saved by Grace," which became one of Moody and Sankey's favorite hymns and for which Stebbins supplied the music, was first published in the *London Christian Paper* (1894). His tune for William Sleeper's "Ye Must Be Born Again" was initially published in *Gospel Hymns No. 3* (1898).

W. K. McNEIL

Reference and Further Reading

Hall, Jacob Henry. *Biography of Gospel Song and Hymn Writers*. New York: AMS Press, 1971 (1914).

Osbeck, Kenneth W. *101 Hymn Stories*. Grand Rapids, MI: Kregel, 1982.

———. *101 More Hymn Stories*. Grand Rapids, MI: Kregel, 1985.

Reynolds, William J. *Companion to the Baptist Hymnal*. Nashville, TN: Broadman, 1976.

Stebbins, George C. *Reminiscences and Gospel Hymn Stories*. New York: G. H. Dorns, 1924.

STONEHILL, RANDY

(b. March 12, 1952, Stockton, CA)

Randy Stonehill's early musical influences were Harry Belafonte, Burl Ives, and the Weavers. He began dreaming about having his own folk group when he was in grade school. When he was ten years old, his father bought him an acoustic guitar and enrolled him in classical guitar lessons. By the time he was fourteen, he formed his first garage band. His ambition at that time was to follow in the success of the San Francisco Bay area rock stars of that time, such as the Grateful Dead, Jefferson Airplane, and Janis Joplin.

After he graduated from high school, Stonehill left home and moved to Los Angeles to pursue his first love, rock 'n' roll. He stayed with Larry Norman, whom he knew from San Jose, and converted to Christianity. His conversion resulted in a new direction in his songwriting, in which he expressed his newfound faith and world view. Norman produced Stonehill's first album, *Born Twice*, in 1971 on his new label, One Way. Throughout the 1970s, Stonehill was managed and produced by Norman, who began Solid Rock Records in 1974. *Welcome to Paradise* was released in 1976 and contained classic songs such as "King of Hearts," and "Keep Me Running." He found himself on the ground floor of the Jesus revolution, and as a result he appeared in Billy Graham's 1971 film *A Time to Run*. After a trip to Haiti, he began to work with Compassion International, a children's relief organization.

In 1980, Stonehill signed with Myrrh Records, a division of Word Records. At the same time he was managed by Steve Ware through Street Level Artist's Agency, which Norman had sold to Philip Mangano. *Equator*, his second album on Myrrh, contained one of his most enduring compositions, "China." At one point during the early 1980s, he was touring with Amy Grant, which resulted in a duet on his *Love Beyond Reason* album, titled "I Could Never Say Goodbye." The song was nominated for a Grammy in 1985. In 1989, thirteen years after his first vinyl volume was released, the long-awaited sequel *Return to Paradise* was released. Stonehill worked with a variety of producers on his albums, including Mark Heard, Barry Kay, and Terry Taylor. His albums often included compositions that used his unique humor on issues such as cigarette smoking, fast food addiction, or an obsession with cosmetic superficiality, in the songs "Lung Cancer Blues," "American Fast Food," and "Cosmetic Fixation."

In 2001, Stonehill and Terry Taylor wrote and produced *Uncle Stonehill's Hat*, which was a children's concept album. On it, Randy created a character reminiscent of Willy Wonka or Pee Wee Herman, from a Christian perspective. Using the Uncle Stonehill character, he began to perform children's concerts. In 2002 he released his nineteenth album, *Edge of the World*, on Fair Oaks Records. It included the song "We Were All So Young" with performances by some of Christian rock's most important pioneers, including Annie Herring, Phil Keaggy, Barry McGuire, Noel Paul Stookey, and Russ Taff.

BOB GERSZTYN

See also Myrrh Records; Word Records

Reference and Further Reading

Ankeny, Jason. "Randy Stonehill Biography." *Rolling Stone* website, http://www.rollingstone.com/artist/bio.asp?oid=1348581 (accessed January 3, 2004).

Balmer, Randall. *Mine Eyes Have Seen the Glory: A Journey into the Evangelical Subculture in America*. New York: Oxford University Press, 1989.

"Jesus Music." One-Way.org website, http://one-way.org/jesusmusic/index.html (accessed January 4, 2004).

Max, Kevin. *Unfinished Work*. Nashville, TN: Thomas Nelson Publishing, 2001.

Music Moz Open Music Project website, http://musicmoz.org/Bands_and_Artists/S/Stonehill,_Randy/Links/ (accessed January 4, 2004).

Pacheco, Brent. "Welcome to Paradise, the Randy Stonehill Page." Nifty Music website, http://www.nifty-music.com/stonehill/ (accessed January 4, 2004).

"Randy Stonehill: At the Edge of the World." Street Level Artists Agency website, http://www.streetlevelagency.com/NewFiles/stonehill.html (January 4, 2004).

Discography

Born Twice (1971, One Way Records); *Get Me Out of Hollywood* (1973, Phonogram); *Welcome to Paradise* (1976, Solid Rock); *The Sky Is Falling* (1980, Solid Rock); *Between the Glory and the Flame* (1981, Myrrh); *Equator* (1983, Myrrh); *Celebrate This Heartbeat* (1984, Myrrh); *Love Beyond Reason* (1985, Myrrh); *Stonehill* (1985, Street Tunes); *The Wild Frontier* (1986, Myrrh); *Can't Buy a Miracle* (1988, Myrrh); *Return to Paradise* (1989, Myrrh); *Until We Have Wings* (1990, Myrrh); *Wonderama* (1992, Myrrh); *Stories* (1993, Myrrh); *The Lazarus Heart* (1994, Street Level); *Our Recollections*

(1996, Word); *Thirst* (1998, Brentwood); *Uncle Stonehill's Hat* (2001, Holy Sombraro); *Edge of the World* (2002, Fair Oaks).

STORY, CARL

(b. May 29, 1916; d. March 31, 1995)

In 1974, Carl Story was given the title "The Father of Bluegrass Gospel Music" by the governor of Oklahoma. Few would argue that Story, whose long career stretched back to the earliest days of bluegrass, did not deserve the title.

Born May 29, 1916, on the edge of Appalachia in Lenoir, North Carolina, he learned to play music from his fiddle-playing father and his guitarist mother. As a teenager, he won a fiddle contest, played for WLVA in Lynchburg, Virginia, and began performing with a local band called J. E. Clark and the Lonesome Mountaineers. Late in 1934, Story and Johnny Whisnant, who played a three-finger banjo style, decided to start their own band, called the Rambling Mountaineers. More than fifty years later, Carl Story and the Rambling Mountaineers were still performing.

Success was slow and gradual. All of the original band members worked long hours in a furniture factory and then, when possible, fit in performances at schools and other local venues. Their first radio job came in 1935 at WHKY in Hickory, North Carolina. They received no money, but the exposure helped them book concerts, and eventually the band members decided to pursue a full-time music career. They performed for WSPA in Spartanburg and WWNC in Asheville, North Carolina, and around 1940 cut eight songs for OKeh Records. Some argue that these songs, which were never released, were the first commercial recordings of bluegrass music.

During World War II, when keeping his band together was difficult, Story had the opportunity to play with Bill Monroe and Earl Scruggs, both of whom would go on to become top artists in the emerging bluegrass music field. In 1943, Story joined the Navy. After the war, he reorganized the Rambling Mountaineers and began working again at WWNC. Soon after that he was invited to join the popular *Mid-Day Merry-Go-Round* program on KNOX in Knoxville. His band members included Red Rector on mandolin and Claude Boone on guitar. Story established himself as a country artist, signed with the Mercury label, and saw his song "Tennessee Border" become a hit.

Story began to focus more on gospel music during the late 1940s. In 1947, the group recorded their gospel songs under the name Carl Story and the Melody Four Quartet, but it appears that since then they have used their regular group name for all of their recordings. The group's first gospel music hit, "My Lord Keeps a Record," was recorded in 1949. It was reported that, at one of Wally Fowler's all-night singings in Birmingham, the band took nine encores for forty-five minutes when they sang the song to a crowd of nine thousand. From that day forward, Carl Story and the Rambling Mountaineers recorded almost exclusively gospel songs.

The 1950s was a decade of much activity and travel and included stints at WCYB in Bristol; WAYS in Charlotte (where he helped establish the *Tar Heel Barn Dance*, later called the *Mineral Springs Music Barn*); WEAS in Decatur, Georgia; KNOX in Knoxville; WLOS in Asheville; and WBIR-TV for the *Cas Walker Show* in Knoxville.

His band during the late 1950s increasingly had a bluegrass sound after previously featuring more mainstream country music instrumentation. Story continued to explore different instrument combinations throughout his career, but this band, which included Clarence "Tater" Tate on fiddle and the Brewster brothers on banjo and mandolin, solidified the group's strong standing in the bluegrass field. For a period, the group recorded a quartet-style gospel song on one side and an instrumental piece (such as their hit "Mocking Banjo") on the other.

Story changed record labels several times. In 1953, he switched from Mercury to the Columbia label. In 1955, he returned to the Mercury label and then to the Starday label when it broke off from Mercury. He stayed with Starday for eighteen years and reportedly recorded a total of sixty-two albums for them. His group also appeared on other labels (often through songs leased from Starday) such as Acme, Spar, Scripture, Sims, Heart Warming, Songs of Faith, GRS, CMH, Rimrock, and Cannon.

Story began to perform less in 1960, and he worked as a deejay for WFLW in Monticello, Kentucky. The growing popularity of folk and bluegrass festivals eventually led various manifestations of the Rambling Mountaineers back to an active performance schedule. During the 1960s, 1970s, and 1980s, Story and his band performed often throughout the United States and Europe. He eventually made Greer, South Carolina, his home base and worked occasionally as a deejay at WCKI. He died on March 31, 1995.

DREW BEISSWENGER

Reference and Further Reading

Rosenberg, Neil V. *Bluegrass: A History*. Urbana: University of Illinois Press, 1985.

Thigpen, Ray. "Carl Story and the Rambling Mountaineers: Golden Anniversary." *Bluegrass Unlimited* (February 19, 1984): 10–16.

Willis, Barry R. *America's Music: Bluegrass.* Franktown, CO: Pine Valley Music, 1998 (1992).

Selected Discography

Gospel Quartet Favorites (1958, Mercury MG-20323, and 1958, Stetson HAT 3128); *America's Favorite Country Gospel Artist* (1959, Starday SLP 107); *Everybody Will Be Happy* (1961, Starday SLP 137); *More Gospel Quartet Favorites* (1961, Mercury MG-20584); *Mighty Close to Heaven* (1963, Starday SLP 219); *There's Nothing on Earth that Heaven Can't Cure* (1965, Starday SLP 348); *Bluegrass Sound of Carl Story* (1966, Spar SP 3000); *My Lord Keeps a Record* (1968, Starday 411); *The Best of Carl Story* (1970, Starday SSLP 455); *Light at the River* (1974, Mercury 71088); *The Early Days of Carl Story* (1980, Cattle 10 [West Germany]); *The Early Years 1953–1955* (1987, Old Homestead Records OHCS-144).

STRYPER

Oz Fox (b. June 18, 1961)
Tim Gaines (b. December 15, 1962)
Michael Sweet (b. July 4, 1963)
Robert Sweet (b. March 21, 1960)

Michael Sweet and his brother Robert formed Roxx Regime in Orange County, California, in 1983. Shortly thereafter, they changed the name to Stryper, which is an acronym for "Salvation Through Redemption Yielding Peace, Encouragement, and Righteousness." They also used Isaiah 53:5 as a biblical reference point, which states "by His stripes we are healed" (KJV).

Oz Fox (guitar), Tim Gaines (bass), Michael Sweet (vocals), and Robert Sweet (drums) were originally inspired by the music of the secular rock band Van Halen, but they wanted to present a more positive message through their lyrics while still maintaining a high-energy show. Their "hair metal" sound and appearance were considered too worldly to some in the church.

While playing the metal club circuit in Los Angeles, they landed a recording contract with Enigma Records. In 1984, their first release was a mini-album titled *The Yellow and Black Attack*, which eventually went gold. In 1985, *Soldiers Under Command* was released and also went gold. It remained on *Billboard*'s top two hundred album chart for nearly a year and even broke into the top one hundred at one point. When *To Hell With the Devil* was released in 1986, it went platinum and earned Stryper a Grammy nomination. The album also produced one of MTV's most requested videos, for the top twenty-five hit ballad "Honestly."

In 1988, they released *In God We Trust*, which went gold and produced another single, "Always There for You." Two thirds of their albums were sold in the mainstream market, which resulted in success for the band on MTV. At the same time, Benson Records distributed their releases to Christian retail stores. In 1990 they released *Against the Law*, which went gold immediately, as a follow-up to their successful concert tour.

In 1991, Stryper signed with Hollywood Records after Enigma Records filed for bankruptcy. After *Can't Stop the Rock* was released, Michael Sweet left the band, in January 1992, to pursue a solo career. The band reunited in May 2000 and performed sporadically during the next few years, as well as releasing a "best of" album in May 2003, which included two new songs.

BOB GERSZTYN

See also Barren Cross; Calvary Chapel, Costa Mesa; Norman, Larry; Petra; Rock Gospel

Reference and Further Reading

Fundamental Baptist Information Service. "The Philosophy of Contemporary Christian Music." Way of Life Literature website, http://www.wayoflife.org/fbns/philosophy.htm (accessed November 12, 2003).

Gaines, Tim. "Sindizzy Fan Page." Sin Dizzy website, http://www.sindizzy.com (accessed November 4, 1999).

Michael Sweet website, http://www.michaelsweet.com (accessed September 8, 2003).

"Stryper." Archived articles from December 1986, August 1988, February 1989, and August 1990. *CCM Magazine* website, http://www.ccmcom.com (accessed November 1, 2003).

"Stryper Biography." *Rolling Stone* website, http://www.rollingstone.com/artists/bio.asp?oid=3473 (accessed November 8, 2003).

Stryper website, http://www.stryper.com (accessed September 8, 2003).

Discography

The Yellow and Black Attack (1984, Enigma).
Soldiers Under Command (1985, Enigma).
To Hell with the Devil (1986, Enigma).
In God We Trust (1988, Enigma).
Against the Law (1990, Enigma).
Can't Stop the Rock (1991, Hollywood).
Stryper-7: The Best of Stryper (2003, Hollywood).

SULLIVAN, JERRY AND TAMMY

Jerry Sullivan (b. November 22, 1933)
Tammy Sullivan (b. October 2, 1964)

The father–daughter duo of Jerry and Tammy Sullivan have worked together since 1979. However, they did not attain wide prominence until the 1990s, when Marty Stuart began producing their recordings. Kinfolk of the well-known traditional bluegrass gospel band the Sullivan Family of St. Stephens, Alabama, Jerry and Tammy play a more contemporary form of bluegrass that still manages to be rooted in what they call "brush arbor–style music."

A native of Wagarville, Alabama, Jerry was attracted to gospel music from childhood but also developed a fondness for blues and rockabilly. He and Tammy made their first recording together in 1978, but they did not go into music full time until after she completed high school in 1982. About 1988, Marty Stuart, who had worked with the Sullivan Family before going to work for Lester Flatt, came back and worked with Jerry and Tammy for about a year and a half. As his career began to regain in stature, he began producing their records. He also cowrote several songs with Jerry, whom he considered a virtual second father.

Tammy's voice has been termed mezzo-soprano, while her dad is a natural baritone. Together, the Sullivans have played everywhere from small rural churches in the deep South to bluegrass festivals and larger coliseums, where they often share the bill with in-law and emerging country star Andy Griggs. Their three compact discs, all produced by Stuart, display considerable versatility and have been well received by reviewers.

IVAN M. TRIBE

See also Sullivans, The

Reference and Further Reading

Allen, Bob. "The Sullivans: Still Making a Joyful Noise." *Bluegrass Unlimited* 35, no. 12 (June 2001): 40–44.

Discography

A Joyful Noise (1991, Foundation CMF 0160).
At the Feet of God (1995, New Haven).
Tomorrow (2000, Ceili CEIL CD 2005).

SULLIVANS, THE

Enoch Hugh Sullivan (b. September 18, 1931, Alabama)
Maggie Louise Brewster Sullivan (b. January 22, 1933, Alabama)
Emmett Austin Sullivan (b. July 25, 1936, Alabama; d. April 10, 1993)

Since 1949, the Sullivan family from Southern Alabama has performed top-flight bluegrass gospel music at concerts, at festivals, via broadcasts, and on more than a dozen recorded albums. Like so much of bluegrass music, their up-tempo style features the acoustic instrumental backing of fiddle, guitar, banjo, mandolin, and bass. The singing, though occasionally done in group harmony, has always featured the lead voice of original member Margie Sullivan, done very much in the strong-voiced country tradition of Molly O'Day and Wilma Lee Cooper.

Enoch Hugh Sullivan and Emmett Austin Sullivan, sons of the Reverend Arthur Sullivan of Washington County, Alabama, grew up with the Pentecostal church music of the region, but they also loved the country music of such artists as Johnnie & Jack and the Bailes Brothers, and the earliest bluegrass recordings of Bill Monroe and his various disciples were special favorites. In 1949, big brother Enoch took to wife a fellow sixteen-year-old, Margaret Louise "Margie" Brewster of Winnsboro, Louisiana, daughter of a Pentecostal evangelist, shortly after their first meeting at an Alabama revival.

Featuring Enoch's new bride as lead singer, the Sullivan Family launched its professional career at WRJW in Picayune, Mississippi. In the early years, father Arthur Sullivan often performed with the family group, as did Jerry Sullivan and Aubrey Sullivan. The group spent six years based on radio in Jackson, Alabama (1950–1956), and then they moved to another station in Thomasville, Alabama. Touring soon eclipsed any broadcast work as the Sullivans found equal acceptance on bluegrass and gospel circuits. Their first recordings were 78-rpm records for the Revival label, but it was with fellow evangelist, revivalist, and broadcast musician Walter Bailes (formerly of the Bailes Brothers) and the Loyal Records label he owned that they made most of their recordings between about 1959 and the early 1970s. "Walking My Lord Up Calvary's Hill" and Margie's original composition "Old Brush Arbor" (also recorded by country legend George Jones) were among their most popular songs.

Talented musicians worked with the family core, including a five-year stint from the versatile Joe Stuart and a year from the young Philadelphia, Mississippi, native Marty Stuart. Enoch and Margie's youngest daughter, Lisa Sullivan, joined the group for a while, and when original member Emmett Sullivan had to leave the group for reasons of health (he died in 1993), Earn Steed, a banjoist formerly with Bill Monroe's Blue Grass Boys, stepped in. Joy DeVille (bass), James Phillips and Joe Cook (both mandolin players), Caleb Dennis, and Alan Sibley are among those who have worked with the group in recent years. The family's recordings made after Walter Bailes's Loyal label folded in the early 1970s have appeared on

Atteiram, Old Homestead, Pioneer, and Homeplace Records, and most of these are still sold in cassette versions at concerts or by mail from the family's home base in St. Stephens, Alabama. The group is featured at the website of the Alabama State Council on the Arts, which recorded them in 1995 at Gadsden for their "Musics of Alabama" series. Their career has been recounted by Enoch and Margie Sullivan in a book cowritten with publisher Robert Gentry and several younger family members, *The Sullivan Family: 50 Years in Bluegrass Gospel Music*.

RONNIE PUGH

Reference and Further Reading

Sullivan, Enoch; Margie Sullivan; et al. *The Sullivan Family: 50 Years in Bluegrass Gospel Music*. Many, LA: Sweet Dreams Publishing Company, 2000.
Tribe, Ivan. "The Sullivan Family." In *Definitive Country: The Ultimate Encyclopedia of Country Music and its Performers*. New York: Bumper Books, 1995.

Discography

LPs

Bluegrass Gospel (Loyal LP-168).
Old Brush Arbors (Loyal LP-231).
The Light in the Sky (Loyal LP-252).
What a Wonderful Savior Is He (Loyal LP-266).
The Prettiest Flowers Will Be Blooming (Atteiram API-1518).
My Old Cottage Home (Atteiram API-1545).
Gospel Warmup (Atteiram API-1599).

Cassettes

The Sullivan Family Remembers the Louvin Brothers (1988, Pioneer).
Live in Philadelphia, Mississippi (1989, Pioneer).
I Have Found the Way (1990, Pioneer).
Pure and Simple (1991, Homeplace).

SUMMERS, MYRNA

(b. March 30, 1949, Washington, DC)

Myrna's uncompromising, fiercely defiant, indefatigable approach to her life and music goes back three generations to her maternal grandmother, Mother Victoria Hill, who left Methodism and pioneered the first Church of God in Christ (COGIC) congregation in Bowman, South Carolina (near Orangeburg). Mother Hill's daughter, Bessie, made her way to Washington, DC, where she married Asbury Summers. It was into this tradition of strong, decisive churchwomen that daughter Myrna was born.

From the age of two, Myrna demonstrated interest and ability in singing and playing the piano (Summers interview, January 12, 2004). However, there was one handicap: shyness. Refreshing Spring COGIC's afternoon program in Summer 1951 was to feature Little Myrna in her debut. Her fiercely determined mother had the perfect cure for stage fright: a "rod" fashioned from an oak tree that stood in the churchyard at 4407 Lee Street N.E. From that time on, Myrna has been blessing audiences regionally and nationally with the gospel in song. Present at the Springs were musical mentors such as the legendary Theodore Alfred King, Refreshing Spring's minister of music who coached her during her formative years. Her formal preparation was with Toutorsky Academy of Music.

Myrna's first group, the Refreshingnettes, was formed during the early 1960s and included Yvonne Bailey (Washington), pianist; Carolyn Gray (DuPree), alto; and Dorothy Felder (Jones) and Ms. Summers, leads. Her first single, "Stay with God," (1970, Hob/Sceptor Records) gave Myrna her first Grammy nomination; the recording from which it came afforded her song and album of the year, awarded by the Gospel Music Workshop of America. In 1979, she took prison ministry to a new level with her live performance of "Give Me Something to Hold On To" in the chapel of the Alderson, West Virginia, Federal Correctional Institution for Women. (Her plans are to return to Alderson during 2005 for a second live concert marking the twenty-fifth anniversary of the project.) This same selection, "Give Me Something to Hold On To," also earned her a Grammy nomination.

Her 1988 album, *We're Going to Make It* (Savoy Records), with guest artist Reverend Timothy Wright, earned her a Stellar Award in the category Best Traditional Gospel Artist (Female). Her biggest hit continues to be "God Gave Me a Song" (1970, Cotillion/Atlantic Records); she is also known widely for *Uncloudy Day* (1976, Savoy; reissued 1990). Another major influence on Myrna's work was the late Donny Hathaway ("Extensions of a Man," 1973, Atlantic Records), whose emphasis on instrumentation almost took her in a different direction had it not been for Arif Mardin, vice president of Atlantic Records. There was no need for overinstrumentation, Mr. Mardin advised. She needed nothing to obstruct nor diffuse that smashing alto voice.

When Summers is not recording, she hones her skills as minister of music, formerly with Bishop Gilbert L. Patterson, Temple of Deliverance COGIC of Memphis, Tennessee, and currently with Reid Temple, AME, in Lanham, Maryland. For its first experiment with gospel music performance, the Inter-American Development Bank's Cultural Center recently invited Myrna and thirty voices of Reid Temple to host a concert at its downtown Washington, DC, location, for a crossroads of International Monetary Fund and World Bank staff, representing cultures and ethnic groups from around the world. With more than fifty albums to her credit, the gospel had yet another hearing from this enterprising, pioneering evangelist, whose compassion and enthusiasm for the things of God continue to propel her music.

EVELYN M. E. TAYLOR

Reference and Further Reading

"Grammy Awards for 1978." Super 70s website, http://www.super70s.com/Super70s/Music/1978/Grammys.asp.

Inter-American Development Bank. "Gospel Singer, Myrna Summers & Reid Temple AME Mass Choir" (announcement flier). December 9, 2004.

"Rev. Timothy Wright: Godfather of Gospel Music." Richard De La Font Agency website, http://www.delafont.com/music_acts/timothy-wright.htm.

Summers, Myrna. Interviews and e-mail with Evelyn M. E. Taylor, Greenbelt, MD, and Washington, DC, January 12, 15, and 19 and February 6, 2005.

———. "Myrna Summers Biographical Statement." December 17, 2004.

Wynn, Ron. "Myrna Summers Biography." Rejoice, All Music Guide website, http://www.mpt.com.

Discography

"God Gave Me a Song" (1970, Cotillion/Atlantic Records)
I Found Jesus (1976, Savoy)
Uncloudy Day (1976, Savoy; reissued 1990)
Give Me Something to Hold On To (1980)
I'll Keep Holding On (1980)
Life Is Fragile, Handle with Prayer (1980)
We're Going to Make It (1989)
You Are My Miracle (1989)
You Don't Have Nothing If You Don't Have Jesus (1990)
I'll Tell the World, Live (1991, Savoy)
Deliverance (1993)
His Mercy Endureth Forever (2000, PGF Records)

Video

Myrna Summers Workshop Choir of Washington, DC (1991).
We're Going to Make It (1991).

SUMNER, JOHN DANIEL "J. D."

(b. November 19, 1924; d. November 16, 1998)

John Daniel "J. D." Sumner was promoted as the world's lowest bass singer, a title he held with the *Guinness Book of World Records* for six years. Although

he had no formal music training, he performed as a member of the Sunshine Boys, the Blackwood Brothers Quartet, and the Stamps Quartet. His contributions as a performer, composer, and businessman have resulted in his induction into the Gospel Music Hall of Fame and the Southern Gospel Music Association Hall of Fame.

J. D. Sumner was born on November 19, 1924, and raised in Lakeland, Florida, as the youngest of four children. He learned to sing in church and at area camp meetings, where legendary bass singer Frank Stamps inspired him. At age eleven, he made his first radio appearance on WLAK Lakeland, singing bass for a quartet from his church. Throughout his amateur career, Sumner performed at the local Polk County Singing Conventions, where he gained respect as an outstanding bass singer. Although he excelled as a singer, he dropped out of school in ninth grade to work and help support his family. At age sixteen, he married Mary Agnes Varnadore and began to raise a family. He was drafted into the army in 1944, where he served as a truck driver because of his flat feet.

When Sumner left the army in 1945, he began his professional singing career as a member of the Sunny South Quartet out of Tampa, Florida. Sumner replaced "Big Chief" James Wetherington, who left to sing bass with the Statesmen Quartet. While in the Sunny South Quartet, J. D. sang with Jake Hess, who would also leave the group to sing lead with the Statesmen. Sumner eventually became the manager of the Sunny South Quartet, which changed its name to the Dixie Lily Harmoneers.

In 1949, Sumner left the Dixie Lily Harmoneers Quartet to sing bass for the Sunshine Boys. While with the Sunshine Boys, Sumner made his first recordings, "Marching Up to Heaven" and "Glad Reunion Day," which were released on the White Church label. The group gained moderate success and signed with Decca Records and Columbia Pictures in 1950. Sumner performed as a singing cowboy in several of the seventeen Westerns in which the group appeared, but he never had a speaking role. After the plane crash that killed bass Bill Lyles and baritone R. W. Blackwood in 1954, J. D. Sumner left the Sunshine Boys to sing with the Blackwood Brothers Quartet.

While with the Blackwood Brothers Quartet, Sumner persuaded the group to buy a bus and customize it to meet their travel needs. So in 1955, the Blackwood Brothers Quartet became the first Southern gospel group to tour in a customized bus. During his time with the group, Sumner was encouraged to write songs and became a prolific composer, writing more than five hundred songs, including "The Old Country Church," "He's All that I Need," "Walking and Talking with My Lord," and "Crossing Chilly Jordan."

To capitalize on the publishing rights to his songs, Sumner formed the Gospel Quartet Music Company and convinced the Blackwood Brothers Quartet to buy the Stamps Music Company in 1963. In addition to the music rights, the Blackwood Brothers bought the rights to the Stamps Quartet name. Sumner took on the role of managing the group and then became the bass singer for the group in 1965. Sumner modernized the Stamps Quartet by adding a guitar, bass, and drums to live performances. This modern sound helped J. D. Sumner and the Stamps Quartet get the job of backing up Elvis Presley in 1971. They toured with Elvis until his death in 1977. While with Elvis, Sumner sang on "Burning Love" and contributed to Grammy-winning performances in 1972 and 1974. In 1981, Sumner returned to traditional quartet singing when he joined the Masters V, a group of legendary gospel performers including Hovie Lister, Jake Hess, Rosie Rozell, and James Blackwood. He remained with this group until 1987.

In addition to his singing contributions, Sumner greatly influenced the gospel music business. He was the owner of several music publishing companies, including the Gospel Quartet Music Company, the Stamps Quartet Music Company (co-owner), and the Temple Music Company. In 1959, he helped the Blackwood Brothers and the Statesmen form the Skylite Recording Company, a pioneering Southern gospel record label. Sumner formed the Sumar Talent Agency, a gospel music booking agency that included clients such as the Imperials, the Stamps Quartet, the Blackwood Brothers, and the Speer Family. Sumner also helped form the National Quartet Convention in 1956 with the Blackwood Brothers.

J. D. Sumner was a charter member of the Gospel Music Association and was inducted into its Hall of Fame in 1983. In 1997, he was inducted into the Southern Gospel Music Association Hall of Fame. J. D. Sumner continued to perform until his death from a heart attack in his sleep on November 16, 1998.

THEODORE E. FULLER

Reference and Further Reading

Davis, Paul. *The Legacy of the Blackwood Brothers: Authorized Biographies of Cecil and James Blackwood.* Greenville, SC: Blue Ridge Publishing, 2000.

Terrell, Bob. *The Life and Times of J. D. Sumner.* Nashville, TN: J. D. Sumner, 1994.

———. *The Music Men: The Story of Professional Gospel Quartet Singing.* Alexander, NC: Mountain Church, 2001.

Discography

Blackwood Brothers Quartet (1954–1965)

His Hands (1958, RCA Victor LPM1705); *I'm Bound for That City* (1958, RCA LPM1488); *The Blackwood Brothers* (1959, RCA Camden CAL 544); *Give the World a Smile* (1959, Skylite SSLP 5966); *Paradise Island* (1959, CA Victor LSP 2093); *The Stranger of Galilee* (1959, RCA Victor LPM1892); *Beautiful Isle of Somewhere* (1960, RCA Victor LSP 2248); *In Concert* (1960, RCA Victor LSP 2137); *Statesmen–Blackwood Favorites* (1960, Skylite SSLP 5980); *Sunday Meetin' Time* (1960, Skylite SRLP 5967); *Pearly White City* (1961, RCA Victor LSP 2397); *On Tour* (1961, RCA Victor LSP 2300); *At Home with the Blackwoods* (1962, Skylite SSLP 5995); *The Keys to the Kingdom* (1962, RCA Camden CAL 618); *Merry Christmas with the Statesmen* (1962, RCA Victor 2606); *Precious Memories* (1962, RCA Victor LSP 2506); *Silver Anniversary Album* (1962, RCA Victor LSP 2585); *The Blackwood Brothers Quartet Featuring J. D. Sumner* (1963, RCA Victor LSP 2752); *Give Us This Day* (1963, RCA Camden CAL 735); *The National Gospel Quartet Convention* (1963, RCA Victor LSP/LPM 2728); *On Stage* (1963, RCA Victor LSP 2646); *The Blackwood Brothers Quartet Featuring James Blackwood* (1964, RCA Victor LSP/LPM 2838); *The Blackwood Brothers Quartet Present Their Tenor Bill Shaw* (1964, RCA Victor LSP 2938); *Blackwood Family Album* (1964, Skylite SSLP/SRLP 6026); *Gloryland Jubilee* (1964, RCA Camden CAL 794); *TV Requests* (1964, Stateswood SW 404); *The Best of the Blackwood Brothers* (1965, RCA Victor LSP 2931); *The Blackwood Brothers Quartet Featuring Cecil Blackwood* (1965, RCA Victor LSP 3439); *Do You Thank the Lord Each Day* (1965, RCA Camden CAS 854e/CAL 854); *Something Old Something New* (1965, RCA Victor LSP 3334).

Masters V (1980–1988)

The Masters V (1981, Skylite SLP6256); *The Legendary Masters V* (1982, Skylite 6282); *Masters V Present* (1982, Skylite SLP6266); *O What a Savior* (1982, Skylite 6265); *Live at the Joyful Noise* (1983, Skylite 6303); *The Master's Hymns* (1985, Skylite 6339); *Sing Sensational Statesmen Hits* (1985, Skylite 6345); *Have a Little Faith* (1986, Merinet 1003); *Great Voices in Gospel Music* (1995, Manna Music; three-tape set of Masters V in concert from 1984 with Doris Akers); *Classics of Yesteryear* (Skylite 6363); *God Made a Way* (Skylite 6377); *Good Things* (Skylite 6333); *The Legend Lives On* (Skylite 8802); *The Original Masters V* (Bibletone 10142; live); *Sing Fabulous Blackwood Brothers Hits* (Skylite 6352); *Thru the Years* (Skylite 6315).

J. D. Sumner & The Stamps Quartet

Elvis Gospel Favorites (1994, K-tel); *Elvis: Walk a Mile in My Shoes—The Essential 70s Masters* (1995, RCA 66670); *Best of Gospel* (1996, Richmond); *20 Southern Gospel Favorites* (1999, Benson Records 8004); *Elvis Presley Collection* (1999, RCA); *Final Sessions* (1999, New Haven); *Elvis: 30 #1 Hits* (2002, RCA 07863 68079-2; "Burning Love" and "Way Down"); *Gospel Gold* (2004, Brentwood 40841).

SUNSHINE BOYS QUARTET

Fred C. Daniel (b. March 29, 1925)
Burl Strevel (b. June 14, 1928; d. November 12, 1981)
Ed Wallace (b. February 2, 1924)
Ace Richman (b. August 14, 1916; d. Unknown)
John Daniel "J. D." Sumner (b. November 19, 1924; d. November 16, 1998)

The Sunshine Boys were formed in the late 1930s as a country and western band. Through the years, they have performed under several names, but they have always been four versatile musicians who were willing and capable of adapting their talents to meet the demands of their market. The Sunshine Boys were one of the few gospel artists to become stars of radio, television, and motion pictures.

During the early years, the group worked for several radio stations as staff musicians performing Western and swing music in addition to their gospel fare. The group consisting of John "Tennessee" Smith, A. L. "Smitty" Smith, Milton "Ace" Richman, and Eddie Wallace was the first that brought gospel music to their fan base.

The Sunshine Boys demonstrated their versatility at this time by performing as two different groups on radio station WAGA. The station needed a Western swing band, so the Sunshine Boys became their alter-ego: the Light Crust Dough Boys. Very few listeners in the Atlanta area realized they were listening to the same group with different names. Their concert performances were always done under the name the Sunshine Boys, where their fare was almost entirely gospel music.

In 1945, the Sunshine Boys traveled to California to act in a series of motion pictures. They appeared with stars including Eddie Dean, Lash Larue, and Smiley Burnette. In these films, the Sunshine Boys would sing Western songs and spirituals in the context of the movie.

In 1949, Ace Richman and Eddie Wallace were joined by J. D. Sumner and Fred Daniel, and the group moved to Wheeling, West Virginia. They quickly built a following for themselves and became regulars on radio station WWVA's *Jamboree*.

The Sunshine Boys were heard on countless radio stations via their transcription services. They recorded several hundred songs for the Lang–Worth Transcription service. These performances were distributed nationwide.

The Sunshine Boys became the first gospel artists to headline in major hotels on the Nevada circuit. Their blend of gospel and Western music made them favorites in that area.

The Sunshine Boys have accomplished many "firsts" in gospel music. They introduced television to the South at WSB-TV in 1948. They also did their own ABC radio network program daily from 1954 to 1959. They still continue to perform on a limited basis in the Atlanta area.

JOHN CRENSHAW

Reference and Further Reading

Terrell, Bob. *J. D. Sumner: Gospel Music Is My Life*, 62–73. Nashville, TN: Impact Books, 1971.
————. *The Music Men: The Story of Professional Gospel Quartet Singing*, 156, 161–163, 190–192. Nashville, TN: Bob Terrell, 1990.
Wallace, Eddie. Interview, November 1999.

Selected Discography

The Sunshine Boys recorded numerous singles on many labels, including Decca, Starday, Dot, and Bibletone, as well as their private label. Included in the Discography are some of their more popular LPs.
Golden Gospel Million Sellers (Starday 156).
Golden Melodies (Starday 129).
Happy Home Up There (Starday 349).
He's Got the Whole World (Starday 290).
Out West (Sing 3051).
Sing Their Most Popular Songs (Dot 3093).
Sing Unto Him (Dot 3189).
The Word (Starday 113).

SWAGGART, JIMMY

(b. March 15, 1935, Ferriday, LA)

Jimmy Lee Swaggart is a pioneering televangelist whose reach was at its broadest in the 1980s. Like his cousins, flamboyant rock 'n' roll pianist Jerry Lee Lewis and the country musician Mickey Gilley, Swaggart was a talented, self-taught pianist. He spent much of his early childhood engaged in secular activities with his cousins but became increasingly drawn to religious life as he aged.

Swaggart's parents, W. L. "Sun" and Minnie Bell Swaggart, were swept up in the religious revivalism of the 1930s. First exposed to the Protestant Pentecostal denomination the Assemblies of God in 1936, when Jimmy was an infant, the family grew increasingly religious during his childhood. Both of his parents had become lay ministers by the time Swaggart reached adolescence. Born again at the age of eight, Swaggart himself was recognized locally as a spiritual prodigy after prophesying in tongues during a church meeting.

Swaggart dropped out of high school at seventeen to marry Francis Anderson, a fifteen-year-old chorister at Sun Swaggart's church. Two years later, in 1954, the couple's only child, Donnie, was born. Swaggart began preaching on streetcorners while supporting his family as a ditchdigger. Despite the concurrent rise to fame of Jerry Lee Lewis, with whom he remained close, Swaggart publicly denounced rock 'n' roll as a tool of Satan and vowed to use his musical talents only in the service of God.

By the time Swaggart was in his early twenties, he and his family had begun traveling the gospel circuit. At tent meeting revivals across the rural South, Swaggart delivered aggressive, fire-and-brimstone–style sermons that he would punctuate by speaking in tongues and breaking frequently into song, dance, and tears. Officially ordained by the Assemblies of God in 1958, he reached beyond rural revival tents during the course of the next decade. He began appearing at increasingly large urban venues through the 1960s. Interested in the disseminatory power of the mass media, he launched a radio show, *The Camp Meeting Hour*, which premiered on January 1, 1969. This successful program was eventually broadcast on hundreds of stations across the country.

Swaggart taped his first television broadcast in Nashville in 1973 and continued to hone his media savvy into the 1980s. Swaggart relied heavily on gospel music to spread his message. Backed by a full band and a mixed choir, he regularly sang gospel songs in his smooth baritone voice during television broadcasts. He has also recorded approximately fifty albums of original gospel music during the course of his career. His ministry claims to have sold more than fifteen million copies of Swaggart's recordings worldwide. These recordings, however, are released on a private label, Jim Records, whose sales are not audited by the Recording Industry Association of America.

By the mid-1980s, the Swaggart Ministries, based in Baton Rouge, Louisiana, claimed seventeen different television programs being carried by more than thirty-two hundred stations to a viewing audience of more than five hundred million in approximately 145 countries. At the height of its reach, Swaggart's organization was bringing in more than a hundred million dollars each year.

Staunchly conservative and hotly judgmental, Swaggart made enemies. His targets included Catholics, lukewarm Protestants, public education, social and political liberals, and homosexuals. In 1987, he publicly accused rival Assemblies of God televangelists Jim Bakker and Marvin Gorman of adultery. Gorman responded to the accusations by hiring a private detective, who photographed Swaggart entering a Baton Rouge motel with a prostitute named Debra Murphree. Murphree acknowledged that Swaggart was a regular customer, who paid her to perform voyeuristic acts.

Branded a hypocrite and an adulterer, Swaggart acknowledged his transgressions during a television broadcast on February 21, 1988. Before a packed studio audience, he tearfully apologized to his family, the Assemblies of God, and Jesus. The Assemblies of God relieved Swaggart of his ministerial duties for one year; Swaggart alienated his denomination further by frequently attempting to ignore the injunction. In 1991, Swaggart was caught driving down the wrong side of a road with another prostitute in his car. This time, the Assemblies of God defrocked him.

In the years since the scandals—and despite the fact that he is no longer recognized by his denomination—Swaggart has attempted to revive his ministry. He claims to have reformed and to have repaired his relationship with God. Along with his son, Donnie, he broadcasts to thirty different countries and continues to record gospel albums. His religious and economic reach, however, have been seriously diminished.

ELIZABETH L. WOLLMAN

Reference and Further Reading

Giuliano, Michael J. *Thrice-Born: The Rhetorical Comeback of Jimmy Swaggart*. Macon, GA: Mercer University Press, 1999.

Jimmy Swaggart Ministries website, http://www.jimmyswaggart.com/exploreJSM.cfm.

Lundy, Hunter. *Let Us Prey: The Public Trial of Jimmy Swaggart*. Columbus, MS: Genesis, 1999.

Nauer, Barbara. *Jimmy Swaggart—Dead Man Rising: On Black Light as a Weapon in the Culture Wars*. Baton Rouge, LA: Glory Arts Productions, 1997.

Seaman, Ann Rowe. *Swaggart: The Unauthorized Biography of an American Evangelist*. New York: Continuum, 1999.

Wright, Lawrence. *Saints and Sinners: Walker Railey, Jimmy Swaggart, Madalyn Murray O'Hair, Anton LaVey, Will Campbell, Matthew Fox*. New York: Knopf, 1993.

Discography

Homeward Bound (1980, Jim Records LP 136).
Living Waters (1984, Jim Records LP 143).
It's Beginning to Rain (1986, Jim Records LP 145).
It Matters to Him About You (1990, Jim Records CD 155).
My God Is Real (1995, Jim Records 169).
You Won't Leave Here Like You Came in Jesus' Name (1998, Jim Records CD 174).
Then Jesus Came (2002, Jim Records CD 178).

SWAN SILVERTONES

Claude A. Jeter (b. October 26, 1914, Birmingham, AL)

One of the earliest quartet groups who ushered in the golden era in 1945 was the Swan Silvertones (the Swans), formed in 1938 by falsetto tenor Claude A. Jeter in Coalwood, West Virginia. His father, a lawyer who held a professional position with the Tennessee Coal and Iron Railroad, died when Claude was eight years old. His mother, Maggie Jeter, was a singer of note. The family moved to Kentucky, where Jeter finished high school. He then went to West Virginia to work in the coal mines.

Singing with quartets and in the church, Jeter organized the Four Harmony Kings, or Kings, with his brother and two miners. The quartet consisted of Jeter, Solomon Womack, John Myles, and Henry Bossard. The Kings performed every Sunday morning on radio WDIR. Initially, the Kings were *a cappella* and not very emotional as they sang. Jeter sang *a cappella* "I'm Coming Home," and "Motherless Child." They were known by fans as a barbershop harmony quartet who performed on weekends.

Slowly, the group became a gospel quartet group in live concert performances. The Swans produced duets, with Jeter and Crenshaw singing "Trouble in My Way" and "I'm A'Rolling." In 1942, the group changed their name to the Silvertone Singers to avoid confusion with the Four Kings of Harmony. The Silvertones moved to Knoxville, Tennessee, becoming full-time professional singers broadcasting five days a week on radio WNOX. They changed their name to the Swan Silvertones to advertise the Swan Bakery that sponsored their broadcasts.

From 1946 to 1951, the Swans produced more than a hundred records. In 1948, the group relocated to Pittsburgh. The membership became Louis Johnson, second lead, Paul Owens as alternative lead, and Myles and William "Pete" Conner as bass. From 1946 to 1952, the Swans recorded on King Records. "I Cried Holy/Go Ahead" was their best seller. Two very famous recordings were "All Alone" in 1947 and "My Rock" in 1950. They recorded "Heavenly Light" on Specialty Records in 1952. The Swans signed with Vee-Jay Records in 1956, recording "Pray for Me/Let's Go to Church Together."

The audiences during the golden era of gospel (1945–1955) and into the 1960s wanted guitars, drums, shouting, moans, and breathtaking blends known as "first class house-wreckin' gospel." The Swans gave them this excitement in 1957, with Claude Jeter and Paul Owens recording the Negro spiritual "Oh Mary Don't You Weep"; it was their greatest hit. Jeter's improvised "I'll Be a Bridge over Deep Water" inspired Paul Simon to compose "Bridge over Troubled Water." In 1959 they recorded an album entitled *The Swan Silvertones* and in 1960, they recorded *Singin' in My Soul.* Hob Records produced many blockbusters for the Swans. In the mid-1960s, Jeter was ordained in Detroit at the Church of Holiness Science.

Jeter retired from the Swans and moved to New York City around 1968. He had been the leader for the Swans group from 1938 to 1968. The group continued with James Lewis and Carl Davis as lead singers. In 1972, Jeter recorded famous gospel composer William Herbert Brewster's (ca. 1898–1987) "Lord, I've Tried." Jeter is currently preaching and continues to sing as a soloist and as a member of reunion quartet concerts. "Love Lifted Me," a long-playing album on Specialty Records produced in 1970, including two great gospel songs entitled "Trouble in My Way" and "Glory to His Name."

The Swans gained national attention with white audiences in around 1953, when they increased travel to other countries, almost instantly becoming a crossover success. The Swans have a large European fan base, with records in the United Kingdom on Ace records. By all accounts, the Swans are quartet pioneers in gospel music. The Swans were inducted by David Gough into the International Gospel Music Hall of Fame and Museum in Detroit in 2003, with "Trouble in My Way" providing background music. The audience stood to sing in a call-and-response style and clap as pictures of the Swans and many accomplishments were shared.

[Call] Trouble in my way [Response] Trouble in my way
[Call] I have to cry sometimes [Response] I have to cry sometimes
[Call] Trouble in my way [Response] Trouble in my way
[Call] I have to cry sometimes [Response] I have to cry sometimes
[Call] I lay awake at night [Response] I lay awake at night
[Call] That is alright [Response] That is alright
[Call] Jesus is goin' to fix it [Response] Jesus is goin' to fix it
[Call] After awhile [Response] After awhile

SHERRY SHERROD DUPREE

Reference and Further Reading

Boyer, Horace Clarence *How Sweet the Sound: The Golden Age of Gospel.* Washington, DC: Elliott & Clark, 1995.

DuPree, Sherry Sherrod *Biographical Dictionary of African-American Holiness-Pentecostals 1880–1990.* Washington, DC: Middle Atlantic Regional Press, 1989.

———; Herbert C. DuPree *African-American Good News (Gospel) Music.* Washington, DC: Middle Atlantic Regional Press, 1993.

International Gospel Music Hall of Fame and Museum website, http://www.gmhf.org (accessed August 28, 2004).

Reagon, Bernice Johnson, ed. *We'll Understand It Better By and By. Pioneering African American Gospel Composers*. Washington, DC: Smithsonian Institution Press, 1992.

Discography

Love Lifted Me (1970, Specialty Records SPS 2122).
Get Right with the Swan Silvertones (Archives Alive 8122-70081; reissue of Vee-Jay release).

SWANEE QUINTET

The "Suwannees" were first a gospel trio formed in Augusta, Georgia, by Charlie Barnwell, Rufus Washington, and William "Pee Wee" Crawford in the mid-1940s. They became the Swanee Quintet when they added two other members, James "Big Red" Anderson and Reuben W. Willingham, on lead vocals in 1945, while Crawford concentrated on his guitar playing, which became the trademark of the group. Like the Harmonizing Four, they stayed an example of the down-home unaffected quartet singing, keeping the same membership for decades. Unlike most groups who gained popularity in gospel, the Swanee Quintet always kept Augusta as their home base, cultivating their rural sound. They were very popular in Georgia and South Carolina.

Like many groups, they were featured daily on a local radio program in Atlanta to spread the gospel message and, most of all, to advertise their singing in churches and performances in auditoriums. They did it with much success for ten years, during which time they won the Golden Cup Award for seven consecutive years; and that is how they came to the attention of Nashboro Records, where they recorded their first session in December 1951. Its success was moderate, and they had to wait until March 1956 to enter the Nashboro recording studios again. Twenty songs were recorded and issued on singles, one of which, "Sit Down Servant," scored a big hit on the gospel market with Crawford's bluesy guitar riffs, Willingham's preaching and singing, and the background vocals of Anderson, Barnwell, and Washington—a dream team bound to enlighten the Swanee Quintet's recordings for more than thirty years of presence on the gospel highway.

A big move happened in October 1956, when the quintet became a sextet (without change of name) with the addition of a second lead singer, "Little" Johnny Jones. His light tenor was a welcome contrast to Willingham's harsh admonitions and personal testimonies, appealing to his audiences because of the references to black people's general experience of hard times in poetic phrases. Jones, influenced by Sam Cooke, could break effortlessly from his tenor solos into melodious falsettos, contrasting with Willingham's growls and baritone.

Between October 1956 and 1964, the group recorded forty-four songs issued on singles; they were sometimes accompanied by piano, organ, bass, and drums, but unobtrusively. Every one of the singles met with great popular success in black communities, and the Swanee Quintet became one of the most celebrated groups in the South. They appeared at the Apollo Theatre in New York in 1955, stealing the show, and at Carnegie Hall in 1957. They toured extensively, performing in forty-four states, with the motto "We put God in everything we do." The best examples of Jones and Willingham's empathy and fascinating complexity from this period are probably "New Walk" and "Lowly Jesus," both on the same single (Nashboro 653), but nearly all of their other songs are worth mention and commendations.

As the years passed, there was little change to the Swanees' personnel and sound; they stayed with Nashboro, keeping up with musical fashion and sounding secular at times (in a bluesy "The Fire Keeps A'Burning," for instance) or even pop (in "Just One More Time" and "Holy Ghost Got Me"). Willingham went on giving out with heavy calls to salvation and Jones continued to combine sweetness with power, occasionally preaching or testifying.

In 1964, the group recorded the first album of a long series for Nashboro and Creed Records, and in 1966 they sang hard gospel songs with the James Brown Road Show; Brown even produced a session for the Swanees in May 1966 with his band's brass section, issued on Federal Records. Shortly after that session, Willingham left the group to enter the ministry and perform as a solo singer for Nashboro, although on his first recordings in 1969, he used the Swanee Quintet as a backing group. Johnny Jones also left to try an unsuccessful and short pop career, and he came back to the Swanees from time to time.

The new leads were Percy Griffin and Clarence Murray, two other tremendous vocalists who kept the group in the fore of modern gospel, but times were changing, and the advent of contemporary gospel in the 1970s put a virtual end to the Swanee Quintet's musical activities.

ROBERT SACRÉ

Reference and Further Reading

Boyer, Horace Clarence. *How Sweet the Sound: The Golden Age of Gospel*. Washington, DC: Elliott & Clark, 1995.

Hayes, J. Cedric; Robert Laughton. *Gospel Records 1943–1969. A Black Music Discography*, 2 vols. London, UK: Record Information Services, 1992.

Heilbut, Tony. *The Gospel Sound: Good News and Bad Times*. New York: Limelight, 1985.

Reagon, Bernice Johnson, ed. *We'll Understand It Better By and By. Pioneering African American Gospel Composers*. Washington, DC: Smithsonian Institution Press, 1992.

Discography

What About Me? Anniversary Album (1992, Ace Records [UK] CDCHD 432).

The Reverend Willingham Collection (1995, Nashboro NASH4622 2).

SWANEE RIVER BOYS

Buford Abner (b. November 10, 1917)

Merle Abner (b. April 25, 1913)

Billy Carrier (b. June 16, 1913)

George Hughes (b. March 1, 1911)

The Swanee River Boys consisted of Buford Abner, lead singer; Billy Carrier, baritone singer and guitarist; Merle Abner, bass singer; and George Hughes, tenor. The Abner brothers, Buford and Merle, were born and reared near Wedowee, Alabama. They met Billy Carrier through their uncle, Stacy Abner. Billy Carrier was born near Arthur, Kentucky.

In 1938, Billy Carrier and Stacy Abner formed a quartet called the Vaughan Four. The quartet was named for the James D. Vaughan School of Music in Lawrenceburg, Tennessee. They performed on radio station WNOX in Knoxville, Tennessee, and they made personal appearances in the area. In 1940, they changed their name to the Swanee River Boys (the Swanees), moved to radio station WDOD in Chattanooga, Tennessee, and added George Hughes, born in Texarkana, Arkansas, who replaced Stacy Abner.

The Swanees made their *Barn Dance* debut in Atlanta, Georgia, on March 22, 1941. In addition to appearing on the *Barn Dance* and the *Georgia Jubilee*, they became the featured artists on the *Little Country Church House*. The Swanees had a unique sound due to their black spiritual sound and smooth harmony. They did some country, folk, and Western music but specialized mostly in soft spirituals. The group was forced to disband in late 1942, when Merle Abner and Buford Abner entered military service. During part of the Abners' absence, they were replaced by Lee Roy Abernathy and Bill Lyles. The original members were reunited in 1946, and two years later they moved to Cincinnati. In 1953, they released on the King label one of their most famous LPs, *Do You Believe*.

Another popular album was *Swanee River Boys' Finest, 1946–48*.

During their career they performed on the NBC radio network and recorded for the King, Skylite, and Zondervan labels. Buford Abner wrote and copyrighted many songs (he has 116 BMI copyrights), including a gospel song called "A Fool Such As I." During the 1960s, the group joined the USO shows performing for the U.S. troops overseas. They sang together for thirty-seven years.

Following their retirement, the Swanees settled in various parts of the country: Billy Carrier in the Atlanta suburb of Smyrna; Buford Abner in Indianapolis, Indiana; Merle Abner in Wedowee, Alabama; and George Hughes in Texarkana, Arkansas. Buford moved back to Alabama from Indiana, where he had lived for many years. Buford sang at the Grand Old Gospel Reunion in Greenville, South Carolina, at eighty-five years of age. The Swanees had a nationwide singing career.

SHERRY SHERROD DuPREE

Reference and Further Reading

Daniel, Wayne W. *Pickin' on Peachtree, A History of Country Music in Atlanta*. Urbana: University of Illinois Press, 1990.

DuPree, Sherry Sherrod; Herbert C. DuPree. *African-American Good News (Gospel) Music*. Washington, DC: Middle Atlantic Regional Press, 1993.

International Gospel Music Hall of Fame and Museum website, http://www.gmhf.org (accessed August 28, 2004).

Discography

"Gloryland Boogie" (1953, King 1254; accessed September 30, 2004, at http://255.128.48.20/MP3/SouthernGospel/SwaneeRiverBoys/SwaneeRiverBoys-glorylandboogie.mp3).

"When I Move" (1953, King 1289; accessed September 30, 2004, at http://255.128.48.20/MP3/SouthernGospel/SwaneeRiverBoys/SwaneeRiverBoys-WhenIMove.mp3).

SWENEY, JOHN R.

(b. December 31, 1837; d. April 10, 1899)

John R. Sweney was one of the most popular song leaders of his day, the author of more than a thousand hymns, and the compiler of more than sixty collections of songs. He was born in West Chester, Pennsylvania, and, at an early age, he developed an enthusiasm for music, becoming so proficient that, by age twenty-two he was teaching the subject in Dover, Delaware. He later taught in various schools and colleges, but during the Civil War he directed the band of the Third Delaware Regiment. Following the war, he entered into a twenty-five–year association with the Pennsylvania Military Academy as a professor of music. In 1886, he received the doctor of music degree from that institution.

For ten years during his association with the military academy, Sweney was music director of the local Bethany Presbyterian Church. Prior to 1871, Sweney wrote several songs, but they were mostly of a secular nature. In that year a spiritual crisis occurred in his life that caused him to focus his efforts on religious songs. For the rest of his life, he devoted himself to Christian ministries and music. Church members knew that they were lucky to have Sweney as music director and leader of Sunday school singing, because his talents as a song leader were in great demand throughout the country. His abilities became widely recognized largely as the result of huge summer assemblies that he directed in places such as Ocean Grove, New Jersey; Lake Bluff, Illinois; and New Albany, Indiana.

Among the gospel songwriters with whom Sweney worked were Fanny J. Crosby, Eliza E. Hewitt, and William J. Kirkpatrick; with the latter he collaborated on forty-nine songbooks, several for Kirkpatrick's own Praise Publishing Company. Hymns that Sweney composed music for that are still occasionally heard today include "Tell Me the Story of Jesus," "I Shall Know Him," "There Is Sunshine in My Soul Today," "Stars in My Crown," and "Beulah Land." The first two were set to texts by Fanny J. Crosby; Eliza Hewitt wrote words for the next two, and her cousin, Edgar Page Stites, supplied lyrics to the last one.

"Beulah Land" was sung by Ira D. Sankey at Sweney's funeral. Its melody, which is essentially the same as that of several earlier secular songs, including "Maryland, My Maryland," "Sweet Genevieve," and the German traditional carol "Tannenbaum," was also utilized for a classic "sodbuster" parody, "Dakota Land," that has been localized in half of the states west of the Mississippi River. "Stars in My Crown" was the theme song and gave the title to a 1950 Joel McCrea–Ellen Drew movie about a frontier community.

W. K. McNeil

Reference and Further Reading

Blackwell, Lois S. *The Wings of the Dove: The Story of Gospel Music in America.* Norfolk, VA: Donning, 1978.

Fife, Austin E.; Alta S. Fife, eds. *Cowboy and Western Songs: A Comprehensive Anthology.* New York: C. N. Potter, 1982 (1969).

Hall, Jacob Henry. *Biography of Gospel Song and Hymn Writers.* New York: AMS Press, 1971 (1914).

Osbeck, Kenneth W. *101 Hymn Stories.* Grand Rapids, MI: Kregel, 1982.

——. *101 More Hymn Stories.* Grand Rapids, MI: Kregel, 1985.

Reynolds, William J. *Companion to the Baptist Hymnal.* Nashville, TN: Broadman, 1976.

SWOPE-DUPREE, SHERYL

(b. November 11, 1948)

Sheryl Swope-DuPree, a musician, songwriter, and singer, is a Chicago native. A graduate of Crane High School, she attended the University of Illinois, Oliva Harvey City College. In 1976, she married Donald DuPree, Sr., a Chicago Gold Coast businessman. They have one daughter, Dana.

DuPree began performing as a singer at two years of age in a contest held at the world famous Club Delisa. As a student at the African American Sammy Dyer School of the Theatre, Sheryl practiced her skills in dance as well as theatrical and social performance. She was under the direction of the late Sammy Dyer, Shirley Hall Bass, and Murial Wilson Foster. Bass also has a Sammy Dyer School in the Bahamas. At thirteen years of age, DuPree became a member of the performance group the Vashonettes, created by Bass. In 1970, the Vashonettes began touring with Sammy Davis, Jr. (b. December 8, 1925; d. May 16, 1990) and Sarah Vaughn (b. March 27, 1924; d. April 3, 1990).

As a young adult, DuPree joined the WVON radio family at the height of its popularity and was adopted by Bernadine C. Washington, general manager. Washington and the "Good Guys" disc jockeys included E. Rodney Jones (b. August 4, 1940; d. January 19, 2004), Ritchie Cordell (b. August 4, 1940; d. April 13, 2004), Ed Cook, Herb Kent "The Kool Gent," and the station's owner, Pervis Spann. DuPree seized this opportunity to learn the inner workings of the music business and a short time later recorded her first single, "Let's Get the Show on the Road," on the Duo Label. Pleased with the response of her first solo effort, DuPree followed with three more singles, "Can't Get Him Off My Mind," "Are You Gonna Do Right This Time," and "One Moment," which did very well on top ten pop charts.

DuPree toured with the Chicago-based performing group the Oncoming Times. They toured throughout South America, Mexico, and the Bahamas, and they recorded two hit singles. DuPree experienced close encounters with celebrities and performers such as Jackie Wilson, Brook Benton, and Walter Jackson of Chicago. She performed background vocals for many artists, and her voice can be heard on several commercial jingles on television and radio. She has returned to her roots and is teaching voice at Sammy Dyer School of the Theatre, the Triumphant Charter School, and Oliver Harvey Middle College.

DuPree has embraced the call to ministry through music and has found new meaning in the expression of her musical gifts. DuPree is committed to God and honors her creator. The call on her life is demonstrated in the musical notes she plays and every lyric sung on the recording *Living for the Lord*. The CD is an inspirational rainbow comprising many musical styles with which God has blessed DuPree to play and sing. Joining DuPree is her uncle, George "Sonny" Cohen, who for thirty years played first trumpet with the world famous Count Basie Orchestra. Cohen began his career in Chicago as a member of the Red Saunders Band, which became a major player in Chicago's musical history as the house band for the internationally renowned Regal Theatre and Club Delisa. Selection five on her latest CD features "Praise His Holy Name," with a moving trumpet accompaniment by her uncle. Blues guitarist Luther Adams, who played with B. B. King and Bobby Blue Bland added a touch to the title tune "Living for the Lord." This experience has given Adams the opportunity to demonstrate his triumphant return to Christian music.

DuPree continues to perform in annual productions celebrating the accomplishments of the Sammy Dyer School of the Theater, which is one of Chicago's oldest theatrical establishments. She continues to perform by dancing, singing, and playing piano. On October 23, 2004, DuPree performed at the Annual Induction Dinner of the International Gospel Music Hall of Fame and Museum in Detroit.

SHERRY SHERROD DUPREE

Reference and Further Reading

Crosby, Keith. "International Gospel Music Hall of Fame and Museum 8th Annual Induction Awards Banquet." Detroit Gospel website, http://www.detroitgospel.com/IGMHFM.htm.

International Gospel Music Hall of Fame and Museum website, http://www.gmhf.org (accessed February 18, 2005).

"Living for the Lord." We Do Pray website, http://www.wedopray.com (accessed February 14, 2005).

"WVON History." WVON website, http://www.wvon.com/aboutus/history.html (accessed February 13, 2005).

Discography

The Sheryl Swope Discography is taken from "Northern & Rare Soul Labels Listings, Duo," Anorak's Corner website, http://capitolsoulclub.homestead.com/DuoListing.html (accessed February 14, 2005):

Sheryl Swope. "Let's Get the Show on the Road"/"How You Feel" (Duo 7448); "Can't Get Him Off My Mind"/"How You Feel" (Duo 7451); "Run to Me Are You"/"Gonna Do Right This Time" (Duo 7453); "One Moment"/"Meet Me" (Duo 7456).

Sheryl Swope-DuPree. *We Do Pray Label* (producer Rhonda D. Hannibal at Blackstone Studio in Chicago, September 2002).

T

TAGGART, BLIND JOE

Blind Joe (Joel) Taggart, an itinerant street singer based in (but not native of) the Greenville, South Carolina, area, was one of the first guitar evangelists on record. Almost all of the biographical information that is known about him comes from Joshua White, who reminisces that Taggart had cataracts but was not completely blind and was one of the meanest of the many visually impaired singers for whom he acted as a lead boy in the 1920s.

Taggart recorded about thirty titles (without alternates), most for Vocalion (1926–1927) and Paramount (1928–1931), and four for Decca (1934). In the first of his three sacred Vocalion sessions, Taggart formed a vocal duet with Emma, presumably his wife, and in the second with James, possibly his son; in the last he accompanied himself on guitar. In 1928, Taggart switched to Paramount, for which he recorded under his real name or with various pseudonyms, first in Chicago and then in Grafton, Wisconsin. With the exception of the last of his five Paramount sessions, where he played unaccompanied and sang, Taggart was backed up by thirteen-year-old Josh White on guitar and vocals.

After a hiatus of three and a half years, Taggart went back to a recording studio, waxing a total of four titles for Decca, three of which he had previously recorded for Vocalion or Paramount, and a new one performed with his daughter Bertha on vocals. From aural evidence and the juxtaposition of matrix numbers, Taggart is almost unanimously thought to have recorded two secular songs for Vocalion under the pseudonym of Blind Joe Amos, "C&O Blues" and "Coal River Blues." The latter side remained unissued (a possible reason for Taggart to change recording companies) and bears the same title as a song later released by Paramount as by Blind Percy and His Blind Band, its flip side being "Fourteenth St. Blues." The identification of Taggart with Blind Percy is strengthened by Jimmy Lee Robinson's assertion that he learned the rudiments of guitar from a guy named Blind Percy when the latter used to live on 14th Street in Chicago. Also possible is that Taggart recorded more secular sides under the name Six-Cylinder Smith.

Regardless of whether all of these speculations are true—and despite the fact that he is known to have played blues at parties—Joe Taggart essentially remains a gospel singer who, especially on his Paramount sides, reached a remarkable sense of involvement. Taggart's religious fervor is unmistakable in songs such as "I Wish My Mother Was on That Train" and "Religion Is Something Within You." His harsh and hoarse—yet flexible and resonant—vocal style is perfectly suited for the material he interpreted, such as "The Storm Is Passing Over," "God's Gonna Separate the Wheat from the Tares" (the latter with its fascinating rolling r's), and the commercially successful "There's a Hand Writing on the Wall." Taggart's essential and repetitive, almost restrained, percussive guitar style adapted well to different musical genres, including hillbilly white music, as evidenced by his recording "Been Listening All Day."

Luigi Monge

Reference and Further Reading

Briggs, Keith. "Separating the Wheat from the Tares." *Blues and Rhythm* 33 (December 1987): 9–12.

Discography

Romanowsky, Ken. *Blind Joe Taggart: Complete Recorded Works in Chronological Order, Vol. 1 (1926–1928) and Vol. 2 (1929–1934)* (1993, Document Records DOCD-5153 and DOCD-5154).

TAKE 6

Alvin Chea (b. November 2, 1967)
David Thomas (b. October 28, 1966)
Claude V. McKnight III (b. October 2, 1962)
Mark Kibble (b. April 7, 1964)
Mervyn Warren (b. February 29, 1964)
Cedric Dent (b. September 24, 1962)

With its signature six-part *a cappella* and instrumental harmonies, Take 6 is a positive, joyous ensemble that has incorporated gospel, jazz, doo-wop, rhythm and blues, rock, 1960s soul, and hip-hop into its music through the years. Take 6 is one of the top *a cappella* groups in the world, commonly recognized by Alvin Chea's bass vocal walking style sound "bangkk."

Take 6 consists of David Thomas, Alvin Chea, Cedric Dent, Mark Kibble, Claude V. McKnight III, and Joel Kibble. The group was established at Oakwood College, a Christian school in Huntsville, Alabama, in 1980 by McKnight. In its original incarnation, the group was called Gentlemen's Estate Quartet. In would take a few personnel changes to come up with the band's roster for the main segment of the group's recording career. A key addition to the band was Mark Kibble, an old childhood friend of McKnight's, who, when hearing the quartet was practicing in the bathroom, wanted to add a fifth vocal part. To wrap up the first full form of Take 6, the last member of the six was Mervyn Warren. With his addition, the band took on the name of Sounds of Distinction and later Alliance, before eventually deciding on Take 6.

Around the same time, in the mid-1980s, the final roster of Take 6 was put together. The core group of McKnight, Mark Kibble, and Warren remained, but then Cedric Dent, David Thomas, and Alvin Chea joined to help bring the group to the regional and national forums. The only other member change would be Warren's departure to become a music producer in 1991, when Joel Kibble joined.

Seeking to move their careers forward with the core group in place, they put together a gospel music showcase at a Christian bookstore in Nashville to court approximately thirty music industry executives. As a result, Jim Ed Norman from Warner Brothers signed the band to a recording deal, also signing them to a separate distribution arrangement with Reunion, which supplies Christian bookstores nationwide.

Their first release, *Take 6*, went gold and won the 1988 Grammy for Best Soul Gospel Performance by Duo or Group, Choir, or Chorus, and it was also rated on *Billboard*'s R&B/hip-hop, gospel, contemporary jazz, contemporary Christian, and top two hundred charts.

With each of its subsequent album releases, the group has won recognition in terms of album sales, awards, and airplay. During their career so far, they have won eight Grammy Awards in total, across such diverse categories as Best Contemporary Soul Gospel Album and Best Jazz Vocal Performance. In addition, they have won ten Dove Awards, for everything from Group of the Year in 1989 to best Contemporary Gospel Album of the Year in 1989, 1991, 1992, 1993, and 1995.

Take 6 has recorded widely, both as a group and with individual contributions to more than 109 different music projects. On a group basis, they have recorded with everyone from Don Henley on the 1989 release *The End of the Innocence* to Randy Travis's 1991 release *High Lonesome* to a compilation of various artists on 1995's *Music of Disney's Cinderella*. Their joint efforts also have garnered industry praise, with Take 6 sharing a Grammy with Stevie Wonder in 2002 for Best R&B Performance By a Duo or Group with Vocal for *Love's in Need of Love Today*. On an individual basis, members have done duets or backup singing with diverse talents, ranging from Whitney Houston to William Aura to Michael McDonald.

Throughout Take 6's success and performance experience, the root of the group's music has been gospel traditions of vocal harmonies and tight musical arrangements. As evidence of the depth of interest in these traditions, Dent earned his MA and Ph.D. degrees in music theory, with his dissertation topic being "Harmonic Development of the Black Religious Quartet Singing Tradition." To bring the tradition to the masses, the group has tried to convey its message through positively messaged vocal performance, superseding specific religious connotation and direct affiliation as Seventh-Day Adventists.

Far past the bounds of their own music recordings and performances, Take 6's vocal grace and technical acumen has paved the way for the success of other modern-day vocal groups, such as Boyz II Men.

MARGARET B. FISHER

Reference and Further Reading

Billboard website, http://www.billboard.com (accessed 2002).
Chea, Alvin. Take 6 website, http://www.take6.com (accessed November 8, 2003).
Ginell, Richard S. "Take 6 Biography." All Music website, http://www.allmusic.com (accessed 2003).
"GMA Music Awards History." Dove Awards website, http://www.doveawards.com/history (accessed 2003).
Grammy Awards website, http://www.grammy.com/awards (accessed December 19, 2003).

Discography

Take 6 (1988, Warner); *So Much 2 Say* (1990, Warner); *He Is Christmas* (1991, Warner); *All I Need (Is a Chance)* (1994, Warner); *Join the Band* (1994, Warner); *Brothers* (1996, Warner); *So Cool* (1998, Warner); *We Wish You a Merry Christmas* (1999, Reprise); *Tonight: Live* (2000, Reprise); *Beautiful World* (2002, Warner).

TALBOT, JOHN MICHAEL

(b. May 8, 1954)

John Michael Talbot was born in Oklahoma City, Oklahoma. Inspired by his older brother Terry, John eventually mastered the guitar, banjo, Dobro, pedal steel, and bass. Influenced by folk artists such as the Chad Mitchell Trio, the New Christy Minstrels, and Peter, Paul, and Mary, John and Terry formed a series of groups, and in the late 1960s they formed Mason Proffit. They became a popular act and performed with many of the top bands of that era, including the Grateful Dead, Iron Butterfly, Janis Joplin, Jefferson Airplane, and Phil Ochs. Along with groups such as the Byrds, the Flying Burrito Brothers, and Poco, they were pioneers of what would later be called country rock.

John and Terry became born-again Christians in 1972, while the group was at its peak of popularity. After playing to crowds numbering more than thirty thousand, John and Terry left the band disillusioned and seeking spiritual direction. The two brothers released *The Talbot Brothers* in 1974 and *Reborn* in 1976 on Warner Brothers Records. John began to study the writings of many of the monastic contemplatives, such as Thomas Merton and Saint John of the Cross. At the same time he met Christian artists such as Barry McGuire (whom he credits as being the one who taught him how to sing for God), Richie Furay, Larry Norman, Nancy Honeytree, Randy Matthews, and record producer Billy Ray Hearn.

John released his self-titled first solo album on Sparrow Records in 1976, and by 1977 he had become an established member of the Christian music scene. John converted to Roman Catholicism on Ash Wednesday in 1978. In July of the same year, John became a Third Order, or Secular Franciscan. He donned a hooded monk's habit made of old army blankets.

He decided to create contemporary Christian music (CCM) for a Roman Catholic audience. Then, inspired by the counterculture of the 1960s and the historical monastic communities of the Benedictines, Cistercians, and Franciscans, as well as Buddhist and other Eastern monastic traditions, John established his own monastic community in Eureka Springs, Arkansas, on land that he had purchased during Mason Proffit's zenith. The community became known as the Little Portion Hermitage and the Motherhouse of the Brothers and Sisters of Charity. It was the first time that a Vatican-sanctioned, self-supporting, indigenous religious community arose in the United States. John was soon featured in a variety of publications, including *People, The Wall Street Journal,* and *The Saturday Evening Post.*

In 1979 and 1980, *The Lords Supper* and *The Painter* were released on Sparrow Records. They combined Gregorian chant with David Crosby–style harmonies, using multiple overdubbing on a twenty-four-track board, to create the effect of four hundred voices. John's albums were a complete departure from anything resembling CCM. *For the Bride* was written as a ballet, which often included performances by Christian dance companies. In 1984 *God of Life* was released, which was the first time that Celtic music was incorporated with Christian—or even pop—music in the United States. In 1988 *The Regathering* was released, combining contemporary orchestra with a chorale, calling Evangelicals and Catholics together in love. *The Master and the Musician* was released in 1992 and was the first album on Talbot's new independent label Troubadour for the Lord.

John was inspired to begin the Catholic Association of Musicians (CAM) in 1996 to give Catholic artists the same opportunities as their CCM counterparts. In 1997, *Table of Plenty* was released; it was the first recording produced at the newly built monastery recording studio. When *Cave of the Heart* was released in 1999, it integrated contemporary folk, rock, and classical musical styles; it also presented an interfaith message by combining portions of text from the holy books of all the major religions of the world.

John performed for Pope John Paul II and was even his guest at the Vatican. He spent time with and performed for Mother Teresa. In Denver, Colorado, on World Youth Day in 2000, John played before a crowd of five hundred thousand people. He played at the inaugural prayer luncheon for President-elect

George W. Bush in 2001. During a nearly thirty-year period, John Michael Talbot has released forty-five albums, selling more than four million copies; written seventeen books, as well as a number of songbooks; and produced concert and teaching videos. His ministry has spanned the globe through his involvement with Mercy Corps, a relief organization that helps the poorest of the poor around the world, and his religious community has grown to more than five hundred members.

BOB GERSZTYN

See also 2nd Chapter of Acts; Calvary Chapel, Costa Mesa; Green, Keith; Hearn, Billy Ray; Norman, Larry; Rock Gospel

Reference and Further Reading

John Michael Talbot website, http://www.johnmichaeltalbot. com (accessed November 21, 2003).

Launchcast, Yahoo Music website, http://launch.yahoo. com/artist/discography.asp?artistID=1026452 (accessed November 21, 2003).

O'Neill, Dan. *Signatures.* Berryville, AR: Troubadour for the Lord, 2003.

Talbot, John Michael. *Blessings.* Berryville, AR: Troubadour for the Lord, 1991.

———. *Changes.* Berryville, AR: Troubadour for the Lord, 1984.

———. *The Joy of Music Ministry.* Berryville, AR: Troubadour for the Lord, 2001.

The Brothers & Sisters of Charity at Little Portion Hermitage website, http://www.littleportion.org/ (accessed November 29, 2003).

The Brothers and Sisters of Charity website, http://bsc. weship4you.com/scripts/prodView.sap?idProduct=172 (accessed November 21, 2003).

Discography

The Talbot Brothers (1974, Warner Brothers); *John Michael Talbot* (1976, Sparrow); *Reborn* (1976, Warner Brothers); *The New Earth* (1977, Sparrow); *The Lord's Supper* (1979, Sparrow); *Come to the Quiet* (1980, Birdwing); *The Painter* (1980, Sparrow); *Troubadour of the Great King* (1981, Birdwing); *Light Eternal* (1982, Birdwing); *The Quiet* (1982, Sparrow); *No Longer Strangers* (1983, Sparrow); *God of Life* (1984, Birdwing); *Be Exalted* (1986, Birdwing); *Empty Canvas* (1986, Sparrow); *Heart of the Shepherd* (1987, Birdwing); *Quiet Reflections* (1987, Sparrow); *The Regathering* (1988, Sparrow); *Songs for Worship, Vols. I & II* (1988, Sparrow); *The Lover and the Beloved* (1989, Sparrow); *Master Collection Vol. I* (1989, Sparrow); *The Birth of Jesus: A Celebration of Christmas* (1990, Sparrow); *Come Worship the Lord, Vols. I & II* (1990, Sparrow); *For the Bride* (1990, Birdwing); *Hiding Place* (1990, Sparrow); *The Master Musician* (1992, Troubadour); *Meditations in the Spirit* (1993, Troubadour); *Meditations from Solitude* (1994, Troubadour); *Chant from the Hermitage* (1995, Troubadour); *The John Michael Talbot Collection* (1995, Sparrow); *The Early Years* (1996, Sparrow); *Troubadour for the Lord* (1996, Troubadour); *Table of Plenty* (1997, Troubadour); *Hidden Pathways* (1998, Troubadour); *Pathways of the Shepherd* (1998, Troubadour); *Pathways to Solitude* (1998, Troubadour); *Pathways to Wisdom* (1998, Troubadour); *Quiet Pathways* (1998, Troubadour); *Spirit Pathways* (1998, Troubadour); *Cave of the Heart* (1999, Troubadour); *Simple Heart* (1999, Troubadour); *Wisdom* (2001, Troubadour); *Signatures* (2003, Troubadour).

TAMBOURINES

One of the oldest instruments, this frame drum with a wooden hoop is known throughout the world. A membrane is pulled over the hoop, with slots—sometimes in two rows—of metal discs, called jingles, carried on wires. This instrument first appeared in the Middle East during the Middle Ages and by the fourteenth century was known in Europe. Its earliest known name was "timbre," from the Latin word *tympanum.* During the early Renaissance in England, it was called the "timbrel." Generally it has been associated with women, but throughout its history it has been played just as often by men. In parts of England it was played to accompany folk dances, some performers striking it with a cow's tail.

There are at least four methods of playing the instrument: (1) striking the head with the fingers, knuckles, palms, or closed fist or hitting the instrument on the knee or back and forth on the knee and hand; (2) shaking the instrument; (3) hitting the rim with the fingertips of both hands, or, when placed in the player's lap, with drumsticks; and (4) rubbing the head with a moist thumb to produce either a thumb roll or recurring strokes. Sometimes colored ribbons are attached to the instrument; the Salvation Army frequently does this. Usually gospel musicians employ one of the first two methods of playing described above.

The tambourine is popular because it is lightweight and can easily be held in one hand. Often it is just a prop to give performers something to do with their hands, this is particularly true in family groups in which the artist is a child. Other performers use the tambourine as a means of keeping time. In the days when most towns had blind street singers playing for whatever money they could get donated, the tambourine occasionally functioned to attract attention to the music and singer. Tambourines have had a long history in both gospel and secular music but, even so, recordings such as the nine sides cut by Elder J. E. Burch and his congregation for Victor in 1927, which prominently features tambourine on each selection, are rare.

W. K. MCNEIL

Reference and Further Reading

Baines, Anthony. *The Oxford Companion to Musical Instruments.* New York: Oxford University Press, 1992.

Blades, James. *Percussion Instruments and Their History.* London: Faber, 1975 (1970).

TAYLOR, STEVE

(b. December 9, 1957)

Soon after his birth in Brawley, California, Roland Stephen Taylor's parents moved to Denver, Colorado, where his father was a Baptist minister. In 1976, after graduating from high school, he moved back to Southern California to study communications and the Bible at Biola University. After his freshman year, he moved back to Colorado, where he earned a BA degree in music, with an emphasis on vocals, at the University of Colorado in Boulder.

After graduating from college Taylor completed a couple of demo tapes bearing titles such as "Whatcha Gonna Do When Your Number's Up?," and "I Want to Be a Clone." He traveled back to California, attempting to market the tapes to mainstream record companies and music publishers, to no avail. In the process he met Jim Chafee, who hired him as the assistant director of both the Continentals, a singing group, and Chuck Bolte's Jeremiah People, a comedy troupe. Impressed with Taylor, Chafee and his wife Janice convinced Continentals founder Cam Floria to allow him to perform a couple of songs at Floria's annual Christian Artists Conference in Estes Park, Colorado. Sparrow Records owner Billy Ray Hearn was present and was impressed by the crowd's reaction to Taylor's performance, and a recording contract resulted.

In 1983, Sparrow released an EP by Taylor, titled *I Want to Be a Clone,* on a seven-thousand-dollar budget. The album contained six songs and sold eighty-five thousand units. His music at that time was influenced by secular groups such as the Cars, the Clash, and the Damned. He was theologically influenced by Evangelical thinker Francis Schaeffer, who encouraged Taylor to press on after hearing the *Clone* EP. His first full-length album, *Meltdown,* was released in 1984. The album contained topical songs, ranging from one about the racist policies of a famous fundamentalist college, titled "We Don't Need No Color Code," to "Over My Dead Body," which addressed the suffering church behind the Iron Curtain. *Meltdown* sold 135 thousand units and got Taylor a gig playing at the Cornerstone Festival in Bushnell, Illinois.

Taylor's next album, *On the Fritz,* was released in the spring of 1985. That summer, he performed at the Greenbelt Festival in England, where he recorded his performance and called the result *Limelight* when it was released in 1986 as a live EP and video. He began working on a new album in 1986, but after numerous delays he switched labels from Sparrow to Myrrh Records. *I Predict 1990* was finally released in late 1987, but it became controversial because the satirical content was misunderstood. Song titles such as "I Blew Up the Clinic Real Good" forced Taylor to take the defensive to explain his motives. The result of all this was his decision to retire from Christian music.

Retirement, however, only meant a change of direction; *Chagall Guevara* was born as a secular incarnation of Steve Taylor and was released on MCA Records. *Rolling Stone* magazine had a review of *Chagall Guevara* that compared them to the Clash, which resulted in a UK tour opening for pop legend Squeeze and a cut on the *Pump Up the Volume* film soundtrack. However, when the album failed to be as successful as any of Taylor's earlier efforts, the group got out of its contract with MCA, and Taylor returned to Nashville.

Taylor began working as a record producer and writer with groups such as the Newsboys; the result was a series of albums, starting with *Not Ashamed.* Soon afterward he decided to create a new solo record, and *Squint* was released in 1993. He went on the road in the fall of 1994, calling it the "Squinternational" Tour. On October 22, 1994, he recorded his performance in Lancaster, Pennsylvania, and released it as a live album titled *Liver.*

In 1997, Taylor became a vice president of Word Records, heading up a new record label called Squint Entertainment. The new label's first release produced by Taylor was a self-titled album by Sixpence None the Richer. His next project was an album and movie called *St. Gimp,* which was to be a stop-action animation film. Neither the film nor the album were finished when the management at Word changed in September 2001. Soon afterward Steve's involvement with the label ended.

After that, other than an occasional concert, Taylor burned his bridges as a musician and began devoting his time exclusively to filmmaking. At the same time he began working with DATA, which is an acronym for Debt relief, AIDS relief, and Trade for Africa, started by Bono, the lead singer of the secular group U2.

BOB GERSZTYN

See also Hearn, Billy Ray; Jars of Clay; Myrrh Records; Newsboys; Norman, Larry; Rock Gospel

Reference and Further Reading

Chattaway, Peter. "Steve Taylor Interview." Peter Chattaway website, http://www.peter.chattaway.com/articles/steve97.htm (accessed November 22, 2003).

Davis, Troy. "A Salute to Steve Taylor." Sock Heaven website, http://www.sockheaven.org/ (accessed December 5, 2003).

Launchcast, Yahoo Music website, http://launch.yahoo.com/artist/discography.asp?artistID=1026602 (accessed December 4, 2003).

Mansfield, Brian. "Steve Taylor Biography." Iceberg Radio website, http://www.theiceberg.com/artist/404/steve_taylor.html (accessed November 21, 2003).

Taylor, Andrew D. "A Biography." Quantitative Roland Stephen Taylor Ubiquitous Volume website, http://www.renc.igs.net/~adt/qrstuv/bio.html (accessed December 4, 2003).

Willman, Chris. "Steve Taylor Biography." Liner notes to *Now the Truth Can Be Told* (1994, Sparrow).

Yaconelli, Mike. "The Door Interview with Steve Taylor." *Wittenburg Door* 81 (October/November 1984).

Discography

I Want to Be a Clone (1983, Sparrow Records, EP); *Meltdown* (1984, Sparrow Records); *On the Fritz* (1985, Sparrow Records); *Limelight* (1986, Sparrow Records); *I Predict 1990* (1987, Myrrh Records); *The Best We Could Find + Three that Never Escaped* (1988, Sparrow Records); *Chagall Guevara* (1991, MCA Records); *Squint* (1993, Warner Brothers Records); *Now the Truth Can Be Told* (1994, Sparrow Records); *Liver* (1995, Warner Brothers Records).

TENNESSEANS QUARTET

Dale Lawrence Shelnut (b. 1935; d. 1983)
Dean Bassham (b. Unknown)
Noel Fox (b. Unknown)
Wally Laxon (b. Unknown)
Jimmy Vassar (b. Unknown)
Eddie Crook (b. Unknown)

The Tennesseans had one of the best quartets on the Southern gospel circuit during the 1960s. Dale Shelnut, their lead vocalist from 1960 to 1962, went on to achieve greater fame with the Dixie Echoes. Fans recall them as quite strong in a musical sense, but they disbanded after a few years. Pianist Eddie Crook later became a noted producer of gospel records in Nashville. Another group, popular in the later 1970s, known as Willie Wynn and the Tennesseans, seems to have had little or no connection to this quartet.

IVAN M. TRIBE

Reference and Further Reading

Sing with the Tennesseans (Heart Warming LPHF 1705). Liner notes.

Southern Gospel Music Association Hall of Fame website, http://www.sgma.org/bios.lasso?id=66.

Discography

Sing with the Tennesseans (Heart Warming LPHF 1705).

THARPE, SISTER ROSETTA

(b. 1915 or 1921, Cotton Plant, AR; d. 1973, Philadelphia, PA)

Sister Rosetta Tharpe, one of gospel's most successful and pioneering artists, was born Rosetta Nubin in Cotton Plant, Arkansas, in 1915 (her date of birth is sometimes placed as 1921). She made her first performance—accompanying herself on guitar, as she would for most of her life—at age six. Tharpe's mother was a mandolin player and evangelist in the Church of God in Christ (COGIC). This church, founded by black Baptist bishop Charles Mason in 1894, encouraged freer physical and musical expression within worship, also allowing women the forum to evangelize. It was the perfect setting for Tharpe's early musical and spiritual development.

Mother and child both moved to Chicago in the 1920s, where they performed regularly at the COGIC church on 40th Street. They also traveled extensively to COGIC services and conventions throughout the country. Continuing through her early adulthood (in the later years with the chaperonage of her first husband, COGIC preacher Thomas J. Thorpe), these tours not only began to build a reputation for Tharpe but also allowed her to experience numerous other musical artists and styles. Thomas Thorpe left the scene within a few years, but Rosetta adapted his name and retained it for the rest of her life.

By the time Tharpe moved to New York and made her first Decca recording in 1938, she was already a musician with a unique, transgressive style. It was extremely rare for a woman instrumentalist to perform in any setting; the practice was particularly frowned upon within the church population. Only Memphis Minnie had received comparable recognition as a guitarist, and this was in the blues field. Tharpe's style of playing was also unusual. She was one of the first to incorporate a melody-driven, city blues style with the folk-blues of old. Her music had a pulsating swing feel that already hinted at the jazz, rock 'n' roll, and boogie-woogie styles with which her music would always flirt.

The four sides recorded for Decca on October 31, 1938 ("Rock Me," "That's All," "The Man and I," and "The Lonesome Road") were the first ever for a gospel artist and were highly successful. On December

Sister Rosetta Tharpe. Photo courtesy Frank Driggs Collection.

23 of the same year, Tharpe performed at Carnegie Hall in John Hammond's Spirituals to Swing concert. Once again, she was trailblazing. Performing gospel outside of the sacred sphere, in front of secular audiences, and side by side with jazz and blues musicians was highly controversial. Tharpe was uncompromising in her transgression: Carnegie Hall was relatively civilized in comparison with her notorious performances with Cab Calloway at the Cotton Club. Despite disapproval from the church, she was a hit, and her move to New York successfully solidified her wide appeal not only within the church population but within the fields of black and white popular music.

In 1941, Tharpe filmed several "soundies" with Lucky Millinder and his orchestra, her now regular music partners. Soundies were very similar to juke box recordings but with accompanying video footage. They enjoyed a brief craze through the 1940s, but again Tharpe's appearance in them—as a mediated and secular form of popular entertainment for bars, cafes, and roadhouses—invited criticism from the religious community. Despite this, her Decca recording of September 5, 1941, "Shout Sister Shout," increased her popularity further, reaching number twenty-one on the Harlem Hit Parade, the black American music chart, in July 1942. By this time, Tharpe's voice had strengthened further, perhaps less infused with country-style blues and influenced by the more declamatory style of the growing gospel movement. Her accompaniment, by Lucky Millinder and his orchestra, provides a contrasting but complimentary jazz swing feel.

A couple of weeks after this recording session, Tharpe recorded a further track with Millinder's orchestra, "That's All." This track, appearing on a Millinder album rather than one under her own name, is notable for featuring the first recorded example of Tharpe's electric guitar playing. In her guitar intro, one can clearly hear the precursors of rock, going a significant way to justifying claims of Tharpe's influence upon the guitar playing of artists as diverse as Chuck Berry, Little Richard, Elvis Presley, and Eric Clapton.

Success with Millinder's orchestra continued to grow, most notably with the completely jazzy and profane "I Want a Tall Skinny Papa" of February 1942. This number, in which Millinder's orchestra provides a vocal call-and-response repartee with Tharpe's energetically mischievous tones, reached number thirteen on in the Hit Parade. Throughout this time, Tharpe was performing in both religious and secular settings. The latter included a week with the Benny Goodman Orchestra in New York's Café Society downtown. Still rare at the time, this highly public interracial mixing was indicative of Tharpe's multiracial appeal and boundary-crossing attitudes.

During the war, Tharpe's following within the white mainstream was demonstrated by recordings she made for the troops. Referred to as "V-Discs" (V being for victory), these were organized by the Armed Forces Radio Services and were particularly coveted due to the contemporaneous ban on all commercial recordings. She was one of only two black religious artists to be invited to record, the other being the tremendously popular Golden Gate Quartet. These jubilee recordings and a six-month sojourn in Los Angeles—first with the Lucky Millinder Orchestra at Casa Manana and later as a soloist at a Hollywood nightclub, the Streets of Paris—represented a period of extended freedom for Tharpe, who had been released from the disapproving eye of New York's religious community. She never moved entirely to secular music, however, and she traveled extensively during this time with several renowned gospel quartets, perhaps most crucially the Dixie Hummingbirds.

Returning to New York in late 1943, Tharpe recorded several solo sides, accompanying herself on guitar; however, even her unusual crossover style was beginning to sound sedate in the face of the rising rhythm and blues movement. Tharpe responded, however, with another musical breakthrough by embarking on what was to be a long-standing partnership with blues piano player Sammy Price and his trio. The house pianist for Decca since the late 1930s, Price was a wonderful pianist with a dancingly punchy touch, whose music wandered comfortably between jazz, blues, and boogie-woogie. The combination of piano and guitar within gospel singing was unprecedented and injected Tharpe's music with an even heavier jazzy inflection that was buoyantly swinging and bordered—for some—on the irreverent.

In her first recording session with Price, in September 1944, Tharpe recorded two immensely successful tracks, "Strange Things Happening Every Day" and "Two Little Fishes and Five Loaves of Bread." Together, they reached number two in the Hit Parade of April 1945. In the wake of ever-increasing popularity from the outside world and criticism from the religious community, Tharpe made the decision to devote herself purely to religious songs over the following years. This did not involve a compromise in her musical style, however, once again demonstrating the ephemeral nature of the boundaries between gospel, blues, jazz, and the nascent influences of rock 'n' roll.

July 1, 1947, marked another important point in Tharpe's musical development, with her first of many collaborations with solo vocalist "Madame" Marie Knight. Knight was younger than Tharpe but had grown up in similar circumstances, singing within the evangelical church. She had a lower and richer-toned voice than Tharpe, her mellow delivery providing the perfect counterpoint for Tharpe's more extroverted, buoyant, and declamatory style. Tharpe's singing with Knight seems to be based much more in the gospel tradition, not only through the forefronting of the voice and its unaffected textural nuance but in often slower, more weighted tempos. This is particularly so for slower numbers such as "Oh When I Come to the End of My Journey" and "Stretch Out," in which Knight's and Tharpe's voices blend in unaffected, free-flowing unison. It is also noticeable in the uplifting, spiritually embedded fervor of faster numbers such as "Up Above My Head I Hear the Music in the Air." This song reached number six on the race charts in December 1948. Note that some of the recordings with Knight from July 1947 with the Down Beat/Swing Time labels give Tharpe the pseudonym of Sister Katy Marie due to the duo being exclusively contracted to Decca at the time.

On July 3, 1951, Tharpe married Russel Morrison. While the details of an artist's wedding would not normally make the pages of an encyclopedia, in this case they are relevant, for Tharpe used the event to push the boundaries of gospel and her own iconic status even further. The wedding was held in Griffith Stadium, the epitome of mass, white secularity: a realm that few black musicians could ever expect to appear in, never mind contract for the day for their personal use. The ceremony, normally the ultimate symbol of intimate religious commitment, was performed in front of paying guests, whose numbers are estimated by different sources as between fifteen and twenty-seven thousand. The event was combined with a gospel concert in which Tharpe performed and played in her wedding gown. The climax was supplied by a fireworks display, in which a model of Tharpe playing the guitar performed a central and explosive role. The event cemented Tharpe's position as gospel royalty while reinforcing her constant transgression of performance and musical spaces.

Tharpe maintained her concentration on religious music until 1953, when she made the decision to record a purely blues album with Marie Knight. This session was to prove damaging for both artists. Knight soon broke entirely into secular fields, but with little success. Tharpe returned to religious forums but was met with severe condemnation, lackluster audiences, and a sharp fall in performance opportunities. It seems that the black religious community had finally tired of Tharpe's flouting of church convention.

Celebrated French jazz critic Hughes Panassie helped Tharpe by organizing an extensive European tour for her in 1957. A significant proportion of this was spent in England, playing with the Chris Barber band, a group that had originated in the New Orleans revival but continually modernized its sound by blending the more recent genres of bebop and rhythm and blues. During the next thirteen years, Tharpe continued a career, principally in gospel, touring Europe and America, but generally with a lower profile than in previous years. Her most prestigious highlights during this time were a 1960 appearance at the Apollo with the Caravans and James Cleveland and a successful 1967 performance at the Newport Jazz Festival.

In 1970, while on a blues tour in Europe with Muddy Waters, Tharpe fell ill and returned to America. She soon suffered a stroke and, due to complications from diabetes, had a leg amputated. Despite these trials, Tharpe continued to perform occasionally, most notably with the Sensational Nightingales. After a second stroke, she died in Philadelphia on October 9, 1973.

Tharpe's career, perhaps above any other of that same period, forced the questions of how to define gospel music and tradition. She broke with numerous conventions by blending the sacred and secular realms, refusing to abandon one for the other and to define herself neatly within preestablished categories. Her lifelong positioning as a female instrumentalist who transgressed borders of convention forms the central tenant of Gayle Wald's article about Tharpe (2003), which is sadly the sole published scholarly work devoted to the artist. Wald defines Tharpe's role not only as a deeply influential musician but as one who redefined the spaces between sacred and secular, black and white, traditional and commercial, and male and female. It is perhaps the very difficulty of defining her musical and ideological realm that has led to her relative neglect in the histories and scholarship of the music.

HILARY MOORE

See also Caravans; Church of God in Christ (COGIC); Cleveland, James; Dixie Hummingbirds; Golden Gate Quartet, The; Knight, Madame Marie

Reference and Further Reading

Boyer, Horace Clarence. *How Sweet the Sound: The Golden Age of Gospel.* Washington, DC: Elliott & Clark, 1995.

Heilbut, Anthony. *The Gospel Sound: Good News and Bad Times.* New York: Simon & Schuster, 1971.

Jackson, Jerma. "Testifying at the Cross: Thomas Andrew Dorsey, Sister Rosetta Tharpe and the Politics of African-American Sacred and Secular Music." Ph.D. dissertation, Rutger's University, 1995.

Reitz, Rosetta. "Sister Rosetta." *Hotwire* (May 1991): 16–20.

Visser, Joop. Liner notes to *Sister Rosetta Tharpe: The Original Soul Sister* (Properbox 51).

Wald, Gayle. "From Spirituals to Swing: Sister Rosetta Tharpe and Gospel Crossover." *American Quarterly* 55 (September 2003): 387–417.

THRASHER BROTHERS, THE

Jim Thrasher (b. Unknown)
Joe Thrasher (b. Unknown)
Andrew "Buddy" Thrasher (b. Unknown)
John Gresham (b. Unknown)
Roger Hallmark (b. Unknown)
Goldie Ashton (b. Unknown)

The Thrasher Brothers of Birmingham, Alabama first came to wide prominence through the syndicated television program *America Sings*, which was produced by Jerry Goff between 1967 and 1971. Among their various achievements, the Thrashers are known for being one of the first gospel groups to appear on national television as contestants on *Ted Mack's Original Amateur Hour* in 1953 and later for introducing the inspirational standard "One Day at a Time" to Southern gospel (it later became a number one country hit for Christy Lane). Using full country and western instrumentation, the Thrashers sometimes crossed over into the secular country field and actually placed five numbers on the *Billboard* charts. However, as one fan put it, they remained about ninety-five percent gospel.

As a quartet, the Thrashers consisted of brothers Jim as tenor, Joe as lead, and Buddy as baritone; John Gresham sang bass. Pianists included the late Randy McDaniel and Steve Payne at various times, while Australia-born "Goldie" Ashton played drums and Roger Hallmark usually played banjo. Jerry Goff, who ultimately led his own group Jerry and the Singing Goffs, had initially played trumpet on *America Sings*. Although primarily a foursome on vocals, other band members—especially Ashton and Hallmark—participated in the singing. Earlier Thrasher Brothers recordings appeared on the Prestige label, while the lion's share of their quality gospel albums were for Canaan.

In December 1979, a patriotic song on the Vulcan label credited to "Roger Hallmark and the Thrasher Brothers" and reflecting on the Iranian hostage crisis, "A Message to Khomeini," made the country charts for five weeks. Soon afterward, the Thrashers signed with MCA and had four additional country songs on the charts from about a dozen singles and two album releases. However, the most successful, "Still the One," peaked at number sixty. Thereafter they returned to the gospel field for the remainder of their active years.

IVAN M. TRIBE

Reference and Further Reading

Anderson, Robert; Gail North. *Gospel Music Encyclopedia.* 179. New York: Sterling Publishing, 1979.

Goff, James D., Jr. *Close Harmony: A History of Southern Gospel*, 194, 230–231. Chapel Hill: University of North Carolina Press, 2002.
Whitburn, Joel, compiler. *Top Country Singles, 1944–1993*, 377. Menomonee Falls, WI: Record Research, 1994.

Discography

The Fantastic Thrashers at Fantastic Caverns (ca. 1969, Canaan CAS 9677).
The Thrasher Brothers Pick These (1973, Canaan CAS 9735).
One Day at a Time (1975, Canaan 9748).
Heart to Heart (1977, Canaan CAS 9770).

TINDLEY, CHARLES ALBERT

(b. July 7, 1851; d. July 26, 1933)

Minister, gospel songwriter, and the first black to publish an original song collection, Charles Albert Tindley was born in Berlin, Maryland. There is some dispute about his year of birth, with some sources giving it as 1859 but most using the year 1851. The son of slaves, he had few educational opportunities and taught himself to read and write. He also listened to spirituals and camp-meeting songs and developed a love of music. This enthusiasm led him to teach himself composition.

After marriage, he moved to Philadelphia in search of better economic conditions. There he worked as a hod carrier until he got a job as sexton at the John Wesley Methodist Episcopal Church. While working, he completed his education via correspondence school; at the same time he studied for the test to become a minister. After passing the examination, he started his pastoral career in 1885, going first to Cape May and Spring Hill, New Jersey, and then to Odessa, Delaware, and Pocomoke and Fairmont, New Jersey. He then moved to Ezion Methodist Episcopal Church in Wilmington, Delaware, eventually becoming elder of the Wilmington District.

In 1902, he moved to Philadelphia to pastor the Bainbridge Street Methodist Church, the new name of the church he had previously served as sexton. He spent the rest of his career there, during which he built up the church's membership to ten thousand. Tindley achieved great fame as a preacher, orator, civil rights worker, and champion of Philadelphia's poor, but his greatest accomplishment was in gospel music. His songs focused on concerns specific to black Christians; they were mostly in the pentatonic scale and allowed for improvisation lyrically, rhythmically, and melodically. In these ways they differed from the songs of white composers such as Fanny Crosby. Most important, these features made Tindley's songs—of which only about fifty are known to exist—eminently singable.

Besides writing songs, Tindley occasionally sang them with his congregation. In 1927 he also formed an important group, the Tindley Gospel Singers (also known as the Tindley Seven), who spread their pastor's songs throughout the country. They were among the first singing groups from the predominant Baptist tradition to be attracted to the new, more emotional music called gospel, and they were the first from this tradition to be accompanied by a piano. In short, they were pioneers who sang some of the earliest gospel songs, including those of Tindley.

Two of Tindley's most popular songs are "We'll Understand it Better By and By" (1905) and "Take Your Burden to the Lord, Leave It There" (1918). Others included "What Are They Doing in Heaven?" (1901), "When the Storms of Life Are Raging, Stand By Me" (1905), "Nothing Between" (1905), "The Storm Is Passing Over" (1905), "Some Day/Beams of Heaven" (1905), "Here Am I, Send Me" (1911), "Let Jesus Fix It for You" (1913), and "I'll Overcome Someday" (1901). As "We Shall Overcome," the latter piece was adopted as the anthem of the Civil Rights Movement of the 1960s.

W. K. MCNEIL

Reference and Further Reading

Boyer, Horace Clarence. "C. A. Tindley: Progenitor of African American Music." In *We'll Understand It Better By and By. Pioneering African American Gospel Composers,* edited by Bernice Johnson Reagon. Washington, DC: Smithsonian Institution Press, 1992.
———. *The Golden Age of Gospel.* Urbana and Chicago: University of Illinois Press, 2000 (1995).
Darden, Robert. *People Get Ready: A New History of Black Gospel Music.* New York: Continuum International Publishing Group, 2004.

TOWNER, DANIEL BRINK

(b. March 5, 1850; d. October 3, 1919)

Towner began musical studies at an early age and soon became involved in teaching and singing. His aspirations for a professional career in singing led him to the Cincinnati Conservatory of Music, where he enrolled as a part-time student. During his studies, he was invited by evangelist Dwight Moody to join his association of evangelists and musicians. During the next three decades, music director Towner was paired with evangelists L. W. Munhall, Dixon C. Williams, B. F. Mills, Dwight Moody, Reuben A. Torrey, and James M. Gray in both the United States and Britain.

When Moody began a school in Chicago to train evangelists and gospel musicians, Towner was selected, in 1893, to head its music department. During the next twenty-five years, Towner developed a music curriculum for preparing gospel musicians and authored numerous textbooks. He stressed employing standard vocal techniques to sing gospel music and using standard conducting techniques to direct both choirs and congregations. (He apparently employed a baton for conducting both choirs and congregations.)

During Towner's years as an evangelistic gospel musician and as a teacher, he composed about two thousand songs, with about half of these being in the gospel song style of verse/chorus. He also edited many gospel music collections and hymnals. These included a large number of his tunes for which he often employed pen names. As an editor, he made a lasting contribution to gospel hymnody, working with the second generation of gospel writers such as Charles Gabriel and E. O. Excell. Towner's 1905 collection *Revival Hymns* opened with "The Glory Song" ("When all my labors and trials are o'er") by Gabriel, becoming one of the most popular songs of the era. The most lasting melodies that Towner contributed to gospel hymnody are connected with the texts "Grace, Greater Than Our Sin," "Trust and Obey"' ("When we walk with the Lord"), and "At Calvary" ("Years I spent in vanity and pride"). Towner's most significant impact on gospel hymnody came, however, through his long tenure at the Moody Bible Institute, where he influenced a generation of leading gospel musicians.

MEL R. WILHOIT

Reference and Further Reading

Hall, J. H. *Biography of Gospel Song and Hymn Writers.* New York: Fleming Revell, 1971 (1914).
Hitchcock, H. Wiley; Stanley Sadie. *The New Grove Dictionary of American Music.* London: Macmillan Press Limited, 1986.

TRACE FAMILY TRIO, THE

Sylvia Justice Trace (b. March 13, 1915, Scioto County, OH; d. May 12, 1989)
Darlene Trace DeAtley (b. May 2, 1932, Scioto County, OH)
Teena Trace Wessel (b. August 5, 1934, Scioto County, OH)

Fans of traditional country gospel music recordings have always had a warm spot in their hearts for the original songs and arrangements of the Trace Family Trio. Consisting of mother-songwriter Sylvia Trace and her daughters Darlene and Teena, the trio had a style and approach with a simple guitar accompaniment (and occasional piano) reminiscent of the Carter Family. Until injury from a fall forced Sylvia's retirement in 1962, the group inspired listeners in church audiences and at gospel songfests throughout Ohio, Kentucky, and West Virginia for more than a decade.

Natives of Scioto County, Ohio, the threesome first developed their trio about 1945. By the early 1950s it had matured into a smooth, high-quality harmony. Darlene furnished guitar accompaniment and Teena played piano. In later years, they had an additional pianist so that Teena could concentrate on her vocals. Although they had no regular radio program, they frequently sang on WPAY in Portsmouth. Their earliest recordings appeared on their own custom label, but late in 1952 King purchased the masters and signed the trio to a regular contract. They had their first studio session on May 17, 1953. During the next six years, they released a total of sixteen sides on King. Their most notable numbers were "The Lord Will Make a Way Somehow," "I'll Be No Stranger There," and "My Title to Heaven," the latter of which has become popularly known as "Clear Title to a Mansion."

In 1962, Sylvia Trace experienced serious injuries when she fell backward ten steps down a flight of stairs. During the next twenty-seven years she was able to sing in public only a few times. The Trace Trio's career as gospel singers had virtually ended. However, their songs continued to have a life and circulate. Eva Mae LeFevre, Wade Mainer, the Happy Goodmans, and the Stanley Brothers, among others, recorded their songs. Darlene reports that she and her sister retain fond memories of their mother, who not only taught them her songs but also gave them a firm moral foundation. Their hope is that their recordings will soon be reissued on CD.

IVAN M. TRIBE

Reference and Further Reading

DeAtley, Darlene Trace. Telephone interview, January 5, 2005.

TRIPP, LAVERNE

LaVerne Tripp (b. April 11, 1944)
Edith Tripp (b. February 12, 1945)
Terry Tripp (b. November 30, 1974)
Robb Tripp (b. December 19, 1964)

During a thirty-five year career in gospel music, LaVerne Tripp has distinguished himself as a vocalist—solo, in duets, and in quartets—as a songwriter, and as an evangelist. A native of North Carolina, he made his first singing appearance at a camp meeting prior to his third birthday. He then sang solo and with local groups, gaining valuable experience. After reaching adulthood, he spent seven years with the Blue Ridge Quartet, beginning in 1969, before going on his own and entering the ministry. His initial recordings appeared on the Queen City label, but in recent years he has operated his own Family Room Recording Studio.

As a member of the Blue Ridge Quartet, it has been said that Tripp brought a new excitement to the group with his original songs and vocal work. The first album made with them had his composition "I've Been Born Again" as the featured cut. Later compositions of note included "I Know," "That Day Is Almost Here," "After Calvary," and "He's Coming Soon." The latter song used the tune of a popular country standard "Ashes of Love," and thus exemplified the old saying, "Why should the devil have all the good tunes?" After seven years with Blue Ridge, LaVerne Tripp "surrendered his will and his life to the care of God and launched out to fulfill God's destiny for his life as an evangelist."

After nearly three decades in the ministry, Tripp has evangelized and sung around the world and continued to write songs and sing often with his wife, Edith. In addition, their two sons, Terry and Robb, have joined their parents on some recordings, and each has also recorded solo CDs. As of February 2005, the Tripps have recorded and released some seventy-six albums and CDs. Their recordings usually contain a mixture of older songs and LaVerne's originals. Some of their best-known new numbers include "Take Me on a Heavenly Trip," "We've Got the Power," and "I'll Be There." LaVerne has also authored the autobiographical and inspirational volume *The LaVerne Tripp Story*.

IVAN M. TRIBE

Reference and Further Reading

LaVerne Tripp website, http://www.lavernetripp.com.
Tripp, LaVerne. *An Offer I Couldn't Refuse: The LaVerne Tripp Story*. Self-published, 1990.

Discography

Take Me on a Heavenly Trip (1979, QCA QC LP 391).
Songs for the New Millenium (2000, CD).
Never Grow Old (2002, CD).
Nothing's Gonna Keep Me Down (2004, CD).

TROMBONE

The history of the modern trombone stretches back to at least the Renaissance in terms of its method of pitch production, which relies on modifying the length of a tube of air by means of a slide. By the late nineteenth century when gospel music came to the fore, the trombone was common in bands (both military and community) and in orchestral music (Beethoven having introduced the trombone in the last movement of his Fifth Symphony). The German culture and its immigrants to the United States (especially Moravians) were also familiar with the *Posaunenchor*, or trombone choir.

The trombone's most conspicuous association with early gospel hymnody came from the leadership of Homer Rodeheaver, the charismatic music director for evangelist Billy Sunday in his national crusades during the early decades of the twentieth century. Rodeheaver often led the singing with the help of his trombone playing. He apparently did not perform gospel solos, but the trombone was a conspicuously visible part of the music of revivalism.

Many of the earliest attempts at arranging gospel music for trombone reflected the same approaches that composers applied to secular music: theme and variations. The tune was played through once, generally unadorned; then it was followed by successive variations modifying the rhythm, meter, or ornamentation, and it generally concluded with a stanza each of double tonguing and triple tonguing—especially if the gospel song suggested a triumphant note. The secular model for this approach can still be attempted as published in the nineteenth-century "bible" of brass pedagogy, *Arban's Complete Conservatory Method for Trumpet* (also transcribed for trombone) in the section "Twelve Celebrated Fantaisies and Airs Varies."

During the early twentieth century, this virtuosic style of trombone playing, usually featuring the theme-and-variation–type arrangements, was made famous by secular trombone soloists such as Arthur Pryor, who often headlined for Sousa's famous bands or led their own. Their example was then imitated by countless religious arrangers and soloists, applying this model to gospel music. The result was a host of solo and duet trombone music with piano accompaniment gracing many a revival and church service. Later secular models influenced aspiring gospel trombone performers as they listened to swing band leaders such as Tommy Dorsey perform his mellow solos with bands on the radio and in recordings during the 1940s and 1950s.

After World War II, published arrangements tended to get a little more sophisticated harmonically as well as giving more importance to the piano accompaniment, although the theme-and-variations model remained strong. Religious recordings made brass gospel music available for repeated listening, especially by artists such as Bill Pearce during the 1960s (on Word Records). With the technological development of tape and CD accompaniment tracks beginning in the 1970s, trombone players gained a new realm of possibility for gospel solo playing as they were no longer limited by the availability or skills of a live piano accompanist. As many of these accompaniment tracks provided orchestral accompaniment, this led to more interesting and sometimes more sophisticated gospel arrangements.

A somewhat separate—but equally vital—tradition of employing the trombone within the context of the Salvation Army brass band movement has also contributed to a century of brass gospel music in the United States and especially Britain. The Army developed an extensive and important body of religious literature featuring brass instruments, but because this music was generally limited to Salvationists, it was often little known outside of those circles in the United States.

As evangelicals began making a greater impact on the classical music world during the last quarter of the twentieth century, professional orchestral players, such as bass trombonist Douglas Yeo of the Boston Symphony, continued to popularize the role of the trombone in gospel music through their performances, recordings, and publications.

MEL R. WILHOIT

Reference and Further Reading

Online Trombone Journal website, http://www.trombone.org.
Pearce, Bill. Interview by Douglas Yeo.

Discography

Recordings of Bill Pearce are available at http://www.nightsounds.org. The Salvation Army Recording Catalog has many examples in this genre.

TRUMPET

Although God commanded Moses to construct two trumpets made of silver (Numbers 10:2) during the Israelite wanderings, the most common instrument described by the word "trumpet" in the Bible is the *shofar*, or ram's horn. Its primary purpose was for signaling rather than musical expression; the same held true for all such later instruments carrying the generic term "trumpet." By the middle ages, a trumpet consisted of a metal tube, variously coiled, with a slightly flared bell on one end and a cup mouthpiece on the other. Available pitches were limited to those of the natural overtone series, such as a modern bugle can play.

During the Baroque era of the seventeenth and eighteenth centuries, composers such as Bach and Handel perfected the use of this instrument, producing such monumental works as Bach's *Brandenburg Concerto No. 2* and "The Trumpet Shall Sound" from Handel's *Messiah.* The Baroque natural trumpet (called clarino) reached its height as a soloistic instrument during the early Classical era (for example, Leopold Mozart's concerto), although its primary musical function came to be for playing supportive loud notes or fanfares in the orchestral literature of Haydn, Mozart, and Beethoven.

After many decades of attempting to make the trumpet chromatic—first by applying keys like clarinets used, then by adding a single valve, and eventually employing three that, in various combinations, produced all the pitches of a scale—the instrument assumed its modern form by about 1820. Slowly, the trumpet and its more popular cousin, the cornet, became instruments that were fully capable of performing complete melodies.

One of the earliest accounts of a cornet (the trumpet's mellower cousin) performing a gospel solo dates from the Moody–Sankey revival meetings in Chicago during the 1890s. Many of the earliest attempts at arranging gospel music for cornet reflected the same approaches that composers applied to secular music—theme and variations. The tune was played through once, generally unadorned; it was then followed by successive variations modifying the rhythm, meter, or ornamentation, and it generally concluded with a stanza each of double tonguing and triple tonguing—especially if the gospel song suggested a triumphant note. The secular model for this approach was the nineteenth-century "bible" of trumpet pedagogy, *Arban's Complete Conservatory Method for Trumpet* in the section "Twelve Celebrated Fantaisies and Airs Varies."

This secular virtuosic style of cornet playing was made famous during the early twentieth century by soloists such as Herbert Clark and Walter Smith who often led their own bands or headlined for Sousa's famous bands. Their example was then imitated by countless religious arrangers and soloists who applied the model to gospel music. Thus, trumpet solos, duets, and trios (an especially popular combination) with piano accompaniment began gracing many revivals and church services.

Published arrangements became a little more sophisticated harmonically after World War II and gave more importance to the piano accompaniment,

although the theme-and-variations model remained strong. By this time, the brassier trumpet had replaced the mellower cornet as the soloistic instrument of choice, and religious recordings made brass gospel music available for repeated listening. The Ohman Brothers were the most successful of many performing and recording soloists and ensembles during the 1950s through the 1970s, publishing trumpet collections with the Singspiration Company and recording for Word Records. Beginning in the 1970s, contemporary Christian music performer Phil Driscoll greatly influenced trumpet and gospel music as he took the instrument to new heights (literally, in terms of range), embracing showbiz styles of playing that reflected more of the jazz and rock traditions.

Beginning in the 1970s, the technological development of tape and CD accompaniment tracks gave trumpet players a new realm of possibility for playing gospel solos, no longer being limited by the availability or skills of a live piano accompanist. These tracks often provided orchestral accompaniment, which led to more interesting and sometimes more sophisticated gospel arrangements.

The Salvation Army has maintained a somewhat separate—but equally vital—brass band tradition that has contributed to a century of brass gospel music in the United States and especially Britain. The Army employed the more mellow cornet, rather than the trumpet, and developed an extensive and important body of religious literature featuring brass instruments. This music was generally limited to Salvationists, however, and thus was often little known outside of those circles in the United States.

Reflecting both the Salvation Army heritage and the trend of evangelicals to make significant contributions to classical orchestral music, Phil Smith, principal trumpet of the New York Philharmonic, has contributed greatly to the instrument's popularity with his gospel performances, recordings, and publications.

MEL R. WILHOIT

Discography

LPs by Chuck Ohman and the Ohman Brothers are out of print. The Salvation Army Recording Catalog has many examples in this genre.

TUTTLE, WESLEY AND MARILYN

Wesley LeRoy Tuttle (b. December 30, 1917; d. September 29, 2003)
Marilyn Myers Tuttle (b. September 3, 1925)

Wesley Tuttle had a lengthy and successful career as a country and western vocalist on radio, television, records, and motion pictures before entering the Christian ministry and the field of sacred music in 1957. His wife, Marilyn Myers Tuttle, worked with him as a vocalist both before and after his conversion. A native of Lamar, Colorado, Tuttle relocated to San Fernando, California, with his parents in 1922. The Western music that flourished on Los Angeles radio had a major influence on him, particularly that of the original Beverly Hillbillies and of Stuart Hamblen's Lucky Stars. The latter provided Tuttle with an entry into show business himself, and he played with Hamblen and other radio acts in the area; except for a brief period that he spent in Ohio, southern California would be his principal musical base.

Tuttle moved from being a band member to leading his own group—the Texas Stars—as support musicians for singing cowboy stars, most notably Jimmy Wakely, in a series of Monogram Pictures, and he also made films with Charles Starrett. He began an association with Capitol Records that extended from 1944 through 1955 and that resulted in such major hits as "With Tears in My Eyes, "Detour," "I Wish I Had Never Met Sunshine," and "Tho' I Tried (I Can't Forget You)." He married his wife Marilyn in 1946, and she was usually part of his musical endeavors from that point onward. Both also appeared on the popular television program *Town Hall Party* for several years, beginning in 1952.

Tuttle's life began to undergo serious changes after June 9, 1954, when his daughter Leslie drowned in a swimming pool accident. That July, he told his biographer, "Packy" Smith:

> I was baptized in the same water my little girl died in. This was very important to me, as previously I did not want to get near that pool, let alone get in it. It was after

that I really began to grow in the Lord. I decided I could not go on the way I was going. I quit the television; I canceled my Capitol Records contract. I made a break from my entertainment career and enrolled in Pacific Christian College to study the Bible and prepare myself for the Christian ministry.

The Tuttles had a second son, Matthew, in 1955, to join Wesley, Jr., and Wesley became known as the Song Minister in the Church of Christ Ministries. During the next two decades, he did some 175 revivals of one and two weeks in length, gave more than 750 musical concerts, and made eight sacred albums for the Sacred and Christian Faith labels. Marilyn and, on occasion, the sons joined in on these recordings. Marilyn operated a Christian bookstore for several years. However, Wesley's eyesight failed, and he retired in 1976, singing but sparingly thereafter; he and Marilyn continued to reside in San Fernando. In 2002, he accepted an award at the Charlotte Film Fair but did not sing. Later that year, Bear Family Records released a boxed set of CDs containing all of Tuttle's Capitol recordings and transcriptions. Wesley Tuttle passed away a year later.

IVAN M. TRIBE

Reference and Further Reading

Smith, Packy. *Detour: Wesley Tuttle.* Hamburg, Germany: Bear Family Records, 2002.

Discography

The Wesley Tuttle Family Album (1966, Christian Faith 5095).
His Name Is Wonderful (Custom Made CD).
Old Fashioned Hymn Sing (Sacred LP 3008).

U

UNSELD, BENJAMIN CARL

(b. October 18, 1843; d. 1923)

Songwriter and singing-school teacher Benjamin Carl Unseld was born in Shepherdstown, Virginia (which later became part of West Virginia). Early in life, he developed an intense love for music. He also demonstrated great talent and sought various means of improving his musical abilities. After obtaining a position in a Pennsylvania railroad office, he took a six-month leave of absence to further his musical knowledge; he never returned to the railroad. He attended the Musical Institute of Providence, Rhode Island, and studied under Dr. Eben Tourjee. When a short time later Tourjee founded the New England Conservatory of Music in Boston, he hired Unseld as the institution's first secretary.

During the early 1870s, Unseld taught music at Fisk University, where he helped develop the Fisk Jubilee Singers. While acquiring his musical expertise, he worked with a number of notables, including Theodore F. Seward, editor of the *New York Musical Gazette*; this contact enabled him to make an important career move. Aldine S. Kieffer was looking for someone to head up a normal school in the Shenandoah Valley. Kieffer saw such a school as the best means of improving music education in the South. Seward recommended Unseld to Kieffer; the two met in 1873 and began making plans for the South's first normal music school.

A genial man and a very knowledgeable student of music, Unseld's only defect, according to George Pullen Jackson, was "that he was a 'round-noter' with a tonic sol-fa hobby." Although Kieffer and Unseld disagreed on the relative importance of round or shape notes, they compromised, deciding that the new school should teach both systems.

The Virginia Normal Music School opened its doors in New Market, Virginia, in August of 1874. It offered instruction in harmony, thorough bass, piano, organ, voice building, reading of round notes and of seven-shape-notes, practice in church psalmody, glee singing, and oratorio. For eight years Unseld served as principal of the school; it then continued under various principals. Eventually, it became affiliated with the music department of Shenandoah Collegiate Institute (later Shenandoah College) in Dayton, Virginia. Unseld continued to teach at normal schools in North Carolina, Kentucky, Missouri, and Tennessee. In 1911, he moved to Lawrenceburg, Tennessee to become dean of a normal school established by a former pupil, James D. Vaughan. Unseld spent the remainder of his life there, serving as dean of the school and also, after 1914, as editor of the company's monthly magazine, *The Vaughan Family Visitor*.

Because of his normal school activities, Unseld is widely regarded as having an influence on nearly all rural singing teachers in the South. Of his several songs, the only one that is still well known is "Twilight Is Stealing."

W. K. McNeil

Reference and Further Reading

Goff, James R., Jr. *Close Harmony: A History of Southern Gospel*. Chapel Hill & London: University of North Carolina Press, 2002.
Jackson, George Pullen. *White Spirituals in the Southern Uplands*. Chapel Hill: University of North Carolina Press, 1933.

V

VAUGHAN FAMILY VISITOR, THE

The Vaughan Family Visitor was an influential periodical published by the James D. Vaughan Publishing Company of Lawrenceburg, Tennessee. A native of Giles County, Tennessee, James D. Vaughan began writing and publishing gospel songs in the late 1890s. In 1900, he published the first of his own songbooks at Cornersville, Tennessee. Later he moved to Lawrenceburg and began a long and successful series of annual paperback songbooks using the shape-note system.

A key innovator in exploring new ways to publicize and sell his books and boost normal school, in 1912 he began publishing a monthly magazine to spread news of singings, upcoming schools, new songbooks, and profiles of singers and composers. At first this magazine was entitled *The Musical Visitor* and was modeled after *The Musical Million,* an earlier magazine published in Virginia by the Ruebush–Kieffer company. In the early 1920s, Vaughan changed the title to *Vaughan's Family Visitor.* For a time, some twenty-six such publications emerged from Southern songbook publishers.

The first editor for the *Visitor* was George W. Sebren, a famed song editor and singer, who served from 1912 to 1914. Later editors included Benjamin C. Unseld, from 1914 to 1923; Charles W. Vaughan (James's brother), from 1923 to 1938; and W. E. B. Walbert (James Vaughan's son-in-law), from 1938 to 1959. The periodical was kept alive through several sales of the company; later editors included Rupert Cravens and Connor Hall.

In all, some eighty-six volumes of the periodical were published, though no complete sets are known to exist. In 1988, the Center for Popular Music at Middle Tennessee State University published on microfilm all of the then-known copies, but even this has gaps (especially in Volumes 34 through 39).

CHARLES K. WOLFE

Reference and Further Reading

Wolfe, Charles. "Introduction" [to microfilm edition of *The Vaughan Family Visitor*]. Murfreesboro, TN: Center for Popular Music, 1988.

VAUGHAN QUARTET

The Vaughan Quartet was a generic name used to describe a variety of different male singing quartets sponsored by the James D. Vaughan Music Company of Lawrenceburg, Tennessee. From 1910 to the 1950s, various groups sent out from Lawrenceburg traveled throughout the United States from Florida to California, but primarily in the South and Midwest. They appeared as guests at singing conventions, church meetings, revivals, and concerts and on radio and records, popularizing the newest songs from the latest Vaughan songbook, selling books, recruiting for the Vaughan Normal Schools, and introducing people to the new seven-shape-note Southern gospel. Many historians and fans credit Vaughan and his quartets with defining gospel music through a quartet format of "four men and a piano"—a format that remains a hallmark of Southern gospel today.

James D. Vaughan got the idea of quartet singing in the late nineteenth century, when he and his brothers would sing informally; after he started his music company, in 1910 he revived the idea and chose four men from the company to go out as the first Vaughan Quartet. The personnel included his brother Charles as bass singer and manager; music editor and composer George W. Sebren as lead or baritone; Ira Foust as alto or high tenor; and Joe M. Allen as tenor. Soon these four were traveling the South in a touring car with the name "Vaughan Quartet" painted on the side. The demand for their appearances became so great that Vaughan soon had to form another quartet, and then yet another. At one time in the 1920s, he had no fewer that sixteen quartets on the road.

Always willing to use the new mass media to publicize his music, Vaughan encouraged his groups to do radio work and to record. In fact, in 1921 he decided to start his own record company under the Vaughan label, and he began releasing and selling records from Lawrenceburg, thus creating the first Southern record company. From 1921 to 1930, the label issued some eighty-three records, each with two songs. Some of the quartets also recorded for commercial labels as well; quartets cut some forty sides for Victor/Bluebird and four for Paramount. "Now you can have a Vaughan Quartet in your home without having to feed them," claimed an ad for the new records, and thousands of fans obliged.

CHARLES K. WOLFE

See also Gospel Quartets; Vaughan, James D

Reference and Further Reading

Fleming, Joe. "James D. Vaughan, Music Publisher." D.S. thesis, Union Theological Seminary, 1972.
Russell, Tony. *Country Music Records: A Discography, 1921–1942.* New York: Oxford University Press, 2004.

VAUGHAN, JAMES DAVID

(b. December 14, 1864; d. February 9, 1941)

Songwriter, publisher, and promoter James David Vaughan was born in Giles County, Tennessee, to George Washington and Eliza Shores Vaughan. He grew up to become a major force in the development of Southern gospel music. At age seventeen, Vaughan attended his first singing school and proved to be an enthusiastic student. Shortly afterward, he taught his first singing school and organized his brothers and himself into a quartet. Then, in 1883, he gained more knowledge as a result of attending the Ruebush–

Kieffer Normal School in New Market, Virginia, where he studied under Benjamin Carl (B. C.) Unseld.

Two years after his marriage in 1890, Vaughan moved to Cisco, Texas, where he attended another singing school, this one taught by Ephraim Timothy (E. T.) Hildebrand, a disciple of Ruebush–Kieffer. Hildebrand was influential on Vaughan, particularly in encouraging him to compose music. Vaughan might have remained in Cisco had not a tragedy occurred there six weeks after the birth of his son, Glenn Kieffer. On March 20, a cyclone hit Cisco, destroying everything Vaughan owned. Reportedly, their house literally fell down around them; fortunately, all family members survived. Thereafter, Vaughan moved his family to Elkmont Springs, Tennessee, where he became a schoolteacher.

Vaughan never lost interest in music, and in 1900 he printed a songbook, *Gospel Chimes*. Two years later, in 1902, he moved to Lawrenceburg, Tennessee, about fifteen miles away, and he founded the James D. Vaughan Publishing Company. His younger brother Charles joined him a year later. The Vaughan brothers were not an overnight success, selling only thirty thousand songbooks in 1909. In 1910, Vaughan hit upon an innovative idea to sell their new collection, *Voices for Jesus*: put a quartet on the road to promote the book. This first quartet consisted of Charles Vaughan, manager; George Sebren; Joe M. Allen; and Ira T. Foust. They sang wherever they could, and their efforts resulted in increased sales for the songbooks and popularity for the quartet.

In 1911, Vaughan started the Vaughan School of Music, which originally moved around in an attempt to reach all interested, promising students, but eventually it was situated in Lawrenceburg. Vaughan had a dual purpose here: he saw the school as a means of supplying trained instructors for rural singing schools, and at the same time as a means to increase sales of his songbooks. He reasoned that teachers trained in his school would naturally recommend his company's books. Vaughan brought in his old teacher, B. C. Unseld, as principal, a position that Unseld held until his death twelve years later, in 1923.

Three years after his arrival, Unseld took over as editor of the company's magazine, *The Musical Visitor*, replacing George Sebren. The monthly publication's name was soon changed to *The Vaughan Family Visitor*. Vaughan advertised it as "the leading music journal of the South" and as "safe, pure, and clean, and should be in every home." Readers found its mix of poetry, music, and good home literature appealing; they found especially interesting the inclusion of words and music to new songs in every issue. These features helped make the magazine very successful.

Vaughan, however, did not rest on his laurels and was constantly searching for new ways to expand his enterprises. In 1921 he established Vaughan Phonograph Records, which he advertised in the *Visitor* and on the back of his songbooks. On this label he made the first gospel quartet recording, "I Couldn't Hear Nobody Pray" and either "Look for Me" or "Steal Away" (sources differ). At its first session, the quartet also recorded four recent songs by William W. Combs, Virgil Oliver Stamps, L. C. Taylor, James Rowe, and Howard E. Smith. These records were advertised—somewhat inaccurately—as the "first and only Southern records to be placed on the market. They are safe for the boys and girls, the kind that Father and Mother will enjoy."

There is some dispute about who made up the quartet heard on the Vaughan label's initial release. According to Bob Terrell, it consisted of Hillman Barnard, Kieffer Vaughan, Walter B. Seale, and Ray Collins, but James R. Goff, Jr., says it more likely was made up of Johnny E. Wheeler, M. D. McWhorter, Adlai Loudy, and Herman Walker, although he admits that Kieffer Vaughan may have also sung with the group.

In any event, the record company and various other enterprises were so successful that Vaughan opened four branch offices, in Arkansas, Mississippi, South Carolina, and Texas. Despite his success, Vaughan had more innovations up his sleeve. Beginning in 1923, his station WOAN (Watch Our Annual Normal), one of the first radio stations in Tennessee, began broadcasting. At first a one-hundred-and-fifty watt station, it was upgraded to five hundred watts in 1925, which, on the sparsely populated radio map of the day, enabled it to reach people hundreds of miles away. Even so, it did not prove to be as lucrative as some of Vaughan's other undertakings. Because it was licensed as a noncommercial station, WOAN was not permitted to sell ads and thus never proved financially viable. It did, however, help to publicize the Vaughan company's activities.

During the 1930s, the station and its equipment were sold; in 1935 Vaughan's record company was discontinued. His songbook publishing, however, continued to be strong; by the time of his death in 1941, ten months before Pearl Harbor, the company had sold more than six million books. Although Vaughan's various activities were intended to financially benefit his company, they also paved the way for others in the field of gospel music.

W. K. MCNEIL

Reference and Further Reading

Goff, James R., Jr. *Close Harmony: The History of Southern Gospel.* Chapel Hill: University of North Carolina Press, 2002.
Terrell, Bob. *The Music Men: The Story of Professional Gospel Quartet Singing.* Nashville, TN: Bob Terrell, 1990.

VIRGINIA NORMAL MUSIC SCHOOL

Although William Walker, author of *The Southern Harmony,* claimed to have taught in normal schools long before the 1870s, it is generally accepted that the Virginia Normal Music School, opened in New Market, Virginia, in August 1874, was the first institution designed for instructing rural singing teachers in the South.

This school, which was based on similar normal music schools established in the Northeast prior to the Civil War, was the brainchild of Aldine S. Kieffer, the "Don Quixote of Buckwheat Notes," as enemies of the shape-note system referred to him. He earned his nickname primarily because of his monthly editorial page in *The Musical Million,* where he frequently attacked the "roundheads"—that is, adherents of conventional notation. For principal of the new school, Kieffer chose Benjamin C. Unseld, an ironic choice because he was a round-noter with a tonic solfa hobby. The two compromised and agreed to teach both systems, a truce that did not work; soon the round-shape system was omitted.

During the school's first year, courses were taught in harmony, bass, piano, organ, voice, reading of round notes and seven-shape notes, church psalmody, glee singing, and oratorio. As the round-noters were driven away, the school's attendance decreased, but Kieffer persisted because he was convinced that prospective teachers of Southern rural singers should be instructed in the Southern musical language. Unseld accepted his fate and remained head of the school, which soon moved to Dayton, Virginia, for eight years.

It would be difficult to overestimate the influence of the Virginia Normal Music School in the South. Among its graduates were teachers and founders of normal schools, songbook compilers, publishers, and composers active in every state south of the Mason–Dixon line. Its best-known alumni are James D. Vaughan and A. J. Showalter. The school was eventually merged into the music department at Shenandoah College of Dayton, Virginia. Although the school exists, it no longer teaches shape notes, confining its instruction to classics and round notes.

W. K. MCNEIL

Reference and Further Reading

Blackwell, Lois S. *The Wings of the Dove: The Story of Gospel Music in America.* Norfolk, VA: Donning, 1978.
Jackson, George Pullen. *White Spirituals in the Southern Uplands: The Story of the Fasola Folk, Their Songs, Singings, and "Buckwheat Notes."* New York: Dover, 1965 (1933).
Suter, Scott Hamilton. *Shenandoah Valley Folklife.* Jackson: University Press of Mississippi, 1999.

WALKER, ALBERTINA

(b. 1930, Chicago, IL)

One of the finest gospel singers of all time, Albertina Walker began singing at West Point Baptist Church when she was eleven. In 1947, she joined the Gospel Caravan, a group led by Robert Anderson. In 1952, she organized her own Caravans with other members of Anderson's group: Ora Lee Hopkins, Elyse Yancey, and Nellie Grace Daniels.

From the beginning, the Caravans were one of the best female groups of their time, producing more gospel superstars than any other group or choir. They recorded a dozen songs for States Records in 1952 and 1953, bearing witness to close, earthy harmony, percussive attacks, and precise rhythm. Walker was the only soloist in the original group, and it was the beauty of her voice (a throaty contralto), her sincerity, and her singing style that drew attention.

By 1953, and with the addition of Bessie Griffin (b. 1927, New Orleans, Louisiana; d. 1990), the Caravans began a long association with Gospel/Savoy Records (while still recording for States) and began to change into an ensemble of soloists. Griffin's light contralto was fluid; she sustained tones for long periods, inserting growls, pitch, and embellishments. She left the Caravans in 1954 to start a successful solo career. She was replaced by Cassietta George (b. 1928, Memphis, Tennessee), whose clear and thin but huge voice astounded the audiences; she also composed more than twenty-five songs while with the Caravans.

Gloria Griffin and James Cleveland joined the Caravans that same year, while Dorothy Norwood (b. 1930, Atlanta, Georgia), the master storyteller, and Imogene Green (b. 1931, Chicago) joined in 1956. Norwood's alto, which was capable of great warmth, graced a lot of songs, but she left during the late 1950s to go solo and to achieve the superstardom that she is enjoying in the 2000s.

In 1957, James Cleveland, pianist and arranger for the Caravans, persuaded Inez Andrews (b. 1929, Birmingham, Alabama) to come and join the group; she was a singer who had a preacher tone, a metallic contralto, and a slow, majestic delivery. This contrasted with the light alto/mezzo-soprano and rapid vibrato of Shirley Caesar ("Baby Shirley," b. 1938, Durham, North Carolina), who was also new to the Caravans and whose extensive range and preacher delivery, dramatization of songs, and intense activity on stage (she might run up and down the aisles on tunes with "run" in the lyrics or mimic sweeping on "Sweeping Through the City") could energize and unleash an audience's passion and enthusiasm. An evangelist since 1961, Shirley Caesar left in 1966 to organize her own groups and choirs and to become the most popular gospel singer and evangelist of the 1990s and 2000s.

From December 1962 to late 1970, Albertina Walker and the Caravans recorded copiously for Vee-Jay, Gospel/Savoy, and Hob Records; then, in the 1980s, Albertina Walker started a very successful solo career, skillfully blending traditional and contemporary gospel according to her audiences. She was named an honorary member of the famed Fisk Jubilee Singers by the president of Nashville University. She has performed all over the United States, Canada, Europe, and the Caribbean Islands; she has received countless honors and awards, including nine Grammy nominations; and she is a favorite of media and show business, appearing in movies such as *Save the Children* and *Leap of Time* and in off-Broadway productions (*The Gospel Truth*), hosting radio and television programs, and recording regularly for Benson Records. She is still a vital force in gospel music.

ROBERT SACRÉ

Reference and Further Reading

Boyer, Horace Clarence. *How Sweet the Sound: The Golden Age of Gospel.* Washington, DC: Elliott & Clark, 1995.

Hayes, J. Cedric; Robert Laughton. *Gospel Records 1943–1969. A Black Music Discography,* 2 vols. London, UK: Record Information Services, 1992.

Heilbut, Tony. *The Gospel Sound: Good News and Bad Times.* New York: Limelight, 1985.

Reagon, Bernice Johnson, ed. *We'll Understand It Better By and By. Pioneering African American Gospel Composers.* Washington, DC: Smithsonian Institution Press, 1992.

Sacre, Robert. "Albertina Walker." *Blues Gazette* (B) no. 3 (Summer 1996): 20.

Discography

The Best of the Caravans (1977, Savoy SCD7012).

Albertina Walker: You Believed in Me (1990, Benson CD 02673).

The Caravans (1993, Vee-Jay NVG2-608).

He Keeps on Blessing Me (1993, Benson S1416-1001-2).

Let's Go Back: Live in Chicago (1996, Benson 84418 4234 2).

WALKER, HEZEKIAH

(b. December 24, 1962, Brooklyn, NY)

Affectionately known as the "Pastor to Hip-Hop," Hezekiah Walker has led the movement in incorporating the urban hip-hop sounds and culture into not only gospel music but into the black church as well. Born in Brooklyn, New York, on December 24, 1962, and raised in the Fort Greene housing projects, Hezekiah Xzavier Walker, Jr., escaped the bitter grips of the streets by seeking refuge at the Greater Bibleway Church in Crown Heights, New York. He began singing at age eight, and by twelve, he began writing songs for a small ensemble that would develop by 1985 into the multi–award-winning Love Fellowship Crusade Choir (LFCC), one of the most important recording choirs since the Chicago-based Thompson Community Choir.

In 1987, Hezekiah and LFCC recorded their first album for the Philadelphia-based Sweet Rain Records

label. In 1991, after nurturing a local following, the group signed with Nashville-based Benson Records. Well known for recording live albums, LFCC won a 1994 Grammy Award for *Live in Atlanta at Morehouse College.* In appreciation for their contribution to the city of Atlanta, the Mayor proclaimed February 5, 1994, Hezekiah Walker Day. In addition, Morehouse College archived footage of the recording in a centennial time capsule. Known for their integration of traditional gospel, R&B, and hip-hop, and for taking the lead as one of the innovative choirs transitioning into the "urban" sound of the late twentieth and early twenty-first century gospel music, Hezekiah and LFCC were awarded a second Grammy for the 2001 recording *Love Is Live!*

Hezekiah Walker accepted his call to ministry at the age of eighteen and was ordained as a Pentecostal minister. After ministering to his choir for numerous years, Walker established the Love Fellowship Tabernacle with less than fifteen members. To date, Pastor Walker leads congregations in Brooklyn as well as in Bensalem, Pennsylvania, with an additional tabernacle slated for New Jersey. Pastor Walker's ministry is committed to assisting folks from the community in need, including drug addicts and dealers, the homeless, convicts, and youth. His commitment to disenfranchised and oppressed people earned him the accolade of "Preacher to the People" by the *New York Daily News* in 1999.

EMMETT G. PRICE III

Reference and Further Reading

Jones, Dr. Bobby; with Lesley Sussman. "Hezekiah Walker." In *Touched By God: Black Gospel Greats Share Their Stories of Finding God,* 38–49. New York: Pocket Books, 1998.

Discography

Live in Atlanta at Morehouse College (1994, Benson CD 4006).

Live in New York by Any Means ... (1995, Benson CD 4168).

Recorded Live at Love Fellowship Tabernacle (1998, Verity CD 43116).

Love is Live! (2001, Verity CD 43157).

Family Affair, Vol. 2: Live at Radio City Music Hall (2002, Verity CD 43176).

WALTER HAWKINS LOVE CENTER CHOIR

The Love Center Choir was founded by Walter Hawkins, pastor and founder of Love Center Ministries located in Oakland, California. Under his able leadership, the choir has recorded a wealth of gospel music hits. From the debut album, *Going Up Yonder* (1975), through each addition to the Love Alive series, the world has come to appreciate the depth of talent in this phenomenal ensemble. The breadth of compositional prowess of its principal songwriter and director is also legend.

Love Alive II (1978) won two Dove Awards from the Gospel Music Association, was nominated for a Grammy Award, and garnered awards from *Billboard, Record World,* and *Cash Box* music trade publications. Six years later, in 1985, *Love Alive III* was finished to rave reviews, earning a Dove Award nomination and record sales. Likewise, *Love Alive IV* was nominated for a Grammy and remained on top of *Billboard*'s gospel chart for an unparalleled thirty-nine weeks. The fifth in the series, *Love Alive V: The 25th Reunion* (1998), on Gospo Centric Records, was a double CD. In it, Hawkins reassembled some of the early singers from the Love Center Choir who had since gone on to award-winning careers of their own. This included Grammy winners Edwin Hawkins and Tramaine Hawkins (Walter's ex-wife and one of the original members of the Love Center Choir who has since become a Grammy Award winner), Lynette Hawkins Stephens, Pastor Yvette Flunder, and Shirley Miller. The concert celebrated the twenty-fifth anniversary of Hawkins's ordination as a pastor and recording artist.

For more than thirty years, the Love Center Choir, under Walter Hawkins's skillful and talented leadership, has had far-reaching influence. Not only have they regularly collaborated with older brother Edwin Hawkins on such projects as his Grammy-winning *Live with the Oakland Symphony* (1982), but they have also appeared on recordings by Celt rocker Van Morrison and Lee Oskar. More than a church ensemble, the Love Center Choir has contributed to the wealth of contemporary and traditional gospel music that is available for churches throughout the world.

DONNA M. COX

WARD TRIO (WARD SINGERS)

Clara Ward (b. August 21, 1924, Philadelphia, PA; d. January 16, 1973)

The Ward Singers were one of the most popular gospel vocal groups of the 1950s. Highly influential thanks to their great showmanship, lavish stage costumes, and incorporation of popular vocal styles into their performances, the group had a lasting impact in the gospel and secular musical worlds.

The family originally hailed from South Carolina, living in relative poverty, and they moved during the early 1920s to Philadelphia in search of better employment. The family matriarch was Gertrude Mae Murphy Ward. She had a vision in 1931 that led her to begin performing gospel music. By the late 1930s, she had brought her young daughters—Clara (b. August 21, 1924, Philadelphia, Pennsylvania) on piano and vocals and Willa on vocals—into the group. Known as the Ward Trio, they made a stunning debut at the 1943 National Baptist Convention, establishing themselves as a major draw on the gospel circuit.

In 1948, two nonfamily members were added to the group, notably dynamic teenaged lead vocalist Marion Williams, and the Ward Singers had hits with "Surely God Is Able" and "Packin' It Up." Williams remained with the group through 1958, with her dynamic performances a centerpiece of their success. However, Clara also showed herself to be a very able vocalist, most notably on the hit "How I Got Over." The Ward Singers are generally credited to be the first to swap lead vocals in a single performance, building intensity as the song progressed. Clara was also responsible for several innovative arrangements, even arranging a gospel waltz for the group's greatest hit, "Surely."

During the 1950s, the group became closely associated with the Reverend C. L. Franklin, whose daughter, Aretha Franklin, credits Ward with influencing her own vocal style. Touring with Franklin and recording major hits, the group enjoyed great popular success. They became famous for their energetic performances, elaborate costumes, and often flamboyant wigs; their sense of showmanship would influence the next generation of gospel and R&B groups, including the Motown hit makers. However, after Williams and the other nonfamily members left in 1958—to protest the fact that they were kept on a low salary while Clara and her mother took the lion's share of the group's earnings—the group struggled. Clara performed as a solo artist through much of the 1960s, recording mainly pop material during this period and performing at nightclubs and in Las Vegas; meanwhile, her mother continued to lead various lineups of Ward Singers. During the later 1960s, Clara returned to recording more traditional gospel material for the small Nashboro label. She suffered a stroke in 1967 but recovered enough to continue performing for a while; eventually, ill health led to her retirement, and Clara died on January 16, 1973.

RICHARD CARLIN

Reference and Further Reading

Heilbut, Anthony. *The Gospel Sound: Good News and Bad Times,* updated and revised edition. New York: Limelight, 1997.

Discography

Down by the Riverside (1958, Dot; live album recorded at New York's Town Hall with the group at the height of its powers).
Lord Touch Me (1965, Savoy; LP reissue of recordings made between 1953 and 1955 for the Savoy jazz label).

WASHINGTON, ERNESTINE B.

"The Songbird of the East"; "Little Momma"
(b. 1914, Little Rock, AR; d. July 1983, Brooklyn, NY)

Ernestine Beatrice Thomas Washington started singing at age four. Her mother was a popular sanctified singer in the Little Rock black community. A friend of Rosetta Tharpe, Ernestine completed high school in Little Rock and was engaged in domestic work while still singing in church. At the annual Conventions of the Church of God in Christ she met and married the Reverend Frederick D. Washington (1913–1988), who then traveled with his wife to Montclair, New Jersey, where he founded the Trinity Temple Church of God in Christ and where Ernestine developed her reputation as a soloist and vocalist, strongly influenced by Arizona Juanita Dranes. She had a high-pitched mezzo-soprano/alto voice with a fast vibrato at range extremes (upper and lower), with a great sense of melody and percussive attacks, setting a rhythm to fit the text and mood of the song.

In the early 1940s the couple moved to Brooklyn, New York, where Washington founded the Brooklyn Church of God in Christ, named the Washington Temple in 1951 in his honor. He was pastor there until his death, also serving as auxiliary bishop of the Jurisdiction of New York. Ernestine first recorded in 1943 (four songs for Regis/Manor/Arco), and she also recorded two tracks in 1944 with the Dixie Hummingbirds (on the same labels).

By 1946, the Reverend Washington had become a fixture in Brooklyn, one of the most respected ministers in the COGIC. Madam(e) Ernestine B. Washington, or the "Songbird of the East" as she was called then, was the featured soloist of the denomination on all official days and the gospel queen of the Washington Temple COGIC, which was in a beautifully remodelled theater and had a large middle- and upper-class and very devout congregation, plenty of instruments (organ, piano, guitars, drums, percussion), and six big choirs.

At the annual November convocation of the Church of God in Christ in Memphis, it was Ernestine's pride to sing the solo before the sermon of the presiding bishop, and she recorded in 1946 with the legendary William Geary "Bunk" Johnson and his New Orleans–style jazz band (four songs for Jubilee/Disc Records). Working with secular musicians was generally subject to the contempt of the church membership, but this time, the people of her church somehow felt complimented that a jazz star was called upon to accompany one of their own.

She made more records for Manor Records with the Heavenly Gospel Singers (1946), the Southern Sons (1947), her singers and/or Reverend Frederick D. Washington (1947–1948), and also with the Milleraires in 1954 (Groove). Her first album, in 1958, showed her in her best sanctified style. With the congregation of Washington Temple COGIC and accompanied by her long-time pianist and organist Alfred Miller and the members of her church choir, she gave way to the full power of her voice and the style that made her famous. This type of performance brought her fame as she toured throughout the United States and abroad (1958–1959). At that time, she recorded a last album for Delden Records with the Celestial Choir directed by Professor Henry O. Coston before devoting the rest of her life to her church and her choirs. At her death, she was mourned in two crowded services at Washington Temple, complete with all the dignitaries of the COGIC.

ROBERT SACRÉ

See also Dixie Hummingbirds; Heavenly Gospel Singers; Tharpe, Sister Rosetta

Reference and Further Reading

Boyer, Horace Clarence. *How Sweet the Sound: The Golden Age of Gospel.* Washington, DC: Elliott & Clark, 1995.
Hayes, J. Cedric; Robert Laughton. *Gospel Records 1943–1969. A Black Music Discography.* 2 vols. London, UK: Record Information Services, 1992.
Heilbut, Tony. *The Gospel Sound: Good News and Bad Times.* New York: Limelight, 1985.

Discography

Sister Ernestine Washington, in Chronological Order 1943–48 (1996, Document Records [Austria] DOCD-5462).

WATERS, ETHEL

(b. October 31, 1896, Chester, PA; d. September 1, 1977)

Ethel Waters was a versatile and influential entertainer and an exceptionally talented and popular singer. She was also a dancer, a Broadway and film actress, and—during the final fifteen years of her career—a highly successful singer of religious music and a witness for her Christian faith with the Billy Graham Crusades.

When Waters joined the Billy Graham Crusades in 1960, she was already famous and a highly respected and influential personality. Her impact in the crusades was a direct outgrowth of the fame and respect she had achieved in her secular career.

Waters was born in Chester, Pennsylvania, when her mother was only thirteen. During Ethel's childhood, she experienced extreme poverty and a troubled and insecure home life. At a young age, she attended a Catholic school in her neighborhood; there she found solace and support and was exposed to discipline and Catholic values (Marks and Edkins, 1999, p. 93). She completed a sixth-grade education, married at the age of thirteen, and began her singing and dancing career around 1917.

Because she came from the Philadelphia area rather than the South, her musical influences were derived more from vaudeville than from the Southern blues and gospel traditions. Around 1917, she began singing and dancing in vaudeville theatres in black neighborhoods in Atlanta, Philadelphia, and Baltimore. As her singing style evolved, rather than the shouting or growling of many blues singers, she incorporated blues and jazz qualities in white vaudeville songs in a more refined style than that of classic blues singers. This had an enormous impact on both black and white singers who followed, such as Sophie Tucker, Billie Holiday, and Ella Fitzgerald (Fabre and Feith, 2001, p. 104).

In the early 1920s, Waters's career was launched, and opportunities kept coming. She entertained in many clubs, large and small. First, Edmonds Cellar in Harlem was important as a place where she honed her craft. Her specialty was the choreography of body shakes, or the "shimmy." Edmonds Cellar was like other "below the street" clubs in Harlem. Waters knew the ways of the patrons, because she understood them and their desire and perhaps need for alcohol, dope, sex, and violence. She had lived within that culture, yet she remained separate from it. She called it "the last stop on the way down in show business" (Krasner, 2002, p. 72). But Waters was on the way up.

Lou Henley was Waters's pianist at Edmonds Cellar. He "encouraged her to add popular tunes to her blues routine" (Pleasants, 1974, p. 86). Earl Dancer, who heard her perform at Edmonds, became her long-time manager. With his encouragement, she became a vaudeville sensation, traveling from coast to coast and becoming the first black entertainer to move successfully from the vaudeville and nightclub circuits to what blacks called "the white time." By the 1930s, she was one of the highest-paid black entertainers on Broadway (Marks and Edkins, 1999, p. 93).

Among Waters's hit songs were "Stormy Weather," introduced in 1935 at a Cotton Club Revue; "Heat Wave," in Irving Berlin's revue *As Thousands Cheer* (1933); "Dinah," introduced at the Plantation Club in 1925; and "St. Louis Blues," "Harlem on My Mind," and "Taking a Chance on Love." During the 1920s and 1930s, she performed and recorded with Fletcher Henderson, Jimmy and Tommy Dorsey, Duke Ellington, and many other jazz greats.

Waters expanded her career to include on- and off-Broadway theater productions, including *Mamba's Daughters* (1939), *Cabin in the Sky* (1940), and *The Member of the Wedding* (1950). In 1943, *Cabin in the Sky* was made into a movie with Ethel Waters, Lena Horne, and Louis Armstrong, and in 1952, *The Member of the Wedding* was made into a movie with Ethel Waters and Julie Harris.

By the mid-1950s, Waters's entertainment career, for the most part, had wound down. However, in 1957, she attended a Billy Graham Crusade in Madison Square Gardens. She was greatly moved by the experience and later joined the choir, even though she did not read music. It was not long before Cliff Barrows, the crusade's music director and song leader, urged Waters to sing a solo with the choir. It was "His Eye Is on the Sparrow," which became her signature song for this final stage of an illustrious career. She became a familiar sight at Billy Graham Crusades for the next fifteen years, singing solos and sharing her faith.

"Ethel Waters never really left show business—she just changed her message" (Knaack, 1978, p.54).

DAVID WILLOUGHBY

Reference and Further Reading

Fabre, Geneviève; Michael Feith, eds. *Temples for Tomorrow: Looking Back at the Harlem Renaissance.* Bloomington: Indiana University Press, 2001.

Gill, Glenda E. *No Surrender! No Retreat!: African-American Pioneer Performers of Twentieth-Century American Theatre.* New York: St. Martin's Press, 2000.

Knaack, Twila. *Ethel Waters: I Touched a Sparrow.* Minneapolis, MN: World Wide Publications, 1978.

Krasner, David. *A Beautiful Pageant: African American Theatre, Drama, and Performance in the Harlem Renaissance, 1910–1927.* New York: Palgrave Macmillan, 2002.

Marks, Carole; Diana Edkins. *The Power of Pride: Stylemakers and Rulebreakers of the Harlem Renaissance.* New York: Crown Publishers, 1999.

Pleasants, Henry. *The Great American Popular Singers.* New York: Simon and Schuster, 1974.

Waters, Ethel; with Charles Samuels. *His Eye Is on the Sparrow: An Autobiography.* Garden City, NY: Doubleday, 1951.

Discography

Am I Blue? (1999, ASV Living Era CD AJA 5290).
The Incomparable Ethel Waters (2003, Columbia/Legacy Recordings CD CK65852).

WATKINS FAMILY, THE

Don Watkins (b. September 12, 1941)
Judy Rumsey Watkins (b. February 5, 1946)
Todd Watkins (b. October 4, 1966)
Shannon Watkins (b. October 4, 1970)
Lorie Watkins (b. April 20, 1972)

The Watkins Family, with their motto "Gospel Because We Believe It—Bluegrass Because We Love It," have been playing their brand of gospel music for some twenty years. Natives of the Appalachian portion of North Georgia, they have proved themselves both a durable and talented group. Two decades as musical professionals with no personnel changes must in and of itself be something of a record.

Don Watkins and his wife Judy Rumsey married in 1965, and they soon put their musical efforts into a local group to play at church, called the Sunshine Trio. When the trio broke up, the three Watkins children were beginning to take an interest in music. Todd Watkins began playing the steel guitar at age four, while Shannon played several instruments but mostly fiddle; little Lorie picked the banjo. Judy played bass fiddle, and Don played the guitar. The Watkins Family converted to bluegrass in 1986, having some "electronic music on them [their first three albums], but they had a bluegrass flavor." After Don retired from his longtime job for General Telephone, the family became a full-time musical group.

The Watkins Family has played and continues to play all over the Eastern United States and in Canada. One highlight performance came in 1988 when they gave a three-hour concert on Capitol Hill in Washington. They have recorded numerous albums, cassettes, and CDs for such labels as Timberline, Cedar Hill, and Makedah during their two decades on the road.

IVAN M. TRIBE

Reference and Further Reading

Powell, Wayde. "The Watkins Family: Gospel Because They Believe It, Bluegrass Because They Love It." *Precious Memories: Journal of Gospel Music* 3, no. 1 (May–June 1990): 5–8.

Selected Discography

Winter to Spring (2000, Makedah MM 01914).
Golden Moments (Cedar Hill).
One Family, One Direction (Cedar Hill).

WATKINS, CHARLES

(b. December 23, 1923, Hopewell, VA; d. October 19, 1988, Cleveland, OH)

Bishop Charles Watkins was a truly unique talent in the gospel music arena. His smooth and soothing voice provided a stark contrast to the traditional gospel quartet and mass choir sound of his day. Despite being a million-selling artist on the Savoy label, his legend has largely escaped the general public. However, his influence is significant among gospel music practitioners.

Born in Virginia but raised in Newark, New Jersey, Watkins was a singer, songwriter, arranger, and choir director whose experimentation with various styles in music raised the eyebrows of his fellow Pentecostal churchmen. A renaissance man in many ways, he pioneered the use of bongos, conga drums, and symphonic accompaniment on recorded gospel music, but he never wavered in his message of gospel truth. Watkins also established two independent labels on which his later works were recorded.

Discovered singing in the gospel choir in 1949, Watkins was initially recorded by Coleman Records. Shortly thereafter, he took his talents to Newark-based Savoy Records and began recording a string of gospel songs that earned the admiration of musicians from various genres. Following an audition at RCA studios in New York, Watkins was approached by both Pearl Bailey and Frank Sinatra. Reportedly Sinatra encouraged him to switch his focus to popular music, noting that his voice was more like Nat King Cole's than those of popular gospel singers.

He recorded "I Must Tell Jesus" and "My Change" in 1952 at Savoy and "What He Done for Me" and "Run, Run, and Tell Him" before introducing bongos on "Don't Let This Harvest Pass" in 1953. In later years, Watkins recalled the fervor with which church leaders took him to task over that innovation when he sarcastically wrote that they "almost put me out of the church." He recorded numerous other gospel favorites for Savoy, despite moving to pastor a church in San Antonio, Texas, and then moving again in 1961 to pastor a Cleveland, Ohio, church. In 1963, Savoy released Watkins's most successful album, *Shady Green Pastures,* on which the million-selling hit "Heartaches" appeared.

His direct musical influence reached a young pianist named Jessy Dixon, who used to visit Watkins's San Antonio church, and Andrae Crouch, with whom he did joint concerts. Upon being introduced to Watkins's youngest daughter years after his death, Edwin Hawkins told her that he had listened to everything Charles Watkins had ever recorded and felt it was a catalyst for his music. Likewise, Charles Fold, reflecting upon "Don't Let This Harvest Pass," called Watkins "contemporary gospel before there was contemporary gospel."

Watkins was the first national minister of music for the Pentecostal Assemblies of the World, one of the largest black Pentecostal organizations in the nation. Like Mattie Moss Clark in the Church of God in Christ, Watkins was the inspiration for a legacy of PAW-nurtured musicians that includes Marvin Sapp, the Debarge family, Angela Winbush, Hammer, Babyface, Fred Hammond, Tonex, Dawkins & Dawkins, and Dietrick Haddon.

After leaving Savoy, Charles Watkins established two independent record labels—Praise Records and then LaCross Records—and recorded for them for the rest of his career. By then the pastor of one of the largest churches in Cleveland, Watkins's musical acumen drew artists from around the nation to his church. Among the personal friends that routinely exchanged visits and performed with his Pentecostal Mass Choir were Sarah Jordan Powell, the O'Neal Twins, Inez Andrews, Doris Akers, Reverend Lawrence Roberts, Edwin and Tramaine Hawkins, and the Banks Brothers.

Watkins continued to perform and record until right before his death. His final album, *Storefront Connection,* was released just months prior to his death. Notable songs he recorded on his labels are "Wake Up in Glory," "Renew," "The Lost Sheep," "By His Spirit," "Oh How Wonderful It Is," "Sometimes I Feel That Way Too," and the "Sound of Pentecost."

Perhaps the greatest tribute to the music of Charles Watkins is the artists who have rerecorded his work. The Rance Allen Group recorded "Heartaches" on the *Up Above My Head* album in 1974. Additionally, Charles Watkins's arrangement of "The Lost Sheep" was rerecorded by the Angelic Choir, the BC&M Mass Choir, Ricky Womack, and Reverend Clay Evans and the AARC Mass Choir. His arrangement of "I Won't Complain" (sometimes titled "God's Been So Good to Me") has become a favorite of soloists in worship services across the nation.

TIMOTHY J. MOORE

Reference and Further Reading

Anderson, Rosetta. Royalty administrator, Malaco Records. Interview, February 14, 2005.
Clark, Rumae. "Lest We Forget ..." *The Christian Outlook* (September/October 2004).
Fold, Charles. Founder, Charles Fold Singers. Interview, February 9, 2005.
Marovich, Bob. "Savoy Records Discography." Gospel website, http://www.island.net/~blues/savoy.htm.
Sanders, Rufus G. W., ed. *The Purpose: 50th Anniversary (1933–1983).* Indianapolis, IN: Pentecostal Assemblies of the World, 1983.
Thomas, Jerry. Producer and Musicians for Bishop Watkins. Interview, February 12, 2005.
Watkins, Charles. "Autobiography of Elder Charles Watkins." *The Christian Outlook* 19, no. 3 (March 1952).
Watkins, Jan. Daughter of and former assistant to Bishop Charles Watkins. Interview, February 3, 2005.

Selected Discography

"Don't Let This Harvest Pass"/"Run, Run & Tell Him" (1953, Savoy Records 4049; 78 rpm).
"Sweet Hour of Prayer"/"What He's Done for Me" (1953, Savoy Records 4054; 78 rpm).
Shady Green Pastures (1963, Savoy Records 4186.)
By His Spirit (1979, Praise Records).
Storefront Connection (1988, LaCross Records).
Always (LaCross Records).

WATTS, ISAAC

(b. July 17, 1674; d. November 25, 1748)

Known as the father of hymn writing in the English language, Watts was born at Southampton, England. His father was an opponent of the state church who was twice thrown into jail for his activities, so among the youth's earliest memories were being carried in his mother's arms to visit his father in prison. This experience perhaps emboldened the young boy to hold to his parent's nonconformist beliefs. In any event, he was a child prodigy who showed a genius for study and writing verse. By age five he was learning Latin; Greek at age nine; French at eleven; and Hebrew at thirteen. His reputation got around, and a wealthy man offered to pay for his university education provided he would become a minister in the established church. This he refused to do and prepared instead for the independent ministry, where he would be allowed to practice his stern Calvinist theology.

Watts gained renown as a student of theology and philosophy, and he produced several influential books on these subjects. However, his most lasting efforts were in hymn writing, which he revolutionized. Dissatisfied with the versified Psalms that the churches of his day used, at age eighteen, he reportedly was challenged by his father to produce something better. His initial effort met with enthusiastic response, leading him to compose a new hymn for his congregation every Sunday for the next two years. In 1707, he published 210 of these hymns in a collection titled *Hymns and Spiritual Songs;* 144 were added in a second edition. These were the first real hymnals in English. Although these songs met with opposition, they became very popular. Watts followed this book with another collection, *Psalms of David Imitated in the Language of the New Testament* (1719). In this volume, he intended to give the Psalms a New

Testament meaning and style, which he did by paraphrasing most of them.

Watts was a little man, only about five feet tall, who was in frail health all of his life. He was, however, gentle and good-natured, and his church members took loving care of him. At his death he was buried in London's Bunhill Fields Cemetery, near the graves of John Bunyan and other dissenters. During his lifetime he was regarded as a radical churchman, but his country eventually honored him by erecting a monument to his memory in Westminster Abbey.

His work did not die with him but lingered on to the present in both black and white gospel. For example, *Gospel Pearls* (1921) includes several of his songs, and they are commonly sung in white churches as well. Many singers refer to them as "Dr. Watts's songs." Some of the best known of Watts's six hundred hymns are "Am I a Soldier of the Cross," "Joy to the World," "When I Survey the Wondrous Cross," and "O God, Our Help in Ages Past." His departure from the traditional metrical Psalms and the use of hymns based entirely on one's own thoughts and words earned him the title of "Father of English Hymnody."

W. K. McNeil

Reference and Further Reading

Boyer, Horace Clarence. *The Golden Age of Gospel.* Urbana and Chicago: University of Illinois Press, 2000 (1995).

Darden, Robert. *People Get Ready: A New History of Black Gospel Music.* New York: Continuum International Publishing Group, 2004.

Osbeck, Kenneth W. *101 More Hymn Stories.* Grand Rapids, MI: Kregel 1985.

Wells, Amos R. *A Treasury of Hymn Stories.* Grand Rapids, MI: 1992 (1945).

WEATHERFORDS, THE (QUARTET AND TRIO)

Earl Henderson Weatherford (b. 1922; d. 1992)
Lily Fern Goble Weatherford (b. November 25, 1928)
Glen Weldon Payne (b. 1926; d. 1999)
Armond Morales (b. February 25, 1932)
Henry T. Slaughter (b. January 9, 1927)
Steve Weatherford (b. ca. 1961)
Kelly Looper (b. Unknown)

For a generation after World War II, the Weatherford Quartet set one of the highest standards in the history of gospel quartet music. They also served as a training ground for individuals who went on to make history as members of other groups. In addition, Lily Weatherford pioneered as a female in what had earlier been an all-male enterprise.

Initially formed in California in the mid-1940s, the Weatherfords shifted their base of operations steadily eastward to Fort Wayne and then to Akron, Ohio, where they had a close association with noted evangelist Rex Humbard. After 1963, they returned to a regular touring schedule. By 1977, they were based in Paoli, Oklahoma. Still built around the remarkable voice of Lily, the group has of recent years been a trio.

Earl Weatherford, the group leader and baritone vocalist, had originally been described as a "diehard" devotee of the four-part-harmony quartet. Lily, a native of Bethanie, Oklahoma, whom he married in 1945, filled in to sing the tenor part only when needed, but by 1948 she had become a regular member, singing alto. At that time, the Weatherfords were part-time singers with a radio program in Long Beach, California, working under Stamps sponsorship. They became full time in 1949, when they secured a radio spot at WOWO in Fort Wayne, Indiana. By the time the Weatherfords went to Akron, their best quartet combination consisted of Earl and Lily on baritone and alto, respectively, with Armond Morales on bass, Glen Payne on lead, and Henry Slaughter on piano. At that point, they recorded for RCA Victor, including their classic album *In the Garden*. During this phase of their career, Lily also worked in an all-female trio with Rex Humbard's wife and sister.

In 1963, Earl and Lily chose to move on, while Slaughter and Morales joined the Imperials, and Glen Payne chose to remain with Humbard, with whom he formed the Cathedral Quartet with two ex-Weatherford members, Danny Koker and Bobby Clark. By the end of the 1960s, the Weatherford Quartet—with all new members except for Earl and Lily Fern—was recording for Canaan. Over the years, others who spent time with the noted quartet included George Younce, James Hopkins, and James Hamill. The best-known original songs associated with the groups were "Tell My Friends" and "What a Precious Friend Is He." After Earl's death, Lily Fern wrote her autobiography, *With All My Heart: A Life in Gospel Music* (1999), with the help of Gail Shadwell. As of 2003, Lily headed the current lineup, which consisted of twenty-year veteran Steve Weatherford on lead vocals and Kelly Looper on baritone.

Ivan M. Tribe

Reference and Further Reading

Gardner, Tim. "Lily Fern Weatherford: A Genuine Lady & Legend." *The Singing News* (March 2003): 64–67.

———; Gail Shadwell. *The Weatherfords: Gospel Music Legend and Legacy.* Carrolton, TX: Alliance Press, 2003.

Discography

Lily Fern Weatherford. *With All My Heart* (CD).

The Weatherfords. *In the Garden* (ca. 1959, RCA Victor); *Listen to Those Smooth Weatherfords* (ca. 1969, Canaan CAS 9635); *Both Sides of the River* (Heartwing CD); *Sprit of the West: Live from Tombstone* (CD); *Standing on Tradition* (CD).

WELLING, FRANK, AND JOHN McGHEE

Benjamin Franklin Welling (b. February 16, 1898; d. January 23, 1957)

John Leftridge McGhee (b. April 9, 1882; d. May 9, 1945)

During the early years of country music recordings, one of the most productive sacred singing teams was the West Virginia twosome of Frank Welling and John McGhee. Although neither exclusively gospel nor what might be termed "hard country," their repertoire had one of the highest percentages of religious songs of any group in the pre-1933 era.

The older McGhee had relocated to the larger city of Huntington from rural Lincoln County about 1900, while the younger Welling migrated to Huntington from just across the Ohio River from Lawrence County, Ohio, somewhat later. Their mutual interest in music drew them together, and they performed in a variety of musical activities around that city from about 1917. Welling had earlier toured in vaudeville with a Hawaiian group, and McGhee played both harmonica and guitar, among other instruments.

The pair began their recording career in 1927 under the direction of W. R. Callaway, and they cut more than two hundred sides during the next six years for such labels as Gennett, Paramount, Brunswick, Vocalion, and the American Record Corporation group. Roughly half of their recordings were of a religious nature. On a few numbers the pair was joined by a third vocalist, such as McGhee's daughter Alma or Welling's wife Thelma. On one occasion in 1928, they split temporarily, with McGhee taking Ted Cogar as a duet partner to the Gennett studio and Welling taking William Shannon to the Paramount studio. Two other early recording artists who were sometime associates of Welling and McGhee were David Miller and Miller Wikel.

Many—if not most—of the Welling and McGhee sacred songs were church hymns that had found favor with both rural and urban congregations over the years. They ranged from such standards as "In the Garden," "The Old Rugged Cross," and "Hallelujah Side" to largely forgotten songs typified by "Get a Transfer," "There's a Great Day Coming," and "Go by Way of the Cross." Sentimental numbers of a quasi-religious nature ranked among their most popular efforts, such as "Picture on the Wall," "Where Is My Mama?," and "A Flower from My Angel Mother's Grave."

After 1933, Welling and McGhee's recording career ended. McGhee remained in Huntington until his death, helping his wife with a wallpaper-hanging business. Welling moved to Charleston, where he worked as a musician and announcer at WCHS radio and later as an announcer at other stations. In later years, he was best known for his characterization of an elderly rustic "Uncle Si"; he helped organize a jamboree-type program at WCHS known as the *Old Farm Hour,* and he even did a final recording session (secular) as such about 1950. Because their musical heritage owes as much to popular and Tin Pan Alley as to pure tradition, their music has been underrepresented in reissues, with only a single album and a few anthologies.

IVAN M. TRIBE

Reference and Further Reading

Tribe, Ivan M. "John McGhee and Frank Welling: West Virginia's Most Recorded Old-Time Artist." *JEMF Quarterly* 17, no. 2 (Summer 1974): 57–74.

Discography

Sacred, Sentimental, and Silly Songs (1987, Old Homestead OHCS 175).

WELLS, KITTY

Muriel Ellen Deason (b. August 30, 1919, Nashville, TN)

Kitty Wells was the first major female country music singer, breaking numerous barriers during the 1950s. Wells proved that women could sell records and draw audiences. Her songs dealt openly with the honky-tonk lifestyle from a woman's viewpoint, and she also enjoyed popularity as a singer of country gospel.

Wells was born Muriel Ellen Deason. At the age of fifteen she began to sing on the radio with her sisters and a cousin as the Deason sisters. Wells married singer Johnnie Wright on October 30, 1937, and the two started performing together. Two years later, Wright and Jack Anglin formed the duo Johnnie and Jack, with Wells as the girl singer of the show. The group did radio work throughout the South during the 1940s, including a memorable stint with KWKH in Shreveport. Early in the 1940s, Wright dubbed his wife "Kitty Wells" after a popular nineteenth-century Southern tune. The group often performed requests for gospel numbers during this period.

Wells's early recordings had little success until 1952, when she recorded "It Wasn't God Who Made Honky Tonk Angels," the popularity of which made Wells a star. Most of Wells's hits explored broken relationships between men and women, which stood in marked contrast to the success of her marriage to Wright. Wells charted thirty-eight top-ten records during her career. Like most country stars of the era, Wells also recorded many gospel songs, including such popular titles as "Dust on the Bible," "Will Your Lawyer Talk to God," and "He Will Set Your Fields on Fire." In 1959 she released an album of gospel songs titled *Dust on the Bible* (Decca DL 8858), a classic of country-style gospel.

Wells headlined television programs in the 1960s and 1970s, and she charted her last hit in 1971. Her later years were marked with numerous honors, including election to the Country Music Hall of Fame (1976) and a Grammy for lifetime achievement (1991)—the first female country artist so honored. She remained an active performer until the beginning of the twenty-first century.

KEVIN S. FONTENOT

Reference and Further Reading

Bufwack, Mary A.; Robert K. Oermann. *Finding Her Voice: The Saga of Women in Country Music.* New York: Crown Publishers, 1993.
Trott, Walt. *The Honky Tonk Angels.* Nashville, TN: Nova Books, 1993.

Selected Discography

Country Music Hall of Fame (MCAO-10081).
Johnnie & Jack with Kitty Wells at KWKH (Bear Family BCD 15791-AH).
Queen of Country Music (Bear Family BCD 15638-01).

WETHERINGTON, JAMES S. "BIG CHIEF"

(b. October 22, 1922; d. October 3, 1973)

Bass singer, songwriter, and publisher James S. Wetherington was born in Ty Ty, Georgia, but he spent much of his life in Atlanta, where he led a choir when he was not on the road singing. Known primarily for his tenure with the Statesmen Quartet, he was earlier with the Melody Masters. Life with that group was hard, and once, to keep from starving, a couple of members stole peaches from an orchard. Things soon brightened financially, but in 1949 Wetherington, who had acquired a reputation as a rhythm bass singer, was invited to join the Statesmen. Soon, other members of the Melody Masters followed suit, and by 1950 three members of the Statesmen were former Melody Masters.

After joining his new quartet, Wetherington acquired the nickname by which he became known. Lee Roy Abernathy suggested that, since he was part Indian, it would be more memorable to call him "Big Chief" than James S. Wetherington. Thereafter, he was Big Chief, and he was one of the reasons for the quartet's great success over the next twenty-five years. In addition to singing, he and Doy Ott started doing most of the group's arrangements; Big Chief also wrote songs. With other members of the Statesmen, he owned the Faith and J. M. Henson Music Company, and he was sole owner of the Lodo Music Company. A genial and kindly man, he helped J. D. Sumner organize the National Quartet Convention. In 1973, while in Nashville to attend the organization's meeting, he collapsed and died of a heart attack.

W. K. MCNEIL

Reference and Further Reading

Taylor, David L. *Happy Rhythm: A Biography of Hovie Lister and the Statesmen Quartet.* Lexington, IN: Taylor-Made WRITE, 1994.
Terrell, Bob. *The Music Men: The Story of Gospel Quartet Singing in America.* Asheville, NC: Bob Terrell, 1990.

WHISNANTS, THE

John L. Whisnant, Sr. (b. April 27, 1930)
Betty Harris Whisnant (b. April 26, 1941)
John L. Whisnant, Jr. (b. August 4, 1962)
Jeff Whisnant (b. September 19, 1964)
Susan Whisnant (b. September 8, 1966)
Aaron Hise (b. February 15, 1977)

The Whisnants began singing in Morganton, North Carolina, in 1970. John Whisnant, Sr., wife Betty, and two sons, John, Jr., and Jeff, mainly traveled locally in the beginning. In 1985, Jeff Whisnant began dating Susan Dry; it was not very long until she was added to the group. After the couple married in 1988, Jeff's parents retired from the road.

The Whisnants did some work with the Eddie Crook Agency, but they did not really sign professionally until 1990, with Sunlight Records. During this time, the group produced hits such as "Homesick Feeling," "Mercy's Child," and "The Greatest Hero." In 1993, John Whisnant, Jr., encountered vocal problems and needed surgery. During this time, John, Jr., felt that

God was calling him to preach. John left the group and eventually became pastor of the Whisnants' home church, Grandview Baptist Church in Morganton, North Carolina. Curt Davis became John's replacement.

In 1996, the Whisnants took another direction: they became a part of the United Independent Agency (UIA). Jeff Whisnant, owner and manager, says, "This just gave us a chance to have more control over the decisions made for the group."

Curt Davis left the group in November 2000. In 2001, Aaron Hise became the third member. He is from DeMotte, Indiana, and he sings tenor for the group. Jeff and Susan's sons, Austin and Ethan, also travel with the group.

The Whisnants have had much success over the years. *The Singing News* nominated them for Horizon Group in 1992; they were also nominated for Favorite Trio. "Is Anything Too Hard for God" is a very special song; it held the number one position on the *Singing News* chart for July and August 2001 and was nominated for Song of the Year. Jeff says, "There is nothing more special than your first number one hit. We were so excited that it stayed on the charts for that long." Other hit songs for The Whisnants are "The Day Will Come," which went to number four on the *Singing News* chart in 2001, "I'll Stand for the Lord," "What You Took from Me," "Woke Up This Morning," "The Next Time That You See Me," and "Even in the Valley."

ANDREA GANNAWAY

Reference and Further Reading

Jones, Danny. "Conversations with Susan Whisnant." *Singing News* (February 2004): 32–33.
Whisnant, Jeff. Personal interview, July 7, 2004.
The Whisnants website, http://www.whisnants.com.

WHITTLE, DANIEL WEBSTER

(b. November 22, 1840; d. March 4, 1901)

Although reared in New England, Daniel Webster Whittle relocated to Chicago, working there until he joined the Union army in 1861. Wounded at the Battle of Vicksburg, "Major" Whittle, as he became known, returned to Chicago and worked in secular employment until 1873, when he became an evangelist for Dwight Moody, who was directing various teams of preachers, often paired with a music director. Whittle's musical assistant was Philip P. Bliss, who conducted music for their series of revival meetings throughout the Midwest and South. Tragically, the highly gifted Bliss was killed in a fiery train wreck in

1876, and Whittle was teamed with musician James P. McGranahan. They worked together for more than a decade, traveling throughout the United States and to England. Whittle's last musical partner was George C. Stebbins.

All of his musical associates were gifted composers of gospel music, producing the most widely sung gospel hymnody of the time. Whittle is credited with about two hundred gospel hymn texts, with James McGranahan being his most successful collaborator. (McGranahan was also an editor of the monumental *Gospel Hymns* series, which contributed to the popularity of Whittle's hymns.) While Whittle's texts contained a limited reliance on poetic symbolism, a strong personal element was often present in the lyrics. One of his most characteristic devices was the use of a highly repetitive refrain or chorus that summarized or answered a question raised in the stanza. Unity between stanzas and chorus was often accomplished through repetition in the chorus of a key word or phrase from the stanza. "I Know Whom I Have Believed" is perhaps the best-known example of this approach. Above all, his lyrics were solidly grounded in Scripture with many allusions or quotations. They were also clearly theological, expounding or teaching a Scriptural doctrine or truth.

His best-known hymns have been "Moment by Moment" (beginning with "Dying with Jesus, by death reckoned mine," for which his daughter composed the music), "I Know Whom I Have Believed," "There Shall Be Showers of Blessing," and "The Banner of the Cross." James McGranahan supplied tunes for all but the first.

MEL R. WILHOIT

See also Bliss, Philip Paul; McGranahan, James; Stebbins, George Coles

Reference and Further Reading

Hall, J. H. *Biography of Gospel Song and Hymn Writers.* New York: Fleming Revell, 1971 (1914).
Schieps, Paul J. *Hold the Fort.* Smithsonian Studies in History and Technology No. 9. Washington, DC: Smithsonian Institution Press, 1971.

WILKINS, REVEREND ROBERT

(b. January 16, 1896, Hernando, MS; d. May 26, 1987)

Wilkins was raised on a small farm twenty miles south of Memphis. At the age of two, he assumed his stepfather's surname of Oliver, from whom he soon learned the basics of playing guitar. By 1910, Tim Oliver (as he was then known) began playing for house parties around Hernando, which is where he first met Jim Jackson, the veteran medicine show entertainer who later recorded for Victor and Vocalion. In approximately 1912, Tim Oliver reassumed the surname Wilkins and moved to Memphis in search of employment; he eventually served in the Army during World War I. Wilkins returned to Memphis in 1919 seeking a career as a professional musician.

Wilkins performed throughout Memphis during the 1920s, often playing with Furry Lewis and Memphis Minnie (whom he claimed to have tutored) as well as a jug band he helped to organize. Along with peers such as "Sleepy John" Estes and Frank Stokes, he performed alone as well as with small ensembles. However, Wilkins's early recordings (1928–1930) for Victor and Brunswick were solo efforts that demonstrated an unusually wide range of tunings, genres, and time signatures on songs such as "Rolling Stone" and "That's No Way to Get Along."

The Great Depression decimated the recording industry, so Wilkins continued to play Memphis during the early 1930s, augmented by stints as a medicine show entertainer. In 1935, he recorded for the Vocalion label at their portable studio in Jackson, Mississippi, with Little Son Joe and "Kid Spoons." Among the songs was "Old Jim Cannan's," which celebrated a notorious gambling parlor formerly located at 340 Beale Street in Memphis. Around 1938, the teetotaling and quiet Wilkins played a house party in Hernando that turned bloody and violent. Partially as a result of this incident, he joined the Church of God in Christ, an important African American Pentecostal sect based in Memphis. Wilkins eventually became a church elder and devoted his musical career to sacred music.

For the next fifty years, "Reverend" Robert Wilkins lived quietly in Memphis, spending much of his time working for and playing at the Lane Avenue Church of God in Christ. He came to the attention of music researchers during the early 1960s as a result of the interest in blues spurred by the folk revival. He was rerecorded, although only in the religious realm. He performed at folk festivals, and he gained nationwide public attention when the Rolling Stones recorded "Prodigal Son" in 1968.

KIP LORNELL

Reference and Further Reading

Wilkins, Mary E. "Lane." *1964: To Profit a Man.* Memphis, TN: Museum Publishing, 1995.

Discography

The Original Rolling Stone (1990, Yazoo 1077).
Memphis Blues 1928–1935 (1994, Document 5014).
Remember Me (1994, Gene's Blue Vault).

WILLIAMS BROTHERS

Leon "Pop" Williams (b. November 24, 1908)
Frank Douglas (b. June 25, 1947)
Leonard Williams (b. July 1, 1951)
Melvin Williams (b. July 21, 1953)

The Williams Brothers were organized in 1960 by their father, Leon "Pop" Williams, with sons Frank Douglas, Leonard Williams, and Melvin Williams, plus nonfamily members Henry Green and Maurice Surrell. The group was known as the Little Williams Brothers, but as they grew in talent, experience, and performance, they changed the name to the Sensational Williams Brothers. The group is now called the Williams Brothers. They are contemporary charismatic artists. They produce songs with easy-to-follow lyrics and music, mixed with rich tenor, baritone, and bass vocals. Their style is Southern down-home family conversations with a call-and-response harmony.

This male gospel quartet uses simple songs such as "Jesus Will Never Say No," and "Cooling Water from Grandmama's Well," which relates how cool water from Grandmama's well is good for the soul. They have been writing and arranging music since 1970, and they recorded their first album, *Jesus Will Fix It*, in 1973 on the Songbird Record label; it became an instant gospel hit. They perform before multiethnic groups. They have recorded more than eighteen albums, with many listed as being among the top ten in *Billboard* and *Cashbox* magazines, and they have received a Grammy nomination. Their hits include "I Won't Let Go My Faith," "He'll Understand," "Sweep Around Your Own Front Door," "God Won't Put No More on You," and "A Ship Like Mine." They performed on the Winans' Grammy-winning song "Ain't No Need to Worry," featuring gospel singer Anita Baker.

In 1989, they won the Traditional Male Group of the Year Award from the Gospel Music Workshop of America. In April 1991, the Williams Brothers formed their own record label, Blackberry Records. It is the first black-owned and -operated recording label in Mississippi. Their first release on the Blackberry label, "This Is Your Night," reached number four on the *Billboard* gospel chart. In 1999, the Williams Brothers were inducted into the International Gospel Music Hall of Fame and Museum in Detroit. A Williams Brothers Road has been named in their honor in Smithdale, Mississippi. They won the most prestigious award in the Stellar Awards gospel music category for "Still Here." On January 15, 2005 in Houston, the Stellar Awards—the longest-running gospel music award show in broadcast television history—celebrated its twentieth anniversary.

SHERRY SHERROD DUPREE

Reference and Further Reading

DuPree, Sherry Sherrod; Herbert C. DuPree. *African-American Good News (Gospel) Music.* Washington, DC: Middle Atlantic Regional Press, 1993.
International Gospel Music Hall of Fame and Museum website, http://www.gmhf.org (accessed August 28, 2004).
Williams Brothers. *Cooling Water* [video]. Blackberry Records, 2002.
Williams, Frank D. "Biographical Sketch." Jackson, MS: Malaco Records, 1993.

Discography

No Ways Tired (1981, Savoy; two LPs, distributed by Suffolk Marketing SMI 2-32H).
The Greatest Hits, Vol. 1 (1991, CD).
The People Empowered to Win Crusade (2002).
Still Here (2004, Blackberry Records).

WILLIAMS, MARION

(b. August 29, 1927, Miami, FL; d. July 2, 1994)

While it is generally conceded that Mahalia Jackson was the greatest gospel *artist* of all time, there are a number of writers who have always maintained that Marion Williams was the greatest gospel *singer.* Her legacy has continued to grow each year, to almost mythic proportions.

Like so many gospel artists, Williams was born in poverty on August 29, 1927, in Miami, exposed not just to gospel and the blues but to calypso and jazz. After leaving school at fourteen to help her mother at a laundry, Williams sang on street corners and in storefront churches. In 1946, while visiting a sister in Philadelphia, she came to the attention of Clara Ward and, as part of the Ward Singers, soon came to dominate the group's solos, including their biggest hit, "Surely God Is Able." Gospel fans called her "Miss Personality." She drew special praise from writers at an early performance with Mahalia at the Newport Jazz Festival in the mid-1950s, and she is featured on the group's classic LPs from the era, including *Lord, Touch Me, That Old Landmark,* and *Down by the Riverside: Live at the Town Hall, New York City.*

Williams, like Mahalia and Aretha Franklin, was one of the foremost proponents of "surge singing," a heavily ornamented, improvised style of singing with its roots in the ancient practice of "lining out" hymns, which was favored by the Baptist church. Williams was able to move effortlessly from bluesy moans to soaring jazz improvisations, fueled by her multi-octave voice and impeccable sense of timing. Even pop artists, including Little Richard, cite Williams's breathtaking vocal swoops and growls as a major influence.

However, Williams—along with Kitty Parham and Henrietta Waddy—eventually tired of the Wards' penurious pay and left to form Marion Williams's Stars of Faith in 1958. Although the Stars of Faith never replicated the Wards' success, Williams's powerful rendition of the Wards' "Packing Up" remains the definitive version. In 1961, she starred off Broadway in Langston Hughes's gospel rendition of the Christmas narratives, *Black Nativity.* A production in London made her a bigger star in Europe than in the United States, and she toured whenever possible overseas, always to rapturous crowds, performing such songs as "Jesus Is All" and "Christ Is All." The album *Prayer Changes Things,* released in 1976, won a Grand Prix du Disque in France that year.

Williams left the Stars of Faith in 1965 and eventually moved to Miami for semiretirement, performing mostly on college campuses, including Harvard and Yale universities, the former of which honored her as an Ellington Fellow. Despite the popularity of her song "Standing Here Wondering Which Way to Go" (which was used in a television commercial), Williams, who struggled with ill health, slowly sank into near obscurity.

In 1991, Bill Moyers's special *Amazing Grace* featured her extraordinary *a cappella* rendition of the title track, and the world discovered Williams's thrilling lyric soprano once again. She appeared in the film *Fried Green Tomatoes* (1992), singing "A Charge I Have to Keep" and was featured on Wynton Marsalis's gospel-jazz suite *In This House/On This Morning.* Williams became the first gospel artist to receive a MacArthur Foundation grant, and she was honored with a performance at the Kennedy Center in Washington, DC. But Williams died shortly thereafter, on July 2, 1994; she was just sixty-six years old.

Writers such as Anthony Heilbut, Sandra Brennan, and Wilfred Mellers frequently cite Williams as the "most lyrical and imaginative singer" in gospel.

ROBERT DARDEN

See also Franklin, Aretha; Franklin, Reverend C. L.; Jackson, Mahalia; Stars of Faith, The; Ward Trio (Ward Singers)

Reference and Further Reading

Boyer, Horace. *How Sweet the Sound: The Golden Age of Gospel.* Washington, DC: Elliott & Clark, 1995.
Erlewine Michael; Vladimir Bogdanov; Chris Woodstra; Cub Koda, eds. *All Music Guide to the Blues,* 2nd ed. San Francisco: Miller Freeman Books, 1999.
Gehman, Richard. "God's Singing Messengers." *Coronet* 44, no. 3 (July 1958): 112.
Harrington, Richard. "Amazingly Graced: The Lord Was Kind to Marion Williams, and Did She Ever Return the Favor." *Washington Post* (July 10, 1994): G4.

Marion Williams, Washington, DC, 1962. Photo by Joe Alper. Photo courtesy Frank Driggs Collection.

Heilbut, Anthony. *The Gospel Sound: Good News and Bad Times*. New York: Limelight Editions, 1997.

"Marion Williams" [obituary]. *The Times of London* (July 8, 1994): B38.

Mellers, Wilfred. *Angels of the Night: Popular Singers of Our Time*. Oxford, UK: Basil Blackwell, Inc. 1986

Moyers, Bill. *Amazing Grace with Bill Moyers*. PBS video directed by Elena Mannes; 88 minutes. Alexandria, VA: Public Affairs Television, 1990.

Oliver, Paul; Max Harrison; William Bolcom. *The New Grove Gospel, Blues, and Jazz, with Spirituals and Ragtime*. New York: W.W. Norton & Company, 1986.

Parles, Jon. "At Gospel Festival, Music Inspired by Hope." *New York Times* (November 11, 1988): C21.

———. "Marion Williams Is Dead at 66: Influential Pioneer of Gospel." *New York Times* (July 11, 1994): 26.

Trescott, Jacqueline. "As the Spirit Moves Him: 'Black Nativity' Producer Mike Malone's Light-Footed Gospel." *Washington Post* (December 24, 1994): Style B1.

Werner, Craig. *A Change is Gonna Come: Music, Race & the Soul of America*. New York: Plume/Penguin Group, 1998.

Zolten, Jerry. *Great God A'Mighty! The Dixie Hummingbirds: Celebrating the Rise of Soul Gospel Music*. Oxford, UK: Oxford University Press, 2003.

Discography

The Clara Ward Singers. *Down by the Riverside: Live at the Town Hall, New York City* (Savoy); *Lord, Touch Me* (Savoy); *That Old Landmark* (Savoy).

Marion Williams. *Born to Sing the Gospel* (Shanachie); *Can't Keep It to Myself* (Shanachie); *God and Me/Let the Words of My Mouth* (Collectables COL 7230); *Gospel Soul of Marion Williams* (Shanachie); *The New Message/Standing Here Wondering* (Collectables COL 7484); *O Holy Night* (Savoy); *Something Bigger Than You and I* (Gospel); *This Too Shall Pass* (Nashboro); *Through Many Dangers* (Shanachie).

The Stars of Faith. *In the Spirit: The Best of the Stars of Faith* (Nashboro); *Go Tell Somebody/Let the Words of My Mouth* (Collectables COL 7230).

WINANS, THE

Delores Winans (b. ca. 1936)

David Winans, Sr. (b. ca. 1934)

BeBe (Benjamin) Winans (b. September 17, 1962)

CeCe (Priscilla) Winans (b. October 8, 1964)

Vickie Winans (b. October 18, 1953)

More than twenty-five years ago, the Winans family—Mom, Pop, and their ten children—rocked the congregation at Detroit's Zion Congregational Church of God in Christ. The children at an early age had visions of winning; having grown up watching the Grammys, the children voted themselves to receive imaginary Grammys—for the best male vocal, the best female vocal, and the best dressed.

Who are the Winans? The ten children grew up and branched out. One group, the Winans, comprised Michael, Ronald, and the twins, Carvin and Marvin; Benjamin and Priscilla became BeBe and CeCe; and Daniel Winans become a solo artist.

The Grammys became a reality. Their first album was completed in 1983, and thereafter they walked away with many Grammys. After a reunion concert, CeCe Winans stated that they were thankful for their parents. The love of their parents and the church sustained them and kept them in church, and they fell in love with the church. CeCe remarked that their parents taught them God's word and values, and they did not represent Christian living as being a boring life. She also stated that they lived in front of the children, showing them that they could be happy. Along the way, Mom and Pop Winans fine-tuned their children to deliver unabashedly evangelistic music in a modern style that attracted not only young people but fans who might not have responded to gospel's more traditional forms.

"For a decade now, the Winans of all ages have been delivering positive and inspirational messages across airwaves both secular and sacred," reported Richard Harrington in *The Washington Post* in 1992, and that is still true. "In the early 1980s the Winans began to bend gospel tradition by writing songs that would not sound out of place on black pop radio." Harrington further states that soul music had come out of the church and that almost every great black vocalist was rooted in some church choir; many soul vocal styles and arrangements can be traced to gospel. He noted that even the greatest gospel singers—from Sam Cooke to Aretha Franklin—found themselves criticized by the hardliners who equated secular music with sin and crossover with the abandonment of the salvation for success. The Winans' music is crossover, and it can be heard on both sides.

Even though the Winans' first commercial album was released in 1983, their career did not soar until 1985, when they connected with Andrae Crouch. The year 1992 marked the Winans' appearance at Culturefest in West Africa. The following year, they were invited to sing at the inauguration festivities.

Mom Winans

An Affair to Remember (*Against the Flow*), an album of hymns and ballads performed by Mom Winans performing with the London Symphony Orchestra, gives listeners insight about the talents of the elders. Mom Winans has stated that it is her task to teach the younger.

Pop Winans

"All aboard, this train is bound for glory" commands Pop Winans on "Uncensored" (*Against the Flow*). "It's an invitation worth heeding," writes Mike Joyce, capturing the essence of this elder. "While his spouse opts for a lushly orchestrated sound, Pop Winans favors pew-rocking gospel quartet music. His raspy baritone is always expressive and easily recognizable as it rises above the harmonies created by his extended family" (Joyce, 1999).

BeBe Winans

BeBe and his sister CeCe, his recording partner, took some time off from each other to discover their individual artistic abilities and dreams. Subsequently, BeBe was involved in production projects and acting roles.

In 1996, BeBe's older brother Ron was diagnosed with a dire heart disease, so severe that they thought his brother would not live to leave the hospital. The family united in prayer, and his brother survived. This life-threatening event changed BeBe's life. When he sees his brother, he is reminded about the greatness of God.

BeBe's special achievements include stage appearances with Whitney Houston, a Grammy Award for Best Contemporary Soul Gospel Album in 1992, and a Dove Award for Best Contemporary Gospel Recorded Song of the Year in 1998.

CeCe Winans

CeCe is the eighth child of Mom and Pop Winans. Equally as talented as her siblings, CeCe has her own musical triumphs. She has hosted a variety series, *CeCe's Place*. Her trove of accomplishments includes authoring an inspirational memoir, *On a Positive Note* (1999, Atria), and creating a nonprofit organization, Sharing the Vision. She is also a spokesman for K-Mart's Share the Word program.

Vickie Winans

Vickie was raised in Detroit and began singing at eight. Coming from a musical and religious family also, Vickie married Marvin and became a part of the Winans' musical legacy. Vickie's first solo album was *We Should Behold Him,* for which she received a Grammy nomination for Best Female Contemporary Soul Album, and she won a Stellar Award for Album of the Year and an Excellence Award for Best Female Contemporary Artist.

Her celebrity status continued as she continued to record and appeared on shows such as *Oprah, The Grammy Awards, Arsenio Hall,* and *The Pat Sajak Show.* She has appeared in a Broadway musical, *Don't Get God Started.* Some of Vickie's other songs are "Daddy Can't Sing," "First Trumpet Sound," "The Diet Medley," "It's Your Thang," "Give It One More Try," and "Sweeter Than the Honeycomb."

The Family

Angie, Debbie, Mario, Carvin, and Marvin are also wonderful vocalists and an integrate part of the Winans dynasty. The family has a strong bond, and they all share the love of music. From the sweet melodic sounds of Mom, to the traditional foot-stomping sounds of Pop, to the rocking hip and contemporary sounds of the children, the Winans have made an immense impact on gospel.

For the Winans, who are often billed as Detroit's first family of gospel music, the sweet dreams of winning and reaching for what appeared impossible became reality. Childhood imagination became an exercise of faith, with the sweet rewards of Grammys and success. In the words of one of their famous renditions, their success can be dubbed as "Oh Happy Day!"

SIMMONA E. SIMMONS-HODO

Reference and Further Reading

"BeBe Winans." Today's Christian Music website, http://todayschristianmusic.com/profile-BeBe.htm (accessed February 21, 2005).

"BeBe Winans: Shaken." Jamsline Christian Music Information Source Library website, http://www.jamsline.com/b_bbwinans.htm (accessed February 21, 2005).

CeCe Winans website, http://cecewinans.com (accessed February 21, 2005).

Considine, J. D. "The Winans Gospel Music Dynasty Is Based on a Strong Family Foundation." *Baltimore Sun* (April 10, 1992): 4.

Estell, Kenneth, editor. *The African American Almanac.* Detroit: Gale Research, 1994.

Harrington, Richard. "First Family of Gospel: The Winans, Raised to Sing the Lord's Praise in Sweet Harmony." *Washington Post* (April 5, 1992): G1.

Joyce, Mike. "CeCe Winans, Answering the Call." *Washington Post* (November 28, 1999): G10.

Owens, Donna M. "Vickie Winans Puts Her Gospel Truths into a Stage Play." *The Baltimore Sun* (April 1, 2004): 12T.

York, Jennifer, editor. *Who's Who Among African Americans.* Detroit: Gale Research, 2003, 2004.

Selected Discography

BeBe Winnans. *BeBe Winans* (1997, Atlantic); *Love & Freedom* (2000, Motown); *BeBe Live and Up Close* (2002, Universal); *I Have a Dream* (2003, Sony).

CeCeWinans. *His Gift* (1998, Atlantic); *Alabaster Box* (1999, Sparrow); *CeCe Winans* (2001, Sparrow); *The Throne Room* (2003, Sparrow).

David Winans, Sr. *The Winanaires* (1999, Diamante).

Delores Winans. *Hymns from My Heart* (2004, EMI Gospel Music).

Vicki Winans. *Lady* (1991, MCA); *Feel the Passion* (1999, CGI Records); *Bringing It All Together* (2003, Verity).

The Winans. *The Great Family of Gospel* (2003, EMI Gospel Music).

WINGS OVER JORDAN

For African Americans in the 1930s and 1940s, there were two significant sources of racial pride: heavyweight boxer Joe Louis and the Wings over Jordan Choir. More than a singing group, Wings over Jordan brought inspiration and social commentary to millions of African Americans during its weekly network radio broadcasts. In the process, the choir introduced people of every race to spirituals as well as gospel songs written by composers such as Thomas A. Dorsey, Lucie Campbell, and Kenneth Morris.

Wings over Jordan was organized in 1937 by Reverend Glenn (also spelled Glynn) T. Settle (1895–1952). Born on a tobacco plantation in North Carolina as one of nine children to sharecroppers Ruben and Mary Settle, the minister described himself as a grandson of slaves whose maternal grandfather was Cherokee Indian and whose paternal grandfather was an African prince. Settle founded the choir after being assigned to Cleveland, Ohio's Gethsemane Baptist Church and learning that the congregation had no music program of significance.

After a short period of rehearsal, Settle felt his new group, Wings over Jordan, was ready to be heard outside the confines of the church. He successfully negotiated a regular spot for the choir on Cleveland radio station WGAR's *The Negro Hour,* a weekly showcase of local African American talent. The station's program manager, Worth Kramer, a man of Jewish heritage, was so taken with the group that he eventually left his radio post to become its producer, arranger, and conductor.

Audiences were swept off their feet by the majestic *a cappella* singing of Wings over Jordan, and the group was soon offered a national broadcast over the Columbia Broadcasting System (CBS) radio network. The choir's Sunday morning program, *Wings over Jordan,* was one of the first national radio shows to feature an African American choir. The program ran from 1937 to 1947 and became a listening staple in pretelevision America. It has been said that one could walk through any African American community on a summer Sunday morning and never miss a moment of the *Wings over Jordan* broadcast, because it could be heard through the open windows of every home in the neighborhood.

In addition to the choir's renditions of spirituals and gospel songs, the *Wings over Jordan* radio program spotlighted guest speakers on a variety of topics. For example, the March 10, 1940, broadcast featured Palmer Memorial Institute founder Charlotte Hawkins Brown on "The Negro and the Social Graces."

As the program's popularity grew, its audience began to include many whites, who were drawn to the choir's distinctive sound. In 1941, a national poll conducted by the Schomburg Collection of the New York Public Library placed *Wings over Jordan* on the Honor Roll of Race Relations for its contribution to "the improvement of race relations in terms of real democracy."

Wings over Jordan even sponsored an annual essay contest in its native Cleveland. A $250 prize was awarded to the person who could best articulate in writing why spirituals ought to be preserved.

The thirty- to forty-member Wings over Jordan traveled from coast to coast in its own bus and also toured internationally as a member of the USO, entertaining troops in the European Theater during World War II and Korea during the early 1950s. It recorded dozens of sides for Columbia, RCA Victor, King/Queen, Dial, and ABC Paramount during the 1940s, 1950s, and early 1960s.

Wings over Jordan's style was more closely aligned with the European classical style of the Fisk Jubilee Singers and the Eva Jessye Choir than the sanctified church choir sound spreading through the country. Dressed in fine clothes, the choir delivered its repertory with superb articulation and breath control, precise harmonies, operatic-quality solos, and a marvelous array of vocal dynamics. Unlike its classical counterparts, however, the choir strived to preserve the folksong quality of the spirituals, eschewing popular arrangements of spirituals for a more organic presentation.

Although its repertory was composed mainly of spirituals, the group included a few gospel songs, such as Kenneth Morris's first songwriting hit, "I'll be a Servant for the Lord," Thomas A. Dorsey's "When I've Done the Best I Can," and Lucie Campbell's "He'll Understand and Say Well Done." Gospel songs were rendered like spirituals, in the chorus's signature refined style, as opposed to the unrestrained sound of the St. Paul Baptist Church Choir and the Voices of Victory.

Many of the group's radio performances and recordings began with its trademark hum, a haunting musical motive akin to old-style Baptist moaning. The hum would be punctuated by the booming voice of Reverend Settle, sounding as if God Himself was speaking. Settle would deliver a short commentary based on the song to be sung, and when he was finished, the choir would launch into the arrangement with verve.

Among the choir's many soloists during its three decades of popularity were Dorothy Clark, Cecil Dandy, Gerald Hutton, Esther Overstreet, and Mildred Pollard. In addition to Kramer, other conductors of the group included Gilbert Allen, James Lewis Elkins, Frank Everett, and Charles King.

Famous members of Wings over Jordan included Specialty recording artist and gospel songwriter Wynona Carr and Voices of Victory director Thurston Frazier. Elizabeth Knight, mother of soul singer Gladys Knight, was a member, as was Ron Townson of the 1960s soul group the Fifth Dimension, Motown Records' songwriter Clarence Paul, and legendary entertainer Sherman Sneed. Many popular singers, including 1950s rhythm and blues diva Ruth Brown, have paid tribute to Wings over Jordan's influence on their artistry and career.

Wings over Jordan members Cecil Dandy, Clarence Smalls, Emory Barnes, and Ellison White took advantage of the gospel quartet craze of the 1940s to form the a cappella Wingmen Quartet. The group recorded two fine but ultimately unsuccessful discs for the Los Angeles–based Down Beat label in March 1948.

Although the original Wings over Jordan has long since disbanded, a new iteration, the Wings over Jordan Celebration Choir, continues to preserve the spirituals by performing in the original style of Reverend Settle's musical ambassadors of African American pride.

ROBERT MAROVICH

See also Gospel Choirs; King Records; Spirituals

Reference and Further Reading

Boyer, Horace Clarence. *How Sweet the Sound: The Golden Age of Gospel*. Washington, DC: Elliott & Clark, 1995.
Edwards, Sam. "Wings over Jordan and Joe Louis: Reincarnated Powers of the Original Spirituals." *The Negro Spiritual* 2 (December 2001): 15–23.
Hayes, Cedric; Robert Laughton. *Gospel Records 1943–1969: A Black Music Discography*. London: Record Information Services, 1993.
Marovich, Robert. "Wings over Jordan on the Internet." *The Negro Spiritual* 2 (December 2001): 24–25.

Discography

Wings over Jordan (ca. 1940s, Columbia Masterworks set M-499).
Amen (1953, King LP 519).
Wings over Jordan Choir (ca. 1958–1959, Dial LP 5163,).
Wings over Jordan Choir (King LP 560; recordings from 1946 sessions).

WINSETT, ROBERT EMMETT

(b. January 15, 1876, Bledsoe County, TN; d. June 26, 1952)

As a gospel song composer, arranger, and publisher, Winsett represented the grassroots nature of gospel music with its focus on a family-run business. From its onset in the 1870s, gospel music reflected both a spiritual dimension and a commercial one. While the spiritual dimension was primarily concerned with the use of gospel music to win the lost and edify the saints, the commercial dimension reflected issues of publication, distribution, and royalties. It was upon these two legs of gospel hymnody that Winsett's career rested.

Winsett received limited formal training in music, but he learned enough to become a successful singing-school teacher in Arkansas, where he had relocated in 1899. As a teacher, Winsett produced instructional materials such as *Standard Rudiments of Music* (1908). He also produced collections of gospel music, such as *Songs of Pentecostal Power* (1908), that proved foundational to the later R. E. Winsett Publishing Company's success. This and similar collections became popular among Free Will Baptists, General Baptists, Holiness churches, and the emerging Pentecostal groups in the Southeastern part of the country.

In addition to Winsett's teaching and music publishing, he was very active in religious work as an evangelistic singer and song leader at camp meetings, churches, and singing conventions. On his thirty-second birthday, Robert married Birdie Harris, and they reared a family of six children. Within three years the family moved to Chattanooga, Tennessee, where the publishing business often shared an address with their residence. Robert's brother William acted as sales manager, adding to the family nature of the business.

Birdie died of cancer in 1927, and by 1929 Robert moved the family and business to an area near Dayton, Tennessee. As a rule, the company issued one or two books per year, which were available with either round or shape notes and in soft or hard cover. The contents reflected a mixture of old favorites of the Northern and Southern Gospel varieties plus new additions by contemporary writers, usually reflecting a decidedly Southern gospel tinge. The songbooks were designed primarily for church use, although they were also popular at singing schools and musical conventions. An informal "gentleman's agreement" among Southern publishers of gospel music—such as Benson, Vaughan, and Stamps–Baxter—allowed the publishing of each other's copyrighted songs without charge.

As a songwriter, Winsett often contributed both words and music. Many of his earliest hymns reflect an interest in the Holiness movement, whereas his later texts reflect more of the Southern gospel traits of longing for heaven and the past. Musically, Winsett's songs embrace the straightforward diatonicism of early twentieth-century gospel hymnody, with the addition of a few secondary dominant or chromatic passing chords. Songs such as "Will You Meet Me Over Yonder?" also employ a triplet rhythm within a common time meter, providing a sense of Southern gospel swing.

His best-known songs include "Jesus Passed This Way Before," "The Message of His Coming," "When I Reach that City," "Lift Me Above the Shadows," "We'll Exchange the Old Cross for a Crown," "Remember," "Will You Meet Me Over There?" "The Half Has Never Been Told," "When He Reached Down His Hand for Me," and "It Is Later Than You Think."

The song for which Winsett achieved his greatest fame—and for which the company received a stream of royalty checks—was "Jesus Is Coming Soon." Written in 1942 and first published in the collection *Joys Supernal*, Winsett's song deals with a staple of Southern gospel music: the Second Coming. It was recorded decades later by the Oak Ridge Boys and a host of others, winning the Gospel Music Association's first Dove Award for Song of the Year in 1969.

Best of All, the company's most successful collection, which eventually sold an estimated six hundred thousand copies, was published in 1951. A year later Robert Winsett died, and the family business was carried on by his second wife, Ruth, whom he had married in 1930. She and a small circle of employees and relatives ran the company until 1979, when it was sold to Ellis Crumb of Kendallville, Indiana, and run by the Sacred Music Trust. It continued to issue a few back titles, especially *Best Loved Songs,* to small churches. By 1980, consolidation within the Christian music industry and the rise of contemporary Christian music had made it nearly impossible for small family businesses to operate. Yet, for nearly seven decades, Robert E. Winsett and the music company that bore his name made a significant and lasting contribution to gospel music.

MEL R. WILHOIT

See also Shape-Note Singing; Stamps–Baxter

Reference and Further Reading

Wilhoit, Mel R. "R. E. Winsett Music Company: A Case Study in Ma and Pa Publishing or The Growth of Grassroots Gospel." In *Hymnology in the Service of the Church: Essays in Honor of Harry Eskew,* edited by Paul Powell (forthcoming).

WLAC AM

Founded November 24, 1926, Nashville, TN

Established as the promotional venue for the Life and Casualty Insurance Company, WLAC became one of the nation's most powerful and influential voices for black gospel and R&B music in the 1940s, 1950s, and 1960s. One of a small number of Class One "clear channel" radio stations in the United States, the fifty-thousand-watt behemoth reached five states during daylight hours but was heard in twenty-eight states and a few foreign countries after dark.

Broadcasting at 1510 on the AM dial, WLAC was bought by businessman J. Truman Ward in 1935. It was during his thirty years of ownership that the station's gospel music legacy was forged. Truman employed a trio of deejays who would later become legendary figures in the history of both gospel and R&B, as well as a fourth deejay who hosted a significant trend-setting gospel show.

The station's foray into gospel music began in 1942, when a popular local quartet began to headline WLAC's daily sunrise broadcast at 6:45 a.m. The group, originally begun as a trio in the basement of Nashville's Fairfield Baptist Church in 1929, sang in church and at social functions around the city before debuting on radio station WSIX AM in 1937. By 1941, Fisk School (University) Professor John Work, on assignment with the Library of Congress, had recorded them. The next year, the group won a local competition, and the prize was a regular spot on a WLAC program that aired nationally on the CBS radio network. The WLAC exposure, sponsored by Nashville-based Sunway Vitamins for fifteen minutes each morning, transformed the Fairfield Four into national celebrities. Musical director and bass vocalist Isaac "Dickey" Freeman recalled, "There was only about four or five major (gospel) groups travelin' back then ... and we were on this fifty-thousand-watt radio station that you could hear pretty much everywhere."

By the mid-1940s, deejay Gene Nobles had begun playing black music on his evening broadcast. The primary impetus for this development was phone requests and records brought to the station by students from Fisk and Tennessee State Agricultural &

Industrial College (now Tennessee State University). When Gallatin businessman Randy Wood purchased a local appliance store in 1946 and began to sell records, he agreed to sponsor Nobles's nightly show. Its success eventually made his Randy's Record Mart the world's largest mail-order record business. Begun as a forty-five–minute show following the 10:00 p.m. news in 1947, Noble's show expanded to a second hour through the sponsorship of the Memphis-based Strickland Company by 1952. The show soon served to usher in a torrent of widely influential gospel programs at WLAC.

In 1950, businessman Ernie Young, who owned a Nashville record store named Ernie's Record Mart, began to sponsor *Ernie's Record Parade* on WLAC. The nightly show was hosted by deejay John Richbourg, known simply as "John R." The distinctive deep, gravelly voice of this beloved show host was so pronounced that it led many listeners to believe he was a black man.

The Ernie's-sponsored show was a one-hour gospel and R&B mix that aired Monday through Friday nights at 9:00 p.m. and from 8 to 9:45 p.m. on Saturday evenings. However, on Sundays, *Ernie's* was an all-spiritual show from 8:30 p.m. to midnight. Its signature opening and closing songs were sung by the venerable Angelic Gospel Singers. Cincinnati-based Savoy recording artist Dr. Charles Fold said, "I still remember listening to *Ernie's* every Sunday night with those theme songs, 'Touch Me Lord Jesus' and 'Milky White Way.'"

The popularity of the show prompted Young to establish the gospel label Nashboro Records in 1951. Nashboro featured such artists as Professor Alex Bradford, Brother Joe May, the Swanee Quintet, the Brooklyn All-Stars, Professor Harold Boggs, Dorothy Love Coates & the Gospel Harmonettes, the Fireside Gospel Singers, the Jewel Gospel Trio (featuring a young Candi Staton), the Angelic Gospel Singers, the Supreme Angels, the Consolers, and the BC&M Mass Choir. In addition, Reverend Cleophus Robinson, the Gospel Keynotes, Clara Ward, Mother Willie Mae Ford Smith, and Reverend Morgan Babb recorded on the Nashboro label. WLAC was the primary vehicle for the promotion of Nashboro albums throughout much of the nation.

The third of WLAC's record-shop–sponsored shows came in the mid-1950s. Nashville-based Buckley's Records sponsored a late-night show that featured a number of gospel artists during the time of greatest strength for the WLAC signal. This show was hosted by the less-ballyhooed deejay Herman Grizzard. However, it was through this show that youthful listeners and insomniacs began to make the overnight timeslot a popular staple of the WLAC lineup.

Bill "Hoss" Allen, who began his on-air career at WLAC by filling in for Nobles, became the host for the Randy's-sponsored show for most of the 1960s and 1970s. Except for a three-year period when Allen took a position with Chicago-based Chess Records and former Jordanaire Hugh Jarrett hosted the show, Hoss Allen was the voice of *Randy's Record Mart*. The program became such a popular part of the WLAC lineup that it was on the air from midnight to 4 a.m. each Sunday, and then eventually each evening.

Hoss Allen, who carried the gospel tradition of WLAC into the 1980s, was such an esteemed figure that Savoy Records released an LP entitled, *Bill "Hoss" Allen Presents: Let's Go to the Program—Twelve of America's Greatest Gospel Groups.*" Likewise, John R. received the 1976 Black Gospel Deejay of the Year Award from the National Gospel Symposium. At his 1986 funeral, Ella Washington sang "Amazing Grace" and "Because He Lives," and Motown songwriter Jackie Beavers sang his favorite song, "His Eye Is on the Sparrow."

WLAC's gospel programming, under J. Truman Ward, became such a part of the fabric of gospel music that it built two enormous record mailing companies and launched three record labels. The gospel label Nashboro, its secular sister Excello Records, and Randy Wood's secular Dot Records were all direct responses to the impact of WLAC AM. An entire generation of listeners referred to deejays Gene Nobles, John R., and Hoss Allen as if they knew them personally, and they nostalgically refer to WLAC's gospel programs as *Randy's* and *Ernie's*— a tremendous legacy from the golden age of gospel music.

TIMOTHY J. MOORE

See also Angelic Gospel Singers; Fairfield Four; Jordanaires, The; Nashboro Records; Swanee Quintet

Reference and Further Reading

Fold, Charles. Founder, Charles Fold Singers. Interview, February 9, 2005.

Friskics-Warren, Bill. "Voices Raised: The Uplifting, Enduring Harmonies of the Fairfield Four." Weekly Wire website, http://weeklywire.com/w/03-02-98/nash_ cover. html (March 2, 1998).

Gray, Michael. Curator, Country Music Hall of Fame. Interview, February 2, 2005.

Lowe, Jim. WLAC Radio Nashville website, http://www. yodaslair.com/dumboozle/wlac/wlacdex.html (accessed May 15, 2003).

"Radio Station WLAC Personalities 1939." World Wide Network Services website, http://wwns.com/wlac/history. html.

Smith, Wes. *The Pied Pipers of Rock 'n' Roll: Radio Deejays of the 50s and 60s.* Marietta, GA: Longstreet Press, 1989.

Ward, Jim. WLAC owner's son. Interview, February 10, 2005.

West, Carroll Van. "WLAC." Tennessee Encyclopedia of History and Culture website, http://tennesseeencyclopedia. net.

Y

YOHE, VICKI

(b. Unknown)

Vicki Yohe has been an active figure in gospel music for more than a decade, averaging some one hundred and fifty concerts yearly. As the child of a minister, she began singing in church at an early age and subsequently spent two years at the Jackson College of Ministries in Mississippi. After that, she accepted a music director position in Louisiana. During that time, her first CD, *Everlasting Love*, was released.

In 1994, Vicki Yohe began recording for the Giant label and subsequently went with Aluminum. Then in 2002, she signed with Wellspring; a year later, that firm released the disc *I Just Want You*. The song "Because of Who You Are" from that project received a 2004 Dove Award nomination. As of February 2005, Yohe and her husband Troy resided in Franklin, Tennessee.

IVAN M. TRIBE

Reference and Further Reading

Vicki Yohe website, http://www.vickiyohe.org.

Discography

Christmas Presence (2000, Aluminum CD).
Beyond This Song (2001, Aluminum CD).
I Just Want You (2003, Wellspring CD).

Z

ZONDERVAN PUBLISHING COMPANY

Zondervan Publishing House was formed in 1931 after P. J. "Pat" Zondervan (b. 1909) was fired from his uncle Bill Eerdman's publishing company. Pat purchased from Harper Brothers remainders, which were Christian books that he sold from the trunk of his car. Shortly thereafter, his mother allowed Pat and his brother, Bernie (b. 1910), to use a spare upstairs bedroom in the family farmhouse in Grandville, Michigan, for their enterprise. Their wares were initially sold through direct mail. The first book they actually published, in 1933, was titled *Women of the Old Testament*, and they began publishing music in 1941.

Pat and Bernie were partners and co-owners of this publishing venture until 1966, when Bernie died and his son, Bernie, Jr., ascended to the position of vice president of the company. Bernie, Jr., died in 1970 at the age of thirty-four. Pat Zondervan retired from the Zondervan Corporation in 1984. He was inducted into the Gospel Music Association's Hall of Fame in 1984, and he died in 1993.

In 1973, Zondervan began publishing the NIV New Testament in partnership with the International Bible Society, and he published the entire NIV Bible in 1978. Because of their mission to engage more people with the Bible, in 2005 Zondervan released the TNIV, an uncompromisingly accurate Bible translation in today's language from the translators of the most trusted Bible translation, the NIV. The TNIV is part of Zondervan and IBS's efforts to reach those eighteen to thirty-four years old with the Bible. Zondervan also holds the exclusive North American publishing rights to the New International Reader's Version, the New American Standard Bible (Amplified), and the Good News Translation of the Bible.

Zondervan became a division of HarperCollins Publishers, one of the largest publishers in the world, in 1988. In 1989, Zondervan's New Media division was formed to publish books and Bibles in an electronic format, becoming the first in the industry to do so. Also, Zondervan released the industry's first two e-books in November 2000, including the first Christian book published exclusively in an electronic format, Leonard Sweet's *The Dawn Mistaken for Dusk*. Zondervan sold its music division in 1992 and has since expanded its electronic product offerings to include curriculum DVDs, reference software, moving and still image CD-ROMs, as well as audio books and e-books. In the spring of 2005, Zondervan introduced a new product category with NOOMAs, a new format of short DVD films, between ten and twelve minutes long, about God and people's lives.

In 1998, Zondervan relaunched its children's product group as Zonderkidz, to publish and market children's products. Emphasizing Zondervan's commitment to the gift category, Inspirio was launched in December 2000, representing a new brand identity for the company's gift group. In 2001, Zondervan took on all publishing responsibilities for Marshall Pickering, the HarperCollins U.K. evangelical imprint, as well as portions of Fount, its largely Anglican publishing list. Also, in 2002, Zonderkidz began partnering with Big Idea, Inc., to publish the popular VeggieTales titles.

Zondervan has more than fifteen hundred writers on its booklist, ranging from homemakers, business people, politicians, and celebrities to theologians, scholars, philosophers, and ministry professionals. Key authors include Billy Graham, Rick Warren, Philip Yancey, Lee Strobel, Karen Kingsbury, Brian McLaren, Ben Carson, Bill Hybels, Joni Eareckson Tada, John Ortberg, Terri Blackstock, Les and Leslie Parrott, Henry Cloud, and John Townsend.

Currently, Zondervan maintains more than two thousand Bible, book, and other product titles in its catalog. Every year Zondervan publishes approximately sixty Bible editions, one hundred and fifty books, eighty gifts, and fifty new media products. These products are sold worldwide in more than sixty countries, and Zondervan's books have been translated into nearly one hundred and thirty languages. Zondervan has forty-one Bibles and books that have each sold more than five hundred thousand copies, including one book with more than thirty million copies in print (*The Purpose-Driven Life*, by Rick Warren).

Zondervan was selected as the Christian Booksellers Association Supplier of the Year in 1978, 1990, 1995, 2003, and 2004. It has earned a total of eighty Gold Medallion awards for its books and Bibles from the Evangelical Publishers Association, which is more than any other publisher.

The Zondervan Corporation's thirty-five thousand square foot glass-enclosed headquarters is built on twenty scenic acres in Grand Rapids, Michigan. The corporate office lobby is highlighted by a life-size bronze sculpture, *The Divine Servant*. Based on Mark 10:43–45 and John 13:3–17, the sculpture by Texas artist Max Greiner, Jr., depicts the biblical scene of Jesus washing the feet of the disciple Peter. Zondervan has a team of more than three hundred and sixty employees, and the company also has offices in Miami, Florida, and Sao Paulo, Brazil.

BECKY GARRISON

See also Gospel Music Association

Reference and Further Reading

Olasky, Susan. "The Battle for the Bible." *World Magazine* (April 19, 1997). Available at http://reformednet.org/salt/970505/battleforthebible.htm.

Zondervan website, http://www.zondervan.com.

INDEX

The terms in *Italics* represent music albums.

INDEX

INDEX

INDEX